W9-CXC-336

American Casebook Series
Hornbook Series and Basic Legal Texts
Nutshell Series
of

WEST PUBLISHING COMPANY
P.O. Box 3526
St. Paul, Minnesota 55165
October, 1978

ACCOUNTING

Fiflis and Kripke's Teaching Materials on Accounting for Business Lawyers, 2nd Ed., 684 pages, 1977 (Casebook)

ADMINISTRATIVE LAW

Davis' Cases, Text and Problems on Administrative Law, 6th Ed., 683 pages, 1977 (Casebook)

Davis' Basic Text on Administrative Law, 3rd Ed., 617 pages, 1972 (Text)

Davis' Police Discretion, 176 pages, 1975 (Text)

Gellhorn's Administrative Law and Process in a Nutshell, 336 pages, 1972 (Text)

Mashaw and Merrill's Introduction to the American Public Law System, 1095 pages, 1975, with 1978 Supplement (Casebook)

Robinson and Gellhorn's The Administrative Process, 928 pages, 1974 (Casebook)

ADMIRALTY

Healy and Sharpe's Cases and Materials on Admiralty, 875 pages, 1974 (Casebook)

AGENCY—PARTNERSHIP

Crane and Bromberg's Hornbook on Partnership, 695 pages, 1968 (Text)

Henn's Cases and Materials on Agency, Partnership and Other Unincorporated Business Enterprises, 396 pages, 1972 (Casebook)

Reuschlein and Gregory's Hornbook on the Law of Agency, Partnership and Other Unincorporated Business Organizations, approximately 750 pages, 1978 (Text)

Seavey's Hornbook on Agency, 329 pages, 1964 (Text)

Seavey and Hall's Cases on Agency, 431 pages, 1956 (Casebook)

Seavey, Reuschlein and Hall's Cases on Agency and Partnership, 599 pages, 1962 (Casebook)

AGENCY—PARTNERSHIP—Continued

Steffen's Cases on Agency-Partnership, 3rd, Ed., 733 pages, 1969 (Casebook)

Steffen's Agency-Partnership in a Nutshell, 364 pages, 1977 (Text)

ANTITRUST LAW

Gellhorn's Antitrust Law and Economics in a Nutshell, 406 pages, 1976 (Text)

Oppenheim and Weston's Cases and Comments on Federal Antitrust Laws, 3rd Ed., 952 pages, 1968, with 1975 Supplement (Casebook)

Oppenheim and Weston's Price and Service Discrimination under the Robinson-Patman Act, 3rd Ed., 258 pages, 1974 (Casebook—reprint from Oppenheim and Weston's Cases and Comments on Federal Antitrust Laws, 3rd, Ed., 1968

Posner's Cases and Economic Notes on Antitrust, 885 pages, 1974 (Casebook)

Sullivan's Handbook of the Law of Antitrust, 886 pages, 1977 (Text)

See also Regulated Industries, Trade Regulation

BANKING LAW

See Regulated Industries

BUSINESS PLANNING

Painter's Problems and Materials in Business Planning, 791 pages, 1975, with 1978 Supplement (Casebook)

CIVIL PROCEDURE

Casad's Res Judicata in a Nutshell, 310 pages, 1976 (Text)

Cound, Friedenthal and Miller's Cases and Materials on Civil Procedure, 2nd Ed., 1186 pages, 1974 with 1978 Supplement (Casebook)

Cound, Friedenthal and Miller's Cases on Pleading, Discovery and Joinder, 643 pages, 1968 (Casebook)

Ehrenzweig and Louisell's Jurisdiction in a Nutshell, 3rd Ed., 291 pages, 1973 (Text)

CIVIL PROCEDURE—Continued

Federal Rules of Civil-Appellate-Criminal Procedure—West Law School Edition, 334 pages, 1978

Hodges, Jones and Elliott's Cases and Materials on Texas Trial and Appellate Procedure, 2nd Ed., 745 pages, 1974 (Casebook)

Hodges, Jones, and Elliott's Cases and Materials on the Judicial Process Prior to Trial in Texas, 2nd Ed., 871 pages, 1977 (Casebook)

Karlen's Procedure Before Trial in a Nutshell, 258 pages, 1972 (Text)

Karlen and Joiner's Cases and Materials on Trials and Appeals, 536 pages, 1971 (Casebook)

Karlen, Meisenholder, Stevens and Vestal's Cases on Civil Procedure, 923 pages, 1975 (Casebook)

Koffler and Reppy's Hornbook on Common Law Pleading, 663 pages, 1969 (Text)

McBaine's Cases on Introduction to Civil Procedure, 399 pages, 1950 (Casebook)

McCoid's Cases on Civil Procedure, 823 pages, 1974 (Casebook)

Park's Computer-Aided Exercises on Civil Procedure, 118 pages, 1976 (Coursebook)

Shipman's Hornbook on Common-Law Pleading, 3rd Ed., 644 pages, 1923 (Text)

Siegel's Hornbook on New York Practice, 1011 pages, 1978 (Text)

See also Federal Jurisdiction and Procedure

COMMERCIAL LAW

Bailey's Secured Transactions in a Nutshell, 377 pages, 1976 (Text)

Epstein and Martin's Basic Uniform Commercial Code Teaching Materials, 599 pages, 1977 (Casebook)

Henson's Hornbook on Secured Transactions under the U.C.C., 2nd Ed., approximately 450 pages, December 1978 (Text)

Murray's Commercial Law, Problems and Materials, 366 pages, 1975 (Coursebook)

Nordstrom and Clovis' Problems and Materials on Commercial Paper, 458 pages, 1972 (Casebook)

Nordstrom and Lattin's Problems and Materials on Sales and Secured Transactions, 809 pages, 1968 (Casebook)

Nordstrom's Hornbook on Sales, 600 pages, 1970 (Text)

Selected Commercial Statutes, 1144 pages, 1976

COMMERCIAL LAW—Continued

Speidel, Summers and White's Teaching Materials on Commercial and Consumer Law, 2nd Ed., 1475 pages, 1974 (Casebook)

Stone's Uniform Commercial Code in a Nutshell, 507 pages, 1975 (Text)

Uniform Commercial Code, Official Text with Comments, approximately 850 pages, 1978

UCC Article Nine Reprint, 128 pages, 1976

Weber's Commercial Paper in a Nutshell, 2nd Ed., 361 pages, 1975 (Text)

White and Summers' Hornbook on the Uniform Commercial Code, 1086 pages, 1972 (Text)

COMMUNITY PROPERTY

Huie's Texas Cases and Materials on Marital Property Rights, 681 pages, 1966 (Casebook)

Verrall's Cases and Materials on California Community Property, 3rd Ed., 547 pages, 1977 (Casebook)

COMPARATIVE LAW

Langbein's Comparative Criminal Procedure: Germany, 172 pages, 1977 (Casebook)

CONFLICT OF LAWS

Cramton, Currie and Kay's Cases-Comments-Questions on Conflict of Laws, 2nd Ed., 1021 pages, 1975 (Casebook)

Ehrenzweig's Treatise on Conflict of Laws, 824 pages, 1962 (Text)

Ehrenzweig's Conflicts in a Nutshell, 3rd Ed., 432 pages, 1974 (Text)

Goodrich and Scoles' Hornbook on Conflict of Laws, 4th Ed., 483 pages, 1964 (Text)

Scoles and Weintraub's Cases and Materials on Conflict of Laws, 2nd Ed., 966 pages, 1972, with 1978 Supplement (Casebook)

CONSTITUTIONAL LAW

Engdahl's Constitutional Power in a Nutshell: Federal and State, 411 pages, 1974 (Text)

Ginsburg's Constitutional Aspects of Sex-Based Discrimination, 129 pages, 1974 (Casebook)—reprint from Davidson, Ginsburg and Kay's Cases on Sex-Based Discrimination, 1974

Lockhart, Kamisar and Choper's Cases-Comments-Questions on Constitutional Law, 4th Ed., 1664 pages plus Appendix, 1975, with 1978 Supplement (Casebook)

CONSTITUTIONAL LAW—Continued

Lockhart, Kamisar and Choper's Cases-Comments-Questions on the American Constitution, 4th Ed., 1249 pages plus Appendix, 1975, with 1978 Supplement (Casebook)—reprint from Lockhart, et al. Cases on Constitutional Law, 4th Ed., 1975

Lockhart, Kamisar and Choper's Cases and Materials on Constitutional Rights and Liberties, 4th Ed., 1244 pages plus Appendix, 1975, with 1978 Supplement (Casebook)—reprint from Lockhart, et al. Cases on Constitutional Law, 4th Ed., 1975

Miller's Presidential Power in a Nutshell, 328 pages, 1977 (Text)

Nowak, Rotunda and Young's Hornbook on Constitutional Law, 974 pages, 1978, with 1978 pocket parts (Text)

Vieira's Civil Rights in a Nutshell, 279 pages, 1978 (Text)

William's Constitutional Analysis in a Nutshell, approximately 360 pages, January 1979 (Text)

CONSUMER LAW

Epstein's Consumer Protection in a Nutshell, 322 pages, 1976 (Text)

Kripke's Text-Cases-Materials on Consumer Credit, 454 pages, 1970 (Casebook)

McCall's Consumer Protection, Cases, Notes and Materials, 594 pages, 1977, with 1977 Statutory Supplement (Casebook)

Schrag's Cases and Materials on Consumer Protection, 2nd Ed., 197 pages, 1973 (Casebook)—reprint from Cooper, et al. Cases on Law and Poverty, 2nd Ed., 1973

Selected Commercial Statutes, 1144 pages, 1976

Uniform Consumer Credit Code, Official Text with Comments, 218 pages, 1974

CONTRACTS

Calamari & Perillo's Cases and Problems on Contracts, 1061 pages, 1978 (Casebook)

Calamari and Perillo's Hornbook on Contracts, 2nd Ed., 878 pages, 1977 (Text)

Corbin's Text on Contracts, One Volume Student Edition, 1224 pages, 1952 (Text)

Freedman's Cases and Materials on Contracts, 658 pages, 1973 (Casebook)

Fuller and Eisenberg's Cases on Basic Contract Law, 3rd Ed., 1043 pages 1972 (Casebook)

CONTRACTS—Continued

Jackson's Cases on Contract Law in Modern Society, 1404 pages, 1973 (Casebook)

Reitz's Cases on Contracts as Basic Commercial Law, 763 pages, 1975 (Casebook)

Schaber and Rohwer's Contracts in a Nutshell, 307 pages, 1975 (Text)

Simpson's Hornbook on Contracts, 2nd Ed., 510 pages, 1965 (Text)

COPYRIGHT

Nimmer's Cases and Materials on Copyright and Other Aspects of Law Pertaining to Literary, Musical and Artistic Works, 828 pages, 1971, with 1977 Supplement (Casebook)

See also Patent Law

CORPORATIONS

Hamilton's Cases on Corporations—Including Partnerships and Limited Partnerships, 998 pages, 1976, with 1976 Statutory Supplement and 1979 Case Supplement (Casebook)

Henn's Cases on Corporations, 1279 pages, 1974, with 1974 Statutes, Forms and Case Study Supplement (Casebook)

Henn's Hornbook on Corporations, 2nd Ed., 956 pages, 1970 (Text)

CORRECTIONS

Krantz's Cases and Materials on the Law of Corrections and Prisoners' Rights, 1130 pages, 1973, with 1977 Supplement (Casebook)

Krantz's Law of Corrections and Prisoners' Rights in a Nutshell, 353 pages, 1976 (Text)

Model Rules and Regulations on Prisoners' Rights and Responsibilities, 212 pages, 1973

Popper's Post-Conviction Remedies in a Nutshell, 360 pages, 1978 (Text)

CREDITOR'S RIGHTS

Epstein's Debtor-Creditor Relations in a Nutshell, 309 pages, 1973 (Text)

Epstein and Landers' Debtors and Creditors: Cases and Materials, 722 pages, 1978 (Casebook)

Riesenfeld's Cases and Materials on Creditors' Remedies and Debtors' Protection, 2nd Ed., 808 pages, 1975, with 1975 Statutory Supplement and 1978 Supplement Update (Casebook)

Selected Bankruptcy Statutes, 486 pages, 1974

CRIMINAL LAW AND CRIMINAL PROCEDURE

Cohen and Gobert's Problems in Criminal Law, 297 pages, 1976 (Problem book)

Davis' Police Discretion, 176 pages, 1975 (Text)

Dix and Sharlot's Cases and Materials on Criminal Law, 1360 pages, 1973 (Casebook)

Federal Rules of Civil-Appellate-Criminal Procedure—West Law School Edition, 334 pages, 1978

Grano's Problems in Criminal Procedure, 171 pages, 1974 (Problem book)

Heymann and Kenety's The Murder Trial of Wilbur Jackson: A Homicide in the Family, 340 pages, 1975 (Case Study)

Israel and LaFave's Criminal Procedure in a Nutshell, 2nd Ed., 404 pages, 1975 (Text)

Johnson's Criminal Law: Cases, Materials and Text on Substantive Criminal Law in its Procedural Context, 878 pages, 1975, with 1977 Supplement (Casebook)

Kamisar, LaFave and Israel's Cases, Comments and Questions on Modern Criminal Procedure, 4th Ed., 1572 pages, plus Appendix, 1974, with 1978 Supplement (Casebook)

Kamisar, LaFave and Israel's Cases, Comments and Questions on Basic Criminal Procedure, 4th Ed., 790 pages, 1974, with 1978 Supplement (Casebook)—reprint from Kamisar, et al. Modern Criminal Procedure, 4th Ed., 1974

LaFave's Modern Criminal Law: Cases, Comments and Questions, 789 pages, 1978 (Casebook)

LaFave and Scott's Hornbook on Criminal Law, 763 pages, 1972 (Text)

Loewy's Criminal Law in a Nutshell, 302 pages, 1975 (Text)

Uniform Rules of Criminal Procedure—Approved Draft, 407 pages, 1974

Uviller's The Processes of Criminal Justice: Adjudication, 991 pages, 1975, with 1977 Supplement (Casebook)

Uviller's The Processes of Criminal Justice: Investigation, 744 pages, 1974, with 1977 Supplement (Casebook)

Vorenberg's Cases on Criminal Law and Procedure, 1044 pages, 1975, with 1977 Supplement (Casebook)

See also Corrections, Juvenile Justice

DECEDENTS ESTATES

See Wills, Trusts and Estates

DOMESTIC RELATIONS

Clark's Cases and Problems on Domestic Relations, 2nd Ed., 918 pages, 1974, with 1977 Supplement (Casebook)

Clark's Hornbook on Domestic Relations, 754 pages, 1968 (Text)

Kay's Sex-Based Discrimination in Family Law, 305 pages, 1974 (Casebook)—reprint from Davidson, Ginsburg and Kay's Cases on Sex-Based Discrimination, 1974

Krause's Cases and Materials on Family Law, 1132 pages, 1976, with 1978 Supplement (Casebook)

Krause's Family Law in a Nutshell, 400 pages, 1977 (Text)

Paulsen's Cases and Selected Problems on Family Law and Poverty, 2nd Ed., 200 pages, 1973 (Casebook)—reprint from Cooper, et al. Cases on Law and Poverty, 2nd Ed., 1973

DRUG ABUSE

Uelmen and Haddox's Cases on Drug Abuse and the Law, 564 pages, 1974, with 1977 Supplement (Casebook)

EDUCATION LAW

Morris' The Constitution and American Education, 833 pages, 1974 (Casebook)

EMPLOYMENT DISCRIMINATION

Cooper, Rabb and Rubin's Fair Employment Litigation: Text and Materials for Student and Practitioner, 590 pages, 1975 (Coursebook)

Player's Federal Law of Employment Discrimination in a Nutshell, 336 pages, 1976 (Text)

Sovern's Cases and Materials on Racial Discrimination in Employment, 2nd Ed., 167 pages, 1973 (Casebook)—reprint from Cooper et al. Cases on Law and Poverty, 2nd Ed., 1973

See also Women and the Law

ENVIRONMENTAL LAW

Currie's Cases and Materials on Pollution, 715 pages, 1975 (Casebook)

Federal Environmental Law, 1600 pages, 1974 (Text)

Hanks, Tarlock and Hanks' Cases on Environmental Law and Policy, 1242 pages, 1974, with 1976 Supplement (Casebook)

Rodgers' Hornbook on Environmental Law, 956 pages, 1977 (Text)

See also Natural Resources

EQUITY

See Remedies

ESTATE PLANNING

Casner and Stein's Estate Planning under the Tax Reform Act of 1976,

ESTATE PLANNING—Continued

456 pages, 1978 (Coursebook)

Lynn's Introduction to Estate Planning, in a Nutshell, 2nd Ed., 378 pages, 1978 (Text)

EVIDENCE

Broun and Meisenholder's Problems in Evidence, 130 pages, 1973 (Problem book)

Cleary and Strong's Cases, Materials and Problems on Evidence, 2nd Ed., 1124 pages, 1975 (Casebook)

Federal Rules of Evidence for United States Courts and Magistrates, 323 pages, 1975

Kimball's Programmed Materials on Problems in Evidence, 380 pages, 1978 (Problem book)

Lempert and Saltzburg's A Modern Approach to Evidence: Text, Problems, Transcripts and Cases, 1231 pages, 1977 (Casebook)

Lilly's Introduction to the Law of Evidence, approximately 500 pages, October 1978 (Text)

McCormick, Elliott and Sutton's Cases and Materials on Evidence, 4th Ed., 1088 pages, 1971 (Casebook)

McCormick's Hornbook on Evidence, 2nd Ed., 938 pages, 1972, with 1978 pocket part (Text)

Rothstein's Evidence in a Nutshell, 406 pages, 1970 (Text)

FEDERAL JURISDICTION AND PROCEDURE

Currie's Cases and Materials on Federal Courts, 2nd Ed., 1040 pages, 1975, with 1978 Supplement (Casebook)

Currie's Federal Jurisdiction in a Nutshell, 228 pages, 1976 (Text)

Federal Rules of Civil-Appellate-Criminal Procedure—West Law School Edition, 334 pages, 1978

Forrester and Moye's Cases and Materials on Federal Jurisdiction and Procedure, 3rd Ed., 917 pages, 1977 (Casebook)

Merrill and Vetri's Problems on Federal Courts and Civil Procedure, 460 pages, 1974 (Problem book)

Wright's Hornbook on Federal Courts, 3rd Ed., 818 pages, 1976 (Text)

FUTURE INTERESTS

See Wills, Trusts, and Estates

HOUSING AND URBAN DEVELOPMENT

Berger's Cases and Materials on Housing, 2nd Ed., 254 pages, 1973 (Casebook)—reprint from Cooper et al. Cases on Law and Poverty, 2nd Ed., 1973

See also Land Use

INDIAN LAW

Getches, Rosenfelt and Wilkinson's Cases on Federal Indian Law, approximately 700 pages, February 1979 (Casebook)

INSURANCE

Keeton's Cases on Basic Insurance Law, 2nd Ed., 1086 pages, 1977

Keeton's Basic Text on Insurance Law, 712 pages, 1971 (Text)

Keeton's Case Supplement to Keeton's Basic Text on Insurance Law, 334 pages, 1978 (Casebook)

Keeton's Programmed Problems in Insurance Law, 243 pages, 1972 (Text Supplement)

INTERNATIONAL LAW

Friedmann, Lissityzyn and Pugh's Cases and Materials on International Law, 1205 pages, 1969, with 1972 Supplement (Casebook)

Jackson's Legal Problems of International Economic Relations, 1097 pages, 1977, with Statutory Supplement (Casebook)

Kirgis' International Organizations in Their Legal Setting, 1016 pages, 1977 (Casebook)

INTRODUCTION TO LAW

Dobbyn's So You Want to go to Law School, Revised First Edition, 206 pages, 1976 (Text)

Kinyon's Introduction to Law Study and Law Examinations in a Nutshell, 389 pages, 1971 (Text)

See also Legal Method and Legal System

JUDICIAL ADMINISTRATION

Carrington, Meador and Rosenberg's Justice on Appeal, 263 pages, 1976 (Casebook)

Nelson's Cases and Materials on Judicial Administration and the Administration of Justice, 1032 pages, 1974 (Casebook)

JURISPRUDENCE

Christie's Text and Readings on Jurisprudence—The Philosophy of Law, 1056 pages, 1973 (Casebook)

JUVENILE JUSTICE

Fox's Cases and Materials on Modern Juvenile Justice, 1012 pages, 1972 (Casebook)

Fox's Juvenile Courts in a Nutshell, 2nd Ed., 275 pages, 1977 (Text)

LABOR LAW

Gorman's Labor Law-Unionization and Collective Bargaining, 914 pages, 1976 (Text)

LABOR LAW—Continued

Oberer and Hanslowe's Cases and Materials on Labor Law—Collective Bargaining in a Free Society, 2nd Ed., approximately 1150 pages, December, 1978, with 1978 Statutory Supplement (Casebook)

See also Employment Discrimination, Social Legislation

LAND FINANCE—PROPERTY SECURITY

Bruce's Real Estate Finance in a Nutshell, approximately 300 pages, March, 1979 (Text)

Maxwell, Riesenfeld, Hetland and Warren's Cases on California Security Transactions in Land, 2nd Ed., 584 pages, 1975 (Casebook)

Nelson and Whitman's Cases on Real Estate Finance and Development, 1064 pages, 1976 (Casebook)

Osborne's Cases and Materials on Secured Transactions, 559 pages, 1967 (Casebook)

Osborne, Nelson and Whitman's Hornbook on Real Estate Finance Law, approximately 900 pages, March, 1979 (Text)

LAND USE

Beuscher, Wright and Gitelman's Cases and Materials on Land Use, 2nd Ed., 1133 pages, 1976 (Casebook)

Hagman's Cases on Public Planning and Control of Urban and Land Development, 1208 pages, 1973, with 1976 Supplement (Casebook)

Hagman's Hornbook on Urban Planning and Land Development Control Law, 706 pages, 1971 (Text)

Wright and Webber's Land Use in a Nutshell, approximately 300 pages, October, 1978 (Text)

See also Housing and Urban Development

LAW AND ECONOMICS

Manne's The Economics of Legal Relationships—Readings in the Theory of Property Rights, 660 pages, 1975 (Text)

See also Regulated Industries

LAW AND MEDICINE—PSYCHIATRY

King's The Law of Medical Malpractice in a Nutshell, 340 pages, 1977 (Text)

Sharpe, Fiscina and Head's Cases on Law and Medicine, approximately 900 pages, October, 1978 (Casebook)

LEGAL RESEARCH AND WRITING

Cohen's Legal Research in a Nutshell, 3rd Ed., 415 pages, 1978 (Text)

LEGAL RESEARCH AND WRITING—Continued

How to Find the Law With Special Chapters on Legal Writing, 7th Ed., 542 pages, 1976. Problem book available (Coursebook)

Rombauer's Legal Problem Solving—Analysis, Research and Writing, 3rd Ed., 352 pages, 1978 (Casebook)

Statsky's Legal Research, Writing and Analysis: Some Starting Points, 180 pages, 1974 (Text)—reprint from Statsky's Introduction to Paralegalism, 1974

Statsky and Wernet's Case Analysis and Fundamentals of Legal Writing, 576 pages, 1977 (Text)

Weihofen's Legal Writing Style, 323 pages, 1961 (Text)

LEGAL CLINICS

Freeman and Weihofen's Cases and Text on Clinical Law Training—Interviewing and Counseling, 506 pages, 1972 (Casebook)

LEGAL PROFESSION

Aronson's Problems in Professional Responsibility, 280 pages, 1978 (Problem book)

Mallen and Levit's Legal Malpractice, 727 pages, 1977 (Coursebook)

Mellinkoff's The Conscience of a Lawyer, 304 pages, 1973 (Text)

Mellinkoff's Lawyers and the System of Justice, 983 pages, 1976 (Casebook)

Pirsig and Kirwin's Cases and Materials on Professional Responsibility, 3rd Ed., 667 pages, 1976, with 1977 Supplement (Casebook)

LEGAL HISTORY

See Legal Method and Legal System

LEGAL METHOD AND LEGAL SYSTEM

Aldisert's Readings, Materials and Cases in the Judicial Process, 948 pages, 1976 (Casebook)

Fryer and Orentlicher's Cases and Materials on Legal Method and Legal System, 1043 pages, 1967 (Casebook)

Greenberg's Judicial Process and Social Change, 666 pages, 1977 (Coursebook)

Kempin's Historical Introduction to Anglo-American Law in a Nutshell, 2nd Ed., 280 pages, 1973 (Text)

Kimball's Historical Introduction to the Legal System, 610 pages, 1966 (Casebook)

Leflar's Appellate Judicial Opinions, 343 pages, 1974 (Text)

LEGAL METHOD AND LEGAL SYSTEM —Continued

Mashaw and Merrill's Introduction to the American Public Law System, 1095 pages, 1975, with 1978 Supplement (Casebook)

Murphy's Cases and Materials on Introduction to Law—Legal Process and Procedure, 772 pages, 1977 (Casebook)

Smith's Cases and Materials on the Development of Legal Institutions, 757 pages, 1965 (Casebook)

Statsky's Legislative Analysis: How to Use Statutes and Regulations, 216 pages, 1975 (Text)

LEGISLATION

Davies' Legislative Law and Process in a Nutshell, 279 pages, 1975 (Text)

Nutting and Dickerson's Cases and Materials on Legislation, 5th Ed., 744 pages, 1978 (Casebook)

Statsky's Legislative Analysis: How to Use Statutes and Regulations, 216 pages, 1975 (Text)

LOCAL GOVERNMENT

McCarthy's Local Government Law in a Nutshell, 386 pages, 1975 (Text)

Michelman and Sandalow's Cases-Comments-Questions on Government in Urban Areas, 1216 pages, 1970, with 1972 Supplement (Casebook)

Stason and Kauper's Cases and Materials on Municipal Corporations, 3rd Ed., 692 pages, 1959 (Casebook)

Valente's Cases and Materials on Local Government Law, 928 pages, 1975 (Casebook)

MASS COMMUNICATION LAW

Gillmor and Barron's Cases and Comment on Mass Communication Law, 2nd Ed., 1007 pages, 1974 (Casebook)

Ginsburg's Regulation of Broadcasting: Law and Policy Towards Radio, Television and Cable Communications, approximately 723 pages, November, 1978 (Casebook)

Zuckman and Gayne's Mass Communications Law in a Nutshell, 431 pages, 1977 (Text)

MORTGAGES

See Land Finance—Property Security

NATURAL RESOURCES LAW

Rodger's Cases on Energy and Natural Resourses Law, approximately 1100 pages, January, 1979 (Casebook)

See also Environmental Law

OFFICE PRACTICE

Binder and Price's Legal Interviewing and Counseling: A Client-Centered Approach, 232 pages 1977 (Text)

Edwards and White's Problems, Readings and Materials on the Lawyer as a Negotiator, 484 pages, 1977 (Casebook)

Freeman and Weihofen's Cases and Text on Clinical Law Training—Interviewing and Counseling, 506 pages, 1972 (Casebook)

Shaffer's Legal Interviewing and Counseling in a Nutshell, 353 pages, 1976 (Text)

Strong and Clark's Law Office Management, 424 pages, 1974 (Casebook)

OIL AND GAS

Hemingway's Hornbook on Oil and Gas, 486 pages, 1971, with 1978 pocket part (Text)

Huie, Woodward and Smith's Cases and Materials on Oil and Gas, 2nd Ed., 955 pages, 1972 (Casebook)

See also Natural Resources

PARTNERSHIP

See Agency—Partnership

PATENT LAW

Choate's Cases and Materials on Patent Law, 1060 pages, 1973 (Casebook)

See also Copyright

POVERTY LAW

Brudno's Poverty, Inequality, and the Law: Cases-Commentary-Analysis, 934 pages, 1976 (Casebook)

Cooper, Dodyk, Berger, Paulsen, Schrag and Sovern's Cases and Materials on Law and Poverty, 2nd Ed., 1208 pages, 1973 (Casebook)

LaFrance, Schroeder, Bennett and Boyd's Hornbook on Law of the Poor, 558 pages, 1973 (Text)

See also Social Legislation

PRODUCTS LIABILITY

Noel and Phillips' Cases on Products Liability, 836 pages, 1976 (Casebook)

Noel and Phillips' Products Liability in a Nutshell, 365 pages, 1974 (Text)

PROPERTY

Aigler, Smith and Tefft's Cases on Property, 2 volumes, 1339 pages, 1960 (Casebook)

Bernhardt's Real Property in a Nutshell, 425 pages, 1975 (Text)

Browder, Cunningham and Julin's Cases on Basic Property Law, 2nd Ed., 1397 pages, 1973 (Casebook)

PROPERTY—Continued

Burby's Hornbook on Real Property, 3rd Ed., 490 pages, 1965 (Text)
Chused's A Modern Approach to Property: Cases-Notes-Materials, 1069 pages, 1978 (Casebook)
Cohen's Materials for a Basic Course in Property, 526 pages, 1978 (Casebook)
Donahue, Kauper and Martin's Cases on Property, 1501 pages, 1974 (Casebook)
Moynihan's Introduction to Real Property, 254 pages, 1962 (Text)
Phipps' Titles in a Nutshell, 277 pages, 1968 (Text)
Smith and Boyer's Survey of the Law of Property, 2nd Ed., 510 pages, 1971 (Text)
Uniform Land Transactions Act, Uniform Simplification of Land Transfers Act, Uniform Condominium Act, 1978 Official Text with Comments, 462 pages, 1978
See also Housing and Urban Development, Land Finance, Land Use

REAL ESTATE

See Land Finance

REGULATED INDUSTRIES

Morgan's Cases and Materials on Economic Regulation of Business, 830 pages, 1976, with 1978 Supplement (Casebook)
Pozen's Financial Institutions: Cases, Materials and Problems on Investment Management, 844 pages, 1978 (Casebook)
White's Teaching Materials on Banking Law, 1058 pages, 1976, with 1976 Statutory Supplement (Casebook)
See also Mass Communication Law

REMEDIES

Cribbet's Cases and Materials on Judicial Remedies, 762 pages, 1954 (Casebook)
Dobbs' Hornbook on Remedies, 1067 pages, 1973 (Text)
Dobbs' Problems in Remedies, 137 pages, 1974 (Problem book)
Dobbyn's Injunctions in a Nutshell, 264 pages, 1974 (Text)
McClintock's Hornbook on Equity, 2nd Ed., 643 pages, 1948 (Text)
McCormick's Hornbook on Damages, 811 pages, 1935 (Text)
O'Connell's Remedies in a Nutshell, 364 pages, 1977 (Text)
Van Hecke, Leavell and Nelson's Cases and Materials on Equitable Remedies and Restitution, 2nd Ed., 717 pages, 1973 (Casebook)

REMEDIES—Continued

York and Bauman's Cases and Materials on Remedies, 3rd Ed., approximately 1200 pages, November, 1978 (Casebook)

REVIEW MATERIALS

Ballantine's Problems
Burby's Law Refreshers
Smith's Review

SECURITIES REGULATION

Ratner's Materials on Securities Regulation, 893 pages, 1975, with 1977 Supplement (Casebook)
Ratner's Securities Regulation in a Nutshell, 300 pages, 1978 (Text)

SOCIAL LEGISLATION

Brudno's Income Redistribution Theories and Programs: Cases-Commentary-Analysis, 480 pages, 1977 (Casebook) —reprint from Brudno's Poverty, Inequality and the Law, 1976
Cooper and Dodyk's Cases and Materials on Income Maintenance, 2nd Ed., 449 pages, 1973 (Casebook)—reprint from Cooper et al. Cases on Law and Poverty, 2nd Ed., 1973
LaFrance's Welfare Law in a Nutshell approximately 435 pages, January, 1979 (Text)
Malone, Plant and Little's Cases on the Employment Relation, 1055 pages, 1974, with 1977 Supplement (Casebook)
See also Poverty Law

SURETYSHIP

Osborne's Cases on Suretyship, 221 pages, 1966 (Casebook)
Simpson's Hornbook on Suretyship, 569 pages, 1950 (Text)

TAXATION

Chommie's Hornbook on Federal Income Taxation, 2nd Ed., 1051 pages, 1973 (Text)
Chommie's Review of Federal Income Taxation, 90 pages, 1973 (Text)
Hellerstein and Hellerstein's Cases on State and Local Taxation, 4th Ed., 1041 pages, 1978 (Casebook)
Kahn and Gann's Corporate Taxation and Taxation of Partnerships and Partners, approximately 1200 pages, January 1979 (Casebook)
Kragen and McNulty's Cases and Materials on Federal Income Taxation, 2nd Ed., 1107 pages, 1974, with 1977 Supplement (Casebook)
Kramer and McCord's Problems for Federal Estate and Gift Taxes, 206 pages, 1976 (Problem book)

TAXATION—Continued

Lowndes, Kramer and McCord's Hornbook on Federal Estate and Gift Taxes, 3rd Ed.,1099 pages, 1974 (Text)
McCord's 1976 Estate and Gift Tax Reform–Analysis, Explanation and Commentary, 377 pages, 1977 (Text)
McNulty's Federal Estate and Gift Taxation in a Nutshell, 343 pages, 1973 (Text)
McNulty's Federal Income Taxation of Individuals in a Nutshell, 2nd Ed., 422 pages, 1978 (Text)
Rice's Problems and Materials in Federal Estate and Gift Taxation, 3rd Ed., 474 pages, 1978 (Casebook)
Rice's Problems and Materials in Federal Income Taxation, 2nd Ed., 589 pages, 1971 (Casebook)
Rose and Raskind's Advanced Federal Income Taxation: Corporate Transactions–Cases, Materials and Problems, 955 pages, 1978 (Casebook)
Selected Federal Taxation Statutes and Regulations, 1321 pages, 1977
Soboloff's Federal Income Taxation of Corporations and Stockholders in a Nutshell, 374 pages, 1978 (Text)

TORTS

Green, Pedrick, Rahl, Thode, Hawkins, Smith, and Treece's Cases and Materials on Torts, 2nd Ed., 1360 pages, 1977 (Casebook)
Green, Pedrick, Rahl, Thode, Hawkins, Smith, and Treece's Advanced Torts: Injuries to Business, Political and Family Interests, 544 pages, 1977 (Casebook)—reprint from Green, et al. Cases and Materials on Torts, 2nd Ed., 1977
Keeton's Computer-Aided and Workbook Exercises on Tort Law, 164 pages, 1976 (Coursebook)
Keeton and Keeton's Cases and Materials on Torts, 2nd Ed., 1200 pages, 1977 (Casebook)
Kionka's Torts in a Nutshell: Injuries to Persons and Property, 434 pages, 1977 (Text)
Prosser's Hornbook on Torts, 4th Ed., 1208 pages, 1971 (Text)
Shapo's Cases on Tort and Compensation Law, 1244 pages, 1976 (Casebook)
See also Products Liability

TRADE REGULATION

Oppenheim and Weston's Cases and Materials on Unfair Trade Practices and Consumer Protection, 3rd Ed., 1065 pages, 1974, with 1977 Supplement (Casebook)

TRADE REGULATION—Continued

See also Antitrust, Regulated Industries

TRIAL ADVOCACY

Hegland's Trial and Practice Skills in a Nutshell, 346 pages, 1978 (Text)
Jean's Trial Advocacy (Student Edition), 473 pages, 1975 (Text)
McElhaney's Effective Litigation, 457 pages, 1974 (Casebook)

TRUSTS

See Wills, Trusts and Estates

WATER LAW

Trelease's Cases and Materials on Water Law, 2nd Ed., 863 pages, 1974 (Casebook)
See also Natural Resources

WILLS, TRUSTS AND ESTATES

Atkinson's Hornbook on Wills, 2nd Ed., 975 pages, 1953 (Text)
Averill's Uniform Probate Code in a Nutshell, 425 pages, 1978 (Text)
Bogert's Hornbook on Trusts, 5th Ed., 726 pages, 1973 (Text)
Clark, Lusky and Murphy's Cases and Materials on Gratuitous Transfers, 2nd Ed., 1102 pages, 1977 (Casebook)
Gulliver's Cases and Materials on Future Interests, 624 pages, 1959 (Casebook)
Gulliver's Introduction to the Law of Future Interests, 87 pages, 1959 (Casebook)
Halbach (Editor)—Death, Taxes, and Family Property: Essays and American Assembly Report, 189 pages, 1977 (Text)
Mennell's Cases and Materials on California Decedent's Estates, 566 pages, 1973 (Casebook)
Powell's Cases on Trusts and Wills, 639 pages, 1960 (Casebook)
Simes' Hornbook on Future Interests, 2nd Ed., 355 pages, 1966 (Text)
Turrentine's Cases and Text on Wills and Administration, 2nd Ed., 483 pages, 1962 (Casebook)
Uniform Probate Code, 5th Ed., Official Text With Comments, 384 pages, 1977

WOMEN AND THE LAW

Davidson, Ginsburg and Kay's Text, Cases and Materials on Sex-Based Discrimination, 1031 pages, 1974, with 1978 Supplement (Casebook)
See also Employment Discrimination

WORKMEN'S COMPENSATION

See Social Legislation

REAL ESTATE FINANCE LAW

By

GEORGE E. OSBORNE
Late Professor of Law, University of California,
Hastings College of the Law

GRANT S. NELSON
Professor of Law, University of Missouri-Columbia
and

DALE A. WHITMAN
Professor of Law and Associate Dean
University of Washington, through 1979
Professor of Law, J. Reuben Clark Law School,
Brigham Young University, 1979–

A Successor to
Handbook on the
Law of Mortgages, 2nd Edition (1970)
by George E. Osborne

HORNBOOK SERIES

ST. PAUL, MINN.
WEST PUBLISHING CO.
1979

Printed in the United States of America

Library of Congress Cataloging in Publication Data

Osborne, George Edward, 1894–
Real estate finance law.

(Hornbook series)

Second ed. published in 1970 under title: Handbook on the law of mortgages.

Includes index.

1. Mortgages—United States. I. Nelson, Grant S., joint author. II. Whitman, Dale A., joint author. III. Title. IV. Series.

KF695.08 1979 346'.73'0436 79-284

ISBN 0-8299-2034-X

Osborne et al. Real Est.Fin.Law HB

To
Judy and Marjorie

*

PREFACE

The task of revising the work of a scholar of George Osborne's stature and reputation is a humbling, even intimidating one. Osborne's Handbook on the Law of Mortgages has been widely regarded as one of the finest works in the hornbook series. First published in 1948 and revised by the author in 1970, it has been relied upon with great frequency by courts and lawyers.

During the period since the book was first printed, the law of real estate finance, once thought staid and dull, has burgeoned. New mortgage forms and techniques have developed, new legal issues have arisen, and a new awareness of the interests of mortgagors as consumers has emerged. Statutes and regulations have multiplied as long-standing lenders' practices have come under question. The work of lawyers who represent borrowers and lenders continues to become increasingly complex; the old issues remain, and new ones are constantly being added. The need for a new edition of the Handbook on the Law of Mortgages was clear.

Our effort has been to retain the best of the previous editions while making the needed additions. To accomplish this within a reasonable span of pages, some editing of Osborne's previous material has been necessary. His meticulous treatment of the historical development of mortgage law, for example, has been drastically shortened. The previous editions are widely available, and those who need the greater depth on such topics can find it in them. We have tried to retain and update the best of Osborne's work which has modern relevance. Still found in this new edition, albeit with some revision and reorganization, is his superb treatment of such topics as the absolute deed as mortgage, the mortgagee in possession, the lien, title, and intermediate theories, receiverships, and transfers by the mortgagor.

At the same time, a large number of traditional topics have been substantially or completely rewritten to provide greater clarity and to take recent developments into account. These include assignments and transfers by the mortgagee, the installment land contract, the effect of defective exercise of a power of sale, antideficiency statutes, and the deed in lieu of foreclosure.

Finally, we have added numerous topics which were barely mentioned or entirely uncovered in previous editions, often because they were simply not relevant issues prior to recent years. We have covered the constitutionality of power of sale foreclosure and mechanics' lien statutes. We have examined such current issues in mortgage drafting as due-on clauses, escrow accounts for taxes and insurance, prepayment fees, late charges, and rights to eminent domain and casualty insurance proceeds. We have dealt with the increasing federalization of mortgage law, as it is reflected in government agency regulation of lenders, prohibitions on lending discrimination, the strengthening of federally-sponsored mortgage market support institutions, and the pre-emption of state mortgage law. We have described the problems associated with the financing of condominiums and cooperative apartments, and we have attempted to analyze the special problems of construction lending.

We hope the present edition represents an optimum combination of old and new, with the inevitable compromises and deletions made on the wisest possible basis. For those who might have wished for a more thorough treatment of one topic or another, our apology must be based on the inherent limitations of a one-volume treatise. Since neither of us worked personally with George Osborne, we can only hope, but cannot be certain, that our work would have met with his approval. For us, the project has been a pleasant and productive experience which has greatly strengthened our mutual friendship and respect.

Much of our work has been done at the J. Reuben Clark Law School at Brigham Young University, Provo, Utah. Both of us have served on the BYU faculty, although neither is a permanent member of that faculty as of the publication date of this book. Our working conditions there have been virtually ideal, with excellent library and staff support. Since BYU's name does not appear on the title page, we feel a special obligation to thank the administration and staff there, as well as our faculty colleagues at BYU, for their support and encouragement. We also express our gratitude to the University of Missouri-Columbia and University of Washington Schools of Law for their significant support.

We have been blessed with research assistants of unusual caliber. They include Karen M. Johnson, N. Gregory Smith, Myrna South, and Grant Walker. The mistakes which may be found by readers must, of course, be laid at our feet and not theirs, but their help was invaluable. Many secretaries have made major contributions to the book, but special thanks must go to Marie Jensen of Brigham Young University for her superb efforts.

Finally, we express our gratitude to our wives, Judy Nelson and Marjorie Whitman, for their patience and forbearance during our travels, hours of telephone conversations, and time spent in collaboration.

G.S.N.
D.A.W.

February, 1979

*

SUMMARY OF CONTENTS

SUMMARY OF CONTENTS

TABLE OF CONTENTS

CHAPTER 1. AN INTRODUCTION TO THE LAW OF MORTGAGES

CHAPTER 2. THE NECESSITY AND NATURE OF THE OBLIGATION

CHAPTER 3. MORTGAGE SUBSTITUTES

A. RESTRICTING THE RIGHT TO REDEEM

B. THE ABSOLUTE DEED

TABLE OF CONTENTS

B. TORTIOUS INJURY TO LAND BY MORTGAGOR OR THIRD PERSONS

C. RIGHTS IN THE PRODUCT OF THE RES

D. ESCROWS OR RESERVES FOR TAXES AND INSURANCE

E. RIGHT TO RENTS

F. MORTGAGEE IN POSSESSION

G. RECEIVERSHIPS

H. ACQUISITION OF TITLE IN BREACH OF DUTY

CHAPTER 5. TRANSFER BY THE MORTGAGOR AND THE MORTGAGEE

A. TRANSFER BY THE MORTGAGOR

E. POWER OF SALE FORECLOSURE

F. DISPOSITION OF SURPLUS

CHAPTER 8. STATUTORY IMPACTS ON FORECLOSURE

A. REGULATION OF DEFICIENCY JUDGMENTS

B. STATUTORY REDEMPTION

C. THE SOLDIERS' AND SAILORS' CIVIL RELIEF ACT

D. BANKRUPTCY

TABLE OF CONTENTS

CHAPTER 9. SOME PRIORITY PROBLEMS

A. PURCHASE MONEY MORTGAGES AND AFTER-ACQUIRED PROPERTY CLAUSES

B. FIXTURES

CHAPTER 10. SUBROGATION, CONTRIBUTION, AND MARSHALING

A. SUBROGATION AND CONTRIBUTION

B. MARSHALING

CHAPTER 11. GOVERNMENT INTERVENTION IN THE MORTGAGE MARKET

CHAPTER 12. FINANCING REAL ESTATE CONSTRUCTION

CHAPTER 13. FINANCING CONDOMINIUMS AND COOPERATIVES

†

REAL ESTATE FINANCE LAW

CHAPTER 1

AN INTRODUCTION TO THE LAW OF MORTGAGES

Table of Sections

§ 1.1 The Basic Mortgage Transaction

The material in this volume focuses upon, in a variety of simple and sophisticated factual settings, the use of real estate as security for obligations. In this connection, there is a substantial emphasis on the real estate mortgage and its functional equivalents. As the term is used in its modern context, a real estate mortgage involves a transfer by a debtor-mortgagor to a creditor-mortgagee of a real estate interest, to be held as security for the performance of an obligation, normally the payment of a debt evidenced by the mortgagor's promissory note.

It is analytically useful, initially, to distinguish the purchase money transaction from other mortgage transactions. As will be seen later in this volume, the distinction between purchase money and non-purchase money mortgages is especially important in determining lien priorities.[1] A purchase money mortgage arises where the mortgagor's acquisition of the mortgaged real estate is financed by the mortgagee-lender. Often a seller of real estate will take back a purchase money mortgage for part of the purchase price. More commonly, however, a third party lending institution will take a mort-

1. See § 9.1, infra.

gage covering real estate acquired by the mortgagor with funds provided by the lending institution. In many states this is also treated as a purchase-money mortgage. Such transactions may be as simple as the purchase of a single family residence by a borrower-mortgagor or as complex and sophisticated as the construction and long term financing obtained by a developer to build a shopping center or an apartment building. In the non-purchase money situation the mortgagee-lender does not provide an acquistion loan but rather lends money on real estate already owned by the borrower-mortgagor. A corporation, for example, may often mortgage previously owned real estate to obtain money for expansion purposes. Or a long-time homeowner may give a mortgage to a lending institution on his home to secure a loan, the proceeds of which will be used to finance the college tuition of his children.

Today most mortgages are amortized or repaid over a substantial number of years. Until the 1930's most mortgages, however, were of the "balloon-note" type. Typically these were short-term mortgages for three or five years, and borrowers made only interest payments until the loan came due. Then if the borrower had not saved enough to pay the entire principal, he would expect the note to be renewed or would attempt to refinance it with another lender. However, during the depression period of the 1930's, many of these lenders were forced to demand full payment and to foreclose on properties when mortgagors could not pay. With the encouragement of the Federal Housing Administration and federal housing legislation, lenders during this period developed the amortized mortgage loan system under which mortgagors were permitted to repay loans over many years by making monthly principal and interest payments. Such loans are common today in both the housing and commercial real estate markets. However, as will be seen, much of the substantive law of mortgages developed prior to the advent of the long-term amortized real estate mortgage. In analyzing this substantive law, we should consider whether many of these principles do or should apply to modern long-term amortized mortgage loans.

Because the level-monthly-payment fully-amortized loan is so commonly employed in modern real estate financing, its characteristics are important to understand. The monthly payment is set so that only a portion (though a large portion in the early years) is needed to cover the interest which has accrued since the last preceding payment; the remainder of each payment is applied to reduce the outstanding principal. Thus, the interest which accrues in each month will be less than the interest for the preceding month, since interest is being computed on a continually declining principal amount.

This is best illustrated by an example. Assume that $36,000 is borrowed at an interest rate of 9%, and is to be paid off in monthly installments over 30 years. The loan proceeds are disbursed by the lender on January 1, 1980, and the borrower will make the first monthly payment one month later. Interest alone at the end of that first month would be $36,000 times ¾ of 1% (the monthly equivalent of 9% per annum), or $270.00. However, consultation of a mortgage payment table reveals that the full payment due (including both interest and amortization) is $289.66. The following table shows the effect of this payment and those which follow it:

Payment Date	Payment Amount	Credited to Interest	Credited to Principal	Principal Balance After Payment
Feb. 1, 1980	$289.66	$270.00	$19.66	$35,980.34
Mar. 1, 1980	289.66	269.85	19.81	35,960.53
Apr. 1, 1980	289.66	269.70	19.96	35,940.57
.	.	.	.	.
.	.	.	.	.
.	.	.	.	.
Jan. 1, 2010	289.66	2.16	287.50	–0–

The last payment, made at the end of the 360th month of the loan, will be approximately the amount necessary to entirely discharge the small sum still remaining on the principal balance. Thus, our choice of the amount originally specified for the monthly payments has been verified. Monthly payment amounts vary according to the original principal lent, loan term, and interest rate.

Several observations can be made about the level-payment amortized loan. The principal balance declines very slowly during the early years. Thus, after five years of regular payments on the loan in the foregoing example, the principal would be reduced to $34,517, a reduction of only $1483. Since principal amortization is in a sense a form of forced savings, some households might prefer to minimize, or even eliminate entirely, the amortization component. If a family wishes to sell the house in our example after five years, it will probably be easier for a prospective buyer to assume or take subject to the loan if its balance is still quite high.

Monthly payments obviously rise if the interest rate is increased; this effect can be quite startling. In our example, an interest rate of 10% (rather than the 9% we assumed) would raise the monthly payment by $26.27, to $315.93. These figures suggest something of the adverse impact high interest rates can have on demand for housing. Lengthening the loan term can reduce the monthly payments, but beyond about 30 or 40 years, the impact is not very great. In our example (with a 9% interest rate), increasing the maturity from 30 to 40 years would lower monthly payments by only $11.97, to $277.69. Further increases in maturity would bring the monthly payments somewhat closer to $270 per month, the interest-only level, which forms a "floor" below which payments cannot go no matter how long the loan term.

The level-payment amortized loan is most widely used in single-family home financing, and somewhat less so with commercial and industrial property. Even in residential financing, both the Federal Home Loan Bank Board [2] and the Department of Housing and Urban Development [3] authorize non-level-payment financing under limited circumstances, and some state regulatory agencies permit the making of variable interest loans which can result in monthly payment modifications over the life of the mortgage. However, these variants are currently being employed only on a modest scale, and the level-payment loan is likely to predominate for some years to come.

When a mortgage loan goes into default, normally the mortgagee has the right to "accelerate," which has the effect of making the entire debt due and payable.[4] The mortgagee may, under some circumstances, simply decide to proceed against the mortgagor personally and forego reliance on the mortgage security. Usually, however, the mortgagee will choose or will be required by law to foreclose the mortgage first. Although methods of foreclosure differ widely, under most circumstances there will be a sale of the mortgaged premises. The proceeds will be used to pay off the mortgage debt and the surplus, if any, will go to any subordinate lien-holders and the mortgagor. If the sale does not yield enough to cover the debt, the mortgagee will often be able to obtain a personal judgment for the deficiency against the mortgagor.

Where more than one mortgage exists on the same property, questions of priority become paramount. Suppose, for example, the mortgagor gave a $45,000 long-term first mortgage to a savings and loan association on Blackacre, which then was worth $50,000. Assume that after paying the mortgage down to about $40,000, the mortgagor borrows $8,000 from another lender and gives that lender a mortgage to secure the $8,000 debt. This is a second mortgage. Suppose that the first mortgage is foreclosed. What will the purchaser get and what will he pay for it? Here it is important to remember one of the basic functions of foreclosure—to put the foreclosure sale purchaser in the shoes of the mortgagor at the time he executed the mortgage being foreclosed. Thus, the purchaser will obtain a title that is free and clear of all mortgages or other liens junior or

2. 12 CFR 541.14(c), 545.6-1.

3. 24 CFR 203.45, added by 41 Fed. Reg. 42948 (Sept. 29, 1976). Unlike the FHLBB program, HUD permits monthly payments during the early years to be less than interest alone, thus necessitating the capitalization (addition to principal balance) of some unpaid interest, c.f., FHLBB Proposed Reg. permitting negative amortization and other innovations, 43 Fed.Reg. 33254 (July 31, 1978).

4. See § 7.6, infra.

subordinate to the mortgage being foreclosed. Accordingly, a sale purchaser, assuming that the market value of Blackacre free and clear of liens is still $50,000, will be willing to pay, at most, $50,000. For this he will get title free of the second mortgage. In other words, any junior liens are wiped out. If, however, the sale brings more than the $40,000 first mortgage debt, the second mortgagee should normally have a claim to the surplus superior to that of the mortgagor.[5]

Suppose, instead, that the first mortgage is not in default but that the second mortgage is and that the second mortgagee forecloses. What will the sale purchaser get and what will he pay for it? Again, remembering one of the basic functions of foreclosure discussed above, the sale should put the purchaser in the shoes of the mortgagor as of the time the mortgage being foreclosed was executed. Thus a purchaser will obtain fee title to Blackacre subject to the first mortgage. In other words, the foreclosure of a junior mortgage normally will not affect the status of a senior mortgage on the property.[6] Therefore, in calculating what a purchaser will bid, he will, at the very least, subtract from the market value of Blackacre free and clear of liens the amount of the first mortgage. Thus, assuming that this market value is still $50,000, the most the purchaser should bid is $10,000, the fair market value less the amount of the senior lien. Although the sale purchaser will not usually be personally liable on the first mortgage debt, if he does not pay it off he runs the risk that the first mortgage will be foreclosed and that he will lose his title to Blackacre.

§ 1.2 The Impact of English History

An understanding of the modern real estate mortgage requires, at least, a limited consideration of its historical antecedents. Although the mortgage has its roots in both Roman law and in early Anglo-Saxon England, the most significant developments for our purposes are the English common law mortgage and the effects on that mortgage of the subsequent intervention of English equity courts. These developments not only substantially influenced the substance of American mortgage law, but they are responsible for much of its terminology as well.[7]

Although the common law mortgage as it developed in the fourteenth and fifteenth centuries varied, in form it was essentially a conveyance of fee simple ownership, but the conveyance was expressly on condition subsequent. For example, assume B loans A $1,000. A

5. See §§ 7.31–7.32, infra.

6. For some instances where the foreclosure by a junior mortgagee may affect the senior mortgagee's options, but not his priority, see § 7.14, infra.

7. For a more complete analysis of the historical development of the modern real estate mortgage, see Osborne, Mortgages §§ 1–7 (2d Ed. 1970).

would convey Blackacre to B and his heirs, but on the condition that, if A repaid the $1,000 to B on a specified day, A would have the right to reenter and terminate B's estate. There were several important attributes to this transaction. B, the mortgagee, received legal title to the land and the normal incidents of that title. Perhaps the most striking and important feature of this mortgage is that the grantee, having legal title from the outset, got the incidents of that title even though unnecessary or even antagonistic to the sole purpose of the conveyance, namely, security for the performance of an act by the grantor. Thus the wife got dower until 1678; [8] the Rule in Shelley's case applied; [9] on the death of the mortgagee the property went to his heirs [10] or devisees; [11] creditors of the grantee could seize the property itself; [12] the mortgagee was entitled to all accretions to the property,[13] to compensation if the land was taken by eminent domain,[14] and to the title deeds; [15] he could bring actions against third parties and defend actions brought by them; [16] he might get the personal privilege of voting if he took possession; [17] his title would escheat; [18] and, most vital of all, he had the right to immediate possession.[19] Originally, the mortgagee used possession and the right to collect rents and profits as a method to get a return on his loan, since the taking of any interest was then considered to be usury and unlawful. Later the custom developed to leave the mortgagor in possession, although the mortgagee nevertheless retained the right to obtain possession. If he did obtain possession, however, he was required to account for the rents and profits on the mortgage debt.

The condition with provision for reentry was gradually displaced by a covenant by the mortgagee to reconvey upon full performance

8. Nash v. Preston, Cro.Car. 190 (1632). This led to the practice of giving mortgages of long terms of years. Co.Litt., § 332 n.; 2 Blackstone, 158. One advantage of these was that on the death of the mortgagee the term vested in the personal representatives instead of the heir. A disadvantage was that on default by the mortgagor the mortgagee did not get the fee.

9. Simes, Future Interests, 2d Ed., § 20 et seq.

10. Ex parte Morgan, 10 Ves. 101 (1804); see 2 Coote, Mortgages, 9th Ed., 863. By statute the legal estate of a deceased mortgagor now vests in his personal representatives. 44 & 45 Vict. c. 41, § 30.

11. A general devise of lands, unless a contrary intention appears, passes the legal interest of the mortgagee. Co. Litt., 205a n. However, see Littleton's Case, 1 Vern. 3 (1681).

12. Turner, The Equity of Redemption, XXXV, 52.

13. Doe v. Pott, 2 Doug. 710 (1781).

14. Ranken v. East and West India Docks Co., etc., 12 Beav. 298 (1849).

15. 2 Coote, supra note 10, at 835.

16. Pomeroy, Eq.Juris. § 1182.

17. 2 & 3 Will. IV c. 45, § 23; 6 & 7 Vict. c. 18, § 74.

18. Semble, Y.B. 5 Ed. IV, 18 pl., 7 b. See Turner, supra note 12, at 55.

19. A thorough discussion of all the cases may be found in Turner, supra note 12, at 88 et seq.

by the mortgagor. This covenant had a double operation. It was effective at law as a condition, and also was a promise which equity would enforce specifically. Its development apparently coincided with that of the equity of redemption referred to below, and its popularity was based upon the practical advantages of getting back by a reconveyance, instead of by reentry, the interest conveyed to the mortgagee. Regardless of which form was used, if the mortgagor failed to perform on the day set, the mortgagee's estate became absolute.

This common law mortgage was especially harsh on the mortgagor. The payment date was called the law day. Under the common law, if for any reason the payment was not made on that day, the mortgagor forfeited all interest in Blackacre. This was an absolute rule. It applied even if the mortgagor could not find the mortgagee to pay him. Time was strictly of the essence.

§ 1.3 The Intervention of Equity

The excesses and harshness of the common law mortgage inevitably yielded to the moderating influence of English Chancery. Intitially, equity intervened to aid the mortgagor who had failed promptly to perform on law day where the mortgagor could establish such traditional equitable grounds for relief as fraud, accident, misrepresentation, or duress. In other words, even though the mortgagee's rights at law were absolute, the mortgagor who had the financial capability to tender the amount due and owing could get his property back after law day so long as he could fit within the grounds described above. However, by the 17th century, the granting of such relief by equity became much more routine so that the mortgagor was able, as a matter of course and right, to redeem his land from the mortgagee if he tendered the principal and interest within a reasonable time after law day. It was no longer necessary to establish the more specific equitable grounds for relief. This right to tardy redemption was referred to as the mortgagor's equity of redemption and became recognized as an equitable estate in land.[20]

The mortgagor's right to tardy redemption obviously created a substantial problem for the mortgagee. Even though the mortgagor had defaulted, the mortgagee could never be reasonably sure that the mortgagor would not sue in equity to redeem. The mortgagee obviously needed to be relieved at some point of the threat of redemption. Thus, this same period saw the concurrent development in equity of the mortgagee's right to foreclosure. When the mortgagor failed to pay on law day or to bring a suit to redeem, at the request of the mortgagee in a bill setting forth the details of the mortgage and default, equity would order the mortgagor to pay the debt, inter-

20. For a more detailed consideration of the development of the equity of redemption, see Osborne, Mortgages, § 6 (2d Ed. 1970).

est and costs within a fixed period. Failure to comply with the decree meant that the mortgagor's right to redeem was forever barred. This type of foreclosure, which is little used today, is known as strict foreclosure because the land is forfeited to the mortgagee no matter what its value in relation to the original mortgage debt. No sale of the land is involved.

Whatever the original reasons for the chancellor's interventions, clearly the later equity view was that the mortgagee's interest was only security and intercession needed no other justification than to limit and protect it for that purpose. It is unlikely that the law courts did not recognize just as clearly as did the courts of equity that the parties intended the transaction to be one for security purposes only. The difficulty was that, although they saw it, they felt powerless to alter the design of the legal device chosen by the parties to achieve their purpose. So far as the law courts were concerned, since the parties had seen fit to have the entire legal title given as security (not absolutely, since the mortgagor could get it back by paying on a certain day), that was that. There were, however, no such limitations felt by the courts of equity, and consequently, they could superimpose upon the legal device various restrictions or additions so as to give to the mortgagee only that protection in regard to the property which they thought it necessary or desirable that he should have for the purpose of security. What this protection should be inevitably would be a compound of conflicting economic interests, contradictory social ideals, business expediency, feelings of "fairness" in the particular case, and attempts, justifiable or otherwise, at logical consistency with other legal rules, plus other miscellaneous considerations.

In developing this view of the mortgage as a security transaction the equitable theory of the nature and incidents of the mortgagor's interest in the property before default underwent considerable change. For one thing, the term "equity of redemption" which had previously and appropriately been applied to the mortgagor's right to get back his property after default was applied somewhat inappropriately to this entirely distinct equitable ownership before default. This, however, is merely a matter of nomenclature. But the analytical nature of the interest itself was the subject of serious and important inquiry and decision.

At first the mortgagor's interest was looked upon as a purely in personam right against the mortgagee, soon was perceived to be in rem, and finally was regarded as an equitable estate, a conception conforming to both popular and legal notions. For example, it could be cut into lesser estates; it had to be conveyed by a formal conveyance with formal limitations; it descended on to the heirs of the mortgagor; it could be devised, mortgaged, or entailed; and it prevailed against heirs, purchasers, and other successors of the mortgagee.

§ 1.4 The American Development

While strict foreclosure is theoretically available in a few states and in some relatively special situations in others, the major method of foreclosure in the United States today involves a public sale of the premises. There are two main types of sale foreclosure used in the United States today. The most common type is judicial foreclosure where a public sale results after a full judicial proceeding in which all interested persons must be made parties. In many states this is the sole method of foreclosure. It is time-consuming and costly. The other method of foreclosure is by power of sale. Under this method, after varying types and degrees of notice to the parties, the property is sold at a public sale, either by some public official such as a sheriff, by the mortgagee, or by some other third party. No judicial proceeding is required in a power of sale foreclosure. It is generally available only where the mortgage instrument authorizes it. As we shall see later in this volume, it raises serious constitutional problems.[21]

It is important to remember that as a general proposition, the mortgagor cannot lose his equity of redemption (or equity of tardy redemption, as it is sometimes called) unless there has been a valid foreclosure of the mortgage. In other words, even though the mortgage is in substantial default, normally no agreement of the parties in the mortgage, or contemporaneous with it, can cut off a recalcitrant mortgagor's rights in the mortgaged property without the mortgagee resorting to foreclosure. This concept, which will be considered in greater detail later, is sometimes referred to as the *prohibition against clogging the mortgagor's equity of redemption.*

Suppose, however, that there has been a valid foreclosure and that the mortgagor's equity of redemption has been cut off. Some states, by a variety of legislative methods, have created something called *statutory redemption.* This type of redemption becomes available *only* when the equity of redemption has been effectively cut off by a valid foreclosure. Statutory redemption, as we will see later, varies widely from state to state.[22] In general, however, these statutes permit the mortgagor and sometimes his creditors and junior lienors to redeem after the sale for various periods of time as short as a few months in some states to as long as 18 months or more in a few others. The statutory right of redemption was created, in part, to afford the mortgagor or other person entitled to exercise the right additional time to refinance and save his property, but mainly to put pressure on the mortgagee to bid the value of the property at the foreclosure sale, at least up to the amount of the mortgage debt. To enforce this purpose the redemption amount is usually the *sale price* and *not the mortgage debt.* A secondary purpose of these statutes in some states is to allow an additional period of possession to a hard-

21. See §§ 7.23–7.30, infra.

22. See §§ 8.4–8.7, infra.

pressed mortgagor. The operation and effectiveness of these statutes will be analyzed in greater detail later in this volume. The important thing to remember at this point is that statutory redemption normally begins *only* after the mortgagor's equity of redemption has been validly terminated by foreclosure.

§ 1.5 The Title, Lien, and Intermediate Theories of Mortgage Law

Three "theories" of mortgage law exist today in the United States. One of these, the *title theory*,[23] has its roots in the English Common Law mortgage discussed earlier. Under this theory, legal "title" is always in the mortgagee until the mortgage has been satisfied or foreclosed. While the states that recognize this theory have for the most purposes treated the mortgagee as simply holding a security interest, the mortgagee's "title" does appear to give him the right to possession. Under the more predominant *lien theory*,[24] however, the mortgagee holds no "title" but has security only. The mortgagor, accordingly, has the right to possession until there has been a valid foreclosure. The so-called *intermediate theory*[25] gives the right to possession to the mortgagor at least until default, and generally to the mortgagee after default. The lien theory states, with such exceptions as New York and South Carolina, tend to be west of the Mississippi, and the title and intermediate theory states in the east. Lien theory states have rejected the mortgagee's possessory rights, either by judicial decision or by statute.[26]

While the three theories have tended to interest academics more than practitioners, in certain situations they can prove to have important practical significance. It may come as a surprise that a mortgagee would want possession of the mortgaged premises prior to foreclosure. Most mortgagees, after all, are primarily in the lending business and do not view themselves as managers of real estate. Indeed, in every jurisdiction the mortgagor, at least initially, is in possession of the premises. Then why is the right to possession significant? Primarily because it carries with it not only the right to protect the premises against waste, but more importantly, the right to collect rents and profits. The mortgagee, however, must *account* for any such rents and profits on the mortgage debt.

There may be occasions when a mortgagee may wish to bring ejectment to obtain possession of the premises. Suppose, for exam-

23. See § 4.1, infra.

24. See § 4.2, infra.

25. See § 4.3, infra.

26. For a consideration of the three theories, see Kratovil, Mortgages—Problems in Possession, Rents, and Mortgagee Liability, 11 DePaul L.Rev. 1 (1961); Gavit, Under the Lien Theory of Mortgages is the Mortgage Only a Power of Sale? 15 Minn.L. Rev. 147 (1931); Sturges and Clark, Legal Theory and Real Property Mortgages, 37 Yale L.J. 691 (1928); Comment, Real Estate Mortgage Theory in Missouri, 6 Mo.L.Rev. 200 (1941).

ple, that the foreclosure proceedings in a particular state are so lengthy that it may take up to three years to bring a foreclosure to successful culmination. Suppose further that a defaulted mortgage on commercial real estate is involved and that the mortgagor is so financially weak as to be judgment-proof. If the mortgagee can gain possession prior to foreclosure, deterioration or destruction of the security can be prevented and the mortgagee will be able to prevent the rents and profits from being diverted to purposes other than payment of the mortgage. Indeed, as we shall see later, the mortgagee may wish to have a receiver appointed to accomplish essentially the same purposes and, to some extent, the mortgage theory followed may influence availability of the receivership remedy. Moreover, many mortgagees attempt to draft around the lien theory by providing mortgage clauses which purport to give the mortgagee a present assignment of the rents and profits. As later material in this volume will illustrate, the seriousness with which a particular jurisdiction views the lien theory will influence the validity of such provisions.

§ 1.6 The Deed of Trust as a Mortgage Variant

In many states the deed of trust represents the most commonly used mortgage instrument. This device normally involves a conveyence of the realty to a third person in trust to hold as security for the payment of the debt to the lender-noteholder whose role is analogous to that of the mortgagee. Deeds of trust will almost always contain a power of sale in the trustee to be exercised after a default at the request of the lender-noteholder. Such a deed of trust is essentially similar to a mortgage with a power of sale. Indeed, in many states the same statutes regulating foreclosure of power of sale mortgages are applicable to deeds of trust as well. Most courts today are inclined to treat a deed of trust like a mortgage for other purposes as well. However, this form of mortgage sometimes can create special problems which force courts into detailed analysis of the similarities and differences between the two types of instruments. The following language of the Supreme Court of California in Bank of Italy National Trust & Savings Ass'n v. Bentley,[27] illustrates some of the problems the use of both the deed of trust and the normal mortgage can pose in a given jurisdiction:

> At common law and, in fact, in nearly every state in the United States, a deed of trust, both in legal effect and in theory, is deemed to be a mortgage with a power of sale, and differs not at all from a mortgage with a power of sale. * * * In Idaho, a state that has adopted nearly all of our Code sections on security transaction, it has been held that a

27. 217 Cal. 644, 20 P.2d 940 (1933), certiorari denied 290 U.S. 659, 54 S. Ct. 74, 78 L.Ed.2d 571.

> deed of trust is a mortgage with power of sale. Brown v. Bryan, 6 Idaho, 1, 51 p. 995. If California had followed this common law rule, there would be no dispute over the question now involved. It would necessarily follow that a deed of trust is a mortgage with power of sale. * * * The real difficulty is caused by the fact that the courts of this state have not followed the common law rule. Although, as already pointed out, this state, at an early date, adopted the "lien" theory of mortgages, it adopted the "title" theory in reference to deeds of trust. In the early case of Koch v. Briggs, 14 Cal. 256, 73 Am.Dec. 651, it was held that mortgages and deeds of trust were fundamentally different, in that in a mortgage only a "lien" was created, while in a deed of trust, "title" actually passed to the trustee. This distinction, although frequently attacked by counsel and often criticized by the courts, has become well settled in our law and cannot now be disturbed. * * * Thus we have in this state a type of instrument partaking of many of the characteristics of a mortgage, but for other purposes treated as a separate type of security. Two lines of authority have developed as a result, one group of cases emphasizing the distinctions between the two types of security, the other group emphasizing the similarity between the two. Thus it has been held that a deed of trust differs from a mortgage in that title passes to the trustee in case of a deed of trust, while, in the case of a mortgage, the mortgagor retains title; that the statute of limitations never runs against the power of sale in a deed of trust, while it does run against a mortgage; and that a mortgagor has a statutory right of redemption after foreclosure (Code Civ.Proc. 702), while no such right exists under a deed of trust. * * *
>
> As opposed to these cases, there have been an increasing number of cases which, although recognizing that "title" passes in the case of a deed of trust, emphasize the fact that the function and purpose of the two types of security are identical, and, for that reason, apply the same rules to deeds of trust that are applied to mortgages. These cases hold that in legal effect, although perhaps not in theory, deeds of trust are similar to mortgages with a power of sale. * * *

It is important not to overemphasize such problems, however, because in most important respects the substantive law of mortgages is equally applicable to deeds of trust. Thus, aside from the foregoing, consideration of deeds of trust will, for the most part, be integrated into our coverage of major problems of mortgage law rather than treated separately. On the other hand, where the substantive law is different from that governing straight mortgages or where there are important problems unique to the deed of trust, those areas will be considered specially.

§ 1.7 Mortgage Substitutes and Clogging the Equity of Redemption

From the mortgagee's viewpoint, the equity of redemption is irritating and undesirable; he would prefer, in the event of the mortgagor's default, simply to have the power to assert and keep fee simple title to the realty. Since the courts do not allow such "clogging" by mortgage language, mortgagees have sometimes resorted to other forms of documents, which we term "mortgage substitutes",[28] to achieve this result. Note, however, that the deed of trust was *not* developed for this purpose; a trustor under a deed of trust has the same equity of redemption as a mortgagee. The rise of the deed of trust is probably attributable to the desire of lenders for legal power to foreclose by power of sale, and simultaneously to be bidders, in effect, at their own sales; the latter power was often prohibited when an ordinary mortgage was foreclosed under a power of sale.[29]

The remainder of this section is concerned with devices which mortgagees do employ in attempts to avoid the consequences of the mortgagor's equity of tardy redemption. For example, a grantee-mortgagee may take an absolute deed on Blackacre from a grantor-mortgagor with the oral understanding that if the underlying debt is paid, there will be a reconveyance of Blackacre to the grantor-mortgagor. In the event the debt is not paid, however, the theory of this device is that the grantee-mortgagee retains title to Blackacre without the problems of foreclosure. This basic transaction may take numerous forms. There may, for example, be a written agreement to reconvey; "such a written agreement to reconvey may take the form of an option to repurchase, an unconditional contract obligating the grantee to reconvey and the grantor to repurchase, or a lease-back to the grantor with an option to repurchase at or before the end of the term." [30] As we shall see later in this volume,[31] however, courts have freely permitted the grantor-mortgagor to establish, by parol testimony or otherwise, that such transactions are actually mortgages, with the result that they are often of dubious value in circumventing the mortgagor's equity of tardy redemption and other substantive mortgage law rights.

The most commonly used substitute for the mortgage or deed of trust as a land financing device is the installment land contract. This device is also known variously as the contract for deed or the long term land contract. The installment land contract and the purchase

28. See Chapter 3, infra.

29. See e. g., Dingus, Mortgages—Redemption After Foreclosure Sale in Missouri, 25 Mo.L.Rev. 261, 282 (1960); § 7.21, infra.

30. Cunningham and Tischler, Disguised Real Estate Security Transactions as Mortgages in Substance, 26 Rutgers L.Rev. 1 (1973).

31. See §§ 3.5, 3.17, infra.

money mortgage carry out the same economic function—the financing by the seller of the unpaid portion of the purchase price of the real estate. Under the installment land contract, the vendee normally goes into possession and agrees to make monthly installment payments of principal and interest until the principal balance is paid off. The vendor retains legal title until the final payment is made, at which time he has a duty to execute a deed to the land. Such contracts may be amortized over varying time periods as short as two or three years or as long as twenty years. During the period of the contract, the vendee will usually be required to pay the taxes, maintain casualty insurance and keep the premises in good repair.

The main advantage to a vendor under a land contract presumably is that upon the default of the vendee, the vendor, by summary proceedings analogous to strict foreclosure, may keep the land and all installments paid, and possibly even sue for future installments as they fall due if the contract so provides, with vendee having no equity of tardy redemption. Because these devices are often perceived to be "pro-vendor," they are used a great deal, especially in states where foreclosure of a straight mortgage is cumbersome and time-consuming. However, as we shall see later in this volume,[32] because statutes and judicial decisions have substantially enhanced the rights of the defaulted vendee it is doubtful in many states that such contracts can achieve their intended purpose for the vendor, at least where there is a vendee actively asserting his rights.

32. See §§ 3.25–3.32, infra.

§§ 1.8–2.0 are reserved for supplementary material.

CHAPTER 2

THE NECESSITY AND NATURE OF THE OBLIGATION

Table of Sections

§ 2.1 Necessity of Obligation

While it is axiomatic that a mortgage is security for the performance of an act, it is not clear whether there must be a personal obligation by someone to perform the act. A personal obligation to perform the act was essential to the classical common law mortgage.[1] Moreover, there is today still substantial case authority holding or stating that a mortgage cannot exist without an obligation which it secures.[2]

1. See generally Osborne, Mortgages, § 102 (2d Ed. 1970).

2. See Morvay v. Drake, 325 So.2d 165 (Ala.1976); Bruckman v. Breitenbush Hot Springs, Inc., 271 Or. 1, 534 P.2d 971 (1975); Coon v. Shry, 209 Cal. 612, 289 P. 815 (1930); Kuhne v. Gau, 134 Minn. 34, 163 N.W. 982 (1917); Tyler v. Wright, 122 Me. 558, 119 A. 583 (1923); Cotten, Trustee v. Graham, 84 Ky. 672, 2 S.W. 647, 8 Ky. Law Rep. 658 (1887); Burr v. Beckler, 264 Ill. 230, 106 N.E. 206 (1914); Beck v. Sheldon, 259 N.Y. 208, 181 N.E. 360 (1932); Baird v. Baird, 145 N.Y. 659, 40 N.E. 222, 28 L.R.A. 375 (1895); Weich v. Graham, 124 N.Y.S. 945 (1910), affirmed 148 App.Div. 900, 132 N.Y.S. 1150 (1911) and 21 N.Y. 637, 105 N.E. 1102 (1914); McCourt v. Peppard, 126 Wis. 326, 105 N.W. 809 (1905); Bernheim v. Pessou, 143 La. 609, 79 So. 23 (1917); Perkins v. Trinity Realty Co., 69 N.J.Eq. 723, 727, 61 A. 167 (1905), affirmed 71 N.J.Eq. 304, 71 A. 1135 (1909).

See also Smith v. Haertel, 125 Colo. 348, 353, 244 P.2d 377, 379 (1952). Cf. Standard Fire Ins. Co. v. Fuller, 90 U.S.App.D.C. 300, 195 F.2d 782 (1952), noted, 101 U. of Pa.L.Rev. 286 (1952), no mortgage interest under the "Standard Mortgage Clause" where note secured is invalid. And see Validity of a Mortgage Intended as a Gift, 39 Iowa L.Rev. 195 (1953), discussing De Penning v. Bedell, 242 Iowa 102, 44 N.W.2d 385 (1950); Sterling, Validity of "Myself" Notes and Deeds of Trust, 30 Rocky Mt.L. Rev. 195 (1958); Karesh, Security Transactions in Survey of South Carolina Law, 10 S.C.L.Rev. 114, 124 (1957), noting Johnston v. Farmers and Merchants Bank, 229 S.C. 603, 93 S.E.2d 916 (1956).

In 1956, the Supreme Court of Indiana, in Egbert v. Egbert, 235 Ind. 405, 132 N.E.2d 910 (1956) criticized by Updike, Mortgages, in 1956 Annual Survey of American Law, 32 N.Y.U.L. Rev. 789, 791 (1957) held that, since a mortgage cannot exist without an obligation to be secured, a deed-in-lieu-of-foreclosure, which operated as an accord and satisfaction of the debt, wiped out the mortgage. That there must be debt as basis of an equitable mortgage under Kansas law, see Note, 13 Kan.L.Rev. 585, 587, 588 (1965).

Some of these cases, however, may be explainable for collateral reasons. For example, some of the cases which hold the mortgage unenforceable because the obligation is invalid for lack of consideration may be explained on the ground that the intention was that the mortgage should secure a certain note or obligation and, consequently, would not be enforceable if that note or obligation failed for want of consideration. The giving of a note or bond along with the mortgage, especially if coupled with the usual recital in the mortgage that it secures the note, or a similar recital in the note that it is secured by the mortgage is, in itself, an indication that this was the intention of the parties.[3]

Cases in which the mortgage is in the form of a deed absolute constitute another group in which the existence of a debt has been held vital.[4] In these cases, since the central question is whether a mortgage is intended in spite of the transaction being cast in the form of an absolute transfer or a transfer with a resale agreement, optional or absolute, there are considerations not present when the transaction takes the regular mortgage form.[5] In them the courts might well insist more rigidly upon a debt as a guarantee of mortgage *intent*. In the latter case, as between the parties, the intent in regard to the nature of the transaction is clear and the questions to decide are whether there can be a mortgage without a personal obligation, or whether, even if there can be, the parties intended this particular mortgage to be binding regardless of the validity of the personal duty. Both of these questions have been obscured in the cases by the entirely distinct one of whether, as between the parties, a mortgage requires consideration, and this, in turn, is confused with problems of precedence and validity against third parties, i. e., matters of priority, actual and constructively fraudulent conveyances, estoppel, and the doctrine of *bona fide* purchase. There is also a failure to segregate the necessity of consideration for the transfer or creation of the security interest in the property from the necessity of consideration for the creation of the obligation secured.[6]

3. Among such cases are Hannan v. Hannan, 123 Mass. 441, 25 Am.Rep. 121 (1877); Saunders v. Dunn, 175 Mass. 164, 55 N.E. 893 (1900); Anderson v. Lee, 73 Minn. 397, 76 N.W. 24 (1898); Brooks v. Owen, 112 Mo. 251, 19 S.W. 723 (1892), reversed on rehearing 112 Mo. 315, 20 N.W. 492 (1884); Cawley v. Kelly, 60 Wis. 315, 19 N.W. 65 (1884).

4. Conway v. Alexander, 11 U.S. (7 Cr.) 218, 3 L.Ed. 321 (1812), (in holding the transaction a conditional sale rather than a mortgage Marshall, C. J., said: "It is * * * a necessary ingredient in a mortgage, that the mortgagee should have a remedy against the person of the debtor"); Henley v. Hotaling, 41 Cal. 22 (1871) (option to repurchase insufficient); Caraway v. Sly, 222 Ill. 203, 78 N.E. 588 (1906) (option to repurchase insufficient); Holmberg v. Hardee, 90 Fla. 787, 108 So. 211 (1925); Holmes v. Warren, 145 Cal. 457, 78 P. 954 (1904); 1 Jones, Mortgages (8th ed.) §§ 309, 311, 316; 3 Pomeroy, Equity Juris. (4th ed.) §§ 1195, 1192, 1196. See 20 Ill.L.Rev. 732 (1926). See Fogelman, The Deed Absolute as a Mortgage in New York, 37 Fordham L.Rev. 299, 306 (1963).

5. See §§ 3.3–3.15, infra.

6. See § 2.3, infra.

Another group of authorities relied upon holds executed and recorded mortgages to secure optional future advances void until the advances are made as against a subsequent purchaser from the grantor on the ground that a debt is essential to a mortgage.[7]

Moreover, the general rule requiring a personal obligation is subject to several qualifications and modifications. "Thus, a mortgage to secure the debt of a third person, the mortgagor being subject to no obligation, is clearly valid." [8] It is also thoroughly settled that an express provision in the mortgage that there shall be no personal liability for the debt or claim on the mortgagor or any other person, the creditor limiting his rights to enforcing his interest in the land under the mortgage, is valid and effective.[9] In these cases, although it is

7. Ladue v. Detroit & Milwaukee R. Co., 13 Mich. 380, 87 Am.Dec. 759 (1865) ("* * * the mortgage instrument, without any present debt, liability or obligation secured by it, can have no present legal effect as a mortgage * * * and it can make no difference in the result whether there has once been a debt or liability which has been satisfied, or whether the debt or liability to be served has not yet been created * * * as in this case. * * *"). See Freutel v. Schmitz, 299 Ill. 320, 323, 132 N.E. 534, 535 (1921) ("A mortgage is security for a debt, and, without a debt, it has no effect as a lien. * * * If there is no mortgage debt in existence, there is nothing for the mortgage to operate on, and the lien begins only when money is advanced or the contemplated debt comes into existence in the course of dealing between the parties.").

However, cf. West's Ann.Cal.Civ.Code § 2884 (A lien may be created by contract to take immediate effect, as security for the performance of obligations not then in existence). Cases like Ackerman v. Hunsicker, 85 N.Y. 43, 39 Am.R. 621 (1881), upholding a recorded mortgage for optional advances to the amount of advances made as against subsequent claims in the property acquired before the advances, are not necessarily opposed. The court in that case admitted that no mortgage existed as a charge upon the land until the optional future obligation arose but, for other reasons postponed it to judgment liens arising after recordation but before the option was exercised. As will be pointed out later, the true situation in these mortgages for future advances is that the obligation secured exists in practically every case, prior to any advances and regardless of whether the advances are optional or obligatory. It is the present binding promise to repay the advances made in the future. If there were no consideration for this promise there would, of course, be no obligation. Seldom, if ever, would this be the case even where the future advances are optional. For further consideration of mortgages to secure future advances and the above problems, see § 12.7, infra.

8. Halderman v. Woodward, 22 Kan. 734 (1879); Garretson Inv. Co. v. Arndt, 144 Cal. 64, 77 P. 770 (1904); Theodore v. Mozie, 230 S.C. 216, 95 S.E.2d 173 (1956), 10 S.C.L.Rev. 114, 123 (1957).

Even though the notes of a third party for which the mortgage was given as security are void because they are in violation of the Bankruptcy Act, the mortgage has been held valid. Amherst Factors, Inc. v. Kochenburger, 4 N.Y.2d 203, 173 N.Y.S. 570, 149 N.E. 2d 863 (1958), discussed in, 8 Buffalo L.Rev. 102 (1958).

9. Seieroe v. First Nat. Bank of Kearney, 50 Neb. 612, 70 N.W. 220 (1897); Weikel v. Davis, 109 Wash. 97, 186 P. 323 (1919); Wells v. Flynn, 191 Iowa 1322, 184 N.W. 389, 17 A.L.R. 710 (1921); Rice v. Rice, 21 Mass. (4 Pick.) 349 (1826), are typical. See 17 A.L.R. 717 (1922); Parks, Cas. on Mort., 96 n. 1. McKinney's Real Property Law of N.Y. § 249, provides that "A mortgage of real property does not imply a covenant for the payment of the sum intended to be secured; and where such covenant is not expressed in the mortgage, or

possible to conceive of the agreement as merely limiting the remedy of collection to certain property or, perhaps, to regard it as creating a duty of imperfect obligation,[10] it is also possible to construe it as negativing the existence of any independent obligation except insofar as the land itself can be looked upon as owing a "real" obligation.[11] Further, barring an action to enforce the personal liability of the mortgagor by the statute of limitations does not affect, in some states, the validity of the mortgage.[12] The same is true of a discharge from personal obligation by bankruptcy proceedings.[13] Finally, there is authority that a mortgage is valid by way of gift where, because of lack of consideration, no personal obligation ever arose or where, for some other reason, it is clear there is in existence no independent obligation for the mortgage to secure.[14] It has been argued

a bond or other separate instrument to secure such payment has not been given, the remedies of the mortgagee are confined to the property mentioned in the mortgage." West's Ann.Cal.Civ.Code § 2928, is similar. See Van Brunt v. Mismer, 8 Minn. 232, Gil. 202 (1863); Demond v. Crary, 9 F. 750, 752 (C.C.N.Y.1882). See also Restatement, Security, § 1(b). A mortgage to secure the obligation of a trustee limited to his liability *qua* trustee is good. In re Robinson's Settlement, 81 L.J.Ch.Div. 393 (1912). See Coote, Mortgages, 9th Ed., 11. In 1956 the Illinois Court of Appeals, in Bedian v. Cohn, 10 Ill. App.2d 116, 134 N.E.2d 532 (1956), commented on by Updike, Mortgages in 1956 Annual Survey of American Law, 32 N.Y.U.L.Rev. 789, 790 (1956), held that documents may effectively provide that the mortgagor shall not be personally liable without affecting the validity of the mortgage.

10. See Williston, and Thompson, Contracts, Rev.Ed., § 16; Restatement, Contracts, § 14. Similar cases of personal substantive obligations recognized as existing but with remedies curtailed or unavailable are (1) mortgages in states with valid "no deficiency" statutes, (2) quasi in rem actions against absent defendants who have property in the jurisdiction, (3) broad exemption statutes covering all of the debtor's property within the jurisdiction, (4) a non-assuming grantee of mortgaged property in the state with the mortgagor-transferor out of the state or with the remedy against him barred by statute of limitations, etc.

11. See 3 Tiffany, Real Property, 2d Ed. § 607 ("the debt being in such case regarded as due by the land itself"); Walsh, Mortgages, § 16 ("a mortgage * * * may create a real obligation in a business transaction with an express provision excluding any personal obligation on which the mortgagor may be held liable.").

12. See § 6.9, infra.

13. Bush v. Cooper, 26 Miss. 599, 59 Am.Dec. 270 (1853), affirmed 59 U.S. 82, 15 L.Ed. 273; Brown v. Hoover, 77 N.C. 40 (1877); Wilson v. Russell, 13 Md. 494, 71 Am.Dec. 645 (1859).

14. Goethe v. Gmelin, 256 Mich. 112, 239 N.W. 347 (1931) (note and mortgage intended as gift, note void for want of consideration. The court placed the decision on the ground that no consideration is necessary for a mortgage and did not discuss the lack of an obligation to be secured). Cf. Cooklin v. Cooklin, 260 Mich. 69, 244 N.W. 232 (1932), in which the court said that "it is not necessary that a mortgage be accompanied by a note provided the mortgage itself contains a promise to pay" and treated the Goethe case, inferentially, as not involving any question other than the necessity of consideration for the mortgage which secures the debt. Other cases more clearly holding no obligation necessary are Cook v. Johnson, 165 Mass. 245, 43 N.E. 96 (1896) (instruction that transaction was a mortgage not inconsistent with verdict that no debt existed because conveyance extinguished the personal obligation); Matthews v. Sheehan, 69

that, regardless of theory and authorities, the existence of a personal obligation in most modern mortgages is of no practical importance and not only should be but is ignored.[15]

It is possible to distinguish between (1) the cases where the mortgage was attempted as a gift and no personal obligation ever arose because of lack of consideration, and (2) those cases in which a debt or other obligation is created with the property as security for it but there is (a) a limitation on the enforcement of the personal duty, by agreement or by rules of law, or (b) a release of the personal obligation with rights in the mortgaged property reserved by agreement, (e. g., (i) the mortgagee releases the mortgagor in the usual two party agreement, (ii) the mortgagee releases the mortgagor after the latter has conveyed to a non-assuming grantee, but by agreement with both mortgagor and grantee reserves all rights against the mortgaged property, (iii) the mortgagee releases the debtor from personal liability in a case in which the property was given in mortgage by a third party, but by agreement with the mortgagor the release of the debt is not to affect the rights of the mortgaged land).

In the gift cases, a suggested test of validity is whether the parties *intended* the mortgage to secure a debt or other personal obligation.[16] Almost universally that is the intent, and in such cases if the obligation does not arise the mortgage should not because that is the intention. The court would never reach the question whether there *could* be a mortgage without a personal obligation. Further, since only a sporadic case could not be decided on this reasoning, the ultimate question in this type of case may be regarded as of theoretical rather than practical importance.

In the second group, the parties' intention usually is express and entirely clear. They mean the mortgage to remain valid in spite of restrictions upon the enforcement or even the complete extinction of

N.Y. 585 (1877) (deed absolute with only an option to repurchase); Rice v. Rice, 21 Mass. (4 Pick.) 349 (1826) (deed absolute, no personal duty to pay); Mooney v. Byrne, 163 N.Y. 86, 57 N.E. 163 (1900) (deed absolute, no covenant to pay and agreement for no deficiency, but court said there was a debt); Niggeler v. Maurin, 34 Minn. 118, 24 N.W. 369 (1885) (deed absolute, no covenant for payment). See Pearson v. Mulloney, 289 Mass. 508, 194 N.E. 458 (1935) (dictum only, second mortgage "subject to" first mortgage estopped to deny validity of first mortgage); Campbell v. Tompkins, 32 N.J.Eq. 170 (1880) (dictum, want of consideration for bond secured held closed to inquiry); Fisk v. Stewart, 24 Minn. 97 (1877) (dictum, debt existed); Campbell v. Dearborn, 109 Mass. 130, 12 Am.Rep. 671 (1872) (dictum in deed absolute case; debt existed); In re Robinson's Settlement, 81 L.J.Ch. 393 (1912) (dictum); Ministers Life & Cas. Union v. Franklin Park Towers Corp., 239 N.W.2d 207 (Minn.1976) (dictum). See also Walsh, Mortgages, 75 n. 2; Coote, Mortgages, 9th Ed., 11; 2 Wis.L.Rev. 60 (1922) 14 Tex.L.Rev. 560 (1936); 31 Mich.L.Rev. 102, 105 (1932); 58 N.J.L.J. 1; 4 St. John's L. Rev. 276 (1930).

15. See Wiltsie, Mortgage Foreclosure, 5th ed., § 1; see also, Ministers Life & Cas. Union v. Franklin Park Towers Corp., 239 N.W.2d 207 (Minn.1976).

16. Walsh, Mortgages, §§ 16, 17d.

the personal obligation which existed at the outset and which the property without question was intended to secure. Whether effect can be given to the intention in this last, extreme case is of more than academic interest. Since there is no guesswork about intention, since the agreement is entered into subsequent to the creation of the mortgage and therefore the most valid reasons for scrutinizing or restricting agreements is absent, and since the problem is clearly presented so that all arguments will be faced squarely, it would seem that only the most rigid, mechanical conceptualism would defeat the agreement.

§ 2.2 Nature of the Obligation

Any obligation capable of being reduced to a money amount may be secured by a mortgage.[17] Thus, unliquidated debts such as open book accounts and contingent obligations that are uncertain in amount, such as indemnity bonds, may be secured by a mortgage on real estate.[18] Moreover, promises to build a driveway and a sewer line on mortgagor's land and to build an apartment house have been held to be mortgagable.[19]

It is doubtful that an obligation that is incapable of reduction to a money equivalent can be secured by a mortgage. There are several reasons for this. First, in the event of a foreclosure sale, the purchaser, of course, would presumably bid what the real estate is worth. However, unless the mortgage debt is reducible to a money amount, it would be impossible to determine a deficiency or to allocate surplus among junior lienors, if any, or to the mortgagor.[20] Second, creditors of the mortgagor would face the same uncertainty in attempting to enforce a judgment against the mortgaged real estate. Third, mortgagees would have difficulty in assigning the mortgagee's interest. Finally, mortgagors would find it extremely difficult to obtain second mortgage financing where potential lenders are unable to ascertain the value of any prior lien against the land.

17. Stub v. Belmont, 20 Cal.2d 208, 124 P.2d 826 (1942) (consignment contract); Cook v. Bartholomew, 60 Conn. 24, 22 A. 444, 13 L.R.A. 452 (1891) (promise to support during life); Dover Lumber Co. v. Case, 31 Idaho 276, 170 P. 108 (1918) (faithful performance of a contract to cut and deliver timber). See West's Ann.Cal. Civ.Code § 2920. Contra, Bethlehem v. Annis, 40 N.H. 34, 77 Am.Dec. 700 (1860) ("Wherever the condition, when broken, gives rise to no claim for damages whatever, or to a claim for unliquidated damages, the deed is not to be regarded as a mortgage in equity * * * ").

18. Merills v. Swift, 18 Conn. 257, 46 Am.Dec. 315 (1847); Emerson v. Knight, 130 Ga. 100, 60 S.E. 255 (1908); McDaniels v. Colvin, 16 Vt. 300, 42 Am.Dec. 512 (1844); Fidelity and Deposit Co. v. Oliver, 57 Wash. 31, 106 P. 483 (1910).

19. Application of Jeffrey Towers, Inc., 57 Misc.2d 46, 291 N.Y.S.2d 41 (1968).

20. Id.

One of the promises in a New York case illustrates this problem. There the mortgagor, among other things, agreed to consent to any applications for variances, changes of zone or special exception uses with respect to the mortgagee's land. The court believed that this promise was not capable of being secured by a mortgage because its monetary value was highly speculative.[21]

Mortgages to secure promises for support pose special problems. Two peculiarities of the normal agreement for support secured by a mortgage of land, i. e., that performance is to be by the mortgagor personally and out of the use of the property, make it inadvisable to apply to it all of the ordinary rules of mortgage law and have even caused some doubt as to whether it should be classified as a mortgage at all.[22] Thus, even if default is unintentional and causes no irreparable harm the mortgagor will not be permitted to redeem.[23] Although the mortgagee may obtain or accept damages in lieu of the promised support, he cannot be forced to take them.[24] The mortgagee cannot assign the mortgage,[25] and not only is the mortgagor unable to transfer the property without the mortgagee's consent[26] but creditors of the mortgagor cannot reach it except subject to possession being retained by the mortgagor until the purpose of the mortgage has been fulfilled.[27]

§ 2.3 The Necessity of Consideration

There is substantial confusion as to the necessity of consideration to support a valid mortgage. The legal mortgage itself is an executed conveyance and no more requires consideration than any other executed transfer of property.[28] This is obviously true of the com-

21. Id.

22. See Bethlehem v. Annis, 40 N.H. 34, 77 Am.Dec. 700 (1861); Soper v. Guernsey, 71 Pa. 219, 221 (1872).

Typically the agreement is an intra-family one with the mortgagee elderly or feeble. And, since to permit the mortgagee to take possession would deprive the mortgagor of the means by which it was contemplated he was to carry out his obligation, the mortgagor is held to have the right to possession. Flanders v. Lamphear, 9 N.H. 201 (1838); Rhoades v. Parker, 10 N.H. 83 (1839); Colman v. Packard, 16 Mass. 39 (1819), contra.

23. Bryant v. Erskine, 55 Me. 153, 157 (1867); Henry v. Tupper, 29 Vt. 358 (1857); Dunklee v. Adams, 20 Vt. 415, 50 Am.Dec. 44 (1848); Rowell v. Jewett, 69 Me. 293, 301 (1879).

24. Cook v. Bartholomew, 60 Conn. 24, 22 A. 444, 13 L.R.A. 452 (1891); Ridley v. Ridley, 87 Me. 445, 32 A. 1005 (1895); Tuttle v. Burgett's Admr., 53 Ohio St. 498, 42 N.E. 427, 30 L.R.A. 214, 53 Am.St.Rep. 649 (1895); Austin v. Austin, 9 Vt. 420 (1837); Joslyn v. Parlin, 54 Vt. 670 (1881) contra.

25. Bryant v. Erskine, 55 Me. 153 (1867).

26. Bethlehem v. Annis, 40 N.H. 34, 77 Am.Dec. 700 (1860); Bryant v. Erskine, 55 Me. 153 (1867); Eastman v. Batchelder, 36 N.H. 141, 72 Am.Dec. 295 (1858); Flanders v. Lamphear, 9 N.H. 201 (1838).

27. Bodwell Granite Co. v. Lane, 83 Me. 168, 21 A. 829 (1891); Greenleaf v. Grounder, 86 Me. 298, 29 A. 1082 (1894).

28. "Consideration has to do with contracts, not executed conveyances."

mon law mortgage conveying legal title, for if an owner may convey the whole title by deed of gift he surely may convey the lesser, security interest in the form of title subject to a condition subsequent.[29] No different rule need apply where the mortgage gives a lien, for, regardless of any controversy over the precise nature of the lien,[30] the transaction is executed. That a mortgage is valid without consideration is evidenced by mortgages given to secure the debts of third persons.[31] Other proof is in the almost universal rule that mortgages may be given to secure preexisting debts.[32]

Nevertheless, numerous cases state that consideration is an essential element of a mortgage.[33] There are several explanations of such statements. Perhaps the most frequent source of confusion is the failure to differentiate between the mortgage and the obligation it secures.[34] "The mortgage itself is an executed conveyance, defeasi-

National City Bank of Chicago v. Wagner, 216 F. 473, 132 C.C.A. 533 (1914), certiorari denied 235 U.S. 698, 35 S.Ct. 199, 59 L.Ed. 431 (1915). See also Perry v. Miller, 330 Mass. 261, 112 N.E.2d 805 (1953), commented on by Updike, Mortgages, in 1953 Annual Survey of American Law, 29 N.Y.U.L.Rev. 829, 830 (1954).

29. "There need not be proven, and there need not exist, as I understand it, any consideration between the mortgagor and the mortgagee for the defeasible conveyance manifested by the mortgage itself." Perkins v. Trinity Realty Co., 69 N.J.Eq. 723, 726, 61 A. 167, 168 (1905), affirmed 71 N.J.Eq. 304, 71 A. 1135 (1909). Actually, of course, mortgages of this sort existed prior to the development of any doctrine of consideration.

30. See Gavit, Under the Lien Theory of Mortgages is the Mortgage Only a Power of Sale? 15 Minn.L.Rev. 147; Durfee, Lien or Equitable Theory of Mortgage, 10 Mich.L.Rev. 587 (1912); Chapter 1, D, supra. See also 2 Wis.L.Rev. 59 (1922); 8 Wis.L.Rev. 184 (1933); 19 Ky.L.J. 146, 155 (1931).

31. Garretson Inv. Co. v. Arndt, 144 Cal. 64, 77 P. 770 (1904); Herron v. Stevenson, 259 Pa. 354, 102 A. 1049 (1918). It is immaterial that the debt of the third party is a pre-existing one. Buck v. Axt, 85 Ind. 512 (1882); Lee State Bank v. McElheny, 227 Mich. 322, 198 N.W. 928 (1924); Lee v. Kirkpatrick, 14 N.J.Eq. 264 (1862) (given in payment of debt of third party); Moore v. Fuller, 6 Or. 272 (1877); Nat. City Bank of Chi. v. Wagner, 216 F. 473, 132 C.C.A. 553 (1914), certiorari denied 235 U.S. 698, 35 S.Ct. 199, 59 L.Ed. 431 (1915); Bynum Mercantile Co. v. First Nat. Bank of Anniston, 187 Ala. 281, 65 So. 815 (1914); Bell v. Bell, 133 Mo. App. 570, 113 S.W. 667 (1908); Kansas Mfg. Co. v. Gandy, 11 Nev. 448, 9 N.W. 569, 38 Am.Rep. 370 (1881); Ray v. Hollenbeck, 42 F. 381 (C.C.N.Y. 1890) (dictum), contra.

32. Bray v. Comer, 82 Ala. 183, 1 So. 77 (1877); Usina v. Wilder, 58 Ga. 178 (1877); Hewitt v. Powers, 84 Ind. 295 (1882); Rea v. Wilson, 112 Iowa 517, 84 N.W. 539 (1900) (valid against subsequent attaching creditor); Barrett v. Weber, 125 N.Y. 18, 25 N.E. 1068 (1890); Lehrenkrauss v. Bonnell, 199 N.Y. 240, 92 N.E. 637 (1910) (valid against creditors even though given while insolvent and with intent to defeat other creditors provided mortgagee not chargeable with notice of such intent); Reeves & Co. v. Dyer, 52 Okl. 750, 153 P. 850 (1915); Richeson v. Richeson, 43 Va. (2 Grat.) 497 (1846) (valid against creditor). See Jones, Mortgages, 8th Ed., § 757; Tiffany, Real Property, 2d Ed., § 606; Walsh, Mortgages, § 14; Campbell v. Bagley, 276 F.2d 28 (C.A.La.1960).

33. See e. g., Morvay v. Drake, Ala., 325 So.2d 165 (1976); see Tiffany, Real Property, 2d Ed., § 606, n. 65 for a collection of cases so stating. See also 31 Mich.L.Rev. 102 (1932).

34. "Such confusion as exists with respect to the right to plead and prove

ble upon the carrying out of an executory contract. This executory contract is subject to all the laws applicable to contracts, and must, of course, be supported by consideration."[35] One reason for this failure to distinguish between the two disparate ingredients is the habit of using the word mortgage to refer indiscriminately to the debt, the property security, or the composite unit of the two.[36] More influential is the requirement that, either because it is the parties' intention or substantive law demands it, there must be an obligation for the mortgage to secure. This makes the validity of the mortgage depend indirectly upon consideration, not for the mortgage itself, but for the obligation upon which it ordinarily depends.[37] In some cases, flowing also from the conception of a mortgage requiring an obligation, the doctrine that a mortgage can be enforced only to the amount of the debt due regardless of the face of the bond, etc., seems to be what the court means by its requirement of consideration.[38] Many other cases which say consideration is necessary are dealing with the validity of the mortgage as against third parties, not as between the mortgagor and mortgagee. In some of these cases the problem of "consideration" really is one of "value" in the doctrine of bona fide purchase.[39] In others the kind and amount of consideration involves doctrines of the law of fraudulent conveyances in determining intent and whether the taker is a volunteer.[40]

no consideration arises, I think, out of the failure to distinguish between the mortgage and the debt which the mortgage is given to secure." Perkins v. Trinity Realty Co., 69 N.J.Eq. 723, 726, 61 A. 167, 169 (1905), affirmed 71 N.J.Eq. 304, 71 A. 1135 (1909). For an example of such confusion, see Barnes, Consideration in Mortgages, 19 Ky.L.J. 146, 148–151 (1931).

35. Perkins v. Trinity Realty Co., note 34 supra, at 727, 61 A. at 168. See Surety Life Ins. Co. v. Rose Chapel Mortuary, Inc., 95 Idaho 599, 514 P. 2d 594 (1973).

36. A striking example of this is the conclusion of the court in Perkins v. Trinity Realty Co., note 34, supra, at 729, 61 A. at 169, that "there was consideration for the mortgage", i. e., the debt.

37. Chesser v. Chesser, 67 Fla. 6, 64 So. 357 (1914); Hall v. Davis, 73 Ga. 101 (1884); Conwell v. Clifford, 45 Ind. 392 (1873); Hannan v. Hannan, 123 Mass. 441 (1877); Saunders v. Dunn, 175 Mass. 164, 55 N.E. 893 (1900); Anderson v. Lee, 73 Minn. 397, 76 N.W. 24 (1898); Brooks v. Owen, 112 Mo. 251, 19 S.W. 723 (1892), reversed on rehearing 112 Mo. 251, 20 S.W. 492; Hughes v. Thweatt, 57 Miss. 376 (1879); Bradshaw v. Farnsworth, 65 W.Va. 28, 63 S.E. 755 (1909); Cawley v. Kelley, 60 Wis. 315, 19 N.W. 65 (1884).

38. E. g., Laylin v. Knox, 41 Mich. 40, 1 N.W. 913 (1879). See Barbour, History of Contract in Early English Equity, 4 Oxford Studies 89; 3 Tiffany, Real Property, 2d Ed. § 606.

39. For example, a legal mortgage given to secure an existing debt is perfectly valid between the parties but the taker could not qualify, in most jurisdictions, as a bona fide purchaser for value under the equitable doctrine or under the requirements in recording acts. See 36 Yale L.J. 564 (1927); 23 Yale L.J. 186 (1913).

40. Lehrenkrauss v. Bonnell, note 32, supra, (mortgage to secure existing debt, given by mortgagor while insolvent, is not voidable as fraudulent conveyance).

§ 2.4 Description of the Debt

There is some difference of opinion as to how precise the mortgage must be in describing the amount of the debt. Cases involving the amount of the debt may be divided into two classes: those in which the amount is omitted entirely, or is expressed in general terms, or by way of reference; and those in which although specified, it is either overstated or understated. The objections to the validity of the first group are the possibilities afforded for the substitution of fictitious claims [41] and the burden of investigations dehors the mortgage to discover what could easily have been inserted in it. Nevertheless, most courts uphold them,[42] although there is a minority view requiring the amount of the debt to be stated as accurately as its nature permits on pain of having the mortgage held void as to third parties.[43]

The divergence in the decisions reflects the courts' attempts to balance interests. The mortgagee wants to be protected as long as the description of the obligation is adequate to warn a person looking at it and to enable discovery of the truth by inquiry. The searcher of records, on the other hand, wants to be able to rely on them; he does not want to make any more inquiries outside the record than absolutely necessary. Even in the majority jurisdictions the claim must be described and defined with such accuracy as to make identification reasonably possible and certain.[44] And, of course, in all jurisdictions the mortgage will operate as security for only those obligations which are covered by the agreement of the parties and identified by it. The problem of extending it to secure other existing or subsequently created debts or claims is dealt with in connection with mortgages to secure future advances.[45]

41. "The incumbrance on the property must be so defined, as to prevent the substitution of everything which a fraudulent grantor may devise to shield himself from the demands of his creditors." Pettibone v. Griswold, 4 Conn. 158, 10 Am.Dec. 106 (1822).

42. Equitable Bldg. & Loan Ass'n v. King, 48 Fla. 252, 37 So. 181 (1904); Hurd v. Robinson, 11 Ohio St. 232 (1860); Goff v. Price, 42 W.Va. 384, 26 S.E. 287 (1896). See Robinson v. Williams, 22 N.Y. 380 (1860). See also 145 A.L.R. 375 (1943).

43. Pearce v. Hall, 75 Ky. (12 Bush) 209 (1876); Hart v. Chalker, 14 Conn. 77 (1840); Bullock v. Battenhousen, 108 Ill. 28 (1883). As to the description of an unliquidated debt, see Stoughton v. Pasco, 5 Conn. 442, 13 Am.Dec. 72 (1825).

44. See Harper v. Edwards, 115 N.C. 246, 20 S.E. 392 (1894). See also 145 A.L.R. 385 (1943); 49 Am.St.Rep. 207 (1896). See additionally Smith v. Haertel, 125 Colo. 348, 353, 244 P.2d 377, 379 (1952).

45. See § 12.7, infra.

46. Nazro v. Ware, 38 Minn. 443, 38 N.W. 359 (1888). See Shirras v. Caig, 11 U.S. (7 Cranch) 34, 3 L.Ed. 260 (1812); Burnett v. Wright, 135 N.Y. 543, 32 N.E. 253 (1892). Cf., contra, Stearns v. Porter, 46 Conn. 313 (1878). See also Thompson, What Description of the Debt is Sufficient in a Recorded Mortgage, 44 Cent.L.J. 490 (1897); Redfield, The Necessity of Describing the Security upon the Registry, 2 Am.L.Reg.,N.S., 1 (1862). If the debt is overstated with the intention of defrauding the mortgagor's creditors, the transaction

Where there is an untruthful statement of the amount it can be urged that actual deception, or the danger of it, should invalidate the mortgage as to creditors and some other third parties. If the amount is overstated there is, in effect, a concealment of an asset to the extent of the overage; and an understatement may be misleading as to the debtor's affluence. In the absence of an actual intent to deceive, however, such mortgages are not void.[46] One reason for this is that the original amount stated, even though correct at the time, is seldom the amount actually due on the mortgage. Usually there will have been payments on the principal or accumulations of unpaid interest, instalments, or taxes; and third parties, whether creditors or subsequent purchasers or encumbrancers would be unjustified in relying on the original statement.[47] Although this is true and although it is customary for purchasers from the mortgagor and subsequent encumbrancers to ascertain the exact amount of the prior mortgage, there seems little reason why they should not be entitled to depend on the expressly stated amount as the correct original indebtedness if there has been actual reliance and if an alteration would be disadvantageous to them. Ordinarily, of course, it will not harm purchasers or subsequent mortgagees to cut down the amount of an overstatement to the actual debt. General creditors, however, may have been harmed through inactivity by them [48] caused by the concealed value of the redemption interest; and the extent of this injury may be difficult to measure and not necessarily cured by revelation of the truth. The problem of an overstatement which is intended to cover future advances involves much the same considerations but, because of certain differences, will be mentioned again later.[49] Where the amount is understated it cannot, of course, be enforced beyond the stated sum as against subsequent purchasers and encumbrancers, and, presumably, any creditors who actually rely on the incorrect amount.[50]

The date of maturity is of importance to transferees or creditors of both the mortgagor or mortgagee in order that they may know when a default may occur, and therefore it should be set forth in the mortgage. A failure to do so will not, however, ordinarily invalidate

will not be sustained. Holt v. Creamer, 34 N.J.Eq. 181 (1881). See Tully v. Harloe, 35 Cal. 302, 95 Am.Dec. 102 (1868).

47. See Bell v. Fleming's Ex'rs, 12 N.J.Eq. 13, 18 (1858), affirmed 12 N.J. Eq. 490.

48. "He [the creditor] finds an encumbrance on record for as much as the debtor's property is worth, and thinks it useless to take legal means to secure his debt; whereas, if the mortgage had truly expressed the debt actually due, the creditor might have secured his debt." Griffin v. New Jersey Oil Co., 11 N.J.Eq. 49, 53 (1855).

49. See § 12.7, infra.

50. Gilchrist v. Gough, 63 Ind. 576, 30 Am.Rep. 250 (1878); Burriss v. Owen, 76 S.C. 481, 57 S.E. 542 (1907). Look at Johns v. Church, 29 Mass. (12 Pick.) 557, 23 Am.Dec. 651 (1832) (personal property, actual amount enforcible against creditors).

the mortgage but instead will be construed at least for purposes of foreclosure as merely making the debt payable on demand.[51]

The failure to include the maturity date in the mortgage may be significant under some statutes of limitation governing foreclosure. For example, under the Missouri statute, "[n]o suit, action or proceeding * * * shall be had or maintained * * * after the lapse of twenty years from the date at which the last maturing obligation secured by the instrument sought to be foreclosed is due on the face of such instrument * * *."[52] If the failure to include the maturity date in fact makes the debt payable on demand for purposes of foreclosure limitations statutes, it could be argued that the statutory period should run from the date of the debt and not the actual maturity date. Thus, in the case of a long term installment type mortgage, the failure to include the ultimate maturity date could mean that the statute of limitations could prevent foreclosure of the mortgage prior to the actual due date of some of the future installments.[53]

51. Green v. Richards, 23 N.J.Eq. 32 (1927), reargument denied 245 N.Y. vanna v. Brooks, 97 N.J.Eq. 329, 127 A. 247, 37 A.L.R. 361 (1925); Ansorge v. Kane, 244 N.Y. 395, 155 N.E. 683 (1927) reargument denied 245 N.Y. 530, 157 N.E. 845; N. E. D. Holding Co. v. McKinley, 246 N.Y. 40, 157 N. E. 923 (1927) semble, accord. See 12 Cornell L.Q. 367 (1927).

52. Vernon's Ann.Mo.Stat. § 516.150. See Note, 19 Mo.L.Rev. 186 (1954).

53. For a further consideration of such statutes, see § 6.12, infra.

§§ 2.5–3.0 are reserved for supplementary material.

CHAPTER 3

MORTGAGE SUBSTITUTES

Table of Sections

A. RESTRICTING THE RIGHT TO REDEEM

§ 3.1 Clogging the Equity of Redemption

When the courts of equity created the equity of redemption, they did direct violence to the explicit intention of the parties. They did this by allowing the mortgagor to regain his property by performing the secured obligation after the legal title to the property had vested absolutely in the mortgagee—vested according to the express language of the parties in the mortgage deed and according to the effect the law courts gave to that language. Following their original intervention equity courts developed the doctrine *prohibiting the clogging of the mortgagor's equity of redemption.*[1] Under this doctrine, even though the mortgage is in default, normally no agreement contained in the mortgage, or contemporaneous with it, can cut off a recalcitrant mortgagor's equity of redemption without the resort to foreclosure by the mortgagee. Stated another way, courts will not enforce attempts by a mortgagee to have the mortgagor at the inception of the mortgage transaction waive his right to be foreclosed in the event of a default.

While the prohibition against clogging has been characterized by a variety of labels, the most common characterization associated with

1. The first use of the term clog is in Bacon v. Bacon, Tot. 133–4 (1639): "Where the mortgagee will suddenly bestow unnecessary costs upon the mortgaged lands, of purposes to clogg the lands, to prevent the mortgagor's redemption."

See Williams, Clogging the Equity of Redemption, 40 W.Va.L.Q. 31, 33 (1933) for various theories as to the origin and historical development of the doctrine against clogging. For other discussions of the problem or some aspects of it, see Wyman, The Clog on the Equity of Redemption, 21 Harv.L.Rev. 459 (1908); Coutts, Once a Mortgage Always a Mortgage—Stipulations in the Mortgage, 50 Cent.L.J. 464 (1900); Coughlin, Clogging Redemption Rights in Illinois, 3 John Marshall L.Q. 11 (1937); Falconbridge, Legal Mortgages in Equity, 54 Can.L.J.N.S., 1 (1918); Turner, The Equity of Redemption, 175–183; E.N. D., The Basis of Relief from Penalties and Forfeitures, 20 Mich.L.Rev. 646 (1922). For a concise résumé of English decisions, see note, 136 L.T. 137 (1913). For an incorporation of the doctrine in a statutory enactment, see West's Ann.Cal.Civ.Code § 2889. For a recent statement of the doctrine see Fratcher, Restraints upon Alienation of Equitable Interests in Michigan Property, 51 Mich.L.Rev. 509, 542 (1953). There are cases both affirming and denying that the mortgagor's statutory right of redemption from a foreclosure sale may be waived. Nippel v. Hammond, 4 Colo. 211 (1878); King v. King, 215 Ill. 100, 74 N.E. 89 (1905) hold that it may; Parmer v. Parmer, 74 Ala. 285 (1883); Lambright v. Bales, 139 Ark. 48, 213 S.W. 2 (1919), contra. See Skilton, Government and the Mortgage Debtor, 23.

the doctrine in the United States is "once a mortgage, always a mortgage." It has been pointed out that this "is only another way of saying that a mortgage cannot be made irredeemable." [2] The clogging doctrine, as a corollary of the original creation of the equity of redemption, was developed to prevent evasion of it by ingenious and determined mortgagees who utilized a wide variety of clauses which, while recognizing the existence of the equity of redemption, in practical effect nullified or restricted its operation.

One of the earliest and crudest of these attempts was the insertion in mortgages of clauses limiting redemption to a certain time after the law day.[3] Equity struck them down automatically. Moreover, when the same attempt took the form of a warranty by the mortgagor not to redeem after the law day [4] or a provision making time of the essence,[5] equity courts reached similar results. In addition, provisions that only the mortgagor himself, as distinct from his executor or heir,[6] or that only the mortgagor and the heirs male of the body [7] might redeem were held invalid, a restriction upon persons who may exercise the right to redeem being as offensive as a time limit within which it may be exercised. By a parity of reasoning, an agreement allowing the mortgagee to keep any part of the mortgaged property, redemption being limited to the balance, fails.[8] Similarly, the doctrine is violated when a mortgagee requires the mortgagor to deliver an executed deed to the mortgaged premises to the mortgagee at the time of the initial mortgage transaction, the mortgagee's purpose being, in the event of the mortgagor's default, to utilize the deed to obviate the need for foreclosure. For example, when an escrow was attempted in which the mortgagor executed a deed at the time the loan and mortgage was given and deposited it in escrow to be delivered to the mortgagee in payment of the debt in the event of default, the court held that the mortgagor still retained the right to redeem and that the arrangement violated the prohibition against

2. Lord Davey in Noakes v. Rice, A.C. 24, 32 (1902). See Fogelman, The Deed Absolute as a Mortgage in New York, 32 Fordham L.Rev. 299, 301 (1963).

3. Bradbury v. Davenport, 114 Cal. 593, 46 P. 1062, 55 Am.St.Rep. 92 (1896) (four months); Heirs of Stover v. Heirs of Bounds, 1 Ohio St. 107 (1853) (before a fixed date); Frazer v. Couthy Land Co., 17 Del.Ch. 68, 149 A. 428 (1929) (three years); Price v. Perrie, Freem.Ch. 258 (1702) and Floyer v. Lavington, 1 P.Wms. 268 (1714) (life of the mortgagor); Jason v. Eyres, Freem.Ch. 69 (1681) (three years "if the mortgagor so long lives"); Salt v. Marquess of Northampton, A.C. 1 (1892) (mortgagor dying in lifetime of his father). But Compare Newcomb v. Bonham, 1 Vern. 7 (1681). See Toomes v. Conset, 3 Atkyns 261 (1745).

4. East India Co. v. Atkyns, 1 Comyns 347 (1740); Cowley v. Shields, 180 Ala. 48, 60 So. 267 (1913).

5. Jackson v. Lynch, 129 Ill. 72, 21 N. E. 580 (1889) rehearing denied 129 Ill. 72, 22 N.E. 246. See note 2 supra.

6. Newcomb v. Bascomb, 1 Vern. 7 (1681).

7. Howard v. Harris, 1 Vern. 33 (1681).

8. Salt v. Marquess of Northampton, A.C. 1 (1892).

clogging.[9] Similarly, courts have utilized the clogging concept to deny specific performance to a mortgagee of an option to purchase the mortgaged premises entered into at the time of the mortgage loan.[10]

Not quite so clear a case, is a stipulation providing for an increase in the interest rate on nonpayment on a fixed law day.[11] The difficulty is that if the higher rate was stipulated for at the outset with a reduction for punctual payment the agreement is valid. Yet in both cases precisely the same amounts of money would be payable at exactly the same times.[12] Of course, situations could be envisaged where the jump in interest rate would be so enormous, or the provision for the payment of a bonus on default so huge, that as a practical matter, the mortgagor would be unable to pay it. This clearly would be recognized as merely a device to make the mortgage irredeemable and therefore in violation of the clogging concept. But quite apart from anything of this sort, and with a relatively mild jump in interest rate, (although any jump does, of course, make it more difficult to redeem), the decisions nevertheless seem based upon a principle which underlies relief from penalties and forfeitures.[13] That principle is that relief will be granted where there has been a misreliance upon a "mirage of hope". Ordinarily, the courts have talked in terms of granting relief because of solicitude for the "impecunious landowner" [14] or "necessitous men [who] are not, truly speaking, free men." [15] But another important factor is the mortgagee's tendency to play upon the mortgagor's natural optimism, the "overconfidence in one's own capacities and faith in a special providence [which] leads us to over-sanguine commitments." [16] Equity takes this human failing into account. Thus where the bargain is expressed in terms of a future increase in the amount due, for which the mortgagor never expects to become liable, rather than a firm commitment to the higher rate at the very outset which he knows he has bound himself to pay but may reduce by future effort, the transaction is invalid. The same applies to a bonus to be paid to the mort-

9. Plummer v. Ilse, 41 Wash. 5, 82 P. 1009, 2 L.R.A.,N.S., 627 (1905). Also see Pollak v. Millsap, 219 Ala. 273, 122 So. 16, 65 A.L.R. 110 (1928).

10. See MacArthur v. North Palm Beach Utilities, Inc., 187 So.2d 681 (Fla.App.1966). See Wilson v. Fisher, 148 N.C. 535, 62 S.E. 622; Note, 20 Col.L.Rev. 920 (1920).

11. Holles v. Wyse, 2 Vern. 289 (1693); Strode v. Parker, 2 Vern. 316 (1694). See Salt v. Marquess of Northampton, A.C. 1, 19 (1892); Firth, Freedom of Contract in Mortgages, 11 L.Q.Rev. 144, 153 (1895). See also Goodyear Shoe Mach. Co. v. Selz, Schwab & Co., 157 Ill. 186, 41 N.E. 625 (1895).

12. See the dubious *quaere* in Strode v. Parker, supra note 11.

13. See note, 20 Mich.L.Rev. 646 (1922). Finger v. McCaughey, 114 Cal. 64, 45 P. 1004 (1896), held valid a jump in the interest rate on a mortgage if not paid, from ten percent to twelve percent.

14. "Impecunious landowner in the toils of a crafty money lender." Samuel v. Jarrah Timber & W. P. Corp., Ltd., A.C. 52, 55 (1904).

15. Vernon v. Bethel, 2 Eden 113 (1761).

16. 20 Mich.L.Rev. 646, 647 (1922).

gagee on redemption under certain conditions.[17] And a stipulation that unpaid interest should be capitalized and interest paid on it also has been held void.[18]

Provisions that the mortgagor shall pay the mortgagee's expenses in collecting the secured debt and that the mortgage shall secure this additional item have been upheld by some courts and disallowed by others.[19] The former seem preferable as the additional amount is merely fair compensation for extra trouble and expense by the mortgagee. Of course if an excessive sum is provided for, the effect of which is to interfere with the mortgagor's right to redeem, it will be disallowed and cut to a reasonable amount.[20]

The rule against clogging has occasionally been expressed by the twin concepts that (1) the mortgagee shall not have a "collateral advantage" and (2) there must be no stipulation in the mortgage which will "fetter" the property on redemption. The first concept has been expressed by the terminology that a person "shall not have interest for his money and a collateral advantage besides for the loan of it, or clog the redemption with any by-agreement." The second concept has been summed up as meaning "that the mortgagee shall not make any stipulation which will prevent a mortgagor, who has paid principal, interest, and cost, from getting back his mortgaged property in the condition in which he parted with it."[21] While these two aspects of the clogging doctrine have at times been important in England, they have never played a significant role in the United States and, accordingly, they are not considered in detail here.[22]

§ 3.2 Subsequent Transactions

The doctrine that the mortgagor's equity of redemption cannot be affected by any agreement contemporaneous with the mortgage is, for the most part, inapplicable to transactions subsequent to the creation of the mortgage. Thus, a subsequent sale of the equity of re-

17. Chapple v. Mahon, Ir.R. 5 Eq. 225 (1870).

18. Chambers v. Goldwin, 9 Ves.Jun. 254, 271 (1804).

19. Valid: Clawson v. Munson, 55 Ill. 394 (1870); Baker v. Jacobson, 183 Ill. 171, 55 N.E. 724 (1899); Weatherby v. Smith, 30 Iowa 131, 6 Am.Rep. 663 (1870); Tholen v. Duffy, 7 Kan. 405 (1871) (but see Foote v. Sprague, 13 Kan. 155 (1874)); Gaither v. Tolson, 84 Md. 637, 36 A. 449 (1897); Pierce v. Kneeland, 16 Wis. 672, 84 Am.Dec. 726 (1863). See Voechting v. Grau, 55 Wis. 312, 13 N.W. 230 (1882). Invalid: Thomasson v. Townsend, 10 Bush 114 (Ky.1873); Kittermaster v. Brossard, 105 Mich. 219, 63 N.W. 75, 55 Am.St.Rep. 437 (1895); Northwestern M. L. Ins. Co. v. Butler, 57 Neb. 198, 77 N.W. 667 (1899); Turner v. Boger, 126 N.C. 300, 35 S.E. 592, 49 L.R.A. 590 (1900); Miller v. Kyle, 85 Ohio St. 186, 97 N.E. 372 (1911); Daly v. Maitland, 88 Pa. 384, 32 Am.Rep. 457, 11 Lanc.Bar. 9 (1879).

20. Daly v. Maitland, 88 Pa. 384, 32 Am.Dec. 457, 11 Lanc.Bar 9 (1879).

21. Opinion of Lord Davey, Noakes and Co. Ltd. v. Rice, A.C. 24, 33 (1902).

22. See Osborne, Mortgages, §§ 98–99 (2d Ed. 1970).

demption to the mortgagee will not normally be considered an invalid clog on the equity of redemption. Indeed, this transaction usually takes the form of a deed in lieu of foreclosure. While the majority of courts today permit the mortgagee to purchase the mortgagor's equity of redemption, they will scrutinize the transaction to insure that it is free from fraud or oppression on the part of the mortgagee and is based on an adequate new consideration, the burden of establishing these requirements being on the mortgagee.[23] Moreover, a deed in lieu of foreclosure may also sometimes be characterized as an absolute deed as a mortgage and, in addition, it can create further problems for the mortgagee where there are intervening liens against the mortgagor. The deed in lieu of foreclosure and its attendant problems are considered in greater detail later in this volume.[24]

While the mortgagor, as noted above, may under some circumstances be permitted to sell his equity of redemption, "he cannot, even after the mortgage has been executed, bind himself by an agreement that, if he does not pay his debt by a certain time in the future, he will forfeit all right to the property." [25] In other words, courts

23. See Note, 31 Mo.L.Rev. 312 (1966); Gould v. McKillip, 55 Wyo. 251, 99 P.2d 67, 129 A.L.R. 1427 (1940) and cases there cited; Earle's Adm'r v. Blanchard, 85 Vt. 288, 81 A. 913 (1911). Cf. Ferris v. Wilcox, 51 Mich. 105, 16 N.W. 252, 47 Am.Rep. 551 (1883) (mortgagor to be given the benefit of any doubt); Odell v. Montross, 68 N.Y. 499 (1877). But see Bailey v. St. Louis Union Trust Co., 188 Mo. 483, 87 S.W. 1003 (1905). Cf. Trull v. Skinner, 34 Mass. (17 Pick.) 213 (1835); Stone v. Jenks, 142 Mass. 519, 8 N.E. 403 (1886) (gift by mortgagor to mortgagee). If the price paid is inadequate, the sale will be set aside. Peugh v. Davis, 96 U.S. 332, 24 L.Ed. 755 (1877). If the mortgagee buys on an execution sale under a judgment recovered by a third person, or upon a judgment recovered by the mortgagee on a debt other than that which is secured by the mortgage, the same rule of scrutiny is not applied. This is "for the very good reason that, at this public sale conducted by an officer of the court, the mortgagee has no opportunity to overreach the mortgagor and take undue advantage of his economic weakness. *Per contra*, to permit to purchase on the same terms as any stranger adds one (and a most important one) to the potential market for the land, to the advantage of the mortgagor as well as the mortgagee." Wheeler and Durfee, Evasion of Mortgage Moratoria by Prosecution of Personal Remedies, 33 Mich. L.Rev. 1196, 1198 (1935). Farmers Union Trading Co. v. Wiggins, 127 Mont. 481, 267 P.2d 117 (1954), noted in Updike, Mortgages, in 1954 Annual Survey of American Law, 30 N.Y.U. L.Rev. 805, 806 (1955), upholds the deed where the consideration is fair and the debt is discharged.

24. See §§ 6.16–6.17, infra.

25. Holden Land & Livestock Co. v. Inter-State Trading Co., 87 Kan. 221, 227, 123 P. 733, 736, L.R.A.1915B, 492 (1912), appeal dismissed 233 U.S. 536, 34 S.Ct. 61, 58 L.Ed. 1083 (1914). Batty v. Snook, 5 Mich. 231 (1858); Tennery v. Nicholson, 87 Ill. 464 (1877); Cohn v. Bridgeport Plumbing Supply Co., 96 Conn. 696, 115 A. 328, 24 A.L.R. 808 (1921), accord.

See notes, 13 Col.L.Rev. 170 (1913); 29 Mich.L.Rev. 757 (1931); 36 Mich.L. Rev. 111 (1937); 22 Harv.L.Rev. 295 (1909); 19 Va.L.Rev. 302 (1933). See also 55 Am.St.Rep. 100 (1897); 2 L. R.A.,N.S., 628 (1906); 65 A.L.R. 120 (1930) for discussions of and collections of cases on the problem presented in the principal case and some analogous situations. Bradbury v. Davenport, 120 Cal. 152, 52 P. 301 (1898) is usually cited as the leading case contra to the Holden case. See also Ravnaas v. Andrich, 60 S.D. 281,

will treat *subsequent* executory agreements as uninforceable clogs on the mortgagor's equity of redemption, even though, under some circumstances, they will treat *executed* transactions as legitimate sales.

This distinction between subsequent executed and executory transactions has been criticized on the ground that a person should be able to contract to sell what he could dispose of at once. Nevertheless, it may be defended. The bases for the policy supporting the rule are the necessity of the borrower to obtain the loan coupled with an optimistic overconfidence in his capacities to surmount future difficulties. The two combine to lead to over-sanguine commitments. Both are present at the time the mortgage is entered into originally. When the transaction is subsequent to the mortgage and is consummated at once, neither exerts any influence. However, if it is a subsequent agreement for *future* forfeiture, the "mirage of hope" is sufficiently strong to bring it under the general ban against forfeitures due to "misreliance upon airy hope." [26] If the reasoning is valid, executory contracts to waive statutory rights of redemption from foreclosure sale should be unenforceable. There are, however, authorities holding such agreements good.[27] It has been suggested that the test should be whether the parties actually intended a sale agreement or whether it was merely an arrangement for additional security for the loan on different terms, one of which involved cutting off by the agreement, the new equity of redemption which arose out of the new or modified mortgage agreement.[28] Since the real question is why such an agreement, whether it is to sell in futuro the redemption interest or to release it in satisfaction of the debt when it comes due and unpaid, should not be valid when it is not a part of the original mortgage, such a suggestion has little merit.

Because the mortgagor's equity of redemption and the prohibition against clogging that equity have become so firmly inbedded in the formal law of mortgages, mortgagees, as we have noted earlier, often resort to other types of land security devices to avoid the consequences of those mortgage law doctrines. As Professor Durfee once

244 N.W. 361 (1932), noted 19 Va.L. Rev. 302; Brockington v. Lynch, 119 S.C. 273, 112 S.E. 94 (1922). See additionally Durfee, Cases on Security, 1951, 167. See also Glenn, Mortgages, § 45, dismissing the rule as unsound in principle and contrary to more recent and better authority.

26. See note, 20 Mich.L.Rev. 646, 648 (1922), arguing that such misreliance is a basis for relief against forfeitures generally with the mortgage cases only one illustration.

27. Nippel v. Hammond, 4 Colo. 211 (1878); Cook v. McFarland, 78 Iowa 528, 43 N.W. 519 (1889); King v. King, 215 Ill. 100, 74 N.E. 89 (1905); U. S. Bldg. & Loan Ass'n v. Stevens, 93 Mont. 11, 17 P.2d 62 (1932) (clause in mortgage waiving right to possession during redemption period valid) semble. On the other hand there is authority that a waiver of such a right contained in the mortgage itself is invalid. Parmer v. Parmer, 74 Ala. 285 (1883); Lambright v. Bales, 139 Ark. 48, 213 S.W. 2 (1919).

28. See note, 13 Col.L.Rev. 171 (1913).

aptly put it, "[T]he big idea is to find a form of a transaction that will have the practical effect of security, yet will be held not to be a security but to belong to a wholly different jural species and so be held immune from security law." [29] Commonly encountered mortgage substitutes include the absolute deed, together with its variations, and the installment land contract. A consideration of these devises and related concepts follow.

B. THE ABSOLUTE DEED

§ 3.3 The Absolute Deed with Separate Instrument of Defeasance

The common law mortgage takes the form of a "deed conveying lands conditioned to be void upon the payment of a sum of money, or the doing of some other act." [30] This condition of defeasance was ordinarily tacked onto the end of what otherwise read as an ordinary straight deed of absolute conveyance. Although there are statutory forms of mortgages in many jurisdictions the language of the traditional deed of conveyance is still commonly used even in lien theory jurisdictions. When it is all put into one document no doubts are raised as to the effectiveness of the instrument to accomplish the intended result. Equity added onto the express terms of the transaction, for reasons which were examined earlier [31] a right in the grantor to tardy redemption even though the terms of the defeasance were not fulfilled and title had vested absolutely in the grantee, and gave a corresponding right to the grantee to foreclose that right of redemption—neither of which rights were founded on any expressed intention of the parties either explicit or implied in fact, and one of them at least, the redemption right, in flat contradiction to the stated terms of the instrument.

Sometimes, however, the defeasance is expressed in a separate instrument and the question arises whether the two can be read together so as to establish a legal mortgage. The practice has not gone uncriticised, one chancellor in the time of George II stating with vigor that "it will always appear with a face of fraud: for, the defeasance may be lost; and then an absolute conveyance is set up. I would discourage the practice as much as possible." [32] Nevertheless the well settled rule is that "the condition may be * * * by a separate deed, executed, or at least taking effect, at the same time [as the deed of conveyance], so as to be part of one and the same transaction. It must be by deed, and cannot be by parol or instrument in writing not under seal. It must take effect at the time the deed of

29. Durfee, Cases on Security, 4 (1951).

30. Lund v. Lund, 1 N.H. 39, 41, 8 Am.Dec. 29, 30 (1817).

31. See § 1.3, supra.

32. Cottrell v. Purchase, Cas.Temp.Talbot, 61, 64 (1732).

conveyance takes effect, and not at a subsequent time."[33] There is some authority that where the instruments are separate the result is not a legal mortgage but an "equitable" mortgage only. "Equitable" mortgage in this connection is used to mean that the *mortgagor* has only an equitable interest which these courts seem to regard, even in title jurisdiction, as different from the redemption right of a mortgage executed as one document, a view that seems illogical and undesirable even though the consequences are of little importance.[34]

The substitution of the proviso for reconveyance for the defeasance clause in the debtor's deed did not alter the fundamental character of the common-law mortgage. The proviso was given a double construction; it operated as a condition subsequent to the grant, and it also was specifically enforceable as a promise.[35] If, instead of one instrument being used, the transaction consisted of a deed of the land, absolute in form, given by the debtor to the creditor concurrently with the execution by the creditor of a bond of defeasance or a sealed promise to reconvey on payment of the debt, the two instruments were construed together and held to create a legal mortgage.[36] Although the requirement that the contemporaneous writing had to be of equal dignity and formality with the original conveyance, i. e., under seal if the deed were so executed, was the rule of the law courts,[37]

33. Lund v. Lund, 1 N.H. 39, 41, 8 Am.Dec. 29, 30 (1817); Sears v. Dixon, 33 Cal. 326 (1867), agreement for reconveyance executed, in accordance with terms of original agreement, after the absolute conveyance. "If the defeasance forms a part of the original transaction, it is not material that it be executed at the same time as the deed."; Cosby v. Buchanan, 81 Ala. 574, 1 So. 898 (1886), agreement subsequent to deed but made in performance of the original agreement by which the deed was executed; Erskine v. Townsend, 2 Mass. 493, 3 Am.Dec. 71 (1807); Waters v. Crabtree, 105 N.C. 394, 11 S.E. 240 (1887), agreement of defeasance made at time of deed but reduced to writing at subsequent time; Van Oehsen v. Brown, 148 Wis. 236, 134 N.W. 377 (1912); Teal v. Walker, 111 U.S. 242, 4 S.Ct. 420, 28 L.Ed. 415 (1884).

34. Williams v. Williams, 270 Ill. 552, 110 N.E. 876 (1915); Ferguson v. Boyd, 169 Ind. 537, 81 N.E. 71 (1907), rehearing denied 169 Ind. 537, 82 N.E. 1064 (1908). See note, 23 Ill.L.Rev. 80 (1928).

35. See Turner, The Equity of Redemption, General Preface, XXXII, XL–XLIV.

36. Sears v. Dixon, 33 Cal. 326 (1867); Ives v. Stone, 51 Conn. 446 (1883); Erskine v. Townsend, 2 Mass. 493, 3 Am.Dec. 71 (1807); Mills v. Darling, 43 Me. 565 (1857). See Williams v. Williams, 270 Ill. 552, 110 N.E. 876 (1915). Equity courts reached the same result. Edrington v. Harper, 3 J.J.Marsh. 353, 20 Am.Dec. 145 (Ky. 1830); Hill v. Edwards, 11 Minn. 22, Gil. 5 (1866); Froidevaux v. Jordan, 64 W.Va. 388, 62 S.E. 686, 131 Am. St.Rep. 911 (1908); Williams v. Williams, supra, note 34. Semble, Brown v. Bement, 8 Johns. 96 (N.Y. 1811); Dickinson v. Oliver, 195 N.Y. 238, 88 N.E. 44 (1909). See Holmes v. Grant, 8 Paige 243 (N.Y.1840). See also Turner, loc. cit. supra note 6. Here, also, some of the cases say that the transaction is technically not a legal mortgage. Furguson v. Boyd, supra note 34; Williams v. Williams, supra note 34.

37. Warren v. Lovis, 53 Me. 463 (1866); Kelleran v. Brown, 4 Mass.

in equity it was not necessary for the separate instrument to be of an equal dignity with the original conveyance.[38]

Oral evidence can always be introduced to establish the fact that the two instruments really constituted one transaction; the parol evidence rule cannot be invoked to bar its admission since it is "not introduced to contradict or vary the writings, but as showing that the papers constituted one arrangement agreed upon at one and the same time." [39] Indeed, it has been held that, where the separate deed and the qualifying defeasance are one single transaction, parol evidence is inadmissible to show that the transaction was intended as a sale or a conditional sale.[40] And, of course, the Statute of Frauds is inapplicable since the defeasance is in writing.

The foregoing statements of law presuppose that the character of the separate instrument, whether it be in the form of a condition subsequent or a proviso for reconveyance as a clause of defeasance on the performance of a secured obligation is clear.[41] In such cases the only problem is to show that the two instruments constitute one transaction and are to be construed together. When, however, the separate instrument is cast in the form of a written option or contract to repurchase the issue is not merely whether the two instruments should be treated as though they had been embodied in one document and to be construed accordingly, but whether what has been stated as, for example, a resale agreement is in actual fact intended

443 (1808); Lund v. Lund, 1 N.H. 39, 8 Am.Dec. 29 (1817); Fitch v. Miller, 200 Ill. 170, 179, 65 N.E. 650, 653 (1902). See Illinois Trust Co. of Paris v. Bibo, 328 Ill. 252, 257, 159 N.E. 254, 256 (1928).

38. See Kelleran v. Brown, 4 Mass. 443 (1808). Cf. Emerson v. Murray, 4 N.H. 171, 17 Am.Dec. 407 (1827); Whitfield v. Parfitt, 4 De G. & Sm. 240 (1851) (a written defeasance on the back of the deed of conveyance, if there when the instrument was executed, will constitute a mortgage at law).

39. Reitenbaugh v. Ludwick, 31 Pa.St. 131, 138, 15 L.I. 101 (1858); Sears v. Dixon, 33 Cal. 326 (1867); First Nat. Bank of Florida v. Ashmead, 23 Fla. 379, 2 So. 657 (1887); Cosby v. Buchanan, 81 Ala. 574, 1 So. 898 (1886), accord.

40. Woods v. Wallace, 22 Pa. 171, 1 P.L.J. 130, 2 Am.L.Reg. 186 (1853); Snyder v. Griswold, 37 Ill. 216 (1865). See Haines v. Thomson, 70 Pa. 434, 440 (1872). But see Gassert v. Bogk, 7 Mont. 585, 19 P. 281, 1 L.R.A. 240 (1888), affirmed 149 U.S. 17, 13 S.Ct. 738, 37 L.Ed. 631 (1893).

41. Where there is a conveyance by deed and a condition of defeasance in a collateral paper, any doubt whether the transaction is a mortgage will be resolved in favor of its character as a mortgage. Hennessey v. Rafferty, 326 Ill.App. 259, 61 N.E.2d 409 (1945). McKinney's New York Real Prop. Law, § 320: "A deed conveying real property, which by any other written instrument, appears to be intended only as a security in the nature of a mortgage, although an absolute conveyance in terms, must be considered a mortgage; and the person for whose benefit such deed is made, derives no advantage from the recording thereof unless every writing, operating as a defeasance of the same, or explanatory of its being desired to have the effect only of a mortgage, or conditional deed, is also recorded therewith, and at the same time." If the defeasance is oral such statutes have been held not applicable. Livesay v. Brown, 35 Neb. 111, 52 N.W. 838 (1892); Kline v. McGuckin, 24 N.J.Eq. 411 (1874).

by the parties to be quite a different thing, namely, a defeasance clause in a mortgage. A later section deals with this and it suffices here to differentiate it from the simple question whether extrinsic evidence can be used to establish the unity in transaction of the two physically separate writings.

§ 3.4 The Absolute Deed Coupled with an Oral Understanding—Reasons for Frequent Use

Frequently a debtor will execute an absolute deed of conveyance to his creditor with only an oral understanding that the latter should hold it as security only and reconvey it to the grantor when the obligation has been satisfied. For the most part, such transactions are utilized to avoid the strict requirements of the law of mortgages. As our succeeding discussion will indicate, the advantages that are sought to be secured by using such transactions frequently are not obtained. Moreover, substantial dangers and disadvantages lurk in such transactions.

Perhaps the most important reason for utilizing such transactions is the desire to avoid what are perceived to be substantial costs and delays in certain types of foreclosure proceedings. Indeed, recent studies have indicated that judicial foreclosure, especially, can be both time-consuming and expensive.[42] However, the grantee runs the risk of a suit to establish that a mortgage was what was really intended by the parties and, if such a suit is successful, the grantee will be faced with the foreclosure difficulties he sought to avoid. Moreover, since the agreement is not in regular mortgage form, there is always the chance that some step in the foreclosure proceedings may encounter judicial disapproval, as well as the hazard of what the mortgagor may swear to, and the trier of fact believe, as to the terms of the oral mortgage. Finally, if the transaction is established as a mortgage and not an absolute deed, foreclosure inevitably must be judicial because the absolute deed will obviously not contain a power of sale.

The supposed ease of conveying the property to a purchaser if the mortgagor acquiesces in the sale and the capacity for informal enlargement of the mortgage to cover future advances are sometimes advanced as additional advantages for the absolute deed type transaction. As to the former reason, the advantage over usual methods is insubstantial. As to the latter reason, the law of future advances seems sufficiently simple and efficient in most jurisdictions to accomplish legitimate financing functions.[43]

42. See McElhone & Cramer, Loan Foreclosure Costs Affected By Varied State Regulations, Mortgage Banker 41 (December 1975).

43. See § 12.7 infra.

Another reason for the absolute deed transaction hinges upon the deed operating to transfer legal title to the grantee. Grantees in lien theory states may utilize the absolute deed to gain the right to possession prior to default that would otherwise not exist in a normal mortgage transaction. As will be seen, the grantee may find that he acquired neither title nor the right to possession. Moreover, even if he does get possession, it will not be free from the onerous duty to account in equity—a duty which usually is a substantial deterrent to exercising the right to possession in title jurisdictions where the mortgagee would get that right in a straight mortgage transaction.

Other miscellaneous reasons are sometimes advanced to justify the absolute deed as a financing device. For example, it is occasionally asserted that the absolute deed will enhance the mortgagee's rights to chattels severed from the realty. In addition, some grantees hope that the absolute deed will avoid the normal consequences of the statute of limitations running on the debt. When all of the foregoing reasons are evaluated it seems doubtful whether there are any substantial benefits to be obtained by the grantee-mortgagee in having the transaction framed in this fashion.[44] Yet creditors in large numbers undoubtedly perceive such advantages. Because they do it is necessary to examine the law which governs these absolute deed situations.

§ 3.5 Parol Evidence—Admissibility

The case law in this country overwhelmingly establishes that parol evidence is admissible in equity to show that a deed absolute on its face was intended as a mortgage even though it was knowingly cast in that form and its execution was in no way affected by fraud, mistake, ignorance, duress or undue influence.[45] In some states statutes authorize proof by parol testimony that such an absolute transfer was a mortgage even though the fact does not appear by the

44. Although the objectives of the grantee are usually dominant, and, as will be seen, the assumption that it is the grantee who forces the grantor to consent to this form has an important bearing on the law, it should be observed that the deed absolute form may serve a deservedly frowned upon purpose of the grantor, i. e., to hide away this asset from his other creditors.

45. In Pierce v. Robinson, 13 Cal. 116, 125 (1859), a leading and typical case, the court said, "I consider parol evidence admissible in equity, to show that a deed absolute upon its face was intended as a mortgage, and that the restriction of the evidence to cases of fraud, accident, or mistake, in the creation of the instrument, is unsound in principle and unsupported by authority."

For an excellent consideration of the area, see Cunningham and Tischler, Disguised Real Estate Security Transactions As Mortgages In Substance, 26 Rutgers L.Rev. 1 (1972). For recent examples of application of the general rule, see Havana Nat. Bank v. Wiemer, 32 Ill.App.3d 578, 335 N.E. 2d 506 (1975); Hansen v. Kohler, 550 P.2d 186 (Utah 1976). Cf. Sorenson v. Olson, 235 N.W.2d 892 (N.D.1975). But see Gajewski v. Bratcher, 221 N. W.2d 614 (N.D.1974).

terms of the instrument.[46] Other states reach similar results through their statutory definitions of a mortgage.[47] On the other hand, a few states require that the plaintiff, in order to introduce evidence of the real purpose of the transfer, must allege and prove that the defeasance clause was omitted by reason of "ignorance, mistake, fraud or undue advantage" or some similar ground which would make out a case for reformation in equity.[48] Moreover, in a few states there are statutory restrictions on the doctrine. Thus, for example, a Georgia statute provides that if the deed is absolute and accompanied by possession of the property, (a circumstance which is both very infrequent in real estate mortgages because ordinarily the reason for mortgaging instead of selling is that the mortgagor wants the use of the property and also extremely misleading), only "fraud in the procurement" will permit the deed to be established as a mortgage by parol evidence.[49] Georgia courts, however, will admit parol testimony to establish an absolute deed as a mortgage in those cases where the grantor retains possession of the real estate.[50] The New Hampshire statute is perhaps the most extreme in prohibiting parol evidence because it provides that for an instrument to operate as a mortgage the agreement to that effect must be "inserted in the condition of the conveyance and made a part thereof", thus striking down even a separate written defeasance.[51]

§ 3.6 Burden of Proof

While a few decisions suggest that a mere preponderance of the evidence is the requisite burden of proof in establishing that an abso-

46. E. g., West's Ann.Cal.Civ.Code § 2925. See Workman Constr. Co. v. Weirick, 36 Cal.Rptr. 17, 223 Cal. App.2d 487 (1963).

47. E. g., see 46 Okl.St.Ann. § 1.

48. Newton v. Clark, 174 N.C. 393, 93 S.E. 951 (1917); Williamson v. Rabon, 177 N.C. 302, 98 S.E. 830 (1919); Waddell v. Aycock, 195 N.C. 268, 142 S.E. 10 (1928). See L.R.A.1916B, 18, 41 et seq. Where the conveyance comes to the creditor from a third person North Carolina seems to dispense with any special showing of fraud, etc. Sandling v. Kearney, 154 N.C. 596, 70 S.E. 942 (1911); Lutz v. Hoyle, 167 N.C. 632, 83 S.E. 749 (1914).

See Fogelman, The Deed Absolute as a Mortgage in New York, 32 Fordham L.Rev. 299, 302 (1963).

49. Georgia Code § 67–104 (1967). Accord, Miss.Code Ann. § 89–1–47 (1973).

50. See Haynes v. Blackwell, 232 Ga. 430, 207 S.E.2d 66 (1974).

51. N.H.Rev.Stats.Ann., ch. 479:1 and 479:2 (1968). Pennsylvania follows New Hampshire with the exception that a separate defeasance "made at the time the deed is made and—in writing, signed and delivered by the grantee in the deed to the grantor" will be given effect although it must be acknowledged and recorded to be effective against any subsequent grantee or mortgagee for value. 21 Pa.S. § 951.

There is early authority that parol evidence can be used to establish an absolute deed as a mortgage only in equity and not in legal actions. Because of the merger of law and equity procedurally in most jurisdictions and other factors, the modern view is that such evidence is admissible whether the proceeding is characterized as legal or equitable. See Osborne, Mortgages, § 73 (2d Ed. 1970).

lute deed is a mortgage,[52] most courts demand that the evidence be clear and convincing.[53] In the absence of such clear and convincing evidence the presumption that the conveyance is what it purports to be prevails.[54] Indeed, a few cases have required that the grantor establish his case beyond a reasonable doubt.[55]

The reason for the generally heavy burden of proof on the party attempting to establish the absolute deed as a mortgage is understandable. There is a general interest in enhancing the security of written real estate transactions and a particular interest in discouraging false swearing by unscrupulous grantors who regret their bargains and seek to avoid them by "redeeming" the property. Moreover, the prevailing burden of proof discourages debtors who wish to conceal their equity in the property from creditors by putting the apparently complete "title" in the name of the mortgagee. Finally, although the absolute deed intended as a mortgage is a frequent occurrence, the great bulk of absolute deed transactions are exactly what they purport to be, final and complete transfers. Consequently, the requirement of greater proof than is usually required in civil cases seems justified.

Although there is authority to the effect that the same degree of proof is required whether the grantor or grantee seeks to

52. Welch v. Thomas, 102 Mont. 591, 61 P.2d 404 (1936). See Campbell, Cas.Morts., 2d ed., 83 n. 1 for a collection of cases. Some of the decisions are not very clear and others are not in harmony with other authorities in the same jurisdiction, e. g., Schmidt v. Barclay, 161 Mich. 1, 125 N.W. 729, 20 Ann.Cas. 1194 (1910), preponderance of evidence is sufficient; Polokoff v. Vebb, 226 Mich. 541, 198 N.W. 194 (1924), "clear, irrefragable and most convincing proof." See Palmer v. Lundy, 293 Ala. 463, 305 So.2d 369 (1974); where the court states that "clear and convincing" is the test, but upholds the finding of a mortgage on a "preponderance of the evidence."

53. See e. g., Havana Nat. Bank v. Wiemer, 32 Ill.App.3d 578, 335 N.E.2d 506 (1975); Sorenson v. Olson, 235 N.W.2d 892 (N.D.1975); Fry v. D. H. Overmyer Co. Inc., 269 Or. 281, 525 P.2d 140 (1974). See Fogelman, The Deed Absolute As A Mortgage in New York, 32 Ford.L.Rev. 299, 303 (1963); Cunningham and Tischler, Disguised Real Estate Security Transactions As Mortgages In Substance, 26 Rutgers L.Rev. 1, 22–23 (1972).

Additional cases attesting the heavy burden upon a claimant in establishing a mortgage transaction by clear and convincing evidence are noted by Updike, Mortgages, in 1956 Annual Survey of American Law, 32 N.Y.U. L.Rev. 789 (1957). See also Karesh, Security Transactions, in Survey of South Carolina Law, 8 S.C.L.Q. 122 (1955); Note, The Equitable Mortgage in Kansas, 5 U. of Kan.L.Rev. 114, 116 (1956); Young, Parol Evidence and Texas Deeds: Some Current Problems, 34 Texas L.Rev. 351, 360 (1956). See Stolk v. Lucas, 146 Cal. App.2d 417, 304 P.2d 33 (1956), and Evans v. Evans, 226 S.C. 451, 85 S.E. 2d 726 (1955), which are in accord. So also are Howard v. Steen, 230 S. C. 351, 95 S.E.2d 613 (1956), noted in Karesh, Security Transactions, in Survey of South Carolina Law, 10 S. C.L.Q. 114, 115 (1957); Kohler v. Gilbert, 216 Or. 483, 339 P.2d 1102 (1959); Child v. Child, 8 Utah 2d 261, 332 P.2d 981(1958).

54. See e. g., Wile v. Donovan, 538 S. W.2d 906 (Mo.App.1976).

55. E. g. Rinkel v. Lubke, 246 Mo. 377, 152 S.W. 81 (1912).

have the deed declared a mortgage,[56] it can be argued that a heavier burden of proof should be required of a grantee who seeks to establish the transaction as a mortgage. It is true, of course, that most such attempts to establish an absolute deed as a mortgage will be by the grantor-mortgagor. However, this will not universally be the case. For example, suppose that the value of the deeded land has dropped so significantly that its value is lower than the debt owing to the grantee-mortgagee. Moreover, suppose that the grantor-mortgagor has enough assets to satisfy any personal liability on a mortgage debt. In such a situation, the grantee-mortgagee may very well want to establish that what appears to be an absolute conveyance is actually a debt transaction. It could be argued that since the grantee-mortgagee in all probability required that the transaction be framed in absolute deed terminology rather than in the traditional mortgage format, he should bear a heavier burden than would a grantor in establishing that the transaction was not what he made it appear to be.

§ 3.7 Factors Establishing an Absolute Deed as a Mortgage

The most important factor in determining whether an absolute deed is a mortgage is whether there is an indebtedness on the part of the grantor to the grantee left unaffected by the conveyance.[57] The debt may either have existed prior to the conveyance or have arisen from a loan made contemporaneous with the conveyance. As one excellent article has pointed out, "[p]roof of a pre-existing debt from grantor to grantee justifies concluding that the deed was given either in satisfaction of the debt or as security therefor. But where no written satisfaction of the debt has been executed and it can be shown that the parties have behaved as though the debt continued after the execution of the deed, it is clear that the deed was given as security not in satisfaction of the debt." [58] On the other hand,

56. See e. g., Holman v. Mason City Auto Co., 186 Iowa 704, 171 N.W. 12 (1919). Cf. Downs v. Ziegler, 13 Ariz. App. 387, 477 P.2d 261 (1971).

See § 3.17, infra note 55.

57. Palmer v. Lundy, 293 Ala. 463, 305 So.2d 369 (1974); Todd v. Todd, 164 Cal. 255, 128 P. 413 (1912); Anglo-Calif. Bank Ltd. v. Cerf, 147 Cal. 384, 81 P. 1077 (1905), future advances as well as existing indebtedness; Holmberg v. Hardee, 90 Fla. 787, 108 So. 211 (1926); Holman v. Mason City Auto Co., 186 Iowa 704, 171 N.W. 12 (1919), retention in grantee's possession, without cancellation, of written evidence of debt raises strong presumption of mortgage; Thomas v. Klemm, 185 Md. 136, 43 A.2d 193 (1945); Dean v. Smith, 53 N.D. 123, 204 N.W. 987 (1924); Corey v. Roberts, 82 Utah 445, 25 P.2d 940 (1933); Hunter v. Bane, 153 Va. 165, 149 S.E. 467 (1929), "a mortgage without debt to support it is a legal solecism"; Hofmeister v. Hunter, 230 Wis. 81, 283 N.W. 330, 121 A.L.R. 444 (1939). See Fogelman, The Deed Absolute as a Mortgage in New York, 32 Fordham L.Rev. 299, 305, 306 (1963).

See also When Is an Absolute Conveyance a Mortgage, 8 U. of Fla.L. Rev. 132 (1955), discussing Rosenthall v. LeMay, 72 So.2d 289 (Fla.1954).

58. Cunningham and Tischler, Disguised Real Estate Security Transactions As Mortgages in Substance, 26 Rutgers L.Rev. 1, 15 (1972).

"[w]here there is no pre-existing debt and the grantee paid value for the land, the amount paid by the grantee can be regarded either as purchase money or as a loan. But where it can be shown that the parties thereafter behaved like debtor and creditor, it is clear that the transaction was a loan on security rather than an absolute sale." [59]

Another significant factor is the adequacy of the amount paid by the grantee as purported consideration for the transfer. If the value of the property is substantially greater than the amount advanced by the grantee this constitutes strong evidence that what was paid was a loan rather than purchase price and therefore there is a strong inference that the transaction was a mortgage.[60] On the other hand, if there is no great disparity between the value of the land and the amount paid, this tends to indicate that the transfer was a sale.[61]

Retention of possession of the land by the grantor also cuts in favor of finding a mortgage transaction.[62] While it is conceivable that a grantor could sell his interest in his real estate and retain possession as a lessee,[63] the retention of possession by the grantor at least indicates that he retained some interest in the deeded real estate. Moreover, when retention of possession is coupled with substantial improvements to the real estate, the grantor's case becomes even stronger. In any event, when retention of possession is coupled with favorable evidence based on the two factors discussed previously, the grantor's case becomes strong indeed.

59. Id. at 15.

60. See Horn v. Ketaltas, 46 N.Y. 605, 42 How.Pr. 138 (1871). The authorities to this effect are numerous. For collections of authorities, see, 90 A.L.R. 1504 (1934); 129 A.L.R. 1504 (1940). See also Fogelman, The Deed Absolute as a Mortgage in New York, 32 Fordham L.Rev. 299, 307 (1963). So too, the negotiations and conduct of the parties which lead to the "deed" are significant in reaching a conclusion as to the character of the transaction. Ibid. The absence of disproportion between the value of the land and the expressed consideration is evidence that the transaction is not a mortgage. Howard v. Steen, 230 S.C. 531, 95 S.E.2d 613 (1956), noted in Karesh, Security Transactions in Survey of South Carolina Law, 10 S.C.L.Q. 114, 115 (1957).

61. Conway v. Alexander, 11 U.S. 218, 3 L.Ed. 321 (1812). So, too, if the grantor made a highly advantageous disposition of his interest by the transaction this indicates that the deed was intended to be absolute. Vinquist v. Siegert, 58 N.D. 820, 227 N.W. 556 (1929).

62. See Fogelman, The Deed Absolute as a Mortgage In New York, 32 Ford. L.Rev. 299, 308 (1963), discussing the significance of retention of possession by the grantor and miscellaneous factors in the transaction.

63. Hopper v. Smyser, 90 Md. 363, 45 A. 206 (1900), in which payment of taxes by the grantee together with transfer of possession to him, making improvements by him and no accounting of any income or recognition of any debt or payment of interest proved that no mortgage existed. Possession in the grantor may be explained by his having taken a lease back. Pancake v. Cauffman, 114 Pa. St. 113, 7 A. 67 (1886); Brickle v. Leach, 55 S.C. 510, 33 S.E. 720 (1899); Edwards v. Wall, 79 Va. 321 (1884). On the other hand, a lease back to the grantor is not conclusive that the conveyance is not a mortgage. See Rogers v. Davis, 91 Iowa 730, 59 N.W. 265 (1894); Bearss v. Ford, 108 Ill. 16 (1883).

Several other factors provide evidence that the transaction was a mortgage: the grantee was a money-lender by occupation;[64] the grantee was not in the business of buying and selling property of the description conveyed;[65] the fact that the transferor was in financial difficulties at the time of the execution of the conveyance, (even though this might instead indicate a forced sale if it stood by itself);[66] prior negotiations for a loan from the grantee of approximately the amount paid;[67] and payment of taxes by the grantor subsequent to the deed.[68]

§ 3.8 Effect of Absolute Deed Between the Parties

Whenever an absolute deed is established as a mortgage, it will be treated, as between the parties, as if it were a mortgage executed in regular form. All the rights and obligations of the mortgage relationship bind the parties.[69] Thus the grantor may maintain an action to redeem.[70] Moreover, even though the grantee obtains possession he will be treated as a mortgagee in possession and be accountable as such.[71] Correspondingly, the grantee may maintain an action to foreclose the grantor's redemption right.[72] This result flows, of course, from the general doctrine that the right to foreclose, like the right to redeem or to compel an accounting, does not depend on any provision in the mortgage, but is simply one of the legal consequences flowing from the general mortgage relationship. Nevertheless, there is authority that this general doctrine will not apply to permit strict fore-

64. Haggerty v. Brower, 105 Iowa 395, 75 N.W. 321 (1898).

65. Desloge v. Ranger, 7 Mo. 327 (1842).

66. Lewis v. Wells, 85 F. 896 (D.C. Alaska 1898); Smith v. Berry, 155 Ky. 686, 160 S.W. 247 (1913).

67. Couts v. Winston, 153 Cal. 686, 96 P. 357 (1908); Evans v. Thompson, 89 Minn. 202, 94 N.W. 692 (1903); Macauley v. Smith, 132 N.Y. 524, 30 N. E. 997 (1892).

68. King v. Crone, 114 Ark. 121, 169 S.W. 238 (1914); Hart v. Randolph, 142 Ill. 521, 32 N.E. 517 (1892). See Karesh, Security Transactions, in Survey of South Carolina Law, 10 S. C.L.Q. 114, 115 (1957).

69. Carr v. Carr, 52 N.Y. 251, 258 (1873). As to differences between a mortgage by deed absolute and a straight form mortgage, see Note, 28 Neb.L.Rev. 481 (1949).

70. Campbell v. Dearborn, 109 Mass. 130, 12 Am.Rep. 671 (1872). A large proportion of the cases brought to establish that the absolute deed was intended as a mortgage are cases of this sort and will be found in other footnotes.

71. Husheon v. Husheon, 71 Cal. 407, 12 P. 410 (1886); Murdock v. Clark, 90 Cal. 427, 27 P. 275 (1891); Miller v. Peter, 158 Mich. 336, 122 N.W. 780 (1909); Pratt v. Pratt, 121 Wash. 298, 209 P. 535, 28 A.L.R. 548 (1922), deed absolute from a third party. Cf., however, Barnard v. Jennison, 27 Mich. 230 (1873), the duty to account is not so stringent as in the case of the ordinary mortgagee in possession.

72. Shadman v. O'Brien, 278 Mass. 579, 180 N.E. 532 (1932); Hughes v. Edwards, 22 U.S. (9 Wheat.) 489, 495, 6 L.Ed. 142 (1824).

For other cases holding that a deed absolute intended as security may be foreclosed in equity as a mortgage, see, 22 L.R.A.,N.S., 572 (1909).

closure of a deed absolute mortgage.[73] Moreover, since foreclosure by the exercise of a power of sale is permitted only when such a power has been expressly provided for in the mortgage itself, and since a mortgage in the form of an absolute deed obviously does not contain such a power, this method of foreclosure is unavailable.

§ 3.9 Grantee's Title

A difference of opinion exists as to whether the grantee under an absolute deed intended as a mortgage gets a "title" type interest in the property different from that received when the regular mortgage form is used. In title theory states the mortgagee gets legal title when the deed is in the form of a conveyance with a defeasance clause and a fortiori would get a like interest where the defeasance clause is omitted but nevertheless the conveyance is for security purposes.[74] On the other hand, if the jurisdiction follows the lien theory, it makes a difference in several directions whether the deed absolute grantee gets title with the mortgagor having only an equitable interest or whether the result is precisely the same as though the conventional form of mortgage was employed. There is good authority for what is the preferable view that the grantee under a deed absolute intended as a mortgage gets only a lien with the grantor retaining title.[75] Nevertheless, there are decisions to the effect that the mortgagee under a deed absolute in a lien jurisdiction does get title.[76]

73. Libel v. Pierce, 147 Or. 132, 31 P. 2d 1106 (1934). But cf. Northwestern State Bank of Hay Springs v. Hanks, 122 Neb. 262, 240 N.W. 281 (1932); and see § 7.10 infra.

In Hermann v. Churchill, 235 Or. 327, 385 P.2d 190 (1963), in a suit to have a deed absolute declared a mortgage, the court decreed strict foreclosure in spite of ORS 88.010 (1963) providing that liens upon real property shall be foreclosed and the property sold by judicial sale.

74. Finlon v. Clark, 118 Ill. 32, 7 N.E. 475 (1886).

75. Jackson v. Lodge, 36 Cal. 28 (1868); California Civil Code §§ 2888, 2924, 2925, and 2927; Brandt v. Thompson, 91 Cal. 458, 27 P. 763 (1891); Shirey v. All Night and Day Bank, 166 Cal. 50, 134 P. 1001 (1913); Hulsman v. Deal, 90 Kan. 716, 136 P. 220 (1913); Flynn v. Holmes, 145 Mich. 606, 108 N.W. 685, 11 L.R.A., N.S., 209 (1906); Shattuck v. Bascom, 105 N.Y. 39, 12 N.E. 283 (1887); Snyder v. Parker, 19 Wash. 276, 53 P. 59, 67 Am.St.Rep. 726 (1898); Clambey v. Copeland, 52 Wash. 580, 100 P. 1031 (1909); Pratt v. Pratt, 121 Wash. 298, 209 P. 535, 28 A.L.R. 548 (1922), deed absolute from a third party to creditor; Dobbs v. Kellogg, 53 Wis. 448, 10 N.W. 623 (1881). A deed absolute mortgage is not an alienation of the title within the meaning of fire insurance policies. Barry v. Hamburg-Bremen Fire Ins. Co., 110 N.Y. 1, 17 N.E. 405 (1888). Cf. Modlin v. Atlantic Fire Ins. Co., 151 N.C. 35, 65 S.E. 605 (1909). See note, 11 L.R.A.,N.S., 209 (1906) for a collection of additional cases as well as cases holding that the grantee gets legal title. See also 28 A.L.R. 554 (1924); Herron v. Millers National Ins. Co., 185 F.Supp. 851 (D.C.Or. 1960); See Fogelman, The Deed Absolute as a Mortgage in New York, 32 Fordham L.Rev. 299, 310 (1963), on the effect of a deed absolute as creating only a lien in New York. Note, 43 Or.L.Rev. 350, 353 (1964).

76. See Moore v. Linville, 352 N.E. 2d 846 (Ind.App.1976), where grantee-mortgagee was successful in an ejectment action to obtain posses-

In considering the merits of the question, it would seem that the parties should not be able to alter the legal character and incidents of the mortgage as developed in a lien jurisdiction by the simple expedient of leaving out the defeasance clause. When the defeasance clause remains in, the deed purports to pass the title but the courts, as we have seen, will not permit such an operation to it. And the same result should follow, regardless of the desires of the parties, once it is established that the intent was to mortgage. To hold otherwise would permit the parties to reinstitute the title theory of the mortgage in a lien jurisdiction by merely buying and using a different form. On the other hand a deed absolute intended as a mortgage and a regular mortgage should not be treated alike, at least in some instances. The latter sets forth the real nature of the transaction; it reveals on its face that there is a property interest—the redemption right—left in the transferor. The former falsely depicts the actual transaction, leaving the true situation to be revealed by oral testimony. They are therefore sufficiently different, certainly as to third parties and to some extent between the parties, to justify the application of different rules. The straightforward way of dealing with the problem would be to face squarely the question as to what extent and in whose favor the usual rights created by a mortgage should be modified by reason of the deceptive form in which this type of mortgage has been cast. Instead the courts have been somewhat inclined to adopt a mechanical attitude and let the solution flow from a determination of whether the grantee got "title" rather than a "lien," or whether the parol evidence would be admissible at law or only in equity. Since in most cases, it is believed, a desirable result will be reached on this type of reasoning, or at least one not particularly undesirable, about the only criticism that can be leveled at the cases which concern themselves with or decide rights on the basis of

sion against a grantor-mortgagor in possession; Woodson v. Veal, 60 Ga. 562 (1878); Gibson v. Hough, 60 Ga. 588 (1878); Shumate v. McLendon, 120 Ga. 396, 48 S.E. 10 (1904); Ferguson v. Boyd, 169 Ind. 537, 81 N.E. 71 (1907) rehearing denied 196 Ind. 537, 82 N.E. 1064 (1908); Burdick v. Wentworth, 42 Iowa 440 (1876); Baxter v. Pritchard, 122 Iowa 590, 98 N. W. 372, 101 Am.St.Rep. 282 (1904), mortgagor's interest being purely equitable may be surrendered by parol; Lindberg v. Thomas, 137 Iowa 48, 114 N.W. 562 (1908); Williams v. Williams, 270 Ill. 552, 110 N.E. 876 (1915), deed absolute with separate written agreement to reconvey, grantor's interest only equitable and therefore transferable without a deed. Illinois, however, is a hybrid state; First Nat. Bank of Plattsmouth v. Tighe, 49 Neb. 299, 68 N.W. 490 (1896) mortgagor's interest being equitable a judgment lien does not attach to it; First Nat. Bank of David City v. Spelts, 94 Neb. 387, 143 N.W. 218 (1913); Northwestern State Bank v. Hanks, 122 Neb. 262, 240 N.W. 281 (1932), mortgagee entitled to strict foreclosure since he had title; Hall v. O'Connell, 52 Or. 164, 95 A. 717, (1908) modified on rehearing 52 Or. 164, 96 P. 1070; dissenting opinion, Pratt v. Pratt, 121 Wash. 298, 209 P. 535, 28 A.L.R. 548 (1922), conveyance from third party and therefore, if grantee got only a lien, it was argued that the third party would still have title, and the mortgagor would have an anomalous right; Beebe v. Wisconsin Mortgage Loan Co., 117 Wis. 328, 93 N.W. 1103 (1903).

whether a deed absolute intended as a mortgage conveys the legal title to the grantee is the mode of reasoning by which they reach their results.

The cases in which the courts have raised the question of title include actions for possession by the grantee-lender, assertion of rights in severed crops, timber or fixtures against third parties, the ability of creditors to reach the interest of the grantor by legal process, the formalities necessary for the transfer or surrender of the grantor's interest, and whether the running of the statute of limitations on the debt will prevent foreclosure of the property as a mortgage.[77] In a case of the last sort the question was complicated by the fact that the deed absolute came to the creditor from a third party thus presenting the difficulty in a lien state of getting title into the borrower-mortgagor who does not appear in the deed or on the record at all.[78] A separate section is devoted to this tripartite type of transaction [79] and the question of whether the running of the statute of limitations on the obligation secured should affect the mortgage is considered later and therefore will not occupy us here.[80] However it may be stated here that the question of whether the running of the statute of limitations on the debt should bar the enforcement of the mortgage ought not to depend upon any legalistic distinction as to whether the mortgagee got a lien or a title by his regular form mortgage, and even less upon whether in a lien jurisdiction a deed absolute intended as a mortgage gave the creditor a lien or title as security, but rather upon an examination of the desirability of permitting the enforcement of the security to survive the barring of a direct action to enforce the obligation secured. Upon this there may be, and are, different views.[81] And further, since the security here rests in oral understanding, the remedy to enforce it, regardless of the effect upon it of the debt being barred, properly may be governed by a different statutory period than where it is in writing.[82]

§ 3.10 Rights of Grantor on Sale by the Grantee

Even courts in lien jurisdictions which, in other connections, say that a grantor under a deed absolute intended as security retains le-

77. See cases cited in the preceding footnotes.

78. Pratt v. Pratt, 121 Wash. 298, 209 P. 535 (1922). See notes, 8 Cornell L.Q. 172 (1923); 71 U. of Pa.L.Rev. 284 (1923); 32 Yale L.J. 611 (1923). See also 28 A.L.R. 554 (1924); 11 L.R.A.,N.S., 209, 825 (1908). See also Coutts, Does a Mortgagee under Deed Absolute in Form Gain Rights Not Incident to an Ordinary Mortgage? 52 Cent.L.J. 360 (1901).

79. See §§ 3.19–3.21, infra.

80. See § 6.9, infra.

81. See note 79, supra.

82. Although there is some authority to the contrary, the general rule is that the equitable rule as to laches may bar the grantor from establishing that the deed absolute was a mortgage even though the delay on his part was short of the statute of limitations period. See 28 A.L.R. 554.

gal title with the grantee getting only a lien, agree that a bona fide purchaser from the grantee will prevail over the grantor.[83] A fortiori, in a jurisdiction following the title theory a purchaser from the grantee for a valuable consideration and without notice that the property has been conveyed for security will hold the land free from any equity of the grantor to redeem.[84] This result, apart from statute, has been explained as resting upon the doctrine of a bona fide purchase of the legal title cutting off equitable rights. Since this is the rationale invoked, the cases preferring the bona fide purchaser are usually cited as establishing that the deed absolute intended as a mortgage gives to the grantee the full legal title and leaves only an equitable interest in the grantor.[85] Estoppel in pais by reason of the grantor having vested apparently complete title in the transferee by a deed of conveyance would seem an equally valid basis for the conclusion that the purchaser prevails and would not require holding that the grantee actually acquired title rather than a lien. In many states statutes provide that the bona fide purchaser shall prevail unless a separate defeasance has been recorded.[86]

Even though the mortgagor's rights in the land may have been cut off by the sale to a bona fide purchaser, he "is not prevented by that wrongful act from any form of redemption now practicable. * * * In order to prevent him [the grantee] from making a profit out of his wrong, the law raises the presumption that he now has the full value of the land as a separate fund in his hands, and, treating it as land, allows the plaintiff to redeem. * * *[87] The value of the land which he is permitted to recover has been held to be that at the time of the redemption action,[88] at the time of tender of payment,[89]

83. Mooney v. Byrne, 163 N.Y. 86, 57 N.E. 163 (1900). See, 32 L.R.A.,N.S., 1046; L.R.A.1916B, 584 (1911). Macauley v. Smith, 132 N.Y. 524, 30 N.E. 997 (1892); Meehan v. Forrester, 52 N.Y. 277 (1873); Pancake v. Cauffman, 114 Pa. 113, 7 A. 67 (1886); Harrington v. Butte & Superior Copper Co., 52 Mont. 263, 157 P. 181 (1916). The grantor's rights continue against a grantee with notice. Graham v. Graham, 55 Ind. 23 (1876); Hadley v. Stewart, 65 Wis. 481, 27 N.W. 340 (1886). Where the grantor under a deed absolute intended as a mortgage remains in possession, he may prove his equity by parol evidence against the grantee and also against a purchaser for value from him who had no actual notice of the occupant-grantor's equity and made no inquiry of him. Williamson v. Floyd C. Wildlife Ass'n, Inc., 215 Ga. 789, 113 S.E.2d 626 (1960), noted by Smith, Security Transactions, 12 Mercer L.Rev. 182, 188 (1960).

84. Hogan v. Jacques, 19 N.J.Eq. 123, 97 Am.Dec. 644 (1868).

85. See Walsh, Mortgages, 37; 5 Pomeroy, Equity Juris., 5th ed., 587.

86. See, e. g., West's Ann.Cal.Civ. Code, § 2950; Carpenter v. Lewis, 119 Cal. 18, 50 P. 925 (1898); Payne v. Morey, 144 Cal. 130, 77 P. 83 (1904). See also Jones, Mortgages, 8th Ed., §§ 304, 631.

87. Mooney v. Byrne, 163 N.Y. 86, 95, 57 N.E. 163, 166 (1900).

88. Mooney v. Byrne, supra note 87; Boothe v. Feist, 80 Tex. 141, 15 S.W. 799 (1891).

89. Clark v. Morris, 88 Kan. 752, 129 P. 1195 (1913). See note, 13 Col.L. Rev. 442 (1913).

and at the time of sale.[90] Of course he is always entitled, at his election, to take the proceeds realized by the sale.[91] However, the action, it should be noted again, even though it will bring only money to the plaintiff, is an action to redeem land from a mortgage and not to recover money and, consequently the statute of limitations fixing the time within which to bring an action to redeem governs.

§ 3.11 Creditors of Grantee

Where recording statutes are inapplicable, the grantor arguably should prevail over creditors of the grantee, the theory being that creditors merely stand in the shoes of their debtors.[92] Moreover, even where there is a statute requiring recordation of a defeasance when the mortgage is by deed absolute, there is authority that in the absence of an express provision that non-compliance will defeat the grantor as against creditors of the grantee, the statute will not be construed to so operate.[93] On the other hand, in some jurisdictions, where the absolute deed is accompanied by an unrecorded collateral defeasance, "creditors of the creditor-grantee obtaining judgements against him while he is record owner will obtain liens valid as against the debtor-grantor." [94]

§ 3.12 The Absolute Deed as a Fraudulent Conveyance

Where the grantor does not retain possession of the land, the recording of an absolute deed intended as security obviously operates to conceal one of the grantor's assets from his creditors. It is true, of course, that a regular form mortgage may be made the vehicle of defrauding creditors and the fact that the value of the mortgaged property is greatly disproportionate to the amount of the debt invites throwing out the mortgage as fraudulent.[95] But when the mortgage is used cooperation by the mortgagee in fabricating fictitious debts is usually necessary to accomplish the purpose and this ordinarily will present difficulties. The mortgage by itself is not inherently deceptive. On the other hand, the creditor very frequently prefers a deed absolute without any collusion with the debtor in respect to the lat-

90. Staples v. Barret, 214 Ala. 680, 108 So. 742, 46 A.L.R. 1084 (1926); Brimie v. Benson, 216 Ill.App. 474 (1920).

91. Staples v. Barret, supra, note 90; Shillaber v. Robinson, 97 U.S. 68, 24 L.Ed. 967 (1877); Meehan v. Forrester, 52 N.Y. 277 (1873).

92. Vallely v. First Nat. Bank of Grafton, 14 N.D. 580, 106 N.W. 127, 5 L.R.A.,N.S., 387, 116 Am.St.Rep. 700 (1905). On the question of priorities of an equitable mortgagee against creditors of the mortgagor, an analogous problem, see Welton v. Tizzard, 15 Iowa 495 (1864).

93. See preceding footnote.

94. Cunningham and Tischler, Disguised Real Estate Security Transactions as Mortgages in Substance, 26 Rutgers L.Rev. 1, 26–27 (1972). See N.J.Stat.Ann. 46:22–1.

95. Butts v. Peacock, 23 Wis. 359 (1868); Jones v. Third Nat. Bank of Sedalia, 13 F.2d 86 (C.C.A.Mo.1926).

ter's creditors, while the form it takes automatically operates to conceal an asset. Consequently many courts treat deed absolute mortgages as constructively fraudulent and, as a matter of law, void even as security, not only as to subsequent but as to prior creditors.[96]

On the other hand, other courts take a more flexible approach. Some hold that the transaction cast in this form is a "badge of fraud," not conclusive, but capable of rebuttal by proof of the actual good faith of the parties.[97] Other decisions require actual fraudulent intent to be established as a fact.[98] In New Jersey, for example, the absolute deed is not fraudulent unless both the grantor and the grantee intended to use that device instead of a regular mortgage to conceal the grantor's equity of redemption from his creditors.[99]

A grantee who is a party to an actual fraudulent design in giving and taking a deed absolute not only loses the property to creditors of the grantor but has no right to reimbursement for the amount loaned when the conveyance is set aside.[1] If the grantor had an actual fraudulent intent he is not entitled to relief against the grantee.[2]

§ 3.13 Recordation

There is diverse opinion as to whether and where a deed absolute mortgage may be recorded effectively. It has been held that it is unrecordable as either a deed or a mortgage and consequently is invalid against creditors of the grantor.[3] There are some authorities, however, which hold it may be recorded as a deed; others that it may or must be recorded as a mortgage. Under statutes providing for the recordation of a separate defeasance for the deed to be valid against third parties a distinction has been drawn between oral and written defeasances, the statute applying to the latter only.[4]

96. Bryant v. Young, 21 Ala. 264 (1852). See Fogelman, The Deed Absolute as a Mortgage in New York, 32 Fordham L.Rev. 299, 312 (1963).

97. McClure v. Smith, 14 Colo. 297, 23 P. 786 (1890), and Hanneman v. Olson, 209 Iowa 372, 222 N.W. 566 (1928) (badge of fraud but not conclusive).

98. Capital Lumber Co. v. Saunders, 26 Idaho 408, 143 P. 1178 (1914); Hutchison v. Page, 246 Ill. 71, 92 N.E. 571 (1910). See note, 2 Am.L.Reg.,N.S., 1, 11 (1862). See also L.R.A.1916B, 576–580. See Glenn, Fraudulent Conveyances, rev.ed., § 299a.

99. See Kline v. McGuckin, 24 N.J.Eq. 411 (Ch.1874); N.J.Stat.Ann. 25:2–3, 25:2–4; Cunningham and Tischler, Disguised Real Estate Security Transactions as Mortgages in Substance, 26 Rutgers L.Rev. 1, 27 (1972).

1. Svalina v. Saravana, 341 Ill. 236, 173 N.E. 281, 87 A.L.R. 821 (1930).

2. Baldwin v. Cawthorne, 19 Ves.Jun. 166 (1812). See 3 Williston, Contracts, rev.ed., 1828.

3. Gulley v. Macy, 84 N.C. 434 (1881).

4. Livesey v. Brown, 35 Neb. 111, 52 N.W. 838 (1892). The following are a few representative authorities on the questions suggested above. Ives v. Stone, 51 Conn. 446 (1883) (agreement to reconvey construed as a defeasance); Clemons v. Elder, 9 Iowa 272 (1859); Marston v. Williams, 45 Minn. 116, 47 N.W. 644, 22 Am.St. Rep. 719 (1890); Kline v. McGuckin, 24 N.J.Eq. 411 (1874); Dey v. Dun-

§ 3.14 Objections to Parol Evidence

Although the authority permitting the use of parol evidence to establish that a deed absolute was intended on a mortgage is overwhelming, there are two objections often raised to the introduction to such evidence that need to be considered. One is the parol evidence rule; the other is the Statute of Frauds. The parol evidence bars extrinsic agreements which would vary the terms of the single written instrument or group of instruments which the parties have executed with the intention that it or they be the complete expression and embodiment of their entire agreement.[5] The Statute of Frauds, on the other hand, is a statutory requirement that certain agreements be in writing.[6] The explanations offered as to why the evidence should not be barred by one or the other of these two rules have varied significantly. Although in many cases there is no clear segregation of the parol evidence rule from the Statute of Frauds, they are considered separately here. While at least some of the same arguments may justify the admission of the evidence under either of the rules, the two are quite independent of each other in their operation and theory.

The simplest explanation for why the admission of parol evidence does not violate the parol evidence rule is that the deed absolute did not embody, and was not intended to embody, the whole agreement of the parties. The oral agreement merely supplements the deed with respect to a matter on which the instrument is silent and with which it does not purport to deal.[7] As stated by Wigmore, "the act of transfer and the user of the property transferred are distinct legal ideas; or, put still differently, the kind of estate—according to the categories of fee simple, life estate, and the like—is a different thing from the quality of the estate, i. e., trust or security. The simple question is, then, whether the parties, under all the circumstances, appear to have intended the document to cover merely the kind of estate transferred, or to cover all possible aspects of the transfer, including that of the quality of the estate, i. e., its subjection to an equity of redemption; in the latter case, no extrinsic agreement can be

ham, 2 Johns.Ch. 182 (N.Y.1816), reversed 15 Johns. 555, 8 Am.Dec. 282, affirmed 16 Johns. 367, 8 Am.Dec. 323; In re Mechanics' Bank, 156 App.Div. 343, 141 N.Y.S. 473 (1913), affirmed 209 N.Y. 526, 102 N.E. 1106; Security Sav. & Trust Co. v. Loewenberg, 38 Or. 159, 62 P. 647 (1900). See L.R.A.1916B, 600; 1 Jones, Mortgages, 8th Ed. §§ 304, 631 (1928). See also White v. Moore, 1 Paige 551 (N.Y.1829). See Fogelman, The Deed Absolute as a Mortgage in New York, 32 Fordham L.Rev. 299, 311 (1963).

5. See 3 Corbin, Contracts § 573 (1963); Calamari & Perillo, Contracts, 99–100 (1977).

6. For the historical connection between the parol evidence rule and the Statute of Frauds, see IX Wigmore, Evidence, 3d ed., § 2426.

7. See Cunningham & Tischler, Disguised Real Estate Security Transactions as Mortgages in Substance, 26 Rutgers L.Rev. 1, 9 (1972).

considered."[8] A few cases have taken this latter view in the deed absolute cases, and if a court does conclude that the parties intended the document to cover the entire scope of the transaction it is difficult to see how parol evidence of a mortgage intent can be received, as one such court said, "without contradicting the instrument, for the reason, that the instrument and the parol testimony both assume to state the transaction; and as they differ, they must naturally be in contradiction. They both historically relate the same transaction, and the one says it was an absolute sale—the other, it was not such, but a mere mortgage, and is not this a plain contradiction? * * *"[9] That court also felt that logic in the matter was reinforced by sound policy. It said, " * * * The general rule, that parol shall not be received to contradict written evidence, is founded in true policy, and in good sense. Why should parties state, in solemn instruments, that which is not true? These instruments assume to state the truth, and the whole truth; and if parties will state that which is untrue, should they not justly suffer the consequences? Is not the rule that parties must be held to mean what they say, the plain, honest, simple, and correct rule at last?" And the same court found a further logical difficulty in another direction. " 'A formal conveyance may certainly be shown to be a mortgage by extrinsic proof, while a formal mortgage may not be shown to be a conditional sale by the same means. * * *' But here, again, I must confess I cannot see the reason of the distinction. To say that a deed absolute is a mere mortgage, is no contradiction—while, to say a mortgage cannot be made a conditional sale, without a contradiction, is making a distinction without a difference." To this last an answer may be given that while a deed absolute can be argued to be silent as to the purpose for which title was conveyed and, therefore, the oral evidence merely supplements and does not contradict, when the instrument expressly states that it is a mortgage it clearly would contradict terms clearly embodied in the agreement as written to put in evidence that it was intended to be a conditional sale. It would be much the same as attempting to show that a deed containing a written trust was not intended to create a trust but to operate as a sale with an option in the grantor to repurchase. In addition it could be urged that there is a technical difficulty at least, in lien jurisdictions certainly, in swelling a mortgage lien interest which was given on the face of the instrument into a fee in the grantee which he would have if it were construed to be a conditional sale. Furthermore, a policy factor which plays an important, in fact, it is believed, a decisive role in permitting the oral agreement to establish a mortgage, is not present when

8. IX Wigmore, Evidence, 3d ed., § 2437. See also Scott, Trusts, § 38; I Bogert, Trusts, 2d ed. 410–412; Smedley and Blunk, Oral Understandings at Variance with Absolute Deeds, 34 Ill.L.Rev. 189, 198 (1939).

9. Lee v. Evans, 8 Cal. 424, 432 (1857). Accord, Gajewski v. Bratcher, 221 N.W.2d 614 (N.D.1974).

the question is one of transforming a mortgage into something else. That policy factor is the traditional solicitude of the courts toward a mortgagor's redemption right a matter which has been stressed earlier and will be mentioned again, and which is a basic consideration in the problems considered in this chapter.

On the other hand, if the former view is taken, there is no objection to proof of an extrinsic agreement so far as the parol evidence rule is concerned.[10] It would seem a proper interpretation of the holding of the cases which freely admit parol evidence in this situation is that they do so on the ground that it was not the intention of the parties that the deed itself tell the entire story and that, consequently, the evidence comes in in accordance with the parol evidence rule itself.

In spite of this rather obvious conclusion, the opinions of many of the cases seem to assume that the rule is applicable to bar the agreement; that is, that the deed did contain and was intended to contain the parties' entire agreement, and then, because the evidence of the oral agreement for the mortgage is nevertheless let in, feel compelled to advance reasons why this can be done. These reasons can be boiled down to two sorts: those that seek to allow it in on the ground that there are present factors which will create an independent equity superior to the written agreement; [11] and those that seem to proceed upon the notion that the evidence comes in as an exception to the parol evidence rule. The first proceeds upon the theory that the written instrument can only be considered to be contradicted when the oral agreement is allowed in to enforce it according to its terms, and if it is allowed in to establish an equity arising by operation of law in the property, such use of the oral agreement is not in conflict with the other words used by the parties and put into the writing even though they intended that writing to be the sole repository and expression of their intention. The latter goes upon the conception that the oral words are admitted to enforce them, that they do contradict or add to the document, but that this is permitted by a flat exception to the rule making it inoperative where certain factors are present.

One of these explanations, which we may consider as possibly applying to explain why the parol evidence rule will not exclude the agreement, although it is usually advanced in connection with the Statute of Frauds objection, is that it is a virtual fraud upon the

10. This same reasoning applies equally to a deed absolute with an oral agreement by the grantee to hold in trust. It has been suggested that the cases barring the oral trust do not do so because of the parol evidence rule but because of the Statute of Frauds covering trusts. See Wigmore, supra, note 8. This seems correct.

11. See, e. g., Pierce v. Robinson, 13 Cal. 116, 131 (1859), "The parol evidence is admitted * * * not for the purpose of contradicting or varying the written instrument, but to show facts *dehors* the instrument creating an equity superior to its terms."

grantor for the grantee subsequently to refuse to perform his promise to treat the conveyance as security.[12] And this fraudulent conduct by the grantee justifies making an exception to the parol evidence rule, or the Statute of Frauds, even if admission of the agreement does contradict the deed. Or, in the alternative it may be argued that the fraud warrants the imposition upon the grantee of a constructive trust founded upon the fraud itself, that the terms of the oral agreement are not being enforced, and, consequently, the parol evidence rule which would bar the oral agreement for the purpose of enforcing it is not involved at all. It has been pointed out in criticism of this explanation that in effect the court is lifting itself by its own bootstraps. For there is no fraud to justify the admission of the parol agreement unless there has been a breach of the parol agreement. And yet the parol agreement is first admitted in order to show a breach of it which will establish the fraud that justifies admitting it.[13] Or, to put the matter in a little different way, the fraud which will justify the admission of the parol evidence, if it is admitted for that reason, must occur when the transaction is entered into. The alleged fraud here consists in later insisting that it was intended as a sale when actually it was intended as a mortgage. The very question at issue before the court, therefore, is whether it was intended to be a mortgage or a sale. Until the court decides that it was intended to be a mortgage there would be no justification in saying that the defendant was fraudulent in insisting that it was a sale. What the court does is to admit the parol evidence to discover what the intention really was, and then, having already admitted the evidence and determined the question in issue, it says that this determination makes the defendant's conduct fraudulent and consequently parol evidence is admissible to decide the question it had already decided, namely, that a mortgage was intended.[14] Another objection to this line of reasoning is that it treats the later breach of the agreement as establishing fraud in the entering into the agreement in the first place. Logically this amounts to converting a subsequent breach of contract into fraud in the inception of the contract, a generalization which should be summarily rejected. But the basic objection, so

12. Strong v. Stewart, 4 Johns.Ch. 167 (1819); Taylor v. Luther, C.C.R.I., 2 Sumn. 228, Fed.Cas.No.13,796 (1835); Jenkins v. Eldredge, 3 Story 299, Fed.Cas.No.7,267 (1845). See Newton v. Fay, 92 Mass. 505 (1865); 4 Pomeroy, Eq.Juris., 5th ed., § 1196.

13. See Smedley and Blunk, supra note 8, 197.

14. A similar criticism was voiced in a leading case where the analogous question of allowing in a parol trust in the face of the Statute of Frauds was involved. The court said, "But it seems apparent to my mind to say, in such a case, it shall be admitted to establish the fraud, is equally a violation of the Statute. Because the fraud consists only in the refusal to execute the trust. The court, therefore, cannot say that there is a fraud, without first saying that there is a trust. And the parol evidence, if admitted, must be admitted to establish the trust, in order that the court may charge the party with fraud in setting up his claim against it." Rasdall's Adm'rs v. Rasdall, 9 Wis. 379 (1859).

far as the argument concerns the parol evidence rule, although not when it is directed at the Statute of Frauds, is a fundamental fallacy in the reasoning. The assumption is that the parol evidence rule does operate to exclude the oral agreement that the property was to be held as security and returned on payment of the debt. If this assumption is true, it means that the court has concluded that the deed itself was intended by the parties to constitute the entire and complete transaction between the parties and consequently the oral agreement was not intended to have any legally operative effect and therefore is excluded from consideration. If this is so, it seems nonsense to predicate fraud upon the violation of an agreement which, by hypothesis, was barred from consideration initially on the ground that it was not intended by the parties to be a legally binding part of their agreement in the matter. If it was not intended to be legally binding the grantee or grantor should be perfectly free to disregard it. It is nonsense to talk of the refusal of the party to perform such an agreement as fraud justifying its admission in order to enforce it in the face of the parol evidence rule which excluded it only because the parties did not intend it to be a part of their bargain; and, for the same reason, it is equally nonsense to argue that non-performance of such an agreement is a fraud justifying the imposition of a constructive trust. Since it was barred because the court believed the parties did not intend it to be legally binding it should continue to be regarded as without legally operative significance for any purpose whatsoever. Actual fraud in the procurement of a deed absolute intended as a mortgage is, it is true, a perfectly good ground for allowing in evidence of a parol agreement for a mortgage which was omitted by reason of the fraud. But the rule which permits parol evidence of the fraud demands that it establish "some independent fact or representation, some fraud in the procurement of the instrument or some breach of confidence concerning its use," and not simply and solely an agreement directly at variance with the terms of the writing.[15] And yet, as we have seen, in most jurisdictions the parol evidence is admitted merely upon a claim, and proof, of an oral agreement that it be treated as security. In such cases, the only oral proof of the so-called fraud would consist solely in the oral agreement itself. And, to repeat, it is the court's initial assumption that that oral agreement is excluded on the ground that the parties had not intended that it be any part of their final, legally operative agreement; that the writing, and the writing alone, contained all of their agreement that they intended to be binding upon them. If this reasoning is correct, the above explanation cannot be valid. On the other hand, if the assumption is incorrect, the explanation is not needed. The

15. Bank of America, etc., Ass'n v. Pendergrass, 4 Cal.2d 258, 263, 48 P.2d 659, 661 (1935). See semble, Newton v. Clark, 174 N.C. 393, 394, 93 S.E. 951 (1917), "the intention must be established, not merely by proof of declarations, but by proof of facts and circumstances, dehors the deed, inconsistent with the idea of an absolute purchase."

oral agreement would come in as fulfilling the test of the parol evidence rule. If it is barred, it is by reason of the Statute of Frauds.

Quite similar to the foregoing is the explanation that, even in the absence of fraud or undue influence, it is permissible to show an oral trust or contract for the purpose of preventing unjust enrichment. Here the transferee would be unjustly enriched if he were allowed to keep the property, and this unjust enrichment should be prevented by compelling the transferee to return the property on payment of the debt by the transferor.[16] But here also, if it is assumed that the parol evidence rule would bar the parol agreement because the parties did not intend that it should be any binding part of their transaction, it balks the intelligence to understand why the non-performance of such an agreement should be considered as establishing unjust enrichment and therefore justify the admission of it in evidence either for the purpose of enforcing it according to its terms or founding upon it a constructive trust or mortgage. And, here, again, if the parol evidence rule does not bar it, there is no need to talk unjust enrichment in connection with its admission unless the Statute of Frauds is urged as an obstacle. If the Statute is set up as a defense the argument seems sound. The only difficulty is that it would be just as applicable to an oral trust. But, as we shall see, the American authorities generally do not accept it in the latter case.

A third explanation, and one which is believed to be the correct one, certainly the one which best distinguishes the oral mortgage from the oral trust case, is one rooted in the history of and policy of the courts toward the mortgagor's equity of redemption. As was pointed out by Field, J., in the leading case of Pierce v. Robinson,[17] which gives one of the best statements of this rationale, "The entire doctrine of equity, in respect to mortgages, has its origin in considerations independent of the terms in which the instruments are drawn. In form, a mortgage in fee is a conveyance of a conditional estate, which, by the strict rules of the common law, became absolute upon breach of its conditions. But, from an early period in the history of English jurisprudence, Courts of Equity interposed to prevent a forfeiture of the estate and gave to the mortgagor a right to redeem, upon payment within a reasonable time, of the principal sum secured,

16. See Scott, Conveyances upon Trusts Not Properly Declared, 37 Harv.L.Rev. 663 (1923). See also Stone, Resulting Trusts and the Statute of Frauds, 6 Col.L.Rev. 326, 339 (1906). "The substanbasis of the jurisdiction is the inequitable conduct of the grantee in receiving property for one purpose, and using it for another, and equity, consequently, imposes upon the grantee, an equitable obligation to restore the property to the grantor upon payment of the mortgage indebtedness. The inequitable conduct of the grantee in retaining the property for his own purposes is sufficient to give equity jurisdiction to declare the deed a mortgage, despite the parol evidence rule, and the provisions of the Statute of Frauds." Ames, Constructive Trusts Based upon the Breach of an Express Oral Trust of Land, 20 Harv.L.Rev. 549, 553 (1907).

17. 13 Cal. 116 (1859).

interest and costs. * * * And when the right to redeem had been once established, to prevent its evasion, the rule was laid down and has ever since been inflexibly adhered to, that the right is inseparably connected with the mortgage, and cannot be abandoned or waived by any stipulations entered into between the parties at the time, whether inserted in the instrument or not. * * * It is against the policy of the law to allow irredeemable mortgages, just as it is against the policy of the law to allow the creation of inalienable estates. Under no circumstances will equity permit this end to be effected, either by express stipulation, or the absolute form of the instrument. * * *" In creating the redemption right the courts clearly recognized that they were defeating the expressed intention of the parties as contained in the instrument. In other words, it involved as much or more of a departure from the terms of the instrument than the conveyance of an absolute conveyance executed as security. "The conveyance upon condition, by its terms, purports to vest the entire estate upon the breach of the condition, just as the absolute conveyance does in the first instance. The equity arises and is asserted, in both cases, upon exactly the same principles, and is enforced without reference to the agreement of the parties, but from the nature of the transaction to which the right attaches, from the policy of the law, as an inseparable incident. * * * Unless parol evidence can be admitted, the policy of the law will be constantly evaded. Debtors, under the force of pressing necessities, will submit to almost any exactions for loans of a trifling amount, compared with the value of the property, and the equity of redemption will elude the grasp of the Court, and rest in the simple good faith of the creditor." [18] This last point particularly, the notion that the mortgagor is in a weak economic position as compared with the mortgagee, a continual object of oppression and therefore the subject of special solicitude and protection of the chancellor, has been stressed over and over again and is a dominant consideration in mortgage law. Typical of this attitude is the much quoted statement of Lord Northington in Vernon v. Bethell that "necessitous men are not, truly speaking, free men; but, to answer a present emergency, will submit to any terms that the crafty may impose upon them." [19] This strong policy in favor of the mortgagor's redemption interest is sufficient to account for the letting in of parol evidence to establish it even if both the parol evidence rule and the

18. Pierce v. Robinson, supra note 17, at 126. See also Glenn, Mortgages, 55; Walsh, Mortgages, 35.

19. 2 Ed. 110, 113 (1762). See also Russell v. Southard, 53 U.S. (12 How.) 139, 13 L.Ed. 927 (1851); Marshall, C.J., in Conway's Ex'rs v. Alexander, 11 U.S. (7 Cranch) 218, 3 L.Ed. 321, 328 (1812), "lenders of money are less under the pressure of circumstances which control the perfect and free exercise of the judgment than borrowers", and they frequently make the effort "to avail themselves of the advantage of this superiority in order to obtain inequitable advantages."; Lord Chancellor Hardwicke in Toomes v. Conset, 3 Atk. 261 (1745); Thomas v. Klemm, 185 Md. 136, 43 A.2d 193 (1945).

Statute of Frauds logically applied to exclude it. It is also sufficient to outweigh any policy objections against countenancing the deed absolute form of mortgage on the ground that it opens an easy way to debtors to conceal their assets from their creditors, a possibility which has been inveighed against and given as a bolstering reason for excluding the oral agreement.[20]

It is worth noting again that the redemption right, as was stated by Field, was created by the court of equity, for reasons of policy, in flat violation of the expressly stated intentions of the parties in the mortgage and for the purpose of defeating those intentions. In the deed absolute case, however, at least when the oral agreement is excluded by the Statute of Frauds, the problem is one of showing the true intention of the parties in spite of a positive rule of law that would prohibit it. Just as the strong policy of equity overrode the express terms of the agreement in the mortgage in the form of a deed with a defeasance, so it may override the positive statutory rule of the Statute of Frauds forbidding the showing of the actual intent when it is expressed orally. So far as the parol evidence rule is concerned, even if the court should find that under its application the parol agreement could not be considered because the parties intended the deed to be the complete expression of the whole transaction, it would do no more violence to either the intention of the parties or the positive rule of law which bars the oral proof in such a case, for the courts to say that they should both be disregarded when a claim of mortgage is made, than the original creation of the equity did to the expressed intention of the parties and the strict workings of real property law.

A final suggestion may be made as to why the evidence is let in. It may be that it is so common an occurrence for parties to enter into transactions of this sort that the courts, recognizing this fact, have established a positive rule of law as a square exception to the parol evidence rule, that when a claim of mortgage is made the issue of whether the claim is borne out by the evidence shall go directly to the trier of fact without any preliminary inquiry by the court into whether the parties intended the written deed to constitute their entire agreement. The courts may well feel that such an exception is sufficiently safeguarded by the usual rule requiring exceptionally strong evidence to establish the claim.

Statute of Frauds

The Statute of Frauds is considerably more of an obstacle to the introduction of the parol agreement of defeasance than is the parol evidence rule. In the latter case, the easiest and soundest view is, as we saw, that the application of the rule does not operate to exclude the evidence. Further, upon the assumption that it did exclude the

20. Lee v. Evans, 8 Cal. 424, 432 (1857).

showing of the agreement, we looked at various justifications for admission in spite of the rule. Three of them have been advanced as reasons for avoiding the prohibition of the Statute of Frauds.[21] The second and third clearly are theories that afford rational grounds for admitting the evidence in spite of the Statute. Although the final stricture on the first explanation would be inapplicable where the Statute of Frauds is the obstacle, the other criticisms of it seem appropriate. Another reason closely connected with this first explanation is most frequently expressed by saying that rules of law designed to prevent fraud must not be used so as to produce fraud, and "that it would be a virtual fraud for the grantee to insist upon the deed as an absolute conveyance of the title, which had been intentionally given to him, and which he had knowingly accepted, merely as security, and therefore in reality as a mortgage." [22] But perhaps the best reason advanced as to why the Statute of Frauds has not prevented showing that the transaction was a mortgage is that it is not violated.[23]

"It is frequently and correctly stated that the statute of frauds has no application to parol proof of an equitable mortgage, but this is for the obvious reason that such proof by establishing an equitable mortgage does not transfer to the mortgagor an interest in land. The oral proof simply limits the effect of a conveyance absolute in form to the agreed effect—a transfer as security." [24]

In other words, the parol evidence merely shows that the grantor *retained* a part interest in the property, namely the beneficial ownership of the property; and parol evidence showing that a person never even purported to part with the beneficial ownership of property does not constitute a transfer or creation of an interest in property.[25]

21. I. e., fraud upon the grantor, unjust enrichment of the grantee, and policy in favor of protecting the redemption interest.

22. See Smith v. Smith, 153 Ala. 504, 508, 45 So. 168, 169 (1907); Pomeroy, Eq.Juris., 5th ed., § 1196. See also 15 Iowa L.Rev. 193 (1929).

23. De Bartlett v. De Wilson, 52 Fla. 497, 42 So. 189, 11 Ann.Cas. 311 (1906). See L.R.A.1916B, 71, 73.

24. Bennett v. Harrison, 115 Minn. 342, 355, 132 N.W. 309, 314, 37 L.R. A.,N.S., 521 (1911).

25. See Smedley and Blunk, Oral Understandings at Variance With Absolute Deeds, 34 Ill.L.Rev. 189, 198 (1940), where the argument was made that such an agreement did not, for this reason, violate either the parol evidence rule or the trust provision of the Statute of Frauds. However, even where there is a special statute, rather than § 4 of the English Statute of Frauds or a paraphrase of it, expressly requiring "mortgages" to be "created, renewed, or extended" by an instrument in writing it has been held that it would be no bar to the admission of oral evidence that a deed absolute was intended as a mortgage. Anglo-Californian Bank v. Cerf, 147 Cal. 384, 81 P. 1077 (1905). See Fogelman, The Deed Absolute as a Mortgage in New York, 32 Fordham L.Rev. 299, 303 (1963); Cunningham and Tischler, Disguised Real Estate Security Transactions as Mortgages in Substance, 26 Rutgers L.Rev. 1, 10 (1972).

§ 3.15 Parol Mortgage vs. Parol Trust Or Parol Condition Subsequent to a Written Contract

A further question arises as to whether an oral agreement to hold an absolute deed as a mortgage should be treated differently from an oral agreement to hold as trustee in so far as the impact of the parole evidence rule or the Statute of Frauds is concerned.[26] This is a potential problem because substantial authority holds that an oral express trust agreement by a grantee under a deed absolute cannot be established in favor of the grantor nor may a constructive trust be imposed.[27] With respect to the parol evidence rule no plausible distinction between the two types of cases has been offered. And, indeed, in spite of some respectable authorities[28] that imply, at least, that the parol evidence rule would bar it if there were no basis for an exception to it, the clearly preferable view, and the one accepted by most cases, is that the rule raises no barrier to the introduction of the oral agreement in either case. The real hurdle is the Statute of Frauds.[29]

At the outset one reconciliation of the two groups of cases so far as the Statute of Frauds is concerned may be suggested. It is that trusts are specifically covered by two sections of the English Statute of Frauds, seven and eight,[30] whereas there are no sections specifically dealing with mortgages and, if they are covered, it is because the general language of section one or four is construed to apply. But there is authority for the view that establishing the mortgage only shows a reservation of an interest in the grantor and the Statute doesn't prevent doing this.[31] This distinction, however, has seldom

26. For a thorough discussion of the whole problem see Smedley and Blunk, Oral Understandings at Variance with Absolute Deeds, 34 Ill.L. Rev. 189 (1939).

27. See Scott, Conveyances Upon Trusts Not Properly Declared, 37 Harv.L.Rev. 653 (1924); Ames, Constructive Trusts Based upon the Breach of an Express Oral Trust of Land, 20 Harv.L.Rev. 549 (1907); Costigan, Trusts Based on Oral Promises to Hold in Trust, to Convey, or to Devise Made by Voluntary Grantees, 12 Mich.L.Rev. 427, 515 (1914); Stone, Resulting Trusts and the Statute of Frauds, 6 Col.L.Rev. 326 (1906).

28. E. g., Pierce v. Robinson, supra note 17.

29. See IX, Wigmore, Evidence, 3d ed. § 2437; Scott, Trusts, § 38; Bogert, Trusts and Trustees, 2d Ed., § 51.

30. In some states in the United States there is no provision in the Statute of Frauds applying to trusts. In these jurisdictions an additional reason exists why the parol evidence rule should not bar the oral trust, because if it did the courts "would be faced with the uncomfortable problem of having a valid oral trust with a destruction of the only means whereby the trust can be enforced. This would be in effect to add a trust provision to the Statute of Frauds by force of judicial decision." Smedley and Blunk, Oral Understandings at Variance with Absolute Deeds, 34 Ill. L.Rev. 189, 197 (1939). The same argument would apply to an oral mortgage to which the Statute of Frauds did not apply.

31. See preceding section. But cf. Anglo-Californian Bank v. Cerf, 147 Cal. 384, 81 P. 1077 (1905), holding that a Statute of Frauds explicitly referring to mortgages would not prevent showing the oral mortgage.

been pointed out [32] and, although some courts simply dismiss the apparent inconsistency by saying, without giving any reasons, that the oral mortgage cases are distinguishable from the oral trust cases,[33] more important authorities have stated flatly that they "can see no distinction between an express trust and a parol agreement making a deed a mortgage," [34] so far as the Statute is concerned. But, even assuming that both trusts and mortgages are governed by the requirements of the Statute of Frauds, there are several gro ınds upon which to reconcile the two lines of cases.

One reconciliation, although that seems scarcely an appropriate term for it, is to say that the problem in the two cases is identical, that the mortgage cases are correct, and that in the oral trust cases the evidence should be let in also, not for the purpose of enforcing it, but to show unjust enrichment of the grantee and forfeiture of the grantor's interest in order to impose a constructive trust; that the policy of the Statute against false claims and any other policy against permitting a transaction which permits the concealment of assets is outweighed by the policy against permitting one person to be enriched at the expense of another plus the general desirability of permitting the intention of the parties to a transaction to be enforced.[35] It has even been urged that the forfeiture in the trust case is greater than in the mortgage case and thus presents an even stronger basis for relief because in the latter "the party would get it for the money he had loaned, while in the latter he would get it for nothing." [36] This seems an error. The establishment and collection of the debt by the grantee would not be affected by the Statute of Frauds or the parol evidence rule; and there is no reason to assume that if the court refused to admit the oral evidence of the mortgage that it would, because of this, prevent the collection of the debt. If so the amount of forfeiture would be the same in both cases.

The most important difference between the two cases is the one which best explains why courts, even though there may be strong objections in the mortgage case to letting in the evidence, neverthe-

32. See, however, Smedley and Blunk, Oral Understandings at Variance With Absolute Deeds, 34 Ill.L.Rev. 189, 204 (1939).

33. E. g., Sturtevant v. Sturtevant, 20 N.Y. 39, 40, 75 Am.Dec. 371 (1859); Patton v. Beecher, 68 Ala. 579 (1872).

34. Rasdall's Adm'rs v. Rasdall, 9 Wis. 379 (1859), a leading case. See Stone, Resulting Trusts and the Statute of Frauds, 6 Col.L.Rev. 326, 341 (1906).

35. See Scott, Trusts, § 44; Stone, Resulting Trusts and the Statute of Frauds, 6 Col.L.Rev. 326, 339 (1906); Ames, Oral Trusts of Lands, 20 Harv.L.Rev. 549, 553 (1906).

36. Rasdall's Adm'rs v. Rasdall, 9 Wis. 379 (1859). See also Scott, Abridgment of the Law of Trusts, § 44.3: "Indeed, the unjust enrichment is greater in the case of an oral trust than in the case of an oral mortgage; for if no relief is given in the former case the whole of the property is lost, while in the latter case only the value above the amount of the debt is lost."

less do allow it. That is the notion which has played such a part in the protection of the mortgagor's redemption interest, namely, that the mortgagor is an economic weakling who must be protected against his own agreements because he makes them under the pressure of necessity. The mortgagee has money and the mortgagor needs it. The mortgagee has a leverage on the mortgagor and can virtually club him into giving a deed absolute with the mortgagor having to rely on the oral agreement. And this strong policy in favor of the mortgagor's redemption right overbalances, as we have suggested, counter policies against both fraudulent claims and possible [37] fraudulent concealment of assets. In the case of the oral trust there is no similar reason to excuse the grantor. And the forfeiture and unjust enrichment, which exists in the mortgage case also, is not sufficient to overcome the opposing considerations.

This deference toward the mortgagor, if it is based upon the assumption that the owner of money is in a strong position, is illogical. A owns Blackacre and is in dire need of money. B has money. A can get money from B either by mortgaging Blackacre to B or selling it to him. If A gives to B a deed absolute, the courts will allow A to show it is a mortgage and get back his property. But if it is a sale A cannot rescind the sale and get back the property on the ground that B drove a hard bargain when A was necessitous. Of course it can be answered that in the mortgage case equity is granting the relief to effectuate the executory intention of the parties as expressed orally while in the sale case it would be defeating an executed intention. Yet this seems only verbally to distinguish the cases for, in pursuance of its solicitude for the mortgagor, as, for example, in the original creation of the redemption right, equity did not hesitate to defeat a completely executed intention of both parties that title should be absolute in the mortgagee if the debt was not paid. Possibly the difference is psychological. In the mortgage case the mortgagee plays not merely upon the *necessities* of A but upon his *hopes* of getting the land back and his hopes lead him to make foolish bargains. In the case of the sale, however, the buyer plays only upon the needs of the other.

There are other distinctions between the mortgage and the trust cases which may play some part in causing the divergent results. For one thing there are no rules of law which prevent proving the existence of a debt which existed before or arose at the time of the conveyance and continued to exist after the conveyance. This observable and independent circumstance gives corroboration to the grantor's story that the conveyance was for security. There is no similar external guarantee for the grantor who claims an oral trust. Again, there were historical precedents permitting the oral mortgage to be

37. See Scott, Conveyances upon Trusts Not Properly Declared, 37 Harv.L.Rev. 653, 663 (1924); Scott, Abridgment of the Law of Trusts, § 44.3.

shown before the enactment of the Statute of Frauds whereas there was no similar power found in the case of oral trust. Although it might not have more sanction than the influence of precedent, the courts may well have coupled the express provisions in the newly enacted Statute covering trusts, the lack of any such explicit coverage of mortgages, and the older mortgages cases to arrive at the conclusion that the oral trust was prohibited but the oral mortgage not.[37a]

It has also been suggested that the cases allowing the oral mortgage to be shown are inconsistent with the well settled rule that an obligor upon a written contract or a negotiable instrument cannot prove an extrinsic condition subsequent. It has been answered that the "distinction must rest on the assumption that A may very likely give an actual conveyance of Blackacre in absolute form when it is agreed that the transfer shall operate merely as a security, but that he is not so likely to make a written contract promising to transfer Blackacre in absolute form when the understanding of the parties is, as before, that the transaction shall be defeasible upon a certain contingency."[38] An acute observation, this, which requires no addition.

C. THE CONDITIONAL SALE

§ 3.16 Nature of the Transaction

Where there is a conveyance by deed absolute on its face and, in addition, executed as part of the same transaction, a separate written agreement, there is no difficulty in construing the two instruments together. If the separate agreement provides by its terms that the deed is to be void on the payment of a debt which was part of the transaction, or that the grantee should reconvey on the same event, the whole transaction is clearly a mortgage. This we have already discussed.[39] But the written agreement may not disclose unambiguously that the property is to go back to the grantor on the payment of a debt, and likewise it may not clearly purport to be a contract or option for a resale of the property to the grantor. In such cases there is a question as to whether the separate writing was a mortgage defeasance or a contract of sale of some sort.[40] To answer this question, extrinsic evidence undoubtedly can be admitted to ascertain the true character of the writing.[41] But there are a large number of

37a. See Smedley and Blunk, supra, note 32 at 202–204.

38. 3 Williston, Contracts, rev. ed., § 635.

39. See § 3.3, supra.

40. There is authority that if the instrument leaves it doubtful, it will be construed a mortgage. Graham v. Mullins, 286 Ill.App. 393, 3 N.E.2d 723 (1936). See Smith v. Swendsen, 57 Idaho 715, 69 P.2d 131, 111 A.L.R. 441 (1937).

41. Keithley v. Wood, 151 Ill. 466, 38 N.E. 149, 42 Am.St.Rep. 265 (1894); Chase Nat. Bank v. Tover, 245 App. Div. 615, 283 N.Y.S. 832 (1935), af-

cases in which the separate instrument without any ambiguity at all professes expressly to be a contract or option to resell to the grantor the property conveyed by the deed.[42] In some instances, indeed, in addition to spelling out the transaction, the parties may insert quite explicit statements negating the existence of a debt as the foundation of a mortgage or affirming the character of the undertaking as a contract.[43] When this is done the question of determining whether, nevertheless, the transaction is a mortgage presents more difficulty and is the subject of our present inquiry.

The historical origin of this type of transaction apparently lies in the social humiliation attached to being forced to mortgage the family estate and to resort to money lenders to do so. "The transaction, then, which will raise the needed money, will leave the way open for a winning back of the family inheritance when its fortunes have been regained, and will at the same time avoid the stigma of being forced by a pecuniary need, is the transaction which will commend itself as the desirable one, * * *. Such a transaction is the sale for repurchase." [44] In other words, it was the borrower historically who often desired this type of transaction.

Today, however, it is usually the lender who dictates this form of transaction and for at least three important reasons. First, as is the case with the absolute deed as a mortgage, the lender seeks to avoid the consequences of the mortgagor's equity of redemption and the accompanying rules of mortgage law.[45] Second, the lender often seeks to avoid the consequences of the usury law.[46] In other words, the lender will seek to characterize the difference between the "sale" price and the repurchase price as simply part of the repurchase price and not as interest. Finally, an income tax motive may be present. For example, the grantee may seek to mask the difference between the sale price and the repurchase price as a capital gain rather than as ordinary interest income.[47] This would, of course, be impossible in a regular mortgage transaction.

Such transactions today take many forms. The most frequent of them are "(1) a sale and conveyance of the land by R to E with option in R to repurchase it; (2) the same as (1) with the addition of

firmed without opinion, 271 N.Y. 518, 2 N.E.2d 674 (1936). See note, 111 A.L.R. 448, 455 (1937).

42. See cases cited in the following footnotes. For a collection of cases, see 79 A.L.R. 937 (1932); 155 A.L.R. 1104 (1945).

43. See, e. g., Downs v. Ziegler, 13 Ariz.App. 387, 477 P.2d 261 (1971).

44. Wigmore, The Pledge-Idea, 10 Harv.L.Rev. 389, 393 (1897).

45. See e. g., Swallow Ranches, Inc. v. Bidart, 525 F.2d 995 (C.A.Nev.1975).

46. See Robinson v. Durston, 83 Nev. 337, 432 P.2d 75 (1967); Kawauchi v. Tabata, 49 Hawaii 160, 413 P.2d 221 (1966); Kjar v. Brimley, 27 Utah 2d 411, 497 P.2d 23 (1972).

47. See, e. g., Robinson v. Durston, 83 Nev. 337, 432 P.2d 75 (1967).

a deed of reconveyance deposited in escrow * * *; (3) a sale and conveyance by R to E and a lease by E to R with option in R to repurchase; (4) a sale and conveyance by R to E with an unconditional contract by E to resell and by R to repurchase the land, that is, the creation of the relation of vendor and purchaser, rather than that of mortgagor and mortgagee, attended with a different right of foreclosure * * *; (5) the same as (4), with the addition of a deed of reconveyance deposited in escrow * * *; (6) a sale and conveyance by R to E with a written agreement that in the event of further sale the proceeds over and above a certain sum should be paid in whole or part to R * * *; (7) a sale and conveyance made by one already a mortgagor to the mortgagee, with a provision that the former should have the same privilege of redemption as would be given by statute in that state after a foreclosure sale." [48] The term conditional sale has been loosely applied to all such arrangements although frequently this description has been restricted to a sale with merely an option to repurchase.[49]

§ 3.17 Extrinsic Evidence

In all of these situations the question again arises whether extrinsic evidence can be introduced to show that the transactions, notwithstanding the terms of the agreements, are mortgages. In spite of some cases holding to the contrary,[50] the authorities in general again answer yes.[51] But there is one striking difference here from the case where the only written instrument is the deed absolute. Here the extrinsic evidence establishing the fact that the parties intended the transaction to be a mortgage collides head on with the written agreement integrated with the deed as the full statement of the parties' agreement. It squarely contradicts it. There can be no explanation here that the oral agreement merely fills out a part of the transaction not covered, and intended not to be covered, by the part which was written. And yet, as was just said, the evidence comes in. Also,

48. Campbell, Cases on Mortgages, 2d ed., 109 n.

49. See Campbell, Cases on Mortgages, 2d ed., 97 n. 1. See also Sargent v. Hamblin, 57 N.M. 559, 564, 260 P.2d 919, 926 (1953); When Is an Absolute Conveyance a Mortgage?, 8 U. of Fla.L.Rev. 132 (1955).

50. Thomas v. Ogden State Bank, 80 Utah 138, 147, 13 P.2d 636, 639 (1932); Carter v. Simpson Estate Co., 103 Or. 383, 388, 391, 193 P. 913, 203 P. 580, 581, 582 (1922) (alternative decision); McMurry v. Mercer, 73 S.W.2d 1087, 1089 (Tex.Civ.App.1934), criticised, 13 Tex.L.Rev. 241 (1934). Cf. Fry v. D. H. Overmyer Co. Inc., 269 Or. 281, 525 P.2d 140 (1974).

51. See Downs v. Ziegler, 13 Ariz.App. 387, 477 P.2d 261 (1971); Robinson v. Durston, 83 Nev. 337, 432 P.2d 75 (1967); Orlando v. Berns, 154 Cal. App.2d 753, 316 P.2d 705 (1957); McKinley v. Hinnant, 242 N.C. 245, 87 S.E.2d 568 (1955), noted in Third Annual Survey of North Carolina Case Law: Credit Transactions, 34 N.C.L.Rev. 35 (1955); Cowles v. Zlaket, 167 Cal.App.2d 20, 334 P.2d 55 (1959); Cunningham & Tischler, Disguised Real Estate Security Transactions as Mortgages in Substance, 26 Rutgers L.Rev. 1, 13 (1972).

although there are many authorities requiring the mortgage intent to be established by clear and convincing evidence,[52] as in the deed absolute cases, others hold that a preponderance of evidence will suffice.[53] Further, in doubtful cases the courts will construe the arrangement as a mortgage [54] and some courts have ruled that if there is any agreement executed contemporaneously with an absolute deed whereby the grantor may, within a limited time, demand a reconveyance the transaction is conclusively a mortgage.[55] In other words the task of establishing the transaction to be a mortgage is distinctly easier than in the straight deed absolute case in spite of an apparently clear encroachment on the parol evidence rule, certainly clearer than in the deed absolute case. At first glance this seems curious and an apparent aberration. As one court said, " * * * it seems illogical to hold that clear and convincing evidence is required to establish that the transaction is a mortgage, where the deed is absolute and there is no collateral writing, but that where there is a contemporaneous agreement to sell the property, less evidence is required

52. See Fry v. D. H. Overmyer Co. Inc., 269 Or. 281, 525 P.2d 140 (1974). Parks v. Mulledy, 49 Idaho 546, 290 P. 205, 79 A.L.R. 934 (1930); Nitkey v. Ward, 199 Minn. 334, 271 N.W. 873 (1937), certiorari denied 302 U.S. 706, 58 S.Ct. 25, 82 L.Ed. 545, rehearing denied 302 U.S. 775, 58 S.Ct. 134, 82 L.Ed. 600; Sargent v. Hamblin, 57 N.M. 559, 260 P.2d 919 (1953); Cowles v. Zlaket, 167 Cal.App.2d 20, 334 P.2d 55 (1959).

53. Westberg v. Wilson, 185 Minn. 307, 309, 241 N.W. 315, 316 (1932). For cases on the quantum of proof, see Updike, Mortgages, in 1953 Annual Survey of American Law, 29 N.Y.U.L.Rev. 829, 830 (1954).

54. "In all doubtful cases a contract will be construed to be a mortgage rather than a conditional sale, because in the case of a mortgage the mortgagor, although he has not strictly complied with the terms of the mortgage, still has his right of redemption; while in the case of a conditional sale, without strict compliance, the rights of the conditional purchaser are forfeited." Matthews v. Sheehan, 69 N.Y. 585, 590 (1877). See, Russell v. Southard, 53 U.S. (12 How.) 139, 13 L.Ed. 927 (1851).

"A matter of intention is entirely one of fact to be determined by the trial court and a finding by it in this regard will not be set aside unless it is clearly or manifestly against the weight of the evidence." Nitkey v. Ward, 199 Minn. 334, 340, 271 N.W. 873, 876 (1937), certiorari denied 302 U.S. 706, 58 S.Ct. 25, 82 L.Ed. 545, rehearing denied 302 U.S. 775, 58 S.Ct. 134, 82 L.Ed. 600.

See also Fogelman, The Deed Absolute as a Mortgage in New York, 32 Fordham L.Rev. 299, 307 (1963) on the significance of the existence of a written defeasance.

55. Kerr v. Gilmore, 6 Watts 405 (Pa. 1837); Brown v. Nickle, 6 Pa. 390 (1847). Only slightly weaker than this is the attitude of a Canadian court expressed in Hawke v. Milliken, 12 Grant Ch. 236, 238 (1866), "when an obligation to purchase and pay the money is exacted from the grantor, that is sufficient to show the real character of the transaction to be a mortgage, though the form of it is a sale."

It has been held that a *grantee* may establish that the transaction was a mortgage if he meets the requirements of proof which would be required of the grantor. Holman v. Mason City Auto Co., 186 Iowa 704, 171 N.W. 12 (1919); Goodbar & Co. v. Bloom, 43 Tex.Civ.App. 434, 96 S.W. 657 (1906); Baldwin v. McDonald, 24 Wyo. 108, 156 P. 27 (1916) (semble); Downs v. Ziegler, 13 Ariz.App. 387, 477 P.2d 261 (1971). See § 3.6, supra.

* * *." [56] Yet the explanation is not difficult. The same solicitude for the redemption right is just as important here to prevent the summary ending of the grantor's right which would occur if he is held to be merely an optionee or vendee of a contract of purchase and to preserve to him the benefits of the mortgagor's right of redemption. This idea was stressed in a leading case, the court saying "it is not to be forgotten, that the same language which truly describes a real sale, may also be employed to cut off the right of redemption, in case of a loan on security; that it is the duty of the court to watch vigilantly these exercises of skill, lest they should be effectual to accomplish what equity forbids; and that, in doubtful cases, the court leans to the conclusion that the reality was a mortgage, and not a sale. * * * It is true [the mortgagor] must have given his assent to this form of the memorandum; but the distress for money under which he then was, places him in the same condition as other borrowers, in numerous cases reported in the books, who have submitted to the dictation of the lender under the pressure of their wants; and a court of equity does not consider a consent, thus obtained, to be sufficient to fix the rights of the parties." [57]

Moreover, since by the evidence the grantor does have a written claim to get the property from the grantee and the only controversy is whether it is to be by virtue of a contract of purchase or by a right to redeem as mortgagor, there is not nearly the violence of alteration of the situation of the parties as there is where the grantor is allowed to take away property from the person who, by the only written evidence, has an absolute and indefeasible title to it. This also cuts in another direction. There is a policy objection in the deed absolute cases both against permitting the grantor to conceal his assets by making a conveyance which does not reveal by a writing that there is a string to it by which the property can be pulled back, and, also, in favor of the grantee, against the possibility of false swearing to do him out of his property. Here the written agreement minimizes both such policies. There is not only a written clue to the grantor's continued interest in the conveyed property for his creditors to follow up, but also no great hardship is going to fall on the grantee if the amount the grantor is to pay is held to be a debt rather than a contract purchase price and his right, consequently, to be one of redemption instead of one upon the grantee's promise to reconvey. The chief inju-

56. Johnson v. National Bank of Commerce, 65 Wash. 261, 275, 118 P. 21, 25, L.R.A.1916B, 4 (1911).

57. Russell v. Southard, 53 U.S. (12 How.) 139, 151, 13 L.Ed. 927 (1851).

"It may be premised that where upon the face of the transaction it is doubtful whether the parties intended to make a mortgage or conditional sale, courts of equity will always incline to consider it a mortgage, because by means of conditional sales oppression is frequently exercised over the needy, and they are too often made the vehicle of extortion." Earp v. Boothe, 24 Gratt. (Va.) 368, 375 (1874).

ry the grantee suffers is in being deprived of his ability to end the grantor's right on default by means other than foreclosure; and it would be difficult to argue that this is of great seriousness; or, if it is, or might be, substantial, that it is not outweighed by the greater possible hardship on the grantor of the opposite result.

§ 3.18 Factors Establishing Conditional Sale as a Mortgage

In determining whether the transaction is a mortgage, or an absolute or conditional sale, the problem is substantially the same as in the straight deed absolute case. It is the intention of the parties at the time the transaction is entered into, as gathered from the writings themselves and from relevant extrinsic evidence, which governs.[58] Many factors enter into the determination of this question of fact. A good summary of some of these essential elements includes, "whether or not there is a continuing obligation on the part of the grantor to pay the debt or meet the obligation which it is claimed the deed was made to secure; the question of relative values; the contemporaneous and subsequent acts; the declarations and admissions of the parties; the form of the written evidences of the transactions; the nature and character of the testimony relied upon; the various business, social and other relationship of the parties; and the apparent aims and purposes to be accomplished." [59] At least a few of these factors, however, need further consideration.

When the agreement gives the grantor only an option to repurchase and it is clear that he has no duty to pay the sum specified as "purchase" money, there is a question as to whether the transaction can be a mortgage. If, for example, a personal obligation is a condition precedent to a valid mortgage,[60] then, of course, there could be no mortgage if the grantor has no such personal obligation. However, in those jurisdictions where a personal obligation on the part of

58. Both parties must intend a mortgage. Douglass v. Moody, 80 Ala. 61, 69 (1885); Nitkey v. Ward, 199 Minn. 334, 271 N.W. 873 (1937), certiorari denied 302 U.S. 706, 58 S.Ct. 25, 82 L.Ed. 545, rehearing denied 302 U.S. 775, 58 S.Ct. 134, 82 L.Ed. 600; Ministers Life And Cas. Union v. Franklin Park Towers Corp., 239 N.W.2d 207 (Minn.1976); Fry v. D. H. Overmyer Co. Inc., 269 Or. 281, 525 P.2d 140 (1974).

59. Corey v. Roberts, 82 Utah 445, 452, 25 P.2d 940, 942 (1933). Another excellent summary of the evidence indicating the factors going into the finding is in Morton v. Allen, 180 Ala. 279, 286, 60 So. 866, 868, L.R.A. 1916B, 11 (1912). See also Gray v. Frazer, 63 Idaho 552, 123 P.2d 711 (1942); Nitkey v. Ward, 199 Minn. 334, 271 N.W. 873 (1937) certiorari denied 302 U.S. 706, 58 S.Ct. 25, 82 L.Ed. 545, rehearing denied 302 U.S. 775, 58 S.Ct. 134, 82 L.Ed. 600; O'Briant v. Lee, 214 N.C. 723, 200 S. E. 865 (1939); Dean v. Smith, 53 N.D. 123, 204 N.W. 987 (1925) discussed in note, 2 Ill.L.Rev. 732 (1926); Selik v. Goldman Realty Co., 240 Mich. 612, 216 N.W. 422 (1927), discussed, 26 Mich.L.Rev. 821 (1928); notes, 16 N. Car.L.Rev. 416, 418 (1938); Robinson v. Durston, 83 Nev. 337, 432 P.2d 75 (1967); Downs v. Ziegler, 13 Ariz. App. 387, 477 P.2d 261 (1971); Kjar v. Brimley, 27 Utah 2d 411, 497 P.2d 23 (1972).

60. See § 2.1, 2.3, supra.

the mortgagor may not be required to establish a valid mortgage,[61] its absence will not automatically bar the establishment of a mortgage in the option to purchase situation.[62] Nevertheless, the absence of a personal obligation in the latter situation is probably strong evidence that the parties did not intend a mortgage transaction.[63] On the other hand, evidence of the existence of a debt is strongly persuasive of a mortgage intent.[64]

As in the absolute deed situation, another significant factor cutting in favor of finding a mortgage transaction is great disparity between the price the grantor receives and the *value* of the land.[65] When a regular mortgage is used, the mortgagor is normally liable to pay the balance of the debt in the event that the mortgaged property is insufficient for that purpose. Where a sale with an option to purchase is used and the disparity referred to above is not great, if the land goes down in value, the grantor will not exercise the purchase option and the grantee will bear the loss. Where, however, the disparity is substantial, even if the value of the land subsequently drops, the grantee has substantial protection even though he has no personal action against the grantor.

It is also often necessary in these repurchase situations to consider the relationship between the amount received by the grantor and the *repurchase* price. For example, if the amount received is $10,000 and the repurchase price is $11,000 one year later, the 10%

61. See, e. g., Ministers Life and Cas. Union v. Franklin Park Towers Corp., —— Minn. ——, 239 N.W.2d 207 (1976); § 2.1, supra.

62. See Robinson v. Durston, 83 Nev. 337, 432 P.2d 75 (1967).

63. "Neither that fund nor the option imposed any obligation to repurchase. It was entirely a matter of choice with the lessee. * * * That is a strong circumstance tending to prove that the conveyance was what it purported to be (see Dixon v. Wright, 175 Miss. 191, 166 So. 374) (1936), * * *." Nitkey v. Ward, 199 Minn. 334, 341, 271 N.W. 873, 877 (1937); Ministers Life and Cas. Union v. Franklin Park Towers Corp., 239 N.W.2d 207 (Minn.1976).

64. O'Briant v. Lee, 214 N.C. 723, 733, 200 S.E. 865, 871 (1939), "If there was a debt, either antecedent or presently created, the instrument must be construed to constitute a mortgage, unless a contrary intent clearly appears upon the face of the instrument." See Hawke v. Milliken, 12 Grant. Ch., Upper Can., 236 (1866). See note, 20 Ill.L.Rev. 732, 733 (1926).

In Investors' Mortgage Security Co. v. Hamilton, 51 Idaho 113, 4 P.2d 347 (1931), discussed in note, 2 Idaho L.J. 151 (1932), the fact that the grantee, who took a conveyance of mortgaged property in purported satisfaction of the grantor's mortgage debt to him, retained the original evidence of indebtedness was thought to be convincing evidence that the conveyance and option to repurchase constituted a mortgage.

65. Courts generally treat inadequacy of price as one of the important facts in determining whether a mortgage was intended. See Glass v. Hieronymus Bros., 125 Ala. 140, 28 So. 71, 82 Am.St.Rep. 225 (1899); Rogers v. Davis, 91 Iowa 730, 59 N.W. 265 (1894); Daniels v. Johnson, 24 Mich. 430 (1872); Lawrence v. DuBois, 16 W.Va. 443 (1880); Carpenter & Carpenter v. Kingman, 56 Wyo. 314, 109 P.2d 463 (1941). See 155 A.L.R. 1109 (1945); 90 A.L.R. 953 (1934), for additional authorities.

premium looks to some extent like a normal interest return on a loan. If the repurchase price at the end of the one year is $14,000, the disparity could represent an attempt to mask a usurious loan and thus arguably could cut in favor of a mortgage transaction. Suppose, however, that the repurchase price is $20,000. Here the substantial disparity could indicate a highly usurious loan or it may simply mean that the land was purchased at a distress sale and that there was no mortgage transaction.

Indeed, it is often necessary to consider all three "disparity" factors in repurchase cases or at least different combinations of them. For example, one court, in holding a transaction to be a loan, gave considerable weight to the fact that the value of the property conveyed greatly exceeded *both* the amount received by the grantor and the repurchase price.[66] In another case, the court was strongly influenced to find a mortgage because the repurchase price was exactly the amount owed by the grantors to the grantee at the time of the conveyance.[67]

D. TRIPARTITE TRANSACTIONS

§ 3.19 Purchase Money Resulting Trusts

Most American jurisdictions recognize the long-established rule that where one person pays the purchase price for land, but legal title is conveyed to another, a presumption is created that the grantee holds the land under a resulting trust for the person paying the purchase price.[68] "The real purchaser of the property is considered as the owner, with the right to control the title in the hands of the grantee, and to demand a conveyance from him at any time." [69] The same rule is applicable "if the money paid by the party taking the title is advanced by him as a loan to the other." [70] In all cases the burden of establishing the resulting trust is on the party asserting it. In the first type of case the alleged real purchaser "must prove not only that the consideration for the conveyance was paid by him or out of his funds, but also that the money was paid as the purchase price and not as a loan" to the grantee.[71] In the second case the fact

66. Orlando v. Berns, 154 Cal.App.2d 753, 316 P.2d 705 (1957).

67. Osipowicz v. Furland, 218 Wis. 568, 260 N.W. 482 (1935), discussed in note, 11 Wis.L.Rev. 118 (1935).

68. See Nelson, Purchase-Money Resulting Trusts In Land In Missouri, 33 Mo.L.Rev. 552, 553 (1968); Scott, Trusts, § 440 (3d Ed. 1967); Bogert, Trusts and Trustees, § 454 (2d Ed. 1964).

69. Campbell v. Freeman, 99 Cal. 546, 34 P. 113 (1893).

70. Campbell v. Freeman, 99 Cal. 546, 34 P. 113 (1893). See Bogert, Trusts and Trustees, § 455 (2d Ed. 1964). Accord: Kohler v. Gilbert, 216 Or. 483, 339 P.2d 1102 (1959).

71. Phillips v. Phillips, 81 N.J.Eq. 459, 461, 86 A. 949, 950 (1913), affirmed 83 N.J.Eq. 345, 91 A. 1070 (1914). See Scott, Cases on Trusts, 2d Ed., §

of loan by the grantee must be clearly proved.[72] In both cases, however, when A establishes the fact that it was his money that paid for the land, regardless of whether it was his before the transaction or borrowed from B, the grantee, to consummate it, the burden of proof is met because, without further evidence, the inference is drawn that B does not take the beneficial interest and, therefore, that B holds on resulting trust for A. B may rebut this inference, but the burden of proof is upon him to do so.[73] Furthermore, in both cases, it is thoroughly settled that Statutes of Frauds do not prevent such trusts arising. It is sometimes stated that this is so because the trust arises by operation of law and therefore is within an express exception of the Statute of Frauds.[74] A better reason, given by an authority in the field, is that although such resulting trusts "arise out of the intention of the parties, that intention is evidenced by the circumstances of the transaction rather than by the language of the parties. There is not, therefore, as a practical matter the same danger of perjured testimony as in cases where the only evidence of intention is the oral language of the parties." [75] Quite obviously the parol evidence rule has no application: the only writing is the deed from the third party and it would not control as the sole memorial of the agreed upon rights between the grantee and the alleged purchaser.[76]

§ 3.20 Purchase Money Resulting Trusts—Security Agreements

Where the grantee of title under a purchase-money resulting trust has loaned the money, it is usual for him to stipulate that the land shall be security for the loan, and such an agreement, even though oral, is recognized.[77] As one court stated, "In such a case the grantee holds a double relation to the real purchaser,—he is his trustee of the legal title to the land, and his mortgagee for the money advanced for its purchase, and, as in the case of any other mortgage which is evidenced by an absolute deed, is entitled to retain the title until the payment of the claim for which it is held as security; and he may also enforce his lien by an action of foreclosure. The conveyance is nonetheless a mortgage because it was conveyed to him directly by a third party, to secure his loan to the purchaser for the

440 et seq. for a collection of authorities on purchase money resulting trusts. See also 42 A.L.R. 10, 21 (1926).

72. McDonough v. O'Niel, 113 Mass. 92 (1873).

73. See Scott, supra note 68; Bogert, supra note 70 § 455.

74. Anonymous, 2 Vent. 361 (1683).

75. Scott, Trusts, 3315 (3d Ed. 1967). "This resulting trust is a form of trust dependent for its existence on the actual intent of the creator, expressed in acts other than writing or talking". Bogert, Trusts and Trustees, 2d Ed., (1964) § 454.

76. See Williston, Contracts, Rev.Ed., § 647.

77. Miller v. Miller, 101 Md. 600, 61 A. 210 (1905). See Note, Equitable Mortgages in Iowa, 44 Iowa L.Rev. 716, 721–723 (1959).

amount of the purchase money, than if the conveyance had been made directly to the purchaser in the first instance, and the purchaser had then made a conveyance to him, as a security for the money that he had previously borrowed with which to make the purchase." [78] It should be noted in this connection that, although the burden of establishing the resulting trust is on the alleged purchaser, including the proof that the money paid by the grantee was in fact a loan, the burden of establishing the mortgage agreement is a separate and distinct question and is on the one asserting its existence. Usually this is the purchaser and, when it is, the courts do not clearly differentiate between the tasks of establishing the resulting trust and the mortgage, saying that both must be proved by strong evidence. Since one element in the security agreement is the loan by the grantee, which must be proved to make out the resulting trust, it is easy to understand why the two problems are not segregated.[79] When the grantee is seeking to foreclose on the property there is a similar overlapping. His main task is to prove the fact of loan as an element in the mortgage; but when he does this he has made out the resulting trust. The additional part of his case, the agreement that the property be security for the payment of the loan, is treated either as controlled by the rules governing the creation of the trust, or as involving precisely the same problem raised in the case of a straight deed absolute from the borrower to the lender.[80] So far as burden and standard of proof are concerned there is no objection to this approach. However, this tripartite situation is different from the two-party one with respect to the possible application to it of the Statute of Frauds.

78. Campbell v. Freeman, 99 Cal. 546, 548, 34 P. 113 (1893).

Accord: Hicks v. Bridges, 152 Cal.App. 2d 146, 313 P.2d 15 (1957).

See Note, 13 Kan.L.Rev. 585 (1965), discussing Duncan v. Essary, 193 Kan. 241, 392 P.2d 877 (1964), in which the court held that equitable mortgages were created by a warranty deed from the defendant of property owned by it and also on property conveyed to the plaintiff from a third party grantor which had been bought by defendant with money loaned by plaintiff for that purpose. The note writer's thesis was that in the tripartite transaction it would be possible, and in some instances advantageous to either creditor or debtor, to choose between advancing the theory that the transaction was a purchase money resulting trust or an equitable mortgage. The Kansas statutes in respect to the existence in Kansas of purchase money resulting trusts was blamed by the writer for what he considered was confusion in the Kansas law on the tripartite problem. See also, Hergenreter v. Sommers, 535 S.W.2d 513 (Mo.App.1976); Scott, Trusts, § 448 (3d Ed. 1967); Nelson, Purchase-Money Resulting Trusts In Land In Missouri, 33 Mo.L.Rev. 552, 576 (1968).

79. Hall v. O'Connell, 52 Or. 164, 167, 95 P. 717 (1908); Jackson v. Maxwell, 113 Me. 366, 94 A. 116, Ann.Cas. 1917C, 966, 970 (1915).

80. Campbell v. Freeman, 99 Cal. 546, 34 P. 113 (1893).

§ 3.21 Statute of Frauds in Tripartite Cases

Although the Statute of Frauds is no objection to the creation of the resulting trust interest in the purchaser in these cases, it is not so clear that the oral agreement between the parties that the grantee-trustee shall hold his title as security for his loan does not fall within its prohibition, and hence some analysis of the matter is in order. It would seem clear that where T is an existing trustee under an express written trust and makes a loan to C, the beneficiary, with an oral agreement that T is to hold title to the trust property as security for repayment of the loan, the Statute of Frauds applies to prevent enforcement of the mortgage agreement by T. The same is true where T holds property as trustee for C under a purchase money resulting trust and later T loans money to C under an oral agreement that the property shall be security.[81] Whether in these cases the Statute would bar T from showing the agreement in case C brought an action to compel a conveyance seems to depend upon the purpose and use of the loan. If the borrowed money went into improvements or the clearing off of other liens, the court will invoke the principle that C must do equity in order to get the aid of the court of equity. As one court said in a case of this sort, "for equity to actively interpose its decree * * * denying to plaintiff all compensation for expenditures in improving and preserving the property is abhorrent, not only to a sense of natural justice, but to those fundamental principles upon which equity grants or withholds its peculiar remedies." [82] On the other hand, where the loan is made for purposes having no relation to the land, C may get the property from T without paying, the Statute of Frauds preventing T from showing the oral agreement.[83]

If the Statute of Frauds applies in the two cases just discussed, it is pertinent to inquire why it does not apply also to the case where T loans C the money with which to buy property from X, taking title in a direct deed absolute from X, but with an oral agreement at the time with C that T is to hold the property as security for the repayment of the loan. One answer is that the agreement is used only to rebut pro tanto the creation of the resulting trust. Parol evidence of the intention of C that T should have the beneficial interest for the limited purpose of security violates neither the Statute of Frauds nor the parol evidence rule. If resulting trusts arise because it is presumed from the facts that the payor of the money intended that the grantee should not have the beneficial interest, if it is shown that he

81. See Warner v. Tullis, 206 Iowa 680, 218 N.W. 575 (1928); Pierce v. Parrish, 111 Ga. 725, 37 S.E. 79 (1900).

82. Warner v. Tullis, supra note 81, 206 Iowa at 692, 218 N.W. at 580.

83. Pierce v. Parrish, 111 Ga. 725, 37 S.E. 79 (1900); Warner v. Tullis, supra, note 81, loan for funeral expenses not included in debts which must be paid as condition to compelling conveyance.

intended that the grantee should have the complete or a limited beneficial interest, the foundation for raising the resulting trust does not exist.[84] Or, if the language of courts holding that purchase money resulting trusts are not under the Statute of Frauds because they arise by "operation of law" is taken at face value, the same result follows. If it arises by "operation of law," it is an interest independent of the intention of the parties and the parol evidence of what the payor's intention actually was is let in, not for the purpose of vitiating rights effectuating anyone's intention, but for the purpose of establishing by this proof that the law, for reasons other than effectuating intent, ought not to operate to create the right, or to create it only to a limited extent. Whichever of these views is accepted, there seems no reason why, on this rationale, the security agreement should not extend not only to the purchase money loan itself but to additional loans.

Another explanation invokes the "do-equity" rationale mentioned before. The idea is that the loan has paid for the property under an agreement that it be so used and, therefore, before the borrower should be allowed to obtain it from the lender under the resulting trust he should pay the loan just as he should have to pay off loans obtained for and used to make improvements. This explanation would confine the enforceable security agreements to those covering loans of purchase money.

A contributing influence, no matter what theory is followed, undoubtedly is the fact that in this sort of transaction there are normally present factors, e. g., the fact of loan, the dealings involving the third party with his story available, the borrower-payor frequently being let into possession and paying taxes, which minimize the evils at which the Statute aims.[85] On the other hand, it should be noted that it differs from the straight deed absolute cases, in which it is clear that traditional solicitude for the hard pressed borrower who has to put up his property at risk of losing it in order to get the money he needs plays a part. Here the borrower is expanding his operations, acquiring new property, not risking old, and pledging as security only the property he never had before and for the money which enabled him to get it. Certainly no very convincing argument can be made for any special tenderness to the mortgagor in cases of this sort.

§ 3.22 Continuing Equitable Ownership in the Borrower

In many cases the borrower-payor, instead of acquiring an interest in the property by way of resulting trust arising for the first time

84. Scott, Trusts, § 441.1 (3d Ed. 1967).

85. A good illustration is Miller v. Miller, 101 Md. 600, 61 A. 210 (1905), in which M, the borrower-purchaser, went into possession, made improvements, paid taxes, and not only paid interest on his loan from E, the grantee, but also the interest on the loan owed by E to T, the grantor.

out of the transaction, had a prior equitable ownership.[86] Instances of this are contracts [87] or options [88] to purchase the property entered into by the borrower before the loan was made or the property conveyed to the lender by the contract vendor. On the question of showing the oral agreement for mortgage in such cases analogy to the two-party deed absolute cases can be invoked here, the prior equitable interest in the borrower giving to him a standing comparable to that of the legal owner-grantor; and the fact that the conveyance is from a third party, but at the direction of the borrower, is insufficient to change the substance of the transaction. Indeed the argument in favor of allowing the oral agreement is stronger here because the borrowed money was used to complete the payments necessary for the borrower to acquire the land. But apart from this, it would seem that the reasoning in the purchase money resulting trust with oral security agreement cases is also applicable here. In both cases it is the borrower's money that pays for the property conveyed to the lender; it should be immaterial to the creation of a resulting trust by reason of this fact that the buyer had a prior equitable interest in the property because of an executory contract for its purchase and that the grantee, not being a bona fide purchaser, would take subject to it.

A still different approach may be suggested. The Statute of Frauds presents no obstacle where an oral agreement for a mortgage is made by one who borrows the money for the purpose of paying the vendor under a contract of purchase, if the money is so used and the conveyance made to the borrower.[89] It would be only a slight extension to apply this to the case we have here in which the conveyance is made to the lender in accordance with the intention of the borrower. If this reasoning is accepted, the grantee-lender would be able to enforce an equitable security interest in the property to which he holds legal title. And, of course the borrower would have to do equity by paying the debt before he would be entitled to a conveyance in enforcement of either his preexisting equitable interest or his interest as beneficiary under a purchase money resulting trust.

86. See generally, Cunningham & Tischler, Disguised Real Estate Security Transactions As Mortgages in Substance, 26 Rutgers L.Rev. 1, 22 (1972).

87. McConnell v. Gentry, 30 Ky.L.Rep. 548, 99 S.W. 278 (1907); Grout v. Stewart, 96 Minn. 230, 104 N.W. 966 (1905); but see Anderson v. Anderson, 81 Minn. 329, 84 N.W. 112 (1900). See also Logue's Appeal, 104 Pa. 136, 40 L.I. 485, 31 P.L.J. 116 (1883), in which A purchased land at a judicial sale and having borrowed from B the money with which to pay the sheriff, had conveyance made to B under an oral agreement for security. See note, 42 A.L.R. 10, 25 (1926).

88. Stitt v. Rat Portage Lumber Co., 96 Minn. 27, 104 N.W. 561 (1905); Welsh v. Griffith-Prideaux, Inc., 60 N.J.Super. 199, 158 A.2d 529 (1960).

89. See Osborne, Mortages, Ch. 2 (2d Ed. 1970).

§ 3.23 Effect of Statutory Abolition of Purchase Money Resulting Trusts

Statutes in several states have abolished the purchase money resulting trust.[90] In general, they provide that in the purchase money resulting trust situation, no trust shall be declared in favor of the payor unless the grantee takes title in his own name without the consent of the payor or the grantee in violation of some trust purchases the land with the money of another.[91] There is a presumption that such conveyances are fraudulent against the creditors of the payor, and unless such fraudulent intent is disproved, a trust results in favor of such creditors to the extent necessary to satisfy their demands.[92] Two states have provisions that purport to abolish purchase money resulting trusts, but these statutes are inapplicable where it can be shown that, absent any fraudulent intent, there is an agreement that the grantee hold the land in trust for the payor.[93] Such agreements need not be written. Essentially, these latter type statutes simply do away with the presumption in favor of a resulting trust and put the burden on the trust claimant to establish the trust intact.[94]

In theory, in those states that clearly have abolished the purchase money resulting trust, an oral agreement for a mortgage in tripartite cases will be invalid under the Statute of Frauds. This is so because, apart from the specific enforcement of the oral agreement, the alleged mortgagor has no interest whatsoever in the property either beforehand or arising out of the transaction, and to permit the purely executory oral agreement to create an interest would squarely contravene the Statute of Frauds.[95]

Some courts stick more closely than others to the language of the statutes barring resulting trusts. Thus, some courts have refused to permit the trust and, consequently, the mortgage, in cases where there is an oral agreement that the grantee shall hold the title as security for the purchase money loan and, subject thereto, for the benefit of the borrower.[96] On the other hand, other courts have held that

90. See Ky.Rev.Stat. § 381.170 (1972); Mich.Stat.Ann. §§ 26.57–26.59 (1974); Minn.Stat.Ann. §§ 501.07–501.09 (1947); N.Y. Estates, Powers and Trusts Law § 7–1.3 (1967); Wis.Stat. Ann. § 701.04 (1977). On the other hand, four states have statutes expressly authorizing purchase money resulting trusts. See Mont.Rev. Code Ann. § 86–103 (1947); N.D.Cent. Code Ann. § 59–01–03(4) (1960); Okla.Stat.Ann. tit. 60, § 137 (1971); S. D.Comp.Laws § 55–1–10 (1967).

91. See Nelson, Purchase-Money Resulting Trusts in Land in Missouri, 33 Mo.L.Rev. 552, 605 (1968); Scott, Trusts, § 440.2 (3d Ed. 1967).

92. See Nelson, Purchase-Money Resulting Trusts in Land in Missouri, 33 Mo.L.Rev. 552, 605 (1968).

93. See Ind.Ann.Stat. §§ 56–606–56–608; Kan.Stat.Ann. §§ 58–2406—58–2408; Scott, Trusts, § 440.2 (3d Ed. 1967).

94. See Nelson, Purchase-Money Resulting Trusts in Land in Missouri, 33 Mo.L.Rev. 552, 605 (1968).

95. See In re Bennett, 115 Minn. 342, 132 N.W. 309 (1911).

96. Anderson v. Anderson, 81 Minn. 329, 84 N.W. 112 (1900), approved in

the resulting trust arises and the oral mortgage is good, the reasoning being twofold: (1) that the statute bars resulting trusts which would arise *solely* from the payment of the purchase money and have no other foundation. It therefore is inapplicable because there is another foundation in the oral agreement and the lending transaction. (2) That the transaction was purely one of oral mortgage.[97] The latter ground was justified on the basis that the title had been taken by the grantee "upon paying a balance due upon a contract of purchase" previously entered into by the borrower with the grantor; [98] in other words it was a case of a previously existing interest in the borrower claimant.

In many cases, even though no resulting trust can be established as an exception to the statutes prohibiting them, the borrower can work out a constructive trust in his favor which will bring him within the requirement of an interest in the property before or at the time of the mortgage transaction as effectively as would the resulting trust. An oral promise by the lender-grantee to hold it for the borrower should be sufficient to accomplish this.[99] Where there is an oral agreement with the borrower to bid in property about to be sold at foreclosure, execution, tax, partition or other judicial sale, coupled with forbearance on the part of the borrower, in reliance upon the agreement, to take steps to protect his interest, the courts have no difficulty in giving relief in spite of the fact the agreement was oral.[1] As one court put it, "where one of the parties to a contract, void by the statute of frauds, avails himself of its invalidity, but unconscientiously appropriates what he has acquired under it, equity will compel restitution; and it constitutes no objection to the claim, that the opposite party may happen to secure the same practical benefit, through the process of restitution, which would have resulted from the observance of the void agreement."[2] The same doctrine has been applied to oral agreements to redeem land for the own-

Nelson v. Nelson, 149 Minn. 285, 288, 183 N.W. 354, 355 (1921); contra, alternative decision, Stitt v. Rat Portage Lumber Co., 96 Minn. 27, 36, 104 N.W. 561, 565 (1905).

97. Carr v. Carr, 52 N.Y. 251 (1873) (there was a prior oral contract of purchase between the borrower and the grantor as well as part payment of the purchase price and taking of possession by the borrower contemporaneously with the conveyance); Widmayer v. Warner, 192 App.Div. 499, 182 N.Y.S. 629 (1920) (alternative decision). See Bogert, Trusts and Trustees, 2d Ed., § 467 (1964); Scott, Trusts, § 440.2 (3d Ed. 1967).

98. Carr v. Carr, supra note 97.

99. See Scott, Trusts, § 440.2 (3d Ed. 1967).

1. Ryan v. Dox, 34 N.Y. 307, 90 Am. Dec. 696 (1866); Congregation Kehal Adath Jeshurun M'Yassy v. Universal Bldg. & Const. Co., 134 App.Div. 368, 119 N.Y.S. 72 (1909); Widmayer v. Warner, 192 App.Div. 499, 182 N.Y.S. 629 (1920), alternative decision. If the borrower did not refrain from taking steps to protect himself no constructive trust will arise. Wheeler v. Reynolds, 66 N.Y. 227, 232 (1876); Southwick v. Spevak, 252 Mass. 354, 357, 147 N.E. 885, 886 (1925). See note, 42 A.L.R. 10, 78 (1926).

2. Ryan v. Dox, supra, note 1, at 319.

er after forced sale on foreclosure or execution.[3] Similarly, if the purchase was made by one standing in a confidential relation to the borrower, or if the purchase was in breach of a fiduciary duty a constructive trust will be imposed.[4]

A preliminary inquiry in all of these cases is whether the arrangement between the parties was for a loan by the grantee to the claimant or whether it was for the grantee to buy the property and then resell it to the claimant. The latter clearly falls within the prohibition of the Statute of Frauds even in jurisdictions where purchase money resulting trusts are not abolished. Since this is so, it is not surprising that where the agreement is for a loan and security, but because of the abolition of purchase money resulting trusts the borrower gets no interest in the property, the courts should say that this is bad because the Statute of Frauds prevents the enforcement of the oral agreement. In other words they treat it the same way that they treat an oral agreement for purchase. This seems sound, for in both cases the claimant can acquire an interest in the property for the first time only by the enforcement of the executory oral agreement. And yet one cannot escape an uneasy feeling that the result may rest more upon adherence to what the courts consider the basic theory of a mortgage than concern with the Statute of Frauds. The usual mortgage involves a prior property interest in the mortgagor which is put up by him as collateral to obtain money and which will be lost if the mortgage is valid and is foreclosed. Starting with this as the norm, it is not difficult to see that courts might establish as an indispensable part of the mortgage concept that there must be property interest in the mortgagor. Where the property interest in the mortgagor is acquired for the first time in and through the transaction which results in the mortgage, the concept still could be held to be satisfied even though the hazard the borrower runs in such a case is only that of losing what he acquired by the use of the loan. But where there exists only an executory right to get an interest in the property the mortgage concept will not stretch and the courts assimilate the case to that of a contract to sell.

§ 3.24 Contract or Option to Purchase

We saw in the two-party deed absolute case that the agreement between the parties may in form be one for an option or a contract to purchase, rather than an oral agreement that the property is to be security. The same may be true here where the deed comes to the

3. Wood v. Rabe, 96 N.Y. 414, 425, 427, 48 Am.Rep. 640 (1884). See note, 42 A.L.R. 10, 118 (1926); 54 id. 1207.

4. Foreman v. Foreman, 251 N.Y. 237, 241, 167 N.E. 428 (1929), is a leading case. See Peppard Realty Co., Inc. v. Emdon, 213 App.Div. 824, 209 N.Y.S. 5 (1925), affirmed 241 N.Y. 588, 150 N.E. 566. See note 42 A.L.R. 10, 28 (1926).

grantee from a third person.[5] Sometimes, indeed, the parties use the utmost care to adopt the form of a sale and purchase and not of a loan and mortgage.[6] When this is done the problem is similar to the two-party cases previously considered in which the deed absolute transaction was accompanied by an agreement or option to resell. In both the question is whether the transaction is what it purports to be or whether it actually is a mortgage. And in both there is no legal prohibition against resolving that question by any relevant evidence that is admissible. Plainly, in these tripartite cases he who would transform the expressed contract for sale into a different one which is supposed to be hidden by it carries a heavy burden.[7]

Two theories are used to justify treating such tripartite transactions as mortgages. First, it has been said that "if a transaction resolves itself into a security, whatever may be its form and whatever name the parties may choose to give it, it is, in equity, a mortgage." [8] Second, as two commentators have pointed out, "it can also be justified on the more complicated theory that the grantee-lender holds the legal title subject to a resulting trust based on the presumption that the lender was not intended to get the entire beneficial interest in the property conveyed to him, and that the security interest of the grantee-lender may be established by parol evidence."[9]

The factors which guide the courts in the two-party transactions are much the same ones that will influence their decisions here. However there is one vitally important point to stress again here: that to find a mortgage there must be in the mortgagor, either prior to, or arising through, the transaction otherwise than by the terms of the agreement that he should get it, an interest in the mortgaged property. As was stated in a penetrating opinion, "So far as we can find, every case in which the existence of an absolute promise by an ostensible vendee to pay the sum involved has been thought to indicate that the transaction was merely a loan instead of having the character in which it was made to appear, is a case where the contract vendee had parted with his recent title and was arranging to get it back again. In no case was the contract one for the purchase of property which he had never before owned." [10] Further, while in the

5. See Pollak v. Millsap, 219 Ala. 273, 278, 122 So. 16, 20, 65 A.L.R. 110 (1929).

6. E. g., Stark v. Bauer Cooperage Co., 3 F.2d 214 (C.C.A.Ohio 1925), certiorari denied 45 S.Ct. 464, 267 U.S. 604, 69 L.Ed. 809.

7. Id. at 215. But cf. the following statement: "all doubts are resolved in favor of it being a mortgage, and not a conditional sale." Pollak v. Millsap, 219 Ala. 273, 278, 122 So. 16, 21, 65 A.L.R. 110 (1929).

8. Welsh v. Griffith-Prideaux, Inc., 60 N.J.Super. 199, 208, 158 A.2d 529, 534 (1960). See also, Miller v. Miller, 101 Md. 600, 61 A. 210 (1905).

9. Cunningham & Tischler, Disguised Real Estate Security Transactions As Mortgages In Substance, 26 Rutgers L.Rev. 1, 21 (1972). See Vreeland v. Dawson, 55 N.J.Super. 456, 151 A.2d 62 (1959). See also, Annot., 27 A.L. R.2d 1285 (1953).

10. Stark v. Bauer Cooperage Co., supra note 6, at 216.

two-party cases the tendency to find the transaction to be a mortgage was observed, the contrary is the general rule in this type of transaction. And the reason for this stems from the fact that in this sort of business deal the hazard is not of losing what the obligor had owned before, but only of failing to get for the first time what he had bargained for.

E. THE INSTALLMENT LAND CONTRACT

§ 3.25 An Introduction to the Installment Land Contract

The installment land contract is the most commonly used substitute for the mortgage or deed of trust. This device is also sometimes referred to as a "contract for deed" or a "long-term land contract." The installment land contract and the purchase money mortgage fulfill the identical economic function—the financing by the seller of the unpaid portion of the real estate purchase price. Under an installment land contract, the vendee normally takes possession and makes monthly installment payments of principal and interest until the principal balance is paid off. The vendor retains legal title until the final payment is made, at which time full title is conveyed to the vendee. Such contracts may be amortized over time periods as short as a year or two or as long as twenty years or more. During the contract period, the vendee normally will be required to pay the taxes, maintain casualty insurance, and keep the premises in good repair.

It is important to distinguish the installment land contract from the ordinary executory contract for the sale of land, variously known as a "binder," a "marketing contract," or an "earnest money" contract. This latter type of contract is used primarily to establish the parties' rights and liabilities during the period between the date of the bargain and the date of closing, usually only a month or two later, on which title passes to the purchaser and security agreements, if any, are consummated. In contrast, the installment land contract governs the parties throughout the life of the debt, while the earnest money contract is completed at closing when the purchaser either tenders the full purchase price of the land or enters into a separate security agreement. Indeed, it is not uncommon for parties to agree to enter into an installment land contract at the closing date of the earnest money contract.

When a vendee defaults under an installment land contract the vendor has several traditional remedies. He may sue "(1) for the installments which are due with interest thereon; (2) for specific performance of the contract; (3) for damages for the breach; (4) to foreclose his vendee's rights; (5) to quiet title; or if he should desire, he may merely rescind the contract." [11] These

11. Comment, Installment Contracts for the Sale of Land in Missouri, 24 Mo.L.Rev. 240, 243 (1959).

remedies, however, often involve litigation that may be too slow or expensive to be practical and some of them depend on the vendee's capacity to satisfy a money judgment. Consequently, only the quiet title action is used with any great frequency. Its assertion is usually an outgrowth of the vendor's claim to his purported rights under a forfeiture clause. This clause, found in virtually every installment contract, typically provides that "time is of the essence" and that when a vendee fails to comply with the contract, including the obligation to pay promptly, the vendor has the option to declare the contract terminated, to retake possession of the premises without legal process, and to retain all prior payments as liquidated damages. Generally, the clause also relieves the vendor from all further obligation under the contract.

As one commentator has aptly pointed out, "[i]f the contract is enforceable as written and if title will not be clouded * * * [the installment land] contract gives the vendor a very favorable remedy, much more advantageous than would be available under a purchase money mortgage or deed of trust." [12] Indeed, under a mortgage or deed of trust, the defaulting mortgagor has a right to redeem (the equity of redemption) which the mortgagee can eliminate only by a foreclosure proceeding should the mortgagor prove to be uncooperative. The forfeiture clause in an installment contract appears to give the vendor a remedy similar to foreclosure without any need for judicial action. For our purposes, however, it is important to emphasize that if the vendee resists forfeiture the installment land contract is advantageous only if it "*is enforceable as written and if title will not be clouded.*"

Installment land contracts have traditionally been used as mortgage substitutes in those states where the substantive law of mortgages and the foreclosure remedies are considered to be heavily pro-mortgagor. For example, in a substantial number of states, judicial foreclosure is the only method of foreclosing a mortgage. This procedure requires a full court proceeding in which all interested persons must be made parties, and is often time consuming and costly. Against a mortgagor who contests the mortgagee's claims, it may take several years to conclude such an action. Thus, utilization of the installment land contract in such states, whatever its risks, is perhaps understandable. But the risks are high, as will be seen below.

§ 3.26 The Forfeiture Remedy—Some General Considerations

Traditionally, installment land contract forfeiture provisions were routinely enforced in favor of the vendor.[13] Enforcement of

12. Id. at 244. See also Comment, Forfeiture: The Anomaly of the Land Sale Contract, 41 Albany L.Rev. 71, 73–74 (1977).

13. See Note, Forfeiture and the Iowa Installment Land Contract, 46 Iowa L.Rev. 786, 788 (1961); Comment, Florida Installment Land Contracts:

such provisions presumably was based on a desire to carry out the intent of the parties, even though forfeiture often resulted in a substantial loss to the vendee and in a windfall gain to the vendor.[14] Enforcement became especially burdensome on the vendee as the contract neared completion and the vendee's cash investment became increasingly substantial. Courts tended to ignore the mortgage substitute aspect of the installment land contract and to treat it instead as an executory contract for the sale of land.

Today, however, the foregoing description of forfeiture clause enforcement at best serves as a point of departure. As has been observed, the law in this area is not susceptible to orderly analysis: "Not only does the law vary from jurisdiction to jurisdiction, but within any one state results may vary depending upon the type of action brought, the exact terms of the land contract, and the facts of the particular case." [15] The interplay of these various factors makes it extremely difficult to predict whether the buyer's interest will be forfeited. While forfeitures are still occasionally judicially enforced,[16] it nevertheless can be safely stated that in no jurisdiction today will a vendor be able to assume that forfeiture provisions will be automatically enforced as written. This change is the result of both legislative and judicial intervention to ameliorate the harsh impact of automatic forfeiture.

§ 3.27 Statutory Limitations on Forfeiture

Several states have attempted to alleviate some of the harshness in forfeiture clauses by enacting legislation regulating the circumstances under which forfeiture is permitted. These statutes often incorporate a "grace period" within which late payments must be accepted. Perhaps the best example of this type of legislation is the Iowa statute.[17] It provides that installment land contracts may be cancelled only by following a specified procedure. The vendor must provide written notification to the defaulting vendee and to the person in possession of the real estate; the notice must identify the real estate, specify the terms of the contract that have not been complied with, and inform the vendee that he has thirty days in which to correct his default. If the vendee performs within this time period, the forfeiture is avoided. If he does not, the notice of forfeiture, together with proof of service, may be recorded to constitute constructive

A Time for Reform, 28 U.Fla.L.Rev. 156, 159 (1975).

14. Note, Forfeiture and the Iowa Installment Land Contract, 46 Iowa L. Rev. 786, 788 (1961).

15. Power, Land Contracts as Security Devices, 12 Wayne L.Rev. 391, 416 (1966) (footnotes omitted).

16. See, e. g., Ellis v. Butterfield, 98 Idaho 644, 570 P.2d 1334 (1977), rehearing denied 98 Idaho 663, 572 P.2d 509 (1978).

17. Iowa Code Ann. §§ 656.1–.6 (West 1950).

notice of the completed forfeiture. Several other states have statutes similar to that of Iowa; [18] the grace period varies from thirty days in Iowa to as long as one year in North Dakota. In Minnesota, the grace period extends up to sixty days depending on the percentage of the contract price the vendee has already paid.[19] Some of these statutes permit nonjudicial forfeiture, while others allow it only by judicial action. It should be emphasized, however, that the purpose of these statutes is not to prevent forfeitures, but to alleviate the harshness of their operation.[20] In this connection several observations should be made.

First, the statutory grace period approach, as a practical matter, is analogous to the mortgage law concept of strict foreclosure. This mortgage foreclosure method, rarely used in the United States, allows a judicial grace period during which the mortgagor either pays the mortgage debt or forfeits the land to the mortgagee.[21] Similarly, if a vendee under an installment contract fails to correct a default within the statutory grace period, he loses the land. It is perhaps ironic that in some respects the statutory contract forfeiture procedures are more "pro-vendee" than the strict foreclosure concept is "pro-mortgagor." Under strict foreclosure, the mortgagor must pay the *accelerated* debt or lose the land. On the other hand, in such states as Iowa and Minnesota, the defaulting vendee need only pay the *arrearages* within the grace period, rather than the accelerated debt, in order to reinstate the contract.[22]

Second, to some degree these statutes have institutionalized or formalized the forfeiture concept and, in so doing, may have tended to discourage judicial interference in those situations where the vendor complies with the statutory forfeiture method.[23] For example, the Iowa and Minnesota cases allowing forfeiture have been concerned for the most part with technical compliance with the statutory procedure and have tended to downplay any independent analysis of the fairness of the forfeiture.[24]

Finally, one practical advantage of statutory regulation is that it encourages the stability of land titles. Whatever the defects in such

18. See, e. g., Minn.Stat.Ann. § 559.21 (West Supp.1977); N.D.Cent.Code §§ 32–18–01 to 06, S.D.Comp.Laws Ann. §§ 21–50–01 to 07.

19. Minn.Stat.Ann. § 559.21 (West Supp.1977).

20. See Note, Forfeiture and the Iowa Installment Land Contract, 46 Iowa L.Rev. 786, 797 (1961).
See §§ 7.9–7.10 infra.

21. See G. Nelson & D. Whitman, Cases and Materials on Real Estate Finance and Development 229 (1976). See §§ 7.9–7.10 infra.

22. See Hampton Farmers Coop Co. v. Fehd, 257 Iowa 555, 559, 133 N.W.2d 872, 874 (1965); Needles v. Keys, 149 Minn. 477, 480, 184 N.W. 33, 34 (1921); 51 Iowa L.Rev. 488 (1966).

23. Note, Forfeiture and the Iowa Installment Land Contract, 46 Iowa L. Rev. 786, 797 (1961).

24. See, e. g., id. at 792; Dale v. Pushor, 246 Minn. 254, 75 N.W.2d 595 (1956).

statutory regulation, title examiners in many of these states apparently routinely approve of the titles derived through the statutory proceedings.[25] There are at least two reasons for this. First, the tendency of the courts to discourage attacks on forfeitures on nonstatutory grounds encourages reliance on a forfeiture proceeding that complies with the applicable statute. Second, many of these statutes provide for the recording of a written and formalized memorial of compliance with the statute.[26] As a result, the title examiner is able to rely on the record for evidence of a permissible forfeiture. This is true even where the original contract is recorded. On the other hand, in states that lack statutory control of the forfeiture process, the recording of a statement that forfeiture has occurred may be regarded by a subsequent title examiner simply as a self-serving assertion that in itself may constitute a cloud on title.

The Maryland statute takes a substantially different approach from those described above.[27] Where an installment land contract for the sale of residential property to a noncorporate vendee is involved, forfeiture is prohibited. The vendor can utilize the land to satisfy the vendee's debt only through a foreclosure sale identical to that used for a mortgage.[28] The vendee is entitled to receive any surplus from the sale—that amount by which the sale price exceeds the unpaid balance of the purchase price. Since installment land contracts are treated like mortgages in residential transactions, there is apparently no incentive to continue their use in the residential setting. On the other hand, the common law rules as to forfeiture presumably still apply to nonresidential installment land contracts.[29]

25. Nelson, The Use of Installment Land Contracts in Missouri—Courting Clouds on Titles, 33 J.Mo.B. 161, 164 (1977).

26. The Iowa statute exemplifies such a provision: "If the terms and conditions as to which there is default are not performed within said thirty days, the party serving said notice or causing the same to be served, may file for record in the office of the county recorder a copy of the notice aforesaid with proofs of service attached or indorsed thereon (and, in case of service by publication, his personal affidavit that personal service could not be made within this state) and when so filed and recorded, the said record shall be constructive notice to all parties of the due forfeiture and cancellation of said contract." Iowa Code Ann. § 656.5 (West 1950).

27. Md.Real Prop.Code Ann. §§ 10–101 to 108 (1974); Md.R.P. W79.

28. Md.R.P. W70 to W72, W77.

29. Ohio legislation governing termination of installment land contracts is also somewhat unique. It combines the "grace period" function with the additional requirement that after either five years or payment of twenty percent of the purchase price, judicial foreclosure is required. Thus, forfeiture is permitted and regulated during the early part of the contract, whereas mortgage law takes over thereafter. See Ohio Rev.Code Ann. §§ 5313.01–.10 (1970). See also Mont.Rev.Codes Ann. §§ 52–401 to 417 (Cum.Supp.1975), in which the Montana Small Tract Financing Act of 1963 made possible an optional power of sale deed of trust mechanism for tracts of 15 acres or less. One commentator has suggested that this legislation makes the installment land contract in Montana unnecessary. See Lohn, Toward Abolishing Installment Land Sale Contracts, 36 Mont.L.Rev. 110 (1975).

Recent Oklahoma legislation constitutes perhaps the most sweeping and decisive statutory regulation of installment land contracts. In one relatively short paragraph, an Oklahoma statute states that installment land contracts

> for purchase and sale of real property made for the purpose or with the intention of receiving the payment of money and made for the purpose of establishing an immediate and continuing right of possession of the described real property, whether such instruments be from the debtor to the creditor or from the debtor to some third person in trust for the creditor, shall to that extent be deemed and held mortgages, and shall be subject to the same rules of foreclosure and to the same regulations, restraints and forms as are prescribed in relation to mortgages.[30]

The effect of this statutory provision is to treat all installment land contracts entailing a transfer of possession to the vendee as mortgages and thus to make the forfeiture remedy unavailable to a vendor. Thus, installment land contracts presumably have been rendered obsolete in Oklahoma. This legislation is especially significant in view of the fact that Oklahoma permits only judicial, and not power of sale, foreclosure of mortgages.[31]

§ 3.28 Judicial Limitations on Forfeiture

Absent statutory regulation, numerous state courts have in recent years refused to enforce against a defaulting vendee forfeiture clauses that the courts have deemed unreasonable or inequitable. These courts have employed several approaches to save the vendee from forfeiture. Some cases, for example, have in effect conferred on the vendee a mortgagor's equity of redemption, permitting him to tender the remainder of the purchase price (or even his arrearages) in a suit or conterclaim for specific performance of the contract. Where the vendee was unable or unwilling to redeem, courts have occasionally ordered the judicial foreclosure of the land contract. Finally, some courts, after determining that a particular forfeiture clause is unfair, have extended to the defaulting vendee the right to restitution–the right to recoup his payments to the extent that they exceed the vendor's damages caused by the vendee's default. Of course, many state courts have not considered the forfeiture clause in all of the remedial contexts described above, nor have they always been theoretically precise. Some courts have utilized contract principles to protect the defaulting vendee from an inequitable forfeiture provision. Other courts have gone a long way toward simply treating the installment land contract as a mortgage—in much the same fashion as does the Oklahoma statute. Still others have employed a

30. Okla.Stat.Ann. tit. 16, § 11A (West Supp.1976).

31. Okla.Stat.Ann. tit. 12, § 686 (West 1960).

confusing amalgam of mortgage and contract law. The following headings examine these various approaches employed by state courts to mitigate the harshness of forfeiture.

Waiver By the Vendor As An Excuse for Delinquency

Frequently a vendor will accept one or several late payments from his purchaser without taking action to declare a forfeiture. When the vendor finally reaches the end of his patience and informs the purchaser that forfeiture has occurred, the purchaser may argue that the vendor's prior behavior constitutes a waiver of the time provisions of the contract and that the vendor is legally bound to accept the late payments. Often this dispute is presented to the court in the context of a purchaser's suit or conterclaim for specific performance of the contract. The vendee may be willing to tender the entire purchase price, or he may insist upon an opportunity to make up his arrearages and resume the original payment schedule.

Many cases have adopted the purchaser's position in this situation.[32] In effect, these cases hold that the vendor's waiver avoids the effect of the forfeiture clause and creates in the purchaser a right analogous to an equity of redemption. According to this view, if the vendor had given the purchaser clear notice that no further delinquencies would be tolerated, and if this notice had been given in adequate time to allow the purchaser to get back on schedule, the vendor might thereby have preserved his right of forfeiture as to future installments. Since he did not do so, the court itself will generally fix a reasonable time within which the purchaser must cure the delinquencies.

The courts of Missouri and Utah have been particularly inclined to employ this technique. One commentator aptly described the Missouri situation:

> Thus, Missouri courts today seem hesitant to give full effect to forfeiture provisions as measures of liquidated damages in installment land contracts. They are likely to find that such provisions have been waived by the vendor due to such acts as his acceptance of late payments of principal or of interest on late payments after the delinquency of those payments. Furthermore, waiver of forfeiture provisions is equally likely to be found in any of the following in

32. See In re Northern Ill. Dev. Corp. 309 F.2d 882 (7th Cir. 1962), certiorari denied 372 U.S. 965, 83 S.Ct. 1090, 10 L.Ed. 2d 129 (1963); Triplett v. Davis, 238 Ark. 870, 385 S.W.2d 33 (1964); Petersen v. Ridenour, 135 Cal.App.2d 720, 287 P.2d 848 (1955); Krentz v. Johnson, 36 Ill.App.3d 142, 343 N.E.2d 165 (1976); Miles Homes, Inc. v. Mintjal, 17 Ill.App.3d 642, 307 N.E.2d 724 (1974); Pierce v. Yochum, 330 N.E.2d 102 (Ind.App.1975); Soltis v. Liles, 275 Or. 537, 551 P.2d 1297 (1976); Stinemeyer v. Wesco Farms, Inc., 260 Or. 109, 487 P.2d 65 (1971); Bradley v. Apel, 531 S.W.2d 678 (Tex.Civ.App.1975); Williamson v. Wanlass, 545 P.2d 1145 (Utah 1976); Paul v. Kitt, 544 P.2d 886 (Utah 1975).

> which a land installment contract is involved: viz., an action for ejectment by a vendor, an action for specific performance by a defaulting vendee, a counterclaim for specific performance by a defaulting vendee who is defendant to an action for ejectment, or even a trespass action by a defaulting vendee against his vendor concerning the land that is the subject of the contract. The finding that such a forfeiture provision has been waived would be very likely if the value of the land subject to the forfeiture provisions substantially exceeded the amount still unpaid under the contract.[33]

The waiver cases tend to be variable and difficult to reconcile. In some cases rather innocuous forbearances by vendors have been translated into favorable holdings for purchasers,[34] while in others quite substantial leniency has been unavailing.[35] In one Utah case,[36] for example, the vendees under an installment land contract for the purchase of a house made sporadic late payments for the first two years of the contract. Some monthly payments were missed entirely. The vendor repeatedly demanded that the contract be paid up to date, but from time to time the vendees were assured that no forfeiture was contemplated "at that time." Finally, more than two years from the date of the contract, the vendor declared a forfeiture and after unsuccessful negotiation brought an unlawful detainer action to have vendees ousted and the contract forfeited. The trial court concluded that the vendor had waived the strict performance of the contract. The Utah Supreme Court reversed the trial court and upheld the forfeiture in the following language: "Under the circumstances of this case, we believe that the buyers * * * were given a reasonable length of time to clear themselves of default * * *. They had not paid the equivalent of the rental value of the property for the time they occupied it."[37]

The quoted language is quite telling. Obviously the amount of the payments in relation to the rental value has nothing at all to do with whether there was an effective waiver by the vendor. It is difficult not to conclude that the court was manipulating the waiver concept as a means of deciding whether, in terms of fairness and economic equity, the purchaser should have another opportunity to make up his missed payments.[38] Such decisionmaking may be entirely salutory, but it should not be disguised.

33. 29 Mo.L.Rev. 222, 226 (1964) (footnotes omitted).

34. See note 22 and accompanying text, supra.

35. See, e. g., Economy Sav. & Loan Co. v. Hollington, 105 Ohio App. 243, 152 N.E.2d 125, 6 O.O.2d 61 (1957); Christy v. Guild, 101 Utah 313, 121 P.2d 401 (1942).

36. Pacific Dev. Co. v. Stewart, 13 Utah 403, 195 P.2d 748 (1948).

37. Id. at 409, 195 P.2d at 751.

38. The court may have been confusing the waiver concept with the principle of equitable relief from forfeiture. See text accompanying notes 31–45, infra.

Recognition of An Equity of Redemption

A number of jurisdictions have taken the view that the purchaser, notwithstanding his default, should be granted a final opportunity to pay the balance owing on the contract or, in some instances, the arrearages, before losing his land. Some courts view this right, analogous to a mortgagor's equity of redemption, as unconditional, while others are inclined to recognize it only if the purchaser's prior payments add up to a substantial investment or "equity" in the property. Sometimes the existence of the right is made to turn on whether the purchaser's payments significantly exceed the property's rental value or some similar test. The critical point is that, unlike the cases discussed in the preceding paragraphs, these opinions do not rely upon a prior waiver by the vendor.

A typical case is Nigh v. Hickman,[39] decided by the Missouri Court of Appeals. There a vendee under an installment land contract covering farmland had paid almost 35% of the total purchase price. The vendee then defaulted on one payment by fifteen days, and the vendor refused to accept the late payment. The vendee sued for specific performance and tendered the balance owing on the contract. The appellate court held that the trial court correctly granted specific performance and that enforcement of the forfeiture clause would have been inequitable. Although the contract contained no "time of the essence" clause, the court indicated that the result would not have been different had such a clause been present.

The relationship between the granting of specific performance to a purchaser and more traditional mortgage concepts is illustrated by the Florida Court of Appeals' opinion in H & L Land Co. v. Warner.[40] There the vendee had made installment payments for about five years, but thereafter a four-year period elapsed during which no payments were made. During this period of nonpayment the vendor remained silent as to the vendee's default. The vendee ultimately sued for specific performance, tendering the balance of the purchase price; the vendor counterclaimed for removal of the contract as a cloud on the vendor's title. The court granted specific performance and stated: "[T]he vendor under a specifically enforceable installment land sale contract, who has received part of the purchase price and has given the vendee possession of the land and the benefits and burdens of ownership, is in essentially the same position as a vendor who has conveyed the legal title and taken back a purchase money mortgage * * *."[41] The court implicitly imposed at least three conditions to be satisfied in order to qualify for specific performance: (1) The

39. 538 S.W.2d 936 (Mo.App.1976). See also Key v. Gregory, 553 S.W.2d 329 (Mo.App.1977).

40. 258 So.2d 293 (Fla.App.1972). See also Huguley v. Hall, 157 So.2d 417 (Fla.1963); Mid-State Inv. Corp. v. O'Steen, 133 So.2d 455 (Fla.App. 1961).

41. 258 So.2d at 295.

vendee must be in possession or have a right to possession; (2) the contract must be specifically enforceable; and (3) the vendee must assert and exercise his right of redemption by tendering full performance.[42]

There are problems with these conditions, especially with the last two. Arguably, tying these latter two requirements together is an inconsistent blending of contract and mortgage law. It is axiomatic that a vendee in default does not have a right to specific performance of a contract. Yet under mortgage law the right to redeem is not exercised until there has been a default. In *Warner*, the second requirement was met because the court found that the vendor had waived the vendee's default. However, as has been pointed out, "By so holding, the court is going in circles. If one must tender the unpaid balance as a condition precedent to the vesting of the right of redemption, then one must exercise this right before one is entitled to it—an anomaly, to be sure. Thus, the rights of mortgagors will not be extended to purchasers in default who are either in straitened circumstances or unaware of the right of redemption—the very individuals whom the mortgage statutes were designed to protect." [43] Notwithstanding this apparent anomaly, a more recent case reinforces the argument that, in general, Florida installment land contracts will be treated as mortgages for redemption purposes. In Hoffman v. Semet,[44] a Florida District Court of Appeals held that a vendee *in default* under an installment land contract had an equity of redemption and that the vendee's successor was entitled to satisfy the total outstanding indebtedness due the vendor under the contract and to receive a conveyance of the real estate. The court cited *Warner* for the proposition that an installment land contract "must be deemed and held to be a mortgage, subject to the same rules of foreclosure and to the same regulations, restraints, and forms as are prescribed in relation to mortgages." [45] Unlike the situation in *Warner,* however, there had been no waiver of the default; therefore, the contract was not specifically enforceable within the implicit requirements of *Warner*. The *Semet* court did not deal with this difficulty. Instead, it simply repeated "equity of redemption" language in referring to the vendee's interest.

The Kansas case of Nelson v. Robinson [46] illustrates how a court can sometimes refuse to enforce a forfeiture provision and in addition can impose a remedy that treats the installment land contract involved as an equitable mortgage. The vendors in *Nelson* brought an action to cancel an installment land contract for the sale of farmland. The vendee was over $1,900 delinquent in back payments, but had paid

42. See Comment, Florida Installment Land Contracts: A Time for Reform, 28 U.Fla.L.Rev. 156, 168–70 (1975).

43. Id. at 170.

44. 316 So.2d 649 (Fla.App.1975).

45. Id. at 651.

46. 184 Kan. 340, 336 P.2d 415 (1959).

nearly one third of the $48,000 purchase price and had made valuable improvements to the land. The trial court refused to permit forfeiture, but rather ordered strict foreclosure of the contract. Under the terms of the decree, the vendee was given six months in which to pay the entire amount remaining due on the contract. Failure to so pay within that period would result in forfeiture of the land and back payments to the vendor. If the vendee paid only the arrearages within ten days of the decree, however, the redemption period would have extended to eighteen months. Interestingly, the vendee, and not the vendor, appealed, and the Kansas Supreme Court affirmed this exercise of equitable discretion of the trial court. It is noteworthy that the court here impossed the relatively rare mortgage remedy of strict foreclosure which was sought by neither party, but in which the vendor acquiesced.[47]

The *Nelson* decision clearly does not mean that all installment land contracts in Kansas will henceforth be treated as mortgages. If, for example, the vendee's stake in the property had been substantially less, perhaps immediate forfeiture would have been ordered.[48] The case, however, does illustrate that Kansas vendors cannot rely on automatic enforcement of the forfeiture clause. Thus, in Kansas, courts may very well apply the law of mortgages to some installment contracts and contract law to others.

In California, the movement toward recognition of a right of redemption for a defaulting vendee has received a considerable impetus from general statutory provisions, although their application was somewhat uncertain until fairly recently.[49] In Barkis v. Scott,[50] the California Supreme Court reevaluated a long line of earlier precedents dealing with forfeiture. The court concluded that when a forfeiture would otherwise result, the vendee can be relieved therefrom under section 3275 of the Civil Code which provides that

> Whenever, by the terms of an obligation, a party thereto incurs a forfeiture, or a loss in the nature of a forfeiture, by reason of his failure to comply with its provisions, he may be relieved therefrom, upon making full compensation to the other party, except in case of a grossly negligent, willful, or fraudulent breach of duty.[51]

The vendor in *Barkis* sought to quiet title and to enforce a forfeiture after the vendees inadvertently overdrew their bank account with

47. This mortgage remedy is apparently the standard method in Wisconsin for terminating a vendee. See Exchange Corp. v. Kuntz, 56 Wis.2d 555, 202 N.W.2d 393 (1972).

48. For a discussion of the significance of the proportion paid, see Croft v. Jensen, 86 Utah 13, 40 P.2d 198 (1935).

49. See Comment, Reforming the Vendor's Remedies for Breach of Installment Land Sale Contracts, 47 S.Cal. L.Rev. 191, 205 (1973).

50. 34 Cal.2d 116, 208 P.2d 367 (1949).

51. Cal.Civ.Code § 3275 (West 1970).

their monthly house payment. The vendees' later efforts at payment were refused by the vendor. The supreme court held that section 3275 should provide relief from forfeiture and that the vendees had established the right to keep the contract in force. Here the default was, at most, negligent and not "grossly negligent, willful, or fraudulent."

In MacFadden v. Walker,[52] the California Supreme Court dealt with the "willful, but repentant defaulting vendee." There an elderly lady vendee had been in willful default over two years, but had paid over half of the purchase price. When the vendor sought to quiet title to the property, she counterclaimed for specific performance, tendering the full amount due and owing on the contract. The court held that the policy against forfeitures includes granting the right to specific performance even when the default is willful, reasoning that, when taken together, the prohibition against punitive damages contained in section 3294 of the Civil Code, the strict limitations on the right to provide for liquidated damages contained in sections 1670–1671, and the provision of section 3369 that "neither specific nor preventive relief can be granted to enforce a penalty or forfeiture in any case * * *" prevented a forfeiture having no reasonable relation to the damage caused by the vendee's breach even when that breach is willful. Although the court noted that "persuasive arguments" had been made by Professor Hetland that installment land contracts should be treated like mortgages and deeds of trust and that willfully defaulting debtors should therefore have the right to redeem, it concluded that because the vendee was entitled to specific performance, "we need not decide whether she might also be entitled to some other remedy under the law governing security transactions."[53]

From the viewpoint of vendors, the trend illustrated above toward recognition of an equity of redemption is rather frightening. In the absence of statute, nothing but a court order can cut off an equity of redemption. In effect, this means that the vendor will be forced to litigate—precisely the thing he hoped to avoid by use of the installment contract. Even if the court will follow the example of the Supreme Court of Kansas, granting forfeiture in the event the purchaser is unable to redeem,[54] the vendor's situation as far less advantageous than he expected when the contract was signed.

Restitution

In a jurisdiction in which no equity of redemption is yet recognized, or in a case in which the purchaser cannot or will not redeem,

52. 5 Cal.3d 809, 97 Cal.Rptr. 537, 488 P.2d 1353 (1971).

53. Id. at 816, 488 P.2d at 1357, 97 Cal.Rptr. at 541. See also Williams Plumbing Co. v. Sinsley, 53 Cal.App.3d 1027, 126 Cal.Rptr. 345 (1975) (where breach not intentional).

54. See notes 46–47 and accompanying text, supra.

traditional analysis would suggest that forfeiture should follow. But along this dimension, too, the courts have been actively reforming the law. Increasingly they are holding that forfeiture may not be "free" and that the vendor must return the payments he has received insofar as they exceed his actual damages. Some courts, such as those of Utah, take this position only in cases in which they conclude that an outright forfeiture would be "unconscionable," [55] but this may simply mean that the purchaser would suffer a substantial net loss if no restitution were ordered.[56]

The Utah cases usually measure the vendor's damages as the fair rental value of the property during the period of the purchaser's occupancy, plus such incidental damages as repairs and a sales commission upon resale.[57] In most of the fact situations presented, courts have concluded that these items exceed the purchaser's payments and that he is not entitled to restitution. For example, in Strand v. Mayne,[58] the vendees under an installment land contract for the sale of a motel had made payments of principal and interest of over $19,000 on a $41,500 purchase price. They also spent $9,500 on repairs on the premises. Upon default, the vendors obtained possession by an unlawful detainer action. The vendees subsequently brought an action to recover the payments made under the contract on the ground that retention by the vendor was unconscionable. The Utah Supreme Court affirmed a summary judgment for the vendor, noting that the fair rental value of the motel up to the date of forfeiture, when added to the down payment the vendees had received on a resale of the property to a third party, exceeded the total of their payments to the vendors. The court observed that "[t]his clearly shows that the amount they have lost under the forfeiture provision is not unconscionable. * * *" [59] Similarly, in Weyher v. Peterson,[60] the Utah court concluded, in affirming a judgment for a vendor under a forcible entry and detainer action based on a forfeiture clause, that the rental value and damages, totalling $10,505, exceeded the $9,387 the vendee had paid on the contract and found no inequity in refusing to allow the vendee to recover some of his payments.

Although vendees have generally not fared well in Utah litigation,[61] the reasoning of the above decisions indicates that com-

55. Jacobson v. Swan, 3 Utah 2d 59, 278 P.2d 294 (1954).

56. The Utah court has had difficulty in reaching a consensus as to what is "unconscionable." See Kay v. Wood, 549 P.2d 709 (Utah 1976).

57. See, e. g., Weyher v. Peterson, 16 Utah 2d 278, 399 P.2d 438 (1965).

58. 14 Utah 2d 355, 384 P.2d 396 (1963).

59. Id. at 357, 384 P.2d at 398.

60. 16 Utah 2d 278, 399 P.2d 438 (1965).

61. One factor contributing to this litigation record is that few Utah vendees appear to record their contracts. Those who do record and subsequently default can probably settle with their vendors for at least the nuisance value of the suit which would be necessary to clear the vendor's ti-

plete vendor reliance on the forfeiture clause is probably misplaced. In the above cases, the court upheld forfeiture because it believed the vendor's actual damages, based on the property's fair rental value, exceeded the vendee's payments. In the few Utah cases in which the vendee's payments exceeded the vendor's damages, the court did order restitution to the vendee of the excess.[62]

Florida cases also appear to impose a burden of showing unconscionability upon a purchaser who prays for restitution. Unfortunately, Florida courts have been less than carefully analytic in articulating the relevant test and thus have made the availability of restitution quite unpredictable. In Chace v. Johnson,[63] for example, the vendee was one year in default and sued to recover money totalling 80% of the contract price. The Florida Supreme Court ordered the vendor to return payments to the vendee that exceeded the vendor's damages. On the other hand, in Sawyer v. Marco Island Development Corp.,[64] where a vendor brought suit to remove from the record the interests of several vendees, one of whom was one year in default and who had paid 90% of the purchase price, a Florida appellate court held that vendee's interest could be extinguished without return of the payments made. Title to thirty-six lots was involved in *Sawyer*. Other vendees were also involved but were represented by a guardian ad litem because they did not appear. None of the vendees so represented had paid over 25% of the purchase price. The vendee who had paid the 90%, however, was personally represented. Despite the special circumstances of this last vendee, the court enforced forfeiture as to everyone, observing:

> We see a substantial difference between the unjust enrichment which would result if a large deposit were forfeited within a short period of time and a situation where a vendor has removed his property from the market for several years while the vendee abandons the contract by ceasing to make further payments . . . .[65]

The purchaser's restitution remedy is perhaps best developed in California. It should be noted first that, under the rule of Venable v. Harmon,[66] a vendor cannot receive a deficiency judgment regardless of his loss. Beyond this, California antiforfeiture cases also compel the vendor to return to the vendee any amount paid in excess of the

tle, since the damages and restitution issues are alway litigable.

62. Kay v. Wood, 549 P.2d 709 (Utah 1976); Jacobson v. Swan, 3 Utah 2d 59, 278 P.2d 294 (1954).

63. 98 Fla.118, 123 So. 519 (1929).

64. 301 So.2d 820 (Fla.App.1974), certiorari denied 312 So.2d 757 (1975).

65. 301 So.2d at 821.

66. 233 Cal.App.2d 297, 43 Cal.Rptr. 490 (1965) (based on West's Ann.Cal. Civ.Proc.Code § 580b (1970).

vendor's damages. In Freedman v. Rector, Wardens and Vestrymen of St. Matthias Parish,[67] for example, the California Supreme Court held that it violated the public policies against forfeitures, penalties, and unjust enrichment to deny restitution, even to a vendee willfully in default. There have been problems, however, in determining the amount of restitution to which the vendee is entitled. Under the reasoning of the California Supreme Court decision in Honey v. Henry's Franchise Leasing Corp.,[68] the vendor apparently has the option of measuring his damages by either the "rental value" (giving restitution of the amount by which the vendee's payments exceed the fair rental value of the property while the vendee was in possession) or the "difference value" (giving restitution of the amount by which the vendee's payments exceed the difference between the current market value and the higher original contract price).[69] Professor Hetland points out that "rarely over the past few decades has the value of the property dropped so that the vendor prefers difference value to his alternative measure—rental value."[70] The choice is the vendor's, according to *Honey*, because permitting the vendee to make it would in effect give all installment vendees an option to convert their contracts into leases—an advantage the court hardly thought appropriate to give to a defaulter.

It is interesting to note that the economic results of the "difference value" measure of restitution are roughly similar to those of a judicial sale, in the sense that the market value of the property is debited against the vendor's claim. Of course, the two approaches are distinct, since in a restitution case the property's value is measured by the court upon the testimony of witnesses, rather than by a sale.[71]

67. 37 Cal.2d 16, 230 P.2d 629 (1951).

68. 64 Cal.2d 801, 52 Cal.Rptr. 18, 415 P.2d 833 (1966).

69. The court noted that since recission was not sought by the vendor, the rental value standard was inappropriate; the court consequently held that the proper calculation involved the difference value.

70. J. Hetland, Secured Real Estate Transactions 52 (1974).

71. If the California Supreme Court's formulation of the "difference value" measure of restitution is taken literally, then it seems subject to serious criticism. The problem is illustrated by the following example.

Assume *P* buys property from *V* under an installment contract. The pertinent facts of the transaction are:

Purchase price	=	$30,000
Down payment	=	2,000
Original debt	=	28,000, 8% interest, 25-year maturity
Monthly payments	=	216.11

Suppose default occurs after five years and that the value of the property has declined, so that:

Value of property	=	$25,000
Balance on debt	=	25,836.58 (based on standard mortgage payment tables)

If foreclosure by judicial sale occurs, and if the costs of foreclosure are neglected and the sale brings fair market value, the sale proceeds will be $25,000; *V* will be entitled to a deficiency judgment of $836.58, assuming no antideficiency statute. (In California, no such judgment will be permitted if a one-to-four-family house is involved. West's Ann.Cal.Civ. Proc.Code § 580b (1970).

Suppose that *V*, instead of seeking foreclosure, elects to terminate *P*'s rights under the contract and to make restitution, as he is permitted to do under *Honey*. *V* must restore to *P* all payments made in excess of *V*'s loss. *V* elects the "difference value" measure of loss.

Payments made	=	$14,966.60	($216.11 per mo. x 60 months) including $2000 down payment
(–) V's loss	=	5,000.00	($30,000 minus $25,000)
Restitution	=	9,966.60	

Thus, instead of being entitled to a deficiency judgment, *V* must pay back to *P* nearly $10,000. This is, to say the least, a strange result.

The problem is that the court, in computing the amount of restitution, has ignored the "time value" of money. In a short-term marketing contract for $30,000, if *P* breaches and *V* must remarket the property one month later for $25,000, it is reasonably accurate to say that *V*'s damages are $5,000. See Jensen v. Dalton, 9 Cal. App.3d 654, 88 Cal.Rptr. 426 (1970). If, however, the period between contract and breach is five years (during which *V* has not had possession), the $5,000 damage figure is completely erroneous. Let us recompute *V*'s damages, but in doing so translate all amounts involved to a single point in time by computing future values for each amount involved, using compound interest tables. We may select any point in time we wish, but a convenient reference point is the fifth anniversary of the sale—which happens to be the date of default. (This is convenient because nothing of financial significance happens thereafter, and whatever *V*'s damages are on that date can easily be translated to their value on the date of judgment simply by adding interest.)

In order to make translations of values to any given date, we must assume some interest or discount rate. Let us use 8%, since it is the figure selected by the parties themselves when they initiated the transaction. Here is what actually happened:

Date		
1–1–0	V gives up $30,000 asset, receives $2,000 cash. Future value of $28,000, as of 1–1–5	= $41,715.66 (+)
2–1–0 through 1–1–5	V receives regular monthly payments of $216.11. Future value of $216.11/mo for 60 months	= $15,879.08 (–)
1–1–5	V receives back the property, worth $25,000	= $25,000.00 (–)
Subtracting what V received from what he gave up, damages		= $ 836.58

Thus the "difference value" approach to restitution, properly computed, yields results exactly equal to a foreclosure sale. Of course, under California law, *V* cannot actually recover the $836.58 deficiency. Venable v. Harmon, 233 Cal.App.2d 297, 43 Cal.Rptr. 490 (1965).

No California case appears clearly to recognize the foregoing problem. Perhaps the closest is Kudokas v. Balkus, 26 Cal.App.3d 744, 103 Cal. Rptr. 318 (1972), a "difference value" case in which the court refused to allow the vendees to claim, as part of their "payments," the interest they

Foreclosure As a Mortgage

The trend of the cases discussed above is clearly toward application of mortgage concepts to aid defaulting purchasers. The logical conclusion of this trend would be an absolute equivalency of installment contracts and mortgages, with foreclosure becoming the exclusive means by which a vendor could realize upon his security interest in the property. For a court to take this position should hardly seem surprising, for the judiciary reached the same conclusion long ago with regard to other forms of mortgage substitutes. Nevertheless, our research has disclosed only two states, California and Indiana, whose courts have indicated an acceptance of this view by judicial action.

California cases actually include no direct holding that foreclosure is a proper remedy in an installment contract default. However, a California Supreme Court decision, Honey v. Henry's Franchise Leasing Corp.,[72] and an opinion by the Ninth Circuit Court of Appeals, Ward v. Union Bond & Trust Co.,[73] imply that a judicial sale would be appropriate if at least one of the parties requests it. To date there appears to be no California appellate opinion in which either purchaser or vendor has sought a judicial sale, and thus the language in the cases mentioned must be regarded as dicta. If taken at face value, however, the language makes California the most protective state from the purchaser's viewpoint, with an equity of redemption, restitution, and judicial sale all available to him.

In Indiana the case for judicial sale is both better defined and less dependent on the wishes of the parties. In Skendzel v. Marshall,[74] the vendor sought a judicial declaration of forfeiture of a vendee's interest where the vendee had already paid $21,000 of a $36,000 contract price. The Indiana Supreme Court applied the concept that "equity abhors a forfeiture" and held that enforcement of the forfeiture clause was "clearly excessive" and "unreasonable." More significantly, however, the court treated the installment land contract as a mortgage:

> The Court, in effect, views a conditional land contract as a sale with a security interest in the form of legal title

had paid prior to default of deeds of trust they had assumed. *Id* at 756; 103 Cal.Rptr. at 325. Even this holding does not address the problem systematically.

The "future value" problem is also raised in "rental value" restitution cases, but its impact is relatively slight if the vendee's payments have been fairly regular prior to default and if they approximate the rental value of the property.

72. 64 Cal.2d 801, 52 Cal.Rptr.18, 415 P.2d 833 (1966).

One other decision by the California Supreme Court suggests the availability of foreclosure in the installment contract context. See MacFadden v. Walker, 5 Cal.3d 809, 97 Cal.Rptr. 537, 488 P.2d 1353 (1971).

73. 243 F.2d 476 (C.A.Cal.1957).

74. 261 Ind. 226, 301 N.E.2d 641 (1973), certiorori denied 415 U.S. 921, 94 S.Ct. 1421, 39 L.Ed.2d 476 (1974), appeal after remand 264 Ind. 77, 339 N.E.2d 57 (1975).

> reserved by the vendor. Conceptually, therefore, the retention of the title by the vendor is the same as reserving a lien or mortgage. Realistically, vendor-vendee should be viewed as mortgagee-mortgagor. To conceive of the relationship in different terms is to pay homage to form over substance.[75]

The court ordered that the contract be foreclosed judicially in accordance with Indiana mortgage procedure. While the court did not absolutely rule out forfeiture in all cases, it did limit application of forfeiture to cases of absconding or abandoning vendees or to situations in which a minimum amount has been paid and the vendee seeks to retain possession while the vendor is making expenditures for taxes, insurance, and maintenance.

Skendzel has been followed in several subsequent decisions by Indiana appellate courts. For example, in Tidd v. Stauffer,[76] a defaulting vendee sought to obtain specific performance by paying the remaining balance where $16,000 out of a $39,000 contract price had been paid. The Court of Appeals of Indiana noted that forfeiture was inappropriate and directed the trial court to order judicial foreclosure of the contract in the event that the vendees failed promptly to pay the balance of the contract price. In Fisel v. Yoder,[77] a vendee in default who had paid one-fourth of the purchase price was allowed to continue to make payments on the contract; the vendor's request for forfeiture was denied. On the other hand, in Donaldson v. Sellmer,[78] the Court of Appeals of Indiana affirmed a trial court's award of forfeiture to a vendor where the vendee had paid $7,000 out of a $23,158 purchase price. There the appellate court agreed that the case fell within an exception to *Skendzel* in that the vendee "had wholly failed to perform his obligation to acquire adequate insurance and had allowed the property to deteriorate to such an extent that substantial repair was necessary before the house would even be habitable." [79]

Thus, in Indiana, in most instances where the defaulting vendee has a substantial equity, installment land contracts are now treated as mortgages. Because of the exceptions noted above, *Skendzel* does not go as far judicially as Oklahoma went legislatively in converting installment land contracts into mortgages. Nonetheless, the case constitutes the clearest judicial statement to date of that principle.[80]

75. Id. at 234, 301 N.E.2d at 646.

76. 159 Ind.App. 570, 308 N.E.2d 415 (1974).

77. 320 N.E.2d 783 (Ind.App.1975).

78. 333 N.E.2d 862 (Ind.App.1975).

79. Id. at 866. In Goff v. Graham, 158 Ind.App. 324, 306 N.E.2d 758 (1974), forfeiture of an installment land contract was upheld because of evidence showing that the vendee had failed to insure as required by the contract, had committed waste, and had deliberately neglected the property. The vendee had paid a down payment of $1,950 and one monthly payment of $562.62 on a contract price of $61,750 amortized over 20 years.

80. For analysis of the Indiana situation, see Bepko, Contracts and Commercial Law, 8 Ind.L.Rev. 116, 117–20 (1974); Polston, Survey of Recent

There is every reason to expect this movement to continue, particularly in states in which there is little or no statutory regulation of land contracts. The same factors that induced the courts to treat other mortgage substitutes as mortgages—particularly the necessitous borrower's willingness to sign anything presented to him and the potential for a harsh and unwarranted loss of his investment as a consequence of his default—should and will almost surely be increasingly persuasive in the installment contract context.

It is sometimes argued that this trend is undesirable and that it is socially advantageous for the law to provide an extremely quick and cheap method for a vendor to terminate his purchaser's interest in the real estate upon default. Such a procedure, it is said, encourages the extension of credit to individuals whose credit-worthiness is so poor that they would otherwise be unable to transact at all. There are, however, two errors in this argument. First, the cases discussed above illustrate that no vendor today can count on forfeiture under a land contract as being either quick or cheap; indeed, it is an invitation to litigation. Second, no procedure, however quick or cheap, can be justified if it amounts to foul play. The solution, of course, is not for the law to ignore the legitimate needs of installment contract purchasers, but to reform the modes of foreclosure commonly used for mortgages to make them as inexpensive and rapid as feasible, consistent with the requirements of fairness and due process. If this is done, land contracts (if they continue to exist at all) can be brought within the ambit of the more efficient mortgage foreclosure proceedings, and no one will have cause for complaint. Perhaps the growing tendency of the courts to treat land contracts as mortgages will bring pressure on state legislatures to accomplish the needed reforms of mortgage law.

In light of the judicial trend outlined above, we must ask why installment land contracts continue to be used. The question is particularly perplexing in those states in which relatively rapid nonjudicial foreclosure is available for mortgages or deeds of trust. The reason given several years ago by Professor Warren may still be applicable: "[T]he vendor continues to use the instalment sale contract despite its deficiencies with regard to remedies because he is willing to gamble that the vendee's rights under this device will never be asserted and his own contractual advantages will not be challenged." [81] In addition, it is possible that neither most vendors nor most real estate brokers have an accurate concept of the risks of litigation that land contracts present today. Whatever the motivations of vendors, it is clear that the risks are inflating rapidly.

Developments in Indiana Law—Property, 10 Ind.L.Rev. 297, 298 n.4 (1976); Strausbaugh, Exorcising the Forfeiture Clause From Real Estate Conditional Sales Contracts, 4 Real Est.L.J. 71 (1975).

81. Warren, California Installment Land Sales Contracts: A Time for Reform, 9 U.C.L.A.L.Rev. 608, 633 (1962).

§ 3.29 Constitutionality of Forfeiture

In recent years power of sale mortgage and deed of trust foreclosure procedures have been under increasing attack as violative of the due process clause of the fourteenth amendment.[82] The constitutional questions presented by these attacks may be raised as well in the context of installment contracts. Space does not permit a detailed discussion of these cases here, but in essence they have focused on two aspects of the foreclosure process: notice and hearing. Many power of sale statutes do not provide for any notice, or only notice by publication or posting, to the debtor and to junior lienors.[83] In addition, the statutes usually make no provision at all for a hearing, either before or after the foreclosure. If the due process clause is applicable to the foreclosure process, it is very clear that many statutes violate the standard articulated by the Supreme Court in Mullane v. Central Hanover Bank & Trust Co.,[84] since the notice they provide is "not reasonably calculated to reach those who could easily be informed by other means at hand." [85] The hearing standard is not quite so clear, but there is a strong possibility that on the merits the total absence of a presale hearing would also be held unconstitutional.[86]

The application of these due process standards to installment contract forfeitures is somewhat uncertain, and no cases seem to have been reported. But some observations may nevertheless be safely made. Many contract forms do provide for direct mail notice to the purchaser as a prerequisite to forfeiture, and this would certainly meet the Mullane standard.[87] However, as in the case of mort-

82. See §§ 7.19–7.30, infra. See Leen, Galbraith, & Gant, Due Process and Deeds of Trust—Strange Bedfellows?, 48 Wash.L.Rev. 763 (1973); Nelson, Deed of Trust Foreclosure Under Powers of Sale—Constitutional Problems—Legislative Alternatives, 28 J.Mo.B. 428 (1972); Pedowitz, Current Developments in Summary Foreclosure, 9 Real Prop. Prob. & Trust J. 421, 425–31 (1974); Comment, The Constitutionality of the California Trustee's Sale, 61 Calif.L.Rev. 1282 (1973); Comment, Due Process Problems of Mississippi Power of Sale Foreclosure, 47 Miss.L.J. 67 (1976); Comment, Notice Requirements of the Non-judicial Foreclosure Sale, 51 N.C.L.Rev. 1110 (1973); Comment, Power of Sale Foreclosure After Fuentes, 40 U.Chi.L.Rev. 206, 217–20 (1972).

83. See, e. g., D.C.Code § 45–615; Miss.Code Ann. § 89–1–55. Cf. Minn.Stat.Ann. § 580.03 (personal service on person in possession only).

84. 339 U.S. 306, 70 S.Ct. 652, 94 L.Ed. 865 (1950).

85. Id. at 319. This conclusion has been reached in three mortgage foreclosure cases. See Ricker v. United States, 417 F.Supp. 133 (D.Me.1976); Turner v. Blackburn, 389 F.Supp. 1250 (W.D.N.C.1975); Law v. United States, 366 F.Supp. 1233 (N.D.Ga. 1973).

86. See United States v. White, 429 F. Supp. 1245 (N.D.Miss.1977); Ricker v. United States, 417 F.Supp. 133 (D. Me.1976); Turner v. Blackburn, 389 F.Supp. 1250 (W.D.N.C.1975); Garner v. Tri-State Dev. Co., 382 F.Supp. 377 (E.D.Mich.1974); Northrip v. Federal Nat. Mortgage Ass'n, 372 F.Supp. 594 (E.D.Mich.1974), reversed on other grounds 527 F.2d 23 (6th Cir. 1975). Contra, Guidarelli v. Lazaretti, 233 N.W.2d 890 (Minn.1975).

87. Junior liens may, of course, be created by contract vendees. For ex-

gages, a contract procedure that provided only publication notice or the like would not. Installment contracts almost never provide for a hearing, and on this point they are as suspect as power of sale mortgages.

Whether it will ever be necessary for the contract forfeiture process to withstand scrutiny on the merits of the due process clause is questionable, however. Two defenses raised, often successfully, by power of sale mortgages appear to be similarly applicable to the contract situation. The first is waiver. If the contract itself contains language by which the purchaser authorizes a forfeiture by the vendor without notice or hearing, can the purchaser later be heard to complain that his constitutional rights were violated? In related contexts, the Supreme Court has held that the efficacy of such a contractual waiver depends on a variety of factors, including the specificity of the waiver, the relative equality of bargaining power of the parties, the sophistication of the waiving party and perhaps whether the waiver was part of a printed contract.[88] Obviously each case must be litigated upon its facts, but in the typical installment contract transaction the waiver is probably not very explicit, is part of the printed form, and is generally not a point of negotiation; the purchaser will often be able to make at least a colorable argument that the purported waiver does not bind him.

The second defense that power of sale mortgagees have asserted in constitutional litigation is that no state action is involved in such foreclosures. State action is, of course, a prerequisite to applicability of the fourteenth amendment; if non-judicial foreclosure is deemed a purely private process, no due process standard need be met. The plaintiffs in these cases have sought to show the presence of state action, pointing out that in most states in which power of sale foreclo-

ample, a vendee may mortgage his contract interest. If such an interest exists and is recorded or otherwise readily identifiable by the vendor, failure of the vendor to provide notice to the junior lienor may raise the same due process issues as in the analogous first mortgage foreclosure situation. But see Kendrick v. Davis, 75 Wash.2d 456, 463–64, 452 P.2d 222, 227–28 (1969) (holding, without discussion of constitutional principles, that the vendee's junior mortgagee was cut off by the vendor's forfeiture notwithstanding lack of notice).

88. Fuentes v. Shevin, 407 U.S. 67, 94 92 S.Ct. 1983, 2001, 32 L.Ed.2d 556, (1972) rehearing denied 409 U.S. 902, 93 S.Ct. 172, 34 L.Ed.2d 165; Swarb v. Lennox, 405 U.S. 191, 92 S.Ct. 767, 31 L.Ed.2d 138 (1972), rehearing denied 405 U.S. 1049, 92 S.Ct. 1303, 31 L.Ed.2d 592; D. H. Overmyer Co. v. Frick Co., 405 U.S. 174, 92 S.Ct. 775, 31 L.Ed.2d 124 (1972). Mortgage foreclosure cases rejecting the mortgagee's waiver argument include Ricker v. United States, 417 F.Supp. 133 (D.Me.1976); Turner v. Blackburn, 389 F.Supp. 1250 (W.D.N.C. 1975); Garner v. Tri-State Dev. Co., 382 F.Supp. 377 (E.D.Mich.1974); Law v. U. S., 366 F.Supp. 1233 (N.D. Ga.1973). Cf. Huggins v. Dement, 13 N.C.App. 673, 187 S.E.2d 412 (1972), appeal dismissed 281 N.C. 314, 188 S.E.2d 898, certiorari denied 409 U.S. 1071, 93 S.Ct. 677, 34 L.Ed.2d 659 (1973) (provision in deed for foreclosure upon default found to constitute sufficient notice for due process requirements); 51 N.C.L.Rev. 1110 (1973).

sure is widely employed, it is authorized and regulated by statute. A few early cases found state action to be present,[89] but the clear trend of recent decisions is against such a finding.[90] There is no Supreme Court decision yet on the point, but the probabilities are that state action will be found absent in the typical power of sale mortgage foreclosure.

Superficially, this conclusion seems equally valid with regard to installment contract forfeitures. By the terms of the typical contract, no judicial action is necessary to effect a forfeiture, and no state official is involved except perhaps the recorder of deeds, whose duties are entirely mechanical. However, both the Iowa-style recording-of-forfeiture statutes and the recent cases discussed above permitting redemption, restitution, or judicial sale at the behest of the purchaser may actually strengthen the state action argument. If the state, through its court system, actively superintends forfeiture procedures generally, its involvement is arguably sufficient to trigger the protections of the fourteenth amendment.[91] The fact that the contract itself says nothing about such state involvement is probably irrelevant. It may seem ironic that the state, by providing certain minimal protections, becomes constitutionally obligated to provide greater ones, but that peculiarity is actually built into the fourteenth amendment state action concept. In any event, these constitutional theories must be taken seriously; plainly, their existence further increases the litigation risk of the vendor who elects to secure his debt with an installment contract.

89. See Turner v. Blackburn, 389 F. Supp. 1250 (W.D.N.C.1975); Northrip v. Federal Nat. Mortgage Ass'n, 372 F.Supp. 594 (E.D.Mich.1974), reversed 527 F.2d 23 (C.A.Mich.1975). *Turner* relies heavily upon the rather peculiar participation of the clerk of the court in nonjudicial foreclosures under the then-applicable North Carolina statute.

90. See Northrip v. Federal Nat. Mortgage Ass'n, 527 F.2d 23 (C.A.Mich. 1975); Barrera v. Security Bldg. & Inv. Corp., 519 F.2d 1166 (C.A.Tex. 1975); Bryant v. Jefferson Fed. Sav. & Loan Ass'n, 166 U.S.App.D.C. 178, 509 F.2d 511 (1974); Y. Aleman Corp. v. Chase Manhattan Bank, 414 F. Supp. 93 (D.C.Guam 1975); Kenly v. Miracle Properties, 412 F.Supp. 1072 (D.C.Ariz.1976); Lawson v. Smith, 402 F.Supp. 851 (N.D.Cal.1975); Global Indus. Inc. v. Harris, 376 F.Supp. 1379 (N.D.Ga.1974); Federal Nat. Mortgage Ass'n v. Howlett, 521 S.W. 2d 428 (Mo.1975), appeal dismissed 423 U.S. 1026, 96 S.Ct. 210, 46 L.Ed. 2d 137, rehearing denied 423 U.S. 1026, 96 S.Ct. 471, 46 L.Ed.2d 400.

91. See Northrip v. Federal Nat. Mortgage Ass'n, 372 F.Supp. 594 (E. D.Mich.1974), reversed 527 F.2d 23 (C.A.Mich.1975), in which the district court held the Michigan power of sale foreclosure procedure to be state action on the ground that the statute encouraged mortgagees to opt for nonjudicial foreclosure. The argument is not, however, a powerful one, and was rejected by the Sixth Circuit. Cf. Moose Lodge v. Irvis, 407 U.S. 163, 92 U.S. 1965, 32 L.Ed.2d 627 (1972) (finding an extensive scheme of state regulation of liquor licenses insufficient to implicate state action in the racial discrimination practiced by a private club.)

§ 3.30 Title Problems for Vendees

When a person purchases property as a vendee under an installment land contract, the chances of title problems with respect to the vendee's interest are greater than if the transaction were cast in the purchase money mortgage setting. This is true, to a large extent, even in those jurisdictions that have reduced the impact of the forfeiture provision by statute or judicial decision.

In the usual purchase money mortgage situation, the chances are extremely high that the purchaser will examine the seller's title and require it to be marketable. Even if the purchaser is not sophisticated enough to have the title checked, any third party lender involved in the transaction will insist upon a title insurance policy or at least upon an attorney's title opinion as evidence that the seller's title is good. On the other hand, in installment land contract situations there is a strong possibility that the vendor's title will not be examined at the time the contract is executed. Here there usually is no third party lender to insist upon title examination—the vendor serves that economic function, and he is unlikely to insist upon an examination of his own title. Moreover, many contract purchasers have low incomes and either cannot afford a title examination or do not recognize the need for it. Accordingly, many purchasers may unknowingly execute the contract, go into possession, and make substantial installment payments when in fact the vendor's title is encumbered by mortgages, judgment liens, or other interests perfected prior to the execution of the contract.[92]

The recording act can also cause substantial problems for an installment land contract vendee. In the usual purchase money mortgage transaction, the deed to the mortgagor and the mortgage or deed of trust will be recorded almost immediately. If there is no third party lender, the purchaser will record his deed as a matter of custom. Any third party lender involved will insist upon and carry out immediate recordation in order to protect itself against subsequent interests and encumbrances that may be created by or rise against the mortgagor. This recording by the mortgagee will also protect the mortgagor against any subsequent interests arising through the former owner of the land. On the other hand, in the installment land contract situation there is no third party stimulus for prompt recording. Many unsophisticated vendees do not record and, as we shall see later, indeed may be prevented from recording by acts of the vendor.[93] Since vendors anticipate a high default rate among vendees, it is in the vendors' interest that the contracts not be recorded so that they may quickly resell to other

92. See generally Mixon, Installment Land Contracts: A Study of Low Income Transactions, With Proposals for Reform and a New Program to Provide Home Ownership in the Inner City, 7 Houston L.Rev. 523, 545–46 (1970).

93. See text accompanying note 14 infra.

purchasers without the necessity of a judicial proceeding to remove a title cloud posed by a recorded contract.[94] Suppose, for instance, that after executing the contract, a vendor either mortgages the land or sells it to another purchaser. While it is true in many jurisdictions that possession by the original vendee will constitute constructive notice to those dealing with the land thereafter and thus will be the equivalent of recording,[95] this is not universally the case. Even if possession does constitute constructive notice, establishing the existence of that possession could require litigation, while the fact of a recorded document would not.[96]

Even if the vendee does receive assurance prior to the execution of the contract that the vendor has good title, and even if the vendee records promptly, the installment land contract transaction could pose additional problems for the vendee that would not be present in a purchase money mortgage transaction. Suppose, for example, that four years into a ten-year installment contract, the vendor goes into bankruptcy. Section 70(b) of the Bankruptcy Act provides that "[t]he trustee shall assume or reject an executory contract." [97] Because of the rule of In re New York Investors Mutual Group, Inc.,[98] this statutory provision presents serious problems for a vendee. In that case, a land contract vendee contended that he was entitled to specific performance against the bankruptcy trustee who had disaffirmed the contract under the above statute. The vendee contended that disaffirmance divested it of its equitable title to the land. The court, however, concluded that any rights of the vendee originated solely in the contract and that section 70(b) apparently did not exclude contracts for the sale of real estate from the trustee's power to reject executory contracts. Professor Warren has commented that

94. See Mixon, supra Note 92, at 547.

95. See, e. g., Drey v. Doyle, 99 Mo. 459, 12 S.W. 287 (1889); Comment, Possession as Notice Under Missouri Recording Act, 16 Mo.L.Rev. 142 (1951).

96. Failure to record an installment land contract may also cause problems for the vendee when the vendor goes into bankruptcy. This is because section 70(c) of the Bankruptcy Act authorizes a bankruptcy trustee in his status as a hypothetical lien creditor to take advantage of state recording statutes to defeat an unrecorded interest. If, under state law, such a contract is recordable (and they generally are) and an unrecorded interest is invalid against creditors who obtain a judgment lien without notice of the unrecorded interest, a bankruptcy trustee may be able under section 70(c) to avoid the contract. In re Sayre Village Manor, 120 F.Supp. 215 (D.N.J.1954); Lacy, Land Sale Contracts in Bankruptcy, 21 U.C.L.A.L.Rev. 477, 493–97 (1973); Lynn, Bankruptcy and the Land Sales Contract: The Rights of the Vendee Vis-A-Vis the Vendor's Bankruptcy Trustee, 5 Tex.Tech.L.Rev. 677, 694–99 (1974). Normally, however, possession will be the equivalent of recording. See Lacy, supra at 496. In some states where possession is not constructive notice, however, a nonrecording vendee in possession may be vulnerable under section 70(c). See note 95, supra. The Bankruptcy Reform Act of 1978 does not alleviate the above problems. See Section 544 (a).

97. 11 U.S.C.A. § 110(b) (1970).

98. 143 F.Supp. 51 (S.D.N.Y.1956).

application of the *New York Investors* rule would leave an installment land contract vendee "with a claim for damages instead of a home." [99] Despite this criticism, subsequent decisions have followed the *New York Investors case.*[1] Professor Lacy, however, has pointed out that the contracts in all these later cases may have been executory or earnest money contracts rather than true installment land contracts.[2] He contends that true installment land contracts are the functional equivalent of purchase money mortgages: [the vendee] has made his payments in reliance on a particular asset belonging to the vendor, and this, taken with his right of possession and the substantial protection against loss of his rights even though he may default, justifies full preservation of his right to the property in the vendor's bankruptcy." [3] Such equities do not exist in the "truly executory" contract contemplating conveyance, payment of the full price, and a closing date in the near future. It remains possible, however, that the principle of *New York Investors* applies to installment land contracts.[4]

The Bankruptcy Reform Act of 1978, which becomes effective on October 1, 1979, appears to have resolved the above problem in favor of the installment land contract vendee. Where the vendee is in possession, the trustee's right to reject the contract will be subject to the vendee's right to obtain title by completing the payments under the contract.[4a] Where the vendee is not in possession, the trustee will be able to reject the contract and leave the vendee with a claim for damages for breach.[4b] While the vendee in this latter situation will have a lien on the contract property to the extent of prior payments under the contract, he will have the status of an unsecured creditor for purposes of recovering other damages.[4c] Since most installment land contract vendees normally are in possession, the 1978 Act thus rejects the implications of *New York Investors* for most installment land contracts. On the other hand, with respect to the normal earnest money contract (where the seller retains possession) and the relatively uncommon installment land contract where the vendor retains possession, the 1978 Act seems to codify the *New York Investors* result.

While vendor bankruptcy presents risks to a land contract vendee, the existence of federal tax liens against the vendor is no longer a problem for the prudent vendee who has title examined prior to con-

99. Warren, California Installment Land Sales Contracts: A Time for Reform, 9 U.C.L.A.L.Rev. 608, 613 (1962).

1. See Gulf Petroleum, S.A. v. Collazo, 316 F.2d 257 (C.A.Puerto Rico 1963); In re Philadelphia Penn Worsted Co., 278 F.2d 661 (C.A.Pa.1960).

2. Lacy, supra note 96 at 483.

3. Lacy, supra note 96, at 483–84 (footnote omitted).

4. Id. at 481.

4a. Bankruptcy Reform Act of 1978, § 365(i).

4b. Id.

4c. Id., § 365(j).

tract execution and who has actually recorded the contract. If the vendor is delinquent in payment of federal taxes, the United States may obtain a lien on "all property and rights to property, whether real or personal, belonging to [the delinquent taxpayer]." [5] This lien is ineffective against "any purchaser, holder of a security interest, mechanic's lienor, or judgment lien creditor until notice thereof * * * has been filed" [6] in a designated place. Thus, for example, if a grantee recorded a conveyance of the taxpayer-grantor's property for adequate and full consideration prior to the filing of a tax lien and without actual knowledge of the lien, the grantee's title would not be encumbered by the lien. A fortiori, if the lien arose after the conveyance, the grantee is protected. Before the 1966 amendments to the Federal Tax Lien Act, however, there was case law indicating that a vendee who had taken possession under an installment land contract, but who had not received legal title, did not come within the statutory definition of a "purchaser" and thus was subject not only to preexisting unfiled tax liens, but also to liens for taxes arising against the vendor after the contract was executed and the vendee went into possession.[7] Now, however, that problem has been largely obviated by the rule which provides that a person who enters into a *written* executory contract to purchase property is afforded the protection of a "purchaser" with title.[8] Thus, in most situations the contract vendee who takes possession pursuant to an installment land contract is protected against unfiled tax liens arising against the vendor before the execution of the contract and against all such liens arising thereafter.

There is still, however, a potential pitfall for some vendees. Under the Federal Tax Lien Act, protection of the contract vendee as a "purchaser" is "conditioned upon his having taken whatever action is necessary under local law to protect his interest against subsequent purchasers without actual notice." [9] In most states the contract vendee's possession qualifies as constructive notice against such subsequent purchasers. However, in those states where possession does not so qualify,[10] recording is necessary. Thus, in view of the fact that many vendees do not record, it is conceivable that a vendee, after properly examining title at the time of execution of the contract and promptly going into possession, may nevertheless be vulnerable not only to preexisting unfiled tax liens, but also to tax liens arising *after* the execution of the installment land contract.

5. I.R.C. § 6321.

6. I.R.C. § 6323(a).

7. See United States v. Creamer Indus., Inc., 349 F.2d 625 (C.A.Tex. 1965), certiorari denied 382 U.S. 957, 86 S.Ct. 434, 15 L.Ed.2d 361; Leipert v. R. C. Williams & Co., 161 F.Supp. 355 (S.D.N.Y.1957).

8. W. Plumb, Federal Tax Liens 73 (3d Ed.1972).

9. Id. at 73.

10. See note 95, supra.

§ 3.31 Title Problems for Vendors

As was pointed out earlier, there have been relatively few title problems for the vendor in those states that specifically regulate forfeiture by statutory procedure. In those states, of which Iowa and Minnesota are typical, the statutory procedure for termination has been institutionalized, and the statutes provide a mechanism for establishing record title in the vendor even if the vendee has recorded the contract. However, in states without such statutory mechanisms, and where the forfeiture clause is governed solely or largely by case law, there are potential title problems for the vendor. Indeed, in many such jurisdictions, the installment land contract "will provide the * * * vendor with an efficient and cheap method of regaining possession of the contract land and a merchantable title *only* if the vendee fails completely to assert his rights." [11] As one commentator has noted:

> Thus, if, after default, the vendee moves out of possession, without protest and without having recorded the contract, the vendor will be able to resell the land to a person who will probably qualify as a bona fide purchaser. In practice this probably often happens and may explain, in part, why the installment land contract is continually used. The thing to remember, however, is that *any* device is practical if the other party does nothing to protect his rights.[12]

On the other hand, suppose the vendee attempts to protect his rights by recording his contract and thereafter goes into default. Even assuming that a court will find that enforcing forfeiture would be valid under the circumstances, it will take a judicial proceeding to make that determination. A statement or affidavit that forfeiture has occurred, recorded by the vendor, will probably not suffice.

> Thus, the vendor is faced with the costly prospect of a quiet title action or some other judicial proceeding to regain a marketable title. The vendee, for settlement purposes, may very well be able to demand much more than what he has invested in the property as the price for a quit-claim deed.[13]

Some vendors try to eliminate such problems by attempting to prevent the recording of the contract. The most common method used to accomplish this is to omit an acknowledgment of the parties' execution of the contract. For any vendee represented by counsel, however, this method is easily circumvented by recording an affidavit in which the vendee refers to the installment land contract and attaches the contract as an exhibit. Or, as a variation, the vendee

11. Nelson, supra note 25, at 165 (emphasis in original).

12. Id. at 165 (emphasis in original).

13. Id.

could execute and record an affidavit that incorporates the essential terms of the contract, including the legal description, the parties, and the important terms. Occasionally, a vendor will attempt to prevent recording by keeping *all* copies of the contract. Again, however, it would seem that the vendee could use the second affidavit method described above. After all, if in fact a land contract exists, it would surely not be improper for a vendee to summarize the terms of that contract in an affidavit. In jurisdictions that do not permit recordation of affidavits, another variant would be to record an acknowledged assignment of the purchaser's interest to a straw party and a reassignment back to the vendee.[14]

Vendors also occasionally attempt to discourage recording by the vendee by including a provision in the installment land contract that makes recording of the contract a ground for default and forfeiture. Such provisions may have a substantial deterrent effect because the risk of forfeiture should never be taken lightly. Nevertheless, such provisions probably violate the public policy of encouraging the recording of interests in real estate. Indeed, Professor Warren has indicated that it is doubtful that such clauses would be effective "to attain anything more than the hostility of the judge who has to interpret the contract." [15]

Stated simply, in states where the above title complications to the vendor can occur, the installment land contract can be a "pro-vendee" financing device. Where, for example, such contracts are used in a wholesale fashion as substitute financing devices in low income, low down payment situations, mass recording of such contracts by vendees could increase the vendees' practical economic interests in the involved real estate and possibly result in pervasive title clouds on substantial amounts of that real estate.

The foregoing, of course, is not intended to deemphasize the risks for the vendee under installment land contracts. Many of these risks have been discussed previously. Where the vendee has paid a substantial amount of the contract and then defaults, the vendor may choose to go to court to seek enforcement of a forfeiture clause. Notwithstanding clouds on the vendor's title, what if the court determines that forfeiture is reasonable? In that event a vendee could lose his entire equity without a public sale. In addition, some local recorders may occasionally block attempts by vendees to record evidence of their contracts.[16] In other words, the installment land contract device means, at best, uncertainty for both sides.

14. Id. at 165–66. As we shall see, a vendee's interest is mortgagable. See text accompanying note 19, infra. Thus, even if a vendee does not record, a recorded mortgage from the vendee will similarly cloud the title. It is unlikely that recording by the vendee under these circumstances will constitute slander on the vendor's title. See Nelson, supra note 25, at 166.

15. Warren, supra note 81, at 629.

16. A recorder who strictly adheres to statutory language defining recorda-

It is perhaps understandable that, notwithstanding the above risks, installment land contracts would be used in states where mortgages must be foreclosed by a costly and time-consuming judicial action. This helps to explain why such contracts are popular in Iowa and Illinois where such a judicial proceeding is the only foreclosure remedy. On the other hand, in many states, of which Missouri and Utah are typical, where the power of sale mortgage or deed of trust is permissible and where foreclosure is efficient and relatively inexpensive, reliance on the installment land contract is difficult to understand or justify.[17] Several possible explanations may be suggested. First, the use of installment land contracts may spill over from states where they have been used successfully for the good reasons discussed above to adjacent states where such use is especially dangerous for vendors. Second, many vendors may use land contracts in low down payment situations and take their chances that the vendees will be too unsophisticated to record or to otherwise protect their interests. Finally, many vendors may simply want to feel assured that they will receive their land back in the event of a default by the vendee. With a mortgage or a deed of trust, of course, the mortgagee must ultimately foreclose against a defaulting mortgagor; a third party could purchase at the sale, and the mortgagee thus could be left with money and not the land. Nonetheless, in view of the uncertainty of the enforceability of the forfeiture clause in many, if not most, jurisdictions that do not regulate installment land contracts specifically by statute, reliance on the forfeiture clause to regain one's land is probably at best misplaced.[18]

§ 3.32 Mortgaging the Vendee's Interest—Problems for Mortgagees

As a vendee pays off his obligations under an installment land contract or if, in any event, the land goes up in value, the vendee's interest can become a significant economic asset. Thus, it is a relatively common practice for a vendee to seek to borrow money by using his interest as security for the loan. Functionally, of course, a mortgage on a vendee's interest is the economic equivalent of a second

ble documents could conceivably justify a refusal to record such evidence of a contract. For example, Utah law provides for the recordation of conveyance instruments, but the definition of "conveyance" arguably eliminates the instrument here in issue:

> The term "conveyance" as used in this title shall be construed to embrace every instrument in writing by which any real estate, or interest in real estate, is created, aliened, mortgaged, encumbered or assigned, except wills, and leases for a term not exceeding one year.

Utah Code Ann. § 57–1–1.

17. While it is true that power of sale foreclosure has been under constitutional attack on fourteenth amendment due process hearing and notice grounds, those attacks have been meeting with diminishing success, primarily due to the reluctance of the courts to find state action in foreclosures by nongovernmental leaders. See notes 81–91 and accompanying text, supra.

18. See Nelson, supra note 25, at 167–68.

mortgage, because the vendor holds an interest analogous to a first purchase money mortgage on the land. Increasingly, the case law recognizes the proposition that the vendee's interest is mortgagable.[19]

To state this latter proposition, however, raises some serious questions. For many courts, the determination that the vendee has an interest which can be mortgaged includes the notion that mortgages of such interests are valueless unless the mortgagee has some way to protect his interest against the vendor's declaration of forfeiture. Thus, a number of cases have held that the vendor could not declare a forfeiture of an installment land contract without giving the vendee's mortgagee both notification of intent to forfeit and an opportunity to protect himself.[20] Furthermore, recording by the vendee's mortgagee constitutes, under the reasoning of these cases, constructive notice to the vendor of the mortgagee's existence and imposes a duty on the vendor to examine the title to the land prior to a declaration of forfeiture in order to insure that notice can be given to any subsequent mortgagee of the vendee's interest. One recent decision, however, has held that, absent actual knowledge of the mortgagee's existence, the vendor is under no obligation to notify the mortgagee of his intention to declare a forfeiture.[21] This case relied on the notion that the recording of an instrument constituted notice only to those acquiring interest in the land subsequent to a recording and not to those whose interest predated that recording. The practical effect of such reasoning will mean that a mortgagee, in order to protect himself, will be required to give actual notice to the vendor at the time the mortgagee takes his security interest.

Assuming that notification of an intent to invoke forfeiture reaches the vendee's mortgagee, how may the latter protect himself? It has been suggested that notification would permit the mortgagee to fulfill the obligations of the vendee under the contract.[22] If this means that the mortgagee may take over the vendee's interest without foreclosure of the mortgage, it would seem to be clearly erroneous, since it would confer on a mortgagee of the vendee greater rights than those possessed by a second mortgagee in the normal mortgage situation. In the normal situation, the second mortgagee, when the senior mortgage goes into default, has two options. First, he may pay off or redeem the senior mortgage and stand in the senior's shoes as an assignee of that mortgage. At that point, the sec-

19. See Davis & Son v. Milligan, 88 Ala. 523, 6 So. 908 (1889); Stannard v. Marboe, 159 Minn. 119, 198 N.W. 127 (1924); Fincher v. Miles Homes, Inc., 549 S.W.2d 848, (Mo.1977); Kendrick v. Davis, 75 Wash.2d 456, 452 P.2d 222 (1969).

20. See, e. g., Stannard v. Marboe, 159 Minn. 119, 198 N.W. 127 (1924). See 45 Wash.L.Rev. 645, 646 (1970).

21. Kendrick v. Davis, 75 Wash.2d 456, 452 P.2d 222 (1969). See also Miles Homes, Inc. v. Grant, 257 Iowa 697, 134 N.W.2d 569 (1965) (interpreting the Iowa statutory termination proceeding).

22. 45 Wash.L.Rev. 645, 646 (1970).

ond mortgagee would own two mortgages on the land and would have to foreclose one or both of them in order to acquire either money or title to the land. Alternatively, the second mortgagee could foreclose his mortgage, and the purchaser at that sale would buy the land subject to the first mortgage.[23] The foreclosing second mortgagee would get title only if he were the successful purchaser at the sale. Otherwise the second mortgagee would have his lien paid off. But in no event can the second mortgagee acquire title to the land without himself foreclosing.

In applying the mortgage analogy to the installment land contract situation, it would seem that the vendee's mortgagee should have no greater rights than a "normal" second mortgagee. In other words, the vendee's mortgagee should have two options. First, he could pay off the defaulted land contract and have all the rights of an assignee of the vendor under that contract. Assuming forfeiture is enforceable in his jurisdiction, the mortgagee-assignee presumably could then himself invoke the forfeiture rights under the contract.[24] But in no event should he be able to eradicate the vendee's interest without invoking the functional equivalent of foreclosure. Second, the mortgagee could choose to foreclose his mortgage on the vendee's interest. In that case the purchaser at the sale would buy the land subject to the vendor's rights.[25] The mortgagee would either purchase the land himself or be paid out of the proceeds of the sale. This second option is, of course, highly risky, because if the vendor is able to invoke forfeiture promptly, the purchaser at the vendee's mortgagee's foreclosure sale may simply be buying nothing.

Very often, mortgagees of a vendee's interest make the mistake of taking an assignment of the vendee's interest and a quitclaim deed from the vendee as security for the loan to the vendee. This transaction, of course, will be treated substantively as a mortgage.[26] The problem is that the use of such documents means that the mortgagee's second option, foreclosure of his mortgage, must be accomplished by a costly and time-consuming judicial action. This is because the assignment and quitclaim deed will contain no power of sale, so that even if the particular jurisdiction permits nonjudicial foreclosure, the mortgagee could not utilize that remedy. Thus, if a mortgage on a vendee's interest is desired and if the applicable jurisdiction permits nonjudicial foreclosure, the mortgagee of the vendee

23. See G. Nelson & D. Whitman, supra note 21, at 242–43.

24. Note, 43 Mo.L.Rev. 371, 376–377 (1978). But see Knauss v. Miles Homes, Inc., 173 N.W.2d 896 (N.D. 1969).

25. Note, 43 Mo.L.Rev. 371, 376–377 (1978).

26. See Kendrick v. Davis, 75 Wash.2d 456, 452 P.2d 222 (1969); Cunningham & Tischler, Disguised Real Estate Security Transactions as Mortgages in Substance, 26 Rutgers L.Rev. 1 (1972).

should utilize a mortgage or deed of trust with an express power of sale instead of the assignment and quitclaim type documents.

F. THE NEGATIVE COVENANT AS A MORTGAGE SUBSTITUTE

§ 3.33 The Negative Covenant and the "Coast Bank" Mortgage

Lenders occasionally, in otherwise unsecured loan transactions, exact a separate negative covenant from the borrower that certain separate real estate will not be encumbered or transferred by the borrower while the debt remains unpaid. Indeed, it has been suggested that such negative covenants have been used by some California creditors to retain the option, in the event of default, of choosing to proceed as either a secured or unsecured creditor.[27] If, for example, at the time of default, a borrower has sufficient assets to satisfy a judgment, the creditor may opt simply to sue as an unsecured creditor on the debt. In so doing, the creditor would presumably avoid the protections that the California mortgage law confers on the borrower. These protections include a "one-action" rule and significant anti-deficiency limitations.[28] Under the "one-action" rule, a debt secured by real estate must be foreclosed in a foreclosure action and any deficiency must be sought in that foreclosure proceeding.[29] On the other hand, if the defaulting borrower lacks other assets, the creditor will attempt to establish the negative covenant as a mortgage. As Professor Hetland has aptly pointed out, this use of a negative covenant represented an "attempted have-a-cake and eat-it-too device." [30]

Traditionally this type of negative covenant not to mortgage specified real estate has not created a security interest in favor of the creditor.[31] "The creation of a lien is an affirmative act, and the intention to do such an act cannot be implied from an express negative." [32] It seems probable that under certain circumstances the debtor might be enjoined from violating his promise and third persons with notice could be prevented from taking a mortgage.[33] This

27. Hetland, Secured Real Estate Transactions, 73 (1974).

28. See §§ 8.2–8.3, infra.

29. Id.

30. Hetland, Secured Real Estate Transactions, 73 (1974).

31. Knott v. Shepherdstown Mfg. Co., 30 W.Va. 790, 5 S.E. 266 (1888); Western States Finance Co. v. Ruff, 108 Or. 442, 215 P. 501 (1923), modified and rehearing denied 108 Or. 455, 216 P. 1020. See Kuppenheimer & Co. v. Mornin, 78 F.2d 261, 101 A.L.R. 75, C.C.A.Iowa 1935.

32. Knott v. Shepherdstown Manufacturing Co., supra note 31, 796.

33. See Kelly v. Central Hanover Bank & Trust Co., 11 F.Supp. 497 (D.C.N.Y.1935). See 49 Harv.L.Rev. 620, 627 (1936). Insolvency at time of suit rather than insolvency at time of breach seems the preferable test. See 36 Col.L.Rev. 319, 320 (1936). On the other hand, in the Kelly case an acceleration clause effective on breach was held to make the remedy

right, however, rests upon the protection of a purely in personam contract right rather than upon an equitable lien or mortgage theory.[34]

The 1964 California Supreme Court decision in Coast Bank v. Minderhout [35] suggested a break with the foregoing analysis. That case held that an equitable mortgage could be established based on a purely negative covenant. The agreement in *Coast Bank* was executed by the borrower together with a note covering some small loans and some contemplated future advances. The agreement provided that the borrower would not sell or encumber certain described real property until he had repaid all present and future advances. It also provided for acceleration of all indebtedness on default in payment or on breach of the property agreement. It gave permission to the bank to record the agreement at such time as the bank saw fit. The agreement was silent as to whether a lien on the property was created. The bank recorded and the borrower, while still indebted, conveyed the property. There was a default on the indebtedness and the bank accelerated and brought an action to foreclose the equitable mortgage that it claimed the agreement created. The defendant demurred generally and failed to answer the plaintiff's allegation that the parties intended to create a security interest in the property. The lower court decreed foreclosure and, on appeal, the judgment was affirmed.

The court based its holding in favor of an equitable mortgage on two grounds: (1) the parties intended to create a security interest, and (2) this intent was "reasonably susceptible" from the face of the executed instruments. While *Coast Bank* was a unanimous opinion by an influential court, much confusion resulted in the wake of that decision.

In 1971, the California Supreme Court again confronted the problem of negative covenants as security in the case of Tahoe National Bank v. Phillips.[36] In *Tahoe* the court clearly seemed uneasy with what it had created in *Coast Bank*. *Tahoe* involved an attempt by the bank to foreclose as a mortgage an "Assignment of Rents and Agreement Not to Sell or Encumber Real Property" that was very similar to the "Agreement Not to Encumber or Transfer Property" used in *Coast Bank*. The court ruled that *Coast Bank* was not controlling. In *Tahoe* the borrower had not conveyed or sold property in question but had declared a homestead exemption on the property.

at law adequate, the obligor being solvent at the time. See 49 Harv.L. Rev. 620, 623 (1936); 22 Va.L.Rev. 440, 448 (1936). Cf. 30 Ill.L.Rev. 487, 490 (1935); 46 Yale L.Jour. 97, 605 (1936).

34. Osborne, Mortgages, § 43 (2d Ed. 1970).

35. 61 Cal.2d 311, 392 P.2d 265, 38 Cal.Rptr. 505 (1964).

36. 4 Cal.3d 11, 480 P.2d 320, 92 Cal. Rptr. 704 (1971).

The court also determined that the form used in *Tahoe* was not generally considered in the trade to be a security agreement.

The *Tahoe* court continued to use the somewhat general and confusing terminology of *Coast Bank* by stating that the language of the instrument was not "reasonably susceptible of interpretation" as a mortgage. This language obviously leaves the door open for an interpretation in favor of an equitable mortgage where the language is "reasonably susceptible" for that result.

The *Tahoe* court concluded that "to permit a creditor to choose an allegedly ambiguous form of agreement, and then by extrinsic evidence seek to give it the effect of a different and unambiguous form, would be to disregard totally the rules respecting interpretation of adhesion contracts, and to create an extreme danger of over-reaching on the part of creditors with superior bargaining positions. Since the bank was the party who selected the documents, it was required to "bear the responsibility for the creation and use of the assignment it now claims as ambiguous; it is only 'poetic justice' . . . if such ambiguity is construed in favor of the borrower. Legal alchemy cannot convert an assignment into an equitable mortgage, violating the customer's reasonable expectation and bestowing upon the bank the riches of an hypothecation of title." [37]

The confusion that resulted from *Coast Bank* and *Tahoe* is evident in two cases from different California Courts of Appeal decided in 1971 after the *Tahoe* decision. In Kaiser Industries v. Taylor [38] the court held that a letter of instructions containing an agreement not to encumber or transfer was sufficient evidence of the parties' intent to make a mortgage. The court followed *Coast Bank* and held that the letter of instructions was "reasonably susceptible" of interpretation as an equitable mortgage. It should be emphasized that because of California's "one-action" rule, the effect of this decision was "pro-debtor". The creditor had initially sued on the debt and secured a judgment against the debtor. On appeal, the Court of Appeal determined that an equitable mortgage existed and that, because of the "one-action" rule, foreclosure was the only remedy permitted.

In Orange County Teachers Credit Union v. Peppard [39] an agreement admittedly similar to the ones both in *Coast Bank* and *Tahoe* was held not to be an equitable mortgage because it was not "reasonably susceptible" as such. The court attempted to follow both *Coast Bank* and *Tahoe* and discovered the problem that the Supreme Court of California had created when it failed to overrule *Coast Bank* in the *Tahoe* decision. The "reasonably susceptible" test had turned out to be no test at all, but instead, a source of confusion.

37. 480 P.2d at 327–328.

38. 17 Cal.App.3d 346, 94 Cal.Rptr. 773 (1971).

39. 21 Cal.App.3d 448, 98 Cal.Rptr. 533 (1971).

The Ninth Circuit Court of Appeals interpreted the California law of negative covenants in 1972 in Browne v. San Luis Obispo National Bank.[40] That court held that the document in that case was similar to the one used in *Tahoe* and that the facts indicated an equitable mortgage was not created. The court still used the language of intent, however, and ruled that there was no evidence of intent to create a mortgage.

The foregoing indicates, at least, that the California creditors will be foolhardy if they believe that such negative covenants will give them a "have their cake and eat it too" option. While courts may, at the creditor's request, occasionally determine that a mortgage exists, and thus give the creditor the advantage of being in a secured position, this advantage is offset by the fact that, if the creditor attempts to enforce the debt alone, the debtor may be able to invoke the "one-action" rule if the court is persuaded that the negative covenant is in fact a mortgage.

The Court of Appeals of Arizona, most likely aware of the confusion in California, specifically declined to follow *Coast Bank* and characterized the *Coast Bank* reasoning as "weak".[41] The Arizona court indicated that an equitable mortgage should be found only where the parties tried to create a mortgage but technically failed to do so. The court declined to apply the "reasonably susceptible" test.

No other states have thus far recognized the *Coast Bank* type of security. From the results of *Coast Bank* in California, it appears doubtful that any states will follow it in the near future. Apparently Professor Gilmore's advice is still good: "Negative covenants should not, it is submitted, be allowed to operate as informal or inchoate security arrangements, even against third parties with notice. If a creditor wants security let him take his security in some recognized form: mortgage, pledge, Article IX security interest or what not. If he wants protection against third parties, let him take possession of the collateral or file. Nothing is to be gained by giving a shadowy effectiveness to informal arrangements which conform to no recognized pattern." [42] According to Professor Gilmore, the "debtor's covenant not to encumber property, * * * should be treated, as on the whole the case law has done, as a covenant 'merely personal'—good enough to give rights against the covenantor for breach, to bring an acceleration clause into play, to constitute 'an event of default' under a loan agreement but not good enough to give rights, whether they be called legal or equitable in the property." [43]

40. 462 F.2d 129 (C.A.Cal.1972).

41. Weaver v. Tri City Credit Bureau, 27 Ariz.App. 640, 557 P.2d 1072 (1976).

42. Gilmore, Security Interests in Personal Property, 1017 (1965).

43. Id.

§§ 3.34–4.0 are reserved for supplementary material.

CHAPTER 4

RIGHTS AND DUTIES OF THE PARTIES PRIOR TO FORECLOSURE

Table of Sections

A. THEORIES OF TITLE AND THE RIGHT TO POSSESSION

B. TORTIOUS INJURY TO LAND BY MORTGAGOR OR THIRD PERSONS

C. RIGHTS IN THE PRODUCT OF THE RES

D. ESCROWS OR RESERVES FOR TAXES AND INSURANCE

E. RIGHT TO RENTS

A. THEORIES OF TITLE AND THE RIGHT TO POSSESSION

§ 4.1 The Title Theory

As mentioned earlier, three "theories" of mortgage law exist in the United States.[1] One of these theories, the title theory, has its origin in the English Common Law Mortgage. Under the title theory, legal "title" is in the mortgagee until the mortgage has been satisfied or foreclosed, whereas the lien theory regards the mortgagee as the holder of a security interest only and the mortgager as the owner of the land until foreclosure.[2] The intermediate theory, as we will observe later in this chapter, represents a compromise between the other two theories.

1. See § 1.5, supra.

2. See Kratovil, Mortgages—Problems In Possession, Rents, and Mortgage Liability, 11 DePaul L.Rev. 1, 4–5 (1961).

Some consideration of English history is helpful in understanding the title theory. When the basic mortgage transaction became the conveyance of the fee on condition subsequent—defeasance being performance on the law day by the mortgagor—possession passed to the mortgagee upon the execution of the mortgage. There were two reasons for this. First, livery of seizen was necessary to the conveyance. Second, possession by the mortgagee was in accord with the practice of the times and theory of the legal rights conferred upon the creditor by the transaction. As late as the beginning of the seventeenth century it was unusual for the mortgagor to be left in possession and it was not until about the middle of that century that it became the general rule to do so. In all probability, the practice of leaving the mortgagor in possession was connected with the creation of the mortgagor's equity of redemption; certainly it coincided with it.[3] Indeed this was natural, for with the recognition of the mortgagor as equitable owner of the property, there was, of course, corresponding understanding that the sole interest of the mortgagee in the property, regardless of his technical legal rights was that of security. With the acceptance of this view the mortgagee who exercises right to possession was held to strict accountability to the mortgagor. The onerous duties of accounting thus became an effective deterrent to mortgagees taking possession. As a result, this right to possession was resorted to infrequently and only in extreme cases.[4] Nevertheless, although seldom exercised, the right to possession, was as it still is, a fundamental incident of the mortgagee's legal title. The mortgagee could maintain ejectment against the mortgagor, or if he entered by self-help he could not be sued by the mortgagor in trespass.

The American states, at least initially, adopted the title theory as it had developed in England.[5] Even though it was the common practice for the mortgagor to remain in possession and although equity courts in both countries viewed the mortgagor as an owner in possession, law courts, because the mortgagee had legal title, attempted to

3. Turner, The Equity of Redemption, 89–91.

4. See Maitland, Equity, 274.

In England, since 1936, actions by mortgagees for possession must be brought in Chancery. In such actions the judge, through the exercise of a discretionary power, not clearly defined, of adjourning the case, may afford a defaulting mortgagor an opportunity to delay or defeat the mortgagee. Robertson v. Cilia, 1 W.L.R. 1502 (1956), commented on in 73 L.Q.Rev. 17 (1957). See also id. at 300.

5. Trannon v. Towles, 200 Ala. 82, 75 So. 458 (1917); Brown v. Cram, 1 N.H. 169 (1818); Gilman v. Wills, 66 Me. 273 (1877) (trespass denied to mortgagor against mortgagee who took possession before default); Doe ex dem. Roby v. Maisey, 8 Barn. & C. 767 (1828) (ejectment by mortgagee against mortgagor); Jamieson v. Bruce, 6 Gill & J. 72, 26 Am.Dec. 557 (1834) (personal property; trespass denied to mortgagor against mortgagee who took possession before default). See Brown v. Loeb, 177 Ala. 106, 58 So. 330 (1912); Green v. Kemp, 13 Mass. 515, 7 Am.Dec. 169 (1816).

fit the mortgagor into an established tenancy category. For example, when there was no agreement about possession, expressed or implied between the parties, there was some attempt to consider the mortgagor as having the status of a tenant at will. Under another mode of analysis, the mortgagor was "a tenant at sufferance."[6] In any event, both of the above attempts at characterization of the mortgagor seem anomalous. It is, after all, difficult to compare a mortgagor who in equity is considered the owner of a real estate and who was left in possession with the consent of the mortgagee, as being on the same basis as a tenant who was holding over wrongfully.

Normally, however, there was an express agreement permitting the mortgagor to stay on the property. If the agreement was that the mortgagor shall have possession until some specified date, a tenancy for a term was sometimes said to be established.[7] On the other hand, if the agreement provided for possession in the mortgagor until default, or without specifying any terminal date, a tenancy at will was said to result.[8] Moreover, even without an express stipulation, courts were quick to find an implied in fact agreement for the mortgagor to remain in possession from provisions of the mortgage or the nature and circumstances of the loan.[9] In any event, even in cases where there is an express agreement between the parties it would seem that the mortgagor in possession should be recognized in modern law as something more than a tenant of the mortgagee at will, at sufference, or even for a set term.

In any event, for the most part title theory states differ in few significant respects from their lien theory counterparts. Title theory states today generally recognize that the mortgagee holds title for security purposes only, and that, except as between the mortgagor and the mortgagee or one claiming under him, the mortgagor, for practical and theoretical purposes, is to be regarded as the owner of the land.[10] In the process of this recognition, title states have whittled away at incident after incident of legal title, although to varying extents in different jurisdictions and often inconsistently in the same jurisdiction. In many states this whittling-away process cut down title so far that the mortgagee's interest was called a chattel interest or even a chose in action.[11] Moreover, the title theory has also been

6. Thunder v. Belcher, 3 East 449 (1803); Doe d. Roby v. Maisey, 8 B. & C. 767 (1828). See Turner, The Equity of Redemption, 103.

7. Gibbs v. Cruikshank, L.R., 8 C.P. 461 (1873); Doe d. Parsley v. Day, 2 Q.B. 147 (1891).

8. Turner, The Equity of Redemption, 93.

9. Hartshorn v. Hubbard, 2 N.H. 453 (1822).

10. Turner, The Equity of Redemption, 103.

11. A good example of this, together with a résumé in the opinion of many of the normal incidents of legal title which are not accorded to the mortgagee's interest in states following the title theory, is Stevens v. Turlington, 186 N.C. 191, 119 S.E. 210, 32 A.L.R. 870 (1923).

tempered by two other developments. First, some title states by statute give possession to the mortgagor until default and second, many commonly used mortgage forms in title states accomplish the same result.[12] Nevertheless, it is important to emphasize that title theory mortgagees still retain the right to possession and rents prior to foreclosure. This right to possession, as we shall see later in this chapter, can still significantly affect certain of the mortgagee's rights against the mortgagor and, in some instances, third parties.

§ 4.2 The Lien Theory

The substantial majority of states follow the lien theory of mortgages.[13] Under this theory, the mortgagor has the legal title until there has been a valid foreclosure and, importantly, has the right to possession prior to foreclosure.[14] The mortgagee has only a security interest which is termed a lien. For the most part, the development of the lien theory was the result of statutory enactments the earliest of which was in South Carolina.[15] This act provided not only that the mortgagee should not be entitled to maintain any possessory action for the mortgaged real estate even after default but explicitly said that the "mortgagor shall be deemed to be the owner of the land." [16] Other statutes phrased in slightly different terminology accomplish the same result. For example, some state that the mortgage shall not be deemed a conveyance so as to enable the mortgagee to recover possession without foreclosure and sale.[17] Others provide that a mortgage does not entitle the mortgagee to possession unless there is an express provision to that effect; some are combinations of

12. Kratovil, Mortgages—Problems In Possession, Rents, and Mortgagee Liability, 11 DePaul L.Rev. 1, 5 (1961).

13. Arizona, California, Colorado, Florida, Georgia, Idaho, Indiana, Iowa, Kansas, Kentucky, Louisiana (Civil Law), Michigan, Minnesota, Montana, Nebraska, Nevada, New Mexico, New York, North Dakota, Oklahoma, Oregon, South Carolina, South Dakota, Texas, Utah, Washington, Wisconsin, and Wyoming are lien states. See Comment, Proposed Changes in Minnesota Mortgage Law, 50 Minn.L.Rev. 331, 339 (1965); Pomeroy, Equity Jurisprudence, § 1188 (1941). Missouri is also probably a lien state. See Sweet Lumber Co. v. Lane, 513 S.W. 2d 365 (Mo.1975); but see In re Stuckenberg, 374 F.Supp. 15 (E.D. Mo.1974), affirmed 505 F.2d 1250 (C. A.Mo.).

14. See Kratovil, Mortgages—Problems In Possession, Rents and Mortgagee Liability, 11 DePaul L.Rev. 1, 5 (1960); Martyn v. First Federal Sav. & Loan Ass'n, 257 So.2d 576 (Fla. App.1971). In some lien states, the right to possession remains with the mortgagor until the period of statutory redemption has run. See Mutual Benefit Life Ins. Co. v. Frantz Klodt & Son, Inc., 237 N.W.2d 350 (Minn. 1975); Woodmen of the World Life Ins. Society v. Sears Roebuck and Co., 294 Minn. 126, 200 N.W.2d 181 (1973).

15. See Lloyd, Mortgages—The Genesis of the Lien Theory, 32 Yale L. Jour. 233, 241 (1922).

16. S.Car., Laws, pp. 32 and 33 (1791); Code §§ 45–51 (1962); Bredenberg v. Landrum, 32 S.C. 215, 10 S.E. 956 (1890).

17. West's Ann.Cal.Code Civ.Proc., § 744; Minn.Stat.Ann. § 559.17; Or.Rev. Stat. 86.010; Rev.Code Wash.Ann. § 7.28.230.

these two.[18] Still others state that the mortgagee shall not be able to maintain an action of ejectment against the mortgagor, or that the mortgagor shall have the right to possession "regardless of the terms of the instrument." [19]

It was a provision denying the mortgagee the right to bring ejectment [20] that transformed New York into a lien state. The history of the conversion is interesting and important because New York is not only a representative, but very influential exponent of the lien theory. An early decision limiting the effect of the legislation by holding that the mortgagor could not oust the mortgagee who got possession peaceably after default because "he is still considered as having the legal estate after condition broken." [21] It took two later developments to establish without question that all that the mortgagee got at any time was a legal lien and that the mortgagor at all times prior to foreclosure was the legal owner. One was a change in the decision as to the circumstances under, and theory upon, which a mortgagee would be considered a "mortgagee in possession" entitled to hold as against the mortgagor, a matter which we will deal with in detail later in this chapter.[22] The other was a holding,[23] under the then New York statute which permitted levy of execution upon legal,

18. West's Ann.Cal.Civ.Code, § 2927; Burns' Ann.Ind.Stats., § 56–701; cf. Ind.Rev.Stats., p. 459 (1843). See also 3 Tiffany, Real Prop., 2d Ed., 2427; Uniform Mortgage Act § 2.

19. Colo.Code Civ.Proc., § 281(1921).

20. Revised Stat. of N.Y., Part 3, Ch. V, § 57 (1828): "No action of ejectment shall hereafter be maintained by a mortgagee, or his assigns, or representatives, for the recovery of the possession of the mortgaged premises."

N.Y.Civ.Prac.Act, Action to Recover Real Prop., § 991: "A mortgagee, or his assignee or other representative, cannot maintain such an action to recover the mortgaged premises." Cf. Harlem Savings Bank v. Cooper, 199 Misc. 1110, 101 N.Y.S.2d 641 (1950) discussed in 52 Col.L.Rev. 150 (1952), holding that a mortgagor in possession was not a "tenant" entitled to protection against eviction under emergency rent laws as against purchaser at foreclosure sale. Since 1963, this provision in slightly different form is in Real Prop.Actions and Proc.Law, Art. 6, § 611, in 49½ McKinney's Consol.Laws of New York, Ann.

21. Phyfe v. Riley, 15 Wend. 248, 256, 30 Am.Dec. 55 (1836). See also Mickles v. Townsend, 18 N.Y. 575, 584 (1859); Packer v. Rochester etc., R. R. Co., 17 N.Y. 283, 287 (1858). And in holding that the right to redeem was limited by the section of the Code governing equitable actions generally, reasoning from the same decision on the mortgagee's right to defeat ejectment by the mortgagor after the mortgagee has possession, it was said that it can "hardly be said that such a mortgagee has no legal title." Hubbell v. Sibley, 50 N.Y. 468, 472 (1872).

22. See §§ 4.27–4.28, infra.

23. Trimm v. Marsh, 54 N.Y. 599, 13 Am.Rep. 623 (1874). Rev.Stats.N.Y., vol. 2, p. 368, §§ 31, 32 (1828); N.Y. Civil Pract.Act, Laws c. 925, §§ 710, 711 (1920), provided that the interest of the mortgagor, his heirs or assigns, should not be sold on execution levied thereon by virtue of a judgment recovered on the mortgage debt. It was recognized that this statute would be applicable in Trimm v. Marsh, 3 Lans. 509, 511 (1874) affirmed 54 N.Y. 599, 13 Am.Rep. 623. The statute was applied in Delaplaine v. Hitchcock, 6 Hill (N.Y.) 14 (1843), and a similar one in Linville v. Bell, 47 Ind. 547 (1874).

but not equitable, interests in land, that a mortgagee who recovers a judgment against his mortgagor on a cause of action other than the mortgage debt, levies execution upon, sells, and buys in the mortgaged property gets the full title thereto which is not subject to redemption by the mortgagor. The reasoning of the court was that, since under the New York statutes the mortgagee had no right to possession, therefore the mortgage "gives the mortgagee no title or estate whatever," that "the mere right, when he goes into possession by consent of the mortgagor, to retain possession, is not an attribute of title" and since the mortgagee does not get legal title it must therefore remain in the mortgagor because title must be somewhere.[24]

In contrast to the doubts and difficulties that accompanied the establishment of the lien theory in New York, courts in many other states that enacted statutes similar to the New York legislation adopted the lien theory without hesitation. Michigan is a typical example.[25] Similarly, under the California legislation, in a leading case, Justice Field stated that "this section takes from the [mortgage] instrument its common law character, and restricts it to the purposes of security. It does not, it is true, in terms, change the estates at law of the mortgagor and mortgagee, but, by disabling the owner from entering for condition broken, and restricting his remedy to a foreclosure and sale, it gives full effect to the equitable doctrine, upon consideration of which the section was evidently drawn. An instrument which confers no right of either present or future possession, possesses little of the character of a conveyance, and can hardly be deemed to pass any estate in the land." [26]

In states where the lien theory is established the courts apply it even though the parties do not use the traditional mortgage format. Thus, under a deed of trust in a lien jurisdiction, the grantor-trustor has the right to possession until the trustee realizes on the security by a foreclosure sale.[27] The same is true of absolute deeds intended as mortgages.[27a]

24. See note 21, supra.

25. The 1843 Act in Michigan was substantially the same as the 1828 statute in New York. For the development of the law in that state see the following cases collected in Campbell, Cases Mortgages, 2d ed., 22, n. 3; Stevens v. Brown, Walk.Ch. 41 (1842); Mundy v. Monroe, 1 Mich. 68 (1848); Crippen v. Morrison, 13 Mich. 23 (1864); Ladue v. Detroit etc. Co., 13 Mich. 380, 87 Am.Dec. 759 (1865); Hogsett v. Ellis, 17 Mich. 351, 363 (1868); Newton v. McKay, 30 Mich. 380 (1874).

26. McMillan v. Richards, 9 Cal. 365, 409, 70 Am.Dec. 655, 661 (1858).

27. Tyler v. Granger, 48 Cal. 259 (1874) (ejectment by the trustee against the grantor-trustor denied); Wisconsin Cent. R. Co. v. Wisconsin River Land Co., 71 Wis. 94, 36 N.W. 837 (1888) (ejectment by grantor-trustor against third party allowed). See Sacramento Bank v. Alcorn, 121 Cal. 379, 384, 53 P. 813, 814 (1898): "* * it would seem that, while we must say that title passes, none of the incidents of ownership attach, except that the trustees are deemed to have such estate as will enable them to convey." Although the California courts constantly state as fundamen-

27a. See note 27a on page 121.

In some states adopting the lien theory it has been held that there is a statutory policy against possession in the mortgagee that invalidates agreements in the mortgage permitting the mortgagee to enter.[28] In other lien states, however, an agreement between the parties, giving the mortgagee the right to possession of the mortgaged premises, is valid.[29] Indeed, in some statutes such agreements are expressly contemplated.[30] Moreover, as we will see in detail later in

tal that in a mortgage there is only a lien created while in a trust deed legal title actually passes (see, e. g., Bayer v. Hoagland, 95 Cal.App. 403, 273 P. 58 (1925)) nevertheless they also have repeatedly come to the conclusion stated in the extract from Sacramento Bank v. Alcorn. Bostwick v. McEvoy, 62 Cal. 496 (1882); McLeod v. Moran, 153 Cal. 97, 100, 94 P. 604 (1908) ("it is practically and substantially only a mortgage with power of sale"); Hollywood Lumber Co. v. Love, 155 Cal. 270, 100 P. 198 (1909); Curtin v. Krohn, 4 Cal.App. 131, 135, 87 P. 243 (1906); Wyser v. Truitt, 95 Cal.App. 727, 273 P. 147 (1928); Wasco Creamery & Const. Co. v. Coffee, 117 Cal.App. 298, 3 P.2d 588 (1931); Wilson v. McLaughlin, 20 Cal.App.2d 608, 67 P. 2d 710 (1937); Pacific States Sav. & Loan Co. v. North American Bond & Mortg. Co., 37 Cal.App.2d 307, 99 P. 2d 355 (1940); C. A. Warren Co. v. All Persons, 153 Cal. 771, 96 P. 807 (1908) (the trustor has an estate of inheritance which may pass by devise or descent against all persons except the trustee); Aitchison v. Bank of Am. Assn., 8 Cal.2d 400, 65 P.2d 890 (1936) (trustor has a legal estate which he may convey subject to the trust deed).

There is some authority drawing a distinction between trust deed mortgages containing a condition subsequent in the conveyance that it was to be void on payment by the trustor and those providing only that the trustee have power to sell on default; the former being construed to leave legal title in the trustor until sale and the latter to reserve only an equitable interest. Martin v. Alter, 42 Ohio St. 94 (1884); National Bank v. Tennessee etc., Co., 62 Ohio St. 564, 585, 588, 57 N.E. 450, 453, 454 (1900); City of Chicago v. Sullivan Machinery Co., 269 Ill. 58, 69, 109 N.E. 696, 700 (1915), all containing defeasance clauses. Morris v. Way, 16 Ohio 469, 479 (1847) (no condition subsequent).

27a. A granted land to B by absolute deed to secure a debt. Held, B, as such grantee, not entitled to possession. Yingling v. Redwine, 12 Okl. 64, 69 P. 810 (1902). See also Hall v. Savill, Iowa, 3 G. Greene 37, 54 Am. Dec. 485 (1851); Flynn v. Holmes, 145 Mich. 606, 108 N.W. 685, 11 L.R. A.,N.S., 209 (1906).

28. Ganbaum v. Rockwood Realty Corp., 62 Misc.2d 391, 308 N.Y.S.2d 436 (1970); Teal v. Walker, 111 U.S. 242, 252, 4 S.Ct. 420, 28 L.Ed. 415 (1884); Hall v. Hall, 41 S.C. 163, 167, 19 S.E. 305, 44 Am.St.Rep. 696 (1893); Orr v. Bennett, 135 Minn. 443, 161 N.W. 165, 4 A.L.R. 1396 (1917); State ex rel. Gwinn, Inc. v. Superior Court, 170 Wash. 463, 16 P.2d 831 (1932), following Western Loan & Bldg. Co. v. Mifflin, 162 Wash. 33, 297 P. 743 (1931); Rives v. Mincks Hotel Co., 167 Okl. 500, 30 P.2d 911 (1934). By statute in 1927, the Oregon policy was modified in certain instances. ORS 86.010. See a full discussion in Investors Syndicate v. Smith, 105 F. 2d 611 (C.C.A.Or.1939).

29. Dick & Reuteman Co. v. Jem Realty Co., 225 Wis. 428, 274 N.W. 416 (1937); Penn Mutual Life Ins. Co. v. Katz, 139 Neb. 501, 297 N.W. 899 (1941); Hulseman v. Dirks Land Co., 63 S.D. 404, 259 N.W. 679 (1935); Kinnison v. Guaranty Liquidating Corp., 18 Cal.2d 256, 115 P.2d 450 (1941). Mich. Trust Co. v. Lansing Lumber Co., 103 Mich. 392, 61 N.W. 668 (1894); Rice v. St. Paul & Pac. R.R., 24 Minn. 464 (1878); Kelly v. Roberts, 93 Mont. 106, 17 P.2d 65 (1932). See Geraldson, Clauses Increasing the Possessory Rights of Mortgagees, 10 Wis.L.Rev. 492 (1935).

30. E. g., West's Ann.Cal.Civ.Code § 2927.

this chapter,[31] if the mortgagee actually goes into possession with the consent of the mortgagor, or even, in many jurisdictions, without such consent but peaceably, or under color of legal right, he may hold onto possession until his debt is paid. The courts differentiate between an executory agreement for such possession and the executed transaction.[32] However, in the absence of such an agreement, wherever the lien theory prevails, a mortgagor, prior to foreclosure, may sue the mortgagee for any illegal interference with his possession of the mortgaged premises as freely as any owner of the land, under similar circumstances, may sue a wrongdoer.[33]

§ 4.3 The Intermediate Theory

Several states have adopted a compromise position between the lien and title theories. In these so-called "intermediate states" the mortgagee's right to possession accrues on default.[34] To justify this position courts have talked in terms of legal title being in the mortgagor until default, and then, "after the condition has been broken, the legal title is in the mortgagee." [35] Other courts more cautiously hold that the mortgagee's right to possession has been limited to cases where the condition of the mortgage has been broken.[36] In some states statutory provisions establish that rule.[37]

The intermediate theory has been vigorously attacked on the basis that the only correct and desirable view of the mortgage relation is that the mortgagor, not the mortgagee, is the legal owner and therefore is alone entitled to possession. Further, it is argued that it is completely indefensible to treat the mortgagor as owner before default and the mortgagee as owner after default since this would be combining two utterly inconsistent theories. Moreover, it has been stated flatly that the lien theory, under which the mortgagee has no

31. See §§ 4.27–4.28, infra.

32. See §§ 4.27–4.28, infra.

33. See Rundle, Mortgages, 9 Wis.L. Rev. 40, 42, 43 (1933); Tiffany, Real Prop., 3d ed., § 1416.

34. See Kratovil, Mortgages, Problems In Possession, Rents and Mortgagee Liability, 11 DePaul L.Rev. 1, 4, 6 (1960); Wells v. Kemme, 145 Ga. 17, 88 S.E. 562 (1916); Cohn v. Plass, 85 N.J.Eq. 153, 95 A. 1011 (1915).

35. Bradfield v. Hale, 67 Ohio St. 316, 65 N.E. 1008 (1902). See also Taylor v. Quinn, 68 Ohio App. 164, 39 N.E. 2d 627 (1941).

36. Kransz v. Uedelhofen, 193 Ill. 477, 62 N.E. 239 (1901).

37. E. g., 12 V.S.A. (Vt.) § 4772. "Every mortgagor shall, until condition broken, have, as against the mortgagee, the legal right to possession to the mortgaged premises, unless it is otherwise stipulated in the mortgage deed." Crahan v. Chittenden, 82 Vt. 410, 74 A. 86 (1909). See also Dickerson v. Bridges, 147 Mo. 235, 48 S. W. 825 (1898); Sanderson v. Price, 21 N.J.L. 637, 646 (1846); Shields v. Lozear, 34 N.J.L. 496, 3 Am.St.Rep. 256 (1869); Cohn v. Plass, 85 N.J.Eq. 153, 95 A. 1011 (1915); Mershon v. Castree, 57 N.J.L. 484, 31 A. 602 (1895); Stewart v. Fairchild-Baldwin Co., 91 N.J.Eq. 86, 108 A. 301 (1919); Steinberg v. Kloster Steel Corp., 266 Ill.App. 60 (1932).

right to possession, fully protects the creditor whose only interest should be recognized to be one of security.[38] In criticism of such unqualified condemnation it may be suggested that the real issue is not whether it is desirable to accord to a mortgagee as part of his security interest in the property the right to take possession at a particular time. If the question is posed in this fashion there is something to be said in favor of permitting a mortgagee to take possession after his debtor has defaulted. Certainly, it is difficult to argue that under no circumstances should the mortgagee be permitted to take possession. To reach this result upon the concept that the mortgagor has legal title is to reason as mechanically as do the courts which allow the mortgagee to have possession because he has title. Moreover, the large number of situations in which the mortgagee may obtain possession, or the fruits of possession, would indicate that, on the merits, a rule permitting him possession cannot be dismissed as completely without merit. As one writer has pointed out "to establish his thesis that nature's livery of seisin pending foreclosure sale is to the mortgagor, [one] must struggle not only with the ejectment cases that begot the 'title' and 'intermediate' theories but also with four other varieties of hostile decision. There are the cases that allow the mortgagee (a) to collect rent from tenants of the mortgagor; (b) merely by adding a few words to the mortgage agreement to obtain possession anytime he wants it; (c) to come in to possession by means of a receiver; and (d) if he has obtained possession peaceably but without valid foreclosure, to stay in until he is paid. Of these decisions at least the (b), (c), and (d) varieties are indigenous to so-called lien jurisdictions." [39] Given this tendency of many of the lien theory states to stray from a purely formalistic notion that a mortgagor always has the right to possession prior to foreclosure, the intermediate theory may come closer than the other theories to reflecting what courts do in practice.

B. TORTIOUS INJURY TO LAND BY MORTGAGOR OR THIRD PERSONS

§ 4.4 Tortious Injury by the Mortgagor

The mortgagor in possession may do such acts on the mortgaged property in the same manner as such property is ordinarily used, or, in the common phrase, are "usual and proper in the course of good husbandry." He may do them even though they involve severance of fixtures or parts of the realty and result in a diminution of the value of the property.[40] In a lien state the ownership and possession being

38. Walsh, Mortgages, 93.

39. McDougal, Review of Walsh, Mortgages, 44 Yale L.J. 1278, 1280 (1935).

40. Searle v. Sawyer, 127 Mass. 491, 34 Am.Dec. 425 (1879).

Cf. Ingell v. Fay, 112 Mass. 451 (1873). See Walsh, Mortgages, 113 and cf.

in the mortgagor would be sufficient justification of the rule, technically at least. In title states it has been thought necessary to rest it upon the terms of a license. The license may be either express or implied from the relations of the parties and the consent of the mortgagee to the mortgagor's retention of possession.[41]

When the limits of permissible use have been exceeded the mortgagee has a right to recover damages for the injury he has suffered by the mortgagor's acts. There are, however, different theories as to the basis of the mortgagee's right and as to the proper measure of damages that he may recover.[42]

One view is that the mortgagor's conduct constitutes legal waste, or a tort in the nature of waste, the mortgagor in possession being treated as a tenant of the mortgagee.[43] "The right of action in such case is based upon the plaintiff's interest in the property; and the damages are measured by the extent of injury to that property. * * * It does not depend upon, and the damages are not to be measured by, proof of insufficiency of the remaining security."[44] Such a solution finds its logical grounding in the title theory of the mortgage but it also provides a simpler and more practical answer to the problem than do the decisions stemming from the lien theory. The mortgagor is protected, for of course any recovery by the mortgagee is applied on the debt or accounted for; and the mortgagee is fully protected in being assured the full benefit of the value of the en-

McDougal, 44 Yale L.J. 1278, 1281 n. 15 (1935).

A, a mortgagor, while in possession of the mortgaged premises, cut a reasonable quantity of wood. B, the mortgagee, thereafter evicted A. Held, A, upon quitting the land, was privileged to remove the wood for use elsewhere. Judkins v. Woodman, 81 Me. 351, 17 A. 298, 3 L.R.A. 607 (1889).

On the exploitation of oil or gas resources of land by the mortgagor, or purchaser, or lessee subsequent to the mortgage as waste as against the mortgagee, see note, 9 Tulane L.Rev. 283 (1935). See also 95 A.L.R. 957 (1935).

41. Smith v. Moore, 11 N.H. 55 (1840); Page v. Robinson, 64 Mass. (10 Cush.) 99 (1852); Searle v. Sawyer, 127 Mass. 491, 34 Am.Dec. 425 (1879).

42. See Leipziger, The Mortgagee's Remedies for Waste, 64 Calif.L.Rev. 1086 (1976).

43. Delano v. Smith, 206 Mass. 365, 92 N.E. 500, 30 L.R.A.,N.S., 474 (1910). Since common law waste is limited to acts by tenants for life or years, unless the mortgagor were left in possession under a tenancy for years his conduct would not accurately be waste but a tort in the nature of waste for which either the action of trespass or case might be brought. Anon., 1589, Savile, 84; West v. Treude, 3 Croke, 187 (1630); Langdon v. Paul, 22 Vt. 205 (1850). Camden Trust Co. v. Handle, 132 N.J.Eq. 97, 26 A.2d 865, 154 A.L.R. 602 (1942) noted, 27 Minn.L.Rev. 407 (1942) allowed recovery for voluntary "waste" but denied it for permissive "waste" against a transferee of the mortgagor who did not assume payment of the mortgage debt.

44. Byrom v. Chapin, 113 Mass. 308, 311 (1873). See also First Nat. Bank of Gadsden v. Sproull, 105 Ala. 275, 16 So. 879 (1894); Scaling v. First Nat. Bank, 39 Tex.Civ.App. 154, 87 S.W. 715 (1905). Cf. Ellis v. Glover & Hobson, Ltd., 1 K.B. 388, 399 (1908).

tire mortgaged property, the very security he bargained for.[45] Other cases, allowing the same recovery, have permitted the mortgagee to sue the mortgagor in trespass [46] for such acts as the removal of buildings although one court found it "difficult to see upon what principle, trespass, an action appropriate only to an injury to the possession of the plaintiff, can be maintained by a mortgagee who has never had possession of the mortgaged property against a mortgagor who is in possession of it, upon the ground that the former, by the cutting of the timber or the like, is exceeding his power over the mortgaged property." * * * [47] It has been suggested that waste committed by a tenant at will is regarded as ending the tenancy and making him liable as a trespasser.[48]

Other cases base the mortgagee's right to recover upon the impairment of his security interest, not upon the damage to the property itself.[49] They represent the lien theory view that the mortgagee, not having title, possession, or the right to possession, cannot maintain an action of trespass against a mortgagor who is guilty of acts of waste but can only recover in an action on the case for the damage to his security interest. It follows that the mortgagee's damages "would be limited to the amount of the injury to the mortgage, however great the injury to the land may be." [50]

Since that is the test, the chief problem is what constitutes an impairment of the security. One rule is the difference in value of the property before and after the wrongful acts.[51] Under this the measure of damages is almost identical with that in title states.[52] Another rule requires that the impairment of the security must go to the extent of reducing the value of the remaining mortgaged property below the amount of the debt secured.[53] This seems objectionable as

45. The claim "when recovered applies in payment *pro tanto* of the mortgage debt, and thus, ultimately for the benefit of the mortgagor if he redeem." Gooding v. Shea, 103 Mass. 360, 4 Am.Rep. 563 (1869). See note, 10 Tex.L.Rev. 475, 476 (1932).

46. Stowell v. Pike, 2 Me. 387 (1823); Page v. Robinson, 64 Mass. (10 Cush.) 99 (1852); Pettengill v. Evans, 5 N. H. 54 (1829); Smith v. Moore, 11 N. H. 55 (1840); cf. Stevens v. Smathers, 124 N.C. 571, 32 S.E. 959 (1899); Hoskin v. Woodward, 45 Pa. 42, 3 Leg. & Ins.Rep. 27 (1863).

47. Waterman v. Matteson, 4 R.I. 539, 543 (1857).

48. Walsh, Property, 2d ed., 78.

49. Heath v. Haile, 45 S.C. 642, 24 S.E. 300 (1896).

50. Van Pelt v. McGraw, 4 N.Y. 110 (1850).

51. President & Directors of Manhattan Co. v. Mosler Safe Co., 264 App.Div. 785, 284 N.Y.S. 145 (1935); Atlantic etc., R. Co. v. Rutledge, 122 Fla. 154, 165 So. 563 (1935); Ogden Lumber Co. v. Busse, 92 App.Div. 143, 86 N. Y.S. 1098 (1904).

52. Under the title theory the mortgagee may recover in trespass or trover the value of the severed property, e. g., gravel, which may either exceed or be less than the diminution in value to the land caused by its removal. Consequently the two measures are not always the same. Bates v. Humboldt County, 224 Iowa 841, 277 N.W. 715 (1938).

53. "The action must rest upon proof that, before the alleged injury, the

unfair to the mortgagee. The interest rate and the discount rate of the debt and mortgage on transfer are both determined in large measure by the amount of property securing the obligation and vary in proportion to the ratio between the debt and the value of the security. If a low rate of interest has been charged because ample security has been given, the mortgagee is forced to bear a risk he did not bargain for if part of the security can be taken away even though what is left still equals the debt.[54] And, also, the sale value of his debt and mortgage similarly will be reduced. It may be pointed out, further, that if the value of the remaining security is to be considered, so too should the solvency or insolvency of the mortgagor. Although one early case,[55] later repudiated, so held, this clearly is a factor which should not determine the extent to which the mortgagee has been injured by wrongful reduction of the value of the property taken in mortgage.[56] A further limitation imposed, whichever rule of damages is followed, is that in no event can the mortgagee recover an amount in excess of his mortgage debt and expenses, or any balance due upon it.[57] Most of the cases have arisen after maturity in connection with foreclosure proceedings[58] but there is authority, on the

mortgaged premises were of sufficient value to pay the plaintiff's mortgage, or a part of it, and that, by reason of such injury, they became inadequate for that purpose." Schalk v. Kingsley, 42 N.J.L. 32, 33 (1880).

Carroll v. Edmondson, 41 S.W.2d 64 (Tex.Com.App.1931), commented on 10 Tex.L.Rev. 475 (1932); Lieberman, etc., v. Knight, 153 Tenn. 268, 283 S.W. 450 (1925); Turrell v. Jackson, 39 N.J.L. 329 (1877).

54. Note, 10 Tex.L.Rev. 475, 478 (1932).

55. Gardner v. Heartt, 3 Denio 232 (N.Y.1846).

56. Ogden Lumber Co. v. Busse, 92 App.Div. 143, 86 N.Y.S. 1098 (1904); Toledo v. Brown, 130 Ohio St. 513 (1936). See Denton, Right of a Mortgagee to Recover Damages from a Third Party, 3 Ohio L.J. 161, 164 (1936).

"It certainly is not just, and cannot be lawful, to leave a mortgagee without redress for the destruction of that substantial security upon the strength of which he loaned his money, because he is unable to show the present insufficiency of that wavering staff, the solvency of his debtor, upon which he never expected to rely". Turrell v. Jackson, 39 N.J.L. 329, 332 (1877).

57. Lavenson v. Standard Soap Co., 80 Cal. 245, 22 P. 184, 13 Am.St.Rep. 147 (1889); Heath v. Haile, 45 S.C. 642, 24 S.E. 300 (1896); Cottle v. Wright, 140 Misc. 373, 251 N.Y.S. 699 (1931); Bowden v. Bridgman, 141 S.W. 1043 (Tex.Civ.App.1911); Edler v. Hasche, 67 Wis. 653, 31 N.W. 57 (1887).

58. E. g., Cottle v. Wright, 140 Misc. 373, 251 N.Y.S. 699 (1931), discussed 32 Col.L.Rev. 146 (1932); Heath v. Haile, 45 S.C. 642, 24 S.E. 300 (1896).

In Cottle v. Wright, supra, note 58, the court said: "The bringing of a separate action at law by a mortgagee for waste presents two difficulties. The basis of his action limits him to damages representing the impairment of his security at the time of the commission of the waste. Yet he is further limited in that he cannot receive more than his mortgage debt and expenses, which can only be determined upon a sale in foreclosure. On the other hand, the amount realized upon the foreclosure sale in no way determines the impairment of his security at the time of the commission of waste for later intervening extraneous conditions such as insolvency of mortgagor or market depression may

theory that the creditor is not injured until the foreclosure sale fails to raise enough money to pay his debt, that the mortgagee must first obtain a deficiency judgment.[59] When this is the case there is no difficulty in both limiting the mortgagee's recovery to an amount not to exceed his deficiency and in compelling him to apply it to his claim. However, this restriction even more than the rule taking into account the value of the remaining property at the time of the wrong, deprives the mortgagee of the benefit of the security he bargained for, and substitutes for it not merely only so much of it as a court may consider adequate, but what the remaining property may bring at a foreclosure sale in the future.[60] Further, a judgment for damages against the mortgagor for taking or injuring the mortgaged property which cannot be brought before default is of no benefit to the mortgagee because he is then able to get a judgment for the entire debt or a deficiency after foreclosing on the remaining property. A second judgment at that time equal to a part or all of the mortgage debt or deficiency would be a completely useless duplication. The clearly preferable view, for which there is ample authority, is that the mortgagee may sue before default or foreclosure and recovery of a deficiency.[61] Although it is urged in such a case that the amount of damage to the security could not be ascertained without difficulty, and that it would be unfair to give it to the mortgagee before his debt is due, neither objection has great weight. On any rule of damages, except the one requiring a foreclosure first, the amount can be ascertained. And, although the mortgagee could not be compelled to accept payment before maturity, or the mortgagor to pay, the mortgagee should be permitted to take payment if he wishes and the mortgagor, who has committed a wrong in injuring the security, ought not to be heard to object. Practically, the mortgagor will have little cause to complain for his debt will be reduced and along with it the amount of interest payments, and it is doubtful whether he could have used the amount he will have to pay to much better advantage. Even if he could, it should be no answer to the mortgagee's claim to redress for the mortgagor's tort.

Other rules of damages for the impairment of the mortgagee's security are the reasonable cost of restoring the land to its former condition when this is less than the diminution in market value of the whole property by reason of the injury; as a minimum, the amount[62]

materially affect the foreclosure sale price."

59. Taylor v. McConnell, 53 Mich. 587, 19 N.W. 196 (1884).

60. See 10 Tex.L.Rev. 479 (1932); 17 N.C.L.Rev. 291, 294 (1939).

61. President & Directors of Manhattan Co. v. Mosler Safe Co., 246 App.Div. 785, 284 N.Y.S. 145 (1935); Hummer v. R. C. Huffman Const. Co., 63 F.2d 372 (C.C.A.Ill.1933); Toledo v. Brown, 130 Ohio St. 513, 200 N.E. 750 (1936); Arnold v. Broad, 15 Colo.App. 389, 62 P. 577 (1900). Cf., however, Aggs v. Shackleford County, 85 Tex. 145, 19 S.W. 1085 (1892).

62. Hartshorn v. Chaddock, 135 N.Y. 116, 31 N.E. 997, 17 L.R.A. 426

received from the sale of wrongfully severed fixtures or part of the realty; [63] and "such an amount to be applied on the mortgage debt as will make the debt after this application bear the same ratio to the mortgaged estate after the injury as the original debt bore to the mortgaged property before the injury."

§ 4.5 Injury by Third Parties

While the authorities are sparse and unclear, it would seem that liability of subsequent grantees for waste normally should be the same as that of the original mortgagor.[64] Where a mortgagor's liability is based on tort or other noncontractual theories, a subsequent grantee's liability should be identical, whether the grantee assumed the mortgage debt or not.[65] Such a result is even more likely where a mortgagee's claim is to some extent buttressed by statute. For example, in one recent decision, the California Supreme Court indicated that Section 2929 of the Civil Code, which prohibits any person whose interest is subject to a mortgage from doing "any act" that would substantially impair mortgage security, could be used to impose liability on nonassuming grantees.[66] On the other hand, because nonassuming grantees do not become personally liable on the debt or mortgage, to the extent that the mortgagee simply is attempting to enforce a specific mortgage covenant, only assuming grantees arguably should be liable.[67]

Where the action for injury to the mortgaged property is against other third parties, the authorities and theories follow substantially the same pattern as in the case against the mortgagor. Thus, in title states the mortgagee is allowed to bring trespass for injuries done to the land [68] and actions of replevin [69] or trover [70] to recover severed

(1892); Cedar Ave. Bldg. etc. v. McLaughlin, 69 Pa.Super. 73 (1918). See Ogden Lumber Co. v. Busse, 92 App.Div. 143, 86 N.Y.S. 1098 (1904).

63. See Cottle v. Wright, 140 Misc. 373, 251 N.Y.S. 699 (1931). Note, 10 Tex.L.Rev. 475, 482 (1932).

64. Leipziger, The Mortgagee's Remedies for Waste, 64 Cal.L.Rev. 1086, 1130 (1976).

65. Id. at 1129–1130.

66. Cornelison v. Kornbluth, 15 Cal.3d 590, 125 Cal.Rptr. 557, 542 P.2d 981 (1975).

67. Camden Trust v. Handle, 132 N.J. Eq. 97, 26 A.2d 865 (1942).

68. Smith v. Goodwin, 2 Greenl., Me., 173 (1822); Frothingham v. McKusick, 24 Me. 403 (1844); Sanders v. Reed, 12 N.H. 558 (1842); Federal Land Bank of Columbia v. Jones, 211 N.C. 317, 190 S.E. 479 (1937) (after default by mortgagor); Jeffers v. Pease, 74 Vt. 215, 52 A. 422 (1902) (after condition broken); Harris v. Haynes, 34 Vt. 220 (1861) (after condition broken only).

69. Dorr v. Dudderar, 88 Ill. 107 (1878).

70. Searle v. Sawyer, 127 Mass. 491, 34 Am.St.Rep. 425 (1879). In Houle v. Guilbeault, 70 R.I. 421, 40 A.2d 438 (1944), noted, 25 Boston Univ.L.Rev. 149 (1945), a junior mortgagee in a title state was held unable to bring an action on the case against a third party for removal of fixtures without joining the first mortgagee.

fixtures or parts of the realty or their value. On the other hand, in jurisdictions where the mortgagee can hold the mortgagor only for impairment of the security, he is similarly restricted against third parties.[71]

There is early authority in lien jurisdictions that before the mortgagee can recover for injury to his security against a third party, he must show that such injury was intentional.[72] Indeed, an early view was expressed in New York that not only must there be knowledge of the fact of the mortgage, but an actual fraudulent design to injure the mortgagee.[73] However, the present trend of the cases is based upon the principle that a person must be deemed to intend the necessary consequences of his voluntary act. This trend holds that such a third person is liable if he can be charged with knowledge of the mortgage and that his act impairs the mortgagee's security.[74] One recent California court of appeals decision exemplifies this approach.[75] There a mortgagee brought suit for damages against third party developers, designers and contractors who allegedly substantially impaired the mortgagee's security as a result of their work on a residential subdivision. The court rejected the "old" New York rule and recognized negligence as a valid basis for an action against such third parties. Moreover, the court imputed a broad knowledge of the existence of the mortgagee's interest to the third party defendants. According to the court, "it is common knowledge that the development of residential subdivisions is accomplished financially by means of loans secured by deeds of trust on the real property involved. Therefore, it was not only reasonably foreseeable that the alleged negligence of respondents would result in impairment of plaintiff's security; such a result was substantially certain to occur." [76]

71. Bates v. Humboldt County, 224 Iowa 841, 277 N.W. 715 (1938); Carroll v. Edmondson, Tex.Com.App., 41 S.W.2d 64 (1931), discussed, 10 Tex. L.Rev. 475 (1932); Federal Land Bank of Columbia v. St. Clair Lumber Co., 58 Ga.App. 532, 199 S.E. 337 (1938), discussed, 17 N.C.L.Rev. 291 (1939). The same conclusion has been reached in some title states on the ground that title is in the mortgagee only for security purposes and in relation to the mortgagor. McKelvey v. Creevey, 72 Conn. 464, 45 A. 4, 77 Am.St.Rep. 321 (1900); Verner v. Betz, 46 N.J.Eq. 256, 19 A. 206, 7 L. R.A. 630, 19 Am.St.Rep. 387 (1890); Cooper v. Davis, 15 Conn. 556 (1843). Some lien states, however, by statute permit the mortgagee to recover from third parties the full value of severed fixtures up to the amount of the mortgage debt. See, e. g., Ky.Rev. Stat. 382.350 (1972).

72. Gardner v. Heartt, 3 Denio 232 (N.Y.1846); Wilson v. Maltby, 59 N. Y. 126 (1874).

73. Id.

74. U.S. Financial v. Sullivan, 37 Cal. App.3d 5, 112 Cal.Rptr. 18 (1974); Van Pelt v. McGraw, 4 N.Y. 110 (1850); Jackson v. Brandon Realty Co., 100 N.Y.S. 1005 (1906); Turrell v. Jackson, 39 N.J.L. 329 (1877).

75. U.S. Financial v. Sullivan, 37 Cal. App.3d 5, 112 Cal.Rptr. 18 (1974).

76. Id. at 37 Cal.App.3d 13–14, 112 Cal.Rptr. 22–23.

§ 4.6 Severed Property—Mortgagee's Rights

To what extent can the mortgagee follow and reclaim or subject to his mortgage fixtures, buildings or other things severed from the mortgaged real property? Here again title and lien theories have affected the opinions of the courts. Thus in Betz v. Verner,[77] the court summarized the two lines of reasoning as follows: "It seems that where the mortgage is regarded as a conveyance of the legal title to the property, giving the mortgagee the right of possession, his legal ownership, and actual or constructive possession, give him the right to follow and recover the property severed. The principle applied is that property severed from the realty, so as to become a chattel, belongs to the legal owner of the land; but where the mortgage is regarded merely as a lien for security, and the mortgagor has the right of possession until ejectment or foreclosure, there the mortgagee has merely the right to restrain the removal of the property by injunction, to protect his lien, or, after the removal, only a right to recover damages for the wrongful diminution of his security." Following this reasoning in title states, since the mortgagee has "legal ownership and right of possession, he may follow things severed from the mortgage lands without his consent wherever he can find them," [78] and recover them by an action of replevin or through the appointment of a receiver, or, in the alternative, recover their value in trover.[78a] On the other hand, the lien view has been followed to deny to the mortgagee any rights in things severed.[79] However, in a few title jurisdictions, the courts have decided that, because title was for the limited purpose of security, severance would divest the title so that no rights could be asserted in the severed article.[79a] On the other

77. 46 N.J.Eq. 256, 19 A. 206, 7 L.R.A. 630, 19 Am.St.Rep. 387 (1890).

78. Betz v. Verner, 46 N.J.Eq. 256, 19 A. 206, 7 L.R.A. 630, 19 Am.St.Rep. 387 (1890).

78a. Dorr v. Dudderar, 88 Ill. 107 (1878) (replevin); Burley v. Pike, 62 N.H. 495 (1882) (replevin); Waterman v. Matteson, 4 R.I. 539 (1856) (replevin against the mortgagor); First Nat. Bank & Trust Co. v. Hagar Oil Co., 105 N.J.Eq. 62, 146 A. 878 (1929), noted 78 U. of Pa.L.Rev. 269 (1929) (receiver); Langdon v. Paul, 22 Vt. 205 (1850) (trover); Searle v. Sawyer, 127 Mass. 491, 34 Am.St.Rep. 425 (1879).

79. Cases denying the mortgagee a right to recover the severed chattel in actions at law are Vanderslice v. Knapp, 20 Kan. 647 (1878) (replevin denied against a purchaser from the mortgagor); Moore v. Moran, 64 Neb. 84, 89 N.W. 629 (1902) (replevin denied against a third party). Odell v. Buck, 5 A.D.2d 732, 168 N.Y.S.2d 756 (3d Dept.1958) noted in 24 Brooklyn L.Rev. 372 (1958). An equitable lien on a leasehold does not extend to oil converted to personal property by severance. Onyx Refining Co. v. Evans Production Corp., 182 F.Supp. 253 (N.D.Tex.1960).

79a. "If the mortgagee have the legal ownership and right of possession, he may follow things severed and removed from the mortgage lands without his consent wherever he can find them. If he holds title under the mortgage only as security for his lien, then the remedies appointed for preserving the security, and compensating for any loss sustained by its diminution, are such, only, as the mortgagee may use. The theory in the latter case is that, as to innocent third parties, the mortgagor is the owner of the property, and may sever

hand there are several lien states that hold that the lien will continue after severance. It can be enforced even though in the hands of a third party provided he took with notice of the mortgagee's lien or acted in collusion with the mortgagor; [80] it will be cut off by a bona fide purchase.[80a] Some of the cases allowing foreclosure on the severed part have been made conditional on the remaining property being insufficient to pay the debt but others have ignored this requirement.[80b] Here, as elsewhere, the rights of the parties ought not to be fixed upon any legalistic reasoning from the concepts of title or lien but upon considerations of how far a secured creditor should have protection. It is believed that the rule allowing him to assert his security interest in the severed property as against all but bona fide purchasers is the preferable view in all jurisdictions, and that the test of how far constructive notice should be invoked to prevent there being such a claimant ought to depend, as previously suggested, upon the character of the severed property. And, indeed, this seems to be the result of a majority of the cases, regardless of the reasoning by which they arrived there.

§ 4.7 Injunction Against Removal of Severed Property

Some authorities, influenced by the title theory, say that a mortgagor who wrongfully severs fixtures, buildings, or part of the land itself is liable for conversion. The reason is found in the view of the

and sell until restrained by injunction, or ejected by entry, or barred by foreclosure." Betz v. Verner, supra, note 77 at 267, 19 A. at 208; Cooper v. Davis, 15 Conn. 556 (1843); McKelvey v. Creevey, 72 Conn. 464, 45 A. 4, 77 Am.St.Rep. 321 (1900); Kircher v. Schalk, 39 N.J.L. 335 (1877) (replevin denied, his remedy being limited to an action for damages).

80. A mortgagor moved a house off the mortgaged premises onto other lands. Held, a decree of foreclosure sale, giving the purchaser leave to remove the house, proper. Turner v. Mebane, 110 N.C. 413, 14 S.E. 974, 28 Am.St.Rep. 697 (1892); Federal Land Bank v. Davis, 228 Ala. 85, 152 So. 226 (1934) (foreclosure), accord; Dakota Loan & Trust Co. v. Parmalee, 5 S.D. 341, 58 N.W. 811 (1894); Campbell, Cas.Morts., 153 n. 5; Hamlin v. Parsons, 12 Minn. 108 (Gil. 59) 90 Am.Dec. 284 (1882) (foreclosure on house on land of a third person who took with notice); Mills v. Pope, 90 Mont. 569, 4 P.2d 485 (1931) (foreclosure permitted); Johnson v. Bratton, 112 Mich. 319, 70 N.W. 1021 (1897); Partridge v. Hemenway, 89 Mich. 454, 50 N.W. 1084, 28 Am.St.Rep. 322 (1891).

80a. "So long as the mortgagor continues in possession, or when the property severed passes into the possession of a person in collusion with him to defeat the lien and security of the mortgagee, whether upon or off the mortgaged premises, it would seem that the rights of the mortgagee would be unaffected. But when the property is severed, and sold to an innocent purchaser, the lien in equity is gone, and the remedy of the mortgagee is an action at law against the mortgagor, and those who act with him to impair or defeat the security of the mortgage." Betz v. Verner, supra, note 77 at 268, 14 A. at 208. In New Jersey, the court, although saying that the mortgagee has title, limits it to security purposes and, on the point involved here, follows the rule of lien jurisdictions.

80b. See Tex.L.Rev. 481 (1932).

mortgagee as having title to the severed product.[81] In these states equity courts hold further that normally the mortgagee cannot have an injunction against the mortgagor to restrain the asportation or other conversion of the severed portion. An injunction will lie only if the mortgagor is insolvent or money damages would be inadequate.[82] In the states in which severance from mortgaged land frees the severed part from the lien of the mortgage so that the mortgagee has no right to sue at law for it, it follows that the mortgagee would have no claim to an injunction to prevent the removal of the severed product. In these latter states even the insolvency of the mortgagor would not be sufficient to warrant an injunction.[83] The result is that in all states the mortgagee's only reliable remedy is to prevent the commission of waste in the first place.[84]

Both lines of cases arguably are wrong. Regardless of whether the state is of lien or title theory persuasion, severance should not shake off the mortgagee's security interest in the severed article. Further, the criterion for issuing an injunction against a mortgagor should not be whether the subject matter of the mortgage is real or personal property, but whether if it is disposed of there will be sufficient property left still subject to the mortgage to leave the plaintiff adequate security.[85]

§ 4.8 Injury by Third Persons—Mortgagor's Rights

A mortgagor in possession, even in title states, is treated as owner of the mortgaged property as to all persons other than the mortgagee or one claiming under the mortgagee, and this is *a fortiori* true in lien states.[86] It follows that he may recover from a third person for injuries done to the premises the full amount of damage done just as though the property were not subject to a mortgage.[87]

81. See § 4.6, supra.

82. See, McClintock, Equity, 2d ed., §§ 45, 47.

83. Ames, Cas.Eq., 484 n. However, see American Trust Co. v. North Belleville Quarry Co., 31 N.J.Eq. 89 (1879); Chanango Bank v. Cox, 26 N.J.Eq. 452 (1875); Ennis v. Smith et al., Del.Ch., 80 A. 636 (1911).

84. Watson v. Hunter, 5 Johns.Ch. 169, 9 Am.Dec. 295 (1821).

See Cooper v. Davis, 15 Conn. 556 (1843); Vanderslice v. Knapp, 20 Kan. 647 (1878); Tomlinson v. Thomson, 27 Kan. 70 (1882). See note, 60 U. of Pa.L.Rev. 135 (1911).

85. Ensign v. Colburn, 11 Paige 503 (N.Y.1885); Hutchins v. King, 68 U.S. (1 Wall.) 53, 17 L.Ed. 544 (1862).

86. Huckins v. Straw, 34 Me. 166 (1852), Campbell, Cases Mortgages, 2d Ed., 13; Cotton v. Carlisle, 85 Ala. 175, 4 So. 670, 7 Am.St.Rep. 29 (1887); Orr v. Hadley, 36 N.H. 575 (1858); Seaman v. Bisbee, 163 Ill. 91, 45 N.E. 208 (1896); Huckins v. Straw, 34 Me. 166 (1852).

87. Hamilton v. Griffin, 123 Ala. 600, 26 So. 243 (1898); Craig v. W. P. Carmichael Co., 271 Mo. 516, 197 S. W. 141 (1917); Watkins v. Kaolin Mfg. Co., 131 N.C. 536, 42 S.E. 983, 60 L.R.A. 617 (1902); Van Dyke v. Grand Trunk R. Co., 84 Vt. 212, 78 A. 958, Ann.Cas.1913A, 640 (1910).

It has been argued that this view is completely inconsistent with the title theory of mortgages and that it is incompatible with the rule in title states that the mortgagee may recover severed parts of the realty or their value from third parties in actions of replevin or trover.[88] If this thesis were carried to its logical conclusion, the mortgagee would be denied any remedy against a third party. But he can always recover to the extent that his security has been impaired even in lien jurisdictions.

There seems little more objection to allowing the mortgagee to recover entire damages without regard to the measure of his own security, or the severed portion itself, and then crediting his recovery on the debt or accounting for it than there is in allowing a partial recovery limited to the extent his security interest is impaired and applying or accounting for it. Further, to restrict any relief of the mortgagee to holding the mortgagor and giving to the mortgagor the sole rights against third parties would pose practical difficulties in forcing the mortgagor to sue. In addition, such a view would permit settlements [89] between the mortgagor and the third party to preclude any recovery by the mortgagee, and, carried to a logical absurdity, deny relief to the mortgagee where the third party has acted to injure the property with the connivance of the mortgagor so that the latter has no action of his own.[90] Such considerations should not merely refute any argument that the sole desirable solution is to vest the right to full recovery against third parties exclusively in the mortgagor, but to lend support to the view that, as a practical solution, permitting the mortgagee not only the right to sue but to recover full damages has considerable merit. Indeed, the vitality of such a view is evidenced by legislation in a number of states altering the rule that restricts him to recovery of the diminution of his security interest.[91]

§ 4.9 Relation of Rights of Mortgagor and Mortgagee Against Third Parties

Another difficulty arises because of the fact that courts have recognized rights by both the mortgagor and the mortgagee against third parties who have injured the property. In states [92] where the mortgagee can have no action unless the remaining property is less than the debt, if the injury has not reduced the security below that mark the mortgagor is the only one injured, and therefore he can recover for the entire damage done. The question of whether there must be two suits, one by the mortgagor and one by the mortgagee,

88. Walsh, Mortgages, § 23.

89. See cases cited Campbell, Cases Mortgages, 2d Ed., 152, n. 4.

90. See Sanders v. Reed, 12 N.H. 558 (1842).

91. See, e. g., Ky.Rev.Stat. 382.350 (1972). See also, note, 53 Harv.L. Rev. 503 (1940).

92. See Garrow v. Brooks, 123 N.J.Eq. 138, 196 A. 460 (1938).

or whether there may be a full recovery in one action by either party, is raised in two situations. (1) Where the injury has impaired the value of the remaining property to such an extent that it is insufficient to pay the debt. (2) In jurisdictions which permit the mortgagee to recover for the injury to the property itself.[93] In a jurisdiction in which the mortgagee's right to recover is a limited one, the mortgagor who sued first was allowed a complete recovery. The court said that the defendant would be protected against an action by the mortgagee because such recovery would be a legal bar to further recovery by either.[94] Further, the judgment recovered by the mortgagor would be subjected to the lien of the mortgage as substitute collateral "to the extent that it may be found the proceeds of the judgment represent the amount of damage sustained by the complainant under the rule as to the measure thereof",[95] i. e., the diminution in value of the security. In a title jurisdiction, the mortgagor's recovery would be subject, on a parity of reasoning, to a lien for the entire amount of the mortgagee's debt claim.

On the other hand, if there has been a settlement without suit between the mortgagor and the third person, the mortgagee will not be barred from recovering against the tortfeasor.[96]

"When the mortgagee has instituted the prior suit, and recovered his damages, as he may, there is no difficulty about the rule. The owner may still maintain an action for the injury, and the trespasser can protect himself by giving in evidence the recovery by the mortgagee in mitigation of damages. The owner has suffered damage to the full extent of the injury, but his claim has been satisfied pro tanto by payment to the mortgagee for his loss." [97] Of course, if the mortgagee had been permitted to recover the entire amount of damage done, this should be a complete bar to the mortgagor's action.

93. See Turner Coal Co. v. Glover, 101 Ala. 289, 13 So. 478 (1892); Paine v. Woods, 108 Mass. 160 (1871). See also Ann.Cas.1913A, 652. Cf. Gooding v. Shea, 103 Mass. 360, 4 Am. Rep. 563 (1869); Jenks v. Hart Cedar & Lumber Co., 143 Mich. 449, 106 N. W. 1119, 114 Am.St.Rep. 673 (1906); Sanders v. Reed, 12 N.H. 558 (1842).

94. Delaware etc., Telephone Co. v. Elvins, 63 N.J.L. 243, 43 A. 903, 76 Am.St.Rep. 217 (1899); Garrow v. Brooks, supra note 92.

95. Garrow v. Brooks, 123 N.J.Eq. 138, 141, 196 A. 460, 462 (1938). "The mortgagee was entitled to the building as part of her security and is now entitled to look to the fund in the hands of the sheriff as converted into its original form." See American Sav. & Loan Ass'n v. Leeds, 68 C.2d 611, 68 Cal.Rptr. 453, 440 P.2d 933, n. 2 (1968).

96. Taylor v. Federal Land Bank, 162 Miss. 653, 657, 138 So. 596, 597 (1932); Guaranty Savings & Loan Ass'n v. Springfield, Mo.App. 113 S. W.2d 147, 154 (1938); Federal Land Bank of Columbia v. Jones, 211 N.C. 317, 190 S.E. 479 (1937).

97. Delaware, etc., Telephone Co. v. Elvins, 63 N.J.L. 243, 245, 43 A. 903, 76 Am.St.Rep. 217 (1899).

§ 4.10 Equitable Relief Against the Mortgagor

It is thoroughly settled that a mortgagee may have an injunction against a mortgagor in possession to prevent him from injuring the mortgaged property under certain circumstances. The only question is what those circumstances are.[98] This is true even though the mortgagee has the right to take possession of the mortgaged premises. The severe rules of accounting, theory to the contrary notwithstanding, make this such an inadequate remedy that it will not prevent the granting of equitable relief in appropriate cases.[99] There is some authority that equity will act to prevent the mortgagor doing any serious injury to the property over and above the normal use of it in the course of good husbandry, as by cutting down an undue amount of timber or the removal of buildings or fixtures.[1] And there is much sense in such a view. If five acres of land have been mortgaged the mortgagor could not sell off, free and clear of the mortgage, one acre even though what is left is more than ample to secure the debt. The mortgagee took the entire five acres and he is entitled to keep all of it. He is not compelled to run the risk that though now the property that is left is ample, it might not be later when the debt is due. And so here. He bargained for the greater amount of security and he should not have to accept anyone else's judgment on whether it, or what is left of it after the mortgagor does an act reducing its value, is adequate.

Most courts, however, follow the rule that the threatened injury must be one that will bring the value of the security down to a point where it is in the danger zone so that it might not be ample.[2] In one of the early and leading cases, the test was put this way: "It is rather a question of prudence than of actual value. I think the question which must be tried is whether the property the mortgagee takes as a security, is sufficient in this sense, that the security is worth so much more than the money advanced that the act is not to be considered as substantially impairing the value, which was the basis of the contract between the parties at the time it was entered into." [3] What is the danger zone will depend on the nature of the property in part. A bigger margin of security must be left if the property is subject to wide and frequent fluctuations in value than if it is of stable value,

98. See generally, Leipziger, The Mortgagee's Remedies For Waste, 64 Cal. L.Rev. 1086, 1099–1100 (1976).

99. See Glenn, Morts., § 211. See §§ 4.30–4.35 infra.

1. Nelson v. Pinegar, 30 Ill. 473 (1863); Williams v. Chicago Exhibition Co., 188 Ill. 19, 58 N.E. 611 (1900).

2. King v. Smith, 2 Hare, 239 (1843); Fairbank v. Cudworth, 33 Wis. 358 (1873); Fidelity Trust Co. v. Hoboken etc. R. Co., 71 N.J.Eq. 14, 63 A. 273 (1906); Coker v. Whitlock, 54 Ala. 180 (1875); Collins v. Rea, 127 Mich. 273, 86 N.W. 811 (1901); Hastings v. Perry, 20 Vt. 272 (1848); Brady v. Waldron, 2 Johns.Ch. 148 (N.Y.1816).

3. King v. Smith, supra note 2 at 243.

but probably in no case would the security have been considered adequate security by a prudent lender unless it was worth one-third more than the amount of the money lent at the time of the mortgage.[4] In no case would it be sufficient that the value of the property was barely equal to the mortgage debt.[5] And, quite properly, the insolvency of the mortgagor is immaterial on this question. The mortgagee demanded the mortgage before making the loan so that he would not have to rely upon the general pecuniary condition of the mortgagor and it would be inequitable to take into account in granting relief a factor which the mortgagee took care to guard against by seeing to it that he was a secured and not a general creditor.[6]

The ability of the court of equity to protect the mortgagee from the commission of waste is not limited to the issuance of injunctions. Although "it is true that in general a receivership is ancillary or incidental to the main purpose of the bill, it does not follow that where a case is presented which demands the relief which can be best given by a receivership, such relief must be refused, because the time has not arrived when other substantial relief can be asked. For example, although as a rule, a mortgagee cannot ask for relief until his mortgage debt has become due, he can go into a court of equity before that time has arrived and ask for an injunction and a receiver to prevent the subject-matter of his mortgage from being impaired and wasted." [7] Nevertheless "the appointment of a receiver and authorizing him to take possession of property is the exercise of a higher and more far reaching power than the granting of an injunction, and should not be resorted to where an injunction will as well serve the purpose of the judicial proceedings, and to the same extent protect the rights of the complainant." [8] This attitude of the courts toward the appointment of a receiver, it should be stressed, leaves out of ac-

4. King v. Smith, supra note 2; Moriarty v. Ashworth, 43 Minn. 1, 3, 44 N.W. 531, 532; 19 Am.St.Rep. 203 (1890). Perhaps a smaller loan to value ratio would be considered acceptable if the loan were originally a high-ratio one with mortgage insurance. See § 11.2 infra.

5. Moriarty v. Ashworth, supra note 4; Beaver Flume and Lumber Co. v. Eccles, 43 Or. 400, 73 P. 201, 99 Am.St. Rep. 759 (1903).

6. Fairbank v. Cudworth, supra note 2; Core v. Bell, 20 W.Va. 169 (1882).

7. Brassey v. New York & N. E. R. Co., 19 F. 663, 669 (C.C.Conn.1884). See also Farmers' Loan & Trust Co. v. Meridian Waterworks Co., 139 F. 661 (C.C.Miss.1905); Davis v. Alton, Jacksonville & P. Ry. Co., 180 Ill.App. 1 (1913). Cf. American Loan & Trust Co. v. Toledo, C. & S. Ry. Co., 29 F. 416 (C.C.Ohio 1886). But see, contra, Houston & B. V. Ry. Co. v. Hughes, 182 S.W. 23 (Tex.Civ.App.1916) (appointment of a receiver must be ancillary to foreclosure, and will not be made where the mortgagor has not defaulted in performance of obligation secured).

8. Schack v. McKey, 97 Ill.App. 460, 465 (1901). See also Original Vienna Bakery Co. v. Heissler, 50 Ill.App. 406, 413 (1893); Clark, Receivers, § 59.

count the appointment of a receiver at the request of a mortgagee who has begun foreclosure. That is considered separately later.[9]

§ 4.11 Enforcing Specific Covenants Against Waste

The mortgage theory followed by an individual jurisdiction, as we have seen, can substantially affect the mortgagee's remedies against waste. In a similar vein, the classification of waste as either "voluntary" or "permissive", when taken in the context of the lien or title theory, can prove significant in weighing the mortgagee's chances for recovery for waste. Voluntary waste entails such activities as excessive cutting of timber and removal or physical destruction of buildings, while permissive waste, on the other hand, consists of failing to repair or allowing the property to fall into disrepair.[10] While a mortgagee stands a good chance of recovering damages for voluntary waste in both title and lien jurisdictions, only in title theory states would recovery be possible for permissive waste.[11]

Thus, for a variety of reasons, mortgagees today generally include specific covenants against waste in the mortgage instrument. First, lien theory mortgagees seek to avoid the limiting consequences of the "substantial impairment" rule. Second, such mortgagees seek to be able to recover for permissive waste, a right their title theory counterparts sometimes enjoy as a matter of law. Similarly, the lien mortgagee seeks protection from "financial waste", such as failure to pay real estate taxes and senior liens. Moreover, both title and lien mortgagees use such covenants to establish that the commission of waste will be a ground for acceleration and foreclosure. While the use of covenants has to some extent enhanced the mortgagee's rights in the financial waste situation, in the other areas of concern referred to above they have not significantly increased the mortgagee's common law rights.[11a]

While covenants against "financial waste" have generally been recognised judicially, practical enforcement methods are limited in both title and lien jurisdictions. There is almost no authority permitting the recovery of damages against the mortgagor who fails to pay real estate taxes.[12] Moreover, such a recovery may not be possible

9. See §§ 4.36—4.46, infra. Where the mortgagee has conveyed the mortgaged premises to a purchaser who assumes or takes "subject to" the mortgage, must the mortgagee bring a suit to enjoin waste by the grantee as a condition precedent to preserving his right to collect the debt from the mortgagor? While there is authority that indicates an affirmative answer, the better view is to the contrary. See Osborne, Mortgages, § 135 (2d Ed. 1970).

10. Leipziger, The Mortgagee's Remedies For Waste, 64 Cal.L.Rev. 1086, 1087 (1976).

11. Id. at 1103–1104.

11a. Id.

12. Wiggin v. Lowell Five Cent. Sav. Bank, 299 Mass. 518, 13 N.E.2d 433 (1938); Camden Trust Co. v. Handle, 132 N.J.Eq. 97, 26 A.2d 865 (Ct.Err. & App.1942).

even after the mortgagee has paid the taxes.[13] As a practical matter, after such financial waste has occurred the only realistic option for the mortgagee is to protect the mortgage security by paying the delinquent taxes or other liens, accelerate the debt, and then either attempt to sue on the entire debt, including advances, or foreclose on the mortgage. Most institutional mortgagees attempt to avoid the above predicament by requiring the mortgagor to make periodic payments into "reserve" or "escrow" accounts to provide a fund for the payment of taxes. Detailed consideration of this practice follows later in this chapter.[14]

Another type of covenant against waste is the "repair covenant". Under such covenants, mortgagees often agree "to maintain [the mortgaged property] in good condition and repair; not to remove or demolish any building or improvement [on the mortgaged property]; to complete promptly in workmanlike manner any improvement hereafter constructed thereon and to restore promptly in workmanlike manner any improvement thereon which is damaged or destroyed, and to pay when due all cost therefor or in connection therewith; to comply with all laws, ordinances, regulations, covenants, conditions and restrictions affecting the property; not to commit, suffer, or permit any waste thereof . . ." [15]

Mortgagors occasionally demolish or remove existing improvements to replace them with newer structures. Courts generally hold that repair covenants are unenforceable unless, after the improvements are made, the market value of the property is lower than prior to the demolition and new improvements.[16] Otherwise, no "damage" would be suffered by the mortgagee. Such cases do not distinguish between the breach of a repair covenant as a basis for a damage action and as a basis for acceleration of the debt and foreclosure of the mortgage. One commentator has criticized the reasoning of these cases as "shallow and unfair to the mortgagee" because while "the absence of damage to the property would indeed be fatal to a suit alleging waste and seeking to collect damages, * * * the mortgagee should have the right to accelerate the debt whenever any condition expressed in the note or the mortgage has failed. For it is reasonable to assume that the parties intended that the prohibition on demolition would give control over development of the property to the mortgagee. . . . If the covenant is not enforced, the mortgagee faces a real risk that the construction that was supposed to follow the demolition will never be completed or that, even if completed, the building will be uneconomic and provide less security than the original structure." [17]

13. Glenn, Mortgages, § 91.1 (1943).

14. See §§ 4.17–4.22, infra.

15. Krone v. Goff, 53 Cal.App.3d 191, 127 Cal.Rptr. 390, n. 1 (1976).

16. See e. g., Heller v. Gerry, 47 A.D. 2d 697, 364 N.Y.S.2d 615 (1975); Bart v. Streuli, 5 Cal.2d 67, 52 P.2d 922 (1935).

17. Leipziger, supra note 10 at 1106.

Courts also construe narrowly and hesitate to enforce repair covenants either by a damage action or by foreclosure where the mortgagor's breach consist of a failure to make repairs.[18] For example one court has refused to permit foreclosure by a federal government mortgagee where the mortgagor violated a covenant to comply with local building, health and other codes and to make all repairs and replacements necessary to preserve and maintain the value of the mortgage security.[19] Because the value of the mortgage property was seven times the mortgage debt, the court determined that the security had not been sufficiently impaired. Moreover, in damage actions for waste, other courts have indicated that security impairment will be required notwithstanding specific repair covenants.[20]

Finally, some repair covenants cases involve fact situations where the mortgagee has a right to compensation from a special fund. For example, where there has been substantial physical damage and the mortgagee is entitled to insurance proceeds, courts have refused to permit foreclosure even though the mortgagor has specifically covenanted to rebuild.[21] In one case, after substantial damage by fire, the property was not rebuilt and was vandalized notwithstanding some attempts by the mortgagor to prevent it. The mortgagee was a named insured under the insurance policy enforced at the time of the fire. The court refused to permit foreclosure, holding that the covenant language "to keep the property in good condition" required only normal maintenance and not rebuilding.[22] Moreover, the court determined that the mortgagor had not "permitted waste" within the covenant language because the mortgagor had attempted to protect the remains and obtain new insurance coverage for them.

C. RIGHTS IN THE PRODUCT OF THE RES

§ 4.12 Eminent Domain

Where mortgaged land is taken by eminent domain the mortgagee's rights in the land follow the award and attach to it.[23] "The underlying theory of the right of a mortgagee to part or all of the award is that, as the parties are powerless to prevent the taking of the property by the public and the mortgagee loses his lien on the part taken, the award equitably stands in the place of the land taken; and, as the mortgage does not cover the award in law, it is held to

18. See, e. g., United States v. Angel, 362 F.Supp. 445 (E.D.Pa.1973); Krone v. Goff, 53 Cal.App.3d 191, 127 Cal. Rptr. 390 (1975).

19. United States v. Angel, 362 F.Supp. 445 (E.D.Pa.1973).

20. See e. g., Krone v. Goff, 53 Cal. App.3d 191, 127 Cal.Rptr. 390 (1975).

21. See Leipziger, supra note 10 at 1107.

22. Erickson v. Rocco, 433 S.W.2d 746 (Tex.Civ.App.1968).

23. Nichols, Eminent Domain § 5.74 (1976); Silverman v. State, 48 A.D.2d 413, 370 N.Y.S.2d 234 (1975).

operate as an equitable lien thereon. This results in two separate encumbrances, the legal mortgage on the remainder of the land and the equitable lien on the award." [24] Where the entire property subject to the mortgage is taken, the mortgagee is entitled to the entire award, or so much of it as is necessary to satisfy his mortgage debt.[25]

Where there is only a partial condemnation, there are at least three views to the mortgagee's rights. One view gives the mortgagee the entire amount of the award without distinguishing whether the mortgage has been foreclosed or even whether it has matured.[26] According to a second view, the mortgagee in a partial taking situation is entitled to that amount of the condemnation award that will compensate him for the impairment of his security.[27] There are varying views as to what constitutes impairment of security. For example, some have said that if the value of the property after condemnation exceeds the amount of the mortgage debt, the entire condemnation award for a partial taking presumably belongs to the mortgagor.[28] On the other hand, it has been stated that "we do not agree that in a case where the mortgagee has bargained for a lien on property valued greatly in excess of the debt, his security may be whittled down in value by partial takings in condemnation . . . to the point where it barely equals the amount of the debt, and there still be no impairment of his security." [29] Whatever the exact parameters of the impairment of security approach, it will be followed even where the mortgage specifically confers on the mortgagee the option of releasing the proceeds of a condemnation award to the mortgagor or applying them to the mortgage indebtedness.[30] The Uniform Emi-

24. Petition of Dillman, 276 Mich. 252, 258, 267 N.W. 623, 625 (1936).

25. Calumet River Ry. v. Brown, 136 Ill. 322, 26 N.E. 501, 12 L.R.A. 84 (1891); Chicago v. Gage, 268 Ill. 232, 109 N.E. 28 (1915); Connell v. Kakauna etc., Co., 164 Wis. 471, 159 N. W. 927, Ann.Cas.1918A 247 (1916), rehearing denied 164 Wis. 471, 160 N.W. 1035. It is immaterial whether the mortgage debt is or is not due. Morgan v. Willman, 318 Mo. 151, 1 S.W.2d 193, 58 A.L.R. 1518 (1927); Federal Trust Co. v. East Hartford Fire Dist., 283 F. 95 (C.C.A.Conn. 1922).

See Teague, Condemnation of Mortgaged Property, 44 Tex.L.Rev. 1535, 1537–1939. (1966).

26. In re Forman, 138 Misc. 501, 240 N.Y.S. 718 (1930), noted 44 Harv.L. Rev. 1142 (1931); In re Public Park, 184 App.Div. 509, 172 N.Y.S. 50 (1918), dismissed, 224 N.Y. 697, 121 N.E. 356 (1918). If not mature, a rebate of interest on the debt must be given. See Teague, Condemnation of Mortgaged Property, 44 Tex.L.Rev. 1535, 1539 (1966).

27. Teague, Condemnation of Mortgaged Property, 44 Tex.L.Rev. 1535, 1540 (1966); Buell Realty Note Collection Trust v. Central Oak Inv. Co., 483 S.W.2d 24 Tex.Civ.App. 1972), refused n. r. e. 486 S.W.2d 87; Swanson v. U. S., 156 F.2d 442 (9th Cir. 1946), certiorari denied 329 U.S. 800, 67 S.Ct. 492, 91 L.Ed. 684.

28. Rayburn, Texas Law of Condemnation, §§ 79, 113 (1960).

29. Buell Realty Note Collection Trust v. Central Oak Inv. Co., 483 S.W.2d 24, 27 (Tex.Civ.App.1972), refused n. r. e. 486 S.W.2d 87.

30. Milstein v. Security Pacific Nat. Bank, 27 Cal.App.3d 482, 103 Cal. Rptr. 16 (1972).

nent Domain Code, approved by the National Conference of Commissioners on Uniform State Laws in 1974, specifically provides that "notwithstanding the provisions of an agreement, if any, relating to a lien encumbering the property: (1) if there is a partial taking, the lien holder may share in the amount of compensation awarded only to the extent determined by the court to be necessary to prevent an impairment of the security * * *"[31] A third suggestion is that the court should allocate to the mortgagee a portion of the award measured by the ratio which the mortgage debt bears to the value of the whole mortgaged land, thus preserving the ratio of debt to security.[32]

Generally the mortgagee must be given notice of a condemnation proceeding and an opportunity to appear in that proceeding. In at least half of the states, this requirement is mandated by statute.[33] Although other state statutes provide that notice shall be given to the "owner" or "parties in interest", judicial interpretation of such statutes has generally resulted in the inclusion of mortgagees within the coverage of one or both of those terms.[34] Nevertheless, there may still be a few jurisdictions that hold, in the absence of express statutory requirements to the contrary, that the mortgagee need not be made a party or given notice of the condemnation proceedings.[35] This result seems in part to stem from the refusal of a few lien theory states to recognise, for purposes of interpreting their condemnation statutes, that the mortgagee has any interest in the mortgaged real estate other than a lien.[36] In such a situation, the mortgagee presumably must recover the award from the condemnor before it is paid to the mortgagor or from the mortgagor if it has already been remitted to him.[37] To the extent that any state law today still fails to require that both notice and an opportunity to be heard be afforded to the mortgagee in a condemnation proceeding, it must surely violate procedural due process requirements of notice and hearing under federal and state constitutions. Whether one characterizes the mortgagee's interest as an estate in land or as merely a lien, the mortgagee's economic stake in the land is often substantial. Accord-

31. Uniform Eminent Domain Code, § 1014.

32. Teague, Condemnation of Mortgaged Property, 44 Tex.L.Rev. 1535, 1543 (1966); Buell Realty Note Collection Trust v. Central Oak Inv. Co., 486 S.W.2d 87 (Tex.1972).

33. Teague, supra note 32 at 1535.

34. See, e. g., Id. at 1535; Calumet River Ry. v. Brown, 136 Ill. 322, 26 N.E. 501, 12 L.R.A. 84 (1891).

35. See, e. g., State Highway Comm. v. District Court of the Thirteenth Judicial District, 499 P.2d 1228, 1234–35 (Mont.1972); Nichols, Eminent Domain, § 5.741 (1976).

36. See Nichols, Eminent Domain, § 5.741 (1976).

37. Whiting v. New Haven, 45 Conn. 303 (1877); Parish v. Gilmanton, 11 N.H. 293 (1840); Read v. Cambridge, 126 Mass. 427 (1879); Goodrich v. Com'rs of Atchison Co., 47 Kan. 355, 27 P. 1006, 18 L.R.A. 113 (1891); Thompson v. Chicago etc., Ry. Co., 110 Mo. 147, 19 S.W. 77 (1892).

ingly, mortgagees may often have a significant economic interest in insuring that the condemnation award be as large as possible. Indeed, in a judicial era when procedural due process rights have been expanded to other areas of mortgage law,[38] it would seem unthinkable such protections should not be afforded to a mortgagee in a condemnation proceeding. In any event it seems undesirable to deprive the mortgagee of his bargained for security and leave him with inadequate protection. Indeed, after the award has been paid over to the mortgagor, the mortgagee is in the same position he would have been in had he never bargained for and obtained security.

When the mortgagee is a necessary party in a condemnation proceeding, what are the consequences of failure to join him? Some courts hold that the land condemned is still subject to his mortgage and the mortgagee can foreclose on it.[39] If the original award has not been paid to the mortgagor, the mortgagee may seek and obtain a revaluation and new award and have this paid to him in amount sufficient to satisfy his mortgage claim.[40] Others hold that even though the full award has been made and paid to the mortgagor, the mortgagee is entitled as against the condemnor to so much of the original award as is necessary to compensate him for his interest in the property taken[41] or to have a new valuation of the property taken and be satisfied out of it.[42]

§ 4.13 Insurance—Some General Considerations

Both the mortgagor and the mortgagee of real property have an insurable interest in the mortgaged property. Hence each may protect himself against loss by his own contract of insurance.[43] The in-

38. See §§ 7.23–7.30, infra.

39. Grigsby v. Miller, 144 Or. 551, 25 P.2d 908 (1933), giving, however, a reasonable time to the condemnor to secure the property by new condemnation or purchase. See also Wilson v. European & N. A. R. Co., 67 Me. 358 (1877); Michigan Air Line Ry. Co. v. Barnes, 40 Mich. 383 (1879); Morgan v. Willman, 318 Mo. 151, 1 S.W.2d 193, 58 A.L.R. 1518 (1927); Wade v. Hennessy, 55 Vt. 207 (1882); Stamnes v. Milwaukee etc., Ry. Co., 131 Wis. 85, 109 N.W. 100 (1907), rehearing granted 131 Wis. 85, 109 N. W. 925, opinion modified 131 Wis. 85, 111 N.W. 62; North Coast Ry. Co. v. Hess, 56 Wash. 335, 105 P. 853 (1909).

40. Seaboard All-Florida Ry. Co. v. Leavitt, 105 Fla. 600, 141 So. 886 (1932), noted, 32 Col.L.Rev. 1240 (1932); Calumet River Ry. Co. v. Brown, 136 Ill. 322, 26 N.E. 501, 12 L.R.A. 84 (1891); Stamnes v. Milwaukee etc. Co., 131 Wis. 85, 109 N.W. 100 (1907).

41. Stemper v. Houston County, 187 Minn. 135, 244 N.W. 690 (1932) noted, 17 Minn.L.Rev. 92 (1932); South Park Com'rs v. Todd, 112 Ill. 379 (1884); Sherwood v. City of Lafayette, 109 Ind. 411, 10 N.E. 89, 58 Am.St.Rep. 414 (1886); note, 58 A.L. R. 1534, 1539.

42. South Park Com'rs v. Todd, 112 Ill. 379 (1884); Gray v. Case, 51 N.J. Eq. 426, 431, 26 A. 805, 807 (1893).

43. Connecticut Mut. Life Ins. Co. v. Scammon, Ill., 117 U.S. 634, 6 S.Ct. 889, 29 L.Ed. 1007 (1885). See Honore v. Lamar Fire Ins. Co., 51 Ill. 409 (1851).

surable interest of the mortgagor is the full value of the property[44] while that of the mortgagee is limited to the amount of the mortgage itself, i. e., the amount of the debt secured.[45] Traditionally courts have insisted that insurance is a purely personal contract of indemnity against diminution in the value of the property;[46] the proceeds of the contract are not regarded as a substitute res for the destroyed property.[47] As a result, if the mortgagor insures his interest in the property and there is a loss, he alone is entitled to payment. The mortgagee has no interest whatsoever in the proceeds in the absence of an agreement to insure for his benefit.[48]

So, too, on the same idea that the contract is a purely personal one of indemnity, a mortgagee who insures his interest at his own expense and with no understanding with the mortgagor, is entitled to recover even though the property remaining undestroyed is fully ample to cover his debt,[49] and the money paid belongs to him alone, the mortgagor being a stranger to the contract and entitled to no benefit under it. Consequently, in such a case, the payment to the mortgagee does not reduce the mortgage debt; but in order to prevent the mortgagee from getting double payment, the insurer, on payment of the loss becomes subrogated *pro tanto* to the mortgage debt.[50] The

44. Florea v. Iowa State Ins. Co., 225 Mo.App. 49, 32 S.W.2d 111 (1930); Strong v. Mfg. Ins. Co., 27 Mass. 40, 20 Am.Dec. 507 (1830).

45. Lockett v. Western Assur. Co., 190 Ark. 1135, 83 S.W.2d 65 (1935); Foster v. Van Reed, 70 N.Y. 19, 26 Am. Rep. 544 (1877); Grevemeyer v. Southern Mut. Fire Ins. Co., 62 Pa. 340, 1 Am.Rep. 420 (1869); Excelsior Ins. Co. v. Royal Ins. Co., 55 N.Y. 343, 14 Am.Rep. 271 (1873); Savarese v. Ohio Farmers' Ins. Co., 260 N.Y. 45, 182 N.E. 665, 91 A.L.R. 1341 (1932); Thompson v. National Fire Ins. Co., 48 S.D. 224, 203 N.W. 464 (1925).

46. See 1 May, Insurance, 4th ed. § 6.

47. There is occasional judicial recognition of the idea that insurance takes the place of the property destroyed. See Gordon v. Ware Savings Bank, 115 Mass. 588, 591 (1874). See note, 19 Va.L.Rev. 508 (1933) advocating the rule that insurance proceeds are a "new form of the old res." See, also, Gilligan, Insurance on Mortgaged Property, 88 U. of Pa.L. Rev. 347 (1940); Glenn, Mortgages, § 27.4.

48. See Walsh & Simpson, Cas. Security Transactions, 184 Note (1) citing, Niagara Fire Ins. Co. v. Scammon, 144 Ill. 490, 28 N.E. 919 (1891) affirmed 144 Ill. 490, 32 N.E. 914, 19 L.R.A. 114; Ryan v. Adamson, 57 Iowa 30, 10 N.W. 287 (1881).

49. Kernochan v. New York etc. Co., 17 N.Y. 428 (1858); Excelsior Fire Ins. Co. v. Royal Ins. Co., 55 N.Y. 343, 14 Am.Rep. 271 (1873); Aetna Ins. Co. of Hartford, Conn. v. Baker, 71 Ind. 102 (1880); Meader v. Farmers' etc. Ass'n, 137 Or. 111, 1 P.2d 138 (1931).

50. Excelsior Fire Ins. Co. v. Royal Ins. Co., 55 N.Y. 343, 14 Am.Rep. 271 (1873); Foster v. Van Reed, 70 N.Y. 19, 26 Am.Rep. 544 (1877); Honore v. Lamar Ins. Co., 51 Ill. 409 (1851); Norwich Fire Ins. Co. v. Boomer, 52 Ill. 442, 4 Am.Rep. 618 (1869); Gould v. Maine Farmers Mut. Fire Ins. Co., 114 Me. 416, 96 A. 732, L.R.A.1917A, 604 (1916); Leyden v. Lawrence, 79 N.J.Eq. 113, 81 A. 121 (1911) affirmed 80 N.J.Eq. 550, 85 A. 1134; Gainesville Nat. Bank v. Martin, 187 Ga. 559, 1 S.E.2d 636 (1937); Le Doux v. Dettmering, 316 Ill.App. 98, 43 N.E.2d 862 (1942). Cf. King v. State Mutual Fire Ins. Co., 61 Mass. 1, 54 Am.Dec. 683 (1851).

only result, so far as the mortgagor is concerned, is that his creditor is changed.[51]

Normally, instead of both mortgagor and mortgagee taking out separate policies, there is an agreement in the mortgage that only one policy shall be taken out but that it shall insure the respective interests of both parties. Usually it is the mortgagor who is bound to take out the policy. If in violation of the agreement the mortgagor only insures his separate interest, the mortgagee may impress an equitable lien on the amount due him under the policy. The extent of the lien is the mortgagee's interest in the mortgaged property covered by the agreement to insure.[52] This equitable lien, it has been pointed out, arises as a consequence of the mortgagee's right to specific performance because of the inadequacy of money damages at law for breach of the contract to insure.[53] The amount realized by the mortgagee upon the lien must be applied in *pro tanto* satisfaction of the mortgage debt. Consequently, the insurer is not entitled to be subrogated to any rights that the mortgagee had against the mortgagor.[54] On the other hand, even though the insurance is taken out by the mortgagee in his own name, if "it has been effected at the request or by the authority of the mortgagor, or under circumstances that would make him chargeable with the premium, the mortgagor, in case of loss, is entitled to have the proceeds of the insurance applied in liquidation of the mortgage debt pro tanto." [55] The consequence again is that subrogation will be denied to the insurer.[56] The same applies where the mortgagor takes out the insurance for the benefit of the mortgagee. The mortgagee is compelled to apply the

51. See Gainesville Nat. Bank v. Martin, 187 Ga. 559, 1 S.E.2d 636 (1937).

52. Nichols v. Baxter, 5 R.I. 491 (1858), Walsh & Simpson, Cas. Security Transactions, 180; Wheeler v. Factors' & Traders' Ins. Co., 101 U.S. 439, 25 L.Ed. 1055 (1879); Grange Mill Co. v. Western Assur. Co., 118 Ill. 396, 9 N.E. 274 (1886), apply the same rule to a vendee. Where insurance had been taken out before the agreement but the mortgagor neglected to have it transferred, the same rule applies. See Walsh & Simpson, Cas. Security Transactions, 184 Note (2), citing Ames v. Richardson, 29 Minn. 330, 13 N.W. 137 (1882); Nordyke, etc. Co. v. Gery, 112 Ind. 535, 13 N.E. 683, 2 Am.St.Rep. 219 (1887).

53. Walsh, Mortgages, § 25.

54. See Glenn, Mortgages § 27.5.

55. Le Doux v. Dettmering, 316 Ill. App. 98, 109, 43 N.E.2d 862, 867 (1942); Elliott v. Pendleton, 67 Mich. 496, 35 N.W. 97 (1887); see Honore v. Lamar Ins. Co., 51 Ill. 409, 413 (1851).

56. Waring v. Loder, 53 N.Y. 581 (1873), true although insurer took assignment; Kernochan v. New York Bowery Fire Ins. Co, 17 N.Y. 428, 441 (1858). See Pendleton v. Elliott, 67 Mich. 496, 498, 35 N.W. 97 (1887). There is authority that in a case of this sort, by agreement with the mortgagee, the insurer can reserve a right of subrogation. Foster v. Van Reed, 70 N.Y. 19, 26 Am.Rep. 544 (1877). As was succinctly observed, "This, however, does not make sense." 1 Glenn, Mortgages, 187, fn. 6. Imperial Fire Ins. Co. v. Bull, 18 Can.S.C. 697 (1889), denied subrogation in spite of a stipulation for it unknown to the mortgagor.

proceeds insofar as the debt is due, and if he fails to do so, the law will make the application.[57]

§ 4.14 Insurance—Types of Policies

Normally one insurance policy is obtained insuring the interests of both parties and, in this connection, one of two types of policy clauses is utilized. One is the older "loss payable" or "open" mortgage policy which is infrequently used today. The other is the "standard mortgage policy" or the "New York standard mortgage policy" which is in common use nationally.[58]

Loss Payable Policy

Under the loss payable policy, the courts were virtually unanimous in holding that the mortgagee is a mere appointee of the mortgagor to receive payment. Therefore his right to recover is completely dependent upon the right of the mortgagor, so that a breach of the conditions of the policy by the mortgagor, which would prevent a recovery by him, bars recovery by the mortgagee.[59] After loss, it has been held that the interest of the mortgagee becomes independent and is not affected by a breach of the policy by the mortgagor subsequent to the loss.[60] And the weight of authority clearly is that the mortgagee is not bound by any settlement of the loss or appraisal agreed upon between the mortgagor and the insurer to which he was not a party and did not consent.[61] However, since the mortgagee is only the appointee to receive what the mortgagor is entitled to under the policy, it follows that on receipt it goes in reduction of what the mortgagor owes on the mortgage debt just as though the

57. Thorp v. Croto, 79 Vt. 390, 65 A. 562, 10 L.R.A.,N.S., 1166, 118 Am.St. Rep. 961, 9 Ann.Cas. 58 (1905); Gordon v. Ware Savings Bank, 115 Mass. 588 (1874).

58. See generally Appleman, Insurance Law and Practice, § 3401 (1970); Comment, Foreclosure, Loss, and The Proper Distribution of Insurance Proceeds Under Open and Standard Mortgage Clauses: Some Observations, 7 Valparaiso L.Rev. 485–487 (1973); Lev, Mortgagees and Insurers: The Legal Nuts and Bolts of Their Relationship, 12 Forum 1012, 1013 (1977); Fred v. Pacific Indemnity Co., 53 Hawaii 384, 494 P.2d 783 (1972); Hartford Fire Ins. Co. v. Associates Capital Corp., 313 So.2d 404 (Miss.1975).

59. Hill v. International Indemnity Co., 116 Kan. 109, 225 P. 1056, 38 A.L.R. 362 (1924); Inland Finance Co. v. Home Ins. Co., 134 Wash. 485, 236 P. 73, 48 A.L.R. 121 (1925); St. Paul Fire & Marine Ins. Co. v. Ruddy, 299 F. 189 (C.C.A.Neb.1924). See 17 Cornell L.Q. 151 (1931). See also 48 A. L.R. 124 (1927); 38 A.L.R. 367 (1925) for collections of cases.

60. McDowell v. St. Paul Fire & Marine Ins. Co., 207 N.Y. 482, 101 N.E. 457 (1913).

61. First Nat. Bank of Duluth v. National etc. Co. of Am., 156 Minn. 1, 194 N.W. 6, 38 A.L.R. 380 (1923). See 38 A.L.R. 383 (1923), for a collection of cases. Officer v. American etc. Co., 175 La. 581, 143 So. 500 (1932), noted, 7 Tulane L.Rev. 449 (1933), holding the mortgagee bound by an appraisal of which he had no knowledge represents a minority view. Of course if he does know and consent, he is bound. Scania Ins. Co. v. Johnson, 22 Colo. 476, 45 P. 431 (1896).

mortgagor had paid him directly.[62] Consequently, even though there was a clause in the policy providing for subrogation of the insurer, it would be unavailing. The mortgagee would have no rights to which to subrogate him.[63] Or, to put it in another way, to permit subrogation would nullify the mortgagor's insurance by preventing the payment of the insurance money from discharging his debt. If, however, the mortgagor's rights have been forfeited, but the policy is continued as to the mortgagee, since the only interest now insured is that of the mortgagee, a clause providing for subrogation of the insurer in case of payment to the mortgagee when no liability existed to the mortgagor will be honored.[64] The same has been held where there was no stipulation for subrogation in the policy.[65]

Standard Mortgage Policy

To have the mortgagee's right to collect insurance dependent upon the right of the mortgagor against the insurer, as it was under the older simple loss-payable policy, was unsatisfactory. So to it was added another clause: "and this insurance, as to the interest of the mortgagee only therein, shall not be invalidated by any act or neglect of the mortgagor." This is the standard mortgage insurance clause which is now in wide-spread use. The effect of the provision is to insure the mortgagee's interest as fully and to the same extent as if he had taken out a separate policy directly from the insurer free from the conditions imposed upon the mortgagor, at least to the extent that no act or neglect of the mortgagor which occurs subsequent to the issuance of the policy will defeat the mortgagee's right.[66] As to

62. Sisk v. Rapuano, 94 Conn. 294, 108 A. 858, 11 A.L.R. 1291 (1920). See 11 A.L.R. 1296 (1921) for a collection of cases.

63. Imperial Fire Ins. Co. v. Bull, 18 Can.S.C. 697 (1889); Burton-Lingo Co. v. Patton, 15 N.M. 304, 107 P. 679, 27 L.R.A.,N.S., 420 (1910); Milwaukee Mech. Ins. Co. v. Ramsey, 76 Or. 570, 149 P. 542, L.R.A.1916A, 556, Ann.Cas. 1917B, 1132 (1915); see Atlantic etc. Bk. v. Farmers' etc. Ass'n, 203 N.C. 669, 166 S.E. 789 (1932).

64. Ins. Co. of N. Am. v. Martin, 151 Ind. 209, 51 N.E. 361 (1898); Washington Fire Ins. Co. v. Cobb, 163 S.W. 608 (Tex.Civ.App.1914).

65. First Nat. Bank v. Springfield etc. Co., 104 Kan. 278, 178 P. 413 (1919) (standard clause).

66. See Fred v. Pacific Indemnity Co., 53 Hawaii 384, 388, 494 P.2d 783, 787 (1973); Savarese v. Ohio Farmers' Ins. Co., 260 N.Y. 45, 182 N.E. 665 (1932); Magoun v. Fireman's Fund Ins. Co., 86 Minn. 486, 91 N.W. 5, 91 Am.St.Rep. 370 (1902); Beaver Falls etc. Ass'n v. Allemania Fire Ins. Co., 305 Pa. 290, 157 A. 616 (1931), noted 16 Minn.L.Rev. 597 (1932); American Building & Loan Ass'n v. Farmers Ins. Co., 11 Wash. 619, 40 P. 125 (1895). See note, 11 Corn.L.Q. 553, 555 (1926). That it is not an independent contract between the insurer and the mortgagee but that it is a contract between the mortgagor and the insurer with the mortgagee as third party beneficiary, see Walker v. Queen Ins. Co., 136 S.C. 144, 134 S.E. 263, 270 (1926); see also Davis v. German-American Ins. Co., 135 Mass. 251, 256 (1883); Union Central Life Ins. Co. v. Codington County Farmers Fire & Lightning Mut. Ins. Co., 66 S.D. 561, 287 N.W. 46, 124 A.L.R. 1027 (1939), creditor beneficiary. This last idea seems incorrect for, if accepted, it would make the mortgagee subject to defenses of the insurance company

misconduct of the mortgagor at the time the policy is issued, the weight of authority protects the mortgagee even here.[67] This is in spite of the argument that, on agency principles, the insurance company should have a defense against the mortgagee, and, although in general it is abhorrent that the mortgagee should be at the mercy of the mortgagor as to whether his insurance is good, there would be no great burden upon him to make the mortgagee check on the mortgagor's conduct at the inception of the contract to make sure that it is valid.[68] The insurance being for the benefit of both the mortgagor and the mortgagee,[69] so long as the insurer remains liable to the mortgagor, any payments for loss made to the mortgagee under the policy must go in reduction of the mortgage debt as being in substance a payment from the mortgagor.[70] This seems an indirect admission that in this situation, at least, the proceeds do take the place of the destroyed property.

If, on the other hand, the policy has been forfeited as to the mortgagor, by reason of the violation of some provision not affecting the mortgagee, the mortgagor, since he is not entitled to recover under the policy, therefore is not entitled to have money paid to the mortgagee under the policy applied in satisfaction of his debt, but rather the insurance company is entitled to be subrogated to the

against the mortgagor, the very thing the standard clause outlaws. Erie Brewing Co. v. Ohio Farmers Ins. Co., 81 Ohio St. 1, 89 N.E. 1065, 25 L.R.A.,N.S., 740, 135 Am.St.Rep. 735, 18 Ann.Cas. 265 (1909), seems to stand alone in holding that the mortgagee's rights under such a policy are derivative through the mortgagor. Since the standard clause only protects the mortgagee against the mortgagor interfering with the mortgagee's rights in the policy, it is possible for the insurer to reserve a power to cancel the policy and, it has been held, to exercise that power in furtherance of an agreement, between the insurer and mortgagor, to cancel on a certain contingency. B. X. Corp. v. Aetna Ins. Co., 187 Misc. 806, 63 N.Y.S.2d 14 (1946), commented on, 47 Col.L.Rev. 153 (1947). The right of the mortgagee to the unearned premiums on cancellation, it was determined under a statute, going to the mortgagor.

67. See Annot., 24 A.L.R.3d 431 (1969).

68. See 55 Can.L.J. 151 (1919); 17 Cornell L.Q. 151, 153 n. 4 (1931). Graham v. Fireman's Ins. Co., 87 N.Y. 69, 41 Am.Rep. 349 (1881), is the leading American case.

69. "The insurance was for indemnity to the mortgagor as well as to the mortgagee." Gordon v. Ware Sav. Bank, 115 Mass. 588, 591 (1874). For an argument that one clause of such a standard policy, that providing for payment of premiums by the mortgagee in case of default by the mortgagor, is construed too favorably to the mortgagee, see Hartnett & Thornton, Is the Mortgagee a Free Rider, 1949 Wis.L.Rev. 714 (1949).

70. See Tarrant Land Co. v. Palmetto Fire Ins. Co., 220 Ala. 428, 125 So. 807 (1930).

Reason also points to the conclusion that when a fire occurs the insurance company must pay the loss to the mortgagee in accordance with its contract with him. The mortgagor benefits by such payment as the insurance money reduces the amount of the mortgage debt. Waring v. Loder, 53 N.Y. 581 (1873). "The value taken out of the property by the fire is taken off the mortgage by the payment of the insurance money, and the parties remain in the same relative position after as before the fire." Savarese v. Ohio Farmers' Ins. Co., 260 N.Y. 45, 53, 182 N.E. 665, 667 (1932).

rights of the mortgagee against the mortgagor.[71] This is true not only where the policy contains a stipulation for subrogation,[72] but also where there is no such agreement.[73] Where there is more than one mortgage on the property and the insurance includes only the first in the mortgage clause, the insurer, if not liable to the mortgagor, is entitled to subrogation not only to the rights of the first mortgagee against the mortgagor but to his priority over the subsequent mortgagee.[74] But when the second mortgagee also is included in the mortgage clause in the policy, the insurer's rights by subrogation are postponed to the second mortgagee's rights.[75] This is right because if the insurer were permitted, through subrogation, to enforce the first mortgage against the property left after the destruction it would result in making the property satisfy the first mortgage twice—once by the destruction of enough of it to justify the insurer in paying off the first mortgage, and again by enforcement of the assigned first mortgage on the property left—before the second mortgagee could enforce his claim. This would impair the second mortgagee's ability to collect his claim and thus violate the provision in a standard mortgage clause that the insurer's subrogation shall not impair the right of the mortgagee to recover the full amount of his claim.[76]

§ 4.15 Insurance—Restoration of Premises

Today most mortgages in common use by institutional lenders specifically provide for the disposition of insurance proceeds in the event of a casualty loss. One commonly used form, for example, provides that "insurance proceeds shall be applied to restoration or repair of the property damaged, provided such restoration or repair is economically feasible and the security of this [mortgage] is not thereby impaired. If such restoration or repair is not economically

71. See cases in next two footnotes.

72. To permit the application of the proceeds of the policy to payment of the mortgagor's debt when the mortgagor has forfeited his rights to any benefit under the policy would render the insurer's declaration of non-liability to the mortgagor futile. The effect of the payment to the mortgagee is not to pay the mortgagor's debt but to give the insurer an equitable proportionate interest in the mortgage as a subsisting obligation. Grangers' Mut. Fire Ins. Co. v. Farmers Nat. Bank, 164 Md. 441, 165 A. 185 (1933); Springfield Fire & Marine Ins. Co. v. Allen, 43 N.Y. 389, 3 Am. Rep. 711 (1871). See note, 52 A.L.R. 278 (1928).

73. First Nat. Bk. v. Springfield Fire & Marine Ins. Co., 104 Kan. 278, 178 P. 413 (1919); Hastings v. Westchester Fire Ins. Co., 73 N.Y. 141 (1878); see Tarrant Land Co. v. Palmetto Fire Ins. Co., 220 Ala. 428, 430, 125 So. 807 (1930). But see 19 Va.L.Rev. 508, 510 (1932).

74. Hare v. Headley, 54 N.J.Eq. 545, 35 A. 445 (1896); Tarrant Land Co. v. Palmetto Fire Ins. Co., 220 Ala. 428, 125 So. 807 (1930).

75. Mutual Fire Ins. Co. v. Dilworth, 167 Md. 232, 173 A. 22 (1934) discussed 19 Minn.L.Rev. 125, 83 U. of Pa.L.Rev. 273 (1934); Perretta v. St. Paul Fire & Marine Ins. Co., 106 Misc. 91, 174 N.Y.S. 131 (1919), affirmed 188 App.Div. 983, 177 N.Y.S. 923.

76. See 83 U. of Pa.L.Rev. 273, 274 (1934).

feasible or if the security of this [mortgage] would be impaired, the insurance proceeds shall be applied to the sums secured by this [mortgage], with the excess, if any, paid to the [mortgagor]."[77] Moreover, even where such language is not contained in the mortgage instrument, mortgagors and mortgagees routinely agree, after a loss, to utilize the insurance proceeds to restore the premises.

However, in the absence of specific mortgage language governing casualty loss, to what extent, if any, will the mortgagor be able to compel the application of the insurance proceeds to rebuild the mortgaged premises? It could be argued that if rebuilding would restore the mortgaged premises to the pre-casualty condition, the mortgagee's security would be fully protected and that the proceeds therefore should be used to rebuild the premises. On the other hand, there is some indication that the mortgagee has a common law choice of either applying the insurance proceeds to the debt or to the restoration of the mortgaged premises.[78] More important, however, case law has consistently recognized that the right of a mortgagee to recover on an insurance policy protecting his interest is not conditioned upon the casualty loss rendering his security inadequate. Normally the mortgagee may recover the full amount of his debt, even though the portion of the premises remaining is greater in value than the mortgage debt.[79] Thus, absent an agreement in the mortgage to the contrary, the mortgagee cannot be forced to apply the insurance proceeds to rebuild the premises. Indeed, the majority of courts have permitted the mortgagee to recover the proceeds even when the mortgagor has rebuilt the premises on his own funds.[80]

77. Federal Home Loan Mortgage Corporation Deed of Trust Form prescribed for use in Colorado. For background on this form, see Federal National Mortgage Association Public Meeting on Conventional Mortgage Form, Senate Banking, Housing and Urban Affairs Comm., 92d Cong., 1st Sess. (1971).

78. Fergus v. Wilmarth, 117 Ill. 547, 7 N.E. 508 (1886). See Glenn, Morts., § 27.4.

79. See e. g., Kintzel v. Wheatland Mut. Ins. Ass'n, 203 N.W.2d 799 (Iowa 1973); Koppinger v. Implement Dealers Mut. Ins. Co., 122 N.W.2d 134 (N.D.1963); Thompson v. National Fire Ins. Co., 48 S.D. 224, 203 N. W. 464 (1925); Meader v. Farmers' Mut. Fire Relief Ass'n, 137 Or. 111, 1 P.2d 138 (1931), loss-payable clause; Excelsior Fire Ins. Co. v. Royal Ins. Co., 55 N.Y. 343, 14 Am.Rep. 271 (1873); Uhlfelder v. Palatine Ins. Co., 44 Misc. 153, 89 N.Y.S. 792 (1904) loss-payable clause; Kent v. Aetna Ins. Co., 84 App.Div. 428, 82 N.Y.S. 817 (1903). But see, Babow v. The Home Ins. Co., 34 Cal.App.3d 304, 109 Cal.Rptr. 858 (1973).

80. Price v. Harris, 251 Ark. 793, 475 S.W.2d 162 (1972); Pink v. Smith, 281 Mich. 107, 274 N.W. 727 (1937); Savarese v. Ohio Farmers' Ins. Co., 260 N.Y. 45, 182 N.E. 665 (1932). Some of the older cases involving loss payable rather than standard mortgage policies reach an opposite result. These, since they are construed as making the mortgagee a mere appointee of the mortgagor with his rights purely derivative through the mortgagor, afforded a basis for permitting the mortgagor by his act of restoration to defeat the right of the mortgagee to collect. See, e. g., Friemansdorf v. Watertown Ins. Co., 1 F. 68 (C.C.Ill.1879); Huey v. Ewell, 22 Tex.Civ.App. 638, 55 S.W. 606 (1900).

At least in the absence of mortgage provisions to the contrary, it would seem that in the modern standard mortgage policy context where the mortgage is not in default, the mortgagor normally should be able, where rebuilding is practical, to insist upon the application of the insurance proceeds to rebuild the premises. To be sure, to permit the mortgagor to defeat the mortgagee's right of recovery by rebuilding may force the mortgagee to litigate the extent and sufficiency of the repairs.[81] On the other hand, it is almost always the mortgagor who is paying the premiums on the casualty insurance policy. Moreover, while permitting the mortgagee to utilize the insurance proceeds to pay the mortgage debt presumably benefits the mortgagor by rendering the property free from the mortgage lien to the extent of the loss, in many cases the mortgagor probably cannot afford to rebuild or is unable to obtain new mortgage financing for that purpose. Thus, on balance, it would seem more equitable in most cases to permit the mortgagor to rebuild and have the insurance applied to that purpose. Indeed, there is some authority for such a result in a case where a mortgagor was allowed to have the insurance money apply to the cost of repairs though the money had previously been paid over to the mortgagee.[82]

Interestingly, one recent California decision endorsed a presumption in favor of using insurance proceeds to rebuild even where the documents specifically gave the mortgagee the option to apply the proceeds to the debt. There, after a fire loss, the mortgagee refused to permit the mortgagor to utilize the insurance proceeds to rebuild and instead insisted on their application to the indebtedness. The mortgagors could not afford to continue to make mortgage payments and pay rent on an apartment. As a result they defaulted on the mortgage debt and foreclosure ensued. The mortgagors then sued the mortgagee for damages. The Court of Appeals held that "the right of a beneficiary to apply insurance proceeds to the balance of a note secured by a deed of trust must be performed in good faith and with fair dealing and that to the extent that the security is not impaired the beneficiary must permit those proceeds to be used for the cost of remodeling."[82a]

Where the loss occurs after the mortgage is either already in default or has matured, the equities probably favor the mortgagee. At that stage, the mortgagee, after all, has the immediate right to receive the mortgage debt and could foreclose to enforce that right. Moreover, by defaulting, the mortgagor arguably has created enough uncertainty for the mortgagee to raise doubts as to the wisdom of

81. "Must the mortgagee litigate the extent and sufficiency of the repairs, or, if partially repaired, is his insurance to be reduced in proportion?" Savarese v. Ohio Farmers' Insurance Co., supra note 80, at 55, 182 N.E. at 668.

82. Cottman Co. v. Continental Trust Co., 169 Md. 595, 182 A. 551 (1936).

82a. Schoolcraft v. Ross, 81 Cal.App. 3d 75, 146 Cal.Rptr. 57 (1978).

continuing the mortgage relationship. Under these circumstances, allowing the mortgagee to apply the insurance proceeds to the mortgage debt may obviate the necessity for foreclosure proceedings.

§ 4.16 Insurance—Effect of Foreclosure Purchase By Mortgagee

Suppose that a mortgagee, either before or after a casualty loss, purchases the mortgaged premises at a foreclosure sale by bidding in the full amount of the debt. Where the insurance policy protecting the mortgagor and mortgagee is a loss payable type, the cases uniformly refuse to permit the mortgagee to collect on the policy.[83] Under the loss payable type policy, as we have noted, only the mortgagor's interest techically is insured, the mortgagee merely being an appointee to collect the proceeds. When the mortgagee bids in the full amount of the debt, the debt is extinguished and the mortgagee's interest in the policy is terminated.[84]

When the commonly used standard mortgage policy is in force, however, the mortgagee's rights to insurance proceeds depends largely on when the loss occurred. If the loss occurs after a foreclosure purchase by the mortgagee for the amount of the debt, courts permit the mortgagee to recover.[85] The reasoning of these decisions has been based on several factors. First, the cases emphasize that the standard mortgage policy creates an independent insurance contract between the mortgagee and the insurer.[86] Moreover, they note that the standard mortgage policy, unlike the loss payable type policy, which refers only to a property interest in the mortgagor, protects the mortgagee's interest in the property.[87] Finally, these courts have noted that "a change in status from mortgagee to owner through foreclosure and purchase does not defeat the mortgagee-owner's right to the insurance proceeds because the provisions of the standard mortgage clause are designed to accommodate such change in status." [88]

When, however, the foreclosure purchase for the amount of the debt follows the loss, courts uniformly deny the mortgagee-purchaser recovery of the insurance proceeds.[89] A variety of reasons for this

83. See Reynolds v. London & Lancashire Fire Ins. Co., 128 Cal. 16, 60 P. 467 (1900); Power Bldg. & Loan Ass'n v. Ajax Fire Ins. Co., 110 N.J.L. 256, 164 A. 410 (1933); Comment, Foreclosure, Loss, And The Proper Distribution Of Insurance Proceeds Under Open And Standard Mortgage Clauses: Some Observations, 7 Valparaiso L. Rev. 485, 490 (1973).

84. Comment, supra note 83 at 490.

85. Guardian Sav. & Loan Ass'n v. Reserve Ins. Co., 2 Ill.App.3d 77, 276 N.E.2d 109 (1971); Shores v. Rabon, 251 N.C. 790, 112 S.E.2d 556 (1960).

86. See, e. g., Shores v. Rabon, 251 N.C. 790, 112 S.E.2d 556 (1960).

87. See Comment, supra note 83 at 494.

88. Id. at 494.

89. See e. g., Northwestern Nat. Ins. Co. v. Mildenberger, 359 S.W.2d 380 (Mo.App.1962); Rosenbaum v. Funcannon, 308 F.2d 680 (9th Cir. 1962); Whitestone Sav. & Loan Ass'n v. Allstate Ins. Co., 28 N.Y.2d 332, 321 N.Y.S.2d 862, 270 N.E.2d 694 (1971).

result have been advanced. One court, for example, believed that the independent contract of insurance under the standard mortgage policy was of limited scope and that the mortgagee's interest was based upon the mortgage debt rather than the mortgaged property.[90] Other courts have emphasized that the value of the property to the mortgagee was presumably reflected by his bid and that the recovery of the insurance proceeds in addition to his purchase for the full debt would be inequitable and result in double recovery for the mortgagee.[91] According to one court, this no-recovery rule was fair and practical because no one "disputes that the mortgagee is entitled to recover only his debt. Any surplus value belongs to others, namely the mortgagor or subsequent lienors. Indeed, it is not conceivable that the mortgagee could recover a deficiency judgment against the mortgagor if it had bid in the full amount of the debt at foreclosure sale. To allow the mortgagee, after effectively cutting off or discouraging lower bidders, to take the property and then establish that it was worth less than the bid encourages fraud, creates uncertainty as to the mortgagor's rights, and most unfairly deprives the sale of what ever leaven comes from other bidders.[92]

The time of loss distinction utilized in standard policy cases is probably reasonable. In the loss after foreclosure sale situation, it is unlikely that the bid is influenced by the possibility of a loss and insurance recovery. On the other hand, in the loss-purchase situation, as the court in the preceeding paragraph pointed out, a mortgagee presumably could bid in the amount of the debt on the damaged premises intending to discourage lower bidders and, ultimately, to collect the insurance proceeds as well. To be sure, in view of the common practice for mortgagees to bid in the amount of the mortgage debt, the full debt bid in the loss-purchase situation may simply be the result of mere inadvertence. However, the prudent mortgagee in this situation can protect himself by bidding what the property is actually worth. If a third party bids more than the debt, the mortgagee will be made whole by the sale proceeds. On the other hand, if the mortgagee or the third party purchases for less than the debt, the mortgagee can normally obtain a deficiency judgment and have it satisfied out of the insurance proceeds.

90. Northwestern Ins. Co. v. Mildenberger, 359 S.W.2d 380 (Mo.App. 1962).

91. See Rosenbaum v. Funcannon, 308 F.2d 680 (9th Cir. 1962); Whitestone Sav. & Loan Ass'n v. Allstate Ins. Co., 28 N.Y.2d 332, 321 N.Y.S.2d 862, 270 N.E.2d 694 (1971).

92. Whitestone Sav. & Loan Ass'n v. Allstate Ins. Co., 28 N.Y.2d at 336, 270 N.E.2d at 697 (1971).

D. ESCROWS OR RESERVES FOR TAXES AND INSURANCE

§ 4.17 Escrow Accounts—Some General Considerations

As we have seen, mortgagees are understandably insistent that mortgagors carry casualty insurance on the mortgaged real estate and that insurance premiums be paid promptly. Insurance, of course, provides protection against the partial or complete destruction of the mortgage security. Mortgagees, moreover, have special concern as to real estate taxes and assessments because, as Professor Durfee once aptly pointed out, "in most tax systems . . . the burden of the ordinary tax on land and the burden of special assessments for local improvements rests on both mortgagor and mortgagee in the sense that unless these charges are satisfied by someone before the axe falls the interest of both parties will be rubbed out. The state goes after the land and its claim overrides *all* prior interests whatever their character." [93] In other words, a "first" mortgage on real estate will be eliminated by a sale under a subsequently arising real estate tax lien. Thus, mortgagees are extremely cautious to protect their security and generally utilize mortgage clauses specifically imposing the duty to pay taxes on the mortgagor and making failure to pay a cause for acceleration of the mortgage debt.

An important additional protection device for the mortgagee today is the "escrow" procedure. Contemporary lending institutions commonly require that one-twelfth of estimated annual taxes and casualty insurance premiums be paid monthly together with the usual payment of principal and interest.[94] Such payments are usually credited to an account variously known as an "escrow," "reserve," or "impound" account. These accounts became widespread after the depression experience of the 1930's when substantial numbers of mortgagors lost their homes, and mortgagees some of their mortgage security, because of real estate foreclosures.[95] As a result, lending institutions adopted the escrow or impound requirement on the theory that mortgagors would have less difficulty paying monthly installments than a year-end lump sum tax payment. This practice was accelerated because the Federal Housing Administration (FHA) made such escrow accounts mandatory for all loans it insured.[96]

93. Durfee, Cases on Security, 136 (1951).

94. Comment, Trusts: Requiring Mortgage Loan Escrow Holders to Account for Profits Earned on Tax and Insurance Prepayments, 28 Okl.L. Rev. 213, 213 (1975).

95. Comment, The Attack Upon the Tax and Insurance Escrow Accounts in Mortgages, 47 Temp.L.Q. 352, 352 (1974).

96. Comment, Trusts: Requiring Mortgage Loan Escrow Holders to Account for Profits Earned on Tax and Insurance Prepayments, 28 Okl.L. Rev. 213, 213 (1975).

While lending institutions do not require an escrow or impound account for all mortgagors, it is common practice as to most conventional loans which exceed 80% of value, and is currently required with respect to loans insured by the FHA.[97] The Veterans Administration (VA) encourages the practice as to VA guaranteed loans[98] and requires it as to its direct loans.[99] The Federal Home Loan Bank Board (FHLBB), which regulates all federally chartered savings and loan associations, authorizes such associations to escrow taxes and insurance,[1] and requires them to do so where the loan to value ratio exceeds 80%.[2]

There are three types of escrow procedures utilized by lending institutions today.[3] First, a few mortgagees deposit escrow funds in a special savings account from which the mortgagee may withdraw to pay taxes and insurance premiums.[4] The mortgagor, under this method, receives the prevailing savings account interest rate on the impounded funds. Second is the capitalization method. "Under this system, all payments, when received, are applied to decrease principal of the loan. When payments * * * are made by the [mortgagee], the outstanding balance is accordingly increased."[5] The net effect is that the mortgagor receives a return on the escrowed funds equal to the interest rate he is paying on the mortgage debt. Since the latter rate is almost always higher than savings account interest rates, the capitalization method is highly advantageous from the mortgagor's perspective. The third and most widespread method, however, is "to deposit escrow payments in noninterest bearing accounts which allow the lender to comingle funds with his own."[6] Any income earned from these funds is retained by the mortgagee.

Because of its failure to pay mortgagors any interest return on escrow accounts, controversy over this last method has been substantial in recent years. This has resulted in considerable litigation and some significant legislative response. The following material considers the major judicial theories of attack utilized thus far and some of the important legislative and regulatory impact on the problem.

§ 4.18 Judicial Scrutiny of Escrow Accounts

Because of the relatively minor amount of interest income that the individual mortgagor loses because of the mortgagee's retention

97. 24 CFR 203.23

98. See V. A. Lender's Handbook § 4150 (1969).

99. 38 CFR 36.4512.

1. 12 CFR 545.6–11(b).

2. 12 CFR 545.6–1 (4) (iii).

3. Comment, Payment of Interest on Mortgage Escrow Accounts, 23 Syracuse L.Rev. 845, 849 (1972).

4. Id. at 849.

5. Buchanan v. Brentwood Fed. Sav. and Loan Ass'n, 457 Pa. 135, 142, 320 A.2d 117, 122 (1974).

6. Comment, Payment of Interest on Mortgage Escrow Accounts, 23 Syracuse L.Rev. 845, 850 (1972).

of escrow profits, judicial challenges to mortgagee escrow practices almost invariably take the form of class actions. A class action requires that the class be numerous, that common questions of law or fact exist, that the claims of the representative parties are typical, and that those parties represent the interest of the class fairly and adequately.[7] Further, the common questions must predominate over other issues, and the class action must be superior to other adjudication methods as to fairness and efficiency.[8] Substantial problems face potential class action mortgagor-plaintiffs. Where, for example, plaintiff seeks to bring a multi-mortgagee class action, mortgage forms and language may differ from mortgagee to mortgagee, making the "common question" issue difficult to resolve.[9] Even where one mortgagee is involved, the mortgagor-plaintiff may have difficulty defining the class. For example, mortgagees often change forms from year to year and different classes may be required as to each period that a different form was used.

§ 4.19 Escrow Accounts—Express Trust Theory

The most common theory utilized in challenging noninterest-bearing escrow arrangements is based on breach of an express trust.[10] The most important early case to utilize this theory was Carpenter v. Suffolk Franklin Savings Bank [11] (*Carpenter I*), in which the Massachusetts Supreme Court determined that the mortgagor's complaint stated a cause of action in trust. The court chose as a standard the following language: "Where the mortgagor pays funds to a bank with an expressed purpose that the funds shall be used for a particular purpose, then the funds may be deemed to be held in trust * * *. We think it is clear from the bill that the tax payments were designated by the mortgagors for a specific purpose, namely, to pay real estate taxes." [12] The Massachusetts Supreme Court did not have the actual written instruments before it, but relied on what the parties pleaded as the legal effect of the documents. In Buchanan v. Brentwood Federal Savings & Loan Association,[13] the Pennsylvania Supreme Court had the written documents before it and reached a result similar to *Carpenter I* on the express trust issue. The court concluded that the mortgagors had alleged sufficient facts, together with the instruments, to afford them the opportunity to prove their claim that funds were paid to the mortgagee with the expressed purpose that they be used for tax payments.

7. Carpenter v. Suffolk Franklin Sav. Bank, 346 N.E.2d 892, 895 (Mass. 1976).

8. Id. at 346 N.E.2d 896.

9. Id. at 346 N.E.2d 896.

10. Note, Tax and Insurance Escrow Accounts in Mortgages—The Attack Presses On, 41 Mo.L.Rev. 133, 133–34 (1976).

11. 362 Mass. 770, 291 N.E.2d 609 (1973).

12. Id. at 778, 291 N.E.2d 614.

13. 457 Pa. 135, 320 A.2d 117 (1974).

There is support in trust law for the notion that acceptance of money "with notice of its ultimate destination creates a trust, as in the case of a deposit for a specific purpose." [14] Nevertheless, with respect to banking type institutions, the usual application of the foregoing rule is that absent an agreement to the contrary, a deposit is considered to be general and not special, and the burden is on the person claiming that the deposit is special to establish that the banking institution received the deposit under an express or clearly implied agreement that the funds should remain separate and not be comingled with the funds of the banking institution.[15]

The *Carpenter I* court also relied upon the so-called "ABC" express trust theory that when A gives money to B to be delivered to C, a trust arises in favor of C.[16] In the *Carpenter I* setting, the argument would be that when A, the mortgagor, gives money to B, the mortgagee, who is to pay taxes to C, the city, failure to pay the city would give C a cause of action against B for breach of trust.[17] However, the essential purpose of this theory is "to protect creditors from middle-men, not to allow mortgagors to recover the profits derived from a mortgagee's wrongful use of escrow funds." [18]

Carpenter II [19] undid much of what *Carpenter I* created. When *Carpenter I* was returned to the trial court, the trial judge concluded that there was no manifestation of intention to create a trust on the part of either of the parties. The court noted that the written agreements were silent as to investment of the payments, as to profits thereon, and as to intention to create a trust. The trial court also determined that the agreements established contractual relationships and not trusts and that the payments constituted general deposits for a special purpose, creating a debtor-creditor relationship, rather than special deposits creating a fiduciary situation. In *Carpenter II*, the Supreme Court of Massachusetts upheld the trial court as not being clearly erroneous.

> "Nothing is said in the statutes or the written agreements of the parties as to interest on the payments or fruits

14. Comment, Trusts: Requiring Mortgage Loan Escrow Holders to Account for Profits Earned on Tax and Insurance Prepayments, 28 Okl.L.Rev. 213, 216 (1975).

15. Id. at 216. See Durkee v. Franklin Sav. & Loan Ass'n, 17 Ill.App.3d 978, 309 N.E.2d 118 (1974); Sears v. First Federal Sav. & Loan Ass'n, 1 Ill.App. 3d 621, 275 N.E.2d 300 (1971).

16. See In re Interborough Consolidated Corp., 288 F. 334 (2nd Cir. 1923), certiorari denied 262 U.S. 752, 43 S.Ct. 700, 67 L.Ed. 1215; Comment, Tax and Insurance Escrow Accounts in Mortgages—The Attack Presses On, 41 Mo. L.Rev. 133, 135 (1976).

17. Comment, Lender Accountability and the Problem of Noninterest-Bearing Mortgage Escrow Accounts, 54 B.U.L.Rev. 516, 522–23 (1974).

18. Comment, Tax and Insurance Escrow Accounts in Mortgages—The Attack Presses On, 41 Mo.L.Rev. 133, 135 (1976).

19. Carpenter v. Suffolk Franklin Sav. Bank, 346 N.E.2d 892 (Mass.1976).

> of the investment. The general understanding and practice in Massachusetts and elsewhere over a period of some forty years has been that the bank has the right to treat the tax payments as its own. We think that a mortgagor who claims that he has made a different arrangement must show a clear understanding to that effect. * * * No such showing was made."[20]

The net result is that the leading "express trust" theory decision was substantially undermined.

Other attempts to utilize the express trust theory have been notably unsuccessful.[21] These decisions emphasize the difficulty of establishing the express trust relationship. The Supreme Court of Illinois, in La Throp v. Bell Federal Savings & Loan Association,[22] for example, held that in the absence of express language by which a mortgagor retains an interest in the escrowed funds, and in view of the common practice for savings and loan associations to commingle escrowed funds with its other funds, there was insuffcent evidence to create an express trust.[23] Moreover, the Arizona Supreme Court concluded that even where, under the terms of the agreement, the mortgagor paid the tax payment to the mortgagee "in trust," an express trust was not created. "The fact that the words 'in trust' are used does not alter the intent of the parties, and the [mortgagor] cannot rely on this phrase to impose a trust on the payment of funds which he does not claim he intended to be held in trust and which [the mortgagee] specifically denies receiving in any trust relationship."[24] Even where a court recognizes an express trust relationship, the mortgagor may nevertheless come up empty-handed. In Marsh v. Home Federal Savings & Loan Association,[25] a California appellate decision, the court determined that the agreement of the mortgagee to pay taxes and insurance from the tax impound account, and the fact that the impound account was substantial, indicated a fiduciary situation rather than an ordinary deposit relationship. However, because the agreement between the parties expressly authorized comingling of the impounded funds with others of the mortgagee and pro-

20. Id. at 900.

21. See Brooks v. Valley Nat. Bank, 113 Ariz. 169, 548 P.2d 1166 (1976); Marsh v. Home Federal Sav. & Loan Ass'n, 66 Cal.App.3d 674, 136 Cal. Rptr. 180 (1977); Tucker v. Pulaski Federal Sav. & Loan Ass'n, 252 Ark. 849, 481 S.W.2d 725 (1972); Lathrop v. Bell Federal Sav. & Loan Ass'n, 42 Ill.App.3d 183, 355 N.E.2d 667 (1976); Surrey Strathmore Corp. v. Dollar Sav. Bank, 36 N.Y.2d 173, 366 N.Y.S. 2d 107, 325 N.E.2d 527 (1975); Richman v. Security Sav. & Loan Ass'n, 57 Wis.2d 358, 204 N.W.2d 511 (1973). But see, Abrams v. Crocker-Citizens Nat. Bank, 41 Cal.App.3d 55, 114 Cal.Rptr. 913 (1974).

22. 68 Ill.2d 375, 12 Ill.Dec. 565, 370 N.E.2d 188 (1977).

23. Id.

24. Brooks v. Valley Nat. Bank, 113 Ariz. 169, 174, 548 P.2d 1166, 1171 (1976).

25. 66 Cal.App.3d 674, 136 Cal.Rptr. 180 (1977).

vided that "no interest would be payable," the court felt compelled to deny a claim for interest, notwithstanding the presence of a trust relationship.

Not only are courts becoming more unwilling to find an express trust where the documents are ambiguous, but the express trust theory has become increasingly vulnerable to redrafted escrow and impound agreements which expressly negate a trust relationship.[26] Moreover, even if the agreement creates a trust relationship, *Marsh* indicates that the inclusion of "no interest" and "comingling permission" language will mean no recovery for a mortgagor. In this connection, it should be noted that the mortgage form utilized by those lending institutions that sell their loans on the secondary market to the Federal National Mortgage Association (FNMA) or the Federal Home Loan Mortgage Corporation (FHLMC), specifically provides that absent a contrary agreement, the "lender shall not be required to pay borrower any interest on the funds." [27]

§ 4.20 Escrow Accounts—Constructive Trust Theory

The *Buchanan* court is the only appellate court thus far to endorse constructive trust as well as express trust theories. Unlike an express trust, a constructive trust is not the creature of an express agreement or the intention of the parties, but is remedial in nature and is utilized to prevent the unjust enrichment of one person at the expense of another.[28] In this connection, *Buchanan* approved three possible constructive trust theories.

First, it was argued in *Buchanan* that a confidential relationship arose between the mortgagors and the mortgagee. The mortgagors claimed that the mortgagee's retention of profits from the escrow account had breached this confidential relationship. The court stated that "the existence, if proved, of a confidential relationship is sufficient justification for imposing a constructive trust, unless the dominating party can prove by clear and satisfactory evidence that the contract was not tainted by his overweening bargaining position." [29]

The *Buchanan* mortgagors also advanced a constructive trust-agency argument based on the alleged agency relationship between the mortgagors and the mortgagee. Under this theory, if an agent uses the principal's money without authority to his own advantage, a constructive trust may be an appropriate remedy. The court concluded that the mortgagors could prevail on this theory if they could

26. Comment, Tax and Insurance Escrow Accounts in Mortgages—The Attack Presses On, 41 Mo.L.Rev. 133, 138 (1976).

27. FNMA/FHLMC Uniform Deed of Trust, 1 to 4 Family, par. 2.

28. Comment, supra note 18, at 136–37; see Restatement, Second, Trusts Ch. 12, at 326 (1959) (Introductory note to topic 1).

29. Buchanan v. Brentwood Sav. and Loan Ass'n, 457 Pa. 135, 143, 320 A. 2d 117, 123 (1974).

prove on remand that the mortgage agreement envisaged an agency relationship.[30]

Finally, the mortgagors claimed that unjust enrichment was a proper basis for the imposition of a constructive trust. The court noted that a constructive trust is appropriate "whenever justice and fair dealing warrant it." [31] Accordingly, the court concluded that the mortgagors were to be given a chance to offer evidence to convince the "conscience of equity" that the mortgagee would be unjustly enriched if it were allowed to retain the profits on the escrowed funds.

Stating valid constructive trust claims and proving them are two significantly different matters. Moreover, while some courts recognize the possibility of proving a constructive trust theory in the escrow context,[32] others seem almost as a matter of law to reject the theory in the usual escrow situation.[33] For example, the trial judge in *Carpenter II* found no basis for the imposition of a constructive trust and the Massachusetts Supreme Court affirmed. While the supreme court admitted that the escrow agreements were "contracts of adhesion," they were not "unconscionable in aspects here in issue." [34] Nor did the supreme court believe that there was the unjust enrichment necessary for constructive trust. According to the court, "most of the unjust enrichment, if any, enriched the bank's depositors at the time." [35] Moreover, because the legislature had acted to require mortgagees to pay interest on escrow accounts at "a rate and in a manner to be determined by the mortgagee," [36] the court noted that even the legislature was not prepared to say how much enrichment was too much; the court was unwilling to go further. The Arizona Supreme Court, in Brooks v. Valley National Bank,[37] emphasized freedom of contract: "The absence of a provision to pay interest on the impoundment funds is equivalent to an agreement that it should not be paid. A person is not entitled to compensation on the grounds of unjust enrichment if he receives from the other that which was agreed between them the other should give in return." [38] In addition, an Illinois appellate court limited the constructive trust remedy to situations involving fraud or an abuse of a confidential relationship.[39]

30. Id. at 144, 320 A.2d at 124.

31. Id. at 145, 320 A.2d at 125.

32. See, e. g., Carpenter v. Suffolk Franklin Sav. Bank, 346 N.E.2d 892 (Mass.1976).

33. See e. g., Brooks v. Valley Nat. Bank, 113 Ariz. 169, 548 P.2d 1166 (1976); La Throp v. Bell Federal Sav. and Loan Ass'n, 68 Ill.2d 375, 12 Ill. Dec. 565, 370 N.E.2d 188 (1977).

34. Carpenter v. Suffolk Franklin Sav. Bank, 346 N.E.2d 892, 900 (Mass. 1976).

35. Id. at 346 N.E.2d 900.

36. Mass.Gen.Laws Ann. c. 183 § 61 (1973).

37. 113 Ariz. 169, 548 P.2d 1166 (1976).

38. Id. at 176, 548 P.2d at 1171.

39. La Throp v. Bell Fed. Sav. and Loan Ass'n, 42 Ill.App.3d 183, 355 N. E.2d 667 (1976).

Where the mortgagee openly admitted that it treated the escrow earnings as its own, the court could find no fraud. Moreover, absent an allegation of specific facts, it simply could not envisage how a relationship of special trust or confidence could be established in the usual mortgagor-mortgagee relationship.[40]

§ 4.21 Escrow Accounts—Other Theories

Although several other theories have been utilized in the judicial attack on noninterest paying escrow arrangements, they have generally proved unsuccessful. For example, numerous unsuccessful attacks have been made under the Federal Truth in Lending Act.[41] Mortgagors frequently allege that interest on the impound or escrow accounts constitutes a "finance charge separately paid" and that failure by the mortgagee to disclose interest earned on such accounts violates the act.[42] In addition, mortgagors argue that the impounds or escrows are "required deposit balances" as to which disclosure under the Act is required.[43] However, courts have uniformly held that the impounds or interest thereon cannot be construed as a "finance charge separately paid" and that escrow and impound accounts are an exception to the concept of "required deposit balances."[44] In short, every court considering the issue thus far has held that interest earned on escrow accounts is exempt from the reporting requirements of the Act.[45]

Noninterest bearing escrow accounts have also been attacked on a resulting trust theory. Unlike an express trust, which is created by a settlor's external expression of intention, "a resulting trust exists if the circumstances show an absence of intention on the part of a transferor to give the beneficial interest in property to one who has received legal title."[46] The closest analogy in the escrow area is the purchase-money resulting trust, in which property is purchased with A's funds, but legal title is taken in B. A presumption of trust in fa-

40. Id. at 190, 355 N.E.2d 673.

41. 15 U.S.C.A. §§ 1601–1665.

42. See Moore v. Great Western Sav. and Loan Ass'n, 513 F.2d 688 (9th Cir. 1975).

43. Id.

44. Id.

45. See Stavrides v. Mellon Nat. Bank and Trust Co., 487 F.2d 953 (3rd Cir. 1973); Moore v. Great Western Sav. and Loan Ass'n, 513 F.2d 688 (9th Cir. 1975); Umdenstock v. American Mortgage & Investment Co. of Oklahoma City, 495 F.2d 589 (10th Cir. 1974); Foster v. Maryland State Sav. and Loan Ass'n, 369 F. Supp. 843 (D.D.C.1974); Kinee v. Abraham Lincoln Federal Sav. and Loan Ass'n, 365 F.Supp. 975 (E.D.Pa. 1973); Munn v. American General Inv. Corp., 364 F.Supp. 110 (S.D.Tex. 1973); Graybeal v. American Sav. and Loan Ass'n, 59 F.R.D. 7 (D.D.C. 1973); Buchanan v. Brentwood Fed. Sav. and Loan Ass'n, 457 Pa. 135, 320 A.2d 117 (1974).

46. Comment, Tax and Insurance Escrow Accounts in Mortgages—The Attack Presses On, 41 Mo.L.Rev. 133, 136 (1976).

vor of A is created.[47] More particularly in point are "those purchase-money resulting trust cases in which two parties are intended to have a beneficial interest in the property, but where one party takes more than his intended share." [48] In the escrow situation, the mortgagor and mortgagee each intend to have an interest in the escrow funds. It could be argued that the mortgagee is intended to have an interest in the escrow payments sufficient to protect his mortgage security and that any other beneficial interest in the escrow payments belongs to the mortgagor.[49] Accordingly, where a mortgagee takes a profit in the form of interest from the escrow funds, he arguably is taking more than he was intended to have and, thus, a resulting trust should be imposed on those profits.[50] In *Carpenter II*, the only reported case in which this theory was advanced, however, the court tersely rejected the resulting trust theory. "The [trial] judge ruled that neither the nature of the transaction between the [mortgagors] and [mortgagee] nor their relationship now calls for the imposition of a resulting trust. We agree substantially for the same reasons that we uphold his finding that there was no express trust." [51] Moreover, since a purchase-money resulting trust is grounded on the presumed intent of the settlor, it would seem that future mortgage forms could obviate the purchase-money resulting trust argument by expressly providing that the mortgagee shall be entitled to have the beneficial interest in the profits from the escrow payments.

In Madsen v. Prudential Federal Savings & Loan Association,[52] a Utah Supreme Court decision, the mortgagors were successful in utilizing a pledge theory, a concept that had not previously been advanced to attack noninterest bearing escrow procedures. The deed of trust in *Madsen* provided for the usual monthly payments of one-twelfth of estimated annual taxes and insurance premiums, but further provided that "said *budget payments are hereby pledged to the beneficiary as additional security for the full performance of this deed of trust and the note secured hereby*." [53] The mortgagors argued that the monthly escrow payments constituted a pledge and that the pledgee was liable to account to the pledgor for profits earned from the pledged property. The trial judge granted the mortgagee a summary judgment, ruling that the funds were not pledged property. The Utah Supreme Court reversed and held that the granting of the summary judgment in favor of the mortgagee was erroneous. The court determined that a deposit of money as security for the perform-

47. See Nelson, Purchase-Money Resulting Trusts in Missouri, 33 Mo.L. Rev. 552 (1968).

48. Comment, Lender Accountability and the Problem of Noninterest-Bearing Mortgage Escrow Accounts, 54 B.U.L.Rev. 516, 527 (1974).

49. Id. at 527.

50. Id. at 527.

51. Carpenter v. Suffolk Franklin Sav. Bank, 346 N.E.2d 892, 900 (Mass. 1976).

52. 558 P.2d 1337 (Utah 1977).

53. Id. at 1338.

ance of a contract can be a valid pledge. Moreover, the court found that the deed of trust agreement established the essential elements of a pledge. In this connection, the court emphasized the existence of a debt and a transfer of property to the pledgee to be held as security and, if necessary, to be used to assure performance of the obligation. Moreover, the court noted that the mortgagee had the discretion to withdraw funds for taxes, insurance premiums or for *any* sum due under the deed of trust or note. The court then cited Section 9-207 of the Uniform Commercial Code (UCC) for the proposition that when collateral is in the secured party's possession, unless otherwise agreed,

> "The secured party may hold as additional security any increase or profits (except money) received from the collateral, but money so received, unless remitted to the debtor, shall be applied in reduction of the secured obligation; * * *."[54]

The opinion is somewhat ambiguous, and could reasonably be read either as holding that the pledge relationship had already been established or that mortgagors had simply properly pleaded a pledge theory and that proof of the pledge relationship was still necessary. However, on remand, the trial court placed the former interpretation on the case and stated that "if there is any 'law of the case' established by the decision of [the Utah Supreme Court] as contended by [mortgagors], it is that the [escrow payments] constitute 'pledged' property under the law and are to be so treated in the proceedings that must follow."[55] According to the trial court, the only further issue to be resolved was whether "profits" existed on the escrow accounts; if so, accounting of them to the mortgagors would be required.[56]

Although the Utah pledge theory is unique, there is some doubt whether it can have substantial impact elsewhere. First, the court emphasized the use of the "pledge" language in the deed of trust, language that is probably not commonly used in other jurisdictions. In any event, just as other courts have rejected an express trust theory even where the words "in trust" are used in the mortgage instrument,[57] so also could another court hold that "pledge" language alone is not significant enough to create a pledge transaction. Finally, mortgagees in Utah and elsewhere will probably delete the pledge language and attempt to negate the pledge by doing what the UCC permits, namely, having the parties specifically agree that the profits from any "pledge"-escrow arrangement are for the benefit of the pledgee-mortgagee.

54. Utah Code Ann. 70A–9–207(2).

55. Madsen v. Prudential Fed. Sav. & Loan Ass'n, Memo Decision 3 (Dist. Ct., 3rd Dist.Utah 1977).

56. Id. at 3.

57. See Brooks v. Valley Nat. Bank, 113 Ariz. 169, 548 P.2d 1166 (1976).

§ 4.22 Statutory and Related Regulation

Several states have enacted legislation regulating escrow accounts and generally requiring the mortgagees to pay interest to the mortgagors on escrowed funds.[58] The legislation varies considerably from state to state. In California, for example, mortgagees of single family, owner-occupied dwellings are prohibited from requiring, as a condition of their loans, an impound for taxes and insurance premiums except where such an impound is required by federal or state regulatory authorities, where the loan is made, guaranteed, or insured by a state or federal lending or insuring agency, where the mortgagor has previously defaulted on the payment of taxes, or where the original mortgage loan is for 90% or more of the sale price or appraised value of the mortgaged property.[59] Where impounds are used and authorized as to one to four family residences, the mortgagee must pay the borrower interest on the impound at the rate of at least 2% per annum.[60] Under the New York statute, the mortgagee is prohibited, as to one to six family owner-occupied residences, from charging a service fee for maintaining escrow accounts as to any loans after the effective date of the law, and mortgage lending institutions must pay interest on escrow accounts (except as to those mortgages existing prior to the date of the legislation which expressly provided for no payment of interest) at the rate of 2% or such rate established by the New York Banking Board, whichever is higher.[61] Minnesota, as to one to four family owner-occupied dwellings, prohibits the imposition of a service fee for escrow services and requires the payment of interest at the rate of 3% or such rate set by the state Commerce Commission, whichever is higher.[62] Massachusetts legislation requires the payment of interest on escrow accounts with respect to mortgage loans on one to four family owner-occupied households, but leaves the amount and manner of payment up to the mortgagee; a mortgagee can obtain from the Commissioner of Banks an exemption from the payment of interest during a particular year if that mortgagee can show that it lost money on escrow fund investment during that year.[63] Connecticut simply requires the payment of

58. See West's Ann.Cal.Civ.Code §§ 2954, 2954.8 (1976); Conn.Gen.Stat. Ann. § 49–2(a) (1975); Mass.Gen. Laws Ann. ch. 183 § 61 (1973); Minn. Stat.Ann. § 47.20 (1976); N.H.Rev. Stat.Ann. § 384:16–c (1974); Neb. Rev.Stat. § 45–105.05–.06 (1976); McKinney's N.Y.Banking Law § 14–b (1974); McKinney's N.Y.Gen.Obligations Law § 5–601 (1974); Or.Rev. Stat. 86.240, 86.245.

59. West's Ann.Cal.Civ.Code § 2954 (1973).

60. West's Ann.Cal.Civ.Code § 2954.8 (1976). See Marantz, Consumerism Reaches the Sacrosanct Trust Deed, 52 Cal.St.Bar J. 203 (1977).

61. McKinney's N.Y.Banking Law § 14–b (1974); McKinney's N.Y.Gen. Obligations Law § 5–601 (1974).

62. Minn.Stat.Ann. § 47.20 (1976). See also Or.Rev.Stat. 86.240, 86.245 (Lender must pay interest on the escrow account at the bank passbook rate minus ¾ of one per cent, but in no event less than 4%).

63. Mass.Gen.Laws Ann. ch. 183 § 61 (1973).

not less than 2% interest on escrow accounts,[64] while New Hampshire sets the rate at 2% below the rate for regular savings deposits in the mortgagee institution.[65] Finally, some statutes merely regulate the method and amount of monthly payments into the escrow account, but do not require the payment by the mortgagee of interest on the account.[66]

Constitutional problems have arisen because statutes mandating the payment of interest on escrow accounts generally require the payment of interest after the effective date of the legislation on all mortgage loans in the mortgagee's portfolio, whether they were executed prior to or after the date of the legislation.[67] The New York legislation was upheld by a three-judge federal court against a broadside attack in Jamaica Savings Bank v. Lefkowitz.[68] The decision was affirmed without opinion by the United States Supreme Court.[69] The bank argued that nonpayment of interest on escrow accounts, though not an express provision of prior mortgage contracts, was a term implied in fact that was unconstitutionally impaired by the legislation. The court rejected this contention, stating that the mere absence of a contract provision does not raise the implication of a term implied in fact, and held that since the escrow fund profits were not *specifically* allocated by contracts, the legislature possessed the authority to allocate those profits to "safeguard the vital interests of the people." [70] Further, the court rejected the bank's claim that payment of interest on escrow accounts constituted a "taking" without due process in violation of the Fourteenth Amendment as "not substantial." [71] Finally, the bank argued that the legislation's distinction between pre-existing mortgage contracts which expressly excluded payment of interest and those which were silent as to such payment, violated the equal protection clause of the Fourteenth Amendment. However, the court rejected this argument and noted that "where by express language mortgagors were made aware of the possibility of interest, and they expressly waived their rights to it, the legislature was entirely rational in not wishing to confront a potential constitutional problem." [72]

This decision did not deal with a situation in which escrow interest legislation attempts to reach mortgages, executed prior to the leg-

64. Conn.Gen.Stat.Ann. § 49–2(a) (1975).

65. N.H.Rev.Stat.Ann. § 384:16–c (1974).

66. Neb.Rev.Stat. § 45–105.05–.06 (1976).

67. See e. g., Conn.Gen.Stat.Ann. § 49–2(a) (1975); Minn.Stat.Ann. § 47.-20 (1976); N.H.Rev.Stat.Ann. § 384:-16–c (1974); McKinney's N.Y.Banking Law § 14–b (1974); McKinney's N.Y.Gen.Obligations Law § 5–601 (1974).

68. 390 F.Supp. 1357 (D.C.E.N.Y. 1975).

69. 423 U.S. 802, 96 S.Ct. 10, 46 L.Ed. 2d 23 (1975).

70. 390 F.Supp. at 1362. See Note, 11 Tulsa L.J. 124, 126 (1975).

71. Id. at 1363.

72. Id. at 1362.

islation, which by express language provide for no payment of interest on escrow funds. To be sure, the majority of older mortgages are probably silent as to payment of interest on escrow accounts. However, the FNMA and the FHLMC forms expressly negate the payment of escrow interest unless there is an express agreement to the contrary.[73] Thus, to the extent that there are pre-legislation mortgages outstanding using such forms, the constitutional argument based on impairment of contractual obligation would be stronger. Nevertheless, even in this situation it could be argued that the express contractual provision waiving any right to escrow account interest should be considered a year-to-year contract to correspond to its purpose of meeting annual tax and insurance requirements. Thus, any legislation arguably would impair no "existing" contracts because the previous years' contracts would have expired prior to the effective date of the legislation. Moreover, even actual impairment of existing contracts may be deemed to be reasonable and hence valid where an important enough state interest justifies the impairment.[74] In this regard, it could be argued that a legislature properly can conclude that because mortgagees possess an overwhelming bargaining position, such mortgage agreements were in all probability not bargained for. Thus, it would arguably be proper for a state legislature to exercise its power to correct an imbalance in the bargaining relationship.

While legislation has occasionally been introduced in Congress,[75] there is currently no federal law or regulation requiring mortgagees to pay interest on escrow accounts.[76] Indeed, as noted earlier, much of the federal or quasi-federal regulation in this area is aimed at encouraging or requiring the establishment of escrow accounts. The Federal Home Loan Bank Board (FHLBB), for example, requires the payment of interest by federally chartered savings and loan associations only where state law requires it.[77]

When a new loan is made, it is usually necessary for the lender to require the mortgagee to make an initial deposit into the escrow account. At a minimum, this deposit must be large enough so that, when added to the amounts which will accumulate through regular monthly payments, it will result in enough money to pay the taxes and insurance premiums when they fall due. Many lenders prefer to require an initial deposit in a larger amount in order to provide a "cushion" against the possibility that the mortgagor will miss a later payment or that the taxes or insurance premiums will be more than

73. See text at note 27, supra.

74. See El Paso v. Simmons, 379 U.S. 497, 85 S.Ct. 577, 13 L.Ed.2d 446 (1965), rehearing denied 380 U.S. 81, 85 S.Ct. 879, 13 L.Ed.2d 813.

75. See Comment, Lender Accountability and the Problem of Noninterest-Bearing Mortgage Escrow Accounts, 54 B.U.L.Rev. 516, 537 (1974).

76. See text at notes 5–8, supra.

77. 12 CFR 545.6–11 (b).

expected. To curb the tendency of some lenders to require excessively large cushions (sometimes as much as a six months' tax and insurance payments), the Real Estate Settlement Procedures Act (RESPA)[78] limits the initial payment into the account to the minimum described above, plus a two-month cushion.[79] RESPA also provides that, after regular monthly payments on the loan have begun, the mortgagor cannot be required to pay more than one-twelfth of the annual taxes and other charges each month, unless a larger payment is needed to make up a deficit in the escrow account or to maintain the two months' cushion referred to above.[80]

E. RIGHT TO RENTS

§ 4.23 General Considerations

The rights to rents of mortgaged property are largely determined by (1) whether the lease precedes or follows the giving of the mortgage and, (2) as a matter of legal right, whether the particular jurisdiction follows the title or lien theory. The importance of this latter factor is minimized in actual practice, as will be seen later, (a) by agreements which are ordinarily entered into by the parties respecting possession, either permitting the mortgagor to remain in possession in title states [81] or the mortgagee to take possession in lien states; (b) by clauses assigning or pledging the rents; (c) by the appointment of receivers; (d) by the practical inefficacy of remedies by which a mortgagee may enforce his rights to possession against a non-cooperative mortgagor or his tenant; and (e) by the burdens and strictness of the accounting to which a mortgagee in possession is subjected. This last is a reality which makes the exercise of the right to possession a matter of last and undesirable resort. Leaving these matters aside for the present, when the lease precedes the mortgage it is clear in all jurisdictions that the tenant's term cannot be affected by the later mortgage.[82] In both title and lien jurisdictions the only interest the mortgagor had to give in security was the reversion. And the difference between the two kinds of mortgages of it is that title to the reversion passes in one case and in the other the

78. 12 U.S.C.A. § 2609.

79. HUD Guide, Settlement Costs, 35 (1976).

80. Id. at 36.

81. See Tefft, The Myth of Strict Foreclosure, 4 U. of Chi.L.Rev. 574, 582 (1937).

82. American Freehold Land Mortgage Co. v. Turner, 95 Ala. 272, 11 So. 211 (1891). 1 Tiffany, Landlord and Tenant, § 146e. See Anderson, The Mortgagee Looks at the Ground Lease, 10 U. of Fla.L.Rev. 1 (1957); Boshkoff, Financing Construction on Long Term Leasehold Estates, 5 Buffalo L.Rev. 257 (1956). That a mortgagee in possession of the mortgaged premises of a lessee in a lien state is not an assignee of the lease and therefore not liable on a covenant for rent was held in Amco Trust, Inc. v. Naylor, 159 Tex. 146, 317 S.W.2d 47 (1958) discussed in 58 Mich.L.Rev. 140 (1959).

mortgagee gets only a lien upon it.[83] This difference is vital, however, on the matter of the legal right to rents.

§ 4.24 Lease Before Mortgage—Title States

In a title jurisdiction the transfer of the reversion carries the right to rent with it and creates a privity of estate between the mortgagee and the tenant of the mortgagor.[83a] In the early law, due to the personal nature of the relation between landlord and tenant, there had to be consent by the tenant to be the tenant of the transferee before the relationship arose.[84] However, this requirement of attornment was dispensed with by the Statute of Anne [85] in England. The same result was reached in this country, either by similar statutes or by decision.[86] The tenant, by a saving provision, is always protected as to rents paid to his original landlord before notice to him of the transfer. Today, therefore, in title jurisdictions, the law is that the "mortgagee has by force of the conveyance a right, which he may exercise or not at his pleasure, to demand and recover all rent which becomes due and payable subsequently to the conveyance. To this end he may give notice, whenever he chooses to do so, of this right to the lessee, who will thereupon become bound to pay the rent to him. This liability however is limited to rent becoming due after execution of the deed of conveyance, and does not extend to that which was then already due, or to that which before notice of the conveyance has been paid to the lessor. For rent which is due and payable at the time when the conveyance is made is a mere chose in action; a debt which the lessee owes to the lessor, and which being disconnected from the reversion does not pass to the grantee by a conveyance of it." [87]

As to rents which become due but unpaid after the mortgage but before notice by the mortgagee, it has been argued that the mortgagee should be entitled to them only if he asserts his right to them in connection with a foreclosure action,[88] in which case the mortgagor is

83. Burden v. Thayer, 44 Mass. (3 Metc.) 76, 37 Am.Dec. 117 (1841), title state; Metropolitan Life Ins. Co. v. Childs Co., 230 N.Y. 285, 130 N.E. 295, 14 A.L.R. 658 (1921), reargument denied 231 N.Y. 551, 132 N.E. 885, lien state: "If a lease is prior to a mortgage, a sale under the latter is but a sale of the reversion."

83a. Moss v. Gallimore, 1 Doug. 279 (1779), a decision by Lord Mansfield is the leading authority.

84. See Litt. § 551; Co.Litt. 309a; 2 Sheppard's Touchstone, c. 13, 253–266.

85. 34 Anne, c. 16, §§ 9, 10.

86. 1 Tiffany, Landlord and Tenant, § 146.

87. Coffey v. Hunt, 75 Ala. 236 (1883); Baldwin v. Walker, 21 Conn. 168 (1851); Noble v. Brooks, 224 Mass. 288, 112 N.E. 649 (1916)—accord. But see St. Louis Nat. Bank v. Field, 156 Mo. 306, 56 S.W. 1095 (1900). See also 14 A.L.R. 640 (1921); Russell v. Allen, 84 Mass. (2 Allen) 42 (1861); King v. Housatonic R. R. Co., 45 Conn. 226 (1877); Burden v. Thayer, 44 Mass. (3 Metc.) 76, 37 Am.Dec. 117 (1841)—accord.

88. Glenn, Mortgages, § 33.4, citing N.Y. Life Ins. Co. v. Fulton Development Co., 265 N.Y. 348, 193 N.E. 169

in no moral position to object. Otherwise the mortgagee should be entitled only to rents which are current or of later maturity than the notice.

The rule is otherwise,[89] however, and both technically and substantially it seems correct. The mortgagee became entitled as transferee of the reversion to all rents accruing after the mortgage, although if paid to the mortgagor the tenant would be protected and the mortgagor would clearly be entitled to keep them. However, if they have not been paid over there seems no reason why the mortgagee should not be able to assert his right to them even though past due and, if the tenant pays the mortgagor thereafter, he should be liable again, for he is outside the protection afforded him by the statute.[90]

The mortgagee's right to collect the rents before enforcement of the mortgage for default has been criticized as in "direct violation of the essence of the transaction which is to give the mortgagee security and security only." [91] But there seems no reason why, if he is entitled to the rents, that right should not extend to unpaid but accrued rent to which he succeeds as mortgagee of the reversion. In addition, although it is arguable that all jurisdictions should adopt the lien view giving to the mortgagor prior to foreclosure all rights in the property including possession and the fruits of possession, the latter covering rents as well as emblements and profits, such is not the law in a good many states. In these states a mortgagee lends in reliance upon being able to reach the lease and rents as part of his security and should be fully protected in reaching the rents to apply to his debt if he wishes to do so, including accrued rents unpaid [92] at the time he asserts his right.

(1934), a receivership case in a lien state in which the court said the receiver might collect rents already accrued but not paid to the mortgagor.

89. King v. Housatonic Ry., 45 Conn. 226, 234 (1877), "he [the mortgagee] becomes entitled to all rents accruing after the execution of the mortgage and in arrear and unpaid at the time of the notice, as well as to those which accrue afterwards. But the rents in arrear at the time the mortgage was executed belong to the mortgagor." But cf., New Order Bldg. & Loan Ass'n v. 222 Chancellor Ave., 106 N.J.Eq. 1, 149 A. 525 (1930), receivership case; Stewart v. Fairchild etc., Co., 91 N.J.Eq. 86, 108 A. 301 (1919), receivership case.

90. Ex parte Wilson, 2 V. & B. 252, 253 (1813): "the mortgagor does not receive the rents for the mortgagee." Payment of rent to record senior mortgagee at a time when he no longer had title to the mortgage is not a defense to the claim of a second mortgagee in possession. Lamson & Co. v. Abrams, 305 Mass. 238, 25 N.E.2d 374 (1940), noted, 53 Harv. L.Rev. 1402 (1940); 26 Va.L.Rev. 1070 (1940). This would be true regardless of whether the lease preceded or followed the first mortgage. However, the decision emphasizes the dilemma of a tenant who must at his peril determine which party to the mortgage transaction he must pay in spite of possibly unascertainable facts and intricate questions of law.

91. Walsh, Mortgages, 95.

92. See Note, 50 Yale L.J. 1424, 1434 (1941).

Further, it would be agreed generally that before default the mortgagor ought to have possession and all income from his property; security for the mortgagee's payment of his money claim does not warrant depriving the mortgagor of any use or fruit of his property before then. Indeed the mortgagee before default rarely wants the rent; what he wants is the interest on his debt. He does not want the trouble of collecting the rents and then being subjected to the strict and burdensome rules of accounting for them. Consequently the usual practice in title states is to permit the mortgagor to stay in possession and to take and keep for himself the rents. Not until default does the picture change and the mortgagee, in spite of the drawbacks, want to reach the rent.[93]

When default is made and the picture does change there is merit in the idea that the mortgagee should be able to take over the property and its income.[94] The experience of mortgagees in the last depression when the capital value of the security asset practically vanished emphasized the importance to mortgagees of having the ability to reach the rents as well as the corpus of the property as part of their security and to be able, on default, to impound it. The title and intermediate theories accord such a right to mortgagees without any stipulation for it. Even in lien jurisdictions it can be and is bargained for with varying success or achieved by means of a foreclosure receivership as we shall see.[95] Since this is so, the difference between the different types of jurisdictions is narrowed to such an extent that, on this point, there seems scant warrant for an all-out assault upon the title theory result. If any criticism of it is to be made, it should be aimed only at the right of the mortgagee to take over before default. But, since in practice this right is seldom exercised, either being bargained away or not exercised because of its burdensome disadvantages to the mortgagee, the objection even here is largely academic.

The tenant of the mortgagor, where the lease precedes the mortgage, is protected in paying his rent to the mortgagor before notice of the mortgagee's claim to it provided he pays in accordance with the provisions of the lease.[96] But he is not protected when he pays his rent in advance when it is not called for by the lease contract even though he did not know of the mortgage at the time.[97] His

93. Note, 80 U. of Pa.L.Rev. 270, 272 (1931).

94. "The fairness of the claim to sequester the rents is generally conceded when default has rendered it imperative to take possession." Note, 45 Harv.L.Rev. 901, 903 (1932).

95. See Note, 50 Yale L.Jour. 1424 (1941).

96. Baltimore Markets v. R. E. etc. Co., 120 Pa.Super. 40, 181 A. 850 (1935).

97. De Nichols v. Saunders, L.R. 5 C. p. 599 (1870). For legislation in New York enacted to prevent mortgagors from "milking" the mortgaged premises by manipulating the terms of the lease and by prepayment of rent, see Norvell, 1959, Annual Survey of New

privilege to pay, and of the mortgagor to receive, rents is only to do so as they fall due. A fortiori it would be no defense to the tenant if he makes payment in advance of the date due after notice of the mortgage but before demand upon him by the mortgagee.

Entirely apart from the operation of technical rules of real property, the rule is fair. The tenant could bargain for the payment of his rent to be made in any way he wished at the time he made the lease. Prepayment of the entire rent may be a stipulation of the lease and, if so, the later mortgagee cannot complain. A mortgage cannot affect a prior lease except to make the lessee pay to the mortgagee rent accruing under the lease after the mortgage is given if the mortgagee demands it. Further, if a prepayment has been made, not in accordance with the terms of the lease, before the mortgage is taken and the mortgagee can be charged with notice of this deviation, the payment should be good against the mortgagee because he has gone ahead and made the loan on that basis. However, in the absence of notice it is reasonable to charge the tenant with knowledge that the property might later be mortgaged, that the rent provisions of the lease would be relied on in part to determine whether the loan should be made, and consequently that a change would prejudice the mortgagee and should not be permitted.[98]

§ 4.25 Mortgage Before Lease—Title States

Where the mortgage precedes the lease the lessee's rights can rise no higher than those of his landlord, the mortgagor. "The mortgagor has no power, express or implied, to let leases, not subject to every circumstance of the mortgage. * * * The tenant stands exactly in the situation of the mortgagor." [99] It follows that if the mortgagee could take possession against the mortgagor, as he can in title states at any time in the absence of agreement to the contrary and in intermediate states after default, he has the same right against a tenant of the mortgagor. And if such a right is exercised the mortgagee can repudiate the lease and treat the tenant as a trespasser subject to eviction by an action of ejectment.[1] Moreover, like all interests in the mortgaged property attaching to it subsequent to the mortgage, the lease can be wiped out by foreclosure in all jurisdictions, title or lien. However, a mortgage transfers no reversion against subsequent tenants and therefore there is no privity of estate

York Law: Property, 35 N.Y.U.L.Rev. 1495, 1507 (1960).

98. See Berick, The Mortgagee's Right to Rents, 8 Cin.L.Rev. 250, 263 (1934).

99. Keech v. Hall, 1 Doug. 21, 22 (1778); Zimmern v. People's Bank, 203 Ala. 21, 81 So. 811 (1919).

1. Keech v. Hall, 1 Doug. 21 (1778); West Side Trust & Savings Bank v. Lopoten, 358 Ill. 631, 193 N.E. 462 (1934); City of Hagerstown v. Groh, 101 Md. 560, 61 A. 467 (1905); Brown to Use of Par Bond & Mortgage Co. v. Aiken, 329 Pa. 566, 198 A. 441 (1938). See note, 4 U. of Newark L. Rev. 183 (1939).

or contract between the mortgagee and the mortgagor's tenant. Consequently the mortgagee "cannot, by mere notice, compel the tenant to pay rent to him," [2] nor exercise any of the remedies of a landlord against the tenant.[3] "Until there has been an actual entry, or some act equivalent thereto has occurred, the mortgagee can maintain no action against him for the recovery of rent, except upon an express promise to pay it." [4]

However, having the right to oust the mortgagor and his tenant, he may assert the right and compel the tenant to agree to pay the rent to him in order to avoid eviction. Such an agreement is commonly referred to as an "attornment" by the lessee.[5] Actually, however, it is the creation of an entirely new lease between the mortgagee and tenant.[6] Such new lease, or "attornment," is "no violation of the principle which estops a lessee from denying his lessor's title" for "by promising to pay the mortgagee upon the latter's rightful entry, the tenant saved the trouble and expense of eviction, which he could not lawfully prevent," [7] and "only recognizes a title which his landlord has granted".[8]

Whether the new lease between the mortgagee and the tenant is for the balance of the original one upon the same terms as were contained in it would seem to be a question of fact in each case.[9] In most cases the parties would have in mind the terms of the original lease. Further, talking of the new lease in terms of attornment by the lessee, although technically incorrect, nevertheless probably is a faithful enough portrayal of the attitude of the parties toward the relationship they are entering into. Yet there is authority that the

2. Kimball v. Lockwood, 6 R.I. 138, 139 (1859); Long v. Wade, 70 Me. 358 (1879); Winnisimmet Trust, Inc. v. Libby, 234 Mass. 407, 125 N.E. 599, 14 A.L.R. 638 (1920); Trask v. Kelleher, 93 Vt. 371, 107 A. 436 (1919).

3. Burke v. Willard, 243 Mass. 547, 137 N.E. 744 (1923). See Teal v. Walker, 111 U.S. 242, 248, 4 S.Ct. 420, 28 L.Ed. 415 (1884).

4. Russell v. Allen, 84 Mass. (2 Allen) 42, 44 (1861); Peoples-Pittsburgh Trust Co. v. Henshaw, 141 Pa.Super. 585, 15 A.2d 711 (1940); noted, 89 U. of Pa.L.Rev. 679 (1941).

5. E. g., "the tenant of the mortgagor may attorn to the mortgagee, and by thus placing him in possession of the mortgaged premises, entitle him to the rents thereof." Kimball v. Lockwood, 6 R.I. 138, 139 (1859). See Anderson v. Robbins, 82 Me. 422, 19 A. 910, 8 L.R.A. 568 (1890).

6. See Berick, The Mortgagee's Right to Rents, 8 Cin.L.Rev. 250, 266 (1934).

7. Anderson v. Robbins, 82 Me. 422, 426, 19 A. 910, 911, 8 L.R.A. 568 (1890); Magill v. Hinsdale, 6 Conn. 464a, 16 Am.Dec. 70 (1827); Smith v. Shepard, 32 Mass. (15 Pick.) 147, 25 Am.Dec. 432 (1833)—accord. See Towerson v. Jackson, 2 Q.B. 484 (1891); Reed v. Bartlett, 9 Ill.App. 267 (1881); note, 1 Harv.L.Rev. 255 (1887); note, 1918, 18 Col.L.Rev. 91; note, 80 U. of Pa.L.Rev. 602 (1932). See 14 A.L.R. 640 (1921); 105 A.L.R. 744 (1936); note, 70 Sol.J. 972 (1926). See also McDougal, Review of Walsh, Mortgages, 44 Yale L.J. 1278, 1280 (1935).

8. Kimball v. Lockwood, 6 R.I. 138, 139 (1889).

9. See Taylor, Landlord & Tenant, § 120; note, 1 J. Marshall L.Quar. 161, 168 (1935).

mere payment and acceptance of rent, without more, creates only a tenancy from year to year.[10]

When the mortgagee takes over possession of the property in the middle of the term of a lease, several questions arise. If the tenant stays on under an agreement with the mortgagee, that agreement usually is called an attornment and normally will provide for paying to the mortgagee rent for the entire term, including that portion of it prior to the mortgagee's entry. Since the lease really is a new one beginning when the mortgagee enters, it would seem that it covers a period of time over which the mortgagee had no rights. The mortgagor, it is arguable, should have a right to hold the tenant for the use and occupation during that portion of the term prior to entry by the mortgagee and this right should not be affected by the new agreement by the tenant with the mortgagee. That is not, however, the law. The new agreement, if it covers the entire term, will bar any recovery by the mortgagor.[11]

But the lessee may refuse to make any agreement with the mortgagee and in such case the mortgagee cannot hold him for rent as such for any period.[12] Rent falling due and paid to the mortgagor prior to taking possession may be kept by the mortgagor.[13] So, too, rent due but not paid to the mortgagor before the mortgagee takes possession belongs to the mortgagor.[14] But there is the portion of the term before the mortgagee entered during which the tenant was in occupation. The mortgagor cannot collect on the lease for this portion because rent is not apportionable.[15] The mortgagee has no claim to payment for it because his rights accrue only on entry and here he gets no payment for it by agreement with the tenant.[16] If the mort-

10. Gartside v. Outley, 58 Ill. 210, 11 Am.Rep. 59 (1871); West Side, etc., Bank v. Lopoten, 358 Ill. 631, 193 N. E. 462 (1934). By statute in Missouri the new tenancy runs from month to month. V.A.M.S. § 441.060; Roosevelt Hotel Corp. v. Williams, 227 Mo. App. 1063, 56 S.W.2d 801 (1933).

11. The cases uniformly hold that the tenant does not have to pay twice. Bulger v. Wilderman, 101 Pa.Super. 168 (1931); Magill v. Hinsdale, 6 Conn. 464a, 16 Am.Dec. 70 (1827); Hinck v. Cohn, 86 N.J.L. 615, 92 A. 378 (1914) are cases so holding in addition to Kimball v. Lockwood, supra note 8, and Anderson v. Robbins, supra note 7

12. The mortgagee, in the absence of an "attornment" by the lessee, cannot enforce any of the terms of the lease against him. Evans v. Elliot, 9 A. & E. 342 (1838); Trask v. Kelleher, 93 Vt. 371, 107 A. 486 (1919); Moran v. Pittsburgh, C. & St. L. Ry. Co., 32 F. 878 (C.C.Ohio 1887); Bessemer Inv. Co. v. Fell, 225 F. 13, 140 C.C.A. 473 (C.C.A.Pa.1915), discussed in note 16 Col.L.Rev. 76 (1916); Mack v. Beeland Bros. Mercantile Co., 21 Ala. App. 97, 105 So. 722 (1925), certiorari denied 213 Ala. 554, 105 So. 725.

13. Kimball v. Lockwood, 6 R.I. 138 (1889).

14. Clarke v. Curtis, 1 Gratt. 289 (1844).

15. Anderson v. Robbins, 82 Me. 422, 19 A. 910, 8 L.R.A. 568 (1890).

16. "The lessee becomes liable to the mortgagee for rent accruing due after the latter's entry and the lessee's promise to pay, but not for rent due before such entry and promise, as prior thereto there would be no privity between them." Anderson v. Robbins, 82 Me. 422, 424, 19 A. 910, 911 (1890).

gagor brings a quasi-contractual action for use and occupation there are difficulties in allowing recovery. If the mortgagor had deliberately brought on the entry by his actions, or had not apprised the tenant of the possibility of such an entry, recovery should be denied. On the other hand, if the mortgagor did inform the tenant of the mortgage and the possibility of entry and did not do things to bring on the entry and it occurred prior to default, it would seem the mortgagor ought to be able to recover.

If the mortgagee enters because of default by the mortgagor the question is closer. Here the lease has been ended by the mortgagee because of the mortgagor's failure to pay and the lessee in such a case can escape any liability to his landlord, the mortgagor, because the mortgagor was responsible for the loss of the lease.[17] In title states where the mortgagee could have entered prior to default and the tenant knew it, to let the tenant acquire such a windfall at the expense of the defaulting mortgagor seems undesirable, at least in cases where the mortgagee was willing to permit the lessee to stay on under the terms of the old lease, as is usually the case.

But the tenant may stay on after the mortgagee takes over, at the same time refusing to come to any agreement with him. The mortgagee may bring ejectment, which is slow and cumbersome,[18] or an action to foreclose, which is also time consuming. Equity would not help him to get possession,[19] the legal remedy being considered adequate, although that adequacy has been described as "Pickwickian", and probably was so considered because equity did not want the mortgagor to be ousted from his property prior to foreclosure.[20] As a result, a recalcitrant tenant might well occupy the property for a considerable period of time without any agreement to pay rent. In such a case the mortgagee should be able to hold him for use and occupation of the premises from the time the mortgagee entered until the tenant departs and collect the fair rental value regardless of the rent reserved in the original lease.[21]

17. Where a receiver disaffirms a lease and demands payment of the value of the use and occupation, this constitutes a breach of the covenant of quiet enjoyment in a lease, releasing the tenant from liability under the lease. In re O'Donnell, 240 N.Y. 99, 147 N.E. 541 (1925); Casassa v. Smith, 206 Mass. 69, 91 N.E. 891 (1910). The tenant can also sue the mortgagor for breach of covenant of quiet enjoyment. Ganz v. Clark, 252 N.Y. 92, 169 N.E. 100 (1929) lease ended by foreclosure.

18. See Tefft, The Myth of Strict Foreclosure, 4 U. of Chi.L.Rev. 575, 583, n. 43 (1937), for authority that eight to eleven months would elapse before the plaintiff would be in possession in an ejectment action.

19. Seton, Decrees, 140, 143. This was true both before and after a foreclosure decree. After decree an order for possession is now obtainable. Keith v. Day, L.R. 39 Ch.D. 452 (1888).

20. See Tefft, supra, note 18, 582. See also notes, 80 U. of Pa.L.Rev. 269, 274 (1931); 50 Yale L.J. 1424, 1436 (1941).

21. Lucier v. Marsales, 133 Mass. 454 (1882). See 1 Tiffany, Landlord & Tenant, § 73a. On the other hand in Burke v. Willard, 243 Mass. 547, 137

It is worth observing here that the doctrine that a mortgagee who takes possession cannot affirm the leases made by his mortgagor subsequent to the mortgage because of lack of privity between him and the lessee is a most dubious one. The mortgagee, although he comes in by paramount title as a technical matter is quite unlike the ordinary third party who enters. This is because in fact and in law the mortgagor still continues to be the substantial owner of the property and the mortgagee has only asserted an additional security right that he had, the right to possession which carries with it the income. Whatever the merits of the rule permitting tenants to disaffirm leases in the ordinary case where his landlord's interest has been completely ended, to permit him to do so here works an impairment not only of the mortgagee's security interest but of the mortgagor's substantial interest.[22] It has been pointed out that the doctrine was extended to the mortgage cases only after considerable controversy and in the face of a line of cases that had held that the mortgagee by giving notice might affirm the mortgagor's leases.[23] A possible justification of the rule, apart from the argument that it is desirable to let the general real property rule as to privity operate mechanically in all cases to achieve the merit of certainty as to rights, is that it would be an additional deterrent to mortgagees' asserting their legal rights to possession and thus bolster the mortgagor's protection. This last reason would be inapplicable to receivership cases in which the same question arises and will be discussed later.

Where a mortgage precedes the lease even if the tenant pays his rent in advance according to the terms of his lease he may nevertheless be ousted by the mortgagee who enters. And, if he stays on in possession, he must either come to terms with the mortgagee or be liable for the fair rental value from the time of the mortgagee's entry.[24]

N.E. 744 (1923), the mortgagee was denied recovery on the ground that the tenant was holding adversely to the mortgagee under the lease from the mortgagor.

Most of the authorities allowing recovery are receivership cases, but the principle is the same. Rohrer v. Deatherage, 336 Ill. 450, 168 N.E. 266 (1929), fair rental value; Monro-King, etc., Corp. v. Ninth Ave., etc., Corp., 233 App.Div. 401, 253 N.Y.S. 303, 32 Col.L.Rev. 144 (1931). A similar right was given to a purchaser on foreclosure sale in Harris v. Foster, 97 Cal. 292, 32 P. 246 (1893).

22. See Tefft, Receivers and Leases Subordinate to the Mortgage, 2 U. Chi.L.Rev. 33, 41 (1934). See also note, 17 Wash.L.Rev. 37, 46 (1942).

23. See Tefft, supra note 22, 42 n. 35, citing Pope v. Biggs, 9 B. & C. 245 (K.B.1829); Waddilove v. Barnett, 4 Dowl. 347 (K.B.1835); Brown v. Storey, 1 Man. & G. 117 (C.P.1840); Underhay v. Read, 20 Q.B.D. 209, 1 Harv. L.Rev. 255 (1887). Cf. Evans v. Elliot, 9 Ad. & El. 342 (K.B.1838); Towerson v. Jackson, 2 Q.B. 484 (1891); 1 Tiffany, Landlord & Tenant, § 73a(6).

24. See note, 46 Harv.L.Rev. 491, 493 (1932). See also Berick, The Mortgagee's Right to Rents, 8 Cin.L.Rev. 250, 271 (1934).

§ 4.26 Lien States

Under the lien theory of mortgages the mortgagor remains the full legal and beneficial owner of the mortgaged property until his rights are ended by foreclosure sale. The mortgagee, having no right to possession prior to foreclosure except where he acquires the status of a "mortgagee in possession", a matter discussed later, is not entitled to rents from the mortgagor's tenants regardless of whether the leases preceded or followed the giving of the mortgage.[25] If he has leased the property before giving the mortgage, the lien acquired on the reversion gives the mortgagee no right to the rents accruing under the lease. If a mortgagor leases the mortgaged premises subsequently to giving the mortgage, he is entitled to the rents until title passes under a decree of foreclosure.[26]

Foreclosure of the mortgage in lien states creates problems similar to those in title jurisdictions when the mortgagee before foreclosure asserts his right to possession against the mortgagor and seeks to reach the rents. If the lease preceded the mortgage and the latter was taken with actual or constructive notice of it, only the lessor's interest can be sold on foreclosure and the tenant's rights under the lease cannot be extinguished.[27] However the purchaser on foreclosure sale has rights analogous to those of a mortgagee in a title state who takes a mortgage on leased property. Where the mortgage precedes the lease, since title remains in the mortgagor until foreclosure, the lease by the mortgagor cannot be affected until foreclosure. Since it depends upon the mortgagor's interest it may, however, be foreclosed along with it if the tenant is properly joined in those proceedings.[28] The purchaser on foreclosure sale acquires rights to rents and in respect to the lease that the mortgagee did not possess.[29]

25. Wagar v. Stone, 36 Mich. 364 (1877).

On the problem of a mortgagee's security interest in crops, with especial reference to California law, see Smith, Security Interests in Crops, 10 Hastings L.J. 23, 156 (1958).

Woolley v. Holt, 77 Ky. (14 Bush) 788 (1879) in which the mortgagor, who leased the property before mortgaging it, transferred the lease to X. Held, on foreclosure, X took free and clear of the mortgage lien.

26. See Mills v. Hamilton, 49 Iowa 105 (1878); Mills v. Heaton, 52 Iowa 215, 2 N.W. 1112 (1879); Orr v. Broad, 52 Neb. 490, 72 N.W. 850 (1897); Mason v. Lenderoth, 88 App.Div. 38, 84 N.Y.S. 740 (1903). The mortgagee of a lessee in possession in a lien state is not an assignee of the lease and thus is not liable on the covenant for rent. Note, 58 Mich.L.Rev. 140 (1959).

27. Possession by the tenant or recordation of the lease will give notice of it. Taylor v. Bell, 129 Ala. 464, 29 S.W. 572 (1900); Tropical Inv. Co. v. Brown, 45 Cal.App. 205, 187 P. 133 (1920); Heaton v. Grand Lodge No. 335, IOOF, 55 Ind.App. 100, 103 N.E. 488 (1913).

28. For the effect of non-joinder in foreclosure proceedings, see § 7.15 infra.

29. E. g., a purchaser at a foreclosure sale may eject the mortgagor's tenant, or make a new lease. McDermott v. Burke, 16 Cal. 580 (1860). See 8 L.R.A.,N.S., 404; 1921, 14 A.L.R. 664 (1907).

If the mortgagor puts the mortgagee into possession with authority to collect the rents this will not affect the leases apart from altering the person to whom the rents are to be paid by the lessee. Although the leases are subject to the mortgage, the mortgagee cannot end them except by foreclosure unless the tenant consents or breaks some condition in the lease.[30] A foreclosure receivership in lien jurisdictions will also alter the simple general rule that the mortgagor is entitled to the rents before foreclosure.[31]

F. MORTGAGEE IN POSSESSION

§ 4.27 "Mortgagee-in-Possession" Rule

The mortgagee may lawfully acquire possession while the mortgage is still subsisting. The courts have developed the doctrine that if he does his security interest as mortgagee in possession generally entitles him to hold the premises until either the mortgagor redeems or the property is foreclosed.[32]

As we have already seen, in jurisdictions following the title theory of mortgages, the mortgagee, in the absence of an agreement or a statutory provision to the contrary, is entitled as a matter of right to possession before or after default.[33] In the "intermediate" jurisdictions the same is true after default.[34] In both types of states, when

30. Fidelity Bond and Mortgage Co. v. Paul, 90 Colo. 94, 6 P.2d 462 (1931).

31. The effect of foreclosure, of receiverships in foreclosure, and of agreements in respect to rents and possession in lien jurisdictions upon leases and the right to rents in those jurisdictions is dealt with in §§ 4.36–4.46 infra.

32. He may, however, be ousted for gross mismanagement, by the extinction of the mortgage through tender, merger, or sale of the property by the mortgagee to a purchaser without notice, or by the assertion of a prior mortgage interest. For cases, see 35 Col.L.Rev. 1248, 1253 notes 31, 33, 34 (1935).

The doctrine that a mortgagee in possession cannot be dispossessed by the mortgagor without payment of the mortgage debt applies although an action on the debt or the right to foreclose the mortgage is barred by the statute of limitations. Jasper State Bank v. Braswell, 130 Tex. 549, 111 S.W.2d 1079, 115 A.L.R. 329 (1938); Spect v. Spect, 88 Cal. 437, 26 P. 203, 13 L.R.A. 137, 22 Am.St.Rep. 314 (1891); Bulson v. Moffatt, 173 Cal. 685, 161 P. 259 (1916), noted in 5 Cal.L.Rev. 258; Kelso v. Norton, 65 Kan. 778, 70 P. 896, 93 Am.St.Rep. 308 (1902). Knight v. Hilton, 224 S.C. 452, 79 S.E.2d 871 (1954) noted by Karesh, Survey of South Carolina Law (1954): Security Transactions, 7 S.C.L.Q. 171. See Burns v. Hiatt, 149 Cal. 617, 87 P. 196, 117 Am.St.Rep. 157 (1906). Nor does a hostile reentry on the land by the mortgagor divest the rights of the mortgagee as mortgagee in possession. Finley v. Erickson, 122 Minn. 235, 142 N.W. 198 (1913); Cory v. Santa Ynez Land, etc. Co., 151 Cal. 778, 91 P. 647 (1907). On the ability of a mortgagee in possession to acquire title by adverse possession, see 6 Minn.L.Rev. 510 (1922), and Cory v. Santa Ynez Land Co., supra.

33. See § 4.1, supra; Cook v. Curtis, 125 Me. 114, 131 A. 204 (1925); Weathersbee v. Goodwin, 175 N.C. 234, 95 S.E. 491 (1918); Brown v. Loeb, 177 Ala. 106, 58 So. 330 (1912).

34. See § 4.3, supra.

the mortgagee exercises his right to enter, his possession is clearly lawful within the scope of the doctrine and he becomes a mortgagee in possession.

In lien states the mortgagor has the right to possession of the mortgaged premises both before and after default until foreclosure and the expiration of the period of redemption from foreclosure.[35] Consequently, on first impression, it would seem that the doctrine of mortgagee in possession would have no place in them. Nevertheless, it has generally been accepted although there is a divergence of view especially as to what will constitute lawful possession making the doctrine operative. One line of cases reconciles it with the lien concept only upon the basis of consent, express or implied in fact, on the part of the mortgagor that the mortgagee be in possession of the mortgaged premises. As one of the leading cases expressed it, "it would seem to follow that when the legislature deprived the mortgagee of the only legal method by which he could get possession of the mortgaged premises without the mortgagor's consent, prior to foreclosure, there was no way left by which the mortgagee could acquire such possession except by the mortgagor's consent." [36] Further, this consent must be to an entry by the mortgagee "under or by virtue of the mortgage," or, at least, "for purposes, or under circumstances not inconsistent with their relative legal rights under the mortgage." [37] Thus when the mortgagee gets possession in a capacity other than that of mortgagee, e. g., as a tenant of the mortgagor, he cannot, during, or after the expiration of his term as lessee, assert a right of possession as mortgagee, without the express or implied consent of the mortgagor.[38] So, too, if he enters as the agent of the mortgagor,

35. See Mutual Benefit Life Ins. Co. v. Frantz Klodt & Son, Inc., 237 N.W.2d 350 (Minn.1975); § 4.2 infra.

36. Barson v. Mulligan, 191 N.Y. 306, 315, 84 N.E. 75, 78, 16 L.R.A.,N.S., 151 (1908). McClory v. Ricks, 11 N. D. 38, 88 N.W. 1042 (1902). Accord: 8 Col.L.Rev. 486 (1908); note by E. N.D., 15 Mich.L.Rev. 58 (1916). A few lien jurisdictions, it is true, invalidate executory agreements for the mortgagee to take possession. See Geraldson, Clauses Increasing the Possessory Rights of Mortgagees, 10 Wis.L.Rev. 492 (1935); Tiffany, Real Prop., 3d ed., § 1416. This result, however, can be regarded as "an extension of the familiar view early developed in equity that the mortgagor shall not be permitted to bargain away his right to redemption as a part of his mortgage contract," Rundle, Work of the Wisconsin Supreme Court—Mortgages, 1933. 9 Wis. 33, 40, and thus distinguished from cases holding that a later actual entry with consent is valid.

For a discussion of the development of the problem of lawful possession after default by a mortgagee in New York, where the doctrine originated, see note, 8 Col.L.Rev. 486 (1908). See also E.N.D., The Mortgagee in Possession in New York and in Michigan, 15 Mich.L.Rev. 58 (1916).

37. Barson v. Mulligan, supra note 36, at 322, 84 N.E. at 81. See 26 Albany L.Jour. 526 (1882); 27 Albany L.Jour. 6 (1883).

38. Barson v. Mulligan, supra n. 36; Robinson v. Smith, 128 S.W.2d 27 (Tex.Com.App.1939), discussed, 24 Minn.L.Rev. 434 (1939); Russell v. Ely, 67 U.S. (2 Black.) 575, 17 L.Ed. 258 (1862), a mortgagee who obtains possession from the tenant of the mortgagor after his lease had expired is not lawfully in possession. See 8 Col.L.Rev. 486 (1908).

he will not be a mortgagee in possession, only an agent with the liabilities of that relation.[39]

Another line of reasoning has sometimes been advanced. It has been asserted that "the possession of the land is a special security for the debt, distinct and separate from the mortgage, which has been conferred by an act of the debtor, and the right to retain the same is independent of and distinct from any right springing from the mortgage." [40] Possession is not an incident of the mortgage in a lien jurisdiction and "the *fact* of possession is entirely distinct from the *contract* of hypothecation. When, therefore, * * * the debtor gives to his creditor the possession of the mortgaged premises, he thereby, in addition to the mortgage which he has executed, also pledges the land to him as security for the debt, and confers on him such rights are are incident to a pledge." [41]

However, there are some objections to such an analysis. It would limit the doctrine to consensual transactions between the mortgagor and mortgagee. Logically, also, it would dispense with the necessity of the existence at any time of a mortgage; and, in place of the requirement that the mortgagee should be in possession as mortgagee, demand that he be in possession as pledgee. This last test, however, is never suggested. This may be because there is no difference between the two. But if this is so it minimizes the utility of the distinction drawn.

The doctrine of mortgagee in possession in lien jurisdictions is not confined, however, to cases where the mortgagee entered with the consent of the mortgagor.[42] In some states a peaceable entry, in good faith, and under color of right, e. g., under a void foreclosure sale, is sufficient to make the possession lawful without any consent whatsoever by the mortgagor.[43] And in others it is enough that the entry was peaceable.[44] But in all such states, in order for the occupa-

39. Realty Inv. & Sec. Corp. v. H. L. Rust Co., 71 App.D.C. 213, 109 F.2d 456 (1939); Ireland v. U. S., etc. Co., 72 App.Div. 95, 76 N.Y.S. 177 (1902) affirmed 175 N.Y. 491, 67 N.E. 1083 (1903); Whitley v. Barnett, 151 Iowa 487, 131 N.W. 704 (1911).

40. Spect v. Spect, 88 Cal. 437, 441, 26 P. 203 (1891).

41. Spect v. Spect, 88 Cal. 437, 441, 26 P. 203 (1891). See Kortright v. Cady, 21 N.Y. 343, 78 Am.Dec. 145 (1860); Brinkman v. Jones, 44 Wis. 498, 512 (1878).

42. See 7 Tex.L.Rev. 170 (1928); 18 N.Car.L.Rev. 61 (1939).

43. Jasper State Bank v. Braswell, 130 Tex. 549, 111 S.W.2d 1079, 115 A.L.R. 329 (1938); Raggio v. Palmtag, 155 Cal. 797, 103 P. 312 (1909); Cameron v. Ah Quong, 175 Cal. 377, 165 P. 961 (1917); Pettit v. Louis, 88 Neb. 496, 129 N.W. 1005, 34 L.R.A.,N.S., 356 (1911); Caro v. Wollenberg, 68 Or. 420, 136 P. 866 (1913). In such states, a mortgagee who entered into possession under an agreement with his mortgagor that he should do so as additional security would be given, *a fortiori*, the status of a mortgagee in possession. Spect v. Spect, 88 Cal. 437, 26 P. 203, 13 L.R.A. 137, 22 Am. St.Rep. 314 (1891).

44. Stouffer v. Harlan, 68 Kan. 135, 74 P. 610, 64 L.R.A. 320, 104 Am.St.Rep.

tion of the premises to entitle him to the status of mortgagee in possession, he must assert his claim to have and to hold them under and by virtue of his lien, i. e., *qua* mortgagee.[45] If he enters as the result of a defective foreclosure sale, the most usual case, this satisfies the requirement.[46] But suppose that, although a mortgagee at the time, he enters peaceably in a capacity other than mortgagee and later claims to hold possession as mortgagee. Or, that he takes possession peaceably under an invalid claim derived from a third party and later, while in possession he thus acquires a subsisting mortgage and then claims as mortgagee in possession. It has been suggested that possession so acquired might be regarded as having been obtained by fraud and thus as illegal as though obtained by force.[47] However, the mortgagee's claim probably will be sustained.[48]

Where the mortgagee in possession is there with the consent of the mortgagor the doctrine of according him rights as such is not inconsistent with lien theory. When, however, consent by the mortgagor to the mortgagee's entry is dispensed with as a necessary ingredient in the doctrine of mortgagee in possession, it becomes more difficult to reconcile it with lien dogma.[49] One explanation of the extension is that "the old rule, existing when a mortgage actually passed the title to the property, kept its hold upon the later opinions when

396 (1903) same case, 84 Kan. 307, 114 P. 385 (1911); Burns v. Hiatt 149 Cal. 617, 87 P. 196, 117 Am.St.Rep. 157 (1906); West v. Middlesex Banking Co., 33 S.D. 465, 146 N.W. 598 (1914); Pierce v. Grimley, 77 Mich. 273, 43 N.W. 932 (1889) (power of sale illegally exercised); Jaggar v. Plunkett, 81 Kan. 565, 106 P. 280, 25 L.R. A.,N.S., 935 (1910). But see State ex rel. Montgomery v. Superior Court, 21 Wash. 564, 58 P. 1065 (1899); Herrmann v. Cabinet Land Co., 217 N.Y. 526, 112 N.E. 476 (1916) (mortgagor not served with process in foreclosure action).

45. Daniel v. Coker, 70 Ala. 260 (1881); Anglo-Calif. Bank v. Field, 154 Cal. 513, 98 P. 267 (1908), in possession under deed of redemption right of mortgagor; Armistead v. Bishop, 110 Ark. 172, 161 S.W. 182 (1913) in possession as tenant; Compton v. Jesup, 68 F. 263, 15 C.C. A. 397 (1895). A mortgagee who, without the consent of the mortgagor, acquires possession after the mortgage lien has become extinguished cannot assert the rights of a mortgagee in possession. Faxon v. All Persons, 166 Cal. 707, 137 P. 919 (1913). See Tiffany, Real Prop., 3d ed., § 1419; Pomeroy, Eq.Juris., 5th ed., § 1215.

46. See note 43, supra. Even though the purchaser under a defective foreclosure sale taking possession under such sale is not the mortgagee himself, he succeeds to the rights of the mortgagee although the sale under foreclosure is void, and he is treated, therefore, as a mortgagee in possession. Bryan v. Brasius, 3 Ariz. 433, 31 P. 519 (1892) affirmed 162 U.S. 415, 16 S.Ct. 803, 40 L.Ed. 1022 (1896); Kaylor v. Kelsey, 91 Neb. 404, 136 N.W. 54, 40 L.R.A.,N.S., 839 (1912).

47. See note 15 Mich.L.Rev. 58, 60 (1916).

48. See, e. g., Jaggar v. Plunkett, 81 Kan. 565, 106 P. 280 (1910).

49. The extension of the doctrine beyond cases of consent by the mortgagor has been vigorously criticized. See Walsh, Mortgages, § 19, which in turn is criticized by McDougal, 44 Yale L.Jour. 1278, 1281 (1935); E.N.D., 15 Mich.L.Rev. 58 (1916); Tiffany, Real Prop., 3d ed., § 1415.

the reason which led to it was gone."[50] In other words, it is just an anachronistic survival of the title view of mortgages. While this may have been the origin of the rule, its vitality and wide acceptance demands a better rationalization. The one most commonly accepted is that the mortgagee's "right to retain possession does not depend upon an estate held by him. His possession is protected by his lien. It is certainly more simple and just that the mortgagee should be left in possession, and the mortgagor forced to redeem, than that the mortgagor should be permitted to recover the possession by an action at law, and be immediately liable to the consequences of a foreclosure suit in equity brought by the mortgagee."[51]

Both the doctrine itself and this last justification of it have been criticized on the ground that, under the lien theory, the right to possession before foreclosure "admittedly belongs to the mortgagor and his suit in ejectment by which he enforces it can hardly be called useless or unnecessary," and that the doctrine gives "the mortgagee a right to possession in fact though acquired without right, and forces the mortgagor to redeem long before he is required to do so under the general principles of equity applying to the action to redeem." The cases following it are called "anomalous, without explanation other than an undefined equity or feeling of abstract justice is the bases of it."[52]

Several answers may be made. One is that, in the face of this strong judicial authority recognizing the right of the mortgagee to hold onto possession, it is difficult to say that "admittedly" possession belongs to the mortgagor under all circumstances before foreclosure is complete. These decisions are square holdings to the contrary, creating an exception to the general rule, and the only question ought to be whether the result is a good one, taking into account not only a mechanical concept of the lien theory, but the practical situation involved in the particular problem. The interest of the mortgagor in having possession after default must be balanced against the mortgagee's interest in continuing in possession of the property he took as security. Before default, it is generally agreed that the mortgagor's interest outweighs any claim the mortgagee may assert. But when the mortgagee has acquired the right, through the default of the mortgagor, to realize on his security, his interest in having possession of the property and getting its proceeds to apply on the debt become very strong. As we shall see, he often can take possession away from the mortgagor by getting a receiver appointed and, although inadequacy of the security or waste are, in theory, essential requirements

50. Stouffer v. Harlan, 68 Kan. 135, 74 P. 610, 64 L.R.A. 320, 104 Am.St.Rep. 396 (1903), attributing it to Howell v. Leavitt, 95 N.Y. 617 (1884). This basis is, however, older and was expressed in Phyfe v. Riley, 15 Wend. 248 (1836). See E.N.D., 15 Mich.L. Rev. 58 (1916).

51. Pomeroy, Eq.Juris., 5th ed., § 1189.

52. Walsh, Mortgages, 100.

for this, in actual practice receivers are sometimes appointed pretty much as a matter of course.[53] The mortgagee in possession has advantages in keeping down costs and, under the requirement of strict accountability, of providing better management than a receivership affords.[54] Further, when the mortgagor's action for possession can be immediately nullified by an action to foreclose by the mortgagee, it can properly be regarded as "useless or unnecessary" unless justified by substantial reasons.[55]

One of the chief arguments for allowing the mortgagor to have possession is that it is the source of his ability to get income with which to pay off the mortgage debt. However, the mortgagee in possession must account for all rents and profits, which will be applied to payment of the mortgage debt, thus accomplishing the same result and benefiting the mortgagor. There exists, of course, the possibility that the mortgagor could have made more out of the property had he been in possession, and thus, it should be assumed, have paid off more of the mortgage debt. No doubt there is some substance to this, but it overlooks the reality that the benefit the mortgagor will receive by any increased earnings will not be by virtue of their reducing the amount of the mortgage debt but by the mortgagor having all of the income from the property to use for other purposes, leaving the debt unpaid except insofar as the sale on foreclosure of the property will do so. The reason for this is plain. The doctrine is seldom invoked except in cases where the mortgagor is in at least a precarious,[56] if not hopeless, condition, for it is applicable in lien jurisdictions only after default, and, practically, occurs most frequently, when consent to entry is not obtained, after a defective foreclosure has taken place. The dangers to the mortgagee, under such conditions, that the mortgagor will resort to "milking" the property if he regains possession, or at least attempt to maintain it at a minimum expense with the result that the property would become run down, are great and the ability of the mortgagee to protect himself is unsatisfactory. To allow the mortgagor to get back possession of the property under these circumstances would amount, in effect, to a judicial exemption founded upon mechanical application of the lien theory and tenderness to mortgagors at the expense of mortgagees. Such considerations serve both to explain and support the desirability

53. See §§ 4.36–4.37, infra.

54. See Note, 35 Col.L.Rev. 1248, 1260 (1935).

55. American Trust Co. v. England, 84 F.2d 352 (C.C.A.Cal.1936); where the mortgagee is in possession after a breach of the conditions in a mortgage, the mortgagor must show affirmatively that his possession is not lawful.

56. "The paucity of redemption cases points to the probability that possession is merely a prelude to foreclosure. In that event, continuation of possession in a mortgagee may be socially desirable, since it gives him control over his security without resort to receivership." 35 Col.L.Rev. 1247, 1254 (1935).

of decisions accepting the doctrine of mortgagee in possession even in cases where there is no consensual basis for it.

§ 4.28 What Constitutes Possession

In order for a mortgagee to become a mortgagee in possession he must have possession of the premises *qua* mortgagee. What constitutes such occupation *qua* mortgagee varies with the nature and condition of the property.[57] Indeed both the words "possession" and "occupation" are somewhat misleading because a mortgagee can be a mortgagee in possession without actually occupying the premises.[58] For example, in the case of urban rental real estate, while merely the collection of rent by the mortgagee may not create a mortgagee in possession,[59] that factor combined with active management will probably be enough.[60] Consequently "exercise of dominion and control" over the property as mortgagee is more descriptive.[61]

§ 4.29 Liability of Mortgagee to Third Parties

When a mortgagee goes into possession questions as to his personal liability to third persons arise. Since he is the person in possession of the premises he is personally liable in tort for injuries resulting either through his actionable fault in utilizing the property or by reason of his failure to perform duties imposed by law upon the owner of land.[62] Even more clearly he is liable for goods and services furnished to him during his occupancy on either an express or implied contract basis.[63]

57. See 35 Col.L.Rev. 1248, 1250 (1935).

58. See cases in 35 Col.L.Rev. 1248, 1250, notes, 14, 15, 16 (1935). Gandrud v. Hansen, 210 Minn. 125, 297 N.W. 730 (1941), discussed, 26 Minn.L.Rev. 880, 887 et seq. (1942).

59. Strutt v. Ontario Sav. & Loan Ass'n, 28 Cal.App.3d 866, 881, 105 Cal.Rptr. 395, 405 (1973); Bank of America Nat. Trust & Sav. Ass'n v. Bank of Amador Co., 135 Cal.App. 714, 28 P.2d 86 (1933); Stephens Invest. Co. v. Berry Schools, 188 Ga. 132, 3 S.E.2d 68 (1939).

60. Ireland v. United States Mortgage & Trust Co., 72 App.Div. 95, 76 N.Y.S. 177 (1902) affirmed 175 N.Y. 491, 67 N.E. 1083; cf. Whitley v. Barnett, 151 Iowa 487, 131 N.W. 704 (1911). See 35 Col.L.Rev. 1248, 1250 (1935); 50 Yale L.Jour. 1427, 1431 n. 42 (1941).

61. Zisman v. City of Duquesne, 143 Pa.Sup. 263, 18 A.2d 95 (1941), noted, 7 Pitts.L.Rev. 345 (1941).

62. See Restatement, Second, Torts, § 329, comments a, c. Zisman v. City of Duquesne, 143 Pa.Sup. 263, 18 A.2d 95 (1941), noted, 7 Pitts.L.Rev. 345 (1941); Daniels v. Hart, 118 Mass. 543 (1875); Rogers v. Wheeler, 2 Lans. 486 (N.Y.1870); affirmed 43 N.Y. 598; Barter v. Wheeler, 49 N.H. 9, 6 Am. Rep. 434 (1869); Sprague v. Smith, 29 Vt. 421, 70 Am.Dec. 424 (1857). The liability is probably exclusive. See Sabiston's Adm'r v. Otis Elevator Co., 251 Ky. 222, 229, 64 S.W.2d 588, 591 (1933). Exceptions to this may be based upon an agency relationship between the mortgagor and the mortgagee in possession as to third persons, Grand Tower Mfg. & Transp. Co. v. Ullman, 89 Ill. 244 (1878), or in the case of a known dangerous condition existing at the time of transfer of possession to the mortgagee, at least if the transfer was consented to. Restatement, Second, Torts §§ 353, 354.

63. Essex Cleaning Contractors, Inc. v. Amato, 127 N.J.Super. 364, 317 A.2d

The liability of a mortgagee in possession on covenants running with the mortgaged land presents some substantial problems. Normally, use restrictions are enforcible *in equity* as equitable servitudes against non-fee holders such as lessees and even licensees.[64] Thus, mortgagees in possession presumably should be subject to equitable relief at least to the same extent as other non-feeholders.

Where, however, money damages are sought for violation of use restrictions, the problems are more complex. This is because "the contractual obligation attaches to the estate of the covenantor, and can run with the land only against one who succeeds to that estate. Succession of estate between the covenantor and his assignee is an absolute essential to the running of the burden at law." [65] If this reasoning is applied to the mortgagee in possession, the title-lien distinction could theoretically become important. For example, in a title theory state it could be argued that the mortgagee in possession should be liable for damages on a covenant running with the land because the mortgagee, as the holder of legal title, has succeeded to the estate of the covenantor. On the other hand, the lien jurisdiction mortgagee in possession, since he holds only a security interest and not legal title, would not be similarly liable.

The few cases in this area have dealt for the most part with the liability of a mortgagee in possession for rent where the mortgaged property consists of a leasehold. There is title theory case law holding the mortgagee liable.[66] Two lines of cases are discernible in lien states. There are New York cases holding that the mortgagee will be bound because "when the mortgagee takes possession he then has all the right, title and interest of the mortgagor." [67] This, of course, runs counter to the usual lien theory concept that the mortgagee can acquire the title to the mortgaged real estate against a recalcitrant mortgagor only by foreclosure. However, there are other, preferable cases holding that the mortgagee never becomes liable even though he has taken possession. This result has been reached on the ground that the "mere act of the parties of going into possession, and consenting to or acquiescing in it can [not] have the effect to pass the mortgagor's estate to the mortgagee" and, therefore, just as he could not sue on a covenant running with the land "because he is not the owner of the land with which such covenants run" so he is not liable

411 (1974) (quoting text with approval); First National Bank v. Matlock, 99 Okl. 150, 226 P. 328, 36 A.L.R. 1088 (1934). He probably can avoid such liability, as can a foreclosure receiver, by express stipulation in the contract with the third person. Cf. Knickerbocker Ice Co. v. Benson, 155 Misc. 738, 741, 279 N.Y.S. 86 (1935).

64. American Law of Property, § 9.31 (1952).

65. Id. at 427.

66. See Gibbs v. Didier, 125 Md. 486, 94 A. 100 (1915), Annot., 73 A.L.R.2d 1119, 1121 (1960).

67. Astor v. Hoyt, 5 Wend. 603, 617 (N.Y.1830); Moffatt v. Smith, 4 N.Y. 126 (1850). Cockrell v. Houston Packing Co., 105 Tex. 283, 147 S.W. 1145 (1912), accord.

on them.[68] A preferable basis, and one that should apply in title states as well, would have been that, whether technically the mortgagee has legal title or lien, his interest is only for security purposes and liabilities that are founded upon full ownership should not attach to it.

§ 4.30 The Mortgagee's Duty to Account—Nature and Scope

Once the mortgagee is in possession, he becomes entitled to the income of the property on the one hand and, on the other, he becomes subject to certain duties in respect to management of the property. These concepts apply equally in title and lien jurisdictions.[69]

The rules of accounting for a mortgagee in possession are harsh. While the parties to some extent may alter the impact of these rules by contract provisions [70] and courts of equity will vary them to avoid hardship,[71] the role of the mortgagee in possession is not an easy one. As was seen in examining the development of the lien theory and in other connections, there is a strong policy in favor of leaving the mortgagor in possession which is furthered by stringent rules discouraging mortgagees from taking over even when they have the legal right to do so. Realization by sale of the capital asset is the essence of the mortgagee's right. To take possession from the mortgagor is justified by the danger of "milking" by a hard pressed mortgagor, and the idea that the mortgagee is entitled not only to the capital asset itself but all it yields in the form of income from the time his right to realize accrues and he starts to exercise it; the time lag between starting and final realization should not defeat his rights. But on both counts possession is purely in the mortgagee's interest and deprives the mortgagor of a source of income and sometimes the means by which he has the best chance of saving his property. Further, the mortgagee in possession holding the property as security has it in his power to prolong the period of his responsibility or to shorten it by foreclosure proceedings. Finally, since the income of

68. Cargill v. Thompson, 57 Minn. 534, 543, 59 N.W. 638, 640 (1894); Johnson v. Sherman, 15 Cal. 287, 76 Am. Dec. 481 (1860). Annot., 73 A.L.R.2d 1119, 1123–1134 (1960).

"We suspect the courts of New York would hesitate to hold that as soon as he gets possession he may sue upon or may release such covenants, which he certainly can do, if he has an estate that makes him the owner of them." Cargill v. Thompson, supra note 33, at 544, 59 N.W. at 640. The mortgagee in possession under an arrangement with the mortgagor to manage the mortgaged leasehold was held not liable to the landlord on the ground that he was acting as agent of the mortgagor in holding possession. Cleveland v. Detroit Trust Co., 264 Mich. 253, 249 N.W. 842 (1933), commented on in 32 Mich.L.Rev. 864 (1934).

69. See Walsh, Mortgages, § 20.

70. See, e. g., Johns v. Moore, 168 Cal.App.2d 709, 366 P.2d 579 (1959).

71. See 35 Col.L.Rev. 1248, 1251 (1935), citing as examples, Madison Ave. Baptist Church v. Baptist Church in Oliver St., 73 N.Y. 82 (1878); Walter v. Calhoun, 88 Kan. 801, 129 P. 1176 (1913).

the property must be applied to the payment of the mortgage debt, the mortgagee who takes control of the source of that income should answer pretty strictly for any conduct that prevents income arising.

The mortgagee in possession is sometimes characterized in semi-fiduciary terminology. In this connection, cases have labeled him as having the "quasi character of trustee or bailiff" [72] or of being a "trustee",[73] a "constructive trustee" [74] or a "pledgee in possession." [75] Actually the mortgagee in possession is not a trustee and he is not truly a fiduciary, and invoking these designations is chiefly by way of analogy and for the purpose of ascribing to him certain rights and duties. It would have been better to have recognized that his position was *sui generis* and then determined what legal incidents should attach to it.

Whatever the label, the mortgagee in possession has a duty of conduct in respect to the mortgaged property which is substantially that of a provident owner—"to manage the property in a reasonably prudent and careful manner so as to keep it in a good state of preservation and productivity" and to use the yield of the property for no other purpose than to credit it upon the mortgagee's claim by way of equitable set-off. However, the mortgagee in possession in the course of his management of the property, in addition to receiving income, will have incurred various expenses for which he is entitled to be reimbursed, or by his affirmative conduct or neglect have subjected himself to charges other than income actually received which will be assessed against him. It is only the balance, after these charges and debits have been cast up and set off against each other, that goes in satisfaction of the debt.

From the foregoing two things are apparent. One is that before it can be known how much of the income is to be applied to the mortgage debt there must be an accounting which can be made only in accordance with equitable theory and practice. The other is that the application in the accounting of the balance when ascertained is in the nature of an equitable set-off when the debt is being paid. This being so, it must be made in a proceeding or transaction directly involving the satisfaction of the mortgage debt.[76] Consequently an account can be called for only when the mortgagee enforces his debt by foreclosure or when the mortgagor seeks to pay it, either by voluntary agreement with the mortgagee or else in an action in equity to

72. Hubbell v. Moulson, 53 N.Y. 225, 228, 13 Am.Rep. 519 (1873).

73. Toomer v. Randolph, 60 Ala. 356, 360 (1877); Anglo-Calif. Bank v. Field, 154 Cal. 513, 98 P. 267 (1908).

74. Real Estate-Land, Title & Trust Co. v. Homer Building & Loan Ass'n, 138 Pa.Super. 563, 10 A.2d 786 (1940); Travis v. Schonwald, 131 S.W.2d 827 (Tex.Civ.App.1939).

75. Spect v. Spect, 88 Cal. 437, 26 P. 203, 13 L.R.A. 137, 22 Am.St.Rep. 314 (1891).

76. Hubbell v. Moulson, 53 N.Y. 225, 13 Am.Rep. 519 (1873).

redeem.[77] Therefore, questions as to the accountability of the mortgagee in possession cannot be raised in actions at law for possession by the mortgagor [78] or by action and garnishment by a junior encumbrancer or any similar action not putting the payment of the mortgage debt directly in issue.[79]

It is elementary that the mortgagor is entitled to an accounting from any mortgagee in possession. So, too, may junior encumbrancers,[80] because they derive their interest from and participate in the mortgagor's right to redeem. And the same is true of transferees of the mortgagor's redemption interest.[81] Similarly, an assignee of the mortgagee in possession will be bound to render an accounting.[82] On the other hand, a senior mortgagee has no right to an accounting from either a junior mortgagee in possession [83] or a transferee of the mortgagor. This follows from the fact that they stand in the same position as the mortgagor and the mortgagee has no right to compel an accounting from the mortgagor in possession.

§ 4.31 The Duty to Account for Rents

A mortgagee in possession may either rent the mortgaged property or occupy it himself. In any event, "with respect to accountability for rents and profits which the mortgagee in possession received or could have received, the general duty of the mortgagee toward the premises is that of an ordinarily prudent owner." [84] In the case where the property is rented the mortgagee must account for the rents and profits actually received.[85] Moreover, if he remits to a tenant part of the rent which he could have collected with reasonable

77. See 23 Harv.L.Rev. 301 (1910); Eisen v. Kostakos, 116 N.J.Super. 358, 282 A.2d 421 (1971).

78. Hubbell v. Moulson, 53 N.Y. 225, 13 Am.Rep. 519 (1873); Green v. Thornton, 8 Cal.App. 160, 96 P. 382 (1908).

79. Toomer v. Randolph, 60 Ala. 356 (1877). See note, 23 Harv.L.Rev. 301 (1909).

80. Landau v. Western Pennsylvania Nat. Bank, 445 Pa. 217, 282 A.2d 335 (1971); Gaskell v. Viquesney, 122 Ind. 244, 23 N.E. 791, 17 Am.St.Rep. 364 (1890); Hirsch v. Northwestern Mut. Life Ins. Co., 191 Ga. 524, 13 S.E.2d 165 (1941); Mallalieu v. Wickham, 42 N.J.Eq. 297, 10 A. 880 (1886), holder of judgment lien. Thus it has been held that a mortgagee in possession is under a duty to a junior encumbrancer to refrain from permitting the mortgagor to receive the rents. Gandrud v. Hansen, 210 Minn. 125, 297 N.W. 730 (1941) discussed at length in note, 26 Minn.L.Rev. 880 (1942).

81. Dicken v. Simpson, 117 Ark. 304, 174 S.W. 1154 (1915); Ruckman v. Astor, 9 Paige 517 (N.Y.1842); Elliott v. Brady, 172 N.Car. 828, 90 S.E. 951 (1916).

82. Strang v. Allen, 44 Ill. 428 (1867); Ackerman v. Lodi Branch R. Co., 31 N.J.Eq. 42 (1879).

83. Leeds v. Gifford, 41 N.J.Eq. 464, 5 A. 795 (1888), affirmed 45 N.J.Eq. 245, 19 A. 621 (1890).

84. Johns v. Moore, 168 Cal.App.2d 709, 336 P.2d 579, 581 (1959). See also, Shaeffer v. Chambers, 6 N.J.Eq. 548, 47 Am.Dec. 211 (1847). See Gerrish v. Black, 104 Mass. 400 (1870).

85. Gerrish v. Black, 104 Mass. 400 (1870).

diligence he will be charged for it.[86] However, the standard itself permits some flexibility in bargaining with tenants as to amount of rent, subordination, extension of time for payment and length of lease and other similar matters[87] and the mortgagee will not be liable if the standard of provident owner is adhered to.[88] Even occasional vacancies will not be charged to him if he has used reasonable diligence to obtain tenants.[89]

When a mortgagee occupies the premises himself instead of leasing them several questions arise. One is whether there is any duty upon him to work or operate it in case he has tried with due diligence to rent it and failed. The answer should be yes and there is authority so holding, at least in the case of a farm.[90] If the mortgagee retains possession when he finds that he cannot rent the property, he should have to work it or, if he does not, he should be held for the fair rental value. Business property would present a more difficult case and it would seem undesirable to force a mortgagee to start a new business on it although there may be a duty to carry on an existing business.[91]

But when the mortgagee does operate it for how much should he be held accountable? The prevailing view is to charge him with the fair rental value no matter what he makes, letting him keep any excess and bear the loss if he makes less. In support of this it is ar-

86. Carroll v. Tomlinson, 192 Ill. 398, 61 N.E. 484, 85 Am.St.Rep. 344 (1901); Miller v. Lincoln, 72 Mass. (6 Gray) 556 (1856), allowing "notoriously insolvent" tenant to remain in possession eighteen months made mortgagee chargeable for the lost rent.

87. Landau v. Western Pennsylvania Nat. Bank, 445 Pa. 217, 282 A.2d 335 (1971) (voluntary subordination of mortgage to existing lease upheld even though junior lienor and mortgagor claimed that this would reduce the value of the premises on a foreclosure sale.); Chapman v. Cooney, 25 R.I. 657, 57 A. 928 (1904), 11% reduction to retain tenant who could not afford former rental; Wilmarth v. Johnson, 124 Wis. 320, 102 N.W. 562 (1905) rent remission to tenant "probably insolvent" when "times were hard" and mortgagor had consented; Eldriedge v. Hoefer, 52 Or. 241, 93 P. 246 (1908), modified 52 Or. 257, 94 P. 563, motion to recall mandate denied 52 Or. 241, 96 P. 1105, ten year lease; Hays v. Christensen, 114 Neb. 764, 209 N.W. 609 (1926), five year lease; Brown v. So. Boston Savings Bank, 148 Mass. 300, 19 N.E. 382 (1889), rent below value stated by expert testimony.

88. "The reasonableness of the mortgagee's action must be tested in light of general economic conditions, the character of the premises, the likely duration of his possession, and the extent of the mortgagor's residual interest." 50 Yale L.Jour. 1424, 1432 (1941).

89. Whitley v. Barnett, 151 Iowa 487, 131 N.W. 704 (1911), recognizing that vacancies might occur despite "the very best management obtainable"; Chapman v. Cooney, 25 R.I. 657, 57 A. 928 (1904); cf. McDonald v. Lingle, 199 N.C. 219, 220, 153 S.E. 848 (1930). Contra: Humrich v. Dalzell, 113 N.J.Eq. 310, 166 A. 511 (1933).

90. Shaeffer v. Chambers, 6 N.J.Eq. 548, 47 Am.Dec. 211 (1847).

91. Baumgard v. Bowman, 31 Ohio App. 266, 167 N.E. 166 (1928), mortgagee in possession must operate oil wells. But see Engleman Transp. Co. v. Longwell, 48 F. 129 (C.C.Mich. 1880).

gued that "The rule is founded in sound policy, for the reason that the particular items of expenditure, in labor or otherwise, as well as the profits received, are wholly within the knowledge of the mortgagee, and if he is not disposed to render a full and honest account, it would be impossible for the mortgagor to show them, or to establish errors in the mortgagee's account." [92] Another possibility is to allow the mortgagor to hold the mortgagee for the fair rental value as a minimum but, in the alternative, the actual net rents and profits.[93] This would be fair enough in case it were established that the mortgagee had intentionally falsified his accounts. It seems unduly harsh upon the hard luck mortgagee to make him liable for all he makes when successful but to hold him for a fair rental even when unsuccessful. The only possible justification for it would be a very strong policy of discouragement to mortgagees taking possession.

Where the mortgagee has entered believing that he is owner and not mortgagee, although in fact the latter is his status, he will be charged only with the rents actually received. The reason is the obvious unfairness of holding a person to a standard of responsibility based upon a conscious occupation of the property of another when no knowledge of the situation on which the liability is founded exists.[94] On the other hand if possession is taken wrongfully and with knowledge of the wrongfulness the least the mortgagee will be charged with is the rental value.[95]

§ 4.32 Maintenance and Improvements

The duty of the mortgagee in possession to maintain the physical condition of the property reflects the fact that, however precarious his financial condition may be, the mortgagor is the beneficial owner of the premises and, as such, is entitled to protection against depletion of its value. Clearly any acts of destruction of the corpus of the property by the mortgagee will be waste for which he will be accountable.[96] Mismanagement of the property is treated as akin to

92. Sanders v. Wilson, 34 Vt. 318, 321 (1861); Barnett v. Nelson, 54 Iowa, 41, 6 N.W. 49, 37 Am.Rep. 183 (1880); Walter v. Calhoun, 88 Kan. 801, 129 P. 1176 (1913); Miller v. Peter, 184 Mich. 142, 150 N.W. 554 (1915); Liskey v. Snyder, 66 W.Va. 149, 66 S.E. 702 (1927)—accord. See, 46 A.L.R. 138, 153 (1927); 4 Am.St.Rep. 69 (1887). See also Shaeffer v. Chambers, 6 N.J.Eq. 548, 47 Am.Dec. 211 (1847), and Moshier v. Norton, 100 Ill. 63, 69 (1881) contra.

93. This seems to be what was done in Engleman Transportation Co. v. Longwell, 48 F. 129 (C.C.Mich.1880), for after an accounting for net rents and profits, of which there were none, the mortgagee was held for fair rental.

94. Parkinson v. Hanbury, L.R. 2 H.L. 1 (1867). Anglo-Cal. Bank v. Field, 154 Cal. 513, 98 P. 267 (1908); Morris v. Budlong, 78 N.Y. 543 (1879).

95. Sedlak v. Duda, 144 Neb. 567, 13 N.W.2d 892, 154 A.L.R. 490 (1944).

96. American Freehold Land Mortgage Co. v. Pollard, 132 Ala. 155, 32 So. 630 (1902), timber removed; Smith v. Stringer, 228 Ala. 630, 155 So. 85 (1934), grapevines destroyed; Whiting v. Adams, 66 Vt. 679, 30 A. 32, 25

impairment of the property itself and the mortgagee will be charged with damage resulting from it.[97] But the mortgagee's duty goes beyond refraining from actively harming the property. He "is bound to use reasonable means to preserve the estate from loss and injury" [98] and one court has gone so far as to state that the mortgagee must "maintain the mortgaged premises in good condition to prevent its deterioration." [99] He must, therefore, conserve its value by making necessary repairs,[1] and this duty is recognized on the one hand by charging him for any loss that flows from his failure to act [2] and, on the other, by allowing him credit for expenditures in carrying it out.[3]

There are, however, limitations on this. For example, he is not bound to dig into his own pocket and so need not expend more than the rents and profits he receives.[4] Moreover, whatever the language

L.R.A. 598, 44 Am.St.Rep. 875 (1894), timber removed; Sandon v. Hooper, 6 Beav. 246 (1843), cottages torn down; Hansom v. Derby, 2 Vern. 398 (1700), wainscoting destroyed; Brown v. Daniel, 219 N.C. 349, 13 S.E.2d 623 (1941), timber removed. The measure of damages will be the diminution in the value of the estate caused by the destruction, Smith v. Stringer, supra; or, in case there is a severance and sale, either the proceeds or market value of the severed portion, Brown v. Daniel, supra.

97. Baumgard v. Bowman, 31 Ohio App. 266, 167 N.E. 166 (1928). The mortgagee's irresponsibility or mismanagement may also be relieved against by the appointment of a receiver. Harding v. Garber, 20 Okl. 11, 93 P. 539 (1907); Brayton & Lawbaugh v. Monarch Lumber Co., 87 Or. 365, 169 P. 528 (1917), rehearing denied 87 Or. 365, 170 P. 717; Gibson v. Hamiltion & Rourke Co., 21 Wash. 365, 58 P. 217 (1899).

98. Barnard v. Paterson, 137 Mich. 633, 634, 100 N.W. 893 (1904); McCarron v. Cassidy, 18 Ark. 34 (1856); Woodward v. Phillips, 80 Mass. (14 Gray) 132 (1859); Eggensperger v. Lanpher, 92 Minn. 503, 100 N.W. 372 (1904)—accord. See Barthell v. Syverson, 54 Iowa 160, 6 N.W. 178 (1880); 1914, 49 L.R.A.,N.S., 122. Cf. Williams v. Rouse, 124 Ala. 160, 27 So. 16 (1899) (statute); Halbert v. Turner, 233 Ill. 531, 84 N.E. 704 (1908).

99. Landau v. Western Pennsylvania Nat. Bank, 445 Pa. 217, 282 A.2d 335, 339 (1971).

1. Shaeffer v. Chambers, 6 N.J.Eq. 548, 47 Am.Dec. 211 (1847), "a mortgagee in possession is not at liberty to permit the property to go to waste, but is bound to keep it in good ordinary repair; and if it be a farm he is bound to good ordinary husbandry." Scherer v. Bang, 97 N.J.Eq. 497, 500, 128 A. 258, 259 (1925) "such repair as is absolutely necessary for the protection of the estate"; Hirsh v. Arnold, 318 Ill. 28, 148 N.E. 882 (1925).

2. Miller v. Ward, 111 Me. 134, 88 A. 400, 49 L.R.A.,N.S., 122 (1913); see S. P. Wragge v. Denham, 2 Younge & C. 117, 121 (1836); Hughes v. Williams, 12 Ves. 493 (1806); Dexter v. Arnold, 7 Fed.Cas. 597, 604 (1834).

3. Burns v. Williams, 147 Ark. 608, 228 S.W. 726 (1921); Hidden v. Jordan, 28 Cal. 301 (1865); Buettel v. Harmount, 46 Minn. 481, 49 N.W. 250 (1891); Mosier v. Norton, 83 Ill. 519 (1876); Miller v. Curry, 124 Ind. 48, 24 N.E. 219 (1889) rehearing denied 124 Ind. 48, 24 N.E. 374; Wise v. Layman, 197 Ind. 393, 150 N.E. 368 (1925); Gordon v. Krellman, 207 App.Div. 773, 202 N.Y.S. 682 (1924); Lynch v. Ryan, 137 Wis. 13, 118 N.W. 174, 129 Am.St.Rep. 1040 (1908).

4. Fidelity Trust Co. v. Saginaw Hotels Co., 259 Mich. 254, 242 N.W. 906 (1932); Carter v. McMillan, 68 Dom. L.R. 653 (1922). See Dexter v. Arnold, 7 Fed.Cas. 597, 604 (1834).

of the general standard, there is some authority that, the mortgagee does not have to compensate for or prevent depreciation caused by ordinary wear and tear—"the silent effect of waste and decay from time." [5] Indeed, a few cases describe the mortgagee's obligation in terms of "gross negligence" or "recklessness and improvidence." [6] In any event, the mortgagee's liability is governed by the condition of the property as of the time he went into possession.[7]

When it is a question, not of duty to make repairs, but of privilege of doing so, there seems to be considerably more latitude in determining what will constitute necessary repairs than when it is a matter of duty to do so.[8]

A mortgagee who obtains possession wrongfully is not entitled to an allowance for repairs.[9] Normally a mortgagee in possession will not be allowed to make improvements on the property and to charge them to the mortgagor, a rule which is in sharp contrast with that governing repairs.[10] The reason for it is simple and sound. It "is a rule to protect the interests of the mortgagor, and to prevent the mortgagee from rendering it more difficult for the mortgagor to redeem

5. Dexter v. Arnold, 2 Sumn. 108 (1834), Fed.Cas.No. 3,858, Story, J.: Brown v. So. Boston Sav. Bank, 148 Mass. 300, 19 N.E. 382 (1889). See also Russell v. Smithies, 1 Austr. 96 (1792); S. P. Wragge v. Denham, 2 Younge & C. 117, 121 (1836).

6. "But where a mortgagee is guilty of wilful default or gross neglect as to repairs, he is properly responsible for the loss and damage occasioned thereby. * * * And there is the stronger reason for this doctrine because it is also the default of the mortgagor himself, if he does not take care to have suitable repairs made to preserve his own property." Dexter v. Norton, 7 Fed.Cas. 597, 604 (1834). Toole v. Weirick, 39 Mont. 359, 102 P. 590, 133 Am.St.Rep. 567 (1909), mortgagee accountable for depreciation resulting from "the reckless or improvident management of the property."

Other cases laying down the test of "wilful default or gross negligence" include: Dozier v. Mitchell, 65 Ala. 511 (1880); Fidelity Trust Co. v. Saginaw Hotels Co., 259 Mich. 254, 242 N.W. 906 (1932); Mosier v. Norton, 83 Ill. 519 (1876). But in Burnett v. Nelson, 54 Iowa 41, 6 N.W. 49, 37 Am.Rep. 183 (1880), the court said the standard the mortgagee must use in keeping up the premises was ordinary care and he is not exonerated because not guilty of fraud or gross carelessness.

7. Barnard v. Paterson, 137 Mich. 633, 100 N.W. 893 (1904).

8. Gordon v. Krellman, 207 App.Div. 773, 202 N.Y.S. 682 (1924), in which new stoves and other items of a permanent nature put in to obtain tenants on advantageous terms was allowed as repairs. On the other hand, in Fletcher v. Bass River Sav. Bank, 182 Mass. 5, 64 N.E. 207, 94 Am.St. Rep. 632 (1902), repairs made for the purpose of enhancing the sale price but not necessary to preserve it from deterioration for the short period it would be occupied by the mortgagee, although of such a nature as ordinarily would be credited to a mortgagee in possession, were disallowed. Today in Massachusetts, by statute, the mortgagee will be permitted to make "reasonable repairs and improvements." Mass.Gen.Laws Ann. c. 244, § 20; McFarlane v. Thompson, 241 Mass. 486, 135 N.E. 869 (1922).

9. Malone v. Roy, 107 Cal. 518, 40 P. 1040 (1895). See Roberts v. Fleming, 53 Ill. 196 (1870).

10. Sandon v. Hooper, 6 Beav. 246 (1843); Schuetz v. Schuetz, 237 Wis. 1, 296 N.W. 70 (1941), discussed, 40 Mich.L.Rev. 133 (1941). See also authorities cited in following footnotes

the premises".[11] The idea is trenchantly expressed by the statement that to permit it might enable the mortgagee "to improve the mortgagor out of his estate." [12] But the line of demarcation between repairs and improvements is wavering and blurred if not, as has been suggested in criticism of the distinction, fictional.[13] Certainly, the rule against improvements is not inflexible.[14]

Although it would be going too far, perhaps, to discard it altogether and substitute for it as a test "the reasonableness of the mortgagee's action in the light of economic conditions, the probable duration of his possession, and the nature of the property and the mortgagor's interest," there are exceptions to it, or at least cases to which it does not apply.[15] For one thing, if the improvements were made in pursuance of an agreement with the mortgagor or with his consent, either express or implied in fact, there can be no question but that the cost is an allowable item.[16] Credit will be given to a mortgagee who completes an unfinished building in order to make it tenantable, something most beneficial to the mortgagor and something he ought to want to have the mortgagee do.[17] However, the charge is justified, not on the ground of the mortgagor's acquiescence, but because the improvement was necessary to prevent deterioration on the one hand and to make it productive of income on the other, both essential to the protection of the interest of the mortgagor and for that reason chargeable to him as a matter of justice and equity. Similarly, the mortgagee may make reasonable improvements which are fairly and competently undertaken for the maintenance or increased income yield of the property.[18] But the character of the property cannot be

11. Miller v. Ward, 111 Me. 134, 138, 88 A. 400, 402, 49 L.R.A.,N.S., 122 (1913).

12. Burns v. Williams, 147 Ark. 608, 228 S.W. 726 (1921); Kinkead v. Peet, 153 Iowa 199, 132 N.W. 1095 (1911); Cook v. Ottawa University, 14 Kan. 548 (1875); Moore v. Cable, N.Y., 1 Johns.Ch. 385 (1815)—accord.

13. See 35 Col.L.Rev. 1248, 1258 (1935).

14. "This rule [against improvements] is not inflexible, for the allowance may be regulated by the justice and equity arising out of the circumstances of each particular case." Wells v. Van Dyke, 109 Pa. 330, 42 L.I. 345, 16 W.N.C. 151 (1885).

15. 35 Co.L.Rev. 1248, 1259 (1935).
"The rule forbidding an allowance for permanent improvements is not an inflexible one, but is suspended in exceptional cases, if justice and the equity of the case require it. 4 Kent. Com. 167, and note." Morgan v. Walbridge, 56 Vt. 405, 409 (1883).

16. Shellnutt v. Shellnutt, 188 Ga. 306, 3 S.E.2d 900 (1939); Fort v. Colby, 165 Iowa 95, 144 N.W. 393 (1913); McGuire v. Halloran, 182 Iowa 209, 160 N.W. 363 (1917) rehearing denied 182 Iowa 209, 165 N.W. 405; Lynch v. Ryan, 137 Wis. 13, 118 N.W. 174, 129 Am.St.Rep. 1040 (1908). See 49 L.R.A.,N.S., 122, 128 (1913).

17. Miller v. Ward, 111 Me. 134, 88 A. 400, 49 L.R.A.,N.S., 122 (1913); Gilpin v. Brooks, 226 Mass. 322, 115 N.E. 421 (1917).

18. Hays v. Christiansen, 105 Neb. 586, 181 N.W. 379 (1921) new boiler; Gordon v. Krellman, 207 App.Div. 773, 202 N.Y.S. 682 (1924), new ranges and other items of permanent nature to keep tenants and attract new ones, the court classifying them as "repairs"; Wells v. Van Dyke, 109 Pa. 330, 42 L.I. 345, 16 W.N.C. 151 (1885) new improved machinery to

altered. It cannot be made into a new and different thing rather than a better and more productive version of the premises taken over. Still another group of cases in which the mortgagee is allowed credit for improvements is where he is in possession believing in good faith that he is the owner or at least free from the possibility of redemption by the mortgagor whereas in truth all he has in his security interest and therefore has, even though he does not know it, only the rights of a mortgagee in possession.[19]

These cases, in addition to pointing to the good faith[20] by the mortgagee, the beneficial character of the improvements and their reasonableness, stress the fact that the mortgagor stood by in silence without asserting his rights while the improvements were being made. This makes the injustice of permitting him to redeem without paying anything for the value added to his property so clear that the ordinary rule against allowances for improvements will not be followed.[21] This conduct by the mortgagor, it

enable mill to compete successfully with other mills; McFarlane v. Thompson, 241 Mass. 486, 135 N.E. 869 (1922), new cesspool, but statute covered case; Shepard v. Jones, 21 Ch.D. 469 (1882), deepening of well increase sale value although purchaser did not use water supply, mortgagee allowed for increased value.

19. Such cases include those in which the mortgagee purchased at a defective foreclosure sale. McSorley v. Larissa, 100 Mass. 270 (1868); Hicklin v. Marco, 46 F. 424 (C.C.Or.1891), affirmed 56 F. 549, 6 C.C.A. 10 (1893); Bradley v. Snyder, 14 Ill. 263, 58 Am. Dec. 564 (1853); Poole v. Johnson, 62 Iowa 611, 17 N.W. 900 (1883). See Martin v. Ratcliff, 101 Mo. 254, 13 S.W. 1051, 20 Am.St.Rep. 605 (1890) (defective exercise of power of sale); Freichnecht v. Meyer, 39 N.J.Eq. 551 (1885); Green v. Dixon, 9 Wis. 532 (1859) (statute). Cf. McCumber v. Gilman, 15 Ill. 381 (1854). Also those in which he was a grantee under a deed absolute given as security, so that by the form of the transaction he has reason to believe he is owner. Gillis v. Martin, 17 N.C. 470, 25 Am.Dec. 729 (1833); Harper's Appeal, 64 Pa. 315 (1870); Liskey v. Snyder, 66 W. Va. 149, 161, 66 S.E. 702, 708 (1909). Miller v. Curry, 124 Ind. 48, 24 N.E. 219, 374 (1889), contra, in spite of good faith by the mortgagee. Cf. Wilson v. Fisher, 148 N.C. 535, 541, 62 S.E. 622, 624–5 (1908), in which it was held that the appreciation was merely deductible from the charge for rents and profits.

20. Where the mortgagee takes possession wrongfully, claiming to be owner although he knows of the mortgagor's claim, there is an absence of good faith and no allowance will be made. Mahoney v. Bostwick, 96 Cal. 53, 30 P. 1020, 31 Am.St.Rep. 175 (1892); Malone v. Roy, 107 Cal. 518, 40 P. 1040 (1895); Bradley v. Merrill, 88 Me. 319, 34 A. 160 (1896); Dougherty v. McColgan, Md., 6 Gill & J. 275 (1834); Sedlak v. Duda, 144 Neb. 567, 13 N.W.2d 892, 154 A.L.R. 490 (1944); Shelley v. Cody, 187 N.Y. 166, 79 N.E. 994 (1907); Cookes v. Culbertson, 9 Nev. 199 (1874); Witt v. Trustees of Grand Grove of United Ancient Order of Druids, 55 Wis. 376, 13 N.W. 261 (1884). By the weight of authority, constructive notice from a record of the existence of a paramount title or interest does not prevent an occupant from being an improver in good faith. See 68 A.L.R. 288 (1930).

21. Hadley v. Stewart, 65 Wis. 481, 27 N.W. 340 (1886); Morgan v. Walbridge, 56 Vt. 405 (1883); Mickles v. Dillaye, 17 N.Y. 80 (1858). Also, basing the allowance on the fact that the mortgagor had permited a long period to elapse without asserting his rights, see Roberts v. Fleming, 53 Ill. 196 (1870); Montgomery v. Chadwick, 7 Iowa 114 (1858); Miner v. Beekman, 50 N.Y. 337 (1872). See

should be observed, is the foundation for imposing a nonconsensual obligation upon him to prevent unjust enrichment rather than the basis for inferring an implied in fact contract to pay for the improvement. Indeed, in an extreme case, the mortgagor's continued passivity over a long time may be so reprehensible in view of the mortgagee's reliance upon it as to estop the mortgagor altogether from redeeming.[22] And, finally, in some states there are statutory provisions making changes in the rule. Thus in Massachusetts improvements which are "reasonable" may be made and charged to the mortgagor.[23] And in Alabama there is a statute permitting the mortgagee to charge for improvements up to the amount of rents charged against him.[24]

Where the property after improvement has been sold, even though the case does not fall under any of the exceptional situations discussed, since the great objection to allowing the mortgagee to charge for improvements, that it will make redemption more difficult, is not present, there is no reason why there should not be allocated to the mortgagee from the proceeds of the sale the amount the property brings in the market because of the improvement over what it would have sold for without it, and it has been so held.[25]

Where improvements are allowed, how should the credit to the mortgagee be calculated? Where they are allowed because of consent by the mortgagor [26] or in order to make or keep the property tenant-

also Morris v. Budlong, 78 N.Y. 543 (1879). There are, however, some cases that require only that the mortgagee believe that he is the owner and make beneficial improvements in good faith. Hicklin v. Marco, 46 F. 424 (C.C.Or.1891) affirmed 56 F. 549, 6 C.C.A. 10 (1893); Ensign v. Batterson, 68 Conn. 298, 36 A. 51 (1896); Liskey v. Snyder, 66 W.Va. 149, 162, 66 S.E. 702, 708 (1909); Green v. Dixon, 9 Wis. 532 (1859).

22. Ferguson v. Boyd, 169 Ind. 537, 81 N.E. 71 (1907), rehearing denied 169 Ind. 537, 82 N.E. 1064 (1908); Purcell v. Thornton, 128 Minn. 255, 150 N.W. 899 (1915). That mere silence by the mortgagor should not work an estoppel, see Glenn, Mortgages, § 220.1, criticizing Purcell v. Thornton, supra. The estoppel in cases of this sort is against showing that the right of redemption exists, either because the foreclosure was defective or because the transaction, although not in form a mortgage, was so intended by the parties, and not against asserting a redemption right already established. It does not, therefore, violate, technically at least, the rule safeguarding the exercise of the equity of redemption once it has been shown to exist. See Glenn, Mortgages, § 220.1.

23. Mass.Gen.Laws Ann., c. 244 § 20; McFarlane v. Thompson, 241 Mass. 486, 135 N.E. 869 (1922).

24. Dozier v. Mitchell, 65 Ala. 511 (1880). For the statutory rule requiring payment for improvements by a redemptioner from a foreclosure sale, Ala.Code 1958, Tit. 7, §§ 732, 740; Rudisill v. Buckner, 244 Ala. 653, 15 So.2d 333 (1944); Ladd v. Parmer, 278 Ala. 435, 178 So.2d 829 (1965). "Betterment" statutes have been enacted in many states protecting the improver in good faith of another's property. See 30 Col.L.Rev. 575, 576 (1930), on the requirement of good faith under "betterment" statutes.

25. Halbert v. Turner, 233 Ill. 531, 84 N.E. 704 (1908).

26. Lynch v. Ryan, 137 Wis. 13, 19, 118 N.W. 174, 176, 129 Am.St.Rep. 1040 (1908), "where the making of the improvements was authorized or consented to * * * the legitimate basis is the reasonable cost, the same as in repairs. * * *".

able or productive, the amount reasonably expended is the criterion, just as in the analogous case of necessary or authorized repairs.[27] However, where the mortgagee acted under an honest belief that he was the owner, or that the redemption interest was barred or would never be exercised—a belief to which the mortgagor's conduct usually contributes—an entirely different principle is operative. It purpose is the prevention of unjust enrichment due to justifiable misreliance because of mistake. Consequently the value added to the property by the improvement, not to exceed its actual cost, is the proper measure of recovery and the one recognized by the courts in such cases.[28] Incidentally, it may be remarked, that the quasi-contractual measure of recovery recognized in these cases is additional proof that the relief is non-consensual and not based upon any theory of implied in fact agreement by the mortgagor to pay for them.

Where the mortgagee is not allowed any charge for improvements, since the mortgagee is going to lose his capital investment, it seems unfair to charge him for any rent other than for the property without the improvement, and this has been held to be the rule.[29] Or, reaching a somewhat similar result when the mortgagee was charged with the full rental value of the property as improved, as an offset, he was held to be entitled to interest upon the cost of the improvement.[30] Indeed, going beyond this, there is authority that, although the full value of the improvement cannot be allowed, the mortgagee will be able to recoup so much of its value as will be covered by the net income of the property for which he is chargeable.[31]

Where the mortgagee is permitted to charge for the improvements, "no interest should be allowed the [mortgagee] appellant on the value of his improvements, as he has had the use of them, and,

27. E. g., Miller v. Ward, 111 Me. 134, 139, 88 A. 400, 402, 49 L.R.A.,N.S., 122 (1913), "the money expended * * * was a proper charge"; Hays v. Christiansen, 105 Neb. 586, 181 N.W. 379 (1921); Gordon v. Krellman, 207 App.Div. 773, 202 N.Y. S. 682 (1924).

28. See Ladd v. Parmer, 278 Ala. 435, 178 So.2d 829 (1965); Hadley v. Stewart, 65 Wis. 481, 485, 27 N.W. 340, 342 (1886), "the sum the improvements enhanced the value of the whole premises, and not their cost, in case the cost exceeds the value which they have added to the premises."; Mickles v. Dillaye, 17 N.Y. 80, 93 (1858), "he should be required to make equitable compensation for the benefits he will receive from the improvements." ; see quotation, s. c., supra, § 169 note 26. Merriam v. Goss, 139 Mass. 77, 28 N.E. 449 (1885); Halbert v. Turner, 233 Ill. 531, 84 N.E. 704 (1908); Moore's Guardian v. Williamson's Ex'r, 201 Ky. 561, 257 S.W. 711 (1923); Howard v. Clark, 72 Vt. 429, 48 A. 656 (1900); see 49 L.R.A.,N.S., 122, 129.

29. Bradley v. Merrill, 91 Me. 340, 40 A. 132 (1898); Gresham v. Ware, 79 Ala. 192; see 49 L.R.A.,N.S., 122, 130 (1885).

30. Lynch v. Ryan, 137 Wis. 13, 118 N.W. 174, 129 Am.St.Rep. 1040 (1908).

31. Dozier v. Mitchell, 65 Ala. 511 (1880); Montgomery v. Chadwick, 7 Iowa 114, 7 Clarke 114 (1858); Wilson v. Fisher, 148 N.C. 535, 62 S.E. 622 (1908).

under the rule of estimating the rent * * * he will not be charged any rent for the use of his improvements." [32]

§ 4.33 Compensation for Services

If the circumstances are such that an owner would be reasonable in employing someone to take care of the premises and do such things as collecting the rents, the mortgagee in possession may hire it done and charge the expense to the mortgagor.[33] However, many American authorities hold that, even though the situation is such that the mortgagee could have hired someone else, he cannot do the job himself and charge the mortgagor compensation or commissions for so doing.[34] One reason advanced is that the mortgagee in possession is comparable to a trustee,[35] and the courts do not want the fiduciary relation which exists under such circumstances to be permitted with the mortgagee having a selfish interest adverse to that of the mortgagor. The interest of the mortgagor is in having the work done for as little as possible; the interest of the employee, is in getting paid as much as possible. The rule as to trustees, however, has been changed either by statute or decision, and since admittedly the mortgagee situation is a weaker one for imposing the restriction, it should be abandoned there also.[36] Another reason given for denying the mortgagee compensation is that he is in possession solely for his benefit and consequently there is no foundation for implying in fact any agreement to charge or to impose a quasi-contractual obligation on the mortgagor.[37] But an answer to this is that the care and man-

32. Hadley v. Stewart, 65 Wis. 481, 27 N.W. 340 (1886); Howard v. Clark, 72 Vt. 429, 48 A. 656 (1900); Poole v. Johnson, 62 Iowa 611, 17 N.W. 900 (1883); see Lynch v. Ryan, supra note 30, 49 L.R.A.,N.S., 122, 130.

33. Turner v. Johnson, 95 Mo. 431, 7 S.W. 570, 6 Am.St.Rep. 62 (1888); Johnson v. Hosford, 110 Ind. 572, 10 N.E. 407 (1887), rehearing denied 110 Ind. 572, 12 N.E. 522; see Harper v. Ely, 70 Ill. 581 (1873). But in American Freehold Land Mort. Co. v. Pollard, 132 Ala. 155, 32 So. 630 (1902), although the mortgagor had voluntarily given possession to a non-resident corporation mortgagee, the court refused to recognize that fact of non-residence as sufficient reason to allow payment of agents to collect the rents.

34. Barnard v. Paterson, 137 Mich. 633, 100 N.W. 893 (1904); Lynch v. Ryan, 137 Wis. 13, 118 N.W. 174 (1908); Wadleigh v. Phelps, 149 Cal. 627, 87 P. 93 (1906); Shaw v. G. B. Beaumont Co., 88 N.J.Eq. 333, 102 A. 151, 2 A.L.R. 122 (1917); Moore v. Cable, 1 Johns.Ch. 385 (N.Y.1815). His own out of pocket expenses incurred in management and collection do not fall under the ban. Harper v. Ely, 70 Ill. 581 (1873); Turk v. Page, 64 Okl. 251, 167 P. 462. See 170 A. L.R. 181 (1917).

35. Bonithron v. Hockmore, 1 Vern. 316 (1685). See Green v. Lamb, 24 Hun 87, 89 (N.Y.1881), "the mortgagee in possession is classed with a trustee; and it is said that neither was entitled to commissions. Plainly the law is changed as to a trustee."

36. In re Hemphill's Estate, 157 Wis. 331, 147 N.W. 1089 (1914); see Green v. Lamb, note 35, supra; Scott, Trusts, § 242.

37. Benham v. Rowe, 2 Cal. 387, 408, 56 Am.Dec. 342 (1852), "his care and trouble are bestowed for the furtherance and protection of his own interests."; Barnard v. Paterson, 137 Mich. 633, 100 N.W. 893 (1904).

agement of the premises is also necessary to preserve the value of the mortgagor's redemption interest.[38]

Other courts permit compensation to the mortgagee. Massachusetts and a few other states allow the mortgagee a reasonable commission for his services.[39] Still others leave the setting of compensation to the discretion of the court.[40]

§ 4.34 Reimbursement for Insurance and Taxes

Today the usual mortgage contains a clause requiring the mortgagor to keep the premises insured for the benefit of the mortgagee, or, more commonly, as their interest shall appear. If there is such a contractual duty and the mortgagor fails to insure, the mortgagee is privileged to do it and charge the expense thereof to the mortgagor as an addition to the mortgage debt.[41] In the absence of such agreement or an authorization by the mortgagor, some older cases hold that a mortgagee may not insure the mortgaged premises and charge the mortgagor.[42] It has been pointed out, however, that some of these authorities represent an attitude toward insurance out of harmony with present day notions, while others are those in which the mortgagee insured only his own interest.[43] Trustees today have a duty to keep trust property insured and are surcharged in their accounts if they do not do so and a loss occurs.[44] The same duty should apply to a mortgagee in possession. As was pointed out in a leading case, "in the light of modern ideas in respect to the reasonable care of property by one in possession thereof in the nature of trustee for another, having a duty or authority to preserve the same, reasonable expenditures for insurance are as legitimate as such expenditures for repairs and to prevent loss by decay or destruction or otherwise." [45]

38. See 24 Col.L.Rev. 318, 319 (1924).

39. See MacNeil Bros. Co. v. Cambridge Sav. Bank, 334 Mass. 360, 135 N.E.2d 652 (1956); Van Vronker v. Eastman, 48 Mass. (7 Met.) 157 (1843); Barry v. Dow, 240 Mass. 419, 134 N.E. 367 (1922); Barry v. Harlowe, 242 Mass. 159, 136 N.E. 105 (1922), possession by consent does not alter the rule; Waterman v. Curtis, 26 Conn. 241 (1857); Bradley v. Merrill, 91 Me. 340, 40 A. 132 (1898).

40. Walter v. Calhoun, 88 Kan. 801, 129 P. 1176 (1913); Massari v. Girardi, 119 Misc. 607, 197 N.Y.S. 751 (1922).

41. Baker v. Aalberg, 183 Ill. 258, 55 N.E. 672 (1899); Jehle v. Brooks, 112 Mich. 131, 70 N.W. 440 (1897); Sanford v. Litchenberger, 62 Neb. 501, 57 N.W. 305 (1901); Hays v. Christiansen, 114 Neb. 764, 209 N.W. 609 (1926). See 20 St. John's L.Rev. 59 (1945).

42. Curtis v. Curtis, 180 Ala. 70, 60 So. 165 (1912); Barnett v. Nelson, 54 Iowa 41, 6 N.W. 49, 37 Am.Rep. 183 (1880); Saunders v. Frost, 22 Mass. (5 Pick.) 259, 16 Am.Dec. 394 (1827); Faure v. Winans, N.Y., 1 Hopk.Ch. 283, 14 Am.Dec. 545 (1824); see United States Trust Co. v. Miller, 116 Neb. 25, 29, 215 N.W. 462, 469 (1927).

43. See Glenn, Mortgages, § 213. Miller v. Ward, 111 Me. 134, 88 A. 400, 49 L.R.A.,N.S., 122 (1913), policy in mortgagee's own name; Wise v. Layman, 197 Ind. 393, 150 N.E. 368 (1926), no showing that payment would be other than to mortgagee's personal favor.

44. Restatement, Second, Trusts § 176; Scott, Trusts, § 176.

45. Lynch v. Ryan, 137 Wis. 13, 23, 118 N.W. 174, 178, 129 Am.St.Rep. 1040 (1908). cf. Land Finance Corp. v. Giorgio, 280 N.Y.S. 924 (1935).

It has been urged that the duty or privilege of insuring should extend beyond that against the hazard of fire to any kind that a reasonable person [46] in charge of his own property would take out. In this connection, some courts have allowed the mortgagee reimbursement for premiums on "property owners liability" insurance.[47]

A mortgagor in possession has the duty of paying all taxes on the mortgaged property.[48] If he fails to do so the law is well settled that the mortgagee may pay them to protect his security interest in the land.[49] If the property has been sold for taxes, the mortgagee may redeem it from the tax sale. In either event he may add the amounts so expended to the mortgage debt.[50] If the mortgagee is in possession, there is a duty upon him, at least to the extent of rents and profits received, to pay taxes.[51] But, since the payment nevertheless inures to the benefit of the mortgagor, the beneficial owner of the property, he can in such cases also demand credit for the payment and add it to his claim.[52] Consequently, whether the payment is made by a mortgagee in possession or out of possession the right clearly is one for reimbursement on quasi-contractual principles because of the benefit conferred upon the mortgagor in relieving his

46. Glenn, Mortgages, § 213.

47. See e. g., State Realty Co. of Boston Inc. v. MacNeil Bros. Co., 334 Mass. 294, 135 N.E.2d 291 (1956); MacNeil Bros. Co. v. Cambridge Sav. Bank, 334 Mass. 360, 135 N.E.2d 652 (1956).

48. Dayton v. Rice, 47 Iowa 429 (1877); Pines v. Novick, 168 App.Div. 155, 153 N.Y.S. 891 (1915).

49. See, e. g., Eisen v. Kostakos, 116 N.J.Super. 358, 282 A.2d 421 (1971).

50. Eisen v. Kostakos, 116 N.J.Super. 358, 282 A.2d 421 (1971); see collection of cases, 60 A.L.R. 425 (1929); 84 A.L.R. 1366 (1933); 123 A.L.R. 1248. The rule extends to cases where taxes were paid in the mistaken belief, bona fide, that the payor held a mortgage on the land. Central Wisconsin Tr. Co. v. Swenson, 222 Wis. 331, 267 N.W. 307, 106 A.L.R. 1207 (1936); see 84 A.L.R. 1366, 1371, 1372 (1933); 123 A.L.R. 1248, 1250, 1252, 1253 (1939). A first mortgagee who pays taxes can add the amount paid to his debt in priority to a second mortgagee. Wiggin v. Lowell Five Cent Sav. Bank, 299 Mass. 518, 13 N.E.2d 433 (1938). Additional authorities include Redic v. Mechanics & Farmers Bank, 241 N.C. 152, 84 S.E.2d 542 (1954), discussed in Third Annual Survey of North Carolina Case Law: Credit Transactions, 34 N.C.L.Rev. 36 (1955); Crofts v. Johnson, 6 Utah 2d 350, 313 P.2d 808 (1957). Although the mortgaged property becomes security for the right to reimbursement for delinquent taxes paid by the mortgagee, this right of repayment is separate and apart from the original mortgage debt. Equitable Life Assurance Soc. of the United States v. Bennion, 81 Idaho 445, 346 P.2d 1053 (1959).

51. Brown v. Simons, 44 N.H. 475 (1863); Shoemaker v. Commonwealth Bank, 15 Pa. 297, 11 W.N.C. 284, 39 L.I. 81 (1881); Ten Eyck v. Craig, 62 N.Y. 406 (1875). Cf. Eisen v. Kostakos, 116 N.J.Super. 358, 282 A.2d 421 (1971).

52. Eisen v. Kostakos, 116 N.J.Super. 358, 282 A.2d 421 (1971); Hays v. Christiansen, 114 Neb. 764, 209 N.W. 609 (1926); Wise v. Layman, 197 Ind. 393, 399, 150 N.E. 368, 371 (1926); Brown v. Berry, 89 N.J.Eq. 230, 236, 108 A. 51, 54 (1918); Johns v. Moore, 168 Cal.App.2d 709, 336 P.2d 579 (1959); United States v. Bond, 172 F. Supp. 759 (E.D.Va.1959), reversed 279 F.2d 837 (C.A.1960), certiorari denied 364 U.S. 895, 81 S.Ct. 220, 5 L.Ed.2d 189.

property of the charge upon it for taxes.[53] However, it is a right which inures to him only in his capacity as mortgagee, for, were it not for the mortgage relationship, the rule would apply that "the payment of the taxes of one man by another without some request, express or implied, would be such a voluntary payment as would not support an action." [54]

Although this is true, it would be in accord with ordinary rules of restitution to permit the right to be enforced either by subrogation to the rights of the taxing power [55] or by a direct independent action, as well as by doing the same thing, in effect, by adding the amount onto the sum of the mortgage debt and treating the mortgage as securing the enlarged sum. Nevertheless, it is also the clear weight of authority that "this claim must be enforced as a part of the mortgage debt, and cannot be made the basis of an independent action against the mortgagor, as for money paid to his use, * * * or * * * by virtue of the law of subrogation." [56] In other words, the mortgagor is limited to reimbursement as part of the action of foreclosure or redemption. The explanation given for this rule is that the amount due for taxes, together with the amount due on the mortgage, constitutes a single, indivisible debt, and "could become a lien only in connection with and because of the mortgage, and could not exist independent of it" and consequently, mortgagees "could not at pleasure split up their demand and make the parts the subjects of separate suits." [57] The plain answer to this is that the debt claim itself is a contract claim and the mortgage securing it is the result of a consensual transaction, while the claim for reimbursement for taxes paid is clearly nonconsensual as is the lien on the property to secure it. It is true that the mortgage must exist, or be honestly thought to exist, at the time of payment in order for the mortgagee not to be classed as a

53. See 90 U.Pa.L.Rev. 90 (1941).

54. Horrigan v. Wellmuth, 77 Mo. 542, 545 (1883).

55. For general collections of cases on the right of subrogation to the right of the taxing power by one who pays taxes, see 61 A.L.R. 587, 601 (1929), payment by mortgagees; 106 A.L.R. 1212, 1217 (1937), payment by mortgagees.

56. Home Owners' Loan Corp. v. Joseph, 306 Ill.App. 244, 28 N.E.2d 330 (1940); Criswell v. McKnight, 120 Neb. 317, 232 N.W. 586, 84 A.L.R. 1361 (1930); The Praetorians v. State, 53 S.W.2d 334 (Tex.Civ.App.1932); Vincent v. Moore, 51 Mich. 618, 17 N.W. 81 (1883); Eblen v. Major's Admr., 147 Ky. 44, 143 S.W. 748 (1912); Stone v. Tilley, 100 Tex. 487, 101 S.W. 201, 10 L.R.A.,N.S., 678, 123 Am.St.Rep. 819, 15 Ann.Cas. 524 (1907). See 1907, 10 L.R.A.,N.S. 679. But see Childs v. Smith, 51 Wash. 457, 99 P. 304, 130 Am.St.Rep. 1107 (1909). Cf. Hill v. Townley, 1891, 45 Minn. 167, 47 N.W. 653 (1891); 84 A.L.R. 1366, 1387 (1933); 123 A.L.R. 1248, 1256 (1939). And, it has been reasoned, that since the mortgagee cannot have an independent action against the mortgagor, even more clearly he should be denied independent relief against a non-assuming grantee of the mortgagor. Citizens Sav. Bank v. Guar. Loan Co., 62 R.I. 448, 6 A.2d 688, 123 A.L.R. 1236 (1939); cf. Conaty v. Guar. Loan Co., 62 R.I. 470, 6 A.2d 698 (1939), noted and criticized, 53 Harv.L.Rev. 144 (1939).

57. Vincent v. Moore, 51 Mich. 618, 17 N.W. 81 (1883).

volunteer and denied recovery altogether. But the existence of the mortgage as a necessary condition to the creation of the non-consensual right to restitution obviously does not make the right so created an integral part of his mortgage debt claim. Rather the rule would seem to rest upon the practical ground that it is so intimately, if not indissolubly, connected with the mortgage debt that the whole matter should be, as a matter of expediency and fairness to the mortgagor, settled in the one suit in which the mortgage debt is enforced; the mortgagee should not be permitted inexcusable tardiness in not presenting his demand at the time the entire transaction was in issue.

So viewed, the rule seems a sound one, certainly as to all taxes paid before the foreclosure decree. If this is the proper basis it should not be applied mechanically. Independent recovery should be and has been permitted where payment is made (1) after entry of a foreclosure decree;[58] (2) after the debt claim has been barred by a statute of limitations or non-claim;[59] or (3) in other situations where hardship on the mortgagee justifies departure from the rule.[60]

§ 4.35 Annual Rests

Rents received by a mortgagee in possession are not automatically applied on the mortgage debt or the interest on it. Before any of the income received by him is appropriated to such a purpose there must be, as was seen, an accounting in which the mortgagee's allowable expenses and charges are first set-off against what he has taken in, and such an accounting is had only when there is either an action to foreclose or to redeem.[61] Consequently the mortgagor cannot omit payments of interest or installments of principal on the ground that the mortgagee has in his hands income from the property more than sufficient to cover them.[62] However, an accounting is a matter of equitable set-off. So when it is taken there is no inherent difficulty in balancing off as of a prior date, if that be desirable, the net rents as they would have been at that time in payment or reduction of princi-

58. Hogg v. Longstreth, 97 Pa. 255, 10 W.N.C. 95 (1881); New Haven Sav. Bank v. Atwater, 51 Conn. 429 (1883); Mut. Life Ins. Co. v. Newell, 78 Hun 293, 28 N.Y.S. 913 (1894), affirmed without opinion, 144 N.Y. 627, 39 N.E. 494. See 90 U.Pa.L.Rev. 90, 93 (1941).

59. Federal Land Bank of Columbia v. Brooks, 139 Fla. 506, 190 So. 737 (1939) noted with approval, 17 N.Y. Univ.L.Q.Rev. 295 (1939), subrogation to lien of state for taxes paid; Catlin v. Mills, 140 Wash. 1, 247 P. 1013, 47 A.L.R. 545 (1926), quasi-contractual recovery; Hill v. Townley, 45 Minn. 167, 47 N.W. 653 (1891), contra.

60. White v. First Nat. Bank, 24 F. Supp. 290 (D.C.Pa.1938); Dunlop v. James, 174 N.Y. 411, 67 N.E. 60 (1903). See cases in two preceding footnotes. See also 123 A.L.R. 1248, 1256 (1939); 17 N.Y.Univ.L.Q.Rev. 295, 297 notes 16, 17 (1939); Restatement, Restitution, § 104, comment *a*, illustration 3.

61. Eisen v. Kostakos, 116 N.J.Super. 358, 282 A.2d 421 (1971); Onderdonk v. Gray, 19 N.J.Eq. 65 (1868); Landau v. Western Pennsylvania Nat. Bank, 445 Pa. 217, 282 A.2d 335 (1971).

62. 4 American Law of Property § 16.-105 (1952) (quoted in Eisen v. Kostakos, supra note 61).

pal and income. And, quite obviously, there would be injustice to the mortgagor if, in any one year, the mortgagee has in his hands a surplus of income over outgo which might be used to pay interest and also to reduce part of the principal debt so that the interest on it for the ensuing year would be less, and it were not so credited. One way of handling such a situation would be to compute on the one side, interest on the debt for the entire period without annual rests together with interest on the various items of expenses allowed to the mortgagee as they accrued, while on the other he would be charged interest on the rents and profits as and when received down to the date of the accounting.[63] Most courts, however, when an account is taken, meet the problem by ordering annual rests in all cases where the net income is in excess of the annual interest.[64] An unsurpassed and frequently quoted statement of this method is that of the great Shaw, C. J., who said, "1. State the gross rents received by the defendant to the end of the first year. 2. State the sums paid by him for repairs, taxes, and a commission for collecting the rents,[65] and deduct the same from the gross rents, and the balance will show the net rents to the end of the year. 3. Compute the interest on the note for one year and add it to the principal, and the aggregate will show the amount due thereon at the end of the year. 4. If the net annual rent exceeds the year's interest on the note, deduct that rent from the amount due, and the balance will show the amount remaining due at the end of the year. 5. At the end of the second year go through the same process, taking the amount due at the beginning of the year as the new capital to compute the year's interest upon. So to the time of judgment." [66]

G. RECEIVERSHIPS

§ 4.36 General Considerations

An equitable receivership normally entails the judicial appointment of a third party to take possession of the mortgaged property to repair or preserve the property and to collect rents. As the following sections will indicate, the grounds for the appointment of a receiver and the scope of a receivership vary substantially from jurisdiction to jurisdiction. Nevertheless, mortgagees generally prefer a receiver-

63. Keeline v. Clark, 132 Iowa 360, 106 N.W. 257 (1906); Morrow v. Turney's Adm'r, 35 Ala. 131 (1859); Walter v. Calhoun, 88 Kan. 801, 129 P. 1176 (1913); cf. Green v. Westcott, 13 Wis. 606 (1861).

64. See, e. g., MacNeil Bros. Co. v. Cambridge Sav. Bank, 334 Mass. 360, 135 N.E.2d 652 (1956).

65. In Massachusetts commissions are allowed. See supra, § 4.33. Of course where not allowed this item would not be deducted.

66. Van Vronker v. Eastman, 48 Mass. (7 Metc.) 157, 163 (1843). Gladding v. Warner, 36 Vt. 54 (1863); Adams v. Sayre, 76 Ala. 509 (1884); MacNeil Bros. Co. v. Cambridge Sav. Bank, 334 Mass. 360, 135 N.E.2d 652 (1956). For further consideration of problems incident to annual rests, see Osborne, Mortgages §§ 175–176 (2d Ed. 1970).

ship over attempting to obtain possession of the mortgaged premises as a mortgagee in possession, even where the latter remedy is available.

The reasons for this preference are not difficult to understand. A title state mortgagee, as we have seen, in theory may successfully obtain possession by an action at law for ejectment. However, this action may sometimes be drawn out and time consuming whereas a receiver may usually be appointed incident to a judicial foreclosure suit. Moreover, by utilizing a receivership, a mortgagee avoids some of the strict accounting responsibilities that, as we have previously noted,[67] are associated with being a mortgagee in possession. While a "mortgagee in possession must credit on the mortgage debt not only all the net rents received, but also all the rents that he might have received by the exercise of reasonable diligence," [68] the mortgagee under a receivership need not shoulder that burden. Moreover, the receivership generally will insulate the mortgagee from tort and related landowner-type liabilities that, as we have seen,[69] are normally imposed on the mortgagee in possession. Finally, of course, in lien theory states, the availability of a receivership may be even more important to the mortgagee because of the unavailability of ejectment as a possessory remedy.

§ 4.37 Basis for Appointment—Title and Lien Jurisdictions

In states following the title theory, and in the intermediate states on default, no question arises as to the right of the mortgagee to take possession and with it the fruits of possession, the rents and profits of the land. Both the corpus and the income from it are part of his security by the creation of the mortgage, and no additional agreements are necessary either to give him the right to possession or the rents of the land that go with it. Earlier we saw that equity, although it would enjoin acts by the mortgagor that would imperil the adequacy of the mortgagee's security before foreclosure and in extreme cases might appoint a receiver, nevertheless took this latter step with the greatest reluctance. In general the court of equity took the position that either the legal remedy of obtaining possession or equitable remedies [70] restraining harmful conduct by the mortgagor were sufficient protection to the mortgagee.[71]

67. See §§ 4.30–4.35, supra.

68. Kratovil, Mortgages—Problems in Possession, Rents, and Mortgagee Liability, 11 DePaul L.Rev. 1, 7 (1961).

69. See § 4.29, supra.

70. See § 4.10, supra.

71. That the chancellor would not appoint a receiver to sequestrate rents and profits preceding foreclosure, Cortelyeu v. Hathaway, 11 N.J.Eq. 39, 64 Am.Dec. 478 (1855); Williams v. Robinson, 16 Conn. 517 (1844); Morrison v. Buckner, Fed.Cas. 9,844 (C.C.Ark.1843). Cf. the early New York rule. Bank of Ogdensburgh v. Arnold, 5 Paige (N.Y.) 38 (1835).

Under early title state decisions, receivership was denied even as an incident to a judicial foreclosure action. The mortgagee was left to his remedies at law. The courts insisted they were adequate despite the facts (1) that ejectment was so far from expeditious that the foreclosure action might well be concluded first, (2) that when pursued it had the unfortunate consequence of destroying leases subordinate to the mortgage and saddling the mortgagee with the hazard and burden of making new agreements for keeping the premises productive of income, and (3) that it subjected the mortgagee to an intentionally severe and strict accounting.[72]

What then will induce a court in a title jurisdiction to appoint a receiver of rents and profits in a foreclosure action? The clue to the solution may be found in the reason invoked in lien jurisdictions to give to the mortgagee a claim to the rents and profits prior to the sale on foreclosure. That reasoning has been expressed by an able court thus: "There can be no doubt, that in a proper case where a bill was filed for specific performance of a contract to convey land, the court might appoint a receiver of the rents accruing during the pendency of the action, for equity treats that as done which ought to be done, and, therefore, considers a conveyance as made at the time when it ought to have been made, and the rents as belonging in equity, to the vendee from the time when he became entitled to the conveyance. On the same principle it may deem the foreclosure of a mortgage completed as of the time when the mortgagee becomes entitled to it. The legal right to the rents, as well as to the possession, continues in the mortgagor until foreclosure and sale, as it does in a vendor until conveyance. But when default has been made in the condition of the mortgage, the mortgagee at once becomes entitled to a foreclosure of the mortgage and a sale of the mortgaged premises. *This process requires time,* and on general principles of equity, the court may make the decree, when obtained, relate back to the time of the commencement of the action, *and where necessary for the security of the mortgage debt,* may appoint a receiver of the rents and profits accruing in the meantime, thus anticipating the decree and sale." [73]

That sort of reasoning, of course, would be applicable in a title jurisdiction just as much as in a lien jurisdiction provided it were needed, or as an additional ground even if it is not needed. And, in fact, that reasoning is not necessary in title jurisdictions to establish a substantive right in the mortgagee to the rents and profits for he has that right as part of his security from the outset, as was previ-

72. See Tefft, The Myth of Strict Foreclosure, 4 U. of Chi.L.Rev. 575, 582, 591 (1937).

73. Hollenbeck v. Donell, 94 N.Y. 342, 347 (1884), opinion by Rapallo, J. The order of the quotation has been altered. The italics are the author's. Bank of Ogdensburgh v. Arnold, 5 Paige 38 (N.Y.1838), was the earlier New York case relied upon. To the same effect is the opinion of Groner, J., in Totten v. Harlowe, 67 App.D.C. 132, 90 F.2d 377, 111 A.L.R. 726 (1937), certiorari denied 301 U.S. 711, 57 S.Ct. 945, 81 L.Ed. 1364.

ously noted. But entirely apart from the question of substantive right to the income the property produces as distinct from the property itself, it nevertheless has pertinency on the point of getting the aid of equity in reaching all the property he is entitled to reach, and of getting it in the foreclosure action itself, i. e., on whether his legal remedy is adequate. It should be as true in a title state as in a lien state that, on default and the beginning of a foreclosure action, the mortgagee is entitled to have applied to his claim as of the date of the beginning of his action all of the property to which he has a right as security, regardless of how that right originated, provided that property is *necessary* to the satisfaction of his claim. To get the aid of equity in the form of a receivership the mortgagee must show that there is a genuine danger that his security will be inadequate without the rents and profits. When he does make such a showing this will be sufficient to make the court undertake the preservation of the entire security through a receivership.[74] When there is a real need for equity's aid all talk of the courts about the mortgagee's remedies at law being adequate are either forgotten or recognized as patently untrue. Further, when the mortgagor is in default and the mortgagee has actually started his realization on the mortgage, the policy which operates in favor of leaving the mortgagor in possession of the property and enjoyment of the rents and profits, a policy that finds expression in title states in holding the remedies of the mortgagee adequate when the contrary is true, and in deterring the exercise of the right by imposing burdensome duties of accountability, is largely vitiated.

While it would appear, based on the foregoing, that inadequacy of the security without the rents and profits should be a sufficent basis for the appointment of a receiver in a title jurisdiction, title states in fact often impose additional requirements such as mortgagor insolvency and "some additional, distinct, equitable ground, such as danger of loss, waste, destruction, or serious impairment of the property." [75]

In jurisdictions following the lien theory the main obstacle to the appointment of a receiver is the mortgagor's right to possession until foreclosure. We have seen that this right is founded upon a policy so strong that a few states even strike down agreements permitting the

74. See Tefft, Receivers and Leases Subordinate to the Mortgage, 2 U. of Chi.L.Rev. 33 (1934).

75. Grether v. Nick, 193 Wis. 503, 508, 213 N.W. 304, 306 (1927). Although the quotation is from a decision in a lien state, it states correctly the requirements which are usually expressed to be essential in all jurisdictions. First Nat. Bank of Joliet v. Illinois Steel Co., 174 Ill. 140, 51 N.E. 200 (1898); Cortelyeu v. Hathaway, 11 N.J.Eq. 39 (1855) (inadequacy and insolvency not sufficient); Broad etc., Bank v. Larsen, 88 N.J.Eq. 245, 102 A. 265 (1917); Totten v. Harlowe, 67 App.D.C. 132, 90 F.2d 377, 111 A.L.R. 726 (1937), are other cases laying down requirements beyond inadequacy of the security.

mortgagee to have possession.[76] On the other hand, the principal difficulty encountered in title states is not present here. That is the objection that the mortgagee has a remedy to get possession which is normally considered adequate. The mortgagee in lien jurisdictions has no remedy to get possession.

The first problem is to find any basis of right in the lien state mortgagee to have the rents and profits of the land, the fruits of possession. This basis must be found in the face of the conflicting right, founded on strong policy, of the mortgagor to have them until foreclosure sale. In the preceding discussion of the situation in title states we considered, incidentally, the theories on which such a right is grounded. As was seen, the common and best explanation is the time lag between the commencement of his action to realize on the security to which he is entitled on default and his ultimate success in that action. We also saw that another basis was offered, either as a supplement or a substitute. It stresses wrongful conduct by the mortgagor in impairing the *res* to which the mortgagee is entitled, or threatening to do so by active misconduct or neglect. Such wrongdoing arguably makes it reasonable to give the mortgagee the yield of the *res* as a sort of compensatory substitute.

The question arises as to why, if it is admitted that the mortgagee has a right on one or the other or both of these lines of reasoning, the lack of a legal remedy to enforce the right—a lack which clearly exists—should not be sufficient to invoke the desired aid of equity. Normally if there is a right but no remedy at law, equity will supply the deficiency. But here something more is required. Generally, just as in title states, the courts in lien states find that additional something in inadequacy of the security in relation to the debt.[77] And the reason is not hard to find. Not only does the receivership fly in the face of policy favoring the mortgagor but it imposes a heavy administrative burden upon chancery which it undertakes reluctantly. Furthermore, receiverships are more costly than if the mortgagor managed the property himself.[78] This is true even if competent receivers are appointed, something which is more than dubious. Consequently it is understandable that equity will not grant the relief unless it is *necessary* to the mortgagee's payment, i. e., unless there is actual or threatened inadequacy of security to meet the debt.

76. See Geraldson, Clauses Increasing the Possessory Rights of Mortgagees, 10 Wis.L.Rev. 492 (1935).

77. See Title Insurance Co. v. California Development Co., 164 Cal. 58, 127 P. 502 (1912).

78. For an example of the difference of cost of administering the property by a receiver as contrasted, for example, with a mortgagee in possession, see Wolkenstein v. Slonim, 355 Ill. 306, 189 N.E. 312 (1934). See also Folk v. U. S., 233 F. 177, 147 C.C.A. 183 (Okl.1916); 50 Yale L.Jour. 1424, 1447; Carey and Brabner-Smith, Studies in Realty Mortgage Foreclosures: III. Receiverships, 27 Ill.L.Rev. 717, 753 (1933).

However, inadequacy of security is not the only condition precedent to the appointment of a lien state receiver. Some courts, for example, maintain that "a mortgagee is not entitled to a receiver if the security is adequate and no waste is threatened." [79] Other jurisdictions specify three requirements. For example, Minnesota decisions require proof that "(1) the mortgagor is insolvent; (2) the mortgagor was committing waste; and (3) the value of the security is inadequate to cover the mortgage debt." [80]

These additional requirements need closer examination. While insolvency of the mortgagor is often stressed in the cases as a condition precedent to a receivership [80a] a good argument can be made that it should be irrelevant. The creditor who takes security is entitled to rely upon it exclusively for the payment of the entire debt without resorting to other assets of the mortgagor, if he so wishes, because that is why he took it in the first place. It is quite true that a solvent mortgagor will pay the debt to save the property if it is worth more than the mortgage debt. And it is equally true that a solvent mortgagor usually will pay the debt even though the property is worth less than the mortgage debt, for in this latter case he would have to pay the difference anyway through a deficiency judgment against him with the property normally bringing, on a forced foreclosure sale, less than the mortgagor could dispose of it for should he redeem. Consequently it would be an extraordinary case in which the question of receivership would arise unless the mortgagor was insolvent. Nonetheless it arguably ought to be no part of the mortgagee's case to have to establish insolvency as a condition to his relief.

The waste requirement is subject to a variety of interpretations.[80b] For example, to the extent that waste simply means conduct that impairs the mortgagee's security, it really is not a separate requirment. Moreover, courts sometimes will characterize as waste the failure to pay taxes or insurance premiums.[81] Also, mere neglect that causes rapid deterioration of the property has been classified as

79. Dart v. Western Sav. & Loan Ass'n., 103 Ariz. 170, 438 P.2d 407 (1968).

80. Mutual Benefit Life Ins. Co. v. Frantz Klodt & Son, Inc., 237 N.W.2d 350, 353 (Minn.1975). See note 91 infra.

80a. E. g., Minnesota Bldg. & Loan Ass'n v. Murphy, 176 Minn. 71, 222 N.W. 516 (1928). A few cases take the position that waste is the *sole* ground for a receivership. See, e. g., First Federal Sav. & Loan Ass'n of Coffeyville v. Moulds, 202 Kan. 557, 451 P.2d 215 (1969). This approach, however, seems to be equating waste with inadequacy of security and, in any event, the receiver may be limited to protecting the property as opposed to collecting rents. See text in this section at notes 83–86, infra.

80b. See Annot., 55 A.L.R.3d 1041 (1974).

81. Grether v. Nick, supra note 75; Shepherd v. Pepper, 133 U.S. 626, 10 S.Ct. 438, 33 L.Ed. 706 (1890); Title Insurance & Trust Co. v. California Development Co., 164 Cal. 58, 127 P. 502 (1912); Larson v. Orfield, 155 Minn. 282, 193 N.W. 453 (1923); Dart v. Western Sav. & Loan Ass'n, 103 Ariz. 170, 438 P.2d 407 (1968); American Medical Services, Inc. v. Mutual Federal Sav. & Loan Ass'n, 52 Wis.2d 198, 188 N.W.2d 529 (1971).

waste.[82] On the other hand, the concept of "committing waste" could very well require proof of affirmative destruction of the property by the mortgagor.

Where a lien mortgagee meets the applicable requirements for a receivership, the receiver generally will be permitted to collect rents and profits and apply them to the mortgage debt.[83] However, there is isolated lien authority that, once appointed, the receiver may be limited to preserving the security *res* against waste by the mortgagor.[84] Under this view the *res* to be preserved is just the property itself and not its yield. The waste, or threatened waste, does not justify giving the mortgagee any additional security but only sanctions the preservation of that security which the mortgagee took originally. It would follow logically from this that the receiver in taking over the *res* should allocate the rents and profits, not to the mortgagee, but to the mortgagor and his general creditors.[85] As one court noted in denying the right of the receiver to collect rents and profits, "The rents and profits of land do not enter into or form any part of the security. At the time of giving the security both parties understand that the mortgagor will and the mortgagee will not, be entitled to the rents, issues or profits of the mortgaged premises, until the title shall have become absolute upon a foreclosure of the mortgage. * * * It would be a novel doctrine to hold that the mortgagee had a right incident to ownership, and yet that he had neither a legal title or right to possession. The legislature, in depriving him of the means of enforcing possession, intended thereby also to cut off and deprive him of all rights which he could have acquired, in case he obtained possession before acquiring an absolute title. To deprive him of this particular remedy, and yet allow him in some other proceeding to, in effect, arrive at the same result, * * * would not be securing to the mortgagor those substantial rights which it was the evident intent he should have." [86]

Many jurisdictions have statutes or other regulations governing the appointment of receivers.[87] For example, California provides for

82. American Medical Services, Inc. v. Mutual Federal Sav. & Loan Ass'n, 52 Wis.2d 198, 188 N.W.2d 529 (1971).

83. See, e. g., Federal Farm Mortgage Corp. v. Ganser, 146 Neb. 635, 20 N.W.2d 689 (1945).

84. Wagar v. Stone, 36 Mich. 364 (1877).

85. Ibid. See Rundell, Work of the Wisconsin Supreme Court: Mortgages, 9 Wis.L.Rev. 40, 43 (1933). There is some authority that the rents may be used, however for preserving the premises. See American Nat. Bank v. Northwestern Mut. Life Ins. Co., 32 C.C.A. 275, 89 F. 610 (1898), certiorari denied 172 U.S. 650, 19 S.Ct. 883, 43 L.Ed. 1184 (1899).

86. Wagar v. Stone, 36 Mich. 364, 366 (1877). In accord with this view, look at Teal v. Walker, 111 U.S. 242, 4 S.Ct. 420, 28 L.Ed. 415 (1884), applying Oregon law; Investors' Syndicate v. Smith, 105 F.2d 611 (C.C.A. Or.1939), reviewing and applying Oregon law; American Investment Co. v. Farrar, 87 Iowa 437, 54 N.W. 361 (1893); Moncrieff v. Hare, 38 Colo. 221, 87 P. 1082, 7 L.R.A.,N.S., 1001 (1906).

87. See e. g., West's Ann.Cal. Code Civ.Proc. § 564(2); Minn.Stat.Ann. §

the appointment of a receiver "where it appears that the mortgaged property is in danger of being lost, removed, or materially injured, or that the condition of the mortgage has not been performed, and that the property is probably insufficient to discharge the mortgage debt." [88] Absent specific rents and profits language in the mortgage, the effect of which we will consider in the next section, California courts strictly adhere to the requirements of the above rule.[89] While statutory provisions sometimes appear to impose relatively mild receivership requirements the case law interpreting them often imposes more substantial conditions precedent. For example, while the Minnesota statute seems to authorize the appointment of a receiver whenever the "property or its rents and profits are in danger of loss or material impairment," [90] the Minnesota courts nevertheless rigorously impose the three part requirement considered earlier in this section.[91]

§ 4.38 Agreements for Rents, Profits, and Receiverships

To enhance the mortgagee's rights, mortgagees normally include in the mortgage two types of clauses. One conveys, pledges, or assigns the rents and profits of the mortgaged land and empowers the mortgagee on default to take possession and collect them.[92] The other provides for the appointment of a receiver on default to collect rents and profits and apply them to the secured debt.[93]

These clauses have two purposes. One is to give the mortgagee a right to the rents and profits as part of his security, distinct from the capital asset, the land. The other is to provide an additional basis for the appointment of a receiver to capture them, or, in the alternative, the privilege of taking possession to achieve the same end. The mortgagee wants this right not only to be able to reach and apply the rents and profits of the land to his debt as against the mortgagor but, also, in priority to other mortgagees and general creditors. And he normally wants the right to exist either completely independent of taking possession,—or at least giving him a right anterior to any dealing with possession—together with the right to enforce it on de-

576.01(1); Reissue Neb.Rev.Stat.1975 § 25–1081.

88. West's Ann.Cal. Code Civ.Proc. § 564(2).

89. See e. g., Barclays Bank of California v. Superior Court, 69 Cal.App.3d 593, 137 Cal.Rptr. 743 (1977); Turner v. Superior Court, 72 Cal.App.3d 804, 140 Cal.Rptr. 475 (1977).

90. Minn.Stat.Ann. § 576.01.

91. See Mutual Benefit Life Ins. Co. v. Frantz Klodt & Son, Inc., 237 N.W.2d 350 (Minn.1975); In response to the latter case, the Minnesota legislature removed most impediments to receiverships as to mortgages in original amount of $500,000 or more executed after August 1, 1977. Minn.Stat.Ann. §§ 559.17 (Subd. 2), 576.01 (Subd. 2) (1977).

92. See May, The Effect and Operation of a Pledge of the Rents and Profits of Real Estate, 21 N.Dame L. 225 (1946).

93. See 50 Yale L.Jour. 1424, 1426 n. 10 (1941); 45 Harv.L.Rev. 902, n. 9 (1932).

fault by acquiring possession either by his own act or through a receivership.

It is often said that a court will not enforce a receivership clause where it would, in its absence, deny the appointment of a receiver.[94] Indeed, as one authority has emphasized, "the answer is that no such contract provision should force a court of equity to exercize its discretion in favor of a party who stands in no need of aid." [95] On the other hand, the fact that the mortgagor consents to a receivership is sometimes considered by courts to be a relevant factor and, in some instances, may favorably influence the appointment of a receiver.[96] This will especially be the case if the receivership agreement is subsequent to the mortgage.[97] Moreover, state statutes sometimes provide for the enforcement of such clauses.[98]

Where the receivership clause is utilized in a federally insured mortgage, it tends to be much more influential. For example, federal courts have indicated that such clauses alone may justify the appointment of a receiver in situations where the mortgagee is unable to meet the traditional requirements for the appointment.[99] It should be emphasized however, that these cases are largely the product of applying a "federal common law" instead of the traditional mortgage rules of the forum state, a problem considered elsewhere in this volume.[1]

The first of the two clauses, the "rents and profits clause," has received varying interpretations and consequences but they boil down

94. "Where a court has no authority under the law to appoint a receiver, such authority cannot be conferred by consent or stipulation of the parties." Baker v. Varney, 129 Cal. 564, 565, 62 P. 100, 79 Am.St.Rep. 140 (1900); Hubbell v. Avenue Inv. Co., 97 Iowa 135, 66 N.W. 85 (1896); Hazeltine v. Granger, 44 Mich. 503, 7 N.W. 74 (1880); Aetna Life Ins. Co. v. Broecker, 166 Ind. 576, 77 N.E. 1092 (1906). Cf. Moncrieff v. Hare, 38 Colo. 221, 87 P. 1082, 7 L.R.A.,N.S., 1001 (1906); Dart v. Western Sav. & Loan Ass'n, 103 Ariz. 170, 438 P.2d 407 (1968); Barclays Bank of California v. Superior Court, 69 Cal.App.3d 593, 137 Cal.Rptr. 743 (1977).

95. 2 Glenn, Mortgages § 1.75.1

96. See Israels & Kramer, The Significance of the Income Clause in a Corporate Mortgage, 30 Col.L.Rev. 489, 492 (1930). See discussion of cases to this effect in Barclays Bank of California v. Superior Court, 69 Cal. App.3d 593, 601, 137 Cal.Rptr. 743, 747 (1977).

97. In some states statutes specifically state that agreements as to the possession of the mortgaged property may be made subsequent to the date of the mortgage. West's Ann.Cal. Civ.Code, § 2927; N.Dak. Century Code 35–02–13; Rev.Code Mont. § 52–107 (1947); Ariz.Rev.Stat. § 33–703.

98. Under McKinney's N.Y. Real Property Law, § 254(10), where the mortgage so provides, the mortgagee may have a receiver appointed on default as a matter of right. See Minn.Stat. Ann. § 559.17 (Subd. 2) (1977) (as to mortgages of $500,000 or more.).

99. See United States v. Mountain Village Co., 424 F.Supp. 822 (D.Mass. 1976); United States v. Queen's Court Apartments, Inc., 296 F.2d 534 (9th Cir. 1961).

1. See § 11.6, infra; View Crest Garden Apartments, Inc. v. United States, 281 F.2d 844 (9th Cir. 1960), certiorari denied 364 U.S. 902, 81 S. Ct. 235, 5 L.Ed. 2d 195.

to three.[2] A few states outlaw them on the ground that they violate a fundamental policy of the law of the state as expressed in statutes banning ejectment, confirming possession in the mortgagor, or declaring mortgages to be liens.[3]

On the other hand, many jurisdictions treat such clauses as transferring the legal right to the rents of the land *in praesenti* subject to a condition precedent that it shall become effective upon default by the mortgagor.[4] Moreover, this approach has been buttressed by recent legislation in lien states that provides that such assignments "shall be valid whether contained in the mortgage instrument itself or in a separate instrument." [5]

This is not to say that all courts purporting to follow this second approach have done so enthusiastically. A few courts have been reluctant to find that there actually was an assignment.[5a] Some courts stress the language used and differentiate between an "assignment" and a "pledge" to arrive at the result. As the court in a leading case said "* * * an examination of the cases cited as authority for the statement that the mortgagor [sic] is not entitled to the rents until he takes possession, or until a receiver is appointed, convinces me that the word 'pledge' was there used as distinguished from the word 'assigned.' There is a marked difference between a pledge and an assignment. Ordinarily a pledge is considered as a bailment, and delivery of possession, actual or constructive, is essential, but transfer of title is not. On the other hand, by assignment, title is transferred although possession need not be. There may, of course, be

2. Decisions holding that the inclusion of the words "together with the rents, issues and profits thereof" in the description of the property mortgaged does no more than describe the lands should, perhaps, be put into a still different category. Myers v. Brown, 92 N.J.Eq. 348, 112 A. 844 (1921) affirmed 93 N.J.Eq. 196, 115 A. 926 (1922); In re Foster, Fed.Cas.No. 4,963, 6 Ben. 268, 10 N.R.B. 523 (D.C. N.Y.1872), affirmed C.C.N.Y., Fed.Cas. No. 4,981, 10 N.R.B. 523.

3. See Comment, Proposed Changes in Minnesota Mortgage Law, 50 Minn.L. Rev. 331, 339–347 (1966); See also Geraldson, Clauses Increasing the Possessory Rights of Mortgagees, 10 Wis.L.Rev. 492 (1935); note, 50 Yale L.Jour. 1424, 1426, 1427 (1941); Israels & Kramer, The Significance of the Income Clause in a Corporate Mortgage, 30 Col.L.Rev. 488, 493 (1930).

4. Kinnison v. Guaranty Liquidating Corp., 18 Cal.2d 256, 261, 115 P.2d 450, 453 (1941); Granniss-Blair Audit Co. v. Maddux, 167 Tenn. 297, 69 S. W.2d 238 (1934); New Jersey Nat. Bank & Trust Co. v. Morris, 9 N.J. Misc. 444, 155 A. 782 (1931); East Grand Forks Federal Sav. and Loan Ass'n v. Mueller, 198 N.W.2d 124 (N. D.1972). But see Smith v. Grilk, 64 N.D. 163, 250 N.W. 787 (1933). Such assignments may be made either by a clause in the mortgage contract or by a separate instrument. Paramount Building & Loan Ass'n v. Sacks, 107 N.J.Eq. 328, 152 A. 457 (1920), clause in mortgage; Harris v. Taylor, 35 App.Div. 462, 54 N.Y.S. 864 (1898), separate clause. That such a clause when it appears in the granting clause of the mortgage is ineffective, being only an extended description of the land, Myers v. Brown, 92 N.J.Eq. 348, 112 A. 844 (1921), affirmed 93 N.J.Eq. 196, 115 A. 926 (1922). That it does operate to transfer a right, see Randal v. Jersey Mortgage Inv. Co., 306 Pa. 1, 158 A. 865 (1932).

5. Minn.Stat.Ann. § 559.17. See, e. g., Rev.Code Wash.Ann. 7.28.230.

5a. Fisher v. Norman Apartments, 101 Colo. 173, 72 P.2d 1092 (1937), is a good example.

pledges accompanied by an assignment where both possession and title are transferred to the pledgee; and there may also be a qualified assignment where neither possession nor complete title passes." [6] As has been pointed out, to achieve such a great difference in result upon such a distinction seems "to place an inordinately high premium upon the phraseology of the instrument. If the rents are available in one case without the requirement of obtaining possession, no policy ground is perceivable for denying them in the other." [7]

Apprehension has also been expressed that if the clause operated automatically to transfer the right to rents, logically the mortgagor would be held subject to the imposition of a constructive trust upon all rents collected and expended by him after default, a result which would "impose unworkable restrictions upon industry." [8] Additionally it has been urged that, since the clause imposes no duty upon the mortgagee to collect rents, to permit these clauses to give automatic accrual would both deprive the mortgagor of his rights to the rents and use of them and give him no assurance that the mortgagee would collect them and apply them to the debt.[9] Even if this were true, as a practical matter the mortgagor would not have to worry that a mortgagee, after default by the mortgagor, would fail to collect any rents if they were available and apply them in payment.[10] But it is not true, as was pointed out by a court in giving one of the best reasons for construing the agreement as stopping short of an assignment. The court said, "the question before us is not dependent upon the power of the parties to the mortgage to contract as to the rents and profits of the mortgaged property, but upon the intention of the parties as expressed by them in the mortgage instrument. We do not think that the parties * * * intended * * * to make an absolute and unqualified assignment of the rent of the mortgaged property * * *. If so, the mortgagee should be charged with the amount of the rents accruing after default, at least if they could have

6. Paramount B. & L. Ass'n v. Sacks, 107 N.J.Eq. 328, 331, 152 A. 457, 458 (1930). For other discussions of the effect of an assignment or pledge of rents and profits to the mortgagee or third persons, see note, 43 Yale L.J. 107 (1933); note, 47 Yale L.J. 1000 (1938); Israels and Kramer, The Significance of the Income Clause in a Corporate Mortgage, 30 Col.L.Rev. 488 (1930); Abelow, An Historical Analysis of Assignment of Rents in New York, 6 Brooklyn L.Rev. 25, 52 (1936); note, 31 Mich.L.Rev. 1124 (1933) (discussion of Michigan statute permitting the assignment of rents and profits to a trustee under a trust deed mortgage); note, 18 Iowa L.Rev. 251 (1933); note, 21 Iowa L.Rev. 646 (1936); note, 50 Harv.L.Rev. 1322 (1937); note, 50 Yale L.Jour. 1424 (1941); note, 21 Notre Dame Law. 225 (1941); Berick, The Mortgagee's Right to Rents, 8 U. of Cin.L.Rev. 250, 283 (1934); Leesman, Corporate Trusteeship and Receivership, 28 Ill. L.Rev. 238, 239 (1933); 4 A.L.R. 1405 (1919); 55 A.L.R. 1020 (1928); 87 A. L.R. 625 (1933); 91 A.L.R. 1217 (1934).

7. 50 Yale L.Jour. 1424, 1428 (1941).

8. Prudential Ins. Co. of America v. Liberdar Holding Corp., 74 F.2d 50 (C.C.A.N.Y.1934).

9. Kidd's Estate, Re, 161 Misc. 631, 292 N.Y.S. 888 (1936).

10. See 50 Yale L.Jour. 1424, 1427 (1941).

been collected with reasonable diligence." [11] Probably most important of all is the policy of protecting the mortgagor's possession prior to foreclosure sale. But the validity of even this reason has been challenged. A defaulting mortgagor is usually insolvent and beset by creditors. Therefore, it has been pointed out, the most likely result of the policy is to deny the mortgagee priority on this contracted for asset—priority to which he should be entitled against general creditors by virtue of his foresight in demanding it.[12]

A third, and probably predominate, approach holds that the rents and profits clause creates in the mortgagee only a security interest in the rents and profits and one which requires some further positive action by the mortgagee before he can harvest the subject matter of his bargain.[13] One explanation of the need for further action is that the clause amounts to an inchoate or executory pledge,[14] thus invoking the analogy of pledges or mortgages of after-acquired chattels.[15] Another is that the security interest the mortgagee acquires in the rents and profits is of like character as that of the mortgage [16] of the real property with the consequence in a lien jurisdiction that no right to possess them vests in the mortgagee prior to foreclosure sale. Coupled with this is the idea that the collection of rents and profits, in the absence of a severance of them from the reversion by a valid transfer of title to them by assignment, is inseparable from the possession of the land. This latter notion is as applicable to a title state as a lien state, the only difference between them being in respect to the right of the mortgagee to obtain possession of the land and, through it, the rents and profits.[17] And they all lead to the same an-

11. Sullivan v. Rosson, 223 N.Y. 217, 223, 119 N.E. 405, 407 (1918).

12. 50 Yale L.Jour. 1424, 1427 (1941). 18; Storke and Sears; Colorado Security Law, 135–145 (1952).

13. See e. g., Wuorinen v. City Federal S & L Ass'n, 52 Wis.2d 722, 191 N.W. 2d 27 (1971); Kratovil, Mortgages—Problems In Possession, Rents, And Mortgagee Liability, 11 DePaul L.Rev. 1, 11 (1961).

14. See Restatement of Security, §§ 1, 10.

15. See Conn. Mut. Life Ins. Co. v. Shelly Seed Corp., 46 Ohio App. 548, 189 N.E. 654 (1933), rent clause referred to as an equitable chattel mortgage of after-acquired chattels; Lincoln Joint Stock Land Bank v. Barlow, 217 Iowa 323, 251 N.W. 501 (1933), mortgage with pledge of rents and profits recorded as both a real estate and chattel mortgage. See Kinnison v. Guaranty Liquidating Co., 18 Cal.2d 256, 261, 115 P.2d 450, 453 (1941). See also Simpson v. Ferguson, 112 Cal. 180, 40 P. 104, 53 Am. St.Rep. 201 (1895); Modesto Bank v. Owens, 121 Cal. 223, 53 P. 552 (1898).

16. "The mortgage as it relates to the real property * * * is * * * but a pledge of property as security for the debt. It would appear that the assignment of rent in this case is of the like character as the conveyance of real property and not intended as an absolute transfer thereof." Sullivan v. Rosson, 223 N.Y. 217, 224, 119 N.E. 405, 407 (1918). See Smith, Security Interests in Crops, 10 Hastings L.J. 156, 161–164 (1958).

17. "In jurisdictions where the mortgagor retains the legal title and right of possession, as here, it follows that the right to collect rents and profits remains in the mortgagor until he is deprived of possession in the manner provided by law, and this notwith-

swer as to just what positive action is required of the mortgagee: he must either take possession of the property himself or get a receiver appointed.[18] This seems definite enough but an examination of the cases where the mortgagee attempted to take possession without the appointment of a receiver makes it "apparent that possession is an elusive quality and that there is no uniform method which is certain to accomplish the desired end." [19] Apparently a physical entry either by self-help or court help such as would be necessary were there no pledge clause is usually required.[20] Consent of the mortgagor to entry has been insisted upon by one decision in which there was only an assignment of the rents.[21] But there is authority that if the clause, in addition to pledging the rents and profits, gives the mortgagee the right to possession, a demand and refusal of possession will enable the mortgagee to collect in spite of an antagonistic mortgagor.[22] It has been suggested that a provision in the pledge agreement carefully stating that the collection of rents would constitute a taking of possession would be advisable as giving a definite test [23]

To what extent does the presence of a rents and profits clause affect the mortgagee's ability to get a receiver appointed? There are cases holding that the pledge of rents and profits is sufficient by itself, without showing inadequacy or waste of the security or insolvency of the mortgagor, to entitle the mortgagee to a receiver.[24] On the

standing the fact that the mortgagee may pledge the rents and profits." Grether v. Nick, 193 Wis. 503, 512, 215 N.W. 571, 572, 55 A.L.R. 525 (1927). The same result is reached in a title jurisdiction. Rohrer v. Deatherage, 336 Ill. 450, 168 N.E. 266 (1929).

18. Wuorinen v. City Federal S & L Ass'n, 52 Wis.2d 722, 191 N.W.2d 27 (1971). Freedman's Savings & Trust Co. v. Shepherd, 127 U.S. 494, 502, 8 S.Ct. 1250, 32 L.Ed. 163 (1887).

19. 43 Yale L.Jour. 107, 112 and cases cited (1933).

20. "All of the authorities agree that a pledge of rents and profits does not create any lien upon the rents and profits until the mortgagee acquires possession * * *." Grether v. Nick, 193 Wis. 503, 513, 215 N.W. 571, 572, 55 A.L.R. 525 (1927); Paramount Building & Loan v. Sacks, 107 N.J.Eq. 328, 331, 152 A. 457, 458 (1930).

Storke and Sears, Colorado Security Law, 141–143 (1952).

21. Dime Savings Bank v. Altman, 249 App.Div. 174, 291 N.Y.S. 417 (1936), affirmed 275 N.Y. 62, 9 N.E.2d 788, 50 Harv.L.Rev. 1322, 7 Brooklyn L. Rev. 115 (1937). Entry by the mortgagee with the mortgagor's consent would be good. 148th Street Realty Co., Inc. v. Conrad, 125 Misc. 142, 145, 210 N.Y.S. 400 (1925).

22. Long Island Bond etc., Co. v. Broson, 171 Misc. 15, 11 N.Y.S.2d 793 (1939); Freedman's Saving and Trust Co. v. Shepherd, 127 U.S. 494, 503, 8 S.Ct. 1250, 32 L.Ed. 163 (1888). See 50 Yale L.Jour. 1424, 1430 (1941).

23. See 43 Yale L.Jour. 107, 113 (1933).

24. Turner v. Superior Court, 72 Cal. App.3d 804, 140 Cal.Rptr. 475 (1977); Barclays Bank of California v. Superior Court, 69 Cal.App.3d 593, 137 Cal.Rptr. 743 (1977); Howard v. Burns, 201 Ill.App. 579 (1916) affirmed 279 Ill. 256, 116 N.E. 703 (1917); Ohio Mut. Savings & Loan Co. v. Public Construction Co., 26 Ohio N.P.,N.S., 371 (1926); see Rhinelander v. Richards, 184 App.Div. 67, 70, 171 N.Y.S. 436, 437 (1918); Berick, The Mortgagee's Right to Rents, 8 Cin.L.Rev. 250, 290 (1934); 45 Harv.L.Rev. 902 n. 10 (1932); 27

other hand, other cases take the position that apart from giving to the mortgagee a clear right to the rents and profits as part of his security,[25] thus clearing the hurdle that faced lien theory states where there was no clause covering them, the same considerations should govern the appointment of the receiver where there is a pledge agreement as where there is none.[26] In other words, if the mortgagee's security, including the right to rents and profits which his agreement gave to him, is adequate, equity should not grant a receivership even though his bargain also expressly purported to give him a right to one. But although it is recognized that a mortgagee can claim no absolute right to a receiver and cannot bind a court by stipulations in the mortgage or separate agreement for the appointment of one, nevertheless, the presence of rent assignment or pledge and receivership clauses in the mortgage increases the chances of a receiver being appointed.[27]

§ 4.39 Ex Parte Receivership—Constitutional Problems

Variations of the two clauses discussed in the previous section can have a significant impact on a related matter—the appointment of receivers by *ex parte* order. Ex parte reciversship involves the appointment of a receiver, usually pending judicial foreclosure, without providing either notice or an opportunity to be heard to the mortgagor.

Standing alone, the practice of appointing receivers *ex parte* arguably violates the constitutional principles of both Mullae v. Central Hanover Bank & Trust Co.[28] and Fuentes v. Sheven [29] and their progeny. The Supreme Court in *Mullane* noted that "where the names and post office addresses of those affected by a proceeding are at hand, the reasons disappear for resort to means less likely than the mails to apprise them of its pendency." [30] Implicit in this, at least, is that *some* notice is required before a court may deprive a person of a significant property interest. In *Fuentes*, the Supreme Court struck

Iowa L.Rev. 627 (1933); 43 Yale L. Jour. 112 (1933).

25. "All authorities agree that a pledge of rents and profits vests in the mortgagee a right thereto which equity will recognize and enforce in a proper manner." Grether v. Nick, supra note 20.

26. See e. g., Mutual Benefit Life Ins. Co. v. Frantz Klodt & Son, Inc., 237 N.W.2d 350 (Minn.1975); Aetna Life Ins. Co. v. Broecker, 166 Ind. 576, 77 N.E. 1092 (1906); Althausen v. Kohn, 222 Ill.App. 324 (1921). But see notes 91 and 98 supra.

27. Martorano v. Spicola, 110 Fla. 55, 148 So. 585 (1933); Pizer v. Herzig, 121 App.Div. 609, 106 N.Y.S. 370 (1907). This statement, of course, does not take into account those jurisdictions which hold void an executory agreement pledging or assigning rents and profits.

28. 339 U.S. 306, 70 S.Ct. 652, 94 L. Ed. 865 (1950).

29. 407 U.S. 67, 92 S.Ct. 1983, 32 L. Ed.2d 556 (1972), rehearing denied 409 U.S. 902, 93 S.Ct. 177, 34 L.Ed.2d 165.

30. 339 U.S. at 318.

down certain state replevin statutes because they did not provide for an opportunity to be heard before chattels were taken from the possessor, even on a temporary basis, pending a trial on the merits. In the *ex parte* receivership situation the mortgagor, of course, can lose both possession of the mortgaged real estate and the ability to direct the disposal of its rents with *no* prior notice or opportunity to be heard. To be sure, this practice may be justified in emergency situations such as where a mortgagor is engaged in removal or destruction of the real estate.[31] A more detailed analysis of *Mullane* and *Fuentes* in the power of sale foreclosure context is provided elsewhere in this volume.[32] Nevertheless, it should suffice here to emphasize that the *ex parte* appointment of a receiver, standing alone, is, at best, certainly constitutionally suspect.[33]

Of course, even if ex parte receivership is constitutionally deficient as to notice and hearing, such rights, in theory at least, are capable of being waived. *Fuentes* and other cases recognize the possibility of waiver, at least where the parties were aware of the significance of the waiver and there was bargaining over contractual terms between parties who were equal in bargaining position.[34] Receivership clauses often provide that a receiver may be appointed "without notice" to the mortgagor for purpose of taking possession of the mortgaged premises and collecting rents and profits therefrom. Recent decisions have upheld waiver based on such clauses.[35] However, these cases have involved sophisticated real estate mortgagors who were deemed to have acted knowingly and from a bargaining position relatively equal to that of the mortgagee. Suppose, however, that the transaction does not involve commercial real estate and that the mortgagor lacks the sophistication, understanding and bargaining position incident to the usual commercial mortgage transaction. In such situations the waiver concept will be much more difficult to sustain.

31. Cf. Ewing v. Mytinger & Casselberry, Inc., 339 U.S. 594, 70 S.Ct. 870, 94 L.Ed. 1088 (1950), rehearing denied 340 U.S. 857, 71 S.Ct. 69, 95 L.Ed 627; North American Cold Storage Co. v. Chicago, 211 U.S. 306, 29 S.Ct. 101, 53 L.Ed. 195 (1909). See Elliot and Smith, 1 West's Texas Forms, § 1.4 (1977).

32. See §§ 7.23–7.30, infra.

33. One case seems to have upheld the constitutionality of ex parte receivership, although it did not consider *Fuentes* and waiver seems to have been an alternative ground. See Security Nat. Bank v. Village Mall at Hillcrest, Inc., 79 Misc.2d 1060, 361 N.Y.S.2d 977 (1974).

34. See Nelson, Constitutional Problems With Power of Sale Real Estate Foreclosure: A Judicial Dilemma, 43 Mo.L.Rev. 25, 33–34 (1978).

35. See United States v. Mountain Village Co., 424 F.Supp. 822 (D.Mass. 1976); Massachusetts Mut. Life Ins. Co. v. Avon Associates, Inc., 83 Misc.2d 829, 373 N.Y.S.2d 464 (1975), noted in 28 Syr.L.Rev. 379, 416 (1977); Security Nat. Bank v. Village Mall at Hillcrest Inc., 79 Misc.2d 1060, 361 N.Y.S.2d 977 (1974).

§ 4.40 Effect of Receivership on Rents—General Considerations

When a receiver has been appointed in a foreclosure action many questions arise as to his rights to rents and profits. One concerns what rents the receiver is entitled to collect. Another is whether he may disaffirm leases and, accompanying this, how far a tenant may be bound on his lease when a receiver has been appointed, or be held liable upon any other basis. Although the most difficult problems have arisen in respect to leases made subsequent to the mortgage, there is also the question of the right of the receiver to rents of leases prior to the mortgage. Still a different matter is involved when the mortgagor himself is in possession and the receiver seeks to hold him for income actually earned or for an occupational rental. Indeed, this goes back to the question of whether a receiver is justified at all in such a case, a point which was not covered in the earlier discussion of the basis for receiverships. Priorities on rents and profits between various mortgagees and other creditors form still another area of controversy. Conduct of the mortgagor, generally classified as "milking" the mortgaged property, also becomes important especially in times of depression. And in all of these cases there is the inquiry as to whether title and lien theories as well as rents and profits and receivership clauses affect the solutions.

More complex problems arise when the mortgagor is involved in a federal bankruptcy liquidation or reorganization. For example, there are often competing claims to both possession and rents of the mortgaged real estate between the judicially appointed receiver and the trustee in bankruptcy. A detailed consideration of these problems follows later in this volume.[36]

§ 4.41 Receivership—Lease Prior to Mortgage

Where the lease is entered into prior to the mortgage both theory and practice are are fairly clear. As was seen earlier,[37] such leases are superior to the mortgage and will not be affected by foreclosure. The purchaser on forclosure sale is bound by them. "It is entirely clear that if a lease is prior to a mortgage a sale under the latter is but a sale of the reversion." [38] It follows that the receiver has no power to disaffirm such leases; all that he can do is to collect the rents from the tenants.

The only question is as to what rent the receiver is entitled, and even this narrows down to rent which had accrued but was unpaid at the time of his appointment, since it is clear that rent accruing between the date of his appointment and the date of sale belongs to

36. See §§ 8.11–8.13, infra.

37. See § 4.24, supra.

38. Metropolitan Life Ins. Co. v. Childs Co., 230 N.Y. 285, 290, 130 N.E. 295, 297, 14 A.L.R. 658 (1921)

him.[39] Thus, for example, a receiver who is appointed before a judgment creditor actually levies on the rents by attachment, has priority over the judgment creditor.[40] While the receiver's claim is generally held to vest at the time of his appointment,[41] there is authority that it relates back to the commencement of the foreclosure action if a receiver is then requested; and if not, to the time in the action when a petition for one is made.[42] This latter rule has the sound merit of not penalizing the mortgagee by delays in appointment beyond his control after he has done all that he can to make his claim to the rents and profits operative.[43]

Where there are no rent clauses in the mortgage, in title jurisdictions the mortgagee may assert his right to possession even before default and the rule gives to the mortgagee accrued and unpaid rent on the date that the mortgagee asserts his right.[44] The receiver, it is true, does not take possession or collect rents under the rights of the mortgagee but as an officer of the court.[45] However, he stands in a stronger position than the mortgagee because he is not appointed until the mortgagor is in default and the mortgagee has started to realize upon his security, which in title states by virtue of the mortgage itself includes not merely the legal title to the reversion carrying the rents but the right to collect them, absent an agreement to the contrary, at any time. The defaulting mortgagor has no standing to insist that he be allowed to collect and keep any part of the property which was subject to the mortgagee's security claim.[46]

The same result should follow in a lien jurisdiction. There the right to collect the rents and profits, as was seen, does not come from the mortgage even though leases prior to the mortgage, being attached to the mortgaged reversion, are under the mortgagee's security in the sense that they will be subject to foreclosure sale in the

39. Argall v. Pitts, 78 N.Y. 239 (1879); Johnston v. Riddle, 70 Ala. 219 (1881); Noyes v. Rich, 52 Me. 115 (1862); Stewart v. Fairchild-Baldwin Co., 90 N.J.Eq. 139, 106 A. 406 (1919), affirmed 1919, 91 N.J.Eq. 139, 106 A. 406.

40. See Connolly v. Plaza Cards & Gifts, 54 A.D.2d 553, 387 N.Y.S.2d 5 (1976).

41. Rankin-Whitham State Bank v. Mulcahey, 344 Ill. 99, 176 N.E. 366 (1931); Rohrer v. Deatherage, 336 Ill. 450, 168 N.E. 266 (1929); Greenwich Sav. Bank v. Samotas, 17 N.Y.S.2d 772 (1940). But see Morris v. Davis, 219 N.Y.S.2d 279 (1961), the court held that the receiver, although duly appointed, was not entitled to collect rents accruing prior to his qualification as receiver.

42. Kooistra v. Gibford, 201 Iowa 275, 207 N.W. 399 (1926).

43. See 27 Iowa L.Rev. 626, 635 (1942).

44. See § 424, supra.

45. See First National Bank of Chicago v. Gordon, 287 Ill.App. 83, 4 N.E. 2d 504 (1936).

46. "Being in default upon the obligation which his mortgage secures, the debtor who starts a quarrel over this point is met by the answer, 'Well, if you pay up, of course you can have the rent. But since you refuse to do that, you are not in a position to demand the rent.'" Glenn, Mortgages, § 181.

same way that the land itself is. Nevertheless, on equitable considerations previously examined,[47] receivers are appointed to collect rents and profits which otherwise belong to the mortgagor up to foreclosure sale or even to the end of the period of redemption from sale. Those equitable considerations apply as much to accrued but unpaid income from the property as to that which accrues after appointment. A clause pledging rents and profits should not alter the situation because such a pledge gives no rights to collect rents prior to the receivership.[48] Whether an assignment of the rents and profits would affect the question depends upon what rents were covered by the assignment. If it covered rents accruing prior to the receivership, even payment to the mortgagor, if with notice of the assignment, would not save the tenant from having to pay again to the mortgagee; and consequently, insofar as the rents have not been paid over to the mortgagee,[49] the receiver should be able to collect them from the tenant dating from the time the assignment transferred the right to them to the mortgagee. On the other hand, if the assignment by its terms were to be operative on the appointment of the receiver, it would confer upon the receiver no rights to rents accruing before that date whether paid or unpaid.[50]

Unfortunately the cases are not as clear on this point as the above analysis would indicate.[51] While there are cases to the effect that the receiver will be entitled, without the aid of rents and profits clauses, to rent accrued but unpaid prior to his appointment,[52] other cases stress the presence of rent clauses in giving the receiver the right to such rent as against the mortgagor[53] and junior mortgagees,[54] and there is still another authority that, in the absence of a clause pledging or assigning the rents, he would have no such

47. See § 4.37, supra.

48. See Paramount Bldg. & Loan Ass'n v. Sacks, 107 N.J.Eq. 328, 331, 152 A. 457 (1930). See § 150, supra.

49. See §§ 4.37–4.38, supra.

50. Paramount Bldg. & Loan Ass'n v. Sacks, 107 N.J.Eq. 328, 152 A. 457 (1930).

51. See 33 Col.L.Rev. 1211, 1216 (1933); 50 Yale L.Jour. 1424, 1440 (1941).

52. Codrington v. Johnstone, 1 Beav. 520 (1838); Russell v. Russell, 2 Ir. Ch.R. 574 (1853); Palmieri v. N. Y. Prep. School, 248 N.Y.S. 934 (1931); see Wychoff v. Scofield, 98 N.Y. 475, 477 (1885); New Way Bldg. Co. v. Mortimer Taft Bldg. Corp., 129 Misc. 170, 171, 220 N.Y.S. 665, 666 (1927); Lofsky v. Maujer, 3 Sandf.Ch. 76, 78 (1845).

53. Touroff v. Weeks, 155 Misc. 577, 278 N.Y.S. 867 (1935); cf. Watts' Adm'r v. Smith, 250 Ky. 617, 63 S. W.2d 796, 91 A.L.R. 1206 (1933).

54. New York Life Ins. Co. v. Fulton Development Corp. 265 N.Y. 348, 352, 193 N.E. 169, 171 (1934), "When the senior mortgagee has a receiver appointed, the lien of the senior mortgagee immediately attaches not only to future rents but also to past rents due and uncollected. As between the equitable liens of the senior and junior mortgagees, that of the senior is superior."; Paramount Bldg. & Loan Ass'n v. Sacks, 107 N.J.Eq. 328, 152 A. 457 (1930), prior mortgagee holding an assignment clause may have receiver appointed who will be entitled to unpaid rent as against junior mortgagee in possession.

right.[55] There is, also, authority that prior attaching creditors of the mortgagor will prevail over the receiver as to back rent.[56]

§ 4.42 Receivership—Lease Subsequent to Mortgage

In order to determine the receiver's rights to affirm or dissaffirm leases that are subsequent to the mortgage, some review of previous material will be helpful. A receiver in foreclosure is appointed in order to conserve and prevent injury to property in which the mortgagee has a security interest. Consequently, in determining the rights of a receiver to rents and profits, there is always the question whether the particular rents and profits constitute a part of the security of the mortgagee which he is entitled to have preserved and protected from injury. Where the lease is subsequent to the mortgage title and lien theories have played a part in the reasoning of the courts in answering this question. In such a lease the tenant's rights are dependent upon those of his landlord, the mortgagor, as against the mortgagee, and this marks the starting point in both types of states. In title states the mortgagee, at least on default, gets the right to possession and with it all of the rents and profits of the land as part of his security. However, while he can assert his right by evicting the mortgagor or his tenant, he does not acquire the mortgagor's rights under the lease against the tenant because, as it is said, he is not in privity with him. His only right against the tenant in such cases is either to come to a new agreement with him or, failing that, to hold him for the occupational use of the property as to such period as the tenant stays on after the mortgagee asserts his rights. And, reciprocal to the right of the mortgagee to oust the tenant, is the tenant's privilege of vacating the property, treating the mortgagee's assertion of rights as an eviction justifying his action and, also, giving him a right to sue the mortgagor for breach of covenant of quiet enjoyment.

Should the mortgage contain an assignment of the rents and profits, this can operate as an automatic transfer in equity of the future leases made by the mortgagor. It gives them to the mortgagee according to the terms of the assignment, usually upon default by the mortgagor, quite independent of rights in the capital asset or flowing from them.

Clauses purporting to transfer rents and profits often are treated as inoperative to give any rights in them until either the mortgagee takes possession or a receiver is appointed. When such an event oc-

55. New Order Bldg. & Loan Ass'n v. 222 Chancellor Ave., 106 N.J.Eq. 1, 149 A. 525 (1930). See also Paramount Bldg. & Loan Ass'n v. Sacks, 107 N.J.Eq. 328, 152 A. 457 (1930), indicating that a pledge of rents would be insufficient.

56. Peoples Trust Co. of Binghamton v. Goodell, 134 Misc. 692, 236 N.Y.S. 549 (1929); In re Barbizon Plaza, 3 F.Supp. 415 (D.C.N.Y.1933). Contra: Donlon & Miller Mfg. Co. v. Cannella, 89 Hun 21, 69 St.R. 8, 34 N.Y.S. 1065 (1895).

curs the agreement can be regarded as giving to the mortgagee at that moment an independent right to the mortgagor's rights against the lessee. It would be the same as though at the time the mortgagee determined to take over he had made an arrangement with the mortgagor whereby the mortgagor then assigned his leases to the mortgagee. Only the most artifical and mechanical sort of reasoning would hold in such an event that the mortgagee's entry into possession necessarily destroyed the interest of the mortgagor in the property and, along with it, the leases dependent upon it so that they could not be preserved to the mortgagee by agreement.[57] The mortgagee really occupied a dual position: (1) he is an assignee of the mortgagor's reversionary interest; [58] (2) he is a mortgagee who has taken possession. He should have his option as to which set of rights he will assert.

What concerns us now is the effect of these principles upon the rights of a receiver when he is appointed. The chief difficulty in title states will be in giving the receiver a right to affirm leases in spite of the lessee's desire to disaffirm them; and, on the other hand, there will be no trouble in permitting the receiver to disaffirm leases regardless of the wishes of the tenant. In lien states, as we shall see, the chief problem is whether the receiver can disaffirm leases by the mortgagor subsequent to the mortgage.

In title states there is no doubt that the receiver may disaffirm all leases subsequent to the mortgage and collect from the tenant the reasonable rental value of the premises for occupancy after the receiver's appointment.[59] This is a conservation measure where the reserved rent is less than occupational rental and the mortgagee's security interest is endangered by the lower yield. Ordinarily however, the lease rental is higher than either an occupational rental or the rent that can be obtained under a new lease negotiated by the receiver, and the receiver consequently wants to hold the tenant to the existing lease.[60]

57. There is good authority that the mortgagee will succeed to the mortgagor's lease rights against the tenant on this reasoning in spite of claiming the rents "as mortgagee." International Paper Co. v. Priscilla Co., 281 Mass. 22, 183 N.E. 58 (1932). Chicago City Bank & Trust Co. v. Walgreen Co., 272 Ill.App. 434 (1933) also gave the mortgagee the right to collect rents from the mortgagor's tenant on the ground that he was a transferee of those rights and claiming them did not constitute an eviction ending the lease.

58. See note, 17 Wash.L.Rev. 37, 41 (1942).

59. Rohrer v. Deatherage, 336 Ill. 450, 456, 168 N.E. 266 (1929); Rankin-Whitham Bank v. Mulcahey, 344 Ill. 99, 176 N.E. 366 (1931); Henshaw, Ward & Co. v. Wells, 28 Tenn. 568 (1848); Lord Mansfield v. Hamilton, 2 Sch. & Lef. 28 (1804).

60. "Not only will the foreclosure ordinarily be commenced when real estate values are depressed, but the receiver's leases will of necessity be forced transactions negotiated under most unfavorable circumstances." Tefft, Receivers and Leases Subordinate to the Mortgage, 2 Chi.L.Rev. 33, 37 (1934).

Two difficulties confront the receiver in such a case if the tenant on his part wants to escape from the lease, as he usually will when he is paying under his agreement more than the fair rental value of the property. One is that there is no privity of estate between the receiver and the tenant any more than there is between the mortgagee who takes possession and the tenant, the receiver being the equivalent of a mortgagee in possession.[61] The other is that since the receiver is not bound by the mortgagor's leases and may hold the tenant for occupational rent if that be higher than the amount reserved in the lease, it is only just that the tenant have a reciprocal power to disavow the lease and either vacate the premises or, if he stays on without a new agreement, be liable only for the fair value of the use and occupation.[62]

A short answer to the first argument is that it is inconsistent with the fundamental nature of receiverships in mortgage foreclosure cases. Rent receivers are appointed as officers of the court to preserve the security interest of the mortgagee in the property subject to his mortgage.[63] And, in the fulfillment of this purpose, the court has the power to direct the receiver to disaffirm the mortgagor's leases in cases where the mortgagee's margin of security cannot be preserved adequately without avoiding them. If the mortgagee's margin of security can be preserved without cancelling the mortgagor's leases, they should continue until wiped out by foreclosure sale.[64] The theory that the appointment of the receiver is the equivalent of entry by the mortgagee, amounting therefore to an eviction of the tenant of the mortgagor and for this reason ending the lease, is so foreign to the true basis of the receivership and the ground on which leases are avoided or affirmed under it that it has been characterized as "both novel and startling." [65] As the same court pointed out, "if that argument were sound no mortgagee would ever take possession of mortgaged premises under the clause giving him a right to do so, nor would any receiver of rents ever be appointed in foreclosure proceedings, as upon such appointment the rental income would

61. See First Nat. Bank of Chicago v. Gordon, 287 Ill.App. 83, 4 N.E.2d 504 (1936), noted, 4 Chi.L.Rev. 151, 504 (1936). Walgreen Co. v. Moore, 116 N.J.Eq. 348, 349, 173 A. 587 (1934).

62. See Holmes v. Gravenhorst, 263 N.Y. 148, 157, 188 N.E. 285, 288, 91 A.L.R. 1230 (1933). Crouch, J., dissenting.

63. Desiderio v. Iadonisi, 115 Conn. 652, 163 A. 254, 88 A.L.R. 1349 (1932); Chicago Title & Trust Co. v. McDowell, 257 Ill.App. 492 (1931).

64. See Tefft, Receivers and Leases Subordinate to the Mortgage, 2 Chi. L.Rev. 33, 35 (1934) citing, In re Newdigate Colliery, Ltd., 1 Ch. 468 (1912); In re Great Cobar, Ltd., 1 Ch. 682 (1915); Stamer v. Nisbitt, 9 Ir. Eq.R. 96 (1846); Murtin v. Walker, Sau. & Sc. 139 (1837); American Brake Shoe & Foundry Co. v. N. Y. R. Co., 278 F. 842 (D.C.N.Y.1922).

65. Walgreen v. Moore, 116 N.J.Eq. 348, 350, 173 A. 587, 588 (1934). Quoted with approval in First Nat. Bank of Chicago v. Gordon, 287 Ill. App. 83, 4 N.E.2d 504 (1936). See comment, 2 Chi.L.Rev. 487 (1935).

cease. But while the possession of a rent receiver has been likened to that of a mortgagee in possession, it is the possession of the court and not of the mortgagee. Such possession does not *terminate* the rights of any party to the proceeding, much less those of one not a party. They are merely held in abeyance and preserved pendente lite. And, moreover, the title of the mortgagor is not 'terminated' until final decree and sale." [66] Furthermore the contention that the appointment of the receiver is really the equivalent of the entry by the mortgagee into possession is not only at variance with an imposing array of decisions dealing with the appointment of receivers,[67] but is also most disadvantageous to the mortgagor and his assigns.[68]

The second argument is more plausible. First, the lessee's plight is the consequence of a risk he voluntarily assumed and could have guarded against. A lessee who takes a lease when there is a prior mortgage on the land knows that his lease may be wiped out by a foreclosure of the mortgage, or, in title states, before that by entry by the mortgagee. And such a lessee can find out whether there is such a mortgage by examining his lessor's title, the most ordinary of precautions. If he failed to investigate he must be regarded as willing to take a blind chance without protecting himself by providing for a covenant against encumbrances with a clause making breach a ground for ending the lease. On the other hand, if he knew of the mortgage, at the time he made the lease he could have insisted that the mortgagee become a party to the lease; [69] or have asked the mortgagee to agree, as part of the consideration for the lease, not to evict him in case of foreclosure; or he might even have got an agreement subordinating the mortgage to the lease. Further, even if the receiver does reject the lease, the hardship on the lessee is mitigated by the rule that the receiver must decide promptly; [70] and, if he does renounce it, the tenant is then free to vacate [71] without liability other than for occupational rent during the period he has stayed on.[72]

66. Id.

67. See Tefft, Receivers and Leases Subordinate to the Mortgage, 2 Chi. L.Rev. 33, 38–42 (1934).

68. The mortgagor is damaged not only because he loses a valuable lease, but also because he will be liable for breach of covenant to the tenant who is evicted. Mack v. Patchin, 42 N.Y. 167, 1 Am.Rep. 506 (1870); Ganz v. Clark, 252 N.Y. 92, 169 N.E. 100 (1929); B. F. Avery & Sons Plow Co. v. Kennerly, 12 S.W.2d 140 (Tex. Com.App.1929).

69. Flynn v. Lowrance, 110 Okl. 150, 236 P. 594 (1924).

70. Central Republic Trust Co. v. 33 So. Wabash Bldg. Corp., 273 Ill.App. 380 (1934).

71. "It would be manifestly unjust to permit a receiver to disaffirm the lease and put new obligations on the tenant without giving the tenant the reciprocal privilege to treat these demands as an interference with his title and equivalent to a constructive eviction." Monro-King & Gremmels Realty Corp. v. 9 Ave.-31 St. Corp., 233 App.Div. 401, 404, 253 N.Y.S. 303, 307 (1931).

72. Sager v. Rebdor Realty Corp., 230 App.Div. 106, 243 N.Y.S. 314 (1930).

Second, if the receiver is allowed to preserve the lease, the tenant's position is in no way jeopardized or made more burdensome than was his hope when he entered into it. His rights and obligations are the same as they would have been had there been no default by his landlord, the mortgagor, and no resulting foreclosure action. The fact that the risk he voluntarily took has been realized would seem no sufficient reason to give him the option of avoiding his bargain.

Third, the tenant's argument of fairness is inconsistent with the rule that the mortgagee, at his option, may have the property sold subject to the lease or free and clear of it. The mortgagee exercises this option by joining or not joining the tenant in the foreclosure action.[73] If the tenant is not joined his lease is unaffected by the foreclosure sale and the purchaser may enforce the lease as a transferee of the reversion.[74] If he is joined, the purchaser takes the property title as it existed at the time the mortgage was entered into, i. e., free of the subsequent lease, and may therefore evict the tenant.[75]

In lien states the mortgagor remains the owner and is entitled to possession, hence to rents and profits, until foreclosure. Therefore, any leases subsequent to the mortgage are also binding as against the mortgagee until then. The logical consequence of this is that the rents and profits of the land where they are subsequent to the execution of the mortgage form no part of the mortgagee's security by virtue of the mortgage alone. Clauses assigning or pledging the rents and profits can, as we have seen, operate to bring them under the security of the mortgage, although not without the mortgagee taking possession or getting a receiver appointed.[75a] Further, even without any agreement in respect to them, by an equity extrinsic to the mortgage terms, the mortgagee under proper conditions is generally held to be entitled to have them collected by a receiver appointed in foreclosure suit even though the mortgagee himself would not have been entitled to them. Also, as was just seen, the mortgagee has the option

73. See notes, 14 A.L.R. 664 (1921); Ann.Cas.1915A, 397; 42 Harv.L.Rev. 280 (1928); 13 Col.L.Rev. 553 (1913); 21 Minn.L.Rev. 610 (1937); 42 Wash. L.Rev. 37 (1942).

74. See Metropolitan Life Ins. Co. v. Childs Co., 230 N.Y. 285, 130 N.E. 295, 14 A.L.R. 658 (1921) reargument denied 231 N.Y. 551, 132 N.E. 885; Commonwealth Mort. Co. v. De Waltoff, 135 App.Div. 33, 119 N.Y.S. 781 (1909); Dundee Naval Stores v. McDowell, 65 Fla. 15, 61 So. 108 (1913); Markantonis v. Madlan Realty Corp., 262 N.Y. 354, 186 N.E. 862 (1933). Contra: McDermott v. Burke, 16 Cal. 580 (1860); really a dictum since the lease was after suit was started and therefore subject to the decree under the doctrine of *lis pendens*; Dolese v. Bellows-Claude Neon Co., 261 Mich. 57, 245 N.W. 569 (1932), discussed in 32 Mich.L.Rev. 119 (1933). See 17 Wash.L.Rev. 37, 41 et seq. (1942).

75. The tenant, as a holder of an interest in the property subject to destruction by foreclosure sale, would have the privilege of redeeming from the mortgage and being subrogated to the mortgagee's rights. In this way he is able to protect his interest from destruction. See Glenn, Mortgages, § 181.1.

75a. See § 4.38, supra.

to determine whether the lease shall survive foreclosure in the sense that if the mortgagee omits the tenant from the foreclosure action, the lease remains in full force in the hands of the purchaser on the foreclosure sale who buys the reversionary interest carrying it.[76]

From the foregoing it is apparent that, in contrast to title states, the chief problem in lien states is not whether the receiver can affirm these leases. Rather it is whether he can disaffirm them and hold the tenant for the reasonable value of the use and occupation of the property, where that is higher than the reserved rental, in the face of the lessee's usual right to have them valid up to the time of the foreclosure sale. It should be scarcely necessary to say that if the mortgagee, or his receiver, cannot repudiate the mortgagor's leases prior to foreclosure sale, the tenant will not be able to do so. And the same is true, even though there might be a power in the mortgagee to reject the lease, if he has acted to preserve it by omitting the tenant from the foreclosure action.[77] In such cases, all the receiver can do is to collect the rents reserved in the leases.

Suppose the mortgagee joins the tenant in the foreclosure suit and thus sells the property free and clear of the tenant's interest. Then the question arises whether the receiver, for the period from his appointment to the foreclosure sale, is entitled only to the rent reserved in the lease or whether he may disaffirm it and either make a new lease with the tenant or hold him for the fair value of the use and occupation. In New York, the doctrine has been established that, barring the presence of fraud and collusion, the receiver on foreclosure sale could not disaffirm the leases entered into by the mortgagor subsequent to the mortgage, but could collect only the rent reserved in the lease itself. The Court of Appeals stated that "Though, during the pendency of the action, a court of equity has power to issue interlocutory orders for the protection of an asserted lien, such orders must be auxiliary to the right to foreclose the lien, and cannot deprive any part of a title or a right, which, though subordinate to the lien of the mortgage, survive and are valid until the lien is foreclosed by a sale under a judgment of foreclosure. * * * Until the lien of the mortgage is foreclosed, the mortgagee has no paramount title which would justify eviction of the occupants or abrogation of the agreements. The order of the court directing the occupants to vacate the premises or pay to the receiver the reasonable value of the use and occupancy deprives the occupants of a right which they have obtained by agreement. It does more than protect the security of the

76. Metropolitan etc. Co. v. Childs Co., 230 N.Y. 285, 130 N.E. 295, 14 A.L.R. 658 (1921), reargument denied 231 N. Y. 551, 132 N.E. 885.

77. Metropolitan etc. Co. v. Childs Co., supra note 74; Hewen Co. v. Malter, 145 Misc. 635, 260 N.Y.S. 624 (1932); Markantonis v. Madlan Realty Corp., 262 N.Y. 354, 186 N.E. 862 (1933); Knickerbocker Oil Corp. v. Richfield Oil Corp., 234 App.Div. 199, 254 N.Y. S. 506 (1931) affirmed 259 N.Y. 657, 182 N.E. 222 (1932); Lynch v. Harrer, 146 Misc. 493, 261 N.Y.S. 565 (1933).

mortgage debt. It gives to the mortgagee a security beyond the stipulations of the mortgage and deprives the occupants of their enjoyment of rights secured by contract." [78]

The logic of the lien theory, and probably its policy also, supports the view which prevailed.[79] Under that theory only the foreclosure sale itself should ever cancel the lease because it is only the sale which will affect the interest of the landlord, the mortgagor. Nevertheless, looking at the problem broadly, there seems no justification for arriving at different results on the basis of title or lien theories. The receivership is granted in any state to preserve the property and to prevent injury to the mortgagee's security. If the rents and profits do not constitute any part of the mortgagee's security, then clearly the receiver should not be able either to collect the reserved rent for the mortgagee or to cancel any of the mortgagor's leases. On the other hand, if they do constitute a part of the mortgagee's security, whether that be by reason of his position *qua* mortgagee, by virtue of clauses assigning or pledging the rents and profits to him, or because the court of equity feels that he should have the produce of the property as of the time he starts to realize on the property itself in which he had his security interest, then, whether or not the receiver should be permitted, or rather, directed, to avoid the mortgagor's leases ought to depend, as has been urged, "upon the answer to a simple question: can the mortgagee's margin of security be preserved adequately without avoiding" [80] them. If the continuance of the leases will render the margin inadequate, the receiver should be directed to avoid them.

The argument that this runs counter to the lien theory is not insurmountable. The appointment of a receiver in a lien state also does violence to the theory by taking possession away from the mortgagor before foreclosure sale. It does so especially when combined with allocation to the mortgagee of the rents and profits that arise and are collected by the receiver before sale. On the lien doctrine these belong to the mortgagor until sale in the absence of an agreement to the contrary. It is true that to allow the receiver, in addition, to disaffirm leases by the mortgagor subsequent to the mortgage would be going beyond this, and, the New York court believed, a step too far. However it really comes down to a question of degree, of how far the court thinks it is desirable to go in contravention of

78. Prudence Co. v. 160 W. 73 St. Corp., 260 N.Y. 205, 211, 183 N.E. 365, 366, 86 A.L.R. 361 (1932). The court was also moved by the unfortunate situation of the tenants under the decisions in New York, pointing out "that, if they vacate they not only lose the rights acquired under their agreements, but remain subject to its obligations, at least until there is a sale under a judgment of foreclosure, and even after that date, if the plaintiff should decide to discontinue the action as to them; if they do not vacate, they can be put out, unless they pay more than they agreed to pay."

79. See Glenn, Mortgages, § 181.1.

80. Tefft, Receivers and Leases Subordinate to the Mortgage, 2 Chi.L.Rev. 33, 35 (1934).

the view that the mortgagor and those claiming under him should be left in undisturbed enjoyment of the property, up to foreclosure sale, on the terms agreed upon between them. The encroachments on the mortgagor's rights under the lien theory which the courts have permitted have been justified on the ground that the protection of the mortgagee's security interest through a receivership was paramount. That same justification would extend to permitting the receiver to nullify any act by the mortgagor subsequent to the execution of the mortgage that operated to impair the adequacy of the mortgagee's security. Leases which fail to bring in the fair value of the use and occupation of the property, when the total security including the rents and profits is inadequate, do operate to impair the mortgagee's interest, and, therefore, if permitted to stand nullify pro tanto the purpose of the receivership. Consequently it boils down to whether it is more desirable to achieve completely the purpose for which the receiver was appointed, a purpose which in the very appointment of the receiver was considered sufficiently important to override the policy and rule in lien jurisdictions that the mortgagor not be ousted before foreclosure sale, or whether it will stop short of that on a combination of reasoning about the lien theory and solicitude for the plight of a tenant who, after all, can be considered to have acted voluntarily at his peril.[81] It is submitted that the former is the better view and that the receiver should have the power to disaffirm leases subsequent to the mortgage on the test suggested and not be confined merely to collecting the rents stipulated for in the leases.

§ 4.43 Receivership—Mortgagor in Possession

Closely related to the foregoing is the question whether a receiver may be appointed when the mortgagor remains in possession of the mortgaged property and uses it as a home or for other non-income producing purpose. There is scattered early authority not only that a receiver may be appointed to take over such property but that the mortgagor can be compelled by the receiver to pay an occupational rental.[82] This was also the law in New York until the case of

81. State ex rel. Coker v. District Court of Tulsa Co., 159 Okl. 10, 11 P.2d 495 (1932).

82. Yorkshire Bank v. Mullan, 35 Ch. D. 125 (1887); Pratchett v. Drew, 1 Ch. 280 (1924); Astor v. Turner, 3 How.Pr. 225 (N.Y.1848); Public Bank v. London, 159 App.Div. 484, 144 N.Y.S. 561 (1913). In New Jersey if the premises are in the possession of the mortgagor, especially if they are occupied by him as a home, the court will be most reluctant to appoint a receiver; and, in such a case will demand a clearer showing of the existence of the reasons for which receivers are appointed. See Rehberger v. Wegener, 107 N.J.Eq. 391, 152 A. 700 (1930), for a review of early and unofficially reported cases on the point. There was no showing that there was any possibility of a deficiency in the foreclosure suit and the receivership was denied. However, it was indicated that in a proper case one would be appointed and the mortgagor ordered to pay occupational rent or vacate. See 91 A.L.R. 1236 (1934), for a collection of cases.

Holmes v. Gravenhorst[83] was decided. In *Holmes* the court heavily stressed the fact that the receiver was appointed under a receivership clause covering rents and profits, and not under the general equity jurisdiction of the court, and the additional fact that there were no rents and profits for the receiver to take under the terms of the contract. The dissenting opinion took the view that "rents and profits" includes the personal occupancy by the mortgagor because that occupancy gives him a "benefit in all respects equivalent to rents and profits".[84]

The distinction stressed by the court makes it possible to distinguish the *Holmes* case from one in which the receiver is appointed on general equity principles. Where the receiver is appointed by virtue of the receivership clause alone without regard to the adequacy of the security there is no necessity for compelling the mortgagor to furnish additional security by way of rent. If the security is not shown to be inadequate, the result normally will be that any rents that the mortgagor is forced to pay as additional security will eventually be returned to him after the foreclosure sale. The imposition of the duty upon him to make payments under such circumstances is unwarranted. Where, however, the receiver is appointed under the general equity jurisdiction of the court because of the inadequacy of the security, the rent exacted from the mortgagor will go in payment or be a guaranty against a threatened deficiency. In such a case the justification for imposing the duty on the mortgagor is the same as that discussed in the preceding section in connection with tenants of the mortgagor. So long as the mortgagor is not in default he is privileged to keep the mortgaged property without regard to whether it

83. 263 N.Y. 148, 188 N.E. 285, 91 A.L.R. 1230 (1933), expressly overruling Citizens Savings Bank v. Wilder, 11 App.Div. 63, 42 N.Y.S. 481 (1896).

The case is discussed in Abelow, The Doctrine of Holmes v. Gravenhorst, 3 Brooklyn L.Rev. 212 (1934); note, 11 N.Y.Univ.L.Q.Rev. 480 (1934); note, 20 Cornell L.Q. 366 (1935); note, 8 U. of Cin.L.Rev. 213 (1934); note 33 Col.L.Rev. 1211 (1933) (a general discussion of the receiver of rents and profits in New York, covering the situation after the decision in the Prudence case and the Appellate Division decision in the principal case); 91 A.L.R. 1236 (1934).

84. "In effect, the mortgagor-occupant charges himself with the value of the space occupied as rent and credits himself with this amount as income. With the appointment of a receiver, the income credit—like the income from any other tenant—goes to the receiver. He continues to charge himself with rent, but he pays it to the receiver instead of to himself. He loses nothing since the rent goes to the receiver's fund to carry the property (a duty resting on him), and thereafter to meet a deficiency, if there be one, otherwise to himself." Crouch, J., dissenting, in Holmes v. Gravenhorst, supra note 83, at 158, 188 N.E. at 288. The Florida Supreme Court has stated that "it should not be lightly presumed that a stipulation for appointment of a receiver without notice is applicable where the property involved is a dwelling house in the actual occupancy of the mortgagors, and not being used nor offered for use as rental property." Martorano v. Spicola, 110 Fla. 55, 148 So. 585 (1933). See also, Grusmark v. Echleman, 162 F.Supp. 49 (S.D.N.Y.1958); Clark, Law of Receivers, § 958*i* (Supp.1969).

produces any income of any sort. When he defaults, however, the mortgagee is entitled to enforce his security and, through the appointment of a receiver, have it produce income from the time he starts to realize on it, provided the security is inadequate without that income. Consequently the mortgagor, if he stays on, arguably should have to pay rent. If he does not wish to do so, he thus should vacate the premises and allow the receiver to obtain income by renting to someone else or utilizing the premises in some other profitable way.

Suppose the mortgagee seeks to avoid the *Holmes* result by including in the receivership clause a provision that the mortgagor pay the receiver a reasonable rent for the mortgagor's occupation of the premises. In a case where the mortgage so provided, a lower New York appellate court cited *Holmes* and held that such a provision was unenforcible at least where the mortgage clause did not also grant the receiver the right of possession.[85]

§ 4.44 Receivership—Mortgagor Conducting Business

Where the mortgagor conducts a business on the mortgaged premises instead of renting them or occupying them as a home the first problem is whether the business is subject to the mortgage either by virtue of its being a product of the land or of an express inclusion under the terms of the mortgage.[86] This is so because it is clear that a mortgage foreclosure receiver cannot take into his possession or control property not covered by the mortgage, and a "mortgage covers the land and building—not the business enterprise housed".[87] The type of business ought to and does make a difference. Where the mortgagor has rented the property—a clear case for receivership—it is nevertheless true that the mortgagor, as landlord, engages in activities that come under the description of business, such as repairs, taking out insurance, paying taxes, getting tenants and executing leases with them and then collecting the rents, or, ousting them if they violate the conditions of the lease.[88] Notwithstanding the contribution to the income from these activities, the entire amount of the rent is regarded as issuing out of the land itself and there is no attempt to allocate the share of the total due to the work

85. Carlin Trading Corp. v. Bennett, 24 A.D.2d 91, 264 N.Y.S.2d 43 (1965); noted in 17 Syr.L.Rev. 774 (1966).

86. "We have, therefore, in the first instance, to ask, before appointing a manger to manage a business whether the business is included in the security." Whitley v. Challis, 1 Ch. 64, 70 (1892).

87. Abelow, The Doctrine of Holmes v. Gravenhorst, 3 Brook.L.Rev. 212 (1933); Scott v. Farmers' etc. Co., 69 F. 17, 16 C.C.A. 358 (N.D.1895); Smith v. McCullough, 104 U.S. 25, 26 L.Ed. 637 (1881); Thomas v. Armstrong, 51 Okl. 203, 151 P. 689, L.R.A.1916B, 1182 (1915). See 14 St.Louis L.Rev. 315. Cf. Muss v. Bergman, 55 A.D.2d 894, 391 N.Y.S.2d 115 (1977) (no authority in receiver to operate business in absence of evidence of waste or impairment of security.)

88. Glenn, Mortgages, § 185.

and abilities of the landlord-mortgagor. When a mortgagor conducts a business of any sort on his own land, the rental value of that land, whether explicitly recognized or not, is one of the elements comprising the gross income of the business, along with other factors such as price of materials, management, and interest on capital. Attempts to segregate from gross income that portion earned by the mortgaged real property can be little more than an arbitrary estimate in most cases.[89] It is not surprising, therefore, to find the courts appointing receivers in cases where the rent element clearly predominates and the services of the mortgagor are essentially the same in kind as those of any landlord, even though accentuated in degree, and the contribution to the income of other conveniences furnished is small.[90] This would cover apartment houses and, probably, a garage or parking lot.[91] Where, in addition to the land and buildings, the business utilizes considerable amounts of chattels, good will is a substantial factor and the part that management plays is large, the propriety of permitting the mortgagee to take over the business through a receiver is dubious. Of course, if the chattels and good will are also given in mortgage, the receivership has more justification.[92] But even without such inclusion, receivers have been appointed for hotels,[93] although there is some authority to the contrary,[94] and one case limited the receivership to that portion of the revenues derived from rent actually paid for rooms occupied.[95] On the other hand a receiver of mortgaged premises on which the mortgagor conducted a dance hall, restaurant and ice cream parlor was denied on the ground that there were no rents and profits within the meaning of the *Holmes* case.[96] Nor is it surprising to find a receiver appointed of property on which the

89. See 50 Yale L.Jour. 1427, 1440 (1941); 44 Yale L.Jour. 701, 704 (1935).

90. See 44 Yale L.Jour. 701, 703 (1935).

91. Garage: Fairchild v. Gray, 136 Misc. 704, 242 N.Y.S. 192 (1930); Title etc. Co. Belgrave Motor Sales Co., Inc., N.Y.L.J., Jan. 27, 1934, at 932, col. 4. Parking lot: City Bank Farmers Trust Co. v. Mishol Realty Co., N.Y.L.J., Jan. 27, 1934, at 441, col. 5.

92. See Cake v. Mohun, 164 U.S. 311, 17 S.Ct. 100, 41 L.Ed. 447 (1896), "furniture, equipment and other personal property" of hotel; Knickerbocker v. McKindley Coal & Mining Co., 172 Ill. 535, 50 N.E. 330, 64 Am. St.Rep. 54 (1898); Pacific N. W. Packing Co. v. Allen, 109 F. 515, 48 C.C.A. 521 (Wash.1901), tools, stock, and "outfit" of cannery. See 44 Yale L.Jour. 701, 702 (1935).

93. Lowell v. Doe, 44 Minn. 144, 46 N.W. 297 (1890); Warwick v. Hammell, 32 N.J.Eq. 427 (1880); Fidelity Trust Co. v. Saginaw Hotels, Inc., 259 Mich. 254, 242 N.W. 906 (1932); see Makeel v. Hotchkiss, 190 Ill. 311, 60 N.E. 524, 83 Am.St.Rep. 780 (1901).

94. Chatham-Phoenix Bank v. Hotel Park-Central, 146 Misc. 208, 261 N.Y. S. 490 (1931), receiver denied, not because the property was a hotel, but because the court thought a receivership could not accomplish the purpose of conservation and preservation any better than well advanced reorganization plans.

95. Stadtmuller v. Schorr, N.Y.L.J., Nov. 3, 1934, at 1633, col. 4.

96. Bartels v. Fowler, 160 Misc. 584, 290 N.Y.S. 908 (1936).

mortgagor has a tree nursery, the trees being treated as part of the realty.[97] Whether or not when the premises are used for a mixed purpose, e. g., a doctor using part of his home as an office, a receiver could compel the payment of some rent has been mooted but not answered by the courts.[98]

A recent California decision illustrates the problems presented where receivers attempt to exercise jurisdiction over the mortgagor's business and chattels.[99] There a rents and profits receiver appointed for a multi-million dollar motel complex attempted to take possession of a liquor license, food and beverage inventories, the furniture and television sets and certain other personal property. The California Court of Appeals noted that the above property was not covered by the deed of trust on the real estate and held that, absent mortgagor consent, the receiver was not authorized to take possession of such property. Having determined that the receiver lacked authority to take possession, it followed that a sale by the receiver of such property without mortgagor consent was prohibited. The court quoted with approval the first paragraph of this section and emphasized the limited role of the mortgage receivership as opposed to the "general" or "equity" receivership. The general or equity receiver often "takes possession of all of the debtor's assets and attempts to satisfy creditors out of those assets" [1] for the purpose of the liquidation or reorganization of the debtor. On the other hand, in characterizing the mortgage receivership, the court used the words of Justice Cardozo to show that "the rents and profits are impounded for the benefit of a particular mortgagee to be applied upon the debt in the event of a deficiency. The [mortgagor] retains its other property, if it has any, unaffected in its power of disposition by the decree of sequestration." [2]

The cases reflect a conflict between penalizing the mortgagor for conducting a business on his property by taking from him the entire profits instead of just that part which represents the share properly allocable to rents, an allocation that cannot be made, as was pointed out, except by arbitrary estimate, and penalizing the mortgagee who, if the property were rented, would be entitled to collect the rents. The policy of the court toward protecting one or the other, as well as its attitude in regard to the desirability or undesirability of receiverships as a remedy are factors that help explain the decisions.[3]

97. Heller v. Amawalk Nursery, Inc., 253 App.Div. 380, 2 N.Y.S.2d 196 (1938), affirmed 278 N.Y. 514, 15 N.E.2d 671, noted, 23 Cornell L.Quar. 614 (1938).

98. See Abelow, The Doctrine of Holmes v. Gravenhorst, 3 Brook.L. Rev. 212, 223 (1934).

99. Turner v. Superior Court, 72 Cal. App.3d 804, 140 Cal.Rptr. 475 (1977).

1. Id. at 72 Cal.App.3d 815, 140 Cal. Rptr. 481.

2. Duparquet Huot & Monevse Co. v. Evans, 297 U.S. 216, 221, 56 S.Ct. 412, 80 L.Ed. 591 (1936).

3. See, 44 Yale L.Jour. 701, 704–705 (1935).

§ 4.45 Receivership—"Milking" by the Mortgagor

When a mortgagor becomes resigned to the eventual loss of the mortgaged real estate, he frequently attempts to squeeze as much money out as possible before surrendering it. This process is often referred to as "milking." The chief devices by which such mortgagors attempt to "milk" the property are leases which require payment in advance for the entire term, the execution of a lease at an inadequate rental in return for a present cash consideration, the assignment of future rents to a third person, and the cancellation of a long term lease favorable to the lessor in exchange for a cash payment to the mortgagor.[4] As one commentator has aptly described the situation, such devices are used by hard-pressed mortgagors to "pocket the future earning capacity of the land and deliver to the mortgagee the empty shell of the mortgaged asset." [5] While the "milking" problem pervades more than receivership cases, the problem is commonly found in the receivership context. Accordingly, receivership situations often provide a useful vehicle for analysis and understanding of the milking concept.

The problem of preventing such undesirable practices necessitates reconciliation of three conflicting interests: safeguarding the mortgagee's security against impairment; protecting a tenant who made a lease in good faith from hardship; and preserving to the mortgagor the benefits of ownership.[6] It is, of course, bound up with the question whether the mortgagee or his receiver may affirm or disaffirm leases made by the mortgagor.[7]

Where the lease is executed prior to the mortgage, if it provides for prepayment, then prepayment in accordance with the terms of the lease is binding on the mortgagee for the simple reason that he took his mortgage subject to that very provision. However, prepayments not in accordance with the terms of the lease, if made with notice of the mortgage, will not be binding on the mortgagee or receiver even in the absence of proof of an actual fraudulent intent by the mortgagor or participation in it by the lessee.[8] This is true even though put in the form of an ageement altering the terms of the original lease.[9] Indeed such cases in most instances might well rest upon a theory

4. See Remedies Against "Milking" of Property by Mortgagors, 46 Harv.L. Rev. 491 (1933); Cancellation of Leases by Mortgagor as Affecting Mortgagee, 12 N.Y.Univ.L.Q.Rev. 501 (1935). There are other ways in which the mortgagor can milk the property. He may collect the rents and use them at the same time failing to pay taxes, keep up insurance, make repairs, etc.

5. Kratovil, Mortgages—Problems in Possession, Rents, and Mortgagee Liability, 11 DePaul L.Rev. 1, 13 (1961).

6. See 50 Yale L.Jour. 1427, 1437 (1941).

7. See § 4.42, supra.

8. See § 4.24, supra. Boteler v. Leber, 112 N.J.Eq. 441, 164 A. 572 (1933).

9. Colter Realty Co. v. Primer Realty Co., 262 App.Div. 77, 27 N.Y.S.2d 850 (1941).

generally more difficult to establish factually, that of setting aside a collusive agreement to defraud the mortgagee. As has been pointed out, any arrangement for prepayment of the rent for the whole term or a large portion of it is abnormal and, if made after a mortgage has attached to the property, indicates clearly a design to defeat the mortgagee's assertion of claim to it on default and foreclosure.[10] Since this is so, the tenant who agrees to such an arrangement must be charged with collusive acquaintance with the scheme[11] and, on this ground, the courts are justified in giving no validity to the prepayment, provided, of course, the tenant knew of the existence of the mortgage at the time.[12]

The cancellation of a favorable lease antedating the mortgage, or a reduction in the rent of such leases for a cash payment to the mortgagor might also be treated as fraudulent conveyances, if, in fact, such was the case.[13] Here, however, there is not present the abnormality of the transaction to charge the tenant with collusion as in the prepayment case, and difficulties of proof would make it an ineffective remedy. However, such acts do constitute a clear injury to the mortgagee's security because they deprive the mortgagee or his receiver of the rents they would be able to collect on entry into possession or on appointment. It is an injury which, looking at the mortgagor's responsibility, may be considered as waste insofar as it threatens to impair the security.[14] However, the mortgagee's remedies against the mortgagor for such a wrong would not be very satisfactory. An action for damages against him, even if allowed and pursued, would probably be worthless since he is likely to be insolvent.[15] An injunction should be allowed, but only against a particular threatened cancellation, and consequently constant vigilance and a series of suits by the mortgagee might be necessary.[16] To be able to hold the tenant on his original lease would give the mortgagee what he really wants. Notice to the tenant of the existence of the mortgage on the reversion should be sufficient to restrict his ability to enter into agreements with the mortgagor that will reduce the value of the security. Proof of actual fraud is unnecessary.[17]

10. See Glenn, Mortgages, § 183.1.

11. See Glenn, Fraudulent Conveyances and Preferences, rev. ed., §§ 299–299b.

12. "The court will take care of a sharper, as landlord, who leases premises for a long term, with rent payable in advance, and lets the mortgagee take the 'empty shell.'" Nerwal Realty Corp. v. 9th Ave.-31st St. Corp., 154 Misc. 565, 278 N.Y.S. 766 (1935). But where the lease is untainted by dishonesty payment in advance will be valid and the lease will stand. See 22 N.Y.Univ.L.Q.Rev. 731 (1947).

13. Sager v. Rebdor Realty Corp., 230 App.Div. 106, 243 N.Y.S. 314 (1930).

14. See 46 Harv.L.Rev. 491, 494 (1933); 50 Yale L.Jour. 1427, 1438 (1941).

15. See § 4.4, supra.

16. See 50 Yale L.Jour. 1424, 1438 (1941); 46 Harv.L.Rev. 494 (1933).

17. Bank of Manhattan Trust Co. v. 571 Park Ave. Corp., 263 N.Y. 57, 188

Where the lease is subsequent to the mortgage, in those jurisdictions, chiefly title states, in which the mortgagee or a receiver in foreclosure may disaffirm the mortgagor's leases, neither a prepayment of the rental, even if in accordance with the terms of the lease, nor a lease calling for an inadequate rental will be binding. In the event that it is disregarded, other questions arise. One is whether the tenant may be held to pay a reasonable rental for the period of his use and occupation from the time that the mortgagee or the receiver takes over rather than being allowed to assert the terms of his agreement with the mortgagor as setting the bounds of his liability.[18] Another is whether, if the prepayment of inadequate rent was by an agreement changing the terms of a previous lease, also subsequent to the mortgage, the tenant could be held to the higher terms of the original lease or whether he could treat the entrance by the mortgagee or appointment of the receiver as an eviction releasing him from his lease.[19]

Where the mortgagee or receiver seeks to take advantage of such a favorable lease by voiding the cancellation of it he is met by arguments that he cannot do so. Lack of privity of title between the mortgagee and tenant together with the notion of eviction of the tenant by superior title are relied upon to block such action. If the cancellation or other agreement altering unfavorably the terms of such a lease can be established to have been effected in anticipation of foreclosure with the intent of defrauding the mortgagee it generally will be set aside. But, as was noted above, proof of this is ordinarily too difficult to make the rule of practical benefit. If the latter is the case, relief from milking operations of this sort may be illusory. If the tenant is unwilling to come to terms on a new lease, at most he can be held only for use and occupation of the premises from the time the rights of the mortgagee or receiver accrue until he moves out, and then a new tenant must be found.

While some lien states hold that the mortgagee or a receiver in foreclosure is bound by the terms of the mortgagor's subsequent leases and cannot disaffirm them, an order appointing a receiver "may [not] be frustrated by a collusive or fraudulent lease for an inadequate rental or advance payment of rent in anticipation of a foreclo-

N.E. 156 (1933) noted, 11 N.Y.Univ.L.Q.Rev. 480 (1934). Cf. Colter Realty, Inc., v. Primer Realty Corp., 262 App.Div. 77, 27 N.Y.S.2d 850 (1941). Both cases involved leases subsequent to the mortgage with clauses making the rents and profits security for the debt. In holding that agreements lessening the yield of the property were invalid the court did so on the ground that, even short of fraud and collusion, the mortgagor and his tenant could not impair the mortgagee's security, with notice of the mortgagee's rights, even though the agreement was made before those rights had become operative. The case of a lease antedating the mortgage would be an *a fortiori* one.

18. Rohrer v. Deatherage, 336 Ill. 450, 168 N.E. 266 (1929).

19. First National Bank of Chicago v. Gordon, 287 Ill.App. 83, 4 N.E.2d 504 (1936). See supra, § 4.42.

sure action."[20] Further, since the mortgagee may preserve favorable leases subsequent to the mortgage and have them sold as part of his security on foreclosure sale, cancellation of such leases can be regarded as an impairment of the mortgagee's security on the same reasoning as in the case of a lease prior to a mortgage, and the same consequences should attend it. In other words, notice of the mortgagee's rights should suffice to prevent a valid agreement being made even though no fraudulent design to defeat his claim can be adduced. This clearly ought to be, and apparently is, true where the milking agreement surrendering or changing the subsequent lease occurs after the date when an assignment or pledge of such rents has become operative.[21] It is also true where it is made after an action for the foreclosure of the property and appointment of a receiver has been begun and notice of *lis pendens* has been filed although the receiver is not appointed until after the agreement and prepayment.[22] It should further be true of agreements made before that time but with notice that under certain contingencies the mortgagee would become entitled to the rent stipulated for in the lease with the mortgagor.

This has been so held in New York where the mortgage contained a pledge of rents and profits, the operative contingency in such a case being the appointment of a receiver. The court, while still affirming its ruling that a "receiver could not require a tenant in occupation under a lease to pay any sum for use and occupation beyond the sum which the lease called for," pointed out that it had not intended by its earlier decision[23] to hold that the mortgagor's agreement was conclusive upon the mortgagee where such agreements were in contravention of the express covenants and the necessary implications of a recorded mortgage prior in lien. The court held that where a mortgagor's agreement is made surrendering the right to receive rent for the mortgaged premises, or for the assignment of rents collectible therefrom, it was an impairment of the lien of the mortgage upon the rent. "The court also held that it was not necessary to find collusion in the making of such an arrangement; that it was beyond the power of the parties to appropriate the pledged rents to a different indebtedness, or defeat the pledge by leasing the premises

20. Prudence Co. v. 160 W. 73d St. Corp., 260 N.Y. 205, 213, 183 N.E. 365, 367, 86 A.L.R. 361 (1932), Hanna, Cas.Security, 983. Webber v. King, 205 Iowa 612, 218 N.W. 282 (1928), Gaynor v. Blewett, 82 Wis. 313, 52 N. W. 313, 33 Am.St.Rep. 47 (1892), might be explained on this same ground although the intent to defraud would have to be based on constructive notice of *lis pendens* of the suit to foreclose.

21. "After the mortgagors' release to the mortgagee of their right to rents under the lease became operative, the landlord had no right to modify the lease or enter into any agreement of modification that would bind the mortgagee without the latter's consent or approval." Franzen v. G. R. Kinney Co., 218 Wis. 53, 57, 259 N. W. 850, 852, 105 A.L.R. 740 (1935).

22. Gaynor v. Blewett, 82 Wis. 313, 52 N.W. 313 (1892).

23. Prudence Co. v. 160 W. 73d St. Corp., 260 N.Y. 205, 183 N.E. 365, 86 A.L.R. 361 (1932).

rent free." [24] The result of such a decision is the recognition of an equitable lien on the rents and profits at least sufficient to prevent arrangements between the mortgagor and the tenant with notice, made prior to the date when the pledge would become operative by the appointment of a receiver, which would impair the mortgagee's security.

On the other hand, in Grether v. Nick,[25] the Wisconsin court, in spite of the presence of a valid pledge of the rents and profits, held that a prepayment of rent by a subsequent lessee was valid against the receiver in foreclosure and the tenant could not be made to pay again. The case, however, can be distinguished from the New York cases even though in its opinion the court emphasized the rule that a pledge of rents and profits does not create any rights in them until a receiver is appointed or the mortgagee takes possession. The right of a receiver to collect rents and profits rests upon the theory that they form part of his security either by express agreement or by an equity extrinsic to the mortgage stipulations.[26] Further, the power of a receiver to disregard various sorts of milking arrangements, or, more broadly, to affirm or disaffirm leases of his mortgagor, rests upon the idea that his action is justified to prevent the security to which the mortgagee is entitled from being impaired. Applying this to the case of prepaid rents, if the mortgagor used them to improve the mortgaged property instead of diverting them to his own pockets, then "the mortgagee enjoys the full benefit of the advanced payment, and * * * a court of equity should not work oppression by requiring its payment a second time." This was the express rationale of Grether v. Nick, the prepaid rent having been used to complete a building on the mortgaged premises.[27]

The question remains whether it is one of the "implications of a prior recorded mortgage" without a rent pledge that the right of a mortgagee to obtain a receiver to collect rents and profits when the mortgagor defaults creates before that time an equitable interest in them as effective, as against anyone charged with notice of the mortgage, as that generated by a pledge clause? If so, then contracts by the mortgagor impairing that interest by surrendering his right to

24. Colter Realty, Inc., v. Primer Realty Co., 262 App.Div. 77, 80, 27 N.Y. S.2d 850, 852 (1941), summarizing Bank, etc. Co. v. 571 Park Ave. Corp., 263 N.Y. 57, 188 N.E. 156 (1933), and holding that the same reasoning invalidated a prepayment arrangement under a lease subsequent to the mortgage in which there was a pledge of the rents, the prepayment occurring before the receiver was appointed and, therefore, before the pledge became operative.

25. 193 Wis. 503, 215 N.W. 571, 55 A. L.R. 525 (1927).

26. See § 4.37, supra.

27. See Glenn, Mortgages, § 183.1. Grether v. Nick was also differentiated from the sort of case in which prepayments of rent were made to enable the mortgagor to appropriate them in fraudulent contravention of the rights of the mortgagee to them. Gaynor v. Blewett, 82 Wis. 313, 52 N.W. 313 (1892), was distinguished on this ground.

receive the rents, collecting them in advance, or assigning them should be invalid as against the receiver in foreclosure.

It ought to be immaterial whether the contingency which would make operative the right of the mortgagee or a receiver to collect the rents under the lease is one provided for and made effective by an assignment or pledge of the rents and profits [28] or one which by a rule of equity is conferred upon a receiver appointed in foreclosure after default by the mortgagor. In either case, while the terms of the lease might be altered for the period up to the time when the rights of the mortgagee or receiver became operative, from that time on the rights on the lease as originally written should be enforced. Nevertheless, in a prior decision in Grether v. Nick,[29] in which the court mistakenly assumed there was no rent pledge, it was held that, although a receiver of rents and profits was appointed, the prepayment of rents by the subsequent lessee before that time was binding on the receiver.[30] The court reasoned that the rent paid in advance bought a leasehold interest in the property which, though subordinate to the mortgage in the sense that it can be ended when the mortgagor's title is divested by foreclosure sale, nevertheless is valid against a receiver of the mortgagor who is entitled only to those rents and profits which become due after his appointment. Further, in Wisconsin, a receiver was appointed only on the ground of prevention of waste, not inadequacy of the security, and this fact made the court reluctant to grant any greater rights to the rents and profits than precedent required. The answer to this is twofold. First, the ground on which the case was put when it was found that there was a pledge of rents and profits, although not mentioned in the first decision, is equally applicable to it. Second, if valid, it would open too wide a door to almost any sort of "milking" by the mortgagor.[31] Certainly a fraudulent prepayment should not be valid [32] and the broader rule of the New York cases hitting agreements that impair the mortgagee's security when made with notice is a desirable one.

28. "These rents were expressly made security for the mortgage indebtedness in the event of default, and the scope of the contracts the mortgagor or its successors might make was necessarily limited to that extent. The pledge of these rents could not subsequently be rendered worthless either by another assignment of rents to be received, or by contracting away the right to collect any rent." Bank of Man. Tr. Co. v. 571 Park Ave. Corp., 263 N.Y. 57, 63, 188 N.E. 156, 158 (1933).

29. 193 Wis. 503, 213 N.W. 304, 215 N.W. 571, 55 A.L.R. 525 (1927).

30. See Berick, The Mortgagee's Right to Rents, 8 Cin.L.Rev. 250, 274 (1934). See also Allen, Appointment of Receivers in Mortgage Foreclosure Cases, 1932, 16 Marquette L.Rev. 168.

31. See Glenn, Mortgages, § 183.1.

32. Webber v. King, 205 Iowa 612, 218 N.W. 282 (1928).

"Even this court [Grether v. Nick], however, would not protect a tenant who pays his rent in advance after the foreclosure is begun. And all the courts in the same group indicate that if an assignment of rent or the prepayment of rent or the execution of a lease upon an inadequate rental, are the result of a deliberate fraud and collusion to defeat the mortgagee, the transaction will not be per-

§ 4.46 Priorities Between Mortgagees as to Rents

Frequently there is a race between different mortgagees to obtain for themselves the rents and profits of the mortgaged property through the appointment of a receiver. When this happens how are the priorities to be determined? The general rule is clear that a first mortgagee, even without a rents and profits clause, who obtains a receiver or takes possession, will prevail as to all rents thereafter [33] to the exclusion of any other claimant whether junior mortgagee,[34] judgment creditor [35] or general creditor.[36] This includes accruing and uncollected back rents. This rule is understandable because, after all, to the extent that the rents reduce the senior lien, the status of the junior lienors often improves. To be sure, there can be situations where the total value of the liens against the property is so high in relation to the value of the property that reduction of a senior lien will have little economic meaning to junior lienors. Even in that situation, however, there seems to be no compelling reason to depart from the consequences of normal priority rules.

Most courts hold that a junior mortgagee who obtains a receiver is entitled to all rents and profits collected by the receiver prior to the assertion of the rights of a senior mortgagee through the extension of the receivership to him,[37] the appointment of a new receiver at his petition, or the getting of possession.[38] This is a reward to the

mitted to prejudice the mortgagee." Berick, The Mortgagee's Right to Rents, 8 Cin.L.Rev. 250, 275 (1934).

33. Both as to income earned prior to default and after default, "it is usually stated as an elementary proposition of law that the mortgagee or trustee [in a trust deed mortgage] has no right to income unless and until he either makes a demand for possession of the mortgaged premises, applies to the court for the appointment of a receiver, or intervenes in a proceeding brought by a junior mortgagee or a general creditor." Israels & Kramer, Income Clause in a Corporate Mortgage, 30 Col.L.Rev. 488, 498 (1930).

34. Last v. Winkel, 86 N.J.Eq. 356, 97 A. 961 (1916), affirmed 86 N.J.Eq. 431, 99 A. 1070; Metropolitan Life Ins. Co. v. Tash-Lap Realty Corp., 138 Misc. 68, 245 N.Y.S. 281 (1930).

35. Central Trust Co. v. Chattanooga R. & C. R. R., 94 F. 275, 36 C.C.A. 241 (C.C.A.Ga.1899).

36. Hayes v. Dickenson, 9 Hun 277 (N.Y.1876). See Israels & Kramer, Income Clause in Corporate Mortgages, 30 Col.L.Rev. 488, 503 (1930).

The mortgagee's ability to obtain the rents of mortgaged property after bankruptcy of the mortgagor is considered in note, 45 Harv.L.Rev. 901 (1932); 50 Yale L.Jour. 1424, 1445 (1941); 18 Col.L.Rev. 91 (1918); Berick, The Mortgagee's Right to Rents, 8 Cin.L.Rev. 250, 292 (1934); 56 Harv.L.Rev. 305 (1942); 75 A.L.R. 1526 (1931); Cf. In re Hotel St. James Co., 65 F.2d 82 (C.C.A.Cal. 1933). For his right to rents and profits during an agricultural composition proceeding, see note, 11 Rocky Mt.L.Rev. 65 (1938).

37. See Yoelin v. Kudla, 302 Ill.App. 413, 24 N.E.2d 67 (1941).

38. Detroit Properties Corp. v. Detroit Hotel Co., 258 Mich. 156, 242 N.W. 213 (1913); Post v. Dorr, 4 Edw.Ch. (N.Y.) 412 (1845); Sullivan v. Rosson, 223 N.Y. 217, 119 N.E. 405, 4 A.L.R. 1400 (1918) noted, 27 Yale L.Jour. 1085 (1918); N.Y. Life Ins. Co. v. Fulton Development Corp., 265 N.Y. 348, 193 N.E. 169 (1934); Goddard v. Clarke, 81 Neb. 373, 116 N.W. 41 (1908); Longdock Mills & Elevator

junior mortgagee for his diligence, for had it not been for his action, the rents up to the time the senior mortgagee asserted his rights, would have gone to the mortgagor-landlord. Or, to put the matter in a different way, in spite of superiority of lien through seniority, a mortgagee who has done nothing to capture the rents arguably should be in no better position than he would have been in had the mortgagor continued in possession.[39]

There is, however, some authority that even though the junior mortgagee obtains a receiver first, if the senior mortgagee intervenes, all of the rents and profits collected by the receiver will be allocated in the order of the priorities of the mortgages, thus depriving the junior mortgagee of his advantage as to the part already collected.[40]

The effect upon these general rules of clauses assigning or pledging the rents and profits has not been definitively settled. Since the first mortgagee without a rents and profits clause will generally prevail as to rents and profits uncollected and accruing from the time he intervenes to assert his rights, *a fortiori* the same would be true if it contained such a clause.[41] It would seem clear, also, that if the first mortgage contained an assignment of rents and profits which operated

Co. v. Alpen, 82 N.J.Eq. 190, 88 A. 623 (1913); Bermes v. Kelley, 108 N.J. Eq. 289, 154 A. 860 (1931); Re Metr. Amal.Ests., 2 Ch. 497 (1912); Re Belbridge Prop.Trust, 165 L.T.Rep. 170 (1941). See 50 Yale L.Jour. 1424, 1442 (1945); 43 Yale L.Jour. 107, 108 (1933); 95 A.L.R. 1050 (1935).

39. "His [the senior mortgagee's] failure to take any action would, or might have been as serious to him if the receiver had never been appointed as he now claims it will be if the money in the hands of the receiver is not paid to him as mortgagee. He is not now entitled to appropriate the proceeds of the diligence of a junior mortgagee." Sullivan v. Rosson, 223 N.Y. 217, 225, 119 N.E. 405, 408 (1918). See Tefft, Receivers and Leases Subordinate to the Mortgage, 2 U.Chi.L.Rev. 33, 41 (1934); 33 Col. L.Rev. 1211, 1218 (1933).

40. Bergin v. Robbins, 109 Conn. 329, 146 A. 724 (1929); Wolkenstein v. Slonim, 355 Ill. 306, 189 N.E. 312 (1934) noted 2 Chi.L.Rev. 149, possibly is susceptible to the same interpretation because the receiver was ordered to pay over to the first mortgagee all of the rents and profits collected by the receiver appointed in the foreclosure action by the second mortgagee. However, the first mortgagee, although he did not know at the time of the prior action by the second mortgagee, began his own foreclosure action on the day that the receiver was appointed in the prior suit and there is nothing in the facts to indicate that any rents had been collected by the receiver before the first mortgagee petitioned to have the receiver turn over to him all of the rents and profits. See, also, N.J. Title & Guarantee Co. v. Cone & Co., 64 N.J.Eq. 45, 53 A. 97 (1902), in which the first mortgagee, who began his foreclosure before the second mortgagee began his and obtained a receiver, was held entitled to all rents and profits, the second mortgagee being denied any priority as to them by securing the appointment of the receiver.

41. Sullivan v. Rosson, 223 N.Y. 217, 119 N.E. 405, 4 A.L.R. 1400 (1918) noted, 27 Yale L.Jour. 1085 (1918), as against junior mortgagee; Atlantic Trust Co. v. Dana, 128 F. 209, 62 C. C.A. 657 (Kan.1903), as against judgment creditor; Newport etc. Co. v. Douglas, 75 Ky. (12 Bush.) 673 (1877) as against judgment creditor; Re Banner, 149 F. 936 (D.C.N.Y.1907), as against general creditor; First Savings, etc., v. Stuppi, 2 F.2d 822 (C.C. A.M.1924), as against general creditors.

to give rights to the mortgagee prior to the appointment of a receiver or taking possession, the first mortgagee should be entitled as against a receiver appointed on the application of a second mortgagee to all rents accruing after the date the assignment become effective even though collected by the receiver prior to intervention by the first mortgagee.[42] On the other hand, if the clause is construed to be only a pledge of the rents and profits any inchoate equitable lien which may be raised by it before being made effective through affirmative action by the mortgagee [43] is insufficient to give him any claim to rents and profits collected by the receiver of a later mortgagee prior to that affirmative action.[44]

The effect upon the rights of a prior mortgagee of rents and profits clauses in a subsequent mortgage has been involved in some of the cases. Where the first mortgage contains no clause and the later one contains a pledge clause, the general rule that the prior one will prevail as to rents and profits from the time of intervention has been followed.[45] The same has been true where there was an assignment of rents and profits in the later mortgage.[46] It would follow that if the prior mortgage contained a pledge of rents and profits the same result would be reached. Where both the earlier and the later mortgages contain clauses that are construed to be pledges only

42. Harris v. Taylor, 35 App.D. 462, 54 N.Y.S. 864 (1898), assignment by separate instrument; John McMenamy Investment & Real Estate Co. v. Dawley, 183 Mo.App. 1, 165 S.W. 829 (1914); Paramount Bldg. & Loan Ass'n v. Sacks, 107 N.J.Eq. 328, 152 A. 457 (1930), clause in mortgage.

43. See § 4.38 supra. Normally this action consists in asking for a receiver, or for the extension of an existing receivership.

44. Sullivan v. Rosson, supra note 41; Abrahams v. Berkovitz, 146 App.Div. 563, 131 N.Y.S. 257 (1911); Prudential Ins. Co. v. Liberdar Holding Co., 74 F.2d 50 (C.C.A.N.Y.1934), clause "assigning" rents and profits on default gave no rights against prior equity receiver for benefit of creditors as to rents collected by the receiver prior to the appointment of the mortgagee's receiver in foreclosure. That a "rents, issues, and profits" clause combined with a receivership clause gives to the mortgagee an inchoate lien valid in Kentucky against general creditors but not against subsequent assignees or specific liens, see Francis, Mortgages on After-Acquired Property in Kentucky, 35 Ky.L.J. 320, 327 (1947). See 50 Yale L.Jour. 1427, 1443 (1941); 30 Col.L.Rev. 488, 503 (1930); 43 Yale L.Jour. 107, 108 (1934).

45. Fidelity Mort. Co. v. Mahon, 31 Ohio App. 151, 166 N.E. 207 (1929). In McBride v. Comley, 204 Iowa 622, 215 N.W. 613 (1927), where both a prior and subsequent mortgagee applied for a receiver, the junior mortgagee was given the prior right to the rents and profits on the ground that it contained a receivership clause while the earlier one did not but based its right to a receiver solely on the ground that the security was inadequate and the mortgagor was insolvent. The court's reasoning was that a receiver appointed on the latter grounds had no power to use the rents to pay the debt of the mortgagee. If the prior mortgagee had obtained a receiver on the ground of waste or impairment of the security, this would carry the right to have the rents applied to the debt, and the court intimates the prior mortgagee would then prevail over the latter one with a clause in it calling for a receiver or pledging the rents.

46. Wiggins v. Freeman, 174 App.Div. 304, 160 N.Y.S. 448 (1916).

of the income, although the first mortgagee will be entitled to priority as to rents and profits from the time he effectively asserts his rights by having the receivership extended to him, a junior mortgagee who previously obtains a receiver is entitled to all rents collected up to the time of the first mortgagee's intervention.[47]

H. ACQUISITION OF TITLE IN BREACH OF DUTY

§ 4.47 Acquisition By Mortgagor

A mortgagor is under a duty to the mortgagee to discharge the secured obligation. Hence he cannot fail to do so, buy the property in on foreclosure, and hold it free of the mortgage. He can do this neither directly nor through intermediaries.

Thus, where there are covenants of title and to defend by the mortgagor in a second mortgage, he cannot acquire title on the foreclosure sale of a defaulted first mortgage so as to cut off a second mortgage by direct[48] purchase or through collusion with another.[49] The same has been held to be true even though the second mortgage was expressly subject to the first mortgage, such a clause being construed as mere identification of a lien already existing and superior

47. Sullivan v. Rosson, supra note 41.

48. Dixieland Realty Co. v. Wysor, 272 N.C. 172, 158 S.E.2d 7 (1967); Home Owners Loan Corp. v. Guaranty Title Trust Co., 168 Tenn. 118, 76 S.W.2d 109 (1934); Hilton v. Bissell, 1 Sandf. Ch. 407 (N.Y.1844).

49. Stiger v. Mahone, 24 N.J.Eq. 426 (1874), no covenant. The result is reached by holding that the purchase was payment of the prior mortgage, that the covenant operated either as an estoppel or a contract which would be given specific effect, or by saying that a title cannot be founded upon the wrong of failing to perform one's duty. See Dorff v. Bornstein, 277 N.Y. 236, 242, 14 N.E.2d 51 (1938), motion granted 278 N.Y. 566, 16 N.E.2d 105; Wood & Oberreich, Revival of a Second or Subsequent Mortgage upon Reacquisition of Title by the Original Mortgagor after Foreclosure of a First Mortgage, 11 Ind. L.J. 429 (1936). See White, Revival of Mortgages, 10 U. of Cin.L.Rev. 217 (1936). 44 Harv.L.Rev. 128 (1930). The doctrine of estoppel has been invoked in behalf of a foreclosing first mortgagee to refasten the lien of his mortgage upon a title obtained by the mortgagor from a third party when the original mortgage given by him was defective. Yerkes v. Hadley, 5 Dak. 324, 40 N.W. 340, 2 L.R.A. 363 (1888). So, too, where a mortgage contained a warranty of title, but before the execution of the mortgage the property, unknown to the mortgagor, had been sold for taxes, a reacquisition by the mortgagor of the title from the state will inure to the benefit of the mortgagee. Jacobsen v. Nieboer, 299 Mich. 116, 299 N.W. 830 (1941), noted, 26 Va.L.Rev. 101 (1941). The doctrine has been held inapplicable in such a situation where the mortgage is given to the vendor for the purchase money. The mortgagee in such a case having first conveyed the defective title to his mortgagor has no standing to invoke the rule. Florida Land Investment Co. v. Williams, 84 Fla. 157, 92 So. 876, 26 A.L.R. 171 (1922). Butterfield v. Lane, 114 Me. 333, 96 A. 233 (1915) accord. But see Clark v. Baker, 14 Cal. 612, 76 Am.Dec. 449 (1860); Toms v. Boyes, 50 Mich. 352, 15 N.W. 506 (1883). See 26 A.L.R. 173 (1923).

See Note, 29 N.D.L.R. 50 (1953), reviewing the different theories on which the courts hold that junior liens revive.

from the standpoint of priority on foreclosure but in no way affecting the covenant between the parties.[50] The same rule has been applied to a grantee from the mortgagor who assumed the payment of the mortgage debt,[51] but not to one who merely[52] took "subject to" it. The distinction is that in the latter case there is no duty on the non-assuming grantee to pay off the mortgage. Whether a mortgagor who reacquires title after foreclosure and sale to an independent third party takes it discharged of a later mortgage is the subject of some difference of opinion. Some courts hold that the mortgagor, on reacquisition, is still subject to the lien of the subsequent mortgage.[53] Others hold that he will take free and clear in the absence of any contract duty or fraudulent conduct by the mortgagor toward the second mortgagee.[54] The protection of the bona fide purchaser in his disposition of the property, he having bought upon the assumption he could sell and convey a title free from subsequent encumbrances to the one foreclosed to anyone, including the mortgagor, seems to be a factor in this result.[55]

Purchase of the mortgaged premises by the mortgagor at a tax sale provides another illustration of the general doctrine. "If a tax deed always conveyed title clear of all past encumbrances, it would be possible for delinquent owners to extinguish outstanding encumbrances by a repurchase of their property at a tax sale."[56] To pre-

50. Martin v. Raleigh State Bank, 146 Miss. 1, 111 So. 448, 51 A.L.R. 442 (1927). See 51 A.L.R. 445 (1927); 111 A.L.R. 1285 (1937); Merchants National Bank of Fargo v. Miller, 59 N.D. 273, 229 N.W. 357 (1930). Contrast Huzzey v. Heffernan, 143 Mass. 232, 9 N.E. 570 (1887); Sandwich Mfg. Co. v. Zellmer, 48 Minn. 408, 51 N.W. 379 (1892); Chamberlain v. Forbes, 126 Mich. 86, 85 N.W. 253 (1901). Federal Farm Mort. Corp. v. Larson, 227 Wis. 221, 278 N.W. 421 (1938), prior mortgage excepted in covenant of warranty; Zandri v. Tendler, 123 Conn. 117, 193 A. 598, 111 A.L.R. 1280 (1937).

51. Beitel v. Dobbin, 44 S.W. 299 (Tex.Civ.App.1898).

52. Searles v. Kelley, 88 Miss. 228, 40 So. 484, 8 L.R.A.,N.S., 491 (1906).

53. Federal Land Bank of Columbia v. Bank of Lenox, 192 Ga. 543, 16 S.E. 2d 9 (1941) discussed, 27 Iowa L.Rev. 482 (1942); Kerr v. Erickson, 24 S. W.2d 21 (Tex.Com.App.1930), noted, 30 Col.L.Rev. 742 (1930); Jensen v. Duke, 71 Cal.App. 210, 234 P. 876 (1921), statute; Johnson v. Clark, 7 Cal.2d 529, 61 P.2d 767 (1936), statute; Jones v. Kingsey, 55 N.C. 463 (1856); Martin v. Raleigh State Bank, 146 Miss. 1, 111 So. 448 (1927) with aid of statute; Merchants National Bank of Fargo v. Miller, 59 N.D. 273, 229 N.W. 357 (1930); Baird v. Chamberlain, 60 N.D. 784, 236 N.W. 724 (1931). See Wood & Oberreich, Revival of a Second or Subsequent Mortgage upon Reacquisition of Title by the Original Mortgagor after Foreclosure of a First Mortgage, 11 Ind.L.J. 429 (1936).

54. Zandri v. Tendler, 123 Conn. 117, 193 A. 598, 111 A.L.R. 1280 (1937); Dorff v. Bornstein, 277 N.Y. 236, 14 N.E.2d 51 (1938) noted, 13 St. John's L.Rev. 182; cf. Schultz v. Cities Service Oil Co., 149 Kan. 148, 86 P.2d 533 (1939) noted, 52 Harv.L.Rev. 1176 (1939). Cf. also McDonald v. Duckworth, 197 Okl. 576, 173 P.2d 436 (1946) criticized 60 Harv.L.Rev. 658 (1947). See also 30 Va.L.Rev. 496 (1944).

55. See 13 St. John's L.Rev. 182, 183 (1938).

56. 46 Yale L.J. 334 (1936).

vent such manipulation, it is the rule that one who owes to another the duty of paying taxes cannot, as to that other at least, default in his duty and then better his title by purchase on the tax sale resulting from his breach of duty.[57] The mortgagor in possession, being bound to pay the taxes as between himself and the mortgagee cannot, therefore, default in his obligation, allow the property to be sold for taxes, which constitute a paramount lien, and then buy in at the tax sale free and clear of the mortgage.[58] He cannot base a title on the violation of his duty [59] and his purchase, so far as the mortgagee is concerned, will be considered a payment of the taxes.[60] The doctrine extends even to the case where the sale is held after the foreclosure of the mortgage,[61] for, even though at the time of purchase the mortgagor-mortgagee relation no longer existed, his title would still be based upon a failure of duty during the time it did exist and one that caused the land on foreclosure to be sold subject to the tax lien rather than free of it, thus reducing the avails from the security accruing to the mortgagee.[62] Further, the great weight of authority holds that a transferee of the mortgagor, whether he assumes the payment of the mortgage debt or merely takes subject to it cannot defeat the lien of the mortgagee any more than could the mortgagor.[63]

§ 4.48 Acquisition of Tax Title by Mortgagee

A mortgagee in possession has the duty of keeping up the taxes and cannot, therefore, after failing to pay them purchase the property on a tax sale brought about by his default and hold the property free of the mortgagor's claim to redeem.[64] Where the mortgagee is

57. 3 Cooley, Taxation, § 1437. It has been pointed out that, since it seems inequitable to permit one to profit by buying in a tax title after neglecting the duty to pay them, regardless of to whom the duty ran, a broader statement is desirable. See 46 Yale L.J. 334, n. 2 (1936).

58. Dayton v. Rice, 47 Iowa 429 (1877); Woodbury v. Swan, 59 N.H. 22 (1879). Cf. Allison v. Armstrong, 28 Minn. 276, 9 N.W. 806, 41 Am. Rep. 281 (1881). See 16 L.R.A.,N.S., 121 (1908).

59. Pines v. Novick, 168 App.Div. 155, 153 N.Y.S. 891 (1915).

60. Waring v. Nat. Sav. & Trust Co., 138 Md. 367, 114 A. 57 (1921); Allison v. Armstrong, 28 Minn. 276, 9 N. W. 806, 41 Am.Rep. 281 (1881). See 90 U.Pa.L.Rev. 90, 94 (1941).

61. Adams v. Sims, 177 Ark. 652, 9 S. W.2d 329 (1928), noted, 42 Harv.L. Rev. 583 (1929). See also 52 L.R.A., N.S., 877, 878 (1914).

62. Barnard v. Wilson, 74 Cal. 512, 16 P. 307 (1888).

63. See 16 L.R.A.,N.S., 121, 124 (1908); 1914, L.R.A.,N.S., 877, 878, (1941) for collections of cases. See also 90 U. Pa.L.Rev. 90, 95. Zuege v. Nebraska Mort. Co., 92 Kan. 272, 140 P. 855, 52 L.R.A.,N.S., 877 (1914), is against the great weight of authority in holding that a purchaser from the mortgagor subject to the mortgage debt may buy a tax title free of the mortgage and seems incorrect. Ownership of the redemption interest, not personal obligation to pay the mortgage debt, is the criterion of duty to pay taxes. And it is the failure of the duty to pay the taxes that prevents the founding of a title on the tax sale purchase.

64. Schenck v. Kelley, 88 Ind. 444 (1882); Dusenbery v. Bidwell, 86

not in possession there is a split in the authorities.[65] Some let him buy in the title on a tax sale and cut off the rights of the mortgagor in the premises. They argue that the mortgagee had no duty to pay the taxes and stood in no fiduciary relation to the mortgagor. A denial of the privilege would let the mortgagor—who did have the duty to pay taxes—force the mortgagee still to hold only as a security claimant. This would allow the mortgagor to take advantage of his own default.[66] Further, the rule does not operate harshly against the mortgagor since, under tax statutes, he can redeem from the tax sale.[67] And, possibly most important, the incentive to the mortgagor and other mortgagees to pay taxes promptly and to purchase at the tax sale would be increased.[68] The clear weight of authority, however, will not permit the mortgagee thus to shake off the claim of the mortgagor.[69] When it comes to the ability of a mortgagee to acquire a tax title which will cut off the rights of a prior mortgagee, although there is authority that he may,[70] most cases hold that a jun-

Kan. 666, 121 P. 1098 (1912); Howze v. Dew, 90 Ala. 178, 7 So. 239, 24 Am.St.Rep. 783 (1889); Brown v. Simons, 44 N.H. 475 (1863); Hall v. Westcott, 15 R.I. 373, 5 A. 629 (1886). See also Moore v. Titman, 44 Ill. 367 (1867). Cf. Beckwith v. Seborn, 31 W.Va. 1, 5 S.E. 453 (1888); Ten Eyck v. Craig, 62 N.Y. 406, 422 (1875). See 140 A.L.R. 294, 318 (1941), for a collection of cases. A mortgagee in possession under an invalid foreclosure sale purchase has been held to be barred from acquiring a valid tax title as against the mortgagor. Nat. Surety Co. v. Walker, 148 Iowa 157, 125 N.W. 338, 38 L.R.A.,N.S., 333 (1910).

65. See 90 U.Pa.L.Rev. 90, 95 (1941).

66. Jones v. Black, 18 Okl. 344, 88 P. 1052, 11 Ann.Cas. 753 (1907); Price v. Salisbury, 41 Okl. 416, 138 P. 1024, L.R.A., 1917D, 520 (1914); Williams v. Townsend, 31 N.Y. 411, 415 (1865), "A mortgage is a mere security for a debt; and there is no such relation of trust or confidence between the maker and holder of a mortgage as prevents the latter from acquiring title to its subject matter, either under his own or any other valid lien. The defendant [mortgagee] had no duty to perform to the plaintiff, or toward the mortgaged premises, that precluded her from buying at the tax sale; she was under no obligation to pay the taxes."; McLaughlin v. Acom, 58 Kan. 514, 50 P. 441 (1898), noted 1898, 11 Harv.L.Rev. 343; Reimer v. Newel, 47 Minn. 237, 49 N.W. 865 (1891). Cf. First Nat. Bank of Rapid City v. McCarthy, 18 S.D. 218, 100 N.W. 14 (1904); see Waterson v. Devoe, 18 Kan. 223 (1877); Beckwith v. Seborn, 31 W.Va. 1, 5 S.E. 453 (1888). See also 140 A.L.R. 294, 311 (1941).

67. 4 Cooley, Taxation, 4th ed. § 1565 (1924).

68. See Baird v. Fischer, 57 N.D. 167, 185, 220 N.W. 892, 899 (1928), Christianson, J., dissenting.

69. Koch v. Kiron State Bank, 230 Iowa 206, 297 N.W. 450, 140 A.L.R. 273 (1941); Hadlock v. Benjamin Drainage Dist., 89 Utah 94, 53 P.2d 1156, 106 A.L.R. 876 (1936), discussed, 46 Yale L.J. 334 (1936); Eck v. Swennenson, 73 Iowa 423, 35 N.W. 503, 5 Am.St.Rep. 690 (1887); Porter v. Corbin, 124 Mich. 201, 82 N.W. 818 (1900). See Shepard v. Vincent, 38 Wash. 493, 80 P. 777 (1905); Burchard v. Roberts, 70 Wis. 111, 35 N. W. 286, 5 Am.St.Rep. 148 (1887); note, 46 Yale L.J. 334 (1936). See also 11 Ann.Cas. 750 (1909); 38 L.R. A.,N.S., 333 (1912); L.R.A.1917D, 522; 140 A.L.R. 294, 302 (1941); Stallings v. Erwin, 148 Mont. 227, 419 P.2d 480 (1966); National Bank of Washington v. Equity Investors, 86 Wash.2d 545, 546 P.2d 440 (1976).

70. Security Mortgage Co. v. Herron, 174 Ark. 729, 296 S.W. 363 (1927); see 140 A.L.R. 294, 329 (1941). Se-

ior mortgagee cannot procure and assert a tax title against a senior mortgage where both mortgages are outstanding.[71] Several reasons have been advanced for denying to a mortgagee the ability to acquire a new and independent title to the mortgaged property good against the mortgagor and other mortgagees. Occasionally it is said that the mortgagee is like a trustee and therefore is debarred from founding a title on the tax sale in opposition to the mortgagor or other mortgagees.[72] But the mortgagee may buy in at even his own court foreclosure sale and, consequently, even if it were true that he is a trustee, which it is not,[73] it is difficult to see why purchase at a tax sale would be in breach of any fiduciary obligation owed to the mortgagor, and, even more so, to other mortgagees. Sometimes the analogy of joint tenants is invoked.[74] But each joint tenant has a duty to pay the taxes and therefore as to them the general principle applies that one cannot profit by failing to do his duty. There is no duty on a mortgagee not in possession, in the absence of an express contract, running either to the mortgagor or to another mortgagee to pay the taxes and, therefore, that reason fails.[75] Still other courts stress the community of interest of the parties in preserving the es-

curity Mortgage Co. v. Harrison, 176 Ark. 423, 3 S.W.2d 59 (1928).

71. Connecticut Mut. Life Ins. Co. v. Bulte, 45 Mich. 113, 7 N.W. 707 (1881); Chrisman v. Hough, 146 Mo. 102, 47 S.W. 941 (1898); Oregon Mortgage Co. v. Leavenworth Sec. Corp., 197 Wash. 436, 86 P.2d 206 (1938), 14 Wash.L.Rev. 231 noted (1939); Baird v. Fischer, 57 N.D. 167, 220 N.W. 892 (1928), 13 Minn.L.Rev. 623 noted (1929); 38 Yale L.J. 263 (1928); 29 Col.L.Rev. 93 (1929). See notes, 14 Wash.L.Rev. 231 (1939); 11 Harv.L.Rev. 343 (1897). See also 11 Ann.Cas. 759 (1909); L.R.A.1917D, 522; 140 A.L.R. 294, 322 (1941); 90 U. of Pa.L.Rev. 90, 96 (1941). That a prior mortgagee cannot cut off a subsequent mortgagee, Anson v. Anson, 20 Iowa 55, 89 Am.Dec. 514 (1866). The junior mortgagee obtains his position in this respect as holder of a security interest in the redemption right of the mortgagor. There is a difference of opinion as to whether the fact that the title had become absolute and irredeemable in the hands of a third person when the mortgagee acquires it alters the result. Safe Deposit and Trust Co. v. Wickhem, 9 S.D. 341, 69 N.W. 14, 62 Am.St.Rep. 873 (1896), rehearing denied 9 S.D. 515, 70 N.W. 654. Contra: Chrisman v. Hough, 146 Mo. 102, 47 S.W. 941 (1898).

72. See, e. g., Finlayson v. Peterson, 11 N.D. 45, 89 N.W. 855 (1902); Ten Eyck v. Craig, 62 N.Y. 406, 422 (1875), mortgagee in possession: "A mortgagee is often called a trustee, and in a very limited sense this character may be attributed to him."

73. See Cholmondeley v. Clinton, 2 Jac. & W. 1, 183 (1820); Ten Eyck v. Craig, supra note 72, at 419 et seq.

74. E. g. Connecticut Mut. Life Ins. Co. v. Bulte, 45 Mich. 113, 122, 7 N. W. 707, 710 (1881), "It is as just and as politic here as it is in the case of tenants in common, to hold that the purchase is only a payment of the tax."

75. "It certainly cannot be said that the second mortgagee owes any duty to the first mortgagee to protect his lien against tax sale. Neither, on the other hand, does the first mortgagee owe any such duty to the second mortgagee, or to the owner. To the state each one of the three may be said to owe the duty to pay the taxes; and the state will sell the interest of all if none of the three shall pay." Connecticut Mut. Life Ins. Co. v. Bulte, 45 Mich. 113, 121, 7 N.W. 707, 710 (1881).

tate by the payment of taxes, drawing the conclusion therefrom that it would be inequitable conduct to acquire and assert a tax title against the others, or that presumably it is paid for the common protection.[76] The last is probably contrary to fact; just why it is inequitable when there is neither a contractual duty or one arising out of their relationship to pay the taxes is not explained; and the common derivation of their interests in the land does not create a common interest but rather antagonistic interests, certainly as between two mortgagees. The courts may be disturbed by the possibility that one who had merely a lien upon the property might obtain a tax deed for a small sum and by it destroy the liens of other mortgagees and the mortgagor; if the payment were viewed as a redemption, "the mortgagee, acquiring a prior lien on the property to the amount expended in that redemption would be placed in a position no worse than that which he occupied prior to the delinquency, while at the same time the other lienors would be materially benefitted." [77] Another suggestion is expressed legalistically by arguing that the rule preventing tax title purchase by one who owes a duty to another person to pay them should be broadened out to include all who owe a duty to the public to pay taxes. Such a duty is then found in the fact that the mortgagee, if he does not pay them, will lose his entire interest in the property.[78] Probably the same idea, but more broadly based, is expressed by saying that it is against public policy to allow the mortgagee to purchase at the tax sale and gain an advantage by so doing in that it would encourage him to fail to take advantage of his privilege to pay taxes. It is to the interest of the state that taxes be paid promptly, and since the mortgagee is fully protected by his privilege of paying when they are due, he should not be encouraged to fail to take advantage of that privilege.[79] But this is an argument that cuts both ways [80] and the incentive in any event is speculative and dubious.

76. Fair v. Brown, 40 Iowa 209 (1875); Woodbury v. Swan, 59 N.H. 22 (1879); Hall v. Westcott, 15 R.I. 373, 5 A. 629 (1886).

77. 46 Yale L.J. 334, 338 (1936).

78. 46 Yale L.J. 334, 337 (1936). See quotation from Connecticut Mut. Life Ins. Co. v. Bulte, 45 Mich. 113, 7 N. W. 707 (1881), supra note 75. But judgment creditors, who also have a security interest in the property, are not subject to the rule. Wilson v. Jamison, 36 Minn. 59, 29 N.W. 887, 1 Am.St.Rep. 635 (1886). "The recognition of a disability to purchase an unencumbered tax title, an issue of policy and not of legal rules, depends on a balancing of social interests that are far from clear; certainly there is no basis for a blanket disqualification of all such lienors." 46 Yale L.J. 334, 337 (1936).

79. See 3 Tiffany, Real Prop., § 616; Baird v. Fischer, 57 N.D. 167, 185, 220 N.W. 892, 899 (1928), Christianson, J., dissenting.

80. See supra, text, where the possibility that one mortgagee might acquire a clear tax title is cited as an incentive to other mortgagees and the mortgagor to see to it that taxes are paid.

§ 4.49 Tax Payment by Subsequent Mortgagee—Effect on Prior Mortgagee

If a second mortgagee pays off the paramount tax lien of the taxing authority, it is quite clear that he can add that amount to his own mortgage debt or be subrogated to the lien of the taxing power as against the mortgagor.[81] Whether he can be subrogated to that paramount lien as against a prior mortgagee is a more difficult question. In Laventall v. Pomerantz,[82] the first mortgage contained a clause accelerating the right to foreclosure on nonpayment of taxes. The New York Court of Appeals held that payment of the taxes by a holder of a subordinate mortgage would give him no right to be subrogated to the priority of the tax lien over the first mortgage. There are, however, cases giving subrogation to the second mortgagee, some of them even where there is an acceleration clause permitting foreclosure on default by the mortgagor in paying taxes, although most of them do not mention whether or not the mortgagor had such a right.[83] In these latter cases there may have been no such right; or it is possible that there was one but it had been so neglected that it could not be and was not seriously urged.[84] In a few jurisdictions the tax-paying junior encumbrancer is given a prior lien by statute.[85]

Where there is an acceleration clause in the first mortgage allowing foreclosure on non-payment of taxes by the mortgagee, the strongest argument against giving subrogation to the paramount lien for taxes as against the first mortgagee is that such payment destroys a most valuable right of the first mortgagee.[86] The right to foreclose on tax default is a valuable one because it is an effective means of forcing the mortgagor to pay the taxes and, also, because it provides a remedy at the first signs of financial irresponsibility of the mortgagor.[87] Consequently a junior mortgagee who destroys that recourse to the detriment of the earlier mortgagee should have no claim to be elevated to priority over the first mortgagee but should be remitted to adding the amount paid to his own mortgage debt,[88] at least

81. See supra, § 4.34.

82. 263 N.Y. 110, 188 N.E. 271 (1933), discussed in notes, 19 Cornell L.Q. 487 (1934); 11 N.Y.Univ.L.Q.Rev. 655 (1934); 1 U. of Chi.L.Rev. 813 (1934); 29 Ill.L.Rev. 123 (1934); 20 Va.L.Rev. 914 (1934). See also notes, 46 Harv. L.Rev. 1036 (1933); 42 Yale L.J. 971 (1937); 17 Tex.L.Rev. 352 (1933).

83. Marks v. Baum Bldg. Co., 73 Okl. 264, 175 P. 818 (1918), acceleration clause; Noeker v. Howry, 119 Mich. 626, 78 N.W. 669 (1899), "usual tax clause"; Ringo v. Woodruff, 43 Ark. 469 (1884); Fiacre v. Chapman, 32 N.J.Eq. 463 (1880). For collections of cases holding both ways, see 84 A.L.R. 1366, 1393 (1933); 123 A.L.R. 1248, 1261 (1939).

84. See 1934, 29 Ill.L.Rev. 123.

85. Ky.Rev.Stat. 134.080; La.Rev.Stat.—Civ.Code art. 2161; see Timken v. Wisner Estates, 153 La. 262, 95 So. 711 (1923).

86. Laventall v. Pomerantz, supra note 82.

87. See 29 Ill.L.Rev. 123 (1934).

88. Sidenberg v. Ely, 90 N.Y. 257, 43 Am.Rep. 163, 11 Abb.N.C. 354 (1882).

in the absence of unreasonable refusal or delay of the prior mortgagee to act for the protection of his own interest. But other reasons have been advanced. It is said that the first mortgagee is not unjustly enriched because he merely got a benefit to which he was entitled, and to grant subrogation would deprive him of a part of the security upon which he based his original loan.[89] The tax lien is the obligation of the mortgagor and if paid by someone else it should not detract from the mortgagee's security any more than if paid by the mortgagor himself.[90] Furthermore, the payment should be considered voluntary because it is made for the purpose of keeping the senior mortgagee from foreclosing, not for the purpose of relieving the estate of any tax liens,[91] and the *quid pro quo* he received was the extinguishment of the prior mortgagee's power to foreclose.[92] Also, where the mortgagor is liable, subrogation cannot be given as against another mortgagee because subrogation cannot be invoked against a third party not liable for the indebtedness discharged.[93] And in any event, a subordinate mortgagee stands in the mortgagor's shoes and gets no better rights than does the mortgagor, his rights being thus limited by reason of his position as mortgagee of the redemption interest. Since it was the mortgagor's duty, owed to all mortgagees, to pay the taxes, although he can add the tax to his claim against the mortgagor, he has no more power to be subrogated to a lien prior to that of the senior mortgagee than would his mortgagor.[94] Moreover, payment of the taxes legally destroys the lien so that there is nothing to which the paying mortgagee can be subrogated.[95] And to grant subrogation would encroach upon the privileges of sovereignty by according to a private individual the privilege of the taxing body's methods of collection.[96]

The chief arguments advanced in favor of permitting subrogation, either made affirmatively or in rebuttal of arguments for the opposite result, are that it would encourage payment of taxes,[97] a socially desirable result; [98] prevent the conferring of an unjust enrich-

89. See 42 Yale L.J. 972 (1932).

90. 20 Va.L.Rev. 914 (1933).

91. Pearmain v. Massachusetts Hospital Life Ins. Co., 206 Mass. 377, 92 N.E. 497 (1910); Fiacre v. Chapman, 32 N.J.Eq. 463 (1880), contra. For a brief discussion of the subrogation of a volunteer, see 40 Mich.L.Rev. 133 (1941).

92. Laventall v. Pomerantz, supra note 82.

93. Lawyers' Title & Guar. Co. v. Claren, 237 App.Div. 188, 260 N.Y.S. 847 (1932). But see 46 Harv.L.Rev. 1036 (1933); 1 U.Chi.L.Rev. 813, 814 (1934); 42 Yale L.J. 972 (1932).

94. Glenn, Mortgages, § 39.2.

95. 11 N.Y.Univ.L.Q.Rev. 655, 656 (1934).

96. Sperry v. Butler, 75 Conn. 369, 53 A. 899 (1903).

97. But it should not go unnoticed that one of the purposes of an acceleration clause is to compel the mortgagor to pay taxes, and encouragement of other mortgagee to pay lessens the pressure on the mortgagor.

98. See 46 Harv.L.Rev. 1037 (1933); 11 N.Y.Univ.L.Q.Rev. 655 (1934); 19 Cornell L.Q. 487 (1934). See also preceding section.

ment on the prior mortgagee because the second mortgagee, by discharging the tax lien, has to that extent increased the proceeds available to the prior mortgagee; the first mortgagee is not injured because otherwise he would be subordinate to the lien of the taxing authority [99]; and not only is the prior mortgagee not injured but he is benefited positively by the prevention of accrual of tax penalties and a sale of the land for taxes [1] and this benefit offsets the value to the prior mortgagee of the right to foreclose under an acceleration clause.[2] Further, there is some doubt whether payment by anyone other than the mortgagor would prevent the acceleration clause from becoming operative.[3] Additionally it is pointed out that subrogation to the lien of the taxing power can be *pro tanto* for the purpose of priority only and need not include granting the state's methods of collection which might be considered a delegation to a private individual of functions reserved to the public government.[4] The absence of personal liability of the prior mortgagee is no bar for the subrogation is to the lien, and not to a right *in personam* against a third party; and further, it is arguable that there is a [5] duty on all mortgagees to pay taxes and the subsequent one therefore is performing that duty.[6] Although the tax lien may be destroyed legally by payment, it is a well settled doctrine that equity can preserve or recreate legal rights that have ceased to exist where it is necessary to prevent unfairness.[7] And finally, the motive of the junior encumbrancer in paying to avoid foreclosure by the first mortgagee rather than of the tax lien ought not to be the test for granting subrogation; even if the primary purpose were to avoid such foreclosure, that is not sufficient cause for conferring so great a benefit on the prior mortgagee at the expense of the subordinate one.[8]

99. See 46 Harv.L.Rev. 1037 (1932); 19 Cornell L.Q. 487 (1934).

1. 11 N.Y.Univ.L.Q.Rev. 655 (1934).

2. See Noeker v. Howry, 119 Mich. 626, 78 N.W. 669 (1899); Fiacre v. Chapman, 32 N.J.Eq. 463 (1880); 1 U.Chi.L.Rev. 813, 814 (1934); 29 Ill. L.Rev. 123 (1934).

3. See 46 Harv.L.Rev. 1037 (1932); 1 U.Chi.L.Rev. 813, 814 (1934).

4. 42 Yale L.J. 971, 972 (1932); 1 U. Chi.L.Rev. 813, 814 (1934).

5. 42 Yale L.J. 972 (1932); 19 Cornell L.Q. 487 (1934).

6. See Connecticut Mut. Life Ins. Co. v. Bulte, 45 Mich. 113, 7 N.W. 707 (1881); 46 Yale L.J. 334, 337 (1936).

7. Title Guar. & Trust Co. v. Haven, 196 N.Y. 487, 89 N.E. 1082, 25 L.R.A., N.S., 1308, 17 Ann.Cas. 1131 (1909). See 11 N.Y.Univ.L.Q.Rev. 655 (1934); 42 Yale L.J. 971, 972 (1932).

8. See 46 Harv.L.Rev. 1037 (1932); 11 N.Y.Univ.L.Q.Rev. 655.

§§ 4.50–5.0 are reserved for supplementary material.

CHAPTER 5

TRANSFER BY THE MORTGAGOR AND THE MORTGAGEE

Table of Sections

A. TRANSFER BY THE MORTGAGOR

B. RESTRICTIONS ON TRANSFER BY THE MORTGAGOR

C. TRANSFER BY THE MORTGAGEE

A. TRANSFER BY THE MORTGAGOR

§ 5.1 Transferability of Mortgagor's Interest

It is axiomatic that a mortgagor's interest in real estate is normally freely transferable. In lien states he is the legal owner subject only to the legal lien of the mortgagee.[1] In title states, regardless of the technical legal title being in the mortgagee, the mortgagor is recognized as the owner in substance.[2] On the other hand, the mortgagor cannot transfer to another the duty of performance. He remains bound by the debt unless it is discharged by payment or by agreement with the mortgagee [3] or, in limited circumstances, by other contractual or suretyship principles.[4]

The transfer, of course, can take place in a variety of ways. "Voluntary inter vivos transfer of the mortgagor's interest is ordinarily effected by a deed of conveyance in the usual form. At the mortgagor's death transfer of his interest may be effected either by a duly executed will or by the statute of descent if he dies intestate. Successive transfers of the mortgaged land may take place in any of these ways or by various modes of involuntary transfer, such as foreclosure, execution, or bankruptcy sale." [5]

The following sections will focus mainly on a variety of voluntary transfers. Indeed, because of the generally rising interest rates of the past two decades, it has become increasingly common for purchasers of land to "take over" the mortgagor-sellers' existing lower than market interest rate mortgage loans. The following material will focus in detail on the methods and implications of "taking over" such existing mortgagees. Many mortgagees often are displeased with the implications of the mortgagor's common law freedom to alienate his interest.[6] Some mortgagees, for example, may believe that particular transferees threaten the security of the mortgage. Many other mortgagees simply want to be able to "call in" existing mortgage loans when there is a transfer in order to facilitate reloaning the money at higher interest rates. Thus we will closely examine the extent to which the mortgagee, by including appropriate language in the mortgage documents, may defeat or a least discourage the transferability of the mortgagor's interest.

1. See § 4.1, supra.

2. See § 4.2, supra.

3. See Prudential Sav. and Loan Ass'n v. Nadler, 37 Ill.App.3d 168, 345 N.E. 2d 782 (1976); U. S. v. Glass, 298 F. Supp. 396 (D.Ala.1969); Adair v. Carden, 29 L.R.Ir. 464, 481 (1892), the mortgagor "cannot get rid of his personal liability as between him and the mortgagee, where such liability exists, in the absence of anything amounting to a complete novation of the contract."

4. See §§ 5.19–5.20, infra.

5. Cunningham and Tischler, Transfer of the Real Estate Mortgagor's Interest, 27 Rutgers L.Rev. 24, 25 (1973).

6. See § 5.21, infra.

§ 5.2 Methods of Sale of Mortgaged Land

There are three basic methods by which a mortgagor sells mortgaged real estate and the purchaser "takes over" the existing mortgage:

1. The purchaser may pay to the mortgagor only the agreed upon value of the redemption interest, i. e., the difference between the amount of the mortgage debt and the amount set by the parties in their sale agreement as the total value of the land.[7] He may not, however, assume any personal liability for the payment of the mortgage debt. He takes, as it is said, "subject" to the mortgage. The effect of such a transaction is considered later.[8]

2. The purchaser may pay to the mortgagor, as in the first transaction, only the value of the redemption interest. In addition the purchaser may promise the mortgagor to pay off the mortgage debt. Such promises are referred to as assumptions of the mortgage and ordinarily the language used says that the transferee "assumes" the debt. The promises do not relieve the mortgagor of his duty of payment to the mortgagee. In addition to giving the mortgagor a personal right against the transferee to have him instead of the mortgagor pay the mortgage debt, it also operates to make the land in the hands of the transferee "subject" to the mortgage debt as in the first case. The promise of the transferee to pay necessarily eliminates any claim between the parties that the transferor should pay instead of having the debt satisfied out of the land. The rights such an assumption gives to the mortgagee are considered in later section.[9] So, too, in more detail, are the rights of the transferor against an assuming grantee.[10]

3. The purchaser may pay the full value of the land, as agreed upon, free from the incumbrance. The mortgagor in return agrees to pay off the mortgage debt when it comes due.[11] This transaction reverses the situation as it exists in the second situation. The land in the hands of the transferee is likened to a real surety with the mortgagor having the primary duty, as principal, to discharge the debt.

7. This amount has been aptly termed the "basic bargain price." See Storke and Sears, Transfer of Mortgaged Property, 38 Corn.L.Q. 185, 187 (1953). See also, Cunningham and Tischler, Transfer of the Real Estate Mortgagor's Interest, 27 Rutgers L. Rev. 24 (1973).

8. See § 5.3, infra.

9. See §§ 5.11–5.15, infra.

10. See § 5.10, infra.

11. "Ordinarily, where the owner of lands subject to a mortgage to secure his debts conveys the mortgaged premises, or any part of the same, to a purchaser, without any express provision with reference to the mortgage debt, such purchaser takes the same subject, of course, to the mortgage, but so far as the rights of the mortgagor and his grantee are concerned with reference to such mortgage debt the mortgagor will be regarded as the principal in such debts, and the land conveyed standing as his surety therefor * * *." Kinney v. Heuring, 44 Ind.App. 590, 596, 87 N.E. 1053, 1055 (1909). See also Van Valkenburg v. Jantz, 161 Wis. 336, 154 N.W. 373 (1915); Wadsworth v. Lyon, 93 N.Y. 201, 45 Am.Rep. 190 (1883).

This transaction normally is unwise from the purchaser's perspective because, while the latter has paid the whole purchase price, he runs the risk that the mortgagor will fail to discharge the mortgage. Of course, if the mortgagor breaks his contract to pay, the transferee has rights against him which will be examined later.[12] However, the mortgagor may not be good for the money personally and since the purchaser is already out of pocket for the mortgage amount, he may not be financially able to prevent foreclosure of the mortgage and loss of the land.

The relationship between the mortgagor and the land in the hands of such a transferee will also affect possible subsequent action by the mortgagee, another matter for subsequent elaboration.[13]

Which one of these three transactions was the one actually entered into presents questions which are considered in the following sections.[14]

§ 5.3 Transfer "Subject To" the Mortgage

Mortgagors commonly transfer real estate "subject" to an existing mortgage. This language goes beyond its apparent meaning that the land in the hands of the transferee can be reached by the mortgagee on default in priority to any right of the former in it. This is always true regardless of any agreement by the parties. What it means in this connection is that the transferee agrees, as between him and his transferor, that the debt is to be satisfied out of the land. Or, as it is frequently put, the land is the principal and the transferor is only in the position of a surety or one secondarily liable.[15]

12. See Chapter 10, infra.

13. See §§ 5.9–5.10, infra

14. See §§ 5.3–5.8, infra.

15. "When the grantee merely takes subject to the mortgage, while it is true that the grantee assumes no personal liability whatever, nevertheless the security in his hands in liable for the payment of the mortgage debt, which liability as between the grantee and the mortgagor is primary. Therefore, to the extent of the value of such security properly applicable to the mortgage debt, the original mortgagor and the grantee subject to the mortgage stand in a relation one to another, which, while not a true suretyship, is nevertheless equitably analogous thereto and subject to the operation of the same principles." Zastrow v. Knight, 56 S.D. 554, 229 N.W. 925, 72 A.L.R. 379 (1930). Accord: North End Sav. Bank v. Snow, 197 Mass. 339, 83 N.E. 1099, 125 Am.St.Rep. 368 (1908); Johnson v. Zink, 51 N.Y. 33 (1873); Howard v. Robbins, 170 N.Y. 498, 63 N.E. 530 (1902), Campbell, Cases on Mortgages, 2d ed., 407; King v. Whitely, 10 Paige 465 (1843); see Wright v. Anderson, 62 S.Dak. 444, 451, 253 N.W. 484, 487, 95 A.L.R. 81, L.R.A.1917C, 592, 593 (1934). If the land is sold "on execution against the mortgagor or under a second mortgage the purchaser acquires only the equity of redemption and the land becomes the primary source from which the mortgage must be satisfied, not the personal responsibility of the mortgagor." Howard v. Robbins, 170 N.Y. 498, 502, 63 N.E. 530, 531 (1902). The concept of a suretyship relation as between the mortgagor on the one side and the land and the transferee on the other is frequently invoked. Both the validity of the concept and its consequences will be considered in later sections, especially in those

Stated in another and perhaps more basic way, the grantee does not become personally liable, without more, to either the mortgagor or the mortgagee.[16] Nor does it affect the obligation of the mortgagor to the mortgagee.[17] But the mortgagor has no obligation to the transferee to pay it for the purpose of relieving the land in the hands of the transferee. And, although he may not be able to compel the mortgagee to proceed first against the land before seeking payment from him,[18] he does have a right against the grantee that the land be first exhausted in payment of the debt.[19] Likewise, if the mortgagor pays, he will be entitled to reimbursement out of the land.[20]

The transferee on his part, although under no personal duty to pay the debt, has the privilege of doing so. If he fails to exercise this privilege he runs the risk of losing his land by having either the mortgagee or the mortgagor apply it to the indebtedness. If he does pay, the mortgage is extinguished and he will hold the land free and clear. He will not, however, be able to obtain any reimbursement from his grantor.[21]

There are cases in which the conveyance in terms is only "subject" to the mortgage where the courts have held that the grantee should be regarded as having assumed the payment of the mortgage debt. They will be considered later in a section dealing with implied personal obligations.[22]

dealing with the effect of extensions of time and other actions by the mortgagee. See § 5.19, infra.

16. See Del Rio Land, Inc. v. Haumont, 110 Ariz. 7, 514 P.2d 1003 (1973); Brice v. Griffin, 269 Md. 558, 307 A.2d 660 (1973); Howard v. Clardy, 29 N.C.App. 570, 225 S.E.2d 149 (1976); Tom Kus v. Parker, 236 Ga. 478, 224 S.E.2d 353 (1976); Andrews v. Robertson, 177 Cal. 434, 170 P. 1129 (1918); First Trust Joint Stock Land Bank of Chicago v. Cuthbert, 215 Iowa 718, 246 N.W. 810 (1933); Chilton v. Brooks, 72 Md. 554, 20 A. 125 (1890); Flynn v. Kendrick, 285 Mass. 446, 189 N.E. 207 (1934); Malcolm v. Lavinson, 110 N.J.Eq. 63, 164 A. 318 (1933); Johnson v. Davis, 146 Okl. 170, 293 P. 197 (1930); Hylands' Estate v. Foote's Estate, 106 Vt. 1, 168 A. 925 (1933); Shepherd v. May, 115 U.S. 505, 6 S.Ct. 119, 29 L.Ed. 456 (1885); see J. H. Magill Lumber Co. v. Lane-White Lumber Co., 90 Ark. 426, 430, 119 S.W. 822, 823 (1909); Comstock v. Hitt, 37 Ill. 542, 548 (1865); Crawford v. Nimmons, 180 Ill. 143, 54 N.E. 209 (1899); Fourth Nat. Bank in Wichita v. Hill, 181 Kan. 683, 314 P.2d 312 (1957).

17. Conway Sav. Bank v. Vinick, 287 Mass. 448, 192 N.E. 81 (1934); Stevenson v. Black, 1 N.J.Eq. 338 (1831); Syracuse Trust Co. v. First Trust & Deposit Co., 141 Misc. 603, 252 N.Y.S. 850 (1931); In re May's Est., 218 Pa. 64, 67 A. 120 (1907).

18. See cases in note 17, supra. But see § 5.9, infra.

19. Syracuse Trust Co. v. First Trust & Deposit Co., 141 Misc.Rep. 603, 252 N.Y.S. 850 (1931).

20. Braun v. Crew, 183 Cal. 728, 192 P. 531 (1920); Harvey v. Lowry, 204 Ind. 93, 183 N.E. 309 (1932), discussed, 42 Yale L.J. 798 (1933); Johnson v. Zink, 51 N.Y. 333 (1873); Murray v. Marshall, 94 N.Y. 611 (1884); Marsh v. Pike, 10 Paige 595 (N.Y. 1844). But see § 5.9 infra.

21. See Wright v. Anderson, 62 S.D. 444, 450, 253 N.W. 484, 487, 95 A.L.R. 81 (1934).

22. See § 5.8, infra.

A clause in a subsequent mortgage that it is subject to a prior one would seem to have no effect other than showing notice of the earlier one.[23] Unlike a purchaser of the property "subject" to a mortgage, a later mortgagee taking "subject" to a prior one receives no consideration by reason of its existence. Hence it is not inequitable, as it would be for a purchaser who has received a consideration, ordinarily a reduction to the extent of the mortgage debt, for him to insist that the mortgagor and not the land should be primarily liable.

§ 5.4 Assumption of the Mortgage—In General

When a purchaser "assumes" an existing mortgage, he becomes personally liable to pay off the mortgage debt.[24] Whether an assumption has actually taken place, however, depends in general on contract principles. The contract need not be formal.[25] The agreement may be contained solely in the deed of conveyance.[26] On the other hand it "may be made orally or in a separate instrument; it may be implied from the transaction of the parties, or it may be shown by circumstances under which the purchase was made, as well as by the language used in the agreement." [27] It must, however, be established by clear and unequivocal proof.[28]

23. Such a clause in a second mortgage of part of the land under the first mortgage has been held to indicate an intention that the part should contribute pro rata to the payment of the prior mortgage. Savings Investment & Trust Co. v. United Realty & Mort. Co., 84 N.J.Eq. 472, 94 A. 588 (1916).

24. Ellickson v. Dull, 34 Colo.App. 25, 521 P.2d 1282 (1974); Nutz v. Shepherd, 490 S.W.2d 366 (Mo.App.1973).

25. Howard v. Robbins, 67 App.Div. 245, 73 N.Y.S. 172 (1901), affirmed 170 N.Y. 498, 93 N.E. 530 (1902).

26. See § 5.5, infra.

27. Hopkins v. Warner, 109 Cal. 133, 138, 41 P. 868, 871 (1895). For New York legislation broadening the requirement that the assumption of the mortgage indebtedness by a grantee of the mortgage must be in writing, see Curtiss, The Commission and the Law of Real Property, 40 Cornell L. Q. 735, 742 (1955). On the other hand, Rosenberg v. Rolling Inn, Inc., 212 Md. 552, 129 A.2d 924 (1957), noted in 18 Md.L.Rev. 138 (1958), held that the Statute of Frauds does not apply to an assuming promise. And Manget Foundation, Inc. v. White, 101 Ga.App. 239, 113 S.E.2d 235 (1960), noted by Smith, Security Transactions, 12 Mercer L.Rev. 182, 188 (1960), held that the Statute of Frauds does not prevent the showing of an oral assumption by a grantee who accepts a warranty deed reciting that the grantee agreed to pay the grantor's debt as part of the consideration.

In Barkhausen v. Continental Illinois Nat. Bank & Trust Co., 3 Ill.2d 254, 120 N.E.2d 649 (1954), reversing 351 Ill.App. 388, 115 N.E.2d 640 (1953), noted in 33 Chi.-Kent L.Rev. 83 (1954), the beneficiaries of a trust were not liable upon an assumption of a preexisting mortgage by a trustee as trustee, that being the intention of all parties to the transaction.

28. Perkins v. Brown, 179 Wash. 597, 38 P.2d 253, 101 A.L.R. 275 (1934). See note, 101 A.L.R. 281 (1934) as to what language amounts to an assumption.

§ 5.5 Assumption of the Mortgage—Deed Provisions

Where the parties intend to create an assumption agreement, it is most commonly found in the deed of conveyance itself. The language will refer to the mortgage and recite that the grantee "assumes and agrees to pay said mortgage according to its terms." The grantee does not have to sign such a deed for him to be bound by the provision.[29] However, assent to the assumption clause must be established as a fact.[30] Consequently the plaintiff must show that the grantee accepted the deed,[31] either with knowledge of the assumption clause in it [32] or under such circumstances as would raise a presumption of knowledge of its existence.[33]

A covenant in the mortgage that it shall bind all persons in whom title to the mortgaged property shall be vested is not a covenant running with the land so as to bind a grantee.[34]

The deed may not contain an assumption clause. It may be in the form of a quit claim deed [35] or it may contain covenants of warranty not only of title but against encumbrances. It may also, whether in form a quit claim or warranty deed, contain a statement that it is conveyed "subject to" the mortgage. In such cases whether there has been an assumption of the mortgage depends upon establishing the fact of an agreement for it by evidence extrinsic to the deed of conveyance. That evidence may consist of either a separate written or oral express agreement. Or it may consist of the circumstances accompanying the transaction, the most important of which is the amount paid by the grantee for the property. These situations

29. Thomas v. Home Mut. Bldg. Ass'n, 243 Ill. 550, 90 N.E. 1081 (1910); Jager v. Volliger, 174 Mass. 521, 55 N.E. 458 (1899); Furnas v. Durgen, 119 Mass. 500, 20 Am.Rep. 341 (1876); Sparkman v. Gove, 44 N.J.Law 252 (1882); Schley v. Fryer, 100 N.Y. 71, 2 N.E. 280 (1885); S. Car. Ins. Co. v. Kohn, 108 S.C. 475, 95 S.E. 65 (1918); Thacker v. Hubbard & Applby, 122 Va. 379, 94 S.E. 929 (1918); Bishop v. Douglass, 25 Wis. 696 (1870); Keller v. Ashford, 133 U.S. 610, 10 S.Ct. 494, 33 L.Ed. 667 (1889).

30. McFarland v. Melson, 323 Mo.App. 977, 20 S.W.2d 63 (1929); see Perkins v. Brown, 179 Wash. 597, 600, 38 P. 2d 253, 256, 101 A.L.R. 275 (1934). See also 13 N.Y.Univ.L.Q.Rev. 486 (1936); 9 Wash.L.Rev. 118 (1934); Acceptance of the conveyance without knowledge of the assumption clause does not bind the grantee who repudiates it on discovery of its presence in the deed. Blass v. Terry, 156 N.Y. 122, 50 N.E. 953, 6 N.Y.Ann.Cas. 79. See L.R.A.1918A, 1003 (1898).

31. Nutz v. Shepherd, 490 S.W.2d 366 (Mo.App.1973).

32. Hamilton Co. v. Rosen, 53 R.I. 346, 166 A. 691 (1933); Magallon v. Schreiner, 97 Wash. 15, 165 P. 1048 (1917).

33. Blass v. Terry, 156 N.Y. 122, 50 N.E. 953, 6 N.Y.Ann.Cas. 79 (1898).

34. Seventeenth and Locust Streets Corp. v. Montcalm Corp., 54 F.2d 42 (C.C.A.Pa.1931).

A covenant by a grantee of an equity of redemption to discharge the mortgage debt does not run with the land. Clement v. Willett, 105 Minn. 267, 117 N.W. 491, 17 L.R.A.,N.S., 1094, 127 Am.St.Rep. 562, 15 Ann.Cas. 1053 (1908). But see Wilcox v. Campbell, 106 N.Y. 325, 12 N.E. 823 (1887).

35. E. g., Howard v. Robbins, note 15, supra.

present several questions. One is whether any or all of this kind of extrinsic evidence is barred by either the Statute of Frauds or the parol evidence rule. Another is, if the evidence is admitted, whether the language used or the facts proved establish that an assumption by the transferee was intended.

§ 5.6 Assumption of the Mortgage—Statute of Frauds

The Statute of Frauds will not be an obstacle to establishing an assumption agreement because the assumption of a mortgage debt is not within that provision of the Statute covering promises to answer for the debt or default of another.[36] The reasons usually advanced are that the promise is to pay the transferee's own debt, or that the promise is not to the creditor, the mortgagee, but to the debtor, the mortgagor. Unless taken out by some doctrine of part performance, it would seem that such a promise would be under that section of the Statute of Frauds relating to contracts not to be performed within a year;[37] the cases, however, have given little consideration to the point. Additional but untenable explanations are that the acceptance of a deed with an assumption clause in it is equivalent to an execution of it by the grantee,[38] or that, by reason of such acceptance, the law imposes an "implied" obligation identical in scope with the provision in the deed.[39] Mere acceptance of the deed seems insufficient to invoke the doctrine of part performance; and the obligation on the transferee is contractual, not non-consensual.

Although cases holding that contracts of assumption are not within the provisions of the ordinary Statutes of Frauds seem correct, there are good reasons why a writing should be required.[40] Such contracts are long term ones with several of them being created during the existence of a mortgage as the mortgaged land is sold to successive buyers. The question of whether there has been an assumption is frequently raised years after the alleged event at a time when recollection is uncertain and intermediate grantees[41] may well

36. White v. Schader, 185 Cal. 606, 198 P. 19, 21 A.L.R. 499 (1921); Herrin v. Abbe, 55 Fla. 769, 46 So. 183, 18 L.R.A.,N.S., 907 (1908); Lamb v. Tucker, 42 Iowa, 118 (1875); Neiswanger v. McClellan, 45 Kan. 599, 26 P. 18 (1890); Strohauer v. Voltz, 42 Mich. 444, 4 N.W. 161 (1880); Langan v. Iverson, 78 Minn. 299, 80 N.W. 1051 (1899); see Enos v. Anderson, 40 Colo. 395, 93 P. 475, 15 L.R.A.,N.S., 1087 (1907); 15 L.R.A.,N.S., 1087 (1908); 25 L.R.A.,N.S., 1202 (1910). Cf. Rooney v. Koenig, 80 Minn. 483, 83 N.W. 399 (1900).

37. See Tiffany, Real Prop., 3d ed., § 1437; Enos v. Anderson, 40 Colo. 395, 93 P. 475, 15 L.R.A.,N.S., 1087 (1907).

38. Foster v. Atwater, 42 Conn. 244 (1875); Schmucker v. Sibert, 18 Kan. 104, 26 Am.Rep. 765 (1877); Baldwin v. Emery, 89 Me. 496, 36 A. 994 (1896).

39. Pike v. Brown, 61 Mass. (7 Cush.) 133 (1851); Urquhart v. Brayton, 12 R.I. 169 (1877). See 14 Bost.U.L.Rev. 692 (1934).

40. See Glenn, Mortgages, § 257.

41. The mortgagee may not only maintain an action against the mortgagor

have lost their copies of the contracts and memoranda. Consequently it is not surprising to find a few statutes explicitly dealing with the matter. For example in California the contract of assumption must be in writing signed by the transferee unless it is specifically provided for in the conveyance of the property.[42] Moreover, in New Jersey no assumption agreement can be effective unless contained in the deed or in a separate written instrument.[43] New York has similar legislation.[44]

§ 5.7 Assumption of the Mortgage—Parol Evidence Rule

Where the conveyance from a mortgagor is by quit claim deed with a recital of a nominal consideration and no other evidence is presented, the presumption is that the land is to be charged primarily with the payment of the mortgage.[45] Since the presumption arises only where there is no other evidence as to intention, if there is a clearly expressed intention in a separate agreement it will control.[46] In such a case there is no question of the extrinsic agreement varying the terms of the deed. The deed neither contained any part of the terms of the contract governing the sale nor was meant to cover the question whether the transferee did or did not assume the mortgage debt. The separate agreement is the sole expression of the contract and supplants the presumption which exists in the absence of affirmative evidence of intent.

However, the deed may contain covenants of warranty against incumbrances without any express provision in respect to the mortgage on the property and without any other evidence as to the parties' intent. In such a case the inference is that as between the grantor and grantee the former is to pay the debt to the exoneration of the land.[47] If, in addition to the covenant against incumbrances,

and his assuming grantee, but also against one or all of successive grantees who assume and agree to pay the mortgage. Baber v. Hanie, 163 N.C. 588, 80 S.E. 57 (1913); Wright v. Bank of Chattanooga, 166 Tenn. 4, 57 S.W.2d 800 (1933); Hofheimer v. Booker, 164 Va. 358, 180 S. E. 145 (1935). An assuming grantee cannot escape liability by transferring it to another. Central Life Ins. Co. v. Thompson, 182 Ark. 705, 33 S.W.2d 388 (1931); McLeod v. Building & Loan Ass'n of Jackson, 168 Miss. 457, 151 So. 151 (1933). But contra, Brinton v. Davidson, 308 Pa. 371, 162 A. 905 (1932).

42. West's Ann.Cal.Civ.Code § 1624(7). See note 11 So.Cal.L.Rev. 109 (1937).

43. N.J.Stat.Ann. 46:9–7.1. See Cunningham and Tischler, Transfer of the Real Estate Mortgagor's Interest, 27 Rutgers L.Rev. 24, 29 (1973).

44. N.Y.Civ.Prac.Act, § 1083c, added by N.Y.Laws 1938, c. 502. See note, 13 St. John's L.Rev. 215 (1938).

45. See Howard v. Robbins, 170 N.Y. 498, 93 N.E. 530 (1902); Scribner v. Malinowski, 148 Mich. 447, 111 N.W. 1032 (1907).

46. Society of Friends v. Haines, 47 Ohio St. 423, 25 N.E. 119 (1890).

47. Maher v. Lanfrom, 86 Ill. 513 (1877); Wadsworth v. Williams, 100 Mass. 126 (1868); Hooper v. Henry 31 Minn. 264, 17 N.W. 476 (1883); Barnes v. Mott, 64 N.Y. 397, 21 Am. Rep. 625 (1876).

the deed also contains a statement that the conveyance is "subject" to a certain mortgage or other explicit statement of intention that the covenant is not to apply to the mortgage specified, the covenant will be nullified as to it.[48] The terms of the deed dealing directly with the mortgage will govern as they would had there been no covenant against incumbrances in the instrument.

Where the deed contains only the covenant against incumbrances the question arises whether extrinsic evidence, in the form of a written or oral agreement or of accompanying circumstances, may be introduced in spite of the covenant to show that the grantee assumed the mortgage. Prima facie such a deed seems to cover exactly the subject with which the extrinsic evidence, if let in, also deals. And the provision in the deed apparently is directly varied and contradicted by the evidence.[49] Nevertheless the evidence is often admitted,[50] although the reasons advanced for doing so have not escaped criticism.[51] Some cases say it is admissible to show the consideration;[52] others feel that the parol agreement is an independent contract neither at variance with the deed nor merged in it.[53] Still others admit the evidence when the mortgagee is plaintiff on the ground that the parol evidence rule is inapplicable to strangers to the deed.[54] The real reason for admission seems to be that if it is excluded the grantee would be unjustly enriched. Properly the evidence should be admitted, not to enforce the agreement to assume, but to recover the amount of enrichment which would otherwise accrue unfairly to the grantee.

48. King v. Whitely, 10 Paige 465 (N.Y.1843); Drury v. Holden, 121 Ill. 130, 13 N.E. 547 (1887); Hopper v. Smyser, 90 Md. 363, 45 A. 206 (1900); Brown v. South Boston Sav. Bank, 148 Mass. 300, 19 N.E. 382 (1889); Fuller v. Devolld, 144 Mo.App. 93, 128 S.W. 1011 (1910); Belmont v. Coman, 22 N.Y. 438, 78 Am.Dec. 213 (1860); Gerdine v. Menage, 41 Minn. 417, 43 N.W. 91 (1889); Calkins v. Copley, 29 Minn. 471, 13 N.W. 904 (1882).

49. In Simanovich v. Wood, 145 Mass. 180, 13 N.E. 391 (1887) parol evidence was excluded on this reasoning; Hicks v. Sullivan, 127 Miss. 148, 89 So. 811 (1921); Patterson v. Cappon, 125 Wis. 198, 102 N.W. 1083 (1905), accord.

50. Bolles v. Beach, 22 N.J.L. 680, 53 Am.Dec. 263 (1850); Hays v. Peck, 107 Ind. 389, 8 N.E. 274 (1886); Laudman v. Ingram, 49 Mo. 212 (1872); Deaver v. Deaver, 137 N.C. 240, 49 S.E. 113 (1904); Johnson v. Elmen, 94 Tex. 168, 59 S.W. 253, 52 L.R.A. 162 (1900).

51. See notes, 12 Wis.L.Rev. 405 (1937); 78 U. of Pa.L.Rev. 432 (1929).

52. Hays v. Peck, 107 Ind. 389, 8 N.E. 274 (1886); Bolles v. Beach, 22 N.J.L. 680, 53 Am.Dec. 263 (1850); Deaver v. Deaver, 137 N.C. 240, 49 S.E. 113 (1904); Johnson v. Elmen, 94 Tex. 168, 59 S.W. 253, 52 L.R.A. 162, 86 Am.St.Rep. 845 (1900). See 50 A.L.R. 1216, 1228 (1927); 84 A.L.R. 347, 358 (1931).

53. Laudman v. Ingram, 49 Mo. 212 (1872); Bolles v. Beach, supra note 52. See 50 A.L.R. 1216, 1229 (1927); 84 A.L.R. 347, 360 (1931).

54. See 50 A.L.R. 1216, 1226 (1927); 84 A.L.R. 347, 358 (1931).

A case of less difficulty is where the deed itself says that the conveyance is "subject" to the mortgage and extrinsic evidence is offered that the grantee assumed the mortgage. The parol evidence rule clearly does not [55] and should not exclude this evidence. The term "subject" to the mortgage deals with and is meant to be limited to part only of the transaction, i. e., the relationship between the grantor and the land. The extrinsic agreement of assumption concerns an entirely separate and independent matter, the personal liability of the transferee to pay the mortgage debt.[56] It does not in any way vary or affect the terms of the instrument of conveyance. It merely creates a quite distinct contract obligation. Other grounds for admitting the evidence are those relied upon where there is only a covenant against incumbrances in the deed, i. e., that it may come in to show the consideration,[57] or, when the mortgagee is suing, that the exclusion rule does not apply to strangers to the deed.[58]

On the other hand, suppose that the deed clearly spells out an assumption agreement. To what extent may extrinsic evidence be used to establish a contrary understanding? Generally, if the deed contains such assumption language and it was known to the grantee, it cannot be contradicted by parol evidence, at least where the grantor sues the grantee.[59] On the other hand, where the mortgagee sues, there is authority that such evidence is admissible, apparently on the theory that because the mortgagee is the plaintiff, the parol evidence

55. White v. Schader, 185 Cal. 606, 198 P. 19, 21 A.L.R. 499 (1921); Herrin v. Abbe, 55 Fla. 769, 46 So. 183, 18 L.R.A.,N.S., 907 (1908); Strohauer v. Voltz, 42 Mich. 444, 4 N.W. 161 (1880); Lamb v. Tucker, 42 Iowa 118 (1875); Langan v. Iverson, 78 Minn. 299, 80 N.W. 1051 (1899); Gustafson v. Koehler, 177 Minn. 115, 224 N.W. 699 (1929); Gilmer v. Powell, 256 S. W. 124 (Mo.App.1923); Ordway v. Downey, 18 Wash. 412, 51 P. 1047, 63 Am.St.Rep. 892 (1898). See Warm, Rights and Liabilities of Mortgagee, Mortgagor and Grantee, 10 Temple L.Quar. 116, 121, 3 Mercer Beasley L.R. 113 (1935); 9 Tex.L.Rev. 453 (1930); 25 L.R.A.,N.S., 1202 (1910); 50 A.L.R. 1220, 1222 (1927); 84 A.L. R. 355, 356 (1931); Hood v. Young, 178 Ark. 439, 11 S.W.2d 767 (1928); Wayne International Bldg. & Loan Ass'n v. Beckner, 191 Ind. 664, 134 N.E. 273 (1922), contra. See 78 U. Pa.L.Rev. 432 (1930), criticizing the grounds of admission.

56. Strohauer v. Voltz, 42 Mich. 444, 4 N.W. 161 (1880); McFarland v. Melson, 323 Mo. 977, 20 S.W.2d 63 (Mo. App. 1929); Ordway v. Downey, 18 Wash. 412, 51 P. 1047, 63 Am.St.Rep. 892 (1898).

57. White v. Schader, 185 Cal. 606, 198 P. 19, 21 A.L.R. 499 (1921); Brosseau v. Lowy, 209 Ill. 405, 70 N.E. 901 (1904); Swarthout v. Shields, 185 Mich. 427, 152 N.W. 202 (1915); Morgan v. South Milwaukee Lake View Co., 97 Wis. 275, 72 N.W. 872 (1897); Wayne International Bldg. & Loan Ass'n v. Beckner, 191 Ind. 664, 134 N.E. 273 (1922), contra.

58. McFarland v. Melson, 323 Mo. 977, 20 S.W.2d 63 (1929) noted, 78 U.Pa.L.Rev. 432 (1930). See 12 Wis. L.Rev. 405 (1937).

59. See Muhlig v. Fiske, 131 Mass 110, 113 (1881); Clark v. Henderson, 62 N.D. 503, 244 N.W. 314, 84 A.L.R. 347 (1931).

rule is inapplicable to strangers to the deed.[60] In any event, such evidence must be clear and convincing.[61]

§ 5.8 Implied Personal Obligations

While the general rule is that a conveyance "subject" to a mortgage creates no personal obligation on the part of the grantee, there are deviations. In Pennsylvania, for example, while such a conveyance creates no direct obligation to the mortgagee on the part of the grantee, the grantee is obligated to indemnify the grantor from the mortgage obligation.[62] This implied obligation has been spoken of variously as "founded on principles of equity and fair dealing," as "purely contractual in nature", and as "impliedly contractual." [63] The Pennsylvania doctrine has been explained as arising out of a misconstruction of early cases in that state in which the conveyance was subject not to the mortgage but to "the payment" of it, a form of expression which understandably could be construed as amounting to an assumption of payment.[64]

Where in addition to a conveyance subject to the mortgage, the full value of the land is agreed on [65] as the purchase price and from it the purchaser has deducted the amount of the mortgage and has paid the balance, there are a good many cases holding that the purchaser has become personally liable.[66] This has been explained on the ground that "His [the grantee's] retention of the vendor's money for the payment of the mortgage, imposes upon him the duty of protecting the vendor against the mortgage debt. This must be so * * * for it would seem to be almost intolerably unjust to permit him to

60. See Nissen v. Sabin, 202 Iowa 1362, 212 N.W. 125, 50 A.L.R. 1216 (1927); Stowers v. Stuck, 131 Neb. 409, 268 N.W. 310 (1936); Page v. Hinchee, 174 Okl. 537, 541, 51 P.2d 487, 491 (1935); Nutz v. Shepherd, 490 S.W.2d 366 (Mo.App.1973). But see Kozan v. Levin, 50 A.D.2d 663, 374 N.Y.S.2d 829 (1975). For a criticism of the distinction, see 12 Wis.L.Rev. 405 (1937).

61. See McFarland v. Melson, 323 Mo. 977, 985, 20 S.W.2d 63, 66 (1929) If the clause was inserted by fraud or mistake there may be relief. See 26 A.L.R. 528; 100 A.L.R. 911; 22 Va.L. Rev. 355 (1935).

62. See Heaney v. Riddle, 343 Pa. 453, 23 A.2d 456 (1942); Masgai v. Masgai, 460 Pa. 453, 333 A.2d 861 (1975).

63. See Moschzisker, C. J., in Dobkin v. Landsberg, 273 Pa. 174, 180, 116 A. 814, 816 (1922).

64. See Tiffany, Real Prop., 3d ed., § 1435.

65. This agreement frequently appears in the deed of conveyance. See cases in note 66, infra. It may, however, be established by admissible extrinsic evidence. E. g., Canfield v. Shear, 49 Mich. 313, 13 N.W. 605 (1882); Hawn v. Malone, 188 Iowa 439, 176 N.W. 393 (1920). See § 5.7 supra.

66. Brice v. Griffin, 269 Md. 558, 307 A.2d 660 (1973). Townsend v. Ward, 27 Conn. 610 (1858); Drury v. Holden, 121 Ill. 130, 137, 13 N.E. 547, 548 (1887); Lamka v. Donnelly, 163 Iowa 255, 143 N.W. 869 (1913); Canfield v. Shear, 49 Mich. 313, 13 N.W. 605 (1882); Sanderson v. Turner, 73 Okl. 105, 174 P. 763, 2 A.L.R. 347 (1918); Parlette v. Equitable Farm Mort. Ass'n, 165 Okl. 155, 25 P.2d 300 (1933).

keep back the vendor's money with the understanding that he would pay the vendor's debt, and still be free of all liability for a failure to apply the money according to his promise." [67] The personal liability so created generally is held to be an assumption of the debt, but in some instances it is one of indemnity as in Pennsylvania.[68] In end result there is little difference between a personal obligation to pay the debt and one to reimburse another person who has had to pay it.

Many states, on the other hand, have specifically rejected the validity of such "implied assumptions." New Jersey, for example, since 1947 has prohibited the concept by statute.[69] Other jurisdictions have reached similar results by judicial decision.[70]

The "implied assumption" decisions have been vigorously criticized.[71] It is a fair enough inference from the fact that the conveyance is subject to a mortgage that the purchaser paid only the value of the redemption interest.[72] And it is a further proper inference that the grantee in such a case, as between him and the grantor, assumes the debt as a charge upon the land he has acquired.[73] Such an interpretation exposes the grantee only to the risk of losing the property and to no additional loss should it prove to be inadequate security for the debt. But to impose upon such a grantee, whether on grounds of implication of fact or ideas of fairness,[74] a duty to recoup

67. Heid v. Vreeland, 30 N.J.Eq. 591, 593 (1879). See Dimmitt v. Johnson, 199 Iowa 966, 969, 203 N.W. 261, 263 (1913), for a similar statement of rationale.

68. Lamka v. Donnelly, 163 Iowa 255, 143 N.W. 869 (1913); Hawn v. Malone, 188 Iowa 439, 176 N.W. 393 (1920); Friedman v. Zuckerman, 104 N.J.Eq. 322, 145 A. 541 (1929); Britton v. Roth, 313 Pa. 352, 169 A. 146 (1933).

69. See N.J.Stat.Ann. 46:9–7.1; Cunningham and Tischler, Transfer of the Real Estate Mortgagor's Interest, 27 Rutgers L.Rev. 24, 29 (1973).

70. See Belmont v. Coman, 22 N.Y. 438, 78 Am.Dec. 213 (1860); Equitable Life Assur. v. Bostwick, 100 N.Y. 628, 3 N.E. 296 (1885); Fiske v. Tolman, 124 Mass. 254, 26 Am.Rep. 659 (1878), (but otherwise if *payment* of the mortgage is stated to be part of the consideration, Jager v. Vollinger, 174 Mass. 521, 55 N.E. 458 (1899), and cf. Flynn v. Kenrick, 285 Mass. 446, 189 N.E. 207 (1934), noted 14 Bost.U.L.Rev. 692 (1934); yet see 101 A.L.R. 281, 283); McFarland v. Melson, 323 Mo. 977, 20 S.W.2d 63 (1929); Redhead v. Skidmore Land Credit Co., 194 Wis. 123, 215 N.W. 937 (1927). For discussions and additional authorities, see Warm, Rights and Liabilities of Mortgagee, Mortgagor, Grantee, 10 Temple L.Quar. 116, 119 (1935); Friedman, Creation and Effect of Personal Liability of Mortgage Debts in New York, 50 Yale L.J. 224, 226 (1940); Walsh, Mortgages 209, note 16; notes, 8 Cal.L.Rev. 447 (1920); 9 Tex.L.Rev. 453 (1931); 18 Minn.L.Rev. 481 (1934); 14 Boston U. L.Rev. 692 (1934); L.R.A.1917C, 592; 111 A.L.R. 1114 (1937).

71. See Warm, Op. Cit. Supra note 70; Walsh, op. cit. supra note 10; Tiffany, Real Prop., 3d ed., § 1435; Glenn, Mortgages § 256.

72. See Adair v. Carden, 29 L.R.Ir. 469, 482 (1892).

73. See Adair v. Carden, note 72, supra; Glenn, Mortgages, § 252.

74. That the obligation is not based upon an implication of fact as to the parties' intention, see Farwell, J., in Mills v. United Counties Bank, 1 Ch. 231 (1912), commented on in 28 L.Q.

his vendor when he has had to pay the mortgage irrespective of the value of the land seems unwarranted.[75] Such a risk should not be imposed upon him in the absence of clear and explicit evidence of an intention to do so.[76] And the same criticism applies to cases which rest the result upon the terms of the agreement as to the purchase price which must be established in addition to the fact of taking subject to the mortgage.[77] As has been pointed out: "In actual fact there is not the slightest difference between a sale of the equity subject to the mortgage for a stated price to be paid for the equity and a sale of the same property by a contract which states the price at the full value of the property unencumbered and provides for payment to the amount of the mortgage by taking subject to the mortgage, the balance to be paid in cash. * * * To say that the purchaser has retained the vendor's money to pay the mortgage is simply contrary to the fact." [78]

The practical solution in those states that recognise one form or another of "implied assumptions" is proper drafting. For example, where an assumption is not intended the drafter could include after the "subject" to language, the following language: "Said mortgage is *not* being assumed by the Grantee."

§ 5.9 Rights of Transferor—Non-assuming Grantee

As against a non-assuming grantee the mortgagor or other transferor has no personal claim to have him pay off the debt.[79] However, as we have seen, the land in the hands of such a grantee becomes the principal fund for payment and the mortgagor stands in the position of a surety.[80] When the debt comes due the mortgagor may pay it and then be subrogated to the rights of the mortgagee in the mort-

Rev. 122 (1912); Adair v. Carden, 29 L.R.Ir. 469, 482 et seq. (1892).

75. Additionally, it has been suggested, that if the obligation is imposed at all it should be to pay the debt, not merely to recoup the transferor to the extent he has had to pay it. See Tiffany, Real Prop., 3d ed., § 1435. This may be correct if the obligation rests upon an implication of fact as to the parties' intention. If however, the basis is unjust enrichment at the expense of the transferor, limiting recovery to the amount of loss established by him can be defended.

76. See Warm, op. cit. supra note 70, 121; Glenn, op. cit. supra, note 73 § 256.

77. See note 70 supra.

78. Walsh, Mortgages, 209 note 16. See also, Warm, op. cit. supra note 70, 120.

79. See § 5.3, supra. Cf. Fitzgerald v. Flanagan, 155 Iowa, 217, 135 N.W. 738, Ann.Cas.1914C, 1104 (1912); Locke v. Homer, 131 Mass. 93, 41 Am.Rep. 199 (1881); Hall v. Morgan, 79 Mo. 47 (1883); Woodbury v. Swan, 58 N.H. 380 (1878); Hoy v. Bramhall, 19 N.J.Eq. 563, 569, 97 Am.Dec. 687 (1868); Faulkner v. McHenry, 235 Pa. 298, 83 A. 827, Ann.Cas.1913D, 1151 (1912). But cf., Glenn, Purchasing Subject to the Mortgage, 27 Va.L.Rev. 853, 865 (1941).

80. See § 5.3, supra and § 10.2, infra.

gage.[81] The mortgagor may then reach the land by using the mortgagee's rights to realize out of it by foreclosure. Since the grantee's duty is limited to having the land in his hands go to pay the debt, this remedy gives the mortgagor adequate relief.

There are difficulties in such a course due to the rule that, technically, payment of the mortgage debt discharges it and releases the mortgage.[82] Consequently, as an alternative, the mortgagor may sometimes ask that the mortgagee assign both the debt and the mortgage to a nominee of the mortgagor so that the lien clearly will be kept alive for his benefit. Since the mortgagee cannot be injured by such action and it is important to the mortgagor's protection, equity will grant specific performance of such a request.[83] A court could, of course, treat such a transaction as ineffective based on a "form over substance" argument. However, it would seem that if the reasons for giving the mortgagor subrogation rights in the first place are persuasive, those rights should not be impaired by an overly technical application of the "no debt, no mortgage" rule.

The above concept of the mortgagor's subrogation rights, however, was recently rejected by the Arizona Supreme Court in Best Fertilizers of Arizona, Inc. v. Burns.[83a] In that case A conveyed land to B, who took "subject" to an existing mortgage in favor of E–1. B then gave a second mortgage to E–2. The E–1 mortgage went into default. A then paid the mortgage debt to E–1, who endorsed the note and assigned the mortgage to A. Several years later, A sold the note and mortgage to D. D then brought foreclosure proceedings. E–2 counterclaimed for foreclosure of its mortgage and for a declaration that its lien had first priority. The Supreme Court of Arizona found in favor of E–2. It held, first, that under Section 3–601(3) of the Uniform Commercial Code (UCC), which provides that "The liability of all parties is discharged when any party who has himself no right of action or recourse on the instrument * * * reacquires the instrument in his own right * * *,"[84] the note and all liability thereon was discharged. Thus, since the debt no longer existed, the mortgage and all rights thereunder were destroyed. Second, and seemingly alternatively, the court rejected the argument that A was, in any event, subrogated to the rights of E–1. It reasoned that there cannot be subrogation rights in a "subject to" situation where the debt paid was the obligation of the person who paid it.

81. University State Bank v. Steeves, 85 Wash. 55, 147 P. 645, 2 A.L.R. 237 (1915). See 2 A.L.R. 242, 243 (1919); see § 5.3, supra and § 10.2, infra.

82. See § 5.3, supra.

83. E. g., Johnson v. Zink, 51 N.Y. 333 (1873); Howard v. Robbins, 170 N.Y. 498, 63 N.E. 530 (1902); see 1919, 2 A.L.R. 242. But see Lamb v. Montague, 112 Mass. 352 (1873).

83a. 116 Ariz. 492, 570 P.2d 179 (1977).

84. Ariz.Rev.Stat. § 44–2568(C)1.

The first part of the Best Fertilizer case needs further analysis. Suppose that instead of taking the note and mortgage directly, A had simply directed that the note and mortgage be endorsed and assigned to a third party. In that event, technically at least, the application of the UCC would arguably not have resulted in the destruction of the debt. However, even if the court had been confronted such a situation and had rejected it as a sham transaction placing form over substance, it still can be argued, in any event, that the UCC should not be utilized as the basis for denying equitable subrogation. To be sure, there was a basis under the Negotiable Instruments Law, the predecessor to the UCC, for the argument that suretyship and subrogation principles had been abrogated with respect to negotiable instruments.[85] However, such sweeping generalizations do not apply to the UCC.[86] Moreover, if the above UCC provision is applicable to destroy subrogation rights of the mortgagor in the "subject" to situation, its language is also literally applicable to destroy the debt and mortgage in the case of an assumption transfer. In both instances, the "liability of all parties is destroyed" when the mortgagor reacquires the note. Surely the UCC provision was not intended to destroy the mortgagor's subrogation rights against an assuming grantee. In any event, the Arizona Supreme Court seemed equally inclined to reject subrogation on the basis that a mortgagor in a "subject" to situation is simply not entitled to subrogation under traditional substantive rules.

This latter position seems incorrect both technically and in terms of fairness. First, it is true that when the mortgagor pays the mortgage debt in a "subject" to transaction, he is, in a sense, paying *his* debt. Indeed, it is also true that he is not a personal surety in the same sense that he would be if the grantee had assumed. Nevertheless, as one noted decision has aptly put it, "when the grantee merely takes subject to the mortgage, while it is true that the grantee assumes no personal liability whatever, nevertheless the security in his hands is liable for the payment of the mortgage debt, which liability as between the grantee and the mortgagee is primary. Therefore, to the extent of the value of such security properly applicable to the mortgage debt, the original mortgagor and the grantee subject to the mortgage stand in a relation one to another, which, while not a true suretyship, is nevertheless equitably analogous thereto and subject to the operation of the same principles." [87] Second, the Best Fertilizer approach can lead to inequitable results. Indeed, in the actual case, E–2 obtained an unexpected windfall in being promoted to senior lien status. Moreover, "subject" to grantees could be the more likely dubious beneficiaries

85. See Osborne, Mortgages § 271 (2d Ed. 1970).

86. See Clark, Suretyship in the Uniform Commercial Code, 46 Tex.L.Rev. 453, 454 (1968). Indeed, the mortgagor is specifically protected by suretyship principles when the mortgagee enters into extension agreements with subsequent grantees. See § 5.19, infra.

87. Zastrow v. Knight, 56 S.D. 554, 560, 229 N.W. 925, 930 (1930).

of the decision. When a "subject" to grantee acquires mortgaged land, while he is not personally liable, it is the expectation of the parties that the grantee will pay off the debt. To be sure, at the time of sale by the mortgagor to the grantee, the mortgage debt is probably subtracted from the sale price in determining the amount of the grantee's cash payment to the mortgagor. Suppose then that the grantee fails to pay off the mortgage and, threatened with a probable personal judgment against him in favor of the mortgagee, the mortgagor reluctantly pays the mortgage debt. What our surprised mortgagor discovers is that, under the Best Fertilizer reasoning, instead of being an assignee of a mortgage, he has just bestowed on the grantee a title free of the mortgage. Thus we are faced with the anamolous result that while normally one acquires land free and clear of a mortgage by paying it off, here the grantee can achieve that result by failing to do so.

Although it has been stated that subrogation by payment of the mortgage debt is the sole remedy available to the mortgagor against the non-assuming grantee, two others are possible. First, the mortgagor may be aided in those jurisdictions with "one action" rules or statutes. Under the one action concept, there can be only one action for the enforcement of a mortgage-secured obligation, that action being a foreclosure proceeding in which a deficiency judgment may be obtained.[88] To the extent that such a concept is applicable to a "subject" to situation, the mortgagor would be able to compel the mortgagee to foreclose first before going against the mortgagor personally. In any event, the personal liability would then be limited to the deficiency, if any, resulting from the foreclosure sale.

Another related and remote possibility is the invocation of the suretyship doctrine of Pain v. Packard [89] in those few jurisdictions in which it may be followed.[90] This would enable the mortgagor after maturity of the debt to demand of the mortgagee that he institute an action of foreclosure so that, to the extent of its value, it would be used to pay the debt. The mortgagor, then, would not have to do so. Failure to comply would result in a discharge to the extent of the loss thereafter sustained. There is considerable doubt as to whether the doctrine applies to a suretyship relation arising subsequent to the mortgage by virtue of the transfer of the property.[91] Nevertheless there is some authority applying it to the case of a non-assuming grantee.[92]

88. See § 9.2, infra.

89. 13 Johns. 174 (N.Y.1816).

90. See Friedman, Discharge of Mortgage Debts, 52 Yale L.J. 771, 796 (1943).

91. See Friedman, supra note 90, 796. Fish v. Glover, 154 Ill. 86, 39 N.E. 1081 (1894), rejects the doctrine in the case of mortgages on the ground it applies only to conventional suretyship.

92. Gottschalk v. Jungmann, 78 App. Div. 171, 79 N.Y.S. 551 (N.Y.1903); 3 Col.L.Rev. 199 (1903); Nat. Sav. Bank of City of Albany v. Fermac Corp., 241 App.Div. 204, 271 N.Y.S. 836

§ 5.10 Rights of Transferor—Assuming Grantee

As against an assuming grantee, the mortgagor has the same rights in respect to reaching the property in his hands as in the case of a nonassuming grantee. In addition, however, he has personal rights against the transferee. One of these is to pay the debt and then sue for reimbursement. Moreover, this right accrues as soon as the mortgagor makes any payment on the mortgage debt, whether the accelerated debt or simply the arrearages.[93] It is self-evident that this right exists under any theory of the nature of the contract of assumption.[94] Furthermore, it could rest upon a quasi-contractual basis, at least in those jurisdictions in which the assumption gives to the mortgagee a personal right against the assuming grantee.[95] In such a case the grantor would be benefiting the grantee by discharging the latter's obligation to pay. The grantor would be privileged to make the payment because he remained liable; the grantee is unjustly enriched because he had the primary duty of payment.

A few jurisdictions have limited the right of the mortgagor to the foregoing relief, holding that the grantor may not sue until he has paid the debt.[96] However, the weight of authority is that the assumption agreement calls for the payment of the debt when it falls due and consequently it is broken when it is not paid.[97] The objec-

(1934) affirmed 266 N.Y. 443, 195 N.E. 145; Osborne v. Heyward, 40 App.Div. 78, 57 N.Y.S. 542 (N.Y. 1899); see cases in Union Trust Co. v. Rogers, 261 App.Div. 882, 25 N.Y.S.2d 120 (N.Y.1941). But see Marshall v. Davies, 78 N.Y. 414 (1879). The Fermac case, supra, was affirmed solely on the ground that the mortgagor had made a tender. National Sav. Bank v. Fermac Corp., 266 N.Y. 443, 195 N.E. 145 (1934).

93. See, e. g., Brice v. Griffen, 269 Md. 558, 307 A.2d 660 (1973).

94. Taintor v. Hemmingway, 18 Hun 458 (N.Y.1879), affirmed 83 N.Y. 610 (1880); Comstock v. Drohan, 71 N.Y. 9 (1877); Evans v. Sperry, 12 F.2d 438 (D.C.Ill.1926). See 21 A.L.R. 504, 520 (1922); 97 A.L.R. 1076, 1079 (1935); 76 A.L.R. 1191, 1196 (1932) for collections of cases. See Restatement, Contracts, § 141(2).

95. Graham v. Burnbaugh, 44 Cal.App. 482, 186 P. 798 (1919); Harvey v. Lowry, 204 Ind. 93, 183 N.E. 309 (1932), semble; Poe v. Dixon, 60 Ohio St. 124, 54 N.E. 86, 71 Am.St.Rep. 713 (1899); see Glenn, Morts. § 260. In some cases the right of reimbursement is regarded as merely a surety's relational right of reimbursement against his principal. See Hildrith v. Walker, 187 S.W. 608, 610 (Mo.App. 1916); Poe v. Dixon, supra, the relational right being looked upon as justified by reason of the conference of a benefit by the surety; John Deere Plow Co. of Moline v. Tuinstra, 47 S.D. 555, 200 N.W. 61 (1924).

96. See Gustafson v. Koehler, 177 Minn. 115, 224 N.W. 699 (1929) 21 A.L.R. 504, 514 (1922); 76 A.L.R. 1192, 1195 (1932); 97 A.L.R. 1076, 1078 (1935). This result is reached on different grounds. E. g., in Sloan v. Klein, 230 Pa. 132, 79 A. 403 (1911), and in Tritten's Estate, 238 Pa. 555, 86 A. 461 (1913), it was so decided partly on the ground that the agreement of assumption, properly interpreted, was merely one of "indemnity," i. e., reimbursement. Other cases arrive at the same result for the reason that the right is not contractual but a surety's relational right to compensation against his principal. See note 95, supra.

97. White v. Schader, 185 Cal. 606, 198 P. 19, 21 A.L.R. 499 (1921); Locke v. Homer, 131 Mass. 93, 41 Am.Rep. 199 (1881); Gustafson v.

tion to the majority rule is that "a grantee might be subjected to two judgments for the same debt; one in favor of the grantor, and the other in favor of the mortgagee. One answer to this is that he has brought this upon himself by not carrying out his agreement. Had he paid the mortgage debt (which is in reality the balance of the purchase price) when it became due, as he agreed, he would not have been sued. And, if sued by the grantor, payment then of the mortgage would be a perfect defense." [98] Further, if the transferor-plaintiff does collect the debt he can be compelled to hold it as trustee for the payment of the mortgage debt.[99]

In addition to the courses previously discussed the mortgagor has open to him a suit in equity to compel an assuming grantee to exonerate him by paying the debt to the mortgagee.[1] In theory this is a completely satisfactory remedy but in practice it is not. The reason is that before the mortgage debt can be paid off by judicial process the amount of the debt then due must be ascertained. To do this requires an accounting to which the mortgagee must be a party. Further if there are several successive grantees all are necessary parties, in addition to the mortgagee. The absence from the state of either the mortgagee or an assuming grantee will make the remedy useless.

The right of a mortgagor to compel the payment of the debt assumed by his grantee extends to a grantee or successive grantees of the first grantee who in their turn assume payment.[2] The fact that a grantee who has assumed the payment of a mortgage has subse-

Koehler, 177 Minn. 115, 224 N.W. 699 (1929) commented on, 13 Minn.L.Rev. 737 (1929); Kirk v. Welch, 212 Minn. 300, 3 N.W.2d 426 (1942); Sanderson v. Turner, 73 Okl. 105, 174 P. 763, 2 A.L.R. 347 (1918).

98. Gustafson v. Koehler, 177 Minn. 115, 118, 224 N.W. 699, 700 (1929). The danger of double payment would not exist in jurisdictions denying to the holder of the mortgage debt a direct right against the assuming grantee. See 38 Harv.L.Rev. 502, 506 (1925).

99. Gustafson v. Koehler, note 98, supra. See Parke, B., in Loosemore v. Radford, 9 M. & W. 657 (1842). See also Heins v. Byers, 174 Minn. 350, 219 N.W. 287 (1928). For various suggested ways of relieving the grantee from risk of further payment see Williston, Contracts, Rev. ed., 1936, § 392; Wilson v. Stilwell, 9 Ohio St. 467, 75 Am.Dec. 477 (1859); Locke v. Homer, 131 Mass. 93, 108, 41 Am.Rep. 199 (1881); 38 Harv.L. Rev. 502, 505 (1925); 13 Minn. 737 (1929); Campbell, Cases on Mortgages, 2d ed., 435 n. 3; Williston, Contracts, Rev. ed., § 392; Restatement, Contracts, §§ 141(1), 136(1)c.

1. Marsh v. Pike, 10 Paige 595 (N.Y. 1844); Mowry v. Mowry, 137 Mich. 277, 100 N.W. 388 (1904), semble; see 41 Mich.L.Rev. 975 (1943); Williston, Contracts, Rev. ed., § 392 n. 3; Restatement, Contracts, § 138.

2. Robson v. O'Toole, 60 Cal.App. 710, 214 P. 278 (1923); Comstock v. Drohan, 71 N.Y. 9 (1877). See 21 A.L.R. 504, 507 (1922); 76 A.L.R. 1191, 1194 (1932); 97 A.L.R. 1076, 1077 (1935). Williston, Contracts, Rev. ed., § 386.

The problem of the rights of a mortgagor against an assuming grantee after a break in the chain is analyzed in Maxwell and Meyers, The Mortgagor's Rights Against Remote Assuming Grantees, 29 Tex.L.Rev. 869, 880 (1952). See also Storke and Sears, Transfer of Mortgaged Property, 38 Corn.L.Q. 185, 198 (1953).

quently sold the land to another is no defense to an action by the grantor for a breach of his contract of assumption.[3]

What rights, if any, does a mortgagor have against a subsequent grantee who in buying from a non-assuming grantee assumes the payment of the mortgage? If the mortgagor has paid off the debt he should be entitled to be subrogated to any rights its holder had not only against the land but against the later assuming grantee.[4] To the extent that he has discharged any personal obligation of such a person or freed his land from the lien of the mortgage he has conferred a benefit upon that person for which he should be able to collect.[5] If the mortgagor has not paid it is doubtful whether he has any rights against such an assuming grantee.[6] It is true that the third party beneficiary doctrine has been held to permit a mortgagee to recover against an assuming grantee after a break in the chain of assumptions.[7] But to extend a similar right to a remote grantor whose immediate grantee did not personally assume the debt is a step beyond this and one which courts seem unlikely to take in the absence of special circumstances indicating that such grantor should be regarded as within the class of third persons who can sue as beneficiaries of a contract to which they are not parties.[8] A non-assuming grantee who in turn sells to one who assumes the payment of the debt has no interest in having the debt paid. He never became personally bound for the debt and he no longer owns land he might lose if the debt is not discharged. Technically he has a contract right against his grantee on which he might sue. Since he suffers no injury his damages should be nominal. As against grantees subsequent to the first one who also assume the mortgage whether or not the non-assuming grantor himself can recover depends upon whether in the particular jurisdiction the rule permitting third party beneficiaries to sue will be extended to such a person.[9]

3. Kollen v. Sooy, 172 Mich. 214, 137 N.W. 808 (1912); Reed v. Paul, 131 Mass. 129 (1881); Kirker v. Wylie, 207 Pa. 511, 56 A. 1074 (1904). The same is true of quasi-contractual liability. Reilly v. Lucraft, 34 Idaho 41, 198 P. 674 (1921), deficiency judgment already paid by grantor. See Williston, Contracts, Rev. ed., § 386. But see Penn.Act of June 12, 1878, P.L. 205 (21 P.S. 655, 656).

4. As to the rights of a mortgagee against one who assumes the mortgage after a break in the chain of assumptions, see § 5.15, infra.

5. Harvey v. Lowrey, 204 Ind. 93, 183 N.E. 309 (1932) discussed, 42 Yale L. J. 798 (1933), is to the contrary, but seems incorrect on this point.

6. Harvey v. Lowrey, supra note 5, holds that he does not have; Carter v. Holohan, 92 N.Y. 498 (1883), accord. Semble, McGinty v. Dennehy, 2 S.W.2d 546 (Tex.Civ.App.1927), noted 7 Tex.L.Rev. 482 (1929). The court put the decision on the ground that the defendant's assumption had not been accepted by the mortgagee.

7. See § 5.15, infra. There is a division of authority on the point.

8. See 42 Yale L.J. 798 (1933), commenting on Harvey v. Lowrey, n. 5 supra.

9. At least one decision has allowed recovery. Calder v. Richardson, 11 F.Supp. 498 (D.C.Fla.1935), commented on, 49 Harv.L.Rev. 652 (1936).

§ 5.11 Mortgagee vs. Assuming Grantee—In General

Where there has been a transfer by the mortgagor to an assuming grantee, the mortgagee continues to have his original right against the mortgagor and his security interest in the land follows it into the hands of the transferee.[10] The mortgagor, as has been seen, acquires personal rights against the grantee upon this undertaking. The question remains whether only the mortgagor can enforce the promise to assume the mortgage, or whether the mortgagee acquires a right to do so.

All American jurisdictions confer on the mortgagee, in some manner, the right to enforce the promise of an assuming grantee. There is, however, diversity of view both as to the substantive basis of the right and the procedural method of enforcing it.[11] Since each view begets its own logical corollaries,[12] it is essential, for an intelligent consideration of a large number of mortgage problems, that these various theories be understood.

As a generalized proposition the bases of recovery by the mortgagee against an assuming grantee are two: (1) by virtue of a direct and independent right of the mortgagee; (2) by virtue of enforcing the promise of the assuming grantee derivatively, i. e., through the right against him of the mortgagor or other transferor. Different reasons are assigned in different states for adopting one or the other of these solutions. Frequently identical results are reached regardless of purported theory. Not only do the theory and rules governing a given rationale vary from state to state, but they have changed in the process of development in the same state.[13] Further, in single jurisdictions there has been a shift from one basis to another and sometimes more than one has been recognized simultaneously.[14] The re-

Recovery should be limited, where allowed, to any actual damage the non-assuming grantor may be exposed to. Id.

10. See § 5.1, supra.

11. Union Mut. Life Ins. Co. v. Hanford, 143 U.S. 187, 189, 12 S.Ct. 437, 438, 36 L.Ed. 118 (1891), "Few things have been the subject of more difference of opinion and conflict of decision than the nature and extent of the right of a mortgagee of real estate against a subsequent grantee who by the terms of the conveyance to him agrees to assume and pay the mortgage."

12. See Berick, Personal Liability for Deficiency in Mortgage Foreclosures, 8 U. of Cin.L.Rev. 103 (1934); 19 Va. L.Rev. 624 (1933); 25 Va.L.Rev. 993, 995 (1939).

13. E. g., see the evolution in Virginia, 25 Va.L.Rev. 993 (1939); Warm, Rights and Liabilities of Mortgagee, Mortgagor, Grantee, 10 Temple L.Q. 116, 130 n. 41 (1936). See 84 U. of Pa.L.Rev. 909 (1936) for the development in Pennsylvania. See also 88 U.Pa.L.Rev. 611, 612 (1940), giving as examples the experience in Minnesota and Rhode Island. For a consideration of the problems in Massachusetts see Note, 8 Suffolk L.Rev. 130 (1973).

14. This seems to be the situation in New York, with some resulting uncertainty as to which rule is to be applied. Seaver v. Ransom, 224 N.Y. 233, 120 N.E. 639, 2 A.L.R. 1187 (1918). See Friedman, Personal Liability on Mortgage Debts in New York, 50 Yale L.J. 224, 231–236, 236 n. 90 (1940); 88 U. of Pa.L.Rev. 611, 612 (1940); see also 25 Va.L.Rev. 993,

sult of such changes is that many of the decisions are outdated. Hence, any precise classification of jurisdictions is difficult, would be transient and not particularly helpful. Nevertheless, an analysis of the theories themselves is important to understanding fundamental mortgage law concepts and, moreover, provides a useful foundation for the consideration of related problems dealt with later in this chapter.

§ 5.12 Mortgagee vs. Assuming Grantee—Third Party Beneficiary

The first and most important view is that the mortgagee is allowed to sue the assuming grantee simply as a third party beneficiary of a contract.[15] The great weight of authority accepts this view [16]

996 (1939), for the law in Virginia. In California by statute, West's Ann. Cal.Civ.Code § 1559, a third party beneficiary may sue the promisor directly. See note, 1938, 26 Cal.L.Rev. 627. A mortgagee may sue an assuming grantee of the mortgagor under this statutory provision. Bank of Alameda County v. Hering, 134 Cal. App. 570, 25 P.2d 1004 (1933); see Alvord v. Spring Valley Gold Co., 106 Cal. 547, 40 P. 27 (1895). Yet he also is able to reach such an assuming grantee from his mortgagor, not under the statute, but on the theory of "equitable subrogation." Hopkins v. Warner, 109 Cal. 133, 41 P. 868 (1895).

15. "Where the performance of a promise in a contract will benefit a person other than the promisee, that person is classified as a * * * beneficiary." Aetna Life Ins. Co. v. Maxwell, 89 F.2d 988, 993 (C.C.A.W. Va.1937). Beneficiaries who may recover are of two kinds, donee beneficiaries and creditor beneficiaries. Id. A person is classified as a creditor beneficiary when "the performance of the promise will satisfy an actual or supposed or asserted duty of the promisee to the beneficiary." Restatement, Contracts, § 133(1)b. In jurisdictions accepting the third party beneficiary rationale the mortgagee as a general proposition normally recovers as a creditor beneficiary. The Restatement Second has dropped the use of the "donee" and "creditor" beneficiary designations because they carried "overtones of obsolete doctrinal difficulties". Instead, the terms "intended" beneficiary and "incidental" beneficiary are used to distinguish those beneficiaries who have rights from those who do not. See Restatement of Contracts, Second, § 133 and Introductory Note thereto. While the older terminology is dropped, the "donee-creditor" distinction is recognised as a factual rather than conceptual distinction. See Calamari and Perillo, Contracts 607 (2d Ed. 1977).

16. See Williston, Contracts, § 383 n. 11 (Jaeger Ed. 1959), listing 36 jurisdictions that appear to give relief to the mortgagee on some version of a third party beneficiary theory. See elaborate compilation of authorities in 21 A.L.R. 439, 454 (1922); 47 A.L. R. 339, 341 (1927).

For analysis of the concept, see Williston, Contracts for the Benefit of a Third Person, 15 Harv.L.Rev. 767 (1902), and Corbin, Contracts for the Benefit of Third Persons, 27 Yale L.J. 1008 (1918). See also Whittier, Contract Beneficiaries, 32 Yale L.J. 790 (1923); Hening, History of the Beneficiary's Action in Assumpsit, 1909, 3 Select Essays in Anglo-American Legal History; Finlay, Contracts for the Benefit of Third Persons, 1939; 26 Va. L.Rev. 778 (1940). For other discussions, dealing primarily with the assuming grantee of a mortgagor, see Friedman, Personal Liability on Mortgage Debts in New York, 50 Yale L.J. 224 (1940); Mechem, Assumption of Mortgages, 18 Cent.L.J. 23 (1884); Tucker, Personal Liability of One Assuming Payment of a Deed of Trust, 4 Va.L.Rev. 464 (1917); Glassie, The Assuming Vendee, 9 Va.L.Rev. 196 (1923); Hand, Purchase of Incumbered Land—Rights and Liabilities of Parties, 48 Cent.L.J. 489 (1899); Warm, Some Aspects of the Rights and Liabilities of Mortgagee, Mortgagor, and Grantee, 10 Temple L.Q. 116 (1936); Berick, Personal Liability for Deficien-

but this fact does not free it from difficulty. The right of recovery depends upon theories and rules of general contract law which are still in a period of growth, not only varying from state to state but within a given jurisdiction.[17] Among the more important points on which there is divergence are whether the promisee must be liable to the mortgagee; [18] when the right vests indefeasibly in him; [19] how far it may be affected by defenses between (a) the assuming grantee and his promisee and (b) the promisee and the mortgagee; [20] the effect of subsequent agreements between the promisor and promisee on the rights of the mortgagee,[21] and the consequences as to a mortgagee's other rights of binding extensions of time or releases by him to an assuming grantee.[22] Where the third party beneficiary doctrine is accepted as the foundation of the mortgagee's right, it is clearly an independent one enforceable by an action at law.[23]

cy in Mortgage Foreclosures, 8 U. of Cin.L.Rev. 103 (1934); notes, 25 Va. L.Rev. 993 (Virginia law) (1939); 13 St. John's L.Rev. 215 (1938); 11 Cal.L.Rev. 139 (1923); 11 Cal.L.Rev. 429 (1923); 26 Cal.L.Rev. 627 (1938); 10 Col.L.Rev. 765 (1910); Note, The Third Party Beneficiary Concept: A Proposal, 57 Col.L.Rev. 406 (1957); 4 Cornell L.Q. 53 (1919); 9 Cornell L.Q. 213 (1924); 84 U. of Pa.L.Rev. 909 (1936); 17 Va.L.Rev. 844 (1931); 19 Va.L.Rev. 624 (1933); 39 Yale L.J. 746 (1930). See also 21 A.L.R. 439 (1922); 47 A.L.R. 339 (1927). As to the right of a mortgagee as creditor beneficiary in Pennsylvania under the statute in that state, see 10 U. of Pitt. L.Rev. 419 1949).

17. "The history of the third party beneficiary doctrine since Lawrence v. Fox has been a checkered one of sorties and retreats." Friedman, supra note 14, 233. 88 U.Pa.L.Rev. 611, 612 (1940); In Berick, Personal Liability for Deficiency in Mortgage Foreclosures, 8 U. of Cin.L.Rev. 103, 112 (1934), the beneficiary cases are grouped into three classes. 1. Those permitting the third person to sue only if the promise was made for his sole and exclusive benefit. 2. Those requiring as prerequisites: (a) a clear intent to benefit the third person, and (b) an obligation owing by the promisee to the third person. These limitations were laid down by the New York courts "because of early efforts to find a justification for the doctrine." See other discussions of the New York cases in notes, 4 Cornell L.Q. 53 (1919); 27 Yale L.J. 1008, 1027 (1918); Friedman, op. cit. supra, this note. Those which do not concern themselves with justifying the rule but accept it as well established, and require only an intent to benefit, with the one limitation that incidental or indirect benefit to the third person is insufficient to confer rights upon him. See Aetna Life Ins. Co. v. Maxwell, 89 F.2d 988, 993 (C.C.A.W. Va., 1937). See also Restatement, Contracts, §§ 133–136, 147.

18. See § 5.16, infra.

19. See § 5.19, infra.

20. See § 5.18, infra.

21. See Restatement, Contracts, §§ 142, 143; Restatement, Second, Contracts, § 142.

22. See §§ 5.20–5.21, infra.

23. "The promise creates a duty which the promisor must perform, and this duty, if not performed, may be made the basis of an action by the beneficiary against the promisor." Aetna Life Ins. Co. v. Maxwell, 89 F.2d 988, 993 (C.C.A.W.Va., 1937). See Williston, Contracts, Rev. ed., §§ 357, 383; Restatement, Contracts, §§ 136(1)a; 135, 141(1).

§ 5.13 Mortgagee vs. Assuming Grantee—"Suretyship" Subrogation

A second group of cases, applying a "suretyship" theory, invoke what is called the doctrine of equitable subrogation. As used here, it means that the mortgagee-creditor is enabled to reach a right in the hands of his debtor, the mortgagor, against a third party, the assuming grantee, on the theory that the mortgagor-debtor has become a surety-debtor.[24] In order for the principle to apply a "suretyship" situation must exist. A suretyship situation requires a triangle with the person at each foot of the triangle being bound to the creditor at the apex by their respective contracts.[25] Where there is only one person owing a single obligation to another person no suretyship situation can exist. For a person's duty to be that of a surety, in addition to his obligation to the creditor, there must be a separate one, the principal, for whose performance it stands surety. In a mortgage, to begin with, there is a personal obligation running between the mortgagor and the mortgagee. There is also, existing between the mortgagee and the land in the hands of the mortgagor, a relationship normally referred to as a security interest in the property. When the land is transferred by the mortgagor to a grantee, as between the continuing personal duty of the mortgagor to the mortgagee and the continuing relationship between the mortgagee and the land now in the hands of another, the situation may be treated with some certainty as one of suretyship. In such a case the mortgagee has two rights, one against the land, the other against the mortgagor. Which one is surety and which is principal depends upon the terms of the transfer.[26] If the mortgagor received the full value of the land and agreed to pay

24. See Williston, Contracts for the Benefit of a Third Person, 15 Harv.L. Rev. 767, 789 (1902). See also Arant, Suretyship, 370 et seq. But see Warm, Rights and Liabilities of Mortgagee, Mortgagor, Grantee, 10 Temple L.Q. 116, 129 (1936). This "suretyship" theory of solution has been accepted in a good many jurisdictions: Hopkins v. Warner, 109 Cal. 133, 136, 41 P. 868 (1895); Crawford v. Edwards, 33 Mich. 354 (1876); Klapworth v. Dressler, 13 N.J.Eq. 62, 78 Am.Dec. 69 (1860); Crowell v. Hospital of St. Barnabas, 27 N.J.Eq. 650, 655 (1876); Willard v. Worsham, 76 Va. 392 (1882); Keller v. Ashford, 133 U.S. 610, 623, 10 S.Ct. 494, 497, 33 L.Ed. 667 (1890). See Warm, Rights and Liabilities of Mortgagee, Mortgagor, Grantee, 10 Temple L.Q. 116, 128 (1936); Friedman, Personal Liability on Mortgage Debts in New York, 50 Yale L.J. 224, 230 (1940); Glassie, The Assuming Vendee, 9 Va. L.Rev. 196, 199 (1923); notes, 17 Va. L.Rev. 844, 847 (1931); 19 Va.L.Rev. 624, 625 (1933); 10 Col.L.Rev. 765, 767 (1910); 4 U. of Chi.L.Rev. 469, 476 (1937); 25 Ill.L.Rev. 721, 723 (1931); 26 Cal.L.Rev. 627 (1938); 25 Va.L. Rev. 993, 996 (1939); 21 A.L.R. 439, 451 (1922); 47 A.L.R. 339, 341 (1927). It has been adversely criticized. See Corbin, Contracts for Benefit of Third Persons, 1918, 27 Yale L.J. 1008, 1015. The grantee has deposited with the grantor nothing except a promise to protect him against the enforcement of the mortgage debt. To treat this as security given to him is at variance with the ordinary understanding of the term. See Arant, Suretyship, 370 et seq.

25. See Glenn, Mortgages, § 268; 4 U. of Chi.L.Rev. 469, 476 (1937).

26. See §§ 5.1–5.3, supra.

the debt he would be principal and the land would be surety. And *vice versa* if the transferee paid only the value of the redemption interest and took "subject" to the mortgage or assumed it.[27]

When the mortgagor transfers to an assuming grantee, the suretyship situation just described will exist as between the mortgagor, the land and the mortgagee.[28] But the suretyship situation to which the cases purport to apply the principle is a different and additional one in which the assuming grantee personally, not the land, is the principal. If the assumption creates a new direct right in the mortgagee against the assuming grantee, a suretyship situation results in which the new right is the principal obligation and the old right against the mortgagor becomes that of a surety. However, unless the mortgagee does acquire such a separate right against the assuming grantee in addition to his continuing personal right against the mortgagor no suretyship relation in the ordinary sense can exist.[29] If the assuming grantee is not personally a principal, i. e., obligated directly to the mortgagee, his promise to the mortgagor to pay the debt cannot be regarded as the collateral security given by him, as principal, to the mortgagor, as his surety, for indemnity against liability to the mortgagee. It follows that, if the situation is really one of suretyship, the courts actually are recognizing that the contract of assumption creates a new right in the mortgagee against the assuming grantee—a result in substance no different from that which recognizes openly that it does so under the doctrine that the beneficiary of a contract may enforce it.[30] In spite of this, the theory on which

27. Id.

28. See § 5.10, supra.

29. 4 U. of Chi.L.Rev. 469, 476 (1937). But see Friedman, Discharge of Mortgage Debts, 52 Yale L.J. 771, 796 (1943), "True, the conventional suretyship triangle is not present but similar logic might once have been urged against the creation of constructive and resulting trusts. * * * Furthermore, the right of subrogation, and the penalty for its impairment, appears in situations other than that of conventional suretyship."

30. "For the mortgagor to be a surety, it is necessary that the mortgagee have an independent right against the grantee. Yet for the mortgagee to get this 'direct' right by the above analogy [i. e., that of suretyship subrogation of the mortgagee to the rights of the mortgagor, it was necessary to assume that the mortgagor was a surety; thus assuming the conclusion." 4 U. of Chi.L.Rev. 469, 476 (1937). "The doctrine of subrogation has no doubt been very beneficial in spite of fiction and artificiality; but in this instance it has been used to confer new security and new rights upon a creditor, as a gift out of a clear sky. In suretyship it is used only as against one who is already legally indebted in order to secure the fulfillment of that legal duty. A doctrine whose purpose was the enforcement of a previously recognized duty cannot properly be given as the sole reason for creating an entirely new duty." Corbin, Contracts for the Benefit of Third Persons, 27 Yale L.J. 1008, 1015 (1918).

"The extension of the subrogation theory to cover this case, where the promisor was not indebted to the third party by reason of any operative fact other than his promise to the promisee, is merely a cumbrous intellectual expedient for holding that a contract between two parties can create an enforceable right in a third." Corbin, supra, at 1016, n. 32.

the process of enforcement goes is that the mortgagee is enforcing his right against the mortgagor-surety and reaching the assuming grantee through the right which the mortgagor as surety has against him. Consequently the mortgagee's right on this theory must be classed as a derivative one.[31] A logical consequence is that, if the promisee-grantor is not bound to pay the debt he is not a surety, the doctrine is inapplicable, and the mortgagee cannot reach the assuming grantee.

§ 5.14 Mortgagee vs. Assuming Grantee—Miscellaneous Theories

There have been several additional bases that have been utilized to justify permitting the mortgagee to recover against an assuming grantee. While these approaches have not commanded a substantial acceptance, they, nevertheless, merit some consideration.

The Equitable Assets Theory

The equitable assets theory was initially advanced by Professor Williston.[32] Under this approach, instead of looking at the assuming grantee's promise to the grantor-promisee as indemnity security in the latter's hands as surety, given to him by the principal obligor, it is regarded as an asset of the mortgagee's only debtor, the mortgagor, of a sort which can be reached only by the aid of equity.[33]

The theory has certain distinct merits. On the one hand it avoids both the difficulty of giving reasons why a person who is not privy to a contract may nevertheless maintain an action on it against the promisor and the practical objection to permitting it that the promisor may be exposed to possible double liability on one promise. On the other hand, it escapes the fictitious, or apparently contradic-

31. See cases, note 24, supra. See also Binns v. Baumgartner, 105 N.J. Eq. 58, 60, 146 A. 879 (1929), "The equity on which his relief depends is the right of the mortgagor against his vendee, to which right the mortgagee is permitted to succeed, by substituting himself in the place of the mortgagor." Duvall-Percival Trust Co. v. Jenkins, 16 F.2d 223, 226 (C.C.A.Kan. 1926).

32. Williston, Contracts for the Benefit of a Third Person, 15 Harv.L.Rev. 766, 767 (1902).

33. "Obviously a promise to pay a debt due a third person cannot be taken on an execution against the debtor, nor is it the subject of garnishment; for the promisor, if he is willing to perform his promise, cannot be compelled to do anything else, and as the promise is not to pay the promisee, the promisor cannot be charged as garnishee or trustee for him. The aid of equity is, therefore, necessary in order to compel the application of such property to the creditor's claim, and acting as it does by personal decree, equity can readily give the required relief." Williston, supra note 32.

The theory was initially adopted in Massachusetts. See Forbes v. Thorpe, 209 Mass. 570, 582, 95 N.E. 955, 959 (1911), for the first recognition. It was also acknowledged as existing in Gillis v. Bonelli-Adams Co., 284 Mass. 176, 187 N.E. 535 (1933); Bloch v. Budish, 279 Mass. 102, 180 N.E. 729 (1932) discussed 1933, 19 Va.L.Rev. 624, 628. However, there is some basis for concluding that Massachusetts today follows the equitable subrogation theory. See Note, 8 Suffolk L.Rev. 130, 145 n. 73 (1973).

tory, aspects of the "suretyship" solution which seems to create, or at least recognize the existence of, a primary personal obligation of the assuming grantee running to the mortgagee and yet holds that the only way to realize on that obligation is by reaching, in equity, security in the form of a promise to indemnify given by the grantee-promisor as principal to his grantor-promisee as surety.[34]

Nevertheless certain aspects of the theory have been criticized. For one thing, the asset is a peculiar sort of one in that, unlike other assets, it is available only to one particular creditor, the mortgagee. This is because the promisor cannot be required to do anything other than what he promised. This feature has caused one critic to assert that "[t]o apply the 'equitable asset' theory is merely to recognize the third party beneficiary's right under another and mis-descriptive name." [35] This is not, of course, entirely true, for the right on this theory is purely derivative, a fact that has important consequences.[36] Another possible criticism of the doctrine is that, by offering a good, if not perfect solution of the problem, it tends to retard the complete triumph of the third party beneficiary direct right rule.

Statutory Bases

In a few jurisdictions, statutes specifically confer on the mortgagee a right against the assuming grantee.[37] It is not entirely clear whether, assuming the mortgagee may bring his action by virtue of a statute, the right he is enforcing is a direct one or a derivative one. It should depend upon whether the statute is interpreted to be merely procedural or whether it creates substantive rights.[38] If the latter, the right so created would seem to be direct. If the former, the substantive law apart from statute would determine.

Some courts have utilized statutes or court rules that provide that actions shall be brought in the name of the real party in interest as a method of giving the mortgagee the right to sue the assuming

34. See § 5.13, supra.

35. Corbin, Contracts for the Benefit of Third Persons, 27 Yale L.J. 1008, 1021 (1918). "By differentiating this particular creditor from other creditors and this particular 'asset' from other assets we are merely recognizing that he has obtained a special right in personam as against the promisor, a right that is created by a contract to which he was not a party. He gains this special right because the contracting parties intended that he should have it, or at least that the performance should go direct to him." Idem. But see Friedman, Personal Liability on Mortgage Debts, 50 Yale L.J. 224, 230 (1940).

36. E. g., on the ability of the promisee to release the promisor, on the availability of supervening defenses of the promisee against the mortgagee, the necessity of the promisee being obligated to the mortgagee, etc. See § 5.17 infra.

37. E. g., Conn.Gen.Stat.Ann. § 52–75; Schneider v. Ferrigno, 110 Conn. 86, 147 A. 303 (1929).

38. See Warm, Rights and Liabilities of Mortgagee, Mortgagor, Grantee, 10 Temple L.Q. 130, n. 42 (1936), criticizing Schneider v. Ferrigno, supra note 37.

grantee.[39] This approach seems to beg at least two questions. The prior question is, of course, whether he is the real party in interest. And that goes back to the question of substantive law as to whether the promise of the assuming grantee creates any right against him in favor of the mortgagee.[40]

Plurality of Actions Theory

Another small group of cases assert that the mortgagee is permitted to reach the assuming grantee to avoid plurality of actions and harassment of the mortgagor.[41] Here again, no new rationale of the substantive right itself is advanced. Rather the existence of the procedural relief is predicated upon the existence of a substantive right by the mortgagee against the mortgagor which in turn makes operative a right over by the mortgagor against his assuming grantee. In other words the right of the mortgagee here, as in the "suretyship" or equitable assets rationales, is derivative.

§ 5.15 Successive Purchasers

It frequently happens that there is a series of sales of the mortgaged property with each grantee in turn agreeing with his immediate grantor to assume the mortgage. In such a case all of them become liable to the mortgage creditor who may successfully invoke as to each one in succession whichever doctrine enabled him to reach the first grantee of the mortgagor.[42] The same reasoning which justifies holding the first grantee by virtue of his promise to the mortgagee's debtor applies to charge the second grantee by reason of his promise to the first grantee and so on down to the last grantee. If the mortgagee reached the first grantee derivatively through the right of the mortgagor against him he can reach the second one derivatively through the right of the first grantee since the mortgagor, whose right he is using could have done so. If his right is a direct one as creditor beneficiary of the contract between his original debtor, the mortgagor, and the first grantee, so too his right will be a direct one against the second grantee as creditor beneficiary of the as-

39. Marianna Lime Products Co. v. McKay, 109 Fla. 275, 147 So. 264 (1933); Cooper v. Bane, 110 Neb. 74, 193 N.W. 97 (1923); see Ellis v. Harrison, 104 Mo. 270, 277, 16 S.W. 198 (1891).

40. See Corbin, Contracts for the Benefit of Third Persons, 27 Yale L.J. 1008, 1029 (1918); Williston, Contracts, Rev.ed., § 366.

41. Y. M. C. A. v. Crofts, 34 Or. 106, 114, 55 P. 439, 441, 75 Am.St.Rep. 568 (1898); Osborne v. Cabell, 77 Va. 462, 467 (1883). While New Jersey apparently earlier followed this theory, it is clear that now a mortgagee in that state has a direct right of action against the assuming grantee based on N.J.Stat.Ann. 2A:15-2. See Cunningham and Tischler, Transfer of the Real Estate Mortgagor's Interest, 27 Rutgers L.Rev. 24, 42-43 (1973).

42. Robson v. O'Toole, 45 Cal.App. 63, 187 P. 110 (1919); Carnahan v. Tousey, 93 Ind. 561 (1883); Corning v. Burton, 102 Mich. 86, 62 N.W. 1040 (1894); Hurst v. Merrifield, 144 Or. 78, 23 P.2d 124 (1933).

sumption contract between his new obligor, the first grantee, and the second grantee. Moreover all who have thus assumed the mortgage are liable regardless of having in turn parted with land to subsequent grantees and even though the later transferees assumed the mortgage.[43] Each one's own valid contract, which is the source of his liability, is not affected by his selling the premises. His protection, in case he is forced to pay, lies in his rights against his own and subsequent grantees and the land.[44]

Where one of the successive transferees takes title without promising his vendor to assume the mortgage he incurs no personal responsibility to anyone for the payment of the debt. If such a purchaser in turn sells to a grantee who promises him to pay the debt, the question arises whether the second purchaser, thus bound to his vendor, is liable also to the mortgage creditor. On this point there is diversity of decision.[45] His liability depends upon the rationale under which the mortgagee is allowed to hold an assuming grantee in the particular jurisdiction and the rules governing liability under the rationale followed in that jurisdiction.

Insofar as the mortgagee's rights against an assuming grantee are derivative, i. e., rest upon the theory that he is allowed to apply the rights of his own debtor through subrogation or as an equitable asset the mortgagee cannot compel payment by any transferee who takes after the break in the chain of assumptions. The assuming vendees in such a case have promised a vendor against whom the mortgage creditor has no right and, consequently, to whose claim against the assuming vendee he can lay no claim. The same would be true of those cases which permit the mortgagee to proceed against the assuming grantee to prevent plurality of actions, for in order to have plurality of actions there must first be a right of action by the mortgage creditor against the promisee-grantor. Hence the rule in all these cases is that the mortgagee's right stops with the last grantee who assumed in direct succession.[46]

43. See note 51, supra.

44. See §§ 5.9–5.10, supra.

45. See Calamari and Perillo, Contracts, § 17.4 (2d Ed. 1977). See cases cited in succeeding footnotes. Also see notes, 11 Cal.L.Rev. 139 (1923); 88 U. of Pa.L.Rev. 611 (1940); 6 U. of Cin.L.Rev. 361 (1932); 8 U. of Cin.L. Rev. 103, 125 (1934); 9 Cornell L.Q. 213 (1924); 16 Minn.L.Rev. 114 (1931); 13 Va.L.Rev. 500 (1927); 17 Va.L.Rev. 844 (1931); 39 Yale L.J. 746 (1930); Restatement, Contracts, §§ 133, 144, Illustration 2; Williston, Contracts, Rev.Ed., § 386A. See also 12 A.L.R. 1528 (1921); L.R.A.1916D, 154.

46. Ward v. De Oca, 120 Cal. 102, 52 P. 130 (1898); Morris v. Mix, 4 Kan. App. 654, 46 P. 58 (1896); Colorado Sav. Bank v. Bales, 101 Kan. 100, 165 P. 843 (1917); Norwood v. De Hart, 30 N.J.Eq. 412 (1879); Eakin v. Shultz, 61 N.J.Eq. 156, 47 A. 274 (1900); Osborne v. Cabell, 77 Va. 462 (1883); see South Carolina Ins. Co. v. Kohn, 108 S.C. 475, 480, 95 S.E. 65 (1917). See also Berick, Deficiency in Mortgage Foreclosures, 8 U. of Cin.L.Rev. 103, 108 (1934).

Dail v. Campbell, 191 Cal.App. 416, 12 Cal.Rptr. 739 (1961), is in accord as to the remote grantee who assumed a purchase price mortgage where an intermediate grantee had not assumed the mortgage.

In those jurisdictions which give the mortgagee a direct right as third party beneficiary of a contract there is a conflict in the decisions as to whether recovery should be allowed. The mortgagee is usually regarded as a creditor beneficiary. Since he actually has no right against the promisee-grantor, those cases that insist that an obligation to pay must exist in order for a creditor beneficiary to have rights against the assuming grantee would deny recovery to him as such.[47] Courts also deny recovery on the ground that there is no intent to benefit the mortgagee.[48] A broader test, adopted by the Restatement of Contracts classifies a person as a creditor beneficiary when the "performance of the promise will satisfy an actual or supposed or asserted duty of the promisee to the beneficiary." [49] If the stipulation was inserted intentionally, it most likely was to guard against a supposed or possible liability of the promisee which did not in fact exist.[50] If so, it would fall under this test of a creditor beneficiary and it is possible to justify a good many decisions allowing recovery on this ground although the opinions in them do not explicitly adopt it.[51]

Some courts deny the mortgagee recovery as a creditor beneficiary and also as a donee beneficiary.[52] There are other courts that apparently recognize a right to recover as a donee beneficiary.[53] Some of them reason that since the non-assuming grantor is not personally liable to the mortgagee and is no longer owner of the premises he has no interest in the performance of the assumption promise. The only object of exacting such a stipulation is to confer a gratuitous benefit or right upon the mortgagee.[54] In others, the courts seem to assume the donative intent, treating it as a question of the power of the promisee to create such a right in the mortgagee. The reasoning on this is that, since the contract is enforceable by the

47. Vrooman v. Turner, 69 N.Y. 280 (1877), Walsh & Simpson, Cases Security Transactions, 312; Wager v. Link, 134 N.Y. 122, 31 N.E. 213 (1892); see Hinckley Estate Co. v. Gurry, 56 Idaho 38, 48 P.2d 1111 (1935); De Leon v. Rhines, 64 App. D.C. 73, 75, 74 F.2d 477, 479 (1934). See also 9 Cornell L.Q. 213 (1923); 39 Yale L.J. 746 (1930).

48. Case v. Egan, 57 Cal.App. 453, 207 P. 388 (1922); Y. M. C. A. v. Crofts, 34 Or. 106, 55 P. 439, 75 Am.St.Rep. 568 (1898); Fry v. Ausman, 29 S.D. 30, 135 N.W. 708, 39 L.R.A.,N.S., 150, Ann.Cas.1914C 842 (1912). See also cases in preceding note.

49. § 133(1) b.

50. See Williston, Contracts, (3d Ed.), § 386A; 39 Yale L.J. 746 (1930); 9 Cornell L.Q. 213 (1923).

51. Scott v. Wharton, 226 Ala. 601, 148 So. 308 (1933).

52. The cases in notes 47, 48, supra, may rest upon this ground. See 39 Yale L.J. 746 (1930); 9 Cornell L.Q. 213 (1923); 88 U.Pa.L.Rev. 611, 613 (1940).

53. Schneider v. Ferrigno, 110 Conn. 86, 147 A. 303 (1929) intent to confer right of action sufficient to make mortgagee a donee beneficiary; South Carolina Ins. Co. v. Kohn, 108 S.C. 475, 480, 95 S.E. 95 (1917). See 25 Ill.L.Rev. 723 (1931). Also cases in following footnotes.

54. Casselman's Adm'x v. Gordon & Lightfoot, 118 Va. 553, 88 S.E. 58 (1916); see 25 Va.L.Rev. 993, 997 (1939).

promisee, he can direct that the performance go to whomsoever he wishes and the promisor cannot object.[55]

The Restatement of Contracts, Second, has abandoned the use of the terms "creditor" and "donee" beneficiary, those beneficiaries that had rights under the original Restatement. Instead, these terms are subsumed under the label of "intended" beneficiaries.[56] Under the Restatement, Second, rights are conferred on "intended" beneficiaries, but not on "incidental" beneficiaries.[57] A person is included as an intended beneficiary if "recognition of a right to performance in the beneficiary is appropriate to effectuate the intention of the parties and * * * the circumstances indicate that the promisee intends to give the beneficiary the benefit of the promised performance." [58] Thus, in the mortgage context, so long as the non-assuming transferor has the requisite intent to benefit the mortgagee, the mortgagee would, if a court adopts the Restatement, Second, probably have a direct right against the assuming grantee.[59]

§ 5.16 Assumption by Second Mortgagee

When a mortgagor, instead of selling the property to a purchaser who assumes the mortgage, gives a second mortgage to one who agrees to pay off the first mortgage, the first mortgagee cannot enforce the assumption agreement against the second mortgagee, at least absent separate consideration flowing from the first mortgagee to the second.[60]

The above rule of law may be significant in connection with the commonly used "wrap-around" mortgage. This transaction entails "a second mortgage securing a promissory note, the face amount of which is the sum of the existing first mortgage liability plus the cash

55. Dean v. Walker, 107 Ill. 540, 47 Am.Rep. 467 (1883); Marble Sav. Bank v. Mesarvey, 101 Iowa 285, 70 N.W. 198 (1897); Clement v. Willett, 105 Minn. 267, 117 N.W. 491, 17 L.R.A.,N.S., 1094 (1908); 127 Am.St.Rep. 562, 15 Ann.Cas. 1053; Crone v. Stinde, 156 Mo. 262, 55 S.W. 863 (1900); Hare v. Murphy, 45 Neb. 809, 64 N.W. 211, 29 L.R.A. 851 (1895); Brewer v. Maurer, 38 Ohio St. 543, 43 Am.Rep. 436 (1882); Mullin v. Claremont Realty Co., 39 Ohio App. 103, 177 N.E. 226 (1930); Walser v. Farmers' Trust Co., 126 Ohio St. 367, 185 N.E. 535 (1933); Merriman v. Moore, 90 Pa. 78, 7 W.N.C. 425 (1879); Title Guaranty etc. Co. v. Bushnell, 143 Tenn. 681, 228 S.W. 699, 12 A.L.R. 1512 (1921); Corkrell v. Poe, 100 Wash. 625, 171 P. 522, 12 A.L.R. 1524 (1918); Enos v. Sanger, 96 Wis. 150, 70 N.W. 1069, 37 L.R.A. 862, 65 Am.St.Rep. 38 (1897); Prudential Ins. Co. of America v. Clybourn Realty Co., 214 Wis. 409, 253 N.W. 397 (1934); Duvall-Percival Trust Co. v. Jenkins, 16 F.2d 223 (C.C.A.Kan.1926).

56. Restatement, Second, Contracts, § 133.

57. Restatement, Second, Contracts, § 133 Introductory Note.

58. Restatement, Second, Contracts, § 133.

59. See Restatement, Second, Contracts, § 144, Illus. 3.

60. Garnsey v. Rogers, 47 N.Y. 233, 7 Am.R. 440 (1872); Walsh & Simpson, Cases Security Transactions, 316; Savings Bank of Southern California v. Thornton, 112 Cal. 255, 44 P. 466 (1896); Downs v. Ziegler, 13 Ariz. App. 387, 477 P.2d 261 (1971).

or equity advanced by the lender. The wrap-around borrower must make payments on the first mortgage debt to the wrap-around lender, who, as required by the wrap-around agreement, must in turn make payments on the first mortgage debt to the third party, the first mortgagee. If the wrap-around mortgagee should fail to perform his obligation to pay off the first mortgage, the wrap-around agreement normally gives the non-defaulting mortgagor the right to pay the interest and principal owing on the first mortgage, reducing his wrap-around obligation pro tanto." [61] While these transactions often entail purchase-money financing, a refinancing situation is more illustrative for our purposes. Suppose a mortgagor owns land worth $200,000 subject to a first mortgage of $90,000 carrying a 7% interest rate. Mortgagor wishes to obtain an additional $75,000 by further encumbering his equity in the land. A second mortgage lender may offer a wrap-around mortgage for $165,000 ($90,000 + $75,000) at a 10% interest rate. If this arrangement is accepted, the wrap-around mortgagee will promise to pay off the first mortgage with funds received from mortgagor's payments on the wrap-around mortgage.

To the extent that the wrap-around mortgagee formally assumes the first mortgage debt, the first mortgagee cannot enforce such an assumption against the wrap-around mortgagee. This is true because the first mortgagee normally will not have parted with any consideration in such a transaction. As a practical matter, however, this problem may not always be significant because the wrap-around mortgagee in any event very often does not unconditionally assume the first mortgage debt. The obligation on the part of the wrap-around mortgagee to pay the first mortgage is often conditioned on the receipt from the mortgagor of the debt service amount.[62]

If, however, the second mortgagee, whether a wrap-around mortgagee or not, actually formally assumes the first mortgage, it does not seem unreasonable to allow the first mortgagee to enforce that assumption. Indeed, most of the case law to the contrary was decided at a time when courts were not overly sympathetic to mortgagee recovery from assuming grantees. It is true, of course, that the usual assuming grantee-purchaser receives real estate and the assumption is part of the purchase price. Moreover, such is not the case with respect to the assuming second mortgagee. On the other hand, mortgagees in general would rarely assume a first mortgage by mistake. The decision, for example, to enter into a wrap-around transaction is presumably based on financially advantageous reasons. Moreover, the mortgagor in such a situation may desire additional assurance that the appropriate part of his payment to the wrap-around mortgagee will be applied to the first mortgage debt. The assumption of that first mortgage debt may very well provide the mortgagor

61. Comment, The Wrap-Around Mortgage: A Critical Inquiry, 21 U.C.L.A. L.Rev. 1529, 1529–1530 (1974).

62. Gunning, The Wrap-Around Mortgage * * * Friend or U.F.O.?, 2 Real Estate Rev. Summer, 1972 at 35.

with that added assurance. Consequently, whether a jurisdiction normally uses a third party beneficiary theory or some derivative theory to find assuming grantees liable to a mortgagee, there seems ample basis to utilize similar reasoning in the second mortgagee assumption situation.

Even under traditional case law, there may be clear situations where a first mortgagee will be able to enforce an assumption against a second mortgagee. These will involve situations where consideration for the assumption flows from the first mortgagee to the second. For example, suppose that a first mortgage goes into default and that the second mortgagee approachs the first mortgagee and offers to assume the first mortgage debt if the first mortgagee forbears for one year in foreclosing.[63] Acceptance of this arrangement by the first mortgagee clearly confers a benefit on the second mortgagee. A year's time could very well mean that the mortgagor will be able to reinstate the defaulted first mortgage. If this does occur, the second mortgagee will have avoided having his mortgage wiped out a first mortgage foreclosure sale.

§ 5.17 Grantee's Defenses Against Mortgagee

Whether the mortgagee can enforce the mortgage or the mortgage debt against a transferee of the mortgagor to a different extent than he could do so against the mortgagor had there been no transfer properly depends upon the terms of the transfer and the intention of the transferor.[64] If the transferee promises to take subject to or to assume a specific mortgage, the amount of which has been deducted from the agreed on purchase price of the property, he becomes bound by contract to have the land in his hands subjected to payment of the full amount of the debt so agreed upon and, where he assumes its payment, to pay it. It is immaterial whether his promisee is actually indebted to that amount by an enforceable obligation.[65] By so including it and making its payment binding on the land, or the land and the transferee personally, he has shown that he intends the obligation to be valid so far as his transferee is concerned, and thus negatives any intention to confer a benefit upon him to the extent that the debt may be invalid or uneforceable. To permit the transferee under such circumstances to defeat the mortgagee on the ground that the mortgagor was not liable in whole or in part would unjustly enrich the transferee by enabling him to get the property for an amount less than he had agreed to pay for it, contrary to the intention of the transfer-

63. See Kozan v. Levin, 50 A.D.2d 663, 374 N.Y.S.2d 829 (1975).

64. See 141 A.L.R. 1184 (1942).

65. "If one assumes to pay a definite amount of the indebtedness of another, it is none of his concern whether the debt thus assumed is greater or less than the actual indebtedness." Oglesby v. South Georgia Grocery Co., 18 Ga.App. 401, 402, 89 S.E. 436 (1917).

or.[66] Where the grantee has assumed or taken subject to a specific mortgage most of the cases refuse to permit him to set up usury [67] or other defenses [68] which would have been available to the mortgagor. A good many of the cases do so, however, on the ground either that the transferee is estopped [69] to deny the validity or extent of the mortgage or that the defense is personal to the mortgagor.[70] Neither doctrine is properly applicable. The amount of the debt is not a term of the mortgage to which estoppel by deed applies and no showing of reliance by the mortgagee upon the terms of the promise, a requirement of estoppel generally, is insisted upon. If the defense were really personal to the mortgagor it should be so in all cases. Yet in cases where the terms of the contract indicate that the transferee is binding himself only to be subject to or to pay the amount of the debt actually due or legally enforceable,[71] no objection is raised to his set-

66. Where, for example, usury that could not be collected from the mortgagor formed part of the consideration for the purchase, it "would be permitting a fraud to allow the grantee to plead usury. If the mortgagor chooses to affirm his contract, and sets apart, out of the purchase price for the complete title, an amount sufficient to pay it, whether with an express agreement of the grantee to make such payment, or with an option to either pay or suffer foreclosure, the grantee cannot question the amount. If the usury has become a part of the consideration in the agreement between the mortgagor and his grantee, it is an affirmance of the debt by the mortgagor; and when the grantee contracts with a view to the payment of the incumbrance, equity demands that he shall pay it, or lose the property." Crawford v. Nimmons, 180 Ill. 143, 54 N.E. 209 (1899); Davis v. Davis, 19 Cal.App. 797, 127 P. 1051 (1912); Trusdell v. Dowden, 47 N.J.Eq. 396, 20 A. 972 (1890); U.S. Bond Co. v. Keahey, 53 Okl. 176, 155 P. 557, L.R. A.1917C (1916), 829, accord.

67. Crawford v. Nimmons, 180 Ill. 143, 54 N.E. 209 (1899); Pinnell v. Boyd, 33 N.J.Eq. 190 (1880), reversed 33 N. J.Eq. 600; Central Holding Co. v. Bushman, 238 Mich. 261, 213 N.W. 120 (1927). See 8 L.R.A.,N.S., 814 (1907); 48 L.R.A.,N.S., 840 (1914); L.R.A. 1917C, 832. See also notes, 67 U.S.L.Rev. 163 (1933); 14 Tex.L.Rev. 559 (1936); 13 Tex.L.Rev. 375 (1935).

68. Freeman v. Auld, 1870, 44 N.Y. 50 (1870), failure of consideration; Davis v. Davis, 19 Cal.App. 797, 127 P. 1051 (1912) (statute of limitations); see Bogart v. Geo. K. Porter Co., 193 Cal. 197, 223 P. 959, 31 A.L.R. 1045 (1924), statute of limitations; Bennett v. Bates, 94 N.Y. 354, 370 (1884), invalidity of mortgage; Exchange Tr. Co. v. Ireton, 88 Okl. 262, 213 P. 309 (1923), forgery in creation of mortgage debt; see Roberts, The Defense of Jus Tertii in Mortgage Cases, 16 Bost.Univ.L.Rev. 644 (1936) for a survey of a large variety of defenses; Cunningham and Tischler, Transfer of the Real Estate Mortgagor's Interest, 27 Rutgers L.Rev. 24, 54–55 (1973).

69. Key West Wharf & Coal Co. v. Porter, 63 Fla. 448, 58 So. 599 (1912); Freeman v. Auld, 44 N.Y. 50, Campbell (1870), Cases on Mortgages, 2d ed., 427; see Bogart v. Geo. K. Porter Co., 193 Cal. 197, 223 P. 959, 31 A.L. R. 1045 (1924). See note, 141 A.L.R. 1184 (1942).

70. Central Holding Co. v. Bushman, 238 Mich. 261, 213 N.W. 120 (1927); Higbee v. Aetna Bldg. & Loan Ass'n, 26 Okl. 327, 109 P. 236, Ann.Cas. 1912B, 223 (1910); see Hartley v. Harrison, 24 N.Y. 170, 172 (1861). See 24 Minn.L.Rev. 124 (1940); 87 U. of Pa.L.Rev. 881 (1939).

71. National Mut. Bld. & Loan Ass'n v. Retzman, 69 Neb. 667, 96 N.W. 204 (1903); Washington Nat. Building & Loan Ass'n v. Andrews, 95 Md. 696, 53 A. 573 (1902); National Loan & Ins. Co. of Detroit v. Stone, 46 S.W. 67 (Tex.Civ.App.1898); Loder v. Hatfield, 71 N.Y. 92 (1877). A general assumption of all liens or debts would be given this interpretation. Purdy v. Coar, 109 N.Y. 448, 17 N.E.

ting up defenses which have been at other times denied as personal to the mortgagor. The same is true if the conveyance is by way of gift.[72] In neither case would the grantee be getting any greater benefit than was intended by being allowed to cut down the mortgagee's recovery out of the land to the amount he could have collected had there been no transfer.

Where the grantee has not withheld any part of the purchase price, the grantee should be permitted to set up defenses to a foreclosure action which are available to the mortgagor.[73] And the same is true *a fortiori* if it is established that the full value of the land was paid with an agreement for the mortgagor to discharge the mortgage. It would be extraordinary to construe such a contract as intended to preclude the mortgagor from using his defenses if he wished to. The grantee is interested only in having the land free and clear of any incumbrance, not in having a portion of the money he has paid being earmarked for the full face of the mortgage debt to go to the mortgagee regardless of his right to it as against the mortgagor. Consequently, the grantee who is in the position of a surety with respect to the mortgagor should be entitled to have the mortgagor exonerate him only to the extent of the valid obligation of the mortgagor. So, too, if he paid the mortgagee, as he may, his right of reimbursement, whether enforced directly or by virtue of subrogation, should be no greater. Since this is so, he should be entitled to discharge the debt by paying only what the mortgagor actually owed or, if the mortgagee sues to collect by foreclosure, limit the foreclosure recovery to the same amount.

A second mortgagee who takes his mortgage subject to a prior one should be permitted, in a foreclosure action by the first mortgagee, to set up defenses available to his mortgagor.[74] There is, however a diversity of view among the cases on the point. Those that deny the privilege do so on the ground that the defense is personal to the borrower and those in privity with him.[75] The cases allowing him to set up the defenses are clearly preferable.[76] The junior mort-

352, 4 Am.St.Rep. 491 (1888); Crowe v. Malba Land Co., 76 Misc. 676, 135 N.Y.S. 454 (1912). See 67 U.S.L.Rev. 164 (1933).

72. First Nat. Bank v. Drew, 226 Ill. 622, 80 N.E. 1082, 10 L.R.A.,N.S., 857, 117 Am.St.Rep. 271 (1907).

73. Grove v. Great Northern Loan Co., 17 N.D. 352, 116 N.W. 345, 138 Am. St.Rep. 707 (1908); see Ford v. Washington Nat. Building & Loan Inv. Ass'n, 10 Idaho 30, 76 P. 1010, 109 Am.St.Rep. 192 (1904).

74. As to the right of a subsequent mortgagee to raise the question of usury in a prior mortgage transaction, see notes, 87 U. of Pa.L.Rev. 881 (1939); 24 Minn.L.Rev. 124 (1939); 30 Col.L.Rev. 902 (1930).

75. Union Nat. Bank v. International Bank, 123 Ill. 510, 14 N.E. 859 (1888); Pritchett v. Mitchell, 17 Kan. 355, 22 Am.Rep. 287 (1876); Richardson v. Baker, 52 Vt. 617 (1872); Ready v. Huebner, 46 Wis. 692, 1 N.W. 344, 32 Am.Rep. 749 (1879). See 24 Minn.L. Rev. 124 (1940); 87 U. of Pa.L.Rev. 881 (1939).

76. Evans v. Faircloth-Byrd Merc. Co., 165 Ala. 176, 51 So. 785, 21 Ann.Cas. 1164 (1910); Pinnix v. Maryland Cas-

gagee has an interest in having the senior mortgage discharged at the least possible cost. Although he would be increasing the value of his security by thus cutting down the amount of the prior lien he would not be unjustly enriched by such a result. He has the right to collect the amount of his debt and will not get more than that in any event. Further, to deny such a right would confer an unwarranted benefit on the prior mortgagee at the expense of the junior encumbrancer. The junior mortgagee may pay off the senior mortgage to protect his own interest and then be subrogated to the senior mortgagee's rights against the mortgagor. The mortgagor could then limit recovery against him on the right to which he is subrogated to the amount that the senior mortgagee could have collected.[77]

A grantee of the mortgagor who assumes or takes subject to a specific mortgage is permitted to set up as against the mortgagee any defenses he could use against his transferor.[78] This clearly is corect where the mortgagee's rights are derived through the mortgagor.[79] But it is equally true where the rights are direct ones as a third party beneficiary.[80] The beneficiary of a contract should take his rights subject to any defects in them as against the promisee who created them in his behalf.

§ 5.18 Subsequent Discharge or Modification of Rights Between Grantor and Grantee

There is great diversity of authority as to the extent to which an assumption may be ended or modified by a transaction between a grantor and an assuming grantee.[81] For the most part this variance stems from the differences in theory upon which the right of the mortgagee is rested.[82] If the security of the land is sufficient to pay the debt, the question is of no practical importance to the mortgagee,

ualty Co., 214 N.C. 760, 200 S.E. 874, 121 A.L.R. 871 (1939). See 24 Minn. L.Rev. 124 (1940); 87 U. of Pa.L.Rev. 881 (1939).

77. 87 U. of Pa.L.Rev. 881 (1939).

78. Dunning v. Leavitt, 85 N.Y. 30, 39 Am.Rep. 617 (1881). On the right of an assuming grantee to set up, as against the mortgagee, defenses which he has against his grantor, see notes 12 N.Car.L.Rev. 383 (1934); 22 Va.L.Rev. 355 (1936); 36 Mich.L.Rev. 847 (1938).

79. Dunning v. Leavitt, note 78, supra; Waddell v. Roanoke Mut. Building & Loan Ass'n, 165 Va. 229, 181 S.E. 288, 100 A.L.R. 906 (1935), noted, 22 Va. L.Rev. 355 (1936).

80. Fulmer v. Goldfarb, 171 Tenn. 218, 101 S.W.2d 1108 (1937), discussed, 36 Mich.L.Rev. 847 (1938).

81. For discussions and collections of authorities see Page, The Power of the Contracting Parties to Alter a Contract for Rendering Performance to a Third Person, 12 Wis.L.Rev. 141, 181 (1937); notes, 7 Boston U.L.Rev. 316 (1927); 13 Cornell L.Q. 123 (1927); 10 Col.L.Rev. 765 (1910); 24 Ill.L.Rev. 828 (1930); 9 Minn.L.Rev. 295 (1925); 8 U. of Cin.L.Rev. 103, 109, 122 (1934). See also 21 A.L.R. 439, 462 (1922); 41 A.L.R. 317 (1926); 47 A.L.R. 340, 342 (1927); 100 A.L.R. 911 (1936).

82. See §§ 5.11–5.15, supra.

for no agreement between the mortgagor or later transferors and grantees can affect his mortgage on the land.[83]

Where the mortgagee's right is held to be derivative, i. e., merely a right to avail himself of the benefit of the contract right of the transferor,[84] it is unquestioned that there can be no rescission or alteration after action has been brought by the mortgagee.[85] Indeed this is the rule without dissent no matter what rationale is followed.[86] But short of bringing an action does the mortgagee have power to prevent the parties wiping out or changing this contract? Most courts permit discharge or variation of the contract by the promisee at any time before suit by the mortgagee [87] with two limitations. 1. The mortgagee must not have materially changed his position in reliance on the assumption before he knows of the discharge or variation.[88] 2. The promisee's action is not in fraud of creditors.[89]

The general rule and first limitation are sound. The mortgagee has admittedly picked up an unexpected windfall in being able to reach the assuming grantee and there is no policy in favor of helping him at the expense of free dealing between the grantee and grantor. If, however, the mortgagee can show material change of position in reliance on the promise, familiar principles would justify preventing the destruction or alteration of the asset.[90] The second limitation, except as to the amount the mortgage debt exceeds the value of the security, is on less firm ground. It has been criticized as invoking in

83. See § 5.1, supra.

84. See §§ 5.13–5.15, supra.

85. Wallace v. Hammonds, 170 Ark. 952, 281 S.W. 902 (1926); Field v. Thistle, 58 N.J.Eq. 339, 43 A. 1072 (1899), affirmed 60 N.J.Eq. 444, 46 A. 1099 (1900); Carnahan v. Tousey, 93 Ind. 561 (1883). See Restatement, Contracts, § 143. See also Morstain v. Kircher, 190 Minn. 78, 250 N.W. 727 (1933) discussed in note, 47 Harv.L.Rev. 1065 (1934), accord.

86. Gifford v. Corrigan, 117 N.Y. 257, 22 N.E. 756, 6 L.R.A. 610, 15 Am.St. Rep. 508 (1889); New York Life Ins. Co. v. Aitkin, 125 N.Y. 660, 26 N.E. 732 (1891); Whiting v. Gearty, 14 Hun 498 (N.Y.1878). See Friedman, Personal Liability on Mortgage Debts, 50 Yale L.Jour. 224, 238 (1940); note 13 Cornell L.Q. 123 (1928). This is on the theory that an acceptance makes the mortgagee's direct right indefeasible and the institution of an action is conclusive evidence of an acceptance. See also West's Ann. Cal.Civ.Code § 1559; Orloff v. Metropolitan Trust Co., 38 Cal.App.2d 688, 102 P.2d 562 (1940).

87. Biddel v. Brizzolara, 64 Cal. 354, 30 P. 609 (1883); Crowell v. Currier, 27 N.J.Eq. 152 (1876) affirmed 27 N. J.Eq. 650; see note, 12 A.L.R. 1528, 1529 (1921). But cf. Willard v. Worsham, 76 Va. 392 (1882); McCown v. Nicks, 171 Ark. 260, 284 S.W. 739, 47 A.L.R. 332 (1926).

88. See n. 85, supra.

89. See Youngs v. Trustees, 31 N.J.Eq. 290, 298–302 (1879). What would constitute fraud of creditors would depend upon the law of fraudulent conveyances in the particular jurisdiction. If the promisee is solvent, has no actual intent to defraud creditors, or, even if insolvent, gives the discharge bona fide for valuable consideration, it would not be in fraud of creditors. See Williston, Contracts, (3d Ed. 1959), § 397.

90. See Gifford v. Corrigan, 105 N.Y. 223, 229, 11 N.E. 498 (1887), "to permit a change * * * while the creditor is relying upon it, would be grossly inequitable."

favor of a secured creditor the doctrine of conveyances in fraud of creditors, which should be restricted to unsecured creditors.[91] If the promisee did not assume the mortgage, he should under a derivative theory be able to release the grantee at any time, even after an action to foreclose is commenced. Since the mortgagee's right to reach the assuming grantee depends upon his having an enforceable claim against the promisee-transferor, he has no ground to object to a release or alteration of the grantee's promise when that claim does not exist.[92]

In jurisdictions that accept the third party beneficiary direct right rationale, the problem would seem to be one of what the basis for according the right is and, consequently, one of when it vests in the mortgagee. A few such courts hold that the mortgagee's right becomes indefeasibly vested immediately upon the assumption.[93] If the argument is that the relationship established is purely contractual, the contract being the offer, acceptance and consideration between the promisor and promisee,[94] such a conclusion would be logical.[95] That contract is complete on the making of the promise of assumption. The weight of authority, however, requires acceptance or adoption by the mortgagee before deeming the right vested.[96] There is divergence as to what will satisfy these requirements. Thus it has been held that acceptance will be presumed and therefore on this ground the right arises at the time the contract is made subject only to disaffirmance by the mortgagee.[97] On the other hand, there is au-

91. See Glenn, Mortgages, §§ 271, 5.1; Restatement, Security, § 140.

92. There are some decisions that apparently consider that "acceptance" by the mortgagee is necessary and sufficient. E. g., Hubard & Appleby v. Thacker, 132 Va. 33, 53, 110 S.E. 263, 21 A.L.R. 423 (1922). Such a requirement seems insupportable, except upon the dubious ground that "from that moment, certainly in equity, even more than at law, the mortgagee must be assumed to have acted or to have omitted to act in reliance upon it." Since the right is an unanticipated bonus, it would seem preferable to require that the mortgagee establish affirmatively that he had actually relied upon it before giving him an indefeasible right to it.

93. Bay v. Williams, 112 Ill. 91, 1 N.E. 340, 54 Am.Rep. 209 (1884); Starbird v. Cranston, 24 Colo. 20, 48 P.2d 652 (1897).

94. Corbin, Contracts for the Benefit of Third Persons, 27 Yale L.J. 1008, 1020 (1918).

95. See 10 Col.L.Rev. 765, 766 (1910); 13 Cornell L.Q. 123, 126 (1927). Friedman, Personal Liability on Mortgage Debts, 50 Yale L.J. 224, 239 (1940).

96. Gifford v. Corrigan, 117 N.Y. 257, 262, 22 N.E. 756, 757, 6 L.R.A. 610, 15 Am.St.Rep. 508 (1889); Smith v. Kibbe, 104 Kan. 159, 163, 178 P. 427, 429, 5 A.L.R. 483 (1919); New York Life Ins. Co. v. Aitkin, 125 N.Y. 660, 675, 26 N.E. 732 (1891); and Hill v. Hoeldtke, 104 Tex. 594, 142 S.W. 871, 40 L.R.A.,N.S., 672 (1912). That the assumption may be revoked any time before the mortgagee brings suit, knowledge or any acceptance or adoption not being shown, Ellis v. Kristoferson, 129 Misc. 443, 222 N.Y.S. 370 (1927), see Wheat v. Rice, 97 N.Y. 296, 302 (1884); 9 Minn.L.Rev. 295 (1925); 47 Harv.L.Rev. 1066, 1067 (1934).

97. Rogers v. Gosnell, 58 Mo. 589 (1875).

thority that notice must be given by the mortgagee to the promisor.[98] Others seem to make the test of acceptance or adoption synonymous with material change of position that will make it inequitable to deprive the mortgagee of the right.[99] These last would seem perfectly sound. If the mortgagee's right is regarded as a contract right arising by conduct between the promisor and the beneficiary, the necessity of an "acceptance" is supportable. But if the analogy on which the right is given is to a trust or an insurance policy without right to change the beneficiary an opposite result would follow.[1] In any event it has been suggested "that no fetish should be made of the mortgagee's 'acceptance,' particularly in those communities where it is the general practice to let mortgages run past due if taxes and interest are paid." [2]

Many courts following the direct right theory have permitted recovery in spite of non-liability of the promisee-grantor to the mortgagee, but it is not altogether clear in all cases whether he does so as a donee or as a creditor beneficiary.[3] If he is classed as the former it does not necessarily follow that the rule generally followed in such cases [4] as to the indefeasibility of the beneficiary's right should apply to the mortgagee. The rule was established in cases in which there are present social considerations which do not exist in mortgage cases.[5] This is especially important because of the extremely dubious basis in fact of a donative intent on the part of either the promisee or promisor.[6] If he is regarded as a creditor beneficiary there seems no substantial reason for treating him, so far as this point is concerned, as in a different position than one to whom the promisee-grantor is liable.

§ 5.19 Extension and Release by Mortgagee—Suretyship and the Mortgagor

In spite of certain conceptual difficulties in those states following a derivative theory of the right of a mortgagee against an assuming

98. Berkshire Life Ins. Co. v. Hutchings, 100 Ind. 496 (1884); see Carnahan v. Tousey, 93 Ind. 561, 562, 564 (1883).

99. Morstain v. Kircher, 190 Minn. 78, 250 N.W. 727 (1933).

1. See Friedman, op. cit. supra note 95.

2. Idem, citing Union Trust Co. v. Kaplan, 249 App.Div. 280, 284, 292 N.Y. S. 152, 159 (1936), judicial knowledge of custom.

3. See § 5.15, supra.

4. See Williston, Contracts, § 396 (3d Ed.1959).

5. See note 13 Corn.L.Q. 123, 128 (1927); Friedman Personal Liability on Mortgage Debts, 50 Yale L.J. 224, 240. It should be noted that the mortgagee, unlike the usual donee beneficiary, already has rights against the mortgagor, even if not the promisee-grantor, and the land. And he differs from most creditor beneficiaries in his security right in the land in the hands of the transferee-promisor in addition to his claim against the mortgagor or other transferor.

6. See § 5.15, supra.

grantee,[7] courts generally agree today that a suretyship relationship is created by a conveyance from a mortgagor to an assuming grantee. The mortgagor is looked upon as a surety while the land and the assuming grantee are regarded as principals.[8] Further, accepting the suretyship concept, they also follow suretyship rules in defining the rights of the mortgagor-transferor with respect to such matters as subrogation and reimbursement.[9] In addition, and this is the problem to which attention is now directed, for the most part they tend to follow uncritically those rules of suretyship which give a defense to the surety, in whole or in part, as a consequence of extension agreements or releases given by the creditor to the principal debtor.[10]

Extensions of Time

Suretyship rules of discharge are invoked in cases where mortgagees give binding extensions of time to grantees of the mortgagor. Transactions in which the grantee assumes the mortgage have to be differentiated from those in which he merely takes subject to it. In the former, by the great weight of authority, if the mortgagee with knowledge of the conveyance and assumption,[11] gives time to an as-

7. See §§ 5.13–5.14, supra.

8. See §§ 5.11–5.14, supra.

9. See §§ 5.9–5.10, supra.

10. Restatement, Security, § 83, Comment on Clause (c). See note, 4 U. of Chi.L.Rev. 469 (1937) for a thorough exposition of the rationales, criticisms, and limitations of the suretyship rule that a binding extension of time to a principal by a creditor without the consent of the surety will release the latter, followed by a critical discussion of its application, by analogy, to mortgage cases. See also Cardozo, Nature of the Judicial Process, 152; Glassie, The Assuming Vendee, 9 Va.L.Rev. 196, 203 (1923); note, 15 Iowa L.Rev. 79 (1929) (discussing the Iowa view which gives the mortgagor no defense); note, 79 U. of Pa.L.Rev. 1151 (1931) (effect of mortgagee's ignorance of the grantee's assumption); 41 A.L.R. 277 (1926); 43 A.L.R. 89 (1926); 72 A.L.R. 389 (1931); 81 A.L.R. 1016 (1932); 112 A.L.R. 1324; Friedman, Discharge of Mortgage Debts, 52 Yale L.J. 771, 796 (1943). Warm, Rights and Liabilities of Mortgagee, Mortgagor, Grantee, 10 Temple L.Q. 116, 136 (1936).

11. Since usually assumption terms will be in the conveyance, of which a mortgagee should be on notice, this requirement normally will be fulfilled in mortgage assumption cases. But see Blumenthal v. Serota, 129 Me. 187, 151 A. 138 (1930). Even if the grantee's deed is silent, it would be an extraordinary case in which the mortgagee has known enough about the grantee to give him an extension of time and yet be able to establish that he was unaware of the existence of the assumption agreement. See Murray v. Marshall, 94 N.Y. 611 (1884), "the fact that he dealt with the grantee for an extension of the mortgage shows that he knew of the conveyance, and that it left the land bound in the hands of the grantee. Knowing this he is chargeable with knowledge of the mortgagor's equitable rights, and meddled with them at his peril." But in some cases the mortgagor is held not to be discharged unless the mortgagee had knowledge that the relationship of principal and surety existed between the grantee and mortgagor. Pratt v. Conway, 148 Mo. 291, 49 S.W. 1028, 71 Am.St.Rep. 602 (1899), in which the agreement of assumption was not contained in the deed of conveyance; Wolfe v. Murphy, 47 App.D.C. 296 (1918), in which the mortgagee was not charged with knowledge although the agreement of assumption was in the deed of conveyance and it was recorded. That the mortgagor is not

suming grantee by a binding agreement with him, the mortgagor is completely discharged regardless of any showing of injury.[12] The same is true as to any intermediate grantees.[13] Moreover, while a reservation of rights against the mortgagor contained in the mortgage itself ironically may sometimes operate to prevent an extension from effecting a discharge of the mortgagor,[14] the inclusion of a similar reservation in the extension agreement generally will not so operate.[15] On the other hand, the mortgagor must establish that a binding extension of time was granted to the assuming grantee—the fact, for example, that the mortgagee merely delayed foreclosure as a temporary expedient or "indulgence" may not establish the existence of an extension agreement.[16] Moreover, there are a few cases that

discharged if the mortgagee did not know of the assumption at the time of the execution of the extension agreement, De Lotto v. Zipper, 116 N.J.Eq. 344, 173 A. 588 (1934), affirmed 120 N.J.Eq. 339, 185 A. 54 (1936). See 79 U. of Pa.L.Rev. 1151 (1931); 41 A.L.R. 277, 302 (1926); 72 A.L.R. 389, 397 (1931); 81 A.L.R. 1016, 1023 (1932); 112 A.L.R. 1324, 1340 (1938).

12. Cunningham and Tischler, Transfer of the Real Estate Mortgagor's Interest, 27 Rutgers L.Rev. 24, 59 (1973); Calvo v. Davies, 73 N.Y. 211, 29 Am.Rep. 130 (1878); Union Mut. Life Ins. Co. v. Hanford, 143 U.S. 187, 12 S.Ct. 437, 36 L.Ed. 118 (1892). See 41 A.L.R. 277 (1926); 72 A.L.R. 389 (1931); 81 A.L.R. 1016 (1932); 112 A.L.R. 1324 (1938).

13. Phoenix Trust Co. v. Garner, 227 Mo.App. 929, 59 S.W.2d 779 (1933); Meldola v. Furlong, 142 Misc. 562, 255 N.Y.S. 48 (1932). Whether an extension to a grantee who assumes but whose grantor had not will discharge the mortgage completely depends on the local law as to whether such an assumption creates a personal liability. See § 5.15, supra.

In DeLeon v. Rhines, 64 U.S.App.D.C. 73, 74 F.2d 477 (1934), an extension to the last grantee whose predecessors had not assumed gave no discharge. Even though the grantee incurred no personal liability the case should be governed by the rule of conveyances subject to the mortgage.

14. Bailey v. Inman, 105 Fla. 1, 140 So. 783 (1932); Continental Nat. Bank & Trust Co. v. Reynolds, 286 Ill.App. 290, 3 N.E.2d 319 (1936); Kent v. Rhomberg, 288 Ill.App. 328, 6 N.E.2d 271 (1937); Mutual Life Ins. Co. v. Rothschild, 160 N.Y.S. 164 (1916), affirmed 226 N.Y. 599, 123 N.E. 880 (1918); Kohn v. Beggi, 147 Misc. 701, 264 N.Y.S. 274 (1933).

15. Calvo v. Davies, 73 N.Y. 211, 29 Am.Rep. 130 (1878), holding that such an agreement is only conditional on the consent to it of the surety; Metzger v. Nova Realty Co., 160 App. Div. 394, 145 N.Y.S. 549 (1915), affirmed 214 N.Y. 26, 107 N.E. 1027; Maier v. Thorman, 234 S.W. 239 (Tex.Civ.App.1921); see 4 A.L.R. 277, 304 (1926); 72 A.L.R. 387, 398 (1931); 81 A.L.R. 1016, 1025 (1932); 112 A.L.R. 1325, 1342 (1938): Such a reservation does not give a grantee an unconditional extension but possibly a mere substitution of creditors. The effect is to leave the mortgagor an unconditional right to pay and enforce subrogation and therefore is without effect on either the rights or liabilities of the mortgagor. This result in mortgage cases is justified. See Glenn, Morts., § 276, "Here [in mortgage transfer cases] an extension may seriously alter the mortgagor's position, inasmuch as meanwhile the assuming grantee is in possession. * * * and so the rule cannot apply that, in other situations, will sanction 'reservation of recourse' in connection with extensions."

16. See Osborn v. Aetna Life and Casualty Co., 308 So.2d 355 (La.App. 1975), writ refused 312 So.2d 340 (Sup.1975). The waiver of an acceleration clause is not an extension of time to a grantee so as to release the mortgagor, see notes, 7 N.Y.Univ.L.Q.Rev. 214 (1929); 31 Col.L.Rev. 328

hold that an extension does not discharge the mortgagor, the theory being that the mortgagee is not bound by the suretyship relation between the mortgagor and the transferee but may treat both as principals severally liable unless he assents to the arrangement.[17]

Two major justifications have been advanced for the general rule of discharge outlined above. First, it is argued that any time extension increases the risk to the surety. The theory is that "the surety calculated and undertook the probability of debtor default on the original term, but did not undertake the supposedly greater probability of default over a longer period." [18] Second, a related justification is that an extension of time impairs the surety's rights by depriving him of his right of subrogation to the creditor's cause of action against the principal debtor.[19]

The general rule of discharge has been subjected to substantial criticism. Some have noted, for example, that no empirical evidence exists to show that extensions of time in fact increase the risk of non-payment by the principal debtor.[20] Indeed, in some instances it could be argued that an extension may enable a hard-pressed principal-debtor-grantee to rehabilitate his precarious financial situation, thus actually decreasing the likelihood of mortgagor-surety liability. In those jurisdictions using subrogation to the mortgagor's rights or other derivative notions on which to found the mortgagee's ability to proceed against the assuming grantee personally, impairment of the power to be subrogated to the mortgagee's rights is manifestly an untenable basis for granting a discharge beyond the value of the mortgaged property. "The only right the mortgagee has is to enforce the obligation of the grantee to the mortgagor, and no action of the mortgagee can deprive the mortgagor of this right. He does not need to be subrogated to the right; he has it without subrogation." [21] In jurisdictions where the mortgagee's right is recognized as direct, dis-

(1931). See Friedman, Discharge of Mortgage Debts, 52 Yale L.J. 771, 782–787 (1943) for other agreements between mortgagee and grantees of the mortgagor that will discharge the mortgagor. But see, Germania Life Ins. Co. v. Casey, 98 App.Div. 88, 90 N.Y.S. 418 (1904), (mortgagor was completely discharged by the acceptance by the mortgagee from the assuming grantee of a payment of the interest for six months one day before it was due, thus extending the time of payment of the mortgage debt by one day.)

17. Bailey v. Inman, 105 Fla. 1, 140 So. 783 (1932); Blank v. Michael, 208 Iowa 402, 226 N.W. 12 (1929). See 81 U. of Pa.L.Rev. 641 (1933); 15 Iowa L.Rev. 79 (1929); 13 N.Car.L. Rev. 337 (1935); 41 A.L.R. 277, 285 (1926); 72 A.L.R. 383, 389 (1931); 112 A.L.R. 1324, 1331 (1938).

18. White and Summers, Uniform Commercial Code, 432 (1972).

19. Id.

20. Id.

21. Williston, Contracts, § 386 (3d Ed. 1959). Restatement, Contracts, § 146, accord. Wolfe v. Murphy, 47 U.S. App.D.C. 296 (1918); see Keller v. Ashford, 133 U.S. 610, 625, 10 S.Ct. 494, 33 L.Ed. 667 (1890). Courts which do not allow the mortgagee to sue the grantee at all, it may be assumed, would not release the mortgagor when there has been an extension of time to the grantee.

charge of the mortgagor to an amount above the value of the mortgaged property has been attacked. It is argued that no possibility of injury exists beyond the value of the property since the extension does not affect his rights other than that of subrogation and they give him in every respect a practical equivalent of it. Any discharge as to this is purely technical.[22] In addition it is urged that, because the mortgagor does not assume his obligation gratuitously, having received a loan or other value and having usually been the principal debtor for some time, he resembles one of the more protected type of sureties commonly described as compensated.[23] Such sureties are not discharged by mere extension of time; they must show injury.[24]

The cases dealing with the effect on the liability of the original mortgagor of an extension given by a mortgagee to a grantee who took subject to, but without assuming, the mortgage have not been entirely unanimous.[25] It has been held that the rights of the mortgagee against the mortgagor are not in any manner affected thereby.[26] It has also been held that, under such circumstances, the mortgagor is released entirely.[27] Another rule of discharge is the amount

22. See Williston, Contracts, Rev. ed., § 386; cf. 15 Iowa L.Rev. 79 (1929).

23. See Stevens, Extension Agreements in the "Subject-to" Mortgage Situation, 15 U. of Cin.L.Rev. 58, 73 (1941) "the 'mortgagor-surety' in such cases is not just compensated but has actually received the *quid pro quo.*" See also 4 U. of Chi.L.Rev. 469, 478 (1937); 42 Harv.L.Rev. 712 (1929); Tiffany, Real Prop., 3d ed., § 445, n. 54. But cf. 29 Harv.L.Rev. 314, 317 (1916).

24. See Arant, Suretyship, § 299.

25. See Stevens, Extension Agreements in the "Subject-to" Mortgage Situation, 15 U. of Cin.L.Rev. 58, 70 (1941) for a critical analysis of the several rules. See also Campbell, Cases on Mortgages, 2d ed., 442, n. 4.

As to the effect of an extension agreement on the rights of junior mortgagees, see Meislin, Extension Agreements and the Rights of Junior Mortgagees, 42 Va.L.Rev. 939 (1956).

26. Chilton v. Brooks, 72 Md. 554, 20 A. 125 (1890); DeLeon v. Rhines, 64 U.S.App.D.C. 73, 74 F.2d 477 (1934); Pfeifer v. W. B. Worthen Co., 189 Ark. 469, 74 S.W.2d 220 (1934), accord. See notes, 15 Iowa L.Rev. 79 (1929); 13 N.Car.L.Rev. 337 (1935). In Maryland and in the federal courts it is held, however, that an extension granted to an assuming grantee will discharge the mortgagor. George v. Andrews, 60 Md. 26, 45 Am.Rep. 706 (1882); Asbell v. Marshall Building & Loan Ass'n, 156 Md. 106, 143 A. 715 (1928); Keller v. Ashford, 133 U.S. 610, 10 S.Ct. 494, 33 L.Ed. 667 (1890). The distinction has been explained as follows: "The argument is that an extension can have no effect unless there is privity between the three parties—mortgagee, mortgagor and grantee; and privity there cannot be unless all three are under contract, which is not the case unless the grantee assumes." Glenn, Morts., § 1201. The distinction is fallacious. The requirement of "privity" is artificial. Even if insisted upon, it can be argued that it is satisfied. "The theorem * * * starts with the land as common security, and this brings the parties into privity; the assumption is merely additional collateral, and naturally the privity remains which always was in effect." Glenn, Mortgages, § 278.

27. Braun v. Crew, 183 Cal. 728, 192 P. 531 (1920), discussed in notes, 5 Minn.L.Rev. 150 (1921); 19 Mich.L. Rev. 351 (1921); 10 Not.D.Law. 83, 84 (1934). A provision in the California Civil Code influenced the decision. See also 41 A.L.R. 277, 292 (1926); 112 A.L.R. 1324, 1334 (1938). A later decision in California rejects

which, due to the extension, the value of the property has depreciated below the mortgage debt.[28] The weight of authority, however, is that, under such circumstances, the mortgagor is released to the extent of the value of the security properly applicable to the mortgage debt in the hands of the grantee at the time the extension is granted.[29]

The right of subrogation of a surety to his creditor's rights gives him nothing of substantial value if the creditor has no security or other priority rights and if he himself has rights over against the principal debtor. The personal right of the creditor against the principal debtor is no better than his own personal rights. But if the creditor has security which the surety might reach by subrogation at the maturity of the debt, it is obvious that his risk has been increased by an extension which prevents him or the mortgagee from realizing on it until later.[30] Thus the cases that deny any discharge would seem to be wrong. But the maximum injury would be the value of the land at the time of the injury and therefore a complete release, unless the land exceeded the amount of the debt, would seem to be unjustified. The burden of proof to establish the elements of the defense in these cases is upon the mortgagor.[31] If it were a difficult and onerous task to establish the actual amount of injury suffered by the extension, the majority rule could be accepted without objection. However, it would seem practicable to prove the extent to which the

this rule where the mortgage secures a negotiable note. Mortgage Guarantee Co. v. Chotiner, 8 Cal.2d 110, 64 P.2d 138, 108 A.L.R. 1080 (1936).

28. North End Sav. Bank v. Snow, 197 Mass. 339, 83 N.E. 1099, 125 Am.St. Rep. 368 (1908). This may be the New York rule. See Syracuse Trust Co. v. First Trust & Deposit Co., 141 Misc. 603, 252 N.Y.S. 850 (1931) commented on in 9 N.Y.Univ.L.Q.Rev. 502 (1932); Feigenbaum v. Hizsnay, 187 App.Div. 126, 175 N.Y.S. 223 (1919).

29. Murray v. Marshall, 94 N.Y. 611 (1884); Spencer v. Spencer, 95 N.Y. 353 (1884); Zastrow v. Knight, 56 S. D. 554, 229 N.W. 925, 72 A.L.R. 379 (1930).

See notes, 22 Va.L.Rev. 964 (1936) (discussing Commercial Casualty Ins. Co. v. Roman, 269 N.Y. 451, 199 N.E. 658 (1936) in which the mortgagor was held for a deficiency equal to the amount that the mortgage debt exceeded the value of the land at the time of the extension); 4 U. of Chi. L.Rev. 469, 478 (1937); 10 Not.D.Law. 83 (1934); 5 Br.Rul.Cas. 633 (1916). See also 41 A.L.R. 277, 292 (1926); 72 A.L.R. 389, 394 (1931); 81 A.L.R. 1016, 1021 (1932); 112 A.L.R. 1324, 1331 (1938). As was stated before, this amount was urged as the proper measure in both assumption and non-assumption cases. Williston, Contracts, § 386 (3rd Ed. 1959). But see Glassie, The Assuming Vendee, 9 Va.L.Rev. 196, 205, n. 36 (1923). "With submission, this [discharge equal to value of land at time of extension] does not help in a practical sense. For it introduces the most gaseous of all questions of fact—the value of land at some time other than that of a sale." See also Stevens, Extension Agreements in the "Subject-to" Mortgage Situation, 15 U. of Cin.L.Rev. 58, 74 (1941).

30. See Zastrow v. Knight, 56 S.D. 554, 564, 229 N.W. 925, 930, 72 A.L.R. 379 (1930).

31. Meldola v. Furlong, 142 Misc. 562, 255 N.Y.S. 48 (1932); Commercial Casualty Ins. Co. v. Roman, 269 N.Y. 451, 199 N.E. 658 (1936), amended 270 N.Y. 563, 200 N.E. 319; Mutual Benefit Life Ins. Co. v. Lindley, 97 Ind.App. 575, 183 N.E. 127 (1933), commented on in, 33 Col.L.Rev. 368 (1933), 81 U. of Pa.L.Rev. 641 (1933).

property has depreciated below the mortgage debt during the extension. Further, whether this rule or discharge to the full value of the land at the date of extension is adopted, a presumption that the land was equal in value to the debt at the time the extension was granted seems justified as founded on normal practice and business common sense.[32]

Releases of Obligation or Security

Release by the mortgagee of the personal obligation of an assuming grantee operates, in jurisdictions following suretyship ideas, to discharge the mortgagor completely.[33] Even if the mortgagor and assuming grantee were regarded as co-principals, the same result would follow from the general rule that the release of one joint and several debtor discharges the others.[34]

The effect of the release of the mortgaged property in the hands of an assuming grantee or one who took it subject to the mortgage is not so clear cut. The general rule of suretyship law is that when a secured creditor surrenders to the debtor, negligently loses, or damages the security it discharges a surety to the extent of the value so lost.[35] This same reasoning has been applied to releases of the mortgaged property, completely or in part, in the hands of grantees who assumed or took subject to the mortgage.[36] Other courts, however,

32. Mutual Benefit Life Ins. Co. v. Lindley, 97 Ind.App. 575, 183 N.E. 127 (1932), noted 33 Col.L.Rev. 368 (1933) and, 81 U. of Pa.L.Rev. 641 (1933). "In fact, one cannot imagine a stronger presumption. Whoever heard of a man deliberately lending upon inadequate security, in the absence of a special reason." Glenn, Mortgages, § 277.

33. Gilliam v. McLemore, 141 Miss. 253, 106 So. 99, 43 A.L.R. 79 (1925); Merriam v. Miles, 54 Neb. 566, 74 N. W. 861, 69 Am.St.Rep. 731 (1898); Insley v. Webb, 122 Wash. 98, 209 P. 1093, 41 A.L.R. 274 (1922). The release from a deficiency judgment of a purchaser who assumed the mortgage discharges the mortgagor. Wagoner v. Brady, 221 App.Div. 405, 223 N.Y. S. 99 (1927), discussed in note, 41 Harv.L.Rev. 261 (1927); note, 93 Cent. L.J. 183 (1921). Getting a deficiency judgment against the mortgagor alone which, under a local statute, barred obtaining a similar judgment against the assuming grantee, is ground for setting aside the judgment. Tousey v. Barber, 132 Misc. 861, 231 N.Y.S. 133 (1928), discussed in note, 42 Harv.L.Rev. 583 (1929). See 41 A.L. R. 277, 311 (1926); 72 A.L.R. 389, 398, 399 (1931); 81 A.L.R. 1016, 1025 (1932); 112 A.L.R. 1324, 1343 (1938). See also, Arant, Suretyship, § 49. It might be expected that jurisdictions following the derivative theory of the mortgagee's personal rights against an assuming grantee would not discharge a mortgagor by reason of a purported release by the mortgagee of his rights against such a grantee since he would not have anything to release. See 88 U. of Pa.L.Rev. 611, 615 (1940). But there are cases to the contrary. Herd v. Tuohy, 133 Cal. 55, 65 P. 139 (1901); Codman v. Deland, 231 Mass. 344, 121 N.E. 14 (1918); Reeves v. Cordes, 108 N.J.Eq. 469, 155 A. 547 (1931).

34. See Williston, Contracts, § 334 (3d Ed. 1959).

35. Security, Restatement, § 132. See Arant, Suretyship, §§ 62, 63.

36. Woodward v. Brown, 119 Cal. 283, 51 P. 2, 63 Am.St.Rep. 108 (1897), modified 119 Cal. 283, 51 P. 542, 63 Am.St.Rep. 108; Mann v. Bugbee, 113 N.J.Eq. 434, 167 A. 202 (1933); see 41 A.L.R. 277, 306 (1926); 72 A.L.R.

refusing to inquire into the extent of the injury caused by the giving up of security, give a complete discharge to the mortgagor even where there has been a release of only part of the mortgaged property.[37] A recent New York decision [38] exemplifies this latter approach. There a mortgagee authorized a subsequent purchaser from an assuming grantee to demolish a building and, in addition, gave a release of the mortgage lien to the assuming grantee as to that part of the mortgaged land that the grantee had not sold. Later the mortgagee foreclosed and sought a deficiency judgment against the original mortgagors. The court held that in view of the fact that the mortgagors had not consented to the building destruction and lien release, they were completely discharged as to the mortgage debt.

§ 5.20 Effect of the Uniform Commercial Code on Suretyship Defences

Where the mortgage secures a negotiable instrument, the impact of an extension or release granted by a mortgagee is governed by Section 3–606 of the Uniform Commercial Code (UCC). Under the Negotiable Instruments Law, the UCC's predecessor, the weight of authority held that the usual suretyship defences were unavailable to the mortgagor.[39] On the other hand, under the UCC those suretyship

389 (1931); 81 A.L.R. 1016, 1025 (1932); 112 A.L.R. 1324, 1343 (1938). Similarly, a mortgagee who fails to record his mortgage and thus permits a grantee of the mortgagor to sell the full title to the property to a bona fide purchaser cannot enforce the mortgage debt against the mortgagor. Hampe v. Manke, 28 S.D. 501, 134 N. W. 60 (1912). However, a mortgagee has been held to have a right to a deficiency judgment against the mortgagor in spite of his knowledge of the commission of waste by the mortgagor's grantee. Damiano v. Bergen County Land Co., 118 N.J.Eq. 535, 180 A. 489 (1935), commented on in 36 Col.Rev. 328 (1936). But the mortgagor was discharged in Lynn Five Cents Bank v. Portnoy, 306 Mass. 436, 28 N.E.2d 418 (1940), where the mortgagee consented to the garantee making wasteful changes in the premises. An increase in the amount of the mortgage debt by an agreement between the mortgagee and the mortgagor's grantee discharges the mortgagor to the extent of the increase. Union Bank of Brooklyn v. Rubenstein, 78 Misc. 461, 138 N.Y.S. 644 (1912), commented on in note, 13 Col.L.Rev. 238 (1913).

37. The release of the mortgaged property in the hands of an assuming grantee on the grantee's paying the full market value of the land to the mortgagee was held to give a complete defense to the mortgagor in Farmers' & Merchants' State Bank v. Tasche, 53 S.D. 603, 222 N.W. 139 (1928), criticized in note, 42 Harv.L. Rev. 712 (1929); Elsey v. People's Bank, 166 Ky. 386, 179 S.W. 392 (1915), noted, 1916, 16 Col.L.Rev. 165; In Re Hunter's Estate, 257 Pa. 32, 101 A. 79 (1917), mortgagee takes risk that unreleased portion is of sufficient value to secure his debt; Albright v. Aliday, 37 S.W. 646 (Tex. Civ.App.1896), part only released; Brown v. Turner, 202 N.C. 227, 162 S.E. 608 (1932), discussed in note, 11 N.Car.L.Rev. 96 (1932) release of part of the mortgaged premises; Restatement, Contracts, § 146, accord. See Glenn, Mortgages, § 281, approving this result.

38. Lundquist v. Nelson, 57 A.D.2d 1045, 395 N.Y.S.2d 568 (1977).

39. Mortgage Guaranty Co. v. Chotiner, 8 Cal.2d 110, 64 P.2d 138, 108 A.L.R. 1080 (1936), commented on, 10 So.Cal.L.Rev. 511 (1937); Continental

defences are available[40] and, for the most part, the rules governing the discharge of the mortgagor are identical to those considered in the preceding section. Section 3–606(1) provides:

> "The holder discharges any party to the instrument to the extent that without such party's consent the holder
>
> (a) without express reservation of rights releases or agrees not to sue any person against whom the party has to the knowledge of the holder a right of recourse or agrees to suspend the right to enforce against such person the instrument or collateral or otherwise discharges such person, except that failure or delay in effecting any required presentment, protest or notice of dishonor with respect to any such person does not discharge any party as to whom presentment, protest or notice of dishonor is effective or unnecessary; or
>
> (b) unjustifiably impairs any collateral for the instrument given by or on behalf of the party or any person against whom he has a right of recourse."

In focusing on the key language of the above provision, note that absent the surety's consent, if the holder "releases or agrees not to sue * * * or agrees to suspend the right to enforce * * * the instrument or collateral * * * or otherwise discharges * * *" the principal debtor, the surety is discharged. Note also that a surety may assert a discharge even though the principal debtor is not a party to the instrument.[41] Thus, Section 3–606 probably authorizes all of the suretyship defences that we considered in the preceding section, including extension of time for payment by the principal debtor, release of the principal debtor from liability and release of the security interest.[42] Moreover, the language "any person against whom the party has to the knowledge of the holder a right of recourse" seems "clearly broad enough to include not only 'personal' principal debtors such as assuming grantees, but also 'real' principal debtors such as

Mut. Sav. Bank v. Elliott, 166 Wash. 283, 6 P.2d 638, 81 A.L.R. 1005 (1932), commented on in, 19 Va.L. Rev. 618 (1933); 2 Idaho L.J. 143 (1932); 17 Minn.L.Rev. 220 (1933); Peter v. Finzer, 116 Neb. 380, 217 N. W. 612, 65 A.L.R. 1418 (1928) noted in 42 Harv.L.Rev. 136 (1928); 6 Neb. L.Bull. 417 (1928); 26 Mich.L.Rev. 929 (1928); 12 Minn.L.Rev. 668 (1928); Washer v. Tontar, 128 Ohio St. 111, 190 N.E. 231 (1934).

40. White and Summers, Uniform Commercial Code, § 13–14 (1972); Clark, Suretyship in the Uniform Commercial Code, 46 Tex.L.Rev. 453, 457 (1968).

41. White and Summer, supra note 40 at 434. Comment 1 to Section 3–606 states: "The suretyship defences here provided are not limited to parties who are 'secondarily liable' but are available to any party who is in the position of a surety, having a right of recourse either on the instrument or dehors it, * * *."

42. Cunningham and Tischler, Transfer of the Real Estate Mortgagor's Interest, 27 Rutgers L.Rev. 24, 68 (1973).

grantees who expressly take subject to the mortgage without assuming it." [43]

The UCC and the suretyship concepts considered in the preceding section differ, however, in one important respect. While an express reservation of rights against the mortgagor included in the original mortgage may operate to prevent discharge of the mortgagor, [44] we saw that a similar reservation in the extension or modification agreement normally will not prevent discharge.[45] On the other hand, where the UCC is applicable, while the blanket mortgage reservation clause is probably ineffective to prevent discharge, the mortgagee can reserve his rights against the mortgagor-surety by adding an "express reservation" of those rights to the extension agreement or agreement releasing the grantee.[46] It should be noted, however, that the mortgagee is not authorized by the UCC to reserve his rights to avoid discharge when he authorizes the impairment of collateral (security).[47]

B. RESTRICTIONS ON TRANSFER BY THE MORTGAGOR

§ 5.21 The "Due-On" Clauses—An Introduction

During the 1960's and 70's two relatively new types of restraints on the mortgagor's ability to transfer or mortgage his property expanded rapidly so that their use today is commonplace, at least as to institutional lenders. The due-on-sale and due-on-encumbrance clauses are specialized types of acceleration clauses that give the mortgagee the option of declaring the entire debt due and payable in the event the mortgagor transfers or encumbers the mortgaged real estate.[48] Both of these concepts are usually contained in the same provision which commonly is in the following or similar form:

> "Should trustor (mortgagor) sell, convey, transfer, dispose of or further encumber said property, or any part

43. Id. at 68–69.

44. See text at note 14, supra.

45. See text at note 15, supra.

46. White and Summers, supra note 40 § 13–15; Cunningham and Tischler, supra note 42 at 69.

47. White and Summers, supra note 40 at 437 n. 132.

48. These concepts have resulted in substantial scholarly commentary. See Ashley, Use of "Due-On" Clauses to Gain Collateral Benefits: A Common Sense Defense, 10 Tulsa L.J. 590 (1975); Bonanno, Due-on-Sale and Prepayment Clauses in Real Estate Financing in California in Times of Fluctuating Interest Rates—Legal Issues and Alternatives, 6 U.San.Fran. L.Rev. 267 (1972); Hetland, Real Property and Real Property Security: The Well-Being of the Law, 53 Calif. L.Rev. 151 (1965); Volkmer, The Application of the Restraints On Alienation Doctrine to Real Property Security Interests, 58 Iowa L.Rev. 747 (1973); Comment, Mortgages—A Catalogue and Critique on the Role of Equity in the Enforcement of Modern-Day "Due-on-Sale" Clauses, 26 Ark.L.Rev. 485 (1973); Comment, Applying the Brakes to Acceleration

thereof, or any interest therein, or agree so to do, without the written consent of Beneficiary (mortgagee) being first obtained, then Beneficiary shall have the right, at his option, to declare all sums secured hereby forthwith due and payable." [49]

Of the two concepts, the due-on-sale clause has been more important. During the period of rising interest rates of the last decade and a half, a common method of financing the sale of real estate, both commercial and residential, has been by the "assumption" process.[50] In such situations purchasers agree to "assume" and thereby become liable personally on the seller's already existing lower-than-market interest mortgage. As part of the process, the purchaser either pays the balance of the purchase price in cash to the seller or gives the seller a combination of a second mortgage and cash.

The due-on-sale clause developed largely to prevent the above type of sale by threatening the seller and potential assuming party with acceleration and foreclosure.[51] Under such provisions, mortgagees often consent to an assumption at a high rate of interest or simply refuse permission for a transfer entirely.[52] In either event, the mortgagee is able to earn market interest rates on money that would otherwise be locked in for long amortization periods at lower fixed interest rates. This ability becomes especially significant when it is realized that in some states, like California, the average house "turns over" every four or five years and that the vast majority of all home loans are paid off before maturity.[53]

Another purpose for the due-on-sale clause is to enable the mortgagee to protect security by regulating who owns or occupies the

Clauses: Controlling Their Misuse in Real Property Secured Transaction, 9 Calif.W.L.Rev. 514 (1973); Comment, Judicial Treatment of the Due-on-Sale Clause: The Case for Adopting Standards of Reasonableness and Unconscionability, 27 Stan.L.Rev. 1108 (1975); Note, Property—The Device of the Due-on-Sale Clause, 64 Calif. L.Rev. 573 (1976); Note, 28 Case. West.Res.L.Rev. 493 (1978). Note, Due-on-Sale and Due-on-Encumbrance Clauses in California, 7 Loyola L.A. L.Rev. 306 (1974); Comment, Beyond Tucker v. Lassen: The Future of the Due-on-Sale Clause in California, 27 Hastings L.J. 475 (1975); Note, Deeds of Trust—Restraints Against Alienation—Due-On Clause is an Unreasonable Restraint on Alienation Absent a Showing of Protection of Mortgagee's Legitimate Interests, 47 Miss.L.J. 331 (1976); Note, Mortgages—Use of Due-on-Sale Clause by a Lender Is Not a Restraint on Alienation in North Carolina, 55 N.Car.L.Rev. 310 (1977).

49. Comment, Judicial Treatment of the Due-on-Sale Clause: The Case for Adopting Standards of Reasonableness and Unconscionability, 27 Stan. L.Rev. 1109, 1110 n. 5 (1975).

50. See §§ 5.1–5.10 supra.

51. Volkmer, The Application of the Restraints on Alienation Doctrine to Real Property Security Interests, 58 Iowa L.Rev. 747, 769 (1973).

52. Id. at 769.

53. Comment, Judicial Treatment of the Due-on-Sale Clause: The Case for Adopting Standards of Reasonableness and Unconscionability, 27 Stan. L.Rev. 1109, 1111, 1111 n. 6 (1975).

mortgaged premises.[54] It is true that certain transferees may pose greater risks to the mortgagee than others. For example, if a purchaser of a home has a poor credit rating or is covering the difference between the existing first mortgage and the purchase price largely by borrowing, the chances of default and foreclosure probably increase. While it is true that the original mortgagor remains liable in the event of a default, he may have moved out of the state and is practically, if not theoretically, judgment proof. Moreover, even though they are ultimately made whole, mortgagees usually desire to avoid an increasing number of foreclosure proceedings. However, while this purpose for the due-on-sale clause is perfectly legitimate the clause did develop largely to serve the interest rate function described above.[55]

The due-on-encumbrance concept, on the other hand, has a more primary security protection function and probably did not develop to deal with the interest market problem.[56] The due-on-encumbrance language does enable a mortgagee to prevent a mortgagor from engaging in second mortgage financing when such financing, for example, would reduce the mortgagor's total investment in the real estate. Suppose a first mortgagee initially required that a mortgagor pay 25% down from his own resources as a condition for the granting of a first mortgage loan. If the mortgagor, two weeks after the closing on the first mortgage, simply borrowed the additional 25% by means of a second mortgage loan, the mortgagor clearly would not have the stake in the property initially envisioned and required by the first mortgagee. Thus, the due-on-encumbrance concept can by utilized to fulfill the first mortgagee's legitimate expectations. It should be pointed out, however, that the due-on-encumbrance language is difficult to enforce because the first mortgagee is often unaware of the further encumbrance, whereas, in the case of a due-on-sale situation, the buyer will normally ask for permission to transfer the property because he realizes that the mortgagee will, in any event, become aware of the transfer since payments will be made by the purchaser and not the original mortgagor. Nevertheless, where due-on-encumbrance language is enforced by the mortgagee, it often does have a secondary effect of allowing the mortgagee to reinvest the money at higher interest rates. Thus, such language does clearly often have an interest rate function.

Because the major judicial attack on these clauses centers on the restraint on alienation doctrine, some examination of that doctrine is necessary at this point. Courts have taken probably three ap-

54. Valensi, The Due-on-Sale Clause—A Dissenting Opinion, 45 L.A.Bar Bull. 121 (1970).

55. Volkmer, The Application of the Restraints on Alienation Doctrine to Real Property Security Interests, 58 Iowa L.Rev. 747, 769–770 (1973).

56. Id. at 770.

proaches to restraints on alienation on real property.[57] The first two approaches deal with direct restraints. Direct restraints are often categorized in three ways: disabling, forfeiture, and promissory.[58] Under disabling restraints the grantee arguably has no power to convey.[59] Forfeiture restraints involve a reversion in the grantor or a gift to a third party in the event of alienation and promissory restraints entail promises not to convey which are specifically enforcible.[60] Under the so-called majority view all direct restraints are invalid per se unless the restraint comes within a certain limited recognized exception.[61] The minority view of direct restraints, on the other hand, is that a restraint is valid when the policy underlying its purpose outweighs the degree of restraint on the real estate interest.[62] Finally, it is sometimes said that only "indirect" restraints are valid, an indirect restraint being defined as arising "when an attempt is made to accomplish some purpose other than the restraint on alienability, but with the incidental result that the instrument, if valid, would restrain practical alienability." [63]

Where the due-on-sale clause fits within the above restraint on alienation analysis is conceptually difficult to determine. It seemingly does not fit exactly within either of the three categories of direct restraints. Clearly, no disability is imposed on the mortgagor with respect to his ability to convey. It is rather the threat of foreclosure that inhibits the transfer. Moreover, no forfeiture of the mortgagor's interest is normally involved in mortgage foreclosure as is sometimes the case where there is a default under an installment land contract. Professor Volkmer has concluded that a due-on-sale clause "is so closely akin to a promissory restraint as to justify designating it as a direct restraint. * * * Although written as an acceleration clause, the due-on-sale clause directly and fundamentally burdens a mortgagor's ability to alienate as surely and directly as a classical promissory restraint. As such, the due-on-sale clause is truly a direct restraint insofar as the category of direct restraints can be articulated.[64] " It could presumably be argued that the due-on-sale

57. Note, Mortgages—Use of Due-on-Sale Clause by a Lender Is Not a Restraint on Alienation in North Carolina, 55 N.C.L.Rev. 310, 311 (1977).

58. Restatement of Property, § 404 (1944).

59. Volkmer, The Application of the Restraints on Alienation Doctrine to Real Property Security Interests, 58 Iowa L.Rev. 747, 748 (1973).

60. Id. at 748.

61. See Note, Deeds of Trust—Restraints Against Alienation—Due-On Clause Is an Unreasonable Restraint on Alienation Absent a Showing of Mortgagee's Legitimate Interests, 47 Miss.L.J. 331, 334, 334 n. 21 (1976).

62. Note, Mortgages—Use of Due-on-Sale Clause by a Lender Is Not a Restraint on Alienation in North Carolina, 55 N.C.L.Rev. 310, 312 (1977); Bernhard, The Minority Doctrine Concerning Direct Restraints on Alienation, 57 Mich.L.Rev. 1173, 1176 (1959).

63. Simes & Smith, The Law of Future Interests, § 1112, at 5 (2d Ed. 1956).

64. Volkmer, The Application of the Restraints on Alienation Doctrine to

clause represents a type of indirect restraint because its purpose is not primarily to restrain alienability; rather, the practical effect of the clause may discourage sale by the mortgagor of the mortgaged premises. However one analyzes the due-on-sale clause, the burgeoning case law of the past few years dealing with the validity of such clauses has not been overly concerned with their technical classification into traditional "restraint" categories. Indeed, some courts merely make passing reference to the doctrine.[65] Rather, whether upholding or invalidating such clauses in individual cases, courts have been more concerned with balancing policy considerations supporting such clauses against the degree or restraint imposed on the mortgagor.

§ 5.22 "Due-On" Clauses—The California Experience

Because California decisions have been influential in the development of the law in other jurisdictions, particular emphasis on the California due-on decisions is important and helpful. The Supreme Court of California first upheld due-on clauses in Coast Bank v. Minderhout,[66] decided in 1964. There the bank had made several home improvement loans to the Enrights, who executed a promissory note for the full amount of the loans. In a separate agreement, the Enrights agreed not to sell or encumber their real estate until payment of the debt. Upon sale of the property to the defendant, the bank accelerated the debt and sought to foreclose an equitable mortgage that it argued was created by the non-encumbrance agreement. The California Supreme Court held that a valid equitable mortgage was created [67] which was not invalidated by conditioning acceleration on a "reasonable" restraint on alienation. In reaching this decision, the court adopted the "minority rule" on restraints on alienation, rejecting the view that due-on clauses are per se invalid and concluded that the validity of a restraint would be tested by its reasonableness in view of the parties' legitimate interests.

Coast Bank was further developed by the Second District Court of Appeals in Cherry v. Home Sav. & Loan Ass'n [68] decided in 1969. In that case, a declaratory judgment was sought to obtain relief from a due-on-sale provision in a deed of trust. The mortgagee had conditioned permission to assume on the new owners' payment of an assumption fee and a higher rate of interest on the assumed note. The court in *Cherry* rejected the argument that the exercise of a due-on-sale clause by the mortgagee must be governed by a rule of

Real Property Security Interests, 58 Iowa L.Rev. 747, 773–774 (1973).

65. See, e. g., First Commercial Title, Inc. v. Holmes, 550 P.2d 1271 (Nev. 1976).

66. 61 Cal.2d 311, 38 Cal.Rptr. 505, 392 P.2d 265 (1964).

67. As to the "negative pledge" aspect of this case, see § 3.33, infra.

68. 276 Cal.App.2d 574, 81 Cal.Rptr. 135 (2d Dist.Ct.App.1969).

reason under the circumstances. Instead, *Cherry* seemed to indicate an apparent approach favoring automatic enforcement of such clauses. Although the court did not require an allegation of the security being threatened, the decision did recognize the twin functions of the clause in protecting security and in insulating the lender against the vagaries of the interest market.[69]

In LaSala v. American Sav. & Loan Ass'n,[70] the California Supreme Court distinguished between due-on-sale and due-on-encumbrance language in holding that due-on-encumbrance language was not entitled to the automatic enforcement that the lower appellate courts had been applying to due-on-sale provisions. Due-on-encumbrance language would henceforth be enforced only when "reasonably necessary to protect the lender's security"[71] and not simply to protect the mortgagee from a rising interest market.

The concept of automatic enforcement of due-on language was further restricted in 1974 by the same court in Tucker v. Lassen Sav. & Loan Ass'n[72] where the court enunciated a new test to determine the validity of due-on language in particular circumstances: "To the degree that enforcement of the clause would result in an increased quantum of actual restraint on alienation in a particular case, a greater justification for such enforcement from the standpoint of the lender's legitimate interest will be required in order to warrant enforcement." [73] The transfer in this case involved a sale by the mortgagor on an installment land contract. In applying the above test to the facts of the case, the court was impressed by the apparent difference in the severity of the restraint when dealing with installment land contracts as opposed to outright sales:

> "From this standpoint the contrast between an outright sale and an executory sale by installment land contract is striking. In the former, as we pointed out in *LaSala,* the automatic application of the 'due-on' clause results in little if any restraint on alienation because the terms of the second sale usually provide for full payment of the prior trust deed. In other words, the trustor-vendor normally receives enough money through the financing of the second sale to pay off his note, and he is normally required to do so. Little if any restraint on alienation results through enforcement of the provision.

69. Id. at 579, 81 Cal.Rptr. at 138. See also, Hellbaum v. Lytton Sav. and Loan Ass'n, 274 Cal.App.2d 456, 79 Cal.Rptr. 9 (Dist.Ct.App.1969).

70. 5 Cal.3d 864, 97 Cal.Rptr. 849, 489 P.2d 1113 (1971).

71. 5 Cal.3d at 880–81 n. 17, 489 P.2d at 1123–24 n. 17, 97 Cal.Rptr. at 850–60 n. 17.

72. 12 Cal.3d 629, 116 Cal.Rptr. 633, 526 P.2d 1169 (1974).

73. 12 Cal.3d at 638, 526 P.2d at 1178, 116 Cal.Rptr. at 641.

> In the case of the installment land contract, however, the matter is otherwise. The trustor-vendor normally receives a relatively small down payment upon execution of the contract, the remainder of the purchase price to be paid through monthly installments. This down payment, like the proceeds of the junior encumbrance involved in *LaSala*, 'does not often provide the borrower with the means of discharge the balance secured by the trustee' * * *. The result is that a conveyance by means of an installment land contract would essentially be precluded in all cases wherein the balance due on the trustor-vendor's note was substantial if the 'due-on' clause were to be given automatic effect. Accordingly, although the trustor-vendor might be willing to accept a rate of interest lower than that currently offered by institutional lenders, the prospective purchaser would be compelled to resort to such lenders to finance the acquisition of the property. The result in terms of restraint on alienation is clear." [74]

The court then considered the possible justifications for the restraint. While it noted that the mortgagor would lose possession of the real estate and that this posed greater risks for the mortgagee than would a junior encumbrance, the mortgagor, as an installment land contract vendor, would retain legal title to the property until the contract was paid off. Thus his financial interest would only slowly diminish until the final payment by the vendee. Hence the court held that a "due-on clause contained in a promissory note or deed of trust is not to be enforced simply because the trustor-obligator enters into an installment land contract * * *." [75] Such a clause will only be enforced where the *mortgagee* can show either danger to the security or such moral risks that transfer by installment land contracts significantly enhance the likelihood of default and foreclosure.

Any apparent distinction between "outright sales" and other types of transfer, however, was ultimately rejected by the California Supreme Court in its 1978 decision in Wellenkamp v. Bank of America.[76] In that case the mortgagor-trustor conveyed real estate to the plaintiff who assumed the balance of a deed of trust held by the defendant. Plaintiff paid the original mortgagor-trustor in cash the difference between the purchase price and the balance on defendant's deed of trust. The defendant refused to accept plaintiff's attempted payment of an installment on the deed of trust and instead offered to approve an assumption of the existing loan at an interest rate higher than the original rate. After the plaintiff refused this

74. 12 Cal.3d at 640, 526 P.2d at 1180, 116 Cal.Rptr. at 643.

75. 12 Cal.3d at 641, 526 P.2d at 1181, 116 Cal.Rptr. at 644.

76. 148 Cal.Rptr. 379 (Cal.1978).

proposal, defendant accelerated and initiated foreclosure proceedings. The California Supreme Court determined that the trial court erroneously dismissed the plaintiff's complaint and held, 6–1, that "a due-on clause * * * cannot be enforced upon the occurrence of an outright sale unless the lender can demonstrate that enforcement is reasonably necessary to protect against impairment to its security or the risk of default." [77] In reaching this result the court specifically disapproved the Cherry decision and overruled the Coast Bank case to the extent that it was inconsistent with its Wellenkamp reasoning.

In supporting its opinion, the Wellenkamp court emphasized that the term "outright sale" is not limited to the "all cash to seller" arrangement referred to in the Tucker case, but in addition includes all sales where the buyer pays the seller the amount of the latter's equity and agrees to assume or take "subject to" the existing mortgage or deed of trust. Further, the court rejected the defendant's argument that the risk of waste and default is substantial in the outright sale situation because the seller-trustor-mortgagor retains neither possession nor title. While the court recognised that seller retention of possession or legal title had been important factors in its earlier La Sala and Tucker decisions, it believed that their absence was not necessarily significant in the outright sale situation. The court noted that the outright sale buyer "in order to pay off the seller's equity, may make a large down payment on the property, thereby creating an equity interest in the property *in him* which is sufficient to provide an adequate incentive not to commit waste or permit the property to depreciate. Moreover, the buyer in such an outright sale may be at least as good, if not a better credit risk than the original borrower/seller." [77a] Finally, the court was unmoved by the defendant's argument that enforcement of due-on clauses in the outright sale situation was justified by the lender's interest in maintaining its loan portfolio at current market interest rates. The court stressed that long term lenders, as a matter of business necessity, should and do take their projections of future economic trends into account in setting interest rates. While these projections sometimes prove inaccurate, the court nevertheless concluded "that it would be unjust to place the burden of the lender's mistaken economic projections on property owners exercizing their right to freely alienate their property through the automatic enforcement of a due-on clause by the lender." [77b]

§ 5.23 "Due-On" Clauses—Other Jurisdictions

During the past five or six years numerous state courts have dealt with the complexities of due-on clauses, with almost all of the

77. Id. at 385–386.

77a. Id. at 384–385.

77b. Id. at 385.

cases involving due-on-sale language. As one commentator has noted, "a great deal of confusion currently marks the area." [78] Indeed, commentators are having a difficult time classifying these state decisions.[79] One fact is strikingly apparent, however. No court thus far has held a due-on clause to be a per se invalid restraint on alienation. Every court has at least recognized that there are some circumstances where such clauses are justifiable.

Notwithstanding the confusion in the area it is safe to say that two broad categories of state decisions are emerging. The first category inclines toward automatic enforcement of due-on-sale clauses, or at least the cases in this category support a strong presumption in favor of their validity.[80] While these decisions do not rule out relieving a mortgagor from unconscionable or inequitable conduct of the mortgagee in an individual case, "the validity of the restraint is not to be determined under the circumstances of each case." [81] A case by case determination of reasonableness of the clauses is discouraged. The cases in this category tend to recognize the validity of protecting the mortgagee from the interest market [82] and seem to put the burden heavily on the mortgagor to establish that enforcement is unfair or unconscionable in the particular case. The second broad category of cases, on the other hand, holds that these clauses can be reasonable in individual cases, but seems to put the burden on the mortgagee to establish that enforcement in a particular case is justified.[83] These cases emphasize a case by case determi-

78. Comment, Judicial Treatment of the Due-on-Sale Clause: The Case for Adopting Standards of Reasonableness and Unconscionability, 27 Stan. L.Rev. 1109, 1117 (1975).

79. Compare Note, 47 Miss.L.J. 331, 342 (1976) with Note, 55 N.C.L.Rev. 310, 312–313 (1977).

80. See Medevoi v. American Sav. & Loan Ass'n, 62 Cal.App.3d 309, 133 Cal.Rptr. 63 (2nd Dist.Ct.App.1976); Malouff v. Midland Federal Sav. & Loan Ass'n, 181 Colo. 294, 509 P.2d 1240 (1973); Baker v. Loves Park Sav. and Loan Ass'n, 6 Ill.2d 119, 333 N.E.2d 1 (1975); First Commercial Title, Inc. v. Holmes, —— Nev. ——, 550 P.2d 1271 (1976); Century Federal Sav. & Loan Ass'n v. Van Glahn, 144 N.J.Super. 48, 364 A.2d 558 (1976); Stith v. Hudson City Sav. Inst., 63 Misc.2d 863, 313 N.Y.S.2d 804 (1970); Crockett v. First Federal Sav. & Loan Ass'n, 289 N.C. 620, 224 S.E.2d 580 (1976); Gunther v. White, 489 S.W.2d 529 (Tenn.1973). Mutual Federal Sav. & Loan Ass'n v. Wisconsin Wire Works, 71 Wis.2d 531, 239 N.W.2d 20 (1976).

81. Baker v. Loves Park Sav. & Loan Ass'n, 6 Ill.2d 119, 124, 333 N.E.2d 1, 5 (1975).

82. See, e. g., Century Federal Sav. & Loan Ass'n v. Van Glahn, 144 N.J.Super. 48, 53, 364 A.2d 558, 562 (1976).

83. First Southern Federal Sav. & Loan Ass'n of Mobile v. Britton, 345 So. 2d 300 (Ala.Civ.App.1977). Baltimore Life Ins. Co. v. Harn, 15 Ariz.App. 78, 486 P.2d 190 (1971); Tucker v. Pulaski Federal Sav. & Loan Ass'n, 252 Ark. 849, 481 S.W.2d 725 (1972); Clark v. Lachenmeier, 237 So.2d 583 (Fla.App.1970); Nichols v. Ann Arbor Federal Sav. & Loan Ass'n, 73 Mich.App. 163, 250 N.W.2d 804 (1977). Sanders v. Hicks, 317 So.2d 61 (Miss. 1975); Fidelity Land Development Corp. v. Rieder & Sons Bldg. and Development Co., 151 N.J.Super. 502, 377 A.2d 691 (1977); Bellingham First Federal Sav. & Loan Ass'n v. Garrison, 87 Wash.2d 437, 553 P.2d 1090 (1976).

nation of reasonableness. They tend to reject the interest market justification for due-on-sale clauses and emphasize that the mortgagee must establish in the individual case that the transfer threatens to impair security or, at least, increases the chances of default and foreclosure. Some of these courts ultimately sustain the application of the clause in the particular case,[84] but more tend to refuse enforcement.

It is useful to examine more carefully certain of the decisions that typify each broad category. Perhaps the most extreme example of the first category is First Commercial Title v. Holmes.[85] There the court considered an action to enjoin enforcement of a deed of trust due-on-sale clause in an outright sale situation and the Supreme Court of Nevada rather tersely "adopted the view that the clause is entitled to automatic enforcement where there is an outright sale by the trustor-vendor." [86] The court then equivocated somewhat by noting that it was not suggesting "that the clause is absolutely enforcible without regard to surrounding circumstances * * * Although enforcibility of the clause is automatic, it is not absolute and may be vulnerable to certain defenses (i. e., waiver). However, we reject the view that imposes upon the Beneficiary the burden of establishing justification for enforcement of the clause." [87]

The Illinois Supreme Court, in Baker v. Loves Park Sav. & Loan Ass'n,[88] was similarly emphatic, if somewhat more analytical, in following the same approach. There the appellate court had remanded a case to determine whether enforcement of a due-on-sale clause was reasonable under the circumstances of the case. The supreme court reversed and stated that "judging the reasonableness * * * under the circumstances of each case would not promote the desired stability of titles and would in fact make it extremely difficult to predict whether a restraint will or will not be upheld." [89] While the court noted that a case by case reasonableness approach may be suitable in other areas of the law, it nevertheless believed that greater certainty and predictability were required when land titles were involved. As in *Holmes*, however, a mortgagor nevertheless could be relieved of "unconscionable or inequitable conduct of a lender." [90]

Certain decisions clearly exemplify the second category of cases. In Baltimore Life Ins. Co. v. Harn,[91] the mortgagee attempted to exercise a due-on-sale clause by foreclosing after the mortgagor had ex-

84. See Bellingham First Federal Sav. & Loan Ass'n v. Garrison, 87 Wash. 2d 437, 553 P.2d 1090 (1976); Note, 12 Gonz.L.Rev. 765 (1977); Mutual Real Estate Inv. Trust. v. Buffalo Sav. Bank, 90 Misc.2d 675, 395 N.Y. S.2d 583 (1977).

85. 92 Nev. 363, 550 P.2d 1271 (1976).

86. 550 P.2d at 1272.

87. 550 P.2d at 1272.

88. 6 Ill.2d 119, 333 N.E.2d 1 (1975).

89. 6 Ill.2d at 124, 333 N.E.2d at 5.

90. 6 Ill.2d at 124, 333 N.E.2d at 5.

91. 15 Ariz.App. 78, 486 P.2d 190 (1971).

ecuted an agreement to sell the premises. The court determined that the agreement to sell constituted a conveyance within the scope of the due-on-sale clause. However, the court refused to permit enforcement of the clause simply upon the allegation that the clause had been violated. The court concluded that in the absence of "an allegation that the purpose of the clause * * * is being circumvented or that the mortgagee's security is jeopardized, a [mortgagee] cannot be entitled to equitable relief." [92]

Tucker v. Pulaski Sav. & Loan Assn.[93] is perhaps the classic example of the case by case reasonableness approach. In that case, the mortgagors, the Tuckers, after more than a year of trying, finally sold an apartment house in a racially changing neighborhood to a black couple, the Belchers. The Belchers agreed to pay $1,500 in cash to the Tuckers and took "subject to" a mortgage in favor of Pulaski in the amount of approximately $20,000. Pulaski accelerated and brought a foreclosure action. The Supreme Court of Arkansas "very quickly [stated] that we agree with the [Tuckers] that the [mortgagee] cannot, simply on the basis of the quoted clause, accelerate the note, declare the indebtedness due and payable, and foreclose the property. This procedure cannot be countenanced in a court of equity." [94] The court noted in this case that even though they had had a car repossessed, the Belchers had never been delinquent in another real estate indebtedness to Pulaski. Moreover, the court noted that the Tuckers were still liable on the note and that Mr. Tucker's father was also liable. Further, other Tucker real estate secured the Pulaski mortgage. Thus, the court held that the trial court "erred, first, in holding the mortgagee had no obligation to justify its refusal to consent to the sale of the mortgage property to the Belchers, and further erred in holding that Pulaski had valid business reasons for withholding its consent." [95]

The most recent, and perhaps the most extreme, example of this approach is Sanders v. Hicks,[96] a 1975 Mississippi Supreme Court decision. This case involved an action to enjoin the foreclosure of a deed of trust on a service station which contained a due-on-sale provision, but which required no payment of interest until maturity. The purchase-money mortgagee refused consent to a sale to the Hicks. The property was sold to the Hicks "subject to" the deed of trust, the mortgagee commenced foreclosure proceedings and the action to enjoin ensued. The trial court denied the injunction and the Mississippi Supreme Court reversed. The supreme court held that due-on clauses were not per se invalid restraints on alienation and that such re-

92. 15 Ariz.App. at 81, 486 P.2d at 193.

93. 252 Ark. 849, 481 S.W.2d 725 (1972).

94. 252 Ark. at 853, 481 S.W.2d at 729.

95. 252 Ark. at 857, 481 S.W.2d at 733.

96. 317 So.2d 61 (Miss.1975). See Note, 47 Miss.L.J. 331 (1976).

straints "may be valid depending upon whether [they are] reasonable under the circumstances." [97] Here the court concluded that the mortgagee had not established that the restraint was related to the legitimate interest of the mortgagee, even though the court left for another case the definition of what those legitimate interests might be. The mortgagee did argue that it was legitimate in this case to accelerate because a grantee of substantial means was simply taking advantage of a no-interest loan that had been given by the purchase-money mortgagee as a contractual concession to the original mortgagor. This factor, however, the court determined to be without merit.

The Washington Supreme Court has created an interesting and anomalous cross-current with respect to and enforcement of due-on sale clauses. In Bellingham First Federal Sav. & Loan Ass'n v. Garrison [98] the court placed Washington squarely in the second category of cases described above by holding that although due-on-sale clauses were not per se invalid as restraints on alienation, nevertheless, the burden was on the mortgagee to show in each case that enforcement was necessary to protect the mortgagee's security. In the *Bellingham* case, however, because the court found that the mortgagor had a questionable credit rating and several other delinquencies, it held that the mortgagee had met its burden of proof. Yet, a few months earlier in Miller v. Pacific First Federal Sav. & Loan Ass'n [99] the Washington Supreme Court upheld, in general, a mortgage provision that *specifically* permitted the mortgagee to raise the interest on the mortgage in the event of a sale of the mortgage real estate. The court qualified the approval of this clause to some extent by suggesting that unconscionable or inequitable conduct by the mortgagee in a particular case could limit or invalidate enforcement. The Miller case, nevertheless, represents an explicit recognition of the validity of protecting the mortgagee against rising interest rates, an interest that most due-on-sale cases in the second category and indeed, *Bellingham*, have rejected. It would thus seem that Washington mortgagees, ironically, will be better able to protect themselves by using an express "increased interest on sale" language than the traditional due-on-sale provision.

Interestingly, one factor emphasized by some courts in both of the above categories is whether the mortgagee imposes a pre-payment penalty on the mortgagor.[1] For example, some courts have noted that by not imposing prepayment penalties, the mortgagee permits the mortgagor to refinance easily when interest rates drop.[2]

97. 317 So.2d at 64.

98. 87 Wash.2d 437, 553 P.2d 1090 (1976). See Note; 12 Gonz.L.Rev. 765 (1977).

99. 86 Wash.2d 401, 545 P.2d 546 (1976).

1. See §§ 6.1–6.3 infra.

2. E. g., Crockett v. First Federal Sav. & Loan Ass'n, 289 N.C. 620, 627, 224 S.E.2d 580, 585 (1976); Note, 13 Wake F.L.Rev. 490 (1977); Century Federal Sav. & Loan Ass'n v. Van Glahn, 144 N.J.Super. 48, 54, 364 A.2d 558, 562 (1976).

"Allowing the lender the same ability to adjust the rates seems equitable."[3] On the other hand, where large pre-payment penalties were involved, that factor has been emphasized as weighing against enforcement of a due-on-sale clause.[4]

Because due-on-sale clauses are primarily aimed at protecting the mortgagee against a rising interest market, their continued use is inextricably bound up with pressures from institutional lenders for variable interest rates, i. e., flexible interest rates which change as prevailing market interest rates change.[5] To the extent that variable interest rates become commonplace, due-on-sale clause enforcement will obviously diminish and the general problem of their interpretation and validity will be much less significant.

However, in the absence of formal and widespread adoption of variable interest rates, the approach of the first category of cases, in which there is a presumption in favor of automatic enforcement of due-on-sale clauses, is, on balance, probably preferable to the case by case reasonableness approach of the second category. At least several strong arguments buttress this position. First, one should focus on the reasonable expectations of the mortgagor at the time a mortgage loan is first made. Usually, at least in the residential setting, the borrower is concerned most with his immediate cost, i. e.—the interest rate and how much his monthly payment is going to be. Normally, he will not be concerned with his mortgage as a method for facilitating a future sale of his home. In other words, perhaps it is simply unwise to conceive of a method utilized to *acquire* a home as also a device to *facilitate its sale.* Hence, when a due-on-sale clause in effect warns the mortgagor that the loan will not be available to finance a future sale, there is, generally, no inequity in enforcing the clause as written. Second, no one seriously questions the proposition that institutional lenders during periods of rising interest rates face a serious dilemma. Because a large portion of their portfolios consist of older, lower yielding mortgages, they have difficulty in paying the higher short-term rates demanded by depositors. Third, the enforcement of due-on-sale clauses tends to reduce the discrimination that otherwise exists in favor of those buyers who are fortunate enough to find a low interest loan to assume against those who are forced to obtain new first mortgage financing. As the California Supreme Court once noted, "[t]o permit the lender to accelerate insures that all buyers of property must finance at the current interest rate, and that none obtain an advantage because of the fortuitous fact that the seller originally purchased during a period of low interest rates." [6] Indeed, be-

3. Note, Mortgages—Use of Due-on-Sale Clause by a Lender Is Not a Restraint on Alienation in North Carolina, 55 N.C.L.Rev. 310, 314–315 (1977).

4. See e. g., Baltimore Life Ins. Co. v. Harn, 15 Ariz.App. 78, 81, 486 P.2d 190, 193 (1972).

5. See § 11.4 infra.

6. LaSala v. American Sav. & Loan Ass'n, 5 Cal.3d 864, 880, 97 Cal.Rptr. 849, 859, 489 P.2d 1113, 1123 (1971).

cause existing low interest loans have been paid down to some extent, and because of inflation in the value of real estate, those who are able to assume an existing loan generally will be those who can come up with a significant amount of cash, whereas those who are not so fortunate in this regard will be forced to obtain new financing at higher market interest rates. Thus, to the extent that due-on-sale clauses are not enforced, an inordinate interest rate advantage may be afforded to higher net worth buyers over those who are less fortunate. Finally, one commentator, in taking note that during one period of the last decade new mortgagors were being charged 9% to make up for those paying 4% on existing loans, argues persuasively that "[t]his would indicate that the real estate brokers' arguments against 'due-on' clauses as inhibitors of home sales are misplaced. While it is true that the prospect of having to assume a mortgage at a rate higher than the borrower/vendor's may deter some potential vendees from buying, it appears that the 'due-on' clauses have actually played a part in holding down overall rates."[7] In other words, absent due-on-sale enforcement, the new financing interest rates would arguably have been driven higher to balance off all of the additional low interest loans that would have remained on the mortgagee's books.

§ 5.24 State Regulation of "Due-On" Clauses

Although due-on clauses have generated substantial litigation, there has been relatively little legislative activity in the area. Some legislatures, however, have attempted to deal with the due-on-encumbrance situation. For example, California prohibits acceleration of a mortgage or a deed of trust on a single-family, owner-occupied dwelling solely because the owner further encumbers the property with a junior mortgage or deed of trust.[8] Virginia, similarly, invalidates restrictions on further encumbrances in any mortgage or deed of trust secured by one-to-four family residential dwelling units.[9]

There are substantial policy problems with such absolute ban type legislation, even if it is applicable only to residential loans. It can be argued that a first mortgagee does have a substantial interest in insuring that the mortgagor retains an economic stake in the real estate. Suppose, for example, that there is a $50,000 first mortgage on real estate having a fair market value of $60,000. Suppose further, that the mortgagor gives a second mortgage to a finance company to secure a $10,000 loan, the proceeds of which the mortgagor uses for personal pleasure or unrelated business purposes. It would seem justifiable to argue that the risk of a default and foreclosure on the first mortgage increases as the mortgagor's economic stake in the

7. Ashley, Use of "Due-On" Clauses to Gain Collateral Benefits: A Common-Sense Defense, 10 Tulsa L.J. 590, 593 (1975).

8. West's Ann.Cal.Civ.Code, § 2949.

9. Va.Code § 6.1–2.5 (1975).

property decreases. On the other hand, if the proceeds of the second mortgage loan are used to improve the mortgaged premises, the first mortgagee should have less complaint, because, presumably, the value of the security increases. Of course, even in that situation, there are occasions when improvements do not always increase the value of the mortgaged premises and sometimes, if they are bizarre enough, they may actually lower the value of the real estate. Thus, it could be argued that the judicial approach of examining the reasonableness of a due-on-encumbrance clause in the particular case is preferable to a flat statutory prohibition, even though such prohibitions operate only in the residential setting.

In addition, California has enacted legislation prohibiting acceleration in certain types of transfers of one-to-four family dwellings.[10] These involve involuntary and other types of transfers other than the typical sale of a dwelling. Specifically, acceleration is prohibited where there is a transfer to the spouse resulting from the death of the mortgagor, to a spouse who becomes a co-owner of the property, to a spouse incident to a marriage dissolution proceeding or settlement, by the mortgagor to an inter vivos trust of which the mortgagor is a beneficiary, and where transfers create junior encumbrances or liens. Interestingly, the latter provision as to junior encumbrances or liens seems to duplicate the earlier enacted California statute discussed above that specifically deals with acceleration based on further encumbrances. Perhaps the intent was to insure that junior encumbrances came within the "transfer" type language of a due-on-sale clause as well as the "encumbrance" type language in such clauses.

The Uniform Land Transactions Act (ULTA), promulgated by the National Conference of Commissioners on Uniform State Laws in 1975, but as of yet not adopted by any state, authorizes the mortgagee to provide for acceleration resulting from a "sale without consent of the secured creditor." [11] While the Act itself uses the word "sale," the Comment states that "the security agreement may contain a 'due-on-sale' clause . . . that the debt is accelerated if a *transfer* is made" [12] without consent. This drafting is ambiguous because it is doubtful that the word "sale" encompasses the language typically found in due-on-sale clauses such as "sell, convey, sell under contract of sale, lease with option to purchase," or "sell, convey, transfer, dispose." [13] The purpose of this provision apparently is to permit mortgagees to utilize due-on-sale clauses to protect themselves against rising interest markets. Indeed, the comment states that the "clause restricts the power of a debtor to sell his favorable interest

10. West's Ann.Cal.Civ.Code, § 2924.5.

11. ULTA § 3–208a (1975).

12. ULTA § 3–208, Comment 1.

13. Comment, Judicial Treatment of the Due-on-Sale Clause: The Case for Adopting Standards of Reasonableness and Unconscionability, 27 Stanford L.Rev. 1109, 1110 n.5 (1975).

rate." [14] The provision also prohibits the mortgagee from collecting a pre-payment penalty where a higher interest rate than that in the mortgage is demanded by the mortgagee as a condition to the mortgagee's consent to sale and the full debt is paid within three months after the mortgagor fails to agree to the higher rate.[15]

§ 5.25 Federal Regulation of "Due-On" Clauses

The most recent regulations issued by the Federal Home Loan Bank Board (FHLBB), whose regulations affect all federally chartered savings and loan associations, regulate to some extent the use of due-on clauses.[16] Such federal associations are authorized to utilize due-on-sale clauses and these clauses presumably are enforceable and govern the rights of the parties notwithstanding state law to the contrary. As to loans made after July 31, 1976, on borrower-occupied homes, a due-on-sale clause cannot be exercised as a result of junior liens, purchase-money security interests in household appliances, devise, descent, or operation of law upon the death of a joint tenant or a leasehold for less than three years with no option to purchase. A pre-payment penalty may not be charged as a result of exercising a due-on-sale clause. While the interest rate can be raised as a condition to a mortgagee's refraining from exercising a due-on-sale clause, the FHLBB "expects that no association will request an increase * * * to a rate in excess of the then prevailing rate on comparable new loans made by the association * * *".[17]

In addition, the standard mortgage form approved by the Federal Home Loan Mortgage Corporation (FHLMC) and the Federal National Mortgage Association (FNMA), both quasi-federal entities, utilize a due on sale clause that is virtually identical to that permitted by the FHLBB and described in the foregoing paragraph. This form also tends to set national standards, because many lenders wish to make their mortgages eligible for FNMA or FHLMC purchase, and these agencies require the form's use for all mortgages they buy.[18]

14. ULTA § 3–208, Comment 1.

15. ULTA § 3–208b (1975).

16. 12 CFR 545.6–11(g).

17. 12 CFR 556.9(e).

18. FNMA does not enforce the clause at all as to single-family homes; it *does* enforce it on planned unit developments and condominiums. See FNMA Conventional Selling Contract Supplement, § 301 (E), (F). FHLMC permits the loan servicing institution to charge (and retain) a fee for the administrative work involved in a transfer of title. The fee may not exceed $50 in a "subject to" transaction, or 1% of the mortgage balance in an assumption transaction. If the loan servicing institution wishes to enforce the due on clause by charging a higher fee, or by raising the interest rate, it must repurchase the loan from FHLMC and reimburse it for all associated costs. FHLMC also imposes a set of credit and underwriting criteria to determine whether the proposed grantee is acceptable and will presumably require a payoff if he is not. See FHLMC Servicer's Guide, § 3.114(b).

§ 5.26 Installment Land Contract Prohibitions on Vendee Transfer

Unlike the relatively recent development of the due-on-sale type clause in the mortgage area, installment land contract vendors have traditionally included provisions prohibiting assignment by the vendee without the vendor's consent. Normally violation of this clause constitutes a default under the contract and therefore, in theory, a ground for forfeiture. In the restraint on alienation terminology discussed earlier, the installment land contract prohibition on assignment clearly can be categorized as a forfeiture type of direct restraint.[19]

Traditionally, however, there was early, non-judicial support for the validity of the forfeiture restraint in installment land contracts. For example, the Restatement of Property,[20] Professors Simes and Smith,[21] Professor Goddard[22] and Professor Grismore[23] all were in essential agreement that such forfeiture restraints were not undue restraints on alienation. Later commentary was more doubtful about the validity of such restraints.[24] Professor Lee, for example, pointed out that "[t]hose authorities which place their emphasis upon the land aspect of the transaction favor freedom of alienation. Those who regard the contract aspect as being of greater weight will uphold a non-assignment clause and deny an assignee the rights of the purchaser. The weight of authority favors freedom of alienation."[25] Moreover, even Professor Grismore conceded that "perhaps * * * it can be properly urged that when the restriction is one which purports to destroy the power to assign or to give the other party the right to forfeit the contract, its operation should be limited; so that in case the vendor has received payment for tender of the full purchase price * * * he cannot * * * refuse to recognize the assignee's rights."[26]

The early case law concerning forfeiture restraints does not seem as unequivocal in upholding forfeiture restraints as some of the above commentators would indicate. One leading Michigan case, Sloman v. Cutler,[27] upholding a forfeiture restraint, should be considered.

19. Volkmer, The Application of the Restraints on Alienation Doctrine to Real Property Security Interests, 58 Iowa L.Rev. 747, 753 (1973). See text at notes 57–65, § 5.21, supra.

20. Restatement of Property, § 416 (1944).

21. Simes & Smith, The Law of Future Interests, § 1164 (2d Ed. 1956).

22. Goddard, Non-Assignment Provisions In Land Contracts, 31 Mich.L. Rev. 1, 9–11 (1932).

23. Grismore, Effect of a Restriction on Assignment in a Contract, 31 Mich.L.Rev. 299, 316–17 (1933).

24. See Fratcher, Perpetuities and Other Restraints, 252 (1955).

25. Lee, The Interests Created by the Installment Land Contract, 19 U.Miami L.Rev. 367, 395 (1965).

26. Grismore, Effect of a Restriction on Assignment in a Contract, 31 Mich.L.Rev. 299, 316–17 (1933).

27. 258 Mich. 372, 242 N.W. 735 (1932).

There, vendees assigned their interest to the defendant and the plaintiff-vendor consented to the assignment. Defendant-assignee assumed the obligations under the contract. However, when the vendor sued the assignee for payments due under the contract, the defendant-assignee argued that the non-assignment clause was an invalid restraint on alienation and therefore the vendor's consent to the assignment was not valid consideration for defendant's assuming the vendee's contractual obligation. The court, in upholding the forfeiture restraint, noted that such a restriction on alienation of an absolute interest would be invalid, but that here the vendor retained an interest in the contract property. Because the vendor's interest was "an important interest, commonly the greatest interest, and near the value of the property," and because the vendor had such an interest, the imposition of such a restriction was permissible "as within his rights to preserve his security under the contract." [28] While there are earlier cases that state that a vendor can enforce a non-assignment clause even against an assignee who tenders the full purchase price,[29] there are also cases that permit the assignee to tender full payment and avoid the forfeiture.[30] In Jankowski v. Jankowski,[31] for example, the vendees sold to assignees without vendor's consent in spite of a non-assignment clause entitling the vendor to declare a forfeiture in the event of its breach. Shortly thereafter the vendor gave notice of forfeiture and sued to recover possession. The vendees and assignees then sued to enjoin vendor's proceeding and tendered the balance due on the contract. The trial judge found in favor of the vendees and assignees. The Michigan Supreme Court affirmed and stated that while such a non-assignment restriction is valid when the contract is executory, because the vendor has a right to make sure that the property is under the control of a responsible person who will take care of it and make payments, where full payment is tendered the "equity court made a proper disposition of the case giving vendors everything to which they are entitled and they have no reason to complain." [32] The willingness of such courts to grant specific performance to the assignee of a vendee in spite of the non-assignment-forfeiture provision indicates a judicial disposition to treat installment land contracts as security devices rather than simple contracts because, in effect, the defaulting vendee and assignee are being permitted to exercise the mortgage equivalent of the right to redeem.[33]

28. 258 Mich. at 375, 242 N.W. at 736.

29. See, e. g., Olcott v. Heermans, 10 N.Y. 431, 3 Hun. 431 (1875); Boyd v. Bondy, 113 Wash. 384, 194 P. 393 (1920).

30. See, e. g., Jankowski v. Jankowski, 311 Mich. 340, 18 N.W.2d 848 (1945); Johnson v. Eklund, 72 Minn. 195, 75 N.W. 14 (1898).

31. 311 Mich. 340, 18 N.W.2d 848 (1945).

32. Id. at 344, 18 N.W.2d at 849. Accord, Coraci v. Noack, 61 Wis.2d 183, 212 N.W.2d 164 (1973); Murray First Thrift & Loan Co. v. Stevenson, 534 P.2d 909 (Utah 1975).

33. 3 American Law of Property, § 11.-36 (Casner Ed. 1952).

Two recent Michigan decisions illustrate how courts are now moving substantially away from any notion of automatic enforcement of non-assignment forfeiture provisions. In Pellerito v. Webber,[34] the vendors had paid $13,500 down on an installment land contract and had made monthly payments for about fourteen years. Vendees then assigned to an assignee and the vendors refused payment from the assignee. Vendors then sought to have a court enforce the forfeiture provision. The trial court denied relief and the court of appeals affirmed and allowed the assignees to continue making the contract payments. While the court did not hold the non-assignment provision to be invalid, the court stated: "Restraints on alienation of property are strongly disfavored in Michigan. Where they are permitted, they are strictly construed to prevent a forfeiture. Here plaintiffs have not made any allegations of waste or impairment or loss of security. * * * Under the facts of this case we will not require a forfeiture; to do so would be to impose an unreasonable restraint on the alienation of an equitable interest in real property." [35] Lemon v. Nicolai,[36] decided a year later, is similar to Pellerito. After fifteen payments the vendees assigned their interest and the vendors declared a forfeiture and brought an action to enforce the forfeiture and recover the land. The Court of Appeals reversed the trial court determination in favor of the vendors. The court relied on Pellerito in emphasizing that the vendors had made no allegation of waste or impairment of security. The court remanded the case for a determination as to the waste or security impairment. If none was found, the court concluded, forfeiture enforcement would be an invalid restraint in alienation. The net effect, again, assuming that the vendor cannot meet such a burden of proof, is to allow the assignee to continue the contract by resuming payments.

Professor Volkmer has pointed out that "the grudging acceptance by the early authorities of the full-tender-by-assignee exception to the general validity of forfeiture restraints seems to have given way to a substantially increased emphasis on free alienability of land and a new focus on the interest of the contract vendee." [37] This is consistent with the recent trend of courts toward treating installment land contracts as mortgages. As more courts tend to apply substantive mortgage law to such contracts, it is understandable that those courts will begin to treat the forfeiture restraints as the functional equivalent of a due-on-sale clause and will tend to apply due-on-sale analysis to such restraints. However, because the forfeiture remedy in the installment land contract situation is a drastic one, courts in

34. 22 Mich.App. 242, 177 N.W.2d 236 (1970).

35. Id. at 245, 177 N.W.2d at 238.

36. 33 Mich.App. 646, 190 N.W.2d 549 (1971).

37. Volkmer, The Application of the Restraints on Alienation Doctrine to Real Property Security Interests, 58 Iowa L.Rev. 747, 767 (1973).

the future will probably be less inclined to enforce a non-assignment provision of an installment land contract than they will be to enforce due-on-sale clauses in a mortgage setting, where the remedy is foreclosure and not forfeiture. If vendors in the installment land contract situation desire to use non-assignment provisions, perhaps they would be wise to provide for acceleration and foreclosure of the land contract as the remedy instead of forfeiture.

C. TRANSFER BY THE MORTGAGEE

§ 5.27 Introduction—Nature of the Mortgagee's Interest

The mortgagee of real property has two things: the personal obligation owed by the mortgagor, and the interest in the realty securing that obligation. This twofold character of the rights of the mortgagee must be kept in mind when transfers by the mortgagee are considered. For a transfer to be complete both the obligation and the security interest must pass to the same person.[38]

The practical context in which these issues arise is the trading of mortgages as investments on the "secondary mortgage market." When a lender, having originated a mortgage loan, sells it to another investor, a secondary market transaction is said to occur, and the act of the original mortgagee is loosely termed an "assignment." Three federally-sponsored agencies, the Federal National Mortgage Association (FNMA), the Federal Home Loan Mortgage Corporation (FHLMC), and the Government National Mortgage Association (GNMA), are actively involved in purchasing assignments of mortgages, primarily on residential properties, from local lenders throughout the nation. Their operations are described elsewhere in this book.[39] In addition, mortgage assignment transactions among private lending institutions are very common, and provide a means of moving mortgage capital from one area of the nation to another. The existence of a smoothly-working national market in mortgages is an important element of national housing policy.[40] Hence, the matters discussed in these sections are of intense practical significance.

While a wide variety of types of obligations may be secured by mortgages,[41] by far the most common is the obligation to repay a debt of money. The debt is usually evidenced by a promissory note executed by the borrower-mortgagor. Whatever the nature of the

38. Subrogation can act as an equitable assignment of a mortgage; see §§ 10.1–10.8, infra. This chapter is concerned only with voluntary assignments.

39. The activities and authority of these agencies are discussed at § 11.-3, infra.

40. See, e. g., Grebler, The "New System" of Residential Mortgage Finance, Mortgage Banker, Feb. 1972, at 4.

41. On the necessity and nature of the obligation, see §§ 2.1–2.2, supra.

obligation, the law applicable to it will determine the method or methods by which it may be transferred. In general the law of contracts applies, but in the special case of promissory notes the Uniform Commercial Code governs transfers. The obligation is correctly regarded as the principal thing being transferred, with the interest in the land attached to it in an extremely important, but subsidiary, capacity.[42] This notion is of fundamental importance. It means that the security is inseparable from the obligation, and that whoever can establish his claim to the obligation gets with it the security interest in the land, provided it is still in existence.[43]

In lien theory jurisdictions, any attempt by the mortgagee to transfer the interest in the land while expressly reserving the obligation simply does not work; the realty transfer is held to be a nullity.[44] In title jurisdictions, it is technically possible for the mortgagee to transfer his land interest and keep the obligation.[45] This may happen, for example, if the mortgagee dies and his land (including the security interest represented by the mortgage) descends to his heir, while the promissory note passes to his personal representative.[46] But whoever takes the realty interest in this fashion cannot assert it in any way; for example, he cannot foreclose if the obligation is in default.[47] Moreover, the holder of the obligation can go into equity and compel a transfer of the security to him. In fact, he may accomplish this by a bill to foreclose the mortgage; [48] if the holder of

42. The classic statement is Carpenter v. Longan, 83 U.S. (16 Wall.) 271, 21 L.Ed. 313 (1872): "All the authorities agree that the debt is the principal thing and the mortgage an accessory." See Bautista and Kennedy, The Imputed Negotiability of Security Interests Under the Code, 38 Ind.L.J. 574 (1963); Note, Transfer of the Mortgagee's Interest in Florida, 14 U.Fla.L.Rev. 98 (1961); Britton, Assignment of Mortgages Securing Negotiable Notes, 10 Ill.L.Rev. 337 (1915).

43. Domarad v. Fisher & Burke, Inc., 270 Cal.App.2d 543, 76 Cal.Rptr. 529 (1969); Kernohan v. Manss, 53 Ohio St. 118, 41 N.E. 258, 29 L.R.A. 317 (1895). See West's Ann.Cal.Civil Code, § 2936: "The assignment of a debt secured by a mortgage carries with it the security."

44. Commercial Products Corp v. Briegel, 101 Ill.App.2d 156, 242 N.E.2d 317 (1968); Bryan v. Easton Tire Co., 561 S.W.2d 79 (Ark.1978); Domarad v. Fisher & Burke, Inc., note 43, supra. There is even some authority, probably erroneous, that an attempted transfer of the security interest alone extinguishes it; see Teas v. Republic Nat. Bank, 460 S.W.2d 233 (Tex.Civ.App.1970).

"Among the 'gems' and 'free offerings' of the late Professor Chester Smith of the University of Arizona College of Law was the following analogy. The note is the cow and the mortgage the tail. The cow can survive without a tail, but the tail cannot survive without the cow." Best Fertilizers of Arizona, Inc. v. Burns, 117 Ariz. 178, 571 P.2d 675 (Ariz.App. 1977).

45. Second Nat. Bank v. Dyer, 121 Conn. 263, 184 A. 386 (1936); Stewart v. Crosby, 50 Me. 130 (1863).

46. Demarest v. Wynkoop, 3 Johns Ch. (N.Y.) 129, 8 Am.Dec. 467 (1897).

47. Only the owner of the debt can foreclose; Swinton v. Cuffman, 139 Ark. 121, 213 S.W. 409 (1919); Stribling v. Splint Coal Co., 31 W.Va. 82, 5 S.E. 321 (1888).

48. Lawrence v. Knap, 1 Root (Conn.) 248, 1 Am.Dec. 42 (1791); Pettus v.

the realty interest is named as a party, the court will impress a constructive trust on his interest and foreclose it in behalf of the noteholder.

The benefit of the security goes to the one who owns the debt, even if he did not realize when he bought it that it was secured.[49] To hold otherwise would give a windfall to the mortgagor, since no one but the holder of the debt could assert the security. Of course, the rule stated gives a windfall, in a sense, to the assignee of the debt, but it has the advantage of consistency and predictability. The debtholder would be able to execute a judgment upon the land in any event,[50] so the real significance of his ability to foreclose the mortgage is its priority against subsequent lienors or encumbrancers. They will have had notice of the mortgage from the chain of title, and so cannot complain.

§ 5.28 Methods of Transfer

The methods of transferring an obligation and the mortgage which secures it depend on the nature of the obligation. To a great extent the Uniform Commercial Code specifies these methods, at least when the obligation in question is a promise to pay money. The Code's treatment of this subject is complex, and we can cover it here in only a sparse way; the reader should refer to works on the Code itself for more detail.[51]

Under the Code a note may either be negotiable or nonnegotiable, depending on factors which we will discuss later. If the note is nonnegotiable, it can be transferred only by assignment, and not by negotiation.[52] The assignment may be carried out in any of several ways: by indorsement on the note by the original payee-mortgagee, by the use of a separate document which the payee-mortgagee executes, stating that his rights under the note are transferred to the assignee, and if the amount is small, even by an oral statement to the

Gault, 81 Conn. 415, 71 A. 509 (1908); Kinna v. Smith, 3 N.J.Eq. 14 (1834); Rembert v. Ellis, 193 Ga. 60, 17 S.E. 2d 165, 137 A.L.R. 479 (1941).

49. Mankato First Nat. Bank v. Pope, 85 Minn. 433, 89 N.W. 318 (1902); Betz v. Heebner, 1 Pen. & W. (Pa.) 280 (1830).

50. It is possible that the mortgagor would file a homestead declaration on the property and thereby defeat the debt-holder's execution, but there can hardly be a public policy favoring such a result if the mortgage had been given at a time when no homestead was on file.

51. See, e. g., Anderson, Uniform Commercial Code § 3–101 et seq. (1971); White & Summers, Uniform Commercial Code (1972), at chs. 13–14. Weber, Commercial Paper (Nutshell Series 1975); Annot., 23 A.L.R. 3d 932 (1969).

52. The basis for the statement in the text is a bit convoluted. UCC § 3–202 (1) provides that "Negotiation is the transfer of an instrument in such form that the transferee becomes a holder." § 3–102(1)(e) in turn defines "instrument" as it is used in Article 3 to mean a negotiable instrument. See White & Summers, Uniform Commercial Code (1972), at Sec. 14–4.

assignee that he is effecting a transfer.[53] To assign a nonnegotiable note, it is not necessary that possession of the note itself be given to the transferee.[54]

On the other hand, if a negotiable note is involved, and if the transferee wants to have the special and desirable status of a holder in due course,[55] the mode of transfer (which is termed "negotiation" in this situation) is much more narrowly constrained. The note must be indorsed by the payee-mortgagee, and it must be physicially transferred into the hands of the new holder.[56] The use of a separate document of assignment is not necessarily objectionable, but it cannot substitute for the indorsement and delivery of the note. If the transferee is willing to forego holder in due course status, or if for other reasons he is ineligible for that status, then the methods discussed in the preceding paragraph as applicable to nonnegotiable notes may be used with negotiable notes as well.

Unfortunately, many of the cases do not distinguish between negotiable and nonnegotiable notes, and they often make statements about assignment which clearly could not be correct as representing attempts to negotiate the note to a holder in due course.[57] This is true, for example, of the two other modes of transfer discussed in this section; they may become the basis of an assignment of the obligation, but they surely cannot, by themselves, amount to a negotiation. The difference lies in the rights which the transferee will have, and these can be of great significance.[58]

53. If the assignment is not evidenced by a writing, it is not enforceable "beyond five thousand dollars in amount or value." U.C.C. § 1–206. It might be argued that all assignments of notes secured by realty mortgages must be in writing, since the assignment of the note automatically conveys an interest in land simultaneously, and therefore should comport with the real estate statute of frauds. A similar argument can be raised with regard to the necessity of delivery, which is ordinarily a prerequisite to an effective conveyance of an interest in realty. Here as in other areas the dual nature of the debt and security creates a conflict, but by far the most common resolution, at least in equity, is to disregard the real estate requirements of writing and delivery if the debt itself is properly transferred and if no rights of third parties are prejudiced. Hebrew Home for Orphans & Aged v. Freund, 208 Misc. 658, 144 N.Y.S.2d 608 (1955); Thatcher v. Merriam, 121 Utah 191, 240 P.2d 266 (1952); Braidwood v. Harmon, 31 Mich.App. 49, 187 N.W.2d 559 (1971) (valid gift by delivery of note and mortgage without writing); Hall v. O'Brien, 218 N.Y. 50, 112 N.E. 569 (1916); Note, 36 Ky.L.J. 121 (1947).

54. Felin Ass'n v. Rogers, 38 A.D.2d 6, 326 N.Y.S.2d 413 (1971); Davin v. Isman, 228 N.Y. 1, 126 N.E. 257 (1920).

55. The advantages of HDC status are discussed at § 5.31, infra.

56. U.C.C. § 3–202(1). A holder must have possession of the note; U.C.C. § 1–201(20). No indorsement is required if the note was originally payable to bearer, but this is very uncommon in mortgage transactions; normally a mortgage note will be payable to the mortgagee, so his indorsement is necessary for negotiation.

57. See, e. g., Phillips v. Latham, 523 S.W.2d 19 (Tex.Civ.App.1975) refuse n.r.e., appeal after remand 551 S.W. 2d 103 (1977); Peterson v. John J. Reilly, Inc., 110 N.H. 1, 259 A.2d 393 (1969).

58. See §§ 5.31, 5.32, infra.

Finally, observe carefully that, as between the parties to a transfer, the assignment or negotiation of the note itself is all that must be done. It is unnecessary to have any separate document purporting to transfer or assign the security interest in the real estate, for it will follow the obligation automatically.[59] Written assignments of mortgages are nonetheless very common, and perhaps the most frequent method of transfer consists of executing a document of assignment of the mortgage and also indorsing the note to the transferee. As against certain third parties, to be discussed later, the execution and even recording of a written assignment may be wise and desirable steps,[60] but they are not essential as between the mortgagee and his transferee.

Conveyance of the Land

Suppose the mortgagee executes to his transferee what purports to be a deed to the land.[61] In title jurisdictions, as we have already noted, it is technically possible to separate the security interest from the obligation it secures, although to do so is an idle act, since one who holds the security without the obligation cannot assert it. But the question with which we are now concerned is this: can the deed of the land be construed as transferring both the security and the obligation? The cases are divided, with some holding affirmatively.[62] Others take the view that the deed is a nullity,[63] or that it transfers a naked legal title to the land which equity will restore to the owner of the obligation.[64] The test should be intent, and it is hard to imag-

59. Domarad v. Fisher & Burke, Inc., 270 Cal.App.2d 543, 76 Cal.Rptr. 529 (1969); Miller v. Frederick's Brewing Co., 405 Ill. 591, 92 N.E.2d 108 (1950); Jones v. Titus, 208 Mich. 392, 175 N. E. 257 (1919); cases cited § 5.27 note 43, supra. If the mortgagee does transfer the realty interest by some written conveyance, equity will impress a trust upon it in favor of the assignee of the obligation. See Powell, Real Property, Par. 455 at note 9 (1966).

60. See § 5.34, supra.

61. An interesting problem arises if the original mortgage is in the form of an absolute deed, and if the mortgagee-grantee executes a further absolute deed to a bona fide purchaser. Since the chain of title to the purchaser appears to be perfect, he will take the fee and divest the original grantor-mortgagor. This is a fundamental and serious risk to one who gives an absolute deed to secure an obligation. Mooney v. Byrne, 163 N. Y. 86, 57 N.E. 163 (1900); see § 3.3 et seq., supra.

62. Welsh v. Phillips, 54 Ala. 309, 25 Am.Rep. 679 (1875), warranty deed; Ruggles v. Barton, 79 Mass. (13 Gray) 506 (1859); Hinds v. Ballou, 44 N.H. 619 (1863), quitclaim. Even a release has been held to be sufficient. Welch v. Priest, 90 Mass. (8 Allen) 165 (1864).

63. "A conveyance of the land does not transfer the debt, because, so long as the mortgage is considered as an incident to the debt it cannot pass without a transfer of the principal." Smith v. Smith, 15 N.H. 55, 65 (1844). See Farnsworth v. Kimball, 112 Me. 238, 243, 91 A. 954, 956 (1914); Devlin v. Collier, 53 N.J.L. 422, 22 A. 201 (1891); Delano v. Bennett, 90 Ill. 533 (1878). For a general discussion of the effect of a conveyance of the mortgaged premises by the mortgagee, see Rollison, Priorities in the Law of Mortgages, 9 Notre Dame Law. 50 (1933).

64. Farrell v. Lewis, 56 Conn. 280, 14 A. 931 (1887); Island Pond Nat. Bank v. Lacroix, 104 Vt. 282, 158 A. 684

ine a situation in which the mortgagee intends either of the two latter results; in most cases he obviously wants to transfer both the obligation and the realty interest, and this should be presumed in the absence of rather clear contrary evidence.

In lien states it is often even more difficult to establish that a deed by the mortgagee acts as a transfer of the note and the security interest; the courts tend to hold it a nullity,[65] or in some cases to recognize it as an effective transfer of the obligation only if the intent to accomplish this is affirmatively shown.[66] There is really no basis for distinguishing between the lien and title theories in this context, and in either type of jurisdiction the natural presumption should be that a full transfer has been accomplished.

Where a purchaser buys at a void foreclosure sale and is given a conveyance in terms of the land, both the mortgage debt and the security are treated as having passed to him even though this was not the intent because it was supposed that full title to the property was being transferred.[67] Also if the purchaser of the property on the void foreclosure sale then conveys it, his deed will operate at least as an equitable assignment of both the mortgage title and the mortgage debt.[68] The last two cases do not depend upon a contractual assignment of the mortgage debt but the result comes by operation of law through the doctrine of equitable subrogation.[69]

(1932). Where the mortgagee has previously disposed of the debt to another this is the only operation the conveyance can have. Wolcott v. Winchester, 81 Mass. (15 Gray) 461 (1860); see Ruggles v. Barton, 79 Mass. (13 Gray) 506 (1859).

See Note, Effect of Assignment Without Assigning the Debt—Formalities Necessary to Transfer the Mortgagee's Title to the Mortgaged Property, 36 N.C.L.Rev. 225 (1958), discussing Gregg v. Williamson, 246 N.C. 356, 98 S.E.2d 481 (1957).

65. "A transfer of the mortgage without the debt is a nullity, and no interest is acquired by it. The security cannot be separated from the debt and exist independently of it. This is the necessary legal conclusion, and recognized as the rule by a long course of judicial decisions." Merritt v. Bartholick, 36 N.Y. 44 (1867); Peters v. Jamestown Bridge Co., 5 Cal. 334, 63 Am.Dec. 134 (1855); Carter v. Bennett, 4 Fla. 283, 347 (1852); Merritt v. Bartholick, 36 N.Y. 44 (1867); Johnson v. Cornett, 29 Ind. 59 (1867); Swan v. Yaple, 35 Iowa 248 (1872); see Devlin v. Collier, 53 N.J.L. 422, 427, 22 A. 201, 203 (1891). Cf. Gottlieb v. City of New York, 128 App. Div. 148, 112 N.Y.S. 545 (1908); Hawley v. Levee, 66 Misc. 280, 123 N.Y.S. 4 (1910).

66. Noble v. Watkins, 48 Or. 518, 87 P. 771 (1906); Greve v. Coffin, 14 Minn. 345, Gil. 263, 269 (1869); Blessett v. Turcotte, 20 N.D. 151, 127 N. W. 505 (1910); McCammant v. Roberts, 87 Tex. 241, 27 S.W. 86 (1894).

67. Muir v. Berkshire, 52 Ind. 149 (1875); Dutcher v. Hobby, 86 Ga. 198, 12 S.E. 356, 10 L.R.A. 472, 22 Am.St.Rep. 444 (1890).

68. Cooper v. Harvey, 21 S.D. 471, 113 N.W. 717 (1907); Lawrence v. Murphy, 45 Utah 572, 147 P. 903 (1915); Lamprey v. Nudd, 29 N.H. 299 (1854).

69. See Rollison, Priorities in the Law of Mortgages, 9 Notre Dame Law. 50, 66 (1933).

Assignment of the "Mortgage"

As we have already noted, it is common for an assigning mortgagee to execute an instrument, usually termed an "assignment", and deliver it to his transferee. If the transferee expects to record this document, as he usually does, it should be in appropriate form to satisfy the local recording act; this generally means that it must identify the parties and the original mortgage, describe the land, and bear an acknowledged signature of the mortgagee.

If the "assignment" also mentions that the debt is being transferred,[70] or if there is a separate indorsement and delivery of the note, the transfer is unquestionably complete. If neither of these is present, however, can the "assignment" of the mortgage alone be deemed to include the obligation as well? While some cases hold the transfer to fail entirely on these facts,[71] and others impose the burden of showing an intent to transfer the debt on the assignee,[72] the preferable rule is to presume that intent in the absence of contrary proof.[73] This approach is more compelling with an "assignment" by the mortgagee than with an absolute deed, since the phrase "assign the mortgage" is so commonly employed among those in the banking and real estate industries to refer to a complete transfer of both the debt and the realty interest.

A final reminder: while a deed or an assignment by the mortgagee can and generally should be deemed to act as a transfer of the note as well, neither of these techniques will result in a negotiation; even if the note is negotiable, the transferee who takes by these means alone will not be a holder in due course. The importance of this status is discussed in the next section.

Assignments for Security Purposes

Lending institutions, particularly mortgage bankers, often seek credit from banks and pledge as security mortgages which they have

70. Geffen v. Paletz, 312 Mass. 48, 43 N.E.2d 133 (1942).

71. Hamilton v. Browning, 94 Ind. 242, semble (1883); Pope & Slocum v. Jacobus, 10 Iowa 262 (1859); Miller v. Berry, 19 S.D. 625, 104 N.W. 311 (1905); see Merritt v. Bartholick, 36 N.Y. 44 (1867). See Note, Transfer of the Mortgagee's Interest in Florida, 14 U. of Fla.L.Rev. 98 (1961).

72. See Fletcher v. Carpenter, 37 Mich. 412 (1877).

73. In Sobel v. Mutual Devel., Inc., 313 So.2d 77 (Fla.App.1975), the court refused to find that an assignment of the mortgage included the note, but observed that such a result might follow if the assignee brought an action for reformation. See Buell v. Underwood, 65 Ala. 285 (1880); Seabury v. Henley, 174 Ala. 116, 56 So. 530 (1911); Andrews v. Townshend, 56 Super. 140, 16 St.R. 876, 1 N.Y.S. 421 (1888); id., 16 N.Y.St.Rep. 876; Loveridge v. Shurtz, 111 Mich. 618, 70 N.W. 132 (1897), semble; Foster v. Johnson, 39 Minn. 378, 40 N.W. 255 (1888), semble. See, also, Rollison, Priorities in the Law of Mortgages, 9 Notre Dame Law. 50, 86 (1933); Note Effect of Assignment Without Assigning the Debt—Formalities Necessary to Transfer the Mortgagee's Title to the Mortgaged Property, 36 N.C.L.Rev. 225 (1958) discussing Gregg v. Williamson, 246 N.C. 356, 48 S.E. 2d 481 (1957).

originated and hold in portfolio. For example, a mortgage banker may deliver to his bank a package of numerous notes and mortgages on a temporary basis in return for a short-term loan or a line of credit. When the mortgage banker has arranged a sale of the same loans to a permanent investor, he will retrieve them from the bank, either replacing them with others or retiring the bank's debt which they secured. The practice is known as "mortgage warehousing." A similar procedure is sometimes used when the mortgage banker has made a construction loan; he may deposit the loan documents with his bank as security for credit advanced to him during the construction period, and will recover and cancel the documents when the project is completed and the permanent or "take-out" loan is made by another lender.[74]

In order to save time and expense, pledges of notes and mortgages of this type are often handled in a very informal way, without either the execution of written assignments or the indorsement of the notes. Sometimes even the physical delivery of the documents to the bank is omitted, with the bank appointing the mortgagee its "custodian" over the papers. Seldom is any assignment to the bank recorded, even if one is executed. The informality of the arrangement is advantageous, but it presents certain risks if third parties intervene.[75]

It is ordinarily assumed that only Article 3 of the UCC, which deals with notes and other commercial paper, has relevance to transfers by mortgagees. Article 9, which concerns transactions secured by chattels or other personal property, does not generally affect real estate mortgages; Section 9–104(j) provides that the Article does not apply "to the creation or transfer of an interest in or lien on real estate * * *." However, when the real estate lien and the associated obligation are themselves being employed as security for a separate debt, it may be argued that the documents (the note and mortgage) are personal property rather than real estate, and that their pledge is covered by Article 9. In fact, the draftsmen of the Code seem to have desired exactly this result, as indicated by the Official Comment to Section 9–102:

> The owner of Blackacre borrows $10,000 from his neighbor, and secures his note by a mortgage on Blackacre. This Article is not applicable to the creation of the real estate mortgage. However, when the mortgagee in turn pledges this note and mortgage to secure his own obligation to X, this Article is applicable to the security interest thus created in the note and mortgage. Whether the transfer of the collateral for the note, i. e., the mortgagee's interest in

74. See Kratovil, Modern Mortgage Law & Practice § 199 (1972).

75. See § 5.35 regarding partial assignments and participations, which may also be given for security purposes.

> Blackacre, requires further action (such as recording an assignment of the mortgagee's interest) is left to real estate law.

If the comment is taken at face value, it has important implications for pledgees of mortgage paper. As between the pledgor and pledgee, no particular formality is required; [76] for example, a written security agreement or assignment would be quite sufficient. However, to "perfect" the pledgee's interest as against a third party (such as a subsequent taker from the pledgor who claims an interest in the same paper), transfer of possession of the paper to the pledgee is absolutely essential.[77] This is clearly necessary if the note is negotiable, and probably if it is nonnegotiable as well.[78] Arrangements in which the documents are left with the mortgagee-pledgor, or with his employee who is designated the pledgee's "custodian", are of dubious validity. Moreover, it seems that even the most formal written "assignment" imaginable will not perfect the pledge if the note is not delivered. The same is true of filing a financing statement under Article 9 with the appropriate governmental office. Only a pledge with possession transferred will suffice.

The commentators have generally concluded that Article 9 was intended to have no effect on pledges of notes and mortgages.[79] A Florida appellate court has agreed, but apparently under the erroneous impression that if the UCC applied, it would require the filing of financing statements to perfect the assignments, a procedure which it thought too foreign to the customs of the mortgage industry.[80] Several California cases have held that the UCC does cover pledges of notes and mortgages, but none of them deal with the proper mode of

76. U.C.C. § 9–201; the general statute of frauds may, however, require a writing.

77. U.C.C. § 9–304(1). Under certain limited circumstances, perfection of a security interest in an instrument may be accomplished without possession for 21 days. See U.C.C. 9–304 (4), (5).

78. U.C.C. § 9–105(g) defines "instrument" to include only a paper which "is of a type which is in ordinary course of business transferred by delivery with any necessary indorsement or assignment." It might be argued that a note secured by a mortgage is not customarily transferred merely by delivery, but that an assignment of the mortgage is also usual. See Rucker v. State Exchange Bank, 355 So.2d 171 (Fla.App.1978). Where this argument leads is not at all clear; perhaps it would mean that filing of a financing statement is necessary to perfect.

79. See, e. g., Coogan, Kripke & Weiss, The Outer Fringes of Article 9: Subordination Agreements, Security Interests in Money and Deposits, Negative Pledge Clauses, and Participation Agreements, 79 Harv.L.Rev. 229, 270 (1965); Gilmore, Security Interests in Personal Property § 10.6 (1965); cf. Comment, An Article Nine Scope Problem—Mortgages, Leases, and Rents As Collateral, 47 U.Colo.L.Rev. 449 (1976).

80. Rucker v. State Exchange Bank, 355 So.2d 171 (Fla.App.1978). See also In re Bristol Associates, 505 F.2d 1059 (3d Cir. 1974), holding an assignment of a landlord's interest in a lease as security for a loan was not covered by Article 9.

perfecting the transfer.[81] From the practitioner's viewpoint, the only safe approach is to comply with both the UCC (by delivery of the note) and real estate law (which for reasons to be discussed later, makes the recording of a written assignment desirable).[82] As a matter of policy, the application of the UCC is not so unreasonable. Delivery of the note to the pledgee is usually easy and inexpensive to accomplish, and most creditors would insist on it in any event.

§ 5.29 Negotiability and Negotiation

We have already indicated that holder in due course status may be exceedingly useful to the transferee of a note secured by a mortgage. The reason why this is so is elaborated in a later section, but in essence it is that the HDC takes free of many defenses to which the note would be subject in the hands of the assignor, including such important defenses as failure of consideration, payment, and even certain tyes of fraud. In this section we explore the prerequisites to achieving HDC status. They are essentially two: the note itself must be in the proper form, that is, *negotiable*; and the process by which it is transferred must be appropriate, that is, a *negotiation*. Works on the UCC or commercial paper discuss these two concepts at length,[83] and we will provide only a brief outline of them here, with special reference to the unique bearing which mortgage security may have on them.

81. Bank of California v. Leone, 37 Cal.App.3d 444, 112 Cal.Rptr. 394 (1974) ("one-action" rule is inapplicable to the pledgee of an assignment for security purposes of a note and deed of trust; the pledgee may seek a personal judgment without first attempting to realize on the security); Black v. Sullivan, 48 Cal.App.3d 557, 122 Cal.Rptr. 119 (1975) (assignees of note and deed of trust for security purposes not bound by California law requiring the beneficiary of a deed of trust to give a statement of balance due on demand); Riebe v. Budget Financial Corp., 264 Cal.App.2d 576, 70 Cal.Rptr. 654 (1968) (pledge of note and deed of trust held proper when made to personal property broker who, by law, could not accept real estate security.) See Stewart, Trust Deed Collateral Loans and the California Commercial Code, 2 West.St. L.Rev. 57 (1974).

82. See § 5.34, infra. An interesting sidelight to the issues discussed in the text is the manner in which the pledgee of a note and mortgage should attempt to realize on his security once the pledgor has defaulted. Under the UCC the creditor is entitled to retain the property in satisfaction of the debt (§ 9–505) or to dispose of it in a commercially reasonable manner (§ 9–504). Presumably this means that the pledgee could treat the note and mortgage as his property and foreclose it without further ado. See Tamiami Abstract & Title Co. v. Berman, 324 So.2d 137 (Fla. App.1975); State Realty Co. v. MacNiel Bros. Co., 334 Mass. 244, 135 N.E.2d 241 (1956). On the other hand, if the pledge is the equivalent of a real estate mortgage (a mortgage of a mortgage?), perhaps judicial foreclosure of the pledge itself would be necessary.

83. See, e. g., White & Summers, Uniform Commercial Code (1972), at ch. 14.

Negotiability

The Code spells out the requirements of negotiability as follows:

> Any writing to be a negotiable instrument within this Article must
>
> (a) be signed by the maker * * *; and
>
> (b) contain an unconditional promise * * * to pay a sum certain in money and no other promise, order, obligation or power given by the maker . . . except as authorized by this Article; and
>
> (c) be payable on demand or at a definite time; and
>
> (d) be payable to order or to bearer.[84]

Mortgage notes are ordinarily signed by the maker, and so requirement (a) poses no particular problem. Requirement (b) obviously means that promises to maintain the property, to insure, to refrain from waste, and the like must not be included in the note; they are typically put in the mortgage itself instead. Moreover, the note must not incorporate the mortgage by reference, with two exceptions: it may refer to the mortgage for rights as to prepayment or acceleration.[85] Any further incorporation will make the note nonnegotiable.[86] There is, however, no objection to a statement in the note that it is secured by a mortgage.[87] These rules may seem unduly technical. They arise out of the idea that the holder of a negotiable instrument should be able to ascertain all of its essential terms from its face.[88] In the mortgage context this makes little sense; no intelligent transferee would take the note without inspecting both it and the mortgage which secures it, and it is hard to see any policy rationale forbidding incorporation, or even placing the documents on the same piece of paper. Still, the law is clear and easy enough to observe, with loss of negotiability the price of a violation.

Requirement (d) is extremely significant: the note must be payable to bearer or to order. Bearer notes are rare in mortgage transactions; the note is ordinarily made payable to the mortgagee. To be negotiable, some "order" language must be included, such as "I promise to pay to the order of John Mortgagee" or "I promise to pay to John Mortgagee or order." "Order" is a magical term in this context. In effect, it warns the mortgagor that he is signing a negotiable instrument, with the potential liabilities which that implies. Perhaps many mortgagors have no idea what this means, but the rule is there, all the same. The official comment indicates that the courts should take

84. U.C.C. § 3–104(1).

85. U.C.C. § 3–105(1)(c).

86. Holly Hill Acres, Ltd. v. Charter Bank of Gainsville, 314 So.2d 209 (Fla.App.1975).

87. U.C.C. § 3–105(1)(c) and comments 3 and 8.

88. U.C.C. § 3–105 at comment 8.

this terminology requirement strictly, and that doubtful cases should be resolved against negotiability.[89]

Negotiation

Once we have determined that the note is in proper form and thus negotiable, we must scrutinize the process by which it is transferred. We have already seen that the transfer must be by indorsement (if the note is in "order" rather than "bearer" form) and that possession of it must be delivered to the transferee.[90] In addition, the transferee, to be a HDC must take it for value, in good faith, and without notice that it is overdue, has been dishonored, or is subject to any defense or claim to it on the part of any person.[91] For our purposes value is not a difficult issue; an executory promise to give value does not count, but giving a negotiable instrument does.[92] Taking the transfer in satisfaction of a pre-existing claim is also value.[93]

The tests of good faith and lack of notice are more complicated. In general they are treated by the courts as much the same thing: if one has notice he cannot take in good faith, and vice versa. One possible distinction has been suggested. Knowledge by the assignee of a pervasive pattern of fraud or misdealing by the assignor might not give him notice of a defect in a particular transaction, but might still make it impossible for him to take in good faith.[94]

The Code defines notice as including both actual knowledge and facts and circumstances which indicate that the assignee "has reason to know." [95] There is an element of objectivity in this test; it suggests that one cannot be wilfully ignorant of information of which an ordinary person would have become aware.[96] While the application of this idea can be quite unpredictable, some cases are easy. The notice may appear on the face of the documents. For example, a note's stated maturity date may show that it is overdue; [97] its stated inter-

89. U.C.C. § 3–104 at comment 5.

90. U.C.C. § 3–202(1); see § 5.28, supra at notes 55–56; Bailey v. Mills, 257 Ala. 239, 58 So.2d 446 (1952) (endorsement on separate piece of paper, clipped to note, insufficient for negotiation); Borgonovo v. Henderson, 182 Cal.App.2d 220, 6 Cal.Rptr. 236 (1960) (unauthorized delivery of note by escrowee to assignee does not result in negotiation).

91. U.C.C. § 3–302(1).

92. U.C.C. § 3–303(a), (c).

93. U.C.C. § 3–303(b). Value does not mean the face amount of the note, and a purchase at a discount does not alone impair the assignee's HDC status; Gribble v. Mauerhan, 188 Cal.App.2d 221, 10 Cal.Rptr. 296 (1961).

94. See Financial Credit Corp. v. Williams, 246 Md. 575, 229 A.2d 712 (1967); White & Summers, Uniform Commercial Code 471 (1972).

95. U.C.C. § 1–201(25).

96. See Woodard v. Bruce, 47 Tenn. App. 525, 339 S.W.2d 143 (1960); cf. New Jersey Mfg. & Inv. Corp. v. Calvetti, 68 N.J.Super. 18, 171 A.2d 321 (1961).

97. Cast Stone Co. v. McGowan, —— Ohio App. ——, 102 N.E.2d 615 (1951); see also Stewart v. Thornton, 116 Ariz. 107, 568 P.2d 414 (1977) (note

est rate may be obviously usurious; it may have erasures, blanks, or visible evidence of forgery or modification.[98] The same problems may be apparent upon an inspection of the mortgage which accompanies the note; if it is actually delivered to the assignee, he will be held to knowledge of its contents, including discrepancies of the type mentioned.[99]

Another type of notice may come from sources outside the documents. If the mortgagor-maker telephones or visits the assignee prior to the assignment and says "Don't buy that note. I signed it under duress (or fraud, or without consideration, or what have you)", the assignee must at least investigate or he will imperil his HDC status. Even information from third parties, if appearing to be reasonably reliable, will have the same effect.[1] Moreover, the information may be about the assignor's objectionable or fraudulent business practices in transactions of this type generally, rather than about the particular transaction in question.[2] This view may seem extreme, but there is little doubt that the courts are moving, if cautiously, in this direction. The maker's case for piercing the HDC veil is strengthened on such facts if it can be shown that the paper was sold to the assignee at an unusually large discount, since that suggests that he recognized the risk of losing his HDC protection.[3]

Finally, the courts are beginning to recognize quite widely the "close-connectedness" promulgated by the New Jersey Supreme Court in 1967 in Unico v. Owen.[4] If the business relationships between assignor and assignee are suspiciously close, notice may be imputed or good faith denied on that basis alone, without any direct showing of knowledge on the part of the assignee. White and Summers suggest

assigned within 48-hour recission period under federal law; assignee held subject to maker's recission.)

98. See U.C.C. § 3–304(1).

99. United States Finance Co. v. Jones, 285 Ala. 105, 229 So.2d 495 (1969) (notice of completion dated simultaneously with promissory note, suggesting that work by assignor on maker's house would not actually be completed); HIMC Investment Co. v. Siciliano, 103 N.J.Super. 27, 246 A.2d 502 (1968) (accompanying documents disclosed payment of commission in violation of N. J. Secondary Mortgage Loan Act.)

1. Financial Credit Corp. v. Williams, note 94, supra (newspaper stories of widespread fraud by assignor.)

2. Id. Local Acceptance Co. v. Kinkade, 361 S.W.2d 830 (Mo.1962); U. S. Finance Co. v. Jones, 285 Ala. 105 229 So.2d 495 (1969); Slaughter v. Jefferson Federal Sav. & Loan Ass'n, 361 F.Supp. 590 (D.D.C.1975), 538 F. 2d 397 (D.C.Cir. 1976).

3. Stewart v. Thornton, 116 Ariz. 107, 568 P.2d 414 (1977); Financial Credit Corp. v. Williams, 246 Md. 575, 229 A.2d 712 (1967); United States Finance Co. v. Jones, 285 Ala. 105, 229 So.2d 495 (1969).

4. 50 N.J. 101, 232 A.2d 405 (1967). The case involved a seller of recordings and record players which took notes from its customers, and then assigned them to a finance company. The assignee was formed for the purpose of taking paper from the particular assignor, and largely controlled the assignor's business. The assignee established all credit guidelines for the assignor and supervised its business and records closely. See 4 UCC Rep.Serv, 542, 551–52 (1967).

the following factors as influential in establishing "close-connectedness",[5] although clearly not all five are simultaneously necessary.

(1) The assignee drafts or provides the forms used by the assignor.

(2) The assignee establishes or approves the assignor's procedures, such as the interest rate, credit standards, or appraisers.

(3) The assignee independently checks the debtor's credit or has other direct contact with the debtor.

(4) The assignee customarily takes all or a substantial part of the assignor's paper.[6]

(5) The assignee and assignor have common or affiliated ownership or management.[7]

Other factors, not always mentioned in the opinions of the courts, also seem to play a role. The HDC doctrine is more likely to be rejected if the debtor is a consumer rather than a business-person,[8] if the debtor has been shamefully and egregiously treated by the assignor,[9] and if the assignee bought the paper at a deep discount. The results of the cases are not wholly consistent, but there is little doubt that the HDC doctrine is easier to overcome now than a few years ago.[10]

§ 5.30 Statutory and Regulatory Limitations on the Holder In Due Course Doctrine

A few scattered states have reversed or modified the holder in due course doctrine by individualized statutes; their details vary and

5. White & Summers, Uniform Commercial Code (1972), at § 14–8; the factors have been revised slightly in the text to focus on transactions secured by mortgages.

6. Financial Credit Corp. v. Williams, supra note 3; United States Financial Co. v. Jones, supra note 3.

7. Home Security Corp. v. Gentry, 235 So.2d 249 (Miss.1970); see also Western Sav. & Loan Ass'n v. Diamond Lazy K Guest Ranch, Inc., 18 Ariz.App. 256, 501 P.2d 432 (1972).

8. Most of the cases involve contests between consumers (as makers) and finance companies (as holders); but see Kaw Valley State Bank v. Riddle, 219 Kan. 550, 549 P.2d 927 (1976), applying the close-connectedness doctrine even though the maker was a businessman and the holder a bank.

9. See Jones v. Approved Bancredit Corp., 256 A.2d 739 (Del.1969).

10. The finding is by no means automatic, and the maker is often expected to produce some evidence of notice, lack of good faith, or close-connectedness; see Ritz v. Karstenson, 39 Ill.App.3d 877, 350 N.E.2d 870 (1976); Jeminson v. Montgomery Real Estate & Co., 47 Mich.App. 731, 210 N.W.2d 14 (1973); Slaughter v. Jefferson Federal Sav. & Loan Ass'n, 538 F.2d 397 (C.A.D.C.1976), all rejecting the "close-connectedness" doctrine for lack of evidence. While the Code indicates that once the maker has shown that he has a defense, the holder has the burden of establishing that he is a HDC, the cases do not always follow this allocation of proof strictly. See, e. g., Austin v. Atlas Subsidiaries of Mississippi, Inc., 223 So.2d 297 (Miss. 1969); cf. Kreutz v. Wolff, 560 S.W. 2d 271 (Mo.App.1977).

space will not permit a complete discussion of them.[11] This section will concentrate instead on three enactments having nationwide importance which in some circumstances alter the normal provisions of the UCC giving HDC status to holders of negotiable notes. The first is the Uniform Consumer Credit Code, adopted by eleven state legislatures at this writing.[12] The second is the Federal Trade Commission's "Holder In Due Course Rule", which has nationwide application. The third is the Uniform Land Transactions Act, recently promulgated by the National Conference of Commissioners on Uniform State Laws and not yet adopted in any state. In all three of these contexts we will concentrate on the impact on mortgage transactions of the rule under discussion.

Uniform Consumer Credit Code

Before we examine the operational aspect of the UCCC, it is first necessary to outline the two major fact situations in which it applies. As the discussion of the negotiability concept in the preceding section shows, many litigated cases have arisen because a home improvement contractor or other vendor of goods or housing has taken from his customer a negotiable note secured by a mortgage on the customer's home. The vendor then negotiates the note to a finance company or institution. When the customer discovers that the vendor will not perform as promised, or finds that the papers he has signed constitute a note and mortgage even though he did not so understand them when he signed, the stage is set for a battle over the assignee's HDC status. For present purposes, we emphasize that the original note and mortgage run to the vendor as payee-mortgagee. We might term this "vendor financing"; in the language of the UCCC, it is a *consumer credit sale.*[13]

Compare the following alternative method of arranging the transaction. The customer is introduced to the financial institution before the documents are signed. The institution gives a loan to the customer, who immediately pays that money to the vendor. The customer also gives a note and mortgage directly to the lender. The vendor, having been fully paid, nonetheless performs his contract in-

11. See, e. g., Md.Ann.Code art. 83, § 147; Mass.Gen.Laws Ann. ch. 225 § 12C; 9 Vt.Stat.Ann. § 2455; Wash. Rev.Code Ann. 63.14.020. See Randolph Nat. Bank v. Vail, 131 Vt. 390, 308 A.2d 588 (1973).

12. The UCCC was originally promulgated in 1968, and that version has been adopted by eight states at this writing: Colorado, Idaho, Indiana, Oklahoma, South Carolina, Utah, Wisconsin, and Wyoming. A new version was released in 1974 and has been adopted by three states: Iowa, Kansas, and Maine. All references in the text are to the 1974 version. Both versions contain the basic prohibition on the use of negotiable instruments in consumer transactions, but the details vary, as do the actual enactments of the states. Space does not permit an elaborate discussion of these variations. See Uniform Consumer Credit Code, Official 1974 Text with Comments, 7 Unif.L.Ann. 158, 164–66 (1977 supp.).

13. U.C.C.C. § 1.301(12).

adequately. The transaction might be referred to as "third-party financing" to distinguish it from the "vendor financing" of the preceding paragraph; the UCCC calls it a *consumer loan*.[14]

The economic effect of these two transactions may be virtually identical, but in legal contemplation they are quite different. In the consumer credit sale, the lender's HDC status is critical to his ability to collect the debt despite the vendor's default. By contrast, the lender in the consumer loan situation appears to have no need at all of the HDC doctrine. Defenses which the customer could raise against the vendor cannot be raised against him, not because he holds in due course, but because he does not hold paper which originally ran to the vendor; the debtor-lender transaction is, at least on its face, entirely separate from the debtor-vendor one. Of course, the lender might later assign the note and mortgage to another financial institution, and it might well be a HDC, but even there HDC status would be relevant only to ward off defenses arising out of the debtor-lender aspect of the transaction.

In the recent past the more disreputable vendors have usually employed the consumer credit sale method of financing, while those of greater honesty have generally used the consumer loan approach. Yet it is clear that either type of transaction can have the same bleak result for the debtor: half-finished or defective workmanship accompanied by an absolute and secured obligation to pay the full price. It is to the credit of the draftsmen of the UCCC that they recognized that either situation can be unfairly disastrous to consumers, and that they took steps to address each.[15]

In the consumer credit sale situation, the UCCC's basic approach is an attack on the HDC doctrine. It provides bluntly that the vendor "may not take a negotiable instrument other than a check * * * as evidence of the obligation of the consumer." [16] In addition, if the vendor violates this provision by taking a negotiable instrument from the consumer, any assignee of the paper is subject to all claims and defenses which the consumer could have raised against the vendor arising out of the sale; [17] the HDC doctrine is abrogated. The underlying assumption of the UCCC seems to be that any lender who buys consumer paper from a vendor should be expected to superintend the vendor's behavior, or omit to do so at its peril. Note that no "close-connectedness" need be shown; in a sense, the Code conclusively presumes the connection from the very fact of assignment of the paper.

14. U.C.C.C. § 1.301(15).

15. See comments to 1974 Official Text, supra note 12, at 165–66; Note, Consumer Defenses and Financers as Holders in Due Course, 4 Conn.L.Rev. 83 (1971); Note, Consumer Notes and Rights of Assignee, 56 Minn.L.Rev. 510 (1972).

16. U.C.C.C. § 3.307.

17. U.C.C.C. § 3.404(1); See Circle v. Jim Walter Homes, Inc., 535 F.2d 583 (C.A.Okl.1976).

In the consumer loan situation the matter is more complicated. In some consumer loan cases the lender and the vendor are actually completely unconnected; for example, the customer may have selected each in an entirely separate shopping effort, and the lender may have no knowledge whatever of the vendor's business operations. Yet the Code's draftsmen wished to subject the lender to claims and defenses arising out of the vendor-debtor transaction if it could be shown that some relationship existed between the lender and vendor which would justify lender liability. They listed the objectionable relationships as follows:

> (a) the lender knows that the seller * * * arranged for the extension of credit by the lender for a commission, brokerage, or referral fee;
>
> (b) the lender is a person related to the seller * * *, unless the relationship is remote or is not a factor in the transaction;
>
> (c) the seller * * * guarantees the loan or otherwise assumes the risk of loss by the lender upon the loan;
>
> (d) the lender directly supplies the seller * * * with the contract document used by the consumer to evidence the loan, and the seller * * * has knowledge of the credit terms and participates in preparation of the document;
>
> (e) the loan is conditioned upon the consumer's purchase * * * of the property or services from the particular seller * * *, but the lender's payment of proceeds of the loan to the seller * * * does not in itself establish that the loan was so conditioned; or
>
> (f) the lender, before he makes the consumer loan, has knowledge or, from his course of dealing with the particular seller * * * or his records, notice of substantial complaints by other buyers * * * of the particular seller's * * * failure or refusal to perform his contracts with them and of the particular seller's * * * failure to remedy his defaults within a reasonable time after notice to him of the complaints.[18]

Where one or more of these features is present, the lender is subject to both defenses and affirmative claims growing out of the transaction. The factors listed are reminiscent of the "close-connectedness" doctrine developed by the courts in some HDC cases, and discussed in the preceding section, but the context is different, for here the lender is not a HDC at all, but the payee-mortgagee under a purportedly separate transaction. The effect of the list is to place the lender in the position of a non-HDC assignee. Indeed, his position may be even worse, for the Code says he is "subject to all *claims* * * * arising from that sale," [19] although only to the extent of the amount

18. U.C.C.C. § 3.405(1).

19. U.C.C.C. § 3.405(1), (2).

owing to the lender when he receives notice of the claim. Suppose a home improvement contractor has properly completed the work, but in the process has damaged some other part of the house. Can this affirmative claim be asserted against the third party lender if his relationship with the contractor fits the list above? Ordinarily even an assignee of a note, whether an HDC or not, is not affirmatively liable for obligations of the assignor not contained in the note; [20] perhaps liability might be extended for obligations set out in the accompanying mortgage, such as a promise to pay interest on a tax impound account or to permit fire insurance proceeds to be used for restoration of the property.[21] But the UCCC, if taken at face value, goes much further; it seems to make the lender the vendor's alter ego for purposes of all liabilities "arising from that sale." The same potential liabilities, incidentally, face an assignee in a transaction of the consumer credit sale type under the Code. He too is subject to "all claims and defenses of the consumer." [22] Perhaps the courts will interpret "claim" or "arising out of" more restrictively; [23] if they do not, the Code has accomplished a rather remarkable extension of the vendor's liability to those who finance his work.

The application of the UCCC to mortgage transactions is limited sharply by the definitions contained in the code. Obviously refinancings and other loans not related to a sale are not covered. In addition the Code will apply only if the debtor is an individual rather than an organization [24] and the debt or sale is primarily for a personal, family, household, or agricultural purpose.[25] The original creditor must be regularly engaged in transactions of the kind involved.[26] If the sale is of goods or services (such as home improvements) rather than an interest in land, the Code applies only if the amount financed

20. Black v. Sullivan, 48 Cal.App.3d 557, 122 Cal.Rptr. 119 (1975); Williams Constr. Co. v. Standard-Pacific Corp., 254 Cal.App.2d 442, 61 Cal. Rptr. 912 (1967). See official comment, Unif. Land Trans. Act § 1–313.

21. A rule imposing affirmative liability on the Department of Housing and Urban Development when it has taken an assignment of an FHA-insured mortgage has been applied on a showing that HUD provided all documentation and closely supervised the making of the original mortgage; see Trans-Bay Engineers & Builders, Inc. v. Lynn, 551 F.2d 370 (C.A.D.C.1975); Lindy v. Lynn, 395 F.Supp. 769 (E.D. Pa.1974); F. W. Eversley & Co. v. East New York Non-Profit HDFC, Inc., 409 F.Supp. 791 (S.D.N.Y.1976). These cases also relieve the original mortgagee of further liability when the assignment has been completed.

22. U.C.C.C. § 3.404; again, liability is limited to the amount owing to the assignee at the time he has notice of the claim.

23. The official comment says cryptically, "Suggestions that * * * lenders should be responsible for * * * product liability that might arise out of the transaction are rejected as neither feasible nor reasonable." Official Comment, supra note 12, at 166. Precisely what is meant by "product liability" we are not told, and there seems to be no warrant in the Code itself for excluding product liability claims.

24. U.C.C.C. § 1.301(12)(a)(ii), (15)(a)(i).

25. U.C.C.C. § 1.301(12)(a)(iii), (15)(a)(ii).

26. U.C.C.C. § 1.301(12)(a)(i), 15(a).

does not exceed a dollar amount which is readjusted biennially in accordance with changes in the Consumer Price Index,[27] and is $45,000 at this writing.[28] Finally, the Code is inapplicable if the debt is secured by a mortgage and the interest rate is 12 percent or lower.[29] Since interest rates on first mortgage loans on homes have virtually never exceeded 12 percent in the United States, the UCCC's principal mortgage law application is in second mortgage transactions which finance the sale of goods or home improvements. The protections given to consumers cannot be waived,[30] and hence are likely to be highly effective in litigated cases. Whether they will bring about widespread changes in the home improvement industry, as the draftsmen hoped, remains to be seen.

Federal Trade Commission Rule

Many of the concepts of the UCCC were borrowed by the Federal Trade Commission in 1975 when it adopted a "trade regulation rule" entitled "Preservation of Consumers' Claims and Defenses." [31] The rule simply makes it an unfair trade practice for a seller of goods or services to finance his sale without including in the "consumer credit contract"—a note or other evidence of debt—language which makes the lender subject to the consumer's claims and defenses. The rule spells out the exact language which must be used.[32] Recovery is limited to the amounts the debtor has paid under the contract,[33] as contrasted with the UCCC which permits recovery up to the amount owing to the lender.[34]

27. U.C.C.C. § 1.301(12)(a)(v), 15(a)(iv).

28. U.C.C.C. § 1.106; the dollar amounts are changed on July 1 of even numbered years; they change only in multiples of ten percent and only if the Consumer Price Index (1967=100) changes by at least ten percent.

29. U.C.C.A. § 1.301(12(b)(ii), (15)(b)(ii), and official comments thereto.

30. "An agreement may not limit or waive the claims or defenses of a consumer under this section." U.C.C.C. § 3.404(4); § 3.405(4).

31. 16 CFR 433.1–.2; 40 Fed.Reg. 53506 (Nov. 18, 1975). See also Guidelines on Trade Regulation Rule Concerning Preservation of Consumers' Claims and Defenses, 41 Fed.Reg. 20022 (May 14, 1976), discussing the background of the rule in detail; Note, The New FTC Trade Regulation Rule on Holder in Due Course, 13 Houston L.Rev. 789 (1976). See generally Report of the National Commission of Consumer Finance, Consumer Credit in the United States (1972).

32. The language must appear in at least ten point bold-face type and reads as follows; "NOTICE. ANY HOLDER OF THIS CONSUMER CREDIT CONTRACT IS SUBJECT TO ALL CLAIMS AND DEFENSES WHICH THE DEBTOR COULD ASSERT AGAINST THE SELLER OF GOODS OR SERVICES OBTAINED WITH THE PROCEEDS HEREOF. RECOVERY HEREUNDER BY THE DEBTOR SHALL NOT EXCEED AMOUNTS PAID BY THE DEBTOR HEREUNDER."

The quoted language applies to consumer loans by third-party lenders; the text applicable to vendor paper which is assigned to a lender is similar.

33. See text quoted in note 32, supra.

34. The questions raised in the text at notes 19–23, supra, regarding the

Both consumer loans and consumer credit sales, in the UCCC's parlance, are covered by the FTC rule. If third-party lender financing is the mode employed (as the FTC rule terms it, a "purchase money loan"), there is a type of "close-connectedness" criterion which must be satisfied, but it is much simpler and looser than the UCCC's. The lender is brought within the rule's ambit if the seller of the goods or services refers consumers to the lender or is affiliated with the creditor by common control, contract, or business arrangement.[35] Another interesting difference between the UCCC and the FTC rule is that the latter does not apply to sales of interests in real estate, irrespective of the amount or interest rate.[36] It does, however, apply to sales of goods or services even if a mortgage on real estate is taken to secure payment of the purchase price.

In most other respects the coverage of the FTC rule and the UCCC are similar. The FTC rule applies only to natural persons who buy goods or services for personal, family, or household use.[37] The lender must be engaged in financing such transactions in the ordinary course of business.[38] By virtue of a reference to the Truth-in-Lending Act and its accompanying Regulation Z, the FTC rule covers only purchases involving an expenditure of $25,000 or less.[39]

Uniform Land Transactions Act

Promulgated in 1975 and extensively amended in 1977, the Uniform Land Transactions Act has not been adopted by any legislature at this writing. Nonetheless, the ULTA provides an interesting treatment of the holder-in-due-course doctrine which may form the basis for future state legislation. Unlike the UCCC and the FTC rule, the ULTA does not attempt to deal with the third party lender who provides purchase money financing to a vendor's customers and who is also closely related to the vendor; it deals only with direct assignment, as by a vendor to the lender. This seems an unfortunate omission, since as we have noted either form of transaction can give rise to the same abuses.

The ULTA's basic position is that, absent a waiver, the debtor may assert against the assignee all claims and defenses which arise

scope of possible claims seem equally applicable, and equally unanswered, here.

35. 16 CFR 433.1(d); a "business arrangement" is further defined as "any understanding, procedure, course of dealing, or arrangement, formal or informal, between a creditor and a seller, in connection with the sale of goods or services to consumers or the financing thereof." This language appears to be broad enough to cover virtually every purchase-money loan in which the lender knows what the use of the funds will be; a more refined definition, like that of U.C.C.C. § 3.405(1), would be preferable.

36. 16 CFR 433.1(c).

37. 16 CFR 433.1(b).

38. 16 CFR 433.1(c).

39. 16 CFR 433.1(d), (e).

before the debtor receives notice of the assignment.[40] The language of the act imposes no specific limit on affirmative claims, but since it provides that the assignee's "rights * * * are subject to" such claims, the courts would probably not permit recoveries against the assignee in excess of the total debt, or perhaps the unpaid balance. The act does not limit claims to those growing out of the same transaction in which the debt was incurred, but this may be largely irrelevant if a limitation on the amount of claims is imposed as suggested above; in effect a "claim" would be viewed as a setoff or counterclaim to the assignee's foreclosure action or suit on the debt, and the act's only effect might be to permit the introduction of otherwise non-germane counterclaims in the lender's action.[41]

The ULTA's protection of debtors from actions by assignees is broader than that of the UCCC and the FTC rule, since it is not on its face confined to consumer debt or to junior mortgages. However the ULTA, unlike the other enactments mentioned, permits the debtor to waive his ULTA protections to an extent which will place the assignee in the same position as a holder in due course.[42] No waiver is permitted in cases in which an owner-occupant of a home[43] gives a mortgage and note to a vendor who is in the business of selling real estate, or gives a junior mortgage on his home.[44] Waivers are allowed in first mortgages, a policy designed to protect the secondary mortgage market and attract investors to home mortgages;[45] presumably waiver clauses will be included in all first mortgages in jurisdictions which adopt the ULTA. The secondary market in junior mortgages is more limited, and is not considered essential to national housing policy. The net result is that the coverage of the ULTA in protecting debtors from the HDC doctrine is roughly equivalent to that of the UCCC and the FTC rule.

40. U.L.T.A. § 3–206(a). The provision is copied essentially verbatim from U.C.C. § 9–318.

41. The official comment to U.L.T.A. § 1–313 states "Some recent acts have subjected the assignee to "all claims and defenses" of a consumer-obligor. This Act, however, speaks only to defenses." The statement is obviously erroneous, since § 3–206 explicitly refers to claims as well as defenses. The same comment also raises, but does not answer, the question whether a consumer can recover payments already made to an assignee; in light of the "claims" language of § 3–206, an affirmative answer seems probable. Compare Bank of Wyandotte v. Woodrow, 394 F.Supp. 550 (W.D.Mo. 1975).

42. U.L.T.A. § 1–314. In effect, this means that an effective waiver clause will still leave the assignee subject to so-called "real" defenses, but not to "personal" defenses; see § 5.31, infra.

43. The act's term is "protected party", which includes an occupying owner or purchaser of a building containing four or fewer dwelling units on not more than three acres.

44. U.L.T.A. § 1–313.

45. Official Comment, U.L.T.A. § 1–313. Whether HDC protection is really necessary to attract investors to the home mortgage market is questionable, but there is, as the comment points out, little evidence of widespread abuses by first mortgage originators. Thus the presence or absence of HDC status probably makes little difference to either debtors or assignees.

§ 5.31 Rights of Holders In Due Course

If the assignee of a note secured by a mortgage is a holder in due course, he is free of most of the defenses which the maker of the note might attempt to assert against collection or foreclosure. The UCC lists certain defenses which even HDC status does not immunize the assignee against; they are traditionally termed "real" defenses:

(a) infancy, to the extent that it is a defense to a simple contract; and

(b) such other incapacity, or duress, or illegality of the transaction, as renders the obligation of the party a nullity; and

(c) such misrepresentation as has induced the party to sign the instrument with neither knowledge nor reasonable opportunity to obtain knowledge of its character or its essential terms; and

(d) discharge in insolvency proceedings; and

(e) any other discharge of which the holder has notice when he takes the instrument.[46]

This definition of the real defenses is largely straightforward. Incapacity, duress, and illegality may make a note void or voidable, depending on the jurisdiction and the circumstances. The Code leaves the void-voidable distinction to other state law,[47] but only facts which would make the note void can be asserted against a HDC; indeed, that is the very definition of a void instrument.

The sort of misrepresentation, described in subparagraph (c) above, which will survive negotiation to an HDC, is roughly equivalent to "fraud in the factum," but the Code attempts a more detailed definition. The official comment suggests that in judging whether the maker had a "reasonable opportunity to obtain knowledge", his age, sex, education, intelligence, business experience, linguistic ability, relationship with the payee, and the urgency of the transaction should all be considered, as should the availability of some other person, perhaps a friend or relative, who might have been able to advise him.[48] It is clear that mere "fraud in the inducement", based on false statements about the underlying performance of the payee-mortgagee rather than about the documents being signed, will not be considered a real defense.[49]

46. U.C.C. § 3–305(2).

47. See U.C.C. § 1–103.

48. U.C.C. § 3–305, official comment 7. See Colburn v. Mid-State Homes, Inc., 289 Ala. 255, 266 So.2d 865 (1972); Gallegos v. Gulf Coast Inv. Corp., 483 S.W.2d 944 (Tex.Civ.App. 1972), set aside 491 S.W.2d 659 (Sup. 1973). Hidalgo v. Surety Sav. & Loan Ass'n, 502 S.W.2d 220 (Tex.Civ.App. 1971); Cranesville Block Co. v. Pentagon Constr. Co., 51 App.Div.2d 610, 378 N.Y.S.2d 127 (1976); cf. Venable v. Payne, 138 Ga.App. 237, 225 S.E.2d 716 (1976); Leedy v. Ellsworth Constr. Co., 9 Ohio App.2d 1, 222 N.E.2d 653 (1966); Burchett v. Allied Concord Financial Corp., 74 N.M. 575, 396 P.2d 186 (1964).

49. See Federal Nat. Mortgage Ass'n v. Gregory, 426 F.Supp. 282 (E.D.

The Code defines "personal defenses"—that is, those cut off by negotiation to an HDC—by exclusion from the list quoted above. Such defenses include fraud in the inducement and some types of incapacity, duress, and illegality, as mentioned. They also include lack of consideration (which would make the note unenforceable on normal contract theory),[50] partial or total failure of consideration (e. g., the failure of the mortgagee-creditor to make the loan of money which the note is supposed to evidence an obligation to repay),[51] accord and satisfaction, waiver,[52] and any sort of setoff or counterclaim [53] which the debtor-mortgagor might raise against the original mortgagee.[54] Payment of the debt by the mortgagor is also regarded as a personal defense; its implications are so important that it is discussed in a separate section, infra.[55]

When a negotiable note is secured by a mortgage, the majority of states considering the question have held that the HDC benefits available with respect to the note apply to the mortgage as well.[56]

Wisc.1977); Citizens Nat. Bank v. Brazil, 141 Ga.App. 388, 233 S.E.2d 482 (1977); Myers v. Bank of Prattville, 341 So.2d 726 (Ala.1977); Austin v. Atlas Subsidiaries of Mississippi, 223 So.2d 297 (Miss.1969).

50. Mozingo v. North Carolina Nat. Bank, 31 N.C.App. 157, 229 S.E.2d 57 (1976), certioriari denied 291 N.C. 771, 232 S.E.2d 204; Manufacturers & Traders Trust Co. v. Murphy, 369 F. Supp. 11 (W.D.Pa.1974).

51. Mecham v. United Bank of Arizona, 107 Ariz. 437, 489 P.2d 247 (1971); Hidalgo v. Surety Sav. & Loan Ass'n, 462 S.W.2d 540 (Tex.Civ.App.1971), appeal after remand 481 S.W.2d 208 (Civ.App.1972), reversed 487 S.W.2d 702 (Sup.1972) appeal after remand 502 S.W.2d 220 (Tex.Cir.1973); Holt v. Queen City Loan & Inv. Co., 377 S.W.2d 393 (Mo.1964).

52. See, e. g., Stern v. Itkin Bros., Inc., 87 Misc.2d 538, 385 N.Y.S.2d 753 (1975), in which the mortgagor and mortgagee executed a side agreement that only the mortgage, and not the note, would be sued upon in the event of default. Such an arrangement is sometimes referred to loosely as a "non-recourse mortgage", and may be desirable for tax reasons when the mortgagor is a limited partnership. The court held that the agreement would be binding against a non-HDC holder, but would not be valid against an HDC.

53. Gramatan Co. v. D'Amico, 50 Misc.2d 233, 269 N.Y.S.2d 871 (1966).

54. Even usury is frequently no defense against an HDC, unless the usurious rate of interest is apparent on the face of the note; Szczotka v. Idelson, 228 Cal.App.2d 399, 39 Cal. Rptr. 466 (1964); cf. Davenport v. Unicapital Corp., 230 S.E.2d 905 (S.C. 1976).

55. See § 5.33, infra.

56. Carpenter v. Longan, 83 U.S. (16 Wall.) 271, 21 L.Ed. 313 (1872), the leading case; American Savings Bank & Trust Co. v. Helgesen, 64 Wash. 54, 116 P. 837, Ann.Cas.1913A, 390 (1911). See Restatement, Security, § 34; Gramatan Co. v. D'Amico, 50 Misc.2d 233, 269 N.Y.S.2d 871 (1966). Courts have held that the same is true even though there has not been an assignment or delivery of the mortgage. Hawley v. Bibb, 69 Ala. 52 (1881); see Morgan v. Farmington Coal & Coke Co., 97 W. Va. 83, 94, 124 S.E. 591, 596 (1924). And it has been held to be unnecessary for the mortgagor to be a party to the note. Gabbert v. Schwartz, 69 Ind. 450 (1880). Where the security takes the form of a trust deed mortgage with the conveyance in trust to a third party as trustee, the holder in due course of the note is held entitled to the security free from defenses. Mayes v. Robinson, 93 Mo. 114, 122, 5 S.W. 611, 613

Thus, a HDC may foreclose the mortgage despite fraud in the inducement, failure of consideration, or other personal defenses. This rule has been criticized as an unwarranted extension of the rights of holders of commercial paper,[57] but it is firmly entrenched and seems entirely justified. To the extent that secondary mortgage market investors regard the HDC doctrine as a significant attraction,[58] for example, it is clear that they do so only because the mortgage remedies are a part of it.

Some limitations exist on this "negotiable mortgage" concept. Obviously the mortgage cannot be asserted by the HDC if by its very terms it is unavailable, even though the note contains no reference to the mortgage's restrictions or conditions. In addition, since the mortgage is a conveyance of or a lien on realty, it is subject to the normal operation of the recording acts and the doctrine of constructive notice. Thus, an adverse conveyance in the record chain of title of a mortgage will be effective even though there has been an assignment of the mortgage to a HDC. To illustrate, if a land owner executes two mortgages, the first is recorded, and the second is subsequently assigned to a HDC, the holder will nonetheless be subordinate to the recorded first mortgage.[59] The result may be explained by saying that the holder has a duty to search the records, and hence cannot claim to lack notice of the prior mortgage.

A final advantage of HDC status should be mentioned: a HDC may further assign the note and mortgage, even to one with notice of defects, and yet the assignee will take free of those defects. If this were not so, the entire HDC concept would be endangered, for the HDC might find himself with an instrument good in his hands only,

(1887); Borgess Inv. Co. v. Vette, 142 Mo. 560, 573, 44 S.W. 754, 757, 64 Am.St.Rep. 567 (1898); Webb v. Hoselton, 4 Neb. 308, 19 Am.Rep. 638 (1876); Buehler v. McCormick, 169 Ill. 269, 48 N.E. 287 (1897). In Gribble v. Mauerham, 188 Cal.App.2d 221, 10 Cal.Rptr. 296 (1961), the holder in due course of a negotiable note secured by a trust deed mortgage was held to take both the note and trust deed mortgage free of the defense of no consideration for the note.

In Carolina Housing and Mortgage Corp. v. Reynolds, 230 S.C. 491, 96 S.E.2d 485 (1957), criticized in Karesh, Security Transactions, in Survey of South Carolina Law, 10 S.C.L.Q. 114, 117 (1957), an assignee for value before maturity of a negotiable note, without actual knowledge of the defense of failure of consideration by the maker, took free of the defense on the note, but, since the mortgage was defectively executed on its face the lower court held, and the holding was not appealed, that he could not enforce the mortgage. See also Note, Transfer of the Mortgagee's Interest in Florida, 14 U. of Fla.L.Rev. 98, 100 (1961); Bautista & Kennedy, The Imputed Negotiability of Security Interests Under the Code, 38 Ind.L.J. 574 (1963).

57. The leading critical case is Baily v. Smith, 14 Ohio St. 396 (1863). Ironically, Ohio has subsequently adopted the majority view; see Dennis v. Rotter, 43 Ohio App. 330, 183 N.E. 188 (1932). Only Minnesota still appears to adhere to the minority rule; see note, 32 Ill.L.Rev. 120 (1937); 127 A.L.R. 190 (1940).

58. See § 5.30, supra, at note 45.

59. Johnson v. Masterson, 193 S.W. 201 (Tex.Civ.App.1917), error refused.

but unmarketable as a consequence of widespread notice of its defects.[60] One exception is made to this "HDC-filter" idea. If the HDC reassigns the instrument to a previous holder who was not a HDC, that assignee is subject to the maker-mortgagor's defenses.[61]

§ 5.32 Rights of Assignees Who Are Not Holders in Due Course

This section is concerned with the rights of non-HDC holders of negotiable notes, and of assignees of non-negotiable notes. Before we can deal with these rights, it is necessary to introduce some basic terminology. Two types of fact situations present themselves. The first is the case in which the maker of the note (who is also the mortgagor of the mortgage which secures it) has some defense which can be raised against its enforcement.[62] Such a defense is sometimes termed a "patent equity." The term is a bit archaic and perhaps not very descriptive, but its meaning can be easily grasped. The assignee of a note who realizes that he will or may lack HDC protection is well-advised to inquire of the maker-mortgagor before accepting the assignment.[63] Such an assignee will commonly request that the maker sign an "estoppel certificate", averring that the note is valid and that the maker has no defenses. Such a certificate is generally effective,[64] and if broadly drafted provides even better protection for

60 U.C.C. § 3–201(1) and official comment 3; this right of the HDC is sometimes termed the "shelter" right. See Brock v. Adams, 79 N.M. 17, 439 P.2d 234 (1968).

61. See Coplan Pipe and Supply Co. v. Ben-Frieda Corp., 256 So.2d 218 (Fla. App.1972).

62. The defense may be either real or personal; in this contest the distinction is unimportant. See § 5.31, supra, at notes 46, 50–54. Claims of the original mortgagee or others in the chain of assignments are also considered "patent" on the same rationale discussed in the text; Stevenson Brewing Co. v. Iba, 155 N.Y. 224, 49 N.E. 677 (1898).

63. Long ago it was stated that though "in fact it does happen that assignments of mortgages are taken without calling upon the mortgagor;" to do so is regarded as "extremely unfit and very rash, and a very indifferent security" and "no conveyancer of established reputation would recommend" it "without making the mortgagor a party and being satisfied that the money was really due." Matthew v. Wallwyn, 4 Ves. 118, 127 (1798). These statements are still true today as applied to mortgages securing non-negotiable notes. Some mortgage forms include language obligating the mortgagor to give an estoppel statement upon request.

64. Harrison v. Galilee Baptist Church, 427 Pa. 247, 234 A.2d 314 (1967). Not only the immediate assignee for whom the certificate is given, but subsequent assignees from him as well, may rely upon the certificate. See generally Griffiths v. Sears, 112 Pa. 523, 4 A. 492 (1886); Nixon v. Haslett, 74 N.J.Eq. 789, 70 A. 987 (1908), affirmed 75 N.J.Eq. 302, 78 A. 1134 (1911); 23 L.R.A.,N.S., 177 (1910). See Smyth v. Munroe, 84 N. Y. 354 (1881) on the establishment of reliance by the assignee on the certificate. Weyh v. Boylan, 85 N.Y. 394, 39 Am.Rep. 669 (1881), second assignee may prevail even though first assignee had notice of the defense of usury.

Estoppel may also arise from oral statements by the mortgagor, or even from his conduct, but the courts are reluctant to imply an estoppel from evidence that is less than clearcut; see Bush v. Cushman, 27 N.J.Eq. 131 (1876), mortgagor affirmatively per-

the assignee than would the HDC doctrine, since it insulates him from both real and personal defenses.[65] By making such an inquiry and obtaining such a statement, the prospective assignee can easily discover the maker's defenses, if any; that is, he can make them "patent."

By contrast, "latent equities" are those which cannot be discovered in this manner. They consist of claims to the instrument, or claims which will defeat it, which are asserted by third parties—persons other than the maker. Two general classes of these claims may be considered. First, there are persons whose rights are prior in time and title to the maker's. The maker, for example, may have obtained the mortgaged land by fraud or other device which makes the conveyance to him subject to being set aside.[66] He may have obtained it without payment of consideration under circumstances which would cause a court to subject it to a constructive trust in his hands.[67] It may even be subject to an express but unrecorded trust of which the maker-mortgagor was the trustee.[68] It may have been conveyed to the maker in fraud on the rights of the previous owner's creditors.[69]

Latent equities may also exist in persons whose interests are derived from the maker of the note and mortgage. The most obvious example is the execution of a previous assignment of the note and mortgage by the mortgagee; that is, he purports to assign the same note and mortgage twice.[70] Similarly, a building contractor may do

suaded the assignee to take the assignment; see Melendy v. Keen, 89 Ill. 395 (1878); Rothschild v. Title Guar. & Trust Co., 204 N.Y. 458, 97 N.E. 879, 41 L.R.A.,N.S., 740 (1912), semble; Pomeroy, Equity Juris., 5th ed., § 704.

Language in the original mortgage itself is unlikely to be considered an effective estoppel. For example, a recitation in the mortgage that the full loan has been disbursed will not prevent the mortgagor from showing later that it was not; the reason is that too commonly future advances mortgages recite the full consideration as though it had been disbursed in its entirety, when in fact it has not. See § 12.7, infra.

Finally, an estoppel certificate may be ineffective if the assignee has actual knowledge of the mortgagor's defenses despite the certificate's contrary statement; Fidelity Trust Co. v. Gardiner, 191 Pa.Super. 17, 155 A.2d 405 (1959).

65. For an more extensive discussion of estoppel against the mortgagor, see Osborne, Mortgages § 228 (2d ed. 1970).

66. Humble v. Curtis, 160 Ill. 193, 43 N.E. 749 (1895); Simpson v. Del Hoyo, 94 N.Y. 189 (1883).

67. Capital Investors Co. v. Executors of Estate of Morrison, 484 F.2d 1157 (C.A.Va.1973).

68. Mott v. Clark, 9 Pa.St. 399, 1 Am. L.J. 379, 49 Am.Dec. 566 (1848).

69. Moffett v. Parker, 71 Minn. 139, 73 N.W. 850, 70 Am.St.Rep. 319 (1898); Danbury v. Robinson, 14 N.J.Eq. 213, 82 Am.Dec. 244 (1862); McMurtry v. Bowers, 91 N.J.Eq. 317, 109 A. 361 (1920).

70. The problem can arise, of course, only if the first mortgage note is not delivered to the first assignee, but an effective assignment without delivery is entirely possible as between the parties if the assignee is willing to forego HDC status; see § 5.28, supra, at notes 52–56; Guaranty Mortgage &

work on the land in question prior to the assignment of the note and mortgage, and his work may give rise to a mechanic's lien which relates back to the time the the work was commenced.[71]

In all of these cases the equities are "latent" because an inquiry of the maker will not necessarily disclose their existence, and because the maker's estoppel statement will not cut them off.[72] From the prospective assignee's viewpoint they are hidden.[73] In some of these cases, the recording acts may come into play. For example, in the two-assignment case mentioned in the preceding paragraph, some jurisdictions hold that the first assignment is subject to the recording acts, and if unrecorded is cut off by the second assignment to a bona fide purchaser.[74] Conceivably the same result would be reached with regard to the maker who got the land as trustee under an unrecorded express trust.[75] But clearly many cases remain—the constructive trust, for example—which are not subject to the recording acts of any jurisdiction.

The question, then, is to what extent an assignee who is not a HDC is subject to the maker's defenses (that is, patent equities), and to the claims of third parties (that is, latent equities). Note that we have said "claims" in referring to third parties; this is not meant to imply that they will necessarily assert their rights by becoming plaintiffs in suits, but merely that they have some affirmative rights to assert; they are not merely using their "equities" to defend against the note and mortgage, since they are not the normal objects of a suit on the note or an action to foreclose the mortgage.

Patent Equities

With regard to the defenses of the maker-mortgagor, the law is clear and simple; the non-HDC assignee is fully subject to them, just as the original mortgagee would be. If the note is negotiable but the holder has notice or fails to pay value, or if the note is nonnegotiable merely because it omits "bearer" or "order" language,[76] the UCC ap-

Ins. Co. v. Harris, 193 So.2d 1 (Fla. 1966) in which the first assignment was a pledge evidenced only by a notation on the books of the assignor corporation.

71. Wilson Bros. v. Cooey, 251 Md. 350, 247 A.2d 395 (1968).

72. "He may inquire of all the persons in the chain of title, but their admissions will not affect a party in possession of an equitable right derived from them." Bush v. Lathrop, 22 N. Y. 535 (1860).

73. See Bautista & Kennedy, The Imputed Negotiability of Security Interests Under the Code, 38 Ind.L.J. 574 (1963); Note, Latent Equities, 20 U. Chi.L.Rev. 692 (1952).

74. See Johnson v. Sowell, 80 N.M. 677, 459 P.2d 839 (1969); cf. Neal v. Bradley, 238 Ark. 714, 384 S.W.2d 238 (1964).

75. See Bogert, Trusts and Trustees §§ 881, 893 (1962).

76. Under U.C.C. § 3–805, a note which is nonnegotiable because of these particular omissions is covered by U.C.C. Art. 3, except that a holder of such a note cannot be a HDC. See Locke v. Aetna Acceptance Corp., 309 So.2d 43 (Fla.App.1975); Jones v. United Savings & Loan Ass'n, 515 S.

plies. It specifically provides that the assignee is subject to "all defenses of any party which would be available in an action on a simple contract." [77] If the note is non-negotiable for other reasons, such as incorporation of the mortgage by reference or language which makes the obligation conditional, the UCC does not control but the common law rule is the same. The assignee is subject to all patent equities [78] when he attempts to enforce either the note or the mortgage.

Latent Equities

When latent equities are asserted by third parties, it is essential to determine whether the UCC governs the transaction. As indicated above, it applies either if the note is negotiable (and the assignee's conduct has deprived him of HDC status), or if it is nonnegotiable because not payable to "order" or "bearer." [79] If the Code does apply, its relevant language states that the assignee is subject to "all valid claims to [the instrument] on the part of any person." [80] This language is startlingly broad, and may well be read to include all latent equities. This conclusion is strengthened by the official comment, which states that the quoted phrase "includes not only claims of legal title, but all liens, equities, or other claims of right against the instrument or its proceeds." [81]

Precisely this view of the Code was taken in Capital Investors Co. v. Executors of Estate of Morrison.[82] Morrison, who owned certain real estate, deeded it to a business associate in an apparent attempt to deprive his wife of any interest in it upon his death.[83] The grantee, without Morrison's authority, retransferred the property and took back a purchase-money mortgage which he then assigned to a person who allegedly had no notice of Morrison's interest. The assignee was not, however, a HDC, since the notes were past due and

W.2d 869 (Mo.App.1974); D. Nelsen & Sons, Inc. v. General American Devel. Corp., 6 Ill.App.3d 6, 284 N.E.2d 478 (1972).

77. U.C.C. § 3–306(b); see § 5.29, supra, at notes 94–10.

78. Sosebee v. Atha, 140 Ga.App. 555, 231 S.E.2d 381 (1976); Bittner v. McGrath, 186 Pa.Super. 477, 142 A.2d 323 (1958); Fidelity Trust Co. v. Gardiner, 191 Pa.Super. 17, 155 A.2d 405 (1959). "The rule is conceded that the assignee of the mortgage takes subject to the equities between the original parties, and has no greater rights than the original mortgagee." Rapps v. Gottlieb, 142 N.Y. 164, 36 N.E. 1052 (1894); Davis v. Bechstein, 69 N.Y. 440, 25 Am.Rep. 218 (1877). See also Karesh, Security Transactions, in Survey of South Carolina Law, 10 S.C.L.Q. 114, 120 (1957), discussing Carolina Housing & Mortgage Corp. v. Orange Hill A.M.E. Church, 230 S.C. 498, 97 S.E.2d 28 (1957).

79. See note 76, supra.

80. U.C.C. § 3–306(a).

81. U.C.C. § 3–306, Official Comment 2.

82. 484 F.2d 1157 (C.A.Va.1973).

83. Further background on Mr. Morrison's dealings appears in Capital Investors Co. v. Devers, 360 F.2d 462 (4th Cir. 1966), certiorari denied 385 U.S. 934, 87 S.Ct. 294, 17 L.Ed.2d 214, rehearing denied 385 U.S. 1021, 87 S.Ct. 702, 17 L.Ed.2d 560, appeal after remand 387 F.2d 591 (4th Cir.1968).

the assignee had notice that they were in default. The court applied the UCC literally and held that the assignee would be subject to the claim of Morrison's executor that the original grant by Morrison was subject to a constructive trust in favor of his estate. The court cannot be faulted for following the Code,[84] but in terms of general policy the result is hard to accept; plainly the assignee is being held subject to rights which no reasonable investigation by him would have disclosed.

In cases in which the instrument is not negotiable for reasons other than omission of "bearer" or "order" language, the UCC has no application and the common law of contracts controls.[85] Should an assignee of such a note, if he pays value and has no notice [86] of the latent equities, take free of them? The cases are badly split, but it is probable that a slight majority take an affirmative view.[87] The ten-

84. The court's opinion may be criticized in the following respect. It persistently speaks of a claim of constructive trust by Morrison's estate on the notes or their proceeds; perhaps more aptly the constructive trust should have been imposed on the real estate which Morrison had transferred in fraud on his wife's rights. Moreover, the UCC refers only to the holder of the "instrument" as taking subject to all claims of other persons (3–306(a)). It makes no reference whatever to the mortgage or land. It might thus have been held that the assignee of the mortgage was, under the common law principles discussed at note 87 infra, free of the latent equity in the mortgage, and that no latent equity properly existed in the note; the assignee would thus prevail. If it is conceded that estate's constructive trust claim is properly asserted against the note, and is supported by the UCC, the assignee might still argue that the realty interest is, under non-Code principles, free of the trust. However, that argument would leave the assignee with a mortgage and no note for it to secure, an essentially meaningless position.

85. See notes 76 and 77, supra.

86. If the assignee has actual notice, or constructive notice from previously recorded documents, of the third party's claim, he should of course take subject to it; the same is true if the third party is in possession of the property. Seymour v. McKinstry, 106 N.Y. 230, 12 N.E. 348, 14 N.E. 94 (1887). An equitable vendor's lien, the vendor remaining in possession after conveyance, has been held to prevail over a bona fide assignee for value of the mortgage given by the vendee to one who had knowledge of the vendor's claim. The mortgage had been recorded but the continued possession of the vendor put the assignee upon notice of his interest. See Fisk v. Potter, 2 Keyes, N.Y., 64 (1865); cf. Bloomer v. Henderson, 8 Mich. 395, 77 Am.Dec. 453 (1860).

87. The leading case is Simpson v. Del Hoyo, 94 N.Y. 189 (1883). See also Robertson v. U. S. Livestock Co., 164 Iowa 230, 145 N.W. 535 (1914); Bloomer v. Henderson, 8 Mich. 395, 77 Am.Dec. 453 (1860); Moffett v. Parker, 71 Minn. 139, 73 N.W. 850, 70 Am.St.Rep. 319 (1898); McMurtry v. Bowers, 91 N.J.Eq. 317, 109 A. 361 (1920). A good many of the cases preferring the assignee have other or additional explanations. Thus Congregational Church Bldg. Soc. v. Scandinavian Free Church of Tacoma, 24 Wash. 433, 64 P. 750 (1901), could rest upon the ground that the latent equity in the land was unrecorded and therefore defeated by the operation of the recording acts; it was also in a jurisdiction rejecting the doctrine giving supremacy to latent equities in choses in action. Mott v. Clark, 9 Pa.St. 399, 1 Am.L.J. 379, 49 Am.Dec. 566 (1848) similarly relies upon the nonrecordation of the latent equitable interest in the land to defeat its owner on the ground of laches.

tative draft of the Restatement of Contracts Second concludes that the assignee should prevail, at least if the latent equities are in the nature of an express or constructive trust, an equitable lien, or a right of avoidance in a third party.[88] Some case law supports the same result in the "two assignments of the same mortgage" case mentioned earlier.[89]

This contrast between Code and non-Code results is exceedingly difficult to justify in policy terms. If the note is nonnegotiable because it omits "bearer" or "order", the assignee will lose; if it is nonnegotiable because it is conditional or incorporates the mortgage by reference, the assignee will probably win, assuming he pays value and has no notice of the latent equity. Since these cases all involve two innocent parties one of which must lose, there seem to be no powerful arguments for either result, but it is anomalous to make consequences turn on such minor fact variations.[90]

At least where notes secured by mortgages are involved, the Restatement position has more to commend it than does the UCC. To subject a mortgage assignee to latent equities is particularly odd in light of the fact that the original mortgagee himself (if a bona fide purchaser) is free of those same equities under well-settled law.[91] Thus the UCC, as interpreted in the Morrison case discussed above, goes well beyond merely placing the assignee in the shoes of the mortgagee; it places him in much worse shoes! Perhaps the UCC draftsmen did not have mortgages in mind, but it now seems clear that an appropriate amendment to the UCC would place all non-HDC assignees of mortgage notes in the same status, and would give them priority over latent equities if they took for value without notice.

§ 5.33 Payment to Assignor as a Defense

After a mortgage has been assigned by the mortgagee, to whom should the mortgagor make further payments? If the assignee gives the mortgagor reasonable notice that the assignment has occurred, it

See generally Note, Latent Equities, 20 U.Chi.L.Rev. 692 (1952); Osborne, Mortgages § 230 (2nd Ed. 1970); 2 Glenn, Mortgages §§ 324, 324.1 (1943).

88. Restatements, Second, Contracts § 175 (tent. draft 1973); the first Restatement, Contracts § 174 took the same position.

89. Guaranty Mortgage & Ins. Co. v. Harris, 193 So.2d 1 (Fla.1966); Wilson Bros. v. Cooey, 251 Md. 350, 247 A.2d 395 (1968).

90. The draftsmen of the Restatement apparently intended to observe this distinction, however; § 175 Comment (c) states "The rule of this Section is negated with respect to negotiable instruments * * * which are transferred but not duly negotiated by Uniform Commercial Code § 3–306 * * *."

91. See Osborne, Mortgages §§ 180, 184–85 (2d ed. 1970); 2 Glenn, Mortgages § 324.1 (1943); International State Bank v. Bray, 87 N.M. 350, 533 P.2d 583 (1975). This is the rule in both lien and title theory states; see Haynsworth v. Bischoff, 6 S.C. 159, 166 (1874); Durfee, Lien Theory of the Mortgage, 11 Mich.L.Rev. 495 (1913).

is clear that further payments made to the original mortgagee do not count against the assignee, and may not be raised by the mortgagor as a defense to foreclosure or an action on the debt by the assignee.[92] This result is unsurprising and entirely acceptable. The bulk of this section, however, deals with the more difficult case in which the assignee gives the mortgagor no notice that he now owns the debt and mortgage, and in which the mortgagor innocently continues paying the original mortgagee.

Negotiable Instruments

If the obligation is represented by a negotiable note and the assignee is a HDC, the UCC provides that the assignee takes it free from "all defenses of any party to the instrument with whom the holder has not dealt",[93] except for real defenses.[94] Payment is clearly a personal defense, and that is apparently the end of the matter: payment to anyone except the holder or his agent does not count.[95] The reasoning behind this result is that the maker of a negotiable note is entitled to demand production of the note before making any payment, and to demand its surrender when making the final payment. Since the maker can protect himself against a secret assignment by this means, he fails to do so at his peril.[96] The fact that no mortgage assignment has been recorded, or that the payment is made to the apparent record holder, is immaterial.[97]

The risk is said to be absolute. If the mortgagor asks for the note, but instead is given a plausible but false explanation for its nonproduction, his payment will still be no defense to the true holder's later claim.[98] A grantee of the original mortgagor is also bound by

92. Wood v. Gulf States Capital Corp., 217 So.2d 257, 269 (Miss.1968); Kaufman v. Bernstein, 100 So.2d 801 (Fla. 1958).

93. U.C.C. § 3–305(2).

94. See § 5.31, supra at note 46.

95. Groover v. Peters, 231 Ga. 531, 202 S.E.2d 413 (1973); Carter v. South Texas Lumber Co., 422 S.W.2d 951 (Tex.Civ.App.1967); American Security & Trust Co. v. John J. Juliano, Inc., 203 Va. 827, 127 S.E.2d 348 (1962); Silver Spring Title Co. v. Chadwick, 213 Md. 178, 131 A.2d 489 (1957). The leading case is Assets Realization Co. v. Clark, 205 N.Y. 105, 98 N.E. 457 (1912), affirming 137 A.D. 881, 123 N.Y.S. 1105 (1909).

A few states follow an intermediate rule in which the note and mortgage are viewed separately; if the note is assigned but no assignment of the mortgage has been recorded, payment to the mortgagee will discharge the mortgage, but personal liability on the note will remain. See Ark.Stat. Ann. § 51–1016, discussed in Neal v. Bradley, 238 Ark. 714, 384 S.W.2d 238 (1964); Bartholf v. Bensley, 234 Ill. 336, 84 N.E. 928 (1908); Johnson v. Howe, 176 Minn. 287, 223 N.W. 148 (1929), discussed in Note, 13 Minn.L. Rev. 622 (1929).

96. Smith v. Jarman, 61 Utah 125, 211 P. 962 (1922); see Annots., 89 A.L.R. 171 (1934); 104 A.L.R. 1301 (1936).

97. City Bank v. Plank, 141 Wisc. 653, 124 N.W. 1000 (1910); Eggert v. Beyer, 43 Neb. 711, 62 N.W. 57 (1895); Smith v. Jarman, note 96, supra.

98. Kellogg v. Smith, 26 N.Y. 18 (1962); cf. Clinton Loan Ass'n v. Merritt, 112 N.C. 243, 17 S.E. 296 (1893).

the same rule, for even though he may not be personally liable on the note and hence may not have the right to demand its surrender upon a final payment, he can still insist upon inspecting it before any payment, installment or final.[99]

The rule stated has great potential for mischief and unfairness, since it produces far different results than most lay mortgagors would expect. Fortunately, its relevance in the world of modern mortgage assignments is fairly limited. While secondary market assignments of mortgages are very common, it is quite generally the practice for the assignee to designate the original mortgagee as his agent for purposes of "servicing" the loan—that is, receiving the payments from the mortgagor.[1] If such an agency relationship exists, it is largely irrelevant whether the mortgagor has notice of the assignment or not; he will be fully credited with the payments made to the agent.[2] If the assignee terminates the agency relationship without notifying the debtor, the agent should surely be deemed to have continuing power to receive payments under an apparent authority or inherent authority principle,[3] and this should follow even if the debtor did not realize that the mortgagor was acting as an agent rather than for its own account.

The problems with the rule arise mainly in transactions among natural persons rather than institutions, and are particularly acute with mortgages calling for a single final payment rather than installments. In such cases an assignment may well be made without notice to the mortgagor and without any appointment of the mortgagee as an agent.[4] These situations represent only a small fraction of all mortgages given, but they are sufficiently troublesome that a change in the law is needed, as discussed below.

Nonnegotiable Notes

If the assignee is not a HDC or the note is nonnegotiable, the UCC[5] and the applicable common law subject the assignee to all the mortgagor's defenses, including payment if made before the mortga-

99. Bautz v. Adams, 131 Wis. 152, 111 N.W. 69, 120 Am.St.Rep. 1030 (1907); Shoemaker v. Minkler, 202 Iowa 942, 211 N.W. 563 (1926). See Ross, Double Hazard of a Note and Mortgage, 16 Minn.L.Rev. 123, 125 (1931).

1. See § 11.1, infra, for a more complete description of servicing.

2. Northside Bldg. & Investment Co. v. Finance Co. of Georgia, 119 Ga.App. 131, 166 S.E.2d 608 (1969); American Security & Trust Co. v. John J. Juliano, Inc., 203 Va. 827, 127 S.E.2d 348 (1962); California Title Ins. & Trust Co. v. Kuchenbeiser, 20 Cal.App. 11, 127 P. 1039 (1912).

3. See Seavey, Agency §§ 50-51 (1964).

4. E. g., Groover v. Peters, 231 Ga. 531, 202 S.E.2d 413 (1973).

5. The UCC applies if the note is negotiable and the holder lacks HDC status, or if the note is nonnegotiable because it lacks "order" or "bearer" language; U.C.C. §§ 3-306, 3-805; see § 5.32, supra at note 76. If the note is nonnegotiable for other reasons the common law applies.

gor was given notice of the assignment.[6] Even here, there is some authority that, if a final payment is being made, it is so customary and natural for the debtor to demand surrender of the physical note that his failure to do so is negligence, and hence that his payment will give him no defense against the assignee.[7] It is difficult to see how this result can follow under the UCC,[8] but it may still be the law with notes which are nonnegotiable due to reasons other than omission of "order" or "bearer" language.[9] To the extent that it is the law, it is tempered in one respect; if the mortgagor demands to see the note and is given a reasonable explanation for the mortgagee's inability to produce it, he may safely make his payment.[10]

Since notice is essential to fully protect the rights of the assignee of a nonnegotiable note, to whom should he give notice when a conveyance of the mortgaged land has occurred? If the assignment occurs and notice is given to the mortgagor before he deeds away his land, that should certainly be sufficient.[11] On the other hand, if the land has been conveyed first, and if the assignee knows or can readily learn from the assignor the identity of the new owner, it seems reasonable to require the assignee to give notice directly to him. The assignee probably should not be required to search the title in order

6. Felin Associates, Inc. v. Rogers, 38 A.D.2d 6, 326 N.Y.S.2d 413 (1971); Kansas City Mortg. Co. v. Crowell, 239 So.2d 130 (Fla.App.1970); Olshan Lumber Co. v. Bullard, 395 S.W.2d 670 (Tex.Civ.App.1965) (in the two preceding cases the note was presumably non-negotiable, although the opinions are not explicit on the point); Northside Bldg. & Investment Co. v. Finance Co. of Georgia, supra note 2; Hand v. Kemp, 207 Ala. 309, 92 So. 897 (1922); O'Maley v. Pugliese, 272 Pa. 356, 116 A. 308 (1922), 42 Harv.L.Rev. 1082 (1929). The question is one of contract law; see Restatement, Contracts § 170; Note, Mortgages: Effect of Failure to Record a Mortgage Assignment in Florida, 7 U.Fla.L.Rev. 93 (1954).

7. Assets Realization Co. v. Clark, 205 N.Y. 105, 98 N.E. 457 (1912), affirming 137 A.D. 881, 123 N.Y.S. 1105 (1909): "[When a final payment is made], the evidence of the debt naturally and ordinarily is produced and delivered, and therefore the failure to do this in the absence of sufficient explanation constitutes notice which makes the payment or transaction unavailing as against a prior assignment although unrecorded."

While the practice as described may have been prevalent in New York in 1912, it is certainly not so in the latter half of the Twentieth Century. Today the note is usually unavailable when the final payment is made. The payment is generally transmitted by an attorney or title company by mail and the mortgagee is trusted and expected to mark the note "paid" and mail it to the mortgagor within a reasonable time after receipt of the payment. Certainly no inference of notice should be drawn from failure to deliver the note immediately upon the tender of the final payment.

8. U.C.C. § 3–306 provides without exception that the non-HDC holder is subject to "all defenses of any party which would be available in an action on a simple contract."

9. See § 5.31, supra at note 46.

10. See Brown v. Blydenburgh, 7 N.Y. 141, 146, 57 Am.Dec. 506 (1852); Clinton Loan Ass'n v. Merritt, 112 N. C. 243, 17 S.E. 296 (1893).

11. To expect the assignee to keep track of all future sales of the property and to keep the grantees informed of his assignment is unrealistic. Recording the assignment easily accomplishes the same purpose; see text at note 17, infra.

to learn whether the title has been conveyed, but the increasingly broad use of due-on-sale clauses [12] means that the original mortgagee will usually know of the land conveyance and can easily inform the assignee of the new owner's identity. The wise assignee of a nonnegotiable note will wish to contact the grantee of the title in any event to obtain an estoppel certificate from him.

If the assignee has recorded his assignment, he might argue that the presence of the document in the public records gives constructive notice to the mortgagor or to grantees from the mortgagor. A few cases [13] and statutes [14] expressly provide that recordation of the assignment will have this effect, but at least as against the mortgagor himself this idea seems totally out of touch with reality, for it implies that the mortgagor will take the trouble to examine the title to his own property before making each payment.[15] This is hardly ever done, and it makes no sense to penalize the mortgagor for failure to do it. The great majority of cases do not do so.[16] As against a grantee from the mortgagor, on the other hand, imputing notice of a previously recorded assignment does make sense, for he will have had occasion to examine the title as part of the purchase transaction, and

12. See §§ 5.21–5.26, supra.

13. The cases usually derive from overenthusiastic interpretations of recording statutes which provide that recordation is "notice to all the world." See, e. g., Ross v. Johnson, 171 Wash. 658, 19 P.2d 101 (1933); Bale v. Wright, 120 Okl. 174, 252 P. 56 (1926). See Annot., 89 A.L.R. 171, 196 (1934). Recordation, in practical terms, can only be notice to takers of *subsequent* interests; the mortgagor has a *prior* interest.

14. N.J.Stat.Ann. 46:18–4 is the most direct illustration, for it expressly provides that recordation of an assignment is notice to all persons; this was held to include mortgagors in Dotto v. Ciamboli, 8 N.J.Misc. 37, 148 A. 197, affirmed 107 N.J.Eq. 596, 154 A. 631 (1931). See also United States v. Goldberg, 362 F.2d 575 (3d Cir. 1966), certiorari denied 386 U. S. 919, 87 S.Ct. 881, 17 L.Ed.2d 790 (1967). The Maryland statute, which formerly provided in substance that ownership of a mortgage shall be conclusively presumed vested in the person having record title to it, was construed to give mortgagors constructive notice of assignments in Sennett v. Taylor, 157 Md. 107, 145 A. 358 (1929); this result has now been reversed by legislation described at note 19 infra. The Kansas statute, K.R.S. §§ 67–321, –322, was similarly construed in Walmer v. Redinger, 116 Kan. 580, 227 P. 329 (1924); see text at notes 18–22, infra.

15. "[I]t would be an intolerable hardship if, every time he may wish to make a payment and obtain a credit on his debt, he should be compelled to visit the recorder's office to ascertain whether or not his mortgage had been assigned." Foster v. Carson, 159 Pa. 477, 28 A. 356 (1894); see also Giorgi v. Pioneer Title Insur. Co., 85 Nev. 319, 454 P.2d 104 (1969). See Md.Code Ann. § 7–103, official comment.

16. In some states statutes expressly provide that recordation gives no constructive notice to the mortgagor; see, e. g., Blumenthal v. Jassoy, 29 Minn. 177, 12 N.W. 517 (1882). Ward & Stewart, Mortgage Assignment and Payment Statutes, 8 J.Bar. Ass'n Kan. 488, 495 (1940), lists 10 states with such statutes: Cal., Id., Kan., Mich., Minn., Mont., N. Y., Neb., Wisc., and Wyo. In other states the result follows from recording act language which states that only "subsequent purchasers and creditors" have constructive notice. See Annot., 89 A.L.R. 171, 197 (1934).

thus will have had ample opportunity and reason to learn of the assignment.[17]

A few jurisdictions have enacted statutes which appear to be aimed at aiding an innocent mortgagor on a negotiable note who pays his original mortgagee. In Kansas and New Mexico the legislatures have expressly provided that if the assignment is unrecorded, the mortgagor may pay the assignor with impunity; [18] the former Maryland statute was interpreted similarly.[19] In the case of a negotiable note such statutes provide a theoretical benefit to mortgagors, but it does not amount to much in practical terms, since examination of the records before making payment, particularly on an installment mortgage, is far more effort than most mortgagors can be expected to go to.[20] Moreover, in Kansas the statute has been interpreteted by the courts as a sword for the assignee; in the case of nonnegotiable instruments it is held that recordation of the assignment gives constructive notice to the mortgagor whether he actually examines the records or not.[21] This is, as noted above, an unrealistic and undesirable viewpoint.[22]

Policy Considerations

The rule that innocent payment to the assignor of a negotiable mortgage note is ineffective is seriously out of touch with modern practices and should be revised. It ignores several changes which have occurred in the mortgage market in the last few decades. First, it assumes that the note can readily be produced by the mortgagee upon the mortgagor's request if it has not been assigned or if the mortgagee is the holder's agent. The expansion of financial institu-

17. Rucker v. State Exchange Bank, 355 So.2d 171 (Fla.App.1978); Gilcrist v. Wright, 167 Neb. 767, 94 N.W.2d 476 (1959); Assets Realization Co. v. Clark, 205 N.Y. 105, 98 N.E. 457, 41 L.R.A.,N.S., 462 (1912); Cornish v. Woolverton, 32 Mont. 456, 81 P. 4, 108 Am.St.Rep. 598 (1905); Viele v. Judson, 82 N.Y. 32 (1880). See Robbins v. Larson, 69 Minn. 436, 72 N.W. 456, 65 Am.St.Rep. 572 (1897). With the exception of New York (McKinney's N.Y. Real Prop.Law § 324), the statutes discussed at note 16, supra, exempting mortgagors from constructive notice of assignments, are inapplicable to grantees of the mortgaged land who take after the assignment is recorded.

18. Kan.Rev.Stat. § 67–321, –322; N.M.Stat.Ann. § 63–402, –403; see Seed, Mortgage "Payment" Statutes in Kansas and New Mexico, 3 Kan.L.Rev. 87 (1954).

19. Nussear v. Hazard, 148 Md. 345, 129 A. 506 (1925). As amended in 1972, however, the Maryland statute provides a far more pro-mortgagor rule: whether the assignment is recorded or not, payment to the assigor is good until the mortgagor is given actual notice of the assignment. Md.Code Ann. Real Property § 7–103(b).

20. But see Pletcher v. Albrecht, 186 Kan. 273, 350 P.2d 58 (1960), where the mortgagor *did* examine the records before each payment!

21. Walmer v. Redinger, 116 Kan. 580, 227 P. 329 (1924).

22. See Seed, Mortgage "Payment" Statutes in Kansas and New Mexico, 3 Kan.L.Rev. 87, 95–96 (1954).

tions, the advent of increased branching in many states, and the widespread assignment of mortgages with the mortgagor designated as servicer, all make this assumption wholly unrealistic. The note usually resides in a vault, often many miles from the location at which the mortgagor makes his payments. Moreover, mortgage payments today are very often made by mailed check or by automatic deduction from the mortgagor's checking account; these convenient procedures would be frustrated if the mortgagor really needed to inspect the note before each payment. In truth, a modern mortgagor who demanded to see his note before each payment would probably be viewed as if he had just arrived from Mars.

A further change of significance is the advent of computerized recordkeeping of mortgage payments. In earlier times it was customary to record each payment on a ledger printed on the reverse side of the note itself; thus, production of the note was natural and caused no inconvenience. This practice has almost entirely disappeared in favor of separate, usually computer-based, accounting of mortgagors' payments. The modern practice is more accurate and saves expense for all parties concerned, but the savings would be negated to the extent that production of the physical note were required.

The law should be changed to make payment to the assignor binding until notice of the assignment has been given. The Uniform Commercial Code takes this position with respect to notes secured by chattel paper in Article 9,[23] and its policy is equally sound with respect to real estate security. Payment as a defense is qualitatively different from other defenses which a mortgagor might raise against a HDC, for it is the one defense which the holder can prevent from arising for the small cost of a form letter and a stamp.[24] A change

23. U.C.C. § 9–318(3). Under the Code it is not enough that the debtor has notice that an assignment has occurred; he must be notified specifically that he is to begin making payments to the assignee.

24. The ease with which this may be done is illustrated by the requirement of the Federal National Mortgage Association (FNMA), applicable to single-family conventional home loans which it purchases, that the originating mortgagee send the mortgagor a letter which reads in part as follows:

> We are pleased to inform you as the owner of the property located at [address] that the mortgage on your property has been purchased by the Federal National Mortgage Association (FNMA). This transaction will in no way affect the amount or method of payment of your monthly mortgage payment; you should continue to submit your payment on or before the first day of each month to the address to which you are currently making your payments.

FNMA Conventional Selling Contract Supplement Sec. 301(F).

It is presumably FNMA's practice to send a letter of its own to the mortgagor in the event the originating mortgagee's servicing contract with FNMA is cancelled. If the servicing were reassigned or taken over directly by FNMA (an unlikely event) without such notification, it is almost impossible to believe that a court would deny the mortgagor credit for further payments innocently made to the original mortgagee.

is needed with respect to both negotiable paper and final payments on nonnegotiable paper; no distinctions between the two types of payments or the two types of notes can be justified. The present law is too far out of touch with the practices and expectations of the participants in mortgage transactions.

An amendment to the UCC would not be necessary to accomplish this suggested change.[25] Several courts have held that when an installment note secured by a mortgage is assigned and the assignor continues to collect the payments and remit them to the mortgage, this course of dealing constitutes the assignor the "secret agent" of the assignee, and payment to the assignor is good though he subsequently defaults in passing it through to the assignee. This interpretation is apparently followed even if there was never any formal agency relationship created.[26] There is no reason the concept should not be extended to single-payment notes as well. Moreover, an agency could well be inferred even if the mortgagee-assignor defaulted at the outset in remitting the payments to the assignee. This theory can be made equally applicable to negotiable and nonnegotiable notes. The agency relationship is too typical, too widely expected, and too consistent with business practices to be denied by the assignee who has not taken the trouble to send an appropriate notice to negate it. Absent such a notice, it should be presumed.

§ 5.34 Impact of Recording Acts

This section is concerned with whether the assignee of a note secured by a mortgage ought to record an assignment of the mortgage, and with the risks to which he may become subject if he does not record. These risks may arise in a variety of fact situations, and each will be discussed in turn. From the viewpoint of counsel for secondary market mortgage investors, however, the proper advice is quite clear: unless there is someoverriding need for secrecy, recordation should always be recommended. The cost and trouble in doing so are trivial, and the risks eliminated by recording are certainly substan-

25. This is not a suggest that amendment is a bad idea. Maryland did so in effect in 1972, enacting a statute which explicitly makes payment to the mortgagee good until actual notice of the assignment is given to the mortgagor. Md.Ann.Code § 7–103(b); the official comment to this statute nicely explains the "intolerable burden" which the prior law imposed on mortgagors.

26. Northside Bldg. & Investment Co. v. Finance Co. of America, 119 Ga. App. 131, 166 S.E.2d 608 (1969); Walmer v. Redinger, 116 Kan. 580, 227 P. 329 (1924); Erickson v. Kendall, 112 Wash. 26, 191 P. 842 (1920). It must be conceded that these cases do not quite go so far as the text suggests the law should go, since they all involve established patterns or practices of collection by the assignor for the assignee, even though the mortgagor was unaware of the assignment. There are also plenty of cases in which the courts have refused to find an agency on rather appealing facts; see, e. g., American Security and Trust Co. v. John J. Juliano, Inc., 203 Va. 827, 127 S.E.2d 348 (1962); Silver Spring Title Co. v. Chadwick, 213 Md. 178, 131 A.2d 489 (1957).

tial. This is indeed the position taken by most responsible mortgage assignees.[27]

One further introductory comment may be helpful. Those who purchase interests in real estate are accustomed to recording. Those who purchase interests in promissory notes generally are not; this is particularly true of negotiable notes, as to which possession of the original note is the essential indicium of ownership. A note secured by a mortgage has one foot in each of these camps,[28] and the law has had considerable difficulty reconciling the expectations associated with the two documents. In general, its approach has been to require recording only if the natural expectations of those dealing with the real estate interest would be seriously frustrated if the recording acts were not applied.[29]

We turn now to a consideration of the classic fact patterns in which recordation or its absence becomes an issue.

As Between Assignor and Assignee

It is clearly unnecessary in the great majority of states for the assignee to record in order to have a completed assignment as against the assignor.[30] This result is not surprising, for it would be reached under the usual rules pertaining to either instruments or real property. The typical recording act makes unrecorded conveyances ineffective only as against "subsequent purchasers and creditors for value and without notice [who record first]", with the bracketed phrase being added in "notice-race" jurisdictions.[31] As between the original parties to the transfer, recordation is almost never required.[32]

27. See, e. g., Federal National Mortgage Ass'n, Conventional Selling Contract Supplement § 604(g) (1977); Federal Home Loan Mortgage Corporation, Sellers' Guide Conventional Mortgages § 3.502(b) (1976). The latter provides that "the assignment of the mortgage is not required to be executed and/or recorded, if such recordation is not necessary under applicable law to perfect FHLMC's first lien interest and is not commonly required by private institutional mortgage investors in the area in which the Mortgaged Premises are located. However, Seller agrees to execute and/or record an assignment of the mortgage at Seller's expense upon request by FHLMC."

28. See § 5.27, supra.

29. See generally Osborne, Mortgages § 234 (2d Ed. 1970).

30. United States v. Goldberg, 362 F. 2d 575 (3d Cir.1966), certiorari denied 386 U.S. 919, 87 S.Ct. 881, 17 L.Ed.2d 790; Wilson v. Pacific Coast Title Ins. Co., 106 Cal.App.2d 599, 235 P.2d 431 (1951).

31. See Powell, Real Property Par. 895, Par. 914 (Rohan ed. 1968).

32. One apparent exception is Md.Ann. Code Real Property § 3–101, which provides that conveyances must be recorded to be valid. However, a conveyance supported by consideration will be given effect as a contract to convey; see Nickel v. Brown, 75 Md. 172, 23 A. 736 (1892). Thus, the only conveyances ultimately made void by non-recordation in Maryland are gifts.

Effect of Recordation on Payment to the Mortgagee

The preceding section[33] has discussed the effect of recordation on the efficacy of payments made by the mortgagor or his grantees to the mortgagee. The applicable rules will be only briefly summarized here. If the note is negotiable and the holder is in due course, a payment made to anyone else (except the holder's agent) is ineffective. This is true whether the assignment has been recorded or not. If the note is nonnegotiable or the assignee is not a HDC, payments made to the mortgagee are good until the mortgagor receives notice of the assignment, but the recording of the assignment gives him no constructive notice. In sum, as between mortgagor and assignee, recording is irrelevant.

If the original mortgagor transfers his land, however, and if the assignment of the mortgage is already on record when this occurs, the assignment will give constructive notice to the grantee of the land. This is unimportant if the assignment is to a HDC, but if it is not, the constructive notice will oblige the transferee to make any further payments to the assignee or fail to do so at his peril. In effect, recordation saves the non-HDC assignee the trouble of giving personal notice to those who might subsequently buy the land. This does not mean, however, that a transferee of the land can safely rely exclusively on the record. If the note is negotiable, he must seek it out and pay its holder or his agent even though the records show no assignment. As was suggested in the preceding section, this burden ought to be confined to negotiable notes, and even there it is not supported by sound policy.

Wrongful Satisfaction by the Original Mortgagee

Suppose a mortgage securing a negotiable note is assigned to a HDC who does not record the assignment. Then the original mortgagor and mortgagee engage in a bit of skullduggery. The mortgagor induces the mortgagee (quite wrongfully) to execute and record the customary form of discharge or satisfaction of the mortgage.[34] Having now ostensibly cleared his title, the mortgagor sells the land to a bona fide purchaser for full value who supposes that the mortgage has been properly discharged.

This case presents a fundamental conflict between the UCC, which protects a HDC in his ownership of the note (and by usual extension, the mortgage also), and the innocent land buyer who has relied on the public records. The cases resolve the conflict in favor of the BFP of the land, and he takes free of the mortgage.[35] Obviously

33. § 5.33, supra, at notes 13–22.

34. If the note has been negotiated, this ploy will be impossible or at least difficult in the few states, like Missouri, which require the note to be presented to the recorder for cancellation before the mortgage can be satisfied of record. See Vernon's Ann. Mo.Stat. § 443.060(1).

35. Fannin Investment & Devel. Co. v. Neuhaus, 427 S.W.2d 82 (Tex.Civ. App.1968); Kansas City Mortgage Co.

the opposite result would seriously jeopardize the usefulness of the entire recording system. In addition, the HDC could easily have prevented the problem from arising by recording his assignment. The original mortgagor, who was far from innocent and who was personally liable on the note, remains so, but the debt is no longer secured by the mortgage.[36]

A similar scheme may be devised by a non-assuming grantee of mortgaged land. If he approaches the mortgagee (who has already assigned) and gets and records a wrongful satisfaction from him, it seems equally clear that further grantees may rely on the record of that satisfaction. But who is personally liable on the note is not so clear. It seems quite unjust to permit the assignee of the note to hold the original mortgagor liable, for the price he received when he sold the land was undoubtedly discounted by the then-outstanding balance on the mortgage, and in addition he cannot claim an equitable subrogation of the assignee's rights in the mortgage; [37] it, after all, is satisfied and no longer binds the land. While there is no obvious legal theory on which the assignee of the mortgage can recover from the wrongdoing non-assuming grantee on the note, he can be held liable on a fraud theory. If recovery from him is impossible, perhaps the assignee of the mortgage should go without further relief as a penalty for his own carelessness in failing to record his assignment.

To return to our first example, in which the mortgagor is the procurer of the fraudulent release, some courts are a bit more troubled if the release is given as a part of the very transaction in which the innocent grantee buys the land. Perhaps the result should be reversed, and the land continue to be subject to the mortgage, if the grantee himself paid off the mortgagee without determining that the mortgagee still possessed the note.[38] On the other hand, if the osten-

v. Crowell, 239 So.2d 130 (Fla.App. 1970); Brenner v. Neu, 28 Ill.App.2d 219, 170 N.E.2d 897 (1960); Henniges v. Paschke, 9 N.D. 489, 84 N.W. 350, 81 Am.St.Rep. 588 (1900); Merrill v. Hurley, 6 S.D. 592, 62 N.W. 958, 55 Am.St.Rep. 859 (1895).

Merrill v. Luce, 6 S.D. 354, 61 N.W. 43, 55 Am.St.Rep. 844 (1894); Marling v. Nommensen, 127 Wis. 363, 368, 106 N.W. 844, 845 (1906), upon an estoppel theory. Cf. Northup v. Reese, 68 Fla. 451, 67 So. 136, L.R.A.1915F, 554 (1914); Note, 5 U.Chi.L.Rev. 151 (1937); 16 Minn.L.Rev. 126 n. 19 (1932). The same principle applies if the BFP takes a mortgage rather than a deed; he will have priority over the previous mortgage.

36. Note that it is most improbable that the grantee will have assumed personal liability on the debt, for the land is represented to him as being debt-free.

37. See § 10.2, infra.

38. Windle v. Bonebrake, 23 F. 165 (C.C.Kan.1885); Note, 5 U. of Chi.L. Rev. 151 (1937); Metropolitan Life Ins. Co. v. Guy, 223 Ala. 285, 135 So. 434 (1931); Heintz v. Kebba, 5 Neb. Unoff. 289, 98 N.W. 431 (1904), seems to be in this category. See 16 Minn. L.Rev. 127, n. 21 (1932), for a collection of cases; Federal Land Bank v. Corinth Bank & Trust Co., 214 Ala. 146, 107 So. 88 (1926). Cf. Beckman v. Ward, 174 Wash. 326, 24 P.2d 1091 (1933), in which the court conceded that the grantee had been negligent in failing to demand the note, but allowed him to take free of the mort-

sible discharge is obtained by the mortgagor-grantor, or by an escrow or title company acting in the transaction as the mortgagor's agent, the grantee can hardly be blamed and should take free of the mortgage.[39]

Finally, note that if the grantee can rely on the records as against a holder in due course of a negotiable note, *a fortiori* he can do so as against a non-HDC. Here there is no competing UCC policy against which the operation of the recording acts must be weighed.

Other Wrongful Acts by Mortgagee

The failure of the assignee of a mortgage to record it places the mortgagee in a position to do a variety of wrongful acts which the law makes binding as against the assignee. Instead of giving a release of the mortgage as discussed above, the mortgagee might obtain from the mortgagor by fraud a renewal note and mortgage, and might then asssign them to a bona fide purchaser. Such a purchaser has been held to have priority over the original assignee.[40] Alternatively, the mortgagee might proceed to foreclose the mortgage (assuming it is in default), thereby passing title to a bona fide purchaser at the sale or buying in the property himself and later selling it to a bona fide purchaser; again, such a purchaser should take free of the mortgage even though the mortgagee had no right to foreclose it.[41] Another possibility is that the government will institute an eminent domain action against the property, naming only the mortgagor and mortgagee as defendants, with the assignee omitted because his name does not appear in the public records. If the condemnation award is paid to the named parties, the land will be taken by the government

gage on the ground that the assignee's failure to record had been more negligent.

39. Bacon v. Van Schoonhoven, 87 N.Y. 446 (1882). Chittick v. Thompson Hill Devel. Corp., 230 App.Div. 410, 245 N.Y.S. 71 (1930), affirmed 259 N.Y. 223, 181 N.E. 458 (1932), after reasonable excuse from non-production of documents had been given; Swasey v. Emerson, 168 Mass. 118, 46 N.E. 426, 60 Am.St.Rep. 368 (1897), (apparently); Heintz v. Klebba, 5 Neb. Unoff. 289, 98 N.W. 431 (1904), contra; Vann v. Marbury, 100 Ala. 438, 14 So. 273, 23 L.R.A. 325, 46 Am.St. Rep. 70 (1893); Lewis v. Kirk, 28 Kan. 497, 42 Am.Rep. 173 (1882); Marling v. Jones, 138 Wis. 82, 119 N.W. 931, 131 Am.St.Rep. 996 (1909); City Bank of Portage v. Plank, 141 Wis. 653, 124 N.W. 1000, 135 Am.St. Rep. 62, 18 Ann.Cas. 869 (1910); see 29 Col.L.Rev. 61, 63 (1929); Foss v. Dullam, 111 Minn. 220, 126 N.W. 820 (1910).

40. Central Trust Co. v. Stepanek, 138 Iowa 131, 115 N.W. 891 (1908); Jackson v. Stickney, 107 U.S. 478, 2 S.Ct. 814, 27 L.Ed. 529 (1882) (secured debt negotiable and in hands of holder in due course); Merrill v. Hurley, 6 S.D. 592, 62 N.W. 958, 55 Am.St.Rep. 859 (1895) (same facts as in preceding case)—accord. See also Havighorst v. Bowen, 214 Ill. 90, 73 N.E. 402 (1905); Torrey v. Deavitt, 53 Vt. 331 (1881). See note, 16 Minn.L.Rev. 123, 127 (1932).

41. Huitink v. Thompson, 95 Minn. 392, 104 N.W. 237, 111 Am.St.Rep. 476, 5 Ann.Cas. 338 (1905). The mortgagor, in such a case, will have a remedy against the mortgagee who foreclosed wrongfully. See 18 N. Car.L.Rev. 61, 65 (1939). See generally 89 A.L.R. 170, 182–83 (1934).

free of the mortgage and the assignee will have no claim against the government for any further money.[42]

Finally, suppose the mortgagee, pretending to continue to hold the note and mortgage after he has assigned them, induces the defaulting mortgagor to give him a deed in lieu of foreclosure. On the face of the record, all interests in the property have now merged in the same person—the mortgagee—and he proceeds to sell the land to a bona fide purchaser. Can such a purchaser take title relieved of the unrecorded assignee's interest? The cases are divided,[43] but the answer plainly should be yes. The purchaser, after all, cannot make any more effective inquiry of anyone. The mortgagee has already lied to him, and may further claim that the mortgage note was destroyed after the alleged merger occurred; such a statement is not implausible. Inquiry of the mortgagor is probably useless, for he is likely to be as ignorant of the assignment as the purchaser. There is really no reason to distinguish this case from the one in which the mortgagee gives a wrongful release of the mortgage. Here, his deed to the purchaser is tantamount to a release. The merger in him seems perfect [44] and it should be so held to protect the reliability of the recording system.[45]

In all of these cases in which the mortgagee has employed his power to mislead others because the assignment was unrecorded, the question arises whether the debt, now unsecured, is still enforceable

42. First Nat. Bank v. Paris, 358 Ill. 378, 193 N.E. 207 (1934).

43. Cases favoring the bona fide purchaser include Gregory v. Savage, 32 Conn. 250 (1864); McCormick v. Bauer, 122 Ill. 573, 13 N.E. 852 (1887), in effect overruling Edgerton v. Young, 43 Ill. 464 (1867); Artz v. Yeager, 30 Ind.App. 677, 66 N.E. 917 (1903); Jenks v. Shaw, 99 Iowa 604, 48 N.W. 900, 61 Am.St.Rep. 256 (1906); Ames v. Miller, 65 Neb. 204, 91 N.W. 250 (1902); see Lands, To Use of Security Savings & Trust Co. v. Robacker, 313 Pa. 271, 273, 169 A. 891, 892 (1933).

Cases allowing the unrecorded assignment to survive include Thauer v. Smith, 213 Wis. 91, 250 N.W. 842 (1933), commented on in 82 U. of Pa. L.Rev. 547 (1934); 29 Ill.L.Rev. 121 (1934); 9 Wis.L.Rev. 408 (1934); 10 Wis.L.Rev. 292 (1935); Merchants' Trust Co. v. Davis, 49 Idaho 494, 290 P. 383 (1930); Purdy v. Huntington, 42 N.Y. 334, 1 Am.Rep. 532 (1869); Curtis v. Moore, 152 N.Y. 159, 46 N.E. 168, 57 Am.St.Rep. 506 (1897), decided not only on the ground of constructive notice arising from non-production of the instruments, but also on the ground that the recording act did not require an assignment to be recorded to be effective against subsequent purchasers of the fee, a curious belief in view of Bacon v. Van Schoonhoven, 87 N. Y. 446 (1882); Zorn v. Van Buskirk, 111 Okl. 211, 239 P. 151 (1925), emphasizing the absence of a recorded release; Howard v. Shaw, 10 Wash. 151, 38 P. 746 (1894), on the ground that assignments were not covered by the recording acts then in force.

44. An exception may be made if a title examination by the purchaser disclosed the existence of junior liens, since their presence may suggest that no merger occurred upon the transfer of the equity of redemption to the mortgagee; see generally § 6.15, infra.

45. See 9 Wisc.L.Rev. 408 (1934); 29 Ill.L.Rev. 121 (1934); 82 U.Pa.L.Rev. 547 (1934).

as before. There is little authority,[46] but the answer would seem to be that it can be asserted only against one primarily liable on it, and even then perhaps, only if the debtor has not made an apparent payment of the debt, as by means of a foreclosure or deed in lieu. Here the distinction between assignees who are HDC's and those who are not again becomes relevant. As against the HDC, the foreclosure or deed in lieu would presumably be an ineffective form of payment, for the debtor would be bound to discover who held his note. But if the assignee were not a HDC, and if the debtor had no actual notice of the assignment, the foreclosure or deed in lieu should be held to satisfy the debt.[47]

Wrongful Acts by Trustee under Deed of Trust

Certain of the wrongful acts in which a mortgagee might engage, as discussed above, might also be perpetrated by the trustee if a deed of trust were employed rather than a mortgage as the security device. In particular, a trustee might, without the assignee's assent, collude with the debtor to release the deed of trust, or he might foreclose wrongfully, and in either case title might then pass to a bona fide purchaser. If the note had been assigned to a new holder who had recorded no assignment, these acts of the trustee would quite clearly deprive him of his security in the real estate, much as would similar acts of a mortgagee as we have already seen.

But the use of the deed of trust introduces a striking new dimension to our analysis: such acts of the trustee are equally devastating to the assignee even if the assignment is recorded! Recording does not improve the assignee's position.[48] The reason for this result lies in the nature of the deed of trust. In most jurisdictions, it is the normal role of the trustee to do two things: to reconvey when the debtor pays off the debt, and to foreclose if he defaults. The trustee has a fiduciary duty to perform these functions properly, and he was originally selected by the parties (practically speaking, by the lender in most instances) because of their confidence that he would carry them out. When the original creditor assigns the note, there is ordi-

46. See Ross, The Double Hazard of a Note and Mortgage, 16 Minn.L.Rev. 123 (1932); Brown and Dougherty, Assignment of Realty Mortgages in Oregon, 17 Or.L.Rev. 83 (1938).

47. See § 5.33, supra.

48. Mann v. Jummel, 183 Ill. 523, 56 N.E. 161 (1900); Lennartz v. Quilty, 191 Ill. 174, 60 N.E. 913, 85 Am.St. Rep. 260 (1901); Vogel v. Troy, 232 Ill. 481, 83 N.E. 960 (1908) discussed in 3 Ill.L.Rev. 97 (1908); Marsh v. Stover, 363 Ill. 490, 2 N.E.2d 559 (1936); Williams v. Jackson, 107 U.S. 478, 2 S.Ct. 814, 27 L.Ed. 529 (1882). See Greeley, Note, 26 Ill.L.Rev. 688 (1931); Leesman, Note, 31 Ill.L.Rev. 352 (1936), See also W.Va.Rev.Code c. 38, art. 12, § 2 (1931), discussed by Carlin, Release of Assigned Liens, 44 W.Va.L.Q. 175, 191 (1938), extending the power of a trustee under a trust deed mortgage to execute a valid release regardless of authority in the deed of trust.

On the rights of a mortgagor not in default against a bona fide purchaser after a wrongful sale under the power of sale by the trustee in a trust deed mortgage, see note, 18 N.Car.L.Rev. 61 (1939).

narily no change of trustees. Rather, the assignee is generally satisfied to have the original trustee continue in his role.

Innocent third parties who deal with the land are entitled to assume that the trustee, whether he is acting to reconvey the property or to foreclose, is performing in accordance with the instructions and wishes of the current holder of the note. They have no duty to contact the holder personally to make certain that the trustee is acting within those instructions. Hence an assignment of the beneficiary's interest, even if recorded, is not of any great interest to third parties, for the assignment will merely indicate to whom the trustee owes his duty, and not whether he is acting within it. As a practical matter, recordation of the assignment is irrelevant so far as the rights of innocent purchasers relying on a reconveyance or foreclosure of the security are concerned. In other contexts, such as that of successive assignments to be discussed below, however, recordation of the assignment of a deed of trust may be of great importance.

Successive Assignments by the Mortgagee: Nonnegotiable Note

We come now to the most complex area of application of the recording acts to mortgage assignments. When a mortgagee, concededly acting unethically, executes two successive assignments of the same mortgage to two different assignees, which will prevail? In the very few jurisdictions in which the recording acts do not apply to mortgage assignments,[49] and assuming that the secured note is nonnegotiable (or that it has not in fact been negotiated to either assignee as a HDC), the common law of contracts will apply. According to the Restatement,[50] the fundamental rule is "first in time, first in right."[51] However, a number of exceptions exist. If the second assignee lacks knowledge of the first and pays value, he will prevail over the first if he receives payment or satisfaction, gets a judgment against the maker of the note, or enters into a novation with the maker. Perhaps most important, a second assignee who is a BFP will prevail if he obtains "possession of a writing of a type customarily accepted as a symbol or as evidence of the right assigned."[52] Almost certainly the note itself, even though nonnegotiable, would be considered such a writing, and if the mortgagee gives possession of the note to the second assignee rather than the first, the second will prevail.

49. Neal v. Bradley, 238 Ark. 714, 384 S.W.2d 238 (1964), construing Ark.Stat.Ann. § 51–1016, the recording act, as inapplicable to assignments of mortgage notes.

50. Restatement, Second, Contracts, § 174 (Tent.Draft 1973). The English rule of Dearle v. Hall, 3 Russ., Ch. 1 (1823), which gives priority to the first assignee who gives notice to the obligor, has been fairly widely adopted in the United States. However, it is rejected by the Restatement, and does not apply to interests in land in any event. See Glenn, Assignment of Choses in Action, 20 Va.L.Rev. 621, 652 (1934).

51. See Neal v. Bradley, note 49 supra.

52. Restatement, Second, Contracts, § 174(b) (iv) (Tent.Draft 1973).

In most jurisdictions, the foregoing is merely academic, for the recording acts do apply to mortgage assignments.[53] They, like other conveyances, are generally made void if unrecorded, as against subsequent purchasers [54] for value and without notice; in some jurisdictions, the subsequent purchaser must also himself record first. Again assuming that the note in question is nonnegotiable, the application of the recording acts generally works as follows. If the first assignee records immediately, he will be fully protected against subsequent assignees, and this is so whether or not he obtained possession of the note.[55] If the first assignee does not record, however, the second assignee will prevail, at least if he *does* get possession of the note.[56] (In race-notice jurisdictions, he will of course also need to record his own assignment in order to prevail.) On the other hand, if the first assignee fails to record but takes possession of the note, the mortgagee's failure to tender it to the second assignee has been held to give him notice that a prior assignment has occurred, and thus to rob him of his BPF status under the recording acts.[57] Whether this much importance should be attached to physical possession of a nonnegotiable note as against the normal operation of the recording acts may be debatable. But here we are dealing with relatively sophisticated business persons in most instances, and there is no doubt that most investors in mortgages consider possession of even a nonnegotiable note to be a highly significant indicator of ownership. Hence the assignor's failure to produce the note would indeed tip off most investors that something is wrong with the deal being offered.

53. See Annot., 89 A.L.R. 170 (1934).

54. The second assignee is generally considered a "purchaser" for purposes of the recording act; Price v. Northern Bond & Mortg. Co., 161 Wash. 690, 297 P. 786 (1931).

55. Crane v. Turner, 67 N.Y. 437 (1876); Stein v. Sullivan, 31 N.J.Eq. 409 (1879), even where the bond and mortgage were obtained from the first assignee and sold to the second; Mott v. Newark German Hospital, 55 N.J.Eq. 722, 37 A. 757 (1897); Murphy v. Barnard, 162 Mass. 72, 38 N.E. 29, 44 Am.St.Rep. 340 (1894), negotiable note involved, redelivered to mortgagee after recorded assignment and then sold to a second assignee; Strong v. Jackson, 123 Mass. 60, 25 Am.St.Rep. 19 (1877).

56. Second Nat. Bank v. Dyer, 121 Conn. 263, 184 A. 386, 104 A.L.R. 1295 (1936); Price v. Northern Bond & Mort. Co., 161 Wash. 690, 297 P. 786 (1931) (second assignee prevailed although he did not demand possession of note); Morrow v. Stanley, 119 Md. 590, 87 A. 484 (1913), decided after amendment of earlier statute made title to the debt secured by a mortgage conclusively presumed to be in the person holding record title to the mortgage; Blunt v. Norris, 123 Mass. 55, 25 Am.Rep. 14 (1877); see 89 A.L.R. 171, 177 (1934); 104 A.L.R. 1303 (1936).

57. Syracuse Bank v. Merrick, 182 N.Y. 387, 75 N.E. 232 (1905); cf. Price v. Northern Bond & Mortg. Co., 161 Wash. 690, 297 P. 786 (1931). If the recording act is worded strongly enough, it may be totally controlling, and may make possession of the note in the first assignee irrelevant if he does not record. The Florida statute may be read to have this effect; see Fla.Stat. § 701.02, discussed in Note, Transfer of the Mortgagee's Interest in Florida, 14 U.Fla.L.Rev. 98 (1961).

Successive Assignments by the Mortgagee: Negotiable Note

Where the mortgage debt is in the form of a negotiable instrument there is greater diversity of opinion as to the effect both of recordation and non-recordation of mortgage assignments. Where the first assignee not only records his assignment but gets and keeps possession of the mortgage documents there would be no question that he would be protected against a later assignee. The controversy arises where, although the first assignment has been recorded, the negotiable note and mortgage has been left in the possession of the mortgagee, redelivered to him, or obtained by him from the assignee wrongfully through fraudulent representations or otherwise, and is then sold to one who, aside from any effect of the recording acts upon the situation, would be a holder in due course entitled to the note and mortgage as against the prior assignee.

On this question there are three views.[58] One is that a promissory note, by virtue of being secured by a real estate mortgage, does not lose its character as commercial paper and imparts its negotiable character to the mortgage, thus bringing them both within the purview of statutes dealing with commercial paper. The result is that recording the prior assignment has no effect upon the later transferee of the note and mortgage security. Any constructive notice from the recordation is insufficient to prevent him being a holder in due course of the note, since actual notice is necessary for that; this appears to be the position of the Uniform Commercial Code.[59] And the same is true as to the mortgage which is regarded as accompanying it as an inseparable incident of it.[60]

A second view, at the opposite extreme from the first, is that the later indorsee of the note takes no title to the note since his vendor

58. For discussions of the problem, see notes, 8 Minn.L.Rev. 347 (1924); 22 Cal.L.Rev. 677, 681, 684 (1934); 10 Jour.B.A.Kan. 282, 284 (1942); Ross, Double Hazard of a Note and Mortgage, 16 Minn.L.Rev. 130 (1932); Brown and Daugherty, Assignment of Realty Mortgages, 17 Or.L.Rev. 83, 91–93 (1938). See semble, note 78 U. of Pa.L.Rev. 108 (1929); 16 Tex.L. Rev. 534, 535 (1938).

59. Although no case is yet decided under the Uniform Commercial Code § 3–302 as to whether a previously-recorded mortgage assignment will deprive a holder of HDC status by giving him constructive notice, the Code provides that "The filing or recording of a document does not of itself constitute notice within the provisions of this Article to a person who would otherwise be a holder in due course." U.C.C. § 3–304(5). In National Surety Fire & Casualty Co. v. Mazzara, 289 Ala. 542, 268 So.2d 814 (1972), the existence of a recorded deed was held not to constitute constructive notice to a mortgagee, to whom an insurance company's draft for fire insurance proceeds was endorsed, that the grantee under the deed might have a claim to the proceeds.

60. Foster v. Augustana College & Theological Seminary, 92 Okl. 96, 218 P. 335, 37 A.L.R. 854 (1923); U. S. Nat. Bank v. Holton, 99 Or. 419, 195 P. 823 (1921); Ross v. Title Guarantee & Trust Co., 136 Cal.App. 393, 29 P.2d 236 (1934), discussed 22 Cal.L. Rev. 677, 681, 684 (1934); 23 Cal.L. Rev. 108 (1934); Security Mortgage Co. v. Delfs, 47 Cal.App. 599, 191 P. 53 (1920), semble; prior assignment recorded first but not until after the second assignment. See 37 A.L.R. 860 (1925); 127 A.L.R. 201 (1940).

in fact had none, and the prior recorded assignment was notice to him of the infirmity so as to preclude him from being a holder in due course.[61] Courts taking this view find it necessary to distinguish between unsecured notes, as to which it is clear that no title examination is necessary to become a HDC, and secured notes, as to which it is supposed that the existence of the mortgage should lead the assignee to search the title.[62]

The third view is that the transferee of the note is a holder in due course as to it; but since the element of negotiability is lacking in mortgages, he takes the mortgage with notice of the prior, recorded assignment and cannot foreclose in the collection of the note.[63] Apart from its holding as to the note, this last solution has little to commend it. It infringes upon the basic principle that the assignment of a debt secured by a mortgage carries with it the right to the security.[64] Further, while giving the indorsee of the note the right to collect the debt, the prior holder's recorded interest as assignee of the mortgage is valueless because he has no right to collect the debt which is essential to its utilization. "Thus, either the mortgage lien is extinguished because there is no one entitled to enforce the security, and the maker of the note gets a windfall in having the premises freed of the lien of the mortgage or deed of trust; or the holder of the prior recorded right to the mortgage, through a power to assign the mortgage to the indorsee of the note, is in a position to use pressure to obtain from the indorsee the practical value of the security." [65]

As between the other two views, the first one seems preferable,[66] and may well be required by the U.C.C.[67] Assignees of mortgages are engaged, dominantly, in buying a debt claim, and therefore the rules applying to that particular form of debt should govern its sale. If it is in the form of a negotiable instrument, just as its negotiability is not affected by the fact that it is secured by a mortgage, neither should it be subject to the hazard of the assignee's having to investigate real property records in order to be sure that he will be a holder

61. Murphy v. Barnard, 162 Mass. 72, 38 N.E. 29, 44 Am.St.Rep. 340 (1894); Strong v. Jackson, 123 Mass. 60, 25 Am.St.Rep. 19 (1877).

62. This supposition can lead to anomalous results. If the assignee does not know that the note is secured by a mortgage, he automatically gets the security anyway. But if he does not realize that it is secured, it can hardly serve to warn him to search the title. See § 5.27, supra.

63. Taylor v. American Nat. Bank, 64 Fla. 525, 60 So. 783 (1912); Wood v. Sparks, 59 S.W.2d 361 (Tex.Com. App.1933), rehearing denied 63 S.W. 2d 1109, discussed in note, 10 Tex.L. Rev. 201 (1932); note, 16 Tex.L.Rev. 534, 537 (1938)—accord. See Note, Transfer of the Mortgagee's Interest in Florida, 14 U.Fla.L.Rev. 98 (1961), recommending this view under the Florida mortgage assignment recording statute.

64. See § 5.27, supra.

65. Note, 22 Cal.L.Rev. 677, 695 (1934).

66. See 2 Glenn, Mortgages § 315.2 (1943).

67. See note 59, supra.

in due course. And this is true even though, in good part, the value of the claim is high because it is secured, and even though title to the security may be investigated in determining whether to buy. If he does not wish to investigate he should not be under compulsion to do so on penalty of not getting the main thing he was bargaining for, the note. As was just pointed out, if he gets the note, he should get the mortgage with it.

Where the assignee of a mortgage securing a negotiable note fails to record his assignment but gets and keeps possession of the note he should, and by what is believed to be the better authority, does prevail over a subsequent purchaser of the mortgage from its record owner.[68] The reason is substantially the same one that should leave the purchaser of the secured negotiable note free to ignore prior recorded assignments of the mortgage, i. e., the principal thing that is being bought is the note itself, not its accessory, the mortgage. At least that is the controlling thought and should prevail in determining the rules governing the priorities of the parties who take successive assignments of it. Commercial policy in the free mobility of the debt is more important in a case of this sort than the land policy. It is true that the assignment transaction may be and is sometimes couched in terms which do not mention the debt as distinct from the security; and when this is the case the agreement nevertheless will carry at least an equitable right to the negotiable note or the bond as well as the security interest in the property.[69] Nevertheless, whenever a purchaser is apprised, whether from recitals in the mortgage or otherwise, that the obligation he is about to buy is expressed in the written form of a negotiable instrument, the natural, and the only prudent, course is to ask for the document, for that is what he wants.[70] Indeed he normally wants both the note and the mortgage. So far as he is concerned they are indispensable documents. If they are not forthcoming, he has adequate warning that something may be amiss. He cannot rely upon the records in such a case any more than can one who goes to pay the debt.[71] And it follows that an assignee who gets and holds onto the negotiable note and mortgage, although he runs some risks if he does not record his mortgage,[72] should not run the hazard of losing to a subsequent assignee from his assignor.

68. Syracuse Sav. Bank v. Merrick, 182 N.Y. 387, 75 N.E. 232 (1905); Barringer v. Loder, 47 Or. 223, 81 P. 778 (1905) Richards Trust Co. v. Rhomberg, 19 S.D. 595, 104 N.W. 268 (1905); Miller Brewing Co. v. Manasse, 99 Wis. 99, 74 N.W. 535 (1898). Adler v. Newell, 109 Cal. 42, 41 P. 799 (1895) under a special recording statute making recordation of a mortgage assignment notice but not requiring recordation for validity as in the case of recording of conveyances.

69. See § 5.27, supra.

70. See Thauer v. Smith, 213 Wis. 91, 250 N.W. 842 (1933).

71. See § 5.33, supra.

72. The risks are those created by wrongful releases or other acts of his assignor. See notes 84–1, supra.

In spite of the foregoing there are several cases in which the failure of a prior assignee who held the negotiable note and mortgage to record his mortgage resulted in a subsequent assignee prevailing. It is possible to account for some of the results on the basis of the language of the statute involved,[73] or special facts justifying reliance upon appearances created by the wrongful conduct of the mortgagee for which, it is true, the assignee was not responsible but which were made possible by the assignee's failure to do the simple act of recordation.[74]

§ 5.35 Partial Assignments and Participations

A mortgage lender may frequently wish to assign partial interests in a loan or a group of loans to one or more investors.[75] Such transactions occur in two common contexts. The first is the case of a very large loan which may be beyond the financial resources of the originating or "lead" lender. The creation of "participation" interests by way of partial assignments which can be sold to one or more other financial institutions allows the lead lender to recoup some of its cash immediately, and at the same time spreads the risk of a possible default on the underlying loan. Participations of this type are sometimes arranged on both construction [76] and permanent loans.

The other context in which participations are frequently employed involves the accumulation by the lead lender of a large group or "package" of relatively small mortgage loans, usually on one-family houses. Here the participation device is used as an alternative to direct sale and assignment of the loans on the secondary mortgage market. A large number of participation interests, perhaps hundreds or thousands, may be created; each interest will represent a small share in each of a large number of loans. The participations may be sold to financial institutions or to individual investors. The Federal Home Loan Mortgage Corporation (FHLMC), for example, has used this type of participation sale very effectively in recent years.[77]

73. Morrow v. Stanley, 119 Md. 590, 87 A. 484 (1913), under a strongly worded statute making record ownership of the mortgage conclusive of ownership of the debt.

74. Blunt v. Norris, 123 Mass. 55, 25 Am.Rep.14 (1877), a new, genuine note obtained by fraud by the mortgagee from the mortgagor and transferred together with an assignment of the mortgage; Second Nat. Bank v. Dyer, 121 Conn. 263, 184 A. 386, 104 A.L.R. 1295 (1936), criticized in note, 6 Pitt.L.Rev. 300 (1940), forged instruments transferred to the second assignee (cf. Morris v. Bacon, 123 Mass. 58, 25 Am.Rep. 17 (1877)).

75. See generally Simpson, Loan Participations: Pitfalls for Participants, 31 Bus.Law. 1977 (1976); Drake & Weems, Mortgage Loan Participations: The Trustee's Attack, 52 Am. Bankr.L.J. 23 (1978).

76. See Arnold, Modern Real Estate and Mortgage Forms 4–29 (1970), for a participation agreement intended for use on a construction loan.

77. See Brinkerhoff, PC's Biggest Year: $5 Billion Worth Sold by The Mortgage Corporation, FHLBBJ, Dec. 1977, at 19; see generally § 11.3, infra.

Generally at least two documents are involved in the sale of participation interests of the latter type: a participation agreement and a participation certificate (PC). The first will set forth the parties' rights and duties in general,[78] while the second will state the particular share or percentage which the investor is receiving, and may also identify the loans which are included in the package. In the first type of participation, involving a single large loan, all of this information will usually be contained in a single agreement. Whatever the format, the documents should be drafted to state the parties' agreement on a number of important issues, including the following.[79] As among the participants, and as against the lead lender, who will have priority in the loan and foreclosure proceeds? Almost always the participants have equal priority; whether the lead lender will share their priority or be subordinate to them as to any retained interest in the loans is a matter for negotiation. The lead lender is generally given the right to retain the notes and other loan documents, to satisfy the mortgages as they are paid, and if the participation is on a package of home loans, to make the necessary decisions concerning acceleration, forbearance, appointment of receivers, foreclosure, redemption, collection of deficiencies, settlement with mortgage insurers, and the like. In the case of a large loan with only a few participants, they may arrange to vote or otherwise collaborate among themselves in the making of such decisions triggered by loan deliquency. The agreement will spell out the liability of the parties for foreclosure and property carrying and disposition costs. It will require the lead lender to remit the participants' shares of mortgage payments to them, and it may constitute him a trustee for the participants' benefit. Finally, the lead lender may or may not guarantee payment of the participants' shares of principal and interest.[80]

Priorities in the Absence of Agreement

The common law rules concerning priorities among participants, and as between the participants and the lead lender, are seldom of much practical importance today. This is because participation agreements nearly always deal with these matters fully and competently, as mentioned above. Hence only a brief outline of these priorities issues will be given here.

78. See, e. g., FHLMC Participation Sales Agreement Series 300 (covering sales of participation interests by FHLMC to investors); FHLMC Mortgage Participation Agreement 210 (covering sales to FHLMC of participations by originating mortgagees).

79. See sources cited notes 76, 78, supra for illustrative coverage of these points. There is no question that an express agreement regarding priority among the participants will control, and the same is presumably true of all other important issues in the management of the loans. See Conway v. Yadon, 132 Okl. 36, 269 P. 309 (1928); Wilson v. Eigenbrodt, 30 Minn. 4, 13 N.W. 907 (1882); Walker v. Dement, 42 Ill. 272 (1866); Note, 25 Cal.L.Rev. 504 (1937).

80. FHLMC's guarantee of its PC's has been an important element in their marketability.

As among the participants, the great majority of courts today would unquestionably grant a pro-rata priority in the absence of agreement.[81] Some earlier cases took the view that the order in which the partial assignments were made controlled the priority of the interests they took;[82] others held that the interests of the participants, if represented by separate notes executed by the mortgagor (an unusual situation in modern times, when a single note is typically employed), were determined by the order of maturity of the notes.[83] The previous edition of this book quite effectively points out the impracticality and irrationality of these views,[84] and they are so unlikely to be advanced by any court today that it does not seem worthwhile to attempt to demolish them further. Quite clearly the rule of pro-rata distribution among the participants is most likely to comport with the intent of the parties.

With respect to priority in the mortgage repayments or foreclosure proceeds as between the lead lender and the participants, the matter is somewhat more open to question. Absent a guarantee of payment to the participants by the lead, the better view is that they have no special priority as against the interest retained by the lead.[85] Con-

81. "It may be said, however, that by the great weight of authority the courts of this country * * * are agreed that as between assignees of notes bearing the same maturity date there is not, in the absence of contract, a preference or priority. Studebaker Bros., Mfg. Co. v. McCurgur, 20 Neb. 500, 30 N.W. 686 (1887); Adams v. Lear, 3 La.Ann. 144 (1848); Burhans v. Mitchell, 42 Mich. 417, 4 N.W. 178 (1880); Penzel v. Brookmire, 51 Ark. 105, 10 S.W. 15, 14 Am.St.Rep. 23 (1889); Smith v. Bowne, 60 Ga. 484; Campbell v. Johnston, 4 Dana, Ky., 177, 178 (1895); Dixon v. Clayville, 44 Md. 573 (1876); Wilson v. Eigenbrodt, 30 Minn. 4, 13 N.W. 907, 908 (1882); Bank of England v. Tarleton, 23 Miss. 173 (1856); Bridenbecker v. Lowell, 32 Barb., N.Y., 9 (1865); Andrews v. Hobgood, 1 Lea, Tenn., 693 (1887); Keyes v. Wood, 21 Vt. 331 (1849); First Nat. Bank v. Andrews, 7 Wash. 261, 34 P. 913, 38 Am.St.Rep. 885 (1893)." Domeyer v. O'Connell, 364 Ill. 467, 4 N.E.2d 830, 108 A.L.R. 476 (1936); see Land Title Bank v. Schenck, 335 Pa. 419, 6 A.2d 878 (1939); Annot., 115 A.L.R. 40 (1938); see Note, 10 Tulane L.Rev. 303 (1936).

82. Cullum v. Erwin, 4 Ala. 452 (1842). This was the earlier rule in Virginia but after vigorous attack upon it by J. W. H. Pilson, 19 Va.L.Rev. 878 (1933), it was changed by statute. Va.Code, § 55–60–1. See also Miami Oil Co. v. Florida Discount Corp., 102 Fla. 209, 135 So. 845 (1931), commented on in, 6 U. of Cin.L.Rev. 247 (1932).

83. In Conway v. Yadon, 132 Okl. 36, 269 P. 309 (1928), the court said that it was "more or less consistently followed in Alabama, Florida, Illinois, Indiana, Iowa, Kansas, Ohio, New Hampshire, and Wisconsin." See Wilson v. Hayward, 6 Fla. 171 (1855). For modifications of the order of maturity rule where accepted, see Campbell, Cases on Mortgages, 2d ed., 586 n. 3.

84. See Osborne, Mortgages § 244 (2d Ed. 1970).

85. Domeyer v. O'Connell, 364 Ill. 467, 4 N.E.2d 830, 108 A.L.R. 476 (1936). This case contains an elaborate discussion of the entire question together with a good collection of authorities. In large part its reasoning is followed in the text. For comments on it see notes, 4 U. of Chi.L.Rev. 502 (1937); 2 John Marshall L.Q. 422 (1937); 31 Ill.L.Rev. 111 (1936). See 50 A.L.R. 543 (1927); 108 A.L.R. 485 (1937); 115 A.L.R. 40 (1938). Look also at Title Guarantee & Trust Co. v. Mortgage Commission, 273 N.Y. 415, 7 N.E.2d 841 (1937), discussed in notes, 37 Col.L.Rev. 1010 (1937); 14 N.Y.Univ.L.Q.Rev. 259 (1937).

trary cases are based on a number of dubious arguments: that the lead is, in effect, a trustee for the participants and should not be permitted to recover from the land at their expense;[86] that the inverse order of alienation rule, which applies to protect the grantee of a portion of a mortgaged parcel of land, should also apply here;[87] and that the partial assignment constitutes an implied promise by the lead lender to give the participants priority over himself.[88] None of these arguments has much persuasive power, and the better cases hold that the assignor and the participants share pro rata if they have not agreed to the contrary.

In cases in which the lead lender has guaranteed payment to the participants, the balance of the authorities clearly shifts to favor the latter, and they are usually held to have first claim on the mortgage payments or foreclosure proceeds as against the lead lender.[89] Such

86. While there is authority for the statement that the lead lender is a trustee, see Robbins v. Wilson Creek State Bank, 5 Wash.2d 584, 105 P.2d 1107 (1940), there is no reason to extend this idea so far as to deny the lead what is, under the apparent terms of the agreement, rightfully his; his trusteeship should extend only to the funds he is obligated to pay over to the participants.

87. See § 10.10, infra. The rule is intended to apply only where the grantee has paid full value for the land without deduction for the mortgage, and thus is entirely inapplicable in the present context.

88. Absent contract language, the supposition is far-fetched. Under ordinary contract law the assignor does not even warrant that the obligor will perform; Restatement, Second, Contracts, § 165(2) (Tent.Draft.1973).

89. If the lead lender makes an explicit guarantee of payment, see Matter of Lawyers Mort. Co., 151 Misc. 744, 272 N.Y.S. 390 (1934); Matter of Lawyers Mort. Co., 157 Misc. 813, 284 N.Y.S. 740 (1936); In re Title and Mortgage Co., 275 N.Y. 347, 9 N.E.2d 957, 115 A.L.R. 35 (1937); Pink v. Thomas, 282 N.Y. 10, 24 N.E.2d 724 (1939) commented on, 26 Va.L.Rev. 825 (1940); Lawyers Title and Guar. Co., In re, 287 N.Y. 264, 39 N.E. 233 (1942) commented on 55 Harv.L.Rev. 882 (1942); Ferris v. Prudence Realization Corp., 292 N.Y. 210, 54 N.E.2d 367 (1944), affirmed on certiorari, Prudence Realization Co. v. Ferris, 323 U.S. 650, 65 S.Ct. 539, 89 L.Ed. 528 (1945); commented on, 32 Va.L. Rev. 176 (1945); In re 1934 Realty Corp., 150 F.2d 477 (C.A.N.Y.1945) commented on, 32 Va.L.Rev. 176 (1945); In re Phillippi, 329 Pa. 581, 198 A. 16 (1938); Cannon v. McDaniel & Jackson, 46 Tex. 303 (1876). For a discussion of problems arising in connection with guaranteed mortgages, see 34 Col.L.Rev. 663 (1934).

If the lead lender indorses particular negotiable notes of the mortgagor to particular participants, and the indorsements are unqualified, they constitute the indorser's contract that he will pay the instruments according to their tenor upon dishonor and any necessary notice of dishonor and protest; U.C.C. § 3–414. In this situation, see Anderson v. Sharp, 44 Ohio St. 260, 6 N.E. 900 (1886); Dixon v. Clayville, 44 Md. 573 (1876); Fourth Nat. Bank's Appeal, 123 Pa. 473, 16 A. 779, 10 Am.St.Rep. 538 (1889); Louisville Title Co.'s Receiver v. Crab Orchard Banking Co., 249 Ky. 736, 61 S.W.2d 615 (1933); Fidelity Trust Co. v. Orr, 154 Tenn. 538, 289 S.W. 500 (1926); Reconstruction Finance Corp. v. Smith, 96 S.W.2d 824 (Tex.Civ. App.1936), noted, 15 Tex.L.Rev. 271 (1937); see 37 Col.L.Rev. 1010 (1937); 31 Ill.L.Rev. 1111, 1114 (1937); 77 U. of Pa.L.Rev. 266, 269 (1928).

Note, however, that in the usual case the note is singular, is not indorsed, and is not delivered to any of the assignees. Hence there is usually no guarantee by the lead lender in the absence of a specific agreement. See also, Restatement, Contracts, note 88 supra.

cases typically arise only when the mortgagee is insolvent and the claim to pro-rata priority is made by his trustee in bankruptcy or his unsecured creditors. The reasoning of the majority cases is that it is unfair for the mortgagee, who has obligated himself to see that the participants' claims are paid, to compete with them for the limited funds available.[90] A minority of cases take the position that the participants' claim based on the guarantee merely gives them an unsecured right to the insolvent mortgagee's general assets, just as other unsecured creditors.[91] An intermediate view, taken by the United States Supreme Court, holds that the priority of the mortgagee depends on whether he retained his participation interests at the outset or acquired them from other participants in free market transactions (in which case he will have an equal priority with the other participants), or whether he repurchased his interests from participants pursuant to his guarantee (in which case he will have a subordinate priority).[92] There has been little development in the law in this area in several decades, and it is difficult to say whether the general rule subordinating the guaranteeing lead lender would still be followed today.

Third Party Attacks on Participations

In recent years concern has been growing that participations may be subject to successful attack by third parties who have some claim on the lead lender or his assets. This concern derives from the looseness and informality with which most modern participations are handled. Specifically, the mortgagor's note, the mortgage, and other individual loan documents are usually left in the lead lender's hands. There is generally no recordation of the participation agreement or certificates, and no filing of a financing statement under Article 9 of the UCC.[93]

90. Reconstruction Fin. Corp. v. Smith, 96 S.W.2d 824 (Tex.Civ.App.1936) noted, 15 Tex.L.Rev. 271 (1937); Pustejovsky, v. K. J. Z. T. Lodge, 124 Tex. 504, 79 S.W.2d 1084 (1935); In re Title and Mortgage Guaranty Co. of Sullivan County, 275 N.Y. 347, 9 N.E.2d 957, 115 A.L.R. 35 (1937) commented on 47 Yale L.Jour. 480 (1938).

91. Kelly v. Middlesex Title Guaranty & Trust Co., 115 N.J.Eq. 592, 171 A. 823 (1934) affirmed 116 N.J.Eq. 574, 174 A. 706; Prudence Realization Corp. v. Geist, 316 U.S. 89, 62 S.Ct. 978, 86 L.Ed. 1293 (1942). Look also at Hinds v. Mooers, 11 Iowa 211 (1860), rule of priority of maturity applied; Wilcox v. Allen, 36 Mich. 160, 172 (1877), pro rata rule applied.

92. Under such circumstances "if the surety were allowed to prove his own claim before the creditor is paid, he would to that extent diminish the creditor's dividends upon his claim, and thus defeat the purpose for which he had given the indemnity." * * * "For like reasons equity requires the surety who holds security of the insolvent principal to give the benefit of it to the creditor for whom he is surety until the debt is paid." Prudence Realization Corp. v. Geist, 316 U.S. 89, 96, 62 S.Ct. 978, 86 L.Ed. 1293 (1942). See also Prudence Realization Corp. v. Ferris, 323 U.S. 650, 657, 65 S.Ct. 539, 89 L.Ed. 528 (1944), concurring opinion of Stone, C. J.

93. See Drake & Weems, Mortgage Loan Participations: The Trustee's Attack, 52 Am.Bankr.L.J. 23 (1978); Simpson, Loan Participations: Pitfalls for Participants, 31 Bus.Law 1977

It is quite clear that the participants in this sort of arrangement are not holders in due course of the mortgage note or notes, even if negotiable. Normally the notes are not indorsed to the participants,[94] and even if they were, physical delivery to the participants is impossible if each mortgage loan is represented by a single note,[95] as is the typical procedure. Indeed, the Code appears to make indorsement of fractional interests in a note to holders in due course impossible.[96]

The continuing presence of the note or notes in the lead lender's hands gives him the power to misdeal with them in several ways. For example, he may reassign them, either as additional participation interests or in toto.[97] He may pledge them to another creditor to secure other debts he owes.[98] He may receive payment from the mortgagors, and may effectively cancel the notes and satisfy the mortgages,[99] even if he fails to pass the participants' shares of the payments through to them. He may cancel the notes and record releases or satisfactions of the mortgages even without payment, and thereby allow bona fide purchasers of the land to take free of the mortgages.[1]

The participants normally have confidence that the lead lender will do none of these things, and they usually take no precautions to prevent them. But the failure of several major commercial banks during the 1970's suggests that such confidence may sometimes be misplaced.[2] The participants might insist that the notes be stamped

(1976); Coogan, Kripke & Weiss, The Outer Fringes of Article 9: Subordination Agreements, Security Interests in Money and Deposits, Negative Pledge Clauses and Participation Agreements, 79 Harv.L.Rev. 229 (1965).

94. Negotiation of order paper can be accomplished only by indorsement and delivery. U.C.C. § 3–202(1). The indorsement must be written on the notes themselves or on a paper firmly affixed to each note. U.C.C. § 3–202(2). The payee's signature on a separate piece of paper cannot constitute an indorsement. Tallahassee Bank & Trust Co. v. Raines, 125 Ga. App. 263, 187 S.E.2d 320 (1972).

95. A holder of an instrument must receive physical possession of it. U. C.C. § 1–201(20); Official Comment, U.C.C. § 3–804; Rex Smith Propane, Inc. v. National Bank of Commerce, 372 F.Supp. 499 (N.D.Tex.1974).

96. U.C.C. § 3–202(3), Official Comment 4 states: Any endorsement which purports to convey to any party less than the entire amount of the instrument is not effective for negotiation. This is true of * * * "Pay A one-half", or "Pay A two-thirds and B one-third", * * * and neither A nor B becomes a holder.

97. U.C.C. § 3–301: "The holder of an instrument whether or not he is the owner may transfer or negotiate it * * *." The original payee may be a holder; U.C.C. § 3–302.

98. See § 5.28, supra, at notes 74–82.

99. U.C.C. § 3–301: "The holder of an instrument, whether or not he is the owner may * * * discharge it or enforce payment in his own name.

1. This is always a possibility, whether the assignment is unitary or in the form of participations, if it is not recorded; see § 5.34, supra, at notes 34–39.

2. Banks which failed or were merged with other banks under FDIC supervision included Eatontown National Bank of New Jersey (1970), U.S. National Bank of San Diego (1973), Franklin National Bank of Chattanoo-

or marked with a notation that they are subject to the interests of the participants;[3] this action would be effective to prevent most of the types of misdealing mentioned in the previous paragraph,[4] but it would also seriously complicate the giving of valid satisfactions to mortgagors who repaid their loans, since it would presumably require the consent of all of the participants to a cancellation of the notes. This approach may make sense in a case in which there are only a few participants on a single large loan, but it is probably impractical with a package of small loans sold to a large number of participants. In the latter situation the participants must take the risk of misdealing by the lead.

Even in the absence of specific improper conduct by the lead lender, it is possible in the event of his insolvency that his general creditors or his trustee in bankruptcy may attack the very essence of the participation transaction, claiming that it is not an effective transfer of ownership in the notes, and thus that they remain part of the insolvent lead lender's estate.[5] This conclusion is a rather shocking one, and it is by no means clear that the courts will accept it. The mere absence of holder in due course status for the participants does not lead to the conclusion that no transfer has occurred. Even if the notes are negotiable, it is clearly possible to transfer partial interests in them by assignment.[6] The question is whether such transfers have in fact occurred in the typical participation.

If a participation is not a transfer of partial ownership of the notes, what is it? Some writers have argued that it is in reality a loan of money by the participants to the lead lender, with the interests in the mortgage notes serving as security for repayment.[7] Under this view either the filing of financing statements under UCC Article 9 or the recordation of assignments in the real estate records would be necessary to perfect the partial assignments as against the assignor's creditors or trustee in bankruptcy; which method should

ga (1974), Security National Bank of New York (1975) and American Bank and Trust of New York (1976). See Ailing Banks are Hard to Spot, Business Week, Nov. 8, 1976, at 108; Digging Out the Bad Debt Mess, Time, Jan. 26, 1976, at 49.

3. Such a notation would presumably give notice to any later taker of the instrument and preclude his becoming a HDC. See U.C.C. § 9–308 and Official Comment 3.

4. It would not of course, prevent a wrongful recording of a satisfaction or release by the mortgagee; see § 5.34, supra, at notes 34–39.

5. The authors are informed that this position has been taken by the trustee in bankruptcy of Franklin National Bank of Chattanooga, but at this writing there is no published decision.

6. Transfers which are not "negotiations" are of course recognized by the U.C.C. even for negotiable instruments; U.C.C. § 3–301. The common law recognizes partial assignments of contract rights; see Restatement, Second, Contracts, § 158(1).

7. Drake & Weems, Mortgage Loan Participations: The Trustee's Attack, 52 Am.Bankr.L.J. 23, 43–54 (1978).

be used is not yet clear.[8] In either event, the filing or recordation is bothersome and inconvenient, especially if the participations are in a package of loans which are secured by property in several counties or states. But if the parties provide in the participation agreement that sales and not loans are intended, it is hard to see why a court would resist following this expressed intention.[9]

Another possible view is that the participants have received only assignments of the proceeds from the ultimate mortgage loan payments or foreclosures, and not property interests in the notes themselves.[10] In support of this position it has been argued that only the assignor, and not the participants, has the right to enforce the mortgage notes, and thus that the participants cannot be considered their owners.[11] But this seems too simplistic. The right of the lead

8. See § 5.28, supra at notes 74–82. Under some recording statutes it may be doubtful that partial assignments of mortgages can be recorded. See 2 Glenn, Mortgages § 317.2 (1943); Osborne, Mortgages § 243 (2d ed. 1970), at n. 59. If the mortgages secure accounts receivable rather than notes, Article 9 filing is clearly required; U.C.C. § 9–102(1)(b), §§ 9–105, –106.

9. As against creditors or a trustee in bankruptcy, a court might have a strong incentive to find that the mortgage notes were still the lead lender's property if the lead had represented them to its creditors (for example, in its financial statements) as its exclusive assets. If the notes were dealt with by the lead lender in a manner consistent with the existence of the ownership in the participants, on the other hand, a court should have no motive on policy grounds to try to pull them back into the lead's estate.

10. Drake & Weems, Mortgage Loan Participations: The Trustee's Attack, 52 Am.Bankr.L.J. 32, 30–32 (1978).

11. Id. Drake & Weems argue that (1) the participants cannot be holders, and (2) that holders cannot enforce the underlying obligations unless they have possession of the notes; In re Investment Service Co. v. Martin Bros. Container & Timber Prod. Corp., 225 Or. 192, 465 P.2d 868 (1970). Both statements are true, but the assignees may still enforce the notes as non-holder assignees. The Code specifically recognizes that an action may be maintained either on the instrument, or if it is dishonored, on the underlying obligation; U.C.C. § 3–802. It seems clear that lack of holder status will not in itself prevent enforcement of the notes by the participants.

Their enforcement, however, encounters another problem. Generally, if partial assignments have been made, no action to enforce the note can be brought by either the assignor or any assignee unless all of the participants are joined. Restatement, Second, Contracts, § 158 (Tent.Draft 1973). An exception is made where joinder is infeasible or it is equitable to proceed without joinder. See Bain v. Financial Security Life Ins. Co., 53 Ill. App.3d 702, 11 Ill.Dec. 415, 368 N.E. 2d 1023 (1977), in which the court permitted an action on a note by the assignees of 119/120 interest in it. But if all of the assignees have made the lead lender their agent for purposes of collection and enforcement of the notes, there is no apparent reason that he cannot act effectively in their behalf. The same may be said if the lead is made a trustee for the participants.

Drake & Weems also argue that the usual participation is not a common law assignment, since the obligors do not have the right to pay the assignees directly; Shiro v. Drew, 174 F. Supp. 495, 498 (D.Me.1959). Indeed, the mortgagors are usually not even informed that an assignment has occurred. But again, if the participants delegate management and collection powers to the lead lender as their agent, as is the usual practice, then they *are* being paid by the obligors. This practice is so efficient and desir-

lender to enforce the various legal remedies on the notes can be readily explained by conceiving him as the agent of the participants, with necessary authority to act in their behalf. Alternatively, the lead may be expressly constituted a trustee for the participants, with authority to hold and enforce the notes for their benefit. Either of these legal formats seems to explain adequately the rights of the parties, and either should be able to survive an attack by the lead lender's creditors or trustee in bankruptcy.[12] There is no reason for the court to characterize the participation as a mere assignment of proceeds if the parties themselves have not done so.

Careful drafting of the participation agreement can strengthen it against such attacks. The agreement should clearly spell out that a transfer of ownership of the notes and mortgages is intended.[13] It should negate the idea of a loan from the participants to the lead lender. It should identify the lead as either an agent or a trustee for the participants, and stipulate his powers and duties in terms which are consistent with the agency or trust theory utilized.[14] Finally, the interest yield to the participants should be computed as the equivalent or composite of the interest yields on the underlying mortgages, less an appropriate fee to the lead lender to compensate him for servicing the loans. If these precautions are followed, the chances of the courts sustaining the participation should be excellent.

able for all parties that no policy ground should be found for defeating it.

Finally, Drake & Weems assert that in some participations the interest rate promised to the participators differs from, and is not merely a composite of, the interest rates payable on the underlying mortgage notes. In cases in which this is so, their point seems valid; the arrangement takes on the appearance of a loan to the lead lender, rather than a sale of interests by him. A true participation (i. e., a transfer of ownership) should probably be found only when the lead lender is obligated to pass through the note proceeds to the participants. His guarantee of collection should not destroy the "sale" interpretation, see Stratford Fin. Corp. v. Finex Corp., 367 F.2d 569 (2d Cir. 1966), but his payment of an arbitrary and unrelated yield to them should.

12. It is well established that if a bankrupt holds title to property as a fiduciary (e. g., a trustee or an agent), that property should be returned to its beneficial owners rather than being pulled into the bankrupt's estate. 4A Collier, Bankruptcy par. 70.25. The difficulties lie in determining whether an ostensible trust or agency is truly what it appears to be. See Todd v. Pettit, 108 F.2d 139 (C. C.A.Tex.1939); In re Petroleum Corp. of America, 417 F.2d 929 (C.A.N.D. 1969); Stratford Financial Corp. v. Finex Corp., 367 F.2d 569 (C.A.N.Y. 1966); cf. In re Alda Commercial Corp., 327 F.Supp. 1315 (S.D.N.Y. 1971). See Simpson, Loan Participations: Pitfalls for Participants, 31 Bus. Law. 1977, 1992–2003 (1976).

13. See, e. g., FHLMC Participation Sales Agreement 300 at (1): "The terms and conditions of this Agreement shall govern the transfer, sale and assignment of * * *" the participation interests.

14. See, e. g., FHLMC Participation Sales Agreement 300 at (6): "FHLMC shall act as the representative of Holders in the control, management and servicing of the Mortgages or property acquired in realization or liquidation."

§§ 5.36–6.0 are reserved for supplementary material.

CHAPTER 6

DISCHARGE OF THE MORTGAGE

Table of Sections

A. PAYMENT

§ 6.1 Prepayment—General Considerations

Contrary to what is probably pervasive popular belief, there is, absent a specific provision in the note or mortgage so providing, no right to pay off a mortgage debt prior to its maturity. This rule is derived from the classic case of Brown v. Cole,[1] where the court stated that if mortgagors "were allowed to pay off their mortgage money at any time after the execution of the mortgage, it might be attended with extreme inconvenience to mortgagees, who generally advance their money as an investment." The mortgagee has a common law right to refuse an early tender of principal and interest and courts

1. 14 L.J. (N.S.) Ch. 167, Chancery, 1845.

will not compel premature discharge of the mortgage.[2] As a matter of practice, however, most mortgagees permit prepayment, but exact a fee or "prepayment penalty" for the "privilege" of prepaying the loan. The prepayment penalty occasionally takes the form of the *non-option* type, where the loan agreement omits any mention of prepayment; when the mortgagor wishes to prepay the mortgagee is then in a position to determine the amount of the penalty.[3] However, the *non-option* situation could sometimes result in the mortgagor being unable to collect a prepayment penalty because a few states prohibit the imposition of such a penalty unless it is specifically provided for in the loan agreement.[4] The common practice, however, is to utilize the *option* type where the penalty is actually spelled out in the loan agreement. A "typical" prepayment clause will often read as follows:

> "Privilege is reserved to make additional payments on the principal of this indebtedness at any time without penalty, except that as to any such payments made which exceed twenty percent (20%) of the original principal amount of this loan during any successive twelve (12) month period beginning with the date of this promissory note, the undersigned agree to pay, as consideration for the acceptance of such prepayment, six (6) months advance interest on that part of the aggregate amount of all prepayments in excess of such twenty percent (20%). The privilege of paying amounts not in excess of said twenty percent (20%) of the original principal sum without consideration shall be noncumulative, if not exercised." [5]

Importantly, some of these clauses, in addition, specify that the prepayment charge "shall be due and payable whether said prepayment is voluntary or involuntary, including any prepayment effected by the exercise of any acceleration clause provided for herein." [6] While the penalty will in rare instances be as low as one or two months' inter-

2. See Comment, Secured Real Estate Loan Prepayment and the Prepayment Penalty, 51 Cal.L.Rev. 923, 924 (1963); Smiddy v. Grafton, 163 Cal. 16, 124 P. 433 (1912); Carpenter v. Winn, 566 P.2d 370 (Colo.App.1977); Bowen v. Julius, 141 Ind. 310, 40 N.E. 700 (1895); Moore v. Kime, 43 Neb. 517, 61 N.W. 736 (1895); Dugan v. Grzybowski, 165 Conn. 173, 332 A.2d 97 (1973); Henderson v. Guest, 197 Okla. 443, 172 P.2d 605 (1946). Peter Fuller Enterprises Inc. v. Manchester Sav. Bank, 102 N.H. 117, 152 A.2d 179 (1959). Florida has repealed the common law rule by statute. See Fla.Stat.Ann. § 697.06.

3. Comment, supra note 2 at 924. See, e. g., Feldman v. Kings Highway Sav. Bank, 278 App.Div. 589, 102 N.Y.S.2d 306, affirmed mem. 303 N.Y. 675, 102 N.E.2d 835 (1951).

4. See, e. g., Beth-June, Inc. v. Wil-Avon Merchandise Mart, Inc., 211 Pa.Super. 5, 233 A.2d 620 (1967); Burks v. Verschuur, 35 Colo.App. 121, 532 P.2d 757 (1975).

5. Lazzareschi Inv. Co. v. San Francisco Federal Sav. and Loan Ass'n, 22 Cal.App.3d 303, 305, 99 Cal.Rptr. 417, 419 (1971).

6. Id. at 305, 99 Cal.Rptr. at 419.

est, the most common maximum is six months or one hundred and eighty days' interest. This is because of a Federal Home Loan Bank Board (FHLBB) regulation, applicable to all federally chartered savings and loan associations, which limits the prepayment penalty for payment of the entire principal balance to a maximum of six months' interest.[7] This regulation also requires penalty-free prepayment of up to 20% of the balance of the mortgage debt in any twelve month period.[8]

The prepayment penalty is utilized by mortgagees for at least two reasons. The traditional justification for such provisions is that the mortgagee's fixed cost of making a loan are not recaptured entirely at the inception of the loan, but are amortized over the life of the loan.[9] Thus, the collection of a prepayment penalty should, in theory, make it possible for the mortgagee to recapture those costs. It has been argued, however, that the closing costs and other charges collected by the mortgagee at the inception date of the loan more than compensate for such fixed costs.[10] Such clauses are also used as an economic complement to the due on sale clause.[11] While the due on sale clause enables a mortgagee to force early payment of lower than market interest rate loans, the prepayment penalty is used to discourage refinancing by the mortgagor when market interest rates fall below the rate on the mortgagor's existing mortgage. The prepayment clause tends to "lock in" loans made at higher than currect market interest rates. As such, it is another imperfect method for achieving a higher longterm return on the mortgagee's loan portfolio. It should be pointed out, however, that the use of the two clauses together does *not* result in an approximation of the functional equivalent of variable interest rates. When variable interest rates are utilized, interest rates on long term mortgages will rise or fall in conjunction with some index that is tied or at least related to market interest rates.[12] On the other hand, when the two clauses are used successfully together, the mortgagee uses due on sale clauses to reloan money at higher rates, but the prepayment penalty is used to keep the mortgagee's portfolio interest return from dropping. In essence, the mortgagee seeks to achieve the effect of variable rates only when market interest rates are going up. When such rates are dropping, the prepayment penalty insulates the mortgagee in part from the economic effect of that downturn, an effect that would not be achieved by variable interest rates.

7. 12 CFR 545.6–12(b).

8. Id.

9. Bonanno, Due on Sale and Prepayment Clauses in Real Estate Financing in California in Times of Fluctuating Interest Rates—Legal Issues and Alternatives, 6 San.Fran.L.Rev. 267, 295 (1972).

10. Id. at 295.

11. See §§ 5.21–5.25, supra.

12. See § 11.4, infra.

§ 6.2 Prepayment Clauses—Judicial Treatment

While mortgagors have sometimes attacked prepayment charges on a usury theory, this attack has been uniformly rejected.[13] The usury argument in theory arises when the sum of the actual interest paid plus the prepayment amount exceed the maximum lawful interest rate calculated to the date of prepayment.[14] In the *non-option* type situation, it is generally held that the prepayment penalty is not interest, but rather represents value given by the mortgagor for a new agreement to terminate the original loan agreement.[15] In the *option* situation, where prepayment is expressly provided for in the loan agreement, courts stress that the mortgagor controls both the timing and the imposition of the prepayment charge.[16] Indeed, these courts have determined that the loan is not rendered usurious where the total interest plus the prepayment amount does not exceed the lawful maximum interest computed from the date of the loan to its final maturity date specified in the loan agreement.[17]

Other avenues of judicial attack have also thus far been unsuccessful. For example, in Lazzareschi Investment Co. v. San Francisco Savings & Loan Association,[18] a California appellate decision, the court upheld the standard six month prepayment penalty provision against the allegation that the prepayment charge constituted an invalid penalty because the damages imposed did not bear a reasonable relationship to the injury caused by the prepayment. There, a purchaser of commercial real estate at a judicial sale sought to refinance an existing 7¾% loan on the premises. The mortgagee insisted on collection of the prepayment charge even though the mortgagee had the ability to reloan the money at a higher interest rate. While the appellate court recognized that the mortgagee could reloan the money at a higher rate, it also noted that if the interest rates fell, many mortgagees would refinance. Under the circumstances, the court con-

13. See, e. g., McCarty v. Mellinkoff, 118 Cal.App. 11, 4 P.2d 595 (1931); Dezell v. King, 91 So.2d 624 (Fla. App.1956); Hanson v. Acceptance Finance Co., 270 S.W.2d 143 (Mo.App. 1954); Marley v. Consolidated Mortgage Co., 102 R.I. 200, 229 A.2d 608 (1968); Bell Bakeries, Inc. v. Jefferson Standard Life Ins. Co., 245 N.C. 408, 96 S.E.2d 408 (1957); Annot., 75 A.L.R.2d 1265 (1961).

14. Comment, Secured Real Estate Loan Prepayment and the Prepayment Penalty, 51 Cal.L.Rev. 923, 926.

15. See, e. g., Abbot v. Stevens, 133 Cal.App.2d 242, 284 P.2d 159 (1955); Webb v. Southern Trust Co., 227 Ky. 79, 11 S.W.2d 988 (1928); Luchesi v. Capitol Loan & Finance Co., 83 R.I. 151, 113 A.2d 725 (1955); Annot., 75 A.L.R.2d 1265, 1267 (1961). But see Lyons v. National Sav. Bank of City of Albany, 200 Misc. 652, 110 N.Y.S. 2d 564 (1951), reversed 280 A.D. 339, 113 N.Y.S.2d 695.

16. Comment, Secured Real Estate Loan Prepayment and the Prepayment Penalty, 51 Cal.L.Rev. 923, 926 (1963).

17. See, e. g., Eldred v. Hart, 87 Ark. 534, 113 S.W. 213 (1908); Redmond v. Ninth Federal Sav. & Loan Ass'n, 147 N.Y.S.2d 702 (1955); Annot., 75 A.L.R.2d 1265, 1268 (1961).

18. 22 Cal.App.3d 303, 99 Cal.Rptr. 417 (1971).

cluded that the clause used here was reasonable, in part, because it complied with the regulation of the Federal Home Loan Bank Board (FHLBB) governing prepayment penalties in the residential loan setting. The court looked to the FHLBB regulation as a guide even though this case involved a non-residential transaction. Thus, the impression left by the court was that this particular mortgagee could have charged a higher penalty had it so chosen because a residential transaction was not involved in the case. Finally, the court concluded that the prepayment charge did not constitute an invalid restraint on alienation because the restraint was not absolute and was considered to be reasonable under the circumstances.

In a more recent California appellate court decision, the court in Meyers v. Home Savings & Loan Association [19] upheld a prepayment provision similar to that in *Lazzareschi* against the argument that the prepayment charge constituted invalid liquidated damages under section 1670 of the California Civil Code.[20] The court noted that the purpose of the provision was to give the mortgagor the option to prepay and that the clause did not penalize for the "breach of an obligation" as contemplated by section 1670. "No breach is involved in the prepayment transaction, only the exercise of the option given to the debtor for an alternative method of paying the debt." [21]

The problem, of course, is that the prepayment penalty is sometimes triggered by a breach of the loan agreement, which breach may be the result of a voluntary or involuntary act of the mortgagor. Most of the time the prepayment penalty does indeed result from the mortgagor's desire to refinance at a lower rate, but it can also arise from a mortgagor's default in the payment of the loan and subsequent acceleration by the mortgagee. For example, once a mortgagor defaults and the mortgagee accelerates and initiates foreclosure proceedings, should the mortgage debt, for purposes of the mortgagor's right to redeem or for purposes of calculating the amount of a possible sale surplus or deficiency, include the amount of the prepayment penalty? If we consider that one of the purposes of such clauses is to enable the mortgagee to recoup fixed loan costs over the life

19. 38 Cal.App.3d 544, 113 Cal.Rptr. 358 (1974).

20. West's Ann.Cal.Civil Code, § 1670 provides: "Every contract by which the amount of damages to be paid, or other compensation to be made, for a breach of an obligation, is determined in anticipation thereof, is to that extent void, except as expressly provided in the next section."

West's Ann.Cal.Civil Code, § 1671 provides: "The parties to a contract may agree therein on an amount which shall be presumed to be the amount of damage sustained by a breach thereof, when, from the nature of the case, it would be impracticable or extremely difficult to fix the actual damage."

21. Meyers v. Home Sav. and Loan Ass'n, 38 Cal.App.3d 544, 546, 113 Cal.Rptr. 358, 359–60 (1974). See Aronoff v. Western Federal Sav. and Loan Ass'n, 28 Colo.App. 151, 470 P. 2d 889 (1970), where the court upheld a prepayment penalty against the argument that enforcement of a prepayment penalty against a subsequent grantee who wished to prepay was "inequitable."

of the loan, then the exaction of the charge is perhaps justified. If the primary purpose of the clause, however, is to discourage mortgagor refinancing at lower interest rates, then the requirement of the penalty cannot be justified, at least when the mortgagor's default is not intentional. At least one commentator has suggested that California courts may permit the exaction of a prepayment penalty when the debt is accelerated upon an installment default, or that at least it would not render the transaction usurious.[22] There is, however, little case law directly in point.

One Oregon case,[23] however, is helpful in this respect. There the mortgagee declared an acceleration and commenced foreclosure proceedings after the mortgagor failed to pay. Then the mortgagor persuaded the mortgagee to cancel the foreclosure proceeding. Thereafter, the mortgagor obtained a potential buyer of the premises who desired to pay off the existing mortgage. The mortgagee demanded the 3% prepayment penalty which the note required for "the privilege of full prepayment within the first ten years" in addition to the balance of principal and interest due and owing. This amount was paid and thereafter the mortgagor sued for a refund of the prepayment penalty, arguing that when the mortgagee declared an acceleration and commenced foreclosure proceedings, that election was irrevocable and could not be rescinded without the mortgagor's consent. Since the entire debt was due, the mortgagor argued, there was no prepayment and, therefore, no contractual basis for the exaction of any prepayment penalty. The Oregon Supreme Court held that the mortgagee had validly waived its right to accelerate and that there was no evidence that mortgagor changed its position or "acted to its prejudice after [mortgagee] gave notice of acceleration and before it rescinded the same."[24] Therefore the collection of the prepayment penalty was appropriate in this case. The implication of this case is that, had there been no rescission of the acceleration, the prepayment penalty could not have been calculated as part of the mortgage debt for redemption purposes or, if foreclosure took place, for the purpose of calculating a possible foreclosure sale surplus or deficiency. The theory apparently would be that when default in payment of the indebtedness occurs and there is an acceleration, no prepayment, as such, can take place. At that stage the mortgagor cannot opt to prepay, but only to exercise his equity of redemption by redeeming from the mortgage.[25]

22. Hetland, Secured Real Estate Transactions, 104 (1974).

23. West Portland Development Co. v. Ward Cook, Inc., 246 Or. 67, 424 P.2d 212 (1967).

24. Id. at 214.

25. See Kilpatrick v. Germania Life Ins. Co., 183 N.Y. 163, 75 N.E. 1124 (1905); where the New York Court of Appeals held that once there had been a default and the mortgage brings a suit to foreclose, it was improper for the mortgagee to include a prepayment penalty in calculating the amount mortgagor needed to pay to redeem from the mortgagee. The court reasoned that since the payment of the mortgage debt was under

Suppose, however, the mortgagee utilizes prepayment clause language that requires a prepayment penalty whether such payment was "voluntary or involuntary, including any prepayment effected by the exercise of any acceleration clause provided for herein." [26] Here the argument that the mortgagor has not chosen to prepay presumably will not prevent calculating the amount of the penalty as part of the mortgage debt because the parties have agreed to its inclusion. On the other hand, where prepayment is involuntary should such language be considered an invalid penalty imposed "for a breach of an obligation" under section 1670 of the California Civil Code? [27] One California commentator has stated: "Perhaps the answer is that the [mortgagee] may so recover when his note and deed of trust say he can. But since this is not an otherwise recoverable item, the clause appears to impose a penalty on the [mortgagor] unrelated to any compensable loss incurred by the [mortgagee]." [28] Nevertheless, if the penalty amount falls within the range imposed by most of the mortgage lending community and, thus, cannot be attacked as exhorbitant or inequitable, does not such a clause serve the arguably valid purpose of compensating the mortgagee for the fixed costs of a mortgage loan that normally are amortized over the life of such loan?

Finally, it is conceivable that a mortgagor could intentionally default and trigger a foreclosure proceeding in order to avoid payment of the prepayment charge. His plan would be to exercise his equitable right to redeem prior to foreclosure by paying an accelerated mortgage debt that would not include a prepayment penalty. Although there is no case law considering this problem, the equities here clearly favor enforcement of the clause against the mortgagor. Assuming the prepayment clause is otherwise valid, the mortgagor would be voluntarily using default as a means of avoiding the application of a valid loan agreement provision. Unlike the situation where a mortgagor defaults in the payment of the loan without the prepayment penalty clause in mind, here the mortgagor *chooses default as his means of prepayment.*

Should the lender be able to collect a prepayment penalty when there has been an involuntary disposition of the mortgage security

the threat of foreclosure the payment of the prepayment penalty was not "voluntary" and therefore not a valid prepayment. "Under these circumstances the compulsion was illegal, unjust, and oppressive, and the [mortgagor], having submitted under protest, had the right to recover [the prepayment amount]." Id. at 167, 75 N.E. at 1125. See also, Bell Bakeries, Inc. v. Jefferson Standard Life Ins. Co., 245 N.C. 408, 418, 96 S.E.2d 408, 417 (1957), where court permitted collection of prepayment penalty after a waiver by mortgagee of past defaults, but stated: "[h]ad defendant * * * declared a default and demanded payment, it would only have been entitled to collect the debt and interest accrued thereon to the date of payment."

26. See note 6, supra.

27. See note 20, supra.

28. Bernhardt in Hetland, California Real Estate Secured Transactions, 200 (1970).

followed by a mortgagee's election to have the proceeds of that disposition apply to pay off the mortgage debt? Suppose, for example, that the mortgage premises have been destroyed by fire and that the mortgagee elects to have the proceeds used to pay off the debt, an option that the mortgagee has under many common mortgage forms. In mortgagor's favor, it can be argued that the prepayment is not voluntary on his part and that, indeed, normally the prepayment is not *by* him, but by the insurance carrier. The mortgagee, on the other hand, can argue that absent the collection of the prepayment penalty, it would not fully recover its fixed cost of making the loan. The closest decided case is Chestnut Corp. v. Bankers Bond & Mortgage Co.[29] There the Pennsylvania Supreme Court held that the mortgagee could not collect an additional 2% prepayment penalty, where the payment of the mortgage had been triggered by the application of fire insurance proceeds to pay off the debt. The court recognized the above arguments on behalf of both of the parties, but noted that "in such a situation both parties suffer, but the owner [mortgagor] suffers most." [30] The above case is not always helpful, however, because, unlike in *Chestnut*, many mortgagees, as we have noted, specifically provide for collection of a prepayment penalty in the event of all involuntary prepayment. Yet it can be argued that while the prepayment is involuntary on the mortgagor's part, it may be voluntary on the part of the mortgagee in the sense that commonly used mortgage forms often give the mortgagee the option to reduce the debt or repair the premises. Thus, it can be argued that "it is the [mortgagee] who is compelling the [mortgagor] to prepay the loan and simultaneously asserting a charge for the [mortgagor's] exercise of his 'privilege' to prepay." [31]

A more common problem seems to be whether prepayment that results from a condemnation of the security permits the mortgagee to exact a prepayment penalty. Where the language of the mortgage does not specifically authorize prepayment penalties for involuntary prepayment, the case law thus far uniformly holds that the mortgagee has no right to collect a prepayment penalty either against the mortgagor or the condemning authority.[32] These cases found persuasive the mortgagor's argument in *Chestnut* that there was no voluntary prepayment on the part of the mortgagor and that the latter was not exercising a "right" or "privilege" of prepayment within the language of the prepayment clause. Suppose, however, as discussed

29. 395 Pa. 153, 149 A.2d 48 (1959).

30. Id. at 157, 149 A.2d at 50.

31. Bernhardt in Hetland, California Real Estate Secured Transactions, 197 (1970).

32. See DeKalb County v. United Family Life Ins. Co., 235 Ga. 417, 219 S.E.2d 707 (1975), on remand 136 Ga. App. 822, 222 S.E.2d 644; Associated Schools, Inc. v. Dade County, 209 So.2d 489 (Fla.App.1968); Silverman v. State, 48 A.D.2d 413, 370 N.Y.S.2d 234 (1975); Jala Corp. v. Berkeley Sav. & Loan Ass'n, 104 N.J.Super. 394, 250 A.2d 150 (1969).

in the fire insurance situation in the preceding paragraph, that the prepayment clause specifically authorizes collection of the penalty in involuntary situations. By partial analogy to the insurance proceeds situation, it can be argued that the mortgagee, nevertheless, should be allowed no prepayment penalty. The mortgagee always has the option in almost all mortgage forms to apply the condemnation award to the debt or to allow the mortgagor to take the award. Thus, in a sense, it is the *mortgagee* who is compelling the mortgagor to prepay and also demanding the payment of a prepayment penalty. On the other hand, a persuasive argument can be made that the insurance and condemnation situations are not analogous. While it can be said that a mortgagee's right in the insurance setting to pay the debt or to rebuild the premises is a "true option," it is much more difficult to conclude that the condemnation mortgagee's ability to pay the debt or give the proceeds to the mortgagor is similarly such a "true option." In the former situation, the mortgagee gets either the debt paid or the security intact whereas in the latter situation, the "choice" is between payment of the debt or loss of a security. Thus, in this latter situation where the loan agreement specifically provides for a prepayment penalty in involuntary situations, and where, as always, the mortgagee can argue that prepayment means less than full recovery of the fixed costs of making the loan, a court is possibly justified in following the loan agreement language.

§ 6.3 Prepayment Clauses—Legislative and Other Nonjudicial Regulation

State legislation regulating prepayment penalties is increasing and varies considerably in substance. The one common element in all such legislation is that it is limited to loans secured by residential real estate, the latter being defined variously by such terminology as: "single family dwellings," "owner-occupied single family dwellings," "one to four family dwellings" or "an owner-occupied one to six family residence." In any event, the legislation thus far has not attempted to regulate prepayment penalties in the context of the larger nonresidential loan transactions.

Within the confines of the above qualifications, the legislation ranges from flat prohibitions on prepayment penalties to relatively mild codification of existing practices. For example, at one extreme is the Pennsylvania statute which simply prohibits all prepayment penalties in residential mortgage obligations entered into after the effective date of the statute.[33] Illinois achieves the same practical effect by prohibiting prepayment penalties in all residential mortgages carrying an interest rate in excess of 8%.[34] Since few, if any, such loans in today's market will have interest rates of 8% or lower, the legislation amounts to a flat prohibition on prepayment penalties in

33. 41 Pa.Stat. § 405 (1974).

34. Ill.Ann.Stat. ch. 74, § 4(2)(c).

residential transactions. Missouri, on the other hand, prohibits the imposition of all prepayment penalties in residential real estate loans after five years from the date of the execution of the loan.[35] Michigan cuts off such penalties after three years for single family dwellings, but limits such charges within three years to 1% of the amount of any prepayment.[36] In New York, any mortgage loan made by a savings and loan association may be prepaid. However, the loan agreement may provide for a period during which prepayment may not be made without penalty. Where the mortgage loan is an owner-occupied one to six family residence, the penalties may be imposed only during the first year of the loan and may not exceed interest for a period of three months on the principal so prepaid, or interest for the remaining months in the first year, whichever is the lesser amount.[37] Similar New York legislation exists for mortgage loans made by mortgagees other than savings and loan associations.[38] New Jersey permits prepayment penalties under the following conditions as to loans on one to four family dwellings in which the mortgagor resides; if prepayment is made within the first year from the mortgage date, 3% of the balance of the mortgage loan is the maximum prepayment penalty; if prepayment is made on or after one year from such date, but within two years, 2% of such balance is the maximum authorized prepayment penalty; if prepayment is made on or after two years, 1% of such balance is authorized; and if prepayment is made after three years, no prepayment penalty may be collected. Prepayment without penalty of up to 20% of the principal balance may be made in each of the first three years.[39] Mississippi legislation is similar to the New Jersey approach.[40]

The California legislation is perhaps the least stringent on the mortgagee.[41] Prepayment charges may be assessed with respect to mortgages on single family owner-occupied dwellings within the first five years. Within such period, 20% of the unpaid balance may be prepaid free of penalty within a twelve month period. However, the

35. R.S.Mo. § 408.036 (1975).

36. Mich.Comp.L.Ann. § 438.31c (1974). Kansas prohibits any prepayment penalty in excess of 1.5% of the prepayment. Kan.Stat.Ann. § 17–5512.

37. McKinney's N.Y. Banking Law § 393(2) (1974). See also R.I.Gen. Laws Ann. 34–23–5 (1974).

38. McKinney's N.Y.Gen.Obl.Law § 5–501(3)(b) (1976). As to first mortgages on mortgagor-occupied dwellings of three or fewer families, Massachusetts permits up to three month's interest prepayment penalty for the first three years of the mortgage loan if the mortgagor refinances; prepayments for other reasons may be made with a maximum penalty of the lesser of three month's interest or the balance of the first year's interest. Apparently, after the first year of the loan prepayment for reasons other than to refinance may be made without penalty. Mass.Gen. L.Ann. ch. 183, § 56.

39. N.J.Stat.Ann. 46:10B–2, 10B–3 (1975).

40. Miss.Code § 75–17–1(11) (1974).

41. West's Ann.Cal.Civil Code, § 2954.-9 (1975). See also West's Ann.Cal. Bus. & Prof.Code § 10242.6 (as to loans negotiated by real estate licensees).

maximum charge on a prepayment in excess of the 20% amount is six months' interest. This legislation is similar to the regulation issued by the Federal Home Loan Bank Board (FHLBB) which governs all federally chartered savings and loan associations and, thus, to some extent, tends to codify existing practices.

The New Jersey type legislation appears to be the most satisfactory in taking into account the valid interests of both mortgagor and mortgagee. First, by permitting the imposition of a flexible prepayment penalty during the early years of the loan based on the age of the loan, it recognizes the mortgagee's interest in preventing the mortgagor from refinancing at lower rates and, in part, the mortgagee's interest in recouping some of the fixed cost that may otherwise accrue if prepayment is permitted with no penalty at all. On the other hand, by setting a fixed and relatively early time after which no penalty may be imposed, the legislation recognizes the fact that residential real estate is typically sold long before the maturity of the mortgage loan which financed its purchase and that prepayment of the loan is often merely incidental to the sale rather than a scheme to refinance because of falling interest rates. While one may argue whether the three year date, after which no penalty may be imposed, is too early, the concept underlying the statute is a desirable one. Many of the other statutes lack the sophistication of the New Jersey approach. The flat prohibition of the Pennsylvania statute, for example, recognizes no legitimate mortgagee interest in utilizing a prepayment penalty. Moreover, the New York prohibition of prepayment penalties after one year is probably also too harsh on the mortgagee. On the other hand, the California six month interest penalty authorized for complete prepayment during the first five years is relatively severe on the mortgagor.

Some of the foregoing states that have general regulation of prepayment penalties in the residential setting, and a few states that do not, specifically regulate a variety of prepayment situations that do not arise from voluntary refinancing by the mortgagor. For example, both New York and Virginia prohibit the enforcement of a prepayment penalty, if the prepayment is triggered by the mortgagee's enforcement of a due on sale clause.[42] In addition, a few states prohibit the collection of a prepayment penalty where such penalty would be caused by the exercise of the eminent domain power.[43]

42. See McKinney's N.Y.Real Prop. Law § 254–a (1974); Va.Code § 6.1–330.33 (1975). The New York statute was upheld against a constitutional challenge in Rogers v. Williamsburgh Sav. Bank, 79 Misc.2d 852, 361 N.Y. S.2d 531 (1974).

43. Mass.Gen.Laws Ann. ch. 183 § 57; West's Ann.Cal.Code of Civil Pro. § 1246.2 (1972); Arizona requires reimbursement to the owner "to the extent [the acquiring agency] deems fair and reasonable * * * expenses [owner] necessarily incurred for * * * [p]enalty costs for prepayment of any preexisting recorded mortgage entered into in good faith encumbering such real property." Ariz.Rev.Stat. § 11–965 (1972).

The Uniform Consumer Credit Code (UCCC), which is in effect in nine states, prohibits the imposition of prepayment penalties, with some qualifications, on real estate loans for personal, family, household or agricultural purpose whose interest rates exceed 12% per annum. This legislation does not affect lending to commercial entities and, because of the above interest rate provision, most first mortgage residential lending.[44]

Finally, regulations issued by federal or quasi-federal agencies regulate or limit, to some extent, the imposition of prepayment penalties. Federal Reserve Regulation Z, enforcing the Federal Truth in Lending Act, requires virtually all mortgage lenders who loan money in the ordinary course of business to disclose to the mortgagor the terms, conditions and method of computation of any prepayment penalty imposed by the mortgagee.[45] As previously noted, a regulation of the Federal Home Loan Bank Board (FHLBB), which regulation governs all federally chartered savings and loan associations, limits those associations from imposing more than a six month interest penalty and permits penalty-free earlier prepayment of 20% of the loan balance in any twelve month period.[46] Since a good deal of residential lending is carried out by federally chartered savings and loan associations, the FHLBB regulations tend to set minimum national standards for prepayment penalties. Moreover, the standard note form approved by the Federal Home Loan Mortgage Corporation (FHLMC) and the Federal National Mortgage Association (FNMA), both quasi-federal entities,[47] limits prepayment penalties to the first five years of the loan and permits imposition of a penalty in the first five years only where the mortgagor prepays as a result of refinancing. This form also tends to set national standards because the above two entities require its use as a condition precedent to their purchase of mortgage loans on the secondary market. This is significant because many lending institutions sell their mortgages on this market. Finally, prepayment penalties in mortgage loans guaranteed by the Veterans Administration and insured by the Federal Housing Administration are prohibited and the loans may be prepaid at any time.[48]

44. U.C.C.C. § 2.509 (1974); the UCCC originally was promulgated in 1968 and, after intervening drafts, the 1974 UCCC was promulgated. The UCCC, in one of the foregoing versions, is in effect with a variety of modifications in at least eleven states including Oklahoma, Utah, Colorado, Idaho, Indiana, Wyoming, Kansas, Iowa, Maine, South Carolina and Wisconsin.

45. 12 CFR 226.8(b)(6).

46. See note 7, supra.

47. FNMA's policy is *not* to enforce the prepayment penalties in its single-family home mortgages. However, if the loan is sold by FNMA to some other investor, that investor might elect to collect the penalty upon prepayment. Moreover, FNMA *does* enforce the penalty on mortgages in condominiums or planned unit developments. See FNMA Conventional Selling Contract Supplement, § 301(D), (F) (July 25, 1975). FHLMC *does* regularly enforce the prepayment penalty clause in its mortgages. FHLMC Servicer's Guide § 4.114 (Mar. 21, 1977).

48. See 38 CFR 36.4310; 24 CFR 203.-22(b).

However, the latter type of loans represent a relatively small percentage of the total national mortgage loan volume.

§ 6.4 Acceptance of Payment—Effect

It has long been established that payment [49] of the mortgage debt on "law day" will extinguish the mortgagee's security interest in the property and restore full legal ownership to the mortgagor without the necessity of a reconveyance, release or any other instrument being executed by the mortgagee.[50] And the same effect is given to payment which is accepted before the law day.[51]

In some respects it is outmoded to speak in terms of payment or tender on or after "law day." It is true that until the late 1930's many, if not most, mortgages called for the payment of all or substantially all of the payment of principal on a certain date. In the cases where this type of mortgage is still utilized, it can be said that there is a law day in the common law sense. However, with the advent of the evenly amortized long term installment mortgage in housing and other real estate financing transactions, the concept of the law day in the traditional sense is significantly less important.[52] Indeed, in a certain sense, the usual installment mortgage has a monthly law day and failure to pay on that monthly date can trigger a range of consequences from the imposition of a late payment charge [53] to the acceleration of the entire mortgage debt.[54] Once an acceleration has taken place, payment on "law day" cannot occur.

Moreover, when we talk today of payment or tender *after* law day, we very often have in mind payment or tender after an acceleration has occurred, but prior to a valid foreclosure. We will consider the consequences of acceleration in substantial detail in the following

49. Payment is here used in a broad and generic sense to include not only the doing of the very act the mortgage was given to secure, whether that act be payment of money or rendering some other performance, but also any other act the operative effect of which is to satisfy the mortgage obligation.

50. In title states this is because the condition on which the conveyance was made is performed. "If the money is paid on the very day appointed for the payment of it, the condition is said to be performed, and the mortgagor, as in any other case where the grantee of land on condition performs the condition, may enter on the land and hold it, as of his former estate." Hargrave & Butler's Note to Coke upon Littleton, § 332. Munson v. Munson, 30 Conn. 425, 437 (1862), accord. In lien states since the mortgage lien is regarded as security only for the performance of an obligation, if the obligation is performed or satisfied in any way, the lien is automatically extinguished. Decker v. Decker, 64 Neb. 239, 89 N.W. 795 (1902); Bogert v. Bliss, 148 N.Y. 194, 42 N.E. 582, 51 Am.St.Rep. 684 (1896); Cumps v. Kiyo, 104 Wis. 656, 80 N.W. 937 (1899).

51. Holman v. Bailey, 44 Mass. (3 Metc.) 55 (1841); Cumps v. Kiyo, 104 Wis. 656, 80 N.W. 937 (1899), lien state, mortgage by deed absolute.

52. See § 1.1, supra.

53. See § 6.6, infra.

54. See § 7.6, infra.

chapter.[55] In any event, we should view payment or tender after law day or after the "maturity date" of the obligation in the context of this and the foregoing paragraph. If we do much of the case law in this area and the analysis in this and the succeeding section will be of continuing significance.

In title and intermediate jurisdictions payment after maturity does not by itself operate to revest title in the mortgagor because the concept of the title theory is that only performance of the condition does that.[56] However payment does discharge all equitable interest of the mortgagee in the property regardless of whether it is made on, before, or after the law day.[57] Hence when the mortgagor pays the mortgagee becomes a holder of the bare legal title in trust[58] for the mortgagor who can require a reconveyance on application to a court of equity.[59] Some courts have departed from the logic of the title concept to permit the mortgagor to recover possession from the mortgagee in an action at law[60] and to deny a similar recovery by the mortgagee from the mortgagor after the debt has been paid.[61] Statutes also have altered the rule as to revesting of title on late payment.[62]

In lien theory states it is held that payment of the mortgage debt, whether made on, before, or after default, extinguishes the mortgage lien at law as well as in equity.[63] This flows from the view that a lien is security only for the performance of an act and if the

55. See §§ 7.6–7.8, infra.

56. Phelps v. Sage, 2 Day 151 (Conn. 1805); Smith v. Vincent, 15 Conn. 1, 14, 38 Am.Dec. 52 (1842); Cross v. Robinson, 21 Conn. 379, 387 (1851). See Moore v. Norman, 43 Minn. 428, 45 N.W. 857, 9 L.R.A. 55, 19 Am.St. Rep. 247 (1890); Farmers Fire Ins. & Loan Co. v. Edwards, 26 Wend. 541 (N.Y.1841).

57. Palmer v. Uhl, 112 Conn. 125, 128, 151 A. 355, 356 (1930), alternative decision; see Desiderio v. Iadonisi, 115 Conn. 652, 655, 163 A. 254, 255, 88 A.L.R. 1349 (1932).

58. Cooper v. Cooper, 256 Ill. 160, 99 N.E. 871 (1912). See Stewart v. Crosby, 50 Me. 130, 134 (1863), approved in Hooper v. Bail, 133 Me. 412, 415, 179 A. 404, 405 (1935).

59. Kelly v. Martin, 107 Ala. 479, 18 So. 132 (1894); Town of Clinton v. Town of Westbrook, 38 Conn. 9 (1871); Parsons v. Welles, 17 Mass. 419 (1821); Stewart v. Crosby, 50 Me. 130 (1863); Gardner v. Buckeye Savings & Loan Co., 108 W.Va. 673, 152 S.E. 530, 78 A.L.R. 1 (1930) accord. And see Holman v. Bailey, 44 Mass. (3 Metc.) 55 (1841).

60. E. g., Perkins' Lessee v. Dibble, 10 Ohio, 433, 434, 440, 36 Am.Dec. 97 (1841).

61. See Stewart v. Crosby, 50 Me. 130, 134 (1863); Baker v. Gavitt, 128 Mass. 93 (1880). Cf., Pollock v. Maison, 41 Ill. 516 (1866).

62. See, e. g., Code of Ala., Tit. 47 § 181. "Alabama nominally classifies itself as a 'title' state, * * * Hence, the necessity for our defeasance statute." Lloyd's of London v. Fidelity Securities Corp., 39 Ala.App. 596, 105 So.2d 729, 733 (1958).

63. McMillan v. Richards, 9 Cal. 365, 70 Am.Dec. 655 (1858); Hendricks v. Hess, 112 Minn. 252, 127 N.W. 995 (1910); Tobin v. Tobin, 139 Wis. 494, 121 N.W. 144 (1909); Decker v. Decker, 64 Neb. 239, 89 N.W. 795 (1902); Wakefield v. Day, 41 Minn. 344, 43 N.W. 71 (1889); Nilson v. Sarment, 153 Cal. 524, 530, 96 P. 315, 317, 126 Am.St.Rep. 91 (1908).

act has been performed there is nothing for the lien to secure and it is, therefore, extinguished.[64]

However, even though payment may extinguish a mortgage, it usually has been recorded and it is necessary to have it discharged of record. This the mortgagor may compel the mortgagee to do by whatever means is required by the state where the property is.[65] Whether a mortgagor has a common law right to recover damages from the mortgagee for failure to cancel of record a satisfied mortgage is doubtful.[66] However in a very large number of states statutes give such a right and impose penalties upon a mortgagee who refuses to give a release, satisfaction piece, reconveyance, or whatever is necessary in that jurisdiction to clear up the record title.[67]

§ 6.5 Tender on or After Maturity

Proper tender [68] on the law day, though not accepted, discharges the mortgage in title and lien states [69], but it does not affect the obliga-

64. "The debt, in the eye of the law, thus becomes the principal, and the landed security merely appurtenant and secondary; * * * Acceptance of payment of the amount due on a mortgage, at any time before foreclosure, has always been held to discharge the incumbrance on the land * * *" Kortright v. Cady, 21 N.Y. 343, 347, 78 Am.Dec. 145 (1860). See Caruthers v. Humphrey, 12 Mich. 270 (1864), accord.

65. See 78 A.L.R. 24, 101 (1932). A tender conditioned upon the execution of a release, etc., is a proper tender. Harding v. Home Invest. & Sav. Co., 49 Idaho 64, 286 P. 920 (1930) rehearing denied, 49 Idaho 75, 297 P. 1101 (1931); Wallowa Lake Amusement Co. v. Hamilton, 70 Or. 433, 142 P. 321 (1914).

66. It has been held that he has such a right in Texas. Mickie v. McGehee, 27 Tex. 134 (1881); Knox v. Farmers State Bank of Merkel, 7 S.W.2d 918 (Tex.Civ.App.1928), commented on in 7 Tex.L.Rev. 323 (1929). But Hasquet v. Big West Oil Co., 29 F.2d 78 (C.C.A.Mont.1928), is contra.

67. See, e. g., Mass.Gen.Laws Ann. c. 183 § 55; Reissue Neb.Rev.Stat.1943, § 76–255; Mr. U Inc. v. Mobil Oil Corp., 197 Neb. 612, 249 N.W.2d 909 (1977); Taylor v. Taylor, 363 N.E.2d 1342 (Mass.App.1977) (statute constitutes sole remedy).

68. What constitutes a proper tender is, for the most part, a matter of general law not peculiar to mortgages. For a recent definition, however, consider the following: "A tender is more than a mere offer to pay. It is an offer to perform coupled with the present ability of immediate performance, so were it not for the refusal of cooperation by the party to whom the tender is made, the condition or obligation would be immediately satisfied. A tender is the offer of a sum of money in satisfaction of a debt and is made by producing and showing the amount to the creditor and expressing verbally a willingness to pay it." Mr. U Inc. v. Mobil Oil Corp., 197 Neb. 612, 617, 249 N.W.2d 909, 912 (1977). Harpe v. Stone, 212 Ga. 341, 92 S.E.2d 522 (1956), noted by Loiseaux, Security Transactions, in Annual Survey of Georgia Law, June 1, 1955—June 1, 1956, 8 Mercer L.Rev. 144, 149 (1956), held that where the amount due on a debt is in dispute, the mortgagor must tender at least the amount admittedly due, even if the creditor is demanding more than that amount.

69. Co.Lit. §§ 338, 209a, 209b. Depon v. Shawye, 263 Mass. 206, 161 N.E. 243 (1928); see Security State Bank v. Waterloo Lodge, 85 Neb. 255, 122 N.W. 992 (1909); West's Ann.Cal. Civ.Code, §§ 1504, 2909. See also 93 A.L.R. 12, 25, 31 (1934). If the mortgagee waives payment at maturity it is not certain that a tender at a later

tion secured [70] except to stop the running of interest and prevent the debtor from being liable for costs, at least if the tender is kept good.[71] Although it is commonly said that such a tender constitutes performance of the condition,[72] this obviously is not so. A more careful and accurate statement would be that, the performance of the condition having been prevented by the mortgagee's refusal to accept payment, it will be excused.

Where tender is made after maturity, in states following the common law title theory of mortgages it does not extinguish the mortgage lien if the mortgagee refuses to accept it.[73] The courts in these states reason logically, if technically, from the legal structure and mechanics of the mortgage as they view it. The concept is that a mortgage is an absolute conveyance defeasible by performance of a condition subsequent in the manner and at the time stipulated for in the defeasance, i. e., the law day. In case of nonperformance as specified the mortgagee's estate becomes absolute, and it cannot thereafter be divested even by a full payment of the mortgage debt. It follows as an obvious consequence that mere tender should not be given greater effect than actual payment. The mortgagor's only remedy, except insofar as he may have relief by statute, is in equity by a bill to redeem.[74] In a few states professing to accept the title theory a tender after maturity suspends the mortgagee's right to exercise a power of sale if the mortgage contains one, a result substantially impairing the mortgagee's security.[75]

date, in reliance on the waiver, will extinguish the mortgage although it will stop interest and costs on the debt. Wood v. Babb, 16 S.C. 427 (1882).

70. See Williston, Contracts, 3d Ed. 1959, § 1817; Co.Lit. 209a, 209b; Bacon's Abridgment, title Tender (f); Dixon v. Clark, 5 C.B. 365, 377 (1848).

71. Lutton v. Rodd, 2 Cas.Ch. 206 (1675), "the plaintiff ought to make oath that the money was kept, and no profit made of it"; Bank of New South Wales v. O'Connor, 14 Ann. Cas. 273 (1889); see Gyles v. Hall, 2 P.Wms. 378 (1726); Crain v. McGoon, 86 Ill. 431, 29 Am.Rep. 37 (1877). See also Note, Comparison of California Mortgages, Trust Deeds and Land Sale Contracts, 7 U.C.L.A.L.Rev. 83 (1960).

72. E. g., "Tender of the mortgage debt on the day named is performance of the condition, and, by force of the terms of the condition, determines the estate of the mortgagee, and the condition being complied with, the land reverts to the mortgagor by the simple operation of the condition." Shields v. Lozear, 34 N.J.L. 496, 504, 3 Am.St.Rep. 256 (1869).

73. Shields v. Lozear, 34 N.J.L. 496 (1869), is the leading case. Davis v. Ashburn, 224 Ala. 572, 574, 141 So. 226, 227 (1932); Stockton v. Dundee Mfg. Co., 22 N.J.Eq. 56 (1871); Sandler v. Green, 287 Mass. 404, 407, 192 N.E. 39, 41 (1934); Maynard v. Hunt, 22 Mass. (5 Pick.) 240 (1827), accord. See 94 A.L.R. 25–30 (1934).

74. For clear statements of the rationale of tender after the law day in title jurisdictions, see Moore v. Norman, 43 Minn. 428, 45 N.W. 857, 9 L.R.A. 55, 19 Am.St.Rep. 247 (1890); Shields v. Lozear, note 73, supra; Farmers' Fire Ins. & Loan Co. v. Edwards, 26 Wend. 541 (N.Y.1841). See also 93 A.L.R. 12, 15, 25 (1934).

75. Garrett v. Cobb, 202 Ala. 241, 80 So. 79 (1918); Greer v. Turner, 36 Ark. 17 (1880); Wingert v. Brewer,

In lien jurisdictions the weight of authority is that an unaccepted tender made after default does discharge the mortgage lien.[76] There are, however, several lien jurisdictions that hold such a tender does not affect it.[77] And in some states the rule is not settled.[78]

Reasons given for the majority rule that a belated, unaccepted tender will discharge the mortgage lien begin with the technical nature of the mortgage in lien states as contrasted with title states. Unlike a title theory mortgage, the technical situation of the lien mortgage remains the same after default as on or before the due day. Failure to perform at maturity does not vest indefeasibly any legal or other interest in the mortgagee as it does in title states. In contrast to a common law mortgage, payment after the law day extinguishes the mortgage just as does payment on the law day. This being so, there is no ground for not giving the same effect to tender made after default as is given to tender on the due day. If it is fair to deprive the mortgagee of his security when he refuses to accept a performance on the law day, it is equally fair to do so when he refuses a performance which would have that effect at a later time. It will be noted that the foregoing reasoning, while logical, does not get to the merits of the rule anymore than does the rule to the opposite effect in title jurisdictions. Both are grounded upon the technical legal structure of the mortgage.

As a practical matter, the major problem with failing to discharge the mortgage on tender boils down to a question of hardship. The hardship problem consists of two factors: the marketability of his property is impaired by the cloud upon it of the continuing lien; he remains exposed to the danger of foreclosure action on the part of the mortgagee. As to the first, the answer is that almost invariably a

116 Md. 518, 82 A. 157 (1911); Tonkel v. Shields, 125 Miss. 461, 87 So. 646 (1921). See Wickhem, Tender in Security Transactions, 27 Iowa L.Rev. 579, 593 (1942); 1934, 93 A.L.R. 12, 30. Contra: Cranston v. Crane, 97 Mass. 459, 93 Am.Dec. 106 (1867); Debnam v. Watkins, 178 N.C. 238, 100 S.E. 336 (1919).

76. Kortright v. Cady, 21 N.Y. 343 (1860), is the leading case. Caruthers v. Humphrey, 12 Mich. 270 (1864), accord. See 93 A.L.R. 31 (1934). Bowman v. Poole, 212 Ga. 261, 91 S.E.2d 770 (1956), noted by Loiseaux, Security Transactions, in Annual Survey of Georgia Law June 1, 1955—June 1, 1956, 8 Mercer L.Rev. 144, 150 (1956), held that a proper tender by a second mortgagee, which was refused, discharged the first mortgage and invalidated the deed executed by the first mortgagee to himself under a foreclosure sale.

77. E. g., Keese v. Parnell, 134 S.C. 207, 132 S.E. 620 (1925); but cf. Peoples Nat. Bank of Greenville v. Upchurch, 183 S.C. 147, 153, 190 S.E. 515, 518 (1937), holding mortgage lien discharged if mortgagor pays money into court. See 93 A.L.R. 12, 38–45 (1934).

78. E. g., Perre v. Castro, 14 Cal. 519, 76 Am.Dec. 444 (1860), and Himmelmann v. Fitzpatrick, 50 Cal. 650 (1875), hold that the mortgage is not discharged. Wiemeyer v. Southern Trust & Commerce Bank, 107 Cal. App. 165, 173, 290 P. 70, 73 (1930), holds that it is. And see Walker v. Houston, 215 Cal. 742, 746, 12 P.2d 952, 87 A.L.R. 937 (1932). See 3 Cal.L.Rev. 336 (1915). See also 93 A.L.R. 12, 46–49 (1934).

land mortgage is recorded and the record mortgage constitutes, practially, as much of a cloud on marketability as does the existence of the lien itself. And, to anticipate, no jurisdiction, even though holding that the substantive lien is gone, will give the mortgagor affirmative relief without payment to the mortgagee or into court in a proceeding which is equivalent to an action to redeem.[79] The mortgagor is always at liberty to bring such an action. Further, not only is the ordinary action in equity available for this purpose, but many states have enacted statutes giving summary relief so as to minimize hardship that might result from the slower equity action. These provide for a short form petition which will result in an order for cancellation of debt and mortgage on the mortgagor paying the money into court.[80] These statutes are in addition to the statutes mentioned earlier giving to the mortgagor a right to damages against a mortgagee who refuses to execute a release, etc., on payment.[81] The availability of such remeties which enable the mortgagor to end any possibility of foreclosure by the mortgagee answers the second objection. Additionally, if the foreclosure is by court action he always can end it by paying into court the amount of the debt.

The strongest argument in favor of the majority rule was advanced in the leading case for the doctrine. The court said, "It is not perceived how the mortgagee is to be embarrassed, or his security impaired by the adoption of this rule. * * * If the mortgagor does not tender the full amount due, the lien of the mortgage is not extinguished. The mortgagee runs no risk in accepting the tender. If it is the full amount due, his mortgage lien is extinguished. * * * His acceptance of the money tendered, if inadequate and less than the amount actually due, only extinguishes the lien pro tanto, and the mortgage remains intact for the residue." [82]

In general this provides a sufficient answer to the claim that the rule is unfair in contrast to the rule of discharge by tender on the law day because at that time the mortgagee would "have anticipated payment and * * * have prepared himself to state the account accurately" [83] whereas at a later time he might not be ready with an

79. Tender cannot be made the basis of an action to cancel a mortgage or for other affirmative relief in equity. Cowles v. Marble, 37 Mich. 158 (1877); Tuthill v. Morris, 81 N.Y. 94 (1880); Nelson v. Loder, 132 N.Y. 288, 30 N.E. 369 (1892); McClellan v. Coffin, 93 Ind. 456 (1883); Murray v. O'Brien, 56 Wash. 361, 105 P. 840, 28 L.R.A.,N.S., 998 (1910). See 10 Col. L.Rev. 252 (1910); 93 A.L.R. 12, 53 (1934); L.R.A.1918C, 186. See also the analogous situation as to the mortgagee in possession in lien states, § 4.26, supra. Cf. also § 6.9, infra.

80. E. g., New York Real Prop. Actions and Proceedings Law § 1921; McKinney's Consol.Laws of N.Y. Book. 49½.

81. See note 67, supra.

82. Kortright v. Cady, 21 N.Y. 343, 354 (1860).

83. Crain v. McGoon, 86 Ill. 431, 434, 29 Am.Rep. 37 (1877).

exact computation of the amount due at that particular moment.[84] However, this is not the only question. The real question is whether, even if the mortgagee will not be harmed by taking whatever payment is offered, the penalty for his failure to do so should be the harsh and drastic one of losing his substantive rights in the security.

Courts in which the majority rule is thoroughly established nevertheless have placed far-reaching restrictions upon the doctrine. The most important of these has already been mentioned. It is the generally held rule that if the mortgagor is seeking affirmative relief, e. g., to remove the cloud of the mortgage on his title or to restrain the exercise of a power of sale, he must "do equity" by paying the principal and, at least, the interest and costs accruing up to the time of tender.[85] In addition, the mortgagee's refusal must be absolute and not in good faith;[86] the proof of a proper tender must be very clear and satisfactory;[87] and the tender must be unconditional, although on this last point there is a dispute.[88] Furthermore only the mortgagor or an assuming grantee can take advantage of the rule; a non-assuming grantee, even though he takes subject to the mortgage cannot.[89] Also, unless the tender is kept good, the mortgagor must pay interest accruing thereafter.[90]

Similar to the last requirement is the rule in some states that for a tender to discharge a mortgage when it is refused it must be kept good.[91] There is some authority that seems to limit this requirement

84. See Hudson Bros. Commission Co. v. Glencoe Sand & Gravel Co., 140 Mo. 103, 41 S.W. 450, 62 Am.St.Rep. 722 (1897); Crain v. McGoon, note 83, supra.

85. Note 79, supra.

86. Myer v. Hart, 40 Mich. 517, 29 Am.Rep. 553 (1879); see Lanier v. Mandeville Mills, 183 Ga. 716, 720, 189 S.E. 532, 535 (1937). Cf. Easton v. Littooy, 91 Wash. 648, 654, 158 P. 531, 533 (1916). See 93 A.L.R. 12, 67 (1934).

87. See Engle v. Hall, 45 Mich. 57, 58, 7 N.W. 239 (1880); Hayward v. Chase, 181 Mich. 614, 618, 148 N.W. 214, 215–216 (1914).

88. There is some authority that a tender on condition that the mortgagee give a release or a receipt in full is effective to discharge the mortgage. E. g., Wallowa Lake Amusement Co. v. Hamilton, 70 Or. 433, 142 P. 321 (1914). See 93 A.L.R. 12, 74 (1934).

89. Harris v. Jex, 66 Barb. 232 (N.Y. 1873), affirmed 55 N.Y. 421, 14 Am.R. 285. See L.R.A., 1918C, 186. As to the place of tender and party to whom it should be made, see Weyand v. Park Terrace Co., 202 N.Y. 231, 95 N.E. 723, 36 L.R.A.,N.S., 308, Ann. Cas.1912D, 1010 (1911); Hopkins Mfg. Co. v. Ketterer, 237 Pa. 285, 85 A. 421, Ann.Cas.1914B, 558 (1912). Bowman v. Poole, 212 Ga. 261, 91 S. E.2d 770 (1956), noted by Loiseaux, Security Transactions, in Annual Survey of Georgia Law, June 1, 1955—June 1, 1956, 8 Mercer L.Rev. 144, 150 (1956), held that a second mortgagee by a proper tender which was refused could discharge a first mortgage.

90. Nelson v. Loder, 132 N.Y. 288, 30 N.E. 369 (1892). See 93 A.L.R. 12, 53 (1934); 39 Yale L.J. 434, 435 (1930).

91. Crain v. McGoon, 86 Ill. 431, 29 Am.Rep. 37 (1877); "In order that the tender may extinguish the mortgage lien, it must be kept up, * * * which is practically much the same thing as a bill in equity by the mortgagor or those holding under him to redeem." Knollenberg v. Nixon, 171 Mo. 445, 455, 72 S.W. 41, 44,

to a tender after the law day [92] but some cases apply it to a tender on the law day.[93] It has been argued that such a requirement is in effect a negation of the rule that tender will operate to discharge a mortgage because until "some action has been brought arising out of the debt or the mortgage and it is shown that the tender has been kept good and the money has been paid into court" [94] the lien cannot be regarded as discharged. The obvious answer is that the same could be said of the requirement of a tender *simpliciter*. Until the fact has been established by an action, it cannot be said with certainty that it has discharged the mortgage even if such was all that the law requires. Of greater validity is the observation that if this is made a requirement, so far as the mortgagor is concerned, the rule operates in substantially the same way as that in title states which says that the mortgage persists in spite of a tender after default until ended by an action to redeem in which he must tender payment. There is one difference which the statement does not take into account. The tender and payment into court will operate to end all power of the mortgagee to foreclose the mortgage without the mortgagor taking any additional affirmative action. Under the other rule the mortgagor must actively bring an action to redeem or to clear his title. The difference is not, however, substantial. If the mortgagor has to put up his money he will want to go ahead and finish the business which will necessitate bringing suit. And even though the act of tendering followed by payment into court may have destroyed a mortgagee's rights, court action is frequently necessary to prevent the attempted exercise of voided rights by persons who persist in asserting them notwithstanding.

§ 6.6 Late Payment Charges—Introduction

A common practice in installment type mortgages is for mortgagees to require the payment of "late payment charges" or "delinquency payments" on the failure of the mortgagor to tender timely payment of a mortgage loan installment.[95] The amount of these charges varies but they are often computed in terms of a fixed percentage either of the principal amount owing or of the late installment. Some-

94 Am.St.Rep. 790 (1902). See Williston, Contracts, Rev.Ed., § 1816; 12 A.L.R. 938 (1921); 93 A.L.R. 12, 50 (1934). Cf., Nelson v. Loder, 132 N.Y. 288, 30 N.E. 369 (1892), tender must be kept good to prevent liability for subsequently accruing interest.

92. E. g., Crain v. McGoon, 86 Ill. 431, 29 Am.Rep. 37 (1877). See Wickhem, Tender in Security Transactions, 27 Iowa L.Rev. 579, 594 (1942); 93 A.L.R. 12, 52 (1934).

93. E. g., see White v. Eddy, 202 Ala. 672, 81 So. 628 (1919). But see, Mitchell v. Roberts, 17 F. 776, 5 McCrary 425 (C.C.A.Ark.1883); Balme v. Wambaugh, 16 Minn. 116, Gil. 106 (1870). See also Storke and Sears, Discharge of Security Transactions, 26 Rocky Mt.L.Rev. 115, 123 (1954).

94. 93 A.L.R. 12, 50 (1934).

95. See Comment, Late-Payment Charges: Meeting the Requirements of Liquidated Damages, 27 Stan.L. Rev. 1133, 1133 n. 1 (1975).

times the charge is simply a fixed dollar amount, but more commonly it is stated in terms of the lesser or greater of a percentage or a fixed dollar amount. Typically, for example, a late charge might be stated as "2% of the late installment or $5 whichever is the greater." Less common today, would be a charge of "additional interest at the rate of 2% per annum on the unpaid balance of this note from the date unpaid interest started to accrue until the close of the business day upon which payment curing the default is received." [96]

§ 6.7 Late Payment Charges—Judicial Interpretation

There traditionally have been two judicial approaches taken toward late payment charges; they are somewhat contradictory in language, if not in theory. Some courts have taken the position that these provisions should be viewed as attempts to provide for liquidated damages and the question in those cases is whether the charge constitutes valid liquidated damages or an invalid penalty.[97] In some of these cases, the court found no invalid "penalty" because the charge was determined to be "increased interest" or an "alternative method of performance." [98] On the other hand, late payment charges are sometimes conceptualized as agreements for additional interest and thus are subjected to analysis under usury principles.[99] In so doing, language difficulties arise. For example, some courts, in upholding late charges against the usury attack, have taken the view that such charges are in the nature of "penalties" for delinquency or non-performance and therefore not usurious.[1] According to the reasoning of these cases, the term "penalty" presumably has a lawful connotation and therefore should not be interpreted as being an "invalid penalty" instead of valid "liquidated damages."

The only major case to confront the above inconsistencies is Clermont v. Secured Investment Corp.,[2] a California appellate deci-

96. Garrett v. Coast and Southern Federal Sav. & Loan Ass'n, 9 Cal.3d 731, 108 Cal.Rptr. 845, 848, 511 P.2d 1197, 1199 (1973). A 1969 survey of late payment charges among California savings and loan associations indicated that a majority of the associations (113) charged between 1% and 10% of the monthly installment as the late payment charge, 21 charged 1% of the unpaid principal balance, and 11 charged a flat fee, usually $5. Id. at 738 n. 6, 108 Cal. Rptr. at 853, 511 P.2d at 1204.

97. See Clermont v. Secured Investment Corp., 25 Cal.App.3d 766, 102 Cal.Rptr. 340 (2nd Dist. 1972); Garrett v. Coast and Southern Federal Sav. & Loan Ass'n, 9 Cal.3d 731, 108 Cal. Rptr. 845, 511 P.2d 1197 (1973).

98. See e. g., Walsh v. Glendale Federal Sav. & Loan Ass'n, 1 Cal.App.3d 578, 81 Cal.Rptr. 804 (2nd Dist. 1969); O'Conner v. Richmond Sav. & Loan Ass'n, 262 Cal.App.2d 523, 68 Cal. Rptr. 882 (1st Dist. 1968).

99. See Annot., 63 A.L.R.3d 50, 61 (1975); Randall v. Home Loan & Investment Co., 244 Wis. 623, 12 N.W. 2d 915 (1944).

1. See, e. g., Hayes v. First Nat. Bank, 507 S.W.2d 701 (Ark.1974); First American Title Ins. & Trust Co. v. Cook, 12 Cal.App.3d 592, 90 Cal.Rptr. 645 (1970).

2. 25 Cal.App.3d 766, 102 Cal.Rptr. 340 (2nd Dist. 1972).

sion. There plaintiffs, in a class action, challenged the imposition of a late payment charge of 1% of the original amount of the loan or $45, whichever was smaller. The plaintiffs contended that while there were cases holding that such charges were not interest and thus not usurious, and while there were other cases holding that such charges were not valid liquidated damages within sections 1670–71 of the Civil Code,[3] such charges had to be either interest or liquidated damages. Thus, plaintiffs argued, such clauses had to be invalid either as usurious or as invalid penalties. The court concurred in recognizing the inconsistency of the prior cases and held that the charge constituted a liquidated damages provision. The court noted that this was a contractually established fee, based strictly on the size of the loan and charged in every instance of tardiness, regardless of the length. "We fail to see how this fixed fee can be characterized as anything but an attempt to provide for liquidated damages."[4] The court then acknowledged that its reasoning was in "apparent conflict" with the California usury line of cases, but it noted that these were decided before passage of the usury law or involved exempt lenders. "While the late charge here * * * must constitute either damages or interest, it may not * * * constitute both."[5] Having determined that the clause was a liquidated damages provision, the court believed it was unnecessary to look at the usury allegation and remanded the case for a determination of the liquidated damages issue.

The leading late payment case, Garrett v. Coast & Southern Federal Savings & Loan Association,[6] accepted the *Clermont* characterization of the late charge. There a class action challenged a late payment fee of 2% per annum assessed against the principal balance. The California Supreme Court rejected the mortgagee's argument that to the extent that the late payment provision required the payment of additional interest, it merely gave the mortgagor the option of an alternative performance of the obligation. The court determined that the only reasonable interpretation of the provision was that the parties had agreed on a basic interest rate that would govern the transaction, and that, recognizing that the mortgagors might fail to make prompt payment, the parties agreed, in addition, that mortgagors

3. West's Ann.Cal.Civ.Code, § 1670 provides:

"Every contract by which the amount of damage to be paid, or other compensation to be made, for breach of an obligation, is determined in anticipation thereof, is to that extent void, except as expressly provided in the next section."

West's Ann.Cal.Civ.Code, § 1671 provides:

"The parties to a contract may agree therein upon an amount which shall be presumed to be the amount of damage sustained by a breach thereof when, from the nature of the case, it would be impracticable or extremely difficult to fix the actual damage."

4. 25 Cal.App.3d at 768, 102 Cal.Rptr. at 342.

5. Id.

6. 9 Cal.3d 731, 108 Cal.Rptr. 845, 511 P.2d 1197 (1973).

were to pay an extra amount as damages for their breach. Since the late payment charge was assessed only after a default, it was invalid unless it qualified as liquidated damages. The court further determined that the parties "made no 'reasonable endeavor * * * to estimate a fair average compensation for any loss that might be sustained' by the delinquency in the payment of the installment." [7] The purpose of such charges, the court concluded, is twofold: (1) to compensate the mortgagee for his administrative expenses and the cost of money wrongfully withheld and (2) to encourage the mortgagor to make timely installment payments.[8] According to the court, if the charge imposed on the mortgagor exceeds substantially the mortgagee's damages, the charge represents an invalid attempt to impose a penalty. While the court recognized that a valid late payment charge can be fixed in advance if the mortgagee can show the damages to be "extremely difficult" or "impracticable" to fix for purposes of sections 1670–71 of the Civil Code, it held that a *charge measured against the unpaid principal balance* was punitive and invalid.[9]

In cases from other jurisdictions, the usury approach has had mixed results. For example, where contract purchasers of a mobile home asserted as a defense to a replevin action that a late charge, equal to the lesser of $5 or 5% of any late payment, rendered the transaction usurious, the Arkansas Supreme Court held that such charges were free from usury because the purchaser had it in his power to avoid the penalty by paying the debt.[10] The Wisconsin Supreme Court, in Randall v. Home Loan Investment Co.,[11] utilized a different usury theory in sustaining a late payment charge. In this case, one of the few non-California late payment decisions involving real estate, the late charge was 1% of the monthly installment. If this charge had been considered as interest, the total interest rate would have been usurious. The court sustained the late payment charge by applying the concept that a provision for an interest rate higher after maturity than would be permissible prior thereto, does not render a loan usurious. Applying this notion to the usual installment mortgage, however, seems questionable because, although late charges are routinely collected after a default in a monthly installment, there usually is not an acceleration resulting in the "maturity" of the entire debt. On the other hand, in Louisiana, a series of recent cases in the chattel security area, have held late charges invalid on a usury theory.[12] For example, one of these decisions has stated

7. Id. at 739, 511 P.2d at 1206, 108 Cal.Rptr. at 854.

8. Id.

9. Id.

10. Hayes v. First Nat. Bank, 507 S.W.2d 701 (Ark.1974).

11. 244 Wis. 623, 12 N.W.2d 915 (1944).

12. See Gordon Finance Co. v. Chambliss, 236 So.2d 533 (La.App.1970), certiorari denied 256 La. 869, 239 So.2d 364; Thrift Funds of Baton Rouge, Inc. v. Jones, 274 So.2d 150 (La.1973), certiorari denied 414 U.S. 820, 94 S.Ct. 115, 38 L.Ed.2d 53.

it to be "settled law in Louisiana that late charges or bonus payments for extension of an indebtedness are tantamount to interest payments and are usurious if they exceed the legal maximum." [13]

Although, nationwide, there are relatively few decisions regarding late payment charges, certain observations are, nevertheless, justified. First, while the California "liquidated damages-penalty" approach is based on specific California statutes, a similar common law approach should be applicable to challenge late charges there or elsewhere. For example, Professor Corbin has stated the general common law rule that to sustain "the payment of a definite sum as a liquidation of damages, it is necessary that at the time the contract is made it must appear that the injury that will be caused by breach will be difficult of estimation." [14] Second, the usury argument will be difficult to sustain, in part because the often harsh penalties imposed on usurious transactions, such as total loss of interest or, sometimes, principal, make courts reticent to take a broad view of the usury approach.[15]

Finally, some generalizations are appropriate as to which type of late payment clauses are most likely to be sustained. Late charges that are calculated as a percentage of the principal balance of the loan will, at best, be suspect, because they bear no rational connection to the mortgagee's actual damages caused by late payment. In the average residential mortgage transaction, the administrative costs caused by a late payment are relatively small and the same for all loans. "The components of servicing a late payment consist of the employee and computer time involved in adjusting the borrower's file to reflect the default and charge, plus the material cost of computer card, envelope, stamp and notice form." [16] One commentator has estimated such administrative cost at less than $5 per late payment, an amount that will rise to some extent with inflation.[17] The mortgagee also deserves to be reimbursed for the interest that would have been earned on the installment had it been paid promptly.[18] To the extent that a mortgagee relies on the above two factors in establishing that its late charge approximates its actual loss, the less inclined a court will be to invalidate it, whatever the legal theory utilized in attacking it.

13. Consolidated Loans, Inc. v. Smith, 190 So.2d 522, 527 (La.App.1966), application denied 249 La. 753, 190 So. 2d 913.

14. 5 A. Corbin, Corbin on Contracts § 1060 (1964).

15. See Comment, Secured Real Estate Loan Prepayment and the Prepayment Penalty, 51 Cal.L.Rev. 923, 927–28 (1963).

16. Comment, Late-Payment Charges: Meeting the Requirements of Liquidated Damages, 27 Stan.L.Rev. 1133, 1141 (1975).

17. Id. at 1141.

18. Id. at 1141.

§ 6.8 Late Payment Charges—Legislative and Other Regulatory Impact

A few state legislatures are beginning to regulate the imposition of late payment charges. To some extent, the *Garrett* philosophy is reflected in this legislation because one common feature to such legislation is that any percentage utilized in determining a valid late payment charge is calculated on the amount of the late installment, rather than on the principal balance of the loan.

The Uniform Consumer Credit Code (UCCC), which is in effect in at least nine states, limits, as to real estate installment loans for personal, family, household or agricultural purposes whose interest rates exceed 12% per annum, the imposition of late charges to the lesser of $5 or 5% of the late installment.[19] There is a ten-day grace period and only one penalty may be assessed for each late installment. Any payment tendered by the mortgagor must be applied to the most recent payment due. This legislation does not affect lending to commercial entities and, because of the above interest rate provision, most first mortgage residential lending.

A few states regulate late payment penalties with specific legislation. New York limits late payment penalties with respect to mortgages on owner-occupied one to six family dwellings to a maximum of 2% of the past due installment and requires a fifteen day grace period after an installment due date before penalty may be assessed. Any late charge must be separately charged and collected and not subtracted from any regular payment.[20] In California, as to loans secured by mortgages on single family, owner-occupied dwellings, the maximum late charge is 6% of each delinquent installment or $5, whichever is the greater, and it may be imposed only after a ten day grace period. Any payment tendered by the mortgagor must be applied to the most recent installment due.[21] Massachusetts limits late penalties on first mortgages on owner-occupied dwellings of four or less households to 3% of the late installment; no penalty may be assessed within fifteen days from the due date.[22]

19. U.C.C.C. § 2.502 (1974). The UCCC originally was promulgated in 1968 and, after intervening drafts, the 1974 UCCC was promulgated. The UCCC, in one of the foregoing versions, with a variety of modification, in Oklahoma, Utah, Colorado, Idaho, Indiana, Wyoming, Kansas, Iowa and Maine. The Uniform Land Transaction Act (ULTA) limits late charges in loans on owner-occupied residences to the greater of $5 or 5% of the late installment, but apparently allows the parties to contract differently. See U.L.T.A. § 3–404. The ULTA is not yet law in any jurisdiction.

20. McKinney's N.Y.Real Prop.Law § 254–b (1974).

21. West's Ann.Cal.Civil Code, § 2954.-4 (1975). See also West's Ann.Cal. Bus. and Prof.Code § 10242.5 (1973) (as to loans negotiated by real estate licensees). Oregon has similar legislation. See Ch. 427, Laws 1977 (Eff. Jan. 1, 1978).

22. Mass.Gen.Laws Ann. ch. 183 § 59 (1977).

Federal agencies to some extent regulate the imposition of late charges. Federal Reserve Regulation Z, enforcing the Federal Truth in Lending Act, requires virtually all mortgage lenders who loan money in the ordinary course of business to disclose to the mortgagor the amount and method of computation of any late payment charge.[23] The Federal Home Loan Bank Board (FHLBB) regulation, which is applicable to all federally chartered savings and loan associations, prohibits, as to all loans on owner-occupied dwellings, prepayment penalties in excess of 5% of the amount of the late installment and their assessment during a fifteen day grace period.[24] Unlike the California statute, the FHLBB regulation provides that "an installment payment made by the borrower shall be applied to the *longest* outstanding installment due." [25] Both the California statute and the FHLBB regulation permit only one late charge for each delinquent installment. Thus, if several installments are in default and the mortgagor makes one regular payment, in California the payment would be applied to the most recent installment due. No penalty could be assessed as to that payment. Under the FHLBB regulation however, if our mortgagor makes the same payment, it will be applied to cover the "longest" outstanding installment due and thus a new penalty will be assessed as to the most recent installment due.

The official policies of the two quasi-federal institutions that purchase first mortgage loans on the secondary market to some extent work at cross purposes. The Federal National Mortgage Association (FNMA) policy as to non-federally insured or guaranteed (conventional) mortgages states that the "note shall provide that the borrower *shall* pay a late charge in the amount of 4%, or such lesser amount as permitted by the laws of the jurisdiction, computed on the monthly installment of principal and interest when such installment is not received on or before the fifteenth day after the installment due date." [26] On the other hand, the Federal Home Loan Mortgage Corporation (FHLMC) *permits, but does not require,* the collection of late charges after a fifteen day grace period in an amount no greater than 5% of the late installment of principal and interest.[27] Thus, FNMA requires a late payment charge while the FHLMC simply authorizes it. Since many lending institutions sell loans on the secondary market, and since these institutions, for purposes of maximum flexibility, will probably want to be able to sell their loans to either of these quasi-federal agencies, the practical effect of these agencies' policies will be that the lending institutions will opt to *require* a late

23. 12 CFR 226.8(b)(4). For an interpretation of this regulation see Vega v. First Federal Sav. and Loan Ass'n of Detroit, 433 F.Supp. 624 (E.D. Mich.1977).

24. 12 CFR 545b–11(e).

25. 12 CFR 545b–11(e)(2) (emphasis added).

26. FNMA Conventional Selling Contract Supplement, § 304 (emphasis added).

27. FHLMC Servicer's Guide § 3.103 (March 21, 1977).

payment penalty.[28] Thus FNMA, in effect, may be setting some type of national norm that requires late payment penalties as to non-federally insured or guaranteed (conventional) first mortgage loans.

Prepayment penalties on federally insured or guaranteed loans are limited by federal regulation. With respect to loans insured by the Federal Housing Administration (FHA), late payment charges are limited to 2% of each installment that is more than fifteen days late.[29] The maximum late charge for loans guaranteed by the Veterans Administration (VA) is 4% of any installment that is delinquent more than fifteen days.[30]

B. STATUTES OF LIMITATION

§ 6.9 Relationship of Obligation and Mortgage

The effect of lapse of time upon mortgages is complicated by the separate existence of the mortgage from the debt that it secures[31] and the availability of separate remedies for the enforcement of each which, in most states, may be pursued independently.[32] The mortgage debt may take several forms. It may be a simple oral or written debt, it may be in the form of a negotiable promissory note or bond, or it may be a covenant under seal either in the deed or apart from it. Quite commonly statutes of limitations provide longer or shorter periods of time depending upon the character of the obligation. And in this connection a point may be disposed of here. Where a mortgage executed to secure a note also contains a covenant in which the mortgagor agrees to pay the loan, even though a shorter statute of limitations has run on the note the mortgagee may still enforce the covenant.[33] The rule illustrates and emphasizes the separate existence of remedies and the rule that barring one has no necessary effect upon another.

The concept of the interest of the mortgagee in the land as giving him legal title or a lien which is accessory to the debt plays an-

28. See § 11.3 infra. Interestingly, the note form prescribed by both FNMA and FHLMC contains a late payment clause. The penalty is stated in terms of a percentage of the late installment but the actual percentage amount is left blank. Thus, both agencies, in effect, tend to encourage late payment penalties because mortgagees are not likely to omit the penalty language from the note form.

29. 24 CFR 203.25.

30. 38 CFR 36.4212(c).

31. See §§ 2.1–2.2, supra.

32. See Chapter 7, infra.

33. Dinniny v. Gavin, 4 App.Div. 298, 39 N.Y.S. 485 (1896), affirmed 159 N.Y. 556, 54 N.E. 1090 (1899); Empire Trust Co. v. Heinze, 242 N.Y. 475, 152 N.E. 266 (1926). See also Harris v. Mills, 28 Ill. 44, 81 Am.Dec. 259 (1862). The mortgagee may foreclose and get a deficiency judgment on the covenant. Holcomb v. Webley, 185 Va. 150, 37 S.E.2d 762 (1946), commented on, 32 Va.L.Rev. 1043 (1946); Guardian Depositors Corp. of Detroit v. Savage, 287 Mich. 193, 283 N.W. 26, 124 A.L.R. 635 (1938), discussed in notes, 87 U. of Pa.L.Rev. 741 (1939); 37 Mich.L.Rev. 1340 (1939).

other part; for the theory of the effect of the running of the statute of limitations upon a chose in action is quite different from that upon rights in real and personal property.[34] Again the mortgagee has different remedies to enforce his right in the land. He may bring an action at law to recover possession in title states; he may use a bill in equity to foreclose; or he may foreclose by exercising a power of sale contained in the mortgage.[35] The effect of the passage of time upon each one of these is a separate and distinct problem. The barring of the right to recover possession of the land is governed by statutes of limitations and doctrines quite distinct from those covering the debt obligation whatever its form.[36] The former have led to a requirement insisted upon by some courts that, in order to bar a mortgagee's right to possession of the mortgaged property in title states there had to be some act by the mortgagor in the nature of a disseizin.[37] The concept behind the reasoning goes back to the early idea in the common law classical form mortgage that the mortgagor in possession was a tenant of some sort of the mortgagee.[38] The rule seems unfortunate. The time should begin to run on any remedy the mortgagee has to recover possession from the time he may exercise it without injecting into its barring ideas of disseizin or adverse possession. The foreclosure action, being in equity, originally was not governed by statutes of limitations, which applied only to actions at law, but, rather, by the doctrine of laches. While this may still be true in some jurisdictions,[39] many states have made their statutes of limitation applicable to equity suits, either by express statutory language or by judicial interpretation.[40] Power of sale mortgages pose still other problems which will be considered later.

In considering the effect of the mortgage debt being barred by the running of a statute of limitations, common law title states must be differentiated from lien jurisdictions.[41] Title states appear to hold that the running of the statute of limitations upon the mortgage debt has no effect upon the existence of or remedies upon the mortgage.[42] Having title, the mortgagee may take possession peaceably or main-

34. See, e. g., Chapin v. Freeland, 142 Mass. 383, 8 N.E. 128, 56 Am.Rep. 701 (1886).

35. See Chapter 7, infra.

36. Chapin v. Freeland, note 34, supra.

37. See note, 25 Ill.L.Rev. 563 (1931).

38. See § 4.1, supra and § 6.10, infra.

39. See Walsh, Equity, 474. See also notes, 49 Sol.J. 181, 201, 215, 233 (1905); 79 U. of Pa.L.Rev. 341 (1930); 77 U. of Pa.L.Rev. 701 (1929); 9 Tex. L.Rev. 93 (1930); 6 Wash.L.Rev. 91 (1931).

40. See Van Hecke, Leavell and Nelson, Equitab'e Remedies and Restitution, (2nd Ed. 1973); Ludwig v. Scott, 65 S.W.2d 1034 (Mo.1933).

41. See notes, 16 Harv.L.Rev. 445 (1903); 13 Col.L.Rev. 442 (1913); 32 Yale L.Jour. 611 (1932).

42. See 161 A.L.R. 886, 887 (1946); Phinney v. Levine, 359 A.2d 636 (N.H.1976); Note, The Statute of Limitations as a Defense to Foreclosure in Illinois, U. of Ill.L.Forum 469 (1957).

tain an action of ejectment or writ of entry.[43] This he may do even though not only action on the debt has been barred but an action to foreclose as well, provided the statute of limitations on the remedy of ejectment has not run.[44] Or he may maintain an action to foreclose.[45] The reasoning usually is that the statute of limitations bars merely the remedy on the debt, not the right. And it does not purport to affect any other independent remedy on the mortgage or the mortgage itself. The debt remaining, the mortgage continues to secure it and is not extinguished indirectly upon any theory that a destruction of the obligation secured necessarily destroys the mortgage securing it.[46]

The lien states are in conflict. Probably the majority follows the reasoning of the courts in title states. There are independent rights and remedies on the debt and the mortgage lien. Barring of a remedy upon the debt does not affect the debt itself, nor does it have any operative effect upon either the lien or the remedy to enforce it. Consequently the mortgagee can foreclose his lien by court action[47] or by exercising a power of sale contained in the mortgage.[48] Moreover, most strikingly, the same result has been reached in a jurisdiction in which the running of the statute on the debt is regarded as extinguishing it, not merely barring the remedy to enforce it.[49] A number of lien states, however, hold that when the remedy on the obligation is barred the remedy on the mortgage goes with it. The reason usually given is that the mortgage is merely an incident of the debt and should not be enforceable if the debt is not.[50] Where

43. Bradfield v. Hale, 67 Ohio St. 316, 65 N.E. 1008 (1902); Taylor v. Quinn, 68 Ohio App. 164, 39 N.E.2d 627 (1941), noted 91 U. of Pa.L.Rev. 85 (1942); Thayer v. Mann, 36 Mass. (19 Pick.) 535 (1837), writ of entry.

44. Bradfield v. Hale, supra note 43; Taylor v. Quinn, supra note 43.

45. Belknap v. Gleason, 11 Conn. 160, 27 Am.Dec. 721 (1836); Elkins v. Edwards, 8 Ga. 325 (1850) and see Ga. Code of § 67–101 (1933); Norton v. Palmer, 142 Mass. 433, 8 N.E. 346 (1886). See 161 A.L.R. 886, 887 (1946). The rule is otherwise in Illinois, an intermediate state. Harris v. Mills, 28 Ill. 44, 81 Am.Dec. 259 (1862); Markus v. Chicago Title etc. Co., 373 Ill. 557, 27 N.E.2d 436, 128 A.L.R. 567 (1940). So too, in Arkansas. Johnson v. Lowman, 193 Ark. 8, 97 S.W.2d 86 (1936).

46. See §§ 2.1–2.2 supra, on the dependence of a mortgage upon the existence of an obligation to secure. See also, 11 Cal.L.Rev. 429 (1923); 8 U. of Cin.L.Rev. 121, 123 (1934).

47. Hulbert v. Clark, 128 N.Y. 295, 28 N.E. 638, 14 L.R.A. 59 (1891); Mich. Ins. Co. of Detroit v. Brown, 11 Mich. 265 (1863); Slingerland v. Sherer, 46 Minn. 422, 49 N.W. 237 (1891).

48. House v. Carr, 185 N.Y. 453, 78 N.E. 171, 6 L.R.A.,N.S., 510, 7 Ann. Cas. 185 (1906); Menzel v. Hinton, 132 N.C. 660, 44 S.E. 385, 95 Am.St. Rep. 647, nullified by N.C.C.S. § 2589 (1903); Grant v. Burr, 54 Cal. 298 (1880), trust deed mortgage. Cf. Faxon v. All Persons, etc., 166 Cal. 707, 137 P. 919, L.R.A.1916B, 1209 (1913); Emory v. Keighan, 88 Ill. 482 (1878).

49. First National Bank of Madison v. Kolbeck, 247 Wis. 462, 19 N.W.2d 908, 161 A.L.R. 882 (1945).

50. Allen v. Shepherd, 162 Ky. 756, 173 S.W. 135 (1915); see Prewitt v. Wortham, 79 Ky. 287, 288, 2 Ky.Law Rep. 282 (1881); 32 Ky.L.Rev. 78

the debt itself is regarded as extinguished by the running of the statute the reason for such a rule is stronger and was persuasive in earlier decisions in a state holding this view.[51] The minority rule has been applied to mortgages by deeds absolute on their face but intended as mortgages.[52] This dependence of the mortgage remedy on that of the debt is provided for by statute in some jurisdictions which bar a remedy upon the mortgage when that on the debt is gone.[53] This view is accompanied by the rule that if the remedy on the debt is revived the mortgage also will again become enforceable.[54] A different type of statute provides that "a lien is extinguished by the lapse of time within which an action can be brought upon the principal obligation." [55] Under this, a mortgage is destroyed by the running of the statute so that it cannot be revived by any act of the mortgagor although the debt can be.[56]

The deed of trust requires separate consideration in connection with the running of the statute of limitations. Although the distinction between a mortgage in such a form and a regular form mortgage has been minimized it has not been obliterated. One of the most important persisting notions is that it, like other trusts, continues until the performance of the trust purpose, viz., the payment of the debt for which the trust was created.[57] One result is that there is no time

(1943); Duty v. Graham, 12 Tex. 427, 62 Am.Dec. 534 (1943). See also note 41, 42, supra. And see 161 A.L.R. 886, 890 (1946). Tennant v. Hulet, 65 Ind.App. 24, 116 N.E. 748 (1917), reached the same result but is superseded by Yarlott v. Brown, 192 Ind. 648, 138 N.E. 17 (1923). Cf., 22 Col.L.Rev. 451 (1922). See 29 Col.L. Rev. 210 (1941), on the methods of pleading the statute of limitations as a bar.

51. Pierce v. Seymour, 52 Wis. 272, 9 N.W. 71, 38 Am.Rep. 737 (1881); Eingartner v. Illinois Steel Co., 103 Wis. 373, 79 N.W. 433, 74 Am.St.Rep. 871 (1899); see, 2 Minn.L.Rev. 218, 219 (1917). But see note-call and note 49, supra.

52. Kern Valley Bank v. Koehn, 157 Cal. 237, 107 P. 111 (1910); Pratt v. Pratt, 121 Wash. 298, 209 P. 535, 28 A.L.R. 548 (1922), discussed in notes, 8 Cornell L.Q. 172 (1923); 71 U. of Pa.L.Rev. 284 (1923); 32 Yale L.J. 611 (1923). See also 11 L.R.A.,N.S., 825 (1908).

53. See, e. g., Vernon's Ann.Mo.Stat. § 516.150.

54. Schmucker v. Sibert, 18 Kan. 104, 26 Am.Rep. 765 (1877); Schifferstein v. Allison, 123 Ill. 662, 15 N.E. 275 (1888). Cf., Clinton County v. Cox, 37 Iowa 570 (1873), extension.

55. West's Ann.Cal.Civ.Code, § 2911.

56. Wells v. Harter, 56 Cal. 342 (1880); Sanford v. Bergin, 156 Cal. 43, 103 P. 333 (1909); San Jose Safe Deposit Bank of Savings v. Bank of Madera, 144 Cal. 574, 78 P. 5 (1904). The destruction of the mortgage by the running of the statute of limitations also destroys any power of sale in the mortgage so that equity, at the request of the mortgagor, will restrain an attempted exercise of it without requiring the mortgagor to tender payment to the mortgagee. Goldwater v. Hibernia Savings & Loan Soc., 19 Cal.App. 511, 126 P. 861 (1912), rehearing denied 19 Cal.App. 511, 126 P. 863. And the mortgagor can quiet title against a purchaser under the sale without paying his debt. Faxon v. All Persons, etc., 166 Cal. 707, 137 P. 919, L.R.A.,1916B, 1209 (1913).

57. See Cunningham v. Williams, 178 Va. 542, 17 S.E.2d 355 (1941); Basye, Clearing Land Titles, § 73 (2d Ed. 1970).

limit on it[58] except as so specifically provided by statute.[59] Barring of the remedy on the debt has no effect upon the trustee's power to sell the property and pay the debt with the proceeds.[60] And this is true under statutes extinguishing the "lien of a mortgage" when the remedy on the debt is barred, a trust deed mortgage not being a "lien" within the meaning of the provision.[61]

There is case law even in lien jurisdictions that a mortgagor may not maintain an action to cancel a mortgage or to quiet title based on the running of the statute of limitations, unless payment of the debt is tendered to the mortgagee.[62] This approach is based on the equitable maxim that those "who seek equity, must do equity," a corollary of which is that the mortgagor should perform his moral obligation to pay as a condition precedent to equitable relief. Whatever the merits of such an approach, the majority of states appear to have reversed it by statute.[63]

Interestingly, prior to statutes of limitations as to debts, a common law presumption existed that a debt was presumed to have been paid if twenty years passed without recognition of its existence by the debtor.[64] The rule was also extended to include mortgages where the mortgagor had been in possession for the full twenty year period.[65] This presumption, for the most part, "has been superceded by statutes of limitations, and the rule is further submerged by stat-

58. A common expression is "that the statute of limitations never runs against the power of sale in a deed of trust." Bank of Italy Nat. Trust & Sav. Ass'n v. Bentley, 217 Cal. 644 20 P.2d 940 (1933). See note, 27 Cal.L.Rev. 66, 67. See also Note, Comparison of California Mortgages, Trust Deeds and Land Sale Contracts, 7 U.C.L.A.L.Rev. 83, 85 (1960).

59. There are now a good many statutes declaring that a deed of trust may not be foreclosed after the time that a mortgage, if it rather than a deed of trust had been given to secure the debt, could be foreclosed by action or after the debt it secures is barred by the statute. See e. g., Vernon's Ann.Mo.Stat. § 516.150.

60. See 58 W.Va.L.Q. 417 (1956), commenting on Kuhn v. Shreeve, 141 W. Va. 170, 89 S.E.2d 685 (1955).

61. Grant v. Burr, 54 Cal. 298 (1880); Travelli v. Bowman, 150 Cal. 587, 89 P. 347 (1907); Sacramento Bank v. Murphy, 158 Cal. 390, 115 P. 232 (1910). Cf. Hurley v. Estes, 6 Neb. 386 (1877). Illogically, however, the danger exists that an action to foreclose a trust deed mortgage, brought and prosecuted to judgment after the statute has run on the debt, may, if the debtor or even a grantee pleads the statute, result in the security interest being extinguished. Flack v. Boland, 11 Cal.2d 103, 77 P.2d 1090 (1938).

62. Tracy v. Wheeler, 15 N.D. 248, 107 N.W. 68 (1906); Phinney v. Levine, 359 A.2d 636 (N.H.1976). Cf. Gibson v. Johnson, 73 Kan. 261, 84 P. 982 (1906); Mitchell v. Bickford, 192 Mass. 244, 78 N.E. 453 (1906). See notes, 15 Col.L.Rev. 720 (1915); 22 Col.L.Rev. 451 (1922) (also discussing the question whether a grantee of the mortgagor may have such relief). See 164 A.L.R. 1387 (1946). But cf., 7 Wash. & Lee L.Rev. 220 (1950).

63. See Bayse, Clearing Land Titles, § 75 and n.4 (2d Ed. 1970).

64. Id. at § 71; See 1 A.L.R. 781 (1919), for an extensive collection of cases on the presumption of payment generally; Wigmore, Evidence, 2d ed. § 2517.

65. Basye, supra note 63 at § 71.

utes that destroy the efficacy of a judgment after the lapse of a certain period." [66] The presumption, nevertheless, is applicable in a few jurisdictions for the purpose of compelling the cancellation of a mortgage after a twenty year lapse.[67] In the absence of proof sufficient to rebut the presumption, the mortgagor "is entitled to have the cloud of the mortgage removed since the underlying issue is whether there has been payment of the mortgage, not whether the statute of limitations has barred the remedy on it." [68]

§ 6.10 Effect of Acts of Mortgagor Upon Junior Interests

Any act of a mortgagor which extends the statute of limitations as to the mortgage obligation also extends it as to the mortgage provided he has retained the property unencumbered by junior liens.[69] Where third parties have acquired junior interests in the property as grantees or lienors, there is great confusion in the cases and lack of agreement as to rationale with the exception of certain propositions.[70] For one thing, the courts generally are in accord that when such persons acquire their rights after the mortgagor has done an act sufficient to extend the period of the statute as to the mortgage debt, it likewise extends the statute as to the mortgage both against the mortgagor and the third parties.[71] And the same is true of an act which revives a debt which had been barred.[72] Again, if the statute has run before the junior interest is acquired, the mortgagor cannot

66. Glenn, Mortgages, § 56 at p. 373 (1943).

67. Kuhn v. Shreeve, 141 W.Va. 170, 89 S.E.2d 685 (1955), commented on in 58 W.Va.L.Q. 417 (1956). Proof that no payment of principal or interest has been received by the mortgagee during more than twenty years after maturity, does not rebut the presumption of payment. Osborne Estate, 382 Pa. 306, 115 A.2d 201 (1955). See Note, Admissibility and weight of admissions and acknowledgments to rebut presumption of payment from lapse of time, 48 A.L.R.2d 868 (1956). See also Plowman, in Mortgages and Security Transactions, in 1956–1957 Survey of Pennsylvania Law, 19 U. of Pitt.L.Rev. 292, 294 (1958) noting Oaks Fire Co. v. Herbert, 389 Pa. 357, 132 A.2d 193 (1957); see, Secured Transactions, in 1957–1958 Survey of Pennsylvania Law, 20 U. of Pitt.L.Rev. 371 (1958), noting Sandman v. Old Delancy Bldg. & Loan Ass'n, 184 Pa.Super. 470, 135 A.2d 819 (1957).

68. Basye, supra note 63 at p. 217.

69. Colton v. Depew, 60 N.J.Eq. 454, 46 A. 728, 83 Am.St.Rep. 650 (1900); Hansen v. Branner, 52 N.D. 892, 204 N.W. 856, 41 A.L.R. 814 (1925). See 41 A.L.R. 822 (1926); Niehaus v. Niehaus, 2 Ill.App.2d 434, 120 N.E.2d 66 (1954), noted, 33 Chi.Kent L.Rev. 82 (1954).

70. For discussions of the problem and collections of cases on it, see notes 49 Harv.L.Rev. 639 (1936); 27 Cal.L. Rev. 66 (1938); 32 Ill.L.Rev. 750 (1938); 9 Col.L.Rev. 718 (1909); 9 Minn.L.Rev. 166 (1924). See also 28 L.R.A.,N.S., 169 (1910); 26 L.R.A.,N.S. 898 (1910); 38 A.L.R. 833 (1925); 41 A.L.R. 822, 827, 828 (1926); 101 A.L. R. 337 (1936). Note, 51 Col.L.Rev. 1031 (1951).

71. See Storke and Sears, Discharge of Security Transactions, 26 Rocky Mt. L.Rev. 115, 131 (1954).

72. Clark v. Grant, 26 Okl. 398, 109 P. 234, 28 L.R.A.,N.S., 519, Ann.Cas. 1912B, 505 (1910). Contra, by statute, Musser v. First Nat. Bank, 165 Miss. 873, 147 So. 783 (1933).

revive the mortgage as against the third party who may have acquired it on the faith of the bar,[73] even though his act may revive the debt and mortgage as to himself.[74] Further, in the great majority of cases, the courts do not attempt to differentiate between the effect upon the statute of the mortgagor's absence from the state and affirmative acts such as part payments of principal or interest or an acknowledgment of the indebtedness.[75] Beyond this harmony ceases.

Where a junior interest in the mortgaged property is acquired before the statute of limitations has run and before the mortgagor has done any act which extends the statute, and thereafter the mortgagor does such act there are two broad lines of authorities. A minority of courts hold that after a third party acquires an interest in the mortgaged property the mortgagor cannot extend or revive the mortgage as to him.[76] The chief argument in favor of this is that it is unfair to allow the mortgagor, after he has conveyed away title or transferred a security interest in the property to another, to increase the burden on the transferred junior interest which he does not own, and an extension of time is an increase of the burden.[77] As applied to a grantee, the point has merit, and a few courts limit the doctrine to such a case.[78] A junior lienor, though, holds through the mortgagor and should be bound by the latter's conduct so far as it affects the first mortgage debt and mortgage.[79] In many cases, however, it is impossible to tell whether the court would distinguish between cases in which the mortgagor has divested himself of all property interest by a conveyance and those in which he has merely subjected the

73. Schmucker v. Sibert, 18 Kan. 104, 26 Am.Rep. 765 (1877); Cason v. Chambers, 62 Tex. 305 (1884); De Voe v. Rundle, 33 Wash. 604, 74 P. 836 (1903); see Kerndt v. Porterfield, 56 Iowa, 412, 9 N.W. 322 (1881). See also 28 L.R.A.,N.S., 169, 170 (1910); 41 A.L.R. 822, 828 (1926); 101 A.L.R. 330, 343 (1936). Note, 32 Ill.L.Rev. 750, 751, n. 6 (1938).

74. Brandenstein v. Johnson, 140 Cal. 29, 73 P. 744 (1903); Colonial & U. S. Mortgage Co. v. Flemington, 14 N.D. 181, 103 N.W. 929, 116 Am.St.Rep. 670 (1905); Cason v. Chambers, 62 Tex. 305 (1884). See 9 Col.L.Rev. 718, 719 (1909).

75. See Wood v. Goodfellow, 43 Cal. 185, 188 (1872). See also 49 Harv.L. Rev. 639, n. 2 (1936). As to the basis for extension because of the mortgagor's absence, see 46 Harv.L.Rev. 703 (1933).

76. Storke and Sears, Discharge of Security Transactions, 26 Rocky Mt.L. Rev. 115, 134 (1954).

77. See Lord v. Morris, 18 Cal. 482, 490 (1861); Wood v. Goodfellow, 43 Cal. 185, 189 (1872); Zoll v. Carnahan, 83 Mo. 35, 43–44 (1884); Consolidated Nat. Bank v. Van Slyke, 27 Ariz. 501, 234 P. 553, 38 A.L.R. 825 (1925). See also 47 Harv.L.Rev. 639, 641 (1936); 27 Cal.L.Rev. 66, 71 (1938).

78. E. g., Hess v. State Bank, 130 Wash. 147, 226 P. 257, 38 A.L.R. 829 (1924), discussed in notes, 9 Minn.L. Rev. 166 (1925); 49 Harv.L.Rev. 639, 642 (1936); 27 Cal.L.Rev. 66, 71 (1938), in which the court draws this distinction; George v. Butler, 26 Wash. 456, 67 P. 263, 57 L.R.A. 396, 90 Am.St.Rep. 756 (1901). Cf. Smith v. Bush, 173 Okl. 172, 44 P.2d 921, 101 A.L.R. 330 (1935). See 27 Cal.L. Rev. 66, 71; 1925, 38 A.L.R. 833 (1938).

79. Hess v. State Bank, note 78, supra.

property to another lien.[80] Some cases clearly indicate no such line of demarcation is drawn.[81] Nor is any distinction drawn between subsequent mortgage liens and any other valid lien (by judgment, attachment, etc.).[82] Additional considerations bolstering the rule are that it enables one taking a junior interest in the mortgaged property to know exactly the extent of the lien; and that there is no hardship on the mortgagee because it does not affect his right to foreclose during the normal period of the statute.[83]

Most minority courts hold that the mortgagee must be given notice of the intervention of the rights of the grantee or the latter will be bound by the acts of the mortgagor. However, the courts generally mention, without distinction, "actual or constructive" notice to the mortgagee [84] and hold that recordation of a subsequent change in the status of the mortgaged property acts as constructive notice.[85] And, occasionally, it is stated flatly that, regardless of notice of any sort to the mortgagee, the mortgagor cannot affect the running of the statute in favor of subsequently acquired interests.[86]

The majority view [87] is that any conduct by the mortgagor that keeps the debt enforceable as to him also keeps the mortgage alive as to grantees and junior lienors.[88] These courts argue, technically, that the mortgage is a mere incident of the debt and therefore anything

80. See, e. g., 27 Cal.L.Rev. 69, 70, n. 24 (1938). See also 32 Ill.L.Rev. 750, 752 (1938).

81. E. g., see Lord v. Morris, 18 Cal. 482, 490 (1861).

82. Brandenstein v. Johnson, 140 Cal. 29, 73 P. 744 (1903); Watt v. Wright, 66 Cal. 202, 5 P. 91 (1884); De Voe v. Rundle, 33 Wash. 604, 74 P. 836 (1903).

83. See 9 Col.L.Rev. 718, 719 (1909).

84. See, e. g., Boucofski v. Jacobsen, 36 Utah, 165, 177, 104 P. 117, 121, 26 L.R.A.,N.S., 898 (1909).

85. E. g., Filipini v. Trobock, 134 Cal. 444, 66 P. 587 (1901).

86. See Benedict v. Griffith, 92 Ark. 195, 199, 122 S.W. 479, 480 (1909); Cook v. Union Trust Co., 106 Ky. 803, 809, 51 S.W. 600, 601–2, 45 L.R.A. 212 (1899).

87. See notes 70, 74 supra.

88. Consolidated Nat. Bank v. Van Slyke, 27 Ariz. 501, 234 P. 553, 38 A.L.R. 825 (1925); Smith v. Bush, 173 Okl. 172, 44 P.2d 921, 101 A.L.R. 330 (1935); Hess v. State Bank, 130 Wash. 147, 226 P. 257, 38 A.L.R. 829 (1924), as to junior mortgagee. In many of the decisions in which the junior interest was acquired before the mortgagor's conduct extending the time or reviving the debt occurred and also before the statute had run, the courts are not concerned with whether the mortgagor's act occurred before or after the statute had run. See 101 A.L.R. 330, 342 (1936). In some cases, however, the fact that the tolling occurred after the bar was complete was important in preventing recovery by the mortgagee. Cook v. Prindle, 97 Iowa 464, 66 N.W. 781, 59 Am.St.Rep. 424 (1896). See 101 A.L.R. 337, 343 (1936). Johnson v. Johnson, 81 Mo. 331 (1884), contra. Similarly, the fact that such tolling was made before the bar was complete has been a decisive factor in a few decisions refusing to permit the junior encumbrancer to plead the statute. Kaiser v. Idleman, 57 Or. 224, 108 P. 193, 28 L.R.A.,N.S., 169 (1910). See 32 Ill.L.Rev. 750, 752; 1925 9 Minn.L.Rev. 166 (1938).

that keeps the debt alive should likewise keep the mortgage alive.[89] The mortgage was not destroyed substantively any more than was the debt. It was still there. If the remedy on the debt is now available, it is argued, so should be the remedy on the mortgage. In skepticism of the validity of this line of reasoning it is suggested that the remedy on the mortgage was available even though the remedy on the debt was barred. Also the remedy on the mortgage might be barred independently of the barring of the remedy on the debt. And if this be so, the question is asked whether the extension or revival of the remedy on the debt should have any effect upon the remedy on the mortgage.

In addition, the majority urge that any purchaser of a junior interest with notice of the paramount mortgage, actual or constructive, must be regarded as taking subject to the mortgage and all of its incidents including the possibility of extension of the debt by conduct of the mortgagor.[90] Further, the mortgagee should be free to deal with his debtor, the mortgagor, without having the burden of discovering and taking into account, until he is ready to foreclose, persons who might have acquired a junior interest in the property in between the taking of the mortgage and bringing an action to foreclose. And such a rule imposes no hardship on a transferee since it merely continues a claim on the land which was taken into account when he acquired his interest.[91]

§ 6.11 Effect of Acts of Grantee or Junior Interests on Mortgagor

Turning around the question in the preceding section, can a grantee or junior lienor of mortgaged property extend the period of the statute of limitations as to the mortgagor by a new promise, acknowledgment of, or payment on the debt? In general, in order for such an act to interrupt or revive the running of the statute of limitations it must be made by the obligor or someone legally authorized to act for him.[92] On this test neither an assuming grantee nor one who takes subject to the mortgage should be able to affect the run-

89. Schmucker v. Sibert, 18 Kan. 104, 26 Am.Rep. 765 (1877); Johnson v. Johnson, 81 Mo. 331 (1884); Smith v. Bush, 173 Okl. 172, 44 P.2d 921, 101 A.L.R. 330 (1935); see Clift v. Williams, 105 Ky. 559, 565, 49 S.W. 328, 329 (1899), rehearing denied 105 Ky. 559, 51 S.W. 821. But see Colonial & U. S. Mortgage Co. v. Northwest Thresher Co., 14 N.D. 147, 103 N.W. 915, 70 L.R.A. 814, 116 Am.St.Rep. 670, 8 Ann.Cas. 1160 (1905), criticizing the incident theory as applied to the statute of limitations.

90. See 49 Harv.L.Rev. 639, 643 (1936); 9 Col.L.Rev. 718, 719 (1909).

91. See Kerndt v. Porterfield, 56 Iowa 412, 415, 9 N.W. 322, 323 (1881). See also 27 Cal.L.Rev. 66, 71 (1938).

92. Woodcock v. Putnam, 101 Minn. 1, 111 N.W. 639 (1907); cf. Brooklyn Bank v. Barnaby, 197 N.Y. 210, 90 N. E. 834, 27 L.R.A.,N.S., 843 (1910), reargument denied, 198 N.Y. 522, 92 N.E. 1079 (1910); Vaughan v. Mansfield, 229 Mass. 352, 118 N.E. 652 (1918). But cf., Innocenti v. Guisti, 71 R.I. 274, 43 A.2d 700, 165 A.L.R. 1394 (1945), criticized in 24 Tex.L. Rev. 390 (1946).

ning of the statute as to the mortgagor. Their obligations, the former binding the grantee personally as well as the land in his hands,[93] the latter binding only the land,[94] are separate and independent and create no power to affect the remedies against their grantor, the mortgagor.[95] Many courts take this view both as to an assuming grantee [96] and one who takes subject to the mortgage.[97] Some courts, however, have held that where a grantee has assumed payment of the mortgage any payments by the grantee are made with the implied authority of the mortgagor and for the benefit of both. Hence these courts hold that interest payments toll the statute on the debt as well as the mortgage and so extend the running of the statute against the mortgagor.[98]

Although a grantee should not be able to bind the mortgagor by any acts that have the effect of extending or reviving the statute of limitations, he clearly should be able to and can bind himself or the property he acquired.[99] If he is an assuming grantee his act will affect his personal liability as well as the time within which the mortgage can be enforced against the property.[1] Indeed, the very act of assuming or of taking subject to the mortgage is one which starts a new period of limitations as to rights against the grantee.[2] A grantee who merely takes subject to the mortgage extends the statute only as to the mortgage on the land.[3]

93. §§ 5.4–5.7, supra.

94. § 5.3, supra.

95. See §§ 5.2–5.7, supra. See also cases in following footnotes.

96. Old Alms-House Farm of New Haven v. Smith, 52 Conn. 434 (1884); Trent v. Johnson, 185 Ark. 288, 47 S.W.2d 12, 80 A.L.R. 1431 (1932); Provident Inst. for Saving in Town of Boston v. Merrill, 311 Mass. 168, 40 N.E.2d 280 (1942); Regan v. Williams 185 Mo. 620, 84 S.W. 959, 105 Am.St.Rep. 600 (1904); Frost v. Johnson, 140 Ohio St. 315, 43 N.E.2d 277, 142 A.L.R. 609 (1942); Cottrell v. Shepherd, 86 Wis. 649, 57 N.W. 983, 39 Am.St.Rep. 919 (1894). See 18 A.L.R. 1027, 1033 (1922); 142 A.L.R. 615, 621 (1943). See also 17 Minn.L.Rev. 97 (1932).

97. Home Life Ins. Co. v. Elwell, 111 Mich. 689, 70 N.W. 334 (1897); Fitzgerald v. Flanagan, 155 Iowa 217, 135 N.W. 738, Ann.Cas.1914C, 1104 (1912), noted, 26 Harv.L.Rev. 89 (1912); Turner v. Powell, 85 Mont. 241, 278 P. 512 (1929); Winter v. Kram, 3 A.D.2d 175, 159 N.Y.S.2d 417 (2d Dept. 1957), approved in Mortgages, in 1957 Survey of New York Law, 32 N.Y.U.L.Rev. 1426 (1957).

98. Biddle v. Pugh, 59 N.J.Eq. 480, 45 A. 626 (1900); Ramsey v. Hutchinson, 117 N.J.L. 222, 187 A. 650 (1936); Guardian Depositors Corp. v. Wagner, 287 Mich. 202, 283 N.W. 29 (1938).

99. Daniels v. Johnson, 129 Cal. 415, 61 P. 1107, 79 Am.St.Rep. 123 (1900); 11 Cal.L.Rev. 429, 431, 432 (1923). See also Fourth National Bank in Wichita v. Hill, 181 Kan. 683, 314 P.2d 312 (1957).

1. Daniels v. Johnson, 129 Cal. 415, 61 P. 1107, 79 Am.St.Rep. 123 (1900); Schmucker v. Sibert, 18 Kan. 104, 112 (1877).

2. Hendricks v. Brooks, 80 Kan. 1, 101 P. 622, 133 Am.St.Rep. 186 (1909); Bement v. Ohio Valley Banking Co., 99 Ky. 109, 35 S.W. 139, 59 Am.St.Rep. 445 (1896). See 142 A.L.R. 615, 616 (1943).

3. Curtis v. Holee, 184 Cal. 726, 195 P. 395, 18 A.L.R. 1024 (1921); Fitzgerald v. Flanagan, 155 Iowa 217, 135 N.W. 738, Ann.Cas.1914C, 1104 (1912). See 142 A.L.R. 615, 619 (1943).

Regardless of what theory enables the mortgagee to reach an assuming grantee, the latter's liability [4] rests upon an agreement separate and independent from that of the mortgagor.[5] It arises at the time he enters into his contract of assumption and not before. If at that time the debt of the mortgagor which he assumed was not yet due, no cause of action would arise until maturity although his obligation became binding at the time of his agreement.[6] In such a case the statute of limitations would begin to run on the grantee's obligation at the same time as on the right of the mortgagee against the mortgagor, viz., at time of default at maturity.[7] This is not because there is only one obligation on which both are bound, but because the maturity date of each separate obligation is the same. If the assumption is after maturity, or even after the statute has run on the mortgagor's obligation, the grantee's obligation arises at that time and becomes enforceable at once because his promise is to pay a debt which is then owing. The statute, therefore, starts to run at once.[8]

Where a grantee takes subject to the mortgage instead of assuming it, his agreement confines his liability to the land he bought as a source of payment.[9] Apart from this more restricted coverage, the foregoing also applies to him.[10] Although the mortgagee's original mortgage rights in the land follow it into the hands of the grantee,[11] the latter's agreement that it shall be subject to the mortgage is a new promise in respect to the land which has an effect upon the period for enforcing the mortgage on the land similar to that of an assumption upon the debt period.[12]

§ 6.12 Statutory Trends

Every state has experienced the problem of a substantial number of old, recorded mortgages that have never been released of record. As Professor Basye has aptly pointed out, "in the normal course of events most mortgages were paid, but there was a tendency to over-

4. See §§ 5.11–5.15, supra.

5. Schmucker v. Sibert, 18 Kan. 104 (1877); Hendricks v. Brooks, 80 Kan. 1, 101 P. 622 (1909). See note 96, supra.

6. Carnahan v. Lloyd, 4 Kan.App. 605, 46 P. 323 (1896); Bogart v. Geo. K. Porter Co., 193 Cal. 197, 223 P. 959, 31 A.L.R. 1045 (1924).

7. See 11 Cal.L.Rev. 429, 431 (1923).

8. See 11 Cal.L.Rev. 429, 432. In a state like California where the running of the statute on the debt extinguishes the mortgage, a contract of assumption made after the statute is run, although it will be effective as to the debt will not revive the mortgage. Cf., Weinberger v. Weidner, 134 Cal. 599, 66 P. 869 (1901).

9. Curtis v. Holee, 184 Cal. 726, 195 P. 395, 18 A.L.R. 1024 (1921).

10. See Schmucker v. Sibert, 18 Kan. 104, 112 (1877).

11. See § 5.1, supra.

12. Curtis v. Holee, 184 Cal. 726, 195 P. 395, 18 A.L.R. 1024 (1921); Fitzgerald v. Flanagan, 155 Iowa 217, 135 N.W. 738, Ann.Cas.1914C, 1104; see Schmucker v. Sibert, 18 Kan. 104, 112 (1877); cf., Daniels v. Johnson, 129 Cal. 412, 61 P. 1107, 79 Am.St.Rep. 123 (1900).

look the necessity of recording a formal discharge. Of those that were not paid some became barred by the passage of time or were abandoned, but others were regarded by the parties themselves as subsisting obligations because of partial payments on them or extension agreements. Passing decades, however, left numerous mortgages unsatisfied of record to become a serious impediment to the transfer of land." [13] This problem was also heightened by the existence of separate periods of limitations for the debt and mortgage and the independence of either in many cases of powers of sale, especially in deeds of trust. As a result, a variety of statutory approaches have been utilized to deal with this problem.

One statutory trend to remedy this situation has been to enact statutes making the period of the statute the same as to both the debt and the lien so that the elapse of the same amount of time would bar both simultaneously. Some of these statutes simply bar the enforcement of a mortgage after the mortgage debt has become barred.[14] Others extinguish the mortgage lien after "the lapse of time within which an action can be brought upon the principal obligation." [15] Along with this development has gone a tendency to shorten the longer periods applicable in the older statutes to foreclosure actions.[16] However, doctrines of tolling statutes of limitations, or of reviving barred obligations together with the mortgages securing them constitute hazards to title completely outside of the record and unaffected by such changes. Further equitable doctrines limit the employment of statutes of limitations and presumptions of payment to use as a shield and prevent them from being employed as an affirmative basis for clearing title. These added to the difficulties of perfecting a marketable title. To remedy these defects many states have adopted additional legislation.

The purpose of the additional legislation was to enable a title examiner to rely entirely on the record in determining whether an unreleased mortgage is still legally alive. While the details of this type of legislation vary, it generally provides that a mortgage shall no longer be a lien and that foreclosure is prohibited after the expiration of a certain number of years from the maturity of the mortgage debt as shown by the record or from the date to which payment thereof has been extended by agreement or other written notice recorded before that period.[17] The Florida legislation, as amended in 1974, is illustrative. It both terminates the lien and bars all actions

13. Basye, Clearing Land Titles, 215 (2d Ed. 1970).

14. See, e. g., Vernon's Ann.Mo.Stat. § 516.150.

15. West's Ann.Civ.Code, § 2911. See Colo.Rev.Stat. '73, 38–40–112; Miss. Code 1972 §§ 15–1–21, 15–1–3.

16. See e. g., McKinney's Civ.Pract. Law and Rules § 213(4) (6 years); Vernon's Ann.Tex.Civ.Stat. art. 5520 (4 years).

17. Basye supra note 13 at 222. See, e. g., Minn.Stat.Ann. § 582.14; Ind. Stat.Ann.1971, 32–8–4–1, 32–8–4–2.

to enforce or foreclose with respect to mortgages and other encumbrances after the expiration of five years from the final maturity of the mortgage debt as evidenced by the record or, if the final maturity date is not indicated in the record, twenty years from the date of the mortgage itself, unless an extension agreement is recorded prior to the expiration of such period.[18] If such a recording takes place the period is extended for a like period of five or twenty years.[19] "Under this type of statute nothing in the way of disability or any other fact not of record is permitted to toll or extend the operation of the statute . . . . By this means a favorable appraisal of title in this respect has finally become a reality in some states." [20]

Other states have adopted statutes which apply ordinary statutes of limitation to the original mortgagor, but provide for a termination of the mortgage lien after the expiration of a fixed period of time as to subsequent purchasers or encumbrancers for value.[21] The purpose of this type of legislation is "to permit such purchasers and encumbrancers in appraising the title, to ignore mortgages whose maturity, as it appears of record, exceeds the statutory period. According to many of these statutes provision is made for extending the mortgage lien by recording an extension agreement or an affidavit of notice as to the amount remaining unpaid on the mortgage debt, or by rerecording the mortgage itself." [22] The effect of this recording will not in itself keep the mortgage lien alive, but rather its purpose is to provide notice to subsequent purchasers or encumbrancers for value "who could otherwise ignore the existence of outstanding mortgages which have ceased to have life as against such purchasers or encumbrancers." [23] This type of statute has not eliminated title problems because the validity of the mortgage lien depends on matters that are not of record such as the state of mind of the purchaser or encumbrancer with respect to unreleased mortgages or whether the purchaser or encumbrancer qualifies as one for value.[24]

Marketable Title Acts in effect in over a dozen states also enable a title examiner to ignore certain old unreleased mortgages of record.[25] For example, the Michigan Act expressly states that its purpose is to allow "persons dealing with the record title owner to rely on the record title covering a period of not more than 40 years

18. Fla.Stat.Ann. § 95.281. See Basye, supra note 13, § 87 (1977 Supp.).

19. Id.

20. Basye, supra note 13 at 223.

21. Basye, supra note 13 at 223 lists the following states as having this type of legislation: Alabama, Alaska, Arkansas, Kentucky, Louisiana, Michigan, Mississippi, Montana, North Carolina, Ohio, Oregon, South Dakota and Texas.

22. Id. at 223.

23. Id. at 223.

24. Note, 38 Harv.L.Rev. 651, 653 (1925); Basye, supra note 13, at 223.

25. See, e. g., Iowa Code Ann. § 614.-29–§ 614.38; Ind.Stat.Ann.1971, 32–1–5–1 to 32–1–5–10; Kan.Stat.Ann. 58–3401–3412; Note, Kansas Marketable Title Act, 13 Wash.L.J. 33 (1974).

prior to the date of such dealing and to that end to extinguish all claims that affect the interest thus dealt with, the existence of which claims arises out of or depends upon any act, transaction, event or omission antedating such 40 year period, unless within such 40 year period a notice of claim . . . shall have been duly filed for record." [26] While the 40 year period is common, 30 [27] or 50 [28] year periods are also found in such legislation. Under such legislation, a mortgage recorded more than 40 years earlier would be barred notwithstanding its maturity date, unless the holder had filed a notice of claim within the 40 year period.[29]

C. MERGER

§ 6.13 Merger—General Considerations

The concept of merger is one of the most complex and confusing areas of the law of mortgages. The basic doctrine itself can be stated in a few sentences and is deceptively simple. The theory is that when a mortgagee's interest and a fee title coincide and meet in the same person, the lesser estate, the mortgage, merges into the greater, the fee, and is extinguished.[30] Courts also state that "whether a merger has occurred depends on the intent of the parties, especially the one in whom the interests unite. If merger is against that party's best interest, it will not be deemed intended by the parties." [31]

Once having stated the basic doctrine, our confusion begins. This is often because the merger doctrine can be utilized either as a defense to the mortgage debt or as an argument that the mortgage no longer exists. For example, suppose that in lieu of a foreclosure proceeding, a mortgagor agrees to convey the mortgaged estate to the mortgagee.[32] Does the merger of the two estates in the mortgagee extinguish the mortgage debt so that the mortgagee will be unable to pursue the mortgagor personally? On the other hand, the same facts may result in a merger problem with the focus on the *mortgage* and not the debt. Suppose that our mortgagee was a first mortgagee and that, through inadvertence, he took a deed in lieu of foreclosure without first checking to see if junior liens existed on the real estate. If such a junior lienor did exist and now claims to be a senior lienor, will our former first mortgagee be able to keep his

26. Mich.Comp.Laws Ann. § 565.101–109.

27. See, e. g., N.C.Gen.Stat. §§ 47B–1 to 47B–9, noted in 10 Wake Forest L.Rev. 312 (1974).

28. See, e. g., Ind.Stat.Ann.1971 32–1–5–1 to 32–1–5–10.

29. Basye, supra note 13 at 248–249.

30. See, e. g., Alden Hotel Co. v. Kanin, 88 Misc.2d 546, 387 N.Y.S.2d 948 (1976); Aladdin Heating v. Trustees of Central States, 563 P.2d 82 (Nev. 1977).

31. Aladdin Heating v. Trustees of Central States, 563 P.2d 82, 85 (Nev. 1977).

32. See § 6.16, infra.

mortgage alive and foreclose it to wipe out the junior, or has merger destroyed it?

It should be pointed out that the merger concept is more often a debt problem when the controversy is between the person who holds the debt, mortgage and title and the person who has the duty of paying the debt. On the other hand, merger arguments more commonly focus on the continued existence of the *mortgage* when the controversy is between the person who is the holder of the debt, mortgage and title and the person who represents an intervening lienor or other third party claimant. While these generalizations, like all generalizations, do not represent universal truth, the two fact patterns underlying them provide a helpful framework and basis for attempting to understand the merger concept.

§ 6.14 Merger—Between the Parties to the Mortgage

The problem of merger as between the holder of the debt, mortgage and title and the person who is liable for the payment of the debt may arise in at least five settings: (1) The mortgagee may acquire the title (redemption interest) from the mortgagor. (2) The mortgagee may acquire the title from a grantee of the mortgagor. (3) The holder of more than one mortgage may acquire title on the foreclosure of one of those mortgages. (4) The mortgagee may transfer the debt and mortgage to the mortgagor. (5) The mortgagee may transfer the debt and mortgage to a grantee of the mortgagor.

Acquisition from Mortgagor by Mortgagee

Where the mortgage creditor acquires the redemption interest from the mortgagor, whether the acquisition will permit enforcement of the debt and mortgage according to the intention of acquisitor, or will preclude such enforcement regardless of intention, will depend upon the terms of the transfer. If it was a gift conveyance by the mortgagor it is obvious that the debt claim of the mortgage creditor would be unaffected and whether there would be a merger of the interests in the land would depend, as previously noted, upon the intent of the mortgage creditor. On the other hand, as, for example, in the deed in lieu of foreclosure situation,[33] if the conveyance is made and accepted as payment of the mortgage debt no question of merger is possible. The debt is discharged by payment, or perhaps more accurately, by substituted performance or accord and satisfaction; but not by merger.[34] The creditor now has full title to the property with no debt in existence for it to secure. If the mortgage debt is extinguished, the mortgage itself is never kept alive. Consequently there is automatic

33. See § 6.13, supra, § 6.16, infra.

34. Dennis v. McIntyre Merc. Co., 187 Ala. 314, 65 So. 774 (1914); McCabe v. Farnsworth, 27 Mich. 52 (1873); see, 95 A.L.R. 89, 95 (1935). If the conveyance is accepted at or before maturity it operates by way of substituted performance; if after maturity, by accord and satisfaction.

merger of the two interests in the property and no intent on the part of the creditor can keep them separate.

What should be the effect if the conveyance from the mortgagor to the mortgagee is accompanied by an assumption of the mortgage? If the mortgagee were permitted to recover from the mortgagor, the latter could turn around and sue him to get back the same amount. Or even more strikingly, when sued, the mortgagor might bring a bill in equity against the plaintiff mortgagee to make him exonerate the mortgagor by paying to himself the debt he is seeking to collect.[35] To prevent this circuity of action a court of equity would give a complete defense to the mortgagor to any action on the debt. If there has been an assumption there is complete merger because there is complete circuity. No intent or self-interest on the part of the mortgage creditor could prevent this ending of the claim against the mortgagor and, with it, any mortgage interest in the property securing it.[36]

More commonly, the conveyance to the mortgagee will be subject to the mortgage either because the deed expressly so states or because of its silence. If the agreement is that it is to be accepted in satisfaction of the mortgage debt it will, of course, so operate.[37] If this is not the agreement there may be, technically, no extinguishment of the mortgage debt.[38] And, if there is an express agreement that it shall not operate to extinguish the mortgage, the agreement will be given effect.[39] Nevertheless, such a conveyance makes the land in the hands of the mortgage creditor the principal and the personal obligation of the mortgagor, up to the value of the land, surety only.[40] Consequently, up to the value of the land, the mortgagor has a defense to any enforcement of the debt against him regardless of whether it is technically alive by agreement or not.[41] And usually the courts treat the situation as one of merger with the debt discharged, as it clearly is, in effect, if the land equals the debt in value.[42] However, if there was no agreement that the conveyance should be a discharge and the value of the land was less than the debt, the mortgage creditor can

35. See § 5.10, supra.

36. Forthman v. Deters, 206 Ill. 159, 69 N.E. 97, 99 Am.St.Rep. 145 (1903); Kneeland v. Moore, 138 Mass. 198 (1884); First State Bank v. Arneson, 109 Wash. 346, 186 P. 889 (1920); see 95 A.L.R. 89, 94 (1935). But see § 6.15, as to whether the mortgage may be kept alive as to third parties.

37. See supra, this section. See also Tiffany, Real Prop., 3d ed., § 1479.

38. Murphy v. Zuigaro, 72 Pa.Super. Ct. 511 (1924); Sheehan Bldg. & Loan Ass'n v. Scanlon, 310 Pa. 6, 164 A. 722 (1933).

39. Sheehan Bldg. & Loan Ass'n v. Scanlon, 310 Pa. 6, 164 A. 722 (1933).

40. See §§ 5.3–5.4, supra.

41. E. g., Eagan v. Engeman, 125 App. Div. 743, 110 N.Y.S. 366 (1908).

42. Cock v. Bailey, 146 Pa. 328, 23 A. 370 (1892); see 8 U. of Cin.L.Rev. 212, 213 (1935); 95 A.L.R. 89, 93 (1935).

maintain an action for the excess of the debt over the land.[43] In such a case there is merger of the debt only up to the value of the land because there is circuity only to this extent.

Acquisition by Mortgagee from Grantee of Mortgagor

The same principles govern where the redemption is obtained by the mortgage creditor from a grantee of the mortgagor, but the application of them becomes somewhat more complicated. There must first be an ascertainment of the terms on which the grantee held the property from the grantor and the legal results of those terms in a particular jurisdiction. Then the terms of acquisition by the creditor from the grantee must be determined. The grantee may have bought from the mortgagor paying full value and with an agreement that the mortgagor was to pay the mortgage when it matured and then made a gift conveyance to the mortgage creditor. The result then would be the same as a gift conveyance directly from the mortgagor to the mortgagee. On the other hand, conveyances in satisfaction of the mortgage debt, or with the mortgage creditor assuming or taking the property subject to the mortgage debt, will operate as would similar direct transactions between the mortgagor and mortgage creditor.[44] If the grantee has taken subject to the mortgage debt the mortgage creditor will also take it in the same way with an automatic merger, at least to the extent of the value of the land.[45] If the grantee has assumed the debt, again the land also would be principal and, if it is acquired by the mortgage creditor, bars the debt up to its value.[46] If, in addition, the mortgage creditor, in his turn, assumes the payment of the debt it will operate to preclude enforcement of any of the debt.

Two Mortgages in Same Hands—Purchase at Foreclosure Sale by Mortgagee

Where the mortgage creditor holds not only a first mortgage but a second as well, questions have arisen as to how the purchase on foreclosure sale of one of the mortgages affects his rights under the

43. " 'The purchase of the equity of redemption by the mortgagee at a sale by the mortgagor's assignee in insolvency, or on execution is not at law a satisfaction of the mortgage debt, and the mortgagee is not estopped from claiming that the property is of less value than the amount of the debt.' " Clark v. Jackson, 64 N.H. 388, 391, 11 A. 59 (1887); Findlay v. Hosmer, 2 Conn. 350 (1817); Marston v. Marston, 45 Me. 412 (1858); Spencer v. Harford's Ex'rs, 4 Wend. 381 (N.Y.1830). Cf. Miller v. Little, 37 N.D. 612, 164 N.W. 19 (1917); Ex parte Powell, 68 S.C. 324, 47 S.E. 440 (1904). See 8 U. of Cin.L.Rev. 213 (1935); 15 Harv.L.Rev. 740 (1902); 95 A.L.R. 89, 94 (1935). But see Glassie, The Assuming Vendee, 9 Va.L.Rev. 196, 205, n. 36, quoted § 250, n. 35 (1923), supra.

44. E. g., Dickason v. Williams, 129 Mass. 182, 37 Am.Rep. 316 (1880); National Investment Co. v. Nordin, 50 Minn. 336, 52 N.W. 899 (1892), assuming grantees of mortgagor conveyed to mortgagee subject to the mortgage and thus extinguished it.

45. Lilly v. Palmer, 51 Ill. 331 (1869), see 95 A.L.R. 89, 95 (1935).

46. Russell v. Pistor, 7 N.Y. 171, 57 Am.Dec. 509 (1852); cases notes 45–46, supra.

other one. The general rule is that the purchase of mortgaged property by the holder of a junior mortgage at a sale on foreclosure of the senior mortgage, does not extinguish the debt secured by the junior mortgage.[47] And the same is true even though the foreclosed first mortgage also was owned by the purchasing second mortgagee.[48] However, if the holder of both a junior and senior mortgage forecloses the junior and buys it in on foreclosure sale it is generally held that, in the absence of an agreement to the contrary,[49] the mortgagor's personal liability for the debt secured by the first mortgage is extinguished.[50] The reason given is that upon a foreclosure sale under a junior mortgage the purchase is subject to the payment of the prior lien with the result that "the mortgagor has an equitable right to have the land pay the mortgage before his personal liability is called upon"[51] and the purchaser, if he owns or acquires the mortgage, will not be permitted to enforce it against the mortgagor personally. Nor will such a purchaser who has been willing to pay money for the redemption interest subject to the mortgage be permitted to say, as against the persons liable on that mortgage, that the land he bought, the primary fund for the payment of the prior mortgage obligation, is not worth its amount.[52]

While this is true if the foreclosure sale under the junior mortgage has the same effect as a sale of the redemption interest on execution under the judgment of a third party creditor,[53] under some second mortgages this is not or should not be true. If the second

47. Ferry v. Fisk, 54 Cal.App. 763, 202 P. 964 (1921). Cf. Miller v. Little, 37 N.D. 612, 164 N.W. 19 (1917).

48. Blackwood v. Sakwinski, 221 Mich. 464, 191 N.W. 207, 29 A.L.R. 1314 (1922); Sautter v. Frick, 229 App.Div. 345, 242 N.Y.S. 369 (1930), affirmed 256 N.Y. 535, 177 N.E. 129 (1931) reversing, 133 Misc. 517, 232 N.Y.S. 529 (1929). Cf. Fischer v. Spierling, 93 N.J.L. 167, 107 A. 420 (1919). See 29 A.L.R. 1318 (1924); 95 A.L.R. 89, 103 (1935). After foreclosure and sale under a first mortgage, a conveyance by the first mortgagee, who bought it in, to the mortgagor will not revive the second mortgage on the land in his hands. See 12 N.Y.U.L.Q.Rev. 319 (1935).

49. Continental Title & Trust Co. v. Devlin, 209 Pa. 380, 58 A. 843 (1904); Toston v. Utah Mortgage Loan Co., 115 F.2d 560 (C.C.A.Idaho 1940); Van Woerden v. Union Imp. Co., 156 Wash. 555, 287 P. 870 (1930).

50. Belleville Sav. Bank v. Reis, 136 Ill. 242, 26 N.E. 646 (1891); Maulding v. Sims, 213 Ill.App. 473 (1919); McDonald v. Magirl, 97 Iowa 677, 66 N.W. 904 (1896); Wright v. Anderson, 62 S.D. 444, 253 N.W. 484, 95 A.L.R. 81 (1934); see 95 A.L.R. 89, 104 (1935). It will not merge the first mortgage, however, as against intervening liens. Citizens State Bank v. Peterson, 114 Neb. 809, 210 N.W. 278 (1926); see Wright v. Anderson, 62 S.D. 444, 450, 253 N.W. 484, 487, 95 A.L.R. 81, 86 (1934).

51. See Wright v. Anderson, 62 S.D. 444, 450, 253 N.W. 484, 487, 95 A.L.R. 81, 86 (1934).

52. Id.

53. Murphy v. Elliott, 6 Blackf. 482 (Ind.1843), "a mortgagee, by purchasing at a sheriff's sale on execution the equity of redemption, thereby extinguishes, to the extent of the value of the mortgaged premises, after deducting the sum paid for the equity of redemption, the mortgage debt."

mortgage is by warranty deed containing covenants covering the first mortgage, on foreclosure sale the covenants in the mortgage pass to the purchaser. He stands as though the mortgagor had conveyed the land to him by deed on the date of the second mortgage with the deed containing the covenants that actually were put in the mortgage.[54] Consequently, the mortgagor would continue to be the principal debtor and purchase by the first mortgagee should not affect his debt claim against the mortgagor.[55]

Where both mortgages are in default, it would seem that a mortgagee should be able to avoid the above merger predicament. For example, if judicial foreclosure is utilized, the court could order both mortgages foreclosed simultaneously. If the mortgagee purchased at that sale and the sale price was for less than the combined mortgage debt, there is no reason why the mortgagee should not be able to obtain a deficiency decree for that difference. The merger concept would simply be inapplicable. This approach will probably not work, however, with power of sale foreclosure. Although a court clearly can approve such a procedure, it is doubtful that the person holding a power of sale would have similar authority, if for no other reason than that power of sale legislation does not ordinarily provide for the foreclosure of more than one mortgage at a time.

Acquisition from Mortgagee by Mortgagor

When the mortgage creditor transfers the debt claim and mortgage securing it to the mortgagor the inevitable result as between them is to extinguish both the debt and, along with it, the mortgage.[56] The same person cannot be both debtor and creditor.[57] This would be true regardless of whether the transfer was by way of gift or for value. In the latter case, especially if the value given was the amount of the mortgage debt, the transaction is likely to be intended to extinguish the debt by payment or an accord and satisfaction. If so, its demise should not be considered as occurring by reason of the doctrine of merger.[58]

Acquisition from Mortgagee by Grantee of Mortgagor

A similar situation occurs where the mortgagor has conveyed to a grantee who assumes the mortgage and the mortgage creditor then

54. Allis v. Foley, 126 Minn. 14, 147 N.W. 670 (1914); Knapp v. Foley, 140 Minn. 423, 426, 168 N.W. 183 (1918); see Ross, Covenants of Title in Mortgages, 12 Minn.L.Rev. 34, 41 (1927).

55. See Ross, Covenants of Title in Mortgages, 12 Minn.L.Rev. 34 (1927). See, semble, White, Revival of Mortgages, 10 U. of Cin.L.Rev. 217 (1936).

56. Hussey v. Hill, 120 N.C. 312, 26 S.E. 919, 58 Am.St.Rep. 789 (1897); Hill v. Hall, 4 Rob. 416 (La.1843).

57. "The fundamental principle is that a man cannot be both debtor and creditor with respect to the same debt at the same time and when a situation arises where the hand that is obligated to pay the debt is the same hand that is entitled to receive it, the debt is extinguished and forever gone." Wright v. Anderson, 62 S.D. 444, 253 N.W. 484, 95 A.L.R. 81 (1934).

58. See Tiffany, Real Prop., 3d Ed., § 1482.

assigns the debt and mortgage to him. He is the principal debtor in such a case and his acquisition of the claim against himself not only extinguishes it as to him[59] but also as to the mortgagor who stands in the position of a surety.[60] This would be true of a gift transfer to him and also if he paid value. The latter case parallels the one considered previously. Here as there, the debt may be regarded as extinguished by payment, substituted performance or accord and satisfaction rather than by merger. If the mortgagor was bound by agreement with the grantee to pay off the debt, an assignment of the debt and mortgage to the latter would not prevent him enforcing it against the principal debtor, the mortgagor.[61] Whether there would be merger as to the land would here again depend upon the intent or interest of the holder of it.

If the grantee had taken subject to the mortgage without assuming its payment the only one personally liable is the mortgagor. Where such a grantee takes an assignment of the mortgage, as a general rule the debt secured by the mortgage is held to be extinguished and personal liability on it cannot be enforced.[62] Up to the value of the land there would seem no question as to the result. The mortgagor is surety only and the land principal with the result that, to prevent circuity the mortgagor could defeat any recovery up to that amount, and this is true regardless of whether the mortgage is acquired for value or as a gift. Where the debt exceeds the value of the land a question may arise as to the right of such a grantee-assignee to recover a deficiency. If the grantee paid the amount of the debt for the assignment, the mortgagor should be able to insist that it constituted payment of the debt rather than purchase of it. The reason is that, although the grantee incurred no personal obligation to pay off the mortgage, nonetheless when he bought the land subject to it, his bargain included as a part of the price the amount of the mortgage debt. As a consequence, even though the mortgagor could not compel him to pay and the mortgage creditor has no right against him personally, yet it is so far his duty to discharge the debt that if he does so he should have no recourse against the mortgagor for reimbursement.[63] It would seem, therefore, that regardless of the

59. Russell v. Pistor, 7 N.Y. 171, 57 Am.Dec. 509 (1852); Barnett & Jackson v. McMillan, 176 Ala. 430, 58 So. 400 (1912); Fouche v. Delk, 83 Iowa 297, 48 N.W. 1078 (1891); Lydon v. Campbell, 204 Mass. 580, 91 N.E. 151, 134 Am.St.Rep. 702 (1910). See 95 A.L.R. 89, 111 (1935); 46 A.L.R. 329 (1927).

60. See §§ 5.17–5.18, supra.

61. Barnett & Jackson v. McMillan, 176 Ala. 430, 58 So. 400 (1912), as to the second mortgage.

62. Baxter v. Redevco, Inc., 279 Or. 117, 566 P.2d 501 (1977) (quoting text); Lilly v. Palmer, 51 Ill. 331 (1869); Atherton v. Toney, 43 Ind. 211 (1873); Price v. Rea, 92 Iowa 12, 60 N.W. 208 (1894); Wonderly v. Giessler, 118 Mo.App. 708, 93 S.W. 1130 (1906); see 95 A.L.R. 89, 107 (1935).

63. Baxter v. Redevco, Inc., 279 Or. 117, 566 P.2d 501 (1977) (quoting text).

value of the land, when a grantee subject to the mortgage buys in the mortgage, he cannot enforce any right on it against the mortgagor.

It has been suggested, however, that if the mortgage creditor assigned the debt and mortgage to such a grantee by way of gift or for less than the amount of the debt it could be enforced by him as to any excess of the debt over the value of the land.[64] An argument can be made in favor of such a result along these lines. The mortgage creditor could have enforced the mortgage debt to the amount of its excess over the value of the land against the mortgagor without the latter having any recourse against the grantee who took subject to the mortgage. If he did so, after collecting it, the creditor could make a gift of those proceeds to anyone he wishes, including the grantee, free of any claim of the mortgagor to it. It would seem to follow that he has equal ability to make a gift of the right to collect the deficiency. Thus he might have given it to third person or to the mortgagor. If, instead, his donee is the mortgagor's grantee subject to the mortgage, it seems logical to say that the mortgagor cannot object to his enforcement of it.

§ 6.15 Merger—Intervening Interests

Merger problems also can occur when a senior lienor acquires title from the mortgagor or his grantee. Here the problem usually is that a junior lienor claims that acquisition of title by the senior has resulted in the destruction of the senior lien so that it can no longer be foreclosed against the junior. If merger has occurred, the junior lien is thus promoted to a higher status. This merger argument is most commonly found in the deed in lieu of foreclosure situation discussed earlier.[65] However, it can arise in other contexts. For example, junior lienors have attempted to utilize merger to destroy a senior mortgage where the senior mortgagee acquired the mortgagor's interest at a bankruptcy sale.[66]

It should be emphasized, however, that whether there is merger as between the mortgage creditor and the mortgagor or a grantee of the mortgagor is not decisive as to whether it also occurs as between the mortgage creditor and holders of junior incumbrances[67] or other interests.[68] When the question arises in the latter situation courts repeat the general merger concept that merger is a question of intention and that intention will be presumed, in the absence of express manifestation, in accordance with the interests of the party in whom

64. See Tiffany, Real Property, § 1432.

65. See § 6.13, supra and § 6.15, infra.

66. See Lampert Yards, Inc. v. Thompson-Wetterling Constr. & Realty, Inc., 223 N.W.2d 418 (Minn.1974).

67. See 39 L.R.A.,N.S., 834 (1909); 95 A.L.R. 628 (1935), for collections of cases. See also Note, The Rights of a Junior Lienholder in Wisconsin, 42 Marq.L.Rev. 89, 94 (1959).

68. See 46 A.L.R. 322 (1927).

all interests in the debt and mortgaged property are united.[69] This statement, while it has certain merits, is an inadequate exposition of the principles governing the decisions. A more satisfactory explanation of the results of the cases requires an analysis of the proper role of actual intention, whether express or implied in fact, and the basis for "presuming" an intention in accordance with interest.

In the first place, in certain cases both intent and self interest will be immaterial. If the mortgage creditor in acquiring the land assumes not merely the first mortgage but also the payment of the junior incumbrance no expression of intent to keep the mortgage alive, or self interest in doing so, will avail as against the junior incumbrancer.[70] A plea of circuity of action by the later mortgagee will effectively preclude enforcement of the earlier mortgage in the hands of such a creditor. The same would be true up to the value of the land if the property were acquired subject to the later mortgage.

It is also clear that if the mortgage creditor knew of the intervening interest and nevertheless clearly indicated an intention that his prior mortgage should be discharged there will be merger and the junior encumbrance will be elevated to priority regardless of his best interests being to the contrary.[71]

Normally, however, courts reject the merger argument and hold that the first mortgage will be preserved or reinstated as against the intervening interest. In some cases the mortgage creditor clearly indicated his intention to keep the first mortgage in existence as against such interests and the courts rest the result upon that ground.[72] For example, it has been noted that having the deed run to a nominee of the mortgagee, rather than to the mortgagee himself, indicated such an intent to keep the mortgage alive.[73] On the other hand, in a large number of cases in which there is no evidence of intention to keep the prior mortgage alive, other than that it would be to the interest of the mortgage creditor to do so, it is held that there is no merger.[74] But the courts go beyond this and hold, in spite of an

69. See, e. g., Aladdin Heating v. Trustees of Central States, 563 P.2d 82 (Nev.1977); McCraney v. Morris, 170 S.C. 250, 170 S.E. 276, 95 A.L.R. 622 (1933); note, 95 A.L.R. 628, 629 (1935).

70. Ernst v. McChesney, 186 Ill. 617, 58 N.E. 399 (1900); Kneeland v. Moore, 138 Mass. 198 (1884); Drew v. Anderson, Clayton & Co., 120 Okl. 250, 252 P. 64 (1927), noted, 27 Col. L.Rev. 609; Bolln v. La Prele Live Stock Co., 27 Wyo. 335, 196 P. 748 (1921); Brown v. Stead, 5 Sim. 535 (1832).

71. Townsend v. Provident Realty Co., 110 App.Div. 226, 96 N.Y.S. 1091 (1905); Beacham v. Gurney, 91 Iowa 621, 60 N.W. 187 (1894); Errett v. Wheeler, 109 Minn. 157, 123 N.W. 414, 26 L.R.A.,N.S., 816 (1909); Stantons v. Thompson, 49 N.H. 272 (1870).

72. Gibbs v. Johnson, 104 Mich. 120, 62 N.W. 145 (1895). See 95 A.L.R. 628, 649, 650 (1935).

73. See Alden Hotel Co. v. Kanin, 88 Misc.2d 546, 387 N.Y.S.2d 948 (1976).

74. See Aladdin Heating Co. v. Trustees of Central States, 563 P.2d 82 (Nev.1977); Lampert Yards, Inc. v.

undisputed intent on the part of the mortgage creditor to discharge the first mortgage, that nevertheless he may use it for foreclosure purposes against junior interests.[75] This is the almost uniform result where the mortgage creditor was ignorant of the intervening lien.[76] Although there is some authority that his negligence in not discovering the existence of the later interest [77] or in mistakenly relying on its not being enforced [78] will prevent him using it against the subsequent claimant, other and, it is believed, better authority holds to the contrary.[79]

Indeed, the rule may be stated broadly that, except for the two cases stated at the outset of this section, merger will not operate to permit a later incumbrance to be elevated to a position of priority over the first mortgage regardless of its fate as between the parties to that first mortgage.[80] Actual intent, where it exists, is an adequate basis for the result. The mortgage creditor has a legitimate interest to protect himself against the elevation of the later interest. By bringing a foreclosure action in which they were joined as parties

Thompson-Wetterling Constr. & Realty, Inc., 223 N.W.2d 418 (Minn.1974). See 18 Col.L.Rev. 280 (1918). See also cases in following footnotes.

75. Brooks v. Rice, 56 Cal. 428 (1880), conveyance by mortgagor to mortgagee in satisfaction of the mortgage held not to operate as a merger against an intervening mortgage; Richardson v. Hockenhull, 85 Ill. 124 (1877); Moffet v. Farwell, 222 Ill. 543, 78 N.E. 925 (1906); Sullivan v. Saunders, 66 W.Va. 350, 66 S.E. 497, 42 L.R.A.,N.S., 1010, 19 Ann.Cas. 480 (1909); Fitch v. Applegate, 24 Wash. 25, 64 P. 147 (1901); See 39 L.R.A., N.S., 834 (1912); 95 A.L.R. 628, 643 (1935).

On this point, I am of the opinion that upon such a state of facts, showing a title intervening between the mortgage and quitclaim deed, it is to be presumed, as a matter of law, that the parties did not intend to extinguish the mortgage. * * * " Stantons v. Thompson, 49 N.H. 272, 276 (1870). See also Wilson v. Vanstone, 112 Mo. 315, 20 S.W. 612 (1892); Grellet v. Heilshorn, 4 Nev. 526 (1869). See note, 18 Col.L.Rev. 280 (1918); note, 12 N.Y.Univ.L.Q. Rev. 317 (1934).

76. Silliman v. Gammage, 55 Tex. 365 (1881); Seiberling v. Tipton, 113 Mo. 373, 21 S.W. 4 (1893); Howard v. Clark and Teachout, 71 Vt. 424, 45 A. 1042, 76 Am.St.Rep. 782 (1899); see Woodhurst v. Cramer, 29 Wash. 40, 48, 69 P. 501, 503 (1902); 95 A.L.R. 628, 643 (1935); 40 W.Va.L.Q. 280 (1934); Frazee v. Inslee, 2 N.J.Eq. 239 (1839), contra. *A fortiori*, the same would be true where the discharge of the prior lien was obtained by fraud. See 95 A.L.R. 628, 647 (1935).

77. See Fort Dodge Bldg. & Loan Ass'n v. Scott, 86 Iowa 431, 434, 53 N.W. 283, 284 (1892), semble. And see Rice v. Winters, 45 Neb. 517, 63 N.W. 830 (1895); Bohn Sash & Door Co v. Case, 42 Neb. 281, 60 N.W. 576 (1894).

78. Woodside v. Lippold, 113 Ga. 877, 39 S.E. 400, 84 Am.St.Rep. 267 (1901); cf. Beacham v. Gurney, 91 Iowa, 621, 60 N.W. 187 (1894); Errett v. Wheeler, 109 Minn. 157, 123 N.W. 414, 26 L.R.A.,N.S., 816 (1909); Frazee v. Inslee, 2 N.J.Eq. 239 (1839); Gainey v. Anderson, 87 S.C. 47, 68 S.E. 888, 31 L.R.A.,N.S., 323 (1910). See 27 L.R. A.,N.S., 816 (1910).

See also note, 27 Col.L.Rev. 609 (1927).

79. McCraney v. Morris, 170 S.C. 250, 170 S.E. 276, 95 A.L.R. 622 (1933); Home Owners Loan Corp. v. Collins, 120 N.J.Eq. 266, 184 A. 621 (1936) semble; see 27 Col.L.Rev. 609 (1927).

80. See 95 A.L.R. 628, 629 (1935).

defendant the property could have been sold free and clear of their interests and he could have bought it in that state. Acquisition of the redemption in any other way should not prejudice his position with respect to such junior interests if he did not intend it to do so and was not under a duty to do acts which would have that result. The owner of the junior interest, under such circumstances, cannot object to being kept or put back into his position in the rear because he never bargained for advancement that would come to him by destruction of the first mortgage. But more generally the decisions may be justified on grounds of unjust enrichment, a doctrine implicit in the rationale of fairness in giving effect to the mortgage creditor's intent when it appears. By the destruction of the prior mortgage, the later lien or interest is elevated to a priority for which its owner paid nothing and hence is, as to him, a pure windfall. And it is a windfall at the expense of the prior mortgagee. If the owner of the prior mortgage knew of the later interest and intended nevertheless to discharge or otherwise wipe out the first mortgage, there is, of course, no injustice to him in permitting the later claimant to take advantage of his unmerited advancement. Where the first mortgagee knew of the second man and intended to prevent him getting this benefit it would be unconscionable to permit him to have it. The same seems true of a case where a mortgagee gave up his mortgage in the mistaken belief that a later one would not be enforced. So, too, if he did not know of the later interest and so didn't know that the result of his action with respect to the first mortgage would be to confer this advantage on it. That the ignorance or mistake was due to negligence on his part should make no difference. The only consequence of the negligence is to confer a benefit upon the later lienors or other claimants which, if taken away, would leave them in no worse position than they were before the occurrence. Since it does not put them at any disadvantage or cause them any loss, it should not prevent the first mortgagee from being restored to his position by reinstating his mortgage.[81] And, it is believed that this principle of restitution to prevent unjust enrichment can be justifiably extended to include all cases in which there is no actual intent with respect to the later interest. And there is no ground for automatic merger of it regardless of intent. Indeed, whether the courts clearly analyse it in this way or not, it would seem to be the best justification of their reiterated statements that in the absence of express intention on the part of the mortgagee his intention will be presumed in accordance with his interests.

Reinstating the lien of a prior mortgagee in cases where he has taken a conveyance in satisfaction of the mortgage is sufficient to protect him against junior incumbrances when the debt is equal to

81. See McCraney v. Morris, 170 S.C. 250, 260, 170 S.E. 276, 280, 95 A.L.R. 622, 627 (1933).

the value of the land when the latter's claim is asserted. It is inadequate where the claim is brought forward years later when, subsequent to the mortgagee's acquisition of title, the land is risen in value. In such cases, there is authority that the conveyance to the mortgagee will be treated as equivalent to a foreclosure cutting off the interests of junior lienors.[82]

D. THE DEED IN LIEU OF FORECLOSURE

§ 6.16 Reasons for Use

As we noted earlier, the rule against contemporaneous clogging of the equity of redemption is generally inapplicable to transactions *subsequent* to the original mortgage transaction.[83] Thus most courts, in theory at least, permit the mortgagee to purchase the mortgagor's equity of redemption; however, such transactions are subjected to careful review to ensure that the transaction is free from fraud, is based on an adequate consideration, and that it is, in fact, actually subsequent to the mortgage and not contemporaneous with it.[84]

Relying on the foregoing subsequent transaction exception, a mortgagee will commonly take a deed from the mortgagor in satisfaction of the mortgage debt. We noted this practice briefly in our preceding sections dealing with merger.[85] The mortgagee engages in this practice, ordinarily, to avoid the further expense of a foreclosure action in which, even though he gets it, a deficiency judgment will often be worthless.[86] The mortgagor on his part is quite frequently glad to give the deed in order to avoid, in states not having anti-deficiency legislation, a possible personal judgment against him which might cause him trouble in the future even though at present it was uncollectable. Also, some mortgagees are actuated either by a genuine desire to aid the mortgagor, an aversion to the publicity and trouble of a court action against him, or both.

§ 6.17 Potential Pitfalls for the Mortgagee

Whatever its seeming simplicity, the deed in lieu of foreclosure can create substantial problems for the mortgagee and is often, from his perspective, a dangerous device. These problems can entail potential clouds on title and possible difficulties with intervening lienors and other interests. The following materials examine some of these problem areas.

First, we have already noted that courts carefully scrutinize subsequent transactions for evidence of fraud and the adequacy of con-

82. Jaubert Bros. Inc. v. Walker, 203 Miss. 242, 33 So.2d 827 (1948). See 48 Col.L.Rev. 955 (1948).

83. See § 3.2, supra.

84. Id.

85. See §§ 6.13, 6.15, supra.

86. See Note, 36 Mich.L.Rev. 111 (1937).

sideration. There is in this scrutiny the underlying notion that the mortgagor and mortgagee do not share equal bargaining strength. Thus it is possible, "especially if the consideration paid is disproportionately less than the value of the equity or if none is paid where the equity has value, that the whole transaction will be construed as unfair and unconscionable." [87] Moreover, if the deed is not by the mortgagor but by a non-assuming grantee of the mortgagor, a release of the debt, since there was no personal liability, would be no consideration for the conveyance to the mortgagee and subject it to being set aside. Where the transaction is subject to being set aside on such grounds, the mortgagor or his grantee will be permitted to redeem.[88]

Second, there is always the possibility that a court will construe the deed in lieu transaction itself as simply another mortgage transaction. As earlier material has explained, grantor-mortgagors are often successful in establishing by clear and convincing evidence that an absolute deed in favor of a grantee-mortgagee was actually intended as a mortgage.[89] Although a mortgagee will, of course, contest the mortgagor's view of the deed in lieu transaction, mortgagors do occassionally succeed in persuading courts to conceptualize it as a mortgage cast in the form of an absolute deed.[90] If the mortgagor is successful, he will be treated as a mortgagor under two mortgages—under the original mortgage which was not eliminated by the deed in lieu and under the deed in lieu treated as a second mortgage.

Moreover, the possibility exists that because of insolvency of the mortgagor or an actual intent on his part to defraud his creditors the conveyance may be subject to avoidance at the suit of creditors outside of bankruptcy or under the bankruptcy laws should the mortgagor go or be forced into bankruptcy.[91]

Finally, the deed in lieu transaction raises the related problems of the intervening lienor and the merger doctrine. If, subsequent to the original mortgage, the mortgagor has voluntarily or involuntarily created other liens, the deed in lieu to the mortgagee will not operate to cut off such intervening liens.[92] Foreclosure will still be necessary to eliminate such interests. Moreover, to make matters worse, the junior lienor may well utilize the merger doctrine to assert that since, as a result of the deed in lieu, the mortgage and the redemption interest are now held by the first mortgagee, the first mortgage has been destroyed.[93] Thus, the junior lienor will argue that his lien has been promoted in priority. While this merger argument, as we noted

87. Note, 31 Mo.L.Rev. 312, 314–315 (1966).

88. Id. at 315.

89. See §§ 3.3–3.8, supra.

90. The classic case is Peugh v. Davis, 96 U.S. 332, 24 L.Ed. 775 (1877). See also, Noelker v. Wehmeyer, 392 S.W. 2d 409 (Mo.App.1965).

91. See § 8.11 infra.

92. See Note, 31 Mo.L.Rev. 312, 314 (1966).

93. See § 6.15, supra.

earlier, will seldom succeed,[94] it is nevertheless often asserted[95] and, for that reason alone, worth avoiding. The problems discussed in this paragraph can be avoided only by a thorough title search by the mortgagee prior to taking the deed in lieu to determine whether such intervening interests exist. If such liens or interests are discovered, the only prudent alternative for the mortgagee is to foreclose. However, even if the result of the title search is negative, that result will do nothing to obviate the other problems inherent in the deed in lieu transaction that were considered in earlier paragraphs of this section.

The practice of taking a deed in lieu of foreclosure is probably understandable in states where a judicial proceeding is the only authorized foreclosure method. In such a situation, the problems and risks discussed above may sometimes be outweighed by the costs and delay inherent in judicial foreclosure. However, where valid power of sale foreclosure statutes exist, foreclosure is relatively quick and inexpensive[96] and compelling reasons for such foreclosure alternatives as the deed in lieu simply do not exist.

94. Id.

95. See, e. g., Lampert Yards, Inc. v. Thompson-Wetterling Constr. & Realty, Inc., 223 N.W.2d 418 (Minn.1974); Aladdin Heating Corp. v. Trustees of Central States, 563 P.2d 82 (Nev. 1977); Alden Hotel Co. v. Kanin, 88 Misc.2d 546, 387 N.Y.S.2d 948 (1976).

96. See § 7.19, infra.

§§ 6.18–7.0 are reserved for supplementary material.

CHAPTER 7

FORECLOSURE

Table of Sections

A. REDEMPTION FROM THE MORTGAGE

B. ACCRUAL OF THE RIGHT TO FORECLOSE

C. STRICT FORECLOSURE

D. JUDICIAL FORECLOSURE

E. POWER OF SALE FORECLOSURE

F. DISPOSITION OF SURPLUS

A. REDEMPTION FROM THE MORTGAGE

§ 7.1 Redemption from the Mortgage and Statutory Redemption—Definitions

Because the concept of redemption is so basic to the law of mortgages and is especially intertwined with the procedural and substantive rules governing foreclosure, it is important at this point to reexamine the concept in some detail. In this connection, it is also necessary to reemphasize the two significantly different types of redemption. The first type is variously referred to as the "equity of redemption", the "equity of tardy redemption" or as "redemption from the mortgage." The second type is referred to as "statutory redemption."

When courts utilize the terminology of the first type of redemption, they are referring to the mortgagor's right after default in every jurisdiction, title, lien or intermediate, to perform his obligation under the mortgage and have the title to his property restored free and clear of the mortgage.[1] The important words to emphasize here are "after default." While there is, as we have seen earlier, no right to prepay a mortgage debt absent mortgage language so specifying, the mortgagor nevertheless has the right to pay or otherwise perform his obligations after default under the mortgage at any time until a valid foreclosure sale. Indeed, it is this right, as we saw in earlier sections, that courts jealously protect against attempts at contemporaneous clogs and other devices aimed at defeating or restricting the right.[2]

Statutory redemption, on the other hand, is, as the name implies, a creature of legislative grace.[3] In about half the states, the mortgagor, his successors in interest and, in many instances, junior lienors are permitted for a specific period after a valid foreclosure sale to redeem "from the sale" by paying to the foreclosure sale purchaser the foreclosure sale price plus, in some instances, certain additional amounts.[4] It is a helpful oversimplification to look upon "redemption from the mortgage" in its variety of terminology as a right that ex-

1. Cf. West's Ann.Cal.Civ.Code, § 2903, "Every person, having an interest in property subject to a lien, has a right to redeem it from the lien, at any time after the claim is due, and before his right of redemption is foreclosed * * *."

2. See § 3.1, supra.

3. See § 8.4, infra.

4. See Wayne Sav. & Loan Co. v. Young, 49 Ohio App.2d 35, 358 N.E.2d 1380, 3 O.O.3d 107 (1976).

ists after default until there has been a valid foreclosure.[5] Statutory redemption rights, on the other hand, ripen only *after* there has been such a valid foreclosure. Detailed analysis of statutory redemption as a matter of logic thus will be deferred until after we have considered the intricacies of foreclosure.[6] On the other hand, proper understanding of the procedure and substance of foreclosure necessitates further exploration of the first category of redemption at this point.

§ 7.2 Who May Redeem

Aside from the mortgagor, numerous other persons have the right to redeem from the mortgage. "Any person who may have acquired any interest in the premises, legal or equitable, by operation of law or otherwise, in privity of title with the mortgagor, may redeem, and protect such interest in the land. * * * But it must be an interest in the land, and it must be derived in some way, mediate or immediate from or through, or in the right of the mortgagor; so as, in effect, to constitute a part of the mortgagor's original equity of redemption. Otherwise it cannot be affected by the mortgage, and needs no redemption." [7] This accurately states the general rule and is supported by numerous cases spelling it out in detail as to particular cases.[8] Among those falling under the test, in addition to the mortgagor so long as he is living and has not completely divested himself of all interest,[9] are purchasers of the equity from the mortgagor,[10] an heir or devisee,[11] or any other person who succeeds to the mortgagor's interest in the mortgaged property, e. g., a purchaser at an execution or judicial sale.[12] Likewise an owner of a limited interest such as a tenant for life or lessee,[13] a remainderman or reversioner,[14] one who has dower even though it be inchoate only,[15]

5. Id.

6. See §§ 8.4–8.7, infra.

7. Christiancy, J., in Smith v. Austin, 9 Mich. 465, 474 (1862). See also, Dawson v. Overmyer, 141 Ind. 438, 431, 40 N.E. 1065 (1895), "A person can only redeem when he has an interest to protect, and where, without such redemption, he would be a loser."

8. See text of rest of this section for many examples of the application of the general rule.

9. See Smith v. Varney, 309 A.2d 229 (Me.1973).

10. Purcell v. Gann, 113 Ark. 332, 168 S.W. 1102 (1914); Loomis v. Knox, 60 Conn. 343, 22 A. 771 (1891); Dunlap v. Wilson, 32 Ill. 517 (1863); Watts v. Symes, 16 Sim. 640 (1849).

11. Hunter v. Dennis, 112 Ill. 568 (1884); Zaegel v. Kuster, 51 Wis. 31, 7 N.W. 781 (1881); Chew v. Hyman, 7 F. 7 (C.C.Ill.1881); Lewis v. Nangle, 2 Ves.Sr. 431 (1752).

12. Dalton v. Brown, 130 Ark. 200, 197 S.W. 32 (1917); Jackson v. Weaver, 138 Ind. 539, 38 N.E. 166 (1894); Millett v. Blake, 81 Me. 531, 18 A. 293, 10 Am.St.Rep. 275 (1889); Hayward v. Cain, 110 Mass. 273 (1872); Isam Mitchell & Co., Inc. v. Norwach, 26 Mass. 33 (1927).

13. G. B. Seely's Son, Inc. v. Fulton-Edison, Inc., 52 A.D.2d 575, 382 N.Y.S. 2d 516 (1976); Big Apple Supermarkets, Inc. v. Corkdale Realty, Inc., 61 Misc.2d 483, 305 N.Y.S.2d 531 (1969).

14. Thielen v. Strong, 184 Minn. 333, 238 N.W. 678 (1931); see Coote, Mortgages 9th ed., p. 723.

15. See note 15 on page 427.

or the holder of an easement.[16] Similarly, joint tenants and the like may redeem.[17] So too, many persons who have become owners of fractional portions of land that are covered by the same underlying mortgage.[18] Junior lienors, whether by reason of a judgment or execution or because of a later mortgagee are also entitled to redemption.[19]

As among several persons who may be entitled to redeem, the one whose interest is superior has priority, e. g., a second mortgagee comes ahead of a third mortgagee.[20] Further, "where there are successive mortgages, any subsequent mortgagee may redeem a prior mortgage and every redeeming party is liable to be redeemed in his turn by those below him, and these latter are all liable to be redeemed by the mortgagor." [21]

As indicated above, only those with an interest in the property that will be prejudiced by foreclosure can redeem. Consequently a mortgagor who has conveyed away or otherwise lost all interest in the property cannot redeem.[22] The same is true of persons who, although they once had an interest giving them a right to redeem, have lost it, e. g., a junior lienor which has been discharged.[23] The principle also excludes interests superior to the mortgage from which redemption is sought, e. g., a lien for taxes, a senior mortgage,[24] or the

15. Mackenna v. Fidelity Trust Co., 184 N.Y. 411, 77 N.E. 721, 3 L.R.A., N.S. 1068 (1906).

16. Dundee Naval Stores Co. v. McDowell, 65 Fla. 15, 61 So. 108, Ann. Cas.1915A, 387 (1913) semble. Bacon v. Bowdoin, 39 Mass. (22 Pick.) 401, 405 (1839).

17. McQueen v. Whetstone, 127 Ala. 417, 30 So. 548 (1900); Titsworth v. Stout, 49 Ill. 78, 95 Am.Dec. 577 (1868); Merritt v. Hosmer, 77 Mass. (11 Gray) 276 (1858); Hubbard v. Ascutney Mill Dam Co., 20 Vt. 402, 50 Am.Dec. 41 (1848).

18. Howser v. Cruikshank, 122 Ala. 256, 25 So. 206, 82 Am.St.Rep. 76 (1899); Douglass v. Bishop, 27 Iowa 214 (1869).

19. See Lyon v. Sandford, 5 Conn. 544 (1825) (judgment creditor); Schuck v. Gerlach, 101 Ill. 338 (1882) (judgment creditor); Hasselman v. McKernan, 50 Ind. 441 (1875) (junior mortgagee); Wright v. Howell, 35 Iowa 288 (1872) (judgment creditor); Long v. Richards, 170 Mass. 120, 48 N.E. 1083, 64 Am.St.Rep. 281 (1898) (junior mortgagee). Cf. Kirkham & Woods v. Dupont, 14 Cal. 559 (1860); Bigelow v. Willson, 18 Mass. (1 Pick.) 485 (1823); Cardwell v. Virginia State Ins. Co., 186 Ala. 261, 65 So. 80 (1914).

20. Wiley v. Ewing, 47 Ala. 418 (1872); Loomis v. Knox, 60 Conn. 343, 22 A. 771 (1891); Moore v. Beasom, 44 N.H. 215 (1862); Wimpfheimer v. Prudential Ins. Co., 56 N.J.Eq. 585, 39 A. 916 (1898).

21. Snell's Equity, 18th ed., 290.

22. Smith v. Varney, 309 A.2d 229 (Me.1973); Cardwell v. Virginia State Ins. Co., 186 Ala. 261, 65 So. 80 (1914); Phillips v. Leavitt, 54 Me. 405 (1867); Ingersoll v. Sawyer, 19 Mass. (2 Pick.) 276 (1824).

23. Colwell v. Warner, 36 Conn. 224 (1869); Thomas v. Stewart, 117 Ind. 50, 18 N.E. 505, 1 L.R.A. 715 (1888); McHenry v. Cooper, 27 Iowa 137 (1869).

24. See Dawson v. Overmyer, 141 Ind. 438, 441, 40 N.E. 1065, 1066 (1895), "The prior or senior lienholder has no right to redeem from the junior, because it does not protect any interest he has." See also Harwood v. Underwood, 28 Mich. 427 (1874).

owner of a dower interest not subject to the mortgage.[25] Such interests cannot be affected by foreclosure and therefore give no right to redemption.

Although redemption from a mortgage operates to extinguish the mortgage so far as the mortgage creditor is concerned, it does not necessarily have that effect as regards the persons making the redemption. They may be entitled to keep the mortgage alive for certain purposes, and to accomplish this equity may subrogate them to the rights of the mortgage creditor, or, instead, may order him to assign the debt and mortgage to the one making payment rather than, strictly speaking, discharging the mortgage as in redemption.[26]

§ 7.3 Amount to Be Paid

The mortgagee is entitled to payment in full and to retain his lien on every part of the land until his debt is completely paid.[27] Therefore, in order to redeem, anyone seeking to do so must pay the entire amount to which the mortgagee is entitled even though the redeeming party owns only a fractional part of the property [28] or a limited interest in it as in some of the cases mentioned above.[29] This amount is the mortgage debt, or so much of it as may be due, plus interest to the time of redemption, costs and such additional items as the mortgagee may be entitled to add onto his debt, e. g., taxes paid.[30] Nor can the owner of only a partial interest compel the owners of the rest of the property subject to the mortgage to contribute their shares of the obligation at the time of payment. He must advance the whole amount and recover from them later, being granted subro-

25. Opdyke v. Bartles, 11 N.J.Eq. 133 (1856); Huston v. Seeley, 27 Iowa 183 (1869). Cf., Smith v. Austin, 9 Mich. 465 (1862), no interest shown.

26. See, e. g., G. B. Seely's Son, Inc. v. Fulton-Edison, Inc., 52 A.D.2d 575, 382 N.Y.S.2d 516 (1976).

27. See Graham v. Linden, 50 N.Y. 547, 550 (1872); Sun First Nat. Bank of Orlando v. R. G. C., 348 So.2d 620 (Fla.App. 1977).

28. E. g., Douglass v. Bishop, 27 Iowa 217 (1869); Street v. Beal, 16 Iowa, 68, 85 Am.Dec. 504 (1861); but cf., Coffin v. Parker, 127 N.Y. 117, 27 N. E. 814, 3 St.R. 143 (1891). See note 18, supra.

29. E. g., Springer Corp. v. Kirkeby-Natus, 80 N.M. 206, 453 P.2d 376 (1969) (junior mortgagee); McGough v. Sweetser, 97 Ala. 361, 12 So. 162, 19 L.R.A. 470 (1893); Gibson v. Crehore, 22 Mass. (5 Pick.) 146 (1827) (dower); a junior mortgage: Smith v. Simpson, 129 Ark. 275, 195 S.W. 1067 (1917); see Titley v. Davis, 2 Eq.Cas. Abr. 604 (1739); and note 19, supra. But cf., Green v. Dixon, 9 Wis. 485, 489 (1859); and see 25 Ill.L.Rev. 720 (1931). Or an owner of a part interest in the right of redemption: Merritt v. Hosmer, 77 Mass. (11 Gray) 276 (1858).

30. In the United States a mortgagor, in order to redeem, generally does not have to pay debts other than that for which the mortgage is given as security. Mackenna v. Fidelity Trust Co., 184 N.Y. 411, 77 N.E. 721, 3 L. R.A.,N.S. (1906), 12 Am.St.Rep. 620, 6 Ann.Cas. 471 (1968). See Mahoney v. Bostwick, 96 Cal. 53, 30 P. 1020, 31 Am.St.Rep. 175 (1892). Cf. Brown v. Coriell, 50 N.J.Eq. 753, 26 A. 915, 21 L.R.A. 321, 35 Am.St.Rep. 789 (1893).

gation to the mortgage lien against them for that purpose as an effective remedy.[31]

The mortgage creditor may, of course, consent to a partial redemption.[32] And the rule goes beyond that; he may *insist* upon only a partial redemption, the right of election as to full redemption or redemption only to the extent of the redeeming party's interest in the property subject to the mortgage resting with the mortgage creditor.[33] Where the mortgage creditor has become owner of the interest in that part or undivided share of the mortgaged property which is primarily or proportionately bound to discharge the mortgage, the rule that the owner of the other part or undivided interest must pay the whole debt is inapplicable. He may have redemption by paying only the amount that his interest in the property would have to contribute.[34]

When subdividing is contemplated at the time of the mortgage a section may be inserted in the mortgage providing for it. Some courts have held that the partial release privilege under such a clause is personal to the mortgagor.[35] Others hold that it runs with the

31. See Chapter 10, infra.

32. Union Mut. Life Ins. Co. v. Kirchoff, 133 Ill. 368, 27 N.E. 91 (1890); Kerse v. Miller, 169 Mass. 44, 47 N.E. 504 (1896). See Quinn Plumbing Co. v. New Miami Shores Corp., 100 Fla. 413, 129 So. 690, 73 A.L.R. 600 (1930).

33. E. g., where the mortgagee has become owner of the redemption interest apart from that share of it belonging to the plaintiff. In such a case, if the plaintiff were required to pay the entire mortgage debt he would at once acquire a right of reimbursement against the mortgagee as owner of the other share of the redemption interest for the amount that share should contribute to the redemption and be subrogated to the mortgage in order to collect it. As a short cut, the rule stated in the text applies. Robinson v. Fife, 3 Ohio St. 551 (1854); Simonton v. Gray, 34 Me. 50 (1852); Gibson v. Crehore, 22 Mass. (5 Pick.) 146 (1827). See Quinn Plumbing Co. v. New Miami Shores Corp., 100 Fla. 413, 129 So. 690, 73 A.L.R. 600 (1930). Cf. Barr v. Van Alstine, 120 Ind. 590, 22 N.E. 965 (1889). But cf. West's Ann.Cal.Code Civ.Proc. § 347.

The same principle has permitted the mortgage creditor a choice between requiring full redemption or releasing from the mortgage the part belonging to the party seeking to redeem or paying its value. Boqut v. Coburn, 27 Barb. 230 (N.Y.1858); Wilson v. Tarter, 22 Or. 504, 30 P. 499 (1892). Cf. Mackenna v. Fidelity Trust Co., 184 N.Y. 411, 77 N.E. 721, 3 L.R.A., N.S., 1068, 12 Am.St.Rep. 620, 6 Ann.Cas. 471 (1906).

Cooper v. Peak, 258 Ala. 167, 61 So.2d 62 (1952), certiorari denied 345 U.S. 957, 73 S.Ct. 939, 97 L.Ed. 1377 (1953), rehearing denied 346 U.S. 842, 74 S.Ct. 14, 98 L.Ed. 362, commented on in 52 Mich.L.Rev. 312 (1953) followed the general rule permitting the mortgagee to insist upon a partial redemption.

34. Bradley v. George, 84 Mass. (2 Allen) 392 (1861); Tillinghast v. Fry, 1 R.I. 53 (1841).

35. Gilman v. Forgione, 129 Me. 66, 149 A. 620 (1930), unless words "or his assigns" are included; Rugg v. Record, 255 Mass. 247, 151 N.E. 95 (1926); Cf. Dimeo v. Ellenstein, 106 N.J.Eq. 298, 150 A. 675 (1930). As to the time within which partial release may be exercised when the covenant for it has no express limitation, see 24 Iowa L.Rev. 176 (1938). Also look at Rosenberg v. General Realty Service, Inc., 231 App.Div. 259, 247 N.Y.S. 461 (1931), commented on in 31 Col. L.Rev. 894 (1931); and 3 Pittsburgh L.Rev. 71 (1936).

land.[36] The latter result is better "since the provision for partial release is made specifically with a view to the sale or further incumbrance of part of the property; and a rule limiting the privilege to the mortgagor will either diminish considerably the sale value of the property, or result merely in the release money changing hands twice." [37]

§ 7.4 The Procedure of Redemption

A person who desires to assert a right of redemption must do so by bringing a bill in equity.[38] In it, first of all, he must set forth the mortgage. Then he must state the facts which show that he is one who is entitled to redeem.[39] Although there is some authority saying that prior to bringing the bill, he must have tendered full performance and so aver in his bill,[40] this is not necessary.[41] Nor is it essential that he make tender or payment into court at the time he brings his action.[42] He may do so, of course, but it is sufficient that he assert that he stands ready and willing to pay the sum.[43] His prayer then is that, upon such payment, the mortgage creditor shall discharge the mortgage and do any other acts necessary to restore completely the mortgagor's full interest in the property. It may be, and frequently is, the case that the amount due is uncertain and can only be ascertained by an accounting, in which case the bill will ask for one.[44]

36. Gammel v. Goode, 103 Iowa 301, 72 N.W. 531 (1897); Vawter v. Crafts, 41 Minn. 14, 42 N.W. 483 (1889); Rosenberg v. General Realty Service Co., 231 App.Div. 259, 274 N.Y.S. 461 (1931); Kerschensteiner v. Northern Mich. Land Co., 244 Mich. 403, 221 N.W. 322 (1928).

37. 31 Col.L.Rev. 894, 895 (1931). See also Storke and Sears, Transfer of Mortgaged Property, 38 Corn.L.Q. 185, 211 (1953).

38. See Hubbell v. Sibley, 50 N.Y. 468 (1872). See Coote, Mortgages, 9th ed., pp. 745–765.

39. See Smith v. Austin, 9 Mich. 465, 474 (1862); Dawson v. Overmyer, 141 Ind. 438, 40 N.E. 1065 (1895). Coote, op. cit. supra note 38, p. 715 et seq. See also § 8.5, infra.

40. E. g., Lumsden v. Manson, 96 Me. 357, 52 A. 783 (1902); cf. Toole v. Weirick, 39 Mont. 359, 102 P. 590, 133 Am.St.Rep. 576 (1909).

41. Daubenspeck v. Platt, 22 Cal. 330, 334 (1863); Aust v. Rosenbaum, 74 Miss. 893, 21 So. 555 (1897); Casserly v. Witherbee, 119 N.Y. 522, 23 N.E. 1000 (1890); Nye v. Swan, 49 Minn. 431, 52 N.W. 39 (1892); Gerhardt v. Ellis, 134 Wis. 191, 114 N.W. 495 (1908); Beach v. Cooke, 28 N.Y. 508, 86 Am.Dec. 260 (1864). But see Higman v. Humes, 133 Ala. 617, 32 So. 574 (1901); Kopper v. Dyer, 59 Vt. 477, 489, 9 A. 4, 59 Am.Rep. 742 (1887); Hudkins v. Crim, 72 W.Va. 418, 427, 78 S.E. 1043 (1911).

42. Casserly v. Witherbee, 119 N.Y. 522, 23 N.E. 1000 (1890).

43. Perry v. Carr, 41 N.H. 371 (1860); Casserly v. Witherbee, 119 N.Y. 522, 23 N.E. 1000 (1890); Kopper v. Dyer, 59 Vt. 477, 9 A. 4, 59 Am.Dec. 742 (1887); Powell v. Woodbury, 85 Vt. 504, 83 A. 541, Ann.Cas.1914D, 606 (1915).

44. See Daubenspeck v. Platt, note 41, supra. Look at Frost v. Beekman, 1 Johns.Ch. 288 (N.Y.1814).

Assuming that all of these allegations are established the court will then enter a decree for redemption "on terms."[45] That is, it will provide that the mortgagor may redeem by paying the amount found due plus costs,[46] and fixes a date in the future on or before which the specified payment must be made.[47] The time so allowed is usually six months, but it rests in discretion [48] and may be more or less as determined by the circumstances of the particular case.[49] And it is further decreed that if the proper payment is made within the time specified the defendant shall discharge the mortgage, give over possession and do whatever else is necessary for a complete redemption. If the mortgagor fails to redeem within the specified time, his bill is dismissed and the mortgagor stands foreclosed.[50] Thus a bill to redeem may turn into a foreclosure and, although this is anticipating a later topic, the reverse also is true. If the mortgagee seeks to foreclose, his bill is granted "on terms", the chancellor again fixing an early day in the future within which the mortgagor may redeem and decreeing that, in default of such redemption, the mortgage be foreclosed.[51]

§ 7.5 Limitations on the Right to Redeem

Foreclosure is the usual method by which a right of redemption is ended. However it may be lost in other ways. Its exercise may be

45. See Coote, op. cit. supra note 38, p. 759.

46. Ryer v. Morrison, 21 R.I. 127, 42 A. 509 (1899). See Daubenspeck v. Platt, note 41 supra.

47. Collins v. Gregg, 109 Iowa 506, 80 N.W. 562 (1899); Dennett v. Codman, 158 Mass. 371, 33 N.E. 574 (1893); Turner v. Turner, 3 Munf. 66 (Va. 1812). See also Durfee and Doddridge, Redemption for Foreclosure Sale—The Uniform Act, 23 Mich.L. Rev. 825, 826 (1925).

48. See Perine v. Dunn, 4 Johns.Ch. 140, 141 (N.Y.1819); Clark v. Reyburn, 75 U.S. (8 Wall.) 318, 322, 324, 19 L.Ed. 354 (1869).

49. See Perine v. Dunn, supra, note 48. Murphy v. New Hampshire Sav. Bank, 63 N.H. 362 (1885), one year; Taylor v. Dillenburg, 168 Ill. 235, 48 N.E. 41 (1897), thirty days too short, ninety days allowed; Lindsey v. Delano, 78 Iowa 350, 43 N.W. 218 (1889), nine months.

50. Flanders v. Hall, 159 Mass. 95, 34 N.E. 178 (1893); Perine v. Dunn, 4 Johns.Ch. 140 (N.Y.1819); Bolles v. Duff, 43 N.Y. 469 (1871); Smith v. Bailey, 10 Vt. 163 (1838); Martin v. Ratcliff, 101 Mo. 254, 13 S.W. 1051, 20 Am.St.Rep. 605 (1890); Sloane v. Lucas, 37 Wash. 348, 79 P. 949 (1905). Cf. Carpenter v. Plagge, 192 Ill. 82, 99, 61 N.E. 530 (1901); Stevens v. Miner, 110 Mass. 57 (1872); Cline v. Robbins, 112 Cal. 581, 44 P. 1023 (1896); Hollingsworth v. Campbell, 28 Minn. 18, 8 N.W. 873 (1881); see Turner v. Turner, 3 Munf. 66 (Va.1812); Inman v. Wearing, 3 De G. & Sm. 729 (1850). Meigs v. McFarlan, 72 Mich. 194, 40 N.W. 246 (1888); Fosdick v. Van Husan, 21 Mich. 567 (1870); Ingram v. Smith, 41 N.C. 97 (1849); Turner v. Turner, 3 Munf. 66 (Va., 1812). Cf. Odell v. Montross, 68 N.Y. 499 (1877).

51. "This is not a caprice of the chancellor, but is a natural consequence of the fact that either bill brought all the parties before the court and sought a solution of the mortgage relation, which is essentially a relation of suspense, looking toward further adjustments. That redemption has, in either case, the right of way over foreclosure, is a necessary consequence of the doctrine of redemption." Durfee and Doddridge, 23 Mich.L.Rev. 825, 827, n. 4 (1925).

barred by estoppel in cases where its owner by conduct or words has induced some one to purchase or make expenditures upon the property in reliance upon representations that no right of redemption exists.[52] And it may be barred by such lapse of time as makes operative an applicable statute of limitations or a doctrine apart from statute the effect of which is to end the right to relief. As a general rule neither sort of bar will arise if the mortgagor is in possession.[53]

Falling within the latter group above is laches. Prior to the enactment of statutes of limitations applying to actions in equity, laches alone affected the time within which such an action could be brought.[54] And laches still continues as a general equitable doctrine which is applicable also to the specific case of actions to redeem from a mortgage.[55] In applying it, a court is bound by no inflexible rules and, looking at the particular circumstances of each case, may deny relief even though the elapsed period is less than that allowed under an analogous statute of limitations, or may grant it even though it is longer.[56] To invoke it, the very staleness of the claim itself may persuade the court that it would be unjust to enforce it, but usually material changes in condition, such as altered value of the property, the state of the evidence or other circumstances must be shown in addition.

More generally, equity courts have barred the right to redeem when the mortgagee is in possession by holding that the action must be brought within the time fixed by a statute of limitations which they regard as providing a good analogy. Statutes of limitations on actions at law to recover land or those fixing the time within which

52. Purcell v. Thornton, 128 Minn. 255, 150 N.W. 899 (1915); Ferguson v. Boyd, 169 Ind. 537, 81 N.E. 71 (1907); Munro v. Barton, 98 Me. 250, 56 A. 844 (1903); Kelly v. Hurt, 61 Mo. 463 (1875); Houston v. National Mut. Bldg. & Loan Ass'n, 80 Miss. 31, 31 So. 540, 92 Am.St.Rep. 565 (1902); Ross v. Leavitt, 70 N.H. 602, 50 A. 110 (1900)—accord. Cf. Mellish v. Robertson, 25 Vt. 603 (1853).

53. Miner v. Beekman, 50 N.Y. 337 (1872); Sumner v. Sumner, 217 App. Div. 163, 164, 216 N.Y.S. 389, 390 (1926); Knowlton v. Walker, 13 Wis. 264, 274 (1860); Waldo v. Rice, 14 Wis. 286 (1861). Cf. Bradley v. Norris, 63 Minn. 156, 167, 65 N.W. 357, 359 (1895).

54. See VanHecke, Leavell and Nelson, Equitable Remedies and Restitution, 107 (2d Ed. 1973).

55. For cases dealing with the matter of laches, see Caudle v. First Federal Sav. & Loan Ass'n of Sylacauga, 295 Ala. 274, 327 So.2d 911 (1976); Lucas v. Skinner, 194 Ala. 492, 70 So. 88 (1915); Askew v. Sanders, 84 Ala. 356, 4 So. 167 (1888); Walker v. Warner, 179 Ill. 16, 53 N.E. 594, 70 Am.St.Rep. 85 (1899); Deadman v. Yantis, 230 Ill. 243, 82 N.E. 592, 120 Am.St.Rep. 291 (1907); Chace v. Morse, 189 Mass. 559, 76 N.E. 142 (1905); Hoffman v. Harrington, 33 Mich. 392 (1876); Walker v. Schultz, 175 Mich. 280, 141 N.W. 543 (1913); Cassem v. Heustis, 201 Ill. 208, 66 N.E. 283, 94 Am.St.Rep. 160 (1903); Mahaffy v. Faris, 144 Iowa, 220, 122 N.W. 934, 24 L.R.A.,N.S., 840 (1909); Tukey v. Reinholdt, Iowa, 130 N.W. 727 (1911).

56. E. g., Askew v. Sanders, 84 Ala. 356, 4 So. 167 (1888); Chace v. Morse, 189 Mass. 559, 76 N.E. 142 (1905); see Kelley v. Boettcher, 85 F. 55, 62, 29 C.C.A. 14 (1898).

an action to foreclose may be brought are the ones usually chosen for this purpose.[57] But more troublesome has been the character of the possession by the mortgagee required during the period in order for the mortgagor's claim to be ended.[58] On this, the cases divide into two main categories. In one, the mortgagee's possession must be actively adverse in the sense that his holding cannot be considered as being under the mortgage but is in pursuance of acts repudiating the existence of the mortgage relationship and in hostility to any claim to redeem by the other party,[59] and these facts are brought to his actual notice.[60] The burden of proving both the fact of actual hostile holding and notice to the mortgagor are on the mortgagee.[61] In states where the mortgagee has no right to possession, such possession may be initiated when it is taken without the consent of the mortgagor.[62] Where the mortgagee is in possession as a mortgagee, other unequivocal acts of repudiation of the mortgage relation are essential.[63]

The other line of authorities find the possession of the mortgagee for the required period to be sufficient to bar redemption, even

57. See Roberts v. Littlefield, 48 Me. 61, 63 (1860). See also Jarvis v. Woodruff, 22 Conn. 548 (1853). Clark v. Hannafeldt, 79 Neb. 566, 113 N.W. 135 (1907) accord. Bradley v. Norris, 63 Minn. 156, 65 N.W. 357 (1895), "The limitation upon the right to redeem, adopted by this court by analogy, is the statutory limitation on foreclosure by action."

58. See 20 Va.L.Rev. 464 (1934); 70 U. of Pa.L.Rev. 239 (1922); note, 52 Can.L.J. 414 (1916); note, 53 Can.L.J. 401 (1917); Pugh, Some Peculiarities of the Ohio Law of Mortgages, 4 U. of Cin.L.Rev. 297, 316 (1930). See also 23 L.R.A.,N.S., 754 (1910); 7 A. L.R.2d 1131 (1949); note, 30 N.C.L. Rev. 310 (1952).

59. Munro v. Barton, 98 Me. 250, 254, 56 A. 844, 846 (1903); Arrington v. Liscom, 34 Cal. 365, 94 Am.Dec. 722 (1868); see Grattan v. Wiggin, 23 Cal. 16, 34 (1863); Becker v. McCrea, 193 N.Y. 423, 86 N.E. 463, 23 L.R.A., N.S., 754 (1908), under statute; Ham v. Flowers, 214 S.C. 212, 51 S.E.2d 753, 7 A.L.R.2d 1124 (1949). See 1949, 7 A.L.R.2d 1131, 1133 (1954); Knight v. Hilton, 224 S.C. 452, 79 S. E.2d 871, noted by Karesh, Survey of South Carolina Law: Security Transactions, 7 S.C.L.Q. 171 (1954).

60. Hurlburt v. Chrisman, 100 Or. 188, 197 P. 261 (1921); cf. Cohn v. Cohn, 7 Cal.2d 1, 59 P.2d 969 (1936). See 7 A.L.R.2d 1131, 1141 (1949).

61. See 7 A.L.R.2d 1131, 1134 (1949).

62. Frady v. Ivester, 129 S.C. 536, 125 S.E. 134 (1924). See 7 A.L.R.2d 1131, 1137 (1949).

63. E. g., Cory v. Santa Ynez Land & Improvement Co., 151 Cal. 778, 91 P. 647 (1907). See 7 A.L.R.2d 1131, 1139 (1949).

Strictly speaking, in title states, since the mortgagee in possession already has legal title as well as possession it would seem to be technically inaccurate to describe his freeing the land of the mortgagor's right of redemption as acquiring title by adverse possession. What he has done, of course, is to bar the mortgagor's equity of redemption. Brown v. Berry, 89 N.J.Eq. 230, 108 A. 51 (1918).

In lien states, however, since the mortgagee has only a lien and the mortgagor has title, it is quite correct to talk in terms of acquiring title by adverse possession. However, in both cases the substantial question should be, and is, what sort of possession by the mortgagee is necessary to end the mortgagor's right to redeem, regardless of the technical nature of his interest in the property. Cf. § 16, supra.

though it be rightfully acquired under the mortgage and continued without active repudiation, provided that the mortgagee during that time has made no acknowledgment of the right to redeem.[64] The party seeking to redeem after the end of the period has the burden of showing such an acknowledgment.[65]

Because it has found recognition by some courts it is necessary to note one additional doctrine. It is that the right to foreclose and the right to redeem are reciprocal, and when one is barred, the other is also barred.[66] The mutuality idea is valid to the extent that " 'it shall not be competent for one party alone to consider it a mortgage.' "[67] Thus, if the mortgagee, through possession of the necessary kind, has been freed from an action to redeem by the mortgagor, and then, in order to clear up his title, brings an action to foreclose, this treatment of the mortgage as a subsisting relationship as to him, involves the consequence that it will be treated also as a mortgage in respect to the mortgagor.[68] If, however, a mortgagee or purchaser on foreclosure sale has thus barred the mortgagor's redemption interest, he is not precluded from clearing his title except at peril of bringing to life the mortgagor's right. He may do so by an action designed for that purpose based, not upon a theory that the mortgage still subsists, as is a foreclosure suit, but upon the idea that the mortgage is gone and the plaintiff is now complete owner.[69]

However the doctrine never required that the rights of the parties should in every respect be on all fours. Certainly that is true as to the time within which the respective rights may be enforced, "for it is every day's practice, that one party may not be able to foreclose when the other may redeem."[70] And it would be objectionable to hold that they must be. For then "a person might one day be a mortgagee, having, in most jurisdictions, a lien merely on the premises, and the next day be their absolute owner,"[71] a result flowing from mere failure to enforce his rights. Additionally "it would give

64. Dexter v. Arnold, 3 Sumner 152, F.Cas.No.3,859 (C.C.R.I.1837). See, 7 A.L.R.2d 1131, 1142 (1949).

65. See 7 A.L.R.2d 1131, 1134 (1949).

66. Fitch v. Miller, 200 Ill. 170, 183, 65 N.E. 650, 655 (1902); Locke v. Caldwell, 91 Ill. 417, 420 (1879); (but compare comment in Walker v. Warner, 179 Ill. 16, 27, 53 N.E. 594, 598, 70 Am.Dec. 85) (1899); Cunningham v. Hawkins, 24 Cal. 403, 85 Am.Dec. 73 (1864); Crawford v. Taylor, 42 Iowa 260, 263 (1875); Adams v. Holden, 111 Iowa 54, 60, 82 N.W. 468, 470 (1900); (but cf. Tukey v. Reinholdt, 130 N.W. 727) (Iowa 1911); Leland v. Morrison, 92 S.C. 501, 75 S.E. 889, Ann.Cas.1914B, 349 (1913); Gould v. McKillip, 55 Wyo. 251, 99 P.2d 67, 129 A.L.R. 1427 (1940). But cf. Bradley v. Norris, 63 Minn. 156, 165, 65 N.W. 357, 358 (1865).

67. Bradley v. Norris, 63 Minn. 156, 165, 65 N.W. 357, 358 (1895).

68. Calkins v. Isbell, 20 N.Y. 147 (1859), affirming Calkins v. Calkins, 3 Barb. 305 (N.Y.1848).

69. Arrington v. Liscom, 34 Cal. 365, 94 Am.Dec. 722 (1868); Chapin v. Wright, 41 N.J.Eq. 438, 5 A. 574 (1886).

70. Bradley v. Norris, 63 Minn. 156, 165, 65 N.W. 357, 358 (1895).

71. Tiffany, Real.Prop., 3d ed., § 1501, citing Bradley v. Norris, 63 Minn. 156, 65 N.W. 357 (1895).

to one claimant the benefit of disabilities to which his opponent is subject." [72]

The rule may correctly apply to redemption by a junior mortgagee; his right of redemption from the senior mortgage, in lien states at least, is dependent upon his right to foreclose his own mortgage and hence, when it is barred he also loses his right to redeem.[73] It has also been suggested that the statement means merely that, in fixing the equitable limitation upon suits to redeem, instead of adopting the statutory period for bringing ejectment, a court will follow the time rule governing the bringing of an action to foreclose as more nearly analogous.[74]

B. ACCRUAL OF THE RIGHT TO FORECLOSURE

§ 7.6 Acceleration Clauses—In General

Most installment payment mortgages today contain acceleration clauses. These clauses empower the mortgagee in the event of a default by the mortgagor to declare the whole amount of the mortgage debt due and payable. Moreover, the general concept of acceleration clauses is universally accepted.[75] Indeed, in the absence of such provisions, mortgagees would be forced to utilize cumbersome and impractical procedures for foreclosing for each installment as it comes due, procedures that we will examine later in this chapter.[76] It is important to recognise that acceleration is permitted not only for failure to pay the debt promptly, but also for such other defaults as the failure to pay taxes,[77] maintain insurance [78] or for the commission of waste.[79]

72. Ibid.

73. Gower v. Winchester, 33 Iowa 303 (1871); Krutz v. Gardner, 25 Wash. 396, 65 P. 771 (1901).

74. Parsons v. Noggle, 23 Minn. 328 (1877). See Bradley v. Norris, 63 Minn. 156, 166, 65 N.W. 357, 359 (1895). Some states have enacted statutes applying specifically to actions to redeem. See e. g., West's Ann.Cal.Code Civ.Proc. § 346 (5 years); McKinney's N.Y.Civ.Prac.Law and Rules § 212(c) (ten years). While these statutes set a definite time limit they do not necessarily dispose of the question of what kind of possession by the mortgagee is necessary for the period to run. See Peshine v. Ord, 119 Cal. 311, 51 P. 536, 63 Am. St.Rep. 131 (1897); Cory v. Santa Ynez Land and Improvement Co., 151 Cal. 778, 91 P. 647 (1907); Cohn v. Cohn, 1936, 7 Cal.2d 1, 59 P.2d 969 (1936); Sumner v. Sumner, 217 App. Div. 163, 164, 216 N.Y.S. 389, 390 (1926).

75. E. g., Saunders v. Stradley, 25 Md.App. 85, 333 A.2d 604 (1975); Campbell v. Werner, 232 So.2d 252 (Fla.App.1970); Poydan, Inc. v. Agia Kiriaki, 130 N.J.Super. 141, 325 A.2d 838 (1974); United States Sav. Bank of Newark, New Jersey v. Continental Arms, Inc., 338 A.2d 579 (Del.Super.1975).

76. See § 7.8, infra.

77. See Saunders v. Stradley, 25 Md. App. 85, 333 A.2d 604 (1975); First Nat. Bank of Atlanta v. Blum, 141 Ga.App. 485, 233 S.E.2d 835 (1977); Ford v. Waxman, 50 A.D.2d 585, 375 N.Y.S.2d 145 (1975); Eisen v. Kostakos, 116 N.J.Super. 358, 282 A.2d 421 (1971).

78. Cf. Strong v. Merchants Mutual Ins. Co., 2 Mass.App. 142, 309 N.E.2d 510 (1974), modified 366 Mass. 751, 322 N.E.2d 765.

79. United States v. Angel, 362 F. Supp. 445 (E.D.Pa.1973).

It is important to emphasize, however, that most acceleration clauses are "optional" as opposed to "automatic" in the sense that they are triggered only after a default by the mortgagor *and* the decision of the mortgagee to accelerate.[80] Absent a mortgage provision to the contrary, notice to the mortgagor is not essential for a valid acceleration. However, the mortgagee "must perform some affirmative, overt act evidencing his intention to take advantage of the accelerating provision. Such affirmative action must be taken before the debtor tenders what is actually due, or the creditor loses his right to treat the entire debt as due because of that particular default."[81] Very often the commencement of a judicial foreclosure proceeding constitutes sufficient evidence of an election to accelerate.[82] In the power of sale context, courts have held that letters to the mortgagor threatening foreclosure unless arrearages are promptly paid coupled with oral expressions to the mortgagor of an intention to foreclose supply the requisite evidence of such an election.[83] Normally, however, prudent mortgagees obviate such problems by mailing to the mortgagor a notice of intent to accelerate unless the default is cured. Moreover, in the event the default is not corrected, such mortgagees will mail a second notice to inform the mortgagor that acceleration has in fact occurred and that foreclosure proceedings will be commenced.

Acceleration of the entire mortgage debt may be triggered, as pointed out above, not only by failure to pay installments of principal or interest, but also by such defaults as failure to pay taxes or insurance premiums. Once acceleration has occurred because of non-debt

80. See Rosenthal, The Role of Courts of Equity in Preventing Acceleration Predicated Upon a Mortgagor's Inadvertent Default, 22 Syr.L.Rev. 897, 899 n. 8 (1971).

81. Spires v. Lawless, 493 S.W.2d 65, 73 (Mo.App.1973). See also Lowry v. Northwestern Sav. & Loan Ass'n, 542 S.W.2d 546 (Mo.App.1976); United States Sav. Bank of Newark, New Jersey v. Continental Arms, Inc., 338 A.2d 579 (Del.Super.1975).

82. United States Sav. Bank of Newark, New Jersey v. Continental Arms, Inc., 338 A.2d 579 (Del.Super.1975); Pizer v. Herzig, 120 App.Div. 102, 105 N.Y.S. 38 (1907); Swearingen v. Lahner, 93 Iowa 147, 61 N.W. 431, 26 L. R.A. 765, 57 Am.St.Rep. 261 (1894). As to what will constitute, for this purpose, the commencement of a foreclosure action, see Trowbridge v. Malex Realty Corp., 111 Misc. 211, 183 N.Y.S. 53 (1920), reversed on other grounds, 198 App.Div. 656, 191 N.Y.S. 97 (1922). See also Walsh v. Henel, 226 App.Div. 198, 235 N.Y.S. 34 (1929) noted 7 N.Y.Univ.L.Q.Rev. 214 (1929). See further Updike, Mortgages, in 1954 Annual Survey of American Law, 30 N.Y.U.L.Rev. 805, 812 (1955) noting Jacobson v. McClanahan, 43 Wash.2d 751, 264 P.2d 253 (1953). But see, Basse v. Gallegger, 7 Wis. 442, 76 Am.Dec. 225 (1858). Look at Albertina Realty Co. v. Rosbro Realty Corp., 258 N.Y. 472, 180 N.E. 176 (1932), affirmed 233 App.Div. 737, 250 N.Y.S. 841, and comment on it in Walsh & Simpson, Cases Security Transactions, 482, Note (2).

83. Lowrey v. Northwestern Sav. & Loan Ass'n, 542 S.W.2d 546 (Mo. App.1976). "It is only necessary that the mortgagee show an unmistakable intention to exercise the option, and this may be done by taking steps for foreclosure, filing foreclosure suit, sale pursuant to the mortgage, or advertisement of the property for sale pursuant to the terms of the mortgage." 2 Jones, Mortgages, § 1512 (8th Ed.).

related defaults, it normally cannot be avoided simply by paying the overdue taxes or by reinstating the insurance, but only by tendering prior to foreclosure the full accelerated mortgage debt.[84]

§ 7.7 Limitations on Acceleration

Once a valid acceleration has occurred, in theory the mortgagor's only recourse normally is to redeem by paying the accelerated debt prior to foreclosure. However, a variety of concepts derived from case law and legislation operate in varying degrees to defeat or at least ameliorate the harsh consequences of acceleration.

Acceleration is sometimes defeated by waiver or related considerations. Acceptance by the mortgagee of the amount in default before he has elected to enforce the acceleration operates as a waiver of the provision. Moreover, a payment or tender before election destroys the right to accelerate.[85] However, a mere failure to foreclose on the first default in payment does not operate as a waiver of the option to foreclose because of later defaults.[86] Further, the mortgagee may take such payment after he has elected in favor of acceleration without waiving his right to foreclose the mortgage for the balance.[87] On the other hand, there are numerous cases in which mortgagors have been relieved for inadvertent defaults in payment of principal or interest because courts have detected a *consistent* prior pattern of acceptance of late payments by the mortgagee.[88] Other courts, however, have refused to find waiver in similar circumstances.[89] Indeed, some such courts look upon such repeated defaults and mortgagee forbearance as factors to be held against the mortgagor.[90]

84. See, e. g., Saunders v. Stradley, 25 Md.App. 85, 333 A.2d 604 (1975); Lotterer v. Leon, 138 Md. 318, 113 A. 887 (1921). But compare Eisen v. Kostakos, 116 N.J.Super. 358, 282 A. 2d 421 (1971); Spires v. Lawless, 493 S.W.2d 65, 72 (Mo.App.1973).

85. Trinity County Bank v. Haas, 151 Cal. 553, 91 P. 385 (1907); Van Vlissingen v. Lenz, 171 Ill. 162, 49 N.E. 422 (1897); Cresco Realty Co. v. Clark, 1908, 128 App.Div. 144, 112 N. Y.S. 550 (1908); Bisno v. Sax, 175 Cal.App.2d 714, 346 P.2d 814 (1960).

86. Dunn v. Barry, 35 Cal.App. 325, 169 P. 910 (1917); Bower v. Stein, 101 C.C.A. 299, 177 F. 673 (1910).

87. La Plant v. Beechley, 182 Iowa 452, 165 N.W. 1019 (1918); Robinson v. Miller, 317 Ill. 501, 148 N.E. 319 (1925); Odell v. Hoyt, 73 N.Y. 343 (1878), See, 53 A.L.R. 525 (1928); 41 A.L.R. 732 (1926); 19 A.L.R. 284 (1925); 5 A.L.R. 437 (1920).

See Mortgages in 1957 Survey of New York Law, 32 N.Y.U.L.Rev. 1426 (1957), noting Mayer v. Myers, 155 N.Y.S.2d 129 (S.Ct.1956) and Clark-Robinson Corp. v. Jet Enterprises, Inc., 159 N.Y.S.2d 214 (S.Ct.1957).

88. Rosenthal, supra note 80 at 907; Scelza v. Ryba, 10 Misc.2d 186, 169 N.Y.S.2d 462 (1957); Edwards v. Smith, 322 S.W.2d 770 (Mo.1959); Short v. A. H. Still Inv. Co., 206 Va. 959, 147 S.E.2d 99 (1966); Annot., 97 A.L.R.2d 997 (1964).

89. See e. g., Federal Nat. Mortgage Ass'n v. Walter, 363 P.2d 293 (Okl. 1961); Campbell v. West, 86 Cal. 197, 24 P. 1000 (1890).

90. See, e. g., Har Rich Realty Corp. v. American Consumer Industries, Inc., 351 F.2d 785 (D.C.Cir. 1965).

Under what circumstances, if any, will a court relieve a mortgagor from the consequences of an acceleration in cases involving extreme hardship to the mortgagor? The general rule is that an acceleration clause works neither a forfeiture nor a penalty but is simply a matter of contract determining when the debt is payable.[91] Consequently, courts often state that a mortgagor will not be relieved against its enforcement for a default occurring by his negligence, mistake or by accident in the absence of fraud, bad faith or other conduct on the part of the mortgagee rendering it unconscionable for him to avail himself of it.[92] Indeed, as one court has pointed out, "mere improvidence or neglect or poverty or illness is not sufficient basis for relief in equity from foreclosure under a mortgage acceleration clause. A mortgagee may be ungenerous, perhaps even uncharitable, but generosity and charity are voluntary attributes and cannot be enforced by the Court." [93] On the other hand, there is a growing number of decisions that a mortgagor will be protected from defaults that are the result of an accident or a mistake while acting in good faith, or unusual circumstances beyond his control.[94] For example, one recent Florida decision is indicative of this trend.[95] There after three years of regular payments, there was one lapse of a month and 20 days in making a payment. That was followed by a three month lapse, but immediately thereafter the mortgagor paid three installments with late charges. The mortgagee accepted these

91. Graf v. Hope Bldg. Corp., 254 N.Y. 1, 171 N.E. 884, 70 A.L.R. 984 (1930). The case, because of an important dissenting opinion by Cardozo, J., was widely discussed. See notes: 40 Yale L.J. 141 (1930); 30 Col.L.Rev. 1064 (1930); 17 Va.L.Rev. 80 (1930); 16 Cornell L.Q. 106 (1930); 10 Boston U.L.Rev. 558 (1930); 29 Mich.L.Rev. 380 (1930); 8 N.Y.Univ.L.Q.Rev. 331 (1930); 79 U. of Pa.L.Rev. 229 (1930); 6 Wis.L.Rev. 45 (1930); 70 A.L.R. 993 (1931). See Poydan, Inc. v. Agia Kiriaki, Inc., 130 N.J.Super. 141, 325 A. 2d 838 (1974); Verna v. O'Brien, 78 Misc.2d 288, 356 N.Y.S.2d 929 (1974); Collins v. Nagel, 200 Iowa 562, 203 N.W. 702 (1925). See further Updike, Mortgages, in 1954 Annual Survey of American Law, 30 N.Y.U.L.Rev. 812 (1955), noting Law v. Edgecliff Realty Co., 133 N.Y.S.2d 418 (S.Ct.1954), and August Tobler, Inc. v. Goolsby, 67 So.2d 537 (Fla.1953). And see A–Z Servicenter v. Segall, 334 Mass. 672, 138 N.E.2d 266, 269 (1956) citing text.

92. Graf v. Hope Bldg. Corp., supra, note 91. See 70 A.L.R. 993 (1931). Jacobson v. McClanahan, 43 Wash.2d 751, 264 P.2d 253 (1953), discussed in 29 Wash.L.Rev. 101 (1953); Home Owners Loan Corp. v. Wilkes, 130 Fla. 492, 178 So. 161 (1934); Campbell v. Werner, 232 So.2d 252 (Fla. App.1970); Buckler v. Davis Sand & Gravel Corp., 208 Md. 162, 117 A.2d 562 (1955).

93. Verna v. O'Brien, 78 Misc.2d 288, 292, 356 N.Y.S.2d 929, 932 (1974).

94. See, e. g., Rockaway Park Series Corp. v. Hollis Automotive Corp., 206 Misc. 955, 135 N.Y.S.2d 588 (1954), affirmed 285 App.Div. 1140, 142 N.Y. S.2d 364, commented on by Million, Property Law, in 1955 Survey of New York Law, 30 N.Y.U.L.Rev. 1065, 1074 (1955); Bisno v. Sax, 175 Cal. App.2d 714, 346 P.2d 814 (1960); Federal Home Loan Mortgage Corp. v. Taylor, 318 So.2d 203 (Fla.App.1975); Middlemist v. Mosier, 151 Colo. 113, 377 P.2d 110 (1963); Rosenthal, supra note 80 at 904–905.

95. Federal Home Loan Mortgage Corp. v. Taylor, 318 So.2d 203 (Fla. App.1975).

payments. However, a payment made on September 10, 1973 did not include the installment that fell due on September 1. This latter installment was paid prior to October 4, but the mortgagee refused to accept it because the October 1 installment was not included. In upholding relief from acceleration, the court noted the general delays in mail delivery caused by the fact that the mortgagor was a serviceman stationed overseas. "It is to be noticed here that the mortgagors were not in the Phillippines by mere choice but due to a military assignment. Though the personal hardship arising from the daughter's need of stateside hospitalization is not a circumstance to excuse payment of a debt when due, the distance between the mortgagor and mortgagee's agent because of military obligations of the mortgagor is not to be ignored as a factor impairing the ability of the parties to communicate demands and responses thereto. The total evidence indicates a good faith effort on the part of the mortgagor to meet the mortgagee's conditions of bringing the account current." [96]

An increasing number of states are enacting "arrearages" legislation permitting the mortgagor to defeat acceleration by curing the default that existed prior to the acceleration.[97] Under the Pennsylvania statute, for example, a residential mortgagor may until one hour prior to the foreclosure sale "avoid acceleration" by paying or tendering "all sums which would have been due at the time of payment or tender in the absence of default and the exercise of an acceleration clause." [98] Moreover, when the acceleration is triggered by such defaults as failure to pay taxes or insurance premiums, it may be defeated by the mortgagor simply by performing the defaulted obligation that caused the acceleration.[99] Other states, moreover, confer the benefits of such legislation on *all* as opposed to just residential mortgagors.[1]

It could be argued that the above statutes are subject to abuse because some mortgagors may default repeatedly, knowing that they can defeat acceleration simply by paying the arrearages. However, many of the statutes, to some extent at least, discourage this behavior by requiring the reinstating mortgagor to pay attorney's fees and other expenses such as the cost of foreclosure publication requirements.[2] Moreover, some statutes limit the number of mortgage reinstatements permitted within specified time periods.[3] Thus

96. Id. at 208.

97. See, e. g., West's Ann.Calif.Civ. Code, § 2924c; Ill.Rev.Stat. Ch. 95, § 57; Minn.Stat.Ann. § 580.30; Purdon's Penn.Stat.Ann. Tit. 41, § 404 (1974); Utah Code Ann.1953, 57–1–31. For an interesting interpretation problem in the Minnesota statute, see Davis v. Davis, 293 Minn. 44, 196 N.W.2d 473 (1972).

98. Purdon's Penn.Stat.Ann. Tit. 41, § 404(b)(1).

99. Id. at Tit. 41, § 404(b)(2).

1. E. g., Minn.Stat.Ann. § 580.30; Utah Code Ann.1953, 57–1–31.

2. E. g., Minn.Stat.Ann. § 580.30; West's Ann.Calif.Civ.Code, § 2924c.

3. See Purdon's Penn.Stat.Ann. Tit. 41, § 404 (1974). (3 reinstatements in one year).

there are probably enough economic and other deterrents to discourage the average home mortgagor from intentionally abusing such statutes. However, many commercial mortgagors may very well be willing repeatedly to accept the relatively mild economic penalties of the statutes as the cost of defeating acceleration, especially where multi-million dollar mortgages are involved. Thus the approach of the Pennsylvania statute limiting reinstatement rights to residential mortgagors may be a desirable ingredient of arrearages legislation.

The Federal Housing Administration (FHA) and the Veterans Administration (VA) have both promulgated guidelines to be followed in the foreclosure of loans which they have insured or guaranteed.[4] The guidelines extend the time which must elapse between default and foreclosure, require the mortgagee to permit reinstatement by payment of arrearages, and set up counselling procedures which are to be followed before foreclosure. Whether these guidelines are legally binding on mortgagees, so that failure to follow them will constitute grounds for enjoining a foreclosure, setting aside a sale, or awarding damages to the mortgagor, has been the subject of considerable litigation. While the earlier cases were divided, it is now the clear weight of authority that the guidelines are only advisory and not a legal condition precedent to foreclosure.[5] Nonetheless, a court may well consider them in reaching a decision as to whether foreclosure would be inequitable or unconscionable, and may, in the exercise of its inherent equitable powers, refuse to order foreclosure if the lender has violated the guidelines in an egregious fashion.[6]

§ 7.8 The Absence of An Acceleration Clause—Effect on Foreclosure

Where an installment payment mortgage does not contain an acceleration clause, mortgagor default poses substantial foreclosure problems. The mortgagee is faced with two undesirable foreclosure

4. See, e. g., HUD Handbook FHA G4191.1 (1974); HUD Housing Management Mortgagee Letter 75–10 (Oct. 4, 1975); VA Lenders Handbook Par. 6011–13. Concerning FHA and VA's mortgage insurance operations generally, see § 11.2, supra.

5. Roberts v. Cameron-Brown Co., 556 F.2d 356 (C.C.A.Ga.1977); Encarnacion Hernandez v. Prudential Mortgage Co., 553 F.2d 241 (C.C.A.Puerto Rico 1977); Brown v. Lynn, 385 F. Supp. 986 (N.D.Ill.1974), 392 F.Supp. 559 (N.D.Ill.1975); Nesmith v. Lynn, 377 A.2d 352 (Del.1977); Federal Nat. Mortgage Ass'n v. Ricks, 83 Misc.2d 814, 372 N.Y.S.2d 485 (1975). Mortgagee Letter 75–10, supra note 4, expressly denies that its procedures are legally mandatory.

6. Compare Federal Nat. Mortgage Ass'n v. Ricks, 83 Misc.2d 814, 372 N.Y.S.2d 485 (1975) (lender's conduct unconscionable; mortgagee's motion to dismiss denied) with Government Nat. Mortgage Ass'n v. Screen, 85 Misc.2d 86, 379 N.Y.S.2d 327 (1976) (lender's conduct reasonable; foreclosure ordered). If the mortgage has been assigned to FHA, its action to foreclose may be dismissed or enjoined unless it can show that foreclosure will advance the objectives of the National Housing Act and is rational and consistent, at least with respect to subsidized multifamily project mortgages; Kent Farm Co. v. Hills, 417 F.Supp. 297 (D.D.C.1976).

alternatives. First, the mortgagee presumably could wait, in some instances for many years, for all of the installments to come due and then foreclose for the total accrued debt. The second alternative is to foreclose based on a default in the payment of one or more installments.

When the mortgagee must follow the second alternative, there are several possible methods for handling the foreclosure. Some courts take the view that the security is indivisible and that a foreclosure action must be of the entire security regardless of whether the default being sued for is of a portion or all of the debt.[7] The result of this harsh doctrine is that if a mortgagee forecloses for an installment or interest he will be barred later from foreclosing for the balance or any other portion of his obligation. But most courts, either by decision or under statutes, arrive at more equitable solutions. Thus, if it is possible, which it usually is not, to divide the property into parcels without injury to the whole a sale will be decreed of only so much of the premises as will be sufficient to satisfy the amount due, and the decree will stand as security on the unsold portion of the property for the balance of the debt as it comes due.[8] Where the property is not susceptible to piecemeal sale without injury to the whole, it may be sold as an entirety free and clear of the entire mortgage debt.[9] The surplus over the amount necessary to satisfy the partial default is then handled in various ways.[10] Even without the

7. Curtis v. Cutler, 76 F. 16, 22 C.C.A. 16, 37 L.R.A. 737 (1896), abrogated by Gen.Stat.Minn., Mason, § 9610 (1927). See Prideaux v. Des Moines Joint Stock Bank, 34 F.2d 308 (D.C. Minn.1929), appeal dismissed 282 U.S. 800, 51 S.Ct. 40, 75 L.Ed. 720 (1930); Rains v. Mann, 68 Ill. 264 (1873); Cf., Wells v. Ordway, 108 Iowa 86, 78 N. W. 806, 75 Am.St.Rep. 209 (1899); Mascarel v. Raffour, 51 Cal. 242 (1876), foreclosing on only one parcel. But cf., Widman v. Hammack, 110 Wash. 77, 187 P. 1091, 42 A.L.R. 468 (1920).

8. Blazey v. Delius, 74 Ill. 299 (1874); Griffin v. Reis, 68 Ind. 9 (1879); Caufman v. Sayre, 2 B.Mon. 202 (Ky. 1841). See Reno v. Black, 59 F. 917 (C.C.Mo.1894); 37 L.R.A. 737, 743 (1905). See also Minn.Stat.Ann., § 580.09, "Where a mortgage is given to secure the payment of money by instalments—each instalment, either for principal or interest may be taken and deemed to be a separate and independent mortgage, and such mortgage for each instalment may be foreclosed in the same manner as if a separate mortgage was given for each subsequent instalment"; West's Ann.Cal. Code Civ.Proc., § 728, "If the debt for which the mortgage, lien, or incumbrance is held is not all due, so soon as sufficient of the property has been sold to pay the amount due, with costs, the sale must cease; and afterwards, as often as more comes due, for principal or interest, the court may, on motion, order more to be sold."

9. A mortgagee foreclosed his mortgage upon the mortgagor's partial default. Held, the premises, when sold under the decree, passed to the purchaser discharged from the mortgage lien. Poweshiek County v. Dennison, 36 Iowa, 244, 14 Am.Rep. 521 (1873); Buford v. Smith, 7 Mo. 489 (1842); Reno v. Black, note 8, supra. But see Borden v. McNamara, 20 N.D. 225, 127 N.W. 104, Ann.Cas.1912C, 841, 846 (1910); Edgar v. Beck, 96 Mich. 419, 56 N.W. 15 (1893).

10. For cases dealing with the disposition of surplus arising from a sale under foreclosure for partial default, see Hatcher v. Chancey, 71 Ga. 689 (1883); Peyton v. Ayres, 2 Md.Ch. 64

aid of statute, it has been held that the chancellor will direct its application to the liquidation of the balance of the debt, with a fair and equitable rebate of interest on it.[11] And the same practice is authorized by statute in some jurisdictions.[12] Others direct that the surplus be held in trust to meet the unmatured portion of the debt.[13] Another proper alternative that would avoid the surplus problem would be to sell the premises at a foreclosure sale subject to the continued lien of the balance of the debt.[14] This is conceptually the same as treating the sale as a second mortgage foreclosure sale with the purchaser buying the premises subject to a first mortgage in the amount of the balance of the debt.

C. STRICT FORECLOSURE

§ 7.9 The Nature of Strict Foreclosure

As mentioned earlier, there are two major methods of mortgage foreclosure in use in the United States and each is accompanied by a foreclosure sale. The most pervasive method is judicial foreclosure in equity. While this type of foreclosure is available in every state, in many states it is the only type permitted. In about half the states, the prevailing method is non-judicial foreclosure under a "power of sale." This power of sale is sometimes vested in the mortgagee, but more often in some public official such as a sheriff. If a deed of

(1849); Fowler v. Johnson, 26 Minn. 338, 3 N.W. 986, 6 N.W. 486 (1880); Cox v. Wheeler, 7 Paige 248 (N.Y. 1838); Schreiber v. Carey, 48 Wis. 208, 4 N.W. 124 (1879.)

11. E. g., Black v. Reno, note 8, supra; 37 L.R.A. 737 (1905).

12. N.J.Stat.Ann., 2A:50—33 (1952), payment with rebate for interest, if mortgagee willing to receive it; Cal. Code Civ.Proc., § 728, rebate of interest where such rebate is proper; McKinney's N.Y. RPAP § 1351(c), payment with rebate for interest, or investment; Wis.Stat.Ann. § 278.07–08, payment with rebate for interest, or investment.

13. Ga.Code, § 67–502. And see New York and Wisconsin statutes—in preceding note.

14. Light v. Federal Land Bank, 177 Ark. 846, 7 S.W.2d 975 (1928); Miami Mortgage & Guaranty Co. v. Drawdy, 99 Fla. 1092, 1097, 127 So. 323, 325 (1930); Hughes v. Frisbie, 81 Ill. 188, 193 (1876); Chicago Title & Trust Co. v. Prendergast, 335 Ill. 646, 167 N.E. 769 (1929); Fremont Joint Stock Bank v. Foster, 215 Iowa 1209, 247 N.W. 815 (1933); McCurdy v. Clark, 27 Mich. 445 (1873); Cary v. Met. Life Ins. Co., 141 Or. 388, 17 P.2d 1111 (1933); McDougal v. Downey, 45 Cal. 165 (1872); Burroughs v. Ellis, 76 Iowa 649, 38 N.W. 141 (1888). See, generally, Leesman, The Effect of Foreclosure of Part Only of a Mortgage Debt, 31 Ill.L.Rev. 1056 (1937); note, 1930, 30 Col.L.Rev. 893. See also, 37 L.R.A. 737 (1897). In New York, by an amendment in 1927, Laws of 1927, c. 683, McKinney's N.Y. RPAP § 1351(c) was changed to permit this as an alternative practice. In the face of the statute it was held improper to decree a sale for the defaulted portion of a debt with a continuing lien for the unmatured balance. Bank of America Nat. Ass'n v. Dames, 135 Misc. 391, 239 N.Y.S. 558, 30 Col.L.Rev. 893 (1930). A later case, however, held the other way, giving effect to the clear language of the act. Prudence Co. v. Sussman, 143 Misc. 686, 258 N.Y.S. 241 (1932).

trust is used, the power of sale is in the trustee. These two methods of foreclosure will receive most of our attention in this chapter.

Another type of foreclosure, limited in use, is strict foreclosure. Unlike the above predominant methods, strict foreclosure entails no foreclosure sale. When it is used, strict foreclosure usually is judicial. However, the defaulting mortgagor is given a period of time by the court to pay the mortgage debt. Failure to do so within the prescribed time will result in title to the mortgaged real estate vesting in the mortgagee without sale. The following section focuses on the limited use of this foreclosure device in the Unted States.

§ 7.10 Use of Strict Foreclosure

In most states strict foreclosure of a mortgagor's interest by a mortgagee is not permitted. However, it is still used in Connecticut [15] even though a statute in that state provides for foreclosure sale on written notice by any party, the granting of which is discretionary with the court.[16] Strict foreclosure is also the customary remedy in Vermont.[17] Illinois is a third state in which strict foreclosure, hedged about by salutary restrictions,[18] remains in common use. Decisions in that state lay down three requirements for its employment, all of which must concur [19]: the premises must not be worth more than the debt plus interest and costs; [20] the mortgagee

15. See Conn.Gen.Stat.Ann. § 49–15 (1975).

16. Conn.Gen.Stat.Ann. § 49–24. See Bradford Realty Corp. v. Beetz, 108 Conn. 26, 31, 142 A. 395, 397 (1928); North End Bank & Trust Co. v. Mandell, 113 Conn. 241, 245; 155 A. 80, 81 (1931).

17. See Vt.Stat.Ann. Tit. 12 § 4531; Vt.R.C.P. 80.1 (Reporter's Notes 1975); Devereaux v. Fairbanks, 52 Vt. 587 (1880); Paris v. Hulett, 26 Vt. 308 (1854); see Hill v. Hill, 59 Vt. 125, 7 A. 468, 471 (1887).

18. See Great Lakes Mortgage Corp. v. Collymore, 14 Ill.App.3d 68, 302 N.E. 2d 248 (1973) (reaffirming the availability of strict foreclosure in Illinois subject to the three restrictions in the text). For the requirements of strict foreclosure in Illinois, see Prather, Foreclosure of the Security Interest, U. of Ill.L.Forum, 420, 446 (1957). See also Brodkey, Current Changes in Illinois Real Property Law, 10 DePaul L.Rev. 566, 580 (1960).

19. See Carpenter v. Plagge, 192 Ill. 82, 99, 61 N.E. 530, 536 (1901); Johnson v. Donnell, 15 Ill. 97, 99 (1853). See also Thomas, Strict Foreclosure in Illinois, 4 Ill.L.Rev. 572 (1910); Anderson, Proposed Mortgage Foreclosure Law in Illinois, 2 John Marshall L.Q. 293, 297 (1936); Carey, Brabner-Smith & Sullivan, Studies in Foreclosures in Cook County: II. Foreclosure Methods and Redemption, 27 Ill.L.Rev. 595, 609 (1933); idem, 870; MacChesney with Leesman, Collaborator, Mortgages, Foreclosures and Reorganizations, 31 Ill. L.Rev. 287, 300; note, 25 Va.L.Rev. 947, 950 (1939); Campbell, Cases on Mortgages, 2d Ed., 247, n. 2. See also Leesman, Corporate Trusteeship and Receivership, 28 Ill.L.Rev. 238, 245 (1933) for the possibility of strict foreclosure in the case of a corporate mortgage by trust deed. A fourth requirement, that there be no junior lienors nor creditors, has practically disappeared. Rexroat v. Ford, 201 Ill.App. 342 (1916); Barnes v. Ward, 190 Ill.App. 392 (1914).

20. Carpenter v. Plagge, 192 Ill. 82, 61 N.E. 530 (1901); Barnes v. Ward, 190 Ill.App. 392, 395, 398, 399 (1914).

must be willing to take the property in full satisfaction of the debt; [21] and the mortgagor must be insolvent.[22]

Two related foreclosure methods authorized, but at most only sporadically used in some of the New England States are *Entry Without Process* and *Actions at Law for a Writ of Entry or Possession.*[23] Under the former method, a mortgagee after a default may take possession of the premises without legal help. Then, after the expiration of a time period varying from one to three years, the mortgagor's equity of redemption is forever barred. The entry must be peaceable; however possession by the mortgagee may be constructive. In other words, in theory the mortgagor can become the tenant of the mortgagee. In the *Action at Law for a Writ of Entry,* the mortgagee goes into court and alleges that the mortgage is in default. There is an accounting for what is due and owing and then a judgment for possession of the premises. Then the mortgagee goes into possession and if possession is maintained for a one to three year period, depending on the jurisdiction, the mortgagor's equity of redemption is barred. Both of these methods result in strict foreclosure.

Except in those few states where strict foreclosure is authorized in normal foreclosure proceedings, the use of the remedy is limited to special situations. For example, some states authorize its use in actions to have absolute deeds declared to be mortgages.[24] Moreover, as we have seen elsewhere, its equivalent is sometimes used in statutory actions to cancel installment land contracts.[25]

21. Griesbaum v. Baum, 18 Ill.App. 614 (1886); Miller v. Davis, 5 Ill.App. 474 (1879).

22. Rabbit v. First Nat. Bank, 237 Ill. App. 289 (1925). The Illinois law has been praised as eliminating the most serious objections to strict foreclosure in America by protecting the mortgager against paying a small debt with property worth much more, losing his property and being saddled besides with a deficiency judgment, or forfeiting his property when he might be able to pay a money judgment. See note, 25 Va.L.Rev. 947, 950 (1939).

23. As to both types of foreclosure, see Mass.Gen.Laws Ann. c. 244 §§ 1–10; N.H.Rev.Stat.Ann. 479:19; R.I. Gen.Laws 34–23–3; Me.Rev.Stat.Ann. c. 14 § 6201. In Maine strict foreclosure may be accomplished by advertisement of service of notice of default and intention to foreclose followed by the passage of one year's time. Me.Rev.Stat.Ann. c. 14 §§ 6203, 6204. This statute may not constitutionally be used by any entity that would constitute the state or federal government under the 14th and 5th amendments of U. S. Constitution. See Ricker v. United States, 417 F.Supp. 133 (D.Me.1976). For further discussion of these types of foreclosure, see Osborne, Mortgages, §§ 314, 315 (2d Ed. 1970).

24. See, e. g., Hermann v. Churchill, 235 Or. 327, 385 P.2d 190 (1963), commented on in Note, 43 Or.L.Rev. 350 (1964), the court held that strict foreclosure may be decreed in a suit to have a deed absolute declared a mortgage, in spite of a statute providing for foreclosure of "all liens" by a foreclosure sale. The court said the statute did not apply to an action to redeem. See also Lenske v. Steinberg, 415 F.2d 711 (C.C.A.Or.1969) (strict foreclosure allowed where mortgagor in possession for two years had made no payments and value of land did not exceed the debt).

25. See § 3.27, supra.

The most common special situation where strict foreclosure is utilized is where a mortgagee has foreclosed by sale but has failed to join some party who has an interest in the property subject to the mortgage. The mortgagee, or a third person, may purchase at the foreclosure sale and thus unite in himself all interest in the property [26] save that of the unjoined party which is of course, unaffected by the action.[27] Where the prior foreclosure is defective because the mortgagor or owner of the property, or part of it, was not joined, strict foreclosure is not allowed, sale being required.[28] In such a case the legal title in whole or in part remains outstanding in the unjoined party; the mortgagee or third party purchaser, who succeeds in such a case only to the interest of the mortgagee and joined parties, is still only a mortgagee and must foreclose by sale in order to protect the title holder.[29] Where the legal title has passed to the purchaser on foreclosure sale, but is still subject to a redemptive right in some person whose interest is subordinate to the mortgage and who was not joined as a party to the foreclosure action strict

26. E. g., Miles v. Stehle, 22 Neb. 740, 36 N.W. 142 (1888); Sears, Roebuck & Co. v. Camp, 124 N.J.Eq. 403, 1 A.2d 425, 118 A.L.R. 762 (1938); noted, 23 Minn.L.Rev. 388 (1939). See 118 A.L.R. 769 (1939); 88 U. of Pa.L.Rev. 994 (1949). The same situation occurs where the mortgagee buys in the premises on an execution sale under a judgment against the mortgagor. Benedict v. Mortimer, 8 A. 515 (N.J. Eq.1887); Eldridge v. Eldridge, 14 N.J.Ch. 195 (1862).

27. In the absence of statute, this is generally true even though the foreclosing mortgagee has no knowledge or notice of the subordinate interest of another person in the mortgaged property. See Haines v. Beach, 3 Johns.Ch. 459, 461 (N.Y.1818); § 7.5, supra; Campbell, Cases on Mortgages, 2d ed., 273 n. 1. However, under recording acts, in accordance with their policy, if a purchaser on foreclosure sale has no actual notice of the existence of such an interest, and is not charged with constructive notice because its holder has failed to record, the latter will be bound by the foreclosure to the same extent as if he had been joined as a party. Sibell v. Weeks, 65 N.J.Eq. 714, 55 A. 244 (1903); Rogers v. Houston, 94 Tex. 403, 60 S.W. 869 (1901); Walker v. Schreiber, 47 Iowa 529 (1877), actual notice; Hoppin v. Doty, 22 Wis. 621 (1868), actual notice. See 88 U. of Pa.L.Rev. 994, 997 (1940). And if the unjoined party held only an equitable interest, it could be cut off by the foreclosure sale purchaser under the doctrine of bona fide purchase if the buyer had no notice of its existence and paid value bona fide.

28. Georgia Casualty Co. v. O'Donnell, 109 Fla. 290, 147 So. 267 (1933); Gamut v. Gregg, 37 Iowa 573 (1873); United States Sav. Bank v. Schnitzer, 118 N.J.Eq. 584, 180 A. 624 (1935); Surety Building & Loan Ass'n v. Risack, 118 N.J.Eq. 425, 179 A. 680, 22 Va.L.Rev. 227 (1935); Mickelson v. Anderson, 81 Utah 444, 19 P.2d 1033 (1933). See 118 A.L.R. 769, 779 (1939).

29. "Conceivably the interest of the omitted party, though he be not a mere encumbrancer, may be so insignificant, remote, or contingent, or be so affected by his inequitable conduct, as to render the requirement of a second foreclosure sale unnecessary, impractical, or unjust." 118 A.L.R. 769 (1939). Kansas courts have held that, in their discretion, they may permit strict foreclosure against a mortgagor or other owner to even a "mortgagee in possession." Bankers' Mortgage Co. of Topeka v. O'Donovan, 137 Kan. 309, 312, 20 P.2d 809, 811 (1933); Sutor v. First Nat. Bank, 146 Kan. 52, 69 P.2d 315 (1937).

foreclosure may be ordered.[30] We will examine further when it may be utilized against such omitted interests, chiefly junior lienors, in a subsequent section that explores all of the available remedies in the omitted party situation.[31a]

D. JUDICIAL FORECLOSURE

§ 7.11 Judicial Foreclosure—General Characteristics

Judicial foreclosure by sale in a court action in equity is the predominent method of foreclosure in the United States. It is the exclusive or generally used method of foreclosure in at least half of the states.[31] Moreover, it is available in every jurisdiction, either by virtue of express statutory enactment or as an incident to the inherent jurisdiction of courts of equity.[32] Even in jurisdictions where power

30. See 88 U. of Pa.L.Rev. 994, 1006 (1940); 25 Va.L.Rev. 947, 951; 118 A.L.R. 769, 770 (1939); Campbell, Cases Mortgages, 248 n. 4. Examples of such interests include: a junior mortgage, Leslie v. Smith, 58 S.D. 14, 234 N.W. 669 (1931); Quinn Plumbing Co. v. New Miami Shores Corp., 100 Fla. 413, 129 So. 690, 73 A.L.R. 600 (1930); Evans v. Atkins, 75 Iowa 448, 39 N.W. 702 (1888); Miles v. Stehle, 22 Neb. 740, 36 N.W. 142 (1888); Shepard v. Barrett, 84 N.J.Eq. 408, 93 A. 852 (1915); Sears, Roebuck & Co. v. Camp, 124 N.J.Eq. 403, 1 A.2d 425, 118 A.L.R. 762 (1938); a judgment lien, Koerner v. Willamette Iron Works, 36 Or. 90, 58 P. 863 (1899); Lockard v. Hendrickson, N.J. Ch., 25 A. 512 (1892); a lease, Mesiavech v. Newman, 120 N.J.Eq. 192, 184 A. 538 (1936); an easement, Hinners v. Birkevaag, 113 N.J.Eq. 413, 167 A. 209 (1933); but cf. Monese v. Struve, 155 Or. 68, 62 P.2d 822 (1936) noted, 50 Harv.L.Rev. 990 (1937); and dower, Northwestern Trust Co. v. Ryan, 115 Minn. 143, 132 N.W. 202 (1911); Loeb v. Tinkler, 124 Ind. 331, 24 N.E. 235 (1890); Eldridge v. Eldridge, 14 N.J.Eq. 195 (1862); Ross v. Boardman, 22 Hun. 527 (N.Y.1880); see 118 A.L.R. 769, 782 (1939).

31a. See § 7.15 infra.

31. As of 1968 judicial foreclosure was the exclusive or generally used foreclosure method in Arizona, Arkansas, Connecticut, Delaware, Florida, Illinois, Indiana, Iowa, Kansas, Kentucky, Louisiana, Montana, Nebraska, New Jersey, New Mexico, New York, North Dakota, Ohio, Oklahoma, Pennsylvania, South Carolina, Utah (mortgates only), Vermont and Wisconsin. See Comment, Cost and Time Factors in Foreclosure of Mortgages, 3 Real Prop.Prob. & Tr.J. 413, 414 (1968). In two of these states, Connecticut and Vermont, the foreclosure is judicial, but it is strict foreclosure. See § 7.10, supra. In Pennsylvania it was by scire facias; however, Purdon's Pa.Stat. Tit. 21 § 791 which authorized scire facias was suspended in 1950 by Rule of Civ.Pro. 1460. As a practical matter, Pennsylvania seems to be a judicial foreclosure state. See 3 Real Prop.Prob. & Tr.J. at 427. Delaware utilizes scire facias. Upon default, the mortgagee may obtain a writ of scire facias directing the mortgagor to appear and show cause why the property should not be seized and sold in satisfaction of the debt. If the mortgagor fails to appear, the court is empowered to enter a judgment by default and direct that the mortgagee is entitled to execution by levari facias. See Gelof v. First Nat. Bank of Frankford, 373 A.2d 206 (Del.1977). For a further consideration of scire facias, see Osborne, Mortgages, § 316 (2d Ed. 1970).

32. Chancellor Kent in Mills v. Dennis, 3 Johns.Ch. 367 (N.Y.1818), sustained the power, and nine years later, in a basic decision, it was recognized as both an inherent part of equity jurisdiction and also authorized by statute. Lansing v. Goelet, 9 Cowen, 346 (N.Y.1827). See Belloc v. Rogers, 9

of sale foreclosure is dominant, judicial foreclosure is required in certain special situations. For example, it will be necessary where the mortgage fails to create a power of sale. This situation will arise where the mortgage form omits any reference to a power of sale. It can also occur where one is seeking to foreclose an absolute deed as a mortgage because, by its very nature, the absolute deed will not contain a power of sale.[33] Finally judicial foreclosure will be required where there is a serious lien priority dispute. In such a situation a judicial determination of lien priority will be enable potential foreclosure sale purchasers to know the state of the title they will be bidding on and thus judicial foreclosure will be encouraged. On the other hand, if power of sale foreclosure were used, the uncertainty as to lien priority would discourage bidding and create title problems for the ultimate sale purchaser.

In spite of being the most pervasive method of foreclosure in America today, justified to an extent by the fact that it is the best method of determining conclusively the rights of all interested parties and, consequently, of producing the firmest and most marketable title, it has serious disadvantages. It is complicated, costly, and time-consuming.[34] A typical action in equity to foreclose and sell involves a long series of steps: a preliminary title search to determine all parties in interest; filing of the foreclosure bill of complaint and lis pendens notice; service of process; a hearing, usually by a master in chancery who then reports to the court; the decree or judgment; notice of sale; actual sale and issuance of certificate of sale; report of the sale; proceedings for determination of the right to any surplus; possible redemptions from foreclosure sale; and the entry of a decree for a deficiency.[35] The following sections focus on some of the more important aspects and problems of judicial foreclosure.

§ 7.12 Parties Defendant and the "Necessary-Proper" Party Distinction

Persons are made parties defendant in a foreclosure action for one of two purposes: one is to give the court jurisdiction to make a valid order to sell the person's interest in the mortgaged property at the foreclosure sale; the other is to obtain a decree against him on the mortgage obligation. Strictly speaking, foreclosure is

Cal. 123 (1858); Sprague, History of Chancery and Advertisement Foreclosures in Michigan, 5 Detroit L.Rev. 63, 64ff (1935).

33. See § 3.8, supra.

34. See Comment, Cost and Time Factors in Foreclosure of Mortgages, 3 Real Prop.Prob. & Tr.J. 413 (1968); McElhone & Cramer, Loan Foreclosure Costs Affected by Varied State Regulations, 36 Mortgage Banker 41 (1975); Comment, Power of Sale After Fuentes, 40 U.Chi.L.Rev. 206, 210–211 (1972); Carey, et al., Studies in Foreclosures in Cook County: Foreclosure Methods and Redemption, 27 Ill.L.Rev. 595, 596–609 (1933); Bridewell, The Effects of Defective Mortgage Laws on Home Financing, 5 Law & Contemp.Probs. 545, 549ff (1938), especially Table I, p. 555.

35. Carey, et al. and Bridewell, supra note 34.

only concerned with the first objective. However, in jurisdictions where a decree for a deficiency may be had in the same equitable action after the property has been sold in the foreclosure suit,[35a] it is a customary feature of the proceeding, even though the nature of that part of the action and decree which seeks to so bind the named defendant is fundamentally different from the foreclosure sale portion of it.

In dealing with the question of who should or may be made parties defendant in a foreclosure action, it is common to draw a distinction between "necessary" and "proper" parties.[36] There is, however, no generally agreed-on meaning for either term.[37] The terminology is useful, however, if it is used in the context of the basic purposes of the foreclosure proceeding. Two such purposes are often articulated. First, it is said that foreclosure should, if successful, terminate the rights of all interested parties who have a right to redeem from or are "subject to" the mortgage being foreclosed.[38] To state this proposition however is to beg the question "why"? The answer is found in the more fundamental and descriptive purpose of foreclosure, which is to give the foreclosure sale purchaser essentially the same title to the land as that possessed by the mortgagor when the foreclosed mortgage was executed.[39] In this sense, then, a party is "necessary" if failure to join him will not accomplish the purposes for foreclosure described above. For example, if a first mortgage is judicially foreclosed and a second mortgagee is not made a party, the foreclosure will not affect or terminate the rights of the junior mortgagee. The latter's mortgage will remain on the land. The sale purchaser will receive a title fundamentally different from the one the mortgagor had when the foreclosed mortgage was executed. It should be emphasized, however, that the failure to join such a necessary party does not render the entire foreclosure proceeding invalid; rather it is deemed to be ineffective only as to those necessary parties who were not joined.[40]

35a. E. g., West's Ann.Cal.Code, Civ. Proc., § 726.

36. E. g., Iowa County Board of Supervisors v. Mineral Point R. R. Co., 24 Wis. 93 (1869). See Terrell v. Allison, 88 U.S. (21 Wall.) 289, 22 L.Ed. 634 (1874); Gage v. Perry, 93 Ill. 176 (1879).

37. "The question as to who may or may not be necessary or proper parties * * * constitutes of itself a title in the law of equity jurisprudence, upon which great learning has been expended, without the ascertainment of any rule of general or universal application." Iowa County Board of Supervisors v. Mineral Point R. R. Co., 24 Wis. 93 (1869). See note, 88 U. of Pa.L.Rev. 994, 996 (1940), bringing out that the tests differ according to the stage at which the question is raised, this being especially true as between the period before and after sale.

38. See § 7.2, supra.

39. See, e. g., Valentine v. Portland Timber and Land Holding Co., 15 Wash.App. 124, 547 P.2d 912 (1976); San Francisco v. Lawton, 18 Cal. 465 (1861). See also, Dye v. Lewis, 67 Misc.2d 426, 324 N.Y.S.2d 172 (1971).

40. E. g., Iowa County Board of Supervisors v. Mineral Point R. R. Co.,

A "proper" party, on the other hand, is one whose presence in the suit is convenient and desirable, and who, if joined, will be bound by the proceedings, but whose absence will not defeat the purposes of foreclosure outlined in the preceding paragraph. It is often said that only those who are subject to the mortgage being foreclosed can properly be joined without their consent.[41] A senior lienor is not a necessary party because he is not subject to or subordinate to the mortgage being foreclosed. To omit him from a foreclosure suit brought by a junior lienor will not defeat the purposes of foreclosure because his lien existed on the land as of the time the mortgage being foreclosed was executed. Nevertheless, there are occasions when it is desireable to make the senior lienor a party, at least for limited purposes. For example, in order that a foreclosure purchase subject to the senior lien be intelligently made and bring a maximum amount, it is important that the senior lienor be made a party for the purpose of making clear and definite the nature and extent of the prior lien.[42] The extent to which such senior interests may be joined and for what purposes will be explored later in this chapter.[43]

A comprehensive catalogue of all the various classes of persons who would qualify under the foregoing principles as necessary defendants in an action to foreclose a mortgage by sale is so formidable[44] that only a few of the more important instances can serve as examples.[45]

First in any list comes one who has title to the general ownership of the property subject to the mortgage or any part of it. The mortgagor so long as he retains the property falls under this category and must be joined.[45a] But the mortgagor frequently sells the property and in that case the purchaser of the entire property or any part of it must be made a party.[46] If the mortgagor has parted with all of the property he is no longer a necessary party for foreclosure

24 Wis. 93 (1869); Spokane Sav. & Loan Soc. v. Liliopoulos, 160 Wash. 71, 294 P. 561 (1930). See 88 U. of Pa.L.Rev. 994 (1940); Hagan v. Gardner, 283 F.2d 643 (C.A.Cal.1960).

41. See § 7.14, infra.

42. See Dye v. Lewis, 67 Misc.2d 426, 324 N.Y.S.2d 172 (1971); § 7.14, infra.

43. See § 7.14, infra.

44. E. g., in Wiltsie, Mortgage Foreclosure, 5th ed., § 329, are listed 51 different classes of persons who, either normally or under certain circumstances or in certain states, may be joined as defendants. 103 pages are devoted to covering parties who are such by having an interest in the property subject to the mortgage. Chs. XX, XXI. An additional 15 pages is devoted to prior lienors and adverse claimants, Ch. XXIII. And another 20 pages to parties who are made defendants because personally liable. Ch. XXIV.

45. Section 7.2, supra, contains a discussion of those who have a right to redeem from the mortgage. By definition, those who have a right to redeem are generally necessary parties.

45a. See Goodenow v. Ewer, 16 Cal. 461, 76 Am.Dec. 540 (1860).

46. Terrell v. Allison, 88 U.S. (21 Wall.) 289, 22 L.Ed. 634 (1874); Walker v. Warner, 179 Ill. 16, 53 N.E. 594, 70 Am.St.Rep. 85 (1899); Fowler v. Lilly, 122 Ind. 297, 23 N.E. 767 (1889); Winslow v. Clark, 47 N.Y. 261 (1872). See Slingluff, The Mort-

purposes.[47] Since he is the obligor, and normally remains such, he is usually joined in order that a personal decree may be entered against him in case of a deficiency. A transferee who in turn has disposed of the property is likewise unnecessary for foreclosure.[48] If he has assumed the mortgage debt he may be joined so as to get a deficiency decree against him as in the similar case of a mortgagor who has divested himself of all interest in the property.[49] On the death of a mortgagor or person in whom the present ownership of the property subject to the mortgage is vested, the persons in whom the title then vests, the heirs or devisees, must be joined in the foreclosure.[50] Where a dower interest is made subject to a mortgage the wife or widow is an essential party to foreclosure.[51] Where there are future interests created in the property subject to the mortgage, there are many statements that contingent remaindermen need not be made parties to a foreclosure action, that it is sufficient to join the first person in being who has a vested estate of inheritance.[52] However, if contingent remaindermen are living and available, they should be joined.[53] Although the general rule is that both trustees and beneficiaries should be made parties,[54] there are important exceptions.[55]

gagee's Right in the Event of a Deficiency, 1 Md.L.Rev. 128 (1937).

47. Smith v. Varney, 309 A.2d 229 (Me.1973); Thompson v. Menfee, 218 Ala. 332, 118 So. 587 (1928); Brockway v. McClun, 243 Ill. 196, 90 N.E. 374 (1909); Fitzgerald v. Flanagan, 155 Iowa 217, 135 N.W. 738, Ann. Cas.1914C, 1104 (1912); Delacroix v. Stanley, 113 N.J.Eq. 121, 165 A. 882 (1933); McNeal v. Moberly, 150 Okl. 253, 1 P.2d 707 (1931).

48. Howell v. Baker, 106 N.J.Eq. 434, 151 A. 117 (1930); James v. Brainard-Jackson Co., 64 Wash. 175, 116 P. 633 (1911).

49. Scarry v. Eldridge, 63 Ind. 44 (1878); Vrooman v. Turner, 69 N.Y. 280, 25 Am.R. 195 (1877). See § 8.1, infra; §§ 5.11–5.16, supra.

50. White v. Rittenmyer, 30 Iowa 268 (1870); Abbott v. Godfroy's Heirs, 1 Mich. 178 (1849); Chadbourn v. Johnston, 119 N.C. 282, 25 S.E. 705 (1896); Chew v. Hyman, 7 F. 7 (C.C.Ill.1881). Cf., Reedy v. Camfield, 159 Ill. 254, 42 N.E. 833 (1896). Statutes sometimes provide that the personal representative rather than the heir or devisee shall be made a party. See Tierney v. Spiva, 97 Mo. 98, 10 S.W. 433 (1888); Kelsey v. Welch, 8 S.D. 255, 66 N.W. 390 (1896). For a holding that the personal representative is a necessary party, apparently in absence of statute, see Citizens Bank, Dumright v. Satcher, 521 P.2d 819 (Okl.1974).

51. Bigoness v. Hibbard, 267 Ill. 301, 108 N.E. 294 (1915), commented on in, 10 Ill.L.Rev. 137 (1915); McArthur v. Franklin, 15 Ohio St. 485, 16 Ohio St. 193 (1865).

52. See Jones, Mortgages, 8th ed., § 1401; Wiltsie, Mortgage Foreclosure, 5th ed., § 362. See also Hanna, Cas. Security, 3d ed., 1019, note, citing, Shackley v. Homer, 87 Neb. 146, 127 N.W. 145, L.R.A.1915C, 993 (1910); McCampbell v. Mason, 151 Ill. 500, 38 N.E. 672 (1894); see Clarke v. Cordis, 86 Mass. (4 Allen) 466, 478 (1862); Powell v. Wright, 7 Beav. 444 (1844).

53. See Hess v. Hess, 233 N.Y. 164, 135 N.E. 231 (1922); N.Y.Real Prop. Actions & Proc.Law, McKinney § 1311 (1963) and N.Y.Estates Powers & Trusts Law, McKinney § 6–5.1 (1967); Mass.Gen.Laws, Ann. c. 244, § 13 (1959).

54. Clark v. Reyburn, 75 U.S. 318, 8 Wall. 318, 19 L.Ed. 354 (1868). See Iowa County Bd. of Supervisors v.

55. See note 55 on page 451.

One of these, "as well established as the rule itself, * * * is, that whenever the parties in interest are, or from the nature of the case, may be, so numerous that it would be difficult or impractical to bring them all before the court, and their rights are such as may be fairly and fully represented and tried without joining them, the application of the rule may be dispensed with." [56]

In addition to the foregoing, all persons who have an interest in the mortgaged premises acquired by or through the owner of the property subject to the mortgage subsequent to its execution must be made defendants.[57] Under this classification fall junior mortgagees, mechanics lienors and holders of other subordinate liens.[58] The owner of an easement or restrictive covenant falls within the same reasoning.[59]

Lessees present special problems in foreclosure proceedings. It is well settled that a lease prior to a mortgage is unaffected by a foreclosure. The purchaser at the sale obtains the mortgagor's interest and becomes the lessee's landlord.[60] Since the lease is unaffected by the foreclosure, the lessee is not a "necessary" party in a judicial foreclosure proceeding. On the other hand, where the mortgage is prior to the lease and the lessee is joined, the foreclosure extinguishes the lease.[61] "There is no privity of either estate or contract between the mortgagee and the lessee of the morgagor to bind either, and the foreclosure of the mortgage avoids the lease and releases the lessee from any obligation. . . . Whenever the estate which the landlord had at the time of making the lease is defeated or determined, the lease is extinguished with it." [62]

Suppose, however, that the junior lessee is not joined. Under the majority rule the lessee's interest remains unaffected by the foreclosure.[63] But what does this mean as a practical matter for the

Mineral Point R. R. Co., 24 Wis. 93 (1869); White v. Macqueen, 360 Ill. 236, 195 N.E. 832, 93 A.L.R. 1115 (1935); Williamson v. Field's Ex'rs & Devisees, 2 Sandf.Ch. 533 (N.Y.1845). First Nat. Bank v. Leslie, 106 N.J.Eq. 564, 151 A. 501 (1930).

55. See Wiltsie, Mortgage Foreclosure, 5th ed., § 360.

56. Iowa County Board of Supervisors v. Mineral Point R. R. Co., 24 Wis. 93 (1869). See State ex rel. Ashley v. Circuit Court, 219 Wis. 38, 47, 261 N.W. 737, 741 (1935). See also 20 L. R.A. 535 (1893); 1908, 16 L.R.A.,N.S., 1006 (1908); 35 L.R.A.,N.S., 196 (1912).

57. See, e. g., Yarbrough v. John Deere Industrial Equipment Co., 526 S.W.2d 188 (Tex.Civ.App.1975).

58. E. g., Yarbrough v. John Deere Industrial Equipment Co., 526 S.W.2d 188 (Tex.Civ.App.1974); Motor Equipment Co. v. Winters, 146 Kan. 127, 69 P.2d 23 (1937) (junior mortgage); Lenexa State Bank & Trust Co. v. Dixon, 221 Kan. 238, 559 P.2d 776 (1977).

59. Rector of Christ Protestant Episcopal Church v. Mack, 93 N.Y. 488, 45 Am.R. 260 (1883); Krich v. Zemel, 99 N.J.L. 191, 122 A. 739 (1897).

60. Annot. 14 A.L.R. 664, 678.

61. Annot. 109 A.L.R. 447, 451.

62. Roosevelt Hotel Corp. v. Williams, 227 Mo.App. 1063, 56 S.W.2d 801, 802 (1933).

63. Metropolitan Life Ins. Co. v. Childs, 230 N.Y. 285, 130 N.E. 295;

lessee and the mortgagee? In theory one compelling upshot of the majority rule is that the mortgagee, at his option, may have the property sold subject to the lease or free and clear of it. The mortgagee exercises this option by joining or not joining the lessee in the foreclosure action.[64] If the lessee is not joined his lease is unaffected by the foreclosure sale and the purchaser may enforce the lease as the transferee of the reversion.[65] If he is joined, the purchaser takes the property title as it existed at the time the mortgage was entered into, i. e., free of the subsequent lease, and may therefore evict the lessee.

To permit the above option results in conferring a bonus on the mortgagee who violates the normal foreclosure maxim encouraging the joinder of all junior interests. Indeed, a mortgagee, operating on the usually sound assumption that he will be the foreclosure sale purchaser, could very well intentionally omit a junior lessee in order to preserve a lease that is substantially more pro-landlord than would be possible if negotiated under current market conditions. Perhaps a preferable approach would be to give the unjoined junior lessee the option of being bound by the lease or of treating it as terminated. Such an approach would tend to encourage pre-foreclosure settlement of lease problems between the lessee and the mortgagee-probable purchaser and would discourage manipulation of traditional foreclosure concepts. There is some case law support for it.[66]

14 A.L.R. 658 (1921), reargument denied 231 N.Y. 551, 132 N.E. 885; Dundee Naval Stores Co. v. McDowell, 65 Fla. 15, 61 So. 108, Ann. Cas.1915A, 387 (1913). See 17 Wash.L.Rev. 37, 43 (1942); 21 Minn. L.Rev. 610 (1937); 8 Wash.L.Rev. 184 (1934). See also 14 A.L.R. 664, 672 (1921); L.R.A.1915C, 190, 204. There is some divergence of opinion as to the effect of nonjoinder. The New York rule is that the purchaser on foreclosure sale takes the property subject to the lease just as though he were a purchaser of the reversion. Metropolitan Life Ins. Co. v. Childs, supra. See 17 Wash.L.Rev. 37, 44 et seq. (1942). Other states leave the status of an unjoined lessee somewhat in doubt. See 21 Minn.L.Rev. 611 (1937). A minority of cases seem to hold that a junior lease is extinguished, whether or not joined. See Dolese v. Bellows-Claude Neon Co., 261 Mich. 57, 245 N.W. 569 (1932) discussed in note, 32 Mich.L.Rev. 119 (1933); McDermott v. Burke, 16 Cal. 580 (1860). See 14 A.L.R. 664, 668 (1921).

64. See notes, 14 A.L.R. 664 (1921); Ann.Cas.1915A, 397; 42 Harv.L.Rev. 280 (1928); 13 Col.L.Rev. 553 (1913); 21 Minn.L.Rev. 610 (1937), 1942, 42 Wash.L.Rev. 37. See generally, Hyde, The Real Estate Lease as a Credit Instrument, 20 Bus.Law, 359, 389 (1965).

65. See Metropolitan Life Ins. Co. v. Childs Co., 230 N.Y. 285, 130 N.E. 295, 14 A.L.R. 658 (1921) reargument denied 231 N.Y. 551, 132 N.E. 885, "If * * * he [the tenant] is not a party to the action, his rights are not affected. There is never an eviction. Until the sale he must pay his landlord. Afterwards the purchaser. As to the latter there is no necessity of attornment." The foreclosure sale "was a grant of what interest the mortgagor had in the property at the time the mortgage was given, less the leased estate—the grant of what was left after the leased estate was subtracted. It is precisely the same so far as the estate granted was concerned as if the lease had been prior to the mortgage."

66. See Dolese v. Bellows-Claude Neon Co., 261 Mich. 57, 245 N.W. 569 (1932), where the court held that a mortgage foreclosure purchaser could

§ 7.13 Joinder—Effect of Recording Acts and Lis Pendens

The general rule is that lack of knowledge or notice of the subordinate interest of another person in the mortgaged land does not excuse a foreclosing mortgagee from making such person a party to his suit. If he fails to do so, the subordinate interest, regardless of whether it be legal or equitable and one of ownership or lien, is not subject to the decree.[67] There are, however, limitations upon the operation of this rule. A purchaser on the foreclosure sale who acquires the legal title for which he pays value without notice of the unjoined interest qualifies as a *bona fide* purchaser and thus will take free of such an interest if it is equitable only.[68] Similarly, under the familiar type of statute avoiding unrecorded conveyances as against subsequent purchasers, a purchaser on foreclosure sale who buys without knowledge or notice of an outstanding but unrecorded interest may take free and clear of it just as effectively as though its holder had been joined in the foreclosure action.[69] Moreover, while there is authority to the contrary,[70] there is recent case law for the proposition that the foreclosing mortgagee can qualify as a bona fide purchaser under such statutes.[71] Other statutes, either explicitly or as

not recover rent from the lessee even though the lessee was junior and not joined in the foreclosure action. See also, New York Life Ins. Co. v. Simplex Products Corp., 135 Ohio St. 501, 21 N.E.2d 585, 14 O.O. 396 (1939); Davis v. Boyajian, Inc., 11 Ohio Misc. 97, 229 N.E.2d 116, 40 O.O.2d 344 (1967).

67. First National Bank v. Leslie, 106 N.J.Eq. 564, 151 A. 501 (1930), commented on, Campbell, Cases Mortgages, 2d ed. 274 n. 3; Pancoast v. Geishaker, 58 N.J.Eq. 537, 43 A. 883 (1899); White v. Melchert, 208 Iowa 1404, 1407, 227 N.W. 347, 348, 73 A.L.R. 595 (1929); Nelson v. First Nat. Bank, 199 Iowa 804, 202 N.W. 847 (1925); Holliger v. Bates, 43 Ohio St. 437, 2 N.E. 841 (1885); Mesiavich v. Newman, 120 N.J.Eq. 192, 184 A. 538 (1936).

68. See First Nat. Bank of Union City v. Leslie, 106 N.J.Eq. 654, 151 A. 501 (1930); Pancoast v. Geishaker, 58 N.J.Eq. 537, 43 A. 883 (1899). See §§ 6.5, 6.9, supra. "*Bona fide suit* in which the legal title is brought before the court is analogous to *bona fide purchase* of legal title, and it may well be asked why the suitor is not equally protected. * * * Yet we know of no case which has extended the equitable doctrine of bona fide purchase to the case of the suitor." Durfee and Fleming, Res Judicata and Recording Acts, 28 Mich.L.Rev. 811, 814, n. 6 (1930).

69. Valentine v. Portland Timber and Land Holding Co., 15 Wash.App. 124, 547 P.2d 912 (1976); Pinney v. The Merchants' Nat. Bank, 71 Ohio St. 173, 72 N.E. 884 (1904); Duff v. Randall, 116 Cal. 226, 48 P. 66, 58 Am. St.Rep. 158 (1897); Shippen v. Kimball, 47 Kans. 173, 27 P. 813 (1891); Ehle v. Brown, 31 Wis. 405 (1872). Possession under some circumstances may give notice. See Ehle v. Brown, 31 Wis. 405, 413 (1872); Hodson v. Treat, 7 Wis. 263 (1858); Noyes v. Hall, 97 U.S. 34, 24 L.Ed. 909 (C.C. Ill.1877). See 89 A.L.R. 171, 182 (1934).

70. See Durfee and Fleming, Res Judicata and Recording Acts, 28 Mich.L. Rev. 811, 819 (1926).

71. "Public policy reasons dictate that the recording statute should protect the foreclosing mortgagee as well as the purchaser at a foreclosure sale against unrecorded and unknown interests." Valentine v. Portland Timber and Land Holding Co., 15 Wash. App. 124, 129, 547 P.2d 912, 916 (1976).

interpreted, go beyond this and have the effect of concluding an unjoined party whose interest was not recorded as effectively as though he had been made a party to the suit.[72] Under the most extreme of these, this is true even though the mortgagee at the time he began his foreclosure action had actual knowledge of the unrecorded interest.[73] It seems highly desirable to protect both the foreclosing mortgagee as well as a purchaser on foreclosure sale against interests that are acquired but remain unrecorded prior to the beginning of a foreclosure action. That protection should extend at least far enough to cut off all such interests of which there was no actual notice before suit, or actual knowledge during the pendency of the litigation.[74]

While the bona fide purchase rule and the recording statutes aid the foreclosing mortgagee, his interests are, in addition, substantially served by the lis pendens doctrine. That doctrine concerns persons who acquire an interest in real estate which is subject to litigation. If the property is specifically described and within the court's jurisdiction, it is taken subject to the final determination in the action; it is immaterial that the person acquiring it is not named as a party or that he has no actual knowledge of either the suit or the claim under litigation.[75] Some cases erroneously fail to differentiate the doctrine from that of actual notice of the plaintiff's rights,[76] which would bind a taker of the property regardless of pendency of litigation, the principle of privity of title which applies to alienees after judgment against a grantor,[77] and the rule that property in custody of the court

72. See Durfee and Fleming, Res Judicata and Recording Acts: Does a Judgment Conclude Non-Parties of Whose Interests the Plaintiff Has No Notice? 28 Mich.L.Rev. 811 (1930). See also Campbell, Cases Mortgages, 2d ed., 277, n. 3; note, 25 Cal.L.Rev. 480 (1937); note 88 U. of Pa.L.Rev. 994, 997 (1940). See Curtis, The Commission and the Law of Real Property, 40 Cornell L.Q. 755 (1955).

73. West's Ann.Cal.Code Civ.Proc., § 726, "No person holding a conveyance from or under the mortgagor of the property mortgaged, or having a lien thereon, which conveyance or lien does not appear of record in the proper office at the time of the commencement of the action need be made a party to such action, and the judgment therein rendered, and the proceedings therein had, are as conclusive against the party holding such unrecorded conveyance or lien as if he had been a party to the action." Hager v. Astorg, 145 Cal. 548, 79 P. 68, 104 Am.St.Rep. 68 (1904); Collingwood v. Brown, 106 N.C. 362, 10 S.E. 868 (1890); cf. Holman v. Toten, 54 Cal.App.2d 309, 128 P.2d 808 (1942).

74. See Valentine, supra note 71, quoting text with approval.

75. See 47 Harv.L.Rev. 1023, 1024 (1934); 25 Cal.L.Rev. 480 (1937).

76. E. g., not observing the distinction between lis pendens and actual notice: Fogg v. Providence Lumber Co., 15 R.I. 15, 23 A. 31 (1885); Dent v. Pickens, 59 W.Va. 274, 53 S.E. 154 (1906). On the other hand, observing the difference: Dillard & Coffin Co. v. Smith, 105 Tenn. 372, 59 S.W. 1010 (1900); People's Bank of Wilkesbarre v. Columbia Collieries Co., 75 W.Va. 309, 84 S.E. 914 (1914).

77. Gale v. Tuolumne County Water Co., 169 Cal. 46, 145 P. 532 (1914); Hungate v. Hetzer, 83 Kan. 265, 111 P. 183 (1910); Comanche Ice & Fuel Co. v. Binder & Hillery, 70 Okl. 28, 172 P. 629 (1917).

cannot be alienated in derogation of the court's later order.[78] Courts frequently speak of the doctrine as resting upon constructive notice,[79] but its true basis is public policy, the necessity of having such a rule in order to give effect to the judgments of courts. Without such a rule, it would be possible to defeat the judgment by a conveyance to some stranger, and the plaintiff would be forced to commence a new action against him.[80]

The hardship of the judicial doctrine of lis pendens upon innocent purchasers of property who, as a practical matter, could not discover pending litigation affecting the property they bought, led to the enactment generally in the United States of statutes compelling litigants to file notice of the pendency of their suits in order for third parties to be bound by the doctrine.[81] Since few of the statutes [82] include the entire field of the judicial doctrine, and since the judicial doctrine is unaffected except to the extent that the statutes apply, there are many situations in which it still operates—a fact that might prove a pitfall to the unwary purchaser who relied solely upon an investigation of the records of notice.[83]

Even as to situations covered by the statutes there are problems as to their effect. Clearly the recorded notice of lis pendens will bind all subsequent mortgagees and grantees of the property, but what is its effect upon prior unrecorded mortgages and other conveyances? There seems no doubt that if a foreclosing party has actual knowledge of the unrecorded mortgage at the time of filing his notice, the mortgagee will not be bound by the foreclosure proceeding unless made a party to the action.[84] Where he learns of the unrecorded

78. E. g., where the property has been attached, sequestered or is in the hands of a receiver. Merchants' Nat. Bank of Omaha v. McDonald, 63 Neb. 363, 88 N.W. 492 (1901) rehearing denied 63 Neb. 363, 89 N.W. 770; Sherburne v. Strawn, 52 Kan. 39, 34 P. 405 (1883); Young v. Clapp, 147 Ill. 176, 32 N.E. 187 (1892), s. c., 35 N.E. 372 (1893).

79. E. g., "A *lis pendens* duly prosecuted is notice to a purchaser so as to effect and bind his interest." Jackson ex dem. Hendricks v. Andrews, 7 Wend. 152, 156, 22 Am.Dec. 574 (N.Y.1831).

80. See Newman v. Chapman, 23 Va. 93, 102, 14 Am.Dec. 766 (1823); Jarrett v. Holland, 213 N.C. 428, 196 S.E. 314 (1938); Brown v. Cohn, 95 Wis. 90, 69 N.W. 71, 60 Am.St.Rep. 83 (1896). "This necessity [of the rule] is so obvious, that there was no occasion to resort to the presumption that the purchaser really had or by inquiry might have had, notice of the pendency of the suit, to justify the existence of the rule. In fact, it applied in cases in which there was a physical impossibility that the purchaser could know, with any possible diligence on his part, of the existence of the suit, * * *." Newman v. Chapman, supra, at 102.

81. E. g., West's Ann.Cal.Code Civ. Proc. § 409; McKinney's N.Y. CPLR 6501.

82. Only three statutes embrace all of lis pendens. Fla.S.A. § 48.23; Mich.C. L.A. § 565.25; Va.Code 1950, §§ 8.01–268, 8.01–269.

83. See 20 Iowa L.Rev. 476, 480–483 (1934).

84. See Munger v. T. J. Beard & Bro., 79 Neb. 764, 113 N.W. 214, 126 Am. St.Rep. 688 (1907); Lamont v. Cheshire, 65 N.Y. 30 (1875).

mortgage after recording notice and before judgment one jurisdiction[85] at least imposes upon him the affirmative duty of joining the holder of the mortgage, but several others merely permit the latter to intervene and, if he fails to do so, he is bound by the judgment.[86]

§ 7.14 Senior Lienors and Adverse Interests

The general rule is that the holder of a paramount lien cannot be made a party to a foreclosure action without his consent.[87] The reasons are both logical and practical in nature. Ultimately the purpose is to place the foreclosure sale purchaser in the position of the mortgagor when the foreclosed mortgage was executed.[88] Thus, the proper object of a foreclosure action is to sell the property given as security by the mortgagor and in doing so cut off the rights of redemption in that property of the mortgagor and everyone claiming under him. A junior mortgagee's security is the property subject to prior encumbrances. That, therefore, is all that can be sold when he forecloses his lien, and only rights of redemption based upon it can be cut off by the sale.[89] Since a senior mortgagee's interest cannot be affected by an action to foreclose a junior lien, it follows that an attempt to join him as a party to such an action can be defeated through timely objection. Such is the logic of the rule. To it is added the practical reason that the prior mortgagee should be able to choose his own time for selling and not be forced to realize in a market that in his judgment is unfavorable.[90] The argument is especially strong when the junior's foreclosure action is brought before the senior lien has matured, and it has force even if it is due.

There are, however, qualifications. One of them is suggested by the rule as stated. There is no reason why, if the first mortgagee is

85. Chaudoin v. Claypool, 174 Wash. 608, 25 P.2d 1036 (1933), note, 8 Wash.L.Rev. 197 (1934).

86. Bristol Lumber Co. v. Dery, 114 Conn. 88, 157 A. 640 (1931); Ayrault v. Murphy, 54 N.Y. 203 (1873).

87. Hudnit v. Nash, 16 N.J.Eq. 550, 560 (1862); Krause v. Hartung, 108 N.J.Eq. 507, 155 A. 621 (1931); Osage Oil & Refining Co. v. Muber Oil Co., 43 F.2d 306, 308 (C.C.A.Okl., 1930); Jerome v. McCarter, 94 U.S. 734, 24 L.Ed. 136 (1876); Cf. Scott & Wimbrow v. Calwell, 31 Md.App. 1, 354 A.2d 463 (1976).

88. See § 7.12, supra.

89. Fendley v. Smith, 217 Ala. 166, 115 So. 103 (1928); Armand's Engineering, Inc. v. Town and Country Club Inc., 113 R.I. 515, 324 A.2d 334 (1974).

90. "Lands which today are a slender security for money which may have been loaned by way of mortgage become amply sufficient tomorrow. But if the plaintiff's [subsequent lienor] theory be correct, the mortgagee, as against a subsequent incumbrancer by way of mortgage, cannot exercise his own judgment as to whether he will retain his lien until the security becomes good. * * * The rights of the parties could not thus be reversed, except with the express consent of the prior incumbrancer." McReynolds v. Munns, 41 N.Y. (2 Keyes) 214 (N.Y.1865). See Campbell, Cases Mortgages, 2d ed., 261 n. 5a, for additional authorities.

willing to be a party to the action, he should not be.[91] Consequently if he becomes a party on his own motion he will be bound by the decree.[92] Furthermore, if he is joined in an action in which the plaintiff alleges that the defendant's lien is a prior one and asks that the property be sold free of it, his failure to appear and object operates as consent and bars his mortgage.[93] In such a case the property is sold free of both liens, but the respective priorities persist as to the proceeds.

The possibility of joinder, however, goes beyond active consent or acquiescence of a prior lienor. The junior mortgagee is seeking a sale, and in order to have one in which possible buyers will participate and pay a proper price for the property, the nature and extent of prior liens should be determined so that a prospective purchaser may know with certainty for what he is paying his money. Consequently, even though the senior lien is not yet due, the foreclosing junior mortgagee may join its owner for the purpose of such determination.[94] Moreover, there is authority that the question of priority of encumbrances, i. e., whether another lien is prior or subsequent to the one being foreclosed, may be litigated in a foreclosure action.[95] Where a paramount mortgage debt is due and payable, or will be before decree and sale, such prior mortgagee may be joined and the property sold under what amounts to a joint foreclosure of both mortgages, the proceeds being used to pay off the mortgagees in the order of their priority.[96] This deprives an earlier

91. "But prior lienors may consent to become parties to such an action, or may be made such, where the object is to ascertain the extent of their claims, and to have the premises sold subject thereto, or absolutely to create a fund out of which the several incumbrances shall be paid in their order; but such purpose or object should clearly appear from the complaint." Foster v. Johnson, 44 Minn. 290, 292, 46 N.W. 350 (1890). Cf. Gargan v. Grimes, 47 Iowa 180 (1877); Champlin v. Foster, 7 B.Mon., Ky., 104 (1846); Cochran v. Goodell, 131 Mass. 464 (1881); Roll v. Smalley, 6 N.J.Eq. 464 (1847); Western Ins. Co. v. Eagle Fire Ins. Co., 1 Paige, N.Y., 284 (1828); Vanderkemp v. Shelton, 11 Paige, N.Y., 28 (1844).

92. See Kraus v. Hartung, 111 N.J.Eq. 531, 533, 162 A. 724, 725 (1932); 89 U. of Pa.L.Rev. 373, 379 (1941). Cf. Palmer v. Guaranty Trust Co., 111 F. 2d 115 (C.C.A.N.Y.1940). But cf., McReynolds v. Munn, 41 N.Y. (2 Keyes) 214 (1865). See note 91, supra.

93. Jacobie v. Wickle, 144 N.Y. 237, 39 N.E. 66 (1894).

94. Missouri K. & T. Trust Co. v. Richardson, 57 Neb. 617, 78 N.W. 273 (1899); see Foster v. Johnson, 44 Minn. 290, 292, 46 N.W. 350, 351 (1890); Jerome v. McCarter, 94 U.S. 734, 736, 24 L.Ed. 136 (1876). But see Kraus v. Hartung, 111 N.J.Eq. 531, 533, 162 A. 724, 725 (1932).

95. Iowa County Board of Supervisors v. Mineral Point R. R. Co., 24 Wis. 93 (1869); see Whipple v. Edelstein, 148 Misc. 681, 684, 266 N.Y.S. 127, 131 (1933); cf. Ruyter v. Wickes, 22 N.Y. S. 200, 4 N.Y.S. 743 (S.Ct.1889) affirmed 121 N.Y. 498, 24 N.E. 791, 31 St.R. 387. Contra, Krause v. Hartung, 1931, 108 N.J.Eq. 507, 155 A. 621 (1931), second mortgage expressly subject to first mortgage. And cf. Dawson v. Danbury Bank, 15 Mich. 489 (1867); Strobe v. Downer, 13 Wis. 11, 80 Am.Dec. 709 (1860). And see note 35, infra.

96. Hagan v. Walker, 55 U.S. (14 How.) 29, 37, 14 L.Ed. 312 (1852);

mortgagee of the privilege of exercising his own judgment as to when he will foreclose and sell his security.[97] It is justified as being, in effect, the enforcement of the junior mortgagee's right to redeem in order to protect his own security; and to do so without the necessity of advancing out of his own funds the amount necessary to do so, a requirement which often makes the right, as a practical matter, illusory.[98] And there are other instances where the interests of the mortgagor and encumbrancers require that a prior mortgagee be joined and the property be sold free and clear of both junior and senior liens.[99]

The holder of a claim in the property adverse to the title of the mortgagor is usually bracketed with senior lienors as one who is not a necessary or proper party to a foreclosure action.[1] If his claim is a valid one, his interest cannot be sold in the foreclosure because it is not under the mortgage sued upon. Whether or not it is valid should not be determined incidentally in an action whose purpose is not to decide such an issue but merely to sell property that secures the plaintiff's claim. Such is, at least, the argument and prevailing view. Yet if the claimant appears and litigates the question of his title he is bound by the decree, the court having power to decide the question if the claimant acquiesces.[2] And the same is true if he is properly

Masters v. Templeton, 92 Ind. 447 (1883); see Emigrant, etc., Sav. Bank v. Goldman, 75 N.Y. 127, 132 (1878).

97. See note 90, supra. See also Three-foot v. Hillman, 130 Ala. 244, 30 So. 513, 89 Am.St.Rep. 39 (1906); Waters v. Bossel, 58 Miss. 602 (1881); cf., Bigelow v. Cassedy, 26 N.J.Eq. 557 (1875).

98. See Hefner v. Northwestern Life Ins. Co., 123 U.S. 747, 754, 8 S.Ct. 337, 31 L.Ed. 309 (1887), "the bill in such a case being in effect both a bill to foreclose the second mortgage and a bill to redeem from the first mortgage." See also Peabody v. Roberts, 47 Barb. 91 (N.Y.1866), "And in Norton v. Warner (3 Edw.Ch. 106) it was held that there is no objection to a second mortgagee's filing a bill for a foreclosure and sale to pay off all the incumbrances according to their respective priorities, * * *. It is very important for the promotion of the interests of junior mortgagees that this right should be carefully maintained; for where they do not possess the pecuniary ability of redeeming the senior mortgage, it is the only means afforded them through which the security can be applied to the payment of the debt it secures."

99. E. g., where the first mortgage extended only to a small part of the property covered by the second mortgage, a sale under foreclosure of the latter could not be made advantageously if a purchase had to take subject to a partial mortgage. Shepherd v. Pepper, 133 U.S. 626, 10 S.Ct. 438, 33 L.Ed. 706 (1890).

1. Gage v. Perry, 93 Ill. 176 (1879); San Francisco v. Lawton, 18 Cal. 465 (1861); Dial v. Reynolds, 96 U.S. 340, 24 L.Ed. 644 (1877); Toucey v. New York Life Ins. Co., 314 U.S. 118, 62 S.Ct. 139, 86 L.Ed 100, 137 A.L.R. 967, 137 footnote 8 (1941); Wells v. American Mortgage Co., 109 Ala. 430, 20 So. 136 (1895); Corning v. Smith, 6 N.Y. 82 (1851)—accord. Provident Loan Trust Co. v. Marks, 59 Kan. 230, 52 P. 449, 68 Am.St.Rep. 349 (1898), contra. See also Masters v. Templeton, 92 Ind. 447 (1884); Bradley v. Parkhurst, 20 Kan. 462 (1878); note, 7 Cent.L.J. 473 (1878); note, 21 Cent.L.J. 223 (1885).

2. See Beronio v. Ventura County Lumber Co., 129 Cal. 232, 61 P. 958,

joined and defaults in a case in which the foreclosing mortgagee sets forth facts from which he claims that the defendant's title is subordinate to his mortgage.[3] Furthermore, it has been urged that there is no good reason why the claimant should ever object to having the validity of his claim passed upon, whereas to exclude the question "has the unfortunate result of requiring a sale of a very uncertain quantity largely defeating the purpose of the change from strict foreclosure to that of sale." [4]

§ 7.15 Omitted Parties

When any party having the right to redeem is omitted from a foreclosure action, his interest is not terminated by that action.[5] So far as he is concerned the foreclosure is void and his rights of redemption are the same as before the foreclosure. The purchaser at the foreclosure sale succeeds to the rights of the mortgagee even though the sale is void as to an omitted party,[6] and he also succeeds to the

79 Am.St.Rep. 118 (1900); Goebel v. Iffla, 111 N.Y. 170, 18 N.E. 649 (1888).

3. "* * * We think that * * * a default ought to be construed, as an admission that, at the time he [the holder of a paramount title] failed to appear as required, he had no interest in the property in question, and hence as conclusive of any prior claim of interest or title adverse to the plaintiff." Barton v. Anderson, 104 Ind. 578, 581, 4 N.E. 420 (1886). It has been held that a purchaser at a tax sale held subsequent to the giving of a mortgage is a proper party to a foreclosure of the mortgage, and the validity of such purchaser's title may be settled in the foreclosure action. Hefner v. North Western Mut. Life Ins. Co., 123 U.S. 747, 754, 8 S. Ct. 337, 31 L.Ed. 309 (1887). See also Upjohn v. Moore, 45 Wyo. 96, 16 P.2d 40, 85 A.L.R. 1063 (1932), commented on in, 33 Col.L.Rev. 543 (1933). But cf., Erie County Sav. Bank v. Shuster, 187 N.Y. 111, 79 N. E. 843 (1907).

4. Durfee, Cases Mortgages, 296 n.

5. Springer Corp. v. Kirkeby-Natus, 80 N.M. 206, 453 P.2d 376 (1969); Quinn Plumbing Co. v. New Miami Shores Corp., 100 Fla. 413, 129 So. 690, 73 A.L.R. 600 (1930); Decker v. Patton, 120 Ill. 464, 11 N.E. 897 (1887); Holmes v. Bybee, 34 Ind. 262 (1870); Arnold v. Haberstock, 213 Ind. 98, 10 N.E.2d 591 (1937) rehearing denied 213 Ind. 98, 11 N.E.2d 682; Peabody v. Roberts, 47 Barb. 91 (N.Y.1866); Mackenna v. Fidelity Trust Co., 184 N.Y. 411, 77 N.E. 721, 3 L.R.A.,N.S., 1668, 12 Am.St.Rep. 620, 6 Ann.Cas. 471 (1906); Monese v. Struve, 155 Or. 68, 62 P.2d 822 (1936); Milmo Nat. Bank v. Rich, 16 Tex.Civ.App. 363, 40 S.W. 1032 (1897); Godfrey v. Chadwell, 2 Vern. 601 (1707). See Haines v. Beach, 3 Johns.Ch. 459 (1818). See Note, Rights of Junior Lienholders in Wisconsin, 43 Marq.L. Rev. 89, 96 (1959).

6. Robinson v. Ryan, 25 N.Y. 320 (1862); Quinn Plumbing Co. v. New Miami, etc. Corp., 100 Fla. 413, 129 So. 690, 73 A.L.R. 600 (1930). In spite of some authority in New York to the effect that the purchaser on foreclosure sale acquires the mortgagee's interest in the mortgage and the debt as well even though the price he paid was less than the amount of the debt, e. g., Brainard v. Cooper, 10 N.Y. 356, 359 (1852), the correct rule is, or should be, that the purchaser is entitled "to be subrogated to the place and rights of the mortgagee *pro tanto*, for the amount so paid to the mortgagee upon the mortgage debt. * * * The residue of the mortgage debt was * * * due to the holder of the bond mentioned in the mortgage." Childs v. Childs, 10 Ohio St. 339, 346, 75 Am. Dec. 512 (1859). Accord: Givins v. Carroll, 40 S.Ct. 413, 18 S.E. 1030, 42

rights of all owners of interests in the property subject to the mortgage who were joined in the foreclosure.[7] If the omitted party is owner of the entire redemption interest, the foreclosure sale is entirely void as to his interest, but the purchaser stands as assignee of the mortgage[8] and subject to an accounting as such.[9] As an omitted owner, he may then redeem the land by paying the mortgage debt to the foreclosure sale purchaser.[10] When he redeems, he redeems the title to *the land,* and in so doing, he cuts off any further interest of the foreclosure sale purchaser in the land. Unlike where the party omitted is a junior lienor, a situation we will examine in detail next, the foreclosure sale purchaser has no right to redeem or pay off the owner-mortgagor.

Where the omitted party is a junior lienor, the situation becomes more complicated. He too has a certain type of equitable redemption right and when he is omitted from a foreclosure proceeding, he does not lose his lien and is generally unaffected by the foreclosure.[11] However, why would it be unfair to terminate his lien even though he was not a party? After all, there has been a judicial sale, and in the great majority of cases, the high bid probably does not exceed the amount of the senior mortgage. Where this is so, is it not proof enough that the property's value was insufficient to cover the amount owing to the junior as well, and therefore that the junior must and should go away empty-handed?

The answer to this is that, while a sale has been held, it is not a sale in which the junior was a participant. He had no opportunity to bid for the property himself, nor to attempt to stir up other bidders in order to maximize the price paid for the property. It is well known that in most judicial sales the bidding is scarcely spirited. Often the foreclosing senior lienor will be the only bidder. Of course, it is possible that even if the junior had been a party and present at the sale, no amount of effort on his part would have resulted in a higher bid. But this is a fact which cannot be established by speculation.

Am.St.Rep. 889 (1894). See Wells v. Lincoln Co., 80 Mo. 424 (1883). Cf., Collins v. Riggs, 81 U.S. (14 Wall.) 491, 493, 20 L.Ed. 723 (1871). See also 73 A.L.R. 612, 630, 633, 635 (1931); Ann.Cas.1917D, 576.

7. Christ Protestant Episcopal Church v. Mack, 93 N.Y. 488, 45 Ab.R. 260 (1883); Smith v. Shay, 62 Iowa 119, 17 N.W. 444 (1883); Ferguson v. Cloon, 89 Kan. 202, 131 P. 144, Ann. Cas.1914D, 281 (1913); Renard v. Brown, 7 Neb. 449 (1878); Dorff v. Bornstein, 277 N.Y. 236, 14 N.E.2d 51 (1938), motion granted 278 N.Y. 566, 16 N.E.2d 105; Murphy v. Farwell, 9 Wis. 102. See 1931, 73 A.L.R. 612, 644 (1859). See Chapter 10 infra.

8. Robinson v. Ryan, 25 N.Y. 320 (1862).

9. See §§ 4.27–4.34 supra. See also Updike, Mortgages, in 1953 Annual Survey of American Law, 29 N.Y.U. L.Rev. 829, 935 (1954).

10. See § 7.3, supra.

11. Akeley v. Miller, 264 So.2d 473 (Fla.App.1972); Lenexa State Bank & Trust Co. v. Dixon, 221 Kan. 238, 559 P.2d 776 (1977); Springer Corp. v. Kirkeby-Natus, 80 N.M. 206, 453 P.2d 376 (1969).

What seems to be needed is a procedure which will duplicate, insofar as possible, the right of which the junior was deprived by his omission from the foreclosure proceeding—the right to have the value of the property tested at a judicial sale *in which he is a participant,* so that he has full opportunity to maximize the price paid by the highest bidder.[12]

How can this result be achieved? There are two principal remedies which the courts have granted to omitted junior lienors: foreclosure [13] and redemption.[14] The first remedy is foreclosure by the junior of his own lien, with a resulting judicial sale. Such a sale will be subject to the first mortgage,[15] which is, in effect, revived for this purpose. Indeed, the courts sometimes say that, as to the junior lienor, the original foreclosure sale has never taken place.[16] Both the mortgagor's and mortgagee's rights have become vested in the buyer at the original sale. If the junior subsequently forecloses his lien, the judicial sale held at his instance will convey the original mortgagor's interest to the buyer at the second sale; but the original mortgagee's interest (revived for this purpose) will remain in the hands of the buyer at the original sale.

It is of course possible that there will be no bidders for the property under these conditions. This will normally be so if the property's value is lower than the amount owing on the senior lien. But even if there are no bidders, the junior lienor has had an opportunity to prove that the property has excess value above the balance owing on the senior lien, and it is this right to which he is entitled and of which he was previously deprived.

Note that the amount of the "revived" first lien is the balance which was previously owing on it prior to the first foreclosure sale. This may be more or less than the amount the purchaser at the first sale bid when he took the property. If it is more, the original purchaser obtains a windfall (assuming that the buyer at the second sale ultimately pays off the senior lien); but this is not surprising, since if the property is more valuable than the price paid by the original

12. See Note, 88 U.Pa.L.Rev. 994, 998–999 (1940).

13. See, e. g., Lenexa State Bank & Trust Co. v. Dixon, 221 Kan. 238, 559 P.2d 776 (1977); Catterlin v. Armstrong, 101 Ind. 258, 263 (1884); see Peabody v. Roberts, 47 Barb. 91, 99 (N.Y.1866). See 88 U. of Pa.L.Rev. 994, 998 (1940); Cronin v. Hazeltine, 85 Mass. (3 Allen) 324 (1862); Vanderkemp v. Shelton, 11 Paige 28 (N. Y.1844); Peabody v. Roberts, 47 Barb. 91 (N.Y.1866).

14. See, e. g., Akeley v. Miller, 264 So.2d 473 (Fla.App.1972); Springer Corp. v. Kirkeby-Natus, 80 N.M. 206, 453 P.2d 376 (1969).

15. Cronin v. Hazeltine, 85 Mass. (3 Allen) 324 (1862); Vanderkemp v. Shelton, 11 Paige 28 (N.Y.1844); Peabody v. Roberts, 47 Barb. 91 (N.Y. 1866).

16. Catterlin v. Armstrong, 101 Ind. 258, 263 (1884); see Peabody v. Roberts, 47 Barb. 91, 99 (N.Y.1866). See 88 U. of Pa.L.Rev. 994, 998 (1940). And see Durfee, Cases on Security, 221 (1951).

sale purchaser, he could have simply sold it for that higher price and gained a similar windfall. On the other hand, if the purchaser at the original sale paid more than the amount of the senior lien, the second foreclosure sale will deprive him of his title to the property, and replace it with a lien for a smaller amount than his original investment. This could be a serious detriment to the original purchaser, and might in general act to discourage buyers at foreclosure sales from bidding more than the amount of the lien being foreclosed. It could be argued that this detriment is a reasonable penalty to impose on the purchaser, who should have discovered the fact that the junior lienor had been omitted before he bid at the first foreclosure sale. This argument proceeds from the theory that in all cases the existence of the junior lien is discoverable by a foreclosure sale bidder from a careful search of the public records. Thus, if the bidder makes no search or searches negligently, he has only himself to blame. This argument appears sound if the junior lienor is the holder of a *mortgage,* since it will be rendered nugatory by the recording act unless it has in fact been recorded, or unless the bidder has other notice of its existence. But it is less valid if the junior lien is a mechanics lien which is unrecorded at the time of the senior foreclosure sale, but which is later recorded and which, by statute, relates back to an earlier time when the mechanic performed work on the property.[17]

The other principal remedy available to the omitted junior is redemption.[18] By this we mean that the junior may tender to the buyer at the senior foreclosure sale the balance which was owed on the senior lien at the time of foreclosure, and by so doing in effect compel an assignment of a "revived" senior lien to the junior lienor. The junior thus becomes the holder of two liens, a senior and a junior, and he may foreclose either or both of them. Note that unlike where an omitted owner redeems, the term "redemption" here does not refer to the vesting of *title* to the property in the junior, but merely to his power to compel an assignment to him of the senior lien.[19] Sometimes it is said that, by tendering payment of the balance owing on the senior lien, he becomes subrogated to the senior mortgagee's rights—rights which have now, by the first sale, been vested in the sale purchaser.[20]

Note that redemption requires that the omitted junior come up with a substantial amount of money, and that he is not in a position to use the property itself as security for the obtaining of that capital

17. See, e. g., Lenexa State Bank & Trust Co. v. Dixon, 221 Kan. 238, 559 P.2d 776 (1977).

18. Note, 88 U.Pa.L.Rev. 994, 1000 (1940).

19. "The owner of a junior encumbrance redeems not the premises, strictly speaking, but the senior encumbrance; and then he is entitled not to a conveyance of the premises, but to an assignment of the security." Pardee v. Van Anken, 3 Barb. 534 (N.Y.1848).

20. See § 7.2, supra.

from some other lender. For this reason, redemption by an omitted junior lienor is probably not very common, and it certainly imposes a burden on the junior lienor which he would not have had if he had been named as a party to the original foreclosure action.

There is yet a third remedy available to the omitted junior lienor, although it is rarely useable in practice. Some jurisdictions hold that, if the foreclosure sale of the senior lien has produced a surplus, and if that surplus is still identifiable in the hands of the original mortgagor or of some lienor who is subordinate even to the omitted junior, the junior can assert a lien on the surplus funds.[21] Obviously, cases in which these circumstances exist will be very rare indeed.

Let us now turn to the methods which the buyer at the senior sale can employ to protect his interests in cases in which an omitted junior exercises one of the two principal remedies (foreclosure or redemption) described above. There seem to be three such techniques available to the original sale purchaser: redemption, re-foreclosure, and in some states, strict foreclosure. Let us look first at redemption. If the omitted junior has not taken any further action, it is obvious that the senior sale purchaser may simply pay off the junior lien and thereby clear his title. This is because, as we noted earlier, the senior foreclosure purchaser succeeds not only to the rights of the mortgagee, but to the rights of the foreclosed mortgagor as well. Since the mortgagor would have had the right to pay off the junior lien, the senior foreclosure purchaser will have the same right.[22] Whether this is an attractive alternative to the senior purchaser obviously depends on how large the junior lien is, but the right to do so is always available to him up until the moment the junior lienor forecloses his own lien. If the senior buyer doubts that the property is worth the additional investment, perhaps he is well-advised to allow the junior to proceed to foreclosure, since the senior buyer will still have a first mortgage on the property in the amount of the original senior lien.

Even if the junior lienor redeems the senior debt from the original sale purchaser, the position of the parties is not really changed significantly. The senior buyer can simply pay off the senior lien in the junior's hands, using the very dollars which the junior paid the buyer when *he* redeemed. The redemption by the senior foreclosure purchaser will have priority simply because he stands in the shoes of the foreclosed mortgagor. Once an owner exercizes redemption rights in equity against a lienor, the lienor no longer has a further interest in the land. His only right is to be paid off. As Professor Glenn has pointed out, the junior lienor "can be met at the gate by the purchaser at the sale * * *. In other words, the purchas-

21. See, e. g., Caito v. United California Bank, 20 Cal.3d 694, 144 Cal.Rptr. 751, 576 P.2d 466 (1978); Soles v. Sheppard, 99 Ill. 616 (1881).

22. See text at notes 6–7, supra.

er at the sale can dispose of the junior mortgagee by redeeming the land from his lien."[23] Thus the transaction is, in effect, a wash, and if the senior buyer is willing to add enough money out of his own pocket, he can also pay off the junior lien at the same time. The result of all this is that redemption by an omitted junior lienor is always an act that the senior sale purchaser can easily nullify if he wishes to do so. If the senior buyer does not wish to take the next step and pay off the junior lien as well, the omitted junior lienor still has the power to compel a test of the property's value in his own foreclosure sale.

An alternative route which the senior sale purchaser may take is to re-foreclose the first mortgage.[24] This time, we may be sure that he will not omit the junior lienor. He takes this action while standing in the shoes of the original mortgagee. The junior will have full opportunity to participate in the sale, and will thus have the right denied to him when the original foreclosure sale was held. The proceeds of the sale will be used to pay off both liens in the order of their priority, with any additional surplus going to the re-foreclosing party.

There are two objections to this procedure from the viewpoint of the original sale purchaser. One is that he stands the risk of losing his title to the property if he is outbid at the second sale. Moreover, if this occurs, and if the successful bid at the second sale does not produce a surplus above the total of both liens, the original sale purchaser stands to lose any amount he bid at the first sale in excess of the balance owing on the senior lien. He may have a right to go back against the original mortgagor for the loss, but we may well imagine that in most cases such a right is not worth much.

The third method available to the senior sale purchaser, when he discovers an omitted junior lienor, is sometimes called strict foreclosure. It is not available in all jurisdictions. In substance it amounts to a judicial decree that the junior lien be cancelled unless the junior pays off the senior debt within a court-determined period.[25]

There is authority that in order to have strict foreclosure against such omitted junior interests the plaintiff must establish both that he bought in good faith without knowledge of the outstanding interest and that its holder knew of the sale and permitted the plaintiff to buy without disclosing his own interest.[26] And it is quite clear that

23. Glenn, Mortgages, § 86.5 (1943); See Portland Mortgage Co. v. Creditors Protective Ass'n, 199 Or. 432, 262 P.2d 918 (1953); Murphy v. Farwell, 9 Wis. 102 (1859).

24. Mortgage Com. Realty Corp. v. Columbia Hts. Garage Corp., 169 Misc. 618, 7 N.Y.S.2d 740 (1938). See note, 88 U. of Pa.L.Rev. 994, 1006 (1940). See 73 A.L.R. 612, 633 (1931).

25. See § 7.9, supra.

26. Moulton v. Cornish, 138 N.Y. 133, 33 N.E. 842, 20 L.R.A. 370 (1893). See note, 88 U. of Pa.L.Rev. 994, 1007 (1940).

if the holder of the junior interest is intentionally omitted from the foreclosure action, the mortgagee cannot later have strict foreclosure to cut off his redemption right.[27] Other cases follow a flexible rule that there must be equitable grounds for relief and, in general, require that the omission must be through inadvertence or mistake untinged with bad faith.[28] In addition, the courts look at the amount the property sold for at the prior foreclosure sale or the value of the property.[29] If the premises are worth no more than the encumbrances prior to the one sought to be foreclosed, it is persuasive that strict foreclosure should be granted.[30]

Until this point, we have assumed that an omitted party, whether owner or junior lienor, if he redeems, is acting under his equitable right to redeem from the mortgage rather than pursuant to statutory redemption.[31] In general, the two rights would not seem to exist simultaneously. The equitable right accrues at mortgage maturity and ends only by a valid foreclosure. On the other hand, statutory redemption begins when a valid foreclosure takes place and ends at the expiration of the requisite statutory period. Thus, since no foreclosure has taken place as to the omitted owner, it is generally assumed that only the equitable right of redemption is available to him.[32]

As to the omitted junior lienor, however, matters are somewhat more complicated. Moreover, there are several reasons why the choice of redemption methods might be especially attractive to him. While statutory redemption will be covered in detail later,[33] several features of that type of redemption need to be briefly considered

27. Indiana Invest. Co. v. Evens, 121 N.J.Eq. 72, 187 A. 158 (1936), denying even a later foreclosure by sale, criticised on this point in 17 Chi-Kent L. Rev. 148 (1938); Moulton v. Cornish, note 26, supra; see 118 A.L.R. 769, 775 (1939). See also Surety Building & Loan Ass'n v. Risack, 118 N.J.Eq. 425, 427, 179 A. 680, 681 (1935), party originally joined but not served.

28. See Sears, Roebuck & Co. v. Camp, 124 N.J.Eq. 403, 407, 1 A.2d 425, 428, 118 A.L.R. 762 (1938), constructive notice insufficient to prevent strict foreclosure even though search was careless; Mesiavich v. Newman, 120 N.J.Eq. 192, 184 A. 538 (1936); Koerner v. Willamette Iron Works, 36 Or. 90, 58 P. 863 (1899), strict foreclosure against a junior lienor although no showing of "good faith." See also note, 88 U. of Pa.L.Rev. 994, 1007 (1940); 118 A.L.R. 769, 774 (1939). "Knowledge of and acquiescence" in the foreclosure by the omitted party is not essential. See Campbell, Cases on Mortgages, 2d ed. 249 n. 4. But cf. Denton v. Ontario County Nat. Bank, 150 N.Y. 126, 44 N.E. 781 (1896).

29. See note, 88 U. of Pa.L.Rev. 994, 1007 (1940).

30. Mesiavich v. Newman, 120 N.J.Eq. 192, 184 A. 538 (1936); Miles v. Stehle, 22 Neb. 740, 36 N.W. 142 (1888); see 25 Va.L.Rev. 947, 953 (1939). But contra, see Denton v. Ontario County Nat. Bank, 150 N.Y. 126, 44 N.E. 781 (1896). Of course if the foreclosure sale produced an excess over the amount of the mortgage debt, a mortgagee-purchaser cannot have strict foreclosure to eliminate junior liens. Pettingill v. Hubbell, 53 N.J.Eq. 584, 32 A. 76 (1895).

31. See § 7.1, supra.

32. Note, 88 U.Pa.L.Rev. 994, 1003 (1940); See Herrmann v. Churchill, 235 Or. 327, 385 P.2d 190 (1963).

33. See §§ 8.4–8.7, supra.

here. For example a junior lienor who redeems under a statutory right of redemption normally gets fee title to the property (rather than merely an assignment of a revived first lien). Moreover, to exercise statutory redemption rights, one must usually pay the price paid at the original foreclosure sale, rather than the balance which was owed on the first lien. One additional point: the statutes sometimes give the original mortgagor a priority right to redeem, with others (presumably including omitted junior lienors) having the right if the mortgagor does not exercise it within a given period of time.

Some have maintained that the omitted junior lienor has the choice of proceeding under either form of redemption.[34] The reasoning, in part, is that whenever the mortgagor has been validly foreclosed, statutory redemption is triggered and, since junior lienors normally have rights under such statutes, "unless it were to be held that the statutes applied only to those subsequent lienors whose liens were cut off by foreclosure, it would seem that the omitted lienor also possesses the statutory right."[35] On the other hand, Professor Glenn has stated that the junior lienor "cannot resort to statutory redemption, because he is not within the terms of the statute. The latter comes into effect at and with foreclosure * * * but the statute envisages those only whom the foreclosure has barred. It follows that one who has never been foreclosed cannot resort to statutory redemption. His remedy remains where it always was, regardless of whether the particular state has provided for statutory redemption. The remedy is redemption in equity after the ancient mode."[36] Moreover, subsequent case authority directly confronting the question has supported the latter view.[37]

§ 7.16 Conduct of the Sale

The method of conducting a foreclosure sale is now largely regulated by statute and is, therefore, mostly a matter of local law which must be consulted in each jurisdiction. Such legislation ordinarily provides for a public sale under the direction of either the sheriff or an officer of the court appointed for that purpose.[38] In the absence

34. Note, 88 U.Pa.L.Rev. 994, 1003 (1940); Cf. Century Enterprises, Inc. v. Butler, 526 P.2d 1350 (Colo.App. 1974).

35. Id. at 1003.

36. Glenn, Mortgages, § 238 (1943).

37. See, e. g., Portland Mortgage Co. v. Creditors Protective Ass'n, 199 Or. 432, 262 P.2d 918 (1953). But cf. Century Enterprises, Inc. v. Butler, 526 P.2d 1350 (Colo.App.1974).

38. Typical statutes are West's Ann. Cal.Code Civ.Proc., §§ 726, 729, incorporating by reference provisions governing the conduct of a sale under execution by a sheriff but authorizing court to appoint a commissioner or elisor to do the job; Ga.Code Ann. § 67–401 (1967), "sold in the manner and under the same regulations which govern sheriff's sales under execution"; Minn.Stats.Ann., § 581.03. See State ex rel. Elliott v. Holliday, 35 Neb. 327, 53 N.W. 142 (1892). As to the practice in federal courts, see Blossom v. Milwaukee & C. R. Co., 70

of statutory provision, a court of equity has ample power to order a master to make a judicial sale. The decree in such cases will commonly contain provisions specifying the giving of notice, the time, place, manner and terms of conducting the sale, and other matters that are generally covered by statutory regulation.[39]

Although under statutory provision, or by provision of a chancery decree, the sale is to be conducted by the sheriff as in sales under execution,[40] it usually differs from such sales in important respects. The most fundamental is that "the whole business is * * * under the guidance and superintendence of the court [of chancery] itself."[41] One consequence of the sale being a judicial one under direction of the court is that the sale is equally for the benefit of all lienholders whose rights have been adjudicated by it.[42] Moreover, foreclosure courts more than occasionally order the sale of property based on the principle of the inverse order of alienation.[43] For example, where a mortgage covers several lots, some of which the mortgagor has already sold, the foreclosure court will order the lots retained by the mortgagor sold first before subjecting the already conveyed lots to sale.[44] In addition, the foreclosure decree may, under some circumstances, as we will note later, fix a minimum or "upset" price under which the property may not be sold at the sale.[45]

The fact that the foreclosure sale is judicial also has a bearing upon when title passes under the sale. In a sheriff's sale usually it passes when the property is struck off at the sale and the successful bidder completes his purchase, there being no need for court approval of either the sale or the sheriff's deed.[46] A foreclosure sale, however,

U.S. (3 Wall.) 196, 18 L.Ed. 43 (1865), "by the marshal of the district where the decree was entered, or by the master appointed by the court, as directed in the decree."

39. See Leesman, Some Considerations Involving the Decretal Parts of the Decree of Sale in a Foreclosure Proceeding, 6 J.Marshall L.Q. 314 (1941).

40. See provisions in statutes, note 38, supra.

41. Blossom v. Milwaukee & C. R. Co., 70 U.S. (3 Wall.) 196, 18 L.Ed. 43 (1865). "The whole proceeding, from the beginning to the final confirmation of the reported sale, and the passing of title to the vendee and the money to the persons entitled to it, was under the supervision and control of the court." Penn's Adm'r v. Tolleson, 20 Ark. 652, 661 (1859). Look at Jones v. Williams, 155 N.C. 179, 71 S.E. 222, 36 L.R.A.,N.S., 426 (1911). Nat. Reserve Life Ins. Co. v. Kemp, 184 Kan. 648, 339 P.2d 368 (1959).

42. Welsh v. Lawler, 73 N.J.Eq. 371, 68 A. 218, 133 Am.St.Rep. 737 (1907). Look also at Laub v. Warren Guarantee etc., Co., 54 Ohio App. 457, 8 N.E.2d 258 (1936). Brant v. Lincoln Nat. Life Ins. Co. of Ft. Wayne, 209 Ind. 268, 198 N.E. 785 (1935).

43. See § 10.10, infra.

44. Season, Inc. v. Atwell, 86 N.M. 751, 527 P.2d 792 (1974).

45. See § 7.16, infra.

46. Coulter v. Blieden, 104 F.2d 29 (C.C.A.Ark.1939) certiorari denied 308 U.S. 583, 60 S.Ct. 106, 84 L.Ed. 488; Glenn v. Hollums, 80 F.2d 555 (C.C.A.Tex.1936); Shreiner v. Farmers Trust Co., 91 F.2d 606 (C.C.A.Pa.1937) certiorari denied 58 S.Ct. 36, 302 U.S. 686, 82 L.Ed. 530; State Bank of Hardinsburg v. Brown, 317 U.S. 135, 63

requires confirmation by the court. Even in states where the foreclosure takes place by way of execution, confirmation may be required by statute [47] or the court may reserve power to confirm the sale when made.[48] And there exists power to set aside a sale under certain circumstances and order a new one.[49]

Certain problems connected with the sale are litigated with some frequency within the context of the judicial foreclosure action. These often include problems associated with notice of the sale, sale by parcel or in bulk, and adequacy of the foreclosure sale price. Moreover, these problems will have their greatest impact in a cumulative sense. While one of these problems may not always be sufficient to set aside a sale, the more of them that are present in one fact situation, the greater the likelihood that a new sale will be ordered.

Notice Problems

The purpose of notice is to inform the public as to the date, place, nature and condition of the property to be sold and terms of the sale.[50] Questions as to the sufficiency and definiteness of notice to accomplish these purposes sometimes are of importance.[51]

For example, where there is a conflict between the foreclosure decree and the notice of foreclosure sale as to whether part of the land is to be sold subject to a prior lien, enough uncertainty among bidders is created to justify setting aside a sale.[52] Moreover, sales also are subject to being set aside where there is a substantial discrepancy between the time of sale specified in the notice of sale and the actual time of sale.[53]

Sales by Parcel or In Bulk

Where the mortgage being foreclosed covers more than one parcel of land, the problem arises as to whether the court should order the land sold in parcels or in bulk. Frequently this problem is regulated by statute.[54] However, in the absence of such regulation, the

S.Ct. 128, 87 L.Ed. 140 (1942), rehearing denied 317 U.S. 712, 63 S.Ct. 432, 87 L.Ed. 567 (1943); Leviston v. Swan, 33 Cal. 480 (1867); Pollard v. Harlow, 138 Cal. 390, 71 P. 648 (1903); Bateman v. Kellogg, 59 Cal. App. 464, 472, 474, 211 P. 46 (1922).

47. E. g., Minn.Stat.Ann. § 581.08.

48. E. g., Laub v. Warren Guar. etc. Co., 54 Ohio App. 457, 8 N.E.2d 258 (1936).

49. Von Senden v. O'Brien, 61 App.D.C. 137, 58 F.2d 689 (1932); Bank of America Nat. Trust & Savings Ass'n v. Reidy Lumber Co., 15 Cal.2d 243, 101 P.2d 77 (1940); Ellis v. Powell, 117 S.W.2d 225 (Mo.1938); Kloepping v. Stellmacher, 21 N.J.Eq. 328 (1871).

50. See Leesman, supra note 39.

51. See notes, 2 Minn.L.Rev. 157 (1918); 5 Minn.L.Rev. 325 (1921); 9 Tex.L.Rev. 454 (1931). See also 120 A.L.R. 660 (1939).

52. See, e. g., Bates v. Schuelke, 191 Neb. 498, 215 N.W.2d 874 (1974).

53. Ohio Realty Investment Corp. v. Southern Bank of West Palm Beach, 300 So.2d 679 (Fla.1974).

54. See Security Sav. Bank of Cedar Rapids v. King, 198 Iowa 1151, 199

court should direct the sale in the manner and mode that is likely to secure the highest price.[55] Normally the presumption is in favor of parcel sales.[56] Moreover, where the sale of one parcel is likely to satisfy the mortgage debt, the decree should direct the sale of such parcel only.[57] On the other hand, some situations may favor the sale in bulk. For example, there is considerable authority that where more than one parcel comprise a farm or other enterprise, a sale in bulk is permitted.[58]

Adequacy of the Sale Price

To some extent, legislation in many states is aimed at encouraging an adequate foreclosure sale price. This is one of the purposes of statutory redemption and a major function of anti-deficiency legislation. Both types of legislation will be considered later in this volume.[59] Absent legislation, however, the rule is well-settled, at least in normal times, that a court will not refuse to confirm a sale or set it aside "on account of mere inadequacy of price unless the inadequacy be so gross as to shock the conscience or raise a presumption of fraud or unfairness." [60] Thus, in the absence of other irregulari-

N.W. 166 (1924); Clark v. Kraker, 51 Minn. 444, 53 N.W. 706 (1892); Thomas v. Thomas, 44 Mont. 102, 119 P. 283, Ann.Cas.1913B, 616 (1911); Miller v. Trudgeon, 16 Okl. 337, 86 P. 523, 8 Ann.Cas. 739 (1905); Person v. Leathers, 67 Miss. 548, 7 So. 391 (1890). See also 8 Ann.Cas. 741 (1908); Ann.Cas.1913B, 619; West's Ann.Cal.Code Civ.Proc. § 726. Wis. Stat.Ann. § 278.06, provides that "the court before rendering judgment shall ascertain by reference or otherwise the situation of mortgaged premises and whether they can be sold in parcels without injury to the interests of the parties; and if it shall appear that they can be so sold the judgment shall direct a sale in parcels * * *." For an interpretation of that statute, see Citizens Bank of Sheboygan v. Rose, 59 Wis.2d 385, 208 N.W.2d 110 (1973).

55. See Semmes Nursuries, Inc. v. McDade, 288 Ala. 523, 263 So.2d 127 (1972); Wiltsie, Mortgage Foreclosure, § 683 (5th Ed.), 61 A.L.R.2d 505, 558.

56. Id.

57. See Dozier v. Farrior, 187 Ala. 181, 65 So. 364 (1914); Blazey v. Delius, 74 Ill. 299 (1874); Hughes v. Riggs, 84 Md. 502, 36 A. 269 (1897); Miller v. Kendrick, 15 A. 259 (N.J. 1888); Guarantee Trust & Safe Deposit Co. v. Jenkins, 40 N.J.Eq. 451, 2 A. 13 (1885). See also Leesman, supra note 39; note, 25 Cal.L.Rev. 469 (1937); L.R.A.1917B, 517. Cf. also 15 S.Cal.L.Rev. 19 (1941).

58. See 61 A.L.R.2d 505, 574, § 17.

59. See §§ 8.4–8.7, 8.1–8.3, infra.

60. George v. Cone, 77 Ark. 216, 91 S. W. 557. See Connecticut Mutual Life Ins. Co. v. Carter, 446 F.2d 136 (C.C. A.Fla.1971), certiorari denied 404 U.S. 857, 92 S.Ct. 104, 30 L.Ed.2d 78, certiorari denied 404 U.S. 1000, 92 S.Ct. 563, 30 L.Ed.2d 553 (1952); Wiesel v. Ashcraft, 26 Ariz.App. 490, 549 P.2d 585 (1976); Speers Sand & Clay Works, Inc., v. American Trust Co., 52 F.2d 831 (C.C.A.Md.1931), certiorari denied 286 U.S. 548, 52 S.Ct. 500, 76 L.Ed. 1284 (1952); Raleigh & C. R. Co. v. Baltimore Nat. Bank, 41 F. Supp. 599 (D.C.S.C.1941); Detroit Trust Co. v. Hart, 277 Mich. 561, 269 N.W. 598 (1936); Graffam v. Burgess, 117 U.S. 180, 6 S.Ct. 686, 29 L.Ed. 839 (1886). See also Durfee and Doddridge, Redemption from Foreclosure Sale—The Uniform Act, 23 Mich.L.Rev. 833 (1925); Vaughan, Reform of Mortgage Foreclosure Procedure, 88 U. of Pa.L.Rev. 957, 963 (1940). The leading American case refusing confirmation because of in-

ties, courts have, for example, upheld a foreclosure sale price of half the fair market value of the property.[61] On the other hand, courts have set aside as "inequitably less than the real value of the property" a sale price of approximately one-seventh of the fair market value.[62] Moreover, where the disparity is substantial, courts will seize upon any other irregularity or misconduct to provide the additional basis for setting aside the sale. For example, where the purchaser bid in $5,000 for property appraised at $73,000, the court set aside the sale and focused on two factors: the foreclosure sale purchaser had persuaded the sheriff to dispense with reading the sale notice at the sale and the mortgagee who arrived a few minutes late had been willing to submit a bid of over $55,000.[63]

Moreover, it is also important to emphasize that in some jurisdictions the vestigial remains of judicial doctrines developed during the depression of the 1930's still linger on. The economic hardship was of unprecedented magnitude. Among the factors affecting real property mortgages were a disastrous decline in cash income from lands, a precipitous drop in land values, the prevailing practice in the majority of cases of lending, not on a long term amortization basis, but on short term mortgages which were periodically refunded, and the collapse of thousands of banks and other lending institutions which necessitated liquidation of mortgages held by them and made refinancing impossible. While the legislatures responded with a variety of statutory approaches,[64] courts became more receptive to the notion that they had inherent power, without the aid of legislation, to develop methods to protect the parties when there was an almost complete lack of a market for real estate. Probably the best known of these methods is that enunciated in Suring State Bank v. Giese.[65] That decision authorized the foreclosure court to do the following: (1) refuse to confirm the sale where the bid is substantially inadequate; (2) in ordering a sale or a resale, in the court's discretion and after a proper hearing, fix a minimum upset price at which the land must be

adequacy of price (property worth seven times the amount bid) is Ballentyne v. Smith, 205 U.S. 285, 27 S.Ct. 527, 51 L.Ed. 803 (1907). See note, 26 Mich.L.Rev. 87 (1927).

61. See, e. g., Guerra v. Mutual Federal Sav. and Loan Ass'n, 194 So.2d 15 (Fla.App.1967).

62. Southern Realty & Utilities Corp. v. Belmont Mortgage Corp., 186 So.2d 24 (Fla.1966).

63. Johnson v. Jefferson Standard Life Ins. Co., 5 Ariz.App. 587, 429 P.2d 474 (1967).

64. See §§ 8.1–8.3, infra.

65. Suring State Bank v. Giese, 210 Wis. 489, 246 N.W. 556, 85 A.L.R. 1477 (1933), commented on in, 33 Col.L.Rev. 744 (1933); 42 Yale L.J. 960 (1933); 81 U. of Pa.L.Rev. 883 (1933); 27 Ill.L.Rev. 950 (1933); 17 Minn.L.Rev. 821 (1933); 8 Wis.L.Rev. 286 (1933); 21 Cal.L.Rev. 522 (1933); 18 St.Louis L.Rev. 265 (1933); 17 Marq.L.Rev. 154 (1933); 85 A.L.R. 1480 (1933). See also Perlman, Mortgage Deficiency Judgments During an Economic Depression, 20 Va.L.Rev. 771, 806 et seq. (1934); 47 Harv.L. Rev. 299, 307 (1934).

bid in if the sale is to be confirmed; and (3) in cases where no upset price has been fixed, establish the value of property at a hearing and require that its fair value be credited upon the foreclosure judgment as a condition to confirmation. Other courts endorsed similar controls to avoid sacrifice prices.[66] While the Suring approach has been restricted by later decisions,[67] it would be a mistake to believe that it has been abandoned. Indeed, its principles are to some extent preserved by statute.[68] Interestingly, the Wisconsin Supreme Court recently appeared to reaffirm the Suring options.[69] Were the inflation of the past few decades to give way suddenly to severe recession or worse, then those or similar options stand available for use.

§ 7.17 Position of Purchaser

A bid at a foreclosure sale is only an offer to buy which is accepted and becomes binding upon the bidder when the officer in charge of the sale strikes it off to him.[70] An accepted bidder, it is usually said, "acquires no independent rights until the sale be confirmed by the court, and * * * the court may exercise a discretion in either confirming or rejecting the sale." [71] What this means

66. Among such cases are Federal Title and Mort. Guar. Co. v. Lowenstein, 113 N.J.Eq. 200, 166 A. 538 (1933), commented on, 19 Cornell L. Q. 316 (1934); Cal.Joint S. L. Bank v. Gore, 153 Or. 267, 55 P.2d 1118 (1936), noted 15 Or.L.Rev. 385 (1936), order of resale proper, but fixing upset price is not; Michigan Trust Co. v. Cody, 264 Mich. 258, 249 N.W. 844 (1933); see Michigan Trust Co. v. Dutmers, 265 Mich. 651, 252 N.W. 478 (1934); Monaghan v. May, 242 App.Div. 64, 273 N.Y.S. 475 (1934). In Home Owners' Loan Corporation v. Wood, 164 Misc. 215, 298 N.Y.S. 427 (1937) noted, 51 Harv.L.Rev. 749 (1938).

67. For example, for limitations on the Suring case, look at Kremer v. Rule, 216 Wis. 331, 257 N.W. 166 (1934); Weimer v. Uthus, 217 Wis. 56, 258 N.W. 358 (1935); Buel v. Austin, 219 Wis. 397, 263 N.W. 82 (1935); Drach v. Hornig, 221 Wis. 575, 267 N.W. 291 (1936); Wahl v. H. W. & S. M. Tullgren, 222 Wis. 306, 267 N.W. 278 (1936); and in New Jersey, the Lowenstein case has been restricted. Young v. Weber, 117 N.J.Eq. 242, 175 A. 273 (1934) see Fidelity Union Trust Co. v. Pasternack, 122 N.J.Eq. 180, 181, 192 A. 837, 838 (1937) affirmed 123 N.J.Eq. 181, 196 A. 469 (1938). See 24 Va.L.Rev. 44, 46–47 (1937); 33 Ill.L.Rev. 299, 310–314 (1938).

68. See, e. g., Rev.Code Wash.Ann. 61.12.060, which provides that the court, "in ordering the sale, may, in its discretion, take judicial notice of economic conditions, and after a proper hearing, fix a minimum or upset price to which the mortgaged property must be bid or sold before confirmation of the sale. The court may, upon application for confirmation of a sale, if it has not theretofore fixed an upset price, conduct a hearing, establish the value of the property, and, as a condition to confirmation, require that the fair value of the property be credited upon the foreclosure judgment." See National Bank of Washington v. Equity Investors, 86 Wash.2d 545, 546 P.2d 440 (1976) for an example of the upset price mechanism.

69. See First Wisconsin Nat. Bank of Oshkosh v. KSW Investments, Inc., 71 Wis.2d 359, 238 N.W.2d 123 (1976).

70. Blossom v. Milwaukee & C. R. Co., 70 U.S. (3 Wall.) 196, 18 L.Ed. 43 (1865).

71. George v. Cone, 77 Ark. 216, 91 S. W. 557, 113 Am.St.Rep. 143, 7 Ann. Cas. 171 (1905).

is that the purchaser has no contract right to have the sale confirmed; and until it is confirmed, the sale agreement is not enforceable by him. Whether it shall or shall not be is to be determined according to whether the terms of the sale conform to certain requirements to be determined by the court in its discretion.[72] The discretion, however, is a judicial, not an arbitrary one, and must be exercised in accordance with legal rules governing it. Consequently, the purchaser may insist that "confirmation must follow unless there exists some reason recognized by law as warranting a refusal to confirm," [73] and, in this sense, he does have a vested right at once. And, for the purpose of encouraging bidding, it is highly important that a bidder should have this degree of certainty of confirmation.[74]

On the purchaser's side, however, once his bid is accepted, "he submits himself to the jurisdiction of the court and becomes a party to the cause in which the sale has been decreed, and he may be compelled to stand by the offer he has made." [75] The court, after confirmation, may compel the purchaser to take title and pay the bid price, or it may order a resale and hold the purchaser liable for any loss that may result.[76] In this respect the purchaser's contract obligations are governed by substantially the same rules that apply to a vendee in the ordinary contract for the sale of land.[77] Consequently he is entitled to a marketable title and has a reasonable time within which to make an examination and raise the question as to defects which he discovers.[78] These are of two sorts: (a) defects in the title the mortgagor possessed at the execution of the mortgage; and (b) those that are the result of flaws in the foreclosure action.[79] There is authority that the doctrine of *caveat emptor* applies to sales in foreclosure action. However, even courts which accept the doctrine as a

72. George v. Cone, note 71, supra; Blossom v. Milwaukee, etc., Ry., note 70, supra; Kable v. Mitchell, 9 W.Va. 492 (1876).

73. Allen v. Martin, 61 Miss. 78 (1883).

74. See Morrisse v. Inglis, 46 N.J.Eq. 306, 19 A. 16 (1890), quoted with approval in George v. Cone, note 71, supra; Stump v. Martin, 72 Ky. 285, 292 (1873).

75. Allen v. Martin, supra note 73; Dills v. Jasper, 33 Ill. 262, 272 (1864); Travellers' Ins. Co. v. Thompson, 140 Neb. 109, 299 N.W. 329 (1941).

76. Camden v. Mayhew, 129 U.S. 73, 9 S.Ct. 246, 32 L.Ed. 608 (1888); Fienhold v. Babcock, 275 Ill. 282, 113 N.E. 962 (1916). See Thomas v. San Diego College Co., 111 Cal. 358, 366, 43 P. 965 (1896).

77. "The Court, however, treats a contract made with one of its officers as being made with the court itself, and will deal with the contractee upon equitable principles,—the same principles, indeed, which govern in all cases of specific performance." Boorum v. Tucker, 51 N.J.Eq. 135, 26 A. 456 (1893), 52 N.J.Eq. 587, 33 A. 50 (1895).

78. E. g., Timmermann v. Cohn, 204 N.Y. 614, 97 N.E. 589 (1912); Raleigh & C. R. Co. v. Baltimore Nat. Bank, 41 F.Supp. 599 (D.C.S.C.1941).

79. See Boggs v. Fowler, 16 Cal. 559, 564, 76 Am.Dec. 561 (1860). For New York legislation establishing procedure by which a purchaser in a defective foreclosure may perfect his title, see Curtiss, The Commisssion and the Law of Real Property, 40 Cornell L.Q. 735, 739 (1955).

general proposition may refuse to apply it to irregularities in the foreclosure proceedings, such as the failure to join the mortgagor or his successors or a party holding a subsequent interest under the mortgagor, which result in the estate directed to be sold not passing, or passing subject to defects due to the irregularity.[80] As to the first type of defect some courts proceed upon the theory that there is no warranty of title by anyone to a purchaser on a judicial foreclosure sale, that what is offered for sale is the interest of the mortgagor, whatever it may be, subject to all defects and that the buyer purchases this at his peril.[81] Coupled with this is the doctrine that the chancellor, if a defect of this sort is discovered and objected to before the sale is completed, will grant relief but that he will not act after the buyer has accepted the deed.[82] The objection to this view is that a would-be purchaser at a foreclosure sale must either make an intensive title search before bidding on property he has no assurance of acquiring or else forego bidding except at a figure that would take into account the hazard he runs. Usually the first course is impracticable, and the second is sure to dampen bidding and result in sacrificing the property at a price below that normally attendant upon a forced sale.[83] The better practice, therefore, is to purport to sell a clear title except as to paramount interests in the property which are definitely stated in the pleadings and notices of sale.[84]

When all the steps of the foreclosure sale, including confirmation, have been completed, the purchaser is invested with title, this being accomplished under the usual practice by a deed executed and delivered to him by the master or other officer under order of the court. The title so acquired, as has been seen in different connections previously, is the "entire interest and estate of mortgagor and mortgagee as it existed at the date of the mortgage." [85] This state-

80. Boggs v. Fowler, 16 Cal. 559, 564, 76 Am.Dec. 561 (1860). See 73 A.L.R. 612, 620 (1931). If a foreclosure sale is irregular, but not void, or caused by the fraud of any of the parties thereto, objection to the irregularity must be made at or prior to confirmation. Watson v. Tromble, 33 Neb. 450, 50 N.W. 331, 29 Am.St.Rep. 492 (1891); Clement v. Ireland, 138 N.C. 136, 50 S.E. 570 (1905); Allison v. Allison, 88 Va. 328, 13 S.E. 549 (1891); Strand v. Griffith, 63 Wash. 334, 115 P. 512 (1911); Core v. Strickler, 24 W.Va. 689 (1884).

81. Farmers' Bank of Ky. v. Peter, 13 Bush 591, 594 (Ky.1878); Brown v. Gilmor's Ex'rs, 8 Md. 322 (1855), accord. Cf. Lawrence v. Cornell, 4 Johns.Ch. 542 (N.Y.1820). See Boggs v. Fowler, note 80, supra.

82. See notes 80, 81, supra.

83. See Walsh, Mortgages, 310.

84. See Walsh & Simpson, Cases Security Trans., 503 Note (3).

85. Rector of Christ Protestant Episcopal Church v. Mack, 93 N.Y. 488, 45 Am.R. 260 (1883); Gem Valley Ranches, Inc. v. Small, 92 Idaho 232, 440 P.2d 352 (1968); Valley Nat. Bank of Arizona v. Avco Development Co., 14 Ariz.App. 56, 480 P.2d 771 (1971). See also Champion v. Hinkle, 45 N.J.Eq. 162, 16 A. 701 (1888); Coomes v. Frey, 141 Ky. 740, 133 S.W. 758 (1911).

A mortgagee may be estopped from setting up a reversionary interest of record unless, at the foreclosure sale, he specifies that the property is to be sold subject to it. Ferguson v. Cloon, 89 Kan. 202, 131 P. 144, Ann. Cas.1914D, 281 (1913). Cf. Young v.

ment, of course, is subject to the qualifications as to defects in joinder of parties [86] and, of course, the immediately preceding discussion.

§ 7.18 Judicial Foreclosure—Defects and Title Stability

As we will note later in this chapter,[87] power of sale foreclosure is subject to attacks on numerous grounds including, among others, chilled bidding, defective notice of sale, failure to comply with statutory requirements, selling in gross rather than by parcel or vice versa, conflicts of interest problems where trustees or mortgagees sell the property, selling at the wrong time or place, and increasingly, constitutional attacks on procedural due process notice and hearing grounds. Of course, because judicial foreclosure affords all interested parties the right to notice and an opportunity to be heard, constitutional attacks are not normally a problem. Some of the other defects listed above, however, can as we have seen,[88] arise in the judicial, as well as the power of sale context.

Nevertheless, judicial foreclosure is significantly less vulnerable than is power of sale foreclosure to such attacks and, as a result, produces a more stable title. There are at least three reasons for this. First, because judicial foreclosure is under court supervision, that very fact will prevent many of the above defects from arising. After all, in the power of sale setting, the mortgagee or the trustee normally controls the steps through foreclosure. Judicial foreclosure, on the other hand, entails judicial second guessing prior to and after the sale. Not only are fewer defects likely to arise when a disinterested party is, in theory, doublechecking the process, but the mere presence of the judge may discourage the more overt and intentional defects that may otherwise occur. Second, because judicial foreclosure is an adversary proceeding, the other parties aid the court in calling its attention to potential defects, a second type of check on the mortgagee not found in power of sale foreclosure. Finally, even if defects do go uncorrected, the normal concepts of judicial finality provide the ultimate insulation from attack for a judicial foreclosure decree. If a party in a judicial foreclosure who feels aggrieved by the trial court's action allows the time period for filing objections with the trial court or for appeal to expire, his chances for a successful collateral attack on the foreclosure proceeding are extremely slim. Indeed, in one recent case where a mortgagor did just that, the reaction of the court is illustrative: "Clearly she knew or should have known the manner in which her real estate was advertised, offered, and sold by the time

Brand, 15 Neb. 601, 19 N.W. 494 (1884).

See additionally Survey of Illinois Law, 34 Chi.-Ken L.Rev. 81 (1954–1955), commenting on Kling v. Ghilarducci, 3 Ill.2d 454, 121 N.E.2d 752, 46 A.L.R.2d 1189 (1954).

86. See § 7.15, supra.

87. See §§ 7.20–7.30, infra.

88. See § 7.16, supra.

the period for filing objections expired. Judicial sales must have finality and judgment debtors may not assert untimely challenges on the basis of irregularities which were readily ascertainable before the close of the statutory period for filing objections." [89] Moreover, if there is an appeal, the ultimate foreclosure judgment will have even more finality. Indeed, one of the few defects that will not so easily be cured by the passage of time is the omitted party problem we considered in a preceding section.[90] An omitted junior lienor, as a necessary party not bound by the judicial foreclosure, can, of course, collaterally attack the validity of that foreclosure even after the time periods for direct review have expired. In any event, with power of sale foreclosure, the security of judicial finality is simply absent. While the passage of time inevitably will help a defective title derived from a power of sale foreclosure, it is largely by means of variable and unreliable concepts such as statutes of limitations, laches and related notions.

E. POWER OF SALE FORECLOSURE

§ 7.19 General Considerations

The other main foreclosure method, permitted in about twenty-five states, is power of sale foreclosure.[91] After varying types and degrees of notice, the property is sold at a public sale, either by a public official, such as a sheriff, by some other third party, or by the mortgagee.

In some states utilizing the power of sale method, the deed of trust is the most commonly used mortgage instrument. The mortgagor-trustor conveys the real estate to a trustee who holds the property in trust for the mortgagee-beneficiary until full payment of the mortgage debt. In the event of foreclosure, the power of sale is exercised by the trustee, who holds a public sale of the mortgaged property; the sale is usually not judicially supervised.

As previously indicated, the notice requirements under power of sale foreclosure vary, but are usually less rigorous than those associated with judicial foreclosure. Notice, as used here, may be simply notice of foreclosure or notice of default or a combination of the two. While some states require that notice by mail or personal service be provided for any person having a record interest in the real estate

89. Virgin Islands Nat. Bank v. Tyson, 506 F.2d 802, 805 (C.C.A.Virgin Is. 1974), certiorari denied 421 U.S. 976, 95 S.Ct. 1976, 44 L.Ed.2d 467 (1975). See Milwaukee Western Bank v. Cedars of Cedar Rapids, Inc., 170 N.W. 2d 670 (Iowa 1969).

90. See § 7.15, supra.

91. As of 1968 power of sale foreclosure was used in Alaska, Alabama, California, Colorado, District of Columbia, Georgia, Hawaii, Idaho, Maryland, Massachusetts, Michigan, Minnesota, Mississippi, Missouri, Nevada, New Hampshire, North Carolina, Oregon, Rhode Island, South Dakota, Tennessee, Texas, Virginia, Washington, West Virginia and Wyoming. Cost and Time Factors in Foreclosure of Mortgages, 3 Real Prop., Prob. & Tr.J. 413, 414 (1968).

junior to the mortgage being foreclosed,[92] many do not. A few states require only notice of publication.[93] This publication sometimes takes the form of newspaper advertisement and sometimes consists only of public posting. Other states, in addition to published notice, require notice either by mail or personal service to the mortgagor and the owner of the mortgaged real estate, but not to junior lienors and others holding an interest subordinate to the mortgage being foreclosed.[93a] A few states attempt to protect those interested parties who are neither mortgagors nor owners by requiring that the notice of foreclosure be mailed to any person who has previously recorded a request for such notice.[94] Finally, almost no power of sale foreclosure statutes provide for an opportunity for a hearing prior to the foreclosure sale.

The Uniform Land Transactions Act (ULTA) [95] authorizes power of sale foreclosure under methods not unlike many of those used in state statutes. After default, a minimum of five weeks must expire before the mortgagee officially notifies the mortgagor of his intent to foreclose.[96] After this official notice, there is an additional minimum three week grace period, after which the mortgagee must inform the mortgagor which default remedy he intends to use.[97] If the mortgagee chooses power of sale foreclosure, there is a requirement of mailed notice to the debtor and to all other parties whose interests would be cut off by foreclosure.[98] If a mortgagor qualifies as a "protected party", basically a person who is an owner-occupant of a residence, certain notice requirements and other protections are somewhat more substantial.[99]

The underlying theory of power of sale foreclosure is simple. It is that by complying with the above type statutory requirements, the mortgagee accomplishes the same purposes achieved by judicial fore-

92. See, e. g., Colo.Rev.Stat. § 38–37–113(2), (3) (1973); Idaho Code § 45–1506 (1967); Wash.Rev.Code § 61.24.-040 (1975); Mont.Rev.Codes Ann. § 93–6005 (1963).

93. See, e. g., Miss.Code Ann. § 89–1–55 (1972).

93a. See, e. g., D.C.Code § 45–615 (1973). Compare Minn.Stat.Ann. § 580.03 (1947) (personal service on person in possession only).

94. See, e. g., § 443.325, R.S.Mo. (Supp.1975). Some states combine required mailed notice to all parties having record interest in the real estate together with mailed notice to any other person who has previously recorded a request for it. See, e. g., Ariz.Rev.Stat. § 33–809 (1974); West's Ann.Cal.Civ.Code, § 2924(b) (1976).

95. The Uniform Land Transactions Act was approved by the National Conference of Commissioners on Uniform State Laws in August, 1975 and recommended for enactment in all of the states. It was amended substantially in 1977, although these amendments for the most part did not effect the foreclosure sections. No state thus far has adopted the ULTA in whole or in part.

96. U.L.T.A. § 3–505.

97. U.L.T.A. § 3–508.

98. U.L.T.A. § 3–508(a).

99. See U.L.T.A. §§ 3–505, 3–507.

closure without the substantial additional burdens that the latter type of foreclosure entails. Those purposes are to terminate all interests junior to the mortgage being foreclosed and to provide the sale purchaser with a title identical to that of the mortgagor as of the time the mortgage being foreclosed was executed.[1] Moreover, where it is in common use, power of sale foreclosure has provided an effective foreclosure remedy with a cost in time and money substantially lower than that of its judicial foreclosure counterpart.[2]

Notwithstanding the fact that power of sale foreclosure generally works and that it is more efficient and less costly than judicial foreclosure, the titles it produces have been somewhat less stable than those resulting from judicial foreclosure. As we noted earlier, there are at least three reasons for this.[3] First, the court supervision involved in judicial foreclosure will prevent many defects from arising. Second, because judicial foreclosure is an adversary proceeding, the presence of other parties who will bring possible defects to the court's attention constitutes added protection against a faulty end product. Finally, the concept of judicial finality provides substantial insulation against subsequent collateral attack even on technically defective judical foreclosure proceedings. None of these protections are inherent in power of sale foreclosure. Moreover, as we will examine in detail later in this chapter, power of sale foreclosure has been subjected recently to the further uncertainty of constitutional attack because of its alleged notice and hearing deficiencies.[4]

§ 7.20 Defective Power of Sale Foreclosure—The "Void-Voidable" Distinction

While we examine in detail in the next section a variety of defects that provide grounds for setting aside power of sale foreclosures, it is important initially to consider those defects from a broader perspective. Generally, defects in the exercise of a power of sale can be categorized in at least three ways. Some defects are so substantial as to render the sale *void*. In this situation no title, legal or equitable, passes to the sale purchaser or subsequent grantees, except perhaps by adverse possession.[5] A forged mortgage, for example, would fall into this category. The most common example, however, of a defect that would render a sale void is where the power of sale is exercised when there has been no default in the mortgage obligation.[6]

1. See § 7.12, supra.

2. See McElhone & Cramer, Loan Foreclosure Costs Affected By Varied State Regulations, 36 Mortgage Banker 41 (1975).

3. See § 7.18, supra.

4. See §§ 7.23–7.30, infra.

5. Dingus, Mortgages—Redemption After Foreclosure Sale in Missouri, 25 Mo.L.Rev. 261, 277 (1960); Tiffany, Real Property, § 1552 (3d Ed. 1939). But cf. Phillips v. Latham, 523 S.W. 2d 19 (Tex.Civ.App.1975), refused n. r. e., appeal after remand 551 S.W.2d 103 (Tex.Civ.App.1977).

6. See, e. g., Bradford v. Thompson, 470 S.W.2d 663 (Tex.1971), certiorari

Most defects that we will examine in the next section render the foreclosure *voidable* and not void. This means that bare legal title passes to the sale purchaser, subject to the rights of redemption of those injured by the defective exercise of the power of sale. A common example of a voidable sale in many jurisdictions is the purchase by a trustee under a deed of trust at his own sale.[7] However, where the defect only renders the sale voidable, the rights of redemption can be cut off if the land falls into the hands of a bona fide purchaser for value.[8] Where this occurs, an action for damages against the foreclosing mortgagee or trustee may be the only remaining remedy. Finally, some defects seem to be treated as so inconsequential as to render the sale neither void nor voidable. Such defects commonly involve minor discrepancies in the notice of sale. For example, where the first of four published notices of sale omitted the place of sale, the court held that since there was "substantial compliance" with the requirements specified by the deed of trust and since the parties were not affected in a "material way", the sale was valid.[9]

Assuming that the defective sale is only voidable, who should be treated as a bona fide purchaser? It would seem that a mortgagee-purchaser would rarely, if ever, qualify as a bona fide purchaser. Indeed, it is normally the mortgagee or his attorney who manages the power of sale foreclosure proceeding and who would be responsible for defects that arise. Moreover, even where a deed of trust is involved, while the trustee presumably is in charge of the proceedings, it is not unlikely that, for purposes of determining BFP status, he will be treated as an agent of the mortgagee. If the sale purchaser has paid value and is unrelated to the mortgagee, it would seem that he should take free of voidable defects if: (a) he has no actual knowledge of the defects; (b) he is not on reasonable notice from recorded instruments; and (c) the defects are not such that a person attending the sale exercising reasonable care would have been aware of the defect. Where a subsequent grantee is involved, BFP status would seem slightly easier to achieve. If that grantee did not attend the sale, he should be treated as a bona fide purchaser unless he had actual notice of the defect or was on reasonable notice from the recorded documents. Where, however, the sale purchaser or some later purchaser is a BFP, but he conveys to a person such as the original

denied 405 U.S. 955, 92 S.Ct. 1174, 31 L.Ed. 232 (1972). "The power of sale is ordinarily conditioned upon a failure to pay the debt at a time named, and consequently a sale before that time would, it seems, ordinarily be invalid for any purpose, even in favor of an innocent purchaser from the purchaser at the sale." Tiffany, Real Property, § 1552 at 637 (3d Ed. 1939).

7. See, e. g., Whitlow v. Mountain Trust Bank, 215 Va. 149, 207 S.E.2d 837 (1974); Dingus, Mortgages—Redemption After Foreclosure Sale in Missouri, 25 Mo.L.Rev. 261, 276–282 (1960).

8. See, e. g., Jackson v. Klein, 320 S.W.2d 553 (Mo.1959); Dingus, supra note 7 at 277, 280.

9. Bailey v. Pioneer Federal Sav. and Loan Ass'n, 210 Va. 558, 172 S.E.2d 730 (1970).

mortgagee who would not otherwise qualify for such status, what should be the result? Most jurisdictions would probably refuse to confer BFP status on the mortgagee (or any intervening purchaser with notice of the defect), since such persons could not reacquire the property in good faith.[10]

§ 7.21 Defective Power of Sale Foreclosure—Specific Problems

In this section we focus on commonly raised grounds for setting aside a power of sale foreclosure. As we will note, some irregularities are considered so prejudicial that the presence of one of them alone may be sufficient to invalidate a foreclosure. Other deficiencies, however, may only be significant if they are found in conjunction with other defects. In any event, it is almost a truism that the chances for reversal of a sale are always strengthened by the cumulative impact of several irregularities in one foreclosure proceeding.

Inadequacy of the Sale Price

All jurisdictions adhere to the recognized rule that mere inadequacy of the foreclosure sale price will not invalidate a sale, absent fraud, unfairness or other irregularity.[11] Stating the rule in a slightly different manner, courts sometimes say that inadequacy of the sale price is an insufficient ground unless it is so gross as to shock the conscience of the court, warranting an inference of fraud or imposition.[12]

Absent the presence of such additional circumstances, it is extremely difficult to get a sale set aside on mere price inadequacy. As one commentator has described the situation, "such sales have been upheld where the price paid for the property was only one-half, one-third, one-fourth, one-fifth, or even one-twentieth of its reasonable value." [13] On the other hand, where other factors are present, such as chilled bidding, unusual hour of sale or any other indicia of unfairness, courts do set sales aside.[14] For example, in a case where the mortgaged real estate sold for 3% of the fair market value, the court set aside the sale because of the additional factor that the mortgagee had informed the mortgagor of the incorrect sale date.[15] Moreover,

10. See McDaniel v. Sprick, 297 Mo. 424, 249 S.W. 611 (1923). See also, 3 Pomeroy, Equity Jurisprudence 55–57 (5th Ed. 1941) (support by analogy to recording act cases).

11. See, e. g., Lippold v. White, 181 Md. 562, 31 A.2d 170 (1943); Gilbert v. Lusk, 123 Ind.App. 167, 106 N.E.2d 204 (1952); Handy v. Rogers, 143 Colo. 1, 351 P.2d 819 (1960); Kouros v. Sewell, 225 Ga. 487, 169 S.E.2d 816 (1969); Tiffiny, Real Property, § 1550 (3rd Ed. 1939).

12. Dingus, Mortgages—Redemption After Foreclosure Sale in Missouri, 25 Mo.L.Rev. 261, 262–263 (1960); Pugh v. Richmond, 58 Tenn.App. 62, 425 S.W.2d 789 (1968). See Anderson v. Anderson, 107 R.I. 202, 266 A.2d 56 (1970) for a situation where this difficult burden was sustained.

13. Id. at 263–264.

14. Id. Blades v. Ossenfort, 481 S.W.2d 531 (Mo.App.1972).

15. Kouros v. Sewell, 225 Ga. 487, 169 S.E.2d 816 (1969).

one further factor needs to be stressed. Where sales *are* overturned, whatever the nature of the additional factors, price inadequacy is the key factor because, after all, had the price been adequate, no prejudice would have existed.

Finally, it should be noted that inadequacy of the sale price looms larger on its own when it is the mortgagee who is seeking to validate it for purposes of seeking a deficiency judgment. In other words, courts scrutinize the sale price much more closely where the mortgagee is seeking a deficiency judgment plus retention of the land.[16] This is especially the case where statutes require confirmation of the price in power of sale foreclosures as a condition precedent to a deficiency judgment.[17]

Time of Sale

The time of the sale can create at least two problems. First, the sale is sometimes held at a different day or hour than specified by the notice of foreclosure. Second, even though the sale is held at the time indicated by the notice, it may not be held at the usual hour for such sales in the particular community involved. The danger, in either event, is that possible bidders will not attend the sale and, thus, that the highest possible price for the property will not be obtained.

In the first situation, the impact of the defect on the sale will obviously depend on how serious the discrepancy is between the advertised date and the actual date of sale. Where the discrepancy is substantial, that alone may be enough to set aside the sale. For example, where a sale was advertised for the first Tuesday of August, but not held until the first Tuesday of September, the court found that the defect not only was sufficient to invalidate the sale, but also to hold it to be void.[18] On the other hand, a few minutes discrepancy between the advertised time and the actual sale time will be considered insubstantial.[19] Obviously, most cases will fall in between these two extremes and whether the sale will be set aside will depend on whether the error prejudiced the parties and whether additional circumstances also weigh in favor of sale invalidation.

Where the sale is held at the time or within the times advertised, but at an unusual time, the cases vary substantially and generalizations are hazardous. However, most require, as an additional factor, inadequacy of the sale price as a condition precedent to setting aside the sale.[20] Moreover, some courts hold that if a statute specifies the

16. See Davis v. Sheffield, 123 Ga. App. 228, 180 S.E.2d 263 (1971).

17. See, e. g., Ga.Code Ann.Tit. 67 §§ 1503–1506. See also, Davie v. Sheffield, 123 Ga.App. 228, 180 S.E.2d 263 (1971); Adams v. Gwinnett Commercial Bank, 238 Ga. 722, 235 S.E.2d 476 (1977).

18. Hood Oil Co. v. Moss, 134 Ga.App. 477, 214 S.E.2d 726 (1975).

19. Silver Spring Development Corp. v. Guertler, 257 Md. 291, 262 A.2d 749 (1970).

20. See Dingus, Mortgages—Redemption After Foreclosure Sale in Missouri, 25 Mo.L.Rev. 261, 266 (1960).

range of sale hours, e. g., "between 10 o'clock A.M. and 4 o'clock P. M.," there is no need to delineate the time of sale more specifically and a sale at any time within the statutory range is acceptable.[21] Indeed, some courts have held that sale on a national holiday is permissible unless expressly prohibited by statute.[22] On the other hand, other courts have held that, absent statutory regulation, sale at an unusual hour coupled with price inadequacy will be sufficient to set aside a sale.[23]

Place of Sale

Normally, statutes require that land be foreclosed in the county where it is located.[24] Thus, for example, where a deed of trust covered noncontiguous parcels of land in two counties, a trustee's sale in one county of both parcels was probably void as to the parcel in the other county.[25] Absent such a statutory requirement, however, some courts indicate that the parties may contract in the mortgage instrument for foreclosure in other than the situs county.[26]

Suppose, however, that the parties do agree in the mortgage instrument on a particular place of sale and that provision is violated by the mortgagee or trustee. There is strong authority that under those circumstances the sale is at least voidable.[27] Moreover, the chances of voidability appear to be enhanced when the place specified in the published notice of sale coincides with that called for in the mortgage instrument.[28]

Indeed, where, as in the preceding sentence, the place of sale described in the published notice varies from the actual place of sale, a stronger case for voidability can be made than when the variance is simply between the actual place and the place specified in the mortgage instrument. In the latter situation, after all, it is only the mortgagor who is likely to be affected. In the former case, however, it is third party potential bidders who most likely would be deterred from attending the sale. Outside pressure to raise the sale price would thus be missing. However, all cases do not necessarily follow this reasoning. For example, in one recent case the published notice specified that the sale was to take place at the "Clark County Courthouse in North Las Vegas". In fact, the courthouse is in Las Vegas and

21. Mabry v. Abbott, 471 S.W.2d 442 (Tex.Civ.App.1971).

22. See Koehler v. Pioneer American Ins. Co., 425 S.W.2d 889 (Tex.Civ. App.1968). But see National Life Ins. Co. v. Silverman, 454 F.2d 899, 915 (D.C.Ct.App.1971).

23. See, e. g., Hanson v. Neal, 215 Mo. 256, 114 S.W. 1073 (1908).

24. See, e. g., Minn.Stat.Ann. § 580.06; Vernon's Ann.Mo.Stat. § 443.310; Utah Code Ann.1953, § 57-1-25.

25. See Dingus, Mortgages—Redemption From Foreclosure Sale in Missouri, 25 Mo.L.Rev. 261, 284 (1960); Metropolitan Life Ins. Co. v. Coleman, 99 S.W.2d 479 (Mo.App.1936).

26. See, e. g., Pugh v. Richmond, 425 S.W.2d 789 (Tenn.App.1968).

27. See Dingus, supra note 25 at 284; Schanawerk v. Hobrecht, 117 Mo. 22, 22 S.W. 949 (1893).

28. See, e. g., Stewart v. Brown, 112 Mo. 171, 20 S.W. 451 (1892).

the sale took place there. The court indicated that, absent proof that bidders went to the wrong place, the sale should not be set aside.[29] Perhaps the real question should have been, however, how many third party bidders might have attended had the notice stated the correct place of sale.

Sale By Parcels or in Bulk

Mortgaged real estate often is capable of being divided into parcels for purposes of foreclosure sale as an alternative to selling it in bulk. This will especially be the case where the land consists of lots in a subdivision or where a large tract of undivided land is readily capable of subdivision. Where a mortgage covers such land, the question becomes which method of sale the mortgagee or trustee should utilize. Substantial authority requires that the party exercising the power of sale adopt the mode of sale that will be most beneficial to the mortgagor.[30] Normally this creates a presumption in favor of selling in parcels because "a sale in parcels or lots opens a field to a greater number of bidders, is conducive to a better price, tends to prohibit odious speculation upon the distress of the debtor, and enables him to redeem some of the property without being compelled to redeem it all." [31] Moreover, a few courts seem to require that only as many parcels as are necessary to pay the mortgage debt be sold, even though selling all of the parcels separately would have yielded more money than one sale in bulk.[32] Sales that are set aside are usually held to be voidable.[33] On the other hand, there is significant, but probably minority, authority that, absent specific direction in the

29. Hankins v. Administrator of Veterans Affairs, 555 P.2d 483 (Nev.1976).

30. See, e. g., J. H. Morris v. Indian Hills, Inc., 282 Ala. 443, 212 So.2d 831 (1968); Thompson, Real Property, § 5182 (1977 Supp.); Dingus, Mortgages—Redemption After Foreclosure Sale in Missouri, 25 Mo.L.Rev. 261, 270 (1960). "Where property is susceptible of division, and it will bring more by being divided and sold in separate parcels or lots than by being sold in a body, or where by a sale of a part of the premises a sufficient amount can be realized to pay off the secured debt, then it is the duty of the trustee to make the division and sell a portion accordingly, and if he fails in this the sale will be held invalid on application of the party aggrieved. There are instances in which the whole of a piece of property will sell for more than it would by being separated, and in all such cases the trustee must exercise a sound discretion." Tatum v. Holliday, 59 Mo. 422, 428 (1875). See also Hill v. Farmers & Mech. Bank, 97 U.S. 450, 24 L.Ed. 1051 (1878); Loveland v. Clark, 11 Colo. 265, 18 P. 544 (1888); Singleton v. Scott, 11 Iowa 589 (1859); Patterson v. Miller, 52 Md. 388 (1879); Terry v. Fitzgerald, 32 Grat. 843; L.R.A.1917B, 526 (Va. 1879).

31. J. H. Morris v. Indian Hills, Inc., 282 Ala. 443, 453, 212 So.2d 831, 843 (1968); See Conway v. Andrews, 286 Ala. 28, 236 So.2d 687 (Ala.1970).

32. See, e. g., Moore v. Hamilton, 151 W.Va. 784, 155 S.E.2d 877 (1967). "If it is sold in parts, no more of the property shall be sold than is necessary to satisfy the lien and the costs and expenses of the proceedings." So.Dak.Compiled Laws, 21–54–9.

33. See Dingus, note 30 at 268; J. H. Morris v. Indian Hills, Inc., 282 Ala. 443, 212 So.2d 831 (1968).

mortgage instrument, the method of sale is discretionary and that sales in bulk will ordinarily be upheld.[34]

A condition precedent, in any event, is that the mortgagor establish that the method of sale utilized caused injury.[35] Normally, this will entail establishing that the property would have brought more money had another method of sale been used. On the other hand, this need not always be the case. Suppose the mortgagor is claiming that the sale should be set aside because, even though a sale in bulk brought more money than would a sale of all of the parcels individually, the sale of only a few of the parcels would have satisfied the mortgage debt. Here the mortgagor should presumably be able to show injury simply by establishing the latter fact, even though he may not have suffered monetary injury because the method of sale actually used may have served his best financial, though not other, interests.

There is considerable statutory regulation of this problem. For example, one typical statute provides that "if the mortgaged premises consist of separate and distinct farms or tracts, they shall be sold separately, and no more farms or tracts shall be sold than are necessary to satisfy the amount due on such mortgage." [36] Some statutes simply appear to give the party exercising the power of sale discretion as to the method of sale.[37] A few states take the rather unique approach of giving the mortgagor the option of determining the method of sale. For example, the Utah statute provides that the mortgagor may, if present at the sale, "direct the order in which the (mortgaged) property shall be sold when such property consists of several known lots of parcels which can be sold to advantage separately and the trustee shall follow such directions." [38] A variation on this type of legislation allows the junior lienors in order of priority to make the choice in the event the mortgagor does not exercise his rights.[39] This type of legislation would seem to bar the mortgagor, and, in some situations, junior lienors from getting the sale set aside based on the method of sale actually used. This, in turn, would tend to increase the stability of power of sale titles obtained under such statutes.

There are nevertheless potential problems with this latter type of legislation. Normally, of course, it has to be presumed that the mortgagor will exercise the choice most beneficial to his interests.

34. See Thompson, supra note 30, § 5182 at 17; 61 A.L.R.2d 505, 515–527; Classic Enterprises Inc. v. Continental Mortgage Investors, 135 Ga.App. 105, 217 S.E.2d 411 (1975).

35. See Bellah v. First Nat. Bank of Hereford, 474 S.W.2d 785 (Tex.Civ. App.1972); Dingus, supra note 30 at 269–70.

36. Minn.Stat.Ann. § 580.08. See, e. g., No.Dak.Cent.Code 35–22–09.

37. E. g., Or.Rev.Stat. 86.755.

38. Utah Code Ann.1953, 51–1–27. See, also, Ariz.Rev.Stat.Ann. § 33–810.

39. E. g., So.Dak.Compiled Laws 21–54–9.

Suppose, however, that for purely spiteful reasons, a judgment-proof mortgagor chooses the method that results either in a deficiency for the foreclosing mortgagee or little or no surplus for the junior lienors. Perhaps a court later would hold that such a choice would be impermissible because it might determine that the parcels could not be "sold to advantage separately" within the meaning of the statute. In any event, such mortgagor activity would be aberrational and thus not a substantial problem under such statutes.

As a practical matter, where a statute does not specifically direct the method of sale, it probably makes sense for the mortgagee or trustee to advertise and conduct the sale both by parcel and by bulk. The property ultimately should be sold to the highest bidder under the particular method most beneficial to the parties.[40] Some courts have looked with approval on this approach.[41] Moreover, where possible, it is a good idea for the party selling to obtain the mortgagor's agreement in advance as to the method of sale. For example, if the mortgagor so specifies in advance, the mortgagee or trustee should sell only so much as is necessary to satisfy the debt, even though a sale in bulk or of all the parcels individually would bring more money for the mortgagor. Ideally, junior lienors should also be consulted. Many times, of course, agreement as to the method of sale will not be possible. However, a good faith effort by the selling party to obtain advance agreement will reduce the likelihood that a court would upset a sale because of the sale method ultimately utilized.

Chilled Bidding

Where the mortgagee or trustee engages in irregular conduct that suppresses bidding, the result is often known as "chilled bidding" and is a ground for setting aside a sale.[42] There can be at least two types of chilled bidding.[43] The first occurs where there is collusion involving the mortgagee or trustee and potential purchasers to hold down the bidding or where the mortgagee or trustee by other actions seek to accomplish the same result. The second type encompasses inadvertent and unintentional acts by the trustee or mortgagee that suppress bidding.

The first type of chilled bidding can be involved in a myriad of fact situations, and it arguably can render a sale void rather than merely voidable.[44] A mortgagee or trustee could, for example, get third parties to agree not to bid at a foreclosure sale either by paying

40. See Dingus, supra note 30 at 271.

41. See Lazarus v. Caesar, 157 Mo. 199, 57 S.W. 751 (1900).

42. Dingus, supra note 30 at 274. See also, Biddle v. National Old Line Ins. Co., 513 S.W.2d 135 (Tex.Civ.App. 1974), refused n. r. e.; Sullivan v. Federal Farm Mort. Corp., 62 Ga.App. 402, 8 S.E.2d 126 (1940); Aultman & Taylor Co. v. Meade, 121 Ky. 241, 89 S.W. 137, 123 Am.St.Rep. 193 (1905); Fenton v. Torrey, 133 Mass. 138 (1882).

43. Dingus, Id. at 274–275.

44. Id.

them off or on the understanding that if the mortgagee purchases, the third parties will share in the resale profits. Or the mortgagee or trustee may discourage bidding by intentionally misrepresenting the state of the title or the physical condition of the mortgaged premises.[45]

A more difficult problem is raised when there is collusion among third parties alone. This could involve an agreement among several third parties that they will discourage others from attending the sale and that they will only bid the property up to a specified price. They might further agree that if one of them actually purchases at the sale, he will, upon resale, split the profits with the others. If, of course, the trustee or mortgagee has advance knowledge of this agreement, the sale should be postponed. On the other hand, if there is no such knowledge and the mortgagee purchases the property in spite of the third party agreement, it would seem unfair to set aside the sale against the mortgagee even though the collusion among the third parties may have meant that the mortgagee was able to purchase for a lower price. However, if one of the third parties is successful bidder, it would seem that the mortgagor should be able to get the sale set aside against the third party purchaser. The collusion, after all, probably kept the price down and setting aside the sale would foster a public policy that encourages open and honest bidding.

The most common example of the unintentional or inadvertent type of chilled bidding involves the erroneous statement in a foreclosure advertisement that the mortgaged premises are being sold subject to a senior lien.[46] This, of course, could very well result in a lower sale price than if the bidders were certain the land was free and clear of senior liens. It should be emphasized, however, that truthful statements that suppress bidding do not constitute chilled bidding. For example, in one case a mortgagor unsuccessfully claimed that bidding was chilled because the trustee stated at the sale that an undivided interest was being sold. The problem was that the statement was correct.[47] In any event, unintentionally chilled bidding probably renders the sale voidable and not void.[48]

The chilled bidding concept normally requires that the mortgagor actually establish that the bidding was suppressed; this is often done by showing inadequacy of the sale price. This clearly makes sense where the chilled bidding claim is based on mere inadvertent

45. For similar fact situations, see McDaniel v. Sprick, 297 Mo. 424, 249 S.W. 611 (1920); Hanson v. Neal, 215 Mo. 256, 114 S.W. 1073 (1908).

46. See, e. g., Hoffman v. McCracken, 168 Mo. 337, 67 S.W. 868 (1902). But see Tifton Corp. v. Decatur Federal Sav. & Loan Ass'n, 136 Ga.App. 710, 222 S.E.2d 115 (1975) (notice of foreclosure and recorded documents held not to suggest property was subject to a first lien).

47. Cleveland v. Cleveland, 235 Ga. 361, 219 S.E.2d 715 (1975).

48. Dingus, supra note 30 at 275–276.

mortgagee or trustee action.[49] However, where the chilled bidding is of the first type, it would seem that public policy, even in the absence of clearly established injury, dictates a presumption in favor of setting aside the sale as a deterrent to such intentional or collusive behavior.

Mortgagee Purchase under Mortgage with Power of Sale

Where a mortgage contains a power of sale in favor of the mortgagee, the mortgagee normally may not purchase at a sale carried out pursuant to that power.[50] As one leading decision stated, "a mortgagee may not purchase at his own sale; if he does so, he does not acquire an absolute estate. The sale does not alter the relation of mortgagor and mortgagee existing between the parties. * * * Such sale is voidable at the election of the mortgagor." [51] Moreover, the prohibition also applies where the purchase by the mortgagee is made indirectly through a third party.[52] A few courts, however, permit a sale to the mortgagee where the terms of the mortgage expressly authorize the mortgagee to purchase.[53] Indeed, at least one jurisdiction appears to permit the mortgagee to purchase even in the absence of such consent.[54]

Some jurisdictions that use the mortgage with power of sale have solved the foregoing problems by legislation that specifies that the power of sale be exercised by a public official, usually the sheriff, and that specifically authorizes the mortgagee to purchase.[55] The practical effect of such legislation is to create a financing device that is functionally the equivalent of a deed of trust with a power of sale in a public trustee, a device that is used in a few jurisdictions.[56]

49. Id.

50. Mills v. Mut. B. & L. Ass'n, 216 N.C. 664, 6 S.E.2d 549 (1940); Jackson v. Blankenship, 213 Ala. 607, 105 So. 684 (1925); Imboden v. Hunter, 23 Ark. 622, 79 Am.Dec. 116 (1861); Dyer v. Shurtleff, 112 Mass. 165, 17 Am.Rep. 77 (1873); Martin v. McNeely, 101 N.C. 634, 8 S.E. 231 (1888); Blockley v. Fowler, 21 Cal. 326, 82 Am.Dec. 747 (1863). See 27 Va.L.Rev. 926, 931 (1941); Dingus, Mortgages—Redemption After Foreclosure Sale in Missouri, 25 Mo.L. Rev. 261, 282–283 (1960).

51. Mills v. Mut. B. & L. Ass'n, 216 N.C. 644, 668, 6 S.E.2d 549, 552 (1940).

52. See Dingus, supra note 50 at 283; Byrne v. Carson, 70 Mo.App. 126 (1897).

53. Brown v. Eckhardt, 23 Tenn.App. 217, 129 S.W.2d 1122 (1940); Dexter v. Shepard, 117 Mass. 480 (1875); Cambridge Bank v. Cronin, 289 Mass. 379, 194 N.E. 289 (1935).

54. See Southern Trust & Mortgage Co. v. Daniel, 143 Tex. 321, 184 S.W. 2d 465 (1943) where the Supreme Court of Texas stated that "the rule is well-settled in this state that a mortgagee with a power to sell may purchase at his own sale made at public auction * * *." See also, Skeen v. Glenn Justice Mortgage, Inc., 526 S.W.2d 252 (Tex.Civ.App.1975).

55. See Minn.Stat.Ann. §§ 580.06, 580.-11; Wyo.Stat.1957, § 34–74; Mich. Comp.Laws Ann. § 600.3216. Massachusetts appears to authorize the mortgagee to purchase without a public official conducting the sale. See Mass.Gen.Laws Ann. c. 183, § 25.

56. See, e. g., Colo.Rev.Stat. '73 §§ 38–37–101 through 38–37–139.

Trustee Purchase at Foreclosure Sale and Related Problems

It is stated so frequently as to be a truism that a trustee in a deed of trust is a fiduciary for both the mortgagor and mortgagee and must act impartially between them.[57] As one leading decision has stated, "the trustee for sale is bound by his office to bring the estate to a sale under every possible advantage to the debtor as well as to the creditor, and he is bound to use not only good faith but also every requisite degree of diligence in conducting the sale and to attend equally to the interest of debtor and creditor alike, apprising both of the intention of selling, that each may take the means to procure an advantageous sale." [58] Yet because he represents two parties whose interests are often antithetical, he is not treated as a traditional trustee for all purposes. For example, while there is authority to the contrary,[59] there is case law that in the absence of fraud or misconduct a foreclosure by a trustee under a power of sale is not invalidated because the trustee owns an interest in the mortgage debt.[60] Moreover, so long as the trustee is not employed by or otherwise associated with the beneficiary (the holder of the note and deed of trust), it is both permissible and a standard practice for the beneficiary to purchase at the foreclosure sale.[61] Indeed, one of the possible advantages of the deed of trust over the mortgage with power of sale is that in the former situation the beneficiary is able to purchase at the sale.[62]

Yet it is equally clear that a trustee, at least without the express consent of the trustor (the debtor) or his successor, may not purchase the premises himself at his own foreclosure sale.[63] As one court has noted, "when a trustee buys at his own sale, a constructive fraud exists; the transaction is voidable; and when attacked, the sale must be set aside." [64] In such a situation, the fact that the trustee

57. See e. g., Spires v. Edgar, 513 S.W.2d 372 (Mo.1974); Whitlow v. Mountain Trust Bank, 215 Va. 149, 207 S.E.2d 837 (1974); White v. Macqueen, 360 Ill. 236, 195 N.E. 832, 98 A.L.R. 1115 (1935). See Spruill v. Ballard, 61 App.D.C. 112, 58 F.2d 517 (1932); 90 A.L.R.2d 501, 505–506.

58. Mills v. Mutual Building & Loan Ass'n, 216 N.C. 664, 670, 6 S.E.2d 549, 554 (1940).

59. Spruill v. Ballard, n. 57, supra; Morgan v. Glendy, 92 Va. 86, 22 S.E. 854 (1895); Spencer v. Lee, 19 W.Va. 179 (1881).

60. Jackson v. Klein, 320 S.W.2d 553 (Mo.1959); Dingus, Mortgages—Redemption After Foreclosure Sale in Missouri, 25 Mo.L.Rev. 261, 281 (1960).

61. Dingus, supra note 60 at 282. See, e. g., Utah Code Ann.1953, 57–1–27.

62. See text at notes 50–56, supra.

63. See Whitlow v. Mountain Trust Bank, 215 Va. 149, 207 S.E.2d 837 (1974); Mills v. Mutual Building & Loan Ass'n, 216 N.C. 664, 6 S.E.2d 549 (1940); Dingus, supra note 60 at 276; 90 A.L.R.2d 501, 567. But see Fuqua v. Burrell, 474 S.W.2d 333 (Tex.Civ.App.1971).

64. Whitlow v. Mountain Trust Bank, 215 Va. 149, 151, 207 S.E.2d 837, 840 (1974).

otherwise acted fairly and with good motives is not controlling.[65] The prohibition applies equally when the purchase is made indirectly through a family member.[66] Moreover courts will set aside a purchase by the trustee from a foreclosure sale purchaser that occurs immediately after the foreclosure sale.[67]

More complex problems arise when, as is common, the beneficiary purchases at a trustee's sale and the trustee is an employee or part owner of the beneficiary. This situation can be treated conceptually in at least two ways. First, where the connection between the trustee and the beneficiary is substantial, courts treat the situation as an indirect purchase by the trustee and thus voidable.[68] For example, in one recent case the court took this approach where the trustee owned 13% of the stock and was vice president of the beneficiary, a closely held corporation.[69] As a second method of analyzing such situations, a few courts have determined that, as a practical matter, the "instrument—in form a deed of trust—executed to the chief executive officer of a corporation is, in effect, a mortgage, and the law relating to foreclosure of mortgage deeds rather than the law relating to trust deeds is applicable." [70] The sale thus becomes voidable because the beneficiary is treated as if he purchased pursuant to his own power of sale.

The problems presented by the foregoing paragraph are not insurmountable. At least one state by statute seems to authorize a bank or savings and loan association to be both a trustee and beneficiary under the same deed of trust.[71] Since another statute states that "any person, including the beneficiary, may bid at the sale",[72] it would seem to authorize such an institution to purchase at a foreclosure sale from itself in its capacity as trustee. In the many states without such legislative authorization, it is a common practice for trustees to be employed by, part-owner of, or be otherwise associated with the beneficiary. This is often done largely for convenience and probably is harmless in most instances because the vast majority of deeds of trust are never foreclosed. As to those deeds of trust that do reach the foreclosure stage, beneficiaries obviously want to be able to purchase at the foreclosure sale. A simple expedient at that stage would be for the beneficiary to have the related trustee resign and to

65. Id.

66. See Lee v. Lee, 236 Miss. 260, 109 So.2d 870 (1959).

67. Smith v. Haley, 314 S.W.2d 909 (Mo.1958).

68. See Whitlow v. Mountain Trust Bank, 215 Va. 149, 207 S.E.2d 837 (1974); Southern Trust and Mortgage Co. v. Daniel, 143 Tex. 321, 184 S.W. 2d 465 (1944).

69. Whitlow v. Mountain Trust Bank, 215 Va. 149, 207 S.E.2d 837 (1974).

70. Mills v. Mutual Bldg. & Loan Ass'n, 216 N.C. 664, 6 S.E.2d 549 (1940).

71. Utah Code Ann.1953, 57–1–21.

72. Utah Code Ann.1953, 57–1–27.

replace him with an independent trustee. This can be accomplished by making sure that the deed of trust specifically authorizes replacement of the trustee or, in most states, by relying on statutory authorization for such replacement.[73]

Statutory Presumptions

Some states have statutes that provide that recitals of statutory compliance contained in a trustee's deed executed upon foreclosure create, in general, prima facie evidence of compliance with statutory requirements "relating to the exercise of the power of sale and sale of the property described therein, including recitals concerning any mailing, personal delivery and publication of the notice of default, any mailing and publication and posting of notice of sale, and the conduct of the sale." [74] As to bona fide purchasers and encumbrancers, some of these statutes also provide that the recitals create conclusive evidence of compliance.[75] A variation on the above statute provides that the trustee's deed *itself* provides the same evidence of compliance.[76]

The above legislation seems to have significant impact in two respects. First, it creates a general rebuttable presumption that the statutory sale requirements have been satisfied and that the sale is valid.[77] This would be available to a foreclosure title holder whether a bona fide purchaser or not. To that extent, the effect of such statutes is to add slightly more stability to foreclosure titles and thus is desireable. Second, and more important, it would seem that any defect in the foreclosure proceeding which is contradicted by a recital in the trustee's deed renders the sale merely voidable and not void. As we noted earlier, if a defect renders a sale void, the sale passes no title even to a bona fide purchaser and thus the defect can be raised against such a purchaser.[78] If, on the other hand, the defect renders a sale voidable, the sale cannot be set aside against a BFP.[79] Under these statutes, the recitals themselves constitute conclusive evidence in favor of BFP's, and hence any sale would be voidable at most. Does this mean that defects which normally render a sale void, such as a forged deed of trust or the absence of a default, could not be raised against a BFP? At least two state statutes seem specifically

73. See, e. g., Vernon's Ann.Mo.Stat. § 443.340.

74. Utah Code Ann.1953, 57–1–28. See, e. g., Colo.Rev.Stat. 38–39–115; Ore.Rev.Stat. 86.780; So.Dak.Compiled Laws 21–48–23.

75. Utah Code Ann.1953, 57–1–28; West's Ann.Cal.Civ.Code, § 2924; Ore.Rev.Stat. 86.780.

76. Ariz.Rev.Stat. § 33–811.

77. See, e. g., New England Loan & Trust Co. v. Brown, 157 Mo. 116, 57 S.W. 760 (1900). See generally, Basye, Clearing Land Titles, § 43 (2d Ed. 1970).

78. See § 7.20, supra.

79. Id.

to go this far.[80] However, the statute quoted above and those similar to it probably do not. Rather these statutes seem to cover defects that arise in connection with the mechanics of exercising the power of sale and not those that relate to whether there was a substantive basis to foreclose in the first place. In any event, it would seem unfair to allow a BFP to prevail over a mortgagor who was not in default or, indeed, over a person who never executed a mortgage to begin with.

§ 7.22 Defective Power of Sale Foreclosure—Remedies

As we have noted, there are numerous grounds which can render a power of sale foreclosure either void or voidable. Moreover, these defective sales give grounds for relief not only to mortgagors, but also to any other party who is junior to the mortgage being foreclosed. The nature and scope of the remedy will depend on several variables. Among these are whether the defect is discovered before or after sale, the nature of the defect, and, importantly, if the sale has already been completed, whether the sale purchaser or any subsequent grantee is a bona fide purchaser.

Injunction against Sale

Where the defective power of sale foreclosure has not yet been consummated, the most common remedy for the mortgagor or other injured party is an injunction suit against it.[81] In theory this relief should be available for any defects that would be serious enough to set aside an already completed sale. However, because the sale will not yet have taken place, and because many of the defects we examined in the preceding section could not yet have occurred, very often the basis for the injunction suit will be substantive defenses to the obligation itself and related matters. For example, injunctive relief will be available where the claim is that the debt has already been paid or tendered,[82] or that, for a variety of reasons, the mortgage is not in default or there is no underlying obligation to support the mortgage.[83] Other grounds have included defective advertisement of the sale[84]

80. See Rev.Code Mont.1947, § 52–410; Nev.Rev.Stat. 107.030(8). See also, Uniform Land Transactions Act (ULTA) § 3–511 (1975).

81. See, e. g., Erickson v. Rocco, 433 S.W.2d 746 (Tex.Civ.App.1968); National Life Ins. Co. v. Cady, 227 Ga. 475, 181 S.E.2d 382 (1971); Nelson, Constitutional Problems with Power of Sale Foreclosure: A Judicial Dilemna, 43 Mo.L.Rev. 25, 32 (1978); Tiffany, Real Property, § 1549 (3d Ed. 1939). The remedy is available to a junior lienor, see F & H Inv. Co. v. Sackman-Gilliland Corp., 232 N.W.2d 769 (Minn.1975).

82. See Miller v. Deering, 209 Ga. 377, 72 S.E.2d 722 (1952).

83. National Life Ins. Co. v. Cady, 227 Ga. 475, 181 S.E.2d 382 (1971); Moore v. Parkerson, 255 N.C. 342, 121 S.E.2d 533 (1965); Jones v. Garcia, 538 S.W.2d 492 (Tex.Civ.App. 1976).

84. See, e. g., Walker v. Boggess, 41 W.Va. 588, 23 S.E. 550 (1895).

and attempting to sell property not covered by the mortgage.[85] Moreover, in a more modern context, relief has been granted on the ground that the mortgage debt should have been paid for a disabled mortgagor by disability insurance that originally had been required by and purchased through the mortgagee.[86]

Often the mortgagor or junior lienor will seek both temporary and permanent relief against the sale. Where temporary relief is sought the petitioner generally must post an injunction bond to protect the mortgagee against injury arising from the improper issuance of the temporary injunction.[87] Moreover, the court must balance the relative hardships to determine whether temporary relief is appropriate.[87a] While the ultimate merits of the controversy affect this process, the focus is on the relative hardship imposed on the parties by granting or refusing temporary relief.[88] On the other hand, as one court noted, "in order for one to be entitled to a temporary injunction, it is not necessary that he sustain the burden of proving that he will ultimately prevail in the dispute. It is sufficient that he show a probable right and a probable injury." [89] In theory, a decision on the actual merits is not reached until the hearing on the permanent injunction. The second alternative for the petitioner is to request a permanent injunction alone. This avoids the expense of an injunction bond. On the other hand, it also means that in principle the mortgagee is free to go ahead with the power of sale foreclosure, since he will not be subject to an injunctive decree as of the time of sale. However, with the cloud of the pending permanent injunction suit hovering over the power of sale foreclosure, many mortgagees may very well postpone the sale.

Some courts require that a mortgagor seeking any type of injunctive relief tender to the court the amount due on the mortgage.[90] Where that amount is in dispute, these courts will at least require that the mortgagor tender what he concedes is due.[91] The theory behind this tender requirement is the concept that one who seeks equi-

85. Preiss v. Campbell, 59 Ala. 635 (1877).

86. Exchange Bank of Milledgeville v. Hill, 236 Ga. 445, 224 S.E.2d 23 (1976).

87. See Dobbs, Should Security Be Required As a Pre-Condition to Provisional Injunctive Relief?, 52 N.C.L. Rev. 1091, 1099 (1974);

87a. See Van Hecke, Leavell and Nelson, Equitable Remedies and Restitution, 436–440 (2d Ed. 1973); Dobbs, Remedies, § 2.10 (1973).

88. Id.

89. Erickson v. Rocco, 433 S.W.2d 746, 749 (Tex.Civ.App.1968): See also Hutchison v. Bristol Court Properties, Ltd., 508 S.W.2d 486 (Tex.Civ.App. 1974).

90. See Tiffany, Real Property, § 1549 (3d Ed. 1939) for a list of cases. See also, Durfee, Cases on Security, 278 (1951); 93 A.L.R. 12, 30–31; Thompson, Real Property § 5179 (1957).

91. Tiffany, Id. See Glines v. Theo R. Appel Realty Co., 201 Mo.App. 596, 213 S.W. 498 (1919).

table relief must do equity.[92] Whatever the underlying historical or equitable basis, the tender requirement is objectionable. This is especially so if the mortgagor is seeking temporary as well as permanent injunctive relief because, in that situation, he will be required to post an injunction bond that protects the mortgagee financially against the wrongful issuance of the temporary injunction. Even if only permanent injunctive relief is sought, the mortgagee is free to go ahead and foreclose and take his chances on the ultimate outcome of the suit. Since the mortgagee will be the likely purchaser at the sale, if the injunction suit proves to have been unwarranted, he will then have clear title to the land. While the mortgagee may have been unable to resell the land during this period because of the cloud of the injunction suit, the mortgagor will also possibly have suffered injury. This is so because, had the foreclosure sale not been clouded more bidding may have resulted and there may have been a surplus for the mortgagor. It is reasonable to conclude that the equities as between the parties are equally balanced, even in the absence of a tender by the mortgagor.

There is a further reason that tender should not be required. The mortgagor is, by hypothesis, in default, and is probably in serious financial straits. The fundamental concept of foreclosure is that, despite his economic condition he is entitled to an orderly liquidation of the security in a manner consistent with law. It is plainly a violation of this concept to enjoin a wrongful foreclosure only if he can tender the balance owing on the debt; if he could do so, it is likely that no foreclosure would have been necessary. Of course, if the debtor wishes to redeem by tendering, that is his right, but he should not be compelled to exercise it in order to prevent an illegal foreclosure sale.

Apparently a few courts also require that a junior lienor tender the amount of the senior debt admittedly owing as a precondition to injunctive relief.[93] This seems equally objectionable as the requirement imposed by some courts on the mortgagor, if for different reasons. Unlike the normal mortgagor, the junior lienor has a right to redeem a senior lien in default, but he normally has no obligation to do so. Moreover, the junior lienor has an additional important right to foreclose his lien. It seems anomalous to require him to pay off a senior mortgage that he claims is being improperly foreclosed in order to preserve his own right to foreclose.

Suits to Set Aside the Sale

After a defective power of sale foreclosure has been consumated, the universal remedy available to mortgagors and junior lienors is a suit in equity to set aside the sale.[94] It is available to a mortga-

92. Id.

93. See Thompson, Real Property, § 5179 (1957).

94. The frequency with which this remedy is utilized is attested to by the fact that Volume 30 of the West Eighth Decennial Digest contains

gor whether in or out of possession of the mortgaged real estate. One deterrent to this remedy in a few states is the requirement that the mortgage debt be tendered as a condition precedent to such equitable relief.[95] As in the injunction situation, the requirement is rationalized by the maxim that doing equity is a pre-condition to obtaining equitable relief.[96] In any event, even if such a tender requirement is imposed, it surely is subject to the limitation that tender be made only of the amount admittedly due.[97] Moreover, it would seem even more difficult to justify the requirement where the grounds for challenging the validity of the sale are the absence of default or the invalidity of the mortgage.[98]

In any event, as in the injunctive setting, the tender requirement is a questionable roadblock to equitable relief.[99] As in that situation, the mortgagor, albeit in default, has a right to an orderly and, more important, a legally correct disposition of his security. It is not only unfair to condition this right on the payment of the debt, it is also illogical, since if he pays the mortgage debt the right to be foreclosed lawfully will have been destroyed. Moreover, the junior lienor, who, as we noted earlier, has a right, but no obligation, to redeem the senior lien also has the additional right to foreclose his lien. More important, he, like the mortgagor, has a right to expect that the senior lienor will follow legally acceptable procedures in dealing with the mortgage security. He should not be compelled to pay an alleged wrongdoer in order to assert those rights. While both the mortgagor and junior lienor may, if successful, choose to redeem, they should have the option simply of forcing reinstatement of the mortgage. The mortgagee could then pursue his remedies again, although this time, one would hope, in a legally correct manner.

Even though a mortgagor should not be required to tender simply to set aside a defective sale, he still may be forced to do so if he wishes to regain possession of the mortgaged real estate. For example, in a title or intermediate jurisdiction, the mortgagee in possession cannot be removed simply by setting an invalid foreclosure sale aside. This is because he has a right to possession, at least after a

over 100 cases dealing with suits to set aside foreclosure sales for the period 1966–1976. See also, Dingus, Mortgages—Redemption After Foreclosure in Missouri, 25 Mo.L.Rev. 261, 262 (1960).

95. See, e. g., Berry v. Government Nat. Mortgage Ass'n, 231 Ga. 503, 202 S.E.2d 450 (1973); Massey v. National Homeowners Sales Service Corp. of Atlanta, 225 Ga. 93, 165 S.E.2d 854 (1969); Pachter v. Woodman, 534 S.W.2d 940 (Tex.Civ.App. 1976), reversed, seemingly, on other grounds 547 S.W.2d 954 (Tex.1977); See also, Dingus, supra, note 94 at 293. Cf., Phillips v. Latham, 523 S.W. 2d 19 (Tex.Civ.App.1975), refused n. r. e., appeal after remand 551 S.W.2d 103 (Tex.Civ.App.1977); Blades v. Ossenfort, 481 S.W.2d 531 (Mo. App.1972).

96. See note 92, supra.

97. See text at note 91, supra.

98. See Massey v. National Homeowners Sales Service Corp. of Atlanta, 225 Ga. 93, 165 S.E.2d 854 (1969).

99. See text at notes 90–93, supra.

default by the mortgagor, until the mortgage debt is satisfied.[1] This may also be the case in those lien jurisdictions that confer valid mortgagee-in-possession status on mortgagees who take possession after a void or voidable foreclosure sale.[2]

The ability to bring a suit to set aside a foreclosure sale and to redeem can be cut off by certain events. When this occurs, the mortgagor or junior lienor will be left with a damages action for wrongful foreclosure against the foreclosing mortgagee or trustee. This can arise, for example, where the defect in the foreclosure sale rendered it voidable and not void and a bona fide purchaser has obtained title to the land.[3] Moreover, even where the defect rendered the sale void, adverse possession by the sale purchaser or his subsequent grantee may defeat any attempt to reach the title. The latter situation may be further complicated by the fact that unless the adverse possession statutory period is relatively short,[4] the applicable statute of limitations will probably also have run on the damages action. Finally, one recent case[5] illustrates how even though a relatively long statute of limitations can run on one's ability to reach the foreclosed title, a damages action may nevertheless still be available. In that case the mortgagors sued the foreclosing mortgagee and his subsequent grantee to recover title on the theory that the deed of trust had been foreclosed without being in default. A ten year statute of limitations precluded any contradiction of the recital of default contained in the trustee's deed. The court held that although the statute barred any attempt to regain the title, a damages action was available against the foreclosing mortgagee because no statute of limitations had been raised against that cause of action. Interestingly, absent the ten-year statute of limitations, the action to set aside probably would have been available because the defect alleged was the absence of a default, which, if proved, would have rendered the sale void.[6] Thus, the mortgagors could have reached the title even if it had been in the hands of a BFP.

Damages

Suppose that for one of the reasons suggested in the foregoing paragraph, a mortgagor brings an action for damages for wrongful foreclosure against a foreclosing mortgagee or trustee. The basic measure of damages is the difference between the market value of the real estate and the aggregate amount of liens thereon as of the

1. See §§ 4.1, 4.3, supra.

2. See § 4.27, supra.

3. See § 7.20, supra.

4. In a few states, however, the statute of limitations for adverse possession may be relatively short. See, e. g., Ariz.Rev.Stat. § 12–523 where under some circumstances the period of limitations can be three years.

5. Calverley v. Gunstream, 497 S.W.2d 110 (Tex.Civ.App.1973), refused n. r. e.

6. See § 7.20, supra.

date of the defective sale.[7] Other courts, using slightly different terminology to state the same rule, refer to the measure of damages as the value of the mortgagor's equity in the property at the time of the foreclosure sale.[8]

It could be argued that the mortgagor should have the option, at least where the mortgagee was the foreclosure purchaser or a subsequent grantee, of valuing the land either as of the date of sale or the date of the damages action. To apply the normal rule, in view of the substantial inflation of the past two decades, would permit the foreclosing mortgagee, a wrongdoer, to gain the benefit of the appreciation of land value between the sale date and the damages action. In the rather unlikely event that the land goes down in value, the mortgagor would have been unable to protect himself by selling the land that was then in the hands of the wrongdoer. Where the damage action is against the trustee, it probably makes sense to value the land as of the sale date, at least where the trustee has not benefitted from being an owner of the land.

Where the junior lienor is bringing the damages action for wrongful foreclosure, the measure of damages is the difference between the market value of the real estate and the aggregate value of the senior liens thereon as of the date of foreclosure.[9] However, in no event may the junior lienor recover more than the value of his lien.[10]

Suppose that a defect renders the foreclosure sale void or, alternatively, that it is only voidable but the purchaser or grantee was not a bona fide purchaser. Should the mortgagor's only remedy be a suit to set aside the sale or should he, alternatively, have the option to bring a suit for damages for wrongful foreclosure? Some courts take the view that "to recover damages at law it is necessary to show that the land went to an innocent holder so that the plaintiff's interest in it was lost." [11] In other words, under this view, the damages remedy is available only when the suit to set aside is not. Most courts, however, allow the mortgagor to pursue the damages remedy whether or not the land is still available to him.[12] Damages are allowed on "the

7. See Munger v. Moore, 11 Cal.App. 3d 1, 89 Cal.Rptr. 323 (1970); Adkison v. Hannah, 475 S.W.2d 39, 43 (Mo.1972). See generally, 97 A.L.R. 1059.

8. See, e. g., Guay v. Brotherhood Bldg. Ass'n, 87 N.H. 216, 177 A. 409 (1935). The damages would presumably be further reduced by any sale surplus which had been paid to the mortgagor.

9. See Munger v. Moore, 11 Cal.App. 3d 1, 89 Cal.Rptr. 323, n. 6 (1970); Howe v. City Title Insurance Co., 255 Cal.App.2d 85, 63 Cal.Rptr. 119 (1967). Stephans v. Herman, 225 Cal.App.2d 671, 37 Cal.Rptr. 746 (1964).

10. Id.

11. Bowen v. Bankers Life Co., 185 Minn. 35, 239 N.W. 774 (1935). Cf. Gonzales v. Gem Properties, Inc., 37 Cal.App.3d 1029, 112 Cal.Rptr. 884 (1974).

12. See, e. g., Rogers v. Barnes, 169 Mass. 179, 47 N.E. 602 (1897); Stansberry v. McDowell, 186 S.W. 757

theory that the wrong committed somewhat resembles that of a conversion of personal property. Conversion of personal property is a tort growing out of the unlawful interference with possession giving the owner a cause of action against the wrongdoer even though the title to the property did not pass." [13] Even if the defective foreclosure sale was void, and not merely voidable, the mortgagor may "elect to let the sale stand and recover at law for damages" because he will then be "forever barred from attacking the trustee's deed." [14] The majority view seems preferable because the mere right to set aside the sale, without the damages alternative, in some instances fails to give adequate protection to the mortgagor. For example, if the real estate goes down in value after the defective foreclosure, "a right simply to set aside the sale does not restore to the debtor what he has lost." [15] After all, had the wrongful foreclosure not taken place, the mortgagor could possibly have sold the property to prevent further loss from a drop in market value.

Damage recoveries may not always be limited to the measure of damages or the theories discussed above. Occasionally, for example, damages may be recoverable ancillary or incidental either to an action to set aside a defective sale or to an action to recover damages for the loss of the mortgagor's equity. This should be the case where the mortgagor has lost possession because of a wrongful foreclosure and has been forced to pay higher rental costs for comparable housing. While the case law is sparse and inconclusive,[16] he may also be able to recover for mental distress and suffering associated with wrongfully being deprived of his house or other property. Where the conduct of the mortgagee or trustee is wilful or wanton, punitive damages may be recoverable.[17] Moreover, there is some authority for damages recovery by parties other than the mortgagor or junior lienors. One recent California Court of Appeals decision is interesting in this regard.[18] There prospective third party bidders sued the beneficiary under a deed of trust and certain employees of the corporate trustee for damages for deceit based on allegations that the beneficiary and other defendants conspired to make sure that the beneficiary purchased and mortgaged property at the trustee's sale

(Mo.App.1916); Owens v. Grimes, 539 S.W.2d 387 (Tex.Civ.App.1976) refused n. r. e.; National Life Ins. Co. v. Silverman, 454 F.2d 899 (D.C. Cir. 1971) see generally, 97 A.L.R. 1059.

13. Owens v. Grimes, 539 S.W.2d 387, 390 (Tex.Civ.App.1976).

14. Id. at 390.

15. National Life Ins. Co. v. Silverman, 454 F.2d 899, 918(D.C.Cir. 1971).

16. See Phillips v. Latham, 523 S.W.2d 19 (Tex.Civ.App.1975). Compare Jarchow v. Transamerica Title Ins. Co., 48 Cal.App.3d 917, 122 Cal.Rptr. 470 (1975).

17. See Gilbert v. Cherry, 136 Ga.App. 417, 221 S.E.2d 472 (1975); Block v. Tobin, 45 Cal.App.3d 214, 119 Cal. Rptr. 288 (1975). Cf. Gonzales v. Gem Properties Inc., 37 Cal.App.3d 1029, 112 Cal.Rptr. 884 (1974).

18. Block v. Tobin, 45 Cal.App.3d 214, 119 Cal.Rptr. 288 (1975).

without competition. It was alleged that after an advertisement of sale was published, the sale was repeatedly postponed and that at the time of the actual sale, a private trustee was substituted for the corporate trustee, and the land was secretly sold for below fair market value. While the court held that the prospective bidders could not recover anticipated profits for resale of the land or maintain an action to enforce the trustee's fiduciary duty to the trustor, it determined that the allegations stated a cause of action for deceit and that recovery was permissible for time and effort expended in reliance on defendants' misrepresentations. Moreover, punitive damages were held to be recoverable.

§ 7.23 Constitutionality of Power of Sale Foreclosure—Introduction

In an earlier section we described in some detail the varying notice requirements of power of sale statutes and noted that rarely does such legislation provide an opportunity for a hearing prior to foreclosure sale. Recent constitutional litigation has focused on whether these notice requirements and the absence of a pre-foreclosure hearing violate the procedural due process requirements of the 14th amendment to the United States Constitution.[19] The following material analyzes these questions in some detail.

§ 7.24 Constitutional Problems—Notice

Until recently, it had been assumed that where a mortgagor gave a power of sale in a mortgage or deed of trust, the specific level of notice required was merely a contractual or statutory consideration, not a constitutional problem. Indeed, in Scott v. Paisley [20] the United States Supreme Court stated in dictum in 1927:

> Plainly the right of one who purchases property subject to a security deed, with a statutory power of sale which must be read into the deed, is no greater than that of one who purchases property subject to a mortgage or trust deed, with a contractual power of sale. The validity of such a contractual power of sale is unquestionable. In Bell Mining Co. v. Butte Bank, 156 U.S. 470, 477, this court said: 'There is nothing in the law of mortgages, nor in the law

19. See Leen, Galbraith & Gant, Due Process and Deeds of Trust—Strange Bedfellows, 48 Wash.L.Rev. 763 (1973); Nelson, Deed of Trust Foreclosure Under Power of Sale—Constitutional Problems—Legislative Alternatives, 28 J.Mo.B. 428 (1972); Pedowitz, Current Developments in Summary Foreclosure, 9 Real Prop., Prob. & Tr.J. 421 (1974); Comment, The Constitutionality of California Trustees Sale, 61 Calif.L.Rev. 1282 (1973); Comment, Power of Sale Foreclosure After Fuentes, 40 U.Chi.L.Rev. 206, 217–20 (1972); Comment, Due Process Problems of Mississippi Power of Sale Foreclosure, 47 Miss.L.J. 67 (1976); Comment, Notice Requirements of the Nonjudicial Foreclosure Sale, 51 N.C.L.Rev. 1110 (1973).

20. 271 U.S. 632, 46 S.Ct. 591, 70 L.Ed. 1123 (1927).

> that covers what are sometimes designated as trust deeds in the nature of mortgages, which prevents the conferring by the grantor or mortgagor in such instrument of the power to sell the premises described therein upon default in payment of the debt secured by it, and if the sale is conducted in accordance with the terms of the power, the title to the premises granted by way of security passes to the purchaser upon its consummation by a conveyance.' In the absence of a specific provision to that effect, the holder of a mortgage or trust deed with power of sale, is not required to give notice of the exercise of the power to a subsequent purchaser or trust deed with power of sale is not required to give no- by the fact that such notice is not given * * *.[21]

Such reasoning, of course, did not take into account the possible impact of Mullane v. Central Hanover Bank & Trust Co.[22] on power of sale foreclosure. That case involved the sufficiency of notice to beneficiaries of a judicial settlement of accounts by a trustee of a common trust fund established under New York banking law. The only notice given the beneficiaries of the proceeding was publication in a local newspaper in strict compliance with the statutory requirements. The Supreme Court held that the type of notice used must be "reasonably calculated * * * to apprise interested parties * * *." [23] The Court also noted that "[w]here the names and post office addresses of those affected by a proceeding are at hand, the reasons disappear for resort to means less likely than the mails to apprise them of its pendency." [24] Assuming that the notice requirements of *Mullane* are applicable to power of sale foreclosure statutes, and absent a valid waiver by the affected parties of such fourteenth amendment notice rights, it is difficult to escape the conclusion that the notice provisions of many state power of sale statutes are unconstitutional. Certainly those statutes that provide only for notice by publication must fail the constitutional test, because *Mullane* requires that when the names and addresses of interested parties are available (as at least the property owner's nearly always is), at least notice by mail is required. Under such state statutes *no* interested party is guaranteed constitutionally acceptable notice.

While one earlier case suggests that a notice by publication provision in a power of sale statute violates the *Mullane* principle,[25] only

21. Id. at 635.

22. 339 U.S. 306, 70 S.Ct. 652, 94 L.Ed. 865 (1950).

23. Id. at 314.

24. Id. at 318. See also, Schroeder v. City of New York, 371 U.S. 208, 83 S.Ct. 279, 9 L.Ed.2d 255 (1962) (advertisement insufficient in condemnation); Walker v. City of Hutchinson, 352 U.S. 112, 77 S.Ct. 200, 1 L.Ed.2d 178 (1956) (advertisement insufficient in condemnation).

25. See Law v. United States, 366 F. Supp. 1233 (N.D.Ga.1973).

three cases have met that issue squarely.[26] In Ricker v. United States [27] the Farmers Home Administration (FmHA), under a Maine nonjudicial foreclosure statute,[28] foreclosed a mortgage securing a direct loan that it had made to the mortgagors. After the proceedings were completed and the FmHA conveyed the land to a subsequent purchaser, the mortgagors sued in federal court to nullify the sale, in part on the theory that the Maine statute's notice requirements did not satisfy the requirements of the due process clause of the fifth amendment. The notice required by statute, and that actually provided, was published notice for three successive weeks. The mortgagors did not see the notices but heard about the proceedings through rumors and other second-hand sources. The court held that the published notice "plainly failed to meet" the *Mullane* standards and emphasized that published notice will not suffice constitutionally where a party's name and address are known or are very easily ascertained.[29] Similarly, in Turner v. Blackburn [30] a three-judge federal court invalidated a North Carolina power of sale statute that provided for notice only by newspaper publication and posting. The court stated: "To propose to a homeowner that he trek to the courthouse or spend 20 cents to examine fine-print legal notices, *daily* for the duration of a twenty-year mortgage, as his sole protection against summary eviction, seems to us to offer him nothing of value." [31]

The statutes that provide for publication plus notice by mail or personal service only for the mortgagor and the owner of the real estate are probably also defective because no provision is made for notice to other interested parties such as junior mortgagees and judgment creditors. It could, of course, be argued that such parties tend to be sophisticated commercial lenders able to keep themselves informed of the status of the senior mortgage. However, it is not clear that even a majority of junior lienors fall into such a class. Moreover, junior lienors often stand to lose more than the mortgagor or the owner. Where junior liens exist it is not uncommon for the mortgagor or the owner to have a smaller economic stake in the mortgaged real estate than that of an individual junior lienor.

Those statutes that provide for notice by mail or personal service both for the mortgagor and the owner and for anyone else who has previously recorded a request for such notice represent a closer case

26. See Ricker v. United States, 417 F.Supp. 133 (D.Me.1976); Roberts v. Cameron-Brown Co., 410 F.Supp. 988 (S.D.Ga.1975); Turner v. Blackburn, 389 F.Supp. 1250 (W.D.N.C.1975).

27. 417 F.Supp. 133 (D.Me.1976).

28. 14 Me.Rev.Stat. tit. 14, §§ 6203–6204 (1965).

29. 417 F.Supp. at 138.

30. 389 F.Supp. 1250 (W.D.N.C.1975).

31. Id. at 1258 (emphasis in original). See Roberts v. Cameron-Brown Co., 410 F.Supp. 988 (S.D.Ga.1975). Cf. Brown v. Federal Nat'l Mtg. Ass'n, 359 A.2d 661 (Del.1976).

constitutionally. It is true that under such legislation an interested party could be wiped out without being provided any notice "reasonably calculated to provide actual notice." On the other hand, perhaps the relative sophistication of junior lienors *as a class* can be recognized in this context; after all, such parties can assure themselves of a constitutional form of notice by simply requesting it. Probably the only notice provisions that are clearly constitutional are those that closely approximate the notice provided to interested parties under judicial foreclosure: at least notice by mail to all parties who have a record interest in the foreclosed property junior to the mortgage being foreclosed. In the last analysis perhaps a finding of constitutionality is justified only as to this latter type of notice provision; whatever the arguments in favor of more limited notice, the cost and time involved in searching the title for those who have a record interest subsequent to the mortgage being foreclosed are minor.

The question remains to what extent a foreclosing mortgagee may remedy the problem of a constitutionally defective notice provision by providing more extensive notice to interested parties than the statute requires. Logically, if such notice was provided to all interested parties, no person would have standing to challenge the foreclosure and the statute because no one would have suffered injury.[32] In one recent federal district court decision, the court specifically held that a power of sale foreclosure complied with *Mullane* where the mortgagee supplied greater notice to the mortgagor than the power of sale statute required.[33] Moreover, the court in *Ricker v. United States*[34] emphasized the fact that the mortgagee did not attempt to notify the mortgagor other than by complying with the statutory requirement. The court implied that had the mortgagee made an effort to give actual notice, the foreclosure would not have been constitutionally defective on notice grounds.

Notwithstanding those cases, because of the United States Supreme Court's decision in Wuchter v. Pizzutti,[35] there is still doubt that a foreclosing mortgagee has the ability to conduct a constitutional power of sale foreclosure by supplying necessary notice not required by the applicable statute. In *Wuchter* the Supreme Court held that a nonresident motorist service of process statute that required only service on the secretary of state violated the fourteenth amendment due process clause even though the secretary of state in that case actually mailed notice to the nonresident defendant. While this

32. See Warth v. Seldin, 422 U.S. 490, 95 S.Ct. 2197, 45 L.Ed.2d 343 (1975); C. Wright, A. Miller & E. Cooper, Federal Practice and Procedure § 3531 (1975 & Supp.1976).

33. United States v. White, 429 F. Supp. 1245, 1250 (N.D.Miss.1977).

34. 417 F.Supp. 133 (D.Me.1976).

35. 276 U.S. 13, 48 S.Ct. 259, 72 L.Ed. 446 (1928).

case seems unsound because no one was injured as a result of the statutory notice provision, its existence should make mortgagees cautious as to their ability to resurrect invalid foreclosure statutes through their own resources.

§ 7.25 Constitutional Problems—Hearing

Independently of the constitutionality of notice provisions, power of sale statutes frequently have been attacked on the ground that the due process clause of the fourteenth amendment requires the opportunity for a hearing before a person may be deprived of a significant property interest. This attack is centered on Sniadach v. Family Finance Corp.[36] and Fuentes v. Shevin.[37] In *Sniadach* the Supreme Court held that, except in exceptional circumstances, prejudgment garnishment without provision for a judicial hearing prior to the garnishment violated the due process clause of the fourteenth amendment. In *Fuentes,* a 4–3 decision, the Court struck down certain state replevin statutes because they did not provide for an opportunity to be heard before chattels were taken from the possessor, even on a temporary basis, pending a trial on the merits. At least three principles were established in *Fuentes*:

1. Procedural due process requires notice and an opportunity for a hearing before the state authorizes its agents, on the application of another, to seize property in the possession of a third person. A bond requirement is not a sufficient substitute for a hearing.

2. The debtors, who had already made substantial payments under installment contracts, had a sufficient property interest to invoke fourteenth amendment protection even though they lacked full title to the goods.

3. The hearing requirement is applicable whether or not the items to be seized are "necessities."

Based on *Fuentes,* a strong argument may be made that power of sale foreclosure statutes which do not provide the opportunity for a hearing prior to the foreclosure sale violate the due process hearing requirement of the fourteenth amendment. If *Fuentes* requires some type of hearing before chattel security may be seized even temporarily, surely it may be argued that the due process clause does not permit the *permanent* taking of real estate security by passage of title with no opportunity for a hearing *at all.* Several courts that have reached the hearing issue directly have utilized *Fuentes* to invalidate

36. 395 U.S. 337, 89 S.Ct. 1820, 23 L.Ed.2d 349 (1969).

37. 407 U.S. 67, 92 S.Ct. 1983, 32 L.Ed.2d 556 (1972), rehearing denied 409 U.S. 902, 93 S.Ct. 177, 34 L.Ed.2d 165.

power of sale provisions.[38] In Turner v. Blackburn,[39] which invalidated the North Carolina power of sale statute, the three-judge federal court held, based on *Fuentes,* that a hearing prior to foreclosure and sale is essential. At a minimum, due process "requires the trustee to make an initial showing before the clerk or similar neutral official that the mortgagor is in default under the obligation; the mortgagor must of course be afforded the opportunity to rebut and defend the charges." [40] In Ricker v. United States [41] the government argued that in the context of a Maine nonjudicial mortgage foreclosure the opportunity to be heard would be "mere surplusage" because the issues were "open and shut": the existence of an overdue debt and a valid mortgage. The federal district court rejected this argument on two grounds. First, the simplicity of issues does not necessarily obviate the constitutional necessity for a hearing. Second, in the case at hand the mortgagors had also challenged the validity of the government's decision to foreclose on the theory that the mortgage notes lacked consideration. The court concluded that, at a minimum, fifth amendment due process requires "a hearing at which [mortgagors] could challenge both the legal right of the [mortgagee] to foreclose and the propriety of the decision to do so." [42]

Some temporary concern existed that a subsequent Supreme Court decision had deprived *Fuentes* of its strength. In Mitchell v. W. T. Grant Co.[43] the Supreme Court upheld the constitutionality of a Louisiana sequestration statute which required the secured creditor to come before a judge who, based on a verified complaint delineating the specific facts supporting the claim, could then issue a writ of sequestration. There was no right to a hearing prior to the seizure of the chattel, but the procedure did provide for an immediate right to a hearing thereafter and dissolution of the writ if the plaintiff failed to establish adequate grounds for its issuance. In a dissenting opinion, Justice Stewart concluded that *Mitchell,* in effect, had overruled the *Fuentes* decision.[44] However, the subsequent decision in North Georgia Finishing, Inc. v. Di-Chem, Inc.[45] made it clear that Justice Stewart's prediction of *Fuentes'* demise was premature. The Court

38. See Ricker v. United States, 417 F.Supp. 133 (D.Me.1976); Turner v. Blackburn, 389 F.Supp. 1250 (W.D.N.C.1975); Garner v. Tri-State Dev. Co., 382 F.Supp. 377 (E.D.Mich.1974); Northrip v. Federal Nat'l Mtg. Ass'n, 372 F.Supp. 594 (E.D.Mich.1974), reversed on other grounds 527 F.2d 23 (C.C.A.Mich.1975); Valley Development at Vail v. Warder, 557 P.2d 1180 (Colo.1976). Contra, Guidarelli v. Lazaretti, 233 N.W.2d 890 (Minn. 1975).

39. 389 F.Supp. 1250 (W.D.N.C.1975).

40. Id. at 1259.

41. 417 F.Supp. 133 (D.Me.1976).

42. Id. at 139.

43. 416 U.S. 600, 94 S.Ct. 1895, 40 L. Ed.2d 406 (1974).

44. Id. at 629–36.

45. 419 U.S. 601, 95 S.Ct. 719, 42 L. Ed.2d 751 (1975).

struck down a Georgia prejudgment garnishment statute that did not provide for a hearing prior to the imposition of the garnishment remedy. The Court distinguished *Mitchell* by noting that, unlike the Louisiana procedure, the garnishment writ was issued by a clerk, not a judge, upon an affidavit stating only conclusory and non-specific supporting grounds for the garnishment.[46] Moreover, the Court noted that, unlike *Mitchell,* there was no opportunity under the Georgia statute for an early post-seizure hearing to demonstrate at least probable cause for the garnishment.[47]

The significance of the foregoing for the power of sale foreclosure hearing problem is two-fold. First, the *North Georgia* decision sets to rest the argument that *Fuentes* has been overruled and therefore has no effect on power of sale real estate foreclosure. Second, in view of the fact that *Fuentes* is still good law, the impact of the *Mitchell* case really does not weaken the lower federal court cases considered earlier that invalidate the power of sale statutes on *Fuentes* hearing grounds.[48] The Louisiana statute was upheld in *Mitchell* in large measure because the statute guaranteed the right to an early post-seizure hearing. Power of sale foreclosure statutes, on the other hand, usually make no provision for a hearing at *any* time, *before or after* the *final* deprivation of the mortgagor's real estate. Thus some type of hearing prior to the foreclosure sale is probably required. Indeed, in Garner v. Tri-State Development Co.,[49] a post-*Mitchell* but pre-*North Georgia* case, the federal trial court held that the Michigan power of sale statute violated the fourteenth amendment due process clause because no opportunity for a hearing was provided *at all.* The *Garner* court focused on the fact that in *Mitchell* a judge issued the writ of sequestration and, more importantly, that there was a right to a hearing immediately after the seizure. Thus, the court concluded: "Evaluated by these criteria the foreclosure by advertisement method now before the court fails to meet due process requirements. The procedure used has no provision for a hearing before or immediately after the seizure." [50]

It has been argued that there is in fact an opportunity for a hearing under most power of sale statutes because a mortgagor has the right, based on either common law or statute, to bring suit to enjoin the foreclosure sale. In some jurisdictions this is a common practice and is a primary vehicle for developing the law of mortgages in the power of sale context.[51] While at least one court has found this

46. Id. at 606–07.

47. Id.

48. See text accompanying notes 36–40 supra.

49. 382 F.Supp. 377 (E.D.Mich.1974).

50. Id. at 380. Accord, Roberts v. Cameron-Brown Co., 410 F.Supp. 988 (S.D.Ga.1975).

51. See Nelson, supra note 19, at 432.

argument persuasive,[52] others have rejected it.[53] To equate the foregoing procedure with the constitutional right to a hearing required by *Fuentes* seems questionable for several reasons. First, what *Fuentes* seems to be saying is that the opportunity for a hearing must be an integral part of any statutory procedure that can be used to deprive a person of a property interest. The mortgagor's ability to bring a separate injunction suit normally exists independently of any power of sale statute. To maintain that the ability to bring such an injunction suit satisfies the constitutional hearing requirement would be analogous to contending that a 42 U.S.C. section 1983 injunction suit filed by a tenured college professor to prevent his termination would be a constitutionally permissible substitute for a hearing requirement as an integral part of the college's termination procedure.[54] One court has aptly characterized the injunction suit as a form of "self-help" that does not meet the requirements of either *Fuentes* or *Mitchell*.[55] Second, where the remedy sought is a temporary injunction, the mortgagor must post an injunction bond.[56] Such a requirement seems to condition unfairly the mortgagor's right to a hearing on his ability to pay. It is true, of course, that a mortgagor could avoid the bond requirement in many jurisdictions by simply bringing an action for a permanent injunction. However, although such an action deters many mortgagees from proceeding with the sale, it does not guarantee such a result. Third, for the mortgagor to bring a separate injunction suit inevitably will require the services of a lawyer. On the other hand, even an impecunious mortgagor at least would be able to answer a summons and appear to state his case without counsel at a hearing required as part of a statutory procedure.

§ 7.26 Constitutional Problems—Waiver

Even if a power of sale foreclosure statute is constitutionally deficient as to notice and hearing, such rights, in theory at least, are capable of being waived. In this connection, several cases are important. A few weeks prior to *Fuentes*, the United States Supreme Court in D. H. Overmyer v. Frick Co.[57] and Swarb v. Lennox [58] reject-

52. See Young v. Ridley, 309 F.Supp. 1308 (D.D.C.1970).

53. See, e. g., Turner v. Blackburn, 389 F.Supp. 1250 (W.D.N.C.1975); Northrip v. Federal Nat'l Mtg. Ass'n, 372 F.Supp. 594 (E.D.Mich.1974), reversed on other grounds 527 F.2d 23 (C.A. Mich.1975).

54. See Perry v. Sindermann, 408 U.S. 593, 92 S.Ct. 2694, 33 L.Ed.2d 570 (1972).

55. Garner v. Tri-State Dev. Co., 382 F.Supp. 377, 380 (E.D.Mich.1974).

56. D. Dobbs, Remedies § 2.10 (1973); Dobbs, Should Security Be Required As A Pre-Condition To Provisional Injunctive Relief?, 52 N.C.L.Rev. 1091 (1974).

57. 405 U.S. 174, 92 S.Ct. 775, 31 L. Ed.2d 124 (1972).

58. 405 U.S. 191, 92 S.Ct. 767, 31 L. Ed.2d 138 (1972), rehearing denied 405 U.S. 1049, 92 S.Ct. 1303, 31 L.Ed. 2d 592.

ed a fourteenth amendment due process argument and sustained the constitutionality of certain state statutes authorizing summary entry of judgment based on confession of judgment clauses contained in promissory notes. These cases stand for the proposition that "under [the] appropriate circumstances, a cognovit debtor may be held effectively and legally to have waived those rights he would possess if the document he signed had contained no cognovit provision." [59] In *Fuentes* itself, the Court recognized that waiver was possible, but rejected it in that case. The *Fuentes* contract provided that "in the event of default of any payment or payments, Seller at its option may take back the merchandise." [60] Other contracts provided that the seller "may retake" or "repossess" the merchandise in the event of a "default in any payment." [61] These "waivers" were ineffectual for several reasons: the contracts did not provide specifically for a waiver of constitutional rights nor did they specify how or through what process "the seller could take back the goods"; there was a lack of awareness by the parties of the significance of the waiver; and there was no bargaining over contractual terms between parties who were equal in bargaining position.[62]

Two pre-*Fuentes* cases determined that the presence of a power of sale in the mortgage or deed of trust constituted the mortgagor's waiver of notice and hearing rights,[63] but subsequent decisions have rejected such an approach.[64] In Turner v. Blackburn,[65] for example, the court emphasized that there was a presumption against waiver. In rejecting waiver, the *Turner* court pointed out that there was no waiver of specific constitutional rights, that the purported waiver language was in fine print, and that there was no evidence that the mortgagor was made aware of the significance of that language. Other courts have stressed that merely consenting to foreclosure pursuant to state law is not a sufficient substitute for a delineation of the specific constitutional rights waived.[66] Moreover, in Ricker v. United States [67], the court noted that even if the waiver of specific rights had been spelled out, the government-mortgagee did not show

59. Id. at 200.

60. 407 U.S. at 94.

61. Id.

62. Id. at 95–96.

63. See Young v. Ridley, 309 F.Supp. 1308 (D.D.C.1970); Huggins v. Dement, 13 N.C.App. 673, 187 S.E.2d 412, appeal dismissed 281 N.C. 314, 188 S.E.2d 898, certiorari denied 409 U.S. 1071, 93 S.Ct. 677, 34 L.Ed.2d 659 (1972).

64. United States v. White, 429 F. Supp. 1245 (N.D.Miss.1977); Ricker v. United States, 417 F.Supp. 133 (D. Me.1976); Turner v. Blackburn, 389 F.Supp. 1250 (W.D.N.C.1975); Garner v. Tri-State Dev. Co., 382 F.Supp. 377 (E.D.Mich.1974); Law v. United States, 366 F.Supp. 1233 (N.D.Ga. 1973).

65. 389 F.Supp. 1250 (W.D.N.C.1975).

66. Ricker v. United States, 417 F. Supp. 133 (D.Me.1976); Northrip v. Federal Nat'l Mtg. Ass'n, 372 F.Supp. 594 (E.D.Mich.1974), reversed on other grounds 527 F.2d 23 (C.A.Mich. 1975).

67. 417 F.Supp. 133 (D.Me.1976).

that the mortgagors "were actually aware or made aware of the fine print now relied on as a waiver of constitutional rights." [68] The court also emphasized that when the mortgage was executed the mortgagors were elderly, ill-educated, and without the services of an attorney.[69]

The foregoing illustrates that the waiver concept will not be a practical solution to the constitutional problems of power of sale foreclosure. If a valid waiver depended only upon ensuring that the waived rights are specified and the mortgagor is aware that he is waiving those rights, a carefully drafted document probably would suffice. For example, the mortgagee could have a mortgagor execute a separate recordable document in bold type that clearly specifies a waiver of constitutional rights to notice and hearing and that further contains a statement by the mortgagor that the waiver has been fully explained to him. Although even this type of document could engender later disputes as to whether the mortgagor *actually* understood the significance of the waiver, most title examiners probably would be willing to rely on such a document in approving a title derived from a power of sale foreclosure. If, on the other hand, as *Fuentes* and other cases suggest, a valid waiver depends on such factors as equality of bargaining position and similar considerations, an impossible burden is placed on the title examiner.[70] How can an examiner, evaluating a five-year-old mortgage foreclosure, determine from the record that there was equality of bargaining position? Is there ever equality of bargaining position? Would a recorded statement contemporaneous with the original mortgage certifying that such equality existed suffice? For title examiners who by nature rely primarily on the record, the waiver concept becomes an almost impossible burden and, to the extent that titles thereby become unmarketable, waiver must be considered an impractical concept.

Even assuming that title examiners could be convinced that a foolproof waiver could be developed to bind a mortgagor, it is doubtful that such a waiver would also be effective against holders of subordinate interests in the mortgaged real estate. If, in fact, there is a presumption against waiver and if a party must be made aware of what rights are being waived, how can waiver be accomplished with respect to subsequent grantees of the real estate or junior mortgagees? They, after all, are not parties to the original mortgage transaction, yet they often have a significant financial stake in the mortgaged real estate. It could be argued that such parties stake their interests on notice of the record and that they therefore implicitly consent to the terms of previously recorded documents.[71] However, it is

68. Id. at 139.

69. Id. at 139–40. See United States v. White, 429 F.Supp. 1245 (N.D. Miss.1977).

70. See Nelson, supra note 19, at 433–34.

71. Id. at 431.

doubtful that constitutional rights can be waived in such a manner. Moreover, whatever the likelihood that subsequent grantees and junior mortgagees will search the record prior to taking their interests in the mortgaged real estate, it is less likely that either judgment creditors or mechanics lienors will make such a search. It would, indeed, be stretching the waiver concept to conclude that these latter parties could have waived notice and hearing rights. Accordingly, since the waiver concept may well prove unworkable as a practical matter with respect to *some* parties, it probably cannot be relied upon at all.

§ 7.27 Constitutional Problems—State Action

The fourteenth amendment requires sufficient notice and an opportunity for a hearing; it is, however, fundamental that state action must be found before the amendment is applicable. Unless sufficient state action is found in connection with power of sale foreclosure, a court will not reach the notice or hearing issues, no matter how deficient a statute may be in those respects. Interestingly, some of the early power of sale fourteenth amendment cases resolved the constitutional issues without a consideration of state action.[72] However, the issue has become increasingly important, and the trend of the case law is clearly against finding state action.[73] This trend is significant because, as a practical matter, it means that power of sale statutes continue to provide an effective foreclosure method for nongovernmental mortgagees even where the statutes are noticeably deficient in the notice and hearing area.

At least five theories have been advanced to find state action in the power of sale foreclosures.[74] These are the "direct" state action theory, the "encouragement" theory, the governmental function theory, the judicial enforcement theory, and the "pervasiveness" theory.

Under the first theory, state action exists when state officials act directly to enforce rights arising from a state statute. *Fuentes* illustrates this theory. State action was found, albeit without analysis,

72. See Young v. Ridley, 309 F.Supp. 1308 (D.D.C.1970); Huggins v. Dement, 13 N.C.App. 673, 187 S.E.2d 412, appeal dismissed 281 N.C. 314, 188 S.E.2d 898, certiorari denied 409 U.S. 1071, 93 S.Ct. 677, 34 L.Ed.2d 659 (1972).

73. See Northrip v. Federal Nat. Mtg. Ass'n, 527 F.2d 23 (6th Cir. 1975); Barrera v. Security Bldg. & Inv. Corp., 519 F.2d 1166 (C.A.Tex.1975); Bryant v. Jefferson Fed. Sav. & Loan Ass'n, 509 F.2d 511 (D.C.Cir. 1974); Kenly v. Miracle Properties, 412 F. Supp. 1072 (D.Ariz.1976); Lawson v. Smith, 402 F.Supp. 851 (N.D.Cal. 1975); Y Aleman Corp. v. Chase Manhattan Bank, 414 F.Supp. 93 (D. Guam 1975); Global Indus., Inc. v. Harris, 376 F.Supp. 1379 (N.D.Ga. 1974); Federal Nat. Mtg. Ass'n v. Howlett, 521 S.W.2d 428 (Mo. En Banc), appeal dismissed 423 U.S. 909, 96 S.Ct. 471, 46 L.Ed.2d 400 (1975); Charmicor, Inc. v. Deaner, 572 F.2d 694 (C.A.Nev.1978). Contra, Turner v. Blackburn, 389 F.Supp. 1250 (W.D. N.C.1975).

74. See Barklage, Constitutional Law —Mortgages—Extra-Judicial Mortgage Foreclosure Not State Action, 41 Mo.L.Rev. 278 (1976).

because the replevin statute provided for the writ to be issued by a clerk of court and the service of the writ and seizure of the property to be carried out by the sheriff. This theory was used in the mortgage context in Turner v. Blackburn.[75] Under the North Carolina power of sale statute, certain relatively unusual powers were conferred on the clerk of court. For example, within thirty days after the receipt of the sale proceeds, the person holding the power of sale had to file a final report with the clerk. The clerk then audited and approved the final report and filed it. The filing of the report and the lapse of a ten-day period was a precondition to the trustee's power to convey to the highest bidder at the foreclosure sale. During the ten-day period the clerk had the authority to reject or accept an upset bid. This was held to constitute direct participation by a state official and thus state action for purposes of the fourteenth amendment. On the other hand, the Missouri Supreme Court rejected this argument in Federal National Mortgage Association v. Howlett[76] because the intervention of public officials was limited primarily to ministerial functions performed by the recorder of deeds.[77] While the direct state action theory was useful in *Blackburn*, its impact in the power of sale area is limited because most power of sale statutes do not inject state officials into the process to the same extent as did North Carolina. In many jurisdictions a power of sale foreclosure will normally be consummated without the knowledge, much less the participation, of any public official other than perhaps the recorder of deeds.[78]

The "encouragement" theory asserts that state action may be found when state statutes tend to "encourage" objectionable, but otherwise private, activity.[79] The case most representative of this concept is Reitman v. Mulkey,[80] where state action was premised on the adoption of a constitutional amendment that protected a person's right to refuse to sell or rent his property to anyone for any reason. The United States Supreme Court, in a 5–4 vote, concurred in the finding of the California Supreme Court that the sole purpose of the amendment was to invalidate state anti-discrimination statutes, to prohibit their future enactment and to create a constitutional right to discriminate.[81] Thus the state became at least a "partner" in racial discrimination in violation of the fourteenth amendment.

75. 389 F.Supp. 1250 (W.D.N.C.1975).

76. 521 S.W.2d 428 (Mo. En Banc 1975).

77. See Northrip v. Federal Nat'l Mtg. Ass'n, 527 F.2d 23 (C.A.Mich.1975); Barrera v. Security Bldg. & Inv. Corp., 519 F.2d 1166 (C.A.Tex.1975). But see Garner v. Tri-State Dev. Co., 382 F.Supp. 377 (E.D.Mich.1974).

78. See, e. g., § 443.320–.330, R.S.Mo. (Supp.1975), Tex.Rev.Civ.Stat.Ann. art. 3810 (Vernon 1966).

79. See Comment, Power of Sale Foreclosure After Fuentes, 40 U.Chi.L. Rev. 206, 217–18 (1972).

80. 387 U.S. 369, 87 S.Ct. 1627, 18 L.Ed.2d 830 (1967).

81. Mulkey v. Reitman, 64 Cal.2d 529, 413 P.2d 825, 50 Cal.Rptr. 881 (1966).

It can be argued that the existence of state power of sale foreclosure statutes encourages this method of foreclosure and therefore is state action for purposes of the fourteenth amendment. However, most courts have rejected this argument,[82] advancing at least three reasons for doing so. First, *Reitman* involved racial discrimination and there is some indication that such cases will receive "special scrutiny" for state action purposes.[83] Second, power of sale statutes do not encourage nonjudicial foreclosure because the method existed prior to its authorization by the legislature.[84] Third, the extension of the "encouragement" theory to power of sale foreclosure would subject a vast range of private conduct to fourteenth amendment coverage, since statutes regulate so many forms of private activity and to some extent encourage such activity.[85]

The governmental function theory would find state action when a private person performs a function that is essentially governmental in nature.[86] Perhaps the classic example of this theory is found in Marsh v. Alabama,[87] where a "company town" was held to the same first amendment standards as a municipal corporation.[88] On the other hand, the Supreme Court recently has refused to expand this concept to such arguably quasi-municipal functions as covered mall shopping centers.[89] It could be argued that power of sale statutes have delegat-

82. See Northrip v. Federal Nat. Mtg. Ass'n, 527 F.2d 23 (C.A.Mich.1975); Barrera v. Security Bldg. & Inv. Corp., 519 F.2d 1166 (C.A.Tex.1975); Bryant v. Jefferson Fed. Sav. & Loan Ass'n, 509 F.2d 511 (D.C.Cir. 1974); Federal Nat. Mtg. Ass'n v. Howlett, 521 S.W.2d 428 (Mo. En Banc 1975).

83. See Northrip v. Federal Nat. Mtg. Ass'n, 527 F.2d 23 (C.A.Mich.1975). See also Comment, supra note 79, at 217–18.

84. See Northrip v. Federal Nat. Mtg. Ass'n, 527 F.2d 23 (C.A.Mich.1975); Barrera v. Security Bldg. & Inv. Corp., 519 F.2d 1166 (C.A.Tex.1975); Federal Nat. Mtg. Ass'n v. Howlett, 521 S.W.2d 428 (Mo. En Banc 1975).

85. See Federal Nat. Mtg. Ass'n v. Howlett, 521 S.W.2d 428 (Mo. En Banc 1975); Comment, supra note 79, at 217–18. Many power of sale cases have utilized decisions under section 9–503 of the Uniform Commercial Code, which permits "self-help" repossession of secured chattels. These cases have found no state action under UCC § 9–503 and, inter alia, have rejected the "encouragement" theory. See Gibbs v. Titelman, 502 F.2d 1107 (C.A.Pa.1974); Turner v. Impala Motors, 503 F.2d 607 (C.A.Tenn.1974); Shirley v. State Nat'l Bank, 493 F.2d 739 (C.A.Conn. 1974); Adams v. Southern California First Nat'l Bank, 492 F.2d 324 (C.A. Calif.1973); Bitchell Optical Labs. Inc. v. Marquette Nat'l Bank, 487 F.2d 906 (C.A.Minn.1973).

86. See Barklage, supra note 74, at 280.

87. 326 U.S. 501, 66 S.Ct. 276, 90 L.Ed. 265 (1946).

88. See Evans v. Newton, 382 U.S. 296, 86 S.Ct. 486, 15 L.Ed.2d 373 (1966), on remand 221 Ga. 870, 148 S.E.2d 329 (private trustees' management of park on segregated basis was determined to be a governmental function); Terry v. Adams, 345 U.S. 461, 73 S.Ct. 809, 97 L.Ed. 1152 (1953) rehearing denied 345 U.S. 1003, 73 S.Ct. 1128, 97 L.Ed. 1408 (pre-primary elections with no apparent state involvement held subject to the fifteenth amendment).

89. See Lloyd Corp. v. Tanner, 407 U.S. 551, 92 S.Ct. 2219, 33 L.Ed.2d 131 (1972), conformed to 463 F.2d 1095.

ed the traditional governmental function of judicial foreclosure to private parties.[90] The Court of Appeals for the Fifth Circuit rejected this argument in confronting the Texas deed of trust power of sale statute in Barrera v. Security Building and Investment Corp.[91] The court found that there was no state action based on a governmental function theory because foreclosure of the mortgagor's equity of redemption had never been the exclusive prerogative of the state. The court noted that extrajudicial foreclosure dated back to 1774. Thus, the trustee exercising a power of sale was not deemed to be performing a governmental function.[92]

Each of the foregoing state action theories was raised, but found inapplicable by the United States Supreme Court in Flagg Brothers, Inc. v. Brooks.[93] In that case the plaintiff challenged section 7–210 of the New York Uniform Commercial Code as being unconstitutional under the procedural due process and equal protection requirements of the 14th amendment. Section 7–210 provides for the private sale of goods by a warehouseman to enforce the warehouseman's lien on goods entrusted to him for storage. The Supreme Court, in a 5–4 decision, refused to find the requisite state action for purposes of the 14th amendment. First, it apparently rejected the "direct" state action theory because no public officials were involved in the sale. Thus, the *Fuentes* line of cases was distinguished. Second, the Court held that the mere enactment of section 7–210 was not within the "encouragement" theory because a state's mere acquiescence in a private action does not convert such action to that of the state. Finally, the governmental function concept was held inapplicable because the statute did not delegate to a private party an exclusive prerogative of the government. The Court noted other private remedies were available for dispute resolution between debtors and creditors. The Brooks case tends to buttress an argument that no state action exists in the power of sale foreclosure setting. First, as we have pointed out earlier, most power of sale statutes do not utilize a public official in any significant manner. At least this is true in most deed of trust power of sale situations. Moreover, it can be argued that power of sale legislation is mere acquiesence by the state in private action, and, as in *Brooks,* therefore not enough state involvement for state action purposes. Lastly, a power of sale statute, like the warehouseman's lien provision, arguably does not delegate an exclusive sovereign prerogative to private parties because, in theory at least,

90. See Muller, Deed of Trust Foreclosure: The Need for Reform * * * Fair Play and the Constitution Revisited, 29 J.Mo.B. 222, 229 (1973).

91. 519 F.2d 1166 (C.A.Tex.1975).

92. See Roberts v. Cameron-Brown Co., 556 F.2d 356 (5th Cir. 1977); Northrip v. Federal Nat. Mtg. Ass'n, 527 F.2d 23 (C.A.Mich.1975); Federal Nat'l Mtg. Ass'n v. Howlett, 521 S.W.2d 428 (Mo. En Banc 1975).

93. —— U.S. ——, 98 S.Ct. 1729, 56 L.Ed.2d 185 (1978).

settlement of disputes between mortgagees and mortgagors also "is not traditionally an exclusive public function." [94] Such disputes are often resolved privately without recourse to power of sale legislation.[95]

Under the judicial enforcement theory state action exists when state courts enforce the rights of private parties. The origin of this theory is Shelley v. Kraemer,[96] in which the Supreme Court held that specific judicial enforcement of a racially restrictive covenant constituted state action and was violative of the fourteenth amendment equal protection clause. If *Shelley* were extended to power of sale foreclosure, it could be argued that judicial enforcement of power of sale mortgages would constitute state action. Where such foreclosures ultimately entail intervention by a court, either in the form of a sheriff ejecting a holdover mortgagor or in a subsequent quiet title suit based on the foreclosure, judicial recognition of the mortgage agreement arguably could be considered state action. However, most power of sale foreclosures are accomplished with no subsequent judicial second-guessing, making the *Shelley* concept inapplicable. The Supreme Court has refused to apply the *Shelley* concept outside of the racial covenant area and to some extent has restricted its scope.[97] The Missouri Supreme Court in *Howlett* refused to apply the *Shelley* theory to power of sale deed of trust foreclosure. It noted that title passed by virtue of the trustee's deed and without judicial intervention; courts were used only when mortgagors did not surrender possession. In such a situation, the court noted, possession is obtained by an unlawful detainer action in which the Missouri courts are not permitted to inquire into the merits of title. Thus, courts are not involved in the process by which title passes.[98] This reasoning is problematic. If a mortgagor brings a subsequent suit in equity to set aside a power of sale foreclosure, a court would be called upon to enforce the private agreement, and the logic of *Shelley* would be inescapable. Perhaps the better approach is simply to say that the *Shelley* concept should not be extended beyond the racial covenant area;

94. Id. at 1736.

95. See § 6.17, supra.

96. 334 U.S. 1, 68 S.Ct. 836, 92 L.Ed. 1161 (1948).

97. The other Supreme Court decision to apply *Shelley* was Barrows v. Jackson, 346 U.S. 249, 73 S.Ct. 1031, 97 L.Ed. 1586 (1953), rehearing denied 346 U.S. 841, 74 S.Ct. 19, 98 L.Ed. 361, a case involving a suit for damages for breach of a racial covenant. The Court avoided *Shelley* in Lombard v. Louisiana, 373 U.S. 267, 83 S.Ct. 1122, 10 L.Ed.2d 338 (1963), a sit-in case involving racial segregation in public accommodations. More recently the Court rejected the application of the *Shelley* concept in Evans v. Abney, 396 U.S. 435, 90 S.Ct. 628, 24 L.Ed.2d 634 (1970), where a state court ruled that a trustor's intention to provide a park for whites only could not be carried out and that therefore the property reverted to his heirs. The Supreme Court held that the state court ruling did not constitute state action under the fourteenth amendment.

98. See Federal Nat. Mtg. Ass'n v. Howlett, 521 S.W.2d 428, 437 (Mo. En Banc 1975).

otherwise judicial enforcement of every private agreement could be brought within the state action ambit.[99]

Finally, state action is sometimes found under a "pervasiveness" theory. Under this concept state action exists when statutory regulation pervasively governs otherwise private conduct. This theory, however, was rejected by the Supreme Court in Jackson v. Metropolitan Edison Co.,[1] where an attempt was made to find state action in a public utility termination of services. According to the Court,

> [the] mere fact that a business is subject to State regulation does not by itself convert its action into that of the State for purposes of the Fourteenth Amendment. Nor does the fact that the regulation is extensive and detailed, as in the case of most public utilities, do so * * *. [T]he inquiry must be whether there is a sufficiently close nexus between the state and the challenged action of the regulated entity so that the action of the latter may be fairly treated as that of the State itself.[2]

The *Barrera* court rejected the application of this theory to the Texas power of sale statutes. It found the nexus between state and private activity required by *Jackson* to be absent and determined that in its absence state regulation alone is not sufficient to establish state action.[2a]

The foregoing illustrates that, absent a rather unusual power of sale situation such as existed in North Carolina [3] (where public officials were significantly involved), it will be difficult to establish the state action required by the fourteenth amendment. By finding no state action, many courts avoid the myriad of complex constitutional issues considered earlier. These include: the form of notice which is required; whether all parties, including junior lienors, should be entitled to notice; and the type of hearing which is required, judicial or otherwise. By avoiding these difficult issues such courts apparently defer to legislatures which are perhaps better equipped to deal with them.[4]

99. See Global Indus., Inc. v. Harris, 376 F.Supp. 1379, 1383 (N.D.Ga.1974).

1. 419 U.S. 345, 95 S.Ct. 449, 42 L.Ed. 2d 477 (1974). See also, Moose Lodge No. 107 v. Irvis, 407 U.S. 163, 92 S.Ct. 1965, 32 L.Ed.2d 627 (1972) (state licensing and regulation of a private club not sufficient to find state action).

2. 419 U.S. at 350–51.

2a. Barrera v. Security Bldg. & Inv. Corp., 519 F.2d 1166, 1171–72 (C.A. Tex.1975).

3. See text accompanying notes 73–76, supra.

4. See Barrera v. Security Bldg. & Inv. Corp., 519 F.2d 1166, 1174 (C.A.Tex. 1975).

§ 7.28 Constitutional Problems—Federal Action

Where power of sale constitutional litigation involves a direct instrumentality of the state or federal government as the mortgagee, courts cannot avoid the constitutional issues of notice and hearing. Even though a court would find that a particular state power of sale statute lacks the requisite state action when a private party is the mortgagee, the presence of the government as a mortgagee provides the "governmental action" necessary to reach the constitutional issues. If the foreclosing mortgagee is a direct instrumentality of the state, the fourteenth amendment state action requirement is readily satisfied. If the foreclosing mortgagee is a direct federal instrumentality, then the requisite "federal action" exists, and a court will apply fifth amendment due process standards to test the constitutionality of the foreclosure.

It is a relatively common practice for a direct instrumentality of the federal government to be a foreclosing mortgagee under local power of sale statutes. This situation will arise, for example, where direct loans made by the Veterans Administration (VA) or the Farmers Home Administration (FmHA) under various government programs are foreclosed.[5] It also could occur where the Federal Housing Administration (FHA) opts to take an assignment of an FHA insured mortgage that is in default and then forecloses.[6] For example, in Ricker v. United States [7] the FmHA foreclosed a mortgage under a Maine nonjudicial foreclosure statute. The mortgagors brought suit to invalidate the foreclosure in federal court. Because the government was the mortgagee, the federal district court went directly to the fifth amendment notice and hearing issue and invalidated the foreclosure. Had this foreclosure involved a private mortgagee, the challenge would have been under the fourteenth amendment. Given the trend of the case law, state action probably would not have been found, and the merits would not have been reached.

Difficult federal action issues arise when the mortgagee is either the Federal National Mortgage Association (FNMA) or the Federal Home Loan Mortgage Corporation (FHLMC). Both entities are quasi-federal and purchase large quantities of mortgage loans on the secondary market.[8] They commonly foreclose mortgages under power of sale statutes with respect to those mortgage loans they have purchased and which subsequently go into default. Are these entities the "federal government" for purposes of the fifth amendment due process clause? Courts thus far have concluded that FNMA is not.[9]

5. See G. Nelson & D. Whitman, Cases and Materials on Real Estate Finance and Development, 511–512 (1976); United States v. White, 429 F.Supp. 1245 (N.D.Miss.1977).

6. See G. Nelson & D. Whitman, supra note 90, at 511.

7. 417 F.Supp. 133 (D.Me.1976). See United States v. White, 429 F.Supp. 1245 (N.D.Miss.1977).

8. See G. Nelson & D. Whitman, supra note 90, at 483–84, 486–87.

9. See Northrip v. Federal Nat. Mtg. Ass'n, 527 F.2d 23 (C.A.Mich.1975);

Until 1968, FNMA was wholly owned and administered by the federal government. In 1968 Congress changed its status to a federally-sponsored private corporation whose purpose was to provide a secondary market for residential mortgages.[10] The stock is completely privately owned, but the President of the United States appoints five of the fifteen members of the Board of Directors.[11] The federal government regulates FNMA in many respects, such as establishing debt limits, approving the sale of stock, and requiring that a certain portion of its mortgage purchases be related to furthering the development of low and middle income housing.[12] In Northrip v. Federal National Mortgage Association,[13] the Court of Appeals for the Sixth Circuit found that FNMA, while evidencing "significant" federal involvement, should not be treated as the federal government for fifth amendment purposes when it forecloses mortgages. The court thought that Jackson v. Metropolitan Edison Co.,[14] which found no state action involved in a public utility's termination of customer service, represented an analogous case. According to the court in *Northrip,* "here as in *Jackson* there is not a 'sufficiently close nexus' between the state and the challenged act of foreclosure." [15]

The FHLMC poses a somewhat more difficult federal action problem. It was created in 1970 by Congress to strengthen the secondary market in federally insured and conventional mortgages. Its stock is wholly owned by the twelve Federal Home Loan Banks.[16] The Board of Directors is composed of the three members of the Federal Home Loan Bank Board, the members of which are appointed by the President of the United States.[17] Although there is no case law in point, FHLMC probably should be treated as the federal government for purposes of the fifth amendment. While Congress clearly intended to make FNMA a private corporation,[18] FHLMC is more substantially tied to the federal government. There is, for example, no private market for FHLMC shares as is the case with respect to FNMA. Moreover, because the directors are Presidentially appointed, FHLMC's day-to-day operations are inevitably more significantly intertwined with the federal government than those of FNMA.

Even where the federal government is not the mortgagee, it has been argued that federal action may exist where the mortgage being foreclosed was initiated pursuant to a federally subsidized and regu-

Federal Nat. Mtg. Ass'n v. Scott, 548 S.W.2d 545 (Mo. En Banc 1977).

10. 12 U.S.C.A. § 1716 (1970).

11. 12 U.S.C.A. § 1723a(b) (1970).

12. 12 U.S.C.A. § 1723a(h) (1970).

13. 527 F.2d 23 (C.A.Mich.1975).

14. 419 U.S. 345, 95 S.Ct. 449, 42 L.Ed.2d 477 (1974).

15. 527 F.2d 23, 32 (C.A.Mich.1975).

16. 12 U.S.C.A. § 1453(a) (1970).

17. 12 U.S.C.A. § 1452(a) (1970).

18. See Northrip v. Federal Nat. Mtg. Ass'n, 527 F.2d 23, 32 (C.A.Mich. 1975).

lated program. Roberts v. Cameron-Brown Co.[19] illustrates this type of situation. The mortgage being foreclosed under a Georgia power of sale statute was initiated under section 235 of the National Housing Act and subsequently sold to FNMA, the foreclosing mortgagee.[20] The section 235 program was designed to encourage homeownership by low income groups; to accomplish this goal, the federal government makes mortgage assistance payments to the mortgagee on the mortgagor's behalf.[21] The economic effect of the program is to reduce the cost of the mortgage to the equivalent of a mortgage with a one percent per annum interest rate.[22] Private mortgagees who take part in the section 235 program are extensively controlled by federal statutes and regulations.[23] In *Roberts* the federal district court concluded that even though no state action existed for purposes of the fourteenth amendment, the combination of federal subsidy to the mortgagor and substantial federal regulation of the mortgage transaction resulted in federal action for purposes of the due process clause of the fifth amendment. In an ambiguous opinion, the Fifth Circuit reversed and determined that the federal government's involvement was insufficient to sustain a finding of federal action.[24] Even though the presence of FNMA as the foreclosing party was not emphasized in the district court's reasoning, the court of appeals stressed the fact that FNMA is not a federal instrumentality. Although the Fifth Circuit rejected the pervasive federal regulation and participation argument, its opinion failed to confront the significance of the financial subsidy provided by the section 235 program.

As more courts invalidate power of sale foreclosures by federal or quasi-federal agencies or if courts become more willing to find federal action in connection with federally subsidized and regulated mortgage programs, an interesting two-tier foreclosure system may develop. Where federal action is found, foreclosures under such state statutes probably will be held to violate the notice and hearing requirements of the fifth amendment. However, continued use of power of sale foreclosures by other mortgagees, at least in non-federally subsidized situations, will be permitted because the statutes themselves probably do not represent state action for purposes of the fourteenth amendment. The result could be that "federal" foreclosures may have to be judicial while "private" power of sale foreclosures may continue.

The "federal" role as mortgagee, either as a result of direct loans or because of activity in the secondary market, is substantial. More-

19. 410 F.Supp. 988 (S.D.Ga.1975).

20. 12 U.S.C.A. § 1715z(a) (1970).

21. See G. Nelson & D. Whitman, supra note 5, at 542.

22. Id.

23. See, e. g., 12 U.S.C.A. § 1715z(b) (1970); 24 CFR § 235 (1977); U.S. Dept. of Hous. & Urban Dev., Handbook No. 4155.1, Mortgage Credit Analysis (July 25, 1972).

24. 556 F.2d 356 (C.A.Ga.1977).

over, federal subsidy programs for privately held mortgages are also significant and, under those programs, even where a private mortgagee forecloses, the costs of foreclosure are usually borne by the federal government.[25] Therefore, federal pressure for constitutional and workable state foreclosure procedures without the full formality of judicial foreclosure may become significant. Local institutional lenders who sell loans on the "federal" market or who participate in federal subsidy programs could also become a force for legislative change of state power of sale statutes.

§ 7.29 Constitutional Problems—Title Difficulties

In the event a court surmounts the state action problem and determines that a particular power of sale statute is unconstitutional, the question arises whether a sale held under such a statute will be classified as void or merely voidable. If the sale is rendered void, no title passes in law or equity. Thus the sale purchaser, whether the mortgagee or a third party, cannot obtain title of any kind and no title would pass to subsequent purchasers.[26] On the other hand, if the constitutional sale is only voidable, the right to set aside the foreclosure and regain the land will be cut off as against any purchaser for value without notice.[27] Few cases have considered this problem. Ricker v. United States,[28] in holding that a nonjudicial foreclosure under a Maine statute violated the notice and hearing requirements of the fifth amendment due process clause, avoided classifying the foreclosure as either void or voidable; instead, the court determined that the subsequent purchasers from the federal government were not bona fide, since the original mortgagors stayed in possession and since recorded documents established that the foreclosure was nonjudicial. "Under Maine law a purchaser at a foreclosure sale cannot claim protection as a bona fide purchaser where, as here, it appears from documents and facts known at the time of purchase that there may be a substantial defect in the seller's claim of title." [29] The court may be correct in its assertion that the mortgagors' continued possession gave subsequent purchasers notice of their claim, thus depriving them of bona fide purchaser status. However, the mere presence in the public records of a document indicating that nonjudicial foreclosure had been employed is hardly tantamount to notice of a defect in the title. At present the law is far from clear on the constitutional issues; if the United States Supreme Court, or a majority of lower federal decisions, firmly establish that foreclosures without notice

25. See generally 24 CFR 203.355–.417 (1977).

26. See § 7.20 supra; G. Nelson & D. Whitman, supra note 5, at 280.

27. Id. at 281. See also, Dingus, Mortgages—Redemption After Foreclosure Sale in Missouri, 25 Mo.L. Rev. 261 (1960).

28. 417 F.Supp. 133 (D.Me.1976).

29. Id. at 140. See § 7.20, supra.

and hearing are unconstitutional, then it will be fair to say that purchasers who trace their titles through foreclosures conducted thereafter lack bona fides. That time is not here yet. The Ricker court's holding would make it virtually impossible for any person to claim BFP status and hence would in effect make all such foreclosures void; that view is simply unreasonable at this stage of the law's development.

For the countless thousands of people in the United States who may "own" land whose title was derived from a foreclosure sale under an arguably unconstitutional power of sale statute, the above problems are hardly theoretical. Unless they have been in possession for the applicable period to establish adverse possession, they may not own their land. The few cases invalidating power of sale foreclosure have not dealt with this problem. However, as a practical matter, if a court is to invalidate a state power of sale statute, it virtually will be compelled to make the decision prospective only. Although it has been the traditional rule that newly announced constitutional doctrines are given retroactive effect, the Supreme Court has been loath to do so when there are important overriding societal considerations.[30] Given the substantial reliance on the power of sale foreclosure method in this country, a retroactive application of unconstitutionality could cloud countless titles and result in enormous volumes of costly litigation.[31] This is especially true in inflationary periods when rising land values will encourage potential claimants to upset past foreclosure sales. In fact, the spectre of retroactivity doubtless encourages courts to find other methods, such as the lack of state action, to avoid reaching the constitutional questions involved in power of sale foreclosure. Whatever standards the United States Supreme Court has applied to the retroactivity question in the past in the criminal and other areas, the practical necessities would seem to dictate prospective application of unconstitutionality in the power of sale situation.

§ 7.30 Constitutional Problems—Conclusion

Assuming fourteenth amendment state action exists, many state power of sale statutes are deficient on notice grounds, and nearly all fail to satisfy the constitutional hearing requirement. As we have seen, waiver of the rights to notice and hearing, as a practical matter, simply will not work.[32] While many courts have avoided the con-

30. See G. Gunther, Constitutional Law 546 (1976); Mishkin, The High Court, the Great Writ, and the Due Process of Time and Law, 79 Harv.L. Rev. 56 (1965); Schwartz, Retroactivity, Reliability, and Due Process: A Reply to Professor Mishkin, 33 U. Chi.L.Rev. 719 (1966); Wellington, Common Law Rules and Constitutional Double Standards, 83 Yale L.J. 221 (1973).

31. See Barklage, supra note 74, at 284.

32. See § 7.26.

stitutional problems by utilizing the "no state action" approach, this cannot be the long-range solution to the problem.

The reason the "no state action" approach can at best be only a temporary expedient is because of the two-tier situation discussed earlier.[33] It is true that if courts continue to follow the "no state action" approach, private mortgagees can in theory continue to utilize current power of sale foreclosure statutes. Moreover, it may be that the Supreme Court will agree that such state statutes lack the requisite fourteenth amendment state action. However, as *Ricker* so graphically illustrates, mortgagees that are federal agencies for purposes of the fifth amendment due process clause will not be able to utilize such foreclosure statutes because such foreclosures will be unconstitutional. These federal mortgagees, as noted earlier, may include such quasi-federal agencies as the Federal Home Loan Mortgage Corporation (FHLMC) as well as direct federal instrumentalities. In addition, federal action may be present where federal subsidy programs are involved. State agencies which hold mortgages, such as state housing finance agencies, will also be subject to analogous fourteenth amendment standards.

In theory, of course, the federal government may be satisfied with judicial foreclosure in foreclosures by federal agencies or under federally subsidized programs, even though private mortgagees continue to use power of sale statutes. However, this is not the likely result, if for no other reason than judicial foreclosure is both more time-consuming and costly than its power of sale counterpart.[34] The more probable result is that there will be federal pressure on large private institutional lenders to encourage the enactment of new foreclosure legislation that meets constitutional standards yet retains the power of sale feature.

It is quite possible to enact workable legislation that meets such standards. First, as has been noted earlier, if a statute requires notice by mail to all parties of record subordinate to the mortgage being foreclosed, the constitutional notice requirement can be satisfied. Such notice could be mailed to each subordinate party at the address provided in the recorded document that evidences such party's interest in the real estate. Moreover, it is possible for the legislation to provide for a hearing and still retain a power of sale feature. For example, the statute could require that a two-part postcard be mailed to all the subordinate parties described above. The postcard would apprise them, in simple nontechnical language, of the foreclosure proceeding, and inform them that if a hearing is desired the second half of the postcard should be returned by mail to the court. If any card is returned, a judicial hearing would be scheduled. How-

33. See § 7.28, supra.

34. See McElhone & Cramer, Loan Foreclosure Costs Affected By Varied State Regulations, 36 Mortgage Banker 41 (1975).

ever, if no cards are returned the mortgagee or trustee would be free to exercise the power of sale contained in the mortgage instrument without any judicial intervention. The latter result would, in fact, be likely; even judicial foreclosure actions culminate with a high percentage of default judgments. Such legislation thus may retain the cost saving advantage of the power of sale foreclosure and yet meet constitutional requirements. Such legislation should be seriously considered.

F. DISPOSITION OF SURPLUS

§ 7.31 Surplus—General Rules

Where the foreclosure sale produces a surplus, the rules governing who participates in that surplus and the priority of that participation are generally clear. The major underlying principle is that the surplus represents the remnant of the equity of redemption and security wiped out by the foreclosure. Consequently, the surplus stands in the place of the foreclosed real estate and the liens and interests that previously attached to that real estate now attach to the surplus.[35] They are entitled to be paid out of that surplus in the order of priority they enjoyed prior to foreclosure.[36] The claim of the foreclosed mortgagor or the owner of the equity of redemption normally is junior to those of all valid liens wiped out by the foreclosure.[37]

Statutes often regulate the distribution of surplus, especially in the power of sale setting. Some simply codify the principles described above.[38] Others seem on their face to give the surplus to the mortgagor and make no reference to the rights of junior lienors.[39] However, these latter statutes have generally been interpreted to give junior lienors rights in the surplus and the priority over mortgagors generally described in the preceding paragraph.[40] A few statutes

35. Western Sav. Fund Society of Philadelphia v. Goodman, 103 N.J.Super. 307, 247 A.2d 151 (1968); Security Trust Co. of Rochester v. Miller, 72 Misc.2d 269, 338 N.Y.S.2d 1015 (1972); Sadow v. Poskin Realty Corp., 63 Misc.2d 499, 312 N.Y.S.2d 901 (1970).

36. Id.

37. See, e. g., Sens v. Slavia, Inc., 304 So.2d 438 (Fla.1974); Note, Rights in the Proceeds of a Foreclosure Sale—The Court Helps Those Who Help Themselves, 51 N.C.L.Rev. 1100 (1973); Imperial—Yuma Production Credit Ass'n v. Nussbaumer, 22 Ariz. App. 485, 528 P.2d 871 (1974).

38. See, e. g., Ariz.Rev.Stat. § 33–727: "If there are other liens on the property sold, or other payments secured by the same mortgage, they shall be paid in their order * * *." See Or.Rev.Stat. 87–765.

39. See, e. g., Minn.Stat.Ann. § 580.10; Ind.Code 1971, 34–1–53–10; Rev.Code Wash.Ann. 61–12–150.

40. See, e. g., Brown v. Crookston Agriculture Ass'n, 34 Minn. 545, 26 N. W. 907 (1886); Fuller v. Langum, 37 Minn. 74, 33 N.W. 122 (1887); White v. Shirk, 20 Ind.App. 589, 51 N.E. 126 (1898).

make no mention of priorities, but simply authorize the mortgagee or trustee to pay the surplus to the clerk of court.[41]

One important corrollary of the above rules needing closer analysis is that only those whose interests were cut off by the foreclosure sale have a right to share in the surplus.[42] The party that comes to mind first as qualifying is the foreclosed owner of the equity of redemption. But some courts have included certain subordinate parties who shared in that ownership interest, such as, for example, a foreclosed easement owner.[43] Moreover, if such easement owners qualify, so, too, should a subordinate lessee to the extent that the fair market value of his destroyed leasehold interest exceeds his obligations under the lease. Another obvious group cut off by the foreclosure sale are junior lienors. In order to qualify for lienor status, it must be established that the claim was reduced to a lien prior to the foreclosure sale.[44] Thus, mere general creditors or those holding contract claims unrelated to the land have no claim to the surplus.[45] Moreover, senior lienors have no right to share in the surplus.[46] In one case, for example, where the foreclosed mortgagor was insolvent, two senior mortgagees attempted to utilize the surplus created by the foreclosure of a third mortgage to pay down part of the senior mortgage debt. The court held that since the senior liens were unaffected by the foreclosure they had no right to the surplus.[47]

Where land sale contracts are destroyed by a foreclosure of a prior mortgage given by the vendor, special problems arise if the foreclosure sale results in a surplus. It is not uncommon for vendees to make substantial payments under such contracts either in ignorance of a prior mortgage on the land or in reliance on the vendor's promise to satisfy it by the time the contract is fully paid. However, it too commonly happens that the mortgage is foreclosed and the contract vendee is wiped out.[48] In the event of a foreclosure surplus,

41. See, e. g., Utah Code Ann.1953, 57–1–29.

42. Sadow v. Poskin Realty Corp., 63 Misc.2d 499, 312 N.Y.S.2d 901 (1970).

43. Anderman v. 1395 E. 52nd Street Realty Corp., 60 Misc.2d 437, 303 N.Y.S.2d 474 (1969).

44. Sadow v. Poskin Realty Corp., 63 Misc.2d 499, 312 N.Y.S.2d 901 (1970). The lien of a judgment docketed after the delivery of the deed of a referee in foreclosure but before the confirmation of the foreclosure sale in New York shares in surplus moneys pro rata with other similar liens without priorities. Id.

45. Sens v. Slavia, Inc., 304 So.2d 438 (Fla.1974); Sadow v. Poskin Realty Corp., 63 Misc.2d 499, 312 N.Y.S.2d 901 (1970) (tenant security deposits not a lien on surplus nor is electric utility bill of the mortgagor). Northwestern Mutual Life Ins. Co. v. Nebraska Land Co., 192 Neb. 588, 223 N.W.2d 425 (1974).

46. See Walsky v. Fairmont Arms, Inc., 27 A.D.2d 671, 276 N.Y.S.2d 931 (1967); Armands Engineering Inc. v. Town and Country Club, Inc., 113 R.I. 515, 324 A.2d 334 (1974).

47. Armands Engineering Inc. v. Town and Country Club, Inc., 113 R.I. 515, 324 A.2d 334 (1974).

48. See § 3, supra.

should the vendee share in it? If so, with what priority? A Maryland case involving a somewhat similar situation is interesting in this regard.[49] In that case a contract for the sale of land was apparently wiped out by the foreclosure of a mortgage that had arisen through the vendor. Under Maryland law a contract vendee obtains a lien on the land to the extent of the payments made under the contract in the event the contract, through the fault of the vendor, is not consummated.[50] The court determined that this equitable lien of the vendee came into existence at least as of the date the vendee filed a lien claim in the foreclosure proceeding. As a result, the vendee was permitted to share in the foreclosure surplus and his claim was deemed to be prior to that of another creditor who obtained a judgment two days thereafter.

An alternative, and perhaps better, method of analyzing the vendee's interest is also available. The vendee, like the subordinate easement holder, can be viewed as owning part of the equity of redemption rather than as a lienor. Indeed, under the doctrine of equitable conversion the vendee is regarded in equity as *the* owner of the land for many purposes.[51] It may sometimes be advantageous for the foreclosed vendee to stake his claim to a foreclosure surplus in his equitable role as owner rather than as an equitable lienor. This would be true if a court were to hold that the equitable lien arises only on the vendor's default rather than as of the date of the land contract. In that event the vendee's claim to any foreclosure surplus may be rendered subordinate to post-contract liens arising through the vendor. Under the "ownership" approach, however, it is clear that the vendee's priority would date from the execution of the contract so as to take precedence over such intervening vendor-caused liens. At least this would be true if the vendee promptly recorded his contract or took equivalent steps to establish constructive notice of its existence.[52] If the vendee's equitable lien is viewed as arising as of the date of the contract rather than later, the theory utilized by the foreclosed vendee to reach the surplus becomes less significant.

§ 7.32 Surplus—Some Special Problems

Suppose that for some reason a senior lien has been foreclosed and a surplus was produced, but a junior lien exists that is not in default. Should that junior lienor be entitled to payment from the surplus? Some courts have said yes.[53] On the other hand, In re Castili-

49. Gribble v. Stearman & Kaplan, Inc., 249 Md. 289, 239 A.2d 573 (1968).

50. The rule is the same in many states. See Whitman, Financing Condominiums and Cooperatives, 13 Tulsa L.J. 15, 30 (1977).

51. See Van Hecke, Leavell and Nelson, Equitable Remedies and Restitution, 78–97 (2d Ed. 1973).

52. See § 3.30, supra.

53. See, e. g., Fagan v. Peoples Sav. & Loan Ass'n, 55 Minn. 437, 57 N.W.

an Apartments[54] is an interesting case in this regard. In that case a senior mortgage was foreclosed and produced a substantial surplus. The junior mortgage was not in default and contained no acceleration clause that would have made it due and payable whenever the senior mortgage went into default. Moreover, because the junior debt had previously been determined to be usurious, under North Carolina law all right to receive interest on it was forfeited. As a result, the North Carolina Supreme Court approved a lower court determination that the surplus should not be paid to the junior lienor and that it instead should be invested in a certificate of deposit for junior lienor's benefit but with interest to be paid to the debtor.

The foregoing situation is relatively uncommon for several reasons. First, when a foreclosure sale results in a surplus, the debts of junior lien claimants normally will be in default. This will be true automatically with respect to junior judgment lienors. Moreover, if the mortgagor has allowed senior debt to go into default, the chances are strong that the junior debt is in default as well.[55] Second, even if the mortgagor has not otherwise defaulted on senior debt, many junior mortgages provide as a ground for acceleration that any default or foreclosure with respect to a senior encumbrance will give the junior mortgagee the option to accelerate the junior debt. Acceleration for such a reason is generally upheld.[56] Finally, a few states appear to give junior lienors that are not in default the right to be paid from a foreclosure surplus.[57]

Although, as we have seen in the preceding section, the foreclosing mortgagee or trustee is guided by relatively clear substantive law governing the rights of those cut off by a foreclosure sale to share in any surplus, certain practical problems nevertheless sometimes remain. If, of course, the foreclosure is judicial, all interested parties normally are before the court and the court will make a determination as to entitlement to surplus.[58] Also, even in the power of sale setting, there very often will be no problems in identifying those entitled to the surplus and their relative priorities. However, there is always the possibility that the foreclosing mortgagee or trustee will be confronted by conflicting claims as to surplus. In this connection suppose that one of two junior liens claiming rights to the surplus had a lien on only part of the foreclosed real estate. Should the lienor that is prior in time, but whose lien only covered part of the real

142 (1893); Moss v. Robertson, 56 Neb. 774, 77 N.W. 403 (1898).

54. 281 N.C. 709, 190 S.E.2d 161 (1972). See Note, Rights in the Proceeds of a Foreclosure Sale—The Court Helps Those Who Help Themselves, 51 N.C.L.Rev. 1100, 1101 (1973).

55. See Note, supra note 54 at 1102.

56. See, e. g., Crescent Beach Co. v. Conzleman, 321 So.2d 437 (Fla.App. 1975).

57. See, e. g., Ariz.Rev.Stat. § 33–727.

58. See, e. g., McKinney's N.Y.Real Prop.Actions & Proc. §§ 1441–1445.

estate be entitled to all of the remaining surplus if there is not enough to cover both liens?[59] Payment of the surplus in such a situation without judicial guidance would be risky at best. Or suppose a foreclosing trustee, in a state where the power of sale statute does not require notice to junior lienors for foreclosure purposes, fails to conduct a title search and pays out the surplus. If, in fact, another junior lien existed, there is authority for holding the trustee personally liable to the junior lienor.[60] A few statutes, as we have noted in the preceding section, attempt to deal with these problems by authorizing the payment of surplus to the court.[61] In any event, where there is any doubt, the prudent person holding the surplus will seek judicial guidance instead of proceeding at his own risk.

59. See Banks-Miller Supply Co. v. Smallridge, 175 S.E.2d 446 (W.Va. 1970). For examples of how courts have resolved similar problems that a trustee would have resolved at his peril, see General Builders Supply Co. v. Arlington Co-op Bank, 359 Mass. 691, 271 N.E.2d 342 (1971); Gribble v. Stearman & Kaplan, Inc., 249 Md. 289, 239 A.2d 573 (1968).

60. See, e. g., W. A. H. Church, Inc. v. Holmes, 46 F.2d 608 (D.C.Cir. 1931).

61. See, e. g., N.C.Gen.Stat. § 45–21.-32; Utah Rev.Code 1953, § 57–1–29. North Dakota legislation instructs the person conducting the sale under a power of sale to wait thirty days after the sale and if no claimants show up he is directed to pay the surplus to the mortgagor.

§§ 7.33–8.0 are reserved for supplementary material.

CHAPTER 8

STATUTORY IMPACTS ON FORECLOSURE

Table of Sections

A. REGULATION OF DEFICIENCY JUDGMENTS

A. REGULATION OF DEFICIENCY JUDGMENTS

§ 8.1 Deficiency Judgments—In General

Generally, the mortgagee has two basic methods of collecting the mortgage debt. The mortgagee may sue and get judgment at law upon the personal obligation and enforce it by levy upon any property of the debtor. Or he may foreclose upon the property. Usually these options may be pursued concurrently or consecutively.[1] In some states, however, while the mortgagee may utilize either of the above options, once he elects one type of action, the prosecution of the other is subject to being dismissed or at least stayed.[2]

1. See Foothills Holding Corp. v. Tulsa Rig, Reel & Mfg. Co., 155 Colo. 232, 393 P.2d 749 (1964); Rossiter v. Merriman, 80 Kan. 739, 104 P. 858, 24 L.R.A.,N.S., 1095 (1909); Jewett v. Hamlin, 68 Me. 172 (1878); Bateman v. Grand Rapids & I. R. Co., 96 Mich. 441, 56 N.W. 28 (1893); Gibson v. Green's Adm'r, 89 Va. 524, 16 S.E. 661, 37 Am.St.Rep. 888 (1893).

2. See 3 Powell, Real Property, 616 (1977). There are some state statutes that provide that if separate actions

Regardless of the method of foreclosure, the mortgagee in most states can obtain a judgment for a deficiency. Where foreclosure is by sale under judicial decree in a court action, the usual method in America and the one under chief consideration here, the amount realized on sale is often an automatic determination of the amount to be applied upon the debt and mortgage creditor, is entitled to recover the balance.[3] Today this ordinarily may be obtained by a deficiency decree given by the equity court in the foreclosure action itself. If there is a power of sale foreclosure the sale price determines the amount to be credited on the debt and the mortgagee can then sue for the balance in an action at law. In those few instances where a mortgagee may obtain strict foreclosure, either by equitable action or by cutting off the mortgagor's rights through taking and holding possession, he can obtain a deficiency judgment for the difference between the value of the land as appraised, normally by the verdict of a jury in the action for the deficiency, and the amount of the debt plus interest and costs.[4] And such a judgment does not reopen the foreclosure so as to give the mortgagor another chance to redeem.

There are a variety of procedural prerequisites to obtaining deficiency judgments.[5] Many states impose strict notice requirements [6] and statutory time limits.[7] The consequences to the mortgagee in failing to comply with such requirements can be harsh. For example, in some states, if the mortgagee fails to seek the deficiency judg-

are brought upon the debt and to foreclose, the mortgagee must elect which he desires to pursue and the other will be dismissed. See Ariz. Rev.Stat.Ann. § 33–722; Iowa Code Ann. § 654.4. Of course, the mortgagee's options will be more substantially limited in those jurisdictions following a "one action" type rule. See the following section.

3. Although the point was considered by Chancellor Kent in Dunkley v. Van Buren, N.Y. 3 Johns.Ch. 330 (1818), and not definitely decided until Lansing v. Goelet, 9 Cow. 346 (N.Y.1827) no case held that a foreclosure sale discharged the personal obligation beyond the amount it produced at the sale. In accord is McKnight v. United States, C.A.9th, 259 F.2d 540 (1958). However, this rule has been substantially altered in those states that have enacted anti-deficiency legislation. See § 8.3, infra.

4. See Tefft, The Myth of Strict Foreclosure, 4 U. of Chi.L.Rev. 575, 594 (1937). See § 7.9, supra.

5. See generally, Comment, The Role of State Deficiency Judgment Law in FHA Insured Mortgage Transactions, 56 Minn.L.Rev. 463, 465–466 (1972).

6. See, e. g., Me.Rev.Stat.Ann. § 6203–E (mortgagee required to give at least 21 days notice of his intention to seek a deficiency judgment); Purdon's Penn.Stat.Ann. tit. 12, § 2621.3 (notice to mortgagor required ten days before hearing).

7. Statutes often require that the deficiency judgment be sought within a certain period after foreclosure. See, e. g., Nev.Rev.Stat. 40.455 (three months); N.J.Stat.Ann. 2A:50–2 (three months); N.D.Cent.Code 32–19–06 (ninety days). See U. S. v. Merrick Sponsor Corp., 421 F.2d 1076 (C.A.N.Y.1970). Moreover some states limit the time for completion of execution on a deficiency judgment. See, e. g., N.D.Cent.Code 32–19–06 (two years); Ohio Rev.Code Ann. § 2329.08 (two years for certain residential and farm property).

ment within the specified time period, the foreclosure sale proceeds are deemed to have fully satisfied the mortgage debt.[8]

§ 8.2 The "One Action" Rule

Deficiency judgment questions are often closely related to the "one action" rule in effect in several states. This rule means, in general, that in the event of a default, the mortgagee's sole remedy is a foreclosure action and that any deficiency claim must be sought in that proceeding.[9] The purpose of this rule is two-fold. One is to protect the mortgagor against multiplicity of actions when the separate actions, though theoretically distinct, are so closely connected that normally they can and should be decided in one suit.[10] The other is to compel a creditor who has taken a mortgage on land to exhaust his security before attempting to reach any unmortgaged property to satisfy his claim.[11] The mortgagee, under these provisions, cannot disregard his security even if he wishes to do so, and sue upon the note or debt.[12] Nor may the requirement of the statute be waived by the mortgagor through a provision in the mortgage.[13] However, the rule does not apply where the security has become valueless.[14]

8. See McKinney's N.Y.Real Prop.Actions § 1371(3); 12 Okl.Stat.Ann. § 686.

9. West's Ann.Cal.Code Civ.Proc., § 726 provides in relevant part: "There can be but one form of action for the recovery of any debt, or the enforcement of any right secured by mortgage upon real property, which action must be in accordance with the provisions of this chapter. In such action the court may, by its judgment, direct the sale of the encumbered property." Four other states, Montana, Nevada, Utah, and Idaho, have a "one action" statute copied from California. Mont.Rev.Codes Ann., 93, 6001 (1947); Nev.Rev.Stat. § 40.430 (1957); Utah Code Ann., Supp.1969, § 78–37–1; Idaho Code Ann., Supp. § 6–101 (1969). See also Note, Anti-Deficiency Judgment Legislation in California, 3 U.C.L.A.L. Rev. 192 (1956).

10. Toby v. Oregon Pac. R. Co., 98 Cal. 490, 33 P. 550 (1893); Felton v. West, 102 Cal. 266, 36 P. 676 (1894).

11. Bank of Italy v. Bentley, 217 Cal. 644, 20 P.2d 940 (1933), noted, (1932), 20 Cal.L.Rev. 318; 5 So.Cal.L.Rev. 227 (1932); 6 ibid. 7 (1932); 8 ibid. 35 (1934). But see, 31 Cal.L.Rev. 429, 431 (1943).

12. Woodruff v. California Republic Bank, 75 Cal.App.3d 108, 141 Cal. Rptr. 915 (1977); Barbieri v. Ramelli, 84 Cal. 154, 23 P. 1086 (1890); Crescent Lumber Co. v. Larson, 166 Cal. 168, 135 P. 502 (1913); Clark v. Paddock, 24 Idaho 142, 132 P. 795 (1913), 46 L.R.A.,N.S., 475; Coburn v. Bartholomew, 50 Utah 566, 167 P. 1156 (1922); Cf., Barth v. Ely, 85 Mont. 310, 278 P. 1002 (1929). See note, 25 Cal.L.Rev. 469, 476 (1937).

13. Winklemen v. Sides, 31 Cal.App.2d 387, 88 P.2d 147 (1939), Sup.Ct. hearing den., commented on 27 Cal.L.Rev. 752 (1939). Cf., California Bank v. Stimson, 89 Cal.App. 552, 201 P.2d 39 (1949), commented on, 22 So.Cal.L. Rev. 502 (1949). In 1937 such a waiver was explicitly prohibited by code amendment. Cal.Civ.Code, § 2953.

14. Hibernia Sav. & Loan Soc. v. Thornton, 109 Cal. 427, 42 P. 447, 50 Am.St.Rep. 52 (1895). See Barbieri v. Ramelli, 84 Cal. 154, 23 P. 1086 (1890); note, 25 Cal.L.Rev. 469, 473 (1937). See also 108 A.L.R. 397 (1937). In Edminster v. Van Eaton, 57 Idaho 115, 63 P.2d 154 (1937), the court noted that where the mortgagee's security becomes valueless, he has a complete and independent action on the note secured by the mort-

Procedurally, a mortgagor may use the rule both defensively and as a sanction. If the mortgagor successfully raises the rule as an affirmative defence, the mortgagee will be required to exhaust the security before obtaining a deficiency judgment.[15] On the other hand, suppose the mortgagor does not raise the rule in the personal action. As the California Supreme Court has stated, the mortgagor "may still invoke it as a sanction against the mortgagee on the basis that the latter by not foreclosing on the security in the action brought to enforce the debt, has made an election of remedies and waived the security." [16]

Some of the states that have "one action" legislation not only apply it to deeds of trust as well as mortgages,[17] but also to power of sale as well as to judicial foreclosure.[18] This means that either judicial foreclosure or the exercise of the power of sale will be a condition precedent to a subsequent action for a deficiency.[19] Where power of sale foreclosure is the predominant method of foreclosure, it is thus perhaps more accurate to refer to the "one action" rule as the "security first" principle.

Interestingly, North Dakota has interpreted its anti-deficiency legislation [20] in such a manner as to create a modified "one action" rule. In that state a mortgagee can either "(1) foreclose without asking for a deficiency judgment, or (2) foreclose, asking for a deficiency judgment in a separate action after the sale of the property, and obtain a judgment for only the difference between the mortgage debt plus costs and the fair value determined by a jury against [the mortgagor] or (3) sue on the note without foreclosure but with recovery limited to the difference between the amount due on the note

gage, and that he may assert his right upon the note independent of the mortgage security.

15. Salter v. Ulrich, 22 Cal.2d 263, 138 P.2d 7 (1943); Walker v. Community Bank, 10 Cal.3d 729, 111 Cal.Rptr. 897, 518 P.2d 329 (1974).

16. Walker, supra note 15 at 518 P.2d 334.

17. See Bank of Italy v. Bentley, 217 Cal. 644, 20 P.2d 940 (1933), certiorari denied 290 U.S. 659, 54 S.Ct. 74, 78 L.Ed. 571; McMillan v. United Mortgage Co., 82 Nev. 117, 412 P.2d 604 (1966), appeal after remand 84 Nev. 99, 437 P.2d 878; Nevada Land & Mortgage Co. v. Hidden Wells Ranch, Inc., 83 Nev. 501, 435 P.2d 198 (1967).

18. See Bank of Italy v. Bentley, 217 Cal. 644, 20 P.2d 940 (1933), certiorari denied 290 U.S. 659, 54 S.Ct. 74, 78 L.Ed. 571; Walker v. Community Bank, 10 Cal.3d 729, 111 Cal.Rptr. 897, 518 P.2d 329 (1974) (where mortgagee sues on the obligation, he thereby "waives his right to foreclose on the security or to sell the security under a power of sale."); Nevada Land & Mortgage Co. v. Hidden Wells Ranch, Inc., 83 Nev. 501, 435 P.2d 198 (1967) (mortgagee may select either judicial foreclosure or power of sale foreclosure under a deed of trust and then bring an action on the mortgage note for a deficiency judgment.) See also Second Baptist Church v. First Nat. Bank, 89 Nev. 217, 510 P.2d 630 (1973).

19. Notes 17 and 18, supra.

20. No.Dak.Cent.Code 32–19–06 and 32–19–07.

plus costs and the fair value of the property determined by a jury." [21] Under this interpretation the mortgagee cannot accomplish what he could under the common law, that is, to recover the full debt in a personal action against the mortgagor.

§ 8.3 Anti-deficiency Legislation

The great depression of the 1930's, as might be expected, produced a substantial amount of varied state legislation to provide relief for mortgagors. Perhaps best-known were the various mortgage moratoria statutes, most of which have lapsed or have been repealed. This legislation differed substantially from state to state.[22] Some statutes gave courts authority to grant foreclosure postponements on petition of mortgagors in individual cases. Other statutes often extended the period of statutory redemption beyond the usual period or stretched out the periods of time in a foreclosure action. While this type of legislation was subjected to substantial constitutional attack, most of it was upheld. The United States Supreme Court, for example, specifically upheld the Minnesota Moratoria legislation against the attack that it unconstitutionally impaired the obligations of contracts under the Contract Clause of the United States Constitution.[23]

However, the great variety of anti-deficiency legislation of the 1930's probably represents the most significant and enduring legislative impact of mortgage law arising out of the great depression. As we noted in an earlier section,[24] a mortgagee traditionally has been able to obtain a deficiency judgment calculated by subtracting the foreclosure sale price from the mortgage debt. This has usually been the case whether the foreclosure is judicial or by power of sale. Normally, a forced sale, even under stable economic conditions, will not bring a price that will reflect the reasonable market value of the property if it were sold outside of the foreclosure context. In times of depression, moreover, mortgaged property often sells for nominal amounts. The result is that the mortgagee can purchase at the sale for less than the mortgage debt, resell the property at fair market value and, in addition, attempt to realize on a deficiency judgment determined by the difference between the mortgage debt and the foreclosure sale price.

The anti-deficiency legislation of the 1930's represented a new approach to this problem. Instead of focusing on measures aimed at insuring an adequate sale price for the property,[25] the price obtained though the foreclosure sale was often abandoned as a test for the de-

21. First State Bank of Cooperstown v. Ihringer, 217 N.W.2d 857, 869 (N. D.1974).

22. For a complete consideration of mortgage moratoria legislation and its problems, see Osborne, Mortgages, § 331 (2d Ed. 1970).

23. See Home Bldg. & Loan Ass'n v. Blaisdell, 290 U.S. 398, 54 S.Ct. 231, 78 L.Ed. 413 (1934).

24. See § 8.1, supra.

25. See § 7.16, supra.

ficiency. The methods employed and the coverage of statutes enacted to cut down the amount of deficiency judgments have been diverse.[26] If the foreclosure is by court action, the court, depending upon the terms of the particular statute, either on the demand of a party, or its own motion, or automatically upon application by the plaintiff for a deficiency, must ascertain the "fair value"[27] of the property and give a decree for the difference between it and the debt.[28] If foreclosure is by sale out of court under a trust deed or power of sale, then similarly the value is to be ascertained in an action at law on the debt with a judgment for the difference only.[29] The "fair value" is sometimes determined by the court,[30] sometimes by a jury[31] and, occasionally, by appraisers.[32]

Some statutes flatly prohibit a deficiency judgment where the foreclosure has been by power of sale.[33] In California, for example,

26. See generally, Comment, The Role of State Deficiency Judgment Law in FHA Insured Mortgage Transactions, 56 Minn.L.Rev. 463, 466–68 (1972); Perlman, Mortgage Deficiency Judgments During an Economic Depression, 20 Va.L.Rev. 771 (1934); Poteat, State Legislative Relief for the Mortgage Debtor During the Depression, 5 Law and Contemp.Probs. 517, 539 (1938); Vaughan, Reform of Mortgage Foreclosure Procedure—Possibilities Suggested by Honeyman v. Jacobs, 88 U. of Pa.L.Rev. 957 (1940); Warm, A Study of Some of the Problems Concerning Foreclosure Sales and Deficiency Judgments, 6 Brooklyn L.Rev. 167 (1936); Skilton, Government and the Mortgage Debtor, Ch. VII; Skilton, Government and the Mortgage Debtor, 1946, 95 U. of Pa.L.Rev. 119, 127. Although earlier decisions sometimes invalidated anti-deficiency statutes on constitutional grounds, later decisions upheld them. Moreover there is little question as to their validity when applied prospectively. See Osborne, Mortgages, § 336 (2d Ed. 1970).

Several states have anti-deficiency legislation. See, e. g., West's Ann.Calif.Code Civ.Proc., § 726; Idaho Code § 6–108; McKinney's N.Y. Real Prop. Actions Law § 1371; N.C.Gen.Stat. § 45–21–36; 12 Okl.Stat.Ann. § 686; 12 Purdon's Penn.Stat.Ann. § 2621.1; S. C.Code 1962 §§ 29–3–660—29–3–760; So.Dak. Compiled Laws 21–47–16, 21–48–15, 21–49–27; Wash.Rev.Code Ann. § 61.12.060; Utah Code Ann. 53, 57–1–32; No.Dak.Cent.Code 32–19–04, 32–19–06, 32–19–07.

27. The statutes use a variety of terms to define the "value" of the property for purposes of a deficiency judgment, including "fair value", "true value," "true market value," "appraised value," "actual value," and "market value." See statutes in preceding footnote. Although indefinite, these terms are intended to convey some amount that is not necessarily the same as the foreclosure sale price. See Comment, 47 Mich.L.Rev. 254, 249 (1948).

28. See, e. g., West's Ann.Calif.Code Civ.Proc., § 726; McKinney's N.Y. Real Prop.Actions Law § 1371; So. Dak. Compiled Laws 21–47–16.

29. See, e. g., So.Dak. Compiled Laws 21–48–15, 21–49–27; Utah Code Ann. 53, 57–1–32. For a recent interpretation of the Utah legislation, see Bullington v. Mize, 25 Utah 2d 173, 478 P.2d 500 (1970).

30. See, e. g., West's Ann.Calif.Code Civ.Proc., § 726; McKinney's N.Y. Real Prop.Actions Law § 1371.

31. See, e. g., No.Dak.Cent.Code 32–19–04, 32–19–06, 32–19–07. For an analysis of this statute, see First State Bank of Cooperstown v. Ihringer, 217 N.W.2d 857 (N.D.1974). See, also, § 8.2, supra.

32. In South Carolina, the value is to be determined by appraisers. See S. C.Code § 29–3–660—29–3–760.

33. See West's Ann.Calif.Code Civ. Proc., § 580(d); Prunty v. Bank of

this prohibition was enacted because of the absence of statutory redemption under power of sale foreclosure. As one commentator pointed out, "by exercizing the power [of sale] instead of foreclosing judicially, the creditor could obtain a deficiency judgment as well as the enhanced proceeds of a redemption-free sale. This procedure allowed the creditor to bid in the property himself at an unfairly low price—or offer that opportunity to someone else—secure in the knowledge that any deficiency would be recoverable in a personal judgment against the [mortgagor]. The absence of a redemption right rendered the [mortgagor] vulnerable to an unrealistically low sales price and prevented * * * him * * * from protecting [himself] by redeeming for the property's true worth. The creditor had an opportunity for a 'double recovery' on the debt." [34]

Some states also prohibit deficiency judgments where the foreclosed mortgage is a purchase money mortgage.[35] While some of these states limit the purchase money concept to where a vendor takes a mortgage,[36] others also include a variety of third party lenders within the statutory prohibition.[37] The Uniform Land Transactions Act (ULTA), promulgated by National Conference of Commissioners on Uniform State Laws in 1975, but as of this writing not adopted by any state, permits deficiency judgments in general, but prohibits them as to purchase money mortgages given by mortgagor-occupants of residential real estate.[38] Purchase money mortgages include both the third party as well as the vendor variety.[39]

If a waiver of the benefit of the anti-deficiency statutes is permitted their effectiveness as a protection to mortgagors may be eroded.[40] There is legislative recognition of such danger in some states in statutes enacted to prevent it.[41] And similar awareness is found

America, 37 Cal.App.3d 430, 112 Cal. Rptr. 370 n. 7 (1974); Rev.Code Wash.Ann. 61.24.010, 61.24.040, 61.-24.100; Helbling Bros. Inc. v. Turner, 14 Wash.App. 494, 542 P.2d 1257 (1975).

34. Comment, Exonerating the Surety: Implications of California Anti-deficiency Scheme, 57 Cal.L.Rev. 218, 232 (1969).

35. See West's Ann.Calif.Code Civ. Proc., § 580(b); Ariz.Rev.Stat. § 33–729(A); N.C.Gen.Stat. § 45–21.38; Rev.Code Mont. § 93–6008; Ore.Rev. Stat. 88.070; So.Dak. Compiled Laws 44–8–20—44–8–25.

36. See N.C.Gen.Stat. § 45–21–38; Childers v. Parkers, Inc., 274 N.C. 256, 162 S.E.2d 481 (1968) (statute inapplicable to non-vendor purchase money mortgagees); Currie and Lieberman, Purchase-Money Mortgages and State Lines: A Study in Conflicts of Laws Method, 1960 Duke L.J. 1 (1960). See So.Dak. Compiled Laws 44–8–25.

37. See West's Ann.Calif.Code Civ. Proc., § 580(b); Ariz.Rev.Stat. § 33–729(A).

38. U.L.T.A. § 3–510(b) (1975).

39. Id. at Comment 2.

40. See Skilton, Government and the Mortgage Debtor, 125.

41. E. g., Pa.Stat.Ann. tit. 12, § 2621.-10 (1967); West's Ann.Cal.Civ.Code, § 2953.

West's Ann.Cal.Civ.Code, § 2953 vitiates "any express agreement made or entered into at the time of or in con-

in some court decisions.[42] However, a distinction between a waiver entered into at the time the mortgage is given and one subsequent in time has been drawn, the former being bad and the latter good.[43] This corresponds to the similar distinction broadly drawn by the courts when the question is one of protecting the mortgagor's right of redemption.[44]

In some states limitations on the amount of a deficiency have been coupled with restrictions on the bringing of an action on the debt alone under which unmortgaged assets can be reached. This is true, of course, in states already having the "one action" rule.[45] But other states have enacted legislation somewhat toward the same end, notably New York.[46] There an action on the note and an action to foreclose cannot be pursued concurrently.[47] If the mortgagee sues upon the debt, he cannot later foreclose until execution has been returned wholly or partially unsatisfied.[48] Conversely, while a foreclosure action is pending or after final decree he cannot bring an action on the debt alone without permission of the court in which the foreclosure action was brought.[49] It has been suggested that this is necessary if the object of the deficiency statute is to be accomplished.[50] If he may sue at law at the same time he

nection with the making or renewing of any loan secured by a deed of trust, mortgage or other instrument creating a lien on real property, whereby the borrower agrees to waive the rights, or privileges conferred upon him by sections 2924, 2924b, 2924c of the Civil Code or by sections 580a or 726 of the Code of Civil Procedure." Even though sections 580(b) and 580(d) are not covered by the above statute, they may not be waived at the time the loan is made. See Freedland v. Greco, 45 Cal.2d 462, 289 P.2d 463 (1955); Valinda Builders v. Bissner, 230 Cal.App. 2d 106, 40 Cal.Rptr. 735 (1964); Hetland, Secured Real Estate Transactions, 220 (1974).

42. Salter v. Ulrich, 22 Cal.2d 263, 266, 138 P.2d 7, 146 A.L.R. 1344 (1943); Morello v. Metzenbaum, 25 Cal.2d 494, 154 P.2d 670 (1944); Cf., Winklemen v. Sides, 31 Cal.App.2d 387, 88 P.2d 147 (1939); Cf. also California Bank v. Stimson, 89 Cal.App. 2d 552, 201 P.2d 39 (1949); commented on 22 So.Cal.L.Rev. 502 (1949). See Notes, 27 Cal.L.Rev. 752 (1939); 31 Cal.L.Rev. 429, 434 (1943); Cf., 31 Cal.L.Rev. 429 (1943).

43. West's Ann.Cal.Civ.Code, § 2953; Salter v. Ulrich, 22 Cal.2d 263, 266, 138 P.2d 7, 146 A.L.R. 1344 (1943); Morello v. Metzenbaum, 25 Cal.2d 494, 499, 154 P.2d 670 (1944). See Russell v. Roberts, 39 Cal.App.3d 390, 114 Cal.Rptr. 305 (1974). But in Pennsylvania a waiver or release is void regardless of whether before, after, or at the time the mortgage is given. Pa.Stat.Ann. tit. 12, § 2621.10 (1967).

44. See § 3.1, supra.

45. See § 8.2, supra.

46. McKinney's N.Y. Real Property Actions and Proc.Law § 1301. See Friedman, Personal Liability on Mortgage Debts in New York, 51 Yale L.J. 382, 387 (1942).

47. See D'Agostino v. Wheel Inn, Inc., 65 Misc.2d 227, 317 N.Y.S.2d 472 (1970); Citibank (Mid-Hudson), N. A. v. Rohdie, 82 Misc.2d 372, 368 N.Y.S. 2d 109 (1975).

48. McKinney's N.Y. Real Property Actions and Proc.Law § 1301(1).

49. Id. at § 1301(3).

50. Skilton, Government and the Mortgage Debtor, 125.

brings his action to foreclose, he may obtain a judgment on the debt prior to his foreclosure decree, levy on any available unmortgaged assets, then get his foreclosure decree for the balance. The debt so reduced may be then so greatly oversecured that even though it is wiped out by crediting the real value of the property on it, he will have made a handsome profit at the expense of the debtor.

The California Anti-deficiency Scheme

Perhaps more than any jurisdiction, California has a complex and pervasive anti-deficiency legislative scheme. First, under its "one action" rule contained in section 726 of the Code of Civil Procedure (CCP), the mortgagee's sole judicial remedy is a foreclosure action and any deficiency judgment must be sought in that action.[51] Moreover, the section 726 bar, as noted in an earlier section,[52] can be used both defensively and as a sanction. The mortgagor may raise it in any proceeding on the debt in order to force the mortgagee to foreclose. However, if the mortgagor does not raise the section 726 defense in the debt proceeding, he nevertheless will be permitted to utilize it in any subsequent foreclosure proceeding to prevent the mortgagee from reaching the real estate security.[53] Second, if the mortgage or deed of trust contains a power of sale, the mortgagee may foreclose nonjudicially. If he elects to do so, however, section 580d of the CCP prohibits any deficiency judgment at all.[54] Third, assuming that the mortgagee chooses instead to foreclose judicially, he nevertheless will be prevented from obtaining a deficiency judgment if he is a purchase money mortgagee of the type that we will consider in succeeding paragraphs. Finally, assuming that our mortgagee both forecloses judicially and has no purchase money mortgage problem, the amount of the deficiency will be governed by "fair value" legislation of the type we considered earlier in this section.[55]

The prohibition on deficiency judgments for purchase money mortgagees has presented special and complex problems. Under section 580b of the CCP, purchase money lenders include all vendors who take back real estate security and those third party lenders who

51. See note 9, supra.

52. See § 8.2, supra.

53. See notes 15, 16, supra. Numerous related problems arise under the "one action" rule when there are multiple security devices and multiple debts or combinations thereof. Problems also are created when debt is secured by both chattel and real property security. See Hetland, Secured Real Estate Transactions, §§ 9.14, 9.6 (1974); Walker v. Community Bank, 10 Cal.3d 729, 111 Cal. Rptr. 897, 518 P.2d 329 (1974). Further complications can arise with piecemeal foreclosure of multiple security devices. See Hetland at § 9.16.

54. Section 580d provides in pertinent part: "No judgment shall be rendered for any deficiency upon a note secured by a deed of trust or mortgage upon real property hereafter executed in any case in which real property has been sold by the mortgagee or trustee under power of sale contained in such a mortgage or deed of trust * * *."

55. See West's Ann.Cal.Civ.Code, § 726.

take a mortgage or deed of trust to secure all or part of the purchase price of purchaser-occupied dwellings of less than five families.[56] The twin purposes of section 580b, according to earlier case law, were "to discourage land sales that are unsound because the land is overvalued and, in the event of a depression in land values to prevent the aggravation of the downturn that would result if defaulting purchasers lost the land and were further burdened with personal liability." [57]

In Brown v. Jensen,[58] the California Supreme Court held that section 580b barred a junior purchase money lender, the vendor, from recovering a personal judgment from the vendee-borrower even though his security had been lost through foreclosure by the senior purchase money deed of trust. The court reached this result notwithstanding the fact that for purposes of section 726, the "one action" rule, it was well settled that if the security has become valueless through no fault of the mortgagor or trustor, the secured creditor may then proceed directly against the mortgagor or trustor.[59] To reach its result, the court held that the section 726 analogy was inapplicable because the action was for a deficiency on a note secured by a purchase money trust deed, stating that "a deficiency is nothing more than the difference between the security and the debt" and therefore may consist of the whole debt.[60] The court said that the nature of the security transaction as a purchase money one is determined and fixed for all time at the time it is executed so that no deficiency judgment may be obtained regardless of whether the security becomes valueless. It also relied on the language of section 580b which states that in *no event* shall there be a deficiency judgment.

Institutional lenders seldom can, or will, take a junior encumbrance. Consequently the vast majority of junior purchase money lenders are individual sellers. Furthermore, the enormous increase in recent years of the use of subordination agreements by sellers who are nonprofessionals in the real property business has resulted in the junior encumbrancer being a seller, frequently a farmer or rancher, who has subordinated his purchase money lien to the construction loan mortgage of the buyer, a real estate promotor or developer.[61]

56. West's Ann.Cal.Civ.Code § 580b, provides:

"No deficiency judgment shall lie in any event after any sale of real property for failure of the purchaser to complete his contract of sale, or under a deed of trust, or mortgage, given to the vendor to secure payment of the balance of the purchase price of real property, or under a deed of trust, or mortgage, on a dwelling for not more than four families given to a lender to secure repayment of a loan which was in fact used to pay all or part of the purchase price of such dwelling occupied, entirely or in part, by the purchaser."

57. Bargioni v. Hill, 59 Cal.2d 121, 28 Cal.Rptr. 321, 378 P.2d 593 (1963).

58. 41 Cal.2d 193, 259 P.2d 425 (1953), certiorari denied 347 U.S. 905, 74 S. Ct. 430, 98 L.Ed. 1064 (1954).

59. See § 8.2, supra.

60. Brown v. Jensen, supra at 195, 198, 259 P.2d at 426, 427.

61. See § 12.9, infra.

The application of Brown v. Jensen to this kind of a transaction results in a patent inequity. "Since the construction loan typically is several times larger than the seller's land loan, the subordinated seller rarely has any hope of reinstating the construction loan in the event of the developer's default. If doing so is a prerequisite to his protection, as it is under Brown v. Jensen, he is without remedy. There is nothing in section 580b that expressly precludes the junior from recovering a judgment against the developer for the amount owing after the construction lender takes the security; only Brown v. Jensen's strained construction of section 580b prevents it." [62]

That "strained interpretation" was rejected by the California Supreme Court in Spangler v. Memel,[63] a case involving the subordinated vendor referred to in the preceding paragraph. There a seller of land to a commercial developer took back a deed of trust which she subordinated to the lien of a construction lender. The construction lien was foreclosed and the vendor's junior lien was thus destroyed. Contrary to Brown v. Jensen, the court held that the sold out purchase money junior lienor was not subject to the deficiency prohibition of section 580b. Although the court emphasized the overvaluation function of section 580b, it "no longer looked at overvaluation from the viewpoint of the seller or lender who would presumably accommodate the buyer/borrower by making an unsound loan. Instead, the court viewed the purchase from the standpoint of the buyer/developer and concluded that the imposition of personal liability, rather than its prevention, would preclude overvaluation!" [64] Because the imposition of personal liability on the developer would reduce the inclination of developers to obtain subordinated financing, the likelihood of overvaluation in subordinated financing devices would be lessened.[65] The Spangler court made it clear, however, that it was not overruling Brown v. Jensen. Rather, section 580b still prevented a deficiency in favor of the sold out junior purchase money lienor in "standard", as opposed to "varietal" purchase money transactions.[66] What this seems to mean is that the residential mortgagor will retain deficiency protection against the sold out junior lienor, whether commercial or otherwise, whereas further protection for the commercial mortgagor vis à vis the sold out junior probably no longer exists.[67] As Professor Hetland has suggested, "the change suggested by *Spangler* is not *Brown's* overruling at all; it is the removal

62. See Hetland, Real Property and Real Property Security: The Well Being of the Law, 53 Cal.L.Rev. 151, 161 (1965).

63. 7 Cal.3d 603, 102 Cal.Rptr. 807, 498 P.2d 1055 (1972). For an excellent consideration of this case, see Hetland, Secured Real Estate Transactions, § 9.24 (1974); Leipziger, Deficiency Judgments in California: The Supreme Court Tries Again, 22 U.C.L.A.L.Rev. 753 (1975).

64. Leipziger, supra note 63 at 766.

65. Id. at 768.

66. Hetland, supra note 63 at 210.

67. Id. at 213–214.

of *Brown* from those secured transactions to which *Brown's* extension of a debtor relief provision seems totally inappropriate—the protection of the commercial purchaser, i. e., of the investor and developer at the expense of the seller—without disrupting *Brown's* consumer protection impact, the protection of the homeowner." [68]

California courts seem to be projecting the "residential-commercial" distinction for purposes of protecting the residential borrower in other section 580b contexts. The Court of Appeal decision in Prunty v. Bank of America [69] illustrates this tendency. In that case the Pruntys borrowed money from the bank to build a single family dwelling on a lot they had acquired earlier. They gave the bank a note and deed of trust on the lot and used the proceeds to build the dwelling. After they moved in, the house and part of the lot were destroyed by a landslide. The Pruntys sought a declaratory judgment that section 580b barred a deficiency judgment in favor of the bank even though the loan proceeds had not been used to acquire the lot. The Court of Appeals held in favor of the Pruntys. It believed that the overvaluation purpose of section 580b was served by applying the statute in this case because it would tend to discourage unsound construction lending where the construction is overvalued.[70] Second, the depression "cushion" function of section 580b was enhanced because the court believed that no distinction should be drawn between devaluation caused by natural acts and that resulting from the economic cycle.[71] Moreover, the court also indicated that, in view of the control the bank exercised over the plans and construction of the Prunty residence, it was not unreasonable for the bank to bear the loss. The court appeared to follow the implications of *Spangler* "by affording section 580b protection to a residential borrower while applying the judicially created policies undergirding the purchase money anti-deficiency legislation to the facts of the case." [72]

Interestingly, the non-purchase money junior lienor whose lien is destroyed by a senior foreclosure is in a stronger position than his purchase money counterpart. Unlike the purchase money anti-deficiency provision, section 580d requires that there have been an actual sale by the mortgagee or trustee under the power, and excludes situations in which the security is exhausted in some other fashion.[73] There is a certain logic to this position. As noted earlier, California power of sale foreclosure legislation does not afford statutory redemption rights to those whose interests are destroyed by foreclosure.[74] As Professor Hetland has pointed out, section 580d

68. Id. at 212.

69. 37 Cal.App.3d 430, 112 Cal.Rptr. 370 (1974). See Leipziger, supra note 63 at 784–785.

70. Hetland, supra note 63 at 215.

71. Id. at 215.

72. Id.

73. See Riesenfeld, California Legislation Curbing Deficiency Judgments, 48 Cal.L.Rev. 705, 722 (1960).

74. See text at notes 33–34, supra.

should "not bar a junior creditor * * * who has not himself had the nonjudicial sale which exhausted the security. A redemption statute substitute should bar no one other than a creditor whose lien is foreclosed; certainly it should not impair the remedy of one who himself would have the right to redeem." [75]

On the other hand, section 580d will probably apply where both junior and senior liens are owned by the same lender and power of sale foreclosure of the senior destroys the junior. A Court of Appeals decision has held that an action to enforce the junior debt in such a situation was barred by section 580d.[76] While the court's reasoning was not completely discernible, two themes clearly emerge. First, the opinion of the court indicated that the junior debt was really secured by the first deed of trust because the latter contained a "dragnet" clause that had the effect of making the first deed of trust security for the debtor's future obligations to the creditor.[77] Second, there is the perhaps more persuasive policy argument of the concurring opinion. That opinion noted that the central question was whether by making two loans on the same security, a lender was permitted, by power of sale foreclosure of the first deed of trust "(1) to obtain title to the real property security, and then (2) hold the borrower liable for a deficiency, * * * the security for which had been rendered valueless by the lender's own act. Such a practice would be contrary to the provisions of section 580d, and to the policy expressed thereby. It would permit the lender to frustrate the statute's purpose by obtaining the real property security at [a power of sale foreclosure] thus denying the borrower any right of redemption, and also obtaining a judgment for the remaining deficiency." [78] Indeed, to place a slightly different emphasis on Professor Hetland's analysis referred to earlier, the application of section 580d in such a situation bars a junior creditor whose *own* nonjudicial sale exhausted the security. Moreover, since a party presumably cannot under statutory redemption redeem from himself as sale purchaser, the bar of section 580d is not here impairing the remedy of "one who himself would have had the right to redeem." [79]

B. STATUTORY REDEMPTION

§ 8.4 General Characteristics

When a valid foreclosure has taken place, the equitable right of redemption or the "right to redeem from the mortgage" ends.[80] However-

75. Hetland, Deficiency Judgment Legislation in California—A New Judicial Approach, 51 Cal.L.Rev. 1, 31 (1963).

76. Union Bank v. Wendland, 54 Cal. App.3d 393, 126 Cal.Rptr. 549 (1976).

77. Id. at 54 Cal.App.3d at 401–407, 126 Cal.Rptr. at 556–558.

78. Id. at 54 Cal.App.3d 409, 126 Cal. Rptr. 561.

79. Hetland, supra note 75 at 31.

80. See § 7.1, supra.

ever, more than half the states authorize a statutory right of redemption which provides an additional time period for mortgagors, their successors in interest, and, in many instances, junior lienors, to pay a certain sum of money, usually the foreclosure sale price, to redeem the title to the property.[81] To some extent we have already considered the impact of such legislation in the context of the omitted lienor situation.[82] The statutory time periods vary greatly from state to state, being as short as six months in a few states[83] and as long as two years in others.[84] Most statutes specify a twelve month period. In the vast majority of states, the mortgagor will have the right to possession during the statutory period,[85] although in one or two states both statutory redemption itself, as well as the right to possession, is conditioned on the posting of a bond by the mortgagor.[86] In most states statutory redemption is available in both judicial and power of sale type foreclosure, although in at least one state it is unavailable in the power of sale setting[87] and in one other it is available *only* with that method of foreclosure.[88] Finally, it should be emphasized that, to some extent, state statutory redemption provisions may be inapplica-

81. See Code of Ala., Tit. 7 § 727; Alaska Stats. 09.45.190, 09.35.250; Ariz.Rev.Stat. § 12–1282; Ark.Stats. § 30–440; West's Ann.Calif.Civ.Code, § 725a; Colo.Rev.Stat. '63, 118–9–2; Smith-Hurd Ill.Ann.Stat. ch. 77 § 18c; Kan.Stat.Ann. 60–2414; Ky.Rev.Stat. 426.220; 14 Me.Rev.Stat.Ann. § 6204; Mich.Comp.Laws Ann. § 600.3140; Minn.Stat.Ann. § 580.23; Iowa Code Ann. § 628.3; Vernon's Ann.Mo.Stat. § 443.410; Rev.Code Mont. § 93–5836(2); N.Mex.1953 Comp.Laws § 24–2–19; N.Dak.Cent.Code 32–19–18; Ore.Rev.Stat. 23.560; So.Dak. Comp. Laws 21–52–1; Utah Rules Civ.Proc. Rule 69(f)(3); Rev.Code Wash.Ann. 6.24.140; Wyoming Stat. § 1–480. See generally, Durfee & Doddridge, Redemption from Foreclosure Sale—The Uniform Mortgage Act, 23 Mich. L.Rev. 825 (1925); Blum, Iowa Statutory Redemption After Mortgage Foreclosure, 35 Iowa L.Rev. 72 (1949); Madsen, Equitable Considerations of Mortgage Foreclosure and Redemption in Utah: A Need for Remedial Legislation, 1976 Utah L.Rev. 327 (1976); Bridewell, The Effects of Defective Mortgage Laws on Home Financing, 5 Law & Contemp.Prob. 544 (1938).

82. See § 7.15, supra.

83. See, e. g., Colo.Rev.Stat. '63, 118–9–2; Minn.Stat.Ann. § 580.23.

84. See Tenn.Code Ann. § 64–801.

85. Cross Companies, Inc. v. Citizens Mortgage Investment Trust, 305 Minn. _11, 232 N.W.2d 114 (1975).

86. See Vernon's Ann.Mo.Stat. § 443.-410. Moreover, redemption rights are applicable only if the mortgagee purchases at the sale.

87. E. g., in California this is so clear in the case of powers of sale in a trust deed mortgage that citation of primary authority is superfluous. See Kidd, Trust Deeds and Mortgages in California, 3 Cal.L.Rev. 381, 387 (1916); Cormack and Irsfeld, Jr., Mortgages and Trust Deeds in California, 26 Cal.L.Rev. 206, 216 (1938). The same rule probably applies to sales under powers of sales in a mortgage. See Cormack and Irsfeld, Jr., supra, 216 n. 59 and 219; Sacramento Bank v. Alcorn, 121 Cal. 379, 384, 53 P. 813 (1898); cf. Cormerais v. Genella, 22 Cal. 116 (1863); Kidd, supra, 388 (1863); See further, Note, Comparison of Mortgages, Trust Deeds and Land Sale Contracts, 7 U. C.L.A.L.Rev. 83, 88, 90 (1960).

88. Vernon's Ann.Mo.Rev.Stat. § 443.-410.

ble when federally-held or insured mortgages are involved. This problem is discussed in detail in another section.[89]

Statutory redemption has engendered both substantial criticism and praise. It has been argued that because a mortgagor knows that he can regain the land even after the foreclosure sale, he will be less responsible in making his mortgage payments.[90] In addition, the availability of statutory redemption means that the foreclosure sale purchaser acquires a defeasible title and this uncertainty may discourage outside bidding. Moreover, the mortgagor may regard the eventual loss of the property as inevitable and the ability in most jurisdictions to retain possession during the statutory period may simply encourage him to milk the property as much as possible prior to surrendering it to the purchaser.[91] On the other hand, such legislation may serve several valid purposes. These include "protecting persons who purchased the property subject to the mortgage, allowing time for the mortgagor to refinance and save his property, permitting additional use of the property by the hard-pressed mortgagor, and probably most important, encouraging those who do bid at the sale to bid in a fair price. By allowing junior lienors to redeem, the statutes permit them to protect the security they would otherwise lose."[92]

Although the various statutes on redemption, in addition to the differences mentioned above, have widely varying phraseology and differ in a multitude of details, nevertheless there are certain main features that are common to all. These are (1) a specification of persons who may redeem, the owner of the equity of redemption being universally included, and most of them also including junior lienors and some others; (2) a specification of the sum which must be paid to redeem, the basic factor in which is the sale price to which is added interest and, in differing detail, usually other items; (3) a fixing of a time limit for redemption, which, in addition to the variations mentioned above often provides different periods for different classes of persons; and (4) provisions as to order and effect of redemption.[93] This last feature especially looms large in importance.

§ 8.5 Who May Redeem—Nature of Interest

Statutes providing for redemption from foreclosure sale usually divide those who may exercise the right into two groups: first, the mortgagor, including by variously worded language, his successors in interest in the whole or in any part of the premises, not including lienors;[94] and second, junior lienors whether by judgment or

89. See § 11.6, supra.

90. Comment, The Statutory Right of Redemption in California, 52 Calif.L. Rev. 846, 848 (1964).

91. Id.

92. Id. at 848.

93. See Durfee and Doddridge, Redemption from Foreclosure Sale—The Uniform Act, 23 Mich.L.Rev. 825, 835 (1925).

94. E. g., Minn.Stat.Ann. § 580.23, "the mortgagor, his personal representatives, or assigns"; Iowa Code

otherwise.[95] Depending on the exact language of the statute, a variety of persons, other than the mortgagor, have qualified for the right to redeem in the first group. These have included the spouses of the mortgagor,[96] life tenants[97] and vendees under an installment land contract.[98] Although under some statutes a mortgagee is permitted to redeem from the sale ordered upon the foreclosure of his mortgage,[99] probably most jurisdictions hold that he cannot do so.[1] The latter is clearly preferable, the former diminishing to an important degree the pressure on the foreclosing creditor to bid more than the minimum necessary to obtain the property.[2] Although there is some divergence of opinion and reasoning in interpreting the language of different statutory provisions, both pre-foreclosure sale transferees[3] and post-foreclosure sale transferees[4] of the mortgagor have been included among those in the first group as ones who may exercise the right of redemption. The mortgagor's statutory right of redemption is usually regarded as alienable.[5] However, it probably cannot be levied on by the mortgagee on an execution under a deficiency judgment in the foreclosure action which resulted in the sale of the property.[6] Tra-

Ann., §§ 628.3, 628.25; West's Ann. Cal.Code Civ.Proc., §§ 725a, 701, "the judgment debtor, or his successor in interest."

95. E. g., Minn.Stat.Ann. § 580.24; "creditor having a lien, legal or equitable"; Iowa Code, § 628.5; West's Ann.Cal.Code Civ.Proc., § 701, "creditor having a lien by judgment or mortgage on the property sold * * * subsequent to that on which the property was sold." In some states, under certain circumstances, the process of redemption entails a public sale at which a redeeming creditor may have to bid against anyone who wishes to compete for the property. See 5 U. of Chi.L.Rev. 624, 628 (1938).

96. Martin v. Sprague, 29 Minn. 53, 11 N.W. 143 (1882).

97. Thielen v. Strong, 184 Minn. 333, 238 N.W. 678 (1931).

98. Pine v. Pittman, 211 Kan. 380, 506 P.2d 1184 (1973).

99. See, e. g., the situation in Illinois under Smith-Hurd Ill.Ann.Stat., c. 77, § 20 (1966). Crowder v. Scott State Bank, 365 Ill. 88, 5 N.E.2d 387, 108 A.L.R. 990 (1936); Strause v. Dutch, 250 Ill. 326, 95 N.E. 286, 35 L.R.A.,N.S., 413 (1911).

1. Hervey v. Krost, 116 Ind. 268, 19 N.E. 125 (1888); San Jose Water Co. v. Lyndon, 124 Cal. 518, 57 P. 481 (1899). See 35 L.R.A.,N.S., 413 (1912); 108 A.L.R. 993 (1937).

2. See Durfee and Doddridge, Redemption from Foreclosure Sale, 23 Mich. L.Rev. 825, 845, n. 59 (1925); 5 U. of Chi.L.Rev. 624, 629 (1937).

3. E. g., Pollard v. Harlow, 138 Cal. 390, 71 P. 648 (1903); Warner Bros. Co. v. Freud, 138 Cal. 651, 655, 72 P. 345 (1903); White v. Costigan, 134 Cal. 33, 66 P. 78 (1901); Willis v. Miller, 23 Or. 352, 31 P. 827 (1893); Cooper v. Maurer, 122 Iowa 321, 98 N.W. 124 (1904).

4. Big Sespe Oil Co. v. Cockran, 276 F. 216, 264 (C.C.A.Cal.1921); Phillips v. Hagart, 113 Cal. 552, 45 P. 843, 54 Am.St.Rep. 369 (1896); Kaston v. Storey, 47 Or. 150, 80 P. 217, 114 Am.St.Rep. 912 (1905).

5. See Southwest State Bank v. Quinn, 198 Kan. 359, 424 P.2d 620 (1967). See cases in preceding footnote. But cf., Mixon v. Burelson, 203 Ala. 84, 82 So. 98 (1919); Smith v. Shaver, 112 Kan. 790, 212 P. 666 (1923); 29 L.R.A.,N.S., 508 (1911).

6. See Kan.Stat.Ann. § 60–2414(k); Wheeler and Durfee, Evasion of Mor-

ditional ideas of protection of the mortgagor against restrictions on his equity of redemption present an objection to permitting the foreclosing mortgagee becoming an assignee of the statutory right to redeem from foreclosure sale by virtue of a contract to assign executed prior to foreclosure, and to some extent to an assignment after foreclosure.[7] In a few states an express waiver of statutory redemption rights is authorized by statute.[8] Moreover, some state statutes permit waiver by a corporate mortgagor.[9] Redemption from foreclosure sale is incompatible with practical realities and necessities of corporate reorganization as worked out through foreclosure proceedings and its elimination would not violate the purposes for which it is created.[10] Consequently, it is not surprising that the courts, on some reasoning or other, find ways to uphold its waiver or termination apart from statute, although a legislative sanction for such a result is preferable.[11] And an individual mortgagor, by incorporating himself, may gain the same privilege.[12]

§ 8.6 Effect of Redemption—By Mortgagor or Successor

Redemption by the mortgagor or his successor is a universal feature of statutes providing for redemption from foreclosure sale. Statutes usually give them a priority in redemption over lienors for a certain period of time.[13] In several states concurrent periods of redemption are provided for both mortgagors and lienors, with the latter subject to a redemption by the former if they should act first.[14] A redemption by the mortgagor is final.[15]

atoria by Prosecution of Personal Remedies, 33 Mich.L.Rev. 1196, 1202 (1935). There seems no reason why execution should not be levied under the deficiency judgment after redemption from the sale. Id. 1205.

7. See note, 5 U. of Chi.L.Rev. 625, 636 (1938).

8. Tenn.Code Ann. § 64–801; Idaho Code § 45–1508.

9. E. g., Ill.Rev.Stat. (Smith-Hurd) 1966, ch. 77, § 18a; Kansas Stat.Ann., §§ 60–2410(d), 60–2414(a).

10. See 4 U. of Chi.L.Rev. 675, 676 (1937).

11. First Nat. Bank v. Bryn Mawr Beach Corp., 365 Ill. 409, 6 N.E.2d 654, 109 A.L.R. 1123 (1937), discussed 4 Chi.L.Rev. 675 (1937). See 5 Univ. of Chi.L.Rev. 625, 636 (1938). See also 31 Ill.L.Rev. 1114 (1937). Cf. note, 47 Harv.L.Rev. 530 (1934).

12. See Palcar Real Estate Co. v. Commissioner, 131 F.2d 210 (C.C.A.Mo. 1942). Cf. Jenkins v. Moyse, 254 N. Y. 319, 172 N.E. 521, 74 A.L.R. 205 (1930).

13. E. g., Minn.Stat.Ann., §§ 80.23, 580.24, 6 months generally but 12 months if prior to July 1, 1967, amount due on date of notice of foreclosure is less than 66⅔% of original principal or the mortgaged premises exceed ten acres in size; Iowa Code Ann. §§ 628.2–3, 628.5 (1950), mortgagor's right exclusive for 6 months and last 3 months of year.

14. E. g., West's Ann.Cal.Code Civ. Proc., §§ 702, 703. See 5 U. of Chi. L.Rev. 624, 630 (1937), for a description of the Illinois law under which redemption by a later judgment or decree creditor may be made during the primary period for redemption but has a different effect than when made later.

15. The same finality should attend a redemption by an assignee of the

While a redemption by the mortgagor is "final", problems nevertheless can arise where two parties claim to be redeeming as "mortgagor." A recent Kansas case is illustrative.[16] There both the assignee of a vendee under an installment land contract and the assignee of the vendor were claiming preemptive redemption rights after a foreclosure sale under a mortgage that antedated the land contract. While under the Kansas statute the "defendant owner" had a superior right to redeem vis à vis lienors, so too did the "holder of the legal title". In view of the fact that the original vendee and his assignee had been in possession of the real estate for over seven years and that the vendor's assignee had only a nominal investment in the real estate, the Kansas Supreme Court determined that the vendee's assignee, as the equitable owner of the real estate, had the superior redemption right and therefore the right to possession during the redemption period.

Irrespective of the particular vagaries of the Kansas redemption statute, the holding is sensible both on theoretical and practical grounds in its implications for redemption statutes generally. Under the theory of equitable conversion, vendees under such land contracts are considered to be owners in equity of the real estate while the vendor's legal title is sometimes viewed as personalty.[17] Moreover, as a practical matter, a vendee under an installment land contract is the functional equivalent of a mortgagor and the vendor, in reality, is like a purchase money mortgagee.[18] Indeed, when there is a superior mortgage on the fee title, the vendor can more accurately be characterized as a second mortgagee. Thus, after a superior mortgage on the fee has been foreclosed, it makes sense, in the statutory redemption setting, to treat the vendee as the mortgagor and the vendor as a junior lienor. As a result, the vendee should normally have a preemptive redemption right over the vendor.

It is usually difficult for a mortgagor to obtain a judicial extension of the statutory redemption period. Normally such an extension is possible only where fraud, accident, mistake or waiver are established.[19] In one case, for example, the mortgagor tendered payment to the purchaser's attorney one day before the statutory period expired. Eight days later the payment was returned with the explanation that it had been tendered to the wrong person and with other technical objections. The court determined that under the circum-

mortgagor. E. g., Iowa Code Ann. § 628.5 (1950); Calkins v. Steinbach, 66 Cal. 117, 4 P. 1103 (1884). But see Tirrill v. Miller, 206 Iowa 426, 429, 218 N.W. 303, 304 (1928).

16. Pine v. Pittman, 211 Kan. 380, 506 P.2d 1184 (1973).

17. See Van Hecke, Leavell and Nelson, Equitable Remedies and Restitution, 78–97 (2d Ed. 1973).

18. See § 3.25, supra.

19. United States v. Loosley, 551 P.2d 506 (Utah 1976); Phoenix Mut. Life Ins. Co. v. Legris, 30 Ill.App.3d 678, 334 N.E.2d 399 (1975).

stances the technical defects had been waived and that redemption would be permitted.[20] Other courts have indicated that late redemption will be permitted where substantial irregularities cause a sale that results in a gross sacrifice of the mortgagor's property.[21] But it should be emphasized that such judicial extensions represent exceptional cases. Indeed, relief has been denied where a foreclosure court erroneously fixed the beginning of the redemption period.[22] Moreover, courts have refused to extend the time for redemption simply because the mortgagee impermissibly had been in possession during the redemption period.[23]

When a mortgagor or his transferee redeems, the effect is to "nullify" the foreclosure sale.[24] No court has gone to the length of treating the sale as avoided for all purposes.[25] On the other hand, it is probable that all courts would agree that the sale is avoided, at least for the purpose of ending the title of the purchaser; that the redeeming owner is restored to the title he had before foreclosure sale; and that he does not become a transferee of the title of the purchaser as does a lienor who redeems.[26] The important question, however, is whether nullification of the effect of the foreclosure sale will be carried to the extent that it will revive previously existing liens insofar as they have not been satisfied by the proceeds of the foreclosure sale.

Courts take a variety of approaches to this question. Some seem to hold that all liens existing prior to the sale are revived, including even the lien of the mortgage under which the property was sold to

20. United States v. Loosley, 551 P.2d 506 (Utah 1976); See also, Skach v. Sykora, 6 Ill.2d 215, 127 N.E.2d 453 (1955).

21. See Mollerup v. Storage Systems International, 569 P.2d 1122 (Utah 1977).

22. Phoenix Mutual Life Ins. Co. v. Legris, 30 Ill.App.3d 678, 334 N.E.2d 399 (1975).

23. See Cross Companies, Inc. v. Citizens Mortgage Invest. Tr., 305 Minn. 111, 232 N.W.2d 114 (1975); Milwaukee Western Bank v. Cedars of Cedar Rapids, Inc., 170 N.W.2d 670 (Iowa 1969).

24. Most statutes so provide explicitly by clauses in which, although the language is not identical, the purport is the same. E. G., West's Ann.Cal. Code Civ.Proc. § 703, "the effect of the sale is terminated and he is restored to his estate"; Ill. Jones & Add., Ann.St.1913, § 6764, "Sale and certificate shall be null and void", the same language has been retained in Ill.Ann.Stat., Smith-Hurd, ch. 77, § 18. Even when the statute has no such express stipulation, courts have reached the same conclusion. E. g., Allen v. McGaughey, 31 Ark. 252, 260 (1876); Fields v. Danenhower, 65 Ark. 392, 46 S.W. 938, 43 L.R.A. 519 (1898). See Storke and Sears, Colorado Security Law, 1952, 1954–59, for Colorado law on redemption by the "owner" or "any person who might be liable on a deficiency."

25. See 9 Cornell L.Q. 208, 209 (1924). To do so would involve holding that the mortgage lien was restored to its original amount and require repayment by the mortgagee of any proceeds he might have received from the sale. See Durfee & Doddridge, Redemption from Foreclosure Sale—The Uniform Act, 23 Mich.L.Rev. 825, 850 (1925).

26. See Durfee and Doddridge, supra note 25.

the extent of the unpaid deficiency.[27] Other courts generally agree with the foregoing, but hold that while redemption will revive the general lien acquired by the personal decree in the foreclosure proceeding to the extent of any deficiency, it will not reinstate the specific mortgage lien.[28] While the distinction between these two approaches may seem at best highly theoretical, it has proved important in some cases. For example, in one case adopting the latter approach, if the revived judgment was a mortgage lien, the redeemed real estate, for purposes of a particular state statute, was not protected against execution by virtue of a homestead declaration; but if the judgment became a general one because of the foreclosure and redemption, the real estate did obtain such protection.[29] At the other extreme is a proposal, not adopted by any legislature, that a redemption by the mortgagor or his successor should be free of all encumbrances existing prior to the sale.[30] The scheme is designed to put pressure on the foreclosing mortgagee at the time of the sale to bid what he thinks the property is worth, up to the amount of his debt; and it puts pressure on a junior lienor during the period of his right to redeem to bid more than the price paid by the senior mortgagee.[31] Iowa at the present time comes closest to this suggested solution.[32] Under its statute the mortgagor's assignee on redemption clearly takes free of all liens against the mortgagor; [33] and the mortgagor takes free of any liability for any deficiency on the judgment under which the property is sold. Further, a redeeming mortgagor takes

27. Although the cases holding that redemption revives the original lien under which the property was sold, except to the extent that the purchase price on the sale discharged it, are those involving judgment liens, no distinctions between them and mortgage liens can be upheld. New York is, perhaps, the leading jurisdiction for the doctrine. See note, 9 Cornell L.Q. 208 (1924); 67 Am.St. Rep. 510 (1899). See also Wheeler and Durfee, Evasion of Mortgage Moratoria by Prosecution of Personal Remedies, 33 Mich.L.Rev. 1196, 1205 (1935).

28. See e. g., Damascus Milk Co. v. Morriss, 1 Wash.App. 501, 463 P.2d 212 (1969).

29. Damascus Milk Co. v. Morriss, 1 Wash.App. 501, 463 P.2d 212 (1969).

30. This result would be accomplished by declaring that upon such a redemption the redeeming party shall acquire such title as would have gone to the purchaser if no redemption had taken place. To this is coupled a proposal that lienors shall be given priority in redemption, but with the owner having finally an opportunity to redeem from the purchaser or re-redeem from a lienor-redemptioner. See Durfee v. Doddridge, supra note 25, 861, 852–3, 854 n. 78.

31. See id., 862–863, for additional details and arguments for the proposal.

32. See Blum, supra note 81, pp. 78–79.

33. Idem, p. 77, citing Tirrill v. Miller, 206 Iowa 426, 218 N.W. 303 (1928), prior judgment against mortgagor; Danforth v. Lindsey, 178 Iowa 834, 160 N.W. 318, deficiency judgment (1916); see Cadd v. Snell, 219 Iowa 728, 734, 259 N.W. 590, 593 (1935); cf. Paulsen v. Jensen, 209 Iowa 453, 228 N.W. 357 (1929). See also Cooper v. Maurer, 122 Iowa 321, 98 N.W. 124 (1904). The above Iowa cases were before the 1934 amendment in that state. That enactment, however, changed the existing rule only as to redemption by the debtor-mortgagor.

free of any junior mortgage lien; although if its holder has obtained a judgment, the judgment lien will attach to the redeemed property just as it would to any other property acquired by the judgment debtor.[34] The statute does not, however, give a period of priority in redeeming to the junior lienor [35] and, consequently, the pressure is strong on him to bid high at the sale, at which time he is at a disadvantage in competing with the foreclosing mortgagee.[36] The latter may bid his debt up to its amount whereas the former must bid cash.[37]

A variety of additional distinctions have been drawn. Some states differentiate between the effect of a redemption by the debtor-mortgagor and one by his transferee, the latter taking free of previously existing liens regardless of whether they might revive as against the former on redemption by him.[38] The distinction has been criticised as violating the fundamental rule that a successor in interest, unless he be a bona fide purchaser for value without notice, "simply occupies the shoes of his predecessor." [39] However, the rule may be a most effective factor in forcing a foreclosing mortgagee to bid

34. Anderson v. Renshaw, 229 Iowa 93, 294 N.W. 274 (1940). See Cooper v. Maurer, 122 Iowa 321, 327, 98 N.W. 124, 126 (1904); Paulsen v. Jensen, 209 Iowa 453, 458, 228 N.W. 357, 359 (1929). See Call v. Jeremiah, 246 Or. 568, 425 P.2d 502 (1967) (junior mortgages not revived—alternative holding).

35. Instead, the mortgagor-debtor has priority for six months and, if he exercises the right, the junior lienor will lose his chance. See Iowa Code Ann. §§ 628.2–.3, 628.5 (1950).

36. See Blum, supra note 81, p. 79.

37. See 5 U. of Chi.L.Rev. 625, 626 (1938); Durfee and Doddridge, op. cit. supra note 25, 852, 854 n. 78. Although a junior lienor will have to pay cash to redeem, giving him a certain opportunity to do so for an extended period of time gives him a better chance to finance the deal. Indem, p. 863.

38. See Madsen, Equitable Considerations of Mortgage Foreclosure and Redemption In Utah A Need for Remedial Legislation, 1976 Utah L.Rev. 327, 335 (1976); Simpson v. Castle, 52 Cal. 644 (1878); Sigler v. Phares, 105 Kan. 116, 181 P. 628, 5 A.L.R. 141 (1919), junior liens cut off as to grantee. See also 47 L.R.A.,N.S., 1048, 1050 (1913), as to liability for a deficiency on indebtedness for which it was originally sold; 128 A.L.R. 796 (1940); 5 A.L.R. 145 (1920), as to subordinate liens. See Call v. Jeremiah, 246 Or. 568, 425 P.2d 502 (1967) (junior mortgages cut off by redemption by grantee—alternative holding).

39. Flanders v. Aumack, 32 Or. 19, 25, 51 P. 447, 449, 67 Am.St.Rep. 504 (1897). While the criticism is valid insofar as it concerns liens existing, even though suspended against the property in the hands of the mortgagor before the transfer, the distinction would seem sound enough as to the lien of a judgment obtained against the mortgagor after the transfer and accruing for the first time, if at all, not before that date.

The question may be asked whether it would not be a fraudulent conveyance to permit an insolvent debtor to transfer his redemption right to one who, on redemption, takes the property free and clear of the debtor's creditors. The question would be even more acute if the debtor claimed exemption of the consideration received for the transfer. See note, 5 U. of Chi.L.Rev. 625, 234 (1928). And look at Kerr v. Miller, 259 Ill. 516, 102 N.E. 1050 (1913), commented on in 9 Ill.L.Rev. 60 (1914). But see Glenn, Mortgages, § 234.

up for the property.[40] Some authority distinguishes between the restoration on redemption of the lien under which the property was sold and liens inferior to it, restoring the latter but not the former.[41]

§ 8.7 Effect of Redemption—By Lienors

Holders of liens junior to that under which the property is sold on foreclosure are empowered to redeem,[42] although their right to do so is usually postponed to a time after that during which the right is exclusively reserved to the mortgagor and his successors in interest.[43] Where there are several junior lienors, although the provisions on the subject are not uniform, they usually are given the privilege of redemption at certain periods of time in accordance with their priority.[44] Further, when there is a redemption by one of the latter, there are provisions, again not uniform, providing for re-redemption by others within a specified period.[45] The terms of such a re-redemption are usually what the prior redemptioner had paid and the amount of the encumbrance held by him, if senior to the re-redemptioner, plus certain other charges.[46]

Under most statutes the effect of redemption by a junior lienor is to transfer to him the rights of the purchaser on foreclosure sale which, if there is not a redemption from him by someone else, will ripen into the same title that the purchaser would have got if no one redeemed.[47] This solution has several advantages. It is fair to the

40. See 5 U. of Chi.L.Rev. 624, 633 (1938).

41. See Rist v. Anderson, 70 S.D. 579, 19 N.W.2d 833, 161 A.L.R. 197 (1945). See also 5 A.L.R. 145, 149 (1920). But contrast Sigler v. Phares, 105 Kan. 116, 181 P. 628, 5 A.L.R. 141 (1919).

"Confining the inquiry to the restoration of liens, it is possible to distinguish between senior liens and junior liens, restoring the latter but not the former, and, with respect to each class, a further distinction is suggested,—as to senior liens, a distinction between mortgage liens and judgment liens, the latter being restored but the former not; as to junior liens, a diversity between a passive lienor and one who, as defendant in a suit to foreclose the senior lien, files a cross bill and obtains a decree enforcing his lien, the latter being classed with the senior lienor." Durfee and Doddridge, op. cit. supra note 58, p. 854.

42. See § 8.5, supra.

43. See § 8.6, supra.

44. E. g., Minn.Stat.Ann. § 580.24; West's Ann.Cal.Code Civ.Proc. § 702. See Blum, Iowa Statutory Redemption After Mortgage Foreclosure, 35 Iowa L.Rev. 72, 75; 5 U. of Chi.L. Rev. 624, 630 (1937).

45. See, e. g., Blum, op. cit. supra note 44, for Iowa law; Iowa Code Ann., §§ 628.8, 628.9, 628.10, 628.14; Minn. Stat.Ann. § 580.24, West's Ann.Cal. Code Civ.Proc. §§ 702, 703. See Sprague v. Martin, 29 Minn. 226, 13 N.W. 34 (1882), for the Minnesota law.

46. E. g., Iowa Code Ann., §§ 628.9, 628.10, 628.14; West's Ann.Cal.Code Civ.Proc. § 703; Durfee and Doddridge, Redemption from Foreclosure Sale—The Uniform Act, 23 Mich.L. Rev. 825, 845 (1925).

47. E. g., Minn.Stat.Ann. § 580.27; Eldridge v. Wright, 55 Cal. 531 (1880). See 135 A.L.R. 196, 198 (1941).

owner; [48] it makes any further proceeding to enforce the rights so acquired unnecessary; and it is in accord with the policy of the statute in that, by providing an incentive to redeem, it increases probability of redemption and, therefore, puts pressure on the foreclosing mortgagee to bid up the price.[49]

In some states, notably Illinois, the effect of redemption is not to transfer the title of the purchaser to the redeeming junior lienor, but merely to avoid it as in the case of a redeeming mortgagor. At the same time the junior lien, which may be considered to be suspended, is revived and to it is added the amount which had to be paid in order to redeem. The junior lienor then has to bring further proceedings to enforce his original mortgage augmented by the sum he has paid out in order to redeem.[50]

The effect of redemption by a junior lienor upon the mortgage debt has received varying answers. In jurisdictions where the effect of redemption is merely to continue or revive the subordinate lien, adding to it the amount paid to redeem, the original indebtedness remains unaffected.[51] In Minnesota, however, the court likened the effect of the statute in this respect to a strict foreclosure. Then, proceeding upon the theory that the policy underlying the legislation, i. e., "to have the property of the debtor applied as it will go—as far as creditors will voluntarily apply it—in satisfaction of the debts of the mortgagor," would be furthered by such a construction, it held that redemption extinguished the debt to the extent that the value of the land exceeded the redemption payment.[52] The argument in favor of no satisfaction is the incentive to redemption thus offered to a junior

48. The owner, being given a prior or subsequent opportunity to redeem, or both, cannot complain. See § 8.1, supra.

49. Durfee and Doddridge, op. cit. supra note 46, 847.

50. Ogle v. Koerner, 140 Ill. 170, 29 N.E. 563 (1892). See 5 U. of Chi.L. Rev. 624, 630 (1937); Durfee and Doddridge, op. cit. supra note 46, 846; 135 A.L.R. 196, 206 (1941). In Illinois priority of redemption rights of creditors rank in the order of their judgments or decrees. Ill.Ann.Stat., Smith-Hurd, c. 77, § 24 (1966). And a judgment or decree under which the property is sold is treated the same for this purpose as any other, such a creditor being permitted to redeem from his own enforcement sale. Crowder v. Scott State Bank, 365 Ill. 88, 5 N.E.2d 387, 108 A.L.R. 990 (1932). As to whether a purchaser at a foreclosure sale can prevent "statutory redemption" by a junior lien holder by tendering payment of the debt which the lien secures, see Note, Effect of Satisfying a Junior Lien on Statutory Right of Redemption, 15 Wyo.L.J. 223 (1961).

51. See note 50, supra.

52. Sprague v. Martin, 29 Minn. 226, 13 N.W. 34 (1882). The decision was approved or followed in Northland Pine Co. v. Northern Insulating Co., 145 Minn. 395, 177 N.W. 635 (1920); Crown Iron Works Co. v. Melin, 159 Minn. 198, 198 N.W. 462 (1924); Work v. Braun, 19 S.D. 437, 103 N.W. 764 (1909), affirmed 23 S.D. 582, 122 N.W. 608. Miller v. Little, 37 N.D. 612, 164 N.W. 19 (1918), commented on in, 16 Mich.L.Rev. 204 (1918), reached a result similar to that in Sprague v. Martin, supra, by invoking the doctrine of merger. Look at Moore v. Penney, 141 Minn. 454, 170 N.W. 599, 3 A.L.R. 161 (1919). See Durfee and Doddridge, supra note 46, 847.

lienor, which in turn spurs bidding by the foreclosing mortgagee.[53] This last may offset the apparent injustice to the mortgagor of not having the real value of the property directly applied to the satisfaction of his mortgage debt by the junior lienor. The uncertain amount by which the redeeming junior encumbrancer's debt will be reduced is left to future litigation, which in itself is a deterrent to taking the action, is a strong objection to the rule, minimizing as it does the policy of the statute.

The Iowa solution on this point, as in the case of redemption by the mortgagor or his successor,[54] seems the more desirable. It provides that, on redemption, the junior lienor may file a statement of the amount which he is willing to credit on his debt and if he does so, that amount only is credited. If he does not file such a statement, the whole debt is satisfied. And the land in his hands, whichever course he follows, is subject to re-redemption upon paying what he paid to redeem plus the amount credited on his debt.[55] This eliminates any litigation over the value of the property which would discourage redemption, permits the redemptioner to fix the amount he will credit on his debt, and safeguards against an undervaluation on this point by permitting redemption against him.[56]

C. THE SOLDIERS' AND SAILORS' CIVIL RELIEF ACT

§ 8.8 General Considerations

The Soldiers' and Sailors' Civil Relief Act of 1940,[57] as amended, ("SSCRA") can substantially affect the options of the real estate mortgagee in proceeding against a mortgagor who is in the military service. However, it is important to emphasize that the Act is primarily significant in its impact on secured real estate transactions entered into *prior* to entry by the debtor into the military service.

The purpose of the SSCRA is to provide "for the temporary suspension of legal proceedings and transactions which may prejudice the civil rights of persons" [58] in the military. While it does not extinguish any rights or obligations of debtors or creditors, certain legal proceedings, actions and transactions may be suspended and remedies altered to assure that certain property relationships remain unim-

53. Durfee and Doddridge, op. cit. supra note 84, 848. See 5 U. of Chi.L. Rev. 624, 628 (1937).

54. See § 8.6, supra.

55. Iowa Code Ann. §§ 628.13, 628.17, 628.19. See Durfee and Doddridge, op. cit. supra note 84, 849, 861; Blum, op. cit. supra note 44. See also Ala.Code, Tit. 7, §§ 729, 735ff.; Kan.Stat.Ann. § 60–2414 (1964).

56. See Durfee and Doddridge, op. cit. supra note 46, note 54, supra.

57. 50 U.S.C.App. §§ 501–48, 560–90 (1970). See generally, 40 A.L.R.2d 462.

58. 50 U.S.C.App. § 511(1) (1970).

paired during military service.[59] Although the Act is complex and affects a myriad of debtor-creditor relationships, we will limit our consideration to some of its more important consequences for the real estate mortgagee.

The SSCRA is intended to protect primarily persons on active duty in military service and defines such persons as enlisted persons and officers of the Army, Navy, Marine Corps, Coast Guard, and officers of the Public Health Service detailed for duty with the military service.[60] "Active duty" means full-time service in one of the above branches, including "training or education * * * preliminary to induction" and time absent from duty due to sickness, wounds, leave, or other lawful cause.[61] Army and Air National Guard members are protected only while performing full-time duty for which they are entitled to pay.[62] Section 591, a Vietnam era amendment, extends powers of attorney executed by servicemen missing in action if a spouse, parent, or other relative was named as attorney in fact.[63] Members of reserve units and retired military personnel not on active duty are not covered.[64] Deserters are not protected, but a serviceman who is absent without leave may still be entitled to relief, depending on the facts of each case.[65]

Protection sometimes encompasses a civilian whose liability is connected with the serviceman's obligation, such as a co-defendant, guarantor, or co-signer.[66] Moreover, a dependent may be granted protection if his ability to pay an obligation is materially affected by military service of the person upon whom he depends.[67] A typical case is where an individual had formerly given a parent contributions which were used to make mortgage payments. After showing that a decreased income during active duty impaired the ability to make contributions, resulting in the parent's inability to make mortgage payments, the parent could be extended the same benefits the serviceman would receive were he liable.[68]

59. Bagley, The Soldiers' and Sailors' Civil Relief Act—A Survey, 45 Mil.L. Rev. 1 (1969); Goldman, Collection of Debts Incurred by Military Personnel: The Creditor's View, 10 Tulsa L.J. 537, 541 (1970).

60. 50 U.S.C.App. § 511 (1970).

61. Id. Goldman, supra note 59, at 544.

62. Bagley, supra note 59, at 3.

63. 50 U.S.C.App. § 591(a)(1)–(3) (1970); Goldman, supra note 59, at 563.

64. Bagley, supra note 59, at 2; Goldman, supra note 59, at 544.

65. Bagley, supra note 59 at 3; Shayne v. Burke, 158 Fla. 61, 27 So. 2d 751 (1946), states that the Act should be liberally construed in AWOL cases. See also Mantz v. Mantz, 69 N.E.2d 637 (Ohio Ct.App. 1946), where five years of confinement by court martial was held to remove SSCRA protection.

66. 50 U.S.C.App. § 513 (1970); Bagley, supra note 59, at 1744.

67. 50 U.S.C.App. § 536 (1970); Bagley, supra note 59, at 3. See Nassau Savings & Loan Ass'n v. Ormond, 179 Misc. 447, 39 N.Y.S.2d 92 (1942).

68. 50 U.S.C.App. §§ 531, 532 (1970); Bagley, supra note 59, at 3–4.

In addition to the "stay" sections discussed hereafter, several general relief provisions are significant for real estate mortgagees. For example, section 525 automatically tolls all statutes of limitations during the period of service that would otherwise run against a serviceman.[69] The broad, self-executing language of this section in theory tolls not only properly denominated statutes of limitations, but any period limited by law, specifically including periods relating to redemption of real property sold or forfeited to enforce any obligation, tax, or assessment.[70] For example, section 525 has been held to extend the time for redemption under state statutory redemption legislation by a period equal to the mortgagor's period of service.[71] Title defects are not curable by adverse possession.[72] Moreover, it also applies to redemption periods after real estate tax sales. Thus, in one case, an acknowledged career officer was allowed to redeem land fourteen years after a sale for delinquent taxes.[73] Several recent cases, however, have held in the tax sale redemption setting that section 525 does not protect "career" servicemen.[74] If the same reasoning is applied to the statutory redemption area, career servicemen-mortagors will also no longer be protected.

In addition, the Act theoretically can also affect mortgage interest rates. Section 526 limits interest to six percent during military service on obligations incurred before entering service, even though a higher rate was originally agreed upon.[75] Interest, which includes all carrying, service, and other charges, is automatically reduced unless the mortgagee proves that military service has no material effect on the ability to pay more than six percent.[76] Thus, for example, if a mortgagor executes a 9% mortgage note and then joins the military, the burden in effect falls on the mortgagee to justify the higher rate of interest. This burden should not be difficult to sustain in view of the fact that normal contemporary interest rates substantially exceed the six percent rate.

§ 8.9 The "Stay" Provisions

The major judicial power granted by the SSCRA is to order stays which suspend enforcement of civil obligations. In discussing

69. 50 U.S.C.App. § 525 (1970).

70. Id., specifies tolling of any period "limited by any law, regulation or order".

71. See Illinois Nat. Bank v. Gwinn, 390 Ill. 345, 61 N.E.2d 249 (1945); Peace v. Bullock, 252 Ala. 155, 40 So.2d 82 (1949). See §§ 8.4–8.7, supra.

72. Comment, 24 Mo.L.Rev. 101, 106 (1959).

73. Hedrick v. Bigby, 228 Ark. 40, 305 S.W.2d 674 (1957).

74. See Pannell v. Continental Can Co. Inc., 554 F.2d 216 (C.A.Ga.1977); King v. Zagorski, 207 So.2d 61 (Fla. App.1968); Bailey v. Barranca, 83 N. M. 90, 488 P.2d 725 (1971).

75. 50 U.S.C.App. § 526 (1970); Bagley, supra note 59, at 18.

76. Goldman, supra note 59, at 551.

provisions affecting land-secured obligations, individual sections are considered specifically, but when applying the SSCRA to actual problems it is important to view the sections of the Act as complementary to each other rather than in isolation. It is important to note that application of one section does not necessarily bar relief based on others. For example, use of section 590, a stay provision for obligations in general, is not necessarily excluded by the application of other stay sections addressed specifically to mortgages or installment land contracts. Likewise, where possible, stay sections should be considered in conjunction with general relief provisions such as those tolling statutes of limitations.

Civil Obligations and Taxes

Section 590 may be the most important stay provision.[77] Under this section, during military service or within six months thereafter, a serviceman-debtor may ask the court to suspend enforcement of (1) any civil obligation which arose prior to military service, or (2) any tax or assessment due either prior to or during military service.[78] However, the debtor must first prove that military service materially affects his ability to pay the obligation.[79]

Several factors distinguish section 590 from other stay sections: [80] (1) While most obligations must have been incurred prior to service, the section is applicable to taxes that may have occurred prior to or during service. (2) Only the serviceman may request relief. He usually takes the initiative by going to court, but this section may be raised defensively. (3) The court has no power to grant relief on its own motion; the desired relief must be affirmatively requested. However, the court is not bound by such request and may grant less or conditional relief. (4) The serviceman has the burden of proving material effect on his ability to pay the obligation. (5) Relief may be requested although no judicial proceeding is pending and even if no default has occurred. (6) The relief granted may extend after the period of service, making section 590 especially effective for ultimate resolution of problems rather than mere postponement. (7) Judicial discretion to impose "such other terms as may be just" allows the court to suspend enforcement of the entire obligation or to condition suspension on terms such as partial payment by the serviceman.

As noted above, section 590 also helps the serviceman to adjust financially *after* service. Because immediate payment of the principal and interest accumulated during the stay can sometimes be difficult at the termination of service, additional time may be provided to allow the orderly liquidation of such arrearages. Post-service exten-

77. Goldman, supra note 59, at 554.

78. 50 U.S.C.App. § 590 (1970). Bagley, supra note 59 at 6.

79. Bagley, supra note 59, at 6; Goldman, supra note 59, at 555.

80. See Bagley, supra note 59, at 7; Goldman, supra note 59, at 555.

sions equal to the time spent in service may be granted for any obligation. However, land-secured obligations may get extensions equal to the time spent in service plus the time yet to run on the obligation as of the date of discharge (or date of application for relief, if made after discharge).[81] For example, suppose that an individual had twelve years of installments remaining on a home mortgage at the time he entered the Army for a term of four years. A stay of principal and interest payments could be granted during the service period, during which time nothing would be paid. After discharge from service, the mortgagor would have twelve years to pay the four year arrearages. This is calculated by adding four years, the time equal to the service period, to the eight years remaining on the mortgage as of the discharge date.[82] This example illustrates the maximum extension, but the court has discretion to grant more modest relief. It should be emphasized that relief by stay and extension applies only to arrearages and not to payments falling due after discharge.[83] After ending service, the mortgagor must make normal payments with respect to the eight years yet to run as of the discharge date while also paying the arrearages within the twelve year extension period.[84] Interestingly, under the above example, the former serviceman obtains a longer period to pay the arrearages than to pay the balance of the original obligation. On the other hand, arrearages must be paid in equal installments. The mortgagor cannot wait and pay a lump sum at the end of the extension.[85] As noted earlier, other conditions may also be imposed, such as granting additional interest on the arrearage during the post-service extension.[86]

Installment Land Contracts

Section 531 governs stays on installment land contracts.[87] If the serviceman defaults on payments or breaches any other term of such a contract during military service it is a crime for the seller to exercise any right or option such as termination of the contract, rescission, or repossession of the land, except by judicial action.[87a] However, the contract must have been made and a deposit or installment paid prior to entering service.[88] If the seller files such a judicial action, the court may condition its order on repayment of all or part of

81. 50 U.S.C.App. § 590(1)(a)–(b) (1970); Bagley, supra note 59, at 8.

82. But note that for personal property, even though more expensive and requiring a 20 year security instrument, such as an airplane, the maximum extension would still be only four years. Goldman, supra note 59, at 556.

83. Bagley, supra note 59, at 9.

84. Id.

85. Id.

86. Id.

87. 50 U.S.C.App. § 531 (1970).

87a. Goldman, supra note 59 at 552; 50 U.S.C.App. § 531(2) (1970).

88. See Ryan v. Bloom, 120 Mont. 443, 186 P.2d 879 (1947).

the deposit and prior installments.[89] If military service materially affected the serviceman's ability to comply with the terms of payment, the court may order a stay, either absolute or conditioned on partial payment by the serviceman. The court in its discretion may even order sale of the property and division of the proceeds.[90]

It is important to emphasize here that section 531 stays differ from section 590 stays in several aspects: (1) Section 531 requires that a stay be granted upon request by the defendant unless the court is of the opinion that ability to comply with the contract was not materially affected by military service. The court also may grant a stay on its own motion if such material effect is found.[91] (2) Violation of section 531 is a crime.[92] (3) Section 590 puts the burden of proving material effect on the serviceman, but section 531 makes no such express provision.[93]

Mortgages and Deeds of Trust

Section 532 governs obligations secured by mortgages and deeds of trust. It is similar in language and effect to section 531.[94] After default in payment or other breach, the mortgagee cannot sell, foreclose, or seize the mortgaged property during the term of service or three months thereafter except by court order or pursuant to a valid waiver by the serviceman.[95] This prohibition on the mortgagee applies only if the mortgagor both owned the land and executed the underlying mortgage obligation prior to military service.[96] In states where power or sale mortgages or deeds of trust are widely used to avoid the expense and delay of judicial foreclosure,[97] section 532 not only defeats this purpose, but makes foreclosure in violation of this provision a crime.[98] In addition, foreclosure without court action is probably void, making it impossible for anyone, including a bona fide purchaser for value, to obtain good title.[99]

89. Goldman, supra note 59, at 552.

90. Bagley, supra note 59, at 10.

91. Id.

92. 50 U.S.C.App. § 531(2) (1970) makes violation a misdemeanor punishable by a $1000 fine, a year in jail, or both.

93. Bagley, supra note 59, at 11.

94. 50 U.S.C.App. § 532 (1970); Bagley, supra note 59, at 11, notes that section 532 mentions nothing about the necessity of a pre-service payment or deposit as does section 531.

95. Goldman supra note 59 at 553.

96. See Brown v. Gerber, 495 P.2d 1160 (Colo.App.1972).

97. See § 7.19, supra.

98. Supra note 95. For an example of how one state has attempted to comply with the SSCRA and retain power of sale for use against servicemen, see Colo.R.C.P. 120.

99. Goldman, supra note 59, at 553, n. 100, notes that a bona fide purchaser for value may obtain good title under some circumstances, at least where the serviceman's interest is unrecorded and the purchaser's duty to ascertain possible military service of any mortgagors has been satisfied. See also 24 Mo.L.Rev. supra note 72 at 105, discussing Godwin v. Gerling, 362 Mo. 19, 30, 239 S.W. 352, 359 (1951) (en banc), where section 525 relief was denied to a serviceman

Once a judicial foreclosure proceeding has begun, as in the installment land contract situation, it is subject to being stayed. As a condition precedent, section 532 requires that: (1) The serviceman owned the property both prior to entering service and at the time relief is sought; (2) the obligation secured by the mortgage, deed of trust, or other similar instrument arose prior to military service; (3) breach of the obligation occurred prior to or during military service; and (4) the proceeding which the serviceman seeks to stay was commenced during military service. As in section 531, the court must grant the stay upon request, absent a finding that military service had no material effect on ability to pay. The court also has discretion to grant a stay on its own motion upon finding material effect.[1]

Judicial Proceedings and Execution of Judgments

Two other SSCRA sections with potential effect on land-secured obligations differ from other stays because they apply to obligations arising either prior to or during military service. Section 521 allows a stay to be granted at any stage of a judicial proceeding if the ability of the serviceman to participate, as either plaintiff or defendant, is materially affected by military service. Section 523 provides that in any action resulting in a judgment or order against the serviceman, a stay of execution may be granted if military service has materially affected ability to comply with the judgment.[2] Under both sections, absent a finding of no material effect, the court must grant the requested stay. The court may also grant the stay on its own motion. Both sections apply to actions commenced during military service or within 60 days thereafter. However, section 523 applies also to actions commenced prior to service so long as the resulting judgment or order is unsatisfied during service or within 60 days thereafter.[3]

§ 8.10 Default Judgments

Section 520 provides servicemen certain protections against default judgments. These protections will, of course, extend to judicial foreclosure actions. Section 520 requires default plaintiffs to file an affidavit indicating whether the defendant is in military service.[4] Although the statute requires such an affidavit in every action where default occurs, failure to file one is not a jurisdictional defect and civilian parties such as co-defendants cannot object to noncompliance.[5] Unless the affidavit shows that the defendant is not in service, the de-

with an unacknowledged, unrecorded deed. But cf. § 7.20, supra.

1. Bagley, supra note 59, at 12.

2. 50 U.S.C.App. §§ 521, 523; Bagley, supra note 59, at 12–13; Goldman, supra note 59, at 549.

3. Id.

4. 50 U.S.C.App. § 560 (1970).

5. Bagley, supra note 59, at 15.

fault judgment will not be entered until after an attorney is appointed to represent the defendant. The attorney may take steps, such as making an investigation, that are clearly in the defendant's interest, but he has no power to waive any rights or otherwise bind the absentee serviceman.[6]

A default judgment may be set aside even after full statutory compliance as to the affidavit and appointment of an attorney. The serviceman must make application to set aside the judgment and reopen the case within 90 days after ending military service and he must establish that (1) military service prejudiced his defense, and (2) a meritorious defense exists for at least some part of the action.[7] It should be noted that any appearance by the serviceman or his attorney, even a special appearance to contest jurisdiction or assert rights under SSCRA, waives section 520 protection.[8]

Interestingly, section 520 specifies that any right or title acquired by a bona fide purchaser for value under the default judgment shall not be impaired if the judgment is set aside.[9] This provision limits the effectiveness of section 520 for the mortgagor or vendee attempting to recover possession of land, whether or not the default was intentional. However, if the purchaser is not a bona fide purchaser for value, the judgment can be vacated and the title of the purchaser invalidated.[10]

D. BANKRUPTCY

§ 8.11 General Considerations

In theory, mortgagees should be unconcerned when insolvency forces mortgagors to file bankruptcy. Indeed, protection from such occurrences is the very reason for creation of mortgage security interests. In reality, however, mortgagees' rights, contractual and statutory, are often substantially affected by federal bankruptcy law, as many learn when they are forced into bankruptcy court to defend their security interests from the trustee's attack.[11] Familiar state laws, requiring minimal time and effort to foreclose, are often neutralized by federal bankruptcy provisions which may freeze property

6. Bagley, supra note 59, at 15–16.

7. Id. at 16.

8. Id.

9. Goldman, supra note 59 at 548.

10. Id. See Flagg v. Sun Inv. & Loan Corp., 373 P.2d 226 (Okl.1962), where a foreclosure and sheriff's sale were set aside because the serviceman had filed a "caveat" after default and before the sale, giving the purchasers (who were also the plaintiffs in the original foreclosure action) notice of his military status.

11. "Everyone who takes a mortgage or deed of trust intended as a mortgage, takes it subject to the contingency that proceedings in bankruptcy against his mortgagor may deprive him of the specific remedy which is provided for in his contract." In re Jersey Island Packing Co., 71 C.C.A. 75, 138 F. 625, 627 (1905).

for years. Bankruptcy encompasses both straight bankruptcy and debtor relief provisions, which are commonly called "chapter proceedings." Some of the concepts that are basic to both straight bankruptcy and chapter proceedings will be discussed at this point to avoid later repetition.[12]

The greatest potential threat to mortgagees are the automatic stays provided in various bankruptcy statutes against mortgage foreclosures or enforcement of liens.[13] Such stays shift the initial burden to produce evidence to the mortgagee, in effect forcing him to prove the validity of his security interest.[14] He must petition for relief by an adversary action in the nature of a new case, whereupon the court must set the earliest possible trial date, with "precedence over all other matters except older matters of the same character." [15] Once this initial burden is met, the ultimate burden to justify continuation of the stay shifts back to the debtor.[16] Absent judicial vacation or modification, stays operate from the date of filing until bankruptcy is (1) dismissed or adjudicated and closed, or (2) the mortgaged property is abandoned by the trustee or declared exempt by the court.[17]

It is also important to emphasize that the bankruptcy court acquires jurisdiction, nationwide, of all of the bankrupt's property on the date of filing.[18] This generally encompasses all property, in the possession of any person, over which the court has power to determine questions of possession, validity of claims, or amount of claims.[19] Jurisdiction, however, normally does not extend to property in which the debtor's only interest is a statutory redemption right from

12. Federal bankruptcy law has two sources: (1) the Bankruptcy Act, codified at 11 U.S.C.A. §§ 1 et seq.; (2) Bankruptcy Rules, with the force and effect of law, which are prescribed by the Supreme Court of the United States and often expand upon the Act.

13. Most citations to particular stay provisions will be found in discussions of specific bankruptcy and chapter proceedings, infra. See generally, the Secured Creditor's Complaint: Relief from the Automatic Stays in Bankruptcy Proceedings, 65 Cal.L.Rev. 1216 (1977).

14. Lifton, Real Estate in Trouble: Lenders' Remedies Need an Overhaul, 31 Bus.Law.1927, 1945, n. 73 (1976); Countryman, Real Estate Liens in Business Rehabilitation Cases, 50 Am.Bankr.L.J. 303, 304 (1976); Kennedy, Secured Creditors: The Impact of Bankruptcy on Their Interests, in Basic Bankruptcy: Alternatives, Proceedings and Discharges, pp. 165–66 (Abramson, 1971).

15. Rules 601(c), 10–601(c), 11–44(d), 12–43(d), 13–401; Lifton, supra note 14, at 1945–46, nn. 73, 74.

16. Nellis, The Mortgagor-Mortgagee Relationship in Bankruptcy: When a Stay is Not a Stay and Other Problems, 12 Real Prop.Prob. & Tr.J. 457, 464 (1977); Countryman, supra note 14, at 304.

17. Id.

18. The court has "exclusive jurisdiction of the debtor and its property wherever located." 11 U.S.C.A. §§ 110, 111, 311, 411; Countryman, supra note 14, at 303; Kennedy, supra note 14, at 168, 178; Nellis, supra note 16, at 459; Countryman, supra note 14, at 315–15.

19. Id.

a foreclosure sale held before the date of bankruptcy.[20] The significance of and exceptions to these general rules will be noted in discussion of specific bankruptcy proceedings.

§ 8.12 Straight Bankruptcy

The purpose of straight bankruptcy is to clear the slate and give the insolvent debtor a new start by discharging his debts.[21] Non-exempt assets are liquidated and distributed to creditors according to the priority and amount of their claims.[22] Individuals, corporations, and partnerships may file voluntarily; filing by creditors is termed "involuntary bankruptcy." [23] A court-appointed trustee administers the estate, his title to the bankrupt's property being effective from date of filing.[24] If, however, a real estate mortgagee has a valid mortgage, he will be a secured creditor for purposes of bankruptcy and, in theory, will be for the most part "outside the scope of the bankruptcy administration." [25] The following material indicates, however, that his involvement nevertheless can sometimes be substantial.

Type of Proceeding

Normally, filing the bankruptcy petition stays continuation or commencement of any proceeding to enforce security interests against property of the mortgagor.[26] However, a major exception mitigates the harshness of this rule: the stay does not prevent continuation of judicial foreclosure proceeding if the foreclosure was initiated before bankruptcy.[27] On the other hand, power of sale foreclosures are automatically stayed, at least where the mortgagor is in possession at the date of bankruptcy filing.[28] It should be pointed out, however, that even if a mortgagee is exempt from the automatic stay and therefore entitled to proceed with a foreclosure pending at date

20. 11 U.S.C.A. § 806(6); Kennedy, supra note 14, at 179. But see In re Thomas J. Grosso Investment, Inc., 457 F.2d 168 (C.A.Ariz.1972). See also Countryman, supra note 14, at 315 and cases cited therein.

21. 11 U.S.C.A. § 32(f); Kennedy, supra note 14, at 169–170.

22. 11 U.S.C.A. § 93.

23. 11 U.S.C.A. § 95.

24. Trustees' right to possession, 11 U.S.C.A. § 110; Trustees' duties, 11 U.S.C.A. § 75; Lifton, supra note 14, at 1948–49.

25. MacLachlan, Handbook of the Law of Bankruptcy, 132 (1956). See Comment, The Mortgagee's Rights to Rents and Profits Following a Petition in Bankruptcy, 60 Iowa L.Rev. 1388, 1389 (1975).

26. Rule 601; supra notes 7–10.

27. Straton v. New, 283 U.S. 318, 51 S.Ct. 465, 75 L.Ed. 1060 (1931), conformed to 49 F.2d 869; see 1 Collier ¶ 2.63(1); Kennedy, supra note 14, at 168; Lifton, supra note 14, at 1945, n. 73.

28. See, e. g., In re Bowden, 274 F.Supp. 729 (D.Me.1967); 1 Collier ¶ 2.62(2); Nellis, supra note 16, at 460; Lifton, supra note 14, at 1945, n. 73.

of bankruptcy, such proceedings may still be temporarily enjoined to preserve the status quo and permit intervention by the trustee to protect the interests of the bankrupt estate.[29]

Rents and Profits

An important question, as between the trustee in bankruptcy, who represents the mortgagor's general creditors, and the mortgagee is who is entitled to the rents and profits of the real estate during the bankruptcy period. Generally, if the mortgagee has gained access to the rents and profits prior to bankruptcy by taking certain lawful affirmative steps under state law, he will continue to be entitled to them during bankruptcy. Such pre-bankruptcy actions would include, for example, securing the appointment of a receiver or otherwise attaching or sequestering the rents and profits under state law.[32] In this connection, there is authority that if the mortgagee becomes a valid mortgagee in possession under state law prior to bankruptcy filing, he will prevail over the trustee with respect to continued access to rents and profits from the mortgaged property.[33]

Suppose, however, that bankruptcy has intervened before such affirmative action by the mortgagee. Under these circumstances the mortgagee's right to rents and profits during bankruptcy will generally be determined with reference to what the mortgagee's rights would have been absent bankruptcy.[34] Thus the mortgagee must take those steps, either by leave of or through the bankruptcy court, as would have been necessary to activate his rights under state law.[35] If, for example, a mortgagee was relying on a rents and profits clause, but state law required the appointment of a receiver for its

29. Straton v. New, 283 U.S. 318, 327, 51 S.Ct. 465, 75 L.Ed. 1060 (1931), conformed to 49 F.2d 869; In re Lustron Corp., 184 F.2d 798 (C.A.Ill.1950), certiorari denied 340 U.S. 946, 71 S. Ct. 531, 95 L.Ed. 682 (1951); Kennedy, supra note 14, at 168.

32. 11 U.S.C.A. § 110; Lifton, id., at 1945, 1948, & n. 81; Collier ¶ 70.-16(7); See, e. g., In re Stuckenberg, 374 F.Supp. 15 (E.D.Mo.1974), holding attornment, "the equivalent" of physical possession, entitled mortgagee to retain possession of the entire five-unit rental property, but rents from only the three tenants who signed written acknowledgments of mortgagee's intent to occupy and subsequently paid rent to mortgagee. See also In re Ventura-Louise Properties, 490 F.2d 1141 (C.A.Cal.1974), where a mortgagee, relying on an assignment of rents provision, prevailed over a bankruptcy trustee where, prior to bankruptcy, the mortgagee had notified the mortgagor's tenants to begin paying rent to the mortgagee.

33. See American Trust Co. v. England, 84 F.2d 352 (C.C.A.Cal.1936); 4A Collier ¶ 70.16(7).

34. See Comment, The Mortgagee's Right to Rents and Profits Following a Petition in Bankruptcy, 60 Iowa L. Rev. 1388, 1399 (1975).

35. Id. See, e. g., Petition of Cox, 15 F.2d 764, 765 (C.C.A.Mass.1926); In re Humeston, 83 F.2d 187, 188 (C.C. A.N.Y.1936); In re American Fuel & Power Co., 151 F.2d 470, 481 (C.C.A. Ky.1945), affirmed 329 U.S. 156, 67 S.Ct. 237, 91 L.Ed.2d 162, rehearing denied 329 U.S. 833, 67 S.Ct. 497–499, 91 L.Ed. 706; Groves v. Fresno Guarantee Federal Sav. & Loan Ass'n, 373 F.2d 440, 442–443 (C.A.Cal.1967).

activation, the majority of federal decisions would require that the bankruptcy court apply the same standard. If the latter court believed that a receiver was justified under state law, it presumably could appoint one or permit the appointment of one in state court.[36] A few federal courts, however, apparently do not apply state law in these situations, but look solely or mainly to the terms of the mortgage itself.[37] Thus, for example, if the mortgagee has literally complied with the requirements of the rents and profits clause, it will be enforced in the mortgagee's favor even though it would not have been under state law.[38]

The Debtor's Equity

In straight bankruptcy, the trustee's legitimate claim to mortgaged property is limited to the value exceeding the amount of the secured debt.[39] If the bankrupt mortgagor has no equity in the property, the trustee should abandon it, allowing the mortgagee to proceed with foreclosure.[40] The Act provides for independent, court-appointed appraisers to determine whether the value of the property exceeds the debt secured, i. e., whether the debtor has equity.[41]

Ideally, appraisal should result in a rapid determination, whereupon if the mortgagor has no equity, the trustee should immediately relinquish possession and allow the mortgagee to proceed with his normal remedies.[42] In practice, however, trustees often delay abandonment in an attempt to divert as much income as possible from the encumbered property.[43] Recognizing this exploitation of mortgagees, a few courts have limited the use of income from mortgaged property to operating expenses of that property, prohibiting application of such income to general administration expenses of the bankrupt estate.[44]

36. Comment supra note 34 at 1400.

37. See, e. g., Central States Life Ins. Co. v. Carlson, 98 F.2d 102 (C.C.A. Colo.1938).

38. Id.

39. Lifton, supra note 14, at 1948; Nellis, supra note 16, at 465.

40. See In re Victor Builders, Inc., 418 F.2d 880 (C.A.Cal.1969); In re Polumbo, 271 F.Supp. 640, 643 (W.D.Va. 1967); In the Matter of Ira Haupt & Co., 398 F.2d 607 (C.A.N.Y.1968); Nellis supra note 16, at 465; Lifton, supra note 14, 15 (1948).

41. 11 U.S.C.A. § 96a; Lifton, id., at 1948, n. 80; 4A Collier ¶ 70.96.

42. Supra note 39.

43. Lifton, supra note 14, at 1948–49; see 4A Collier ¶ 70.16(7). "It would be an abuse of discretion to stall a secured creditor where there is no real equity in the property for the sole purpose of enabling the trustee to derive as much income as possible from the encumbered properties," Pasky, Some Procedural Aspects of Administering Encumbered Properties and the Treatment of Secured Creditors in Ordinary Bankruptcy, 44 Ref. J., 54, 55 (1970).

44. In re Franklin Garden Apartments, Inc., 124 F.2d 451 (C.C.A.N.Y.1941); In re Bernhard Altmann Int'l Corp., 226 F.Supp. 201, 205 (S.D.N.Y.1963); In re Ventura-Louise Properties, 490 F.2d 1141 (C.A.Cal.1974). Nellis, supra note 16, at 471 argues that an unreasonable delay in obtaining the income by the mortgagee constitutes

If the mortgagor has equity the trustee, in theory, still has the option to vacate the stay and permit the mortgagee to sell the real estate outside of bankruptcy. However, he more likely will require that it be sold in bankruptcy. If it is sold subject to the mortgage, no court approval is required.[45] However, despite the mortgagee's objections, with judicial permission, the trustee may sell free of the mortgage and transfer the security interest to the proceeds.[46] The effect is involuntary submission to foreclosure at a time and manner decided by a bankruptcy court.[47] The aggrieved mortgagee is also penalized by deduction of sale expenses from the proceeds.[48] If the property is subject to multiple security interests, the court must determine priority to the proceeds according to state law.[49] If a sale free and clear of the mortgage is ordered, the mortgagee usually protects himself by bidding at the sale. As in normal foreclosure, he may bid up to the amount of the mortgage debt without tendering cash.[50]

Generally, straight bankruptcy culminates in discharge of the debtor.[51] However, mortgagees are not barred from enforcing valid security interests that either were not attacked or survived attack during bankruptcy proceedings. Discharge bars only deficiency claims that arise if the security is insufficient to cover the mortgage debt.[52]

§ 8.13 Bankruptcy "Chapter" Proceedings

While straight bankruptcy normally results ultimately in the liquidation of the debtor, chapter proceedings, on the other hand, preserve bankrupt estates during the formulation and operation of arrangements which contemplate the debtor's rehabilitation. Since reorganization necessarily entails extension of debts and broad judicial control over secured and unsecured creditors, the ramifications of chapter proceedings are often more troublesome for mortgagees than straight bankruptcy. Reorganization of insolvent business entities

an unconstitutional taking of the property for the benefit of the debtor and other creditors. See text at notes 80–84 infra.

45. Lifton, supra note 14, at 1948, n. 79.

46. Van Huffell v. Harkelrode, 284 U.S. 225, 52 S.Ct. 115, 76 L.Ed. 256 (1931); Lifton, id., Nellis, supra note 16, at 468–70. See 4A Collier ¶¶ 70.97–90.99.

47. A sale free and clear should not be permitted unless equity exceeding liens, taxes and all other charges against the property can be shown. A sale free and clear where there is no apparent equity and the mortgagee's lien is valid is an abuse of discretion, Federal Land Bank v. Kurtz, 70 F.2d 46 (C.C.A.W.Va.1934); Nellis, supra note 16, at 469; Kennedy, supra note 14, at 167.

48. Kennedy, Id.

49. Kennedy, Id.

50. Nellis, supra note 16, at 470; see 4A Collier ¶ 70.98, for general procedure for sales by the trustee, including measures for the mortgagee's protection.

51. Kennedy, supra note 14, at 167.

52. Kennedy, Id.

may take years, freezing vast amounts of mortgaged property, including rents and profits.[53] Under Chapters X and XII, security rights may even be modified or partially eliminated notwithstanding the mortgagee's objections.

Until recently, chapter stays were virtually incomprehensible. Most were discretionary and cases delineating the bankruptcy court's power conflicted radically. Recent amendments provide automatic stays for all chapters, governed by the general provisions set out in the introductory section. Additionally, chapter proceedings allow ex parte relief to a mortgagee upon showing of immediate, irreparable harm.[54] However, being within the broad discretion of the court, such relief will seldom be granted.[55]

Chapter X

Reorganization and the revision of the capital structure of debtor corporations by adjustment and redistribution of secured and insecured debt is the purpose of Chapter X.[56] Proceedings are initiated voluntarily by the insolvent corporation or involuntarily by creditors.[57] An automatic stay bars both judicial and power of sale foreclosure of mortgages, even though commencement of such proceedings predated the Chapter filing.[58] Although the stay arises automatically, continuation must be predicated upon proof of (1) good faith in filing, (2) absence of jeopardy to the mortgagee's rights, and (3) the reasonable possibility of successful reorganization.[59] The court is required to determine the practicability of reorganization at the outset of Chapter X proceedings.[60]

53. In Chicago, Rock Island & Pacific Ry. v. Fleming, 157 F.2d 241 (C.C.A. Ill.1946), certiorari denied 329 U.S. 780, 67 S.Ct. 201, 91 L.Ed. 669, the stay lasted 10 years.

54. Rules 10–601(d), 11–44(e), 12–43(e).

55. Nellis, supra note 16, at 464.

56. 11 U.S.C.A. §§ 501–676.

57. Lifton, supra note 14, at 1963.

58. Rule 10–601 (August, 1975) supersedes the former discretionary stay at 11 U.S.C.A. § 516(4). But foreclosure of a mechanic's lien was not subject to the automatic stay where final judgment would be against a surety on his bond and not against the debtor. Matter of Stanndco Developers, Inc., 534 F.2d 1050 (C.A.N.Y.1975); Assets of a wholly or partially owned subsidiary are exempt from the stay in the absence of fraud. Parkview-Gem, Inc. v. Stein, 516 F.2d 807 (C.A.Mo.1975); Property in Canada is subject to the automatic foreclosure. Detroit Trust Co. v. Campbell River Timber Co., 98 F.2d 389 (C.C.A.Wash.1938).

59. In re 235 West 46 Street Co. Inc., 74 F.2d 700 (C.C.A.N.Y.1935); First Nat. Bank v. Conway Road Estates Co., 94 F.2d 736 (C.C.A.Mo.1938), certiorari denied 304 U.S. 578, 58 S.Ct. 1047, 82 L.Ed. 1541 (1938); see also, In re U. S. Realty & Improvement Co., 153 F.2d 853 (C.C.A.N.Y.1946); In re Marietta Cobb Apts. Co., 2 CCH Bankr.L.R. ¶ 66, 516, 3 Bankr.Ct.Dec. 720 (S.D.N.Y.1977); In re Pine Gate Assoc.'s Ltd., 2 CCH Bankr.L.R. ¶ 66,340, 2 Bankr.Ct.Dec. 1478 (N.D. Ga.1976); Lifton, supra note 14, at 1955; Nellis, supra note 16, at 464–465; Countryman, supra note 14, at 305–07; Murphy, Restraint and Reimbursement: The Secured Creditor in Reorganization and Arrangement Proceedings, 30 Bus.Law 15, 31 (1975); 6 Collier ¶¶ 3.32, 6.12.

60. 11 U.S.C. § 546(3); Nellis, supra note 16, at 465.

Subsequent occurrences also may result in vacation of the stay.[61] For example, refusal to vacate a stay when six months have elapsed without preparation of a plan has been held an abuse of discretion.[62] In marginal situations, courts have conditioned continuation of the stay on attainment of specified results by the debtor within a certain period.[63] Moreover, a mortgagee might also argue that exemption from the stay will not materially affect chances of successful reorganization if his security is not integral to the debtor's business operation, but held only for investment or sale.[64] However, present case law determines materiality by value of the property, not by its operational necessity to the insolvent corporation.[65] Because a trustee is entitled to "immediate possession" of all the debtor's property, whether or not in custody, he can force mortgagees or state-appointed receivers and trustees to surrender possession. In contrast to straight bankruptcy and Chapter XI, delivery can be compelled even though (1) commencement of foreclosure antedated the Chapter filing, or (2) the nonbankruptcy receiver or trustee was appointed more than four months prior to filing.[66] This provision can irreparably damage mortgagees. For example, in a construction loan situation where a large project is halted, mounting costs and deterioration of the unfinished structure can make resumption of construction impossible.[67] Authorities emphasize the court's duty to refrain from ordering delivery absent proof of the debtor's equity in the property, adequate safeguards for the mortgagee, and a reasonable likelihood of successful reorganization.[68]

61. Nellis, Id., at 467; Caplan v. Anderson, 256 F.2d 416 (C.A.Fla.1958), held that after nine months, where vacation of the stay had been sought and no plan had been submitted, a full hearing was necessary, not just a disposition on affidavits.

62. In re Holiday Lodge, Inc., 300 F.2d 516 (C.A.Ill.1962), certiorari denied, 371 U.S. 824, 83 S.Ct. 43, 9 L.Ed. 263; In re Empire Steel Co., 228 F.Supp. 316 (D.C.Utah 1964).

63. In re Stevens Enterprises, 148 F. Supp. 12 (E.D.Pa.1957), held that a stay of a mortgage foreclosure should be vacated unless default was cured and enough money for operating costs for the next nine months plus $5,000 for attorney and trustee fees was obtained within eight days.

64. Lifton, supra note 14, at 1951–55; Countryman, supra note 14, at 305; see Caplan v. Anderson, 256 F.2d 416 (C.A.Ill.1958).

65. Lifton, id., at 1955.

66. 11 U.S.C. § 657; Reconstruction Finance Corp. v. Kaplan, 185 F.2d 791 (C.A.Mass.1950); John Hancock Mutual Ins. Co. v. Casey, 134 F.2d 162 (C.C.A.Mass.1935), certiorari denied 319 U.S. 757, 63 S.Ct. 1176, 87 L.Ed. 1709 (1935); In re Franklin Garden Apartments, 124 F.2d 451 (C.C.A.N.Y. 1941); see also the following Chapter XII cases: In re Colonial Realty Investment Co., 516 F.2d 154 (C.A.Mass. 1965); In re Samoset Assoc.'s CCH Bankr.L.R. ¶ 66,112 (D.Me.1976); 6 Collier ¶ 3.05.

67. Lifton, supra note 14, at 1950, 1957.

68. In re Georgetown on Delaware, Inc., 466 F.2d 80 (C.A.Pa.1972), reversed a turnover, entered two weeks after filing where no plan had been submitted and the debtor had only $20,000 equity in a 3.5 million dollar apartment complex; Nellis, supra note 16, at 461.

A corollary to the trustee's power to demand possession is his right to rents and profits of the property. This, of course, can further erode the mortgagee's security interest.[69] The court has discretion to order payment of income to the mortgagee or at least limit use of income to operation of the secured property, but absent such discretionary order, the trustee is free to apply rents and profits to general administration expenses.[70] Such diversion of income fosters deterioration of the property, as in the construction loan situation, and could result in insufficient assets to satisfy the mortgagee's secured claim if reorganization fails and liquidation ensues.[71] Moreover, the mortgagee's claim under an assignment of rents clause is generally ineffective against the trustee's right to the income.[72]

After the initial automatic stay, the mortgagee enters a second critical phase when a reorganization plan is finally submitted. Case law has spawned the "fair and equitable" test, purporting, by application of the "absolute priority" rule, to prevent coercion of mortgagees into unfair arrangements.[73] Confirmation of a plan must guarantee senior secured creditors absolute priority: beginning with the most senior class of creditors and working down to the least, claims of each higher class must be given full compensation before the next lower class gets any payment. The plan must also have the written consent of creditors holding ⅔ of the total debt of their class.[74]

However, these safeguards are often illusory because of an extremely controversial exception known as the "cram-down".[75] Cram-down allows confirmation without the requisite written consent of the affected class of creditors if the court finds that "adequate protection" is provided from (1) sale or transfer subject to the mortgage; (2) sale free of the mortgage, at a price not less than the debt, with transfer of the lien to the proceeds; (3) cash payment of the value of the debt as determined by appraisal; or (4) such other

69. In re Colonial Realty Investment Co., 516 F.2d 154 (C.A.Mass.1975); In re Samoset Assoc.'s, CCH Bankr.L.R. ¶ 66,112 (D.Me.1976); Lifton, supra note 14, at 1955–57.

70. "An explicit preliminary finding of probable benefit, or at least, no probable injury" should precede any diversion of rents. Colonial Realty Investment Co., id.; see also, In re Ventura-Louise Properties, 490 F.2d 1141 (C.A.Cal.1974); In re Pittsburgh-Duquesne Development Co., 482 F.2d 243 (C.A.Pa.1973); In re Franklin Garden Apts., 124 F.2d 451 (C.C.A.N.Y.1941); Lifton, at 1952–53.

71. Supra note 59; Lifton, id. at 1956.

72. Federal Shopping Way, In re, 457 F.2d 176 (C.A.Wash.1972); In re Pine Gate Assoc.'s Ltd., 2 CCH Bankr.L.R. ¶ 66,340, 2 Bankr.Ct.Dec.1978 (N.D. Ga.1976).

73. Northern Pacific Ry. Co. v. Boyd, 228 U.S. 482, 33 S.Ct. 554, 57 L.Ed. 931 (1913); Case v. Los Angeles Lumber Products Co., 308 U.S. 106, 60 S.Ct. 1, 84 L.Ed. 110 (1939); Lifton, supra note 14, at 1957–58.

74. Marine Harbor Properties v. Manufacturers Trust Co., 317 U.S. 78, 63 S.Ct. 93, 87 L.Ed. 64, rehearing denied 317 U.S. 710, 63 S.Ct. 254, 87 L. Ed. 566 (1942); 6A Collier ¶ 11.06.

75. 11 U.S.C.A. § 579; Lifton, supra note 14, at 1957–58.

method as equitably and fairly provides protection under the circumstances.[76]

These alternatives, especially the nebulous provisions of (3) and (4), permit courts to coerce mortgagees into acceptance.[77] Theoretically, the "fair and equitable" test governs application of the four cram-down alternatives, thus preventing confirmation of a plan to favor junior creditors and deprive senior classes of all full compensation.[78] However, while courts assert that Chapter X cannot be exploited for the mortgagor's convenience as a "moratorium on foreclosure" to hold creditors at bay, they also concede that general creditors might manipulate a cram-down forcing senior lienors into a prejudicial plan.[79]

Constitutional arguments have been asserted against stays and reorganization plans that mortgagees and other secured creditors have believed unduly threatened their security. The two main constitutional theories advanced are that such proceedings constitute a "taking" without just compensation under the 5th Amendment and that they unconstitutionally impair the obligations of contracts. For example, the Court of Appeals for the Third Circuit has indicated that when reorganization plans go beyond mere postponement of the secured creditor's rights so as to constitute an erosion of the security, a taking may occur.[80] However, even if a reorganization plan did go so far as to constitute a taking, the Supreme Court has indicated that the Court of Claims, and not the Bankruptcy Court, is the proper forum to raise that constitutional issue.[81] The impairment of contracts argument has generally failed, either because courts did not believe that postponement constituted an impairment[82] or because secured

76. 11 U.S.C.A. § 616(7); see Cumberland, Recent Bankruptcy Decisions Alarm Lenders, Mortg. Banker, Dec. 1977, at 24, for discussion of the lending community's abhorrence of the cram-down.

77. See In re Murel Holding Corp., 75 F.2d 941, 942 (C.C.A.N.Y.1935), emphasizing that the vague "adequate protection" provision must meet constitutional standards and be fully compensatory when judicially exercised; Lifton, supra note 14, at 1959–60; 6A Collier ¶ 10.12.

78. See In re Pinegate Assoc.'s Ltd., 2 CCH Bankr.L.R. ¶ 66,340, 2 Bankr.Ct. Dec.1978 (N.D.Ga.1976), stating that "adequate protection rather than consent of the creditor is the keynote" in refusing to release mortgagees from a Chapter XII stay pending submission of a plan, even though mortgagees had announced the intent to refuse any plan submitted; Lifton, id., at 1960.

79. Lincoln-Alliance Bank & Trust Co. v. Dye, 115 F.2d 234, 235 (C.C.A.N.Y. 1940); Lifton, supra note 14, at 1960–61, n. 113.

80. In re Penn Central Transportation Co., 494 F.2d 270 (C.A.Pa.1974), certiorari denied 419 U.S. 883, 95 S.Ct. 147, 42 L.Ed.2d 122. For a thorough consideration of this case and the constitutional claims, see Countryman, Real Estate Liens in Business Rehabilitation Cases, 50 Am.Bankr.L. J. 303, 334–339 (1976). See also, Murphy, supra note 59, 17, 34; Nellis, supra note 16 at 466.

81. Regional Rail Reorganization Act Cases, 419 U.S. 102, 95 S.Ct. 335, 42 L.Ed.2d 320 (1974); See Countryman, supra note 80 at 338.

82. See Chicago, Rock Island & Pacific Ry. v. Fleming, 157 F.2d 241, 247 (C.

creditors were on notice of the bankruptcy reorganization powers when they took their security.[83] A third constitutional argument has been that the automatic stay violates 5th Amendment procedural due process rights of the secured creditor in that the stay becomes effective without notice or an opportunity to be heard. This argument has been rejected on the theory that the bankruptcy proceeding provide for prompt notice and hearing after the stay becomes effective.[84]

Because straight bankruptcy and Chapter proceedings pose substantially different problems for mortgagees, a fact situation at this point should enhance the reader's understanding. Assume that in three different states three corporations, Ajax, Bold, and Comet, each owned similar apartment complexes. Mortgagee held identical valid long term mortgages with unpaid balances of $500,000 on each.

Defaults on all three mortgages occurred and Mortgagee commenced the following proceedings on January 15: (1) judicial foreclosures were initiated on the Ajax and Comet mortgages; (2) power of sale foreclosure was commenced on the Bold mortgage. Mortgagee did not utilize judicial foreclosure on the Bold mortgage since, in Bold's state, power of sale normally provides quick, inexpensive foreclosure. On March 15, all three mortgagees filed bankruptcy petitions in federal district courts of their respective states: (1) Ajax and Bold filed straight bankruptcy; (2) Comet filed under Chapter X. To sum up the situation at this point: (1) Ajax's judicial foreclosure action on January 15 was followed by straight bankruptcy on March 15; (2) Bold's power of sale foreclosure was followed by straight bankruptcy; and (3) Comet's judicial foreclosure was followed by a Chapter X filing.

The Ajax mortgage is exempt from both the initial stay and ultimate bankruptcy court jurisdiction since judicial foreclosure antedated filing.[84a] Thus, Mortgagee may continue these two proceedings unaffected by Ajax's bankruptcy, subject only to the possibility that discharge will wipe out Ajax's personal liability.

In contrast, Bold's mortgage is subject to both the stay and full straight bankruptcy jurisdiction because foreclosure was by power of sale.[84b] The ultimate decision as to Bold's foreclosure will be made by the bankruptcy court and trustee. The court may be persuaded to release the property to Mortgagee on the ground that Bold has no equity in it.

C.A.Ill.1946), certiorari denied 329 U.S. 780, 67 S.Ct. 201, 91 L.Ed. 669.

83. In re Prima, 88 F.2d 785, 788–789 (C.C.A.Ill.1937). For an example of a plan that one authority deems unconstitutional, see In re Yale Express System, Inc., 384 F.2d 990 (C.A.N.Y. 1967). See Murphy, supra note 59, at 34.

84. See Fidelity Mortgage Investors v. Camelia Builders, Inc., 550 F.2d 47 (C.A.N.Y.1977).

84a. See text at note 27 supra.

84b. See text at note 28 supra.

Despite the contrasting results of the Ajax and Bold mortgages, straight bankruptcy actually harbors few unpleasant surprises. Since ultimate liquidation is always the sole purpose, mortgagees are, or at least should be, cognizant that the court may very likely determine not only when, but if there will ever be a foreclosure or only a trustee's sale. Moreover, relatively quick proceedings in straight bankruptcy minimize danger of prolonged deterioration and depreciation.

The status of Comet's mortgage differs substantially since uncertainty is inherent in Chapter proceedings. That judicial foreclosure preceded filing is irrelevant; filing invoked both the initial stay and full Chapter X jurisdiction. Thus, Mortgagee may be subjected to years of an infinite range of "plans." Furthermore, indeterminate cram-down powers nullify Mortgagee's right to refuse consent, allowing judicial approval of a plan if Mortgagee's rights are deemed "adequately protected." For example, a plan might mandate little or no payment of interest for a period of several years during which Comet will likely be given possession and the rents and profits of the premises. If the plan fails after several years, proceedings will probably convert to straight bankruptcy for estate liquidation. Meanwhile, several years of depreciation have certainly eroded the value of Mortgagee's security interest. Extensive deterioration or structural damage may have even rendered the apartments substantially less valuable as security. This passage of time may have the practical effect of forcing Mortgagee into the ranks of unsecured creditors.

Chapter XII

The purpose of Chapter XII is to formulate rehabilitation plans that extend payments or modify rights of real estate mortgagees.[85] Only individual or partnership debtors who are legal or equitable owners of encumbered property can file.[86] No relief is available if the only interest is statutory redemption from a foreclosure sale that preceded filing.[87]

Many provisions and problems of Chapter XII, including the following, basically duplicate those in Chapter X: the automatic stay, grounds for vacating or continuing the stay,[88] the trustee's right to divest other receivers or trustees and compel delivery of property,[89] the use of rents and profits,[90] the alteration of rights without the

85. 11 U.S.C.A. §§ 801–926 generally; 11 U.S.C.A. § 806(1) regarding alteration of land-secured creditors' rights.

86. Lifton, supra note 14, at 1962 & n. 116; 9 Collier ¶ 4.02.

87. 11 U.S.C.A. § 806(6); cf. In re Samoset Assoc.'s CCH Bankr.L.J. ¶ 66,112 (D.Me.1976), and In re Colonial Realty Investment Co., 516 F.2d 154 (C.A.Mass.1975).

88. Rule 12–43; supra notes 58–65.

89. 11 U.S.C.A. § 907; supra notes 66–68.

90. Supra notes 69–72.

mortgagee's consent,[91] possible constitutional limitations,[92] and the general effect of extension on mortgagees. Because eligibility requirements under Chapter XII used to be very stringent there was little case law development. Thus, authorities often analyze Chapter XII in accordance with cases decided under Chapter X.

Bankruptcy Rule changes have made Chapter XII often more advantageous to debtors than Chapter X: (1) the debtor is permitted to remain in possession during the plan formulation stage; [93] (2) appointment of a trustee is not required; [94] (3) rehabilitation plans formerly had to accompany filing of the petition, but now time is given, as in Chapter X, to formulate and submit plans after filing.[95] However, failure to submit a plan within a reasonable time may result in vacation of the automatic stay against foreclosure, dismissal of proceedings, or conversion to straight bankruptcy.[96]

Chapter XII prohibits extension or impairment of mortgages insured pursuant to the National Housing Act, or held by any Federal Home Loan Bank.[97] However, this limitation is not interpreted to exempt such mortgages from the automatic stay or strip the bankruptcy court of jurisdiction. Rather, they are exempted only from inclusion in the final plan.[98]

As in Chapter X, judicial confirmation of an arrangement requires the written consent of land-secured creditors holding ⅔ of the debt in the affected class, but a cram-down provision permits confirmation despite lack of such consent if adequate protection is provided.[99] The mortgagee is in a difficult position because the "fair and equitable" test is not applied to Chapter XII cram-downs.[1] A

91. Supra notes 73–79.

92. Supra notes 80–84.

93. Lifton, supra note 14, at 1961–63.

93. Rule 12–17(b); 11 U.S.C.A. § 832; see In re Walker, 93 F.2d 281 (C.C. A.N.Y.1937), equating debtors in possession with trustees; Lifton, supra note 14, at 1961, 1964, nn. 114, 123.

95. Rule 12–36; Lifton, id. at 1963.

96. Authority suggests that Chapter XII is perhaps less lenient than Chapter XI, limiting the debtor to a shorter period of time to formulate a plan. See Nellis, supra note 16, at 468 & n. 57; Sumida v. Yumen, 444 F.2d 1281 (C.A.Hawaii 1971), certiorari denied 405 U.S. 964, 92 S.Ct. 1168, 31 L.Ed. 2d 240 (1972); In the Matter of Taylor, 458 F.2d 15 (C.A.Cal.1972).

97. 11 U.S.C.A. § 917, thus FHA insured mortgages are immune.

98. In re Consolidated Motor Inns, 5 Collier Bankr. Cases 301 (W.D.Ga. 1975); In re Hall Assoc.'s 8 Collier Bankr. Cases 290 (E.D.Pa.1976); 9 Collier ¶ 14.02; but see Monte Vista Lodge v. Guardian Life Ins. Co., 384 F.2d 126 (C.A.Cal.1967), certiorari denied 390 U.S. 950, 88 S.Ct. 1041, 19 L.Ed.2d 1142, where total exemption was decreed.

99. 11 U.S.C.A. § 861; supra notes 73–79; Cumberland, supra note 76, discussing cram-down from the lender's perspective. Lifton, supra note 14, at 1964–47; Miller & Goldstein, Chapter XII—Real Property Arrangements: Is "Cram-Down" A Debtor's Panacea?, 12 Real Prop.Prob. & Tr.J. 695 (1978).

1. The 1952 Chandler Act Amendment, Pub.L.No. 456, 66 Stat. 579, eliminated the "fair and equitable" test from Chapter XII; Lifton, id., at 1965–67.

lesser standard of protection is specified, requiring only that confirmation be "for the best interests of the creditors." [2]

Some commentators have questioned whether an intransigent mortgagee, after stating his refusal to comply, can be forced to accept a Chapter XII plan merely because it is deemed by the court to provide adequate protection.[3] Although language in several cases indicates that mortgagees cannot be coerced into a plan, it is noteworthy that in every case the recalcitrant mortgagee was the only creditor.[4] If so easily thwarted, cram-down provisions would be superfluous; thus, where other creditors are involved, it seems likely that a single mortgagee cannot resist the plan.[5] In any event, by pre-filing manipulation, the insolvent mortgagor may be able to outmanuever the mortgagee. For example, a debtor could purposely incur other secured obligations before filing, even mechanics' or materialmen's liens, and thus prevent an otherwise sole mortgagee from refusing the plan in order to keep his sizeable security interest intact.[6]

Prompted by the new rules, use of Chapter XII will probably accelerate since partnerships and limited partnerships are increasingly popular devices for the ownership of real property.[7] One reason is that partnerships incurring severe losses on real estate held for tax shelter often seek to avert foreclosure through Chapter XII. Otherwise, previous years' accelerated depreciation would be recaptured in the year of foreclosure and treated as ordinary income to the partners.[8]

Chapter XI

Individuals, partnerships, or corporations can file under Chapter XI in order to formulate plans for the extension and alteration of unsecured debts.[9] By its terms, this proceeding should not affect mort-

2. 11 U.S.C.A. § 872; Lifton, id.

3. Lifton, id. at 1967, Countryman, supra note 14 at 307.

4. Kunze v. Prudential Ins. Co., 106 F.2d 917 (C.C.A.Ga.1939); Meyer v. Rowen, 195 F.2d 263 (C.A.Utah 1952); Taylor v. Wood, 458 F.2d 15 (C.A.Cal.1972). But see In re Marietta Cobb Apts. Co., 2 CCH Bankr.L.R. ¶ 66,516, 3 Bankr.Ct.Dec. 720 (N.D.N.Y.1977), and Miller & Goldstein, supra note 99 at 704–5.

5. Sumida v. Yumen, 409 F.2d 654 (C.A.Hawaii 1969), appeal after remand 444 F.2d 1281, certiorari denied 405 U.S. 964, 92 S.Ct. 1168, 31 L.Ed.2d 240; Lifton, supa note 14 at 1967–68; 6 Collier ¶ 6.09.

6. Lifton, id. at 1968.

7. Lifton, id. at 1961; see, e. g., In re Colonial Realty Investment Co., 516 F.2d 154 (C.A.Mass.1975), where 7,000 limited partners invested $30,000,000 in 9,000 apartments subject to 100 mortgages; see Arey & Russell Lumber Co., Inc. v. American Nat. Bank & Trust Co., 201 F.2d 508 (C.A.Va.1953) and Lifton, id. at 1971–72, regarding bad faith filings by corporations which transfer all their assets to bogus limited partnerships solely to invoke Chapter XII protection.

8. Cumberland, supra note 76 at 26; Lifton, id. at 1962–63 & n. 119.

9. 11 U.S.C.A. §§ 702–799; Lifton, id. at 1949.

gage foreclosure. Nevertheless, although the real estate mortgagee is presumably immune from the plan submitted, courts still prohibit mortgagees from exercising their right of foreclosure during the formulation of plans.[10] A discretionary stay under old rules was applied to mortgagees while the plan for unsecured creditors was being prepared.[11] However, case law was inconsistent as to whether the mortgagee was free to foreclosure without court permission in the absence of a stay.[12] New rules now automatically stay commencement or continuation of any foreclosure or enforcement proceeding, even though initiated before filing.[13] Relief from such a stay is governed by the same considerations considered earlier.

There is debate as to whether a Chapter XI trustee has power to compel delivery of mortgaged realty.[14] Since real estate mortgagees are ultimately exempt from the plan, jurisdiction of the court and powers of the trustee are perhaps construed more conservatively than under Chapters X and XII.[15] Traditionally, Chapter XI has followed the concepts applied in straight bankruptcy. Thus, the trustee can obtain delivery only if the debtor had real or constructive possession on the filing date.[16] Accordingly, nonbankruptcy receivers and trustees cannot be ousted if appointed more than four months prior to filing or pursuant to a foreclosure pending at filing.[17] In contrast, Chapters X and XII reach all property, wherever located, and possession can be wrested from any nonbankruptcy receiver or trustee, regard-

10. In re Consolidated Motor Inns, 5 Collier Bankr. Cases 301 (W.D.Ga. 1975), states that although Chapter XI arrangements "cannot affect secured debts of any kind, the courts have consistently recognized that a debtor under Chapter XI is entitled to an injunction against foreclosure of its properties by secured creditors while a plan of arrangement is being formulated"; Countryman, supra note 14, at 313 and cases cited therein; Lifton, id., at 1949; 8 Collier ¶ 2.-06(3).

11. 11 U.S.C.A. § 714.

12. Lifton, supra note 14 at 1946 n. 74, discusses conflicts in case law under the old stay.

13. Rule 11–44 (July, 1974); In re Victor Builders, 418 F.2d 880 (C.A.Cal. 1969), held that nonjudicial foreclosures were also subject to automatic stays, U. S. v. Mel's Food Lockers, Inc., 346 F.2d 168 (C.A.Utah 1965), held that foreclosure by the Small Business Administration is wholly exempt from an automatic stay under 15 U.S.C.A. § 634(b).

14. Nellis, supra note 16 at 461–62.

15. Countryman, supra note 14 at 304–05; Nellis, id. at 462; Murphy, supra note 52 at 42; see, e. g., In re Presidential Homes, Inc., 1 Bankr.Ct. Dec. 983 (D.N.J.1975).

16. See Wikle for Nevada Henderson Land Co. v. Country Life Ins. Co., 423 F.2d 151 (C.A.Cal.1970), where a trustee's possession and sale were void because the receiver was appointed more than four months before filing in Chapter XI proceedings which were converted to straight bankruptcy.

17. Yoshinmau v. Oberdorfer Ins. Agency, 136 F.2d 460 (C.C.A.Ga. 1943), certiorari denied 320 U.S. 785, 64 S.Ct. 189, 88 L.Ed. 472 (1943); Smith v. Hill, 317 F.2d 539 (C.A.Cal. 1963); Lifton, supra note 14 at 1947 n. 76.

less of when or why he was appointed.[18] Some commentators detect a trend in Chapter XI courts to order such surrender of possession.[19] However, income should still be immune from the trustee's diversion for general expenses since realty is not subject to the final plan for rehabilitation.[20]

Since mortgaged realty is ultimately exempt under Chapter XI, criteria for continuation of automatic stays are amorphous beyond the basic consideration of balancing the mortgagee's harm against the necessity of the stay for successful effectuation of a plan.[21] One theory proposes that judicial attention be directed to the distinction between property essential to business operations and that held merely for investment.[22] Case law emphasizes that a stay must be justified by reasonable expectations of a workable plan.[23] An extended stay cannot be used as a general moratorium to alleviate foreclosure pressure by restless mortgagees.[24]

A mortgagee is entitled to immediate appraisal of the property, and if the debtor has no equity the stay should be lifted.[25] The debtor may sell the property and realize his equity if it is determined to exist, but if no sale occurs within a reasonable time, the stay should be lifted.[26] The mortgagee should not be unduly affected since a sale would be subject to the mortgage.

Some courts allow mortgagees to foreclose in state courts simultaneously with Chapter XI proceedings.[27] The stay is invoked only to enjoin execution of foreclosure judgments until final resolution of Chapter XI proceedings.[28] The court also has discretion to order debtors to indemnify or otherwise protect mortgagees against potential loss during a stay. Failure to comply may result in vacation of the stay, dismissal of proceedings, or conversion of proceedings to straight bankruptcy.[29]

18. Werth and Reed, the Chapter XI Stay Order and The Secured Creditor, 38 Ohio St.L.J. 33, 46–47 (1977).

19. Nellis, supra note 16 at 462.

20. Lifton, supra note 14 at 1952–53.

21. Nellis, supra note 16, at 466–67 and cases cited in nn. 49, 50; Countryman, supra note 14 at 313; 8 Collier ¶ 3.22.

22. Lifton, supra note 14 at 1951–54.

23. Lance, Inc. v. Dewco Services, Inc., 422 F.2d 778 (C.A.Nev.1970); In re Holiday Lodge, 300 F.2d 516 (C.A. Ill.1962), certiorari denied 371 U.S. 824, 83 S.Ct. 43, 9 L.Ed.2d 63 (1962).

24. In re Empire Steel Co., 228 F. Supp. 316 (D.Utah 1964).

25. In re Hull, 311 F.Supp. 197 (E.D. Calif.1970); Lifton, supra note 14 at 1952; Nellis, supra note 16 at 468–69 for discussion of sales in Chapter XI proceedings. See also 4A Collier ¶¶ 70.97–99.

26. Lifton, id. at 1952.

27. Lifton, id. at 1950–51.

28. Rule 11–20(d). But see In re Marietta Cobb Apts. Co., 2 CCH Bankr. L.R. ¶ 66,516, 3 Bankr.Ct.Dec. 720 (S. D.N.Y.1977), and In re Pinegate Assoc.'s Ltd., 2 CCH Bankr.L.R. ¶ 66,340, 2 Bankr.Ct.Dec.1978 (N.D. Ga.1976).

29. Rule 11–42(b).

Chapter XIII

Chapter XIII [30] will be only briefly summarized since its provisions and ramifications generally duplicate Chapter XI. This chapter entails "wage earner plans" which provide for extension of debts in contemplation of payment out of future wages and earnings.[31] Only individual debtors with income from wages and salaries can file.[32] Real estate mortgagees are exempt from the final plan unless they consent to be a part of it.[33] Because of this exemption, such mortgagees are only temporarily affected, being curtailed by an automatic stay during formulation of the plan.[34] For explanation of the automatic stay, and other general considerations, the previous discussion of Chapter XI is applicable.

§ 8.14 The Bankruptcy Reform Act of 1978

While this volume was in the proof stage, the Bankruptcy Reform Act of 1978 ("New Act") was enacted. The substantive provisions of the New Act become effective October 1, 1979. While much of the substantive law and most of the bankruptcy concepts considered in the previous three sections will continue to be applicable after the New Act becomes effective, the New Act does make numerous significant changes in existing law and practice. Some of the more important of these changes that are especially significant for the real estate mortgagee are considered below.

Straight Bankruptcy

Perhaps the most significant impact of the New Act on real estate mortgagees will be on the scope of the automatic stay. Under the New Act the stay will be applicable to any foreclosure proceeding, judicial or otherwise, whether commenced prior to bankruptcy or not.[35] The only significant exemption from the stay is for foreclosure "actions" brought by the Secretary of HUD on federally insured mortgages on property consisting of five or more living units.[36] Under current law and practice the stay was effective against most previously commenced power of sale foreclosure proceedings, but not against such previously commenced judicial proceedings.[37] Under the New Act the

30. 11 U.S.C.A. §§ 1001–1086.

31. Kennedy, supra note 14 at 180.

32. Income from social security payments and retirement benefits is included. 11 U.S.C.A. § 1006.

33. 11 U.S.C.A. §§ 1006(1), 1046(2); Chatman v. Daugherty, 527 F.2d 691 (C.A.Tenn.1975); In re Hawks, 471 F.2d 305 (C.A.Va.1973); In re Townsend, 348 F.Supp. 1284 (W.D.Mo. 1972); In re Howard, 344 F.Supp. 1138 (E.D.Ark.1971).

34. Rule 13–400; stays were discretionary under the old provision, 11 U.S.C.A. § 1014. See also 15 Collier ¶ 13–401.01–4.

35. Bankruptcy Reform Act of 1978 § 362(a)(1). The Bankruptcy Reform Act of 1978 will hereinafter be referred to as the "New Act."

36. New Act § 362(b)(7).

37. See § 8.12 supra.

stay will be effective both as to previously commenced judicial, as well as power of sale, foreclosure proceedings.

Chapter Proceedings

The New Act makes significant procedural and substantive changes in the Chapter proceedings. The most significant departure from the current law involves the consolidation into one new "Chapter 11" of the existing Chapters X, XI and XII.[38] This new Chapter not only incorporates existing concepts from the current Chapter proceedings, but adds some new innovations as well.

While the requirements for confirmation of a reorganization plan under the current law vary to some extent from Chapter to Chapter, the new Chapter 11 prescribes a one basic confirmation procedure. In this connection, the New Act avoids the automatic use of either the "absolute priority" rule or the "fair and equitable" test currently associated with Chapter X.[39]

To accept a reorganization plan, two-thirds of creditors in amount and over one-half in number of those voting must vote affirmatively.[40] If all classes of creditors approve the plan, the bankruptcy court need determine only that any dissenting creditors are receiving no less than they would have received in a straight bankruptcy liquidation.[41] Consequently, the absolute priority rule will not be applied.[42]

In the event, however, that a class of creditors refuses to accept the plan, the bankruptcy court, in order to "cram down" the plan, must determine that the dissenting class is not impaired[43] or that the plan is fair and equitable.[44] The "no impairment" requirement is satisfied if the claim holder is paid in cash.[45] A plan will be considered fair and equitable if "the dissenting class is receiving that to which it is entitled under an absolute priority rule, and if it receives nothing, under the plan no junior class may receive anything."[46]

A dissenting real estate mortgagee is in a stronger position under the New Act than under the current law. For example, as we noted earlier, there is case law under the current Chapter XII indicating that a plan can be crammed down notwithstanding the objection of a sole mortgage creditor.[47] Under the new Chapter 11, acceptance by at least one class of creditors is required for confirmation of the plan.[48]

38. King, The New Bankruptcy Code: Many Improvements Over Earlier Law, National Law Journal, Vol. 1, No. 8, 26, 27 (1978).

39. Id. at 27.

40. New Act § 1126.

41. New Act § 1131; King, supra note 38 at 27.

42. King, supra note 38 at 27.

43. New Act § 1124.

44. New Act § 1129.

45. New Act § 1124; King supra note 38 at 27.

46. King, supra note 38 at 27.

47. See § 8.13, supra.

48. New Act § 1129(a)(10).

The current Chapter XIII proceeding is retained and, to some extent, expanded by the New Act and is designated as "Chapter 13." The impact of the New Act on real estate mortgagees is apparently minimal. As under the current law,[49] mortgagees may be made part of the final plan only if they consent to be included within it.[50]

49. See § 8.13 supra.

50. New Act §§ 1301–1330.

§§ 8.15–9.0 are reserved for supplementary material.

CHAPTER 9

SOME PRIORITY PROBLEMS

Table of Sections

A. PURCHASE MONEY MORTGAGES AND AFTER-ACQUIRED PROPERTY CLAUSES

A. PURCHASE MONEY MORTGAGES AND AFTER-ACQUIRED PROPERTY CLAUSES

§ 9.1 Purchase Money Mortgage Priority Concepts

The vendor of land may have security in the property for the payment of the purchase price in a variety of ways. He may frame the transaction in the form of an installment contract for the sale of the land, retaining the legal title in himself.[1] At the opposite extreme, he may have conveyed the property before receiving payment without any agreement for security, in which case he nevertheless may be given an equitable grantor's lien.[2] Or, in this second sort of transaction, he may expressly reserve to himself a security interest which will give to him a consensual equitable mortgage.[3] Finally, he may, either in pursuance of a prior contract or without one, convey title to the buyer, receive at the time part of the purchase money and receive back as part of the same transaction a mortgage upon the property to secure the balance of the purchase money. This last is the ordinary purchase money mortgage and it merits attention because of the special priority accorded it.

It is familiar learning that a purchase money mortgage, executed at the same time with the deed of purchase of land, or in pursuance of agreement as part of one continuous transaction, takes precedence over any other claim or lien attaching to the property through the

1. See § 3.25, supra.

2. See Pomeroy, Equity Juris., § 1250, for a catalogue of the states accepting or rejecting the doctrine. See also, Patterson, Annual Survey of Georgia Law, 7 Mercer L.Rev. 151, 153 (1957).

3. Id.

vendee-mortgagor.[4] This is so even though the claim antedates the execution of the mortgage to the seller.[5] It will also have priority if it is in favor of a third person who advanced the purchase money paid to the vendor,[6] provided the money was loaned for this purpose only. In some states the priority of the purchase money mortgage is provided for by statute.[7] These apply, of course, to the mortgage executed to the grantor and there is a little authority construing them as limiting priority to such mortgages,[8] but the better view and authority extends them to the third party lender of the price.[9] Thus the purchase money mortgage will prevail over a claim of dower,[10] community property,[11] or homestead.[12]

One of the frequent and important instances of its superiority is over liens arising under judgments against the grantee-mortgagor under a judgment obtained and docketed or recorded before the purchase money mortgage is executed.[13] It is given preference also over

4. County of Pinellas v. Clearwater Federal Sav. & Loan Ass'n, 214 So.2d 525 (Fla.App.1968); Royal Bank of Canada v. Clarke, 373 F.Supp. 599 (D.Virgin Islands 1974); Stewart v. Smith, 36 Minn. 82, 30 N.W. 430 (1886).

5. See 29 Va.L.Rev. 491 (1943).

6. Hand Trading Co. v. Daniels, 126 Ga.App. 342, 190 S.E.2d 560 (1972); County of Pinellas v. Clearwater Federal Sav. & Loan Ass'n, 214 So.2d 525 (Fla.App.1968); Stewart v. Smith, 36 Minn. 82, 30 N.W. 430, 1 Am.St.Rep. 624 (1886); Protestant Episcopal Church of the Diocese of Ga. v. E. E. Lowe, 131 Ga. 666, 63 S.E. 136, 127 Am.St.Rep. 243 (1908); Laidley v. Aikin, 80 Iowa 112, 45 N.W. 384, 20 Am.St.Rep. 408 (1890); Hill v. Hill, 185 Kan. 389, 345 P.2d 1015 (1959).

7. E. g., West's Ann.Cal.Civ.Code, § 2898.

8. Heuisler v. Nickum, 38 Md. 270 (1873) and Stansell v. Roberts, 13 Ohio 148, 42 Am.Dec. 193 (1844), where the court relied upon the statutory definition of purchase money mortgages to give the judgment priority. But see, Mut. Aid Bldg. & Loan Co. v. Gashe, 56 Ohio St. 273, 46 N.E. 985 (1897); Ward v. Carey, 39 Ohio St. 361 (1883).

9. Hopler v. Cutler, 34 A. 746 (N.J.Ch. 1896); Bradley v. Bryan, 43 N.J.Eq. 396, 13 A. 806 (1887), semble; Home Owners Loan Corp. v. Humphrey, 148 Kan. 779, 85 P.2d 7 (1938); Kneen v. Halin, 6 Idaho 621, 59 P. 14 (1869); Jackson v. Austin, 15 Johns., N.Y., 477 (1818). See 36 Georgetown L.J. 676 (1948); Mercantile Collection Bureau v. Roach, 195 Cal.App.2d 355, 15 Cal.Rptr. 710 (1961).

10. Stow v. Tift, 15 Johns. 458, 8 Am. Dec. 266 (N.Y.1818); Clark v. Munroe, 14 Mass. 351 (1817); Gilliam v. Moore, 4 Leigh (Va.) 30, 24 Am.Dec 704 (1832); McKinney's N.Y.Real Prop.Law, § 193. In all but two states, Georgia and Kentucky, the former by statute, this is the rule. See Note, 52 L.R.A.,N.S., 541 (1915).

11. Kneen v. Halin, 6 Idaho 621, 59 P. 14 (1899); Davidson v. Click, 31 N.M. 543, 249 P. 100, 47 A.L.R. 1016 (1926).

12. Martin v. First Nat. Bank of Opelika, 279 Ala. 303, 184 So.2d 815 (1966); Lassen v. Vance, 8 Cal. 271, 68 Am.Dec. 322 (1857); Foster Lumber Co. v. Harlan County Bank, 71 Kan. 158, 80 P. 49, 114 Am.St.Rep. 470, 6 Ann.Cas. 44 (1905); Powers v. Pense, 20 Wyo. 327, 123 P. 925, 40 L.R.A.,N.S., 785 (1912). But see Eyster v. Hathaway, 50 Ill. 521, 99 Am. Dec. 537 (1864), with which compare Jones v. Parker, 51 Wis. 218, 8 N.W. 124 (1881); 29 Va.L.Rev. 491, 495 (1943).

13. The cases are numerous. See, e. g., Hand Trading Co. v. Daniels, 126 Ga.App. 342, 190 S.E.2d 560 (1972); Scott, Carhart & Co. v. Warren, 21

other mortgages which have been executed prior to or simultaneously with the purchase money mortgage and fasten upon the property when it is acquired by the mortgagor. Thus it wins over after-acquired property clauses in previously executed mortgages that would cover the subject matter of the purchase money mortgage.[14] This is clear enough because such clauses operate only to create equitable mortgages and consequently cover only the property as it lies in the hands of the mortgagor.[15] Even more clearly this is true if such a mortgage was taken with knowledge that the grantee-mortgagor did not yet have title.[16]

Several rationales have been advanced for this favoritism for the purchase money mortgagee. The most venerable and frequently stated explanation is that of transitory seizin. The idea is that title shot into the grantee and out of him again into the purchase money mortgagee so fleetingly—*quasi uno flattu*, in one breath, as it were—that no other interest had time to fasten itself to it: the grantee-mortgagor must be regarded as a mere conduit.[17] Such a theory breaks down in lien states where the fee remains permanently in the grantee-mortgagor. It also is inconsistent with the cases of quite common occurrence in which some considerable time elapses between the conveyance to the mortgagor and the execution of the mortgage. If the reason were to be taken literally it would require the execution of the deed of purchase and the execution of the mortgage to be practically simultaneous, something that is ordinarily not feasible and not required by the cases. As was said by an able judge in a leading case, "An examination of the cases will show that the real test is not

Ga. 408 (1857); Stewart v. Smith, 36 Minn. 82, 30 N.W. 430, 1 Am.St.Rep. 624 (1886); Joseph v. Donovan, 118 Conn. 80, 171 A. 24 (1934); Holland Jones Co. v. Smith, 152 Va. 707, 148 S.E. 581 (1929).

14. U. S. v. New Orleans R. R., 12 U. S. (12 Wall.) 362, 20 L.Ed. 434 (1870); Faulkner County Bk. & Trust Co. v. Vail, 173 Ark. 406, 293 S.W. 40 (1927); see Chase Nat. Bk. v. Sweezy, 281 N.Y.S. 487 (1931), affirmed, 261 N.Y. 710, 185 N.E. 803 (1933); Pinellas v. Clearwater Savings & Loan Ass'n, 214 So.2d 525 (Fla.App.1968). Louisiana holds the other way. Equitable Securities Co. v. Talbert, 49 La. Ann. 1393, 22 So. 762 (1897).

15. See § 9.3, supra.

16. Fecteau v. Fries, 253 Mich. 51, 234 N.W. 113 (1931), comment, 17 Iowa L.Rev. 99, Hanna, Cas.Security, 3d ed., 867 (1931); Hoffman v. Kleinjan, 54 S.D. 634, 224 N.W. 187 (1929), matter of notice in doubt.

17. The principle is stated in Nash v. Preston, 3 Cro.Car. 190 (1631) and is found in Coke, Litt. § 31a who is cited as authority in early and leading American cases. Stow v. Tift, 15 Johns. 458, 8 Am.Dec. 266 (N.Y. 1918); Scott, Carhart & Co. v. Warren, 21 Ga. 408 (1857). Other important cases accepting the doctrine are Holbrook v. Finney, 4 Mass. 566, 3 Am.Dec. 243 (1808); Adams v. Hill, 29 N.H. 202 (1854); Wheatley's Heirs v. Calhoun, 39 Va. (12 Leigh) 264, 37 Am.Dec. 654 (1841); see Kent, Com., 5th ed., 173, 174. The theory of transitory seizin is also used as an explanation of the priority of the mortgage to a third party lender of the purchase money. Protestant Episcopal Church of the Diocese of Ga. v. E. E. Lowe, 131 Ga. 666, 63 S. E. 136, 127 Am.St.Rep. 243 (1908); Marin v. Knox, 117 Minn. 428, 136 N.W. 15, 40 L.R.A.,N.S., 272 (1912).

whether the deed and mortgage were in fact executed at the same instant, or even on the same day, but whether they were parts of one continuous transaction, and so intended to be, so that the two instruments should be given contemporaneous operation in order to promote the intent of the parties." [18] Again, if the theory has validity, it would seem it should apply to any case where the grantee mortgaged the property the instant he got the conveyance rather than confining it to mortgages for the purchase price in favor of the vendor or a third party lender. And, further, some theory other than transitory seizin would seem necessary to explain the priority of the vendor's purchase money mortgage over that of the third party lender of part of the purchase money insofar, at least, as the latter's priority is said to rest upon the same doctrine.[19] For when this last is this case, the title could just as readily shoot through the grantee-mortgagor as a conduit into the third party as to double back on its course and return to the vendor.

A better statement of the reason for the rule is that the title comes to the purchaser already charged with the encumbrance in favor of the grantor-mortgagor; that regardless of the form all that the transaction ever transfers is the redemption right.[20] While such a conclusion would square with the decisions where the purchase money mortgage goes to the vendor, it is more difficult to apply it to the mortgage going to a third party lender of the purchase price, although it has been advanced in such a case.[21] Furthermore, it would seem that the opposite conclusion could have been reached just as easily. Indeed, it would have been easier to do so, since in form there is a transfer of the full title without reservation, and the grantee then by a separate mortgage instrument creates the charge on it. So, unless the matter is dug into more deeply, one is left unsatisfied as to

18. Mitchell, J., in Stewart v. Smith, 36 Minn. 82, 84, 30 N.W. 430, 431, 1 Am.St.Rep. 624 (1886).

In Wheatley's Heirs v. Calhoun, 12 Leigh 264, 37 Am.Dec. 654 (Va.1841), a purchase money mortgage to the vendor, executed ten months after the conveyance, was held to have priority over the dower rights of the widow of the grantee.

In Ray v. Adams, 4 Hun 332 (N.Y.1875), about a year elapsed after the vendee received title before he executed the previously agreed upon mortgage to secure E, who had loaned part of the purchase price; nevertheless E prevailed over a judgment obtained against the vendee before he obtained title. See, also, Demeter v. Wilcox, 115 Mo. 634, 22 S.W. 613, 37 Am.St. Rep. 422 (1893).

19. And there are cases stating that it does so rest. Moring v. Dickerson, 85 N.C. 466 (1881); Demeter v. Wilcox, 115 Mo. 634, 22 S.W. 613, 37 Am.St.Rep. 422 (1893).

20. See N. J. Bldg., Loan & Inv. Co. v. Bachelor, 54 N.J.Eq. 600, 603, 35 A. 745, 747 (1896).

21. "One who executes a purchase-money mortgage is not regarded as obtaining the title and then placing an incumbrance on it. He is deemed to take the title charged with the incumbrance, which has priority over preexisting claims. And a mortgage given to a third person to orbtain the money used in buying the porperty is entitled to the same preference." Warren Mortgage Co. v. Winters, 94 Kan. 615, 619, 146 P. 1012, 1013, Ann.Cas.1916C, 956 (1915).

why this one of two perfectly possible conclusions has been chosen. A little delving, though, does give more illuminating answers. One is somewhat technical and legalistic, the other more satisfactorily deals with it as a matter of intrinsic fairness based upon the just expectations on the part of the purchase money mortgagee. The first answer suggests that the purchase money mortgage always takes the place of an equitable interest in the property that precedes any lien or interest of any kind attaching to the purchaser's estate at the time of acquiring title.[22] Where there is a prior contract of sale this equitable interest consists of a specifically enforceable contract right to have the purchase money mortgage given on taking title and the equitable estate under the purchase contract is subject to this right. Where there is no prior contract the vendor has left in him on conveying title without receiving payment an equitable vendor's lien. When the purchase money mortgage is given it merely replaces and takes the priority of one or the other of these prior equities, and this is so whether it is given at once or subsequently, provided it is part of the same transaction. The prevalence of the third party lender of the purchase money is an extension of this. He is said to be in the position of an assignee of prior equitable rights of the vendor.[23]

The other answer justifies the doctrine on the equity and justice of protecting one who has parted with his property on the faith of having a security interest in it until the money for which he was exchanging it is received as against persons who, for different reasons, have inferior claims.[24] Certainly the vendor should prevail over claimants of dower, curtesy, community property or homestead rights, for any of these would be acquiring a pure windfall for which he paid nothing and would be getting it out of the unpaid for property of the vendor.[25] As against judgment lien creditors he should win because they have not extended their credit in reliance on the right to be repaid out of *any* specific property, much less out of property previously owned by another and coming to the debtor unpaid for, with the seller of it relying upon that very property he has parted with for his payment. Furthermore, their judgments are obtained before their debtor receives the property to which it attaches on acquisition so they could not have relied upon it in getting their judgment lien. In such a case the general rule that such creditors' rights should rise no higher than their debtors' seems clearly appropriate. As against other mortgagee claimants to the property, especially those who have

22. See Boorum v. Tucker, 51 N.J.Eq. 135, 26 A. 456 (1893), affirmed 52 N.J.Eq. 587, 33 A. 50 (1895); Davidson v. Click, 31 N.M. 543, 249 P. 100, 47 A.L.R. 1016 (1926); Walsh, Mortgages, 168.

23. Protestant Episcopal Church of the Diocese of Ga. v. E. E. Lowe Co., 131 Ga. 666, 63 S.E. 136, 127 Am.St.Rep. 243 (1908); Laidley v. Aikin, 80 Iowa 112, 45 N.W. 384, 20 Am.St.Rep. 408 (1890).

24. See Tiffany, Real Prop., 3d ed., § 1462.

25. See Davidson v. Click, 31 N.M. 543, 249 P. 100, 47 A.L.R. 1016 (1926).

made their loan for the purpose of paying part of the purchase price, the question is closer; for these, unlike the others, have relied upon getting paid out of the same specific property and have parted with value on that reliance. Moreover, third party purchase money mortgagees, especially in residential transactions, often acquire a substantially greater economic stake in the mortgaged property than that retained by the vendor. Even so, the vendor has the edge because the property he is relying on for payment was previously his up to the time of sale and mortgage back; there was never an instant when he relinquished a hold on it; and he would never have parted with it at all except upon the belief and faith that if his buyer defaulted he could either recapture his property or get paid out of it. And this is normally so even though he may know that his buyer is going to finance the deal in part by borrowing some of the purchase money from another and give him a mortgage on the property. Other mortgagees, on the other hand, even including lenders of purchase money, parted only with money in which they retained no interest whatsoever, and placed their reliance for repayment of their debts on getting a security interest in other property not only never previously owned by them but not even owned by the mortgagor at the time the money was loaned, even though they might not have known that fact. This difference in attitude toward the hazard of losing property previously owned and that of not getting an interest in property which had never before belonged to the claimant is an old and important one. Here it justifies preferring the vendor purchase money mortgagee over even the third party lender of the purchase money as well as the mortgagee under an after-acquired property clause. Much the same reasoning applies to the money-lending purchase money mortgagee to give him priority over all but the vendor who comes into competition with him. He relied upon getting security upon this very property and his money went into the payment of it. Without his advance of money, the mortgagor would never have received the property. It is this last feature that serves to bring him in ahead of other mortgagees whose loans were not limited in their use to the acquisition of the property which was to security for repayment. *A fortiori* he prevails over the other types of claimants.

§ 9.2 Purchase Money Mortgages—Recording Act Problems

The priority of a purchase money mortgage is subject to being defeated by the operation of the recording acts. Under most recording acts a mortgagee is protected against a *prior* unrecorded mortgage if he took his mortgage without knowledge and, in some states, if he recorded it first.[26] If the subsequent mortgagee so qualifies, the

26. The two major recording act types in use in the United States are: (1) those which "invalidate or subordinate an unrecorded conveyance as against the rights of a subsequent bona fide purchaser and (2) those which thus protect a subsequent bona fide purchaser provided his convey-

fact that the prior mortgagee was for part of the purchase money is irrelevant. For example, suppose a vendor conveys title and takes back a mortgage, but does not record it. The mortgagor then gives a mortgage to a different mortgagee who takes and records his mortgage without knowledge of the earlier unrecorded mortgage. The subsequent mortgagee will have priority whether or not the subsequent mortgage is for part of the purchase money.[27] Moreover, an anomalous situation can arise where, because of the interplay of the purchase money doctrine and the recording acts, a negligent purchase money mortgagee can create a situation that results in his mortgage being superior to a prior judgment against the mortgagor but not to a subsequent mortgage. For example, suppose J has an outstanding judgment lien against P. L lends money to P to purchase Blackacre from V. V conveys Blackacre to P, which deed is recorded. At the same time P gives a mortgage for the purchase money to L. A few days later X lends money to P and takes and records a mortgage on Blackacre, X having no actual knowledge of L's mortgage; L then records his mortgage. In all probability, L's purchase money mortgage will be prior to J's lien because of the general priority rules governing purchase money mortgages, but junior to X's subsequent mortgage because of the operation of the recording act.[28]

It is common, especially in residential transactions, for purchase money mortgages to be given to both the vendor and to a third party institutional lender. Usually the third party lender finances the bulk of the transaction and the vendor lends a portion of the normally-required down payment. Notwithstanding this greater financial stake of the third party lender in the mortgaged property, the presumption rules regarding purchase-money mortgages produce a result the parties may not anticipate. As between a purchase money mortgage to a third party lender and one to a vendor, the vendor's lien will be superior to that of the third party lender.[29] Most such institutional lenders either are required to, or at least desire to hold first mortgages.[30] The third party lender cannot, however, guarantee this

ance is the first to be recorded." Simes, Handbook for More Efficient Conveyancing, 18–19 (1961). The first type is referred to as a "notice" type statute and the second as a "notice-race" statute. A third type of statute, in effect in only a few states is the "pure race" statute. In this type of statute, priority of right is given to the purchaser who secures priority of record. In this situation, it "is a pure question of race to the records; the purchaser who first records, wins." Id.

27. See, e. g., Royal Bank of Canada v. Clarke, 373 F.Supp. 599 (D.Virgin Islands 1974); Kemp v. Zions First Nat. Bank, 24 Utah 2d 288, 470 P.2d 390 (1970); Jackson v. Reid, 30 Kan. 10, 1 P. 308 (1883). See generally, 26 A.L.R. 171, 173.

28. See, e. g., Thorpe v. Helmer, 275 Ill. 86, 113 N.E. 954 (1916) (intervening judgment lien); Trigg v. Vermillion, 113 Mo. 230, 20 S.W. 1047 (1892) (intervening mortgage). Cf. "So the last shall be first, and the first last." Holy Bible, King James Version, Matt., ch. 20, v. 16.

29. See text at note 25, supra.

30. See § 11.1, infra.

priority status simply by making sure that its mortgage is recorded first, unless, of course, the land is in one of the few jurisdictions having a "race" recording act,[31] under which merely being the first to record assures priority. A couple of hypotheticals will illustrate why this is so. Suppose, for example, that vendor, purchaser and third party lender are each aware that the purchase price will be financed by two purchase money mortgages. Where two such mortgages are going to be utilized, it normally will be known by all of the parties because they will be referred to in the earnest money contract, a copy of which the third party lender routinely requires and examines before approving a loan. In this situation the third party lender cannot gain priority simply by recording first because it will have taken and recorded with knowledge of the vendor's mortgage. While recording first will not, for the same reason, give the vendor priority, the general presumption in favor of vendor purchase money mortgagees probably will.[32] Moreover, even if the third party lender takes and records its mortgage prior to the execution of the vendor's mortgage and without knowledge of it, it cannot rely on the recording act to achieve priority because such legislation normally protects only those without notice who take *subsequent* to an unrecorded instrument.[33] While the vendor will, because of the recording by the third party lender, have at least constructive knowledge of its mortgage and thus will not be protected by the recording act, he nevertheless will again prevail because of the purchase money presumption in his favor. While some courts in the latter situation, at least if the vendor has actual knowledge of the third party mortgage, may be inclined to find an implied agreement on the part of the vendor to subordinate his mortgage to that of the third party lender, the implied agreement must be clearly established.[34]

How then can the third party lender be assured of priority over the vendor? The normal method is to have the vendor subordinate his lien to that of the third party lender.[35] This is usually done by including language in the vendor's mortgage specifically referring to the third party lender's mortgage and declaring its subordination to it. Normally, a vendor will agree to this for at least two reasons. First, he wants the third party mortgage transaction to be approved so that he can sell his property. Second, a vendor who takes a mortgage under such circumstances probably assumes, at the time of the initial transaction at least, that his will be a second mortgage.

31. See note 26, supra.

32. See Schoch v. Birdsall, 48 Minn. 441, 51 N.W. 382 (1892). See also, Note, 40 Harv.L.Rev. 499 (1927); Fecteau v. Fries, 253 Mich. 51, 234 N.W. 113 (1931).

33. See note 26 supra.

34. Ex parte Johnson, 147 S.C. 259, 145 S.E. 113 (1928); Walter v. Kressman, 25 Wyo. 292, 169 P. 3 (1917); Truesdale v. Brennan, 153 Mo. 600, 55 S.W. 147, (1899); Boies v. Benham, 127 N.Y. 620, 28 N.E. 657, 14 L.R.A. 55 (1891).

35. See § 12.9, infra.

Residential transactions also commonly involve two third party purchase money mortgagees, one institutional and one private. The private lender is very often a relative of the purchaser. Suppose, for example, the purchaser is able to supply only five percent of the purchase price himself. Then he arranges for an institutional loan for eighty per cent of the purchase price and a mortgage loan for the remaining fifteen percent from a relative. Both loans are secured by third party purchase money mortgages. Unlike the vendor-third party mortgagee situation discussed in the preceding pargraph, neither lender is benefitted by a legal presumption in his favor. The institutional lender, of course, for the same reasons indicated above, wants to ensure first mortgage status for its loans. Normally simply recording its mortgage first will not achieve this result. In the usual situation, because of questions on its loan application, the institutional lender will be aware of the other third party mortgage. Thus, when it takes its mortgage it will be on notice of the other mortgage. On the other side, of course, the relative's mortgage will likewise not have first mortgage status because at the time the mortgage to the relative is executed, the relative will obviously be aware of the institutional financing. In any event, a prior recording by the institutional lender will provide constructive notice to the relative. Thus neither mortgage will have the benefit of the recording act. If such a situation arises, a court could treat each as a coordinate first lien or alternatively, allow priority to be governed by common law principles and confer first mortgage status on the first mortgage to be delivered.[36]

If, in the above situation, neither the loan application nor other investigation by the institutional lender discloses the existence of another third party purchase money mortgage, the institutional lender will be in a stronger position. This at least will be true where a mortgage has in fact been executed in favor of the relative, but not yet recorded. In such a situation the institutional lender takes its mortgage without knowledge of a prior unrecorded mortgage and, by recording first, its mortgage will prevail. On the other hand, if the institutional mortgage is executed first, the recording act alone cannot be relied upon to confer first mortgage status on that mortgage because the institutional lender will not have taken it *subsequent* to an unrecorded mortgage.[37] Neither will the relative be able to rely on the recording act, because again he will either have actual notice of the institutional mortgage or be on constructive notice of a prior institutional recording.

When the institutional lender is aware of the existence of the mortgage to the relative, the safest course, as in the vendor-mortgagee situation, is to condition the institutional loan on the relative sub-

36. See Browder, Cunningham & Julin, Basic Property Law, 858 (2d Ed.1973).

37. See text at note 33, supra.

ordinating his mortgage in the manner described earlier.[38] Moreover, the relative will probably accede to this condition because he probably assumed in the first place that his would be a second mortgage. In any event, he will agree to subordinate if he really wants his relative to be able to obtain the institutional loan.

§ 9.3 After-Acquired Property Clauses

Traditionally some mortgages have commonly included not only a description of the specific real estate being mortgaged, but also a clause purporting to mortgage all after acquired realty and personalty as well. Although the history of these clauses is long, complex and sometimes contradictory,[39] two commentators have summarized their current status as follows: "In * * * some * * * states, the after-acquired property clause is effective to create an equitable lien upon both real and personal property subsequently acquired by the mortgagor regardless of the character of the business in which the mortgagor is engaged, provided the new property bears a functional relation to the property originally mortgaged. In other states the after-acquired property clause is effective to create an equitable lien upon both realty and personalty if the mortgagor is a railroad or other public utility company, but is effective only with respect to realty if not within that class." [40] Moreover, there are some jurisdictions that seem to recognize the validity of such clauses with few, if any, of the qualifications mentioned above.[41] It should be noted that the equitable lien created by the clause arises only when the property is acquired and it is subject to any liens placed on it prior to the mortgagor's acquisition of it.[42] In addition, the lien of the clause will nor-

38. See text at note 35, supra. See § 12.9, infra.

39. See Cohen and Gerber, The After-Acquired Property Clause, 87 U. of Pa.L.Rev. 635 (1939); Glenn Mortgages, § 409; Durfee, Cases on Security, 457–459 (1951); Francis, Mortgages of After-Acquired Property in Kentucky, 35 Ky.L.J. 320 (1947); Ethridge, The After-Acquired Property Doctrine and Its Application in Mississippi, 17 Miss.L.J. 153 (1945); After-Acquired Property Clauses—51 Tulane L.Rev. 314 (La.1941); Note, Mortgages—After-Acquired Property Clause in Mortgage Is Valid, 28 Rocky Mt.L.Rev. 432 (1956), commenting on United States v. Westmoreland Manganese Corp., 134 F. Supp. 898 (E.D.Ark.1955); Note, After-Acquired Property and the Title Search, 24 Ford.L.Rev. 412 (1955), commenting on Fries v. Clearview Gardens Sixth Corp., 285 App.Div. 568, 139 N.Y.S.2d 573 (2d Dept.1955). See also, Arnold, After-Acquired Property as Mortgage Security in Maryland, 19 Md.L.Rev. 294 (1959). For a thorough examination of the problem of after-acquired property clauses in mortgages, see Cunningham and Tischler, Equitable Real Estate Mortgages, 17 Rutgers L.Rev. 679, 715–723 (1963).

40. Cunningham & Tischler, supra note 39 at 718.

41. See Rose v. Lurton, 111 Fla. 424, 149 So. 557 (1933); American Nat. Bank of Jacksonville v. International Harvester Credit Corp., 269 So.2d 726 (Fla.App.1972), modified in part 296 So.2d 32 (Sup.1974); Hickson Lumber Co. v. Gay Lumber Co., 150 N.C. 281, 63 S.E. 1048 (1909); Note, 28 Rocky Mtn. L.Rev. 432, 433 (1956).

42. Central Trust Co. of New York v. Kneeland, 138 U.S. 414, 423, 11 S.Ct. 357, 359, 34 L.Ed. 1014 (1891).

mally be subordinate to any purchase money mortgage given by the mortgagor to acquire the property.[43]

While several theories supporting the validity of after-acquired property clauses have been advanced,[44] the one most commonly adopted is the "specific performance" theory. Under this theory, the clause is treated as a promise to mortgage after-acquired property which will be specifically enforced when the mortgagor later acquires the property.[45] As one New Jersey case noted, "it is familiar learning, found in all cases, that a mortgage upon after-acquired property cannot rise higher than a contract to convey the title to that property when acquired, and a suit for its enforcement is, in effect, a suit for the specific performance of a contract." [46]

The Uniform Commercial Code, with minor exceptions, formally authorizes the use of after-acquired property clauses in chattel security agreements.[47] Thus, today where a lien on after-acquired chattels is desired, the more common practice is to perfect a chattel security agreement containing such a clause rather than to rely on a real estate mortgage to accomplish that purpose. Accordingly, our further consideration of the after-acquired property concept will focus primarily on the real estate setting.

In considering the impact of after-acquired property clauses on real estate, it is important to distinguish between the mortgagor's placing of improvements on *Blackacre*, the land specifically described in the mortgage, and the subsequent acquisition by the mortgagor of *Whiteacre*. While an after-acquired property clause is necessary to reach Whitacre it is not with respect to the subsequent improvements on Blackacre. To the extent that such improvements are considered fixtures or, as Professor Glenn has pointed out, "if the mortgagor brings upon the premises a thing which by its very nature becomes a part of the land by virtue of the law of real property, the mortgagee may enjoy the resulting benefit without the need of an after-acquired property clause." [48] To state the foregoing, however, does not answer numerous and substantial priority questions, which would not be necessarily altered or resolved even if an after-acquired

See Cunningham and Tischler, Equitable Real Estate Mortgages, 17 Rutgers L.Rev. 679, 721 (1963).

43. See § 9.1, supra; Comment, Mortgages—After-Acquired Property Clause in Mortgage is Valid, 28 Rocky Mtn.L.Rev. 432, 433 (1956).

44. See 4 American Law of Property, § 1634.

45. See Cunningham & Tischler, supra note 39 at 718–719.

46. Daly v. New York & G.L.R. Co., 55 N.J.Eq. 595, 603, 38 A. 202, 205 (1897).

47. With certain exceptions relating to consumer goods, "a security agreement may provide that any and all obligations covered by the security agreement are to be secured by after-acquired collateral." U.C.C. § 9–204(1) (1972). See also § 9–204(3) of the 1962 Code.

See Bailey, Secured Transactions, 71–73 (1976).

48. 3 Glenn, Mortgages, 1450 (1943).

property clause is used. Suppose, for example, a house is built on vacant land on which there is a preexisting mortgage. To say that the house becomes covered by that mortgage does not resolve the problem of what happens if the building contractor is not paid. The question then becomes one of priority between the mortgage and a possible mechanics lien, a problem we study in detail in a later section.[49] Or suppose that a furnace is installed in a house on which there is a pre-existing real estate mortgage. Again, to say that, as a fixture, the furnace is covered by the real estate mortgage, does not answer the difficult question of who has priority, as between the real estate mortgagee and the holder of a purchase money security interest in the furnace.[50]

The use of after-acquired property clauses to obtain a lien on the mortgagor's subsequently acquired Whiteacre is subject to a substantial and, perhaps, overriding difficulty because the nature of the recording acts. While the mortgagee's equitable lien is valid as to parties subsequently acquiring an interest in Whiteacre with notice of the after-acquired property clause, the problem, of course, is to determine what constitutes constructive notice under state recording acts. Suppose, for example, that R gives a mortgage on Blackacre to X containing an after-acquired property clause. R then acquires Whiteacre and later borrows money from Z and gives Z a mortgage on Whiteacre as security. If Whiteacre is not in the same county as Blackacre, unless a court is willing, as one has, to say that the recording of the Blackacre mortgage "is effectual notice against the world," [51] it should not constitute constructive notice to Z because the records in each county relate only to land within that county.[52]

Suppose, however, that Blackacre and Whiteacre are in the same county. It is often said that a party does not obtain constructive notice of a recorded document that could not have been discovered by a reasonably diligent search or, as it is sometimes said, a document that is not in his chain of title.[53] The problem then is to determine what constitutes a reasonable search in the after-acquired property clause context. All jurisdictions presumably have grantor-grantee indexes in each county and, in theory, in examining title to Whiteacre, a person could examine every mortgage given at any time by all grantors in the chain of title or, at least, every mortgage that the proposed borrower may have executed previously. Such a search would seem to be unrealistically burdensome and unreasonable. As commentators have pointed out, "it is not customary to attempt to check the grantor index against any former owner *before* he acquired

49. See § 12.4, infra.

50. See §§ 9.4–9.7, infra.

51. Hickson Lumber Co. v. Gay Lumber Co., 150 N.C. 281, 63 S.E. 1048 (1909).

52. 3 Glenn, Mortgages, 1657 (1943).

53. Storke and Sears, The Perennial Problem of Security Priority and Recordation, 24 Rocky Mtn.L.Rev. 180, 194 (1952).

title or *after* he parted with it." [54] Moreover, the situation is not improved in those states that maintain an official tract index. Since the mortgage containing the after-acquired property clause will not contain a legal description of the subsequently acquired Whiteacre, it cannot show up in a tract index that deals with Whiteacre. Thus, Professor Glenn was surely correct when he stated that "the mortgage [containing the after-acquired property clause] is of record all right, but the difficulty is that it will not show up in the chain of title that relates to the new property." [55] Although there is some division of authority,[56] it seems difficult to visualize a court determining that the effort necessary to discover an after-acquired property clause is part of a reasonable title search.

Professor Glenn has suggested that where the mortgagor is a large corporation, subsequent parties ought to be on notice that the corporation probably has outstanding a general corporate mortgage containing an after-acquired property clause.[56a] Presumably he is suggesting that the party examining title in such a situation be required to examine every document given by the corporate mortgagor, including even those given prior to its acquisition of title to the parcel in question, to determine whether such a clause exists.

The Uniform Land Transactions Act (ULTA), promulgated in 1975 by the National Conference of Commissioners on Uniform State Laws, but as of this writing not adopted by any state, expressly recognises the validity an after-acquired real estate clause except in certain situations where the mortgagor is giving real estate security for residential real estate that he will or does occupy.[57] In the latter situation an after-acquired property clause will not attach to subsequently acquired real estate unless it is contiguous to the parcel described in the mortgage or unless the subsequently acquired property is itself described in the original mortgage.[58] While the explicit recognition of the validity of after-acquired property clauses is welcome, the ULTA can be criticized for not dealing with the problems of constructive notice discussed in the preceding paragraphs. Until those problems are resolved, the after-acquired property clauses will pose hazards not only for title examiners, but for the parties relying on the clauses as well.

54. Id. at 194. See also, Cunningham & Tischler, supra note 39 at 721.

55. 3 Glenn, Mortgages, 1658 (1943).

56. See Glenn, supra note 55 at § 418.

56a. Id. at § 418. See Cunningham & Tischler, supra note 39 at 721–722.

57. U.L.T.A. § 3–205(b) (1975).

58. Id.

B. FIXTURES

§ 9.4 Introduction

Conflicts in priority often arise between real estate mortgagees and claimants of chattel interests in goods attached to the real estate that are classified as "fixtures". What is classified as a fixture varies widely from state to state. Perhaps no more precise definition is available than this: "a fixture is a former chattel which, while retaining its separate physical identity, is so connected with the realty that a disinterested observer would consider it a part thereof." [59] Suppose that a real estate mortgage is executed and recorded, and the mortgagor purchases central air conditioning or a furnace or some other item that becomes a "fixture". If it becomes a fixture, under the normal rules of real property it becomes part of the real estate and therefore covered by the real estate mortgage.[60] However, to state that, as a fixture, the air conditioning or the furnace is covered by the real estate mortgage, does not answer the difficult question of who has priority, as between the real estate mortgagee and the holder of a purchase-money security interest in the air conditioning apparatus or the furnace. This type of problem and numerous variations thereon are considered in the following sections.

Fixture provisions in the Uniform Commercial Code have ameliorated the historically inconsistent treatment of fixture conflicts between chattel and real estate mortgagees.[61] However, the status of these mortgagees still varies according to jurisdiction because many states have not yet replaced the original 1962 UCC provisions with the amendatory 1972 version.[62] Familiarity with both versions is necessary at this time, but ultimately the 1972 version is more important.[63] Rather than detail both versions, the following format will be used: (1) law prior to the UCC will be surveyed to establish the historical derivation of the code and the problems it was intended to remedy; (2) general aspects of both the 1962 and 1972 fixture provisions will be examined; and (3) specific priority problems will be analyzed, including major distinctions between the initial and revised codes where appropriate, to clarify the current status of fixture law.

59. 5 American Law of Property § 19.-1 at 3–4 (1952).

60. Nelson & Whitman, Real Estate Finance & Development 421 (1976).

61. See generally, Hawkland, The Proposed Amendments to Article 9 of the UCC—Part 3: Fixtures, 77 Com. L.J. 43 (1972); Berry, Priority Conflicts Between Fixture Secured Creditors and Real Estate Claimants, 7 Memphis St.U.L.Rev. 209 (1977).

62. As of 1978, the 1972 revision of § 9–313 governing fixtures has been adopted in Arizona, Arkansas, California, Illinois, Iowa, Kansas, Nevada, North Carolina, North Dakota, Oregon, Texas, Virginia, West Virginia, and Wisconsin.

63. Because of its shortcomings, the 1962 version was simply omitted from the UCC enactments in California and Iowa.

§ 9.5 Fixtures—Pre-UCC Law

In theory, a few major doctrines summarize pre-UCC law. In reality, however, fixture conflicts were resolved on an ad-hoc case law basis regardless of the particular rule a state purportedly followed. Moreover, it is important to emphasize, at this stage, that these common law methods normally did not rely on recording statutes or concepts in resolving priority conflicts between chattel and real estate mortgagees. As a result, chaos often prevailed not only among the states, but also within the case law of each state.

One approach was represented by the Massachusetts Rule.[64] Under this rule there was a strong presumption that articles affixed to real estate became a part of that real estate. Moreover, once an item was classified as a fixture, in conflicts between the chattel and real estate mortgagees, the latter normally prevailed. The doctrine was originally based on the severely legalistic ground that the mortgagee got legal title and consequently acquired all additions which became a part of the realty, the mortgagor having no power "by any agreement made with a third person after execution of the mortgage, to give to such person the right to hold anything to be attached to the freehold, which as between mortgagor and mortgagee would become part of the realty." [65] The purchase money chattel mortgagee was not simply relegated to a subordinate lienor's position. His security interest was instead rendered non-existent since the chattel was deemed likewise non-existent. The rule was a harsh one, giving to mortgagees, when strictly applied, some substantial windfalls. It was not surprising, therefore, to find courts avoiding the rule by going to extremes in declaring heavy and firmly affixed objects not to be fixtures at all.[66] Indeed Professor Gilmore suggested perhaps the Massachusetts rule did not exist at all or that the cases all "involve a factual variant which is not present in the majority cases or that accident rather than design has led some courts to accept a deviant formulation of a rule." [67]

The great weight of authority rejected the Massachusetts approach. Although the rationale for the results often varied, the majority approach was more pro-chattel mortgagor. When an attached

64. Clary v. Owen, 81 Mass. (15 Gray) 522 (1860); Berry, supra note 61 at 210.

65. Clary v. Owen, 81 Mass. (15 Gray) 522, 525 (1860). See Niles, The Intention Test in the Law of Fixtures, 12 N.Y.U.L.Q.R. 66, 73, 91 (1934).

66. Carpenter v. Walker, 140 Mass. 416, 5 N.E. 160 (1886), engine and boiler weighing 5600 pounds, and heavy planing and joining machinery fastened to the floor and connected with a central power shaft; Commercial Credit Corp. v. Gould, 275 Mass. 48, 175 N.E. 264 (1931), frigidaire system in apartment building, including compressor in basement with pipes to units in each apartment; Medford Trust Co. v. Priggen Steel Garage Co., 273 Mass. 349, 174 N.E. 126 (1930), sheet metal garages on cement pillars, one with cement floor; part of mortgage money even expressly advanced to pay for garages.

67. Gilmore, Security Interests in Personal Property, 759 (1965).

article became a fixture, the majority approach favored the purchase money chattel mortgagee over the prior real estate mortgagee so long as removal of the chattel did not substantially injure the real estate.[68] When the real estate mortgage was subsequent to the purchase money chattel mortgage, the real estate mortgagee prevailed if he had no notice of the chattel mortgage and if he could reasonably have believed that the object in question was within the coverage of his mortgage.[69] Courts differed substantially, however, as to what constituted notice and while the majority approach seemed somewhat uniform, results varied from jurisdiction to jurisdiction.

The Uniform Conditional Sales Act (UCSA) emerged from this case law as precursor of the UCC. Unlike its common law predecessors the UCSA utilized real property recording procedures to resolve fixture priority.[70] The UCSA left state law fixture definitions intact. Section 7 of the act divided chattels sold on conditional sale which have been affixed to realty so as to become a part thereof into two classes: those that could and those that could not be severed "wholly or in any portion without material injury to the freehold." If they fell into the first class, the reservation of title was void against subsequent purchasers, who included mortgagees of the land for value and without notice of the vendor's title, unless the sales agreement, describing briefly the realty and stating that the goods are to be affixed to it, is recorded in the realty records before the purchase.[71] If they fell into the second class, they could not be removed without the consent of any person who has not assented to the reservation, a catego-

68. See Storke and Sears, The Perennial Problem of Security Priority and Recordation, 24 Colo.L.Rev. 180, 203–205 (1952).

69. "The exact question has often arisen in other states, and the overwhelming weight of authority is to the effect that the title of the seller of personal property of this character, which title is to be held by him until the price thereof is paid, and which is afterwards affixed to land of the vendee, so as to become part of the realty, is subject to the lien of a subsequent mortgagee in good faith without notice of the reserved title. This is fully shown in the elaborate note of Mr. Freeman to Fuller-Warren Co. v. Harter, 110 Wis. 80, 85 N.W. 698, 53 L.R.A. 603 (1901) in 84 Am.St.Rep. at pages 892 and 893, and also in the notes to Muir v. Jones, 23 Or. 332, 31 P. 646 (1893) in 19 L.R.A. 444, and Lawton, etc., Co. v. Ross-Kellar, etc., Co., 33 Okl. 59, 124 P. 43 (1912) in 49 L.R.A.,N.S., at page 396, to which we refer for a list of the cases." Oakland Bank of Savings v. California Pressed Brick Co., 183 Cal. 295, 302, 191 P. 524, 527 (1920), commented on 8 Cal.L.Rev. 442 (1920); Alf Holding Corp. v. American Stove Co., 253 N.Y. 450, 171 N.E. 703 (1930), noted 5 St. John's L.Rev. 120, semble. See notes, 23 Geo.L.J. 563 (1935); 1 Idaho L.J. 199 (1931); 16 Iowa L.Rev. 116 (1926); 1927, 21 Ill. L.Rev. 517 (1927); 10 Minn.L.Rev. 348 (1930); 32 Harv.L.Rev. 732 (1919).

70. See Hawkland, supra note 61.

71. In his notes on this provision of the Uniform Act (2–A Uniform Laws, Annotated, § 64), George G. Bogert says: "The theory of the Act is that a conditional seller of a fixture should be given protection and allowed to retain title as security for the payment of the price of the fixture, but that in order to retain such title he should be required to give notice adapted as nearly as possible to reaching dealers in real property." * * *

ry that included prior mortgagees of the land and subsequent mortgagees with notice. Recordation by the conditional vendor was immaterial because in such cases the attempt to reserve title was itself ineffectual.

As to subsequent mortgagees, if the annexed chattel was in the first class, those that could be removed without material injury to the freehold, the conditional vendor prevailed if the contract was properly recorded in the realty books; but if it was not, the reservation of title was void if the subsequent mortgagee took without notice and for value.[72]

The UCSA was adopted by only a dozen states. Moreover, UCSA issues were rendered moot due to immediate, widespread acceptance of the UCC's initial fixture provisions in 1962.[73]

§ 9.6 Fixtures Under the UCC

The purpose of both the 1962 original and 1972 amended UCC fixture provisions of the UCC was simply to specify the order of priorities, based on state law definitions of what is a fixture. In theory, there was no intent to promulgate a uniform definition of fixtures which would encroach upon local realty laws.[74] Thus, much of the pre-UCC case law is still relevant.[75] Two reasons were asserted for perpetuating this local law: (1) the generalized nature of a uniform law was inadequate to meet the needs of diverse local circumstances; and (2) laws pertaining to traditionally unique real property were deeply entrenched; a wholesale attempt at displacement would simply have caused omission of the fixture provisions from states' enactments of the UCC.[76]

It should be noted that UCC provisions govern priorities only when a chattel security interest is involved.[77] However, the influence

72. American Laundry Mach. Co. v. Larson, 217 Wis. 208, 257 N.W. 608 (1934). See 19 N.D.Law. 254 (1944). As to subsequent mortgages under the Massachusetts act, look at Security Co-op. Bank of Brockton v. Holland Furnace Co., 274 Mass. 389, 174 N.E. 721 (1931).

73. For thorough discussions of the fixture provisions in Article 9 of the Uniform Commercial Code are Coogan, Security Interests in Fixtures Under the Uniform Commercial Code, 75 Harv.L.Rev. 1319 (1962); Gilmore, Purchase Money Priority, 76 Harv.L. Rev. 1333 (1963); Shanker, Fixture Security Interests, 73 Yale L.Jour. 788 (1964); Shanker, A Further Critique of the Fixture Section of the Uniform Commercial Code, VI Boston College Industrial and Commercial L. Rev. 61 (1964); Kripke, Fixtures Under the Uniform Commercial Code, 64 Col.L.Rev. 44 (1964); Coogan & Clovis, The Uniform Commercial Code and Real Estate Law, 38 Ind.L.J. 535 (1963); Coogan, Public Notice and Chattel Security Law, 47 Iowa L.Rev. 289, 326 (1962); Hollander, Imperfections in the Perfection of Ohio Fixture Liens, 14 W.Res.L.Rev. 633 (1963); Project: California Chattel Security and Article Nine of the Uniform Commercial Code, 8 U.C.L.A.L. Rev. 812, 931–942 (1961).

74. U.C.C. § 9–313(3) and Comment 3 (1972).

75. White & Summers, Uniform Commercial Code 927 (1972).

76. See note 63, supra.

77. U.C.C. § 9–313 Comment 4 (1972).

reasonably to be expected from virtual nationwide adoption would seem likely to affect case law concerning conflicts between real estate mortgagees and chattel claimants other than secured parties. To maximize understanding of the ensuing topics the 1972 draft of UCC 9-313 should be read carefully before proceeding further.[78] In addi-

78. Reading of both the 1962 and 1972 versions is strongly advised. The full text of the 1972 provision is set cut herein:

§ 9–913. Priority of Security Interests in Fixtures

(1) In this section and in the provisions of Part 4 of this Article referring to fixture filing, unless the context otherwise requires

(a) goods are "fixtures" when they become so related to particular real estate that an interest in them arises under real estate law.

(b) a "fixture filing" is the filing in the office where a mortgage on the real estate would be filed or recorded of a financing statement covering goods which are or are to become fixtures and conforming to the requirements of subsection (5) of Section 9–402.

(c) a mortgage is a "construction mortgage" to the extent that it secures an obligation incurred for the construction of an improvement on land including the acquisition cost of the land, if the recorded writing so indicates.

(2) A security interest under this Article may be created in goods which are fixtures or may continue in goods which become fixtures, but no security interest exists under this Article in ordinary building materials incorporated into an improvement on land.

(3) This Article does not prevent creation of an encumbrance upon fixtures pursuant to real estate law.

(4) A perfected security interest in fixtures has priority over the conflicting interest of an encumbrancer or owner of the real estate where

(a) the security interest is a purchase money security interest, the interest of the encumbrancer or owner arises before the goods becomes fixtures, the security interest is perfected by a fixture filing before the goods become fixtures or within ten days thereafter, and the debtor has an interest of record in the real estate or is in possession of the real estate; or

(b) the security interest is perfected by a fixture filing before the interest of the encumbrancer or owner is of record, the security interest has priority over any conflicting interest of a predecessor in title of the encumbrancer or owner, and the debtor has an interest of record in the real estate or is in possession of the real estate; or

(c) the fixtures are readily removable factory or office machines or readily removable replacements of domestic appliances which are consumer goods, and before the goods become fixtures the security interest is perfected by any method permitted by this Article; or

(d) the conflicting interest is a lien on the real estate obtained by legal or equitable proceedings after the security interest was perfected by any method permitted by this Article.

(5) A security interest in fixtures, whether or not perfected, has priority over the conflicting interest of an encumbrancer or owner of the real estate where

(a) the encumbrancer or owner has consented in writing to the security interest or has disclaimed an interest in the goods as fixtures; or

(b) the debtor has a right to remove the goods as against

tion, the following UCC terminology must be distinguished:[79] (1) "attach": fulfillment of requisites specified in UCC 9-204 for creation of an enforceable security interest in personalty; (2) "affix": the physical act of joining or fastening personalty to land; (3) "perfect": unless noted otherwise, the act of filing in order to establish priority;[80] and (4) "fixture filing": the filing of notice in the same office and by the same procedure used for recording real property interests.[81]

Although local law defining fixtures is still applicable,[82] the UCC has to some extent influenced these local fixture concepts by its apparent recognition of three classes of goods. Authorities uniformly accept this so-called "tri-partite" concept, which consists of the three following classes situated on a continuum: (1) incorporated building materials; (2) fixtures; and (3) purely personal property.[83]

Under the UCC, "ordinary building materials incorporated into an improvement on land" are deemed fixtures,[84] in spite of its avowed intent not to define but only to establish priority. However, there is no change in result since the UCC specifies that these fixtures may not be the subject of a chattel security interest after incorporation.[85] It should be emphasized that this prohibition does not affect rights of

the encumbrancer or owner. If the debtor's right terminates, the priority of the security interest continues for a reasonable time.

(6) Notwithstanding paragraph (a) of subsection (4) but otherwise subject to subsections (4) and (5), a security interest in fixtures is subordinate to a construction mortgage recorded before the courts become fixtures if the goods become fixtures before the completion of the construction. To the extent that it is given to refinance a construction mortgage, a mortgage has this priority to the same extent as the construction mortgage.

(7) In cases not within the preceding subsections, a security interest in fixtures is subordinate to the conflicting interest of an encumbrancer or owner of the related real estate who is not the debtor.

(8) When the secured party has priority over all owners and encumbrancers of the real estate, he may, on default, subject to the provisions of Part 5, remove his collateral from the real estate but he must reimburse any encumbrancer or owner of the real estate who is not the debtor and who has not otherwise agreed for the cost of repair of any physical injury, but not for any diminution in value of the real estate caused by the absence of the goods removed or by any necessity of replacing them. A person entitled to reimbursement may refuse permission to remove until the secured party gives adequate security for the performance of this obligation.

79. See White & Summers, supra note 75, at 927 n. 64.

80. U.C.C. § 9–313(4)(b) (1972).

81. U.C.C. §§ 9–313(1)(b), 9–401, 9–402, 9–403 (1972).

82. White & Summers, supra note 75 at 927.

83. U.C.C. § 9–313 Comment 3 (1972); Hawkland, supra note 61 at 46; Adams, Security Interests in Fixtures Under Mississippi's Uniform Commercial Code, 47 Miss.L.J. 831, 836 (1976).

84. U.C.C. § 9–313(2) and Comment 2 (1972).

85. Id.

enforcement against the debtor personally as opposed to against the actual materials.[86]

At the opposite extreme of the continuum is purely personal property. Upon first reading the UCC fixture scheme, one may form a common misconception that realty claimants can somehow prevail as to such property. Goods that are purely personal property do not become part of real estate mortgage, even though a chattel security interest is never perfected, merely because the goods are located on the mortgaged property.[87] For example, personalty such as stereo components or household furniture would not be subject to a real estate mortgage simply because they were situated inside a mortgaged home.

Fixtures, the dual-natured intermediate class, are thus the only items of concern under the UCC priority system. Rather than usurp local fixture definitions, the UCC draftsmen attempted to leave law untouched and focused instead on the concept of fixture filing as the method to regulate priorities.[88] In contrast to the common law, this system is based on filing and certain preferred status classes. It favors chattel mortgagees in most instances. This is predicated on the drafters' belief that fixture priority for real estate mortgages would generally be an undeserved windfall not contemplated in original mortgage agreements. Chattel mortgagees can usually assure priority by filing, thus undercutting the importance of preserving state law definitions which formerly tended to favor realty interests. Note that the act of fixture filing is not an admission or inference of fixture status.[89] Chattel security holders are encouraged to file according to both chattel and fixture rules, so the filing of notice in real estate records may be merely a precaution.

In order to accommodate real estate lending interests, one of the primary changes in the 1972 code was to increase the importance of fixture filing, as will be explained in greater detail below. Under the 1962 provisions, basic priority was given to unperfected chattel interests in most situations. Perfection by fixture filing under the 1962 version merely reinforced the chattel claimants' relative superiority.

Subsequent Real Estate Mortgages

As stated in the official comments, the basic rule of the 1972 code is identical to the usual conveyancing rule for real property: as between a subsequent mortgagee and a prior chattel security interest in fixtures, the first party to fixture file or record his real estate mortgage attains priority.[90] Under this general tenet, a subsequent realty mortgagee cannot obtain priority over fixtures (with the ex-

86. Id.

87. U.C.C. § 9–313 Comment 4 (1972).

88. The Priority Rules of Article Nine, 62 Cornell L.Rev. 834, 920 (1977).

89. U.C.C. § 9–313 Comment 1 (1972).

90. Id. Comment 4(b).

ception of incorporated building materials) so long as the antecedent chattel claim was properly perfected by a fixture filing. Such notice of a fixture interest in the chain of title alerts subsequent purchasers and mortgagees. The fixture filing is an absolute requirement. Otherwise, this provision of the 1972 code will not operate to prefer chattel lienors over realty mortgagees. Thus, this basic priority rule favoring chattel financers requires the goods to (1) become fixtures, and (2) also be perfected by fixture filing, both occurring before the subsequent realty mortgage is recorded.

In comparison, the 1962 code initially specifies that even unperfected chattel security interests are superior to subsequent real estate interests.[91] It then qualifies this priority, however, by a broad exception: if not perfected by fixture filing, the priority is lost to subsequent good faith purchasers for value, i. e., bona fide purchasers, and lien creditors without knowledge of the unrecorded fixture security interest.[92]

Prior Real Estate Mortgagees

Even though a real estate mortgage precedes a chattel mortgagee's interest, the 1972 code nevertheless awards priority to the chattel claim if (1) it is a purchase money security interest, and (2) a fixture filing was made before or within ten days after the goods were affixed to the premises so as to become fixtures.[93] Several justifications were offered for this subordination of the realty mortgagee and these center on an historical preference for purchase money interests. Commentators note that the real estate mortgagee normally did not rely on the fixture as being part of his security in the original agreement. Moreover, the improvement often enhances the real estate value and, thereby, benefits the real estate mortgagee. To award the mortgagee priority over the subsequently installed fixture would arguably give him an undeserved, unbargained-for windfall.[94]

However, suppose the chattel security interest arises after the goods become fixtures. Since no purchase money security interest is involved, the real estate mortgagee receives priority under both the 1962 and 1972 codes.[95] The debtor is not buying and affixing new goods to improve the freehold, but, rather, he is attempting to borrow against existing property on which the real estate mortgagee may have relied.[96]

In contrast to the 1972 requisite of fixture filing within a ten day grace period, the 1962 code specifies priority for purchase money

91. Schroeder, Security Interests in Fixtures, 1975 Ariz.St.L.J. 319, 321 (1975).

92. Id.

93. U.C.C. § 9–313(4)(a) and Comment 4(a) (1972): Schroeder, supra note 91 at 320–329.

94. Supra note 94.

95. Schroeder, supra note 91 at 320–321.

96. Id. at 321.

security interests in fixtures even though the security interests were never perfected.[97] This rule, especially, was one that upset real estate lending proponents.[98] The 1972 code prefers chattel financers, only if they file within ten days after the fixtures in question are affixed to the realty.

Construction Mortgages

Construction mortgagees, for a variety of reasons, pay out the proceeds of their loans on an installment basis as the construction of the building progresses.[99] In an attempt to ensure that these subsequent advances relate back to the original date of the mortgage for priority purposes, construction mortgagees include "future advances" clauses in construction mortgages. Thus, construction mortgagees claim to give new value in the form of these future advances to a much greater extent than chattel mortgagees of fixtures installed during construction. Naturally, therefore, the construction mortgagees want to claim such fixtures as part of their security.

The 1962 code was unfavorable towards the interests of the construction lender. Under the 1962 version, "a creditor with a prior encumbrance of record on the real estate [will take priority] to the extent that he makes subsequent advances if * * * the subsequent advance under the prior encumbrance is made or contracted for without knowledge of the security interest and before it was perfected."[1] As a result of this provision, where a construction mortgagee advances money to the mortgagor-owner who then, instead of using the money to pay cash for certain articles needed for the building project, buys them on credit subject to purchase money security interests, if the articles become fixtures, the chattel security will have priority over the construction mortgage.[2] The underlying premise is that the "construction mortgagee must protect himself by policing the debtor's use of advances or by withholding part of the loan to discharge the liens of unpaid suppliers." [3] On the other hand, if the advance by the construction mortgagee is made *after* the articles have been installed as fixtures, the construction mortgage will have priority over the chattel security unless, prior to the advance, he knew of the chattel security interest or the chattel security interest has been perfected.[4] The theory here was to protect the construction mortgagee "from a danger against which he could not effectively guard—

97. Id. at 320; Funk, The Proposed Revision of Article 9 of the Uniform Commercial Code, 26 Bus.Law. 1465, 1471 (1972).

98. Funk, supra note 97 at 1471.

99. See §§ 12.7, 12.1, infra.

1. U.C.C. § 9–313(4)(c) (1962). See The Priority Rules of Article Nine, 62 Cornell L.Rev. 834, 924 (1977).

2. Adams, Security Interests in Fixtures Under Mississippi's Uniform Commercial Code, 47 Miss.L.J. 831, 852 (1976).

3. Id. at 852.

4. Id. at 852; U.C.C. § 9–313(4)(c) (1962).

making an advance on the supposedly existing security of additions already made to the land when there are unknown and undiscoverable claims against those additions in favor of others." [5]

The 1972 code provides special protection for the construction mortgagee. As one commentator has noted, "as to any goods that become fixtures during the course of construction, the construction mortgagee enjoys priority to the extent of all advances made under the mortgage to finance the construction, including the cost of acquiring the land." [6] Such advances even prevail over purchase money security interests in such goods [7] and, moreover, it makes no difference whether the advances are "optional" or "obligatory." [8] The benefit of this priority is available to both assignees of the construction mortgage and to refinancing mortgagees.[9]

Exceptions Favoring Fixture Financers

A real estate mortgagee with priority may consent to subordinate his claim to the security interest of the fixture financer.[10] Whether to avoid costly litigation, because he is fair-minded, or for other reasons as to which one might speculate, a mortgagee might give such consent if, for example, he had priority because a subsequent fixture financer did not file his purchaser money interest within the ten day grace period. Under the 1962 code, the situation might arise where

5. Adams, supra note 2 at 853.

6. Id. at 908. In order to qualify as a construction mortgage, a mortgage must secure "an obligation incurred for the construction of an improvement on land." 1972 Official Text with Comments, § 9–313(1)(c).

7. See Funk, The Proposed Revision of Article 9 of the Uniform Commercial Code, 26 Bus.Law. 1465, 1472 (1972).

8. Comment 4(e), § 9–313 (1972).

9. Schroeder, Security Interests in Fixtures, 1975 Ariz.St.L.J. 319, 332 (1975).

To what extent does an after acquired property clause in the real estate mortgage strengthen the real estate mortgage vis a vis subsequent chattel security interests? While such clauses do generally give the real estate mortgagee a lien on the after acquired property of the mortgagor, fixtures installed on the mortgagor's real estate would in any event come within the coverage of the realty mortgage. See § 9.3, supra. Under the UCC the presence of the after acquired property clause probably does little to enhance the priority status of the real estate mortgagee. Under the 1962 code, a real estate mortgagee prevails only to the extent that he makes additional advances, even though the subsequent chattel mortgagee never perfects his fixture security interest. See U.C.C. § 9–313(4)(c); Berry, Priority Conflicts Between Fixture Secured Creditors and Real Estate Claimants, 7 Memphis St.L.J. 209, 230 (1977). Indeed, this would seem to mean that the presence of the after acquired property clause is irrelevant in its effect on priority. Berry, supra at 230–231. The same is also probably true under the 1972 code. Because of its emphasis on recording, the previously recorded realty mortgage will generally attain priority over a subsequently filed fixture interest whether or not an after acquired property clause is involved. Moreover, even if the real estate mortgage contains such a clause, in the case of a *purchase money* fixture interest (as the majority probably are), the chattel claimant will be given priority, as explained earlier, if he fixture files within the requisite ten day period.

10. U.C.C. § 9–313(5)(a) (1972).

the mortgagee or a subsequent bona fide purchaser of the real estate has priority over an unperfected antecedent fixture interest. Consenting to removal of an inconsequential fixture might be less troublesome than contending with the junior chattel lienor's claim if the real estate mortgagee foreclosed.

In addition, under the 1972 code a perfected security interest in fixtures has priority over a real estate mortgagee with respect to readily moveable office equipment and replacements for domestic appliances which are subject to chattel security interests perfected by any method permitted in the UCC.[11] This provision was included to alleviate the confusion in various jurisdictions as to whether these types of items are fixtures or pure personalty. Again, undermining the supposedly inviolate status of local laws, the UCC drafters decided the inherent chattel nature of office machines, stoves, refrigerators, and other similar domestic appliances warranted a guarantee of chattel priority in case conservative realty laws defined them as fixtures.

Perfection by fixture filing is not required under this exception due to the confusion over the fixture status of these items.[12] Moreover, since consumer goods in the debtor's hands, such as domestic appliances, are otherwise excused from any filing requirements in all other UCC provisions, the exemption was extended to this provision in the event a court would determine that such appliances are fixtures. Note, however, that the priority guarantee for chattel lienors applies only to replacement appliances. Thus, ordinary consumer purchases to replace worn out appliances do not require recording in the chain of title of underlying realty. In the official comments, the UCC drafters note that other relevant law, such as that governing construction mortgages, applies to original installations of domestic appliances.[13] The comments further state that appliances installed in commercial buildings, whether as originals or replacements, are normally regarded as fixtures unless they are merely domestic appliances installed by a tenant.[14]

The final aspect of this exception concerns possible conflicts with the construction mortgage exception discussed previously. Commentators theorize that this office equipment and appliance replacement exception is largely illusory, since most states consider such items personalty anyway.[15] However, in the event of conflict between the construction mortgage provision and the moveable office equipment clause, the construction provision controls if such equipment is held to be fixtures.[16]

11. U.C.C. § 9–313(4)(c) and Comment 4(d) (1972).

12. Id.

13. Id.

14. Id.

15. Id.

16. Id.

If fixtures are installed by a mortgagor's tenant, the UCC gives priority to the tenant/debtor's fixture claimant as against the realty mortgagee if the tenant has the right to remove the fixtures from the mortgaged property.[17]

Remedies

In the few instances where a real estate mortgagee is awarded priority under the UCC, the debtor, chattel mortgagee, or other claimant of a chattel interest is absolutely prohibited from removing the fixture from the real estate.[18] On the other hand, the chattel mortgage should be deemed subordinate to the realty mortgage, thus entitling the chattel lienor to payment from any surplus that may exist in the event of a foreclosure sale. However, some courts have erroneously extinguished the chattel security interest rather than designating it second in priority.[19] Alternatively, the chattel claim may always be enforced against the debtor personally rather than against the fixtures from a subordinate's status.

In contrast, where the chattel mortgage is granted priority, the holder of the interest has an absolute right to remove the fixture despite damage to the premises.[20] The UCC limits the fixture claimant's liability to the damage incurred in removal; he is not liable for any loss of value to the real estate resulting from removal of the fixture.[21] Real estate mortgages are clearly prejudiced by this absolute right of removal. Their only recourse is to demand a bond to cover the expected damage. This limited protection may reimburse adequately for the dismantling of an enclosure or the nail holes and tool marks left on a wall. However, no such meager remedy can compensate for the unexpected loss of a major improvement which contributed substantially to the value of mortgaged real estate.

17. U.C.C. § 9–313(5)(b) (1972); White & Summers, supra note 75 at 933–34; 62 Cornell L.Rev. at 926; Berry, supra note 9 at 237.

18. See Berry, supra note 9 at 232; Schroeder, supra note 9 at 322.

19. See In re Foskett, 7 U.C.C.Rep. Serv. 267 (W.D.Wis.1970).

20. U.C.C. § 9–313(8) and Comment 9 (1972); Hawkland, supra note 61 at 43, 44; Berry, supra note 9 at 232; Schroeder, supra note 9 at 322.

21. Supra note 20.

§§ 9.7–10.0 are reserved for supplementary material.

CHAPTER 10

SUBROGATION, CONTRIBUTION AND MARSHALING

Table of Sections

A. SUBROGATION AND CONTRIBUTION

A. SUBROGATION AND CONTRIBUTION

§ 10.1 General Principles

Subrogation is the substitution of another person in the place of a creditor whose claim he has satisfied so that the person subrogated (the subrogee) succeeds to all the rights, priorities, liens and securities of the creditor in relation to the debt.[1] It amounts to an assignment by operation of law of the original creditor's position to the subrogee. Subrogation is derived from Roman and civil law,[2] but there is some doubt as to how much those systems have influenced the Anglo-American development of the doctrine.[3] It is an equitable

1. Stafford Metal Works, Inc. v. Cook Paint & Varnish Co., 418 F.Supp. 56 (D.C.Tex.1976); First Nat. City Bank v. United States, 548 F.2d 928 (Ct.Cl. 1977); Liberty Mutual Ins. Co. v. Davis, 52 Misc. 26, 368 N.E.2d 336, 6 O.O.3d 108 (1977).

2. United States v. Commonwealth of Pa., Dept. of Highways, 349 F.Supp. 1370 (E.D.Pa.1972); D. W. Jaquays & Co. v. First Security Bank, 101 Ariz. 301, 419 P.2d 85 (1966); 24 Va.L.Rev. 771 (1938).

3. Marasinghe, An Historical Introduction to the Doctrine of Subrogation: The Early History of the Doctrine, 10 Valpariso University L.R. part 1 at 45, part 2 at 275 (1975–76); Jones, Roman Law Bases of Suretyship in Some Modern Civil Codes, 52 Tulane

doctrine designed to prevent unjust enrichment and is closely related to the principles of suretyship and restitution.[4] Like the doctrine of constructive trust,[5] it is a device designed "to compel ultimate payment of a debt by one who in justice, equity and good conscience should pay it." [6] The facts and circumstances of each case determine whether the doctrine is applicable.[7]

The question of subrogation arises in mortgage law in three different types of situations: (1) When a person who is obligated as a surety for a mortgage debt pays that debt; (2) when a person pays a debt for which he is not liable for the purpose of protecting some interest of his own in the property; and (3) when a person makes a payment voluntarily or at the request of the principal obligor to pay off another mortgage or encumbrance on the property. Subrogation in the first two situations has been categorized as legal subrogation and is said to arise by operation of law.[8] Subrogation in the third example is called conventional subrogation and is sometimes said to arise from contract, the agreement between the subrogee and either the debtor or creditor,[9] but there is serious doubt that its real basis is contractual.[10] An agreement between the debtor and the person

L.R. 129 (1977); Comment, 31 Mich. L.Rev. 826 (1933).

4. Rock River Lumber Corp. v. Universal Mortgage Corp. of Wisconsin, 82 Wis.2d 235, 262 N.W.2d 114 (1978); Reese v. AMF–Whitely, 420 F.Supp. 985 (D.Neb.1976); Garrity v. Rural Mutual Ins. Co., 77 Wis.2d 537, 253 N.W.2d 512 (1977).

5. Cole v. Morris, 409 S.W.2d 668 (Mo. 1966). "The doctrines of subrogation and constructive trust are analogous. The creditor is regarded as holding his claim against the principal debtor and his securities therefor in trust for the subrogee." New York Cas. Co. v. Sinclair Refining Co., 108 F.2d 65, 71 (C.A.Okl.1939).

6. Skauge v. Mountain States Telephone & Telegraph Co., 565 P.2d 628 (Mont.1977).

7. Cagle, Inc. v. Sammons, 198 Neb. 595, 254 N.W.2d 398 (1977); U.S. Fidelity and Guaranty Co. v. Maryland Cas. Co. 186 Kan. 637, 352 P.2d 70 (1960); Burgoon v. Lavezzo, 92 F.2d 726, 113 A.L.R. 944 (C.C.A.D.C.1937).

8. See Skauge v. Mountain States Tel. & Tel. Co., 565 P.2d 628 (Mont.1977); Lawyers' Title Guaranty Fund v. Sanders, 571 P.2d 454 (Okl.1977).

9. Rock River Lumber Corp. v. Universal Mortg. Corp. of Wisconsin, 82 Wis.2d 235, 262 N.W.2d 114 (1978); Lentz v. Stoflet, 280 Mich. 446, 273 N.W. 763 (1937).

"From our study we may draw the following conclusions: (1) That where a lender, in no way related to the property nor in any way required to protect an interest, advanced the money to pay off a lien, it could not be a case for legal subrogation, but must, if anything, come within the principles of conventional subrogation. (2) That in conventional subrogation there must be an agreement, express or implied, that the lender whose money pays off a lien will have the same status as the lien his money releases to the extent of the debt secured by that lien. (3) That equity applies the doctrine of subrogation in such cases, not in exacting a performance of the contract, but as a matter of doing justice under the circumstances; the so-called agreement only being of value showing such a situation where the doctrine should be applied in order to do justice and as evidence that the lender was not a volunteer." Martin v. Hickenlooper, 90 Utah 150, 179, 59 P.2d 1139, 1152, 107 A.L.R. 762 (1936), rehearing denied 90 Utah 185, 61 P.2d 307.

10. "[S]ubrogation arises, not as a direct legal consequence of the con-

claiming subrogation clearly does not in itself transfer the right of the creditor to such person.[11] And if there is really a contract between the subrogee and the creditor, the result may be an assignment or an agreement to assign enforceable in equity, of either a legal or an equitable chose in action—a perfectly valid idea, but not a part of the doctrine of subrogation.[12] In some cases equity will take into consideration the presence of an agreement in determining whether to allow subrogation,[13] and the extent of the right will be determined by the agreement.[14] But unless a formal assignment has been executed, subrogation is always by operation of law.

§ 10.2 Payment as Surety

Where a principal obligor and a surety are liable on a debt, if the surety pays the debt, he is clearly entitled to be subrogated to the rights of the creditor against the principal obligor.[15] Thus if a mortgagor sells the property to a grantee who assumes the mortgage and then the mortgagor has to pay off the mortgage, he is entitled to be subrogated to all rights of the mortgagee both against the assuming grantee personally and against the mortgaged property.[16] Similarly,

tract of the parties, but rather as a matter of doing justice after a balancing of the equities, and * * * the agreement is merely a consideration—although an important consideration—in determining whether subrogation is appropriate." Rock River Lumber v. Universal Mortgage Corp. of Wis., 82 Wis.2d 235, 241, 262 N.W. 2d 114, 117 (1978). "Even when there is an agreement to subrogate, the so-called right of subrogation is not one inherent in the contract, but arises in equity and can therefore be withheld or applied as in equity seems meet according to sound judicial discretion, which is another way of saying, according to the dictates of justice. The doctrine of subrogation has its roots in the soil of justice and equity, and not in contract." Martin v. Hickenlooper, 90 Utah 150, 161, 59 P.2d 1139, 1143, 107 A.L.R. 762 (1936), rehearing denied 90 Utah 185, 61 P.2d 307.

11. "Even where a definite agreement for subrogation is shown, therefore, subrogation will be denied where it would lead to an uncontemplated and inequitable result." Rock River Lumber Corp. v. Universal Mortgage, note 10, supra, at 117.

12. The difference between subrogation and assignments is illustrated by the question discussed, § 10.8, infra, as to whether one who is entitled to subrogation may compel an assignment.

13. "In the case of *conventional* subrogation, equity says: Where the lender of money did it with the intention and understanding that he was to be placed in the position of the creditor whose debt he paid, but without taking an assignment of the credit, equity, where no innocent parties will suffer or no right has intervened, will treat the matter as if an assignment had been executed." Martin v. Hickenlooper, 90 Utah 150, 157, 59 P.2d 1139, 1141, 107 A.L.R. 762 (1936) rehearing denied 90 Utah 185, 61 P.2d 307. See Note 10, supra. Note, 21 Col.L.Rev. 470 (1971).

14. Millers Mutual Fire Ins. Co. of Tex. v. Farmers Elevator Mutual Ins. Co., 408 F.2d 776 (C.A.Tex.1969); Tennessee Farmers' Mutual Ins. Co. v. Rader, 219 Tenn. 384, 410 S.W.2d 171 (1966).

15. Barnes v. Hampton, 198 Neb. 151, 252 N.W.2d 138 (1977); Langeveld v. L.R.Z.H., 74 N.J. 45, 376 A.2d 931 (1977).

16. Konoff v. Lantini, 111 R.I. 691, 306 A.2d 176 (1973); French v. May, 484

if he sells the property subject to the mortgage and is forced to pay, he is subrogated to the creditor's security interest in the property now owned by the grantee—the property being regarded as the principal and the mortgagor the surety.[17] The suretyship relation can run the other way as well: Suppose the purchaser has paid the full value of the property, with the mortgagor being bound to pay off the mortgage. Should the purchaser be forced to pay, he is entitled to subrogation to the mortgagee's claim against the mortgagor.[18]

It is equally clear that a principal obligor who pays is not entitled to subrogation against a person acting as surety. Such a payment would be merely the performance of his own duty. So neither an assuming grantee [19] nor a mortgagor who had agreed to pay the mortgage to protect his grantee [20] would be entitled to subrogation upon paying the mortgage. A grantee subject to the mortgage who pays cannot have subrogation as against the mortgagor unless the amount of payment exceeds the value of the land, for up to that extent, clearly, he is paying on behalf of the principal, the land.[21] Whether he may have subrogation as to the excess of the debt he pays over the value of the land would seem to be governed by the

S.W.2d 420 (Tex.Civ.App.1972); Malone v. U.S., 326 F.Supp. 106 (N.D. Miss.1971) affirmed 455 F.2d 502 (C. A.Miss.1972); Toler v. Baldwin County Sav. & Loan Ass'n, 286 Ala. 320, 239 So.2d 751 (1970); Sanders v. Lackey, 59 Tenn.App. 207, 439 S.W. 2d 610 (1968); Finance Co. of America v. Heller, 247 Md. 714, 234 A.2d 611 (1967).

17. "This relation between the mortgagor and his grantee does not deprive the obligee from enforcing the bond against the obligor. He is entitled to his debt, and has a right to avail himself of all his securities. Equity however requires that the obligor, on the payment of the debt out of his own funds, should be subrogated to the rights of the obligee, so that he can reimburse himself by a recourse to the mortgaged premises for that purpose. This cannot prejudice the creditor, and it is clearly equitable as between the debtor and the owner of the land." Johnson v. Zink, 51 N.Y. 333, 336–37 (1873); Howard v. Burns, 279 Ill. 256, 116 N.E. 703 (1917); Woodbury v. Swan, 58 N.H. 380 (1878); University State Bank v. Steeves, 85 Wash. 55, 147 P. 645, 2 A.L.R. 237 (1915), accord.

18. Simpson v. Ennis, 114 Ga. 202, 39 S.E. 853 (1901); Hazle v. Bondy, 173 Ill. 302, 50 N.E. 671 (1898); Wadsworth v. Lyon, 93 N.Y. 201, 45 Am.R. 190 (1883); Hudson v. Dismukes, 77 Va. 242 (1883).

19. Dodds v. Spring, 174 Cal. 412, 163 P. 351 (1917); Drury v. Holden, 121 Ill. 130, 13 N.E. 547 (1887); Lydon v. Campbell, 204 Mass. 580, 91 N.E. 151, 134 Am.St.Rep. 702 (1910); cf., Lackawanna Trust & Safe Deposit Co. v. Gomeringer, 236 Pa. 179, 84 A. 757 (1912). See 15 Col.L.Rev. 171 (1915).

20. Wadsworth v. Williams, 100 Mass. 126 (1868); Byles v. Kellogg, 67 Mich. 318, 34 N.W. 671 (1887); Hooper v. Henry, 31 Minn. 264, 17 N.W. 476 (1883).

21. Drury v. Holden, 121 Ill. 130, 13 N.E. 547 (1887); Northwestern Nat. Bank v. Stone, 97 Iowa 183, 66 N.W. 91 (1896); In re Wisner's Estate, 20 Mich. 442 (1870); Guernsey v. Kendall, 55 Vt. 201 (1880). Cf. Fortier v. Fortier, 200 So.2d 901 (La.App.1967), writ refused 251 La. 59, 202 So.2d 661, appeal after remand 221 So.2d 653, application refused 254 La. 292, 223 So.2d 412 (Sup.1969); See 5 Houston L.R. 230 (1967) for catalogue of surety-principal relationships in all types of sales of encumbered property.

same principles previously discussed in connection with merger.[22] It is believed he should not. The amount of the debt was figured in on the original purchase price of the land. Even though the agreement imposed no personal duty to pay, nevertheless the payment of the mortgage was a condition to his retention of the land and he should not be able, by paying it, to recover any portion of it from his vendor, the mortgagor, through the agency of subrogation or otherwise. The fact that at the time the mortgage has to be paid the land is no longer equal in value to the amount of the debt would not justify him being able to recover from his seller, in the face of his original bargain, any excess paid over its then value.

Where the debt is in the form of a negotiable instrument, the UCC may arguably prevent subrogation in any case in which the ownership of the instrument passes into the hands of its maker; the Code (§ 3–601) indicates that when this occurs the debt no longer exists. However, the draftsmen of the Code almost certainly did not intend to affect subrogation rights by this provision, and it should not be so read.[23]

§ 10.3 Payment to Protect an Interest—Contribution

Another instance in which the right of subrogation is not questioned is where a person, although not personally bound to pay, is compelled to do so in order to protect some interest of his own.[24] There is a variety of interests in property subject to a mortgage to which the right might apply.[25] Following are some examples:

1. A junior mortgagee may pay off a prior mortgage and be subrogated to all rights under it against the mortgagor.[26]

22. See § 6.14, supra.

23. In Best Fertilizers of Arizona, Inc. v. Burns, 116 Ariz. 492, 570 P.2d 179 (1977), subrogation was denied where the mortgagor-maker paid the holder of the note and took an assignment of it after an assuming grantee had defaulted. The court held that under the UCC all liability on the note was discharged when the maker reacquired the note and therefore the mortgage was released. See § 5.9 for summary of the case and authors' view that the case was decided erroneously.

24. Cagle, Inc. v. Sammons, 198 Neb. 595, 254 N.W.2d 398 (1977); Cobb v. Osman, 83 Nev. 415, 433 P.2d 259 (1967).

25. See Hope, Officiousness, 15 Corn. L.Q. 25, 205, 239 (1930), for a survey of such interests. See also 1934, 93 A.L.R. 89 for a collection of authorities on the right to compel an assignment by one who has an interest to protect and pays.

In In re Keil's Estate, 51 Del. (1 Storey) 351, 145 A.2d 563, 76 A.L.R.2d 996 (1958), reargument denied 51 Del. (1 Storey) 351, 146 A.2d 398, discussed in 58 Mich.L.Rev. 137, 1959, 73 Harv. L.Rev. 425, the surviving mortgagor of entireties property given to secure a joint debt, the proceeds of which were used to improve the property, was held entitled to contribution against the estate of the deceased tenant.

26. Rock River Lumber v. Universal Mortgage Corp. of Wisconsin, 82 Wis.2d 235, 262 N.W.2d 114 (1978); In the Matter of Forester, 529 F.2d 310 (C.A.Cal.1976).

2. A wife who has joined in the mortgage, thus subjecting her dower interest to it, may pay off the entire mortgage but keep the mortgage alive through subrogation as against the other owners who have been benefitted by her payment.[27]
3. A remainderman may pay off the mortgage, where both the life interest and remainder were mortgaged, and be subrogated as against the life tenant.[28]
4. A creditor of the mortgagor who has levied an attachment or execution on the redemption interest may pay off the debt and have subrogation.
5. A cotenant of the mortgaged property whose cotenancy is subject to the mortgage is entitled to pay and be subrogated for the purpose of obtaining contribution from his fellow cotenant.[29]
6. A lessee may pay off a mortgage debt to prevent foreclosure and may be subrogated to the rights of the holder of the lien.[30]

Since the payor as well as the other parties holding interests in the property benefits by the payment, he does not have a claim for the entire amount paid. He will be entitled to recover a ratable contribution from the other parties proportional to the value of the interest in the property from which the mortgage has been removed.[31] The problem of evaluation of the interest is not always easy although the right to contribution is well-recognized.[32]

27. Swaine v. Perine, N.Y., 5 Johns. Ch. 482, 9 Am.Dec. 318 (1821), Osborne, Cases Property Security, 2nd Ed., 546; cf. Gibson v. Crehore, 22 Mass. (5 Pick.) 146 (1827); Fitcher v. Griffiths, 216 Mass. 174, 103 N.E. 471 (1913).

28. See Mosely v. Marshall, 22 N.Y. 545 (1860), life tenant; Wunderle v. Ellis, 212 Pa. 618, 62 A. 106 (1905), tenant for years pays; cf. also Federal Land Bank v. Newsom, 175 Miss. 114, 166 So. 346 (1936), discussed, 50 Harv.L.Rev. 534 (1937).

29. Aiello v. Aiello, 268 Md. 513, 302 A.2d 189 (1973); Taylor v. Jones, 285 Ala. 353, 232 So.2d 601 (1970); A.F. C., Inc. v. Brockett, 257 Cal.App.2d 40, 64 Cal.Rptr. 771 (1967); Eloff v. Reisch, 14 Wis.2d 519, 111 N.W.2d 578 (1961) holds that right of subrogation exists even where joint tenants are husband and wife. In Walters v. Walters, 1 Wash.App. 849, 466 P.2d 174 (1970), subrogation was denied where one tenant in common was made primarily liable for obligations by divorce decree.

30. G. B. Seely's Son, Inc. v. Fulton-Edison, Inc., 52 A.D.2d 575, 382 N.Y.S. 2d 516 (1976); Dominion Financial Corp. v. 275 Washington St. Corp., 64 Misc.2d 1044, 316 N.Y.S.2d 803 (1970).

31. "What rule should then govern the parties in adjusting the common burdens resting upon the property, in different parts of which they have respectively acquired an interest? We think the parties should contribute to the payment of the burden in proportion to the value of the property in which they are respectively interested." Tarbell v. Durant, 61 Vt. 516, 519, 17 A. 44, 45 (1889). See Carpenter v. Koons, 20 Pa. 222 (1852). Cf. McLaughlin v. Estate of Curtis, 27 Wis. 644 (1871).

32. E. g., the evaluation of a dower interest. See Swaine v. Perine, supra note 27. Similarly where the question arises between a life tenant and remainderman. "A tenant for life is bound to keep down the current interest, * * * but not to pay any part of the principal. Now if, for ex-

§ 10.4 The Volunteer Rule

Courts repeatedly state that a volunteer is not entitled to subrogation.[33] A person who is obligated as a surety or who pays to protect his own interest is not a volunteer.[34] Even a moral obligation has been considered sufficiently compelling to entitle the payor to subrogation,[35] but one who pays with no obligation but merely to preserve his goodwill will be held to be a volunteer.[36] Where the payment was made pursuant to an agreement or understanding with the debtor or creditor, the court may deny subrogation on the ground that the payor was a volunteer unless the particular agreement is one which falls within the limits of "conventional subrogation" as recognized in that jurisdiction.[37] It is therefore necessary to determine just which agreements will bring about subrogation. For example, it is sometimes held that the person paying the debt must have believed that he would receive the prior security.[38] If the payor was denied his security by fraud or was induced by fraud, he is not a volunteer.[39]

ample, there is a tenant for life, and a remainderman in fee of an estate, subject to a mortgage which is due and must be paid at once to save foreclosure, and the remainderman, to save the estate, pays the mortgage, he is not obliged to take the share of the tenant for life in annual installments of interest to continue as long as he shall live. He is entitled, as equitable assignee of the mortgagee, to immediate payment; and the sum which he thus has a right to claim is whatever the present worth of an annuity equal to the amount of the annual interest would be, computed for the number of years which the tenant will live." 2 Washburn, Real Prop., 6th Ed., § 1142. See also Todd's Ex'r v. First Nat. Bank, 173 Ky. 60, 67, 190 S.W. 468 (1917); Damm v. Damm, 109 Mich. 619, 67 N.W. 984, 63 Am.St.Rep. 601 (1896); Tindall v. Peterson, 71 Neb. 160, 98 N.W. 688, 99 N.W. 659, 8 Ann.Cas. 721 (1904); Moore v. Simonson, 27 Or. 117, 39 P. 1105 (1895); Wilder's Ex'x v. Wilder, 75 Vt. 178, 53 A. 1072 (1903); 3 Pomeroy, Eq.Jur., 4th Ed., § 1223. Cf. Leach v. Hall, 95 Iowa, 611, 619, 64 N.W. 790 (1895).

33. Lawyers Title Ins. Corp. v. Edmar Constr. Co., 294 A.2d 865 (D.C.App. 1972); Southwest Title & Trust Co. v. Norman Lumber Co., 441 P.2d 430 (Okl.1968); Zapata v. Torres, 464 S. W.2d 926 (Tex.Civ.App.1971).

34. Cagle, Inc. v. Sammons, 198 Neb. 595, 254 N.W.2d 398 (1977); Cobb v. Osman, 83 Nev. 415, 433 P.2d 259 (1967); First Nat. City Bank v. U. S., 537 F.2d 426 (Ct.Cl.1976); Indemnity Ins. Co. v. Lane Contracting Corp., 227 F.Supp. 143 (D.Neb.1964).

35. Commercial Standard Ins. Co. v. American Employers Ins. Co., 209 F. 2d 60 (C.A.Ky.1954).

36. Lawyers Title Ins. Corp. v. Edmar Constr. Co., 294 A.2d 865 (D.C.App. 1972).

37. "[T]he facts or circumstances from which the agreement will be implied vary in the different courts, some requiring evidence from which an actual understanding between the parties may be inferred, while others hold that payment under such circumstances as show that the lender "supposed" or "intended" to get security of the same dignity as that released by his payment is sufficient; and some go as far as holding that such intention may be inferred from the mere fact that the money was advanced for the purpose of paying off another lien." Martin v. Hickenlooper, 90 Utah 150, 179, 59 P.2d 1139, 1152, 107 A.L.R. 762 (1936), rehearing denied 90 Utah 185, 61 P.2d 307.

38. Metropolitan Life Ins. Co. v. First Security Bank, 94 Idaho 489, 491 P.2d 1261 (1971), rehearing denied 94 Idaho 527, 492 P.2d 1400; Southwest Title & Trust Co. v. Norman Lumber Co., 441 P.2d 430 (Okl.1968).

39. Rees v. Craighead Investment Co., 251 Ark. 336, 472 S.W.2d 92 (1971);

The limits as well as the rationale of the volunteer rule are a matter of dispute. It has been asserted that, whenever courts for any reason deny subrogation, they characterize the unsuccessful applicant as a volunteer.[40] Even when used with more discrimination it has sometimes been unclear whether subrogation was denied because the court found that the plaintiff did not intend any legal consequences to flow from his act, e. g., he intended a gift, or that his intervention was unsolicited and therefore officious.[41] A critical examination of the reasons [42] offered for using the rule to deny subrogation on payment of a creditor by a third person has revealed them to be so lacking in force as to make reasonable the suggestion that, in order for such a payment to be officious, it must be unnecessary and confer no benefit.[43] Because of the variety and unpredictability of its application,[44] the voluntary payment test is of little value. Except in cases in which the payor clearly intended a gift, it should be discarded.

§ 10.5 Loans to Pay the Mortgage

The problem of the volunteer rule and subrogation in mortgage law has occurred most frequently in the case of lenders whose money is used to pay off a mortgage or other encumbrance. Where the pay-

Bunge Corp. v. St. Louis Terminal Field Warehouse Co., 295 F.Supp. 1231 (N.D.Miss.1969).

40. Pomeroy, Equity Juris, 4th ed., § 2348n.

"A good deal of the confusion concerning the volunteer rule has arisen because courts have carelessly termed the payor a volunteer in cases involving a situation where payment would ordinarily be considered not voluntary but subrogation is denied because of a superior intervening equity. It is submitted that these cases have misapplied the term and must be sharply distinguished." 32 Minn. L.Rev. 183, 185 (1948).

41. See 31 Mich.L.Rev. 826, 830 (1933).

42. The three basic reasons for not permitting subrogation on the ground that the person asking it is a volunteer are "(1) he is able to elect whether he is to pay or not, and knowing the facts he should protect himself by contract, (2) a debt paid without any agreement to keep it alive is extinguished, and (3) one cannot become a creditor of another against the other's will." 32 Minn.L. Rev. 183 (1948), citing Hope, Officiousness, 15 Corn.L.Q. 25 (1929), and note 24 Va.L.Rev. 771, 776 (1938).

43. Hope, Officiousness, 15 Cornell L. Q. 25, 205 (1929). A comment on this as a criterion stated, "Indeed, there would seem to be no great difference in principle in the case where a person theretofore unconnected with a transaction purchases a debt, which he can obviously do against the express will of the debtor, and where he pays the debt absent any intention to make a gift." 24 Va.L.Rev. 771, 776 (1938).

44. "All courts subscribe to the rule that subrogation will not be permitted a mere 'volunteer'. But there is no general agreement as to the personification of the word. A minority of courts is prone to call everyone a volunteer who was not in the position of a surety or who did not have some previous interest to protect in the subject matter in question. At the other extreme, the liberal view leads to the result that the only volunteer would be one who, without invitation from any other party and purely as a philanthropist, relieved another from an obligation. Note, 48 Yale L.J. 683, 686 (1939).

or already holds a lien junior to that of the creditor being paid off, the payment obviously protects the payor's own position and the courts have no difficulty giving subrogation. In other cases whether subrogation will be given depends both on the terms of the arrangement and the attitude of the particular court toward subrogation.[45] Subrogation of the lender is based on the general principle that one who advances money upon a justifiable expectation of receiving security is entitled to the security.[46] When the question is one of the lender's rights as against the parties to the mortgage, the outcome depends on whether the lender relied only on the general credit of the mortgagor,[47] or whether the loan was made on the understanding that the lender was to have the benefit of the existing mortgage or a mortgage having at least equal rank with that which was paid.[48]

Even if the lender pays off a prior encumbrance and receives a void or defective mortgage, he will be subrogated to the discharged encumbrance.[49] Subrogation has also been invoked where the loan which pays off the old mortgage is on the faith of a promise of a new mortgage which the owner refuses to execute,[50] or an oral agreement to convey title of the land to the lender.[51] Going beyond these are

45. See Burgoon v. Lavezzo, 68 App. D.C. 20, 92 F.2d 726, 113 A.L.R. 944 (1937); Martin v. Hickenlooper, 90 Utah 150, 59 P.2d 1139, 107 A.L.R. 762 (1936), rehearing denied 90 Utah 185, 61 P.2d 307.

46. Rock River Lumber Corp. v. Universal Mortgage Corp. of Wisconsin, 82 Wis.2d 235, 262 N.W.2d 114 (1978).

47. Southwest Title & Trust Co. v. Norman Lumber Co., 441 P.2d 430 (Okl.1968); Citizens State Bank v. Pittsburg County Broadcasting Co., 271 P.2d 725 (Okl.1954), commented on by Updike, Mortgages, in 1954 Annual Survey of American Law, 30 N.Y.U.L.Rev. 805, 809 (1955), followed this test in a chattel mortgage case.

48. Hughes Co. v. Callahan, 181 Ark. 733, 27 S.W.2d 509 (1930); Home Owners Loan Corporation v. Collins, 120 N.J.Eq. 266, 184 A. 621 (1936); Federal Union Life Ins. Co. v. Deitsch, 127 Ohio St. 505, 189 N.E. 440 (1933); Martin v. Hickenlooper, 90 Utah 150, 59 P.2d 1139, 107 A.L.R. 762 (1936), rehearing denied 90 Utah 185, 61 P.2d 307; discussed in notes, 36 Mich.L.Rev. 151 (1937); 6 Fordham L.Rev. 138 (1937); 107 A.L.R. 785 (1937); Federal Land Bank of Baltimore v. Joynes, 179 Va. 394, 18 S.E.2d 917 (1942); Home Owners Loan Corporation of Washington, D. C. v. Dougherty, 226 Wis. 8, 275 N. W. 362 (1937). Cf. Boley v. Daniel, 72 Fla. 121, 72 So. 644, L.R.A.1917A, 734 (1916), denying recovery because lender did not stipulate for the original mortgage, only a "first lien." Where a lender advanced money to pay a valid encumbrance on a homestead, "under circumstances from which an understanding is to be implied that at least part of the advancement made is to be secured by a first lien on the land encumbered," he was subrogated to rights of prior encumbrancer which were superior to homestead rights and was allowed to foreclose the homestead. Means v. United Fidelity Life Ins. Co., 550 S. W.2d 302, 309 (Tex.Civ.App.1977).

49. Union Savings Bank of Patchogue v. Dudinee, 40 Misc.2d 155, 242 N.Y. S.2d 692 (1963); Means v. United Fidelity Life Ins. Co., n. 48, supra.

50. Smith v. Sprague, 244 Mich. 577, 222 N.W. 207 (1928); Baker v. Baker, 2 S.Dak. 261, 49 N.W. 1064, 39 Am. St.Rep. 776 (1891); see 21 Cal.L.Rev. 471 (1921); 31 Mich.L.Rev. 826, 835 (1933).

51. Dobbs v. Bowling, 339 So.2d 985 (Miss.1976).

cases in which the money is loaned and used for the express purpose of paying off an encumbrance but the expectation of security does not relate to the particular property freed from the prior lien.[52] Finally, the most liberal cases allow subrogation simply where money is loaned and used for paying off an encumbrance.[53]

While lenders who have advanced money to pay the claims of laborers and suppliers on construction projects have sometimes been subrogated to their claims,[54] other cases have denied them subrogation rights on the ground that the mechanics lien statutes were not intended to protect them.[55]

§ 10.6 Loans to Pay the Mortgage—Subrogation Against Intervening Interests

A more difficult question is whether the lender who has loaned money to pay off an encumbrance will be subrogated to the encumbrance when there are intervening junior liens on the property. Since the basis for subrogation in this context is the lender's justified expectation of receiving security, actual knowledge of the intervening lien will bar subrogation.[56] Where there is constructive notice, the courts are divided.[57] The better view is that constructive notice

52. In Elmora & West End Bldg. & Loan Ass'n v. Dancy, 108 N.J.Eq. 542, 155 A. 796 (1931), commented on in 45 Harv.L.Rev. 390 (1931), M loaned the widow of his mortgagor, A, money, part of which was used to pay off the mortgage held by him, taking as security a mortgage on her dower interest in the property. M marked the mortgage "paid" and sent it to his solicitor for cancellation but it was never cancelled of record. Before the new debt was paid the widow died, thus extinguishing the security. M sued to foreclose on his original mortgage, and the land was sold. A's heirs petitioned to open the decree and set aside the sale. Held, that M was entitled to foreclose the original mortgage to the extent that the money borrowed from him was applied thereto.

53. Chrisman v. Daniel, 134 Neb. 326, 278 N.W. 565 (1938); see Martin v. Hickenlooper, 90 Utah, 150, 170, 178, 59 P.2d 1139, 1148, 1152, 107 A.L.R. 762 (1936), rehearing denied 90 Utah 185, 61 P.2d 307; 36 Mich.L.Rev. 151, 152 (1937).

54. Contractor who paid material men and laborers was subrogated to their claims under the material payment bond in Cagle, Inc. v. Sammons, 198 Neb. 595, 254 N.W.2d 398 (1977).

55. "The object of the Legislature was to secure to a very meritorious but helpless class of persons the payment of the wages of their toil, and to that end to give them, personally, a paramount lien on the assets of the employer. It did not contemplate giving to creditors from whom the company might borrow money on its own credit with which to pay its workmen, such a lien or the assets for their reimbursement." Board of Educ. of City of Bayonne v. Kolman, 111 N.J.Super. 585, 270 A.2d 64 (1970) citing In re North River Constr. Co., 38 N.J.Eq. 433, 437–438 (Ch. 1884), affirmed 40 N.J.Eq. 340 (E & A 1885).

56. See 70 A.L.R. 1396, 1414 (1931); but see Providence Institution for Savings v. Sims, 441 S.W.2d 516 (Tex.1969). "We hold that under these circumstances neither actual nor constructive knowledge of the intervening lien will defeat the right of subrogation to which the debtor agreed in the later deed of trust." Id. at 520.

57. Id.; Castelman Constr. Co. v. Pennington, 222 Tenn. 82, 432 S.W.2d 669

should be disregarded as it is irrelevant to the question whether the lender actually expected to get priority of security in the property.[58]

Where the lender's ignorance is a result of his own negligence, many courts will consider that factor in balancing the equities between the lender and the parties holding intervening liens.[59] Some courts distinguish between negligence that is inexcusable and negligence that is only ordinary.[60] In connection with the negligence issue courts will consider whether the intervening lienors will be prejudiced by the subrogation.[61] One court held, for example, that intervening lienors would be prejudiced simply because subrogation would

(1968); Peterman-Donnelly Engineers & Contractors Corp. v. First Nat. Bank, 2 Ariz.App. 321, 408 P.2d 841, (1965). See Pipola v. Chicco, 274 F. 2d 909 (C.A.N.Y.1960), granting subrogation; Cheswick v. Weaver, 280 S.W.2d 942 (Tex.Civ.App.1955), subrogation denied; Carl H. Peterson Co. v. Zero Estates, 261 N.W.2d 346 (Minn.1977), subrogation denied even where the lender refinanced a prior mortgage held by himself.

58. See 48 Yale L.J. 683, 688 (1939); 21 Col.L.Rev. 471, 472, (1921) n. 18. But cf. 31 Mich.L.Rev. 826, 834 (1933). Potter v. United States, 111 F.Supp. 585 (D.C.R.I.1953) follows the preferable view.

See 21 Col.L.Rev. 471, (1921) "Constructive notice, which is intended to protect the rights of an equitable lienor, cannot be invoked to increase those rights by imputing to the new mortgagee a knowledge of facts and a consequent expectation which he did not in fact possess." Id. at 472 n.18.

59. Negligence on the part of one seeking subrogation is of some importance when the right is wholly dependent on equitable principles. Providence Institution for Savings v. Sims, 441 S.W.2d 516 (Tex.1969); ordinary negligence of subrogee may be taken into consideration in ascertaining whether he be entitled to equitable relief of subrogation, but "[o]rdinary negligence alone will not be held as a complete bar to subrogation where in spite of such negligence the equities are still in favor of the subrogee." Castelman Constr. Co. v. Pennington, 222 Tenn. 82, 432 S.W.2d 669, 677 (1968).

60. Castelman Constr. Co. v. Pennington, 222 Tenn. 82, 432 S.W.2d 669 (1968). "[A]ccording to the modern view, indiligence in searching the record will not prevent equity from applying the doctrine unless it is culpable or unjustifiable negligence." Martin v. Hickenlooper, 90 Utah 150, 178, 59 P.2d 1139, 1152, 107 A.L.R. 762 (1936), rehearing denied 90 Utah 186, 61 P.2d 307. See also Banta v. Vreeland, 15 N.J.Eq. 103, 82 Am.Dec. 269 (1862).

61. See Fed. Land Bank v. Joynes, 179 Va. 394, 18 S.E.2d 917 (1942), "the negligence should be chiefly of significance when there are subsequently intervening rights involved which would be prejudiced if subrogation were allowed."

"[I]n a case where the court feels the negligence so culpable that the junior lienor should advance to the senior position in preference to the payer, it will refuse to imply an agreement for subrogation of the payer; but where no harm is done and the payer's negligence only 'ordinary,' the courts are prone to find an implied agreement. * * * That is, in a case involving no change of position by the junior lienor in reliance on the discharge of the original first lien, the courts will strain the concept of implied intent to the breaking point in order to prevent the junior lienor from claiming a windfall and advancing to the position of first encumbrancer, whereas their real reason for giving subrogation to the payer is that they feel he has superior equities on his side." Note, 36 Mich.L.Rev. 151, 153–154 (1937).

prevent their being able to enforce their liens.[62] However, most cases have held that the junior lienors are not prejudiced unless they have changed their position in reliance of extinguishment of the debt.[63] Where the junior lienor occupies the same position he occupied before the prior lien was paid and discharged, to deny subrogation and permit the lienor to advance would give him a windfall advantage at the expense of the justifiable expectation of the lender.[64] This would defeat the purpose of subrogation, which is to prevent unjust enrichment and grant an equitable result between the parties.

The volunteer rule is not an obstacle where the lender paid at the request of the mortgagor. If he has advanced money with the understanding or under circumstances which would give rise to an understanding that the loan would be secured by a first lien on the property, he is not a mere volunteer and should be subrogated to the prior liens his advance was made to discharge.[65]

§ 10.7 Payments by Grantees—Subrogation Against Intervening Interests

Where a grantee of the mortgagor assumes the payment of a prior mortgage in actual ignorance of the existence of a later incumbrance, even though it might be of record, the question arises as to whether, on paying the earlier lien he is entitled to be subrogated to it as against the later lienors.[66] A strong line of cases permits subro-

62. Carl H. Peterson Co. v. Zero Estates, 261 N.W.2d 346 (Minn.1977).

63. Rock River Lumber v. Universal Mortgage Corp. of Wisconsin, 82 Wis.2d 235, 262 N.W.2d 114 (1978); Credit Bureau Corp. v. Beckstead, 63 Wash.2d 183, 385 P.2d 864, 866 (1963): "The doctrine however will not be applied if it would work injustice to the rights of those having equal or superior equities; nor will it be enforced against a bona fide purchaser for value without notice or one who, in good faith, has changed his position in reliance upon the act which subsequently is claimed to have been a mistake."

64. Where intervening lienor remains with a lien prior to all claims except a mortgage given before he began work on the project, "Equity requires that appellee be afforded that security for which he obviously bargained." Peterman-Donnelly Engineer & Contractor Corp. v. First Nat. Bank, 2 Ariz.App. 321, 408 P.2d 841, 846 (1965). "There is no reason for advancing [the junior lienor] to the position of a senior lienor, since all he ever contracted for was a junior encumbrance." 21 Col.L.Rev. 471, 472 (1921). "His advancement to first mortgagee on extinguishment of the prior lien is a purely fortuitous benefit, to which he has no equitable or legal right." Id. fn.20.

65. Blaylock v. Dollar Inns of America, Inc., 548 S.W.2d 924 (Tex.Civ. App.1977). See 48 Yale L.J. 683, 686; 1933, 31 Mich.L.Rev. 826, 830 (1939). The same is true of one who pays as part of the purchase price. Burgoon v. Lavezzo, 92 F.2d 726, 113 A.L.R. 944 (C.A.D.C.1937).

66. See 113 A.L.R. 958 (1925); 87 U. Pa.L.Rev. 1012 (1939); 48 Yale L.J. 683 (1939). The same question is involved if the grantee, rather than assuming the senior debt, simply discharges it as part of the purchase transaction, provided he is unaware of the existence of intervening liens. See Burgoon v. Lavezzo, 92 F.2d 726 (C.A.D.C.1937).

gation in such a case.[67] There are, however, a considerable number of authorities that refuse it.[68]

Those denying subrogation do so on several grounds. One is that the assuming grantee has become primarily liable for the debt and the general rule applies that one paying his own debt is not entitled to subrogation. Coupled with this is the idea that by assuming the mortgagor's debt he must be regarded as having stepped into his grantor's shoes and therefore the payment has the same effect as if it had been made by the grantor before he parted with the property.[69] Where the grantee assumes any junior mortgages as well as a senior mortgage, as is the case when the assumption is of "all" encumbrances, no objection can be taken to this reasoning and the courts uniformly deny subrogation in such cases.[70] Since he has a duty to pay the junior liens he cannot complain if his payment and discharge of the earlier mortgage advances them in priority. If the first mortgage only is assumed and the grantee has actual knowledge of the junior liens at the time of assumption, it is arguable that the same result is justified,[71] although there are authorities to the contrary.[72]

67. E. g., Johnson v. Tootle, 14 Utah 482, 47 P. 1033 (1897); Capitol Nat. Bank v. Holmes, 43 Colo. 154, 95 P. 314, 16 L.R.A.,N.S., 470, 127 Am.St. Rep. 108 (1908); Young v. Morgan, 89 Ill. 199 (1878); Smith v. Dinsmore, 119 Ill. 656, 4 N.E. 648 (1887), recorded junior incumbrance; Federal Land Bank v. Smith, 129 Md. 233, 151 A. 420 (1930); Dixon v. Morgan, 154 Tenn. 389, 285 S.W. 558 (1926).

Compare the discussion of merger in §§ 6.13, 6.15, supra.

68. Citizens' Mercantile Co. v. Easom, 158 Ga. 604, 123 S.E. 883, 37 A.L.R. 378 (1924) noted in 38 Harv.L.Rev. 266 (1924); Goodyear v. Goodyear, 72 Iowa 329, 33 N.W. 142 (1887); Kuhn v. National Bank, 74 Kan. 456, 87 P. 551, 118 Am.St.Rep. 332 (1906); Smith v. Feltner, 259 Ky. 833, 83 S. W.2d 506 (1935).

69. Kuhn v. National Bank, 74 Kan. 456, 87 P. 551, 118 Am.St.Rep. 332 (1906); Goodyear v. Goodyear, 72 Iowa 329, 33 N.W. 142 (1887); Poole v. Kelsey, 95 Ill.App. 233 (1900). See also a similar line of reasoning in 87 U. of Pa.L.Rev. 1012 (1939).

70. E. g., Stastny v. Pease, 124 Iowa 587, 100 N.W. 482 (1904); Martin v. C. Aultman & Co., 80 Wis. 150, 49 N. W. 749 (1891); Morris v. Twichell, 63 N.D. 747, 249 N.W. 905 (1933), commented on in, 19 Iowa L.Rev. 629 (1934), denied subrogation to a purchaser who assumed the first mortgage with knowledge of the second mortgage and who, when he paid the first mortgage, asked for and thought he had received an assignment instead of the cancellation which actually was executed. Although the purchaser did not expressly assume payment of the second mortgage the court stressed the fact that its amount had been deducted from the purchase price. The court said, "The rule is that when payment has been made by one primarily liable, it operates as an absolute satisfaction. * * * Neither by assignment nor by subrogation can he keep the mortgage alive as against other liens on the land."

71. In some of the cases in which the courts stress the grantee's assumption as the basis of the decision the grantee had actual notice of the intervening liens. E. g., Lackawanna Trust & Safe Deposit Co. v. Gomeringer, 236 Pa. 179, 84 A. 757 (1912); De Roberts v. Stiles, 24 Wash. 611, 64 P. 795 (1901); Willson v. Burton, 52 Vt. 394 (1880); Cady v. Barnes, 208 F. 361 (D.C.Ohio 1913), reversed 232 F. 318, 146 C.C.A. 366; cf. Kitchell v. Mudgett, 37 Mich. 81 (1877).

72. Joyce v. Dauntz, 55 Ohio St. 538, 45 N.E. 900 (1896); see Young v. Morgan, 89 Ill. 199, 202 (1878); cf.

In such a case he pays under no mistake, and the view that it would not be unfair for the same consequences to follow payment by him as would flow from payment by the mortgagor, namely elevation of the junior lienors, is not an unreasonable one.

The same is not true when his assumption is of the first mortgage only and he pays and discharges it without knowledge of a junior lien. In such a case the grantee owes a duty to the mortgagor to pay off the first mortgage, but he has entered into no agreement with the second mortgagee to discharge it for his benefit. The only possible claim to rise that the second lienor may urge is through the duty of the mortgagor to pay off prior mortgages for his benefit. But between the mortgagor and the grantee the mortgagor has a duty to pay off the second mortgage entirely, not to let it rise to a position of priority on the land now owned by the grantee. This being so, it would seem to follow clearly that the mortgagor could not claim that the grantee owed any duty to him, which could accrue derivatively to a second mortgagee, to pay off the first mortgage in order that the second mortgage, which he was bound to pay for the benefit of the grantee, might rise to a preferred position on the land. To permit the second mortgagee to rise to priority under these circumstances would give him an unwarranted enrichment at the expense of the grantee.[73]

Cases sometimes arise in which the grantee has no actual knowledge of the intervening liens, but either failed to search the records or searched them negligently under circumstances in which a careful search would have disclosed the liens in question. By analogy to the discussion of loans to pay mortgages in the preceding section, negligence [74] or constructive notice [75] should be irrelevant. Here, as

Stantons v. Thompson, 49 N.H. 272 (1870). See § 10.2, supra.

73. Tibbitts v. Terrill, 26 Colo.App. 64, 140 P. 936 (1914), commented on in 15 Col.L.Rev. 171 (1915), in which an assuming grantee was subrogated to the lien of the first mortgage which he paid, although he had actual knowledge of the recordation of a lis pendens claim against the property at the time he bought it but bona fide, after legal advice, thought the claim invalid. The court made the point that to allow subrogation would work no hardship to the junior claimant. His security interest in the property when he acquired it was subject to this superior lien, and he should not reap the benefit of the other man's innocent mistake.

74. Lamoille County Sav. Bank & Trust Co. v. Belden, 90 Vt. 535, 98 A. 1002 (1916); see Burgoon v. Lavezzo, 68 App.D.C. 20, 23, 92 F.2d 726, 729, 113 A.L.R. 944 (1937).

75. Ragan v. Standard Scale Co., 128 Ga. 544, 58 S.E. 31 (1907); Goodyear v. Goodyear, 72 Iowa 329, 33 N.W. 142 (1887); Kitchell v. Mudgett, 37 Mich. 81 (1877); see Stastny v. Pease, 124 Iowa 587, 591, 592, 100 N. W. 482, 483, 484 (1904). In Duke v. Kilpatrick, 231 Ala. 51, 163 So. 640 (1935), criticized in note, 14 N.Car.L. Rev. 295 (1936), subrogation for the purpose of obtaining contribution from his co-owner was denied to an assuming grantee who paid off the entire first mortgage on property which he had bought honestly thinking that he was getting full title when actually he was obtaining only a one-half interest in it. The fact of joint ownership of his grantor with another was on record and also ap-

there, the issue is only whether the payor expected that his payment would free the property; [76] if he did, subrogation should be available to him. A contrary result would give the intervening lienors an unjustified and unearned windfall, advancing their priority for no good reason. Clearly this should be done only when the payor actually knew of them and failed to protect himself against them by obtaining an appropriate assignment of the senior debt.

The same principles discussed above with respect to assuming grantees apply equally, and perhaps even more readily, to grantees who merely take subject to the senior mortgage.[77] On these facts it cannot even be argued that the grantee is paying off his own debt when he discharges the senior mortgage, since he has no personal obligation to do so. At the same time, both assuming and "subject to" grantees must be considered well outside the "volunteer" classification, since they clearly have a property interest to protect by payment.[78]

§ 10.8 Compelling an Assignment

Subrogation is similar to an assignment of the mortgage creditor's rights, but since it is only an equitable right, it does not give as complete protection as does an assignment.[79] Therefore, frequently one who has a right to be subrogated upon payment of the mortgage

peared in the deed he received. Other courts allowing subrogation have expressly considered constructive notice as an obstacle and rejected it. E. g., see Prestridge v. Lazar, 132 Miss. 168, 177, 95 So. 837, 838 (1923); Burgoon v. Lavezzo, 68 App.D.C. 20, 24, 92 F.2d 726, 730, 113 A.L.R. 944 (1937). Look also at Smith v. Dinsmore, 119 Ill. 656, 4 N.E. 648 (1887); Neff v. Elder, 84 Ark. 277, 105 S.W. 260, 120 Am.St.Rep. 67 (1907). Compare Belcher v. Belcher, 161 Or. 340, 87 P.2d 762, 89 P.2d 893 (1939), noted 24 Minn.L.Rev. 121 (1939).

76. See § 10.6, supra.

77. Darrough v. Herbert Kraft Co. Bank, 125 Cal. 272, 57 P. 983 (1899), recorded junior encumbrance; Barnes v. Mott, 64 N.Y. 397, 21 Am.R. 625 (1876), recorded junior encumbrance; Ryer v. Gass, 130 Mass. 227 (1881); Hudson v. Dismukes, 77 Va. 242 (1883); see Burgoon v. Lavezzo, 68 App.D.C. 20, 23, 24, 92 F.2d 726, 729, 730, 113 A.L.R. 944 (1937). See also 14 N.Car.L.Rev. 295, 297 (1936); 15 Col.L.Rev. 171 (1915). *Contra:* Hayden v. Huff, 60 Neb. 625, 83 N.W. 920 (1900) affirmed 63 Neb. 99, 88 N.W. 179, negligence in failure to examine records; cf. Storer v. Warren, 99 Ind.App. 616, 192 N.E. 325 (1934).

78. Kahn v. McConnell, 37 Okl. 219, 220, 131 P. 682, 47 L.R.A.,N.S., 1189 (1913); Clute v. Emmerich, 99 N.Y. 342, 2 N.E. 6 (1885); cf. Weidner v. Thompson, 69 Iowa 36, 28 N.W. 422 (1886).

79. Liberty Mutual Ins. Co. v. Thunderbird Bank, 113 Ariz. 375, 555 P.2d 333, (1976). See § 10.1, supra. See also, Pardee v. Van Anken, N.Y., 3 Barb. 534, 541 (1848). "When there is an assignment of an entire claim there is complete divestment of all rights from the assignor and a vesting of those same rights in the assignee; but, in a case of subrogation, only an equitable right passes to the subrogee and the legal right to the claim is not removed from subrogor." Cantor v. Union Mutual Life Ins. Co., 547 S.W.2d 220, 225 (Mo.App.1977).

debt desires instead a formal assignment. The question arises whether he is entitled to it.

The objection to compelling a mortgage creditor to execute an assignment under such circumstances is that his only duty under his mortgage agreement is to cancel the debt upon payment and to discharge the mortgage on the land—not to keep the mortgage alive by assigning it. But there are many legal incidents which attach to a relationship regardless of the agreement between the parties, simply because equity courts have believed it desirable and fair. In certain circumstances where the claimant shows a substantial need for an assignment as opposed to subrogation an assignment should be compelled.[80] The burden on the mortgagee under an assignment as compared to subrogation is not onerous and the duty to transfer the debt and mortgage without recourse imposes no additional risk on him.

While courts have given varying answers on the question of compelling an assignment,[81] most of the cases have granted it if the person paying the mortgage debt stands in the relation of surety for its payment.[82] Some courts have gone beyond this and granted it where the person paying did so to protect an interest [83] and even in favor of lenders who are entitled to subrogation.[84] On the other hand some courts deny the assignment even though the payment was made to

80. "[W]here justice requires, the payment of a mortgage note will be considered not as a discharge, but as an assignment of both instruments; [particularly if] it is the intention of the person making payment to take an assignment of the instruments for his own protection." United States v. Boston and Berlin Transportation Co., 237 F.Supp. 1004, 1008 (D.N.H. 1964).

81. For collections of authorities, see Ann.Cas.1914B, 562; 2 A.L.R. 242 (1919) (chattel mortgage); 93 A.L.R. 89 (1934).

82. E. g., Johnson v. Zink, 51 N.Y. 333 (1873). See 93 A.L.R. 89, 99 (1934).

83. Tenant who held valuable long term lease which was subordinate to second mortgage was entitled upon payment or tender of amount due on mortgage to demand an assignment of bond and mortgage from its holder. Global Realty Corp. v. Charles Kannel Corp., 9 Misc.2d 241, 170 N.Y.S.2d 16 (1958). Where remainderman tendered payment he could compel life tenant's execution and delivery of an assignment of mortgage rather than a discharge. Payne v. Foster, 284 App.Div. 1058, 135 N.Y.S.2d 819 (1954). E. g., Averill v. Taylor, 8 N.Y. 44 (1853). In Simonson v. Lauck, 105 App.Div. 82, 93 N.Y.S. 965 (1905), the mortgagor, owner of the fee simple as tenant-in-common with four others, obtained an assignment to a third person who had tendered payment of the entire mortgage at the request of the mortgagor. Roberson, 133 Ala. 630, 32 So. 225 (1902), accord. Cf. Fears v. Albea, 69 Tex. 437, 6 S.W. 286, 5 Am.St.Rep. 78 (1887). In Bayles v. Husted, N.Y., 40 Hun. 376 (1886), the widow of a deceased mortgagor tendered to the mortgagee the amount of the secured debt and demanded that the mortgage be assigned to X. Held, the mortgagee should be compelled to make the assignment.

84. French v. Grand Beach Co., 239 Mich. 575, 215 N.W. 13 (1927), noted, 12 Minn.L.Rev. 189 (1927). Cf. Arant, Suretyship, 360–367; 34 Harv.L.Rev. 792 (1921); 20 Va.L.Rev. 917 (1934). Lackawanna Trust & Safe Deposit Co. v. Gomeringer, 236 Pa. 179, 84 A. 757 (1912) is contra.

protect an interest in the property[85] or when the payor was in the position of a surety.[86]

B. MARSHALING

§ 10.9 General Principles

Marshaling is an equitable principle applied by the courts to adjust the rights of the various parties having an interest in mortgaged property.[87]

Frequently a single tract of land consisting of several lots or parcels is mortgaged to secure one debt. Or it may be that two or more separate tracts are subject to a single mortgage debt. The various lots or tracts may then be sold or mortgaged to different parties either simultaneously or successively and one or more of the lots or tracts may be retained by the mortgagor. In such cases there are two or more pieces of property as security for the same debt and more than one person has an interest in the properties under the mortgage. For convenience in the following discussion the foregoing situation may be stated in hypothetical terms in which R is the mortgagor and E the mortgagee of the single tract, Blackacre, which is composed of three lots, X, Y and Z. T–1 and T–2 represent later purchasers or second mortgagees, as the case may be, of lots X and Y. Lot Z remains in the hands of R. If the transfers of X and Y are by sale, T 1 and T–2 may have bought upon any one of the three terms examined earlier. That is, they may have assumed the mortgage, taken subject to it, or paid the full value of the parcel with R bound to pay off the mortgage on it. Or there may be agreements apportioning the debt in specified amounts or percentages among the various parcels transferred or retained by the mortgagor. The transfer to T–1 may or may not have been recorded. T–2, whether he is purchaser or mortgagee, may have actual notice of the prior transfer to T–1.

85. Lamb v. Montague, 112 Mass. 352 (1873); Butler v. Taylor, 71 Mass. (5 Gray) 455 (1855); Hamilton v. Dobbs, 19 N.J.Eq. 227 (1868). Cf. Holland v. Citizens, etc., Bank, 16 R.I. 734, 19 A. 654, 8 L.R.A. 553 (1890). See Updike, Mortgages, in 1954 Annual Survey of American Law, 30 N.Y.U.L.Rev. 805, 812 (1955), noting Marine View Sav. & Loan Ass'n v. Andrulonis, Ch., 31 N.J.Super. 378, 106 A.2d 559 (1954).

86. Fitcher v. Griffiths, 216 Mass. 174, 103 N.E. 471 (1913). Cf. Heighe v. Evans, 164 Md. 259, 164 A. 671, 93 A.L.R. 81 (1933).

87. Marshaling is "the ranking or ordering of several estates or parcels of land for the satisfaction of a judgment or mortgage to which all are liable." 1 Black, Judgments, § 440. For collections of authorities on various aspects of the problem of marshaling see, 5 L.R.A. 280 (1889); 12 L.R.A.,N.S. 965 (1908); id. 359 (1912); id. 302 (1914); Ann.Cas.1914A., 715; id. 1916D, 1119; 35 A.L.R. 1307 (1925); 44 id. 608 (1926); 77 id. 371 (1932); 101 id. 618 (1936); 106 id. 1102 (1937); 110 id. 65 (1937); 119 id. 1109 (1939); 131 A.L.R. 4 (1941). This last is a long and comprehensive survey of the inverse order of alienation rule.

If there were no principles of marshaling, in the event there was a default on the mortgage, E could proceed against the three parcels in any order he wished. This would endow him with the power, to be exercised at his whim, of wiping out the interest of T–1, T–2, or R in the parcel held by one or another of them by going against it rather than against another or all of them. The purpose and effect of marshaling is to prevent this result.

The term marshaling is used to cover two principles which are commonly given the separate titles of the "inverse order of alienation" rule and the "two funds" doctrine.[88] Under the inverse order of alienation a mortgagee holding a paramount lien on an entire tract of land which has been sold successively in separate parcels must satisfy his debt out of the land retained by the mortgagor-grantor, if possible, and if that is insufficient must resort to the parcels aliened in the inverse order of their alienation.[89] The rule has been traced back to Coke in England,[90] and was first enunciated in this country by Chancellor Kent [91] and later approved by the great weight of authority.[92]

The two funds rule requires that where two creditors have claims upon the assets of a common debtor and one of the creditors can resort to two funds but the other can reach only one, the doubly secured creditor must first seek satisfaction out of the fund which he alone can reach before resorting to the fund upon which both creditors have claims.[93] For example, lots X and Y are mortgaged to E. T–1 then takes a second mortgage on lot X. Unless lot X is sufficient

88. See Fidelity & Casualty Co. v. Massachusetts Mut. Life Ins. Co., 74 F.2d 881 (C.C.A.1935). For applications of the principles of marshaling in subdivision financing, see Melli, Subdivision Control in Wisconsin, Wis.L.Rev. 389 (1953). See additionally, Green, Marshaling Assets in Texas, 34 Texas L.Rev. 1054 (1956). For a discussion of subdivision financing problems, see Storke and Sears, Subdivision Financing, 28 Rocky Mt.L. Rev. 1 (1956). See Note, The Rights of a Junior Lienholder in Wisconsin, 43 Marq.L.Rev. 89, 94 (1959).

89. Bartley v. Pikeville Nat. Bank & Trust Co., 532 S.W.2d 446 (Ky.App. 1976); Seasons, Inc. v. Atwell, 86 N. M. 751, 527 P.2d 792 (1974); Taylor v. Jones, 285 Ala. 353, 232 So.2d 601 (1970); Broughton v. Mt. Healthy Flying Service, Inc., 104 Ohio App. 479, 143 N.E.2d 597 (1957).

90. Harbert's Case, 3 Co.Rep. 11b (1584). Cf. Lord Eldon in Aldrich v. Cooper, 8 Ves. 382 (1803), and Sugden, in Averall v. Wade, Ll. & G. 252 (1825), on the "two funds" doctrine. See Clowes v. Dickenson, N.Y., 5 Johns.Ch. 235 (1821). See also Sanford v. Hill, 46 Conn. 42 (1878); National Sav. Bank of District of Columbia v. Creswell, 100 U.S. 630, 25 L.Ed. 713 (D.C.1880).

91. In Clowes v. Dickenson, supra note 90.

92. Brown v. Simons, 44 N.H. 475 (1863); Cumming v. Cumming, 3 Ga. 460 (1847); Clowes v. Dickenson, note 90, supra; Sanford v. Hill, note 90, supra; National Sav. Bank v. Creswell, note 90, supra; see Iglehart v. Crane & Wesson, 42 Ill. 261, 265, 269 (1866). See 5 L.R.A. 276, 282 (1889); Ann.Cas.1916D, 1119.

93. Community Bank v. Jones, 278 Or. 647, 566 P.2d 470 (1977); Bartley v. Pikeville Nat. Bank & Trust Co., 532 S.W.2d 446 (Ky.App.1976); Waff Bros., Inc. v. Bank of North Carolina, N.A., 289 N.C. 198, 221 S.E.2d 273 (1976); In re Beacon Distributors, Inc., 441 F.2d 547 (C.A.R.I.1971); 76 A.L.R.3d 327 fn. 2 (1977).

to pay both mortgages, if E should foreclose by taking payment out of it first there will be nothing left for T–1 and he will be reduced to the status of an unsecured creditor. On the other hand, if E takes his payment out of Y first before resorting to X, some or all of the latter is likely to be available for T–1. To prevent the caprice of the doubly secured creditor, E, from determining where the loss shall fall in such a case, the "two funds" rule may be invoked by T–1 to compel E to realize first on Y.[94]

In application the two rules are not always clear and separable. The doctrine of inverse alienation, while generally thought of in situations where the mortgagor-owner has sold parcels successively, may also apply in other circumstances. As one court noted, it "not only applies to a vendee, but to any one having a substantial and valuable interest in any of the separate parcels of land. It has been applied in favor of the wife's dower and her homestead right. It has been applied in favor of judgment creditors, and in fact to almost all the transactions of business in which the rights of creditors, mortgagees, grantees, and lienees are involved before a court of equity." [95] There are times when the court discusses the "two funds" rule but where more than one junior mortgagee is involved may consider the inverse order of their encumbrances.[96] The court may recognize the inverse order rule as valid between grantees but refuse to apply it between junior mortgagees.[97]

94. "Its purpose is to prevent the arbitrary action of a senior lienor from destroying the rights of a junior lienor or a creditor having less security." Meyer v. United States, 375 U.S. 233, 237, 84 S.Ct. 318, 321, 11 L.Ed.2d 293 (1963). The rule goes back to Culpepper v. Aston, 2 Ch.Cas. 115, 117 (1682). As to the justice of this rule which operates to the prejudice of general creditors, see Langdell, A Brief Survey of Equity Jurisdiction, 15; note, 43 Harv.L.Rev. 501 (1930).

95. Mack v. Shafer, 135 Cal. 113, 67 P. 40, 41 (1901). See 53 Am.Jur.2d, Marshaling Assets § 61.

96. See § 10.13. Indeed some states have statutes providing that the order of inverse alienation be applied within the two funds rule.

West's Ann.Cal.Civ.Code § 2899 provides that "Where one has a lien upon several things, and other persons have subordinate liens upon, or interest in, some but not all of the same things, the person having the prior lien, if he can do so without risk of loss to himself, or of injustice to other persons, must resort to the property in the following order, on the demand of any party interested:

"1. To the things upon which he has an exclusive lien;

"2. To the things which are subject to the fewest subordinate liens;

"3. In like manner inversely to the number of subordinate liens upon the same thing; and,

"4. When several things are within one of the foregoing classes, and subject to the same number of liens, resort must be had—

"(1) To the things which have not been transferred since the prior lien was created;

"(2) To the things which have been so transferred without a valuable consideration; and,

"(3) To the things which have been so transferred for a valuable consideration in the inverse order of the transfer."

See also 42 Okl.Stat.Ann. § 17.

97. Bryson v. Newtown Real Estate & Development Corp., 153 Conn. 267, 216 A.2d 176 (1965). See also Platte Valley Bank of North Bend v. Kracl, 185 Neb. 168, 174 N.W.2d 724 (1970).

Because of this confusion the orthodox classifications have been criticized and some commentators have suggested that the cases be grouped under the two heads, "Suretyship Marshaling" and "Lien Marshaling". "The first group is made up of cases in which there are two owners of separate tracts liable for the same mortgage debt, with a real suretyship relation existing between the owners. The second group consists of cases in which there are two mortgages, one of whom has a mortgage on two tracts, and the other a junior mortgage on one of these tracts."[98] These commentators recognize that there may be complex cases which would involve both suretyship marshaling and lien marshaling.

Regardless of which of these two marshaling principles is applicable, it is clear that marshaling will not be applied in such a way as to prejudice the rights of the paramount mortgagee to have his debt satisfied. All fractional interests remain bound by the first mortgage. The mortgagor can no more divest a portion of the mortgaged property by conveying it away or giving a second mortgage on it than he can free the entire property by the same means[99] (provided that the first mortgage is properly recorded). And although restrictions may be placed upon E's enforcement of his rights for the purpose of ordering or ranking the relative positions of T–1, T–2 and R, those restrictions must stop short of prejudicing E's paramount rights as first mortgagee.[1] Even risk of loss to E will preclude marshaling.[2] It has been held that the junior creditor has the burden to show that the senior creditor has sufficient collateral to satisfy his claims.[3] In some cases the protection to the mortgagee can be ac-

98. Storke and Sears, Transfer of Mortgaged Property, 38 Corn.L.Q. 185, 201 et seq. (1953).

99. "[E]very portion of the real estate embraced within the mortgage was equally burdened with the debt. No part could be relieved of the burden without consent of the mortgagee." Broughton v. Mt. Healthy Flying Service, Inc., 104 Ohio App. 479, 481, 143 N.E.2d 597, 599 (1957).

1. Caplinger v. Patty, 398 F.2d 471 (C.A.Ark.1968); First Nat. Bank of Omaha v. First Cadco Corp., 189 Neb. 553, 203 N.W.2d 770 (1973). "The doctrine is never enforced where it will operate to suspend or put in peril the claim of the paramount creditor, or cause him risk of loss, or where the fund to be resorted to is one which may involve such creditors in litigation, especially if final satisfaction is somewhat uncertain." Platte Valley Bank of North Bend v. Kracl, 185 Neb. 168, 174, 174 N.W.2d 724, 729 (1970) citing 55 C.J.S. Marshaling Assets and Securities § 4, p. 963. In S. Lotman & Sons, Inc. v. Southeastern Financial Corp., 288 Ala. 547, 263 So.2d 499 (1972), the court would not require creditor to attempt satisfaction from 3rd mortgage on land where he also held security interest in equipment. See Matter of St. Cloud Tool & Die Co., 533 F.2d 387 (C.A.Minn.1976), holding that the creditor requesting marshaling must act promptly so as not to prejudice others by inaction.

2. Victor Gruen Ass'n, Inc. v. Glass, 338 F.2d 826 (C.A.Cal.1964).

3. Id. Grise v. White, 355 Mass. 698, 247 N.E.2d 385 (1969) record did not establish existing collateral. But see Continental Oil Co. v. Graham, 8 S.W.2d 719 (Tex.Civ.App.1928) where mortgagee failed to show that marshaling would cause hardship.

complished by the decree itself.[4] After directing that the parcels shall be offered for sale in the inverse order of alienation, beginning with that part of the tract still in the hands of the mortgagor, it may then provide that " '[I]f the aggregate amount bid for the said lands so offered in severalty shall be insufficient to satisfy this decree, then the said master shall offer for sale said lots * * * together as one parcel * * *; and if the amount bid for the said lands so offered together shall exceed the aggregate of the amounts bid for said lands when offered in severalty * * * then said master shall sell said lands together' ".[5] It may be that such a procedure would add to the costs of the action. If so, it could be allocated to those for whose benefit the marshaling is ordered.

It is generally held that one entitled to marshaling has a right only to require a certain order of realization out of the various parcels under the mortgage when foreclosure occurs. Consequently a grantee or junior encumbrancer who has such a right must properly assert his equity before sale or other foreclosure of his parcel takes place.[6] This he may do by bill in equity if the attempted foreclosure is under power of sale,[7] or by cross-bill, answer or the like, in case of judicial foreclosure.[8] Even where the mortgagee's suit is for strict foreclosure the same result can be obtained. In such an action an equity court will always order a sale if the equities of the junior parties in interest require it. And it has even been held that a grantee of one of two mortgaged tracts, in a proper case for marshaling, may require the mortgagee who is seeking strict foreclosure to confine his remedy to the other tract where the net value of that tract is clearly equal to the mortgage debt.[9]

While the foregoing are the most usual ways in which principles of marshaling are worked out others should be mentioned. One is to

4. E. g., Hyde Park Thomson-Houston Light Co. v. Brown, 1898, 172 Ill. 329, 50 N.E. 127.

5. Id. This procedure was followed even in the absence of the contractual provision in Conneaut Bldg. and Loan Co. v. Felch, 100 Ohio App. 52, 135 N.E.2d 480 (1955).

6. Monegan v. Pacific Nat. Bank of Washington, 16 Wash.App. 280, 556 P.2d 226 (1976); Vines v. Wilcutt, 212 Ala. 150, 102 So. 29, 35 A.L.R. 1301 (1925).

7. Vines v. Wilcutt, n. 6, supra.

8. Black v. Suydam, 81 Wash. 279, 142 P. 700 (1915), Ann.Cas.1916D, 1113. See 35 A.L.R. 1307, 1310 (1924). Control of all of the parcels by the foreclosing court is essential. Hence marshalling cannot be ordered if part of the mortgaged property is outside of the state. Drexler v. Commercial Sav. Bank, 5 F.2d 13 (1925), noted, 25 Col.L.Rev. 974 (1925).

9. Markham v. Smith, 119 Conn. 355, 366, 367, 176 A. 880, 885 (1935); New England Mortgage Realty Co. v. Rossini, 121 Conn. 214, 183 A. 744 (1936). "On the other hand, the mortgagor, or a grantee or junior incumbrancer of *both* tracts, not being entitled to marshalling, is denied such relief on the ground that application should have been made to the court for an order of foreclosure by sale, in which event, by the usual practice, the tracts would have been sold separately, unless used as a whole." Campbell, Cases Mortgages, 2d ed., 620 n. 7, citing New Haven Bank N. B. A. v. Jackson, 119 Conn. 451, 453, 455, 177 A. 387, 388 (1935).

utilize the right of subrogation. Instead of having the land sold on foreclosure by the mortgagee in the order to which a subsequent grantee or mortgagee is entitled, such a transferee may elect to pay off the underlying first mortgage and be subrogated to his rights.[10] Those rights are, however, subject to control according to the principles of marshaling just as they were in the hands of the first mortgagee. Another is by an action to redeem, in which the reciprocal rights of the parties may be adjusted by the decree.[11] Or, the mortgagee may be permitted to sell all of the mortgaged property and the subsequent grantee or mortgagee may assert his priority right to the proceeds after the foreclosing mortgagee has been satisfied and before general creditors are paid.

With this much of the problem and principles of marshalling before us we may now turn to specific instances and applications in the following sections. In doing so we shall consider the problem as it arises where subsequent purchasers from the mortgagor are concerned, where junior encumbrancers are interested, where general creditors assert a claim, and the occasional case where the mortgagor himself is seeking protection, e. g., in a homestead subject to the mortgage.

§ 10.10 Grantees—Inverse Order Rule

The basis of the inverse order of alienation rule is that each of the successive purchasers has bought his parcel on terms which impose upon the mortgagor and the remaining property in his hands the primary obligation of paying the mortgage debt, the property in the hands of the grantee, although still liable, standing merely in the position of surety.[12] This situation occurs where the full price of the parcel is paid without deduction of the whole or any part of the debt secured by the blanket mortgage.[13] Persons who have notice of the

10. Taylor v. Jones, 285 Ala. 353, 232 So.2d 601 (1970); Sanders v. Lackey, 59 Tenn.App. 207, 439 S.W.2d 610 (1968); Cobb v. Osman, 83 Nev. 415, 433 P.2d 259 (1967). See §§ 10.2, 10.3, 10.7.

11. Taylor v. Jones, n. 10, supra. See §§ 7.1–7.3, supra.

12. Gribble v. Stearman & Kaplan, Inc., 249 Md. 289, 239 A.2d 573 (1968). "[T]he doctrine of marshaling confers upon the grantee . . . an equitable right to require the mortgagee to seek satisfaction of the underlying obligation from the mortgagor's remaining properties which are subject to the blanket mortgage, before resorting to the premises conveyed. This equitable right on the part of the grantee is, of course, independent of and in addition to its rights against the grantor mortgagor." In re Penn Central Transportation Co., 346 F.Supp. 1323, 1326 (E.D.Pa.1972), motion denied 346 F.Supp. 1333. See also Storke & Sears, Transfer of Mortgaged Property, 38 Cornell L.Q. 185, 202 n. 69 (1953).

13. This is true even though the purchaser does not receive a deed until after sale of a second parcel. The equity attaches when the consideration is paid. Libby v. Tufts, 121 N.Y. 172, 24 N.E. 12 (1890). This equity would be defeated, of course, if the purchaser of the second parcel did not have notice and could qualify as a bona fide purchaser in other respects.

underlying mortgage through searching the records or otherwise [14] would not enter into such a transaction if they possessed business experience or had consulted a competent lawyer.[15] But one having done so has a right to have the remaining property in the hands of the mortgagor exonerate the parcel he bought.

It has sometimes been asserted that the right of grantee to have marshaling is dependent upon having received a deed with covenants of warranty.[16] Historically this has not been true,[17] and indeed this view does not seem proper. Since it is an equitable concept, the vital question is whether the duty of paying off the debt rests upon the mortgagor rather than the grantee.[18] On that question, the presence

14. Their ignorance is as to the existence of the mortgage, not its legal consequences. It cannot, therefore, be urged against helping them that their plight is the result of a mistake of law. See note, 23 Va.L.Rev. 298 (1937).

15. In subdivision financing it is customary to provide in the underlying mortgage agreement that the mortgagee is required "to release any lot from the lien of the mortgage on payment of a specified amount . . . . The contract between the subdivision company and the purchaser should contain a clause requiring the former, upon full payment by the latter, to pay the mortgagee the required amount and procure the release of lien. It is unwise to purchase a lot in a subdivision without first checking the mortgage and contract to see that these provisions are present." Storke and Sears, Transfer of Mortgaged Property, 38 Cornell L.Q. 185, 211 (1953). The language of such provisions has not been standardized and in construing them there is a divergence of authority as to whether the partial release privilege is personal to the mortgagor or can be taken advantage of by purchasers of portions of the property. See 31 Col.L.Rev. 894, 895 (1931). Agreement between mortgagee and mortgagor gave grantee mortgagor's rights in Conway v. Andrews, 286 Ala. 28, 236 So.2d 687 (1970).

16. See, e. g., Pomeroy, Equity Juris, 5th ed., § 1225, "This relation * * * results from the form of the conveyance, which, being a warranty deed, or equivalent to a warranty, shows conclusively an intention between the two that the grantor is to assume the whole burden of the encumbrance as a charge upon his own parcel, while the grantee is to take and hold his portion entirely free."

17. "We are unable to find a case deciding, . . . that the equity could not be founded upon a quitclaim deed; * * * neither can we find a case which affirmatively decides that the rule depends upon the existence or nonexistence of covenants of warranty.' Biswell v. Gladney, 182 S.W. 1168, 1172 (Tex.Civ.App.1916), modified on other grounds 213 S.W. 256 (1919). In Wadsworth v. Lyon, 93 N.Y. 201, 45 Am.Rep. 190 (1883), in spite of the absence of covenants of title, the grantee of mortgaged property who had paid the full value of the property was held entitled to exoneration. In Wilcox v. Campbell, 106 N.Y. 325, 12 N.E. 823 (1887), although the grantee took a quitclaim deed he was held entitled to marshal against a prior grantee of another parcel who assumed the mortgage.

18. "It [the rule requiring sale in inverse order of alienation] rests chiefly, perhaps, upon the grounds that where one who is bound to pay a mortgage confers upon others rights in any portion of the property, retaining other portions himself, it is unjust that they should be deprived of their rights, so long as he has property covered by the mortgage, out of which the debt can be made. * * * The rule cannot, therefore, depend upon the existence or nonexistence of covenants of warranty. Cooper v. Bigley, 13 Mich. 463, 474 (1865). See 131 A.L.R. 103 (1941).

or absence of covenants in the deed has value as evidence in determining the question of fact,[19] but otherwise it is immaterial.

The agreement of purchase having created an equity of marshaling which attaches to the rest of the property under the mortgage remaining in the mortgagor's hands, that equity will follow it into the hands of anyone who has notice of it.[20] When T–2 buys Y with notice of T–1's equity he will, of course, take subject to it. Thus after T–1 bought parcel X, parcels Y and Z are subject in R's hands to T–1's equity that they shall be applied to E's debt before X is touched. But if T–2 bought on the same terms as T–1, he, in turn, has a similar equity against Z which stays in R's hands. Or, if R sells Z to T–3 who takes with notice, T–3 will take it subject to the prior equitable rights of T–1 and T–2. Thus when E seeks to foreclose, T–1 can compel him to proceed first against Y and Z before seeking to realize on X; and T–2 in turn can demand that, as between Y and Z, Z go first. Thus we have the rule of inverse order of alienation, which is, as was stated earlier, the great weight of authority in the United States.[21]

While the courts in Iowa and Kentucky will apply the doctrine of marshaling to the extent that the residue of property remaining in

19. A warranty deed may show intent of the mortgagor to remain liable on the whole mortgage. Seasons, Inc. v. Atwell, 86 N.M. 751, 527 P.2d 792 (1974); Taylor v. Jones, 285 Ala. 353, 232 So.2d 601 (1970).

20. Taylor v. Jones, 285 Ala. 353, 232 So.2d 601 (1970). "The second purchaser sits in the seat of his grantor, and must pay the whole value of what he bought towards the extinguishment of the mortgage, before he can call on the first purchaser to pay anything. The first sale having thrown the whole burden on the part reserved, it cannot be thrown back again by the second sale. In other words the second purchaser takes the land he buys subject to all the liabilities under which the grantor held it." Carpenter v. Koons, 20 Pa. 222, 226 (1852). Brown v. Simons, 44 N.H. 475 (1863). National Sav. Bank v. Creswell, 100 U.S. 630, 637, 25 L.Ed. 713 (D.C.1879); Clowes v. Dickenson, 5 Johns, Ch. 235 (N.Y.1821). "In the case of the sale by the mortgagor of all the mortgaged property to different purchasers at the same time, their equities must be regarded as equal, and each must contribute ratably to the discharge of the common burthen * * *." Brown v. Simons, 44 N.H. 475, 478 (1863).

21. Seasons, Inc. v. Atwell, 86 N.M. 751, 527 P.2d 792 (1974); Taylor v. Jones, 285 Ala. 353, 232 So.2d 601 (1970); In re Penn Central Transportation Co., 346 F.Supp. 1323 (E.D.Pa. 1972); Ellickson v. Dull, 34 Colo.App. 25, 521 P.2d 1282 (1974); In Voltin v. Voltin, 179 N.W.2d 127 (N.D.1970) portion given to wife in divorce decree to go last; In Broughton v. Mt. Healthy Flying Service, Inc., 104 Ohio App. 479, 143 N.E.2d 597 (1957) where parcels had been leased, creditor must look first to residue. See 131 A.L.R. n. 11 for collection of authorities applying the rule.

"It appears from the precedents and authorities dealing with the Rule of Inverse Order of Alienation that whether jurisdictions have adopted the rule in its entirety or with some modifications, they are virtually unanimous in holding that where a mortgagor conveys a portion and retains a portion of the encumbered property, the property so retained should first be subjected to the payment of the debt before resorting to the portion conveyed." Seasons, Inc. v. Atwell, 86 N.M. 751, 756, 527 P.2d 792, 797 (1974).

the hands of the mortgagor will be used to exonerate a grantee or second mortgagee, they reject the doctrine which would require that the debt be satisfied out of portions of the property sold or mortgaged in the order of inverse alienation. Instead the debt is pro-rated against the two tracts or their proceeds proportionate to their respective values.[22] The argument in favor of this minority attitude is that "as between two grantees purchasing different parcels of the incumbered premises at different times, there is no more moral obligation on the one to pay than on the other. Both of them have purchased premises that are alike affected by a lien which neither created nor undertook to pay. The purchased premises are liable to be sold because of the failure of their grantor to discharge his undertaking, and not because of any failure on their part. In such cases, their interest is common, their rights are equal, and there should be equality of burden." [23]

The argument is plausible but there are answers to it. First, a grantee, unless he can qualify as a bona fide purchaser, takes the property subject to the equities held therein by third persons.[24] Thus T–2 takes parcel Y subject to an existing equity in favor of T–1 which arose when T–1 bought X. Second, a mortgagor who by transferring a part of his mortgaged land established an equity in his grantee to have the residue applied first in satisfaction of the debt could divest this equity at pleasure by transferring such residue to another.[25] This would be an undesirable and anomalous result.

Going back to the majority view, if T–2 and T–3 have actual notice there is no question but that the rule operates. If they do not have actual notice will they be charged with constructive notice by reason of the fact that T–1 recorded the conveyance to him? Most states say yes.[26] The rule has been criticized, however, as placing an undue burden upon later purchasers, and as being contrary to the spirit of the recording acts.[27] There is an additional objection where

22. Bartley v. Pikeville Nat. Bank & Trust Co., 532 S.W.2d 446 (Ky.App. 1976); Bronaugh v. Burley Tobacco Co., 212 Ky. 680, 280 S.W. 97 (1926); Bates v. Ruddick, 2 Iowa 423, 2 Clarke 423, 65 Am.Dec. 774 (1856); Huff v. Farwell, 67 Iowa 298, 25 N.W. 252 (1885). "Even in Kentucky marshaling is granted if the mortgagor agreed with the first grantee to confine the mortgage to the retained tract by procuring a release from its operation (Calhoun v. Federal Land Bank, 230 Ky. 460, 465, 20 S.W.2d 72, 74 [1929]), or, probably, if the mortgagor expressly agreed with him that he might have marshaling, and the subsequent grantee or mortgagee had knowledge of the agreement." Campbell, Cases Mortgages, 2d ed., 619 n. 6.

23. Bates v. Ruddick, 2 Iowa, 423, 430, 65 Am.Dec. 774, 779 (1856).

24. Huston, Enforcement of Decrees in Equity, 127–131.

25. See Tiffany, Real Prop., 3d ed., § 1446. Cf. Shenkin, Marshaling of Securities, 79 U. of Pa.L.Rev. 785, n. 14 (1931).

26. Brown v. Simons, 44 N.H. 475 (1863); see Iglehart v. Crane & Wesson, 42 Ill. 261, 265, 269; Ann.Cas. 1916D, 1119 (1866).

27. "The court, in effect, is imposing upon C [the subsequent grantee from the mortgagor of a part of the mortgaged property] a duty of running back every chain of title connected

the terms of conveyance between the mortgagor and his first grantee did not make clear whether the grantee was entitled to exoneration against the remainder. Should a later purchaser of part or all of the rest of the property be put upon inquiry to find out, at his peril, the real terms of the bargain? If so, and this is applied also to cases where notice of the prior conveyance is only constructive (because the prior conveyance is recorded), the objections stated above become stronger.[28]

Where the first grantee failed to record and T–2 took his land without actual or constructive notice of T–1, it has been held that T–2 has an equity to have X sold before Y.[29] This seems correct if the rule of constructive notice by recordation is accepted. Since T–2 has no notice of a prior conveyance, he has no reason to believe that he is not the first grantee and he would justifiably expect to be exonerated out of the land he believed was a residue in the hands of the grantor.

There is, however, a situation in which it would seem that T–1's failure to record should not cause T–2 to advance to T–1's position. Where E has a mortgage on two separate parcels of land securing one debt and T–1 takes a second mortgage on parcel X, his recording of the lien on X would have nothing to do with parcel Y and would not put T–2 who takes a second mortgage on Y on notice. Therefore the recording acts would not apply to T–1's recording as giving notice to T–2 and if T–1 fails to record, T–2 should not be given a windfall by advancing to T–1's priority position. It would seem that the proper result in this case would be to pro-rate the debt between the two parcels according to their respective values.

§ 10.11 Effect of Assumption or Taking "Subject" to the Mortgage

Where a mortgagor sells part of a mortgaged tract to a grantee who assumes the payment of the mortgage, the parcel conveyed becomes primarily liable for the payment of the mortgage and the part retained is only secondarily liable.[30] The grantee is also personally

with a blanket mortgage, to ascertain whether any latent equities exist. To impose such a duty is contrary to the spirit of our Recording Acts, the policy of which is to remove secret liens. * * * Prospective purchasers or mortgagees of real estate are rightly considered to be on notice of prior liens on the property concerned, but the equity to marshal is one that can only be uncovered after, what may be in some cases, a most exhaustive and unreasonable search." Note, 79 U. of Pa.L.Rev. 782, 787 n. 28 (1931).

28. See note 27, supra.

29. In Gray v. H. M. Loud & Sons Lumber Co., 128 Mich. 427, 87 N.W. 376, 54 L.R.A. 731 (1901), the lower court had pro rated the mortgage between two tracts, each of which had been sold by warranty deed with each purchaser paying the full value of the property. The first grantee failed to record, and the subsequent grantee had no actual notice of the first. The upper court reversed the decision and held that the entire mortgage should be paid out of the part first sold. Look also at LaFarge Fire Ins. Co. v. Bell, 22 Barb. 54 (N.Y.1856); Bode v. Rhodes, 119 Wash. 98, 204 P. 802 (1922).

30. Sanders v. Lackey, 59 Tenn.App. 207, 439 S.W.2d 610 (1968); Cobb v. Osman, 83 Nev. 415, 433 P.2d 259

liable as principal for the payment of the debt and the mortgagor and the rest of the mortgaged land is surety only as to this personal obligation.[31] As a consequence, not only does the inverse order of alienation rule not apply [32] but the rule is reversed. Since not only the grantee but the parcel conveyed to him have the duty to exonerate the residue in the hands of the mortgagor, the mortgagee can be compelled to foreclose first on the parcel transferred to the grantee.[33] Where the mortgagor afterwards sells the remainder of the tract to a subsequent purchaser who pays the full price on the remaining portion, all of the mortgagor's rights with respect to the assuming grantee's duty in respect to this remaining part inure to the benefit of the second purchaser.[34]

These rights give the subsequent purchaser a choice of several courses. In a foreclosure action by the mortgagee he may have the parcel held by the assuming grantee sold before that held by himself.[35] If the proceeds of this sale are insufficient to pay the mortgage he may, at his option, either pay the balance due upon the mortgage in order to save his land, or let the land be sold.[36] In either event he

(1967); Chancellor of New Jersey v. Towell, 80 N.J.Eq. 223, 82 A. 861, 39 L.R.A.,N.S., 359, Ann.Cas.1914A, 710 (1912); Wilcox v. Campbell, 106 N.Y. 325, 12 N.E. 823 (1887); Reid v. Whisenant, 191 Ga. 503, 131 N.E. 904, 44 A.L.R. 599 (1926).

31. Id. Prudential Sav. and Loan Ass'n v. Nadler, 37 Ill.App.3d 168, 345 N.E. 2d 782 (1976); Toler v. Baldwin County Savings & Loan Ass'n, 286 Ala. 320, 239 So.2d 751 (1970); Smith v. Olney Federal Savings & Loan Ass'n, 415 S.W.2d 515 (Tex.Civ.App. 1967).

32. In re Beacon Distributors, Inc., 441 F.2d 547 (C.A.R.I.1971); Cobb v. Osman, note 30 supra; Sanders v. Lackey, note 30, supra. See 131 A.L.R. 4, 62 (1941). Where the first grantee of a portion of mortgaged land assumes or takes subject to the mortgage and other parcels are then sold to grantees who pay full value with an agreement that the mortgagor shall pay off the mortgage, although the parcel in the hands of the first grantee is subject to being sold first, the inverse order of alienation rule would apply to the other grantees. Moore v. Shurtleff, 128 Ill. 370, 21 N.E. 775 (1889).

33. Chancellor of New Jersey v. Towell, 80 N.J.Eq. 223, 82 A. 861, 39 L.R. A.,N.S., 359, Ann.Cas.1914A, 710 (1912); Epperson v. Cappellino, 113 Cal.App. 473, 298 P. 533 (1931). Contra: Ewing v. Bay Minette Land Co., 232 Ala. 22, 26, 166 So. 409, 413 (1936), on ground marshaling cannot be invoked by a debtor. See § 10.14, post. This right of the mortgagor to marshaling will be available against subsequent transferees from the grantee if they are not bona fide purchasers. E. g., Costa v. Sardinha, 265 Mass. 319, 163 N.E. 887 (1928).

34. Sanders v. Lackey, note 30, supra; Reid v. Whisenant, note 30, supra. See 1926, 44 A.L.R. 608.

35. Wilcox v. Campbell, 106 N.Y. 325, 329, 12 N.E. 823, 826 (1887); Dieckman v. Walser, 114 N.J.Eq. 382, 386, 168 A. 582, 583 (1933); affirming 112 N.J.Eq. 46, 163 A. 284; Union Central Life Ins. Co. v. Cates, 193 N.C. 456, 463, 464, 137 S.E. 324, 327, 328 (1927); Welch v. Beers, 90 Mass. 151 (1864). Although the subsequent grantee may compel the mortgagee to foreclose first on the property held by the assuming grantee, in the event of a deficiency the mortgagee may sell the remainder of the tract in the hands of the mortgagor or subsequent grantee. Vanderspeck v. Federal Land Bank, 175 Miss. 759, 765, 167 So. 782, 783 (1936). See 39 L.R. A.,N.S., 359, 360 (1912).

36. See Wilcox v. Campbell, n. 35, supra. He might also pay off the en-

has an action against the grantee for failing to perform his promise to pay the mortgage.[37] His damages, depending upon which option he selected, would be the amount he paid,[38] or either the value of the parcel in his hands [39] or the amount of the proceeds from its sale that were applied in discharge of the mortgage foreclosure decree.[40]

As stated by one court: "[W]here the mortgagor sells part of the mortgaged property 'subject to' the pre-existing mortgage without an agreement about payment of the mortgage, it is generally held that the mortgage lien remains an equal charge against all the mortgaged tract and that either mortgagor-vender or his vendee may enforce pro-rata application of the separate tracts to the satisfaction of the mortgage." [41] If it were clear that the purchase of the part was subject to the entire amount of the mortgage which was deducted from its purchase price, the part sold would be primarily liable for the entire debt. In such a case the mortgagor and subsequent purchasers for full value of portions of the tract left in the hands of the mortgagor could insist that the mortgagee, on foreclosing, resort first to the parcel sold subject to the mortgage.[42] Or if there is an explicit provision or clear evidence that the conveyance of a parcel is subject to a specified portion of the mortgage, the parties' intent will govern.[43] In many cases, however, there is no evidence of any express or implied agreement about payment of the mortgage. When such is the situation, where one parcel of a mortgaged tract is sold subject to the mortgage and a later portion is also sold subject to the mortgage, the weight of authority is that the debt will be prorated between the two grantees in proportion to the value of their respec-

tire mortgage before any of the property is sold. In that case he would be subrogated to the rights of the mortgagee and could enforce the mortgage against the assuming grantee and, if the property is insufficient, take a judgment for the deficiency.

37. Sanders v. Lackey, note 30, supra.

38. See Cooley v. Murray, 11 Colo. App. 241, 52 P. 1108 (1898); Wilcox v. Campbell, 106 N.Y. 325, 12 N.E. 823 (1887).

39. Reid v. Whisenant, 161 Ga. 503, 131 N.E. 904, 44 A.L.R. 599 (1926).

40. Wilcox v. Campbell, 106 N.Y. 325, 12 N.E. 823 (1887). The various alternative remedies are not only set forth clearly but the underlying reasons for them are stated accurately by the court in its opinion.

41. Sanders v. Lackey, 59 Tenn.App. 207, 219, 439 S.W.2d 610, 616 (1968).

42. See 39 L.R.A.,N.S., 361 (1912);

43. Mickle v. Maxfield, 42 Mich. 304, 3 N.W. 961 (1879); Engle v. Haines, 5 N.J.Eq. 186 (1845) 43 Am.Dec. 624, affirmed 5 N.J.Eq. 632; Moore v. Shurtleff, 128 Ill. 370, 21 N.E. 775 (1889); New England Loan & Trust Co. v. Stephens, 16 Utah 385, 52 P. 624 (1898). If such an agreement is put into the mortgage it clearly will be binding upon all later transferees of any part of the property. Mickle v. Maxfield, supra; Maurer v. Arab Petroleum Corp., 134 Tex. 256, 135 S.W.2d 87, 131 A.L.R. 1 (1940). The same result can be accomplished by inserting a common provision in all deeds transferring fractional interests in the property. Moore v. Shurtleff, supra; New England Loan & Trust Co. v. Stephens, supra.

tive lots.[44] And the same has been held where the mortgagor first conveyed one parcel of the mortgaged land to T–1 who assumed the payment of the mortgage and later conveyed another parcel to T–2 subject to it.[45]

§ 10.12 Gift Conveyances

Where the mortgagor makes a gift conveyance of a portion of a mortgaged tract with no covenants protecting the grantee against the mortgage, it has been held that the donee will take it subject to a primary liability for a proportional part of the mortgage debt.[46] It has been questioned whether this should be true where the grantor is personally liable for the debt.[47] In such cases, it is urged, the presumption should be that the transferor is to pay his own debt and, consequently, the land retained would be primarily liable.[48] If there is a covenant against encumbrances covering the mortgage, this has been held to be sufficient evidence of intention that the land under the gift conveyance shall not be liable for the debt as to throw the primary liability upon the residue in the hands of the grantor.[49]

§ 10.13 Second Mortgages

Reverting to our hypothetical of Blackacre, if T–1 is a mortgagee rather than a purchaser, T–1 and E are both creditors of a com-

44. Briscoe v. Power, 47 Ill. 447 (1868); Carpenter v. Koons, 20 Pa. 222 (1852); Stephens v. Clay, 17 Colo. 489, 30 P. 43 (1892); Hooper v. Capitol Life Ins. Co., 92 Colo. 376, 384, 20 P.2d 1011, 1014 (1933); Markham v. Smith, 119 Conn. 355, 363, 176 A. 880, 884 (1935); Hall v. Morgan, 79 Mo. 47 (1883); Hog v. Bramhall, 19 N.J.Eq. 563, 97 Am.Dec. 687; Stuyvesant Security Co. v. Dreyer, 103 N.J.Eq. 457, 461, 143 A. 616, 617 (1929), affirmed 105 N.J.Eq. 585, 148 A. 920, values at time of conveyance taken; Dieckman v. Walser, 112 N.J. Eq. 46, 53, 55, 163 A. 284, 287, 288 (1932), affirmed 114 N.J.Eq. 382, 168 A. 582. Cf. Savings Investment & Trust Co. v. United Realty & Mortgage Co., 84 N.J.Eq. 472, 94 A. 588 (1915), Ann.Cas.1916D, 1134, "subject to" clause in second mortgage.

45. Pearson v. Bailey, 177 Mass. 318, 58 N.E. 1028 (1901).

46. Mills v. Kelley, 62 N.J.Eq. 213, 215, 50 A. 144, 145 (1901) ("Where the conveyance is voluntary, and there are no covenants, then equality is equity. There is no reason why the voluntary grantee should not take the land with any charge that may rest upon it, except in so far as the parties themselves have otherwise stipulated."); Jackson v. Condict, 57 N.J.Eq. 522, 526, 41 A. 374 (1898). But see 131 A.L.R. 4, 88 (1941).

47. See Tiffany, Real Property, 3d ed., § 1446.

48. Id. In re Darby's Estate, 2 Ch. 465 (1907) (devisees of balance of mortgagor's property denied contribution against donee-grantee of mortgaged property by deed containing no reference to the mortgage and no covenants for title, express or implied).

49. Harrison v. Guerin, 27 N.J.Eq. 219 (1876). See Howser v. Cruikshank, 122 Ala. 256, 25 So. 206, 82 Am.St. Rep. 76 (1898). The covenant would serve only as evidence of intent. See 5 Houston L.R. 221 (1967). Since covenants cannot be effective without consideration, a warranty deed without exception is unenforceable and the donee has no recourse against mortgagor should mortgagee foreclose and cut out donee.

mon debtor and this is a situation to which the two funds rule applies.[50] In the simple example where R has made only one conveyance to T–1 or given one second mortgage to T–1 the result is the same, but it is reached by a different rationale. Under the inverse order doctrine it is that the mortgagor who incurred the debt should be the one to pay it. Under the two funds doctrine it is that the senior encumbrancer should not be able to foreclose on the only fund available to T–1. However the equities which really must be considered are not between E and T–1. E will be paid in any case and it does not matter to E whether he proceeds against the property upon which T–1 has a second mortgage or the property upon which he alone holds a mortgage. So the equity to be considered is actually the same as that considered under the inverse rule of alienation—should R, who incurred the debt, bear the burden of paying it off as opposed to T–1, who took the second mortgage as security expecting that R would pay off the first mortgage. Where there are no other junior lienholders involved or where their rights will not be prejudiced, the two funds rule will be applied.[51]

50. Generally the funds must be in the hands of a common debtor of both creditors. Dixieland Realty Co. v. Wysor, 272 N.C. 172, 158 S.E.2d 7 (1967); Little v. United Investors Corp., 157 Conn. 44, 245 A.2d 567 (1968); Markman v. Russell State Bank, 358 F.2d 488 (C.A.Okl.1966). See 135 A.L.R. 739–40 for additional cases. But there are exceptions. See Charles Constr. Co., Inc. v. Leisure Resources, Inc., 1 Mass.App. 755, 307 N.E.2d 336 (1974); the court found the reasoning underlying the two funds doctrine had equal application where there is only one fund. See also 8 L.R.A.,N.S., 965 (1912).

51. Associates Realty Credit Ltd. v. Brune, 89 Wash.2d 6, 568 P.2d 787 (1977); In the Matter of Forester, 529 F.2d 310 (C.A.Cal.1976); Zellerback Paper Co. v. Valley Nat. Bank of Arizona, 18 Ariz.App. 301, 501 P.2d 570 (1972); Charles Constr. Co., Inc. v. Leisure Resources, Inc., 1 Mass.App. 755, 307 N.E.2d 336 (1974); In Waff Bros., Inc. v. Bank of North Carolina, N.A., 289 N.C. 198, 221 S.E.2d 273 (1976) a preliminary injunction was granted so that the trial court could determine whether the creditor did have security in a second fund. In Columbia Bank for Cooperatives v. Lee, 368 F.2d 934 (C.A.N.C.1966), certiorari denied 386 U.S. 992, 87 S.Ct. 1308, 18 L.Ed.2d 338 (1967), the doubly secured bank was required to satisfy its debt from the stock rather than the real property because the stock was worth more in the bank's hands than it would be in the hands of the competing creditor. In United States v. Herman, 310 F.2d 846 (C.A. N.Y.1962), certiorari denied 373 U.S. 903, 83 S.Ct. 1291, 10 L.Ed.2d 199 (1963) and United States v. Stutsman County Implement Co., 274 F.2d 733 (C.A.N.D.1960) the courts refused to subject the government to the requirement to marshal assets in favor of junior lienors. But the court enforced the requirement in United States v. LeMay, 346 F.Supp. 328 (E. D.Wis.1972), citing United States Fidelity & Guar. Co. v. Long, 214 F. Supp. 307, 319 (D.Or.1963), "In the application of the doctrine, the United States and its agencies are on an equal basis with other creditors."

For an excellent collection of authorities, see 106 A.L.R. 1102 (1937). See Gest, Marshalling Assets with Reference to the Rights of Successive Part Purchasers and Incumbrancers, 27 Am.L.Reg.,N.S., 739 (1888); Strachan, The Marshalling of Mortgages, 22 L. Q.Rev. 307 (1906); See also notes, 79 U. of Pa.L.Rev. 782 (1931); 18 Harv.L. Rev. 453 (1905); 24 Iowa L.Rev. 328 (1939); 106 A.L.R. 1102 (1937); 5 L. R.A. 280 (1889); 12 L.R.A.,N.S., 965 (1908); 119 A.L.R. 1109 (1939).

If there has been a subsequent second mortgage or conveyance to T–2, does T–1 have the same right to marshal as against T–2 that he would have under the inverse order rule if he had paid full value with the agreement that the duty of discharging the mortgage would fall upon the residue of the land retained by R? Where the question involves competing holders of second mortgages or a second mortgagee and a later transferee, two divergent lines of authority have developed. The major difference between the two lines of cases under the two funds rule is the same distinction that has been offered to explain the difference between the inverse order rule and the two funds doctrine.[52] One group of courts holds that T–1 acquires a fixed and established right in equity at the time he takes his second mortgage on lot X to require E to look primarily to lots Y and Z when he forecloses and to sell them before he resorts to lot X held by T–1,[53] provided that E's rights will not be prejudiced by so doing.[54] Or where both lots must be sold to satisfy E's mortgage T–1 will have a right to any surplus from the sale.[55] This equity would be the same as the equity acquired by T–1 if T–1 were a purchaser rather than a second mortgagee, and under this line of authority the inverse order of alienation is applied.[56] Consequently any subsequent taker of lots X or Y by way of purchase for full value or as second mortgagee will take subject to T–1's prior equity unless he can qualify as a bona fide purchaser for value without notice.[57] Courts adopting this view also hold that T–1 can effectively guard against such a possibility by re-

52. "[T]he two doctrines are quite distinct. The equity of marshaling, until it is asserted, is a mere inchoate equity subject to displacement, whereas the equity of the purchaser of land subject to a lien to have that lien satisfied out of land remaining in the grantor and then out of the parcels subsequently conveyed in inverse order of alienation, where it exists at all, is a fixed indefeasible right." Fidelity & Casualty Co. v. Massachusetts Mutual Life Ins. Co., 74 F.2d 881, 884 (C.C.A.N.C.1935).

53. See note 56, infra.

54. See note 1, § 10.9, supra.

55. Banks-Miller Supply Co. v. Smallridge, 154 W.Va. 360, 175 S.E.2d 446 (1970).

56. Sibley v. Baker, 23 Mich. 312 (1871); Hunt v. Townsend, 4 Sandf. Ch. 510 (N.Y.1847); Riverside Apartment Corp. v. Capital Constr. Co., 107 N.J.Eq. 405, 413, 152 A. 763, 769 (1930), affirmed 110 N.J.Eq. 67, 158 A. 740, probably constructive notice from recording; Fidelity & Cas. Co. v. Mass. Mut. Life Ins. Co., 74 F.2d 881 (C.C.A.N.C.1935), paramount tax lien on the various parcels; Bank of Commerce of Evansville v. First Nat. Bank of Evansville, 150 Ind. 588, 594, 50 N.E. 566, 568 (1898), senior judgment lien on both properties; mortgage on one, followed by conveyance of other to trustee to pay creditors; Sanborn, McDuffie Co. v. Keefe, 88 N.H. 236, 187 A. 97, 106 A.L.R. 1097 (1936); Ingersoll v. Somers Land Co., 82 N.J.Eq. 476, 89 A. 288 (1913); Robeson's Appeal, 117 Pa. 628, 12 A. 51 (1888), senior judgment lien on both properties; recorded mortgage on one followed by mortgage on the other; later mortgagee charged with constructive notice of the earlier. See 76 A.L.R.3d 333, § 4.

57. As to the rule where the transferees of other parcels have not parted with value cf. quotation from Newby v. Fox, n. 69, infra, decided in a jurisidiction following the second view in respect to marshaling by a junior mortgagee on the first parcel.

cording his second mortgage on X which will then give constructive notice of his equity to any later taker of Y or Z.[58] If the subsequent taker is not a bona fide purchaser, the priority of T–1 over him is said to rest upon the fact that his equity is not only prior in time but that the later equity is inferior to his either by reason of notice or lack of value being given for it.[59] If T–2, the subsequent purchaser or mortgagee of Y or Z, can qualify under the bona fide purchase rule, he would then stand on an equality with T–1 and the paramount mortgage would then be apportioned between them according to the value of their respective lots.[60]

The rule in England [61] and that followed by many cases in this country [62] is that the equity of marshaling acquired by T–1 when he takes his second mortgage on X is not a fixed equitable right when T–1 acquires his lien, but remains inchoate until the right is invoked by actual proceedings to enforce it; [63] and if at that time the rights

58. Harron v. Du Bois, 64 N.J.Eq. 657, 54 A. 857 (1903); Ingersoll v. Somers Land Co., note 56, supra; Appeal of Robeson, note 56, supra. If T–1 fails to record he cannot invoke the doctrine against one without actual notice. Birch River Boom & Lumber Co. v. Glendon Boom & Lumber Co., 71 W.Va. 139, 76 S.E. 167 (1922). Some cases do not even mention notice. See 106 A.L.R. 1102, 1103 (1937).

If the paramount lien arises against each of the two or more parcels by separate instruments only most exhaustive search of all deeds or mortgages to or from the mortgagor could reveal to T–2 the prior junior mortgage on lot X to T–1. See 5 Duke B.A.J. 35, 39 (1937), such a burden is much too onerous to impose. Green v. Ramage, 18 Ohio 428 (1849).

59. Conrad v. Harrison, Va.1882, 3 Leigh 532 (Va.1882); Ingersoll v. Somers Land Co., 82 N.J.Eq. 476, 89 A. 288 (1913), constructive notice by record and later mortgage of other parcel was to secure pre-existing debt; Harron v. Du Bois, 64 N.J.Eq. 657, 54 A. 857 (1903), later encumbrance was judgment lien acquired with constructive notice of prior recorded mortgage. See Newby v. Fox, 90 Kan. 317, 319, 133 P. 890, 891 (1913); Bank of Commerce v. First Nat. Bank, note 56, supra, second parcel conveyed to trustee to pay creditors; Sanborn, McDuffie Co. v. Keefe, 88 N.H. 236, 187 A. 97, 106 A.L.R. 1097 (1936). See also 106 A.L.R. 1102, 1103 (1937). Cf. Sager v. Tupper, 35 Mich. 133 (1876); Reilly v. Mayer, 12 N.J.Eq. 55 (1858).

60. Cf. Green v. Ramage, 18 Ohio 428 (1849). Of course both T–1 and T–2 would have an equity to have lot Z in the hands of R sold before touching either X or Y. In such a case any deficiency would be prorated between the latter. See Newby v. Fox, quoted n. 69, infra.

61. Aldrich v. Cooper, 8 Ves. 381 (1803); Barnes v. Racster, 1 Younge & C.Ch.Cas. 401 (1842); Bugden v. Bignold, 2 Y. & C.C.C. 377 (1843). "This disposition of the problem * * * is perhaps attributable to the absence of a recording system at the time the law crystallized. This fact kept the English courts from dealing with the question of presumed notice * * *." Shenkin, Marshaling of Securities, 79 U. of Pa.L.Rev. 782, 784 (1931). See Kay, L.J., in Flint v. Howard, 2 Ch. 54, 73 (1893); Barnes v. Racster, 1 Younge & C.C.C. 401 (1842). See also 106 A.L.R. 1102, 1109 (1937). But cf. Falconbridge, Mortgages, 2d ed., 1931, § 139.

62. "The decided cases in this country are in conflict. Many jurisdictions adopt the English view, while equally as many courts * * * have reached a contrary result, and have practically accorded the equity to marshal the effect of a lien." Shenkin, op. cit. supra note 61.

63. In some cases either of two junior creditors is in a position to demand

of third persons are involved, it will not be enforced to their prejudice.[64] As a consequence, the paramount mortgage is prorated between the two junior mortgagees in proportion to the value of the parcel to which each has claim.[65] In some of the American cases marshaling is refused by simply denying that when T–2 takes his interest in Y he is charged with constructive notice of the inchoate equity of T–1 through his recorded second mortgage on X.[66]

The English courts prorate even though the later second mortgagee of lot Y has actual notice of the prior junior lien on lot X.[67] There is American authority that T–1's prior equity, even though regarded as inchoate, will prevail over T–2 if the latter did not part with value for it.[68] However, if T–2 paid value, doubt has been ex-

marshaling. In In the Matter of Forester, 529 F.2d 310 (C.A.Cal.1976), a junior lienor was competing with the trustee in bankruptcy (in behalf of the mortgagor's creditors) where each had claims against one fund and the bank as paramount mortgagee had claims against two funds. The majority held that the junior lienor's right to marshaling became vested at the point when he demanded that the first mortgagee marshal its liens. The dissent pointed out that the trustee had already demanded of the bank that it marshal its liens in favor of the bankruptcy estate and that the junior lienor should lose the marshaling contest because its demand for marshaling was later in time than the trustee's and its equities were inferior to those of the trustee. The dissent continued: "The demand is an essential step in perfecting a right to marshal, good against a superior lienor or creditor upon whom the demand is made and against others who are also entitled to marshaling, but the demand does not itself create a lien or interest in any asset. A right to marshal does not ripen into an interest in the nature of an equitable lien until the court, applying equitable principles, enforces it." Id. at 319. Both majority and dissent cite Harrington v. Taylor, 176 Cal. 802, 169 P. 690 (1917) which states: "This inchoate right or equity is not a lien, and is therefore subject to defeat at any time before it is attempted to be enforced."

64. Vandever Investment Co., Inc. v. H. E. Leonhardt Lumber Co., 503 P. 2d 185, 76 A.L.R.3d 315 (Okl.1972); Platte Valley Bank of North Bend v. Kracl, 185 Neb. 168, 174 N.W.2d 724 (1970); St. Clair Sav. Ass'n v. Janson, 40 Ohio App.2d 211, 318 N.E.2d 538, 69 O.O.2d 196 (1974). Two funds denied when it would prejudice general creditors, Langel v. Moore, 119 Ohio St. 299, 164 N.E. 118 (1928); Bronaugh v. Burley Tobacco Co., 212 Ky. 680, 685, 280 S.W. 97 (1926), junior mortgage on one tract, followed by execution lien on other tract; Richards v. Cowles, 105 Iowa 734, 75 N. W. 648 (1898).

65. Vandever Investment Co., Inc. v. H. E. Leonhardt Lumber Co., n. 64, supra; Bryson v. Newtown Real Estate and Development Corp., 153 Conn. 267, 216 A.2d 176 (1965); Conneaut Bldg. & Loan Co. v. Felch, 100 Ohio App. 52, 135 N.E.2d 480, 60 O.O. 15 (1955); Green v. Ramage, 18 Ohio 428, 51 Am.Dec. 458 (1849). See 76 A.L.R.3d 351, § 5 (1977).

66. See Gilliam v. McCormack, 85 Tenn. 597, 4 S.W. 521 (1887); Bronaugh v. Burley Tobacco Co., note 64, supra; Cf. last sentence quoted from Shenkin, note 61, supra.

67. Barnes v. Racster, 1 Younge & C. C.C. 401 (1842). See n. 61, supra.

68. E. g., Ingersoll v. Somers Land Co., 82 N.J.Eq. 476, 89 A. 288 (1913), later mortgage of other parcel was to secure preexisting debt; Harron v. Du Bois, 64 N.J.Eq. 657, 54 A. 857 (1903), later encumbrance was judgment lien; Humphries v. Fitzpatrick, 253 Ky. 517, 69 S.W.2d 1058 (1934), attachment creditor as to second parcel; Bank of Commerce of Evansville v. First Nat. Bank of Evansville, 150 Ind. 588, 594, 50 N.E. 566, 568 (1898), later conveyance of second parcel to

pressed as to whether T–1 should prevail over him even if he actually knew of the existence of T–1's mortgage but had no reason to anticipate that T–1 would invoke the doctrine of marshaling.[69] Even if T–2 is a purchaser for value but has notice of a proceeding by T–1 to enforce his equity he will take subject to it.[70]

The doctrine of the first group of cases has been vigorously criticised as a mistaken and improper application of the doctrine of sale in the inverse order of alienation.[71] It is said that a second mortgagee on X, unlike a purchaser of it for full value, does not pay to get the land free and clear of the first mortgage. He merely bargains for a security interest in it subordinate to the first mortgage. So far as other portions of the tract are concerned, since he did not stipulate for any security interest in them, it even has been argued that as to them he should have no better right than general creditors and should come in, *pari passu*, with them.[72] And it is contended that he should have no priority over T–2 who has acquired an interest in those other parcels without notice as purchaser for full value or as mortgagee.

In answer it is urged that "Second mortgages upon portions of mortgaged premises are rarely taken without considering and relying upon the equity which will arise in favor of the second mortgagee to

trustee to pay creditors. See quotation from Newby v. Fox, note 69, infra. General creditors of the mortgagor have been regarded as falling within this class, First Nat. Bank of Boston v. Proctor, 40 F.2d 841 (1930), in spite of a suggestion that this was unfair to them. See Langdell, A Brief Survey of Equity Jurisdiction, 15. Compare Langel v. Moore, 32 Ohio App. 352, 168 N.E. 57 (1928), affirmed 119 Ohio St. 299, 164 N.E. 118, commented on, 43 Harv.L.Rev. 501 (1930). Cf. Shewmaker v. Yankey, 23 Ky.L.Rep. 1759, 66 S.W. 1 (1902), general creditors for whose benefit an assignment has been made; Bronaugh v. Burley Tobacco Co., 212 Ky. 680, 280 S.W. 97 (1926), judgment creditor.

69. "One who acquires title through the debtor without parting with value (as a judgment creditor or a grantee in a voluntary conveyance) cannot thereby gain any superior standing. Even a purchaser for value who becomes such with notice of a proceeding to enforce the right to have the securities marshaled must be deemed to have acted at his peril. But it might unduly extend this merely equitable right to allow its enforcement against one who has bought and paid for the singly mortgaged land, knowing, to be sure, of the existence of the two mortgages, but having no particular reason to anticipate that the doctrine of marshaling securities will ever be invoked." Newby v. Fox, 90 Kan. 317, 323, 133 P. 890, 892 (1913). Cf. notecall 57, supra.

70. Id.

71. "If this doctrine is applied to successive second mortgages in these cases, and the second lot so mortgaged is sold first on foreclosure of the blanket mortgage to the exoneration of the second mortgage on the first lot, the result is almost surely to destroy altogether the second mortgage on that lot. * * * It should be clear that it never can be applied without such injury where the second parcel has been mortgaged instead of conveyed outright." Walsh & Simpson, Cas. Security Transactions, 376. See also Newby v. Fox, 90 Kan. 317, 325, 113 P. 890, 893 (1913).

72. "As between secured and unsecured creditors, equity clearly ought to favor the latter class, if either." Langdell, A Brief Survey of Equity Jurisdiction, 15.

have the first mortgage charged upon the residue of the property; * * *." [73] Furthermore, it has been pointed out that the English rule opens a door to the practice of fraud by the mortgagor-transferor.[74] And apart from this, it has been difficult for one scholar to understand how the right of a second mortgagee to marshaling, which at the time he takes his mortgage exists against his mortgagor and the owner of the paramount mortgage of the whole tract,[75] "can be lost by the intervention of a second mortgagee, over whom, and over the mortgagor, the second mortgagee has no control; nor is it easy to understand why a second mortgagee should be obliged to keep constant watch upon the registry of deeds and assert his equity by litigation against every casual purchaser who records a deed fixing a later lien upon the mortgaged land." [76]

The English rule of pro-ration even though the subsequent second mortgagee of Y had notice of the prior junior mortgage on X seems wrong. Very clearly T–1 did acquire an equity of marshaling against lots Y and Z at the time he took his second mortgage on X. The equity he acquired at that time may well be regarded as "so weak that the rights of a bona fide purchaser for value without notice could displace it, but the equity should be sufficiently virile not to be defeated by the rights of a subsequent taker with notice of its existence." [77] On the other hand, the rule of pro-ration if T–2 takes without notice of any sort seems entirely fair and prevents the caprice of E from determining where any loss shall fall. If notice is only constructive through recordation of T–1's second mortgage, it is difficult to decide between the two results. The preferable solution would seem to be a compromise. Where the "two funds" rule of marshaling is proper it should not be regarded as creating in the first sub-mortgagee of a parcel a fixed indisplaceable equity as does the inverse order of alienation rule in ties having "jarring liens." [78] To this extent there is merit in the attitude of the courts in the second group of cases. So regarded, however, it seems desirable to accept the view of the first group to the extent that T–1's right to marshaling against the other parcels be recognized as the general rule but that relief will be refused in the particular case if it would work

73. La Farge Fire Ins. Co. v. Bell, 22 Barb. 54, 65 (N.Y.1856). As to the duty of a mortgagor to pay off a first mortgage for the benefit of a second mortgagee and the latter's justifiable expectation of advancement in that event see § 10.6, supra.

74. "There is nothing to stop him from giving C, a friend, a mortgage on the second property, reducing to that extent the amount that B would otherwise get. Of course, if a court of equity even suspects the presence of fraud in the case, B and C will not be treated equally, but the possibility is still present, and it may be for this reason that a number of American jurisdictions have reached an opposite result." Shenkin, op. cit. supra note 61, 785 n. 14.

75. See n. 69, supra.

76. Keigwin, Cas.Morts., 583 n. 49.

77. Shenkin, Marshaling of Securities, 79 U. of Pa.L.Rev. 782, 787 (1931).

78. Shenkin, op. cit. supra note 77, at 785.

injustice.[79] This gives to the "two funds" doctrine to some extent the greater certainty of the inverse order rule and yet preserves to it sufficient flexibility to deal with the individual case, if this should be necessary, at the date the right is invoked by action. This flexibility, unimportant where the inverse rule is properly applicable, i. e., in case of successive purchases of portions of the mortgaged property for full value, is of consequence where sub-mortgages on different parcels are concerned. As has been pointed out, the reason is that the lienor on lot X may be amply secured whereas the lienor on lot Y is insufficiently margined.[80]

The last point has relevancy also where one of the sub-mortgagees of part of the property subject to a paramount mortgage has taken, in addition, a piece of property not under that mortgage.[81] That is, lots X and Y only are mortgaged to E. T–1 takes a second mortgage on lot X and also takes a first mortgage on lot Z. T–2 then takes a second mortgage on lot Y with knowledge of the situation. T–1 as well as E is a doubly secured creditor and any equity of marshaling he may have as against E and Y would seem to be limited to the excess of his debt over the value of his outside security, Z. T–2, if T–1 is disregarded, has an equity to have E go first against X. The proper solution, therefore, would seem to be that T–2 should be able to have marshaling, limited only by T–1's superior claim to be able to reach X ahead of T–2 as to any deficiency he would have after applying the value of lot Z. If T–1 is amply secured by Z alone, there is authority for the indicated result.[82] Even if he is not, the principle suggested seems properly applicable and could be used without difficulty if T–1's debt was due at the time of E's foreclosure. Even if it was not, T–1 might be protected by requiring clear proof of the minimum amount Z would yield and reserving out of the sale of X an amount equal to the difference until T–1's debt matured.[83]

79. E. g., Bernhardt v. Lymburner, 85 N.Y. 175 (1881), although recognizing the general rule of marshaling as being established, refused to apply it where it would work injustice. See also, Sternberger v. Sussman, 69 N.J. Eq. 199, 60 A. 195 (1905), affirmed 85 N.J.Eq. 593, 98 A. 1087. Look also at Payne v. Avery, 21 Mich. 524 (1870); Milligan's Appeal, 104 Pa. 503 (1883).

80. Glenn, Morts., § 298. The learned author adds: "The fact that one may have such a case in front of him does not require a general rule that there shall never be marshalling in the case of liens, but it will justify an exception in this case of hardship." Ibid.

81. In general assets will not be marshaled where there are different funds, or the funds are not in the hands of a common debtor, but there are exceptions to this. See n. 50, supra.

82. Worth v. Hill, 14 Wis. 559 (1861). See Glenn, Morts., § 299.

83. Cf. Worth v. Hill, 14 Wis. 559 (1861). The court said that where the adequacy of T–1's outside security could not be tested by sale, the court might nevertheless grant marshaling to T–2 upon testimony of witnesses provided that such testimony clearly established the entire adequacy of lot Z.

§ 10.14 Marshaling by Mortgagor—Exemptions

In general a debtor is not entitled to invoke the doctrine of marshaling,[84] but there are many circumstances in which the mortgagor can compel a doubly secured creditor to resort to one fund rather than to another. Even where the mortgagor is primarily liable for the debt he can restrict the mortgagee to selling only so much of the property as is necessary to pay off the mortgage.[85] And he can compel the selling of the property by parcels or en masse as will be most advantageous to him.[86] If the mortgagor is only secondarily liable he can force the mortgagee to proceed against the person or property primarily liable if that will not prejudice the mortgagee.[87] Similarly, if the mortgagor in selling part of a mortgaged tract takes back a mortgage on the portion sold so that he now occupies the position of a singly secured creditor as well as being debtor-mortgagor of the doubly secured creditor, he is entitled to marshaling under the two funds doctrine.[88]

Perhaps the most frequent case where the question of a mortgagor's right to marshal has arisen is where one of the mortgaged parcels, X, is subject to a homestead exemption which was waived[89] in favor of E when R gave the mortgage on the entire tract of which X is a part.[90] Later R may have given a second mortgage on parcel Y on which R had no exemption. Where the question arises between the two creditors E and T–1, the weight of authority refuses to apply the usual two funds rule of marshaling in favor of T–1 even though

84. See Dolphin v. Aylward, 4 Eng. & Irish.App.L.Rev. 486, 505; Newby v. Fox, 90 Kan. 317, 320, 133 P. 890, 891 (1913); Rogers v. Meyers, 68 Ill. 92, 97 (1873). See Schwartz, Marshaling Assets for Benefit of Mortgagor, 5 Not.D.Law. 208 (1930); 47 L.R.A.,N.S., 302 (1914).

85. See text at § 7.21, notes 30–32, supra.

86. Id Security Savings Bank v. King, 198 Iowa, 1151, 199 N.W. 166 (1924); McClintic-Marshall Co. v. Scandinavian-American Bldg. Co., 296 F. 601 (C.C.A.Wash.1924).

As to the right of the maker of a negotiable instrument to compel the marshaling of securities in his favor, look at Sowell v. Federal Reserve Bank of Dallas, 268 U.S. 449, 45 S.Ct. 528, 69 L.Ed. 1041 (1925), discussed in note, 39 Harv.L.Rev. 256 (1925). See also note, 34 Col.L.Rev. 779 (1934).

87. Konoff v. Lantini, 111 R.I. 691, 306 A.2d 176 (1973); Bartley v. Pikeville Nat. Bank & Trust Co., 532 S.W.2d 446 (Ky.App.1976); Cook v. American States Ins. Co., 150 Ind.App. 88, 275 N.E.2d 832 (1971); Sanders v. Lackey, 59 Tenn.App. 207, 439 S.W.2d 610 (1968); Champlain Valley Federal Sav. & Loan Ass'n v. Ladue, 35 A.D. 2d 888, 316 N.Y.S.2d 19 (1970).

88. Newby v. Fox, n. 84, supra.

89. A debtor may waive his homestead in property so far as the mortgage goes when he gives property on which he has declared it as security for a debt. See Thomas v. Wisner, 65 Colo. 243, 180 P. 744 (1919); Cleve v. Adams, 222 N.C. 211, 22 S. E.2d 567 (1942).

90. For discussions and collections of cases, see 46 Harv.L.Rev. 1035 (1933); 12 Tex.L.Rev. 514 (1934); 23 Minn.L. Rev. 692 (1939), reprinted, 23 Or.L. Rev. 204 (1944); 44 A.L.R. 758 (1926); 77 A.L.R. 371 (1932); 17 Ann.Cas. 1061; 47 L.R.A.,N.S., 302, 303 (1913).

the result may be that E will collect out of Y leaving T–1 unsecured.[91] The justification for this result is found in the policy of protecting homesteads from forced sales. In some states legislation expressly protects the mortgagor and his family in such a situation.[92] There are, however, some cases which have held that T–1 may have marshaling even against X, the homestead parcel, this being the fund to which he had no access.[93]

Where the question arises between the mortgagor and his creditors, E and T–1, the majority rule is that he may compel E on foreclosure to sell first the property to which the homestead exemption does not apply, i. e., that he may have marshaling against T–1.[94] And there are statutory provisions to the same effect.[95] There is, however, authority that the mortgagor cannot compel marshaling in such a case.[96]

Where the case arises only between R and E, the majority rule permitting R to save his homestead if E can get paid out of non-exempt property seems a desirable result.[97] Where exercise of the

91. McLaughlin v. Hart, 46 Cal. 638 (1873), approved on its special facts by Glenn, Mortgages, § 37.3; Bowers v. Norton, 175 Minn. 541, 222 N.W. 71 (1928), T–1 being an attaching creditor; McArthur v. Martin, 23 Minn. 74 (1876). See 44 A.L.R. 758 (1926); 77 A.L.R. 371 (1932).

92. E. g., Smith-Hurd Ill.Ann.Stat. ch. 52 § 4; S.C.Const.1895, Art. 3, § 28; Wis.Stat.Ann. § 272.20; Iowa Code of 1950, § 561.21. See 1926, 44 A.L.R. 758, 761; 1932, 77 A.L.R. 371, 372.

93. E. g., State Sav. Bank of Anderson v. Harbin, 18 S.C. 425 (1883); cf. Plain v. Roth, 107 Ill. 588 (1883). See 44 A.L.R. 758, 761, 762 (1926). Statutory enactments have overcome most of this authority. E. g., White v. Polleys, 20 Wis. 503, 91 Am.Dec. 432 (1866), later nullified by Wis. Stat.Ann. § 272.20.

94. Alston v. Bitely, 252 Ark. 76, 477 S.W.2d 446 (1972). In Sims v. McFadden, 217 Ark. 810, 233 S.W.2d 375 (1950), the state refused to apply marshaling where exemption would be destroyed even though it entailed a loss to general creditors. Boykin v. First State Bank, 61 S.W.2d 126 (Tex.Civ.App.1933), T–1 being a second mortgagee; In re Tucker's Estate, 160 Or. 362, 85 P.2d 1025 (1938); Frick Co. v. Ketels, 42 Kan. 527, 22 P. 580, 16 Am.St.Rep. 507 (1889). See 44 A.L.R. 758, 763 (1926); 77 A.L.R. 371, 373 (1932).

Where there are other interests exempt under state policy or statute, courts will protect such interests held by a mortgagor by refusing to apply the principle of marshaling in favor of a junior lienor. Dower was protected in Alston v. Bitely, supra this note; Bowen v. Brockenbrough, 119 Ind. 560, 20 N.E. 534 (1889); Stokes v. Stokes, 206 N.C. 108, 173 S.E. 18 (1934). Beneficiaries of life insurance policies may have the right to protection, Meyer v. United States, 375 U.S. 233, 84 S.Ct. 318, 11 L.Ed.2d 293 (1963); Barbin v. Moore, 85 N.H. 362, 159 A. 409, 83 A.L.R. 62 (1932). Marshaling was not applied where the effect would have been to defeat rights of survivorship of debtor's widow in mortgaged realty held in tenancy by the entirety; see First Nat. City Bank v. Phoenix Mutual Life Ins. Co., 364 F.Supp. 390 (S.D.N.Y.1973).

95. See note 92, supra. See 44 A.L.R. 758, 766 (1926); 77 A.L.R. 371, 374 (1932).

96. Booker v. Booker, 225 Ala. 626, 144 So. 870 (1932), discussed 46 Harv.L.Rev. 1034 (1933); Searle v. Chapman, 121 Mass. 19 (1876). See 44 A.L.R. 758, 766 (1926).

97. See 46 Harv.L.Rev. 1035 (1933); 12 Tex.L.Rev. 515 (1934).

right to compel marshaling will result in saving the mortgaged homestead at the expense of a creditor whose hold is on non-exempt property the question moves into doubtful area. Perhaps T–1 should be granted marshaling against a homestead if he is a second mortgagee of Y but not if he acquired his lien by way of judgment or attachment lien.[98]

§ 10.15 Effect of Release by Mortgagee

The paramount mortgagee of a tract, having knowledge of parcels which have been transferred or mortgaged to persons under circumstances giving to them a right of marshaling against other portions of the property, must not do anything to defeat the rights of such persons.[99] The knowledge must be actual, not constructive through the recordation of subsequent conveyances or mortgages of portions of the mortgaged property.[1] If the paramount mortgagee does have actual notice of subsequent alienations of mortgages of parcels of the mortgaged property he acts at his peril in releasing from the mortgage any part of the property against which the marshaling equity runs.[2] Hence if he releases a part under such circumstances, he must deduct from the debt, before enforcing his lien against the property in the hands of these persons, the value of the property released which they had a right to have him apply to the debt before resorting to the property held by them.[3] If the right was to have the en-

98. E. g., in Merchants Nat. Bank v. Stanton, 55 Minn. 211, 56 N.W. 821, 43 Am.St.Rep. 491 (1893), a mortgagee was granted marshaling on the ground that his interest arose by contract and not *in invitum*. But cf. Boykin v. First State Bank, 61 S.W. 2d 126, 129 (Tex.Civ.App.1933).

99. See Broughton v. Mt. Healthy Flying Service, 104 Ohio App. 479, 143 N.E.2d 597, 5 O.O.2d 224 (1957). In General Builders Supply Co. v. Arlington Co-op Bank, 359 Mass. 691, 271 N.E.2d 342 (1971) reformation of release was denied where it would prejudice rights of subsequent lienors.

1. Iglehart v. Crane & Wesson, 42 Ill. 261, 268 (1866); Woodward v. Brown, 119 Cal. 283, 51 P. 2, 63 Am.St.Rep. 108 (1897), modified 119 Cal. 283, 51 P. 542, 63 Am.St.Rep. 108; Ocean County Nat. Bank v. J. Edwin Ellor & Sons, Inc., 116 N.J.Eq. 287, 290, 173 A. 138, 139 (1934); Balen v. Lewis, 130 Mich. 567, 90 N.W. 416, 47 Am. St.Rep. 499 (1902); Bridgewater Roller Mills Co. v. Strough, 98 Va. 721, 37 S.E. 290 (1900); Clarke v. Cowan, 206 Mass. 252, 92 N.E. 474, 138 Am. St.Rep. 388 (1910), accord. See also Stuyvesant v. Hall, 2 Barb.Ch. 151, 158 (N.Y.1847); 110 A.L.R. 65, 70 (1937); 131 A.L.R. 4, 109 (1941); Ann.Cas.1916D, 1119, 1133; Bridgewater Roller Mills v. Receivers of Baltimore Bldg. & Loan Ass'n, 124 F. 718 (1903). See 110 A.L.R. 65, 70, 75 (1937).

2. Charles Constr. Co., Inc. v. Leisure Resources, Inc., 1 Mass.App. 755, 307 N.E.2d 336 (1974). See Brooks v. Benham, 70 Conn. 92, 97, 38 A. 908, 910, 66 Am.St.Rep. 87 (1897).

See also Green, Marshaling Assets in Texas, 34 Texas L.Rev. 1054 (1956).

3. The discharge has been rested upon an impairment of the grantee or mortgagee's right of subrogation. Brooks v. Benham, n. 2, supra. Cf. §§ 5.19, supra, for the cognate problem where not just a portion, but the entire property has been sold. The doctrine of discharge here rests upon an application of the same basic principles applied, however, pro tanto. Junior encumbrancer is entitled to have proceeds of sale of mortgaged

tire parcel applied first, its entire value must be deducted.[4] On the other hand, if the right was only that the released lot should be used to satisfy its pro rata share of the debt, the mortgagee must abate the debt only to such a proportion of it as the value of released parcel bore to the value of the entire tract.[5]

If the property released is one against which there is no right of marshaling, e. g., if it is the parcel first aliened in cases where the inverse order of alienation rule applies, the mortgagee does not have to make any deduction of its value before he can enforce the mortgage against the other parcels.[6] Further, if in giving a release of a parcel the mortgagee received a consideration which he applied upon the mortgage debt, he may enforce the balance of the debt against the remaining property provided the amount received was equal to the fair value of the lot in question.[7] And if, as is provided in modern mortgages in which subdivisions are contemplated, the mortgagee is given permission to execute partial releases, he may release portions without further liability to other holders if he adheres to the terms of authorization.[8]

property applied upon the senior indebtedness, even though the property sold was not covered by the junior mortgage. See Continental Supply Co. v. Marshall, 152 F.2d 300 (C.C.A. Okl.1945), certiorari denied 327 U.S. 803, 66 S.Ct. 962, 90 L.Ed. 1028.

4. Brown v. Simons, 44 N.H. 475 (1863); Hill v. Howell, 36 N.J.Eq. 25 (1882); Schrack v. Shriner, 100 Pa. 451 (1882); New South Bldg. & Loan Ass'n v. Reed, 1898, 96 Va. 345, 31 S.E. 514, 70 Am.St.Rep. 858 (1898); Schaad v. Robinson, 50 Wash. 283, 97 P. 104 (1908); Deuster v. McCamus, 14 Wis. 307 (1861)—accord. See also Iglehart v. Crane & Wesson, 42 Ill. 261 (1866); Pomeroy, Eq.Jur., 4th Ed., § 1226, note 4; 110 A.L.R. 65, 67, 73 (1937); 131 A.L.R. 4, 108, 109 (1941). Cf. Gaskill v. Sine, 13 N.J.Eq. 400, 78 Am.Dec. 105 (1861); Snyder v. Crawford, 98 Pa. 414 (1881). Contra: McCoy v. Wynn, 215 Ala. 172, 174, 110 So. 129, 130 (1926).

5. Home Unity Savings & Loan Ass'n v. Balmos, 192 Pa.Super. 542, 162 A. 2d 244 (1960); Brooks v. Benham, 70 Conn. 92, 97, 38 A. 908, 910, 66 Am. St.Rep. 87 (1897). See Taylor v. Short's Adm'r, 27 Iowa 361, 1 Am. Rep. 280 (1869); Parkman v. Welch, 36 Mass. (19 Pick.) 231 (1837).

6. Clark v. Kraker, 51 Minn. 444, 53 N.W. 706 (1892); Lyman v. Lyman, 32 Vt. 79, 76 Am.Dec. 151 (1859). As to the effect the mortgagee's release of the mortgagor's personal liability by dealings with a purchaser of part of the mortgaged property who assumed the mortgage debt has upon the lien of the mortgage upon another part which has been conveyed by the mortgagor to a third person, see 101 A.L.R. 618 (1936).

7. Beardsley v. Empire Trust Co., 96 N.J.Eq. 212, 124 A. 457 (1924), noted 24 Col.L.Rev. 804. See Taylor v. Short's Adm'r, 27 Iowa 361, 362, 1 Am.Rep. 280 (1869).

8. Thompson v. Thomas, 43 Cal.App. 588, 185 P. 427 (1919). See 110 A.L. R. 65, 72, 77 (1937).

§§ 10.16–11.0 are reserved for supplementary material.

CHAPTER 11

GOVERNMENT INTERVENTION IN THE MORTGAGE MARKET

Table of Sections

§ 11.1 The Mortgage Market, Institutional Lenders, and Their Regulators

Of the roughly three trillion dollars in outstanding debt in the United States, about thirty percent is secured by real estate mortgages.[1] Because the United States is a nation of homeowners, it is not surprising that nearly two-thirds (62.5%) of this mortgage debt is secured by 1-to-4 family homes. (Loans on buildings containing four or fewer residential units are conventionally lumped together and termed "home loans.") Another 19.4% of this mortgage debt is secured by commercial properties, 11.5% by multifamily apartment buildings, and 6.6% by farm properties. Mortgage financing is particularly important in the development of new real estate projects and those constructed without mortgage debt are relatively rare.

Nearly three quarters of the mortgage debt in the United States is held by private institutional lenders. Federally-supported agencies account for another 13.2%, with various miscellanous lenders, including individuals, holding the remainder. Since private lending institutions are so important in the American mortgage market, they

1. Most economic data in this section are taken from United States League of Savings Associations, Savings and Loan Fact Book (1977), and reflect conditions in the mortgage market as of the end of 1976. The Fact Book data, in turn, are derived from information supplied by the Federal Home Loan Bank Board, the Federal Reserve Board, and the United States League of Savings Associations. Because market conditions change continually, the data in the text will be somewhat outdated by the time this treatise appears in print; yet the changes are likely to be relatively small for at least several years, and the discussion in the text will probably remain fairly accurate. The United States League publishes a new Fact Book each year and will supply single copies free; it is an excellent source of current information about the mortgage market. The Annual Economic Report of the President is another valuable source, as is the Annual Report issue (generally April) of the Federal Home Loan Bank Board Journal.

and the regulatory agencies under whose rules they operate are the subject of this section; a subsequent section will discuss the federally-supported agencies active in the mortgage market. There are four principal types of institutions active in mortgage lending in the United States. They are listed below, along with the share of total mortgage debt held by each.

1.	Savings and Loan Associations	36.5%
2.	Commercial Banks	16.7%
3.	Life Insurance Companies	10.3%
4.	Mutual Savings Banks	9.2%
	Total	72.7%

There are fairly wide differences in the preferences for mortgage investments among these four types of institutions. For example, the proportions of mortgages on 1-to-4 family homes held by commercial banks and mutual savings banks are roughly equal to their shares of the over-all mortgage market listed above. Savings and loan associations, however, exhibit a definite preference for home mortgages (i. e., those on 1-to-4 family dwellings); their loans account for nearly half (47.3%) of all home mortgages. Life insurance companies, by comparison, have been steadily withdrawing from the home mortgage market since about 1968, and now account for only about 3% of all home loans.

On the other hand, apartment lending has continued to be quite attractive to life insurance companies; they hold about 19% of all loans on multi-family buildings. Mutual savings banks and savings and loan associations are also active in multi-family lending, holding about 14% and 28% of such loans respectively. Commercial banks are relatively inactive in permanent lending on apartments, holding only about 5% of all such loans. Institutions exhibit similar preferences for commercial loans as for apartment loans as discussed above, except that savings and loan associations are a much smaller factor in the commercial real estate market.

The foregoing discussion has focused on permanent or long term lending. Construction lending, which ties up the institution's funds for a relatively short time but requires close on-site supervision, is handled by commercial banks and savings associations to a very substantial extent.[2] Real estate investment trusts are also active in the construction lending field, but life insurance companies, lacking the

2. As of the end of the fourth quarter of 1972, savings and loan associations held 43.1% of construction loans, commercial banks held 32.6%, mortgage investment trusts held 15.7%, and mutual savings banks 3.9%. U. S. Dep't of Housing and Urban Development, Housing in the Seventies 56 (1974); see also Mason & Leaffer, The Preferences of Financial Institutions for Construction and Permanent Mortgage Lending, 4 Am. Real Est. & Urb. Econ. Ass'n J. 41 (1976).

necessary local officers and personnel, are almost totally absent from construction lending.

One type of lending organization not mentioned above is the mortgage banker (sometimes called a mortgage company or mortgage broker). This sort of institution is organized to originate loans, not for retention in its own portfolio, but almost exclusively for sale or assignment to other investors or government-sponsored agencies which will hold the loans for the long term. All of the four types of financial institutions discussed above are active from time to time in transactions with mortgage bankers, as investors purchasing loans which mortgage bankers have originated. They may also act, in effect, as mortgage bankers themselves, originating loans which they do not expect to hold in portfolio, but rather which will be sold to other investors.

An important feature of a mortgage banker's activity (as well as that of any other financial institution which happens to be acting in a mortgage banking capacity) is the "servicing" of the loan. Most investors which purchase mortgage loans on the secondary market lack local offices in the area in which the real estate is located. Consequently they usually contract with the originating lender for "servicing" to be provided by that local organization. Servicing includes collecting the regular payments of principal and interest, maintaining an appropriate escrow account for taxes and insurance, following up on any delinquency, and if necessary, arranging for foreclosure. The servicer maintains proper records, remits the loan payments to the investor which holds the loan, and communicates with the investor if problems arise. For performing this work the servicer receives a fee from the investor, commonly an annual amount of three-eighths of one percent of the average outstanding balance of the loan—for example, $150 on a $40,000 loan. Servicing is considered a profitable and attractive activity by mortgage bankers, and they are usually eager to retain servicing when a loan is sold.

The lending activities of mortgage bankers are relatively unregulated; they must, of course, comply with applicable state law, the requirements and guidelines set down by the investor institutions to whom they sell loans, and the requirements of FHA and VA to the extent that they originate loans of those types. However, they are not subject in most jurisdictions to the supervision of any specialized regulatory agency.[3] For the four major types of institutional mortgage holders, the contrary is true. Each of them must comply with the requirements of at least one, and sometimes several, specialized regulatory agencies at the federal or state level. A brief review of this regulatory system follows.

3. One exception is Illinois, which in 1976 created a regulatory agency for the mortgage banking industry. See Smith-Hurd Ill.Ann.Stat., titl. 16½, § 601 (supp.1978).

Savings and Loan Associations

The Federal Home Loan Bank Board (FHLBB) is the national regulator of savings associations.[4] Such associations may be either federally or state chartered; all federal charters are issued by the FHLBB, and federal associations are closely supervised by the FHLBB in virtually all areas of activity. The FHLBB also exercises considerable authority over most state-chartered savings and loan associations by virtue of their membership in the Federal Savings and Loan Insurance Corporation, an entity controlled by the FHLBB which insures depositors against loss up to a statutory maximum, currently $40,000. This deposit insurance is, of course, an extremely attractive drawing card for institutions seeking deposits, so most state-chartered institutions obtain it, as do all federal associations. The scope of the regulations governing state-chartered institutions through the FSLIC is somewhat more limited than the regulations governing federal associations; for example, the FHLBB's regulations governing lending powers (i. e., loan types, loan-to-value ratios, etc.) apply to federal but not state institutions.[5] Nevertheless, the scope of FHLBB regulation over state-chartered FSLIC-insured associations is significant.

In most states, state-chartered associations are also subject to the supervision of a state banking or savings and loan commission or board. This agency or applicable state statute often controls lending powers and other operational activities of state-chartered associations which are not governed by the FSLIC regulations. In many states, state-chartered associations are subject to periodic on-site examinations by both the federal and state authorities. In other states, however, a cooperative arrangement has been negotiated under which the state supervisory agency merely receives copies of the federal examiners' reports and does not attempt to perform independent examinations except in unusual or emergency cases.

All federal associations must be initially chartered in mutual form; that is, there is no outstanding stock, and in principle the institution is owned by its depositors and borrowers. In many states, however, state-chartered institutions may be owned in either mutual or stock form. Stock ownership clearly creates additional profit opportunities for the management and organizers of a savings association, and arguably provides a broader and more stable capital base as

4. General descriptions of the FHLBB include Biederman & Tuccillo, Taxation and Regulation of the Savings and Loan Industry (1975); U. S. Dep't of Housing and Urban Development, Housing in the Seventies 73–74 (1974); Gerloff, The Federal Home Loan Bank System (FHLBB 1971); Clarke, The Regulatory and Housing Functions of the FHLBB, 26 Bus.Law. 37 (1970). The Annual Report (April) issue of the Federal Home Loan Bank Board Journal will provide a current summary of the FHLBB's activities.

5. 12 CFR 545.6; see Earthman, Residential Mortgage Lending: Charting a Course through the Regulatory Maze, 29 Vand.L.Rev. 957 (1976).

well. In recent years there has been considerable interest in the conversion of both federal and state mutual institutions to stock form.[6] The FHLBB has approved a number of such conversions for federal institutions while permitting them to retain their federal charters.[6a] The FHLBB has also sought legislation permitting the initial creation of federal stock associations, but thus far has not gained such authority from congress.

The dual system of regulation of savings and loan associations produces some interesting and arguably irrational distinctions. For example, federal associations were not permitted by FHLBB regulations to make variable-rate mortgages (VRM's), until 1979, although in a number of states, state-chartered institutions could previously do so. The FHLBB promoted the VRM concept in congress, but was reluctant for several years to confront the intense political opposition to the VRM idea.[7]

Mutual Savings Banks

These institutions are exclusively state-chartered and exist in only eighteen states, mostly in the New England and Mid-Atlantic regions.[8] As the name implies, they are owned by their depositors and borrowers, and have no capital stock. They typically have lending powers which are somewhat broader than those of savings and loan associations, and engage in considerable commercial mortgage lending as well as residential activity. In general their activities are quite similiar to those of savings and loan associations. Mutual savings banks are typically regulated by a state banking board or commission. However, about two-thirds of the MSB's have their deposits insured by the FSLIC, and some of them are also members of the federal home loan bank system (permitting them to receive "advances" or loans from their regional Federal Home Loan Bank). MSB's which enjoy these advantages are also subject to the limited set of FHLBB regulations applicable to such institutions. Some MSB's are insured by the Federal Deposit Insurance Corporation and thus are subject to its regulations.

Commercial Banks

The regulation of commercial banks is far more complex than that of savings and loan associations or mutual savings banks. Part

6. The FHLBB's regulations governing conversion are found in 12 CFR, Part 563b, as amended, 43 Fed.Reg. 49956 (Oct. 10, 1978). See generally Allen, Capital Adequacy Problems of S&L's —And the Changes Needed to Meet Them, 10 FHLBBJ 2 (Feb. 1977); Allen, Stock Conversions: Where We Are Now, 9 FHLBBJ 2 (Mar. 1976).

7. See 37 Fed.Reg. 16201 (Aug. 11, 1972); 40 Fed.Reg. 6870 (Feb. 14, 1975).

8. An excellent source of current information on mutual savings banks, published annually by the National Association of Mutual Savings Banks, is the National Fact Book of Mutual Savings Banking.

of the complexity derives from the fact that both federal and state charters are possible, a feature commonly termed the "dual banking" system.[9] More important is the fact that three federal agencies (rather than a single agency as with savings and loan associations) are charged with commercial bank supervision.[10] All federally-chartered (so-called "national") banks are supervised by the Comptroller of the Currency, a division of the U.S. Treasury Department. State-chartered banks which are members of the Federal Reserve System, and are thereby privileged to draw funds at the credit windows of the Federal Reserve Banks, are supervised by the Board of Governers of the Federal Reserve System, commonly called the Federal Reserve Board (FRB) or the "Fed." [11] Many large state banks fall in this category, and all federally-chartered banks are automatically members of the Federal Reserve System. State-chartered banks which are not members of the Federal Reserve System ("non-fed-member" banks) may nonetheless have their deposits insured (currently up to $40,000) by the Federal Deposit Insurance Corporation (FDIC), which in turn exercises supervisory authority over them. The great majority of state-chartered non-fed-member banks are FDIC-insured as are all fed-member banks and national banks.

In addition to this complex federal regulatory structure, state-chartered banks are all at least potentially subject to regulation by a state agency.[12] In some jurisdictions the state supervision is intense, while in others the state regulators rely principally upon the examination and supervision efforts of the relevant federal agencies except with respect to the small number of banks which are not even FDIC-insured.

The banking regulatory system has fairly been called "baffling." [13] It is quite possible, for example, for a fed-member state bank to be subject to the regulations of at least three agencies—the FRB, the FDIC, and the state banking commissioner—with respect to various phases of its operations. Coordination among the multitude of agen-

9. See Scott, The Dual Banking System: A Model of Competition in Regulation, 30 Stan.L.Rev. 1 (1977); Brown, The Dual Banking System in the United States (American Bankers Assoc. undated), reprinted in Subcomm. on Financial Institutions, Senate Comm. on Banking, Housing and Urban Affairs, Compendium of Issues Relating to Branching by Financial Institutions, 94th Cong., 2d Sess. (1976) at 239.

10. See Via, Some Thoughts on Evaluating the Tripartite Federal Bank Regulatory System, 93 Banking L.J. 509 (1976); Kreider, American Banking: Structure, Supervision, and Strengths, 92 Banking L.J. 437 (1975).

11. See Murane, The FDIC and Bank Regulation, 89 Banking L.J. 483 (1972); Scott & Mayer, Risk and Regulation in Banking: Some Proposals for Federal Deposit Insurance Reform, 23 Stan.L.Rev. 857 (1971).

12. See Vestner, Trends and Developments in State Regulation of Banks, 90 Banking L.J. 464 (1973); Bell, State Regulation of Commercial Banks, 26 Bus.Law. 109 (1970).

13. See Hackley, Our Baffling Banking System, Part I, 52 Va.L.Rev. 565 (1966); Part II, 52 Va.L.Rev. 771 (1966).

cies involved is not as extensive as might be desired.[13a] The system has obvious inefficiencies built into it, and it is not unusual for an institution to engage in a sort of "agency-shopping", changing its status in order to align itself with a regulatory agency that will better fit its desires.[14]

So far as real estate lending powers are concerned, national banks are governed by Section 24 of the Federal Reserve Act [15] and the rules and interpretations thereof issued by the Comptroller of the Currency.[16] Neither the FRB nor the FDIC regulate lending powers, so lending activities of state banks are subject only to applicable state statutes and regulations. At both the federal and state levels, commercial banks are usually granted greater discretion in real estate lending than are, for example, savings and loan associations. There is, however, wide variation from state to state.

A large number of proposals for reform of the federal banking regulatory system have been made in recent years, although none has been adopted at this writing. The most radical reform would collapse both banking and savings and loan regulators into a single federal agency. Less far-reaching proposals would leave the savings and loan industry separately regulated as at present, but would merge the three banking regulators into one or two agencies.[17] A strong case

13a. But see the Federal Financial Institutions Examination Council Act of 1978, H.R. 14279, Tit. X, 95th Cong., 2d Sess., which is designed to improve coordination among the banking agencies.

14. See Changing Charters—Did the Bank Switch Rather Than Fight the Fed. Examiners? Wall St.J., Apr. 26, 1976, at p. 1, col. 6.

15. 12 U.S.C.A. § 371; the Comptroller of the Currency is responsible for interpreting section 24; see 12 C.F.R. § 7.2000 et seq., as amended, 43 Fed. Reg. 6801 (Feb. 16, 1978); interpretive regulations, 43 Fed.Reg. 43289 (Sept. 25, 1978).

16. 12 CFR 7.2000 et seq.

17. See Report of the President's Commission on Financial Structure and Regulation (the "Hunt Commission", after its chairman, Reed O. Hunt) (1972), at 87–95, recommending that two federal agencies, governing national and state banks respectively, be created to replace the present three; the Federal Bank Commission Act, S. 684, 95th Cong., 1st Sess. (1977), proposing a single federal banking agency. See Note, The Federal Bank Commission Act: A Proposal to Consolidate the Federal Banking Agencies, 25 Cleve.St.L.Rev. 475 (1977); Keeffe and Head, What is Wrong with the American Banking System and What to do About It, 36 Md.L.Rev. 788 (1977); Verkuil, Perspectives on Reform of Financial Institutions, 83 Yale L.J. 1349 (1974). See also Hearings on Financial Institutions and the Nation's Economy (FINE) "Discussion Principles" before the Subcomm. on Financial Institutions, House Comm. on Banking, Currency and Housing, 94th Cong., 1st & 2d Sess., pts. 1–4 (1975); Hearings on the Financial Institutions Act of 1975 before the Subcomm. on Financial Institutions, Senate Comm. on Banking, Housing and Urban Affairs, 94th Cong., 1st Sess. (1975); Compendium of Papers Prepared for the FINE Study, House Comm. on Banking, Currency and Housing, 94th Cong., 2d Sess., Books I and II (1976). Although the Chairman of the FHLBB announced at the close of 1977 that he believed restructuring of financial institutions was a dead issue, it is likely to arise again in the future. See Financial Restructuring Dead, Chairman Tells U.S. League, 10 FHLBBJ 2 (Dec. 1977).

can be made for such reorganization, but members of the affected industries have been reluctant to embrace changes which, although theoretically desirable, would disturb relationships which they have come to understand and find manageable.

Life Insurance Companies

Of the four principal types of institutional mortgage lenders, only life insurance companies are not depository institutions. Instead, their assets come from premium payments on life policies, a relatively stable and predictable source of funds compared with bank or savings deposits. Hence, they have a preference for long-term large-dollar mortgage loans. Since life companies are regulated only at the state level by insurance commissions or departments, and since the legal constraints on their lending are not very restrictive, they are generally able to make loans of precisely this type. Moreover, in most jurisdictions life companies are permitted to invest in real estate financings other than standard mortgage loans. These include sale-leasebacks, sale-salebacks, leasehold mortgages, and other innovative financing methods. These investments are often called "basket" loans since the applicable law or regulation usually provides for a maximum percentage of assets which can be devoted to these relatively unusual types of financings.[18]

Real Estate Investment Trusts

A real estate investment trust (REIT) is much like a mutual fund, except that it invests in mortgages or equity positions in real estate rather than in securities. If seventy-five percent of the trust's income is derived from real estate, and if 95 percent of its profits are distributed annually to shareholders, the trust is taxed only on its retained earnings; in effect, the profits can be passed through to the shareholders without tax.[19] REIT's have been a major factor in recent years in construction lending, especially on income properties, but they have made few long-term loans. Shares of REIT's are generally traded on the national and regional stock exchanges and are widely held.

During recent history many REIT's have experienced financial difficulties. To a great extent they employed bank lines of credit as a source of capital from which to make construction loans. Increases in their cost of funds, construction delays and cost overruns, and inability of their developer-borrowers to market the projects they had financed were all important factors in producing losses. While many trusts became insolvent, those which survived are likely to adopt

18. See Gunning and Roegge, Contemporary Real Estate Financing Techniques: A Dialogue on Vanishing Simplicity, 3 Real Prop.Prob. & Tr.J. 322, 325 (1968).

19. See Englebrcht and Kramer, Tax Breaks for REITs Under the Tax Reform Act, 7 Real Est.Rev. 33 (No. 1, Spring 1977).

more conservative practices and to be a long-term force in the mortgage lending industry.[20]

§ 11.2 Mortgage Insurers and Guarantors

From the viewpoint of a mortgage lender, each loan represents a potential risk of loss. In order for an actual loss to be sustained, two or perhaps three occurrences must eventuate. First, there must be a default in payment by the mortgagor or his successor which he is unable or unwilling to cure. Second, the foreclosure of the mortgage (and the ultimate marketing of the property by the lender if he is the successful bidder at the foreclosure sale) must produce insufficient funds to cover the outstanding debt, accrued interest, and costs and fees associated with the foreclosure. Third, in jurisdictions in which deficiency judgments are available, the deficiency must be uncollectable or inadequate to cover the loss resulting from foreclosure.[21]

Lenders attempt to assess the risk of loss for each loan they make. This process is termed "underwriting" the loan; it consists of appraising the property, obtaining a prior credit history on the borrower, verifying the borrower's employment and income, and obtaining a variety of other information thought to be useful in predicting risk. While this process is routinized in the offices of most institutional lenders, and while various rules of thumb have been developed to determine whether a proposed borrower is acceptable, the scientific basis for mortgage risk assessment is surprisingly rudimentary. Some factors commonly considered—length of time on the present job or in residence in the community, for example—are probably of marginal relevance. However, the evidence strongly supports the conclusion that the higher the loan-to-value ratio, the greater the risk.[22]

This relation between loan-to-value ratio and risk is intuitively easy to understand. If the borrower has little or no "equity"—that is, excess value above the mortgage debt—in the property, it is relatively easy for him to decide simply to walk away when financial difficulties arise; he has nothing to protect by sticking it out. He is unlikely to attempt to sell the property in the event of trouble, since the sales proceeds would be inadequate, after payment of the mortgage, to cover a brokerage commission and other selling expenses. Finally, if the lender forecloses or obtains a deed in lieu, there is obviously a strong chance that the ultimate marketing of the property will produce insufficient funds to cover the debt, interest, and expens-

20. See Stevenson, Lessons From the Mortgage Trust Experience, 6 Real Est.Rev. 72 (No. 3, Fall 1976).

21. On antideficiency statutes, see generally § 8.3, supra.

22. See, e. g., von Furstenberg & Green, Estimation of Delinquency Risk for Home Mortgage Portfolios, 2 Am.Real Est. & Urban Econ. Ass'n J. 5 (Spring 1974); von Furstenberg, Technical Studies of Mortgage Default Risk (1971); Herzog and Earley, Home Mortgage Delinquency and Foreclosure (1970); Kendall, Anatomy of the Residential Mortgage (1964).

es. For these reasons, loan-to-value ratio is highly correlated to mortgage risk.

Logically, lenders which make a high volume of mortgage loans might simply charge a somewhat increased interest rate on loans which they judge to be relatively risky, thus hedging against the losses which they expect will result. In modern American mortgage lending, however, lenders attempt to do this only to a modest extent. For reasons of preference and regulation, they tend to a much greater degree to rely on contracts of indemnification with outside entities, usually termed mortgage insurers, to shift the risk of loss.[23] Such insurance contracts are commonly executed on loans in which the loan-to-value ratio exceeds eighty percent, although some lenders employ an even lower threshold ratio. Mortgage insurers charge premiums for executing these contracts,[24] and the cost is usually passed on to the mortgagor, even though the mortgagee is the insured.

Three types of mortgage insurance are commonly written in the United States. The first and oldest is provided by the Federal Housing Administration (FHA), established in 1934 by the National Housing Act [25] and currently a part of the Department of Housing and Urban Development (HUD). The Veterans Administration was given authority to guarantee home loans for GI's by the Servicemen's Readjustment Act in 1944.[26] (Technically, the VA program is termed guaranty rather than insurance, since the agency charges no premiums and maintains no reserves as such to pay future claims.) Finally, private mortgage insurance companies (PMI's) have become a major force, beginning with the chartering of Mortgage Guaranty Insurance Company in Wisconsin in 1957; [27] by 1978 there were more than twenty such companies writing mortgage insurance on a national scale. The Farmers Home Administration (FmHA), a division of the Department of Agriculture, also operates home mortgage insurance and guaranty programs.[28] However, FmHA mortgage insurance is available only in towns of 20,000 or less, and the program is relatively small in scale; it will not be discussed in further detail.

FHA's mortgage insurance programs are much more complex than the activities of VA and the PMI's for two reasons. First, VA

23. See generally Rapkin, The Private Insurance of Home Mortgages (1973); Griffith, Mortgage Guaranty Insurance is What?, 48 Cal.B.J. 683 (1973).

24. The notable exception being the Veteran's Administration.

25. 12 U.S.C.A. §§ 1701–42.

26. 38 U.S.C.A. § 1801 et seq. The VA also has authority to make direct loans to veterans under 38 U.S.C.A. § 1811, but few such loans are made.

27. See Rapkin, supra note 23, at 38ff; The Arthur D. Little Study of the Private Mortgage Insurance Industry (1975); Graaskamp, Development and Structure of Mortgage Loan Guaranty Insurance in the United States, 34 J. Risk & Ins. 47 (1967); Reppe, Why Residential Lenders Like Mortgage Guaranty Insurance, 3 Real Estate Rev. 58 (No. 3, Fall 1973).

28. See Sec. 417, Housing Act of 1949, 42 U.S.C.A. § 1487.

and PMI's confine themselves almost exclusively to mortgages on homes (i. e., one-to-four family buildings) and condominiums, while FHA has a vast range of programs covering homes, condominiums, cooperatives, apartment buildings, hospitals, and other types of real estate. FHA's programs are commonly identified by the relevant sections of the National Housing Act: Section 203(b) for ordinary home loans, Section 207 for apartments, Section 234 for condominiums, and so on.[29] A second reason for FHA's complexity is that congress has given FHA legislative authority to combine mortgage insurance with certain types of housing subsidy programs for low and moderate income families. Perhaps the two best-known examples of this subsidy-mortgage-insurance concept are Section 235 (of the National Housing Act) for assisting moderate income home purchasers, a program created in 1968 which is still operational at this writing, and Section 236, a rental housing subsidy program also created in 1968 and now virtually phased out as to new projects. The details of such subsidy programs are beyond our present scope; they tend to change frequently, and the reader should refer to current HUD litera-

29. The following more complete listing of FHA and HUD programs by statute section number is taken from the glossary of House Comm. on Banking, Currency and Housing, Basic Laws and Authorities on Housing and Community Development, 94th Cong., 1st Sess. (1975), at 1269.

Title I—Block grant program for community development (Housing and Community Development Act of 1974.)

Title I—Urban renewal program—being terminated by Housing and Community Development Act of 1974 (Housing Act of 1949).

Title I—Loan insurance programs, HUD—primarily property improvement loans (National Housing Act).

Sec. 8—"Assistance payments" to owners or prospective owners of rental housing to cover part of rent of low-income tenants (Housing and Community Development Act of 1974).

Sec. 23—Low-rent housing provided by public housing agencies in housing leased from private owners (U.S. Housing Act of 1937 prior to amendment by the Housing and Community Development Act of 1974).

Sec. 202—Loans by HUD for rental housing for the elderly and handicapped (Housing Amendments of 1955).

Sec. 203—Regular mortgage insurance for 1- to 4-family homes, HUD, continuing the original FHA program for such housing.

Sec. 207—Regular mortgage insurance for multifamily housing, HUD, continuing traditional FHA program for such housing.

Sec. 213—Mortgage and loan insurance, HUD, for cooperative housing (National Housing Act).

Sec. 221(d)(3)—HUD-insured mortgages bearing below market interest rates and financing new or rehabilitated rental housing for displaced families or low or moderate income families (National Housing Act).

Sec. 223(e)—The 1968 liberalization of traditional underwriting standards in HUD mortgage insurance for properties in older and declining neighborhoods deemed "reasonably viable."

Sec. 231—Mortgage insurance, HUD, for new or rehabilitated rental housing for the elderly or handicapped (National Housing Act).

Sec. 232—Mortgage insurance, HUD, for new or rehabilitated nursing homes (National Housing Act).

ture for further information.[30] In 1974 congress began to move away from the subsidy-mortgage-insurance idea, enacting Section 8 of the U.S. Housing Act of 1937 [31] which provides for rental apartment subsidies irrespective of whether the projects assisted by the subsidies are also financed with FHA-insured mortgages or not. Whether subsidies and mortgage insurance will be further disconnected in federal housing policy remains to be seen.[31a]

It is instructive to see how the market in home mortgages is divided among the major groups of mortgage insurers.[32] More than three-quarters of the home loans outstanding are "conventional"—that is, neither insured by FHA nor guaranteed by VA. Roughly 25% to 30% of all conventional loans have loan-to-value ratios exceeding 80%, and it is probable that the great majority of this group are PMI-insured. FHA and VA each insure about 12% of all outstanding home mortgages. The annual volume of home mortgages insured by FHA and VA has fluctuated widely. FHA reached a peak of more than $10 billion in new insurance in 1971, but declined sharply to a low of $3.9 billion by 1974; it has since risen somewhat. VA has generally grown fairly steadily during the 1960's and 1970's, exceeding $10 billion in new guaranties in 1976. It will be recalled that

Sec. 235—Interest reduction payments by HUD and FmHA on home mortgages of lower income families (National Housing Act).

Sec. 236—Interest reduction payments by HUD and FmHA for rental and cooperative housing for lower income families (National Housing Act).

Sec. 312—Rehabilitation loans by HUD for owners or tenants of homes or business properties in deteriorating areas where applicants are unable to secure funds from other sources upon comparable terms and conditions (Housing Act of 1964).

Sec. 701—Grants to public agencies to assist comprehensive planning (Housing Act of 1954).

A-95—Circular issued by Office of Management and Budget to coordinate Federal assistance programs to States and local governments which have "significant impact on area and community development."

30. These programs are described in detail in U. S. Dep't of Housing and Urban Development, Housing in the Seventies 104–18 (1974); see also Comptroller General of the U. S., Section 236 Rental Housing—An Evaluation with Lessons for the Future (1978).

31. 42 U.S.C.A. § 1437f; the reference to the U. S. Housing Act, originally enacted in 1937, is misleading, since Section 8 in its present form is a 1974 creation. On the operation of Section 8, see Comptroller General of the U. S., Major Changes Are Needed in the New Leased-Housing Program (1977); U. S. Dep't of Housing and Urban Development, Office of Policy Development and Research, Lower Income Housing Assistance Program (Section 8): Interim Findings of Evaluation Research (1978).

31a. See Whitman, Federal Housing Assistance for the Poor: Old Problems and New Directions, 9 Urb.Law 1 (1977); Kanner, The Future of Public Housing, 6 Real Est.L.J. 34 (1977).

32. The data in this paragraph are derived from U. S. Dep't of Housing and Urban Development, 1976 Statistical Yearbook, and monthly data published in the Federal Home Loan Bank Board Journal. The data reflect year-end 1976 conditions, and the reader may readily update them from more recent publications of the same sources.

FHA also insures mortgages on multifamily rental buildings; it accounts for about 20% of all such mortgages outstanding.

The major classes of institutional lenders have definite preferences for particular types of mortgage insurance. Savings and loan associations, for example, have generally had little interest in making FHA and VA loans, but have been very active customers of the PMI's.[33] Mortgage bankers, by contrast, have been strong participants in the FHA and VA markets for many years, in part because they sold many mortgages to the Federal National Mortgage Association (FNMA) during the pre-1972 period when it did not purchase conventional loans. In more recent years, mortgage bankers have also become active in PMI useage. Mutual savings banks have been historically strong users of FHA and VA, and have now expanded their PMI participation as well.[34] In general, PMI useage has greatly increased during the 1970's as FHA activity has declined; VA's importance has remained roughly constant as its dollar volume has grown with the overall expansion of the mortgage market.[35]

Lending institutions and particular loans must meet relevant criteria and rules in order to be eligible for mortgage insurance through any of the three main types of insurers. First, the institution must be approved as such by the insurer or insurers with which it wishes to do business. In the case of FHA and VA, this poses little problem for most financial institutions; a minimum net worth of $100,000 must be demonstrated, as well as compliance with certain internal financial procedures.[36] PMI's are usually eager to attract new institutional customers and their requirements for approval are not difficult to meet.

In addition, the particular loan in question must conform to the applicable insurer's guidelines. For example, a single-family FHA loan cannot exceed $60,000, and the loan-to-value ratio cannot be greater than 97% of the first $25,000 of value and 95% of the excess above $25,000.[37] VA has no specific limits on loan amount, and loans for 100% of value (i. e., with no down payment) are common. However, the VA's maximum guarantee is the lesser of $25,000 or 60% of

33. Savings and loan associations accounted for 63% of all loans insured by Mortgage Guaranty Insurance Co., the largest PMI, at the end of 1972. Rapkin, supra note 23, at 38. At that same date only 14.2% of all residential mortgages held by S&L's were federally-insured or guaranteed. Federal National Mortgage Ass'n, A Guide to Fannie Mae 41 (1974).

34. The residential portfolios of MSB's were almost equally divided between FHA/VA and conventional mortgages as of the end of 1972; A Guide to Fannie Mae, supra note 33, at 41.

35. U. S. Dep't of Housing and Urban Development, Housing in the Seventies 62 (1974).

36. 24 CFR 203.4; Members of the Federal Reserve System and institutions whose deposits are insured by FDIC or FSLIC are not even required to meet these standards; 24 CFR 203.2.

37. 24 CFR 203.17.

the mortgage amount.[38] For large loans, the $25,000 figure is controlling, and acts in effect as a substitute for the veteran's down payment. Hence, most lenders are unwilling to make a no-down-payment VA loan for more than about $100,000. PMI's may impose maximum loan amounts or loan-to-value ratio limits as a consequence of their own internal policies or the statutes and regulations of the states in which they are chartered and operate.[39] In addition, PMI-insured conventional loans must comply with the regulations governing the financial institutions which make them, and with the guidelines of the purchasing investor if they are sold on the secondary mortgage market. For these reasons, PMI loans are generally limited to 95% loan-to-value ratios or lower.

Both FHA and VA fix a maximum interest rate on the loans they insure or guarantee.[40] In recent years the two agencies have acted simultaneously to raise and lower their maximum rate as the market has fluctuated. However, they have consistently set their maximum at a level below current interest rates on conventional loans, and at too low a level to represent an attractive yield to mortgage lenders.[41] This policy is said to act as a brake on interest rates when they are generally rising, and it has some political attractiveness. However, lenders would simply refuse to make FHA or VA loans under these circumstances unless they had some alternative method of increasing their return on such loans. The method employed is termed the "discount point" system; [42] it works as follows. The lender demands a cash payment as a condition of making the loan. This cash payment effectively reduces the lender's net disbursement of loan proceeds at the closing. Since the monthly payments made by the borrower are based on the full or gross loan amount, they represent a higher effective yield than the stated interest rate and make the loan attractive to the lender. The cash payment is called a "discount", and is commonly stated in terms of "points"—with one point being one percent of the nominal loan amount. FHA and VA regulations prohibit the payment of the discount by the borrower-mortgagor,[43] so someone else, usually the seller of the house, pays it.

38. 38 CFR 36.4302.

39. See Rapkin, supra note 23, at 31–37.

40. 24 CFR 203.20 (FHA); 38 CFR 36.-4311 (VA).

41. 12 U.S.C.A. § 1709–1 instructs the Secretary of HUD to set FHA's maximum interest rate "as he finds necessary to meet the mortgage market." In fact, FHA rates in recent years have usually been set .25% to .75% below the yields demanded by investors on FHA and VA mortgages.

42. See Hood & Kushner, Real Estate Finance: The Discount Point System and its Effect on Federally Insured Home Loans, 40 U.Mo.K.C.L.Rev. 1 (1971).

43. 24 CFR 203.27 (FHA); 38 CFR 36.4312 (VA). Both agencies permit the borrower to be charged a 1% fee (usually called an "origination fee") which is supposed to cover the lender's cost of originating the loan; the

The following example will illustrate the discount point system in operation. Assume that current mortgage market yields are 10%, but the FHA-VA interest ceiling is 9.5%. The mortgagor applies for and is granted a loan of $50,000. The lender informs the seller that a discount of four points or $2,000 is required; the seller is in no position to object if he wishes to sell the house with FHA or VA financing. At the closing the seller gives the lender a check for $2,000; the lender disburses $50,000 to the borrower, but has incurred a net outlay of only $48,000. The borrower's monthly payments are based on a $50,000 loan at 9.5% interest.

The impact on effective yield which a given discount will have depends on whether and when the loan will be prepaid prior to maturity. The earlier the prepayment, the greater the boost in yield produced by the discount. To visualize the importance of the time of prepayment on the loan's yield, suppose in the example in the preceding paragraph the loan were prepaid, for some reason, only a week after it was made. The lender, who was out-of-pocket only $48,000 when the loan was made, would receive the full $50,000 balance in payment. Thus, the lender would receive a clear $2,000 profit. Of course, very few loans are prepaid within a week after they are made, but on the other hand, few are held to maturity either. It is commonly assumed that the average life of a mortgage loan will be twelve years. Under this assumption, mathematical tables can be derived which will show the precise impact of any given discount on the loan's yield.[44] A simple rule of thumb which gives results approximating these tables is this: one discount point will increase the yield by about one-eighth of one percent. Thus in the example above, four discount points ($2,000) would increase the loan's yield by about one-half of one percent, from 9.5% to 10%.[45]

This discount point system permits FHA and VA to maintain the fiction of low interest rates while providing actual yields which are high enough to attract institutional investors, but it has several adverse side-effects. Obviously, sophisticated home sellers will attempt to build the expected discount into the price of the house in order to receive the net sale price they desire. Unfortunately, inexperienced sellers may fail to do so, and hence may receive far few dollars than

origination fee may be higher (2.5% for FHA, 2% for VA) if the loan involves construction advances. The borrower is permitted to pay the discount points if he is building his own house or is refinancing an existing loan, since there is no seller in such cases to pay the points.

44. Such a table is reproduced in Federal Home Loan Mortgage Corporation, Sellers' Guide FHA/VA Mortgages 41–42 (various dates).

45. The rule of thumb given in the text is quite accurate at somewhat lower interest rates—say, in the 7% to 8% range—but overstates the discount necessary to produce a desired increase in yield at higher nominal rates, such as the 9.5% example given. The precise discount necessary to produce a 10% yield in the example in the text is $1672.16, not $2000 as the rule of thumb would indicate.

they expected when the sale is completed. The problem is compounded by the fact that many printed sales contract or earnest money forms do not mention payment of the discount points by the seller if the buyer obtains an FHA or VA loan; thus, the stage is set for a dispute as to whether the seller is contractually obligated to do so.

The system also appears to have the effect of lessening competition in the mortgage market, as the seller who will pay the discount is often not actively involved in arranging and negotiating the loan. Moreover, to the extent that discounts are built into sales prices, they probably have the effect of raising overall housing costs. This follows because appraisers pick up FHA and VA transaction prices and use them as comparables in appraising houses which are not being sold with FHA or VA financing. Finally, during periods of increasing interest rates, the FHA and VA ceilings have often been allowed to lag so far behind market yields that huge discounts—as great as eight or ten points—have been necessary.[46] It is extremely difficult for sellers to build such large discounts into their prices. Instead, they tend to refuse to sell with FHA or VA financing during such periods, thus denying to their purchasers the advantages of these programs.

The system also creates an incentive for FHA or VA mortgagees to foreclose at the earliest possible moment against delinquent mortgagors, rather than to attempt to work out the problem through forbearance or modification of payment schedules. Foreclosure is the equivalent of prepayment from the mortgagee's viewpoint, since FHA or VA ordinarily reimburses the mortgagee for the full debt balance and expenses immediately upon transfer of the house to the government.[47] The sooner the foreclosure, therefore, the greater the impact on yield which the discount will have. There is little question that this factor played an important part in the large volume of foreclosures which FHA experienced in many inner-city areas during the late 1960's and early 1970's.[48] While FHA guidelines ostensibly encourage forbearance and workout arrangements, the discount point system encourages a precisely opposite attitude on the part of mortgagees.[49]

In all, it is hard to avoid the conclusion that the FHA/VA administered interest ceilings are counterproductive. They have been widely criticized, and at least four prestigious governmental commis-

46. Hood and Kushner, supra note 42, cite several examples of discounts ranging from 11 to 13 points; id. at 16 n. 63.

47. See text at notes 53–55, infra.

48. See, e. g., Hearings on Interim Report on HUD Investigation of low- and Moderate-Income Housing Programs before House Banking and Currency Comm., 92nd Cong., 1st Sess. (1971); Hood and Kushner, supra note 42.

49. See § 7.7, supra, for discussion of the legal effect of HUD's forbearance guidelines; see 24 CFR 203.600–.616.

sions or task forces have recommended their abolition.[50] Yet congress has been reluctant to do away with them, perhaps because a vote against the ceilings may be seen as a vote for higher interest, and thus a political liability. PMI financing, incidentally, involves no interest ceilings and raises none of these problems.

The premiums charged for mortgage insurance are generally paid by the mortgagor, and are either paid in cash at the time the loan is made or are divided into twelve equal monthly installments and paid along with the principal and interest payments. FHA charges no front-end fee except a nominal amount for appraisal and application, and its annual premium is one-half of one percent of the average outstanding balance of the loan.[51] Thus, in the example of the $50,000 loan above, the first year's premium would be about $250, paid in monthly installments of $20.83. VA charges no premium at all. It is a free benefit to veterans, with the cost of the program being paid from congressionally-appropriated funds. Premiums charged by the PMI's vary from one company to another, and also depend on whether the loan-to-value ratio is below 90% or between 90% and 95%. Many PMI's give the borrower a choice between a total front-end charge with no payments thereafter and a combination of front-end and monthly charges.[52] For example, on a 90% loan-to-value ratio loan, a common premium charge would be two percent of the loan amount at closing with no further payments; alternatively, the borrower could pay one-half percent of the loan amount at closing and one-fourth percent each year (in monthly installments) for the next ten years. Slightly higher premiums usually apply for loan-to-value ratios between 90% and 95%.

Claims procedures.

The objective of all mortgage lenders in participating in mortgage insurance programs is to shift loss. When default and foreclosure result in a loss, the lender wishes to make sure that the incidence of that loss falls on the insurer. Some claims procedure is necessary to accomplish this. FHA's procedure differs from those of VA and the PMI's, and of the three FHA's is most likely to shift fully even the most severe losses to the insurer. The VA and PMI

50. See U. S. Dep't of Housing and Urban Development, Final Report of the Task Force on Housing Costs 54, 62 (1978); Testimony of Secretary James Lynn, Hearings on Administration's 1973 Housing Proposals before the Senate Banking, Housing, and Urban Affairs Comm., 93d Cong., 1st Sess. (1973), at 8 (recommendation derived from National Housing Policy Review Task Force); Report of the President's Commission on Financial Structure and Regulation 77 (1972); Report of the Commission on Mortgage Interest Rates 10 (1969).

51. 24 CFR 203.22.

52. See Rapkin, supra note 23, at 135. Some variation in premium is made by some insurers depending on whether the top 20% or 25% of the loan is insured; see text at note 57, infra.

procedures are similar, and leave open a greater potential for loss by the lender.

In order to make a claim against FHA, the lender must either assign the mortgage itself to the government, or must foreclose, acquire title, and transfer the property to FHA.[53] If the lender chooses to assign the mortgage (a procedure to which FHA must consent under most programs),[54] FHA will pay 99% of the loan balance and will handle the foreclosure itself. However, much more frequently the lender acquires title by foreclosure or a deed in lieu; upon receipt of title, FHA reimburses the lender for the entire outstanding principal balance. Whether the loan is foreclosed or assigned FHA also pays the expenses of the lender for taxes, assessments, insurance, repairs, and other out-of-pocket costs.[55] FHA also pays two-thirds of the foreclosure expenses if the lender forecloses.

FHA pays claims either in cash or in the form of debentures. Cash payment is more desirable from the lender's viewpoint, since the debentures carry interest rates, fixed by FHA, which are typically lower than those of comparable government obligations; they must therefore be sold by the lender at a discount if he wishes to liquidate them. The option to pay in debentures is intended to help FHA avoid large and unanticipated lump sum cash outflows. At this writing FHA is paying claims on single-family home loans in cash, but that policy is subject to change.

Upon acquiring the property, FHA has the option to hold and rent it, or to place it on the market for sale; the former is generally done only in the case of multifamily projects which are already tenanted, and for which no responsible buyer is immediately available. Single-family homes are usually marketed as rapidly as possible, often at a substantial loss. In theory FHA is subrogated to the lender's right to seek a deficiency judgment against the mortgagor in states where this is permitted, but as a practical matter FHA seldom exercizes this right.

VA's claim procedure is quite different than FHA's. Upon notification by the lender that it intends to foreclose, VA appraises the property and advises the lender of the "specified amount"—that is,

53. 24 CFR 200.155; See generally Note, 49 Bos.U.L.Rev. 717, 722–23 (1969); Melody, FHA–VA Foreclosure and Claim Procedures (Mortg. Bankers Ass'n 1967).

54. Under the single-family programs, FHA will approve an assignment of a mortgage only if the default was due to circumstances beyond the mortgagor's control; 24 CFR 203.350. The apparent purpose of permitting assignment on such facts would be to permit forbearance or recasting of payments under circumstances in which the mortgagee is unwilling to do so.

55. 24 CFR 203.402. Accrued interest is not a direct element of the claim but is accounted for to some extent by the fact that the debentures issued, if any, are backdated to one month following the date of the first delinquent payment. See 24 CFR 203.410, 203.331.

VA's estimate of the property's current value.[56] When the lender acquires title by foreclosure or deed in lieu, it may then transfer the property to VA and receive credit in the specified amount; in effect, the lender is selling the property to VA for that amount. VA then pays the lender's claim, which is equal to the entire outstanding balance, accrued interest, and expenses. However, in no event will the VA payment exceed the sum of (1) the specified amount and (2) the maximum VA guarantee, currently the lesser of $25,000 or 60% of the original loan amount.

To illustrate VA's procedure, assume a loan with an original balance of $75,000, a current balance including interest and expenses of $70,000, and a specified amount or property value of $50,000. The VA guarantee would be $25,000 on these facts. Upon conveyance of the property to VA, the lender would receive the full $70,000 claim. On the other hand, suppose the property had been badly vandalized by the mortgagor, and the specified amount were only $42,500. VA's payment to the lender would be limited to $25,000 plus the specified amount, or a total of $67,500; the lender would suffer a net loss of $2,500. Obviously the VA system will result in a loss to the lender only when the property has dropped rather severely in value, but it can happen. Incidentally, the lender is not required to convey the property to VA in order to make a claim; it may instead retain the property and have the claim payment reduced by the specified amount; this would make sense to the lender if it felt that it could market the property at a net sale price greater than the specified amount. However, in most cases the property is conveyed to VA, which then attempts to market it in much the same fashion as FHA.

PMI claims procedures are roughly similar to VA's. The maximum PMI loss or guarantee is fixed at 20% (or if an extra premium is paid, 25%) of the current loan balance plus costs and expenses.[57] Upon foreclosure or the taking of a deed in lieu, the lender will contact the PMI for further instructions. The PMI has two choices: either to take a conveyance of the property (or authorize the lender to sell it as the PMI's agent) and pay the lender the full loan balance plus costs and expenses, or to pay the guarantee amount and allow the lender to keep the property. Obviously the PMI will elect the latter route only if the lender's total claim exceeds the property's current value plus the guarantee.

While the basic economic decisions which PMI's must make are similar to those of VA, the guarantee amount is usually smaller with PMI insurance. Consequently the potential for unreimbursed lender is greater. In the VA claims example given above, if PMI insurance had been employed instead the guarantee amount would be only

56. 38 CFR 36.4320. See Melody, FHA–VA Foreclosure and Claim Procedures (Mortg. Bankers Ass'n 1967).

57. See, e. g., Mortgage Guar. Ins. Corp., Default and Claims Manual (1969).

$14,000 (assuming a 20% policy) and the lender would sustain a loss if the property's value dropped below $56,000. Of course, even value diminutions of this magnitude are quite rare in the current inflationary economy, a fact which may explain why most lenders seem to perceive little difference in effective coverage as among FHA, VA, and the PMI's.

In principle, a mortgage insurance system in which the risk is shared between insurer and lender, as is the case to some degree with VA and the PMI's, can reasonably delegate more underwriting responsibility to the lender than can a system like FHA's in which the lender has virtually no risk. This is so because the lender can be expected to exercise more care in appraising, checking credit, and so forth if its determinations bear on its own potential loss. In fact, VA and the PMI's do delegate more underwriting decision-making to mortgagees than does FHA. Since such delegation seems likely to be efficient and to reduce processing time, FHA instituted an experimental coinsurance program in 1976.[58] It provides for FHA payment of 90% of the usual FHA claim amount, with the lender at risk for the other 10%. The program has attracted little interest on the part of lenders for a variety of reasons: stiffer requirements for lender approval, provisions for a lender's reserve account to be set up with FHA, and other complexities. The program does in fact delegate significant underwriting power to the lender, but this has not proven a sufficient incentive to overcome its disadvantages.

§ 11.3 Government-Sponsored Mortgage Market Support Agencies

In an effort to improve the functioning of the market for residential mortgages, the federal government has created several agencies and institutions. Among these are FHA and VA, discussed in the preceding section; other entities, which do not insure or guarantee mortgages, will be described here.[59] They include the Federal National Mortgage Association (FNMA or "Fannie Mae") and the Federal Home Loan Mortgage Corporation (FHLMC or "Freddie Mac"), both of which purchase mortgage loans on the secondary market. This section will also discuss the Government National

58. See 24 CFR, Part 204.

59. An excellent work describing the development and economic significance of the federal mortgage support institutions is Grebler, The "New System" of Residential Mortgage Finance, 32 Mortgage Banker 4 (No. 5, Feb. 1972), also reprinted in Federal Reserve Staff Study, Ways to Moderate Fluctuations in Housing Construction 177 (1972) under the title "Broadening the Sources of Funds for Residential Mortgages." The annual reports of the entities discussed in the text are highly useful sources of information about their operations, and most of the data in the text are derived from those reports. See also Friedman, Secondary Market Behavior and Analysis, FHLBBJ, May 1973, at 6.

Other institutions supporting the mortgage market, not discussed in the text because of their relatively small impact, include the Federal Land Banks, Federal Intermediate Credit Banks, Banks for Cooperatives, and Farmers Home Administration.

Mortgage Association (GNMA or "Ginnie Mae"), which operates several mortgage market assistance programs, and the Federal Home Loan Bank System, which makes loans to its member institutions, primarily savings and loan associations. Finally, state agencies which provide support for the residential mortgage market will be described.

Secondary Market Agencies—FNMA and FHLMC

Both of these agencies are primarily engaged in purchasing on the secondary market residential mortgages originated by local lending institutions. FNMA is by far the older, having been organized in 1938 as a corporation wholly owned and administered by the federal government.[60] In 1954 it became a "mixed ownership" corporation, owned partly by private shareholders.[61] Finally, by the Housing and Urban Development Act of 1968, FNMA was divided into two separate entities, each of which inherited a portion of the original FNMA's duties.[62] One of these was the Government National Mortgage Association (GNMA), which became a pure federal agency within the Department of Housing and Urban Development, and which retained the management of FNMA's pre-1954 mortgage portfolio and took over certain of its "special assistance" functions, as described below. At the same time, FNMA was re-created as a privately owned and managed corporation, although with certain ties to the federal government; its function is to continue to purchase residential and other mortgages from originating institutions.

Two years after the "privatization" of FNMA, FHLMC was created by the Emergency Home Finance Act of 1970.[63] Its mission is substantially similar to that of FNMA, although it carries out its functions in a somewhat different fashion. Both FNMA and FHLMC are expected to improve the operation of the mortgage market in several ways:[64] (1) They facilitate the flow of capital from areas of the country where funds are plentiful to places in which mortgage money is in short supply. (2) By means of the sale of debt paper and other instruments to persons and institutions who would not ordinarily invest in mortgages, they divert capital from other sectors of the national economy into the mortgage market. (3) By issuing advance commit-

60. FNMA's original charter was contained in Title III of the National Housing Act, 48 Stat. 1246 (1938).

61. Title II of the Housing Act of 1954, 68 Stat. 612.

62. Title VIII of the Housing and Urban Development Act of 1968, 82 Stat. 503, 536. The FNMA General Counsel's Office provides a booklet entitled "Federal National Mortgage Association Charter Act" which contains complete legislative history details of the Association. The charter's present citation is 12 U.S.C.A. § 1716ff. An excellent historical summary of FNMA is found in 43 Fed. Reg. 36200 (Aug. 15, 1978).

63. 12 U.S.C.A. § 1451.

64. See Federal National Mortgage Ass'n, A Guide to Fannie Mae 9 (1975).

ments to purchase mortgages at fixed interest rates or yields, they assist local lenders and homebuilders in hedging against the risk of rising interest rates in the future. (4) By purchasing mortgages when credit is tight and selling them when funds are readily available, they may assist in smoothing the flow of mortgage funds during the extreme cycles of credit fluctuation which have characterized the post-war American economy.

While FNMA and FHLMC are expected to carry out a similar function, the administrative and regulatory relationships which the two agencies have with the federal government are widely different. FNMA is operated largely like a private corporation. It has outstanding more than 50 million shares of common stock, actively traded on the New York and other exchanges. Until recently, it imposed on lending institutions selling mortgages to it an obligation to purchase its stock, and it continues to require stock holding by its servicers;[65] thus, many of its shares are held by lenders. FNMA's board of directors consists of 15 persons, 5 of whom are appointed by the president of the United States and the other 10 elected by the shareholders in the conventional corporate manner. In addition, the Secretary of Housing and Urban Development holds a variety of regulatory powers over FNMA.[66] These include the authority to fix the association's aggregate annual dividends, to approve increases in its total debt and the issuance of particular debt or equity securities, and the authority to promulgate rules and regulations and to require that a reasonable portion of the corporation's mortgage purchases be related to the national goal of providing adequate housing for low and moderate income families. In addition, the debt securities of the corporation are subject to approval by the Secretary of the Treasury.

The regulatory authority of the Secretary of HUD was regarded as having relatively little significance until 1978, when the secretary proposed a set of far-reaching regulations which would, among other things, have operated to allocate a certain portion of FNMA's mortgage purchase activity for inner-city and other low-income areas.[67] FNMA, which had already created certain inner-city programs, vigorously opposed the regulations, and their more objectional features were ultimately withdrawn by HUD.[67a] The precise legal scope of HUD's regulatory power over the corporation was thus not tested by litigation, and still remains uncertain.

The federal government's control over FHLMC is much more straightforward. The corporation is under the direct control of the

65. The holding of stock by servicers is mandated by statute, but may not be required to exceed 2% of the principal balance of the loans being serviced by a particular lender; 12 U.S.C.A. § 1718(c). The purchase of stock by mortgage sellers to FNMA is not statutorily required and was dropped with respect to commitments issued after Feb. 7, 1977.

66. 12 U.S.C.A. § 1723a(h).

67. 43 Fed.Reg. 7659 (Feb. 24, 1978).

67a. 24 C.F.R. Part 81, as amended 43 Fed.Reg. 36200 (Aug. 15, 1978).

Federal Home Loan Bank Board, and the three members of the board are by statute the directors of FHLMC.[68] Since the board members are presidential appointees, FHLMC is for most practical purposes considered a direct federal agency. The corporation's capital stock, in an amount of 100 million dollars, was subscribed by the twelve Federal Home Loan Banks, and in effect represents a portion of their earnings from their transactions with their member institutions.

Another important difference between the two agencies is the fact that FHLMC is permitted by law to purchase mortgages only from federally-chartered or federally-insured financial institutions.[69] As its affiliation with the Federal Home Loan Bank Board suggests, it is strongly oriented toward service to the savings and loan industry, although some sales of mortgages are made to it by commercial banks and mutual savings banks. FNMA, by contrast, imposes no such limitations. Virtually any FHA or VA-approved lender may do business with FNMA, and a large share of its mortgage purchases are from mortgage bankers who are, of course, not federally insured or regulated. The mortgage banking industry has long sought statutory approval to sell loans to FHLMC as well, and after a lengthy controversy FHLMC in 1978 agreed to submit legislation to congress which, if adopted, would make such a change.[70]

To judge from the relative sizes from their mortgage portfolios, FNMA appears a far larger organization than FHLMC. At the end of 1976, for example, FNMA held nearly 32 billion dollars in mortgage loans, while FHLMC held only 4.2 billion. But this comparison is in part misleading. The accumulation of FNMA's portfolio began in 1955, while FHLMC's commenced in 1970. Moreover, FNMA has sold over the years since 1955 only a tiny proportion of the mortgages it has purchased. Thus, in most years its entire purchase volume has constituted a net addition to its mortgage portfolio. In order to finance this growing volume of mortgage holdings, FNMA has been required to issue an exceptionally large volume of debentures, notes, and other debt securities. Indeed, FNMA is second only to the United States treasury in amount of debt securities issued. This policy of buying but rarely selling mortgages has been criticized in recent years as representing a failure by FNMA to properly carry out the countercyclical credit function for which it was created.[71]

FHLMC has followed a very different policy. After building up a substantial portfolio of mortgages during the 1970-1974 period, it

68. 12 U.S.C.A. § 1453(a).

69. 12 U.S.C.A. § 1455(a)(1).

70. See Should Mortgage Bankers Be Given Servicing Access to the Mortgage Corporation?, 38 Mortgage Banker 12 (No. 9, June 1978); Update on FHLMC Access, id. at 14.

71. See, e. g., New FNMA Programs Won't Go Forward Until Growth and Sales Issues Are Resolved, 5 BNA Hsg. & Devel. Rptr. 50 (No. 4, June 27, 1977), reporting that FNMA was considering implementation of a participation certificate sales program similar to FHLMC's.

began in 1975 to sell mortgages at approximately the same rate at which it was acquiring them. To a very large extent these sales have been in the form of participation certificates (PC's), each of which represents an undivided interest in a package of mortgages which FHLMC has accumulated. The PC's are unconditionally guaranteed by the corporation, and pass through interest and principal payments monthly as they are received from the mortgagors. FHLMC also sells Guaranteed Mortgage Certificates (GMC's), which also represent ownership in a pool of mortgages; GMC's, however, do not pass through monthly payments; instead, they pay interest semi-annually and return a portion of the principal annually, thus resembling ordinary corporate bonds. Like PC's they are guaranteed by the Mortgage Corporation. They are intended to be attractive to institutional investors who are accustomed to purchasing bonds.

For accounting and legal purposes, the mortgages represented by PC's and GMC's are treated as no longer part of FHLMC's portfolio. For this reason, the corporation's mortgage holdings seem rather small in comparison to those of FNMA, but its impact on the mortgage market is very substantial. In 1977, for example, the mortgage corporation purchased more than 5 billion dollars in mortgages and sold an equivalent amount of PC's. It was thus able to outstrip FNMA in mortgage purchases during the same period without any increase in its debt obligations.[72]

Both FNMA and FHLMC have been authorized to purchase FHA/VA and conventional mortgages since 1970, when FHLMC was created. Prior to that time, FNMA was permitted to purchase only government-guaranteed mortgages. The authority to purchase conventional loans has had several important consequences. FNMA and FHLMC cooperated during 1970 in developing a set of standard forms for use with conventional mortgages throughout the United States. These forms have gained wide-spread acceptance and are now often used even in transactions in which the lender does not anticipate a sale of the loan to either FNMA or FHLMC.[73] Another consequence has been the reviewing and approval of private mortgage insurance companies by FNMA and FHLMC. Each agency maintains an approved list, an essential activity since weak or unreliable private

72. See Brinkerhoff, PC's Biggest Year: $5 Billion Worth Sold by The Mortgage Corporation, FHLBBJ, Dec. 1977, at 19. FNMA's total mortgage purchases during 1977 were $4.779 billion; see FNMA Annual Report, 1977.

73. See Federal National Mortgage Ass'n Public Meeting on Conventional Mortgage Form, Committee Print, Senate Comm. on Banking, Housing and Urban Affairs, 92d Cong., 1st Sess. (1971). In 1978 FNMA and FHLMC proposed an interesting revision of their standard mortgage form for New York to comply with that state's "Plain Language Law", Ch. 747, 1977 N. Y. Laws, requiring that consumer agreements be "written in a clear and coherent manner using words with common and every day meanings." The act and the FNMA–FHLMC response to it may well be the harbinger of radical change in the drafting of mortgages on a national scale.

mortgage insurers could endanger the security of the conventional mortgages which the two secondary market entities purchase. For both agencies, private mortgage insurance is legally essential on any portion of a loan which exceeds an 80% loan-to-value ratio.

As one might expect from an understanding of its constituency, FHLMC has tended to emphasize the purchase of conventional rather than government-guaranteed loans. In recent years, the same has been true of FNMA, although in the pre-1970 period, its purchases were entirely government insured. By 1976, FNMA was purchasing conventional loans at about four times the rate of government-insured mortgages. While the agencies have been criticized for their lack of support for the government loan market, the diminution in their activity in this respect is accounted for to a great extent by the increase in GNMA mortgage-backed securities discussed below. Nonetheless, FNMA purchased 24% of all FHA-insured and VA-guaranteed loans made between 1969 and 1977. FNMA has been particularly active in supporting the HUD housing subsidy programs which were operated on a large scale in the early 1970's. At the close of 1976, FNMA had provided 86% of all permanent financing for Section 236 projects and 45% of all financing for Section 235 homes.

Both FNMA and FHLMC purchase multi-family apartment loans as well as home loans. FNMA is also active in purchasing other types of FHA-insured loans, including those on nursing homes, hospitals, and mobile home parks. Both agencies have also cooperated with GNMA in participating in the "tandem plan", discussed below.

An important aspect of the operation of both FNMA and FHLMC is the issuance of advance commitments to purchase mortgage loans in the future. Both agencies make some such commitments through an auction process, in which lending institutions wishing to purchase commitments make offers to FNMA or FHLMC on a designated day, stating the dollar amount of the commitments desired and the yield which the mortgages delivered under the commitment will produce. The agency then grants the total number of commitments which it desires. Usually not all requested commitments are issued, and the agency accepts first those which will carry the highest yield. The successful institutional bidders must then pay a commitment fee, but they are not obligated actually to deliver the mortgages in question, and will usually not do so if market interest rates fall so that another investor will be willing to buy the mortgages at a lower yield. The term of the commitments issued under these programs varies from as short as 4 months to much longer periods, but the programs have varied in detail from time to time, and the current literature of FNMA and FHLMC should be consulted for up-to-date information.[73a]

73a. See § 12.3, infra, for a discussion of FNMA's commitment programs.

The Government National Mortgage Association (GNMA)

When FNMA was re-organized as a private corporation in 1968, GNMA was created simultaneously to take over the "special assistance" functions which FNMA had previously handled, and also to manage and liquidate the existing FNMA portfolio of special assistance loans.[74] For example, during the 1961–1968 period FNMA had purchased a large number of below-market-interest-rate mortgages under FHA's 221(d)(3) moderate-income subsidized apartment program. These mortgages, most of which bore only a 3% interest rate, were transferred to GNMA, which continues to hold many of them today. GNMA also holds and continues to purchase from time to time mortgages of a variety of types which are deemed important to national housing policy but would have difficulty attracting private investors. These include loans in urban renewal projects, in disaster areas, on Indian reservations, and in Guam.[75] Today, however, GNMA's most important activities are in two other "special assistance" areas: The tandem plan and the GNMA mortgage-backed security. Each of these will be explained below.

The tandem plan concept originated in late 1969 when extremely tight money market conditions drove up the discount points on FHA mortgages to very high levels. The problem was particularly troublesome for HUD's subsidized programs under Sections 235 and 236. Under the tandem program then devised, GNMA began issuing commitments to purchase mortgages under these programs at favorable prices; for example, it purchased mortgages on newly-constructed Section 235 homes at 97% of face value, requiring only a 3-point discount. GNMA then immediately resold these mortgages to FNMA and other private mortgage investors at market prices, which at that time were in the range of 92 to 93 percent of face value. Since GNMA was reselling the mortgages at prices below its cost, it sustained a substantial dollar loss on each mortgage handled in this fashion. This loss, which was financed directly by the U.S. treasury[76] (since GNMA is a government agency), was seen as a desirable and worthwhile federal expenditure in order to stimulate the housing market.

Over the years since 1969 when the tandem plan was originated, a variety of modifications have been made in it. GNMA now transfers its loan commitments, rather than the loans themselves, to FNMA or other investors. The tandem program has not been operated continuously but rather has been turned on and off as money mar-

74. See 12 U.S.C.A. § 1717(a)(2)(A).

75. See generally GNMA Annual Report 1977; U. S. Comptroller General, Examination of the Government National Mortgage Association's Financial Statements For The 15-Month Period Ended September 20, 1976 (1977).

76. The tandem plan and GNMA's other operational losses are financed by borrowings from the U. S. Treasury rather than from appropriated funds; U. S. Comptroller General, supra note 75, at 1, 4.

ket conditions and national housing policy seemed to require. Some tandem programs have been exclusively devoted to multi-family mortgages; in recent years most have not been limited to subsidized mortgages, but have included non-assisted loans as well. In 1974 congress authorized GNMA to operate a tandem plan for conventional (non-FHA/VA) mortgages, and the agency has done so.[77] The tandem plan has concentrated heavily on new construction rather than existing housing. On single-family loans, GNMA's tandem plan commitment period is one year, permitting builders to obtain analogous commitments from their mortgage lenders that tandem financing at favorable interest rates and discounts will be available to the builder's home purchasers when his houses are completed. Longer commitment terms are available on multifamily projects.

The tandem plan has involved very large sums of money. For example, during fiscal year 1977, GNMA issued tandem plan commitments totaling nearly 2 billion dollars and sustained a loss of about 166 million dollars in operating the plan. During 1976 the tandem plan came under serious criticism on the ground that it constituted a subsidy to many home-buyers whose incomes were sufficiently high that they could have readily afforded to purchase homes without the implicit assistance of the tandem plan.[78] The evidence seems to support this assertion, but the rationale for the plan is to stimulate housing construction and sales; the subsidy to the home-owners who receive advantageous loans is seen by the plan's proponents as only a side benefit. It is nevertheless questionable whether such large subsidy amounts can justifiably be used to benefit middle and upper-middle income households.

The GNMA activity which has had the greatest impact on the mortgage market in recent years is its program for guaranteeing mortgage-backed securities.[79] These securities are issued by mortgage lending institutions; about 90% of the 800 issuers thus far have been mortgage bankers. The securities are in registered form and are actively traded among investors. They represent the obligation of the issuer, collateralized by a pool of FHA-insured or VA-guaranteed mortgages. The GNMA guarantee behind such securities represents the full faith and credit of the United States government, so the securities are considered highly reliable and desirable.

77. § 313, National Housing Act, 12 U.S.C.A. § 1723e, added by § 3, Emergency Home Purchase Assistance Act of 1974, 88 Stat. 1364. Conventional loans which exceed 80% loan-to-value ratio must be PMI-insured.

78. A statistical analysis of a large group of tandem plan loans purchased by FHLMC disclosed by the mortgagors had an average income of $21,516, about $9,000 above the national median. The average purchase price of the homes was $42,720 and the average down-payment was $8,347. Congressman Thomas Ashley, a ranking member of the House Housing Subcommittee, criticized the use of GNMA funds to subsidize such persons. See Housing Affairs Letter, Jan. 9, 1976, at 7.

79. 12 U.S.C.A. § 1721(g).

Several types of GNMA-guaranteed securities have been issued, but by far the largest volume has been of the "fully modified pass-through" type.[80] This means that GNMA guarantees that the holders of the securities will receive their respective shares of the regular monthly principal and interest payments which are due and owing on the underlying mortgages, even if the mortgage payments are in fact delinquent or the issuer fails to remit the payments to the holders. All additional payments resulting from the mortgage foreclosures or prepayments are also passed through to the holders immediately. The minimum size of a pass-through issue is one million dollars, with minimum individual security denominations of 25 thousand dollars or more.

The mortgages which collateralize a GNMA-backed issue must all be federally insured or guaranteed, must all bear the same interest rate, and must have approximately the same maturity. The mortgages themselves are transferred to a bank or trust company to hold as a custodian. In the event the issuer of the securities defaults in payments, the mortgages are transferred to GNMA, which may in turn place them with another lender to manage and service. The diagram below indicates the relationships of the various parties in a GNMA-backed security issue. The great majority of the securities issued thus far have been collateralized by single family mortgages, but multi-family project and mobile home loans have also been used.

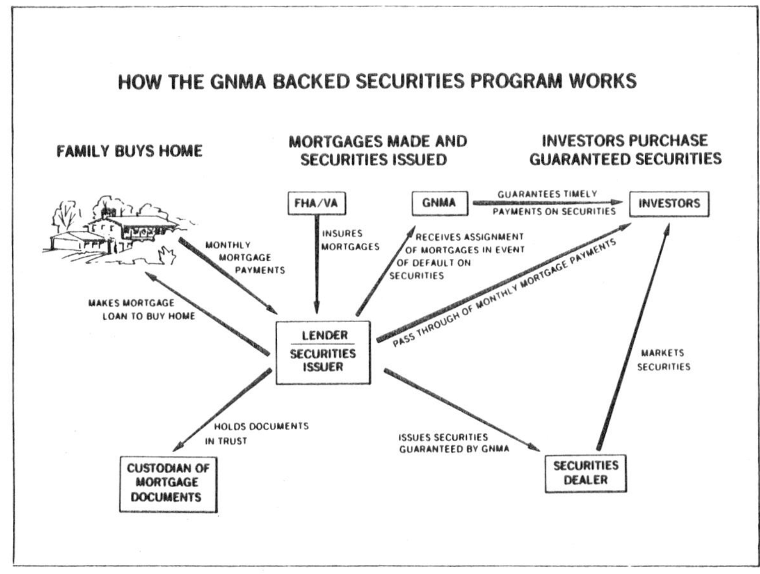

80. See Boileau, GNMA Pass Through: Overwhelming Success Story, 37 Mortgage Banker 20 (No. 5, Feb. 1977).

The program's impact has been very great, and it must be regarded as an outstanding success. More than 80% of all FHA-insured home loans currently originated are funded through GNMA-guaranteed securities. During fiscal year 1977, GNMA guaranteed 17 billion dollars in these securities, bringing the cumulative amount of guarantees to 47.3 billion dollars. Many of the securities are purchased by institutions which are already in the mortgage lending business, but nearly half are bought by pension funds, trusts, profit-sharing plans, and other entities which seldom invest directly in mortgages. In this way the program has been successful in attracting large quantities of new funds to the mortgage market. The fact that the securities carry monthly payments of principal and interest is attractive to many investors, such as pension funds, who have monthly cash flow needs. At the same time, the securities are far simpler investments than mortgages themselves, and require no effort on the part of the investor to satisfy himself with regard to title, appraised value, credit worthiness, or the other factors about which a direct investor in mortgages must be concerned. In addition, the securities are highly liquid, and a secondary market for them is made by many investment banking houses.

The success of the GNMA mortgage-backed pass-through securities has stimulated the issuance of similar securities, without a government guarantee, by several large lending institutions. The first of these was a 150 million dollar issue by the Bank of America in late 1977; [81] several other large institutions have followed suit. These securities are not the obligation of the issuer, but are collateralized only by the mortgages in the pool; the Bank of America's issue, for example, was backed by about 3,000 conventional mortgages in California with loan-to-value ratios of 80% or less. The issue was insured by Mortgage Guaranty Insurance Corporation in an amount equal to 5% of the original mortgage pool balance, insuring both against payment defaults and against such catastrophic physical hazards as earthquakes, floods, mudslides and the like. It is probable that this new form of security, modeled after the GNMA-guaranteed security, will find broad acceptance in the capital markets.[82]

81. See New Attraction for Large-Investor Portfolios: Private Mortgage-Backed Pass-Through Paper, Wall St. J., Aug. 29, 1977, at 22 col. 1.

82. The Federal Home Loan Bank Board has also authorized FSLIC-insured savings and loan associations to issue mortgage-backed bonds. These bonds differ from the mortgage-backed securities discussed in the text in several significant ways. They are not pass-through types, and ordinarily would pay interest installments semiannually. They are, unlike the pass-throughs discussed in the text, the obligation of the issuing institution. The mortgages which collateralize the bonds are maintained in a pool, but the issuer may make substitutions from time to time. See 24 CFR 563.8; Allen, The Mortgage-Backed Bond Regulations: How They Work, FHLBBJ, June 1975, at 13; Adams, The Thrifts Seek Capital With Mortgage-Backed Bonds, 6 Real Estate Rev. 38 (No. 1, Spring 1976).

The Federal Home Loan Bank System

The Federal Home Loan Bank System is organized in a manner similar to the Federal Reserve System. It consists of the Federal Home Loan Bank Board, located in Washington D.C., twelve Federal Home Loan Banks located in districts covering the United States, and the member institutions, most of which are savings and loan associations.[83] The district banks serve as central credit banks for the member institutions and do not do business directly with the public. The banks are instrumentalities of the federal government, and their basic policies are fixed by the Federal Home Loan Bank Board. However, each of the banks has issued capital stock which is owned by its members. Hence the banks are an unusual hybrid of federal control and private ownership. Each bank has its own staff and board of directors; six of the board members of each bank are appointed by the Federal Home Loan Bank Board to represent the public interest, while the other directors are elected by the member institutions.

The banks provide a variety of benefits to their members, including the acceptance of interest-bearing deposits and the provision of computer services. By far the most important activity of the banks is the making available of credit to their members. Loans from the banks to their members are known as "advances". The savings and loan industry has tended to use these advances as a substitute for funds withdrawn by depositors from savings accounts when tight credit and high interest rates in other markets have resulted in reductions in savings account balances. For this reason the total level of advances has fluctuated widely, tending to reach peak levels when interest rates are highest and dropping off as credit becomes more available. At the close of 1976 nearly 16 billion dollars in advances was outstanding. The banks raise the funds with which to make these advances by the sale of debt obligations in the general capital markets. The instruments sold usually take the form of consolidated obligations of the bank system and are issued by the Bank Board and marketed by its Office of Finance in Washington. Since these obligations are purchased by a wide variety of institutional investors, most of which are not primarily mortgage investors, the bank system has the effect of shifting funds from the general capital markets into the mortgage market. In this respect, and also in its countercyclical tendencies, the bank system serves much the same function as FNMA and FHLMC. However, it differs from the secondary market agencies in that no mortgages are actually purchased by the Federal Home Loan Banks from their member institutions. The associations which borrow from the banks continue to hold the mortgages

83. See the Federal Home Loan Bank Act, 47 Stat. 725 (1932), 12 U.S.C.A. § 1421. The system is thoroughly discussed in U. S. League of Savings Associations, Savings and Loan Fact Book 94 (1977).

which exist in their portfolios, although these mortgages serve as collateral for advances made.

Many savings and loan associations make relatively little use of the advances, and in the aggregate they have never been as great as 10% of the members' total savings balances. The highest level of advances at the end of any calendar year occurred in 1974, a period of extreme monetary stringency, when nearly 22 billion dollars was outstanding.

State Housing Finance Agencies

The creation by state governments of mortgage market support agencies is a relatively recent phenomenon. In 1960 New York became the first state to do so; by 1970 twelve more states had acted, and there are now more than forty such agencies.[84] The underlying concept of all of the agencies is similar. They sell bonds and other debt issuances which, because of their state government status, are exempt from federal and often state income taxation, and which therefore bear relatively low interest rates. The funds raised by these bond and note sales are then used to finance housing for low-income and moderate-income families and individuals, with the lower interest rates being passed on in the form of lower mortgage interest to the home-buyers (in the case of single-family housing) or sponsors (in the case of rental apartments).

The mechanisms by which the state agencies funnel their money into the residential mortgage market are varied. Some make direct loans to housing developers, sponsors, and individual buyers. Others act as secondary market purchasers, issuing advance commitments to lending institutions to purchase loans which meet prescribed criteria. Still others make loans to lending institutions on the condition that the funds be employed in mortgage lending on housing of the type the agency desires to assist. Some employ two or more of the foregoing methods. Whether single-family or multi-family housing is involved, the agencies usually impose limitations on the household income of the occupants and on the cost of the housing.

Other programmatic variations exist. In a few states, legislatures have appropriated subsidy funds which the agencies administer, sometimes employing them to further lower interest rates. In addition, many of the agencies have worked cooperatively with the De-

84. See State Housing Finance Agencies: The Iowa Blueprint, 62 Iowa L. Rev. 1524 (1977); Blew, Future Management Directions for HFA's, 36 Urban Land 7 (Apr.1977); Stegman, State Housing Finance Agencies: The American Experience, 4 Local Finance 3 (No. 3, June 1975); Stegman, Housing Finance Agencies—Are They Crucial Instruments of Government?, 40 J.Am.Inst. of Planners 307 (1974); Timilty, State Role in Housing, Neighborhood Improvement Probed, 33 J. Housing 437 (1976). The BNA Housing and Development Reporter contains a thorough summary of state agency techniques and a current listing of the individual agencies and the programs they operate.

partment of Housing and Urban Development, supplying mortgage loans for projects subsidized by HUD under Section 236 or, more recently, the Section 8 program.[85] The advantage of the state agency's lower interest rate when used in conjunction with HUD subsidies is that it may make otherwise infeasible projects feasible by lowering the sponsor's debt service, or may permit the construction of apartment buildings with somewhat greater amenities than would otherwise be possible.

The state agencies have not been free from problems. Many state constitutions include prohibitions on the pledging of the credit of the state for any private enterprise. Most of the state housing agencies have attempted to avoid violations of these clauses by issuing debt paper which is only the obligation of the agency itself, and does not carry the full faith and credit of the state. Since it is understood that the legislature may nonetheless appropriate additional funds if the agency is unable to meet its obligations, the issues are often called "moral obligation" bonds.[86] Despite this sort of attempt to insulate the agency from the state's credit, a few state supreme courts have held the arrangement unconstitutional.[87] A court test of the validity of the legislation has been necessary in most states to satisfy the concerns of bond counsel and investors on this ground.

Operational difficulties have also plagued a few of the agencies, particularly in the making of construction loans on apartment projects. Some agencies which financed construction lending by issuing short term notes found that building delays and cost overruns made refinancing of the notes necessary under unfavorable market conditions.[88] Delays also contributed to increased total costs; some

85. See Sangster, For Section 8 Housing—New Financing Relationship Between LHA's and State Housing Finance Agencies Proposed, 32 J. Housing 67 (1975).

86. The great majority of courts have upheld state housing agencies against this sort of attack. See, e. g., Utah Housing Finance Agency v. Smart, 561 P.2d 1052 (Utah 1977); Huber v. Groff, 558 P.2d 1124 (Mont.1976); California Housing Finance Agency v. Elliott, 17 Cal.3d 575, 131 Cal.Rptr. 361, 551 P.2d 1193 (1976); Rich v. Georgia, 237 Ga. 291, 227 S.E.2d 761 (1976); In re Constitutionality of ORS 456.720, 272 Or. 398, 537 P.2d 542 (1975); West v. Tennessee Housing Development Agency, 512 S.W.2d 275 (Tenn.1974); Warren v. Nusbaum, 59 Wis.2d 391, 208 N.W.2d 780 (1973); Maine State Housing Authority v. Depositors Trust, 278 A.2d 699 (Me.1971); Martin v. North Carolina Housing Corp., 277 N.C. 29, 175 S.E. 2d 665 (1970); Vermont Home Mortgage Credit Agency v. Montpelier Nat. Bank, 128 Vt. 272, 262 A.2d 445 (1970); Bauer v. South Carolina State Housing Authority, 246 S.E.2d 869 (S.C.1978).

87. See Witzenburger v. Wyoming, 575 P.2d 1100 (Wyo.1978), describing the "moral obligation" concept as "a sales gimmick" and "misleading"; Brown v. Beard, 48 Ohio St.2d 290, 358 N.E.2d 569 (1976). After the foregoing decision by the Ohio Supreme Court, the voters of the state rejected a constitutional amendment which would have authorized the creation of a state housing finance agency; see 5 BNA Hsg. & Devel.Rptr. 577 (Nov. 14, 1977).

88. See Now New York State Heads Toward Default, Business Week, Nov. 17, 1975, at 116; Hershman, What Went Wrong with UDC?, 36 Urban Land 3 (Apr.1977).

projects were ill-planned and difficult to market, with rent-up progressing slowly despite the low rents produced by the state's participation and the associated HUD subsidies. The lessons the agencies learned from these experiences were costly, but most have now adopted more cautious practices designed to minimize such mistakes in the future.

In general, the state housing finance agencies have been highly successful. They have generally been able to market bonds at interest rates roughly two percent below the prevailing mortgage market rates. Even after adding an "override" to cover their operating costs, they have usually been able to make or buy mortgage loans at least one percent below conventional rates. In most states they are politically popular and fill a clear-cut need.[89] Their role is likely to expand in the future.[90]

§ 11.4 Alternative Mortgage Instruments

The great majority of mortgage loans made in modern times are of the level-payment self-amortizing type described in Section 1.1. Interest is fixed for the life of the loan and payments are the same each month or other period, and amortize the debt with no "balloon" payment upon maturity. While this format has resolved the problem of mandatory refinancing which existed in pre-depression mortgage loans, in which only interest was paid monthly,[91] it also has certain

89. The political picture is not uniformly rosy. In a few states private lenders have questioned or attacked the state agencies as unwanted competitors who have an unfair advantage. See, e. g., Peterson, Has Michigan Housing Authority Encroached into Private Business?, 35 Mortgage Banker 42 (No. 2, Nov. 1974).

90. HUD provides an additional benefit to state housing agencies. Under Section 244 of the National Housing Act, added by the Housing and Community Development Act of 1974, 12 U.S.C.A. § 1715z–9, HUD is authorized to co-insure with such agencies mortgage loans which would otherwise be fully FHA-insured. In return for acceptance of a portion of the risk, the agencies are given fairly broad powers to process loan applications without direct HUD involvement, thus speeding the processing and making it more efficient. HUD's final regulations under Section 244 were published in 41 Fed.Reg. 43068 (Sept. 29, 1976), codified in 24 CFR, Part 250. Most state agencies found the regulations cumbersome and unsatisfactory, and at this writing only one state, Missouri, has received HUD approval to make loans under Section 244. Negotiations between HUD and the Council of State Housing Agencies are likely to result in significant modifications in the regulations to make them more palatable to the states. See HUD, CSHA Form Separate Groups to Make Major Revisions in Coinsurance Program, 5 BNA Hsg. & Devel.Rptr. 766 (Jan. 9, 1978); Hance & Duvall, Coinsurance: The Key to the Future For State Housing Finance Agencies?, 8 Urban Law. 720 (1976).

91. Pre-depression mortgages were usually written for relatively short periods—five to fifteen years—and made no provision for amortization of principal balance; thus, when the loan matured, the borrower was expected either to pay the principal out of savings he had accumulated, or to refinance for an additional period with the same or another lender. During the depression many borrowers found both alternatives impossible, and large-scale foreclosures resulted. See Harr, Federal Credit and Private Housing 58 (1960). As Harr

disadvantages. The disadvantages fall into two basic categories, as do various proposals for reform.

The first troublesome aspect of the standard loan format is its failure to take into account changes in the ability of the mortgagors to make payments over their life spans. For example, young families purchasing a first house are likely to experience significant increases in income as they grow older.[92] Yet the standard loan provides for level payments in terms of dollars; in an inflationary economy, the real value of the monthly payments will decline over time, even though the mortgagors' ability to pay will probably be increasing. Hence their maximum initial loan amount will be fixed by an income which rapidly becomes irrelevant with the passage of time; [93] after a few years they will easily be able to afford payments on a larger home, but can make such a change only through the rather costly method of selling the existing house and buying another.

At the other end of the mortgagors' life span an opposite mismatch occurs. The mortgagors frequently retire and experience a sharp drop in income, but their monthly mortgage payment obligation remains constant despite the fact that principal amortization and inflating house values have combined to produce a very low loan-to-value ratio. The mortgagors might prefer to reduce their payments, or even to stop them entirely, but the standard loan format makes no provision for doing so.

The second major problem with the standard loan relates not to the preferences and incomes of mortgagors, but to the ability of lenders, particularly thrift institutions, to retain deposits and hence to continue lending during periods of sharply increasing interest rates. The United States economy has experienced a series of large fluctuations in interest rates during the post-war period, especially since 1966. These credit cycles are largely produced by the periodic efforts of the Federal Reserve Board to tighten the supply of money in the economy in order to slow inflation. Interest rate peaks can be clearly discerned in 1966, 1969–70, 1974, and 1978. In each case rates have subsequently fallen, but usually not as low as pre-peak levels.[94]

describes, the FHA was primarily responsible for popularizing the long-term, level-payment, fully-amortizing loan.

92. Life-cycle incomes are discussed in Weinrobe, Whatever Happened to the Flexible Payment Mortgage?, FHLBBJ, Dec. 1975, at 16.

93. Lenders usually "qualify" borrowers by permitting them to borrow only the amount which can be repaid by monthly installments (including principal, interest, taxes, and insurance) no larger than 25% of monthly income. See, e. g., Federal Home Loan Mortgage Corp., Sellers' Guide Conventional Mortgages § 3.403(a) (1977), at 141. Thus income often fixes the maximum amount which a mortgagor can borrow, even if he would prefer a larger loan.

94. See U. S. League of Savings Ass'ns, Sav. and Loan Fact Book 34 (1977); future editions will update this data.

The effect of these credit cycles on thrift institutions such as savings and loan associations and mutual savings banks is highly damaging. When short-term rates on alternative investments, such as Treasury bills and commercial paper, rise above the rates being paid on savings deposits by thrift institutions, many sophisticated depositors withdraw their funds from savings accounts and place them in these alternative investments. The institutions may literally run out of money to lend, and the housing market suffers. This phenomenon is known as disintermediation, since it involves the removal of funds from the thrift institutions, which are financial intermediaries.[95] To forestall disintermediation, the thrifts might attempt to raise their own deposit interest rates, thereby inducing depositors to keep their deposits in place. Two factors militate against this. One is Regulation Q,[96] by which the Federal Reserve Board and the Federal Home Loan Bank Board set legal limits on deposit rates for both commercial banks and thrift institutions. In principle, Regulation Q is supposed to prevent damaging rate wars; it also maintains an interest spread between commercial banks and thrifts, permitting the latter to pay somewhat higher deposit interest (typically one-fourth of one percent) in order to divert funds toward housing.[97] The regulatory agencies have usually been unwilling to amend Regulation Q to permit substantial rate increases when other market rates are rising, although they did authorize several small increases during the decade beginning in 1966.

Even if Regulation Q were not a barrier, mortgage lending institutions would still be largely unable to raise their deposit rates to competitive levels during tight money periods. The reason is that their main source of income, out of which they must pay their depos-

95. Disintermediation and its effects are discussed in Klaman, Maintaining Deposit Inflows When Interest Rates Rise: The Impossible Dream, 38 Mortgage Banker 46 (No. 7, Apr. 1978); Edwards, Can Savings and Loan Associations Survive as Specialized Financial Institutions?, MGIC Newsletter, March 1978; Gramley, Short-Term Cycles In Housing Production: An Overview of the Problem and Possible Solutions, in Federal Reserve Staff Study: Ways to Moderate Fluctuations in Housing Construction (1972), at 1; Schechter, The Residential Mortgage Financing Problem, Committee Print, House Housing Subcommittee, 92d Cong., 1st Sess., 1971.

96. See 12 U.S.C.A. § 1425b(a), added by Pub.L. 89–579, 80 Stat. 824 (1966); see 12 CFR 217 (Federal Reserve Bd.); 12 CFR 329 (Federal Deposit Ins. Corp.); 12 CFR 526 (Federal Home Loan Bank Bd.). All federally-chartered and federally-insured state-chartered banks and S&L's are controlled by these regulations.

97. See, e. g., Kaufman, A Proposal for Eliminating Interest-Rate Ceilings on Thrift Institutions, 4 J. Money, Credit & Banking 735 (Aug. 1972). The Report of The President's Commission on Financial Structure and Regulation (the "Hunt Commission") (1972) recommended abolition of Regulation Q; id. at 23. Cf. Dunne, Scott & Barrett, The Swan Song of Regulation Q—A Rejoinder, 92 Banking L.J. 219 (1975). The thrift institutions have been notably unenthusiastic about the elimination of the rate differential protection which regulation Q gives them as against commercial banks, and the pages of the Federal Home Loan Bank Board Journal and Savings and Loan News are replete with defenses of Regulation Q.

itors, is their mortgage portfolios. These portfolios consist of mortgages made in prior years as well as those made in the current year. Even if the institution raises the interest rates on mortgage loans currently being made to very high levels, that action has relatively little impact on the overall yield of the portfolio, since it consists largely of fixed-interest loans made in earlier periods when rates were lower. This "portfolio lag" phenomenon virtually precludes the institutions from raising deposit interest rates quickly, no matter how much they would like to do so. The thrift institutions are caught in a fundamental structural dilemma; by their nature they violate the well-known axiom of finance: "Never borrow short and lend long." In an economy characterized by volatile interest rates, their problem is an acute one.[98]

Two approaches to this problem can be taken, and the thrift institutions and their regulators have moved toward both. The first is to change the maturity structure of the institutions' liabilities—that is, their deposits—in order to make them less volatile. Several efforts have been made in this direction, including the authorization of longer-term certificate accounts with substantial penalties for early withdrawal,[99] so-called treasury bill accounts with six-month maturities and yields keyed to the rates on current Treasury issues,[1] and the introduction of mortgage-backed bonds and other securities as alternative capital sources to savings deposits.[2]

The other approach is to shorten the effective maturity of the institutions' assets, their mortgage loans. Although most home mortgages today have nominal maturities of twenty-five to thirty years, they are typically prepaid in ten to twelve years or less.[3] These early payments are due in part to rapidly inflating housing prices, which tend to make assumptions and subject-to transfers impractical within a few years after a mortgage loan has been placed on a home. The widespread use of due-on-sale clauses is also an important factor in causing early payoffs, at least in those jurisdictions in which the clauses are enforceable by the lender without a showing of jeopardized credit or security.[4] Many lenders, however, would prefer to shift toward broader use of mortgage instruments with variable or fluctuating interest rates, or with more frequent mandatory refinanc-

98. The portfolio lag concept is developed in Ashley, Use of "Due-On" Clauses to Gain Collateral Benefits: A Common-Sense Defense, 10 Tulsa. L.J. 590 (1975).

99. See regulations cited note 96, supra.

1. See 43 Fed.Reg. at 21435 (Federal Reserve System), 21436 (FDIC), and 21438 (FHLBB) (all May 18, 1978), permitting the offering of such accounts to the public in minimum denominations of $10,000.

2. See § 11.3 n. 82, supra.

3. See Boykin, Implications of the 12-Year Prepayment Assumption, Mortgage Banker, Nov. 1976, at 38; Kinkade, Mortgage Prepayments and Their Effects on S&L's, FHLBBJ, Jan. 1976, at 12.

4. See generally §§ 5.21, 5.23, infra.

ing. Such mortgages would tend to be viewed as the economic equivalent of short-term loans, even though their monthly payment schedules might continue to be based on twenty-five or thirty year amortization of principal.

There are, then, two reasons for experimentation in recent years with alternative mortgage instruments: the desire to conform payment schedules to borrowers' abilities to pay over the life cycle, and the desire to make mortgage loans which are not locked into fixed interest yields for long time periods, but on which yields will tend to match those available in the current market from time to time. Certain types of new mortgage formats are associated with each of these two objectives, and it is important, in analyzing any proposal, to see clearly which objective it is aimed at achieving.[5]

Life-Cycle Mortgages—The GPM and RAM

The graduated payment mortgage (GPM) is intended to be attractive to young mortgagors who expect to have rising incomes in the immediate future. The interest rate on a GPM is fixed, but the payments start out at a relatively low level and gradually rise to a predetermined higher amount. The payments are not keyed to the borrower's actual income, but rather follow a rising schedule which the parties feel he will probably be able to meet without difficulty. The objective is to permit the borrower to qualify for a larger loan than would be permitted if the payments were level.[6]

The first federal encouragement for the GPM came in 1974, when the Federal Home Loan Bank Board authorized federal savings and loan associations to make "flexible payment mortgage loans." [7] Such loans were required to be structured so that each payment would cover at least the entire interest due. In addition, by the end of the fifth year the payments had to be high enough for the loan to be fully self-amortizing. The full-interest requirement meant, for example, that the initial payments on an 8.5 percent "flexible payment" mortgage could, at best, be about 8% lower than payments on a standard mortgage. The reduction in payments was not very great, and the program was not widely used.[8]

5. See generally Federal Home Loan Bank Board, Alternative Mortgage Instruments Research Study (3 vols. 1977) (hereafter cited AMIRS Study); Smith, Reforming the Mortgage Instrument, FHLBBJ, May 1976, at 2; Follain & Struyk, Homeownership Effects of Alternative Mortgage Instruments, 5 Am. Real Est. & Urb. Econ. Ass'n J. 1 (1977).

6. See note 93, supra.

7. 12 CFR 541.14(c); see Cassidy & McElhone, The Flexible Payment Mortgage: An Opportunity for Experimentation by S&L's, FHLBBJ, Aug. 1974, at 7.

8. See Weinrobe, Whatever Happened to the Flexible Payment Mortgage?, FHLBBJ, Dec. 1975, at 16.

The enactment of the Housing and Community Development Act of 1974 added a new Section 245 to the National Housing Act,[9] authorizing HUD to insure mortgages "with provisions for varying rates of amortization corresponding to anticipated variations in family income." After some uncertainty as to how to proceed,[10] HUD in 1976 issued regulations under the authority of Section 245,[11] approving the insurance by FHA of graduated payment mortgages. The regulations permit monthly payments to be increased in annual steps over the first five years or the first ten years of the loan; under the five-year plan the payments may rise by 2.5%, 5%, or 7.5% each year, while under the ten-year plan payments may increase annually by either 2% or 3%. There is no requirement that all payments cover interest owed, and the FHA program often involves "negative amortization" in the early years. If the early payments do not cover the full interest, the difference is added to principal; thus, it is entirely possible for the outstanding balance to rise rather than be reduced for a few years. The program requires that the outstanding balance never exceed 97% of the original appraised value of the property; to account for the negative amortization, a somewhat larger down-payment than 3% is generally necessary. The table below illustrates the impact of the various GPM plans on monthly payments and required income.[12]

Monthly Mortgage Payments and Estimated Income Required for Graduated Payment and Level Payment Mortgages
30–Year, 8.5 Percent and $30,000 Original Obligation

Plan Type (rate of increase)	Required Income *	Monthly Princ. & Int. Payments			Percent Reduction in 1st yr. payments from level payment mortgage
		First Year	Sixth Year	Eleventh Year	
5–Year Increasing Payments – 2½%	$13,400	$209.76	$237.33	Same as 6th year	9%
– 5%	12,500	190.83	243.57	" " " "	17%
– 7½%	11,700	173.73	249.42	" " " "	25%
10–Year Increasing Payments – 2%	$13,100	$203.64	$224.82	$248.22	12%
– 3%	12,500	191.13	221.55	256.83	17%
Level Payments	$14,400	$230.70	Same as 1st year		

* Assumes the mortgagor could pay 25 percent of income for principal, interest, MIP, taxes and insurance. Taxes and insurance were estimated to cost $57 per month.

9. 12 U.S.C.A. §§ 1715z–10.

10. See 40 Fed.Reg. 34625 (Aug. 18, 1975), in which HUD solicited public comments as to what it should do under its Section 245 authority.

11. 12 CFR 203.45, 203.436; condominium financing is also made available under the CPM by virtue of 12 CFR 234.75, 234.259.

12. The table is adapted from Foster, The HUD–FHA GPM Experiment, AMIRS Study at V–15. Note that the precise amount of initial payment reduction available under the GPM is dependent on the interest rate.

The FHA GPM program offers borrowers a much greater initial reduction in monthly payments than did the FHLBB's flexible payment mortgage. It has been very popular, with Plan III, which provides the greatest first-year payment reduction, being selected most often.[13] A question was raised concerning the validity of the negative amortization feature in numerous states having usury laws which prohibit "interest on interest", but in 1977 congress enacted legislation preempting this issue and expressly approving negative amortization.[14]

The success of the FHA GPM program has awakened considerable interest on the part of conventional lenders in making similar loans without FHA mortgage insurance. With respect to state-chartered institutions the matter is one of state law or regulation, and many states do not currently permit GPM's. That situation is likely to change as legislatures and banking commissioners come under increasing pressure to accede to consumer wishes. Effective January 1979, the FHLBB authorized federal savings associations to grant GPM's on greatly liberalized terms similar to those approved by FHA.[14a]

A second type of new mortgage instrument has been proposed for the other end of the life cycle: retirement. Its thesis is that many persons reaching retirement age have accumulated large equity values in their homes, but will suffer substantial income reductions upon retirement. Under the reverse annuity mortgage (RAM),[15] the mortgagor in this situation would be given a large cash advance by the lender, and would immediately use this cash to purchase an annuity. The monthly cash flow from the annuity would be used, in part, to pay the interest (and perhaps some principal amortization) on the enlarged mortgage debt; the remainder of the annuity stream would be paid directly to the mortgagor to augment his income.

As an alternative, the mortgagee might make monthly payments directly to the mortgagor, thereby regularly increasing the outstanding balance on the debt; interest would also continue to accrue and be added to principal. Obviously this approach would result at some future point in the reaching of an unacceptable loan-to-value ratio if the mortgagor lived long enough; the lender would demand payoff, presumably achieved only by selling the house, or would foreclose.[16] The

13. Id. at V–7; see Kidd, FHA 245, Mortgages May Be A Two-edged Sword for Mortgage Bankers, Mortgage Banker, May 1978, at 65.

14. § 310, Housing and Community Development Act of 1977, Pub.L. 95–128.

14a. 12 CFR § 545.6–2(b), 43 Fed.Reg. 59338 (Dec. 20, 1978).

15. See Edwards, Reverse Annuity Mortgages, AMIRS Study at XIX; Guttentag, Reverse Annuity Mortgages: How S&L's Can Write Them, AMIRS Study at XVIII; West's Ann. Calif. Financial Code, § 7153.9 (supp. 1978), authorizing the savings and loan commissioner to issue regulations permitting both GPM's and RAM's on an experimental basis.

16. See Quinn, Let the Mortgagor Beware, Forbes, Mar. 20, 1978, at 77, criticizing this type of RAM.

advantage of the annuity approach, by contrast, is that it will continue to pay as long as the mortgagor lives, so there is no risk of the mortgagor being forced to vacate the property.

A variety of other variants on the RAM are possible. For example, under the so-called "split equity contract" [17] the homeowner might sell his house to an investor (possibly his mortgagee), reserving a life estate. The sale proceeds could be paid in installments over a number of years, or the vendor might take the proceeds in cash and purchase an annuity. Numerous other permutations may also be conceived.

The RAM is not a popularly-used concept at this point, although it would appear to serve a genuine need for older persons. One barrier has been the regulatory prohibition against the making of non-amortized loans having terms exceeding 5 years, applicable to federal savings and loan associations; [18] many state laws impose similar limitations. Moreover, the RAM is far more complex and unconventional than the other alternative mortgage instruments discussed in this section, and it may have trouble finding broad public acceptance. Its use is likely to grow slowly. However, it has now been expressly authorized by the FHLBB for federal savings associations.[18a]

Solving the portfolio-lag problem: the VRM, ROM, and PLAM. At least three alternative mortgage instruments have been proposed which would maintain lenders' portfolio yields at or near current market levels. The most widely analyzed and used of these in the United States is the variable rate mortgage (VRM).[19] It provides for periodic readjustments to the interest rate, based on fluctuations in some external index, such as the institution's cost of funds or the

17. See Edwards, Reverse Annuity Mortgages, AMIRS Study, at XIX–5.

18. 12 CFR 545.6–1(3).

18a. 12 CFR § 545.6–2(d); 43 Fed. Reg. 59340 (Dec. 20, 1978).

19. The literature is abundant, since the VRM is by far the most widely discussed alternative instrument. See, e. g., Comment, Variable Rate Mortgages: The Transition Phase, 61 Marquette L.Rev. 140 (1977); Epley, Variable Mortgage Plans and Their Unsolved Issues, The Appraisal Journal, April 1977, at 242; Stansell & Millar, How Variable-Rate Mortgages Would Affect Lenders, 5 Real Estate Rev. 116 (No. 4, Winter 1976); Matthews, Investors Are Key to VIR Loan Expansion, Mortgage Banker, Oct. 1976, at 44; Cassidy & McElhone, The Pricing of Variable Rate Mortgages, Financial Management, Winter 1975, at 37; Millar & Stansell, Variable Rate Mortgage Experience of the Farm Credit System, Financial Management, Winter 1975, at 46; Comment, Adjustable Interest Rates In-Home Mortgages: A Reconsideration, 1975 Wisc.L.Rev. 742; Edwards, Variable Rate Home Mortgages and the Public Interest, MGIC Newsletter, April 1974; Matthews, Two Major Lenders Report Variable Rate Acceptance, Mortgage Banker, Oct. 1974, at 72; Newton, Some Unanticipated Problems With Variable Rate Home Mortgages, MGIC Newsletter, Oct. 1973 (discussing British VRM experience); Comment, The Variable Interest Rate Clause and Its Use in California Real Estate Transactions, 19 U.C.L.A.L.Rev. 468 (1972); Comment, The Variable Interest Note: An Answer to Uncertainty in a Fluctuating Money Market, 1971 Law & Soc. Order 600.

current rates on Treasury debt issues of some prescribed maturity.[20] The mortgagor may pay the increased interest rate (if it does indeed increase, as has been the net trend during the past decade or more) either by making larger monthly payments or by extending the maturity of the loan. However, only modest interest rate increases can be accommodated by maturity extensions; for example, the regular monthly payment on a 30-year loan at 8% will be sufficient to cover only an 8.8% rate even if the maturity is extended to infinity—that is, if the entire payment is allocated to interest.[21] In addition, many regulators limit the maturities of loans made by institutional lenders. For these reasons, significant rate increases will frequently result in higher monthly payments.

It is generally agreed that some legislation or regulation is necessary to protect consumers from unfair or unduly burdensome provisions in variable rate mortgages.[22] The regulations which the Federal Home Loan Bank Board (FHLBB) proposed for federal savings and loan associations in 1972 [23], 1975 [24], and 1978 [24a] and the relevant statutes in California [25] and Wisconsin [26] provide a useful checklist of such protective features. They include a maximum frequency of change of interest rates such as semiannually or annually; a maximum percent change per year (such as .5% or 1%); a maximum overall change (such as 2.5%); a minimum percent change to avoid trivial or harassing changes; and a provision for some minimum notice prior to a rate increase. Other such pro-borrower clauses include a right in the mortgagor to elect extended maturity (if feasible) or increased monthly payments in the event of a rate increase, and a right to prepay the loan without penalty whenever the current rate exceeds the initial rate. Some sort of special disclosure to the borrower at the time he

20. The choice of index is an important and controversial matter; see Comment, Adjustable Interest Rates in Home Mortgages: A Reconsideration, 1975 Wisc.L.Rev. 742, 762–65; Powell v. Central California Federal Sav. & Loan Ass'n, 59 Cal.App.3d 540, 130 Cal.Rptr. 635 (1976). In California the usual index for S&L's is the weighted cost of funds for all California S&L's as published by the Federal Home Loan Bank of San Francisco. See Thompson, All Quiet on the Western VRM Front, FHLBBJ, Oct. 1978, at 10. The FHLBB has adopted a similar index for federal S & L's; 12 CFR § 545.6–2(c)(3).

21. See Stansell & Millar, How Variable-Rate Mortgages Would Affect Lenders, 5 Real Estate Rev. 116 (No. 4, 1976).

22. See Weinrobe, Analysis of Consumer Safeguards for AMI's, AMIRS Study at XXI; compare The Unvariable Rate Mortgage, Savings and Loan News, July 1974, at 40, for the view that the safeguards are likely to be so extensive as to make the VRM unattractive to lenders.

23. 37 Fed.Reg. 16201 (Aug. 11, 1972).

24. 40 Fed.Reg. 6870 (Feb. 14, 1975).

24a. 43 Fed.Reg. 33254 (July 31, 1978; 43 Fed.Reg. 59339 (Dec. 20, 1978) (final regulations).

25. West's Cal.Civ.Code, § 1916.5 (Supp.1978).

26. Wis.Stat. § 138.055 (1975).

arranges the loan may also be appropriate in order to apprise him fully of the unusual nature of the contract.[27]

Until 1979, FHLBB regulations effectively prohibited federal savings associations from making VRM's on single-family homes.[28] The Board has now decided to permit such loans in states in which they are necessary to permit federal associations "to maintain competitive balance with other financial institutions lending in such state." [28a] State associations are governed only by state law in this respect, and many states permit them to make VRM loans. VRM's have been most common in the New England states, where they have been widely used since the 1960's,[29] and in California, where they date largely from the mid-1970's.[30] The rate at which a lender's mortgage portfolio can be converted to VRM's in a highly mobile state like California is astounding; two large California savings associations which began using VRM's at the beginning of 1975 reported 47% of their portfolios consisted of VRM's by mid-1977.[31] Such portfolios should be quite able to follow fluctuating rates, and the lenders might well argue for exemption from Regulation Q to permit them to pay higher deposit rates in order to prevent disintermediation in high interest periods.

27. See Herbst v. First Federal Sav. & Loan Ass'n, 538 F.2d 1279 (C.A.Wis. 1976), holding that it is unnecessary to make a separate Truth-In-Lending disclosure prior to each interest rate change; Federal Reserve Board Regulation Z, § 226.8, 42 Fed.Reg. 20455 (Apr. 20, 1977).

28. Under 12 CFR 541.14(a), as amended in 1972 (37 Fed.Reg. 5118, Mar. 10, 1972), federal associations may not increase the amount of the monthly payment on a home loan; see FHLBB Interpretive Memorandum T–56, Feb. 12, 1974. Hence, a VRM could be employed to raise the interest only by extending the maturity. However, home loans are limited to 30-year maturities by 12 CFR 546.6–1a, and most loans are made for initial terms of 25 to 30 years. The regulations thus effectively prohibit VRM's and other instruments, such as PLAM's, which involve payment increases or significant maturity extensions. Pre-1972 loans are not subject to the restriction against payment increases; FHLBB Interpretive Memorandum, supra; Vanguard Investments v. Central California Sav. & Loan Ass'n, 68 Cal.App.3d 950, 137 Cal.Rptr. 719 (1977).

28a. 12 CFR § 545.6–2(c); 43 Fed.Reg. 59339 (Dec. 20, 1978).

29. See Variable Rates on Mortgages: Their Impact and Use, New England Economic Review, Mar./Apr.1970, at 3.

30. See Matthews, VIR Mortgages Gain Acceptance Among Lending Institutions But Need Washington Approval, Mortgage Banker, Oct. 1977, at 48.

31. Id. The VRM's written by California S&L's are tied to a rather stable index provided by the Federal Home Loan Bank of San Francisco, and were not subjected to any change between 1975 and mid-1978. A fairly small change in August, 1978, produced little adverse consumer reaction; see Thompson, note 20 supra. If significant rate increases occur, it would not be surprising for the California legislature to take further action limiting them. Such a situation is reportedly responsible for the Wisconsin statute, supra note 26.

Lenders have generally been enthusiastic proponents of the VRM concept, while advocates of consumers and the poor have been sceptical.[32] The latter have argued that the VRM's possibility of increased payments will cause lenders to be more conservative in their initial underwriting, and may induce them to screen out persons of relatively low income who would otherwise qualify for standard format loans; this objection might be resolved by requiring lenders to offer standard loans as an alternative.[33] Some have also asserted that the VRM's effect is to place the risk of fluctuating market rates on unsophisticated consumers, who are least able to predict and hedge against them, rather than on financial institutions whose professional staffs can do so with much greater facility. The available evidence from California suggests that consumers do not like VRM's as well as standard loans, but that they find them reasonably acceptable.[34] While VRM's comprise only a small fraction of all home mortgage loans originated nationally, the proportion is growing as greater regulatory flexibility is given to lenders.[35]

Two other forms of mortgage instrument which are intended to solve the portfolio lag problem are worthy of brief description, although neither is widely used in the United States. The roll-over mortgage (ROM),[36] which is virtually universally employed in Canada, is structured to resemble a standard mortgage with one exception: periodically, perhaps every five years, the mortgagor and mortgagee renegotiate the interest rate. It is assumed that the mortgagee will not refuse to leave the loan outstanding if a satisfactory rate can be

32. See testimony of various consumer group representatives, Hearings on the Financial Institutions Act of 1975 before the Subcomm. on Financial Institutions, Senate Banking, Housing, and Urban Affairs Comm., 94th Cong., 1st Sess. 1975, at 725–49; Center for National Policy Review, Comments on Proposed Amendments Relating to Variable Interest Rate Mortgage Loans (submitted to FHLBB, Oct. 16, 1972).

33. The FHLBB's final VRM regulation does this; 12 CFR § 545.6–2(c)(5)(v). It may, however, be practically impossible for VRM's and standard mortgages to coexist in the same institution; see Epley, Can Variable-Rate and Fixed-Rate Mortgages Coexist?, 5 Real Estate Rev. 119 (No. 4, Winter 1976).

34. See Albaum & Kaufman, How Consumers See the VRM: Results of a Survey, FHLBBJ, Aug. 1977, at 11; Colton, Lessard, Solomon & Modest, National Survey of Borrowers' Housing Characteristics, Attitudes, and Preferences, AMIRS Study at III. The latter study suggests that favorable attitudes toward VRM's may be correlated with expected household mobility, with persons who expect not to move in the foreseeable future preferring fixed-interest mortgages; id. at III–25. See also Thompson, note 20 supra.

35. In 1972 HUD General Counsel David Maxwell opined to Secretary George Romney that FHA had no authority to insure variable-interest mortgages; Letter of Aug. 18, 1972. HUD has shown no disposition to change this position, and no significant legislative activity to modify it has occurred.

36. See Unger, The Canadian Mortgage Market and the Renegotiable Term Mortgage, AMIRS Study at VII. Many New England "variable rate" mortgages are actually structured as ROM's; see Variable Rates on Mortgages: Their Impact and Use, New England Economic Review, Mar./Apr. 1970, at 3.

agreed upon for the next 5-year period, but the mortgagor may prepay at that point without penalty if he prefers to refinance with another lender. In economic terms, the ROM is like a VRM with a long period between rate reevaluation dates, and is subject to many of the same legal and policy debates as VRM's.

Finally, the price-level adjusted mortgage (PLAM)[37] is an attempt to solve the inflation problem directly. Since inflation reduces the value to a lender of all loan repayments, it is generally assumed that lenders add to their interest rates an increment to compensate for the inflation which they anticipate will occur over the life of the loan. For example, if the interest rate for a given loan in a non-inflationary economy would be 3 percent (in light of the maturity, risk, and liquidity aspects of the transaction), and if inflation at a 6 percent rate is anticipated, the lender will presumably demand a 9 percent interest rate. The PLAM, however, takes a different tack: rather than attempting to predict future inflation and build it into the interest rate, the lender charges only the "non-inflationary" rate (say, 3 percent), but the principal balance of the loan is readjusted periodically (say, annually) in accordance with some index of inflation, such as the Consumer Price Index.

This system has several intriguing features. Payments in the early years are very low because of the low nominal interest rate. The real value of the payment stream remains relatively constant over the years, but it rises sharply in terms of dollars if significant inflation actually occurs. This result may or may not be attractive to borrowers, depending on their current and future income prospects. For younger borrowers with strong potential for increased earnings, the PLAM may be even more attractive than the GPM in solving the "life cycle" problem and permitting earlier home ownership. The PLAM also has the effect, perhaps even more directly than the VRM, of shifting the risk of inflation from lender to borrower.

PLAM's are not at all common in the United States, although they and other "indexed" loan plans have been widely employed in other countries, particularly those in which inflation has been rampant.[38] The Tennessee Supreme Court[39] held the PLAM concept to violate the Gold Clause Resolution,[40] by which congress in 1933 prohibited loan clauses requiring payment in a particular form of cur-

37. See Tucker, the Variable-Rate Graduated-Payment Mortgage, 5 Real Estate Rev. 71 (No. 1, Spring 1975); Robinson, Readjustable Mortgages in an Inflationary Economy, FHLBBJ, Feb. 1971, at 19.

38. See Robinson, supra note 37.

39. Aztec Properties, Inc. v. Union Planters Nat. Bank, 530 S.W.2d 756 (Tenn.1975), certiorari denied 425 U.S. 975, 96 S.Ct. 2175, 48 L.Ed.2d 799, discussed in Hyer & Kearl, Legal Impediments to Mortgage Innovation, 6 Real Estate L.J. 211, 228–31 (1978).

40. 48 Stat. 113 (1933); 31 U.S.C.A. § 463.

rency or coin. The clause was surely not intended to prohibit indexing of mortgage loan principals, and the case is wrongly decided, but it represents a litigation risk to any lender considering the use of a PLAM. This legal cloud, when added to the problems of gaining consumer acceptance of PLAM's, probably means that their widespread use is not likely in the near future in the United States.

The foregoing discussion by no means exhausts the possibilites for alternative mortgage instruments, but it represents the major forms discussed in the lending industry at this time. Other innovations will surely arise.[41] We have attempted no detailed consideration of the legal issues which each of the alternative instruments might raise, since space would not allow more than superficial treatment. The following listing of possible areas of controversy may, however, be a useful guide to those who wish to evaluate the legal implications of alternative instruments:[42] The Truth-In-Lending Act; [43] usury statutes; [44] negotiability and the holder-in-due-course doctrine; [45] priority as against intervening lienors; [46] federal and state income tax deductibility of interest; [47] federal and state regulation of institutional lenders; availability of government and private mortgage insurance; [48] acceptability on the government sponsored and private secondary mortgage market; [49] and application of such doctrines as unconscionability and contracts of adhesion.[50] Little le-

41. See, e. g., Lusht, A New Twist to the Variable Payment Mortgage, 7 Real Estate Rev. 72 (No. 2, Summer 1977); Tucker, The Variable Rate Graduated-Payment Mortgage, 5 Real Estate Rev. 71 (No. 1, Spring 1975); statement of Sen. Edward Brooke introducing the "Young Families' Housing Act," Cong.Rec. S12171 (Daily ed., July 22, 1976).

42. See generally Hyer & Kearl, note 39 supra; Ege, Legal Analysis of AMIs, AMIRS Study at XX.

43. See Herbst v. First Federal Sav. & Loan Ass'n, 538 F.2d 1279 (C.A.Wis. 1976); Landers & Chandler, The Truth In Lending Act and Variable Rate Mortgages and Balloon Notes, 1976 A.B.F.Res.J. 35 (1976).

44. See Olwine v. Torrens, 236 Pa.Super. 51, 344 A.2d 665 (1975) (VRM violates usury statute): Werner, Usury and the Variable-Rate Mortgage, 5 Real Estate L.J. 155 (1976).

45. Under the Uniform Commercial Code a note must be for a "sum certain" in order to be negotiable; UCC § 3–104(1). On negotiability generally, see § 5.29, supra.

46. If a mortgage involves future advances by the lender which are not obligatory, and which are made after the lender acquires notice of intervening lienors, the advance is subordinated to those liens; see generally § 12.7, supra.

47. See Rev.Rul. 77–135, 1977–1 Cum. Bull. 133, regarding deductibility of accrued and unpaid interest under a GPM; Peat, Marwick, Mitchell & Co., Accounting, Taxation, Origination, and Servicing Implications of AMI's, AMIRS, Study at XII.

48. See Swan, Private Mortgage Insurance Companies and AMIs, AMIRS Study at X.

49. See Plant & Jannuzzi, Secondary Mortgage Market Analysis of AMIs, AMIRS Study at XI.

50. See Vanguard Investment v. Central California Sav. & Loan Ass'n, 68 Cal.App.3d 950, 137 Cal.Rptr. 719 (1977); Powell v. Central California Sav. and Loan Ass'n, 59 Cal.App.3d 540, 130 Cal.Rptr. 635 (1976) (both holding VRM's valid as against contract of adhesion arguments.)

gal authority exists on many of these points, and further development will have to await the expansion of alternative mortgage instruments in the marketplace.

§ 11.5 Discrimination in Mortgage Lending

A wide range of federal statutes prohibit racial discrimination in mortgage lending. Some of these statutes also bar discrimination on other bases, such as sex, as well; the coverage of each will be described in turn. The oldest statutory provisions are those of the Civil Rights Act of 1866, now codified in 42 United States Code at Sections 1981 and 1982. Section 1982 provides that "all citizens * * * shall have the same right * * * as is enjoyed by white citizens * * * to inherit, purchase, lease, sell, hold and convey real and personal property." Section 1981 makes similar provisions regarding the right to make and enforce contracts. Until 1968 it was generally assumed that these statutes applied only to actions of the federal or state governments, but in Jones v. Alfred H. Mayer Co.,[51] the Supreme Court held them applicable to private acts of discrimination as well. There is little question that the language of these sections would ban racial discrimination by a mortgage lender.[51a] They apply to all transactions, not merely those relating to housing; a commercial mortgage loan, for example, would be covered. However, they provide no administrative enforcement mechanism, and a suit for damages or conceivably an injunction would be the only remedy. Note also that they apply only to discrimination based on race.

Two more recent enactments also prohibit racial discrimination in the provision of mortgage financing. Section 805 of the Civil Rights Act of 1968 (the "Fair Housing Act")[52] makes illegal the discriminatory denial of a loan or discrimination in respect to loan amount, interest rate, duration, or other terms or conditions. Under the original version of the statute, only discrimination based on race, color, religion, or national origin was barred, but a 1974 amendment[53] included sex as well, and also required all persons making "federally related mortgage loans" to married couples to "consider without prejudice the combined income of both husband and wife for the purpose of extending mortgage credit." This last clause was inserted to stop the prevalent practice of discounting a working wife's income in determining the amount of loan for which the couple was qualified.

Section 805 does have certain inherent limitations. It applies only to institutional lenders and others in the business of making real estate

51. 392 U.S. 409, 88 S.Ct. 2186, 20 L. Ed.2d 1189 (1968).

51a. See Baker v. F & F Investment Co., 489 F.2d 829 (C.A.Ill.1973).

52. 42 U.S.C.A. § 3605. Discriminatory enforcement of mortgages, as by selective foreclosures, is also illegal; Harper v. Union Sav. Ass'n, 429 F. Supp. 1254 (N.D.Ohio 1977).

53. § 808, Housing and Community Development Act of 1974, Pub.L. 93–383, 88 Stat. 633, 728, adding § 527 to the National Housing Act.

loans. In addition, the loan in question must be "for the purpose of purchasing, constructing, improving, repairing, or maintaining a dwelling." Thus, non-housing loans are not covered. The statute expressly directs all federal agencies to administer their programs in a manner which will further the objectives of the law,[54] and it gives the Department of Housing and Urban Development authority to administer the act and to receive, investigate, and attempt to resolve complaints of violations.[55] United States district courts are given jurisdiction over suits for violations,[56] and the Attorney General is empowered to file injunctive actions when he has reasonable cause to believe a person or group is engaged in a pattern or practice of resistance to the act.[57]

A third statute explicitly prohibiting mortgage credit discrimination is the Equal Credit Opportunity Act (ECOA).[58] Originally enacted in 1974 to prohibit discrimination based on sex or marital status, it was expanded in 1976 [59] to cover race, color, religion, national origin, and age discrimination as well. Unlike the Fair Housing Act, ECOA is not confined to housing finance, but applies to all extensions of credit, whatever the purpose. Violations may result in civil liability in federal or state courts. The Federal Reserve Board is given the general power to enact regulations under ECOA, and the principal enforcement power is given to the Federal Deposit Insurance Corporation and the Federal Home Loan Bank Board with respect to banks and savings associations respectively.[60] Only persons and institutions which "regularly" extend or renew credit and their assignees are covered by ECOA.

Under the three statutes discussed above, both racial and sex discrimination in lending are broadly prohibited, and it is likely that in their most overt forms they have to a great extent disappeared from the American scene. Two significant issues remain, however. The first is the general problem of loan underwriting criteria which are facially neutral but which in fact have a disproportionate impact on one race or sex; the second is the problem of refusals by institutional lenders to make loans, or the willingness to make loans only on more onerous terms, in certain geographic areas, a practice often termed "disinvestment" or "redlining." The second issue is sometimes an illustration of the first, for a refusal to lend in an area of residential

54. § 808(d), Fair Housing Act, 42 U.S.C.A. § 3608(d).

55. §§ 808, 810, Fair Housing Act, 42 U.S.C.A. §§ 3608, 3610.

56. § 810(d), Fair Housing Act, 42 U.S.C.A. § 3610(d).

57. § 813, Fair Housing Act, 42 U.S.C.A. § 3613; see, e. g., United States v. American Institute of Real Estate Appraisers, 442 F.Supp. 1072 (N.D.Ill. 1977) (suit by Dep't of Justice; settlement agreement; discriminatory appraisal practices violate Fair Housing Act.)

58. 15 U.S.C.A. § 1691ff.

59. Equal Credit Opportunity Act Amendments of 1976, Pub.L. 94–239, 90 Stat. 251.

60. § 704, Equal Credit Opportunity Act, 15 U.S.C.A. § 1691c.

concentration by a minority racial group will plainly have a disproportionate impact on members of a particular race, but redlining may also be considered objectionable as a consequence of its impact on the housing stock and property values, even when no minorities are affected.

The concept that a disproportionate racial *effect* may be illegal, even absent intent to discriminate, is derived from Griggs v. Duke Power Co.,[61] in which the Supreme Court in 1971 considered certain intelligence and aptitude tests administered by an employer to its employees as a condition of promotion. Black employees generally made lower scores on the tests than whites, and hence were not promoted as frequently, but there was no evidence that the employer intended to use the tests to screen out blacks. In response to an attack based on Title VII of the Civil Rights Act of 1964, the Court held that a violation had been made out. The Court's opinion articulated what is commonly called the "effects test": if the plaintiffs can show that the defendant's practices have the effect of disproportionately barring minorities in a substantial manner, the burden shifts to the defendant to show that those practices are required by "business necessity" or "genuine business need." [62] Later cases have generally held that to make a successful defense, the defendant must show that no other procedure with a lesser discriminatory impact could be used to accomplish the same business goal.[63]

For some time after *Griggs* there was doubt as to whether it applied to the Fair Housing Act or other non-employment discrimination statutes,[64] but the Supreme Court has now resolved that issue affirmatively.[65] However, there are still no reported cases dealing di-

61. 401 U.S. 424, 91 S.Ct. 849, 28 L.Ed.2d 158 (1971).

62. 401 U.S. at 432.

63. See, e. g., Williams v. Matthews Co., 499 F.2d 819 (C.A.Ark.1974), certiorari denied 419 U.S. 1021, 95 S.Ct. 495, 42 L.Ed.2d 294 and 419 U.S. 1027, 95 S.Ct. 507, 42 L.Ed.2d 302: to rely on the "business necessity" defense the defendant must show "the absence of any acceptable alternative that will accomplish the same business goal with less discrimination." But see Albemarle Paper Co. v. Moody, 422 U.S. 405, 425, 95 S.Ct. 2362, 2375, 45 L.Ed.2d 280 (1975), which seems to place the burden of showing the availability of less discriminatory alternatives on the plaintiff, and treats such a showing as merely some evidence of an illegal discriminatory intent, but not conclusive. See Perry, The Disproportionate Impact Theory of Racial Discrimination, 125 U.Pa.L.Rev. 540 (1977).

64. Compare United States v. City of Black Jack, 508 F.2d 1179 (C.A.Mo. 1974), certiorari denied 422 U.S. 1042, 95 S.Ct. 2656, 45 L.Ed.2d 694, rehearing denied 423 U.S. 884, 96 S.Ct. 158, 46 L.Ed.2d 115 (1975) and Stingley v. City of Lincoln Park, 429 F.Supp. 1379 (E.D.Mich.1977) (applying *Griggs* to housing discrimination) with Boyd v. Lefrak Organization, 509 F.2d 1110 (C.A.N.Y.1975), certiorari denied 423 U.S. 896, 96 S.Ct. 197, 46 L.Ed.2d 129 (*Griggs* inapplicable to housing). See Note, Applying the Title VII Prima Facie Case to Title VIII Litigation, 11 Harv.Civ.Rts—Civ.Lib.L.Rev. 128 (1976).

65. In Metropolitan Housing Development Corp. v. Village of Arlington Heights, 429 U.S. 252, 97 S.Ct. 555, 50 L.Ed.2d 450 (1977), the town had refused to rezone certain land on which the plaintiffs proposed to build a low-income housing project. The evidence showed no discriminatory purpose or intent on the part of the

rectly with loan underwriting practices which have a discriminatory impact. Clearly many common underwriting rules [66] do so, including the usual 25% housing expense-to-income ratio and probably such requirements as previous homeownership, a specific time in the present residence or on the present job, and the like. The relatively lower incomes and higher mobility of minorities in the United States mean that such criteria will result in more loan rejections than will be experienced by whites. The issue then becomes the nature of the proof which a lender must offer to rebut the prima facie case. Virtually all of the underwriting guidelines now in use have *some* predictive validity in assessing risk of future default, but some of them are far weaker than others.[67] No one alone or in combination is perfectly accurate, of course.

A court confronting this issue is faced with serious problems. Should the judicial standard of business necessity be implemented by inquiring whether the underwriting standards in question are "reasonably predictive" of default, or some such test? [68] What is a reasonably acceptable level of default risk? Suppose it is shown that use of a few relatively noncontroversial criteria, such as loan-to-value ratio, income, and credit rating, provide reasonably adequate predictability, but the addition of other, more objectionable factors such as those mentioned in the preceding paragraph make the underwriting process more accurate. What is called for here is the drawing of fine lines based on complex empirical evidence—a task for which administrative agencies are much better equipped than courts. Yet the most comprehensive federal regulations on the subject, promulgated by the Federal Home Loan Bank Board (FHLBB) and applicable to all federally-insured savings and loan associations, stop short of drawing the necessary lines. Instead, they merely warn that lenders should "take into consideration" the fact that some common underwriting standards, including favoring previous homeowners, those with high educational attainments, those with stable job or residence histories, and those who have previously done business with the lender, may be

town, but it did show a discriminatory impact, since 40% of the population eligible for the project were black, as opposed to only 18% of the overall area population. The Court held that the Fourteenth Amendment did not prohibit municipal actions with such discriminatory effects unless intent were also shown, citing its previous opinion in Washington v. Davis, 426 U.S. 229, 96 S.Ct. 2040, 48 L.Ed.2d 597 (1976). However, it remanded the case for further consideration as to the application of the Fair Housing Act to the town's action, thus clearly implying that a racial effect could form the basis for a Fair Housing Act complaint. See 558 F.2d 1283 (7th Cir. 1977) (on remand to Seventh Circuit Court of Appeals), holding that the town's action may violate the Act if certain additional facts are shown, and applying *Griggs*. See also Resident Advisory Board v. Rizzo, 564 F.2d 126 (C.A.Pa.1977).

66. See § 11.2, supra at note 22 and accompanying text.

67. Id. The Arthur D. Little Study of the Private Mortgage Insurance Industry (summary 1975), at 11–14.

68. Cf. Bishop v. Pecsok, 431 F.Supp. 34 (N.D.Ohio 1976), holding that criteria imposed by a landlord on tenant applicants must be "reasonable measure of the applicant's ability to be a successful tenant."

legally questionable.[69] The guidance provided by the regulations on these points is ambiguous, although they might conceivably provide some evidence of improper practices in a litigated case. The lenders themselves would probably have preferred a clear cut statement of permissible and impermissible practices. The validity of many frequently-employed standards is still open to doubt. The FHLBB's regulation is, however, quite helpful in another way; for the first time, it requires lenders to prepare written loan underwriting standards, review them annually, and make them available to the public.[70]

The regulations promulgated by the California Savings and Loan Commissioner provide an instructive point of comparison with those of the FHLBB. The "effects test" is explicitly stated in the California regulations,[71] and an accompanying set of guidelines [72] lists a number of common practices which are deemed to have a disproportionate racial impact and to lack business justification, and hence to be impermissible. These include the rejection of persons who have had isolated credit problems in the past, those with prior arrest records, those who have not previously owned a home, and those below a certain minimum income or who are buying houses below a specific purchase price or loan amount. Housing expense-to-income ratios below 25% are prohibited, and income from overtime, part-time or other usual work or from alimony or child support payments may not arbitrarily be disregarded. Some ambiguities exist in the California regulations, but they have rather explicit coverage and appear to be readily enforceable.[73]

Redlining

Much of the thrust of recent legislation and regulation has been to combat geographically-based discrimination or redlining. This issue is complicated by the difficulty of separating cause and effect. To some extent, withdrawal by mortgage lenders is a cause of neighborhood deterioration and ultimate abandonment, for the lack of

69. 12 CFR 531.8(c)(5), added by 43 Fed.Reg. 22338 (May 25, 1978). Compare the regulations issued by the Federal Reserve Board under ECOA, which recognize the "effects test" but make no effort to implement it; 12 CFR 202.6(a), footnote 7.

70. 12 CFR 528.2a(b), added by 43 Fed.Reg. 22335 (May 25, 1978); see also Mich.Comp.Laws Ann. § 445.-1601.

71. 10 Cal.Admin.Code § 245.2(c); the regulation imposes upon the lender employing an underwriting policy with a discriminatory effect the burden to "demonstrate that such * * * policy * * * is required to achieve an overriding legitimate business purpose."

72. 10 Cal.Admin.Code § 246.3.

73. See generally, Wisniewski, Mortgage Redlining (Disinvestment): The Parameters of Federal, State and Municipal Regulation, 54 U.Det.J.Urb.L. 367 (1977); Comment, Redlining in Mortgage Lending: California's Approach to Getting the Red Out, 8 Pac.L.J. 699 (1977); Comment, Redlining: Why Make A Federal Case Out Of It?, 6 Golden Gate U.L.Rev. 813 (1976); Renne, Eliminating Redlining by Judicial Action: Are Erasers Available?, 29 Vand.L.Rev. 987 (1976); Comment, Attacking the Urban Redlining Problem, 56 B.U.L.Rev. 989 (1976).

mortgage financing impedes market sales transactions and makes maintenance and rehabilitation more difficult. But other factors also operate to cause neighborhood decline: crime and social disorder, lack of maintenance of public services and facilities such as street cleaning and lighting, trash removal, schools and parks, and the general aging of a housing stock which may have been substandard even when constructed.[74] Some areas which lenders have abandoned are sound and attractive (although now threatened by the lack of mortgage funds), while others are so dilapidated and dangerous that lending on properties there would be insane. In an era in which the supply of mortgage funds has rarely been adequate to meet demand, lenders have generally preferred "safe" loans in the suburbs to loans of even moderate and manageable risk in inner-city neighborhoods.

The articulation of a workable distinction between reasonable and unreasonable geographic discrimination in mortgage lending is no simple matter, and it is doubtful that any existing law or regulation has yet done so successfully. Some principles, however, are clear. One of these is that a refusal to lend because of the race of the neighborhood's occupants is illegal; this follows from the Fair Housing Act and from a number of state statutes as well.[75] In Laufman v. Oakley Building and Loan Co.,[76] the lender declined to loan to a white applicant because the neighborhood in which he proposed to live was racially integrated. The court found violations of both Section 805 of the Fair Housing Act, discussed above, and Section 804, which prohibits the making "unavailable" of housing because of race. The point is virtually incontestible that racially-motivated redlining, if proveable, is prohibited.

In many cases, however, no evidence of the type of racial motivation shown in *Laufman* will be available, and the plaintiff will be left with an argument based on the "effects test"; the area being excluded "happens" to be populated by minorities, but it is also characterized by deteriorated or abandoned housing or other structures, poor public facilities, and the like. Refusal to lend in such an environment, absent a showing of racial motives, has not yet been tested judicially in any reported case. Presumably the lender would be obliged to offer business justifications for his decision, and the court would be faced with deciding whether they were sufficiently compelling to justify the withdrawal of financing. Again, the question "how compelling?" is presently unresolved.[76a]

74. See Sangster & Whitman, Financial Institutions Have An Expanding Role in Revitalizing Cities, 4 J. of Housing 183 (1972); Toward A National Urban Policy: What Will It Take To Rejuvenate Our Cities?, Mortgage Banker, June 1978, at 29.

75. See, e. g., Smith-Hurd Ill.Ann. Stat. ch. 95 § 301 et seq.; West's Ann.Cal. Health & Safety Code § 35812; Mich.Comp.Laws Ann. § 445.-1601.

76. 408 F.Supp. 489 (S.D.Ohio 1976).

76a. The application of the "effects test" to redlining having a racial impact was endorsed by Charles Allen, FHLBB General Counsel, in a written

Both the FHLBB and several state legislatures or regulatory agencies have promulgated rules which attempt to deal with the red-lining problem. Their thrust is generally to prohibit discrimination based on property age or location, and to require lenders to focus on the particular real estate which will secure the proposed loan, rather than on the characteristics of the neighborhood as a whole. In simplistic terms, then, a lender may be expected to make a loan on a good house in a bad neighborhood. But the problem is more complex, for it is well known that neighborhood factors have a strong influence on the value of any given parcel of land, and neighborhood trends can reasonably be expected to bear on its future value.

A comparison of the FHLBB and California regulations on this issue is enlightening. The FHLBB specifically prohibits discrimination based on the age or location of the dwelling, but it concedes that numerous neighborhood factors may properly be considered in appraising the dwelling:

> Loan decisions should be based on the present market value of the property offered as security (including consideration of specific improvements to be made by the borrower) and the likelihood that the property will retain an adequate value over the term of the loan. Specific factors which may negatively affect its short-range future value (up to 3–5 years) should be clearly documented. Factors which in some cases may cause the market value of a property to decline are recent zoning changes or a significant number of abandoned homes in the immediate vicinity of the property. However, not all zoning changes will cause a decline in property values, and proximity to abandoned buildings may not affect the market value of a property because of rehabilitation programs or affirmative lending programs, or because the cause of abandonment is unrelated to high risk. Proper underwriting considerations include the condition and utility of the improvements, and various physical factors such as street conditions, amenities such as parks and recreation areas, availability of public utilities and municipal services, and exposure to flooding and land faults. However, arbitrary decisions based on age or location are prohibited, since many older, soundly constructed homes provide housing opportunities which may be precluded by an arbitrary lending policy.[77]

The terms of the California regulation, now adopted by statute in that state, are considerably stronger:

> No financial institution shall discriminate in the availability of, or in the provision of, financial assistance for the purpose of purchasing, constructing, rehabilitating, improv-

opinion dated Mar. 21, 1974, adopting the "no alternative" theory discussed in the text at note 63, supra.

77. 12 CFR 531.8(6)(c)(6), as amended, 43 Fed.Reg. 22338 (May 25, 1978).

> ing, or refinancing housing accommodations due, in whole or in part, to the consideration of conditions, characteristics, or trends in the neighborhood or geographic area surrounding the housing accommodation, unless the financial institution can demonstrate that such consideration in the particular case is required to avoid an unsafe and unsound business practice.[78]

The California Savings and Loan Commissioner's regulations interpret the "unsafe or unsound business practice" rather narrowly:

> If an association can document that one or more factors relating to the geographic area closely surrounding the security property are such that, even assuming the availability of nondiscriminatory financing in the geographic area, it is probable that such factors will cause the fair market value of the security property to decrease during the early years of the mortgage term, then the association, in determining whether and under what terms and conditions to grant a mortgage loan may do either or both of the following:
>
> (1) Make an adjustment in the loan to value ratio it considers appropriate for the property; or
>
> (2) Require that a shorter term to maturity be used.
>
> Provided, however, that no adjustment or requirement made pursuant to this subsection shall exceed the minimum required for the security property to continue to be a reasonable security for the loan.[79]

Further guidelines [80] discuss the necessary documentation to establish the probability of value declining over time, the radius within which negative neighborhood factors may be considered, the availability of federal, state, or local rehabilitation or neighborhood improvement programs, and other such matters. Great emphasis is placed on obtaining comparable sales prices on similar properties as the basis for a sound appraisal. The overall tone is strongly oriented toward disregarding neighborhood influences which are not clearly and demonstrably related to the property's value.

The other financial regulatory agencies at the federal level have promulgated regulations prohibiting racial discrimination in lending,[81] and several other states have statutes or regulations dealing with discrimination and redlining.[82] None of these, however, are as comprehensive and explicit as the FHLBB and California rules discussed above. These latter rules are particularly significant because they do not rely on proof of racial motivation or even disproportionate racial

78. West's Ann.Cal.Health & Safety Code § 35810.

79. 10 Cal.Admin.Code § 245.3(b).

80. 10 Cal.Admin.Code § 246.1.

81. See sources cited note 73, supra.

82. See statutes cited note 75, supra.

impact, but are based on appraisal and underwriting concepts which are, on their face, racially neutral.

Two federal statutes enacted in the mid-1970's also bear on the redlining problem. The first is the Home Mortgage Disclosure Act,[83] which requires depository financial institutions to maintain and publish records showing, by census tract, the locations of the properties which secure their residential loans. The Act's thesis is that local citizens and groups will, by analyzing this data, be able to identify lenders guilty of redlining and will apply the pressures of publicity and deposit withdrawals to bring them into line. Whether this will turn out to be effective, and whether it may produce undesirable overreactions in some cases, remains to be seen.[84] The data are also useful to the federal and state agencies which examine depository institutions, and complement the requirements of the Community Reinvestment Act of 1977.[85] This statute requires the federal financial regulatory agencies to consider, in their examinations and in evaluating applications by lenders for new deposit facilities, the institution's record in meeting the credit needs of its entire community, including low- and moderate-income neighborhoods. Presumably lenders who have been guilty of unjustifiable redlining will be subject to criticism by the federal examiners, and may not be able to get permission to open new branches, close offices, or take other actions they desire.

Similar provisions have been made a part of state or local law in many areas. Some states and cities have disclosure laws which go further than the Home Mortgage Disclosure Act, which specifically recognizes local law except to the extent of direct inconsistency with the federal law.[85a] Other local efforts to stop redlining also show promise. In some cities, lenders have voluntarily (or acting under pressure from local governments or state regulators) created review boards to which one may appeal if his loan application is rejected.[86] In some cases the appeal board may order the original in-

83. 12 U.S.C.A. § 2801ff.

84. See Witnesses Differ Over Mortgage Disclosure Act's Effectiveness, 4 Housing & Devel.Rptr. 559 (Nov. 29, 1976) (community groups call for expansion of the act, while a university professor questions its basic premise.)

85. 12 U.S.C.A. § 2901ff.

85a. The exemption from federal preemption applies only to state-chartered institutions; see Glen Ellyn Sav. & Loan Ass'n v. Tsouman, 71 Ill.2d 493, 17 Ill.Dec. 811, 377 N.E.2d 1 (1978), holding the Illinois statute entirely void because it purported to bind federal financial institutions and was not severable by its terms; 12 U.S.C.A. § 2806, which also authorizes the Federal Reserve Board to exempt institutions in a state or locality which has adopted a substantially similar disclosure rule which has adequate provisions for enforcement. Four states have been granted such exemptions: Massachusetts, California, New York, and Illinois; 4 BNA Housing & Devel.Rptr. 666 (Dec. 27, 1976). However, Illinois' exemption was withdrawn after the decision in Glen Ellyn Sav. & Loan Ass'n, supra.

83. The Michigan statute expressly authorizes the creation of such review boards; Mich.Comp.Laws Ann. § 445.1609(1). The Boston Board is described in Comment, The Home Mortgage Disclosure Act of 1975: Will It

stitution to grant the loan; alternatively, it may refer the applicant to a pool of funds set up by the lenders of the area for the purpose of making higher-risk loans.[87]

Rules against discrimination or redlining are only useful if their enforcement is effective. The information assembled by lenders under the Home Mortgage Disclosure Act is useful as a general indicator of lending practices, but to identify patterns of discrimination in a conclusive way, information on the nature of loan applications received by lenders is necessary. The most recent FHLBB regulations require the keeping of a "loan application register" listing each application received, along with such information as the race and sex of the applicant, the property's location, the disposition of the application by the lender, and the final loan terms if a loan is made.[88] This data should permit examiners to discern patterns of discrimination with relative ease, and can also be expected to sensitize lenders to the necessity of acting in an objective, rational manner in making underwriting decisions. Much depends, however, on the commitment of the examination staff of the federal agency to fair enforcement of the law.

§ 11.6 Federal Preemption of State Mortgage Law

Under the Supremacy Clause of the United States Constitution, federal law which is validly adopted and within the constitutional

Protect Urban Consumers From Redlining?, 12 N.Eng.L.Rev. 957, 988 (1977).

87. The Neighborhood Housing Services concept, in which a local office provides some financing to high-risk borrowers and assists others in finding and qualifying for commercially-available loans, is also a promising approach to the red-lining problem. The Urban Reinvestment Task Force, a federal entity sponsored by HUD, the FHLBB, and other agencies, assists and funds the creation of Neighborhood Housing Services offices. See Hood & Neet, Redlining Practices, Racial Resegregation, and Urban Decay: Neighborhood Housing Services as a Viable Alternative, 7 Urban Law. 510 (1975); Widener, Neighborhood Housing Services, A Cooperative Venture in the Inner City, Mortgage Banker, July 1978, at 18.

88. 12 CFR 528.6, as amended, 43 Fed.Reg. 22335 (May 25, 1978). A previous record-keeping proposal by the FHLBB, 37 Fed.Reg. 811 (Jan. 13, 1972), was withdrawn in the face of much opposition from lenders. The agency promulgated an experimental record-keeping requirement in 39 Fed.Reg. 12110 (April 3, 1974).

In 1976 a group of civil rights organizations filed a suit against the Federal Home Loan Bank Board, seeking an order compelling it to collect racial and sex information on loan applicants and to analyze and use the data to identify institutions guilty of discrimination. Although the FHLBB had been by far the most energetic of the four banking regulatory agencies in opposing discrimination, it was nonetheless selected as a target because the plaintiffs felt it would be more likely than the other agencies to cooperate. On March 22, 1977, a settlement agreement was signed between the FHLBB and the planitiffs and the suit was dismissed. The agreement is reproduced in 44 Legal Bull. 39 (1978). The 1978 regulations discussed in the text go considerably beyond the undertakings of the FHLBB in the settlement agreement, but some of the provisions clearly have their genesis in that agreement.

power of the federal government is the supreme law of the land and supersedes state law.[89] This preemption concept has several applications in mortgage law. The most clearcut is the situation in which a congressional enactment or a valid regulation of a federal agency speaks directly to the point. Numerous illustrations may be cited. The Home Mortgage Disclosure Act requires institutional lenders to assemble and release to the public certain data on the amounts and locations of their residential loans.[90] The Fair Housing Act limits lenders' discretion in rejecting loan applicants because of race or sex,[91] and the Federal Home Loan Bank Board's regulations supplement the Act by requiring the maintenance of records on loan applications and by delimiting the criteria which can be employed by savings associations in screening applicants and properties.[92] The Truth-In-Lending Act [93] mandates that certain disclosures concerning interest and finance charges be made to borrowers, and the Real Estate Settlement Procedures Act (RESPA) [94] requires disclosures concerning settlement charges, prescribes a standard form of settlement statement, and prohibits certain types of kickbacks and rebates between mortgage lenders and other providers of settlement services. In 1973 congress considered, but did not enact, a comprehensive federal mortgage foreclosure bill which would have applied to all federally-owned, -insured, or -guaranteed loans; [95] the bill would have preempted state foreclosure procedures in numerous respects, and would perhaps have represented the high-water mark in this area.[96]

Most of the existing statutes mentioned above do not seriously impinge on the operation of state law, but merely add further requirements which must be fulfilled by lenders; thus, they do not raise the preemption issue in its starkest context. However, numerous federal regulations issued by administrative agencies (which have

89. U.S. Const. Art. VI, § 2; see McCulloch v. Maryland, 17 U.S. (4 Wheat.) 316, 4 L.Ed. 579 (1819).

90. 12 U.S.C.A. § 2801; see Comment, The Home Mortgage Disclosure Act of 1975: Will It Protect Urban Consumers From Redlining?, 12 N.Eng. L.Rev. 957 (1977); § 11.5, supra, at notes 83–85a. See also Glen Ellyn Sav. & Loan Ass'n v. Tsouman, 71 Ill. 2d 493, 17 Ill.Dec. 811, 377 N.E.2d 1 (1978).

91. 42 U.S.C.A. § 3605; § 11.5, supra, at note 52ff. See also Equal Credit Opportunity Act, 15 U.S.C.A. § 1691 et. seq.

92. 12 CFR 528.6, as amended, 43 Fed.Reg. 22335 (May 25, 1978); § 11.-5, supra, at note 88. The preamble to the regulations states that federal savings associations are not required to observe more stringent state law regarding lending discrimination, and one court has so held; Conference of Federal Savings and Loan Associations v. Silverman, —— F.Supp. —— (1978).

93. 15 U.S.C.A. § 1601 et seq.; 12 CFR Part 226.

94. 12 U.S.C.A. § 2601 et. seq.; 24 CFR, Part 3500. See generally Field, RESPA in a Nutshell, 11 Real Prop. Prob. & Trust J. 447 (1976); Payne, Conveyancing Practice and the Feds: Some Thoughts About RESPA, 29 Ala. L.Rev. 339 (1978).

95. The Federal Mortgage Foreclosure Act, Title IV, S. 2507, 93d Cong., 1st Sess., 1973.

96. See Pedowitz, Current Developments in Summary Foreclosure, 9 Real Prop. Prob. & Trust J. 421, 422–25 (1974).

the same weight as statutes for preemption purposes) directly contradict state law. The most significant of these are promulgated by the Federal Home Loan Bank Board (FHLBB) [97] and apply to federally-chartered savings and loan associations. It is well-established that federal law governs the internal affairs of such associations "from the cradle to the grave",[98] fully occupying the field. If there is no specific regulation on a matter affecting the internal governance of an association, such as branching,[99] proxy solicitations,[1] employment of officers,[2] or directors' fiduciary duties,[3] the federal courts will supply a rule of federal common law.[4] In external transactions, such as the content and enforcement of mortgages and notes, however, state law probably governs unless there is an explicit FHLBB regulation. In recent years the FHLBB has been quite active in attempting to resolve by regulation certain controversial issues in mortgage law as applied to federal associations. Its regulations concerning prepayment penalties [5] and interest on tax escrow accounts [6] on home loans have been held to prevail over contrary state law, and presumably the same would be true of its regulations on due-on-sale clauses [7] and late charges.[8]

There is some authority that the FHLBB has completely occupied the field of relations with borrowers, thereby making state law respecting the content of notes and mortgages inapplicable. In Kaski v. First Federal Savings and Loan Association,[9] the plaintiffs were

97. See generally § 11.1, supra, at notes 4–7; Bartlett, The Federal-State Preemption Conflict, 44 Legal Bull. 1 (1978).

98. See Meyers v. Beverly Hills Federal Sav. & Loan Ass'n, 499 F.2d 1145 (C.A.Cal.1974). When state courts "deal with the internal affairs of federal savings and loan associations * * * they are nonetheless applying federal law." Murphy v. Colonial Federal Sav. and Loan Ass'n, 388 F. 2d 609, 612 (C.A.N.Y.1967).

99. Washington Federal Sav. and Loan Ass'n v. Balaban, 281 So.2d 15 (Fla. 1973); Springfield Inst. for Sav. v. Worcester Federal Sav. & Loan Ass'n, 329 Mass. 184, 107 N.E.2d 315 (1952), certiorari denied 344 U.S. 844, 73 S. Ct. 184, 97 L.Ed. 684.

1. Kupiec v. Republic Federal Sav. & Loan Ass'n, 512 F.2d 147 (C.A.Ill. 1975); Murphy v. Colonial Federal Sav. & Loan Ass'n, 388 F.2d 609 (C. A.N.Y.1967).

2. Community Federal Sav. & Loan Ass'n v. Fields, 128 F.2d 705 (C.C.A. Mo.1942).

3. Rettig v. Arlington Heights Federal Sav. & Loan Ass'n, 405 F.Supp. 819 (N.D.Ill.1975); City Federal Sav. and Loan Ass'n v. Crowley, 393 F.Supp. 644 (E.D.Wis.1975).

4. In Murphy, supra note 1, the court was obliged to devise a common-law rule regarding the availability of lists of members to persons planning a proxy fight; by the time Kupiec, supra note 1, was decided, the FHLBB had promulgated a regulation on the point, thereby superseding the Murphy court's common-law rule.

5. Meyers v. Beverly Hills Federal Sav. and Loan Ass'n, 499 F.2d 1145 (C.A.Cal.1974); see generally § 6.3, supra.

6. Greenwald v. First Federal Sav. and Loan Ass'n, 446 F.Supp. 620 (D. Mass.1978); see generally § 4.22, supra.

7. See § 5.25, supra.

8. See § 6.8, supra.

9. 72 Wis.2d 132, 240 N.W.2d 367 (1976).

borrowers who sought to have a variable interest rate clause in their mortgage declared invalid under the Wisconsin statute regulating such clauses.[10] The loan had been made prior to the 1972 FHLBB regulatory amendments which effectively prohibited variable rate clauses,[11] and the parties conceded that there was no FHLBB regulation dealing with the subject. Nonetheless, the Wisconsin Supreme Court held that the scheme of federal regulations was pervasive and fully occupied the field, thereby making the Wisconsin statute inapplicable. Virtually all of the cases cited by the court involved the internal governance of associations rather than relationships with borrowers, but the court thought the two spheres of activity were intimately tied together: "The regulation of loan practices directly affects the internal management and operations of federal associations and therefore requires uniform control. The present litigation ought, therefore, be resolved as a matter of federal law." [12] The case was remanded for a determination of the content of the federal (presumably common) law and an assessment of whether exhaustion of FHLBB remedies, if any, should be required.

Kaski is anomalous and should not be followed. The FHLBB regulations governing dealings between associations and borrowers are far from comprehensive,[13] and actually reflect ad hoc responses by the Board to a few specific issues raised by consumer advocates during the mid-1970's. They do not purport to exhaust the field, and leave far more issues uncovered than covered. State law has customarily governed such matters as the interpretation of notes and mortgages, the negotiability of notes, and procedures for foreclosure, redemption, and collection of deficiencies by federal associations. To invent federal common law to control all of these issues would require extensive litigation and introduce great uncertainty, and it would be entirely unnecessary. There is no significant need for uniformity in such matters, since most federal associations originate few loans across state lines, and their secondary market purchasing activity is generally quite modest in scope. The training of employees and the education of customers are both likely to be simplified by the application of state law. To infer a new legal basis for more than one-fourth of all home loans made in the United States from the FHLBB's silence is absurd.[14] Federal law should prevail only when there is an applicable FHLBB regulation.[15]

10. Wis.Stat. § 138.055 (1975).

11. See § 11.4, supra, at note 28. The loan in the Kaski case was made in 1967.

12. 240 N.W.2d at 373.

13. The principal regulations are those discussed in the sources cited at notes 5 through 8, supra, and those dealing with security property, loan-to-value ratios, and maturities; see 12 CFR 541.

14. S & L's make 47% of all home loans, and federal S & L's have 58% of the assets of all associations; see U. S. League of Sav. Ass'n, 1977 Fact Book, at 29, 50.

15. The FHLBB's position on the scope of its preemption of state mortgage

Perhaps the most perplexing cases in which federal preemption of state mortgage law is asserted are those in which the United States is the plaintiff, usually as holder and forecloser of the mortgage. Often the government appears in the guise of the Federal Housing Administration (FHA), the Veterans Administration (VA) or the Small Business Administration (SBA); the mortgage may have been originally made to the federal agency, or it may have been assigned to the agency upon the mortgagor's default. It is well-settled that the federal courts have jurisdiction to foreclose mortgages held by the government.[16] The question arises, however, to what extent state rules governing such matters as appointment of receivers, redemption following sale, and protection against deficiency judgments are binding against the government, which frequently would prefer to be unfettered by them.

law is ambiguous. In Schott v. Mission Federal Sav. & Loan Ass'n, Civ. 75–366, D.Cal.1975 (unreported), the plaintiffs attacked the due-on-sale clause in a federal association's mortgage; at that time there was no express FHLBB regulation on the subject. The Board filed an advisory opinion with the court arguing that the topic was preempted because it related to the "internal" affairs of the association. This assertion was based principally on the view that only by use of due-on-sale clauses could federal associations provide the maximum amount of financing at reasonable interest rates to credit-worthy borrowers, thus fulfilling the purpose of their charters. The case was settled, and the FHLBB subsequently issued regulations explicitly preempting the due-on clause issue, so the particular issue is moot. The Board's distinction between internal and external affairs, as expressed in its advisory opinion in *Schott*, is nonetheless interesting:

> We are discussing here only Board regulation and control over the affairs, business, business powers and authority, internal and external expansion, supervisory matters, internal operations and affairs, relationships between the association, its management and its members, and all similar and related matters respecting federal associations. The Board does not seek to regulate wholly unrelated matters of purely local concern, such as zoning for federal association property, methods of recording title, etc., which are left by the Board to state and local authorities, since they do not impinge upon the regulatory areas under Board control, or interfere with the Board's overall regulatory scheme.

As a statement of the delineation between preempted and non-preempted matters, the foregoing is incredibly inept and offers no meaningful guidance for the courts. Since the Board can readily preempt any matter within its competence merely by issuing a regulation (as it ultimately did regarding due-on-sale clauses), it can hardly expect the courts to read its collective mind and to decide matters which the Board itself has not articulated. It is hard to avoid the conclusion that the Board's position in the Schott case was inconsistent with its own statement quoted above, and was merely result-oriented; that is, that it had concluded that due-on-sale clauses were desirable by the time the litigation was filed.

For sources of the foregoing materials, see Bartlett, The Federal-State Preemption Conflict, 44 Legal Bull. 1, 8–13 (1978).

The FHLBB successfully argued for preemption in its amicus brief in Glen Ellyn Sav. & Loan Ass'n v. Tsouman, § 11.5 supra at note 85a, but there the federal interest was based on an explicit act of Congress rather than any supposed general occupation of the field by FHLBB regulations.

16. See 28 U.S.C.A. § 1345 (jurisdiction over cases in which the United States is a plaintiff.)

The preemption concept asserted by federal agencies in these cases originated in Clearfield Trust Co. v. United States,[17] in which the government sought recovery from Clearfield on account of a check, issued by the United States and drawn on the Treasury, which Clearfield had collected. An endorsement had been forged on the check, but under state law the government had not given notice of the forgery in a timely fashion after its discovery, and hence would have been barred from recovery against Clearfield. The Supreme Court, however, held that the federal common law preempted the state rule:

> The application of state law, even without the conflict of laws rules of the forum, would subject the rights and duties of the United States to exceptional uncertainty. It would lead to great diversity in results by making identical transactions subject to the vagaries of the laws of the several states. The desirability of a uniform rule is plain.[18]

The *Clearfield Trust* holding was first applied to a mortgage transaction in 1959 in United States v. View Crest Garden Apartments, Inc.[19] There an FHA mortgage had been assigned to the government after default. The government filed an action in federal court to foreclose the mortgage and sought the appointment of a receiver pending foreclosure. The trial court held that under the law of Washington State, no sufficient showing had been made to justify a receiver, but the Ninth Circuit reversed. It held that after default the question of remedies should be determined by federal law, and remanded the case for a determination as to whether federal law would justify appointment of a receiver. The court purported to reach its conclusion by weighing the policies underlying the state and federal rules, but it strongly emphasized the federal need to protect the treasury and promote the security of the federal investment, and it gave little weight to the policies underlying the Washington law of receiverships.

Following *View Crest* numerous other federal courts held that state foreclosure-related doctrines were inapplicable to the government. The Ninth Circuit itself, in United States v. Stadium Apartments,[20] weighed and rejected the Idaho post-sale redemption statute as against the federal government's need to obtain and liquidate security property speedily. Other courts held that deficiency

17. 318 U.S. 363, 63 S.Ct. 573, 87 L.Ed. 838 (1943).

18. Id. at 367.

19. 268 F.2d 380 (C.A.Wash.1959), certiorari denied 361 U.S. 884, 80 S.Ct. 156, 4 L.Ed.2d 120 (1960); see also United States v. Queen's Court Apartments, Inc., 296 F.2d 534 (C.A.Alaska 1961); United States v. Mountain Village Co., 424 F.Supp. 822 (D.Mass. 1976).

20. 425 U.S. 358 (C.A.Idaho 1970), certiorari denied 400 U.S. 926, 91 S.Ct. 187, 27 L.Ed.2d 185.

judgments were available to the government despite state anti-deficiency legislation.[21] A state statute authorizing credit terms on foreclosure sales was held inapplicable to the government.[22] The United States was held not subject to a state statute requiring deficiency actions to be brought within a specified time.[23] The local law of coverture was held not a defense to a personal judgment based on a note secured by a federal mortgage.[24]

For a time, it appeared that state law respecting mortgage remedies was entirely preempted by the federal government when acting as mortgage holder. However, the seeds of a reconsideration of this trend were sown in 1966 in United States v. Yazell,[25] in which the SBA had made a disaster loan secured by a chattel mortgage to a Texas couple. Upon default and foreclosure, the wife claimed that the Texas law of coverture insulated her separate property from execution by the government to satisfy the deficiency. The Supreme Court agreed, rejecting the SBA's claim that federal common law (which presumably would not recognize the coverture defense) should apply. The Court relied to some extent on the fact that the loan had been individually negotiated with specific reference to state law, and that the documents gave no clue that the government would attempt to overcome the coverture doctrine; in this way it distinguished the View Crest case. But the Court's principal rationale involved a weighing of the respective interests of state and federal governments. It held the state law was a significant manifestation of Texas' overall allocation of family property rights and obligations, and noted that the coverture doctrine could hardly be a serious impediment to SBA collections generally, since it was obsolete in most states. The Court thus concluded that Texas law should apply, although it declined to decide whether through adoption into federal common law or of its own force.[26]

21. Branden v. Driver, 441 F.2d 1171 (C.A.Cal.1971); United States v. Wells, 403 F.2d 596 (C.A.Fla.1968); McKnight v. United States, 259 F.2d 540 (C.A.Cal.1958); but see United States v. Stewart, 523 F.2d 1070 (C. A.Wash.1975) (California anti-deficiency law applied where deed of trust states it is to be construed under state law).

22. United States v. Thompson, 438 F. 2d 254 (C.A.Ark.1971).

23. United States v. Merrick Sponsor Corp., 421 F.2d 1076 (C.A.N.Y.1970); see also Ricks v. United States, 434 F.Supp. 1262 (S.D.Ga.1976) (federal government not bound by state law requiring report of foreclosure sale to be made to court within 30 days as a condition of obtaining deficiency judgment); United States v. McIntyre Veneer, Inc., 343 F.Supp. 1095 (D.La. 1972) (government entitled to deficiency notwithstanding lack of appraisal as required by state statute).

24. United States v. Helz, 314 F.2d 301 (C.A.Mich.1963).

25. 382 U.S. 341, 86 S.Ct. 500, 15 L.Ed. 2d 404 (1966).

26. See Note, The Role of State Deficiency Judgment Law in FHA Insured Mortgage Transactions, 56 Minn.L. Rev. 463 (1972), arguing that in such cases state law should be deemed "selectively incorporated" into federal law rather than applied of its own force.

Yazell was largely ignored by the courts in federal mortgage foreclosure cases until the Ninth Circuit decided United States v. MacKenzie [27] in 1975. That case also involved SBA loans, and the issue was whether state antideficiency and post-sale redemption statutes applied against the government. The court undertook a new evaluation of the competing state and federal interests. It held that state law, which was intended to aid debtors and fulfilled significant state objectives by encouraging higher bidding at foreclosure sales, also tended to fulfill the federal program's goal of helping small businesses! The court saw no compelling need for national uniformity, and thus concluded that state law should apply. The court's assessment that state law would best advance the federal program is rather astonishing, since the SBA itself, normally considered the best authority on how its own programs should be administered, obviously thought otherwise.

Of perhaps greater significance was the court's effort to distinguish *Stadium Apartments*.[28] It noted that the documents in *MacKenzie*, like those in *Yazell*, were individually negotiated and yet made no reference to any federal preemption of state remedies; hence the debtors were entitled to rely on the implicit representation that state law would apply. In *Stadium Apartments*, by contrast, the contract specifically purported to waive the state-law debtor protections.[29] More recent Ninth Circuit cases have placed continuing reliance on the language used by the parties in the documents, applying the California antideficiency statute when the deed of trust stated that California law should control,[30] but choosing federal law and rejecting the Alaska antideficiency statute in another case in which the documents stated federal law would govern.[31] In these cases the court seemed to regard the documents (invariably prepared by government lawyers, whether individually or on a nationwide basis) as tantamount to regulations of the agency, and consequently binding. However, cases in which the documents are silent as to applicable law still require a careful balancing of interests. In United States v. Haddon Haciendas Co.,[32] the Ninth Circuit considered an action by FHA for waste following its foreclosure of an apartment building.

27. 510 F.2d 39 (C.A.Nev.1975).

28. United States v. Stadium Apartments, Inc., 425 F.2d 358 (C.A.Idaho 1970), certiorori denied 400 U.S. 926, 91 S.Ct. 187, 27 L.Ed.2d 185, holding post-sale redemption statutes inapplicable as against FHA.

29. This distinction between individually-negotiated and state- or nationwide documents is flimsy and unconvincing. Judges Ely and Browning, concurring in *MacKenzie*, opined that the court had in reality overruled *Stadium Apartments*. See also Judge Wallace's opinion in United States v. Haddon Haciendas Co., 541 F.2d 777 (C.A.Cal.1976); United States v. Marshall, 431 F.Supp. 888 (N.D.Ill.1977).

30. United States v. Stewart, 523 F.2d 1070 (C.A.Wash.1975).

31. United States v. Gish, 559 F.2d 572 (C.A.Alaska 1977).

32. 541 F.2d 777 (C.A.Cal.1976).

Under a recent California case [33] the former owner could be held liable in damages only if the waste had been committed in bad faith; otherwise, the California Supreme Court had held, recovery by the mortgagee would violate the antideficiency statute. In the case before the Ninth Circuit there was no evidence of bad faith, but the court nevertheless permitted the FHA to recover. It discussed and weighed the competing interests and held that the federal program's objective of eliminating slums and substandard housing would be defeated if the landlords of FHA projects were free of liability for waste, and that such a result would not be unduly intrusive on the state statutory scheme.

As applied to the federal government as mortgage holder, the law of preemption is still far from settled. If the parties contract with explicit reference to either state or federal law, it is entirely reasonable to apply that law upon default. There is no reason to deny the agency the right to accomplish by drafting what it could readily do by regulation.[34] Where there is no such statement in the documents, however, the courts should give great weight to state law and policy, and should devise a federal rule, in the absence of regulations or federal statute, only when it is clearly needed to effectuate an important federal interest which state law would defeat.[35] It is doubtful that there is any such need with regard to antideficiency or redemption statutes, notwithstanding *View Crest* and *Stadium Apartments*. In those cases the only significant federal interest [36] is in collecting more money more quickly,[37] and that interest should not be

33. Cornelison v. Kornbluth, 15 Cal.3d 590, 125 Cal.Rptr. 557, 542 P.2d 981 (1975).

34. But see United States v. Marshall, 431 F.Supp. 888 (N.D.Ill.1977), in which the SBA note and mortgage purported to waive the debtor's post-sale redemption rights, despite the fact that they are non-waivable under Illinois law. The court disregarded the waiver and applied state law, following the balancing approach outlined in *MacKenzie*. However, it indicated that if SBA had promulgated a regulation having content similar to the language of the documents, a different result would obtain. This distinction between drafting and regulating has little to commend it, but perhaps the outcome of the case can be explained on the ground that the documents did not explicitly state that federal law would govern. Whether the documents were individually-tailored or were printed forms prepared by the government should be immaterial; see note 29, supra.

35. The test, as articulated by Judge Ely in his dissent in Stadium Apartments, is

> "whether the state law can be given effect without either conflicting with federal policy or destroying needed uniformity in the pertinent federal law in its operation within the various states."

425 F.2d at 368. See also Dalton Motors, Inc. v. Weaver, 446 F.Supp. 711 (D.Minn.1978), holding that by electing a power of sale foreclosure under Minnesota law, the SBA had waived its right to a deficiency judgment.

36. A federal interest might also be asserted in simpler administration nationally, but this must be regarded as of minor importance, especially if the agency has local offices and personnel.

37. See United States v. Haddon Haciendas, Inc., 541 F.2d 777 (C.A.Cal. 1976).

held to override state debtor-protection statutes. On the other hand, if the government wishes to obtain the appointment of a receiver or recover for waste, its actions may have important implications for the occupants of the buildings involved, and hence may warrant preemption.[38]

38. Id.

§§ 11.7–12.0 are reserved for supplementary material.

CHAPTER 12

FINANCING REAL ESTATE CONSTRUCTION

Table of Sections

§ 12.1 Construction Lending—An Overview

The purpose of a construction loan is to provide funds with which the owner of a parcel of land can construct improvements upon it.[1] The construction loan is superficially similar to a long-term mortgage loan; the borrower's obligation to repay will be represented by a promissory note or similar document, and will be secured by a mortgage, deed of trust, or comparable instrument. In addition, the lender and borrower will usually enter into a construction loan agreement, spelling out the obligations of each with regard to the construction process. The borrower (who is usually the owner of the land on which the project will be built) may perform the construction himself—acting, in effect, as his own general contractor. Alternatively, he may employ a separate general contractor with whom he enters into a construction contract. The discussion below will refer to the borrower as a "developer," and will assume that no separate general contractor is involved unless specifically mentioned. Most of this chapter is equally applicable to construction projects which will be sold upon completion (such as detached-house subdivisions) and to projects which the developer will retain upon completion, either for his own use (such as an individual's own home or a business warehouse

1. See generally U.S. League of Sav. Associations, Constr. Lending Guide; Storke & Sears, Subdivision Financing, 28 Rocky Mt.L.Rev. 549 (1956); Albright, Processing the Constr. Mortgage, 3 Real Est.Rev. 72 (No. 3, Fall 1973); Gallaher, Protecting the Construction Loan, 5 Real Est.Rev. 114 (No. 1, Spring 1975); Tockarshewsky, Reducing the Risks in Construction Lending, 7 Real Est.Rev. 59 (No. 1, Spring 1977); Hall, How to Build Lender Protection into Construction Loan Agreements, 6 Real Est.L.J. 21 (1977).

or office) or for rental purposes (such as the usual apartment building). Where distinctions among these types of projects are important, they will be noted.

Construction lending is far more critical and exacting, and presents far greater risks to the mortgagee, than does lending on completed structures. This is so because the value of the real estate for security purposes is entirely dependent upon the happening of a future event: the completion of the building or project as agreed by the parties. If the construction is not completed by the mortgagor, or is completed late or defectively, or if the project's value upon completion is less than anticipated, the construction lender may find himself in the unhappy position of being inadequately secured. Such a situation is viewed even more seriously by junior lienors, such as the vendor from whom the present owner purchased the land (and who has not yet been fully paid), or claimants under mechanics and materialmen's liens. These parties are frequently present in construction lending situations, and their roles will be discussed subsequently. Because of their junior security position, their risk of being wiped out by the mortgagor's failure to complete the project as agreed, or the project's lack of value despite its completed status, is even more serious than that of the construction lender.

A critical concern of every construction lender (and of knowledgeable junior lienors as well) is that the funds disbursed by the lender actually find their way into labor and materials used in the project. To some extent this is a matter for negotiation between the borrower and lender; in addition to covering the "hard costs," such as materials and direct labor, the construction lender may be willing to cover certain "soft costs" such as legal and accounting services directly related to the project, insurance, real estate taxes, and possibly even interest on the construction loan itself, as well as charges made by permanent lenders for their commitments. Other negotiable points include whether the construction loan will cover any portion of the land acquisition or site development costs, such as the extension of utility lines, roads and streets, storm and sanitary sewers, and the like to the project. The most conservative position, taken by many construction lenders, is to insist that all land acquisition, site development, and "soft" costs be covered by the developer through cash outlays or other financing separate from (and junior to) the construction loan. In many cases the lender is required by law to limit its construction loans to "hard" construction costs.[2]

The construction lender will be particularly concerned that no construction loan funds be diverted to other uses. Such diversions often occur, and can obviously be devastating to the construction

2. See, e. g., Sharp Lumber Co. v. Manus Homes, Inc., 189 N.E.2d 447, 90 O.L.A. 421 (Ohio App.1961), holding a construction loan valid despite its noncompliance with an applicable regulation limiting such loans to construction costs.

lender, since they greatly increase the probability that the property's security value will be less than the indebtedness it secures. Diversion of funds by a developer does not always imply outright dishonesty. In some cases, the developer may have other projects under construction which are in serious trouble, and he may be tempted to "rob" one project in order to "bail out" another. Diversion of funds is almost always a sign of serious trouble to the construction lender, and wise lenders take careful precautions to insure that it does not occur.

Institutional Construction Lenders

Construction lending cannot be successfully handled by remote control. The lender must be intimately familiar with local circumstances and practices, and must be represented by an on-site inspector. In addition, construction loans tend to be of relatively short duration, since the construction periods for most types of real estate projects are measured in months or small numbers of years. Finally, construction lending tends to be risky but profitable, with fees and interest rates significantly higher than are normally expected on long-term loans on completed real estate developments. Given these constraints, it is not surprising that the two principal types of local lending institutions, commercial banks and savings and loan associations, together account for roughly three-fourths of all construction lending in the United States.[3] These two types of lenders are roughly equal in aggregate amounts of construction lending, with commercial banks displaying some preference for loans on commercial property and savings and loan associations having a somewhat heavier activity in the residential construction area. The remaining one-fourth of all construction lending has been attributable largely to real estate investment trusts in recent years, although these entities have often suffered significant losses on such loans, largely as a consequence of poor underwriting and inspection.[4]

The authority of national banks to make real estate construction loans secured by first liens is derived from Section 24 of the Federal Reserve Act.[5] While the Act generally imposes rather rigid requirements with respect to loan-to-value ratios and amortization payments on real estate loans, it provides an exception for construction loans. In substance, those loans are not considered "real estate loans" if their maturities do not exceed sixty months. In order to qualify for this exception, loans to finance the construction of commercial or industrial buildings must be supported by a permanent or "take-out" loan commitment in an equal amount from a financially responsible

3. See U.S. Dept. of Housing and Urban Devel., Housing in the Seventies 3–4 to 3–8 (1973).

4. See, e. g., Stevenson, Lessons from the Mortgage Trust Experience, 6 Real Est.Rev. 72 (No. 3, Fall 1976).

5. 12 U.S.C.A. § 371; 12 CFR 7.2000 et seq.

lender to take effect upon the completion of construction; no such agreement is legally required for loans on residential or farm buildings, although many banks routinely require such a commitment as a matter of policy. The effect of the Act is to entirely eliminate any requirement of amortization during the construction period; in theory, the loan-to-value ratio is also unlimited, but as a practical matter it is constrained by the willingness of permanent lenders to give high-ratio loans when construction is completed; again, individual commercial banks may adopt more conservative policies.

Federal savings and loan associations are subject to the regulations of the Federal Home Loan Bank Board with respect to their lending powers. Such associations are permitted to make construction loans secured by first liens with no amortization payments, and with interest paid semi-annually. Construction loans on detached homes are limited to eighty percent of value and eighteen months maturity.[6] On other dwelling units, such as apartments, the maturity may be as long as thirty-six months.[7] The thirty-six month maturity limitation is also applicable to construction loans on non-residential real estate improvements, but in such cases the loan-to-value ratio may not exceed seventy-five percent.[8] Federal savings and loan associations are also permitted to make loans for land acquisition, or for combined land acquisition and construction of single-family homes.[9] The total of loans in these categories may not exceed five percent of the association's savings accounts. For loans to finance land acquisition only, the current limits are seventy-five percent of completed value and five years maximum maturity. If the loan is made to finance both land acquisition and construction of homes, the loan-to-value ratio may be as high as eighty percent and the maturity as long as six years, but the regulations require some amortization payments during the period that the loan is outstanding.

Each state regulates the lending powers of state-chartered banks and savings and loan associations, as well as mutual savings banks in those states in which they are authorized. The construction lending powers of these institutions are usually roughly similar to those of the federally chartered institutions discussed above, but vary considerably from one jurisdiction to another.

Neither the Federal Housing Administration (FHA) nor the Veterans Administration (VA) normally insures or guarantees construction loans to developers of single-family homes.[10] However, under Ti-

6. 12 CFR 545.6–1(a)(7).

7. 12 CFR 545.6–1(b)(3)(ii).

8. 12 CFR 545.6–1(c)(5).

9. 12 CFR 545.6–14.

10. The Veterans Administration will issue a loan guaranty to permit an eligible veteran to construct a home for his own occupancy; interestingly, such a loan may include land acquisition as well as construction costs; 38 CFR 36.4301.

tle X of the National Housing Act,[11] enacted in 1965, FHA may insure land development loans to finance the installation of such improvements as water and sewer systems, other utilities, street paving, and facilities for public or common use by the residents of the development. Such loans must be secured by first mortgages, although FHA will permit the existence of junior financing, such as a subordinated lien representing the unpaid acquisition cost of the land. Title X cannot be used to finance the construction of dwelling units; the developer must obtain a separate construction loan for that purpose, and it will usually be necessary to release lots from the Title X mortgage as they are placed within the coverage of the construction loan, since most construction lenders require that their loans be secured by first liens.

FHA also insures construction loan mortgages on multi-family housing projects under many of its programs.[12] In such cases, a single set of mortgage documents is frequently used for both the construction and permanent loan periods. In FHA's terminology, the agency's activity during the construction period is known as "insurance of advances." Generally, developers (or "sponsors," as they are called by FHA) who wish the advantages of permanent financing under one of the FHA multi-family programs may elect insurance of advances or not, as they choose.

Despite the fact that FHA does not insure construction loans on housing subdivisions which are to be owner-occupied, the agency nonetheless is sometimes heavily involved in the construction of such projects. This occurs because, under applicable statutes, a house is eligible for a permanent FHA-insured loan with a 97% loan-to-value ratio on the first $25,000 *only* if it was "approved for mortgage insurance prior to the beginning of construction" or is more than one year old.[13] The maximum loan-to-value ratio for a house which has not received such approval is only 90%. Thus, if a builder wishes the advantage of offering his customers high-ratio FHA financing, he must obtain advance approval of his development, with its attendant paperwork (which is substantial) and FHA inspections during construction. The advent of 95% privately-insured conventional permanent financing[14] has made FHA a less attractive approach to many developers,[15] but some are still willing to seek the FHA's "conditional commitment" and concomitant involvement.

11. 12 U.S.C.A. § 1749aa et seq.

12. These include Section 207 (unsubsidized rental projects); Section 213 (cooperative housing projects); Section 221(d)(2) and 221(d)(4) (moderate-income rental projects); and Section 236 (subsidized rental projects for lower-income families). The numbers refer to sections of the National Housing Act.

13. National Housing Act § 203(b)(2), 12 U.S.C.A. § 1709(b)(2).

14. See e. g., 12 CFR 545.6–1(a)(5), permitting federal savings and loan associations to make permanent home mortgage loans up to 95% of value with private mortgage insurance.

15. Only 69,000 mortgages on new homes under Section 203 were in-

The Farmers Home Administration (FmHA), a division of the U. S. Department of Agriculture, operates several programs to finance both single-family and multi-family housing in rural areas.[16] FmHA guarantees loans made by other institutional lenders, and also makes some direct loans. FmHA will provide necessary construction financing for developers, although it strongly prefers that construction loans be made by other institutions.[17]

Underwriting Construction Loans

From the mortgagee's point of view, successful construction lending depends on the interplay of several activities, including thorough underwriting of the proposed loan, inspection during the construction period, and the use of careful controls to insure that disbursed funds are not diverted away from the construction project. "Underwriting," as used in this context, means a careful evaluation of all of the factors which could result in a risk of loss to the construction lender. Not all of these factors are legal in nature, although many have legal ramifications. Underwriting a construction project is complex, and the material given here should be taken only as a brief summary of the items with which the lender will be concerned.

The proposed borrower's reputation, experience, credit rating, and capitalization are highly important to the lender. Success in previous smaller projects is usually a prerequisite to obtaining financing for a major enterprise. If the borrower is a closely-held corporation, its shareholders will usually be asked to take personal liability for the debt. Most lenders will require that the borrower put a substantial amount of his own cash—in many cases on the order of ten percent of the project's construction cost—rather than borrowing the entire amount. This cash investment requirement may be a result of the regulations applicable to the particular lender, or it may derive from the lender's internal policies; in either event, the assetless developer or one whose assets are illiquid (such as other land holdings) does not present an attractive risk.

The marketability of the project is also critical. If the completed structures will be sold or rented, the lender needs some assurance that they will be in demand. A careful market survey will usually be required for a large project.[18] In the case of a project which can be leased to an identifiable business tenant prior to construction (as is

sured by FHA in 1975, a year in which 960,000 one-to-four family private housing units were started; FHA thus captured only about 7.2% of the market. See U.S. Dept. of Housing & Urban Devel., 1975 Statistical Yearbook 258–59.

16. The principal programs are Section 502 (rural home loans) and Section 515 (rural rental project loans) of the Housing Act of 1949, 42 U.S.C.A. §§ 1472, 1485.

17. 7 CFR 1822.7(g), 1822.94(a).

18. See Etzel, Good Data In * * * Good Loans Out, Savings & Loan News, Oct. 1972, at 74, for a thorough discussion of market studies of condominium projects.

often the case with large store space in shopping centers), the lender will usually wish to verify the tenant's credit worthiness.

The architectural and engineering design and the soil tests for the project will be carefully reviewed by the construction lender to make sure that they are technically sound, in compliance with local codes, and will result in a marketable project. The lender will perform an appraisal of the project prior to granting the construction loan, and will carefully analyze the developer's proposed budget and schedule of costs to determine that the project can be completed with the available funds. The lender will also give close scrutiny to the developer's proposed timing and completion date.

A variety of legal matters will be of direct interest to the construction lender, including the quality of the developer's title and his compliance with local zoning and building codes, environmental regulations, and all other local, state, and federal laws which might bear on the construction. The lender will usually require a survey and a plot plan to verify that the property's location and size are as represented by the developer and that the project will comply with any applicable set-back lines.

Finally, the lender will wish to review other documents associated with the project, including the construction contract if the developer is not serving as his own general contractor, the lease forms if the project is to be rented after completion, the forms of any bonds required, and the permanent loan commitment if the construction lender is not also to carry the permanent financing.

Of course, not all construction lenders are as uniformly careful and deliberate as the foregoing list suggests. Some are willing to take underwriting shortcuts when dealing with developers with whom they have had prior good experience. But failure to consider any of these details increases the potential risk.

Documentation

When the underwriting process has been completed and the construction lender has determined to make the loan, it will usually execute, with the developer, three basic documents: a promissory note or bond, a construction loan mortgage or deed of trust, and a construction loan agreement. This agreement [19] will generally incorporate by reference the entire plans and specifications for the project, will contain a budget to which the developer agrees to adhere, and will fix a completion date for the project. The specific "hard" and "soft" costs which the loan will cover are identified. It will explain the method of disbursing funds as construction progresses; events

19. Examples of two construction loan agreements are reprinted in J. Krasnowiecki, Housing and Urban Development Cases and Materials 30, 82 (1969). See also Florida Bar, I. Florida Real Property Practice § 17.56 (1965); Calif.Cont.Ed. of Bar, California Land Security and Development § 30.29 (1960).

which may constitute a default on the part of the borrower will be set forth in detail, and the agreement will specify the lender's remedies for such defaults. The developer's responsibility for such matters as bonds, insurance, and permits from government agencies will be spelled out in detail. The lender's draw inspector may be identified and his right of access to the project assured.

The agreement will usually create a construction loan account out of which funds will be disbursed as construction moves forward; the developer may also be required to deposit an agreed amount of his own cash in this account, as discussed above. From the lender's viewpoint, it is essential that the account, including the loan amount plus the developer's deposit, contain sufficient funds at the commencement of construction to complete the project, and that this sufficiency continue throughout the construction period. The agreement may contain language requiring the borrower to deposit additional funds at any time if the account becomes inadequate to complete construction. The account itself will usually be assigned to the lender as additional security for the loan.

Control of Disbursements

Several methods have been developed by which the construction lender may insure that the funds being disbursed under the loan are in fact being used for improvements in the project. Perhaps the oldest method, now commonly used alone only for the construction of detached houses, is the "progress payment" method under which some previously agreed fraction of the funds is disbursed as each stage of construction is completed. This approach requires periodic inspections by the lender. A more sophisticated method, termed the voucher system, requires the lender to disburse funds only when presented with bills or vouchers for work actually done on the site. The lender may require the developer to pay the bills directly and may issue a single check, say monthly, to the developer to cover them, or it may issue separate checks to the suppliers and subcontractors directly. On large projects, the voucher system is usually supplemented by site inspections by the lender. None of these methods are foolproof, but they tend to discourage attempts by the developer to divert loan funds to non-construction uses.

§ 12.2 Construction Contracts and Bonds

Both of the topics covered in this section are very broad and can be treated only briefly here. They are mentioned primarily because of their relation to financing issues and in order to present a reasonably comprehensive picture of the construction process.

Construction Contracts

It is very rare for a landowner to have the skills and the personnel to construct substantial improvements on his land. Occasionally an owner will build his own house, but for larger projects, some form of construction contracting is almost always necessary.[21] A principal decision which the owner must make is whether he should delegate total responsibility for construction to a single entity—a prime or general contractor—or whether he has the skill and time to assume overall management and should enter into separate contracts with those who will perform the major elements of work, such as structural, electrical, plumbing and heating, and the like. The separate contract system has several advantages: (1) The owner is given the opportunity to select individual firms which are, in his opinion, best qualified; (2) He can pay them directly for their work or arrange for disbursements to them from the construction lender, thereby obviating the possibility that the funds will be diverted by a general contractor; and (3) He need not be concerned that a general contractor will attempt to "squeeze" them to do more work for less money, increasing the general contractor's profits at the expense of quality.

Despite these advantages, the single contract system, involving a general contractor, is much more widely used. As suggested, the primary reason is that it permits full delegation of responsibility to a single entity to whom the owner can look in the event there are problems. If the general contractor is honest, competent, and financially responsible, the owner can sign the contract and then forget about the project until it is finished—in theory, at least. In major projects, the owner's architect or engineer will inspect the work frequently, call discrepancies to the general contractor's attention, and inform the owner if they are not corrected. Thus, the single contract system isolates the owner fairly well from continual administrative concerns with the construction work.

Pricing and Bidding

By far the most widely used pricing system is the fixed price or "lump sum" contract. The general contractor contracts that the project will be built for an agreed dollar figure. If the work costs less than anticipated, the contractor pockets the savings; if it costs more, his profits are reduced and he may ultimately sustain a loss. In principle, this provides maximum protection to the owner; in practice, however, if cost overruns threaten to force the general contractor into insolvency or induce him to abandon the project, the owner may be virtually compelled to increase the contract price; a lawsuit, particularly against a financially disabled contractor, is a poor substitute for a completed building.

21. The discussion here is drawn heavily from J. Sweet, Legal Aspects of Architecture, Engineering, and the Construction Process 307ff (1970). See also Sweet, Your First Construction Contract, 21 Prac.Law. 27 (No. 2, Mar. 1975); E. Colby, Practical Legal Advice for Builders and Contractors 19 (1972); Prac.L.Inst., Construction Contracts 1–58 (1977); Prac.L.Inst., Real Estate Construction Current Problems 45–174 (1973); Simpkin & Nielsen, The Rise of Project/Construction Management, 6 Real Est.Rev. 46 (No. 4, Winter 1977).

An alternative form of contract in fairly wide use is the "guaranteed maximum," in which the owner cannot be charged more than an agreed amount, but if the contractor's costs are lower than estimated, the owner and contractor share in the savings according to some agreed percentage—often 50–50. This gives the contractor an incentive to hold costs down, and at the same time protects the owner to some degree against extravagant overruns.

Another approach is the "cost-plus" contract, in which the owner agrees to pay the contractor's costs plus some agreed percentage or dollar amount. This sort of arrangement is rarely used in real estate development; unless coupled with some maximum or "upset" price it obviously has the potential for wreaking financial devastation on the owner since it gives the contractor no incentive to watch his costs carefully. The cost-plus contract is usually found only in projects which are so unusual or technologically innovative that no reasonable advance estimate of their costs can be made.

All of the types of contracts discussed above may be entered into either through bidding or negotiation. Normally negotiation is feasible only if the owner or his staff are themselves quite skilled in construction matters; otherwise they will have difficulty in knowing whether the contractor's proposed price is a reasonable one. The competitive aspect of bidding tends to eliminate this problem. On the other hand, bidding has its disadvantages. It is often slower and requires more administrative effort to get the contract executed. Additionally, bidders may tend to reduce their bids below feasible levels in order to get the job, anticipating that they will be able to get additional money from the owner when it becomes apparent that the work cannot be completed for the original price. Nonetheless, bidding is more widely used than negotiation.

The owner usually solicits bids through some sort of invitation or advertisement. Often he will limit the invitations to contractors who, on the basis of reputation, experience, and financial position, appear to have the capacity to do the job well. Each prospective bidder will be given a package consisting of the complete plans, specifications, and drawings for the project; the proposed construction contract; and a set of rules outlining the bidding process itself—telling when bids are due, whether the owner is obligated to select the lowest (or any) bid, etc. Bidders may be required to post some security to assure that they will actually enter into the contract if their bid is accepted. All of these matters are often covered by statutes on public contracts, frequently in rather inflexible terms.

Obviously, bidding a general contract requires that detailed plans and specifications have first been developed. This is less true in a negotiated contract, in which the prospective contractor may actually work with the owner's architects and engineers in producing the final plans and specifications. A radically different approach is the "package" or "turnkey" contract, in which the owner provides merely a set of general performance specifications. The contractor is responsible for the detailed design as well as the construction of the buildings. In such a transaction he may even supply the land and may be expected to obtain his own financing during construction. In effect, the owner is purchasing a completed building which meets his needs and which was designed especially for him.

Construction bonds—An Introduction

Construction is a volatile and uncertain business; perhaps more than any other, it follows Murphy's Law: If anything can go wrong, it will.[22] Some types of problems are clearly attributable to the contractor: weak capitalization, poor planning or management, and outright dishonesty are illustrative. Other perils are beyond the contractor's control: strikes, shortages, natural disasters, concealed soil problems, changes in government regulations—all may slow construction or make it more costly. In many cases general contractors are financially weak and are unable to respond in damages even when it is clear that they have breached their contracts. Thus, owners and lenders frequently seek the participation of some financially responsible third party who can step in to rectify the contractor's breach or compensate them for the damage it causes.[23]

The third party is usually a commercial surety company, and the instrument which binds it is a surety bond. Several types of surety bonds are commonly used in construction. These are described below, but first some basic terminology is necessary.[24] In the usual case, it is the general contractor whose default is to be protected against;[25] he is termed the *principal.* The owner of the land on which the project is to be constructed, and who employs the contractor, is the *obligee,* for it is to him that the principal's obligation is owed. The *surety* is obligated to perform if the principal does not,[26]

22. An axiom of engineers and scientists whose origin is obscure; see American Heritage Dictionary of the English Language 863 (1973).

23. Bonds are often required by statute on public projects, but seldom on private work; an exception is Utah Code Ann. § 14–2–1.

24. See generally J. Sweet, Legal Aspects of Architecture, Engineering, and the Construction Process 363 (1970); Prac.L.Inst., Construction Default: The Contractor's Bond (1976); Surety Ass'n of America, Bonds of Suretyship (1959); R. Kratovil, Modern Mortgage Law & Practice § 218 (1972); G. Osborne, Law of Suretyship (1966); L. Simpson, Suretyship (1950).

25. On a large project, the general contractor may also insist that the major subcontractors obtain bonds to protect him; in that case, the general contractor is the obligee and the subs are principals.

26. Technically, a surety's obligation may or may not be conditioned upon the default of the principal; if it is so conditioned, it is properly termed a guaranty. See L. Simpson, Suretyship §§ 4–6 (1950). The typical construction bond is conditioned upon the principal's default; see, e. g., American Institute of Architects Document A311, Performance Bond and Labor and Material Payment Bond, Feb. 1970 edition, reprinted in Prac. L.Inst., Real Estate Construction Current Problems 525–28 (1973).

or to pay damages instead. The bond will contain a "*penal sum,*" the maximum amount the surety company will be obliged to pay out. The amount is usually as high as the price affixed to the underlying contract between owner and contractor, but it may be less—perhaps only 50 percent or 25 percent. This is a point of negotiation between the contracting parties, except in some public or governmentally-financed projects, in which it is fixed by statute or regulation.[27]

Construction bonds are generally purchased directly by the contractor, who pays the premium (a lump sum amount) and who usually selects the surety (although the construction contract may give the owner a veto or approval power). The premium is usually stated as a percentage of the contract amount, which may vary with the size and type of project, as well as other factors, including the surety company's perception of the risk the particular contractor presents.[28] From the contractor's viewpoint, the bond premium is a cost of constructing the project, and he will therefore take it into account in preparing his bid on the job. The owner thus pays it indirectly. Some contractors may be deemed so unreliable, inexperienced, or financially weak that they cannot qualify for a bond from any company at any price; indeed, this is usually the case with small home-building companies, which consequently are seldom required by their customers to obtain bonds. In a project of substantial size, however, a prospective contractor's inability to obtain a bond is an important warning signal to the owner.[29]

Three principal types of bonds are used in the modern construction industry: the bid bond, the performance bond, and the payment bond. Each of these is explained briefly below.[30]

27. See, e. g., the Miller Act, 40 U.S.C.A. § 270a–d (1964), requiring both a payment and a performance bond in federal construction projects; the amount of the latter is in the discretion of the contracting officer, but the payment bond is fixed by statute at 50 percent of the contract amount for contracts under $1 million, 40 percent for contracts between $1 million and $5 million, and $2.5 million for larger contracts.

28. A typical fee is 1 percent of the first $100,000 (of contract amount), 0.65 percent of the next $2.4 million, and 0.525 percent of the next $3.5 million. On this basis the fee for a $5 million bond would be $29,725. Both payment and performance bonds would be provided for this single fee; a bid bond, if required, would be priced and obtained separately. See Prac.L.Inst., Real Estate Construction Current Problems 231 (1973).

29. Sometimes an owner will attempt to save the expense of the bond by requiring that the contractor qualify for it and then waiving it. The thesis is that if the contractor qualifies, he is sufficiently responsible that the bond itself adds little to the owner's protection. If the surety's evaluation was incorrect in such a case, however, the owner will have learned a costly lesson. Id. at 213.

30. An excellent summary of these types of bonds and their legal aspects is Pierce, Rights and Responsibilities of the Contractor's Surety—What Happens When the Contractor Defaults, in Prac.L.Inst., Construction Contracts 435 (1977); see also Rodimer, Use of Bonds in Private Construction, 7 Forum 235 (1972).

The bid bond. The purpose of this bond is to pay the damages if the contractor who is awarded the contract does not enter into it or if he is unable to obtain the other bonds required for the job. In some cases a bid bond is not used; instead each bidder is required to post a cash deposit to assure that he will enter into the contract if he is selected. The bond, however, has the added advantage of serving as a screening mechanism, since bidders who are seriously underqualified probably will not be able to obtain bonds.

The amount of the claim which the owner may make in the event of a default varies with the provisions of the bond. In some cases the bond or the applicable statute provides that the entire penalty amount is forfeited, irrespective of the owner's ability to show actual damages in that amount.[31] Other bond forms limit the owner to actual damages,[32] with the penal sum as a maximum.[33]

In some circumstances the law will excuse a bidder from liability for an inadvertent mistake in his bid. Typically, the courts require proof that the mistake was unintentional and of substantial size, that the owner was notified of the mistake as early as possible, and that he will not be irreparably injured by the court's excusing the bidder.[34] In such cases, the owner is usually denied recovery, both against the bidder himself, and also upon the bid bond.[35] Such holdings follow the general rule that a surety can raise all defenses which would have been available to the principal.[36] From the owner's viewpoint, however, this doctrine makes the bid bond less satisfactory and inclusive than he would prefer.

The performance bond. In the event that the contractor fails to complete the project as agreed, the surety under a performance bond must make good his default. The surety usually has the option of

31. See, e. g., City of Lake Geneva v. States Improvement Co., 45 Wis.2d 50, 172 N.W.2d 176 (1969), holding valid as liquidated damages both bond and statutory clauses which provided for forfeiture of the full bond amount, irrespective of actual damages.

32. See Board of Educ. v. Sever-Williams Co., 22 Ohio St.2d 107, 258 N.E.2d 605 (1970), in which the bond's terms limited the obligee's recovery to its actual damages, measured by the difference between the bid amount and the amount of the contract ultimately entered into with another contractor.

33. The claim cannot exceed the penal sum, even if actual damages are greater. Bolivar Reorg. School Dist. No. 1 v. American Surety Co., 307 S.W.2d 405 (Mo.1957).

34. Ruggiero v. United States, 190 Ct. Cl. 327, 420 F.2d 709 (1970); See Smith & Lowe Constr. Co. v. Herrera, 79 N.M. 239, 442 P.2d 197 (1968); M. F. Kemper Constr. Co. v. City of Los Angeles, 37 Cal.2d 696, 235 P.2d 7 (1951). Grimes & Walker, Unilateral Mistakes in Construction Bids: Methods of Proof and Theories of Recovery—A Modern Approach, 5 B.C.Indus. & Com.L.Rev. 213 (1964); Annot., 52 A.L.R.2d 792 (1957). Cf. Board of Education v. Sever-Williams Co., supra note 32.

35. White v. Berenda Mesa Water Dist., 7 Cal.App.3d 894, 87 Cal.Rptr. 338 (1970); See Boise Jr. College Dist. v. Mattefs Constr. Co., 92 Idaho 757, 450 P.2d 604 (1969).

36. See L. Simpson, Suretyship §§ 52–62 (1950).

taking over the construction and completing it (usually hiring a new general contractor) or of paying for the completion by the owner or a new general contractor hired by him. The surety's liability, of course, does not exceed the bond's penal sum. In addition, the surety has a legal right to the undisbursed portion of the contract price; [37] otherwise the owner would get a windfall, having his building completed without paying the price he originally agreed upon.

Common types of contractor defaults which will trigger the performance surety's obligation include serious delays in the scheduled progress of the work, abandonment by the contractor, and failure to pay for labor and materials in order to keep the property lien-free. Since the surety is only obligated to the performance originally agreed to by the contractor, not all problems in construction will necessarily give rise to bond claims. The construction contract or applicable law, for example, may excuse the builder (and the surety) for defaults resulting from natural calamities [38] or undisclosed subsoil conditions which make the project more costly.[39] The surety may have a defense based on the owner's fraud,[40] the illegality of the contract,[41] or most other standard contract defenses. The owner may also be denied recovery on the bond if he has failed to perform conditions precedent to the contractor's duties [42] or has made advances to the contractor without the surety's consent for work not yet done.[43] Such premature or excessive payments, particularly if they are not actually used in the construction work, harm the surety's position, both by reducing the contractor's incentive to perform and by diminishing the fund which will be available to complete the building if the contractor defaults.

37. Henningsen v. United States Fidelity & Guar. Co., 208 U.S. 404, 28 S.Ct. 389, 52 L.Ed. 547 (1908); Mid-Continent Cas. Co. v. First Nat. Bank & Trust Co., 531 P.2d 1370 (Okl.1975).

38. See Barnard-Curtiss Co. v. United States, 257 F.2d 565 (C.A.N.M.1968), certiorari denied 358 U.S. 906, 79 S. Ct. 230, 3 L.Ed.2d 227, and 358 U.S. 906, 79 S.Ct. 233, 3 L.Ed.2d 227 (1958); Cf. Barnard-Curtiss Co. v. United States, 157 Ct.Cl. 103, 301 F. 2d 909 (1962).

39. See Scherrer Constr. Co. v. Burlington Memorial Hospital, 64 Wis.2d 720, 221 N.W.2d 855 (1974).

40. See United Bonding Ins. Co. v. Donaldson Engineering, Inc., 222 So. 2d 447 (Fla.App.1969).

41. See Wheaton v. Ramsey, 92 Idaho 33, 436 P.2d 248 (1968). Medina v. Title Guar. & Surety Co., 152 App. Div. 307, 136 N.Y.S. 786 (1912), affirmed 211 N.Y. 24, 104 N.E. 1118 (1914).

42. See Kanters v. Kotick, 102 Wash. 523, 173 P. 329 (1918).

43. National American Bank v. Southcoast Contractors, Inc., 276 So.2d 777 (La.App.1973), writ refused 279 So.2d 694 (La.1973); Gibbs v. Hartford Accident & Indemnity Co., 62 So.2d 599 (Fla.1952); Pacific Coast Engineering Co. v. Detroit Fidelity & Surety Co., 214 Cal. 384, 5 P.2d 888 (1931). The more recent cases tend to discharge the surety only pro tanto, to the extent of the harm caused by the advance payment; see L. Simpson, Suretyship § 78 (1950). Some cases treat advance payments as a species of the contract modification problem (see text at note 45, infra), but this may be misleading; the discharge occurs even if the overpayment was unilateral and voluntary.

Another defense available to the surety is the existence of facts, known to the owner and not revealed to the surety, which materially increase the risk of default. If the owner should have perceived the increased risk, realized that the facts were unknown to the surety, and had a reasonable opportunity to reveal them, his inaction may bar his recovery on the bond.[44]

A recurring problem in the enforcement of performance bonds is the modification of construction contracts as work progresses. In every large project numerous changes are made as a result of unavailability of materials, impracticalities in the original design, or innovations which will improve the building's usefulness. Traditionally the law of suretyship provided for a complete release of the surety in the event of any unconsented material alteration in the principal's contract with the obligee.[45] In theory, the modification increased the surety's risk unjustifiably. Courts today have grown less receptive to this doctrine. Only major changes in the scope of work are likely to result in a release of the surety, and even then, it will probably be held a pro tanto release, only to the extent that the change caused damage to the surety, rather than a complete discharge.[46] Additionally, many performance bonds contain language which expressly permits changes in details of the project, so long as the overall concept remains the same.[47]

The performance bond should not be confused with the completion bond, an instrument which is now largely obsolete. The completion bond differs in two important respects.[48] First, the surety is absolutely bound to complete the project; it has no option to pay a penal amount to the obligee instead. Second, completion bonds are normally written in favor of lending institutions and obligate the surety irrespective of the performance or good faith of the owner himself. Thus, the surety is bound even if the owner has squandered or divert-

44. See Sumitomo Bank v. Iwasaki, 70 Cal.2d 81, 73 Cal.Rptr. 564, 447 P.2d 956 (1968); Rocky Mountain Tool & Machine Co. v. Tecon Corp., 371 F.2d 589 (C.A.Colo.1966).

45. See United States v. Freel, 186 U. S. 309, 22 S.Ct. 875, 46 L.Ed. 1177 (1902); Hall & Co. v. Continental Cas. Co., 34 A.D.2d 1028, 310 N.Y.S.2d 950 (1970), affirmed 30 N.Y.2d 517, 330 N.Y.S.2d 64, 280 N.E.2d 890 (1972) (extension of time discharges surety).

46. See, e. g., Zuni Constr. Co. v. Great American Ins. Co., 86 Nev. 364, 468 P.2d 980 (1970); Verdugo Highlands, Inc. v. Security Ins. Co., 240 Cal.App.2d 527, 49 Cal.Rptr. 736 (1966); Hochevar v. Maryland Cas. Co., 114 F.2d 948 (C.C.A.Ohio 1940); cf. Brunswick Nursing & Convalescent Center, Inc. v. Great American Ins. Co., 308 F.Supp. 297 (S.D.Ga.1970).

47. See, e. g., the unusually pro-obligee language in the performance bond appearing at Prac.L.Inst., Real Estate Construction Current Problems 522–25 (1973):

> The Surety hereby waives notice of any and all modifications, omissions, additions, changes and advance or deferred payments in and about the Agreement and agrees that the obligations of this Bond shall not be impaired in any manner by reason of any such modifications, omissions, additions, changes or advanced or deferred payments.

48. Id. at 224, 229–30.

ed the construction funds. The obvious risks associated with this sort of instrument have led most commercial sureties to discontinue issuing them.

The payment bond. This is an undertaking by the surety that all persons supplying labor or materials to the project will be paid. It is arguable that the contractor's duty to pay such persons is a part of his obligation under the construction contract and hence is guaranteed by the performance bond.[49] However, the payment bond obviates the need for this argument and also makes it clear that subcontractors and material suppliers themselves may bring an action on the bond.[50] Thus the bond serves two purposes: it assures the owner a lien-free project, and it induces suppliers and subcontractors to accept work on the project, perhaps at a lower price, because of the assurance that they will be paid. Since no additional charge is generally made for a payment bond when a performance bond is being purchased, the two are usually issued simultaneously.

In public projects, in which the filing of mechanics and materialmen's liens is usually prohibited, the payment bond is even more important and is frequently required by statute.[51] It provides a fund for payment if the general contractor has been dishonest, and thus avoids petitions by subcontractors to legislative bodies for more money to cover the contractor's default.

It is necessary for the payment bond to define the extent of its coverage in terms of layers of subcontractors and suppliers. The 1970 AIA form, for example, defines a "claimant" as "one having a direct contract with the Principal or with a Subcontractor of the Principal for labor, material, or both * * *."[52] Thus, second-tier claimants (sub-subs) are covered, while third-tier claimants (sub-sub-subs) are not.

The payment bond surety is generally entitled to raise as against the owner-obligee the various defenses discussed above in connection with performance bonds. Against third-party beneficiaries of the bond, such as subcontractors and suppliers, however, it is likely that only defenses as to which the claimant has some fault can be asserted. For example, a subcontractor can generally maintain an action on a payment bond despite the fraud of the general contractor or the

49. See Amelco Window Corp. v. Federal Ins. Co., 127 N.J.Super. 342, 317 A.2d 398 (1974).

50. See R. C. Mahon Co. v. Hedrich Constr. Co., 69 Wis.2d 456, 230 N.W.2d 621 (1975); Byler v. Great American Ins. Co., 395 F.2d 273 (C.A.Okl.1968). There is no necessity that the claimant even knew of the bond at the time he supplied his work or materials; Air Temperature, Inc. v. Morris, 469 S.W.2d 495 (Tenn.App.1970). See also Sukut-Coulson, Inc. v. Allied Canon Co., 85 Cal.App.3d 648, 149 Cal.Rptr. 711 (1978) (public project).

51. See note 27, supra.

52. See note 26, supra.

owner in inducing the surety to write the bond, or the default of the owner in complying with the bond's terms.[53]

The dual obligee bond. Construction lenders sometimes feel a need for the same type of protection which performance and payment bonds afford to owners. The dual obligee bond, which names both the lender and the owner as obligees, accomplishes this.[54] However, nearly every dual obligee bond contains a so-called "savings clause" or "Los Angeles clause," which in substance provides that any default by either obligee will release the surety from its obligation to both.[55] The surety's main concern here is the same as that which led to the disuse of the completion bond—that one of the obligees will interfere with the flow of funds to the contractor. The surety fears that the construction lender might refuse to make proper disbursements, or the owner might intercept disbursements and divert them. The consequence of the savings clause is that the dual obligee bond protects the lender against the defaults of the contractor, but not those of the owner. This fact has great impact, since trouble on the job may well lead the owner to commit a technical default as well: he may advance funds to the contractor prematurely, or may grant a contract modification or extension of time without the surety's consent. Although there are few cases,[56] it seems probable that under the savings clause this sort of behavior will discharge the surety (at least

53. See United States Fidelity & Guar. Co. v. Borden Metal Products Co., 539 S.W.2d 170 (Tex.Civ.App.1976); Guin & Hunt, Inc. v. Hughes Supply, Inc., 335 So.2d 842 (Fla.App.1976); Filippi v. McMartin, 188 Cal.App.2d 135, 10 Cal.Rptr. 180 (1961); Williams v. Baldwin, 228 S.W. 554 (Tex.Comm.App.1921); Culligan Corp. v. Transamerica Ins. Co., 580 F.2d 251 (C.A.Ind.1978).

54. Other parties may also be made obligees, although the practice is infrequent: a title company, a major tenant of the project, or a permanent lender. See Leake, Contract Bond Co-obligees—Rights and Responsibilities, 37 Ins.Counsel J. 554 (1970).

55. A simple, although quite ambiguous, form of the clause states:

> Any default by either or both of the obligees will automatically relieve the principal and the surety from the performance of the contract.

A more comprehensive form is:

> The surety shall not be liable under this bond to the obligees, or either of them unless the said obligees, or either of them, shall make payments to the principal, strictly in accordance with the terms of said contract as to payments and shall perform all other obligations to be performed under said contract at the time and in the manner therein set forth.

See R. Kratovil, Modern Mortgage Law & Practice 145–46 (1973); Robinson, The Multiple Obligee Construction Bond: A Problem for the Surety, 15 So.Tex.L.J. 181 (1974); Franklin, Dual Obligee Bond—What Constitutes "Default" of an Obligee, 17 Federation Ins.Coun.Q. 51 (No. 4, Summer 1967). The latter clause above was used in the bond litigated in New Amsterdam Cas. Co. v. Bettes, 407 S.W.2d 307 (Tex.Civ.App.1966).

56. In New Amsterdam Cas. Co. v. Bettes, 407 S.W.2d 307 (Tex.Civ.App. 1966), the court held that the owner's knowledge that funds were being disbursed to the contractor on the basis of falsified affidavits would not be attributable to the lender; thus, the lender's rights against the surety on the dual obligee bond were preserved.

pro tanto, and perhaps absolutely) as to both obligees. To the lender, then, the dual obligee bond does not constitute very adequate protection.[57]

Surety's priority in undisbursed funds. Space does not permit comprehensive treatment here of another common problem with construction bonds: the priority as between the surety and other claimants with respect to the undisbursed construction funds. Frequently the other claimant is a lending institution (not the construction lender) which has advanced money to the contractor. The issue may arise as follows. The contractor is midway through the project and finds that, despite the receipt of regular progress payments from the owner or construction lender, he is unable to meet his obligations to his workmen or suppliers. To solve this problem he obtains a bank loan, assigning as security for its repayment the payments he expects to receive in the future from the owner. Subsequently he is unable to complete the job or to pay his subcontractors, and the surety steps in and does so. As between the surety and the bank, which is entitled to first priority in the remainder of the contract price, as represented by the balance in the construction loan account?

In Prairie State Bank v. United States,[58] the Supreme Court held for the surety on similar facts, reasoning that the surety was subrogated to the rights of the owner against the defaulting contractor, and that this subrogation dated, in effect, from the time the contract and bond were signed, thus being prior to the bank's assignment.[59] The bank's argument, however, is also appealing, particularly if it can show that the loan it made was used to pay for labor or materials on the job, and perhaps was even required by the bank to be so used. On these facts, the bank loan has reduced the surety's potential liability. This argument, however, is typically rejected on the ground that the bank was a mere volunteer in this role, while the surety was contractually bound by its bond.

57. See Kratovil & Werner, Mortgages for Construction and the Lien Priorities Problem—the "Unobligatory" Advance, 41 Tenn.L.Rev. 311, 321 (1974); sources cited note 55, supra.

58. 164 U.S. 227, 17 S.Ct. 142, 41 L.Ed. 412 (1896). See also Henningsen v. United States Fidelity & Guar. Co., 208 U.S. 404, 28 S.Ct. 389, 52 L.Ed. 547 (1908) and Pearlman v. Reliance Ins. Co., 371 U.S. 132, 83 S.Ct. 232, 9 L.Ed.2d 190 (1962), reaffirming the rule of *Prairie*. The development of the law in the federal courts is well summarized in American Fidelity Fire Ins. Co. v. Construcciones Werl, 407 F.Supp. 164, 191–97 (D.St.Croix 1975). See also Dauer, Government Contractors, Commercial Banks, and Miller Act Bond Sureties—A Question of Priorities, 14 B.C.Indus. & Com.L. Rev. 943 (1973); Rudolph, Financing on Construction Contracts Under the Uniform Commercial Code, 5 B.C.Indus. & Com.L.Rev. 245 (1964); Jordan, The Rights of a Surety Upon the Default of its Contractor-Principal, 41 Ore.L.Rev. 1 (1961).

59. The bond or bond application will frequently contain language by which the contractor purports to assign to the surety the funds he expects to receive under the contract, but even in the absence of such language the subrogation theory of *Prairie* still obtains.

While the federal courts have followed *Prairie* quite consistently,[60] state courts have shown more variability. Surveying these cases, one commentator concluded that "while the surety generally wins, assignee banks prevail just often enough to maintain the flow of litigation." [61] It now is settled that the surety need not file a financing statement under the Uniform Commercial Code, even if the competing creditor does so.[62] Cases sometimes turn on whether the surety knew of or approved the obtaining of the bank loan, whether the fund being contested consists of percentage retainages or of earned but undisbursed progress payments, whether the bank insisted that its loan be used on the job, or whether the project is public or private.[63] Since both claimants are innocent, and both have contributed to the completion of the work, a choice between them is difficult.

The surety may sometimes find itself in a contest with others for the undisbursed contract funds. Mechanic's and materialmen's lien claimants may assert a priority, particularly in those states which give such claimants a statutory right in the undisbursed contract funds.[64] Other creditors of the contractor may make similar claims; even the owner himself may seek a setoff against the contract price, perhaps because of defective work done or damage caused by the contractor.[65] Again, these cases defy generalization, and the reader is referred to detailed discussions of them in the literature.[66]

60. See, e. g., Great American Ins. Co. v. United States, 203 Ct.Cl. 592, 492 F.2d 821 (1974); Framingham Trust Co. v. Gould-National Batteries, Inc., 427 F.2d 856 (C.A.Mass.1970); American Fidelity Fire Ins. Co. v. Construcciones Werl, supra note 58 and cases cited therein.

61. Rudolph, Financing on Construction Contracts Under the Uniform Commercial Code, 5 B.C.Indus. & Com.L.Rev. 245 (1964); see First Vermont Bank v. Village of Poultney, 134 Vt. 28, 349 A.2d 722 (1975).

62. See First Alabama Bank v. Hartford Accident & Indemnity Co., Inc., 430 F.Supp. 907 (N.D.Ala.1977); Finance Co. of America v. United States Fidelity & Guar. Co., 277 Md. 177, 353 A.2d 249 (1976); Argonaut Ins. Co. v. C and S Bank of Tipton, 140 Ga.App. 807, 232 S.E.2d 135 (1976); Note, Equitable Subrogation—Too Hardy a Plant to be Uprooted by Article 9 of the UCC? 32 U. of Pitts.L.R. 580 (1971).

63. See Rudolph, supra note 61 at 248–49. See, e. g., First Nat. Bank v. McHasco Electric Inc., 273 Minn. 407, 141 N.W.2d 491 (1966). In Nat. Surety Co. v. State Nat. Bank, 454 S.W.2d 354 (Ky.App.1970), the court held for the assignee bank on the ground that the surety had acquiesced in the contractor's seeking the bank loan, which occurred after the surety had taken over the project.

64. See § 12.4, infra.

65. In United States v. Munsey Trust Co., 332 U.S. 234, 67 S.Ct. 1599, 91 L.Ed. 2022 (1947), the Court held that the set-off claim of the United States as owner had priority over the claim of the surety; see also Safeco Ins. Co. v. State, 89 Misc.2d 864, 392 N.Y.S.2d 976 (1977); American Fidelity Fire Ins. Co. v. Construcciones Werl, supra note 58 and cases cited therein.

66. See sources cited note 58, supra

§ 12.3 Mortgage Loan Commitments

A loan commitment is a promise by a lender to make a loan at some future time. Both construction and permanent loans are frequently preceded by written commitments.[67] For the developer of a new project, the construction loan commitment is a signal that the search for construction financing is over. Before the commitment is issued, the developer has usually completed most or all of the other arrangements for construction, including land acquisition, basic project design, and the preliminary negotiation of the construction contract. Thus, construction will typically commence within a short time after the commitment is issued, after the developer has made whatever modifications and final touches the committing lender requires.

The permanent loan commitment, a promise by a lender to make a long-term loan on the property when construction is completed, is of critical importance. From the developer's viewpoint, it represents assurance that marketing of the project can be financed (if sales-type development, such as a residential subdivision, is involved), or that funds will be available to pay the construction loan when it is due at the time of completion. This sort of assurance is at least as important to the construction lender as to the developer. As a result of regulatory requirements,[68] internal policies, or both, the great majority of construction lenders will not issue *their* commitment until a permanent or "take-out" loan commitment has first been obtained.[69]

The permanent loan commitment will usually be based on the same underwriting considerations as the construction loan: the borrower's credit, the project's design and technical feasibility, an appraisal of its completed value and marketability, and the satisfaction

67. Calif.Cont.Ed. of Bar, California Real Estate Sales Transactions § 10.-42 (1967). A writing is probably required under the Statute of Frauds in most jurisdictions; compare Fremming Constr. Co. v. Security Sav. & Loan Ass'n, 115 Ariz. 514, 566 P.2d 315 (1977), with Martyn v. First Federal Sav. & Loan Ass'n, 257 So.2d 576 (Fla.App.1971). The person issuing the commitment must be authorized to do so; Labor Discount Center, Inc. v. State Bank & Trust Co., 526 S.W.2d 407 (Mo.App.1975). In Walter Harvey Corp. v. O'Keefe, 346 So.2d 617 (Fla.App.1977), the construction lender advanced an additional $450,000, over and above its original loan commitment, in order to cover cost overruns. Even this amount was not sufficient to complete the project, and the developer claimed that the lender was legally obligated to advance even more funds. The court held that the making of one optional advance did not impliedly obligate the lender to make another, and that the lender was entitled to foreclose.

68. See, e. g., Federal Reserve Act § 24, 12 U.S.C.A. § 371; McKinney's N.Y. Banking Law § 103:4(c)(3)(iv). See text § 12.1 at notes 5–9, supra.

69. Haggerty, Procedures, Forms and Safeguards in Construction Lending with a Permanent Takeout, 85 Banking L.J. 1035 (1968). Alternatively, the construction lender may accept a commitment from a high-credit purchaser to *buy* the project (not merely the mortgage) upon completion.

of various title and other legal requirements.[70] Neither the construction nor permanent lender can afford to leave the evaluation of these matters to the other; both must do a thorough underwriting job if they are prudent, since it is impossible to tell at the commitment stage which of them might eventually foreclose on the property. The requirements of the two lenders must not be inconsistent, and the construction commitment will usually require that the developer comply with all terms of the permanent commitment.

Loan commitments are usually hedged with numerous conditions to protect the lender's interests.[71] In a sales-type project such as a subdivision or a condominium, the evaluation of the credit-worthiness of the future purchasers of the units is impossible at the outset of construction; thus the permanent loan commitment for such a project is invariably conditioned upon the purchasers' compliance with the lender's customary standards (which may be articulated in the commitment itself), or the standards of the Federal Housing Administration or other insurance or guaranty agency.[72] Other common conditions include submission to the lender of final plans and specifications (if the commitment is issued on the basis of preliminary versions or if the lender has required changes) and submission of other documentation, including the executed construction contract, the documents creating the developer entity (if a corporation, partnership, or trust), leases executed by the major tenants, the title insurance report and binder, the permanent loan commitment if a construction loan is being made, the building permit, and perhaps an opinion of counsel respecting the validity of the developer entity's creation, its power to undertake the project, and validity of the other documents. In a permanent loan commitment on a project to be built, lien-free completion in accordance with the agreed plans and specifications will be made a condition.

The permanent commitment on a rental project, such as an apartment building or office building, may also be conditioned upon some specified fraction of the project being rented. More complex arrangements are sometimes used, so that a portion of the permanent loan will be funded at a given rental level (the "floor"), and the remainder when a higher rental level (the "ceiling") has been achieved.

70. See text, § 12.1 at note 18, supra.

71. See R. Kratovil, Modern Real Estate Documentation 185–197 (1975).

72. The FHA itself issues conditional commitments to insure permanent loans based on its approval of plans and specifications and its inspections as houses are constructed. The relevant form, FHA 2800–5, provides:

"The mortgage amount and term set forth in the heading are the maximum approved for this property assuming a satisfactory owner-occupant mortgagor. The maximum amount and term in the heading may be changed depending upon FHA's rating of the borrower, his income and credit. * * * A firm commitment to insure a loan will be issued upon receipt of an Application for Credit Approval, FHA form 2900, executed by an approved mortgagee and a borrower satisfactory to the Commissioner."

Obviously a permanent commitment conditioned upon rent-up is less satisfactory to the construction lender than an unconditional commitment, but such conditions are commonly accepted. If the construction lender demands payment before a sufficient number of tenants has been found to meet the permanent lender's rent roll requirements, the developer may be able to obtain an interim or "bridge" loan to carry him through the rent-up period.

The commitment will, of course, fully identify the project and the parties, including the general contractor, if any. It will state the amount of the loan and the period within which the loan closing must occur. The plans and specifications, the construction loan agreement, and the form of note and mortgage which the lender proposes to require will usually be incorporated by reference in the commitment on a construction loan. The interest rate and fees to be charged for the loan will be specified, as well as the fee for the commitment itself. Such fees vary with the duration, type, and amount of the commitment, but are frequently in the 1 to 2 percent range. In some cases permanent loan commitments on residential subdivisions are issued and are acceptable to construction lenders without stipulation of the interest rate. Since such commitments do not shift the risk of fluctuating rates to the permanent lender, they may be obtained at a lower cost than is usually charged for a fixed-interest commitment and may even be issued free or at a nominal charge.

Many lenders who issue fixed-interest permanent loan commitments do soon the basis of commitments which they, in turn, have obtained from the Federal National Mortgage Association (FNMA) to purchase mortgages to be made in the future. FNMA has used a variety of advance commitment programs in the past,[73] and at this writing has two such programs in operation.[74] Under its four-month commitment program, interested mortgage lenders "bid" for available funds from FNMA in a bi-weekly telephone auction; thus yields on mortgages are fixed by the forces of supply and demand in the auction, which FNMA terms its "free market system." [75] A commitment

73. Gladhill, FMS Action Rates: Do They Lead or Follow the Market?, FNMA Seller/Servicer, Mar.–Apr. 1977, at 13.

74. FNMA Selling Agreement Supplement §§ 203–04. The Federal Home Loan Mortgage Corporation (FHLMC) has also experimented with advance commitment mortgage purchase programs. On the general operation of both of these agencies, see § 11.3, infra.

75. An illustration of the telephone auction may be helpful. In one recent auction FNMA received telephone bids for $93.5 million in FHA/VA mortgages. Each bidder states the yield (effective interest rate to FNMA) which the mortgages he proposes to sell will carry. Naturally, FNMA accepts the bids bearing the highest yields; it does not necessarily accept all bids made. In the illustrative auction, it accepted $60 million, with the highest-yielding bid at 8.939 percent and the lowest accepted bid at 8.787 percent. The average yield of all bids accepted was 8.828 percent. In that auction, FNMA received 176 bids and accepted 140. FHA/VA and conventional mortgages are handled in separate

fee of 0.5 percent is charged. FNMA's other program makes available 12-month "standby" commitments at higher-than-current-market yields which are announced periodically by the Association.[76] This program's principal purpose is to assist builders in obtaining construction financing by providing a permanent commitment. In many cases the commitment will not actually be used, and it may be converted to a four-month commitment at then-current auction yields. The stand-by commitment costs 0.5 percent when issued, and an additional 0.5 percent when and if mortgages are actually delivered under it. These fees are paid directly by the lending institution obtaining the commitment, but are usually passed on immediately to the builder if new housing construction is to be financed by the commitment. The commitment issued to the builder by the lender is usually on terms substantially identical to the lender's commitment from FNMA.

The standby commitment concept is not limited to home loans on subdivision tracts. In commercial or income-producing properties as well, the developer may seek a standby commitment from an interim lender on very onerous terms in order to give himself more time to locate permanent financing.[77] The standby commitment will often carry a costly fee, as much as 3 to 5 percent of the amount committed, and will bear a high interest rate and a short maturity if it is

auctions, although they are usually held on the same day. The interest rates mentioned above may seem confusing since they are carried to three decimal places. However, the actual mortgage notes which borrowers will sign under these commitments will carry interest rates stated in eighths, or tenths of a percent, and in the case of FHA/VA mortgages, will normally be made at the maximum currently permitted by FHA and VA (8.5 percent at the time of the auction described above). The yield to FNMA produced by the mortgage is increased by FNMA's purchasing the loan at a discount—that is, by paying less than the face amount of the outstanding balance at the time the mortgage is delivered to FNMA. Obviously, if FNMA pays less than 100 percent of the face amount of a loan which nominally produces 8.5 percent interest, the effective yield to FNMA is greater than 8.5 percent.

A standard set of tables is used to convert yields on accepted commitments into equivalent discount prices. The prices are usually expressed as percentages of face value. Thus, if FNMA were committed to pay a price of 95 on a $30,000 mortgage, the dollar price would be $28,500. The conversion tables are based on the assumption that the loan will be prepaid in 12 years. To illustrate their operation, a yield of 8.828 percent (the average bid in the auction discussed above) converts to a price of 97.70, or a discount of 2.30 percent. The lending institution which originates the loan normally does not absorb the discount, but instead passes it on (along with the FNMA commitment fee) to the builder or seller of the house. Under current law and regulations it cannot be paid by the borrower on an FHA or VA loan, but there is generally no such restriction on conventional loans. See § 11.2, infra, concerning FHA and VA programs.

76. For example, at the time of the free market auction described in the preceding footnote, which resulted in average yields of 8.828 percent (FHA/VA) and 9.004 percent (conventional), the corresponding yields fixed by FNMA for standby commitments were 9.550 percent and 9.700 percent.

77. See, e. g., Prac.L.Inst., Real Estate Financing: Contemporary Techniques 313 (No. 14, 1973).

ever actually funded. But its real purpose is to satisfy the construction lender's requirement that a take-out commitment exist; the developer has no intention of using it. He may well feel that more attractive permanent financing will be available when construction is completed, either because of changes in money market conditions or because the building will then be fully built and rented and thus appear less risky to a permanent lender. The standby lender's position is obviously risky, and this fact accounts for the high cost of his involvement. Sometimes a construction lender will itself issue a standby commitment as well; in substance, this is its way of contracting for substantially increased interest and fees if the construction loan is not paid off immediately upon completion.[78]

Lender's fees and enforcement rights. The cost to the prospective borrower of obtaining a loan commitment varies widely. On permanent commitments for existing owner-occupied houses, some lenders charge nothing and others charge only an appraisal fee of, say $50 to $75. At the other extreme are construction and permanent loan commitments on large income-producing properties where the borrower will usually be required to cover all of the lender's out-of-pocket costs, such as the appraiser's, attorney's, architect's and engineer's fees. These fees are typically nonrefundable, irrespective of whether a satisfactory commitment is ever issued or a loan ever made. Since such fees can add up substantially, a developer is often well-advised to obtain the appraisal as early as possible, so that he can seek other financing without much loss if the appraisal is too low to make possible an attractive loan.[79]

Another type of fee, which must be paid by the borrower upon the issuance of the commitment, is the nonrefundable commitment fee. Its apparent purpose is to compensate the lender for the opportunity cost and administrative burden of underwriting the loan and holding the funds available for the borrower's use.

Finally, many lenders, especially permanent lenders on new income-properties, require that the borrower post a "good faith deposit," sometimes termed a "security" or "standby" deposit, when the commitment is issued.[80] If the loan is actually made, the deposit is refunded or applied against the borrower's obligations toward interest and loan fees; but if the borrower does not draw down the loan, the deposit will be forfeited. Obviously, the deposit is intended to discourage the borrower from "walking away"—i. e., seeking financing from another source on more attractive terms.

78. See Prac.L.Inst., Real Estate Construction 225 (No. 5, 1969).

79. R. Kratovil, Modern Real Estate Documentation § 434 (1975).

80. See Prac.L.Inst. Real Estate Construction 327–31 (No. 5, 1969); Levenson v. Barnett Bank of Miami, 330 So.2d 192 (Fla.App.1976); White Lakes Shopping Center, Inc. v. Jefferson Standard Life Ins. Co., 208 Kan. 121, 490 P.2d 609 (1971).

The commitment-related fees just discussed should not be confused with interest and fees on the loan itself.[81] In many cases the lender will charge a "processing fee" or "origination fee" if and when the loan is made, ostensibly to cover the administrative cost and overhead of putting the loan "on the books." In some cases, however, these fees substantially exceed the lender's costs, and amount to a form of prepaid interest, raising the lender's overall yield on the loan. Such fees are common in a wide range of loan types, from single-family residences to large commercial projects. In addition, in FHA or VA transactions, in which the face interest rate on the note is limited to a below-market level by government regulation, the lender will usually charge "discounts" or "points" to the builder or seller in order to raise the effective yield on the loan to a competitive level.[82]

A loan commitment usually makes it clear that the lender is legally obligated to loan in the event all of the stated conditions are fulfilled. Rather surprisingly, many commitments are so poorly drafted that they leave unclear whether the borrower has a corresponding obligation to follow through and obtain the loan. In most single-family home loan commitments, commitments issued to lenders by FNMA, and in standby commitments,[83] it is apparent that the party receiving the commitment has no obligation to use it, so in effect, the commitment gives the prospective mortgagor an option to borrow. But in loans on income properties, it is often ambiguous whether the borrower has an obligation to borrow the funds.[84]

If a developer to whom a commitment has been issued declines to borrow (presumably because he has found a better deal elsewhere), what remedies can the lender assert? If the loan applicant has deposited fees which by the commitment's terms are nonrefundable, the courts have uniformly allowed the lender to retain them.[85] But if the

81. The distinction between commitment fees and loan fees was significant for usury purposes in Gonzales County Sav. & Loan Ass'n v. Freeman, 534 S.W.2d 903 (Tex.1976), holding the former outside the usury statute. See also Meadow Brook Nat. Bank v. Recile, 302 F.Supp. 62 (E.D.La.1969).

82. See note 75, supra; § 11.2 infra.

83. See Prac.L.Inst., Real Estate Financing: Contemporary Techniques 177–78 (No. 14, 1973).

84. See, e. g., Lowe v. Massachusetts Mutual Life Ins. Co., 54 Cal.App.3d 718, 127 Cal.Rptr. 23 (1976); Goldman v. Connecticut General Life Ins. Co., 251 Md. 575, 248 A.2d 154 (1968). Both cases hold the commitment to be an option to the borrower, but with no clear language in the documents to support the conclusion. A set of letters which reads much like a construction loan commitment was held too vague to be enforced in Willowood Condominium Ass'n, Inc. v. HNC Realty Co., 531 F.2d 1249 (C.A.Tex.1976); see also Wheeler v. White, 385 S.W.2d 619 (Tex.Civ.App.1964) reversed 398 S.W.2d 93.

85. Lowe v. Massachusetts Mut. Life Ins. Co., 54 Cal.App.3d 718, 127 Cal.Rptr. 23 (1976); Suitt Constr. Co. Inc., v. Seaman's Bank for Sav., 30 N.C.App. 155, 226 S.E.2d 408 (1976), holding the applicable law is that of the

lender seeks additional relief, he has several barriers to overcome. First, he must persuade the court that the borrower has an affirmative obligation to borrow, and not merely an option; this is typically a matter of construction of the commitment.[86] Second, he may be faced with the argument that the "good faith deposit" is, in substance, a liquidated damages clause, and that its retention is the sole valid remedy at law for the prospective borrower's default. The situation is arguably analogous to a buyer's "earnest money deposit" in a contract to purchase a house; if the seller reserves the right to retain the deposit, it is often held that he can recover no additional damages.[87] In principle, this issue is also a matter of interpretation of the commitment agreement,[88] but if the good faith deposit is substantial, it would not be surprising for a court to hold it is the lend-

place at which the lender receives the borrower's signed acceptance of the commitment. Other cases are collected in Groot, Specific Performance of Constructs to Provide Permanent Financing, 60 Cornell L.Rev. 719, 729 n. 49. In Levenson v. Barnett Bank of Miami, 330 So.2d 192 (Fla.App. 1976), the court held that the developer could recover his "standby" deposit if he could show that the lender had not in fact been able and prepared to make the loan, since the very purpose of that deposit had been to compensate the lender for holding itself "in readiness." The court distinguished and denied the developer's attempt to recover his commitment fee, which the agreement expressly made nonrefundable; it found that this fee's purpose was to compensate the lender for its time and expense in underwriting the loan.

86. The "option" interpretation has been adopted frequently; see Financial Federal Sav. & Loan Ass'n v. Burleigh House, Inc., 305 So.2d 59 (Fla.App.1974) certiorari denied 429 U.S. 1042, 97 S.Ct. 742, 50 L.Ed.2d 754; D & M Development Co. v. Sherwood & Roberts, Inc., 93 Idaho 200, 457 P.2d 439 (1969); cases cited note 84, supra.

87. See, e. g., Brewer v. Myers, 545 S. W.2d 235 (Tex.Civ.App.1976); Coca-Cola Bottling Works (Thomas) Inc. v. Hazard Coca-Cola Bottling Works, Inc., 450 S.W.2d 515 (Ky.App.1970); Alois v. Waldman, 219 Md. 369, 149 A.2d 406 (1959); Andreason v. Hansen, 8 Utah 2d 370, 335 P.2d 404 (1959); C. McCormick, Damages § 152 (1935). Of course, this conclusion is easy if the contract provides that the vendor's sole damages remedy is retention of the deposit, as is usually the case in California, see Calif.Cont.Ed. of Bar, California Real Estate Sales Transaction §§ 4.67, 11.50 (1967), or if the contract provides that the vendor must elect between retention and other remedies, and he in fact retains the deposit, see G. H. Swope Bldg. Corp. v. Horton, 207 Tenn. 114, 338 S.W.2d 566 (1960); McMullin v. Shimmin, 10 Utah 2d 142, 349 P.2d 720 (1960). See generally M. Friedman, Contracts and Conveyances of Real Property § 12.1(c) (3d ed. 1975); D. Dobbs, Remedies § 12.5 (1973), at 825.

88. In well-drafted commitments, language is employed to clarify the existence of additional remedies (usually in favor of their existence, since the lender is the draftsman). For example:

> It is understood that the foregoing provision for retention of the deposit shall not constitute an option on Borrower's part not to complete the Loan transaction herein contemplated, but that Lener reserves any and all rights which it may have in law or in equity, including but not limited to specific performance.

ABA Sec. of Real Prop., Probate & Trust Law, The Lawyer's Role in Financing the Real Estate Development 36 (Probate & Prop. Cassette Series, Vol. 1, No. 3, 1975). See also Goldman v. Connecticut General Life Ins. Co., 251 Md. 575, 248 A.2d 154 (1968).

er's exclusive remedy. It appears that no reported case deals with this point.[89]

Assuming the lender can overcome these barriers, he is rather clearly entitled to damages against the defaulting commitment-holder. Presumably damages can be shown only if mortgage market conditions have changed so that the lender must place the loan funds with another borrower at lower interest or fees. Damages would then be computed as the difference between the discounted present values of the stream of loan fees and payments the lender would have received if the original loan had been made and the stream of such fees and payments it will be able to earn on alternate investments available at the time of the breach. Discounting should be at the interest rate prevailing in the relevant mortgage market at the date of the breach.[90] Interest on the sum thus computed should be added, again preferably at prevailing mortgage market rates, to the date of judgment.[91] The formulation suggested here presumes that the lender has mitigated its damages by re-lending at prevailing rates the money which the original loan applicant did not draw down; whether the lender actually re-lends at inferior rates, or not at all, is immaterial. The lender can presumably claim its out-of-pocket expenses, such as legal and architect's fees, as additional damages, but it must obviously offset against this claim all such amounts paid to or for it by the loan applicant.

The fact that damages are readily computable suggests that specific performance will not be available to the lender; [92] its remedy at

89. See Groot, Specific Performance of Contracts to Provide Permanent Financing, 60 Cornell L.Rev. 718, 730 n. 50 (1975).

90. The cases which deal with discounting of future income streams contribute little on the appropriate discount rate. See generally D. Dobbs, Remedies 178 (1973). Some courts use statutory or arbitrary rates, but when the breach is so intimately tied to a particular money market, it seems fairest to use the rate prevailing in that market. One may think of the lender as receiving his damages award at the moment of breach and immediately investing it at the then-available rate. In addition, the rate at the date of breach will usually be lower than the rate specified in the commitment (the fall in rates frequently being the very reason for the commitment-holder's breach); the lower rate will produce a larger measure of damages for the lender, which seems reasonable, since the lender is the non-breaching party. Cf. Groot, supra note 89, at 732, advocating interest at mortgage market rates as of the date of judgment.

91. The damages in this sort of case are sufficiently analogous to "liquidated" damages that a court should have no difficulty in awarding interest on them from the date of breach to the date of judgment; see D. Dobbs, Remedies 165–74 (1973). Again, the prevailing rate for mortgages of the type involved should be used in computing interest on the damages, since this is precisely how the lender would have invested the funds if he had been awarded them on the date of breach.

92. An argument that the good faith deposit is a liquidated damages clause, and thus bars other remedies, will be unavailing as a defense to a specific performance suit by the lender; only damages actions are barred by this theory. See cases cited note 87, supra; D. Dobbs, Remedies § 12.5 (1973), at 825.

law is usually entirely adequate.[93] The lender might argue that it had bargained for an interest in land, and that by analogy to land contract cases which hold every parcel of realty to be unique, specific performance should be granted.[94] But the situations are not analogous, for the lender's concern is only with the land's value as security, and not with its individual characteristics as such. Even an express clause in the commitment making it enforceable in specie is unlikely to impress an equity court. Perhaps the only situation imaginable in which specific performance should be awarded is upon a showing by the lender that no comparable investment alternatives were available to it at the time of the breach. If this is the case (which is exceedingly improbable), damages will be more difficult to compute and specific performance arguably the only feasible remedy. Even here, specific performance is both literally impossible and nonsensical if the developer has actually obtained a permanent first mortgage loan from another lender, so that the original lender cannot have the prior lien for which it contracted, or if the project has been abandoned prior to completion, so that the conditions of the original commitment cannot be fulfilled.

Lenders rarely sue holders of loan commitments for breach. Possible reasons are that the right to recover is tenuous under many commitment forms, the fees and deposits retained by lenders are often adequate recompense for their damages, and in the case of incompleted projects, the prospective borrowers are usually insolvent. In an effort to avoid the necessity of suit, while maximizing the probability that the permanent loan will actually be drawn down, some lenders enter into a "buy-sell agreement" rather than issuing a loan commitment.[95] The buy-sell agreement contemplates that upon completion of construction, the construction loan itself will begin to require regular payments of interest and amortization and will be purchased by the permanent lender from the construction lender. The permanent lender has the added advantage of a priority dating from the commencement of construction, which means that any mechanics' liens filed during construction will be subordinate if all con-

93. See Groot, supra note 89, at 727–36; cf. Draper, The Broken Commitment: A Modern View of the Mortgage Lender's Remedy, 59 Cornell L. Rev. 418 (1974). Groot effectively dispatches Draper's arguments that damages are an inadequate remedy.

94. See D. Dobbs, Remedies § 12.10 (1973); Kitchen v. Herring, 42 N.C. 190 (1851). Cf. Centex Homes Corp. v. Boag, 128 N.J.Super. 385, 320 A.2d 194 (1974), denying specific performance to the vendor-builder of a unit in a large condominium project on the ground that the property was not unique.

95. See Haggarty, Procedures, Forms and Safeguards in Construction Lending with a Permanent Takeout, 85 Banking L.J. 1035, 1053 (1968); Prac. L.Inst., Real Estate Construction 327 (No. 5, 1969). The buy-sell agreement is executed by the construction and permanent lenders, and is usually endorsed by the borrower. Such an agreement is illustrated in Equity Associates v. Society for Savings, 31 N.C.App. 182, 228 S.E.2d 761 (1976) certiorari denied 291 N.C. 711, 232 S.E.2d 203, in which the permanent lender refused to purchase the loan.

struction advances have been obligatory.[96] There is thus no opportunity for the developer to find better permanent financing during the construction period; he is locked into the agreement contained in the original documents. If the permanent lender must sue, it will do so to recover on the note or to foreclose the mortgage; a "walk away" by the developer is most unlikely. From the construction lender's viewpoint, the buy-sell agreement is as satisfactory as a permanent loan commitment in most respects, although it does mean that the construction loan documents must be fully acceptable to the permanent lender. There is rarely a problem of unwillingness of the construction lender to sell the loan upon completion since most construction lenders have little desire to get into the long-term loan business. Finally, it should be noted that loan commitments and buy-sell agreements are fundamentally different types of contracts, and a court is unlikely to rewrite the former to make it the latter.[97] The permanent lender should make it perfectly clear whether it is promising to make a new loan or purchase an existing one.

Borrower's enforcement rights. Suppose a lender, despite having issued a loan commitment to a borrower, refuses to make the loan. Assuming that the borrower has met all conditions in the commitment, so that the refusal constitutes a breach, what remedies are available to the borrower? The answer seems to depend on whether the borrower has obtained another loan from an alternate source. If he has done so, and if the interest and fees on the new loan are not higher than under the old commitment, the borrower needs no remedy, aside from possible compensation for incidental or consequential damages. More frequently, however, the new loan will carry higher interest and fees, a reflection of the fact that market rates have risen since the commitment was issued—the very fact which may have induced the committing lender to breach. On these facts damages are an appropriate and adequate remedy. Their computation is similar to the calculation of lender's damages discussed above: the difference between the present values of the payments the borrower would have made under the original commitment and those he must make under reasonable alternative financing.[98] Obviously, the terms of the actual

96. See Selective Builders, Inc. v. Hudson City Sav. Bank, 137 N.J.Super. 500, 509 N. 4, 349 A.2d 564, 570 N. 4 (1975); § 12.7, infra.

97. See Exchange Bank & Trust Co. v. Lone Star Life Ins. Co., 546 S.W.2d 948 (Tex.Civ.App.1977).

98. See text at notes 90–91, supra; Pipkin v. Thomas & Hill, Inc., 33 N.C.App. 710, 236 S.E.2d 725 (1977); Annot., 36 A.L.R. 1408 (1925); 44 A.L.R. 1486 (1926). Many of the cases state the measure of damages too loosely, as the "difference in the interest rates" or the "increased interest," and provide no discussion of the present value aspect of the computation. See, e. g., Consolidated American Life Ins. Co. v. Covington, 297 So.2d 894 (Miss.1974); Archer-Daniels-Midland Co. v. Paull, 188 F.Supp. 277 (W.D.Ark.1960) reversed 293 F.2d 389, on remand 199 F.Supp 319, affirmed 313 F.2d 612 (C.A.Ark.1963); Annot., 36 A.L.R. 1408 (1925). At least one opinion expressly approves discounting the stream of damages to present value, but provides no indica-

substitute loan obtained will usually be excellent evidence of what is reasonably available in the market, particularly if the borrower shopped diligently for it.

The cases dealing with consequential damages suffered by erstwhile borrowers display a surprising diversity. Each element of damages must meet three initial tests: (1) it must have been "foreseeable" or "within the contemplation" of the parties to the loan commitment, (2) it must have been caused by the lender's breach, and (3) it must be proveable with reasonable precision. Clearly the borrower should recover commitment fees already paid to the breaching lender. Direct loan-related expenditures, such as architects', abstract, and title attorneys' fees, recording and notary charges, etc., usually qualify without difficulty.[99] Lost rents or profits have been allowed,[1] but usually only upon rather convincing proof that they would have been earned if the loan had been granted.[2] More remote damages,[3] such as the loss of favorable relations with subcontractors, damage to the borrower's credit standing, loss of a contractor's license, and even mental suffering,[4] are conceivable, though difficult to prove.

If the prospective borrower has been unable or unwilling to obtain another loan, his remedial picture is quite different. He may, of course, seek damages, and they will presumably be measured in the same fashion as described above.[5] It is more probable, however, that he will pray for specific performance of the commitment, hoping thereby to salvage his interest in the property. Manifold authorities hold that this remedy is unavailable for breach of a loan commitment, the remedy at law being fully adequate,[6] but in fact numerous

tion of the appropriate interest rate or method; Financial Federal Sav. & Loan Ass'n v. Continental Enterprises, Inc., 338 So.2d 907 (Fla.App.1976); see particularly the dissent of Pearson, J., arguing that the discount should not be at the statutory rate, but at a rate which is fair and just under the circumstances, taking into account current rates in the relevant money market.

99. Pipkin v. Thomas & Hill, Inc., 33 N.C.App. 710, 236 S.E.2d 725 (1977); Culp v. Western Loan & Bldg. Co., 124 Wash. 326, 214 P. 145 (1923) affirmed 127 Wash. 249, 220 P. 766.

1. Pasadena Associates v. Connor, 460 S.W.2d 473 (Tex.Civ.App.1970) refused n.r.e.; Archer-Daniels-Midland Co. v. Paull, 188 F.Supp. 277 (W.D.Ark.1960), reversed in part, 293 F.2d 389 (C.A.Ark.1961), order on remand affirmed 313 F.2d 612 (1963).

2. Such proof has often been unconvincing to the courts; see Davis v. Small Business Investment Co., 535 S.W.2d 740 (Tex.Civ.App.1976); Stanish v. Polish Roman Catholic Union, 484 F.2d 713 (C.A.Ind.1973); St. Paul at Chase Corp. v. Manufacturers Life Ins. Co., 262 Md. 192, 278 A.2d 12, certiorari denied 404 U.S. 857, 92 S.Ct. 104, 30 L.Ed.2d 98 (1971); Archer-Daniels-Midland Co. v. Paull, note 1, supra.

3. See Bank of New Mexico v. Rice, 78 N.M. 170, 429 P.2d 368 (1967), modified after remand, 79 N.M. 115, 440 P.2d 790 (1968).

4. See Westesen v. Olathe State Bank, 78 Colo. 217, 240 P. 689, 44 A.L.R. 1484 (1925).

5. See text at note 98, supra.

6. The classic case is Rogers v. Challis, 54 Eng.Rep. 68 (Ch.1859). See In-

cases have granted specific performance. Nearly all of these can be explained by the fact that the lender had already closed the loan, recorded his mortgage, and even made some disbursements before closing his credit window.[7] On such facts, the lender's actions will have made alternative first mortgage financing impossible; the mortgage encumbers the borrower's title, and no other lender will be able to secure a prior lien until the old mortgage is satisfied. Several of these cases have involved construction loans, with the attendant difficulty of refinancing a partially completed project. If the borrower is precluded from access to the mortgage market, the traditional measure of damages, which requires proof of the availability and cost of alternative loans, becomes meaningless, and specific performance is entirely appropriate.

Even if the prospective borrower has not executed a mortgage to the committing lender, he might be able to obtain a decree of specific performance if his efforts to obtain an alternate loan have been unsuccessful. It is difficult to apply the traditional measure of damages with confidence on these facts. Moreover, if the breached commitment is for a permanent loan at the completion of construction, the lender's default may result in consequential damages which will be difficult to quantify but are nonetheless harsh, including the besmirching of the developer's reputation and credit, and the possible inability of subcontractors and materials suppliers to collect for their contributions to the project.[8] The court seemed to recognize these factors in Selective Builders, Inc. v. Hudson City Savings Bank,[9] apparently the only American case granting specific performance when no mortgage had been executed to the lender.[10]

vestment Service Co. v. Smither, 276 Or. 837, 556 P.2d 955 (1976); Kent v. Walter E. Heller Co., 349 F.2d 480 (C.A.Ga.1965); Steward v. Bounds, 167 Wash. 554, 9 P.2d 1112 (1932), modified 170 Wash. 698, 15 P.2d 1119.

7. Vandeventer v. Dale Constr. Co., 271 Or. 691, 534 P.2d 183 (1975) appeal after remand 277 Or. 817, 562 P.2d 196; Cuna Mutual Ins. Society v. Dominguez, 9 Ariz.App. 172, 450 P.2d 413 (1969); Southhampton Wholesale Food Terminal, Inc. v. Providence Produce Warehouse Co., 129 F.Supp. 663 (D.Mass.1955); Jacobson v. First Nat. Bank, 129 N.J.Eq. 440, 20 A.2d 19, affirmed, 130 N.J.Eq. 604, 23 A.2d 409 (1941); Columbus Club v. Simons, 110 Okl. 48, 236 P. 12 (1925).

8. See generally Groot, Specific Performance of Contracts to Provide Permanent Financing, 60 Cornell L. Rev. 718, 741 (1975). Other damages in this situation, such as the loss of the project due to construction loan foreclosure, and a possible deficiency judgment, are more readily measurable. See St. Paul at Chase Corp. v. Manufacturers Life Ins. Co., 262 Md. 192, 278 A.2d 12, certiorari denied 404 U.S. 857, 92 S.Ct. 104, 30 L.Ed.2d 98 (1971).

9. 137 N.J.Super. 500, 349 A.2d 564 (1975).

10. In Leben v. Nassau Sav. & Loan Ass'n, 40 A.D.2d 830, 337 N.Y.S.2d 310 (1972), affirmed 34 N.Y.2d 671, 356 N.Y.S.2d 46, 312 N.E.2d 180 (1974), the permanent lender insisted on a higher interest rate at closing than had been agreed to in the commitment. The borrower signed the documents, but sought and obtained judicial reformation to readjust the interest rate downward. Some dicta in the opinion might to read as approving specific perform-

Not many specific performance cases have been decided, probably because the remedy is usually unattractive from the borrower's viewpoint. The delay inherent in litigation suggests that it is economically feasible only if the borrower has access to some interim financing while the case is pending (such as a construction loan which can be extended until the permanent financing becomes available as a result of the court's decree.)[11] Generally, an alternative loan and a suit for damages are more appealing, and if the project or the borrower is so weak that no other financing can be obtained, a court might infer that a decree of specific performance would also be inefficient and bad policy, constituting a futile effort to shore up an economically fatal situation; this risk would have to be balanced against the arguments favoring specific performance mentioned in the preceding paragraph.

The Securities and Exchange Act of 1934

In United States v. Austin,[12] the Tenth Circuit Court of Appeals considered a charge of criminal fraud against a lender based on the antifraud provisions of Section 10(b) of the Securities and Exchange Act of 1934.[13] In substance, the government argued that the lender had issued a mortgage loan commitment and charged a commitment fee with no intention of ever making the loan. The court concluded that the commitment letter was a "security" within the meaning of the Act, and upheld the defendants' conviction. If the holding were sound, civil remedies would be available as well.[14]

The decision, however, is of dubious validity, and its logical implications would cut a wide swath indeed: virtually every executory bilateral contract in which one party pays money consideration in return for the other's future performance would be a security. Plainly the commitment fee paid by a loan applicant is in no sense an "investment"; the applicant does not expect "profits to come solely from the efforts" of the lender.[15] Indeed, the lender's performance of its

ance, but on the facts the case is similar to those cited in note 6, supra, with reformation of future payments as a substitute for damages. See Groot, supra note 8, at 725–27.

11. Compare Selective Builders, Inc. v. Hudson City Sav. Bank, 137 N.J.Super. 500, 349 A.2d 564 (1975), in which the construction lender gave such an extension, making a specific performance suit feasible, with St. Paul at Chase Corp. v. Manufacturers Life Ins. Co., 262 Md. 192, 278 A.2d 12, certiorari denied 404 U.S. 857, 92 S.Ct. 104, 30 L.Ed.2d 98 (1971), in which the construction lender foreclosed and purchased the project, leaving the developer with only a suit for damages against the reneging permanent lender.

12. 462 F.2d 724 (C.A.Kan.1972), certiorari denied 409 U.S. 1048, 93 S.Ct. 518, 34 L.Ed.2d 501 (1972).

13. 15 U.S.C.A. § 78j(b) (1970).

14. See J. I. Case v. Borak, 377 U.S. 426, 84 S.Ct. 1555, 12 L.Ed.2d 423 (1964); Kardon v. National Gypsum Co., 73 F.Supp. 798 (E.D.Pa.1947), supplemented 83 F.Supp. 613.

15. S.E.C. v. W. J. Howey Co., 328 U.S. 293, 301, 66 S.Ct. 1100, 1104, 90 L.Ed. 1244 (1946).

commitment will ordinarily be entirely independent of its internal profitability during the commitment period. The commitment will yield the applicant neither capital appreciation nor a participation in earnings, but only a loan of money upon previously agreed terms. Any profits earned by the borrower will be attributable to his own entreprenurial and managerial efforts, not those of the lender.[16]

The Tenth Circuit appears to have repented of its holding in *Austin.* In McGovern Plaza Joint Venture v. First of Denver Mortgage Investors,[17] it held that neither the construction loan nor permanent loan commitments on hotel construction project were securities, lamely distinguishing *Austin* on the ground that it involved a "large-scale, advance fee loan swindle" in which the "entire procedure was fraudulent." It is difficult to see the relevance of the scale or gravity of the fraud in determining whether a security is being sold. *Austin* must be regarded as overruled,[18] but it contains a useful lesson. The issuance of a loan commitment may well be fraud under state law, if at the time of issuance the lender intends to breach. Both criminal and civil penalties may be applicable in many jurisdictions.

§ 12.4 Mechanics' Liens

Mechanics' and materialmen's liens, created by statute, give unpaid contractors, workmen, and materials suppliers a security interest in the real estate which they have improved; they may foreclose such liens as an aid to the recovery of the payment owed them. Although the legal scholar can find authority that a form of mechanics' lien existed in the Roman law,[19] was well developed in the civil law [20] and was incorporated in the Code Napoleon,[21] it was unknown in England, either at common law or in equity [22] and, so far as our

16. See United Housing Foundation, Inc. v. Forman, 421 U.S. 837, 95 S.Ct. 2051, 44 L.Ed.2d 621, rehearing denied 423 U.S. 884, 96 S.Ct. 157, 46 L.Ed.2d 115 and 423 U.S. 884, 96 S.Ct. 157, 46 L.Ed.2d 115 (1975).

17. 562 F.2d 645 (C.A.Colo.1977).

18. The *Austin* holding is rejected explicitly by Lee v. Navarro Sav. Ass'n, 416 F.Supp. 1186 (N.D.Tex.1976), and FBS Financial, Inc. v. Clevetrust Realty Investors, CCH Fed.Secur. Rptr. Par. 96,341 (1977), and implicitly by McClure v. First Nat. Bank, 352 F.Supp. 454 (N.D.Tex.1973). See also Sanders v. John Nuveen & Co., Inc., 463 F.2d 1075 (C.A.Ill.1972), certiorari denied 409 U.S. 1009, 93 S.Ct. 443, 34 L.Ed.2d 302.

19. Mackeldy, Handbook of the Roman Law, Dropsie's Translation, 274.

20. See Canal Co. v. Gordon, 73 U.S. (6 Wall.) 561, 571, 18 L.Ed. 894 (1867). Jones v. Great So. Fireproof Hotel Co., 86 F. 370, 386 (C.C.A.Ohio 1898), reversed 177 U.S. 449, 20 S.Ct. 690, 44 L.Ed. 842 (1900); 1 Domat, Civil Law, 1861 ed., 681–4, arts. 1736, 1741–5.

21. Code Napoleon, Privileges and Mortgages, § 2 (2103).

22. See Canal Co. v. Gordon, 73 U.S. (6 Wall.) 561, 571, 18 L.Ed. 894 (1867); Van Stone v. Stillwell & Bierce Mfg. Co., 142 U.S. 128, 136, 12 S.Ct. 181, 183, 35 L.Ed. 961 (1891). "Mechanic's liens on buildings and land, though recognized and favored by the civili-

present laws are concerned, is of native origin in the United States, dating back to the Maryland statute of 1791.[23] Today in every state in the Union such legislation exists,[24] but because the liens are wholly statutory, because the laws creating them are extremely varied both in their provisions and in the courts' construction of them, and because legislatures have been prolific with amendments, generalizations are extremely difficult and always must be checked against local enactments.[25] Furthermore, case law is unreliable in the field because the decisions are meaningful only with reference to the particular statute under which each arose and the precise language of the act at that time. This variability has been justified on the ground that the problems involved are dissimilar in different parts of the country,[26] even perhaps from state to state. This assertion is du-

ans, had no place in the common law, which, from its feudal character, was reluctant to subject realty to the payment of any claims other than feudal." Durling v. Gould, 83 Me. 134, 137, 21 A. 833 (1890).

23. Acts of General Assembly of Maryland, c. 45, § 10 (1791). "The origin of such laws, in America, arose from the desire to establish and improve, as readily as possible, the city of Washington. In 1791, at a meeting of the commissioners appointed for such purpose, both Thomas Jefferson and James Madison were present, and a memorial was adopted urging the General Assembly of Maryland to pass an act securing to *master-builders*, a lien, on houses erected, and land occupied. The requested law was enacted December 19, 1791." Moore-Mansfield Const. Co. v. Indianapolis N. C. & T. R. Co., 179 Ind. 356, 369, 101 N.E. 296, 44 L. R.A.,N.S. 816, Ann.Cas.1915D, 917 (1913). The next statute was in Pennsylvania in 1803. Act of April 1, 1803, P.L. 791; see Cushman, Proposed Mechanics' Lien Law, 80 U.Pa. L.Rev. 1083 n. 3 (1932).

24. See Armour & Co. v. Western Const. Co., 36 Wash. 529, 78 P. 1106 (1905). In at least two states mechanics' liens are provided for by constitution. Cal. Const. Art. XX, § 15; Tex. Const. Art. XVI, § 37; see Youngblood, Mechanics' and Materialmen's Liens in Texas, 26 Sw.L.J. 665, 687 (1972).

25. General (and necessarily cursory) summaries of mechanics' lien law from a national perspective include Introductory Comment, Art. 5, Uniform Simplification of Land Transfers Act, 13 Uniform Laws Annot. 197 (Supp.1977); Comment, Mechanics' Liens and Surety Bonds in the Building Trades, 68 Yale L.J. 138 (1968); Report of the Standard State Mechanics' Lien Act Committee of the U.S. Dept. of Commerce 19–25 (1932). Numerous articles and comments analyze the mechanics' lien laws of particular states. Among these (omitting title and author for the sake of brevity) are: 6 Cumb.L.Rev. 243 (Ala.1975); 7 Ariz.L.Rev. 296 (Ariz. 1966); 25 Hast.L.J. 1043 (Cal.1974); 47 L.A.Bar.Bull. 299 (Cal.1972); 9 Santa Clara L. 101 (Cal.1968); 39 U.Colo.L.Rev. 105 (Colo.1966); 29 U.Fla.L.Rev. 411 (Fla.1977); 47 Chi-Kent L.Rev. 157 (Ill.1970); 36 Ind. L.J. 526 (Ind.1921); 51 Iowa L.Rev. 862 (Iowa, 1966); 47 Iowa L.Rev. 144 (Iowa 1961); 62 Ky.L.J. 278 (Ky. 1972); 44 Tul.L.Rev. 326 (La.1970); 6 U.Balt.L.Rev. 180 (Md.1977); 28 Md.L.Rev. 225 (Md.1968); 37 Miss. L.J. 385 (Miss.1966); 42 Mo.L.Rev. 53 (Mo.1976); 12 Wake For.L.Rev. 283 (N.C.1976); 3 Akron L.Rev. 1 (Ohio 1969); 29 Ohio St.L.J. 917 (Ohio 1968); 74 Dick.L.Rev. 740 (Pa. 1970); 35 U.Pitt.L.Rev. 265 (Pa.1963); 25 S.C.L.Rev. 817 (S.C.1974); 6 Memph.St.L.Rev. 519 (Tenn.1976); 5 Memph.St.L.Rev. 359 (Tenn.1975); 26 Southwest L.J. 665 (Tex.1972); Ut.L. Rev. 181 (Utah 1966); 49 Wash.L.Rev. 685 (Wash.1974).

26. See Glenn, Mortgages § 351.

bious, but efforts to secure the adoption of uniform legislation on the subject have thus far failed.[27] Because of the resulting state-by-state complexity, a comprehensive treatment of mechanics' liens is impossible here. However, the principal groups of statutes and their general features can be outlined.

The basic idea of the mechanics' lien is that those whose work or materials go into an improvement to real estate should be permitted, in fairness, to satisfy their unpaid bills out of that real estate. Beginning with the original Maryland statute, "[t]hese laws grew, and their validity became established, as the courts held that the building business did not have the protection inherent in the widespread distribution of credit risk common to other businesses, and therefore needed this broader and special protection. Contractors, subcontractors, materialmen, and other building groups were frequently obliged to extend credit in larger amounts, and for longer time, than other businesses. Such parties might have their entire capital, or a substantial part of it, tied up in one or two, or ten or twenty, projects under construction." [28]

To begin with only general contractors or master-builders were given protection under the acts.[29] But by a process of amendment and enlargement of the similar acts that were passed in other states, today "practically every segment composing the construction industry —including contractors, subcontractors, material dealers, laborers, artisans, architects, landscape architects, engineers, surveyors—is granted liens of varying extent under varying conditions for the labor, services, or materials furnished or contracted to be furnished for the particular improvement." [30]

27. The proposed Uniform Mechanics Lien Law, drafted by the Commissioners on Uniform State Laws in 1932, was adopted only by Florida, and was withdrawn in 1943; see Handbook of Comm. on Uniform State Laws 150 (1943); Cushman, The Proposed Uniform Mechanics' Lien Law, 80 U.Pa.L.Rev. 1083 (1932); the Florida law, which persists today with modifications, is discussed in Note, Lien Rights and Construction Lending: Responsibilities and Liabilities in Florida, 29 U.Fla.L.Rev. 411 (1977). In 1976 the Commissioners on Uniform State Laws promulgated the Uniform Simplification of Land Transfers Act, Article 5 of which deals with "construction liens," and is partially based, in turn, on the Florida statute. This new proposal, as yet unadopted by any legislature, contains some of the features of the 1932 Act, including a requirement that the lien claimant give notice to the owner of his potential claim.

28. Stalling, Mechanics' Lien Laws As They Exist Today, 4 F.H.L.B.Rev. 232 (1938); see Cook v. Carlson, 364 F. Supp. 24 (D.S.D.1973).

29. Acts of General Assembly of Maryland, c. 45, § 10 (1791).

30. Stalling, supra note 28.

"It has long been the theory justifying the granting of a mechanics' lien that the labor, services, or materials of the lien claimant have so gone into the structure created on the land as to make it impossible for him to secure the return thereof in case of non-payment and, except for a suit for the contract price, the lien claimant would be destitute of remedy unless some form of statutory lien be authorized in his behalf. If, by reason of a contract, the claimant would be entitled to recapture the improvement made, the theoretical basis for the lien would then be removed. Hence, it has been held that no statu-

If the mechanics' lien were limited to those with whom the owner dealt with directly little question would arise as to the amount of the lien upon the property—it would be for the unpaid amount still owing under the contract. When the acts extended the coverage to persons who had no direct dealings with the owner, the statutes divided into two main classes. One, generally designated the "Pennsylvania" type,[31] gives the subcontractor or materialman a direct right of his own regardless of the existence of any indebtedness between the owner and general contractor [32] and measured by the value of his contribution. Conceivably,[33] under such statutes the claims of the ancillary contractors could exceed the contract price or would still exist even though the owner had paid the general contractor in full; nevertheless they are generally upheld when attacked as unconstitutional.[34] The other type of statute, usually referred to as the "New York" system, measures the liability of the owner's property by the price stated in the original contract with the general con-

tory mechanic's lien may be claimed where personal property has been sold on conditional sale basis, even though the personal property has become incorporated into the realty or in the improvements made thereon." Survey of Illinois Law, 1951–1952: Mechanics Liens—Fixtures, 31 Chi.-Kent L.Rev. 71 (1952). As to the right to mechanic's lien as for "labor" or "work" in case of preparatory or fabricating work done on materials intended for use and used in particular building or structure, see, 25 A.L.R.2d 1370 (1952). In Nolte v. Smith, 189 Cal.App.2d 140, 11 Cal. Rptr. 261 (1961), a civil engineer who surveyed, planned and prepared a subdivision map for recording and erected permanent markers and monuments on the property was held to be entitled to a mechanic's lien. Engineers' and architects' liens are sometimes provided by statute; see, e. g., Utah Code Ann § 38–1–3 (1974).

A surveyor who had cut brush to get to site lines, staked a road, established location for a channel and constructed iron pipe monuments at lot corners in connection with subdivision of land into saleable lots was not entitled to a mechanic's lien against a partnership and subsequent purchasers under Minnesota's lien law. The Supreme Court of Minnesota, opinion by Justice Frank T. Gallagher, stated that the surveyor's recovery must be on the basis of a personal judgment against the partners by whom he had been employed. Anderson v. Breezy Point Estates, 283 Minn. 490, 168 N. W.2d 693 (1969).

31. See Pa.Stat.Ann., tit. 49, § 21. Approximately 30 states adopt the Pennsylvania approach; see Comment, Mechanics' Liens and Surety Bonds in the Building Trades, 68 Yale L.J. 138, 144 n. 30 (1968).

32. Cf. Baldwin Locomotive Works v. Edward Hines Lumber Co., 189 Ind. 189, 125 N.E. 400 (1919), holding that an express stipulation between owner and general contractor could negative a direct lien.

33. Statutes usually fix the contract price as the uppermost limit for such claims. See Prince v. Neal-Millard Co., 124 Ga. 884, 53 S.E. 761, 4 Ann. Cas. 615 (1906).

34. E. g., Jones v. Great Southern Fireproof Hotel Co., 86 F. 370, 30 C. C.A. 108 (1898), certiorari granted 173 U.S. 704, 19 S.Ct. 885, reversed 177 U.S. 449, 20 S.Ct. 690, 44 L.Ed. 842; Hightower v. Bailey, 108 Ky. 198, 56 S.W. 147, 22 Ky.Law Rep. 88, 49 L.R.A. 255, 94 Am.St.Rep. 350 (1900); Becker v. Hopper, 22 Wyo. 237, 138 P. 179 (1914), Ann.Cas. 1916D, 1041, affirmed on rehearing 23 Wyo. 209, 147 P. 1085, Ann.Cas. 1918B, 35. But, contra, Selma Sash, Door & Blind Factory v. Stoddard, 116 Ala. 251, 22 So. 555 (1897).

tractor less payments properly made to the contractor.[35] The theory of these statutes is that all lien rights are based directly or derivatively upon the contract between the owner and general contractor.[36]

The procedure which a lien claimant must follow varies widely, but he is typically required to file a notice of his claim within some fixed period of time, such as sixty days, after completing his work.[37] The notice is usually required to be recorded, served personally on the owner, published in a newspaper, or made effective by some combination of these methods. If the claim is not paid within some additional period, the claimant must usually bring a judicial action to foreclose the lien in a manner similar to mortgage foreclosures.

When the lien is perfected by the giving of appropriate notice, however, its date for priority purposes generally relates back to some earlier time. This concept is critically important to mortgagees, who frequently must attempt to establish their own priority as against competing mechanics' liens. Nearly half of the states treat the lien as taking its priority from the time of commencement of the building.[38] In theory this rule seems unobjectionable, since an inspection of the property will presumably disclose whether construction has begun or not.[39] As a practical matter, however, commencement is often an ambiguous event, with courts disagreeing as to whether it has occurred when lumber is piled on the property,[40] clearing of trees and brush or grading has begun,[41] or an electrical service

35. See N.Y.Cons.Laws, Cahill, c. 34, §§ 4, 14 (now McKinney's Lien Law, §§ 4, 14) (1930).

36. See Lurton, J., in Jones v. Great So. Fireproof Hotel Co., 86 F. 370, 379, 30 C.C.A. 108, (1898), certiorari granted 173 U.S. 704, 19 S.Ct. 885, reversed 177 U.S. 449, 20 S.Ct. 690, 44 L.Ed. 842 (1900). Commonly there are additional provisions making it the duty of the owner, on notification to him of unpaid obligations by the contractor to subcontractors, to withhold payments to the contractor for the benefit of the notifying lien claimant. Other statutes make it the duty of the owner, on making payments under the contract, to require a statement under oath from the contractor of the sums owed to subcontractors and then to withhold those sums.

37. The date of completion is not always easy to determine. Suppose the owner calls the mechanic back to correct defective workmanship which has been discovered after nominal completion? See Southwest Paving Co. v. Stone Hills, 206 Cal.App.2d 548, 24 Cal.Rptr. 48 (1962). A sale of the property was held not tantamount to completion in Anderson v. Taylor, 55 Wash.2d 215, 347 P.2d 536, 78 A.L.R.2d 1161 (1959). See Hartman, Creditors' Rights and Security Transactions, 8 Vand.L.Rev. 989 (1955).

38. See Kratovil, Modern Mortgage Law and Practice § 214 (1972).

39. A common, but not universal, requirement is that the work of improvement must be "visible"; see Kloster-Madsen, Inc. v. Tafi's, Inc., 303 Minn. 59, 226 N.W.2d 603 (1975); Cook v. Carlson, 364 F.Supp. 24, 29 D.S.D.1973).

40. Compare James v. Van Horn, 39 N.J.L. 353, 363 (1877), with Kansas Mortgage Co. v. Weyerhauser, 48 Kan. 335, 29 P. 153 (1892).

41. See Diversified Mortgage Investors v. Gepada, Inc., 401 F.Supp. 682 (S.D. Iowa 1975); Clark v. General Electric Co., 243 Ark. 399, 420 S.W.2d 830 (1967); Rupp. v. Earl H. Cline & Sons, Inc., 230 Md. 573, 188 A.2d 146, 1 A.L.R.3d 815 (1963).

pole and box are erected.[42] Well-advised construction lenders often photograph the property on the date they record their mortgages in order to establish that construction has not commenced; thus they hope to ensure their priority over mechanics' liens which might be filed later.[43]

The second most popular priority date is the time at which the particular lienor begins his service or furnishing of materials.[44] The difficulties under such statutes of determining commencement of services or supplies are considerably greater than those of being sure when the whole building operation started. There is also the possibility of an intervening mortgage dividing the lien claimants into prior and subsequent groups, creating a problem of concern where the mechanics' lien statute provides that all lien claimants shall, as among themselves, be on a parity.[45] In third place come some half dozen jurisdictions that make the lien attach from the time of filing the claim. In a few states the liens attach at the date of the general contract, or the lienor's contract, or when notice of contract is recorded. In some states the liens attach at different times depending upon various factors involved.

The statutes usually provide that property is lienable only if the improvements were constructed with the consent of the owner.[46] "Owner" is variously defined, and often a lease-holder or life tenant will not have the requisite power to consent.[47] With respect to "consent", it is obviously present if the owner has signed a construction contract, but some courts hold that no formal contract is required, and that the owner's acquiesence or even mere knowledge of the con-

42. Jim Walter Homes, Inc. v. Bowling, 521 S.W.2d 828 (Ark.1975).

43. See Reuben E. Johnson Co. v. Phelps, 279 Minn. 107, 156 N.W.2d 247 (1968).

44. See Comment, Mechanics' Liens and Surety Bonds in the Building Trades, 68 Yale L.J. 138, 152 n. 69 (1968); Geiser v. Permacrete, Inc., 90 So.2d 610, 612 (Fla.1956).

45. Pacific States Sav., Loan & Bldg. Co. v. Dubois, 11 Idaho, 319, 83 P. 513 (1905); Ward v. Yarnelle, 173 Ind. 535, 91 N.E. 7 (1910); Henry & Coatsworth Co. v. Fisherdick, Adm'r, 37 Neb. 207, 55 N.W. 643 (1893), and Meister v. J. Meister, Inc., 103 N.J. Eq. 78, 142 A. 312 (1928), permit the intervening encumbrance to create two different classes of mechanics' liens. See, accord, Conn.Pub.Acts, 3905–6, (now Conn.G.S.A. § 49–33) (1925). Gardner v. Leck, 52 Minn. 522, 54 N.W. 746 (1893), preferred all the lien claimants to the mortgagee. Cf. Finlayson v. Crooks, 47 Minn. 74, 49 N.W. 398, 645 (1891), rehearing denied 47 Minn. 74, 49 N.W. 645.

46. See R. Powell, Real Property, Par. 486 (1977).

47. Express language in the lease may authorize the tenant to consent for the landlord, see American Seating Co. v. City of Philadelphia, 434 Pa. 370, 256 A.2d 599 (1969), or the court may imply such authority from the fact that the lease requires the tenant to construct the improvements, see Ott Hardware Co. v. Yost, 69 Cal. App.2d 593, 159 P.2d 663 (1945); cf. Landas Fertilizer Co. v. Hargreaves, 206 N.W.2d 675 (Iowa 1973); see note, 1952 Wash.U.L.Q. 453 (1952). The lien may well be valid against the limited interest of the tenant, even absent the landlord's consent; see Tropic Builders, Limited v. United States, 52 Hawaii 298, 475 P.2d 362 (1970).

struction will suffice.[48] A number of these latter jurisdictions incorporate procedures under which an owner who has not contracted for the improvement may, within some fixed time after commencement of construction, file of record or post on the property a notice or disclaimer of responsibility.[49] The effect of such a notice, depending on the statute, may be to shift to the lienor the burden of proving actual consent, or entirely to bar the filing of liens on the owner's interest.[50]

Waivers of mechanics' liens are widely permitted, but must be analyzed in two separate contexts. The first is the purported waiver or "no-lien" clause in the original general contract. States which follow the Pennsylvania theory of lien liability generally enforce such clauses, treating them as barring liens filed both by the general contractor and by subcontractors and materialmen.[51] States which follow the New York rule usually treat no-lien clauses as unenforceable.[52] There is a rough justice in the distinction made by these two classes of states, since the owner's potential liability is so much greater in the Pennsylvania-type jurisdictions; yet the Pennsylvania solution seems too extreme in both directions, with vast liability in the ab-

48. See Crowley Bros. v. Ward, 322 Ill.App. 687, 54 N.E.2d 753 (1944); cf. Petrillo v. Pelham Bay Park Land Co., 119 Misc. 146, 196 N.Y.S. 124 (1922).

49. See, e. g., Minn.Stat.Ann. § 514.06; similar provisions are found in California, Nevada, New Mexico, Oregon, and South Dakota. See comment, supra note 44, at 158 n. 99; Calif. Cont. Ed. of Bar, California Mechanics' Lien §§ 6.4–6.10 (1972); Annot., 123 A.L.R. 7. In some states, such as California, the owner is aided in learning of the proposed construction by the requirement that subcontractors and materials suppliers send him written notice of their activities within 20 days after commencement of the work or supplying of materials; West's Ann.Calif.Civ.Code, § 3097; see Calif. Cont. Ed. of Bar, California Mechanics' Liens §§ 3.8–3.15 (1972); Note, 21 Hast.L.J. 216 (1969).

50. Under some statutes, however, the lienor may be permitted to remove the improvement notwithstanding the owner's notice of nonresponsibility; in effect, this may compel the owner to pay for the improvement in order to keep it. See, e. g., American Transit Mix Co. v. Weber, 106 Cal. App.2d 74, 234 P.2d 732 (1951).

51. In addition to Pennsylvania, other jurisdictions recognizing such contractual waivers include Connecticut, Illinois, Indiana, Iowa, Maryland, Minnesota, Missouri, Nebraska, Oregon, and Wisconsin. Such clauses are binding as to subcontractors but not as to the general contractor in Idaho, Illinois, and Massachusetts. See Comment, supra note 44, at 158 n. 102; Annot., 76 A.L.R.2d 1097.

New Jersey law permits the owner to avoid all liens merely by filing for record his contract and specifications. However, subcontractors and suppliers may file "notices of intention" to furnish materials or labor, and the owner is then legally bound to ensure that such claimants receive what is due them from each construction disbursement. See Solondz Bros. Lumber Co. v. Piperato, 28 N.J.Super. 414, 101 A.2d 33 (1953). A similar procedure is followed in Florida, although recordation of the contract is not required; see Fla.Stat. § 713.06; Note, Lien Rights and Construction Lending: Responsibilities and Liabilities in Florida, 29 U.Fla.L.Rev. 411, 417–21 (1977).

52. McKinney's N.Y. Lien Law § 34; prior to amendment in 1975, this statute permitted waiver by contractual language, although interpretations were varied. The present statute makes all waivers of this type unenforceable. See E. Marks, Jensen on Mechanics' Liens § 100 (1963, supp. 1976).

sence of a no-lien clause and no liability with one. An intermediate group of states recognizes the validity of the no-lien clause as binding the contractor, but as having no effect upon subcontractors or materialmen unless they have clearly assented to be bound by it.[53]

Waivers given by individual lien claimants during the course of construction are unquestionably valid,[53a] and are extremely useful to owners and construction lenders. It is a wise and common practice for the owner to insist upon a sworn list of subcontractors and suppliers from the general contractor, and to require partial lien waivers from each party on the list prior to each disbursement of construction funds. Construction lenders also usually require such waivers, which serve to indicate that the prospective claimant has been fully paid for work done or materials furnished to that date. When construction of the project is completed, the owner will usually require a final waiver, the effect of which will be to bar the filing of any lien on the project, even if the particular subcontractor must return to the site later to correct defects in his workmanship, for example.[54]

Sometimes waivers obtained during the course of construction are broadly worded to cover not only work performed to date but also all work to be done in the future. The cases are divided on the validity of such prospective waivers; some courts readily hold them valid,[55] while others construe them strongly against the party obtaining the waiver [56] or hold them unenforceable as against public policy.[57]

§ 12.5 Mechanics' Liens—Constitutionality

Several courts have examined the constitutionality of mechanics' lien statutes; most have held them constitutional. In recent years, constitutional attacks on these statutes have featured a due process analysis of the variety involved in the line of Supreme Court cases

53. See Higby v. Hooper, 124 Mont. 331, 221 P.2d 1043 (1950).

53a. Some courts regard the recitation of nominal consideration as adequate support for a lien waiver; see Ramsey v. Peoples Trust and Sav. Bank, 148 Ind.App. 167, 264 N.E.2d 111 (1970). In jurisdictions in which this is not sufficient, the cases are divided as to whether a waiver is valid in favor of the owner of the property if the subcontractor has not actually been paid; compare Gerard C. Wallace Co. v. Simpson Land Co., 267 Md. 702, 298 A.2d 881 (1973) (waiver valid) with Cook v. Metal Bldg. Products Inc., 297 Minn. 330, 211 N.W.2d 371 (1973) (waiver invalid absent detrimental reliance). Most courts would probably hold the waiver valid in favor of the construction lender on detrimental reliance grounds if it released funds on the basis of the waiver.

54. See R. Kratovil, Modern Mortgage Law and Practice § 214 (1972).

55. Townsend v. Barlow, 101 Conn. 86, 124 A. 832 (1924).

56. Southwestern Electrical Co. v. Hughes, 139 Kan. 89, 30 P.2d 114 (1934); Bruce Constr. Corp. v. Federal Realty Corp., 104 Fla. 93, 139 So. 209 (1932).

57. Boise Cascade Corp. v. Stephens, 572 P.2d 1380 (Utah 1977); Brimwood Homes v. Knudsen Builders Supply Co., 14 Utah 2d 419, 385 P.2d 982 (1963).

beginning with Sniadach v. Family Finance Corp.[58] and running through North Georgia Finishing, Inc. v. Di-Chem, Inc.[59] However, mechanics' lien statutes were subjected to constitutional scrutiny long before *Sniadach*. The older cases generally found the statutes to be constitutional [60] as against a variety of constitutional objections, including ones based on due process,[61] equal protection,[62] freedom of contract,[63] and impairment of contractual obligations.[64] The early

58. 395 U.S. 337, 89 S.Ct. 1820, 23 L.Ed.2d 349 (1969).

59. 419 U.S. 601, 95 S.Ct. 719, 42 L.Ed.2d 751 (1975). The other cases in the series of Supreme Court decisions articulating notice and hearing standards in the debtor-creditor context are Fuentes v. Shevin, 407 U.S. 67, 92 S.Ct. 1983, 32 L.Ed.2d 556 (1972), rehearing denied 409 U.S. 902, 93 S.Ct. 177, 34 L.Ed.2d 165, and Mitchell v. W. T. Grant Co., 416 U.S. 600, 94 S.Ct. 1895, 40 L.Ed.2d 406 (1974).

60. Cases holding mechanics' lien statutes constitutional include: Jones v. Great Southern Fireproof Hotel Co., 86 F. 370 (C.C.A.Ohio 1898), reversed on other grounds 177 U.S. 449, 20 S.Ct. 690, 44 L.Ed. 842 (1900); Hollenbeck-Bush Planing Mill Co. v. Amweg, 177 Cal. 159, 170 P. 148 (1917); Stimson Mill Co. v. Nolan, 5 Cal.App. 754, 91 P. 262 (1907); Chicago Lumber Co. v. Newcomb, 19 Colo.App. 265, 74 P. 786 (1903); State v. Tabasso Homes, Inc., 42 Del. (3 Terry) 110, 28 A.2d 248 (1942); State v. Chillingworth, 126 Fla. 645, 171 So. 649 (1937); Summerlin v. Thompson, 31 Fla. 369, 12 So. 667 (1893); Prince v. Neal-Millard Co., 124 Ga. 884, 53 S.E. 761 (1906); Boyer v. Keller, 258 Ill. 106, 101 N.E. 237 (1913); Barrett v. Millikan, 156 Ind. 510, 60 N.E. 310 (1901); Smith v. Newbaur, 144 Ind. 95, 42 N.E. 40 (1895), rehearing denied 144 Ind. 95, 42 N.E. 1094; Aalfs Wall Paper & Paint Co. v. Bowker, 179 Iowa 726, 162 N.W. 33 (1917); Stewart v. Gardner-Warren Implement Co., 70 S.W. 1042 (Ky.1902) 24 Ky. Law Rep. 1216; Hightower v. Bailey, 108 Ky. 198, 56 S.W. 147 (1900); Bardwell v. Mann, 46 Minn. 285, 48 N.W. 1120 (1891); Chears Floor & Screen Co. v. Gidden, 159 Miss. 288, 131 So. 426 (1930); Colpetzer v. Trinity Church, 24 Neb. 113, 37 N.W. 931 (1888); Baldridge v. Morgan, 15 N.M. 249, 106 P. 342 (1910); Gardner & Meeks Co. v. New York, Cent. & H. R. R. Co., 72 N.J. Law 257, 62 A. 416 (1905); Chapel State Theatre Co. v. Hooper, 123 Ohio St. 322, 175 N.E. 450, affirmed 284 U.S. 588, 52 S.Ct. 137, 76 L.Ed. 508 (1931); Title Guarantee & Trust Co. v. Wrenn, 35 Or. 62, 56 P. 271 (1899); Cole Mfg. Co. v. Falls, 90 Tenn. 466, 16 S.W. 1045 (1891); Spokane Mfg. & Lumber Co. v. McChesney, 1 Wash. 609, 21 P. 198 (1889); Mallory v. La Crosse Abattoir Co., 80 Wis. 170, 49 N.W. 1071 (1891).

Cases finding provisions of mechanics' lien statutes unconstitutional include: Selma Sash, Door & Blind Factory v. Stoddard, 116 Ala. 251, 22 So. 555 (1897); Stimson Mill Co. v. Braun, 136 Cal. 122, 68 P. 481 (1902); Santa Cruz Rock Pavement Co. v. Lyons, 117 Cal. 212, 48 P. 1097 (1897); Cameron-Schroth-Cameron Co. v. Geseke, 251 Ill. 402, 96 N.E. 222 (1911); Kelly v. Johnson, 251 Ill. 135, 95 N.E. 1068 (1911); John Spry Lumber Co. v. Sault Sav. Bank, Loan & Trust Co., 77 Mich. 199, 43 N.W. 778 (1889); Meyer v. Berlandi, 39 Minn. 438, 40 N.W. 513 (1888); Masterson v. Roberts, 336 Mo. 158, 78 S.W.2d 856 (1934); Waters v. Wolf, 162 Pa. 153, 29 A. 646 (1894).

61. See, e. g., Stimson Mill Co. v. Nolan, 5 Cal.App. 754, 91 P. 262 (1907); State v. Chillingworth, 126 Fla. 645, 171 So. 649 (1937); Baldridge v. Morgan, 15 N.M. 249, 106 P. 342 (1910).

62. See, e. g., Hollenbeck-Bush Planing Mill Co. v. Amweg, 177 Cal. 159, 170 P. 148 (1917); Barrett v. Milliken, 156 Ind. 510, 60 N.E. 310 (1901).

63. See, e. g., Jones v. Great Southern Fireproof Hotel Co., 86 F. 370 (C.C.A.Ohio 1898), reversed on other grounds 177 U.S. 449, 20 S.Ct. 690, 44 L.Ed. 842 (1900); Boyer v. Keller, 258 Ill. 106, 101 N.E. 237 (1913).

64. See, e. g., State v. Tabasso Homes, Inc., 42 Del. (3 Terry) 110, 28 A.2d

due process cases are perhaps the most interesting. Typically it was asserted that allowing a subcontractor not in contractual privity with the landowner to assert a lien on the owner's property amounted to an unauthorized deprivation of property in violation of due process. Cases holding the statutes constitutional frequently responded that authorization was implicit in the owner's formation of the original construction contract, with statute becoming in effect part of the contract.[65]

Some of these early cases did find certain statutory provisions unconstitutional. In Kelly v. Johnson,[66] for example, the statute was held unconstitutional as depriving a landowner of liberty of contract to the extent it vested a subcontractor with the right to a lien despite a lien waiver agreement in the construction contract. In Meyer v. Berlandi,[67] a provision of Minnesota's statute was held unconstitutional that conclusively presumed the landowner's consent to a subcontractor's work if the landowner failed to enjoin the work. The court reasoned that the provision violated due process because it permitted a lien to be filed even when no actual consent to work had been given. In Selma Sash, Door & Blind Factory v. Stoddard,[68] the Alabama statute was found violative of due process because it permitted subcontractors to have a lien on property even when the owner fulfilled his contractual duties to the general contractor.

Notwithstanding these holdings, the vast majority of the older cases upheld the validity of lien statutes. Regardless of the results, however, the older cases have had little precedential impact on recent court considerations of the constitutionality of mechanics' liens. The reason for this is that modern attacks on constitutionality have exclusively featured a due process analysis unknown in earlier years. Between 1969 and 1975, the Supreme Court examined statutory prejudgment procedures in the debtor-creditor context and established notice and hearing standards that must be met for such procedures to comport with due process. In three of these cases—Sniadach v. Family Finance Corp.;[69] Fuentes v. Shevin,[70] and North Georgia Finishing, Inc. v. Di-Chem Inc.[71]—prejudgment procedures were found violative of due process. In one case—Mitchell v. W. T. Grant Co.[72]—due process standards were found to be met. There is considerable

248 (1942); Colpetzer v. Trinity Church, 24 Neb. 113, 37 N.W. 931 (1888); Chapel State Theatre Co. v. Hooper, 123 Ohio St. 322, 175 N.E. 450, affirmed 284 U.S. 588, 52 S.Ct. 137, 76 L.Ed. 508 (1931).

65. See, e. g., Stimson Mill Co. v. Nolan, 5 Cal.App. 754, 91 P. 262 (1907).

66. 251 Ill. 135, 95 N.E. 1068 (1911).

67. 39 Minn. 438, 40 N.W. 513 (1888).

68. 116 Ala. 251, 22 So. 555 (1897).

69. 395 U.S. 337, 89 S.Ct. 1820, 23 L.Ed.2d 349 (1969).

70. 407 U.S. 67, 92 S.Ct. 1983, 32 L.Ed. 556 (1972), rehearing denied 409 U.S. 902, 93 S.Ct. 177, 34 L.Ed.2d 165.

71. 419 U.S. 601, 95 S.Ct. 719, 42 L.Ed.2d 751 (1975).

72. 416 U.S. 600, 94 S.Ct. 1895, 40 L.Ed.2d 406 (1974).

uncertainty as to the precise state of the law in this area—even among justices of the Court [73]—but at least this much seems clear: absent extraordinary circumstances, statutory prejudgment creditor remedies which deprive a debtor of a significant property interest without notice and a prior opportunity for hearing are unconstitutional unless sufficient safeguards are present to ensure that the debtor's interests are protected.[74]

The Supreme Court has not yet issued an opinion on the application of these due process standards to mechanics' liens; [75] consequently, it is not entirely clear what safeguards would be required. Other courts, however, have struggled with the constitutional issue. Most have upheld the statutes examined,[76] but two have held otherwise.[77] To some extent, of course, the differences in result reflect differences in the statutes examined, but they also reflect differences in approach. A brief survey of prominent cases will make this clear.[78]

73. Compare North Georgia Finishing, Inc. v. Di-Chem, Inc., 419 U.S. 601, 608–09, 95 S.Ct. 719, 723, 42 L.Ed.2d 751 (1975) (concurring opinions) with Mitchell v. W. T. Grant Co., 416 U.S. 600, 623–29, 629–36, 94 S.Ct. 1895, 1907–10, 1910–14, 40 L.Ed.2d 406 (1973) (concurring and dissenting opinions).

74. See, e. g., North Georgia Finishing, Inc. v. Di-Chem, Inc., 419 U.S. 601, 95 S.Ct. 719, 42 L.Ed.2d 751 (1975); Catz & Robinson, Due Process and Creditor's Remedies: From Sniadach and Fuentes to Mitchell, North Georgia and Beyond, 28 Rutgers L.Rev. 541 (1975).

75. The Court did, however, summarily affirm the decision of a three judge district court upholding the constitutionality of Arizona's mechanics' lien statute. See Spielman-Fond, Inc. v. Hanson's, Inc., 379 F.Supp. 997 (D.Ariz.1973) (per curiam), affirmed 417 U.S. 901, 94 S.Ct. 2596, 41 L.Ed. 2d 208 (1974). The degree to which this summary affirmance should be binding on other courts has been the subject of considerable discussion. See, e. g., B & P Development v. Walker, 420 F.Supp. 704 (W.D.Pa.1976); Bankers Trust Co. v. El Paso Pre-Cast Co., 560 P.2d 457 (Colo.1977); Barry Properties, Inc. v. Fick Bros. Roofing Co., 277 Md. 15, 353 A.2d 222 (1976).

76. See B & P Development v. Walker, 420 F.Supp. 704 (W.D.Pa.1976); In re Thomas A. Cary, Inc., 412 F.Supp. 667 (E.D.Va.1976); Ruocco v. Brinker, 380 F.Supp. 432 (S.D.Fla.1974); Spielman-Fond, Inc. v. Hanson's Inc., 379 F.Supp. 997 (D.Ariz.1973) (per curiam), affirmed 417 U.S. 901, 94 S.Ct. 2596, 41 L.Ed.2d 208 (1974); Cook v. Carlson, 364 F.Supp. 24 (D.S.D.1973); Nelson-American Developers, Ltd. v. Enco Engineering Corp., 337 So.2d 729 (Ala.1976); Connolly Development, Inc. v. Superior Court, 17 Cal. 3d 803, 132 Cal.Rptr. 477, 553 P.2d 637 (1976), appeal dismissed 429 U.S. 1056, 97 S.Ct. 778, 50 L.Ed.2d 773 (1977); Bankers Trust Co. v. El Paso Pre-Cast Co., 560 P.2d 457 (Colo. 1977); Tucker Door & Trim Corp. v. Fifteenth Street Co., 235 Ga. 727, 221 S.E.2d 433 (1975); Carl A. Morse, Inc. v. Rentar Industrial Development Corp., 56 A.D.2d 30, 391 N.Y.S.2d 425 (1977); Silverman v. Gossett, 553 S. W.2d 581 (Tenn.1977).

77. Roundhouse Constr. Corp. v. Telesco Masons Supplies Co., 168 Conn. 371, 362 A.2d 778 (1975), vacated and remanded 423 U.S. 809, 96 S. Ct. 20, 46 L.Ed.2d 29 (1975), reaffirmed 170 Conn. 155, 365 A.2d 393, certiorari denied 429 U.S. 889, 97 S. Ct. 246, 50 L.Ed.2d 172 (1976); Barry Properties Inc. v. Fick Bros. Roofing Co., 277 Md. 15, 353 A.2d 222 (1976).

78. Some commentators have discussed the issue. See Frank & McManus, Balancing Almost Two Hundred Years of Economic Policy Against Contemporary Due Process

The leading case upholding the constitutionality of a mechanics' lien is Spielman-Fond, Inc. v. Hanson's, Inc.[79] In that case, a three-judge district court evaluated the Arizona mechanics' lien statute in light of *Sniadach* and *Fuentes*. The court focused on whether the filing of a mechanics' lien constituted a constitutionally cognizable deprivation of property that would require proper notice and hearing. While the court conceded that a mechanics' lien reduced the owner's ability to alienate his property, it ruled that lien filing did "not amount to a taking of a significant property interest." [80] Accordingly, said the court, due process was not violated by the absence of notice and hearing prior to lien filing. The Supreme Court summarily affirmed the ruling of this three-judge panel.[81]

Several cases have followed the *Spielman-Fond* decision in finding that a mechanics' lien filing does not involve the taking of a significant property interest.[82] One of the most recent opinions in this class of cases is that of a New York appellate court in Carl A. Morse Inc. v. Rentar Industrial Development Corp.[83] The due process challenge to the New York statute was asserted by a landowner whose property was subjected to lien claims of over a million dollars. The court analyzed the *Sniadach* line of cases through *North Georgia*, focusing particularly on how the New York statutory scheme differed from the one invalidated in the *North Georgia* case. The court averred that the New York provision effected no deprivation of use or possession of property. Although it admitted that a mechanics' lien impinges on the economic interests of a landowner, the court found this insufficient to bring the Fourteenth Amendment into play. It was, said the court, a "minimal intrusion." In addition, the court reasoned that even though the value of the property is diminished by the amount of a lien, the loss is offset by the value of the improve-

Standards—Mechanics' Liens in Maryland after Barry Properties, 36 Md.L. Rev. 733 (1977); Levine, Due Process of Law in Pre-Judgment Attachment and the Filing of Mechanics' Liens, 50 Conn.B.J. 335 (1976); Note, The Constitutional Validity of Mechanics' Liens Under the Due Process Clause —A Reexamination after Mitchell and North Georgia, 55 B.U.L.Rev. 263 (1975); Note, Mechanics' Liens Subject to Fourteenth Amendment Guarantees, 26 Cath.U.L.Rev. 129 (1976); 8 Conn.L.Rev. 744 (1976).

79. 379 F.Supp. 997 (D.Ariz.1973) (per curiam), affirmed, 417 U.S. 901, 94 S. Ct. 2596, 41 L.Ed.2d 208 (1974).

80. Id. at 999.

81. 417 U.S. 901, 94 S.Ct. 2596, 41 L. Ed.2d 208 (1974).

82. See B & P Development v. Walker, 420 F.Supp. 704 (W.D.Pa.1976); In re Thomas A. Cary, Inc., 412 F.Supp. 667 (E.D.Va.1976); Ruocco v. Brinker, 380 F.Supp. 432 (S.D.Fla.1974); Bankers Trust Co. v. El Paso Pre-Cast Co., 560 P.2d 457 (Colo.1977); Tucker Door & Trim Corp. v. Fifteenth Street Co., 235 Ga. 727, 221 S.E.2d 433 (1975); Carl A. Morse, Inc. v. Rentar Industrial Development Corp., 56 A. D.2d 30, 391 N.Y.S.2d 425 (1977); Silverman v. Gossett, 553 S.W.2d 581 (Tenn.1977).

A pre-*Spielman-Fond* decision upheld the constitutionality of the South Dakota mechanics' lien provisions on the grounds that the deprivation of property was de minimus. See Cook v. Carlson, 364 F.Supp. 24 (D.S.D.1973).

83. 56 A.D.2d 30, 391 N.Y.S.2d 425 (1977).

ments contributed by a lienor. The court also examined the particular provisions of the lien statute, and found them to constitute a constitutional accommodation of the competing interest of owners, materialmen, and purchasers. Among the safeguards contained within these provisions, the court noted that the lienor was required in filing the lien to state under oath the facts giving rise to his claim, that the owner could discharge the lien by posting a bond, that the owner could compel an expeditious determination on the merits by demanding foreclosure, and that the lien could remain in force no longer than a year from filing unless a foreclosure action were commenced or a continuance granted.[84]

A different analytical approach to the due process question was taken by the California Supreme Court in Connolly Development, Inc. v. Superior Court.[85] The statutory scheme under attack in *Connolly* required a potential lienor to follow certain procedures in order to obtain a lien. One such requirement was the filing of a preliminary notice of claim with the owner, general contractor, and construction lender within twenty days of furnishing materials. In addition, the actual lien claim had to be recorded within ninety days after completion of the improvement or within thirty days after recordation of a notice of completion of the project. The lien could be released if the owner posted a bond, and it was discharged unless a foreclosure suit was begun within ninety days of recordation. These particular provisions ultimately convinced the court to conclude that a constitutional accommodation of competing interests was achieved by the California lien provisions.

Unlike the other two cases discussed, the court in Connolly determined that a constitutionally cognizable taking of property was involved in the recordation of a mechanics' lien. "A deprivation," said the court, "need not reach the magnitude of a physical seizure of property in order to fall within the compass of the due process clause." [86] Here, the constraints imposed on the owner's ability to sell or encumber his property were held sufficient to constitute a taking under the Fourteenth Amendment.

Having crossed this threshold, the court was then forced to decide whether state action was present. The court had no difficulty finding state action—not only is a mechanics' lien a creature of statute, but it can only be recorded and enforced under the power of the state.

84. The court did not mention the fact that a lien could be filed up to four months following completion of the contract or the furnishing of materials. Id. at 35–36, 391 N.Y.S.2d at 432 (dissenting opinion).

85. 17 Cal.3d 803, 132 Cal.Rptr. 477, 553 P.2d 637 (1976), appeal dismissed 429 U.S. 1056, 97 S.Ct. 778, 50 L.Ed. 2d 773 (1977). The case also deals with the constitutionality of California's statutory "stop notice" provision.

86. Id. at 812, 553 P.2d at 643, 132 Cal.Rptr. at 483.

The final question before the court was whether the statutory provisions comported with due process. The court held that they did. In reaching this conclusion, the court noted that California law provided more safeguards than the Arizona statute upheld in *Spielman-Fond.* It also observed that the problematic garnishment provisions invalidated in *North Georgia* were different from the provisions of California law. In this regard, the court emphasized that the California statute did not effect a total deprivation of the owner's property, that the lienor had a legitimate interest in that property, and that the landowner had adequate statutory protection. The court noted that modern due process analysis was flexible, basically constituting a consideration of affected interests. In light of the statutory safeguards, the balance of interest weighed in favor of constitutionality.

Two courts have held mechanics' lien provisions unconstitutional under due process analysis. The first decision was handed down by the Supreme Court of Connecticut in Roundhouse Construction Corporation v. Telesco Masons Supplies Company.[87] The Maryland Supreme Court decided the second in Barry Properties Inc. v. Fick Bros. Roofing Company.[88] Each of these decisions merits discussion.

Beginning its analysis in *Roundhouse*, the Connecticut court reviewed the statutory provisions under attack. These provisions required that, in order to have a valid lien, a potential lienor must file a sworn statement of amount claimed with the town clerk within sixty days after his work. The provisions also required subcontractors and materialmen not privy to the original construction agreement to give notice to the owner against whose property liens are claimed. The owner could apply for dissolution of the lien by filing a bond, or request a discharge on grounds of invalidity. If the request were not honored within thirty days, the owner could then bring a court action for discharge. In no case could a lien remain in force longer than four years unless the lienor commenced a foreclosure action within two years of filing.

The court found that these provisions failed to meet due process hearing standards. Although acknowledging that an early post-taking hearing instead of a prior hearing seemed acceptable after *North Georgia*, the court was concerned that it was possible for a lien to continue for two years without any hearing at all. This was different, said the court, from the Arizona statute upheld in *Spielman-Fond*, under which the lien could last no longer than six months without a foreclosure action. "Such a provision," said the court, "would seem to offer the bare minimum of due process protection consistent with the extent of deprivation present." [89] On the issue of deprivation

87. 168 Conn. 371, 362 A.2d 778, vacated and remanded, 423 U.S. 809, 96 S.Ct. 20, 46 L.Ed.2d 29 (1975), reaffirmed 170 Conn. 155, 365 A.2d 393, certiorari denied 429 U.S. 889, 97 S. Ct. 246, 50 L.Ed.2d 172 (1976).

88. 277 Md. 15, 353 A.2d 222 (1976).

89. 168 Conn. at 381, 362 A.2d at 783. The court was also concerned that the lien statute permitted the ex parte filing, without judicial supervision, of

itself the court noted that even though a mechanics' lien does not prevent the alienation of property, it does restrict the opportunity to alienate. This was sufficient, according to the court, to constitute a significant taking of property.

A similar analysis pointed to unconstitutionality in *Barry Properties.* The Maryland statutory provisions under attack allowed for creation of a mechanics' lien by a general contractor without prior notice to the owner. Although a subcontractor was required to give the owner a notice of intent to make a lien claim, the claim could be filed before the notice was given. In any case, this notice had to be given within ninety days after furnishing work or material.[90] No hearing was required concerning the lien prior to foreclosure. After recordation, the lien could last for one year, unless enforcement were sought within that period. During this year, the owner could sue to compel the claimant to prove the lien's validity or he could post a bond and secure a release. The court, in reasoning reminiscent of *Connolly,* found that state action was involved and that there was a significant taking of property.[91] The only remaining question was whether the statutory scheme provided "protections such as those discussed in *Mitchell* and *North Georgia Finishing* or is deemed to be within the 'extraordinary circumstances' exception." [92]

The court noted that there was no requirement of a sworn statement by the creditor, setting forth facts upon which the lien was based, that there was no requirement of a bond to protect the debtor, nor was there an opportunity for a prompt post-lien hearing. The owner's opportunity to compel the claimant to prove the lien's validity was subject to the usual strictures of the trial calendar. In view of these findings, the court said the requirements of *Mitchell* and *North Georgia* were unmet. It also concluded that the extraordinary circumstances exception did not apply. *Spielman-Fond* was distinguishable, said the court, because the Arizona statute provided for safeguards not reflected in Maryland law.[93]

Modern due process challenges to statutory provisions have usually failed, either because courts have been unwilling to find a sig-

a conclusory statement and that there was no requirement of posting a bond by the lienor.

90. A general contractor was not required to give any such notice, but had to file a lien claim within 180 days of the completion of work or the furnishing of materials. 277 Md. at 19–20, 353 A.2d at 226.

91. The court said that the existence of a lien diminishes an owner's equity, severely impairs alienability of property, and makes additional financing problematical.

92. 277 Md. at 31, 353 A.2d at 232.

93. The court specifically referred to the Arizona provisions requiring that the claimant make a sworn statement upon filing his lien claim, that the owner be notified within a reasonable time of the filing, that the claimant institute enforcement proceedings within six months of filing, and permitting the owner to discharge the lien by filing a bond. Id. at 34, 353 A.2d at 233–34.

nificant deprivation of property or because appropriate constitutional accommodations have been found within the statutory scheme itself. Some well reasoned recent opinions, however, have discerned a significant deprivation of property in the imposition of mechanics' liens. Once this threshold is crossed, state action is easily found; the remaining question is whether adequate safeguards exist. Precisely what safeguards will be found adequate is not clear, but it appears that a statute may be in constitutional trouble if it permits a potential lienor to file without notice long after work's completion or if it allows a lien to subsist beyond six months without requiring a hearing. The *Spielman-Fond* case has become something of a standard in this area; courts have thus far been unwilling to invalidate statutory provisions like those upheld in that case.

§ 12.6 The Stop Notice and the Equitable Lien

The mechanics' lien, the traditional refuge of unpaid subcontractors and suppliers, is largely useless to them in construction projects. Increasingly construction lenders have learned to record their mortgages before any work is done,[94] and to avoid optional advances;[95] under these circumstances the mechanics' lien claimants are almost certain to be subordinate to the construction loan, and its foreclosure will seldom produce any surplus for them. An alternative source of payment to the subcontractors and suppliers is the payment bond, but its use is generally confined to large commercial projects and those being built with public funds.[96] In residential subdivisions and small apartment projects, neither the lien nor the bond is likely to be available.

At least ten states have attempted to provide another route to the unpaid subcontractors and suppliers: the stop notice.[97] In essence, it is a right to make and enforce a claim against the construction lender (and in some states, the owner)[98] for a portion of the un-

94. Mechanics' liens generally relate back in priority to the time the work was commenced; if the construction loan mortgage is recorded first, it will have priority over such liens. See § 12.4, supra, at notes 38–43.

95. An optional advance under a construction loan, if made by a lender having actual notice of intervening liens, will generally be subordinate to them. See § 12.7, infra.

96. See § 12.2, supra, at notes 50–53.

97. Ala.Code, tit. 33, § 37; West's Cal.Civ.Code, §§ 3156–72; Colo.Rev. Stat.Ann. § 86–3–2; Burns Ind.Ann. Stat. § 32–8–3–9; Miss.Code Ann. § 85–7–181; N.C.Gen.Stat. § 44A–18; N. J.Rev.Stat. §§ 2A:44–77, 78; Vernon's Ann.Texas Civ.Stat.Ann. § 5463; Wis. Stat.Ann. § 289.03; Wash.Rev.Code § 60.04.210. See generally Comment, Mechanics Liens: The "Stop Notice" Comes to Washington, 49 Wash.L. Rev. 685, 694 (1974); Comment, California's Private Stop Notice Law: Due Process Requirements, 25 Hast.L.J. 1043, 1054–57 (1974).

98. See, e. g., West's Cal.Civ.Code, §§ 3158–59; under California law, the claimant need not file a bond if his notice is directed to the owner. Some of the statutes also provide for the filing of stop notices against governmental entities for whom public works projects are being constructed.

disbursed construction loan proceeds, if any. It is somewhat like a garnishment of the loan funds, although the analogy is not entirely accurate; a stop notice may be effectively filed, for example, even if the borrower-developer has defaulted and is therefore not entitled to any further construction draws.[99] Obviously the stop notice is effective only if some funds remain in the lender's or owner's hands. The remedy is statutory, and specific time requirements must be met; [1] often the claimant must file a bond to indemnify the lender against damages which might result from a wrongful claim.[2] The lender may simply pay the claim and discharge the stop notice,[3] but if the claim is disputed or there are insufficient funds to pay all stop notice claims, litigation may be necessary.[4]

The statutes commonly deny availability of the stop notice if a payment bond has been filed, and some also do so if conventional mechanics' lien recovery is available.[5] Thus the foreclosure of the construction loan is not a bar to the assertion of a stop notice, and in some states may actually be helpful by establishing that the mechanics' lien has been destroyed.

One effect of the stop notice remedy is generally to make lenders more careful in administration of construction loans. There are two reasons for this. One is that if claimants are unpaid and therefore file stop notices, they may bring the entire project to a halt; [6] this is especially true if it is necessary to litigate the validity of the claims and there are many of them, for they may tie up the entire construction loan account for a long period.[7] A second reason is that negli-

99. See A-1 Door & Materials Co. v. Fresno Guarantee Savings & Loan Ass'n, 61 Cal.2d 728, 40 Cal.Rptr. 85, 394 P.2d 829 (1964).

1. See, e. g., Moss, The Stop Notice Remedy in California—Updated, 47 L.A.Bar.Bull. 299 (1972).

2. E. g., West's Cal.Civ.Code, § 3083. In order to free up the funds which the stop notice has frozen, the lender or owner can file a corresponding bond and discharge the stop notice; id. at § 3171.

3. The lender is generally personally liable if he fails to set aside, from the construction loan account, the amount claimed by the stop notice (or the amount set by the statute, if different from the claim; see Wash. Rev.Code § 60.04.210(4), setting forth a rather complex and confusing formula for determining the amount to be withheld; see, Comment, Wash.L. Rev., supra note 97, at 697 n. 68.)

4. The stop notice claimants usually share pro-rata if the funds are insufficient to pay all claims. The statutes may provide a procedure for adjudication of disputed claims; see, e. g., West's Cal.Civ.Code, §§ 3172–73.

5. See Colorado, New Jersey, and Wisconsin statutes, supra note 97.

6. See Idaco Lumber Co. v. Northwestern Sav. & Loan Ass'n, 265 Cal.App. 2d 490, 71 Cal.Rptr. 422 (1968); Ilyin, Stop Notice—Construction Loan Officer's Nightmare, 16 Hast.L.J. 187 (1964).

7. The California statute provides a speedy summary procedure for litigating the validity of stop notices on public projects, but it does not apply to private projects; West's Cal.Civ. Code, §§ 3197–3205. In Connolly Development, Inc. v. Superior Court, 17 Cal.3d 803, 132 Cal.Rptr. 477, 553 P. 2d 637 (1976), appeal dismissed 429 U.S. 1056, 97 S.Ct. 778, 50 L.Ed.2d 773 (1977), the court expressed ap-

gent or wrongful disbursal of funds may come back to haunt the lender; the stop notice claimants may assert that such money should be regarded, for stop notice purposes, as still held in the hands of the lender and amenable to the claims.[8] Lenders in stop notice jurisdictions are likely to take a fairly active role in project supervision, and often use the voucher or direct-payment system of loan disbursement rather than the looser progress-payments system.[9] By this they hope to make certain that all subcontractors and suppliers are paid on time, and that no funds are diverted to non-construction uses.

Since the stop notice amounts to a garnishment of funds without a prior notice or hearing, it might be held a violation of due process under the *Sniadach-North Georgia* line of cases discussed in Section 12.5, supra. The California Supreme Court held its state's statute valid against such an attack in Connolly Development, Inc. v. Superior Court.[10] While the court conceded that the stop notice resulted in more than *de minimis* takings of property, and that it involved state action, it concluded that the interest of stop notice claimants in a rapid and efficient remedy outweighed the relatively limited deprivation visited upon the owner. In other states, however, this issue may yet be resolved differently.

The Equitable Lien

It often happens that neither the stop notice nor the mechanics' lien provides an adequate remedy to one who has supplied labor or materials to a construction project. As we have already indicated, foreclosure of the construction loan mortgage will usually wipe out the mechanics' lien, and the stop notice may be unavailable because the claimant omitted some essential procedural element in his filing or because he is outside the scope of the statute. For example, he may be a remote materialman (one who has supplied materials to another materialman), an architect (in a jurisdiction in which architects are protected by neither mechanics' liens nor stop notices, as is common), or a general contractor[11] (a class not covered by most stop notice

proval of the summary procedure and suggested that the statute might be amended to cover private work as well, but concluded that its unavailability on private projects did not make the stop notice unconstitutional; id. at 17 Cal.3d 828 n. 26, 132 Cal.Rptr. at 494 n.26.

8. See Moss, The Stop Notice Remedy in California—Updated, 47 L.A. Bar Bull. 299, 303–04 (1972); Miller v. Mountain View Sav. & Loan Ass'n, 238 Cal.App.2d 644, 48 Cal.Rptr. 278 (1965).

9. See Lubell, Changes in Construction Lenders' Policies—1958–1969, A Lender's Viewpoint, 44 L.A.Bar Bull. 346 (1969).

10. 17 Cal.3d 803, 553 P.2d 637, 132 Cal.Rptr. 477 (1976), appeal dismissed, 429 U.S. 1056, 97 S.Ct. 778, 50 L.Ed.2d 773 (1977).

11. General contractors are usually within the class of persons who can claim equitable liens of the type described in the text below; see Swinerton & Walberg Co. v. Union Bank, 25 Cal.App.3d 259, 101 Cal.Rptr. 665 (1972).

laws). Or he may simply live and work in a state having no stop notice statute.

On such facts, the claimant who has supplied materials or labor may assert an equitable lien on either the land itself or the undisbursed portion of the construction loan funds, if any. Several barriers exist which may cause this claim to fail, however. One is the argument that the mechanics' lien and stop notice statutes were intended by the legislature to constitute the sole remedies for such claimants, and that any extra-statutory remedy is out of order. This argument is sound if the legislature has said as much,[12] but in most jurisdictions there is no indication that the statutory remedies are intended to be exclusive, and such a result should not be easily inferred.[13]

To analyze the other barriers to recovery on an equitable lien theory, we must focus on lien claims to the undisbursed loan funds. While claims to a lien on the land itself are also entirely possible,[14] they are analytically much simpler and will be discussed later. Courts dealing with lien claims to the loan funds have explained the lien as based on either of two theories: the equitable concept of unjust enrichment or the contract doctrine of third-party beneficiary, with the lien claimant as the beneficiary of the construction loan agreement. Some courts have dealt with these concepts separately while others have merged them together; the cases are difficult to synthesize. Depending on which of these theories is employed, the equitable lien claimant may be required to satisfy one or more of the criteria discussed below.

Commonly, the courts will recognize an equitable lien only if the construction lender has made some representation to the claimant during the course of construction. One type of representation, sometimes considered sufficient, is an assurance that the claimant will be paid, or that he will be "made whole" or "taken care of." [15] Such a

12. See West's Cal.Civ.Code § 3264, enacted in 1967, which expressly declares the stop notice the exclusive remedy as against undisbursed construction loan funds, thereby wiping out a long line of California equitable lien cases; see Boyd & Lovesee Lumber Co. v. Modular Marketing Corp., 44 Cal.App.3d 460, 118 Cal.Rptr. 699 (1975).

13. See Crane Co. v. Fine, 221 So.2d 145 (Fla.1969), conformed to 222 So. 2d 36, recognizing the equitable lien as an alternative to the mechanics' lien.

14. See note 18, infra.

15. See F. W. Eversley & Co. v. East New York Non-Profit HDFC, Inc., 409 F.Supp. 791 (S.D.N.Y.1976); J. G. Plumbing Service Co. v. Coastal Mortgage Co., 329 So.2d 393 (Fla.App. 1976); Wahl v. Southwest Sav. & Loan Ass'n, 12 Ariz.App. 90, 467 P.2d 930 (1970) (representations by borrower not sufficient; lender must make representations to lien claimant); United Plumbing v. Gibralter Sav. & Loan Ass'n, 7 Ariz.App. 540, 441 P.2d 575 (1968); G. L. Wilson Bldg. Co. v. Leatherwood, 268 F.Supp. 609 (W.D.N.C.1967); Demharter v. First Federal Sav. & Loan Ass'n, 412 Pa. 142, 194 A.2d 214 (1963); cf. Morgen-Oswood & Ass'n, Inc. v. Continental Mortgage Investors,

statement seems to satisfy the supposed requirement, in third-party-beneficiary law, that the parties have intended the claimant to have the benefits of the contract. Yet this test reflects a misconception, for the modern majority view is that only the obligee to whom the direct promise was made must have intended that the third party be benefitted by it; [16] under this view the intent of the obligor—the construction lender in the present discussion—is immaterial, and his statements to the lien claimant should be deemed irrelevant. Since in virtually every case all of the parties understand from the outset that the owner or developer plans to contract for the construction of the improvements and to pay for them with borrowed funds, it is crystal clear that the owner intends to benefit the contractor and his subcontractors and suppliers.[17] No further demonstration of intent should be required.

Other courts tend to focus on whether the construction lender has made some false statement to the lien claimant which has misled him to continue to furnish labor or materials. The usual statement of this type is an assurance that sufficient funds remain in the construction loan account to complete the project or to pay the claimant.[18] Such a statement, if false, seems to satisfy the "unjust" element of the unjust enrichment concept. Here again, however, the lender's statement is quite arguably irrelevant. The essence of unjust enrichment is that the lender is receiving something (in this case, the improvements on the real estate, upon foreclosure) for which he has not paid (as is shown by the presence of undisbursed loan funds.) The enrichment, it would seem, is equally unjust whether the lender duped the lien claimant or not. The equitable lien claim should not be dependent upon a showing of false communications by the lender to the contractors or suppliers.

If the third-party-beneficiary theory is employed by the court, the lien claim may be barred by the owner-borrower's default. Such a default—for example, failure to obtain a permanent loan commit-

323 So.2d 684 (Fla.App.1975) (equitable lien imposed with no discussion of lender's representations). Compare Chase Manhattan Bank v. S/D Enterprises, Inc., 353 So.2d 131 (Fla.App.1977), in which a statement of precisely this type was held to be insufficient to establish a lien; see also Palmer First Nat. Bank v. Rinker Materials Co., 348 So.2d 1234 (Fla.App.1977); Coke Lumber Co. v. First Nat. Bank, 529 S.W.2d 612 (Tex. Civ.App.1975).

16. Williston, Contracts § 356A (3d Ed. 1959).

17. The later California cases took this position; see McBain v. Santa Clara Sav. & Loan Ass'n, 241 Cal.App.2d 829, 51 Cal.Rptr. 78 (1966); but see note 12, supra. See also Trans-Bay Engineers & Builders, Inc. v. Hills, 551 F.2d 370 (C.A.D.C.1976) (no express representation, but "expectation" of lien claimant was reasonable.)

18. Chase Manhattan Bank v. S/D Enterprises, Inc., 353 So.2d 131 (Fla. App.1977); Hall's Miscellaneous Iron Works, Inc. v. All South Investment Co., 283 So.2d 372 (Fla.App.1973) (lien on land imposed; misrepresentations by general contractor.)

ment or failure to pay interest on the construction loan when it begins to accrue under the terms of the loan agreement—may permit the lender to argue that he no longer has any obligation to pay out additional disbursements of loan funds; since this is true as against the owner-borrower, the lender will assert this is also true of third party beneficiaries, since their rights are derivative of the owner-borrower's.[19] This defense by the lender is a formidable one. Some courts have thought it inapplicable if the lien claimant completed his work before the borrower's default, so that the right to payment could be said to have "vested."[20] If the lender has encouraged the contractors and suppliers to continue with their work on the project despite the default, the court might find that the lender waived the default, at least so far as the lien claimants are concerned.[21] And at least one court has quite consciously disregarded the borrower's default and granted a lien on a third-party-beneficiary theory.[22] Yet it must be conceded that such a default is in general a serious impediment to the establishment of a lien on this theory. By comparison, the unjust enrichment theory is not impaired by the borrower's default, so long as it can be shown that the foreclosing lender will nonetheless get more than he has paid for while the lien claimants go unpaid.

Some Florida courts have imposed the requirement that the project have been substantially completed as a condition of imposing a lien on the loan funds.[23] The rationale seems to be that if the project is incomplete, the lender will be forced to foreclose and liquidate the property at a loss; hence he will not be enriched at all, and no lien should be imposed. This analysis is far too simplistic, however. In some cases, the lender will himself complete the project before liquidating it, and may eventually earn a tidy profit from doing so. And even if the project is immediately resold by the lender at a price below the outstanding balance on the debt, that by no means establishes that the lender has not been enriched; but for the labor or materials contributed by the lien claimant, the project would almost certainly have sold for an even lower price, and the lender would have sustained a greater loss. In effect, the lender is mitigating his loss at

19. Trans-Bay Engineers & Builders, Inc. v. Hills, 551 F.2d 370 (C.A.D.C. 1976); Pioneer Plumbing Supply Co. v. Southwest Sav. & Loan Ass'n, 102 Ariz. 258, 428 P.2d 115 (1967).

20. See Trans-Bay Engineers & Builders, Inc., supra note 61; Travelers Indemnity Co. v. First Nat. State Bank 328 F.Supp. 208 (D.N.J.1971).

21. Spring Constr. Co. v. Harris, 562 F.2d 933 (C.A.Va.1977).

22. Bennett Constr. Co. v. Allen Gardens, Inc., 433 F.Supp. 825 (W.D.Mo. 1977).

23. J. G. Plumbing Service Co. v. Coastal Mortgage Co., 329 So.2d 393 (Fla.App.1976). The California courts rejected this requirement; Miller v. Citizens Sav. and Loan Ass'n, 248 Cal.App.2d 655, 56 Cal.Rptr. 844 (1967); McBain v. Santa Clara Savings & Loan Ass'n, 241 Cal.App.2d 829, 51 Cal.Rptr. 78 (1966). But see note 12, supra.

the expense of the unpaid contractor or supplier. It may well be that the lender's enrichment is less than the unpaid bill, and perhaps the former figure should serve as an upper limit of the lien, but the fact that the project is uncompleted should not act as an absolute barrier to imposition of the lien.

The foregoing discussion assumes that the lender has not disbursed the funds which would have gone to pay the lien claimant. Suppose the lender has in fact done so, but the disbursement was made in a fashion which allowed the owner-borrower or some other person, such as the general contractor, to divert the money. On these facts, one of two innocent parties must bear the loss. Neither the lender nor the lien claimant is at fault. It might be argued that the lender has a better opportunity to control the ultimate disposition of the funds or to select reliable borrowers, or that he should have employed a more reliable (although probably more costly) disbursement system—perhaps the voucher system rather than progress payments. Still, it is hard to maintain that unjust enrichment of the lender has occurred. Perhaps the lien should still be imposed, in effect throwing the loss onto the lender's shoulders, in order to encourage lenders to use the best feasible methods of controlling funds and to mitigate damages in the event of default. Yet some authors have argued that lenders are likely to be little influenced in either respect by the decisions of the courts in this matter.[24] In cases in which the lender has not been enriched, and where a default bars the third-party-beneficiary theory, the imposition of the lien should probably depend on whether the lender acted in accordance with reasonable standards in administering the loan; if he did, no lien should be found to exist. From a policy viewpoint, this case is much like that of the priority dispute between the construction lender and the mechanics' lien claimant, discussed in § 12.7, below.

As indicated above, equitable liens can also be asserted against the improved real estate.[25] In this context the equitable lien is merely being employed as a substitute for a conventional mechanic's lien. The analysis is relatively straightforward, since in most cases there is a contractual relationship between the owner of the land and the lien claimant or those with whom he dealt. So long as the debt is proved and the land which was improved is identifiable, no great difficulty should be experienced in obtaining a judgment imposing the lien. The problems arise in determining its priority. As against bona fide purchasers of the land, the equitable lien is not discoverable through the public records and must consequently take a subordinate

24. Lefcoe & Schaffer, Construction Lending and the Equitable Lien, 40 So.Cal.L.Rev. 439 (1967).

25. See Architectronics v. Salem-American Ventures, Inc., 350 So.2d 581 (Fla.App.1977); Syring v. Sartorious, 28 Ohio App.2d 308, 277 N.E.2d 457, 57 O.O.2d 477 (1971). See generally Note, The Equitable Lien Alternative in Ohio, 44 U.Cin.L.Rev. 265 (1975).

position.[26] As against the construction lender, the lien is also likely to be subordinate unless there is evidence that the lender's misrepresentations induced the claimant to refrain from filing an ordinary mechanic's lien,[27] and that such a lien, if filed, would have had priority.

§ 12.7 Future Advances

There are many transactions in which it is desirable from a business viewpoint for the parties to enter into a present mortgage even though some portion of the loan funds is not to be advanced to the mortgagor until some future date.[28] The most common examples are construction loans and other loans to improve real property, in which the funds are advanced in installments as work progresses and the property becomes more valuable security.[29] Another illustration is the "open-end" mortgage, typically a permanent home loan in which the lender reserves the option, after the principal balance has been partially reduced, to advance additional funds up to the original balance to pay for needed remodeling of the house or other purposes.[30] Other transactions involving future advances include mortgages to secure prospective indorsements, guarantees, or accommodations of commercial paper to be issued by the mortgagor; [31] fluctuating balances under lines of credit established with an institutional lender,

26. Divine Homes, Inc. v. Gulf Power Co., 352 So.2d 115 (Fla.App.1977); Jacobsen v. Conlon, 14 Ill.App.3d 306, 302 N.E.2d 471 (1973).

27. Architectronics v. Salem-American Ventures, Inc., 350 So.2d 581 (Fla. App.1977); Hall's Miscellaneous Ironworks, Inc. v. All South Investment Co., 283 So.2d 372 (Fla.App.1973). In Indiana Mortgage & Realty Investors v. Peacock Constr. Co., 348 So.2d 59 (Fla.App.1977), the lender's telephone statement to the contractor that sufficient funds remained in the construction loan account to complete the project was held insufficient to give the contractor an equitable lien on the property superior to that of the lender.

28. See Comment, Future Advances Under the ULTA and USLTA: The Construction Lender Receives a New Status, 34 Wash. & Lee L.Rev. 1027 (1977); Urban, Future Advances Lending in North Carolina, 13 Wake For.L.Rev. 297 (1977); Comment, Mortgages to Secure Future Advances: Problems of Priority and the Doctrine of Economic Necessity, 46 Miss.L.J. 433 (1975); Comment, The Priority Problem Between Construction Mortgages and Mechanics' Liens in Alabama, 6 Cumb.L.Rev. 243 (1975); Kratovil & Werner, Mortgages for Construction and the Lien Priorities Problem—The "Unobligatory" Advance, 41 Tenn.L.Rev. 311 (1974); Meek, Mortgage Provisions Extending the Lien to Future Advances and Antecedent Indebtedness, 26 Ark.L.Rev. 423 (1973); Note, Mortgages for Future Advances: The Need for Legislation in Wisconsin, 1965 Wisc.L.Rev. 175 (1965); Blackburn, Mortgages to Secure Future Advances, 21 Mo.L. Rev. 209 (1956).

29. See § 12.1, supra; Lefcoe & Schaffer, Construction Lending and the Equitable Lien, 40 So.Cal.L.Rev. 439 (1967).

30. See Note, the Open-End Mortgage —Future Advances: A Survey, 5 DePaul L.Rev. 76 (1955); Note, Refinements in Additional Advance Financing: The "Open End" Mortgage, 38 Minn.L.Rev. 507 (1954).

31. See Ackerman v. Hunsicker, 85 N. Y. 43, 39 Am.Rep. 621 (1881); Robinson v. Williams, 22 N.Y. 380 (1860).

such as a bank; [32] and as security for a corporate bond issue, or series of issues.[33]

The advantages of such arrangements, in which the borrower takes only a fraction of the loan to begin with but will receive more in the future, are substantial. The mortgagor saves interest on the surplus until he is ready to use it, and escapes the burden of proper investment of it for the interim. Both parties avoid the expense and paperwork inherent in refinancing the initial loan, or in executing a series of junior mortgages. Particularly with construction loans, the mortgagee has the advantage of seeing that construction is progressing satisfactorily before committing large sums of money to the project, and of making sure that the growth in value represented by the construction is reasonably adequate to secure the additional advances.

Ideally, construction loans and other mortgages to secure future advances should state explicitly the amount initially advanced, the amounts of additional advances to be made in the future, and the terms and conditions on which those advances will be made. Frequently, however, neither the mortgage nor the bond or note is so specific. Instead, two other forms are common. (1) The mortgage may name a certain total sum as if it were being advanced simultaneously with the execution of the mortgage, although in reality (and as may be shown by extrinsic, perhaps oral, evidence) some of the funds are not intended to be advanced until a later time. (2) The mortgage may name only the amount of the initial advance but state that it secures future advances as well, although their amounts and the conditions on which they will be made are left indefinite. One common version of the latter type is the "dragnet" or "anaconda" clause, which purports to make the mortgaged land security for "all debts, past, present, or future, which the mortgagor may owe to the mortgagee." Dragnet clauses are discussed in the next section. In construction lending, there will commonly be a separate written construction loan agreement which fills in the terms and conditions of the future advances which both of these forms omit.

The first form, which seems to pretend that the whole amount has already been advanced, is misleading. Nevertheless, in the absence of fraud, it is clearly enforceable between the parties, although only for the amount actually advanced plus interest, of course.[34] It is valid even as against third party creditors or encumbrancers.[35] This makes sense with respect to subsequent creditors; they can hardly complain of the fact that the mortgage overstated the debt, since the

32. McDaniels v. Colvin, 16 Vt. 300, 42 Am.Dec. 512 (1844).

33. Reed's Appeal, 122 Pa. 565, 16 A. 100 (1888); Claflin v. South Carolina Ry. Co., 8 F. 118, 4 Hughes 12 (C.C. S.C.1880); In re Sunflower State Refining Co., 183 F. 834 (D.Kan.1911), 11 Col.L.Rev. 459.

34. See Note, Future Advance Clauses in Tennessee—Construction and Effect, 5 Memphis St.L.Rev. 586 (1975); Note, 23 U.Kan.L.Rev. 745 (1975).

35. Hemmerle v. First Federal Sav. & Loan Ass'n, 338 So.2d 82 (Fla.App. 1976).

usual effect will have been to make them even more conservative in giving the mortgagor further credit. On the other hand, there is a real danger to pre-existing unsecured creditors; because the recorded mortgage gives them the misimpression that the mortgagor's property is fully encumbered, they may forego efforts to obtain judgment liens or otherwise improve their position.[36] Nonetheless, the law has generally disregarded this problem and upheld the mortgage as against all creditors.

The second format, which states no total debt at all, might be thought open to attack on grounds of its vagueness. However, the courts have been abundantly willing to admit extrinsic documents (i. e., a construction loan agreement) or parol evidence in order to clarify the parties' obligations, and to enforce the mortgage as the parties are found to have intended.[37] One reason for the courts' willingness to enforce such broad mortgage language is that it is often difficult to predict at the outset the exact amount which will be needed in a complex construction job; the same is true of mortgages given to secure performance of public obligations, such as those given by land developers to local governments to guarantee completion of street paving and other required improvements. Moreover, the very vagueness of the mortgage is a warning to third party creditors that they had better inquire of the mortgagee about the status of the debt. Hence, there is little or no risk that they will be misled.

36. Shirras v. Caig, 11 U.S. (7 Cranch) 34, 3 L.Ed. 260 (1812); Griffin v. New Jersey Oil Co., 11 N.J.Eq. 49 (1855); Whelan v. Exchange Trust Co., 214 Mass. 121, 100 N.E. 1095 (1913); Witczinski v. Everman, 51 Miss. 841 (1876); Kramer v. Trustees of Farmers' & Mechanics' Bank of Steubenville, 15 Ohio 253 (1846); Savings & Loan Society v. Burnett, 106 Cal. 514, 39 P. 922 (1895) (trust deed); Tully v. Harloe, 35 Cal. 302, 95 Am.Dec. 102 (1868); Straeffer v. Rodman, 146 Ky. 1, 141 S.W. 742, Ann.Cas.1913C, 549 (1911); Merchants' State Bank of Fargo v. Tufts, 14 N.D. 238, 103 N.W. 760, 116 Am.St.Rep. 682 (1905)—accord. Cf. Youngs v. Wilson, 27 N.Y. 351 (1863); Winchell v. Coney, 54 Conn. 24, 5 A. 354 (1886)—(contra.)

37. The courts are liberal in construing the parties' agreement as including future advances. See House of Carpets Inc. v. Mortgage Investment Co., 85 N.M. 560, 514 P.2d 611 (1973); Industrial Supply Corp. v. Bricker, 306 So.2d 133 (Fla.App.1975); Potwin State Bank v. J. B. Houston & Son Lumber Co., 183 Kan. 475, 327 P.2d 1091 (1958); McDaniels v. Colvin, 16 Vt. 300, 42 Am.Dec. 512 (1844); Citizens' Sav. Bank v. Kock, 117 Mich. 225, 75 N.W. 458 (1898); Huntington v. Kneeland, 102 App.Div. 284, 92 N.Y.S. 944 (1905), affirmed 187 N.Y. 563, 80 N.E. 1111 (1907); Blackmar v. Sharp, 23 R.I. 412, 50 A. 852 (1901); Lamoille County Sav. Bank & Trust Co. v. Belden, 90 Vt. 535, 98 A. 1002 (1916). Cf. Hendricks v. Webster, 159 F. 927, 87 C.C.A. 107 (1908); First Nat. Bank v. Manser, 104 Me. 70, 71 A. 134 (1908). See also 1 A.L.R. 1586 (1919). Parol evidence may be used to show that future advances are included. Langerman v. Puritan Dining Room Co., 21 Cal.App. 637, 132 P. 617 (1913). See Mortgages for Future Advances: The Need for Legislation in Wisconsin, 1965 Wis.L.Rev. 175, 179; Thomson, Titles as Affected by Liens: Open-End Mortgages and Mortgages to Secure Future Advances, 28 Tenn.L.Rev. 354 (1961); Comment, The Extent of the Debts Secured By a Mortgage in Arkansas, 9 Ark.L.Rev. 45 (1954). A few cases are contra; see Akron Sav. & Loan Co. v. Ronson Homes, Inc., 15 Ohio St.2d 6, 238 N.E.2d 760, 44 O.O.2d 4 (1968); Matz v. Arick, 76 Conn. 388, 56 A. 630 (1904).

The courts' liberality with regard to the validity of mortgages securing future advances is not boundless, however. If the mortgage neither states the full amount (including future advances) nor warns that future advances are contemplated, it will probably be held unenforçeable, at least as against third party creditors.

Optional vs. obligatory advances. Thus far we have not discussed whether advances made in the future under a mortgage are obligatory or optional. Certainly the mortgage itself or collateral documents (such as a construction loan agreement) can be drafted to read either way. If the mortgagee has no such contractual duty, but may elect to make the additional advances and include them within the security of the mortgage if he chooses, they are said to be optional. The distinction seems simple, but in practice it is often hard to draw, as will be discussed below.

So far as enforcement between the parties is concerned, the obligatory-optional distinction is irrelevant. Even if the advance is clearly optional, its acceptance by the mortgagor signifies his willingness to have it included in the mortgage. However, when a subsequent third-party creditor enters the picture, it becomes critically important to determine whether the advance is obligatory or not. The rule widely followed in the United States is this: if the advance is obligatory, it takes its priority from the date of the original mortgage, and the subsequent creditor is junior to it.[38] (This is, of course, subject to the operation of the recording acts; it is assumed in this discussion that the mortgage was recorded immediately upon execution.) However, if the advance is optional, and if the mortgagee has notice when the advance is made that a subsequent creditor has acquired an interest in the land, then the advance loses its priority to that creditor.[39] "Notice", as used here, is a concept requiring further explanation and will be discussed later.[40]

38. Kemp v. Thurmond, 521 S.W.2d 806 (Tenn.1975); House of Carpets, Inc. v. Mortgage Investment Co., 85 N.M 560, 514 P.2d 611 (1973); Earnshaw v. First Federal Sav. & Loan Ass'n of Lowell, 109 N.H. 283, 249 A.2d 675 (1969); Western Mortgage Loan Corp. v. Cottonwood Constr. Co., 18 Utah 2d 409, 424 P.2d 437 (1967); Thompson v. Smith, 420 P.2d 526 (Okl.1966); Potwin State Bank v. J. B. Houston & Son Lumber Co., 183 Kan. 475, 327 P.2d 1091 (1958); The English roots of the doctrine are found in Lord Chancellor Campbell's opinion in Hopkinson v. Rolt, 9 H. of L. 514, 11 Eng.Rep. 829 (1861). See generally Annot., 80 A.L.R.2d 179 (1961).

39. Trustees of C. I. Mortgage Group v. Stagg of Huntington, Inc., 247 Pa.Super. 336, 372 A.2d 854 (1977); National Bank of Washington v. Equity Investors, 81 Wash.2d 886, 506 P.2d 20 (1973), appeal after remand 83 Wash.2d 435, 518 P.2d 1072; J. I. Kislak Mortgage Corp. v. William Matthews Builder, Inc., 287 A.2d 686 (Del.Super.1972), affirmed 303 A.2d 648 (Del.1973); Wayne Bldg. & Loan Co. v. Yarborough, 11 Ohio St.2d 195, 228 N.E.2d 841, 40 O.O.2d 182 (1967); Housing Mortgage Corp. v. Allied Constr., Inc., 374 Pa. 312, 97 A.2d 802 (1953); Yost-Linn Lumber Co., v. Williams, 121 Cal.App. 751, 9 P.2d 324 (1932); Home Sav. & Loan Ass'n v. Sullivan, 140 Okl. 300, 284 P. 30 (1929).

40. See text at notes 58–59, infra.

How can this rule be explained? Some earlier decisions and texts employed a highly formalistic approach: in a mortgage to secure future advances, each advance is in reality a separate mortgage which would normally take its priority only from the date it was made, but an equitable "relation back" will occur to the date of the original mortgage if the advance was obligatory or if the mortgage lacked notice of the intervening creditor.[41] This explanation is highly dubious; realistically, there is only one mortgage involved.[42] But more important, the "relation back" concept has no policy rationale. Why should obligatory advances be treated as relating back, while optional ones are not? What does notice to the mortgagee have to do with whether relation back will occur?

Perhaps the best explanation attributes the rule permitting the ending of the first mortgagee's priority as to later advances to a concern over the marketability of the mortgagor's title either for the purpose of additional mortgages by others or of sale. This concern is compounded by the traditional solicitude of the courts for the mortgagor as a person who needs unusual protection, the deepseated policy in favor of free alienability of land, and, most of all, by a desire to make the device an effective one in securing the various economic and business advantages for which it was invented. This rationale, particularly the last ingredient, supplemented or modified by the preceding ones in some instances, provides the most satisfactory explanation of the decisions. It makes understandable the latitude allowed to these transactions in spite of features quite likely to work disadvantageously as to some creditors. It permits treating the mortgage as legal from the outset and as securing the promise made then to repay all advances because the restrictions are imposed for policy reasons and not technical or legalistic ones. Because there is ample room for difference of opinion as to how much weight should be accorded various factors of policy, the operation of settled general rules of law, and arguments of relative merits of the opposing parties, the divergence of view in the cases as to just where the line should be

41. Ladue v. Detroit & Milwaukee R. Co., 13 Mich. 380, 87 Am.Dec. 759 (1865), is probably the leading authority for this view. See also Ter-Hoven v. Kerns, 2 Pa. 96 (1845) ("Every future advancement is, in reality, a new debt . . . "); Walsh, Mortgages, 77 (Mortgages given to secure advances to be made in the future create no lien either at law or in equity until such advances are made. As money is advanced under a mortgage of this kind of lien at law arises thereunder to the extent of the advance actually made. This lien relates back in equity to the original date of the mortgage * * *."); 4 Pomeroy, Eq.Juris. 594. Bank of Montgomery County's Appeal, 36 Pa. 170, 3 Grant 300 (1860); Alexandria Sav. Institution v. Thomas, 70 Va. (29 Grat.) 483 (1877) are to the same effect. See also 11 Col.L.Rev. 459 (1911). Similarly, Second Nat. Bank of Warren v. Boyle, 155 Ohio St. 482, 99 N.E.2d 474, 44 O.O. 440 (1951), noted, 13 U. of Pitt.L.Rev. 431 (1952), took the position that a mortgage for optional future advances was only an offer to provide security if and when such advances were made. Further, such advances must be made in reliance upon the mortgage.

42. See Osborne, Mortgages 114–17 (2d Ed. 1970).

drawn in ending priorities and the resort to artificial and conflicting explanations of the results is natural. And, finally, the distinction drawn by most American courts between obligatory and non-obligatory advances is made sensible. On this last matter, it is pointed out that if optional advances had an absolute preference, the mortgagor, although having no right to demand the contemplated additional loan funds, would be unable to obtain financing elsewhere for no one else would lend on a security which could be cut down by subsequent action by the first mortgagee. And, for like reason, the mortgagor would be unable to sell the property. It is true that even if the advances are obligatory he may find himself with a claim which is quite empty practically. Nevertheless he does have a legal right to performance by the mortgagee and as great, or probably a far greater actual probability of getting it from his mortgagee than he would from another lender even though this other were given power to end the priorities of the first. So long as the mortgagor and his property constitute a good risk, the mortgagee will fulfill his contract; when the risk becomes so bad that the mortgagee refuses to continue, the chance of successful financing elsewhere would be remote.

While this argument has much merit, it is a bit difficult to apply in the context in which the optional-obligatory dispute most often arises: a contest between a construction lender who recorded before work commenced, but has made some optional advances, and a group of unpaid subcontractors or suppliers who have filed mechanics' liens. In effect, the lien claimants have supplied credit to the mortgagor, albeit in the form of labor and materials rather than cash. They have usually done so with full knowledge that there is a prior construction mortgage on record, and with no expectation that the lender would take any action which would subordinate his mortgage to their liens. In effect they have, to paraphrase the argument of the preceding paragraph, lent on a security which they knew could be cut down by subsequent action by the first mortgagee. Why are they willing to assume such a risk? The answers are several: custom in the industry dictates it; they trust the developer's honesty and business judgment; and they expect that the construction lender will carefully supervise the job and the loan disbursements to guard against difficulty. When they are disappointed in these expectations, perhaps because the developer and lender underestimated costs or construction problems, or because the developer was able to divert funds away from the project, they try to advance their priority by showing that some of the loan advances were optional. If they succeed in finding such evidence, they thereby enhance their chances of collecting on their lien claims. Yet this success can only be regarded as a windfall —indeed, a fluke. It is most improbable that its eventuation was a factor in inducing them to work on the project in the first place, or that the owner would have been in a weaker position to obtain labor and materials for his project if the law gave original priority to all construction loan advances, optional or not.

Most construction lenders and their title insurers, as might be expected, despise the optional advance doctrine.[43] They argue that it tends to drive out construction capital and thereby to discourage needed real estate development. It is hard to show that this is so in the real world, however; the legal interpretations of the doctrine in particular states do not appear to have much bearing on the decisions of financial institutions to make or not to make construction loans there.

The one feature of the doctrine that cannot be doubted is its uncertainty in application; as will be seen below, it is often hard to tell whether an advance is obligatory or not, and litigation frequently results. Professor Grant Gilmore has argued that this very uncertainty is the principle virtue of the rule:

> Nevertheless, the conceptually nonsensical distinction between "obligatory" and "voluntary" has had the result (which is not in the least nonsensical) of preserving (or creating) a wide area of judicial discretion. There are few, if any, future advance clauses which an astute judge cannot, at will, classify on one side or the other of the line between obligatory and voluntary. When he has picked his label, he has also picked his priority rule. The distinction amounts to an absence of rule; the judges are invited to pick and choose, case by case, ad hoc or ad hominem. This is a recurrent phenomenon in a common law system when the arguments for or against a given position balance each other exactly. There is much to be said for giving the mortgagee an absolute priority. There is much to be said for allowing other creditors a chance at the assets (or the debtor's equity in the assets). There is much to be said for allowing the mortgagor freedom to choose new sources of financing and for allowing new lenders to come in with secure liens. Only a very wise or a very foolish man would be willing to state, categorically, where truth lies and to propose a rule for application in all possible situations. There is, then, much to be said for having no rule at all, or only a make-believe rule, and for letting the judges decide: judges are not necessarily wiser than other people, but they are paid to decide things.[44]

Gilmore's argument is appealing but ultimately unconvincing. The cost of learning the answer in a particular case, stated in terms of attorneys' fees, court costs, and the time of witnesses, is far too

43. See Skipworth, Should Construction Lenders Lose Out on Voluntary Advances If a Loan Turns Sour?, 5 Real Est.L.J. 221 (1977); Kratovil & Werner, Mortgages for Construction and the Lien Priorities Problem—The "Unobligatory" Advance, 41 Tenn.L. Rev. 311 (1974).

44. G. Gilmore, Security Interests in Personal Property 35.4 (1965).

high. A rule which could be applied with certainty, whatever its content, would be preferable.

As between construction lenders and mechanics' lien claimants, there is really no ground for a strong preference; each is usually innocent of any wrongdoing, and each is a potential victim of the poor judgment, bad luck, or dishonesty of the developer/mortgagor. The lender is usually in a better position to guard against these misfortunes,[45] but on the other hand if he has made advances which were genuinely optional, he has typically done so in a good faith effort to stave off the developer's default and the foreclosure of the mortgage, an effort which surely redounds to the benefit of the prospective lien claimants as well. In an ideal world perhaps the law would grant the lienors and the lender equal priority, allowing them to share pro-rata in the foreclosure proceeds,[46] but no American statute or case seems to take this view. An arbitrary rule favoring either the lender or the lien claimants, irrespective of the obligatory character of the advances, would be much more desirable than the unpredictability and ultimate fortuity of the present system.

What is an "optional" advance? Construction lenders frequently attempt, by language in their construction loan agreements, to reserve fairly broad discretion in making later determinations as to whether a mortgagor/developer is making satisfactory progress on the project. While lenders are generally not eager to cut off further payments or to foreclose, they often prefer to have the apparent right to do so if they sense trouble developing. This is well illustrated in National Bank of Washington v. Equity Investors,[47] in which the agreement made the bank's duty to advance the construction loan conditional upon a current appraisal, retention of an architect, and progress on the project, all of which were to be "satisfactory" to the bank. Moreover, funds were "to be advanced at such times and in such amounts as the Lender shall determine." No advance was due unless, in the judgment of the lender, all work which the advance covered had been done in a good and workmanlike manner. The Washington Supreme Court concluded that under this language the bank had no definite obligation to advance *any* funds; hence all advances were optional. By reserving too much discretion, the bank had defeated its own priority. The discretionary language may have represented sound banking practice, but the court found legally insufficient to obligate the bank.

45. But see Skipworth, supra n. 43, at 224; Lefcoe & Schaffer, Construction Lending and the Equitable Lien, 40 So.Cal.L.Rev. 439, 447–49 (1967); First Nat. State Bank of N.J. v. Carlyle House, Inc., 102 N.J.Super. 300, 246 A.2d 22 (1968), affirmed without opinion 107 N.J.Super. 389, 258 A.2d 545 (1969).

46. This suggestion is advanced in Comment, The Priority Problem Between Construction Mortgages and Mechanics' Liens in Alabama, 6 Cumb.L.Rev. 243 (1975).

47. 81 Wash.2d 886, 506 P.2d 20 (1973), appeal after remand 83 Wash. 2d 435, 518 P.2d 1072 (1974).

A different problem is represented by J. I. Kislak Mortgage Corp. v. William Matthews Builder, Inc.,[48] in which the lender's agreement provided that it was not obligated to make construction advances unless the mortgagor provided evidence that all of the preceding advances had actually been disbursed to subcontractors or materialmen. Notwithstanding this language, the lender made advances without requiring receipts or other such evidence; the court held that these advances were optional and consequently subordinate to filed mechanics' liens.

These and similar cases can be synthesized into three principles which a construction lender should carefully observe. First, he must not reserve too much discretion, but must have a genuine contractual obligation to lend; if he makes the obligation conditional, the conditions must be objectively defined and not subject to the lender's control or whim. Second, the lender must use the controls and assert the conditions which he has reserved for himself in the loan agreement. Even if those procedural controls and conditions are far more restrictive than most prudent lenders require, so that his failure to assert them could in no wise be regarded as negligence, he may still be charged with making optional advances if he does not make the mortgagor hew to the line.[49] Third, the lender must make no further advances after the occurrence of any event which is defined by the documents as a default of the mortgagor; if the lender has the *right* to cease making advances, he had better exercise it.[50] Since the construction loan agreements frequently contain broad and ambiguous pro-lender language, it is frighteningly easy to make, in the ordinary course of business, what turns out to be an optional advance. Better drafting may help, but it is only a partial solution.[51]

48. 287 A.2d 686 (Del.Super.1972), affirmed 303 A.2d 648 (Del.1973); see also Trustees of C. I. Mortgage Group v. Stagg of Huntington, Inc., 247 Pa.Super. 336, 372 A.2d 854 (1977).

49. For example, if progress payments are made ahead of schedule, they are optional; Housing Mortgage Corp. v. Allied Constr., Inc., 374 Pa. 312, 97 A.2d 802 (1953).

50. New York & Suburban Federal Sav. & Loan Ass'n v. Fi-Pen Realty Co., 133 N.Y.S.2d 33 (Sup.Ct.1954); Planters' Lumber Co. v. Griffin Chapel M.E. Church, 157 Miss. 714, 128 So. 76 (1930). It is quite likely that any advance made after exhaustion of the originally-committed construction funds will be held optional, even in the absence of relevant contractual language, since the law does not obligate the lender to fund the building to completion; Walter Harvey Corp. v. O'Keefe, 346 So.2d 617 (Fla.App.1977); Kinner v. World Sav. & Loan Corp., 57 Cal.App.3d 724, 129 Cal.Rptr. 400 (1976). See also First Federal Sav. & Loan Ass'n of Rochester v. Green-Acres Bldg. Corp., 38 Misc.2d 149, 236 N.Y.S.2d 1009 (1963), holding that a charge against the loan account to cover interest or fees on the loan is *per se* optional, since the lender could not sue itself for them. Cf. Mortgage Guarantee Co. v. Hammond Lumber Co., 13 Cal.App.2d 538, 57 P.2d 164 (1936).

51. One approach is to provide in the construction loan agreement that no default will be deemed to exist until the lender sends a formal notice of default to the borrower; another is to provide that all advances reasonably made by the lender to complete the improvements or to protect his security are deemed optional. The

The lender may be put to an extremely difficult choice even if it is obvious that any further advances will be optional. If construction is only partially completed and the construction loan account has been exhausted, it may make excellent business sense for the lender to provide further funds in the hope of getting the building completed; the increment in value which can be added by the investment of further money may far outstrip the amount invested. Moreover, completing the project so that it can be marketed is in everyone's interest if it can be accomplished at a reasonable added cost; the developer, the lender, prospective lien claimants, and the public at large will be benefitted. But if the optional/obligatory rule induces the lender to foreclose at that point the lien claimants will be wiped out (as will the developer), to no one's advantage. Hence, the net result of the rule which deprives optional advances of their priority may well be to give a few lien claimants windfalls (in cases in which the lender is ignorant of the rule or misjudges its applicability), but to harm the great majority of lien claimants by encouraging knowledgable lenders to foreclose immediately when a default occurs or the loan account is exhausted.

In a case in which further (albeit optional) advances represent the only sensible course to the lender, he may argue that those advances are economically if not contractually obligatory,[52] and should therefore retain their priority. Some support for this view may be drawn from the cases which hold that advances to cover delinquent property taxes or insurance, or to pay for necessary repairs, are deemed obligatory because they are essential to protect the lender's security.[53] Over-budget advances to complete construction might conceivably be viewed in a similar light.[54] One commentator has even recommended that before a construction lender makes an op-

success of either of these techniques is problematic; see Skipworth, supra note 43, at 226–27.

Still another approach is to place the entire construction loan amount in an escrow or trust account, thus giving the appearance that the lender has made only a single obligatory advance; the trustee or escrowee is then charged with administration of the loan. The Maryland courts have accepted this technique enthusiastically, probably as a reaction to the extremely restrictive Maryland statute regarding future advance mortgages which prevailed until 1972; see Toney Schloss Properties Corp. v. Union Federal Sav. & Loan Ass'n, 233 Md. 224, 196 A.2d 458 (1964); text at notes 69–72 infra. However, if the lender has effective control of the trustee, the ruse is so obvious that its success in other jurisdictions is doubtful.

52. See Skipworth, supra note 43; Comment, Mortgages to Secure Future Advances: Problems of Priority and the Doctrine of Economic Necessity, 47 Miss.L.J. 433 (1975).

53. See United States v. Seaboard Citizens Nat. Bank, 206 F.2d 62 (C.A. Va.1953); Blackburn, Mortgages to Secure Future Advances, 21 Mo.L. Rev. 209, 220–21 (1956); Gilmore, Security Interests in Personal Property 929 (1965); but see Heller v. Gate City Bldg. & Loan Ass'n, 75 N.M. 596, 408 P.2d 753 (1965).

54. A few cases adopt this view; see First Nat. Bank v. Zook, 50 N.D. 423, 196 N.W. 507 (1923); Hyman v. Hauff, 138 N.Y. 48, 33 N.E. 735 (1893); Rowan v. Sharps Rifle Mfg. Co., 29 Conn. 282 (1860). There are also numerous cases upholding the priority of optional advances to farm-

tional advance, he should obtain an appraisal of the property in order to show that the advance does make business sense and is in effect economically compelled.[55] Unfortunately, most courts which have considered the economic compulsion argument have rejected it.[56] If a lender acts in an economically reasonable manner to protect or enhance the security by making further advances, and makes them by means of a non-negligent mechanism—that is, one reasonably calculated to ensure that the funds are actually employed in improvements to the realty—the courts ought to protect loan's priority irrespective of the optional nature of the advances. Such a rule would better serve all parties, although only a few cases thus far support it.[57]

Notice. An optional advance loses its priority only to intervening liens of which the mortgagee has notice at the time the advance is made. By the weight of authority, the notice must be actual; [58] in the case of mechanics' liens, this presumably means not merely knowledge that contractors have done work or supplied materials to the site, but that they are unpaid and their bills are overdue. A minority view holds that the mortgagee is also charged with constructive notice from the public records, so that recordation of the appropriate form of notice of lien would postpone the priority of all further advances whether the lender had actual knowledge or not.[59] The basic policy

ers to prevent loss of growing crops; see Cedar v. W. E. Roche Fruit Co., 16 Wash.2d 652, 134 P.2d 437 (1943); Hamilton v. Rhodes, 72 Ark. 625, 83 S.W. 351 (1904); Comment, supra note 52, at 446–47.

55. Skipworth, supra note 43, at 238–39.

56. See, e. g., Elmendorf-Anthony Co. v. Dunn, 10 Wash.2d 29, 116 P.2d 253 (1941); Althouse v. Provident Mutual Bldg. Loan Ass'n, 59 Cal.App. 31, 209 P. 1018 (1922).

57. The Mississippi cases require that the mortgagee use reasonable diligence to ensure that the funds advanced actually pay for improvements to the property, but this requirement is in addition to, not in lieu of, the requirement that they be obligatory; see Wortman & Mann, Inc. v. Frierson Bldg. Supply Co., 184 So.2d 857 (Miss.1966); Southern Life Ins. Co. v. Pollard Appliance Co., 247 Miss. 211, 150 So.2d 416 (1963); Comment, supra note 52 at 458–60. Under the Arkansas rule, the lender must disburse the advances for construction purposes, but has no absolute duty to ensure that they are so used; see House v. Scott, 244 Ark. 1075, 429 S.W.2d 108 (1968). The California statute gives even optional advances on a construction loan priority if they are applied against filed mechanics' lien claims or actually used to pay for improvements to the realty; West's Ann.Cal.Civ.Code, § 3136; see Turner v. Lytton Sav. & Loan Ass'n, 242 Cal.App.2d 457, 51 Cal.Rptr. 552 (1966). Concerning the general duty of construction lenders to use reasonable care in disbursing advances, see § 12.10, infra.

58. See McMillen Feed Mills, Inc. v. Mayer, 265 S.C. 500, 220 S.E.2d 221 (1975); Alston v. Bitely, 252 Ark. 76, 477 S.W.2d 446 (1972); Pike v. Tuttle, 18 Cal.App.3d 746, 96 Cal.Rptr. 403 (1971); Leche v. Ponca City Production Credit Ass'n, 478 P.2d 347 (Okl. 1970); Biersdorff v. Brumfield, 93 Idaho 569, 468 P.2d 301 (1970); Rochester Lumber Co. v. Dygert, 136 Misc. 292, 240 N.Y.S. 580 (1930); Annot., 138 A.L.R. 566 (1942).

59. See, e. g., People's Sav. Bank v. Champlin Lumber Co., 106 R.I. 225, 258 A.2d 82 (1969), following Ladue v. Detroit & Milwaukee R.R. Co., 13 Mich. 380, 87 Am.Dec. 759 (1865).

choice regarding notice is whether it is more reasonable to impose on the lender the burden of searching the records before each disbursement which might be deemed optional, or to impose on the intervening lienor the duty to inform the lender of this claim? Technical arguments, based on whether each advance is the equivalent of a new mortgage, are of only academic relevance, and do not assist in the resolution of the policy question.

From the viewpoint of the intervening lienor, it may be observed that the title search which the lender would be required to make before each advance under the minority rule is not a very extensive one; he would need only to update his examination from the date of the previous advance. Moreover, there may be cases in which the junior lienor cannot readily locate the senior in order to give him actual notice, so that recording is the only practical alternative. Such cases must, however, be quite rare; the vast majority of mortgages to secure future advances, and particularly construction loans, are made by institutional lenders to whom notice may readily be given. From the lender's perspective, there can be no doubt that there is a real cost implicit in the necessity of making even a partial title search. The burden is magnified by the difficulty of knowing whether an advance is optional, probably causing most conservative lenders to obtain such searches before every advance in minority rule states.[60] The cost, of course, will be passed on to the developer and ultimately to the public. A more even-handed rule would require that actual notice be given except in cases in which the junior lienor could show inability to locate the lender by a reasonable effort; the needs of both parties would thereby be accommodated.

Waiver. Even if the advances made by a construction lender are clearly obligatory, several cases indicate that the lender's priority may be lost if he makes statements to prospective lien claimants which mislead them with respect to potential problems with the project.[61] For example, suppose a subcontractor, in the midst of construction, inquires of the lender about the economic soundness of the project, and is told that sufficient funds remain in the construction loan account to permit completion; in fact, the account is badly depleted and it is unlikely that the project can be completed with the funds available. Relying on the false impression he has been given, the subcontractor

60. See Note, Mortgages for Future Advances: The Need for Legislation in Wisconsin, 1965 Wisc.L.Rev. 175, 181 (1965).

61. See Trout's Investments, Inc. v. Davis, 482 S.W.2d 510 (Mo.App.1972); H. B. Deal Constr. Co. v. Labor Discount Center, Inc., 418 S.W.2d 940 (Mo.1967). Cases recognizing the principle, but finding no estoppel on the facts, include Palmer First Nat. Bank v. Rinker Materials Corp., 348 So.2d 1234 (Fla.App.1977); Gancedo Lumber Co. v. Flagship First Nat. Bank, 340 So.2d 486 (Fla.App.1976); First Nat. State Bank v. Carlyle House, Inc., 102 N.J.Super. 300, 246 A.2d 22 (1968), affirmed without opinion 107 N.J.Super. 389, 258 A.2d 545 (1969); Utah Sav. & Loan Ass'n v. Mecham, 12 Utah 2d 335, 366 P.2d 598 (1961).

continues his work, in effect throwing good money after bad. On such facts, it is hard to deny that the liens ultimately filed [62] should have priority over advances made after the misleading statement. A duty of candor to junior lienors should accompany the right of priority which the law awards to the construction lender.

Statutory modifications. A number of states have reversed the traditional doctrine by legislation and permit future advances to take the same priority as the original mortgage regardless of their optional character.[63] Most of these statutes also require a definite statement in the mortgage of the maximum amount which will be advanced under it, and withdraw priority for advances which exceed the amount stipulated together with costs, fees, and accrued interest.[64] The statutes usually exalt the mortgage above all types of intervening liens; the California statute appears on its face to grant priority only over mechanics' liens, but has been held to give a construction loan priority over a vendor's purchase money mortgage as well.[65] While some of the statutes apply only if the future advances are for improvements to the real estate or for similar purposes,[66] others make no requirement concerning the use of the advances.[67]

The Maine and Nebraska statutes [68] are particularly interesting; they permit the mortgagor to file a notice limiting the amount of the advances having priority to not less than the amount which has actually been disbursed to him to date. These statutes provide an ingenious answer to the argument, discussed previously, that if optional advances are given priority the debtor may be entirely foreclosed from obtaining additional financing, having no right to demand more funds

62. The representations may be so convincing that the subcontrators or suppliers do not file their liens until after the applicable statutory period has run; they should nonetheless be granted liens (and priority) as against the construction lender. See also § 12.6, supra, regarding the possibility of such lien claimants being awarded equitable liens on any undisbursed construction loan funds.

63. West's Adm.Cal.Civ.Code, § 3136; Conn.Gen.Stat.Ann. § 49–3; Fla.Stat. Ann. § 697.04; Ga.Code Ann. § 67–1317; Md.Ann.Code § 7–102 (1974); Maine Rev.Stat.Ann. Tit. 9B, § 436 (Supp.1977); Mont.Rev.Codes Ann. §§ 45–506, 52–201; Neb.Rev.Stat. § 76–238.01; S.C.Code § 29–3–50; Wash. Rev.Code § 60.04.220.

64. Of the statutes cited supra, n. 63 only Georgia's does not require some binding statement of the maximum loan amount. Under the Connecticut statute, however, the parties may amend the advances schedule (including, presumably, the maximum amount) at any future time. The Florida statute appears to require an express statement that the mortgage is given for future advances, but a mortgage referring only to a stated principal sum, with no reference to further advances, was given priority over intervening liens in Snead Constr. Co. v. First Federal Sav. & Loan Ass'n, 342 So.2d 517 (Fla.App. 1977). For a general review of the Florida law, see Silver Waters Corp. v. Murphy, 177 So.2d 897 (Fla.App. 1965).

65. Turner v. Lytton Sav. & Loan Ass'n, 242 Cal.App.2d 457, 51 Cal. Rptr. 552 (1966).

66. E. g., Conn., Cal., Ga.

67. E. g., Fla., Me., Md., S.C.

68. See note 63, supra.

from the original mortgagee and no apparent equity to pledge as security with a new lender. The Maine or Nebraska borrower who finds himself in such a predicament can file the applicable notice, thereby freeing his equity in the property for junior financing.

Another feature shared by the Maine and Nebraska statutes is their provision that written notice be given to the mortgagee by persons furnishing labor or materials to the realty. All optional advances made after the receipt of such notice are deemed inferior to resulting mechanics' or materialmen's liens. This provision roughly codifies the common law with respect to a particular type of intervening lien, while clarifying the nature of the notice required. However, the statutes do not define "optional" and consequently leave construction lenders in much the same dilemma discussed previously.

The Maryland statute has a fascinating and checkered history. It was originally enacted in 1825,[69] apparently because of serious abuses of the future advances mortgage. Language in such mortgages was so broad as to permit the mortgagee to acquire the mortgage, then proceed to buy up at depreciated prices debts owed by the mortgagor to third parties, and assert them against the mortgagor's land.[70] The statute, which was modified numerous times, in effect held that no future advance, optional or obligatory, would have priority but from the date it was made. By its terms the law did not apply to Baltimore or Prince George's counties, and in the rest of the state a practice grew up among construction lenders, sanctioned by the courts, of evading the statute by depositing the entire loan amount into an escrow or trust account from which the escrowee or trustee would administer the disbursements.[71] Finally in 1972 the statute was repealed and replaced with an express endorsement of priority for all future advances, irrespective of their obligatory character.[72] The Maryland statute thus shifted from one of the most restrictive (although easily evaded) in the country to one of the most liberal.

All of these statutes represent legislative recognition of the economic compulsion concept [73] and the need for reasonable discretion on the part of lenders in making optional advances to protect their interests in construction projects. These same concepts are carried over, although with greater precision and complexity, to the Uniform Land Transactions Act (ULTA) and the Uniform Simplification of Land Transfers Act (USLTA), adopted by the National Conference of

69. Md. Laws, 1825, c. 50; Md. Code, art. 66, §§ 2, 3 (1957) (repealed).

70. Watkins, Maryland Mortgages for Future Advances, 4 Md.L.Rev. 111 (1940); comment, Md.Ann.Code § 7–102 (1974).

71. See, e. g., Toney Schloss Properties Corp. v. Union Federal Sav. & Loan Ass'n, 233 Md. 224, 196 A.2d 458 (1964); Comment, Md.Ann.Code § 7–102 (1974).

72. Md.Ann.Code § 7–102 (1974).

73. Comment, Md.Ann.Code § 7–102 (1974).

Commissioners on Uniform State Laws. As these uniform acts are organized, it is necessary to consider mortgages for future advances in three distinct contexts: (1) as between mortgagee and mortgagor; (2) as between mortgagee and intervening claimants other than those claiming "construction liens" (the term ULTA and USLTA use for mechanics' and materialmen's liens); and (3) as between mortgagee and intervening construction lien claimants.

As between the mortgagor and mortgagee, mortgages for future advances are valid, but are limited to the maximum aggregate amount stated in the mortgage unless the advance is made to protect the security (as by paying property taxes, etc.) or to complete the improvements under a construction agreement,[74] in which cases the stated maximum amount may be exceeded.[75] There is no requirement that the mortgage state that it secures future advances.[76]

When a contest arises between the mortgagee and intervening claimants other than those claiming construction liens, the issue is one of priority. The ULTA grants full priority to the mortgagee who advances funds to complete improvements under a construction loan; the lender's knowledge of the intervening lien, the maximum amount stated in the mortgage, and the obligatory or optional nature of the advance are all irrelevant.[77] If the loan is for any other purpose, the lender will have priority only if the advance is made to protect the security,[78] or is made or committed to before he receives actual notice of the intervening lien.[79] In the language of the ULTA, an advance is made "pursuant to a commitment" if the lender has promised to advance the funds, even though a default by the borrower or some other extrinsic condition may excuse or has excused him from his legal duty to do so.[80] Thus, even on a non-construction loan, the lender may well have priority over intervening liens despite the fact that they were disbursed after the borrower's default. However, if the advance is not for completion of improvements or protection of the security, it can have priority only to the extent that it does not exceed the maximum amount stated in the mortgage.[81]

Finally, a somewhat different scheme of priorities is established as between the mortgagee and construction lien claimants. Such liens take priority over all future advances under non-construction

74. U.L.T.A. § 3–205(e).

75. U.L.T.A. § 3–205(c).

76. This statement is clearly correct with respect to construction advances and advances to protect the security; U.L.T.A. § 3–205(e). Whether it is also true of other types of future advances is unclear under the ULTA; the matter would presumably be governed by the common law, which has generally permitted such advances notwithstanding the lack of reference to them in the mortgage. See text at notes 34–37, supra.

77. U.L.T.A. § 3–301(b)(4).

78. U.L.T.A. § 3–301(b)(3).

79. U.L.T.A. § 3–301(b)(1)(2).

80. U.L.T.A. § 1–201(14).

81. U.L.T.A. § 3–301(b)(1), (2)

loans, even if the lender has made the advance or commitment before learning of the lien.[82] However, they are inferior to advances under construction loans if the advances are paid toward improvements on the real estate, the discharge of prior construction liens, or protection of the security interest (again, such as payment of taxes.) [83] Even if none of these three criteria are met, the construction loan will have priority to the extent of advances made before the lender had actual knowledge that a mechanics' lien had attached.[84]

In sum, the ULTA and USLTA give construction lenders considerable advantages not made available to other lenders of future advances. The construction lender is not limited to the maximum amount stated in the mortgage; this provision is reasonable, since inflating construction costs can make the parties' original cost estimate inadequate even though additional advances to complete the project are socially highly desirable. Construction loan advances made to enable completion of the improvements have priority over most types of intervening liens, even if they are clearly optional. Even as against mechanics' liens, construction loan advances are given priority if they are "made in payment of the price of the agreed improvements." [85] This last phrase may have important connotations, for it can be read to impose an absolute duty on the part of the lender to make certain that the funds are not diverted to non-construction purposes. Compare the language employed in describing the priority of construction loan advances over *non*-mechanics' lien claims: "made * * * to enable completion of the agreed improvement." [86] This terminology does not seem to require that the funds in fact be used to purchase the improvements, but only that they be advanced to the owner or developer with that purpose in mind. Diversion of the funds would not, under this view, be fatal to the lender's priority.

Whether any distinction along these lines was intended by the Commissioners is hard to say. It is not easy to see why a mechanics' lien claimant should be entitled to a higher standard of care or performance from the construction lender than, say, a junior mortgagee or a subordinated purchase-money vendor. In any event, to impose absolute liability on the lender seems excessively harsh; a standard of reasonable care in selecting and implementing a method of disbursal of funds would give adequate protection for all types of intervening lienors. However, speaking generally, the Commissioners have achieved a reasonable balance between the needs of construction lenders and other claimants, and they have acted wisely in granting construction lenders the flexibility they need to complete troubled projects without undue fear of loss of priority.

82. U.S.L.T.A. § 5–209(a).

83. U.S.L.T.A. § 5–209(c).

84. U.S.L.T.A. § 5–209(b).

85. U.S.L.T.A. § 5–209(c)(1).

86. U.S.L.T.A. § 3–301(b)(4).

§ 12.8 Dragnet Clauses

The dragnet clause is a mortgage provision which purports to make the real estate security for other, usually unspecified, debts which the mortgagor may already owe or may owe in the future to the mortgagee. The clause is not functionally related to construction lending and is discussed at this point only because it is conceptually a mortgage to secure future advances. In a sense the dragnet clause is just the opposite of a construction loan; the lender usually has no particular future advances in mind, and merely "throws in" the clause in the hope that it might come in handy later.

A simple form of dragnet clause reads as follows:

> "This mortgage is given to secure the payment of a promissory note (described in detail), and also the payment of any additional sums and interest thereon now or hereafter due or owing from mortgagor to mortgagee." [87]

A more carefully-drafted form, which attempts to resolve some questions implicit in the foregoing clause, is:

> "This mortgage is given to secure the payment of a promissory note (described in detail), and any other indebtedness or obligation of the mortgagor, or any of them, and any present of future demands of any kind or nature which mortgagee or its successor may have against the mortgagor or any of them, whether created directly, or acquired by assignment, whether absolute or contingent, whether due or not, whether otherwise secured or not, or whether existing at the time of the execution of this instrument or arising thereafter." [88]

Dragnet clauses are frequently included in the printed language of mortgages drafted by mortgagees. They are seldom the subject of negotiation, and may go entirely unnoticed by the mortgagor until the mortgagee asserts them. The rule making optional advances subordinate to intervening liens [89] is highly relevant in this context. Advances secured by dragnet clauses are almost never obligatory; the only factual issue is generally whether the mortgagee had the requisite notice of intervening liens, and this is usually not hard to determine.[90] Moreover the rule, which was severely criticized in the

87. The language is adapted from Union Bank v. Wendland, 54 Cal.App.3d 393, 126 Cal.Rptr. 549 (1976). See Emporia State Bank & Trust Co. v. Mounkes, 214 Kan. 178, 179, 519 P.2d 618, 620 (1974); Note, Future Advance Clauses in Tennessee—Construction and Effect, 5 Memph.St.L. Rev. 586 (1975).

88. Wong v. Beneficial Sav. & Loan Ass'n, 56 Cal.App.3d 286, 128 Cal. Rptr. 338 (1976).

89. See § 12.7, supra, at notes 39–41.

90. See Bank of Ephriam v. Davis, 559 P.2d 538 (Utah 1977), requiring actual notice on the part of the lender to subordinate its lien deriving from a dragnet clause. Since no such notice was shown, the lender was held to have priority despite the optional nature of the advances.

preceding section as applied to construction loans, makes rather good sense in the dragnet clause case; in its absence, a mortgagor might naively execute upon his house a mortgage containing a dragnet clause and consequently find himself locked to that particular lender for the rest of his life.[91] Dragnet clauses are generally upheld,[92] but because their apparent coverage is so broad, and because the mortgagor is often unaware of their presence or implications, the courts tend to construe them narrowly against the mortgagee.[93] Generalizations are difficult, since the language of the particular clause may be a decisive factor. However, the following illustrations show numerous ways in which the courts have narrowed the application of dragnet clauses. Sometimes such holdings are said to be based on the intention of the parties, but in reality they usually represent the court's conceptions of fairness and equity. These illustrations are not intended to represent any majority rule, as there are many conflicting or contrary cases. They merely show the sort of judicial treatment dragnet clauses often receive.

1. The mortgage will only secure advances made or debts incurred in the future. If the mortgagor already owes debts to the mortgagee at the time the mortgage is executed, it would supposedly be easy enough to identify those existing debts specifically; if they are not so identified, it is assumed that the parties did not intend to secure them.[94]

2. Only debts of the same type or character as the original debt are secured by the mortgage.[95] For example, if the original loan is

91. See Meek, Mortgage Provisions Extending the Lien to Future Advances and Antecedent Indebtedness, 26 Ark.L.Rev. 485 (1973).

92. First Nat. Bank v. Rozelle, 493 F.2d 1196 (C.A.Okl.1974); Lammey v. Producers Livestock Credit Corp., 463 P.2d 491 (Wyo.1970).

93. First v. Byrne, 238 Iowa 712, 28 N.W.2d 509 (1947); Annot., 172 A.L.R. 1072 (1948). The courts of Tennessee tend to be an exception, construing dragnet clauses rather consistently in favor of the lender; see Note, Future Advances Clauses in Tennessee—Construction and Effect, 5 Memph.St.L.Rev. 586 (1975).

94. Durham v. First Guar. Bank, 331 So.2d 563 (La.App.1976), writ denied 334 So.2d 431; National Bank v. Blankenship, 177 F.Supp. 667 (E.D.Ark.1959), affirmed sub nom National Bank v. General Mills, 283 F.2d 574 (C.A.Ark.1960); First v. Byrne, 238 Iowa 712, 28 N.W.2d 509 (1947); Bank of Searcy v. Kroh, 195 Ark. 785, 114 S.W.2d 26 (1938); Farmer's Nat. Bank v. DeFever, 177 Okla. 561, 61 P.2d 245 (1936); Iser v. Mark Bldg. Corp., 253 N.Y. 499, 171 N.E. 757 (1930). Cf. United States v. Automatic Heating & Equipment Co., 181 F.Supp. 924 (E.D.Tenn.1960), affirmed 287 F.2d 885 (C.A.Tenn.1961).

95. Emporia State Bank & Trust Co. v. Mounkes, 214 Kan. 178, 519 P.2d 618 (1974), noted 23 U.Kan.L.Rev. 745 (1975) (original mortgage loan apparently to purchase realty; note signed eight years later to buy car and start son in restaurant business not covered by dragnet clause); Airline Commerce Bank v. Commercial Credit Corp., 531 S.W.2d 171 (Tex.Civ.App.1975), refused n.r.e.; Akamine & Sons, Ltd. v. American Security Bank, 50 Hawaii 304, 440 P.2d 262 (1968); Hendrickson v. Farmers' Bank & Trust Co., 189 Ark. 423, 73 S.W.2d 725 (1934). Cf. Wong v. Beneficial Sav. & Loan Ass'n, 56 Cal.App.3d 286, 128 Cal.Rptr. 338 (1976);

for home repairs, a future loan or advance for more repairs would be secured by the mortgage but a loan for an automobile purchase would not. It is easy to imagine grey areas in such a test. For example, what if the second loan were for adding a room to the house? The resolution of the matter is made easier if the documents on the second loan state that it is to be secured under the dragnet clause of the existing mortgage.

3. As an extension of the foregoing concept, it is sometimes held that the dragnet clause will cover future debts only if the documents evidencing those debts specifically refer back to the clause.[96]

4. If the future debt is separately secured, whether by another mortgage or by a personal property security agreement, it may be assumed that the parties did not intend that it also be secured by the dragnet mortgage.[97]

5. The clause is inapplicable to debts which were originally owed by the mortgagor to third parties, and which were assigned to or purchased by the mortgagee.[98]

6. If there are several joint mortgagors, only future debts on which all of the mortgagors are obligated [99] (or at least of which all were aware) [1] will be covered by the dragnet clause.

7. Once the original debt has been fully discharged, the mortgage is extinguished and cannot secure future loans.[2]

First Nat. Bank v. Rozelle, 493 F.2d 1196 (C.A.Okl.1974); In re Dorsey Electric Supply Co., 344 F.Supp. 1171 (E.D.Ark.1972); Hamlin v. Timberlake Grocery Co., 130 Ga.App. 648, 204 S.E.2d 442 (1974); Murdock Acceptance Corp. v. Jones, 50 Tenn.App. 431, 362 S.W.2d 266 (1961); Thorp Sales Corp. v. Dolese Bros. Co., 453 F.Supp. 196 (W.D.Okla.1978).

96. Stockyards Nat. Bank v. Capitol Steel & Iron Co., 201 Kan. 429, 441 P.2d 301 (1968).

97. Vaughn & Co., Ltd., v. Saul, 143 Ga.App. 74, 237 S.E.2d 622 (1977); Moran v. Gardemeyer, 82 Cal. 102, 23 P. 8 (1889); Second Nat. Bank v. Boyle, 155 Ohio St. 482, 99 N.E.2d 474, 44 O.O. 440 (1951).

98. Hudson v. Bank of Leakesville, 249 So.2d 371 (Miss.1971); Wood v. Parker Square State Bank, 400 S.W.2d 898 (Tex.1966); Thorp Sales Corp. v. Dolese Bros. Co., note 95 supra. See also Bowen v. Kicklighter, 124 Ga. App. 82, 183 S.E.2d 10 (1971) (assignee of mortgage may not assert dragnet clause to secure advances made to mortgagor before assignment.)

99. Holiday Inns, Inc. v. Susher-Schaefer Investment Co., 77 Mich.App. 658, 259 N.W.2d 179 (1977); United States v. American Nat. Bank, 255 F.2d 504 (C.A.Fla.1958), certiorari denied, 358 U.S. 835, 79 S.Ct. 58, 3 L.Ed.2d 72, rehearing denied 359 U.S. 1006, 79 S. Ct. 1135, 3 L.Ed.2d 1034; First v. Byrne, 238 Iowa 712, 28 N.W.2d 509 (1947). Cf. Newton County Bank v. Jones, 299 So.2d 215 (Miss.1974); Wright v. Lincoln County Bank, 62 Tenn.App. 560, 465 S.W.2d 877 (1970); Martin v. First Nat. Bank, 279 Ala. 303, 184 So.2d 815 (1966).

1. Lomanto v. Bank of America, 22 Cal.App.3d 663, 99 Cal.Rptr. 442 (1972); Gates v. Crocker-Anglo Nat. Bank, 257 Cal.App.2d 857, 65 Cal. Rptr. 536 (1968).

2. Jacobs v. City Nat. Bank, 229 Ark. 79, 313 S.W.2d 789 (1958); cf. Central Production Credit Ass'n v. Page, 268 S.C. 1, 231 S.E.2d 210 (1977) (dragnet clause remains valid even after principal debt is fully paid.)

8. If the real estate is transferred by the mortgagor to a third party, any debts which the original mortgagor incurs thereafter are not secured by the mortgage.[3] This is the position taken by the draftsmen of the Uniform Land Transfer Act.[4]

In addition to these judicial limitations, most of the statutes relating to future advances discussed in the preceding section [5] limit the amount of such advances to the maximum amount stated in the original mortgage. This limitation is important in the construction of dragnet clauses since the clauses on their face are usually unlimited as to amount.

While the dragnet clause is usually regarded as advantageous to mortgagees, that is not necessarily the case. One reason is that the types of judicial limitations on the clause discussed above are very much open to debate and further development in most states; in this sense, the clause is an invitation to litigation. Moreover, even if the clause is held to be valid, it may be turned against the mortgagee. Union Bank v. Wendland,[6] a California intermediate appellate decision, provides an interesting example. Somewhat simplified, the Wendlands borrowed a sum from the bank and gave a deed of trust (containing a dragnet clause) on their house as security. Subsequently, they borrowed an additional amount from the same bank to remodel the house, giving a second note and another deed of trust on the same real estate. Upon their default the bank foreclosed the first deed of trust by power of sale. It then brought a suit upon the second note. The antideficiency statute, by its terms, barred any personal judgment on a note secured by a deed of trust which had been foreclosed by power of sale.[7] The Wendlands argued, and the court held, that the second note was in fact secured by the first deed of trust (through the operation of its dragnet clause) and thus could not be collected by way of personal suit.

Dragnet clauses can also be dangerous to title insurers. In Southwest Title Insurance Co. v. Northland Building Corporation,[8] the title company issued a policy which specifically excepted two existing mortgages which the company's search had disclosed. The policy language recited that those mortgages secured certain specific promissory notes which were carefully identified in the policy. However, the mortgages also contained dragnet clauses which caused them to secure other loans made to the mortgagors as well, a fact not mentioned in the policy. The Texas Supreme Court held that, as to the loans covered by the dragnet clauses, the policy exceptions were ineffective and the title company was liable. More careful drafting of

3. Vaughn v. Crown Plumbing & Sewer Service, Inc., 523 S.W.2d 72 (Tex. Civ.App.1975), refused n.r.e.

4. U.L.T.A. § 3–205(d).

5. § 12.7, supra, at notes 63–86.

6. 54 Cal.App.3d 393, 126 Cal.Rptr. 549 (1976).

7. West's Ann.Cal.Civil Proc.Code, § 580 (d); see § 8.3, supra.

8. 552 S.W.2d 425 (Tex.1977).

the policy exceptions could probably have produced a different result, but the case illustrates how dragnet clauses can have unanticipated and undesired results.

§ 12.9 Subordination Agreements

By subordination agreements mortgagees may agree to alter the relative priorities that the applicable law and documents would otherwise give their mortgages.[9] Subordination agreements are subject to recording statutes and are used in many kinds of transactions. It is well established that parties may use a subordination agreement to establish the priority of mortgages executed on the same property at the same time.[10] And a senior mortgage can be subordinated to specific junior mortgage.[11] If a first mortgage is subordinated to a third mortgage, the first mortgage becomes subordinate to the second mortgage.[12] However, as this section will explain, an agreement to subordinate a mortgage to an undefined future mortgage may not be enforceable.

Subordination of Vendors to Construction Lenders

Subordination agreements are frequently used in mortgages relating to new real estate developments because they make it possible for developers to finance subdivisions and other construction projects without investing large amounts of their own capital. First, the developer persuades the original land seller to accept a purchase money mortgage or trust deed for all or a large part of the purchase price.[13]

9. A mortgagee must personally agree to be subordinated. The trustee under a trust deed has no power to subordinate without the consent of the beneficiary unless the trust instrument so provides. Belknap Sav. Bank v. Lamar Land and Canal Co., 28 Colo. 326, 64 P. 212 (1901). Persons dealing with a trustee must take notice of the scope of his authority. But if the trustee has power to subordinate, a third party acting in good faith is protected unless apprised of facts that should reasonably put him on notice that a breach of trust is involved. Dye v. Lincoln Rochester Trust Co., 40 A.D.2d 583, 334 N.Y.S.2d 402 (1972), affirmed 31 N.Y.2d 1012, 341 N.Y.S.2d 619, 294 N.E.2d 207 (1973).

10. Gautney v. Gautney, 253 Ala. 584, 46 So.2d 198 (1950); Collins v. Home Sav. & Loan Ass'n, 205 Cal.App.2d 86, 22 Cal.Rptr. 817, 822 (1962); Hagen v. Butler, 83 Idaho 427, 363 P.2d 712 (1961).

11. Olds Bros. Lumber Co. v. Marley, 72 Ariz. 392, 236 P.2d 464 (1951); State Sav. & Loan Ass'n v. Kauaian Dev. Corp., 50 Hawaii 540, 445 P.2d 109 (1968); Landau v. Western Pennsylvania Nat. Bank, 445 Pa. 217, 282 A.2d 335 (1971).

12. Shaddix v. National Surety Co., 221 Ala. 268, 128 So. 220 (1930); Ladner v. Hogue Lumber & Supply Co., 229 Miss. 505, 511, 91 So.2d 545, 547 (1956).

13. Sellers are often willing to accept a purchase money mortgage because of the tax benefits from receiving payments spread over a number of years (I.R.C. § 453). Sellers will subordinate their purchase money mortgages if they are convinced that the sale depends upon the developer being able to obtain first lien construction financing. And usually sellers are compensated by receiving a higher purchase price. See generally Note, The Subordination of Purchase-Money Security, 52 Cal.L.Rev. 157 (1964). See Statland Holliday, Inc. v. Stendig Development Corp., 46 A.D.2d 135, 362 N.Y.S.2d 2 (1974).

Then, using the land as security, the developer arranges a construction loan from an institutional lender to finance the construction of the houses, apartments, or condominiums that he plans. A subordination agreement with the seller makes this financing scheme possible by reordering the lien priorities between the purchase money mortgage and the construction loan. Institutional lenders are required by law to secure real estate loans with first liens,[14] but in the absence of an explicit reversal of priorities, the law presumes that the purchase money mortgage is intended to have priority.[15] The purchase money mortgage is usually recorded first, so an enforceable subordination agreement is necessary to give the institutional lender the first lien.

Much of the recent litigation relating to subordination agreements has centered on their enforceability, especially in relation to indefiniteness.[16] The validity and effectiveness of subordination agreements have been challenged at two points in the transaction: (1) while the agreement is still executory and (2) after the construction loan has been made and a contest over priority develops between the seller and the construction lender after a default.

The most common way for litigation to arise while the agreement is still executory is for a developer to bring suit against a seller seeking specific performance of a contract for the sale of land. This usually occurs when it is not feasible to negotiate the terms of the construction loan at the time the contract for the purchase of the land is entered into. As a result, the subordination clause of the contract is left more or less indefinite concerning the terms of the construction loan to be obtained. Then the seller sours on the whole transaction or refuses to enter into a specific subordination agreement that would subordinate his lien to the particular loan that the purchaser has arranged.[17] When the purchaser seeks specific per-

14. National banks are required to take first liens under 12 U.S.C.A. § 1371, federal savings and loans under 12 U.S.C.A. § 1464(c), and most state-chartered institutions under state laws.

15. See § 213; West's Ann.Cal.Civ. Code, § 2898.

16. See generally Annotation, Requisite Definiteness of Provision in Contract for Sale or Lease of Land, that Vendor or Landlord Will Subordinate His Interest to Permit Other Party to Obtain Financing, 26 A.L.R.3d 855 (1969); Miller, Starr and Regalia, Subordination Agreements in California, 13 U.C.L.A.L.Rev. 1298 (1966).

17. "The agreement altering priority may be contained in a separate writing or it may be set forth in the recorded security instrument. In either case the provisions of the subordination agreement are regulated, in part, by statute, and it must be recorded in order to impart constructive notice of its contents. By the terms of the 'automatic' subordination agreement the seller's lien is recorded with an agreement that the lien of a subsequent lender will automatically be senior to the seller's lien without further acts on his part. By the terms of the other common form, the seller promises to execute a subsequent instrument which will subordinate his lien to that of the lender. However, even under the 'automatic' subordination agreement, a title company will usually require the seller to execute another document at the time the new lien is recorded, in order specifi-

formance of the contract, the seller usually attempts to avoid performance by showing that the subordination clause is too vague and indefinite to be enforced. In the cases in which the courts have ruled for the seller, the entire contract has become unenforceable, since the clause is considered a material part of the contract. However, it has been suggested that an absolute and unconditional waiver of the subordination clause by the purchaser could save the rest of the contract.[18]

In addition to the defense of indefiniteness, sellers have successfully raised defenses based on the Statute of Frauds.[19] And in California sellers have used a statute that prohibits the enforcement of a contract by specific performance against a party if the contract is not, "as to him, just and reasonable." [20]

When the subordination agreement is challenged after a default has occurred and a contest over priority has developed, sellers attempt to raise these same arguments. But because the contract has been at least partially performed, other issues prevent the question from being decided simply by determining if the contract is indefinite or unjust and unreasonable on its face.

Actions to Enforce Executory Subordination Agreements

In California, where most of the litigation related to subordination agreements has occurred, the courts have been sympathetic to the seller, generally regarding him as an unsophisticated party in need of protection. They have held that "an enforceable subordination clause must contain terms that will define and minimize the risk that the subordinating lien will impair or destroy the seller's security." [21] Although the California courts have not specified a

cally to subordinate the seller's lien to the new lien." Miller, Starr and Regalia, Subordination Agreements in California, 13 U.C.L.A.L.Rev. 1298, 1299 (1966).

18. Spellman v. Dixon, 256 Cal.App.2d 1, 4, 63 Cal.Rptr. 668, 671 (1967).

19. Troj v. Chesebro, 30 Conn.Sup. 30 296 A.2d 685 (1972).

20. West's Ann.Cal.Civ.Code, § 3391 (2). See also West's Ann.Cal.Civ. Code, §§ 2953.1–2953.5 which provides that where the secured loan to be subordinated is less than $25,000, the subordination agreement or clause must contain a prominent warning that the agreement may subordinate the holder of the note to another security which would normally have a lower priority. If the warning is not given and the subordinating party has no actual knowledge of the subordination, he can void the agreement anytime within two years by recording notice.

21. Handy v. Gordon, 65 Cal.2d 578, 55 Cal.Rptr, 769, 422 P.2d 329, 26 A. L.R.3d 848 (1967). See Stockwell v. Lindeman, 229 Cal.App.2d 750, 40 Cal.Rptr. 555 (1964); Magna Development Co. v. Reed, 228 Cal.App.2d 230, 39 Cal.Rptr. 284 (1964); Burrow v. Timmsen, 223 Cal.App.2d 283, 35 Cal.Rptr. 668, 100 A.L.R.2d 544 (1963); Roven v. Miller, 168 Cal.App.2d 391, 335 P.2d 1035 (1959).

minimum set of terms that will make a subordination agreement enforceable, they have provided some guidance.[22]

In 1967 the California Supreme Court was asked to decide in Handy v. Gordon if a subordination clause specifying maximum loan amounts per unit, maximum interest rates, and maximum loan periods could be enforced by specific performance. In addition to arguing that the subordination clause was too indefinite to enforce, the seller raised a defense based upon a statute [23] which prohibited the enforcement of a contract by specific performance if the contract is not just and reasonable to the party against whom enforcement is sought. The court denied the suit for specific performance, saying that the contract was not fair and reasonable to the seller because it did not adequately define and minimize his risk. Specifically, the clause did not limit the buyer's use of the loan proceeds to construction on the land. Nor did it provide assurance that the amounts of the loans would not exceed the value which the improvements added to the land; the loan maximums were expressed in terms of absolutes and did not limit the loan amounts to percentages of the building costs. Finally, the loan limits were maximums per lot and the developer had discretion to determine the number of lots.

While the court in Handy v. Gordon appeared to decide the case on the basis of whether the contract was just and reasonable to the seller, it would seem that the subordination clause was not just and reasonable because it was too indefinite. Thus in subordination agreement cases it probably makes no difference that the statutory defense relied upon in Handy v. Gordon technically applies only to suits for specific performance: if a subordination agreement is so indefinite that it is unfair to require a seller to perform under it, it probably would not be definite enough to support a suit for damages.

In Malani v. Clapp [24] the Supreme Court of Hawaii followed *Handy*, holding that a subordination agreement must adequately protect the subordinating party. There a lessor sued a lessee for breach of contract, and the lessee tried to avoid the contract by showing that

22. In Stockwell v. Lindeman, supra note 21, a California court of appeals held that a subordination clause which specified a maximum loan amount and a maximum interest rate and provided that repayment should be made upon the terms required by the lender, could be enforced by specific performance. The court said that the terms of repayment could be supplied by the lender or by custom but that the contract would not be valid if the terms of repayment were left for future agreement between the parties themselves. Although Stockwell is cited with apparent approval in Handy v. Gordon, supra note 21, Stockwell's reliance on custom or the future loan agreement to supply additional terms providing essential protection to the vendor is of questionable validity after Handy.

23. See note 20, supra.

24. Malani v. Clapp, 56 Hawaii 507, 542 P.2d 1265 (1975).

the subordination clause [25] was too indefinite to enforce. The subordination agreement limited the term of subordination to two years, required the lessee to be personally liable to the lessor, and required the lessee to show an aggregate net worth of $2,000,000. In addition to the clause itself, the court looked at the entire context of the transaction to determine if the lessor was adequately protected. The court felt that because of the protections in the subordination clause and because the type of construction was specified in a building permit, the lessor was adequately protected.[26]

Most of the other courts which have been asked to decide the validity of subordination agreements have similarly held that terms limiting the seller's risk are necessary to make the agreement enforceable. While these courts have not uniformly designated certain terms as essential, the terms which they most often mention are maximum loan amounts, maximum interest rates, maximum loan periods, and limitations on the use of the loan proceeds.[27] Despite the general trend toward requiring terms of limitation in subordination agreements, there are a few recent cases in which courts have ruled that construction loans do not have to be described in detail.[28]

Action to Reverse Priorities After a Default

A contest over priorities after a default is quite different from an action to enforce an executory subordination agreement. First, the parties usually have executed a second subordination agreement describing the specific construction loan, thus curing any indefiniteness in the original agreement. Miller v. Citizens Savings and Loan Association [29] provides an example of such a situation. In this case the question revolved around a term limiting the use of the loan proceeds that was in the first agreement but not in the second. The

25. Under this agreement the lessor would subordinate her fee estate to a construction loan to be procured by the lessee. While this type of agreement is commonly called a subordination agreement, it is technically inaccurate to call it such since subordination agreements alter the priorities between mortgages and there is only one mortgage involved in this case. In reality the "subordination clause" is an agreement by the lessor to join in the lessee's mortgage, thereby subjecting the fee title to the mortgage. See Committee on Leases, Ground Leases and Their Financing, 4 Real Prop.Prob. & Trust J. 437 (1969).

26. The court might not have been so willing to find that the lessor was adequately protected if it had been the lessor who was trying to avoid the contract.

27. Lahaina-Maui Corp. v. Tau Tet Hew, 362 F.2d 419 (C.A.Hawaii 1966); Troj v. Chesebro, 30 Conn.Sup. 30, 296 A.2d 685 (1972); Hux v. Raben, 74 Ill.App.2d 214, 219 N.E.2d 770 (1966), affirmed 38 Ill.2d 223, 230 N.E.2d 831 (1967); Grooms v. Williams, 227 Md. 165, 175 A.2d 575 (1961).

28. Rivers v. Rice, 233 Ga. 819, 213 S.E.2d 678 (1975); Ideal Realty Co., v. Reese, 122 Ga.App. 707, 178 S.E.2d 564 (1970); White & Bollard, Inc. v. Goodenow, 58 Wash.2d 180, 361 P.2d 571 (1961).

29. 248 Cal.App.2d 655, 56 Cal.Rptr. 844 (1967). See discussion in The California Supreme Court 1966–1967: X. Secured Transactions A. Subordination Agreements, 1967, 55 Cal.L. Rev. 1184–1187.

court merged the agreements and enforced the clause in the first agreement that required the construction loans to be used only for certain purposes.[30] But even absent the first agreement, the court noted that "a subordination agreement should be construed, unless it expressly provides otherwise, as permitting the loan proceeds to be used only for * * *" purposes which will improve the seller's security position.[31] The seller was granted reestablishment of the superiority of his lien over that part of the construction loan not used for authorized purposes.[32]

Even when a second agreement has not cured indefiniteness, courts have held that the seller was estopped from asserting that the subordination agreement was invalid. In First Connecticut Small Business Investment Company v. Arba [33] the seller contended that a subordination agreement violated the Statute of Frauds because it contained neither the interest rate nor the maturity date of the construction loan. Although Connecticut courts had earlier accepted the Statute of Frauds as a defense against the enforcement of a similar subordination agreement,[34] in *Arba* the court held that the seller was estopped because the agreement had been executed and a lender had relied to his detriment on the subordination.[35]

Florida and Georgia courts have differed from the other state courts in the treatment of executed agreements. A Georgia court simply required no specificity in the description of the construction loan.[36] In a Florida case a seller sought to reestablish the priority of his lien over a construction loan on the grounds that the loan proceeds were not used for the purpose specified in the subordination agreement. The court held that the construction lender was not bound by the agreement because he was not a party to it.[37]

Drafting Subordination Agreements

The developer will want a self-executing subordination agreement that contains enough terms to be enforceable. To be safe the

30. But see Fandel, Inc. v. First of Denver Mortgage Investors, 522 S.W. 2d 721 (Tex.Civ.App.1975).

31. Miller v. Citizens Sav. and Loan Ass'n, 248 Cal.App.2d 655, 663, 56 Cal.Rptr. 844, 851 (1967).

32. For a more thorough discussion of diversion of funds see § 12.10, infra.

33. 170 Conn. 168, 365 A.2d 100 (1976).

34. Troj v. Chesebro, supra note 19.

35. See also, American Century Mortgage Investors v. Unionamerican Mortgage and Equity Trust, 355 A.2d 563 (D.C.App.1976).

36. In Rivers v. Rice, 233 Ga. 819, 213 S.E.2d 678 (1975), a seller brought suit to reestablish the priority of her mortgage. She attacked the three subordination agreements which she had executed on the grounds that they did not describe the subordinating loans. The court held that the subordination agreements were valid because they showed her intention to subordinate her mortgage. The court recited the rule in Ideal Realty Co. v. Reese, supra at note 28, which states that it is not necessary to set forth with particularity the terms of the construction loan in a subordination agreement.

37. Roberts v. Harkins, 292 So.2d 603, (Fla.App.1974), certiorari denied 302 So.2d 417 (Fla.1974).

developer should see that the agreement includes (1) the maximum loan amount both as an absolute and as a percentage of the cost of construction, (2) the maximum interest rate, (3) the minimum and maximum terms of years over which the construction loan is to be repaid, and (4) a clause stating the purpose for which the loan will be used. The terms should not be so restrictive that the developer cannot obtain financing meeting the conditions described.

The seller will want all of the terms mentioned above, and he may also bargain for other safeguards that will protect him from unreasonable risk. He should consider prohibiting refinancing, future advances, dragnet clauses and assignments of the senior loan. He will certainly wish to require that all proceeds be used for permanent improvements on the land.[38] He may want to require that all documents, plans and specifications be submitted for his approval, or that the lender make all disbursements through a voucher or progress payment system that assures that the funds pay only for material and labor. The seller may want to reserve the right to inspect the premises or the records of the other parties at any time. He may also want to require the construction lender to give him some reasonable notice—say, 30 days—before the lender files a notice of default, thus giving the seller an opportunity to cure the default. The seller should make sure that the subordination agreement is recorded in full, and he should try to get the construction lender to sign it. In sum, he should investigate the project thoroughly and bargain for any safeguards that will insure the project's successful completion.

Subordination Between Mortgages and Leases

The priority relationship that exists between a lease and a mortgage usually depends upon the order in which they are recorded,[39] unless their priorities have been altered by a subordination agreement. In large developments such as shopping centers that involve mortgages and leases, subordination agreements are frequently negotiated because the priorities of the mortgages and leases are very important to the parties involved. For instance, an institutional lender is required by law to have a first lien on the property securing his mortgage, and while a lease is an encumbrance rather than a lien, the lender may still be in violation if his mortgage is junior to a lease. On the other had, because foreclosure of a senior mortgage will usually destroy all leases subordinate to it, a major tenant in a shopping center may have a great deal to lose if his lease is subordinate to a mortgage.

38. A lawyer was successfully sued by the seller he had represented for failing to draft a subordination agreement that required that all loan proceeds be used for permanent improvements on the property. Starr v. Mooslin, 14 Cal.App.3d 988, 92 Cal. Rptr. 583 (1971).

39. Notice also plays a role in determining priorities, of course. A recorded mortgage may not have priority over an unrecorded prior lease if the mortgagee has notice of the lease. Republic Nat. Life Ins. Co. v. Marquette Bank and Trust Co., 251 N.W.2d 120 (Minn.1977).

In some states the mortgagee has the option of keeping junior leases in force by not joining the lessees in the foreclosure proceeding.[40] In these states it is never a disadvantage for a mortgagee to be senior to important leases.[41] But in other states where foreclosure permits omitted junior lessees to terminate, it may be a serious detriment to a mortgagee to have his mortgage senior to important leases. The leases of major tenants often form a very important part of the security value of a shopping center. A mortgagee may desire to have his mortgage subordinate to important leases so that he can foreclose without losing these leases. It is possible for a mortgagee to agree with a tenant to subordinate his mortgage to a lease after the mortgagor is in default,[42] but he cannot do so unilaterally.

Before a mortgagee chooses to have his mortgage subordinate to a lease on the mortgaged premises, he should examine the lease carefully to be sure that it does not contain onerous duties for the landlord to perform.[43] He should also be sure that the lease does not give the lessee an option to buy that will cut off his mortgage if the option is exercised.

If the lender does assume priority, whether by order of recording or by agreement, he can insure that he will have the option of keeping the leases in force by having the mortgagor procure attornment agreements from the lessees. In an attornment agreement the lessee agrees to accept the purchaser at a foreclosure sale as his landlord and to be bound to him by the lease. Yet attornment agreements usually do not bind the mortgagee or the sale purchaser to refrain from cancelling junior leases.

It is a simple matter for the lessor to put a subordination clause and an attornment clause in the form leases signed by minor tenants who have little bargaining power. But it is more difficult to negotiate an attornment clause or subordination clause in a lease with a major tenant. Nonetheless it is often less expensive to negotiate the clauses into the original lease than to get a lease amendment from a

40. See § 7.12, supra; Hyde, The Real Estate Lease as a Credit Instrument, 20 Bus.Law. 359, 389 (1965).

41. Anderson, The Mortgagee Looks at the Commercial Lease, 10 U. of Fla. L.Rev. 484, 495 (1957).

42. Landau v. Western Pa. Nat. Bank, 445 Pa. 217, 282 A.2d 335 (1971).

43. If the mortgagee feels that some of the landlord's covenants in the lease would be objectionable, he may be able to reach an agreement with the tenant that those clauses will not be enforceable against the mortgagee if he takes possession, or against a buyer at the mortgage foreclosure sale. The tenant, in turn, may bargain with the mortgagee for notice of the landlord's default and some reasonable time period in which the tenant may cure it, thus minimizing the risk of default to the tenant. This right to cure, however, is attractive to the tenant only if the debt service on the mortgage plus the other operating and carrying costs of the building do not exceed the rent which the tenant is obligated to pay under the lease. Moreover, the right to cure is binding against the landlord only if he expressly agrees to it in the lease or in a later agreement. Anderson, supra note 41, at 495.

powerful tenant.[44] In order for the mortgagor to get a subordination agreement from a major tenant he may have to get the mortgagee to agree to a nondisturbance clause which guarantees that as long as the lessee conforms to the lease he will be allowed to remain in possession of the property even if a foreclosure occurs. If the lessee is given a nondisturbance clause, the mortgagee should make sure that the lessee also has an obligation to remain bound by the lease after a foreclosure.[45]

As was mentioned earlier, a major tenant may lose a great deal if his lease is destroyed by a foreclosure, especially if he has made expensive improvements on the property. If the tenant is powerful enough, he may be able to demand that his lease be prior to all mortgages on the property. But if it is not practical for the tenant to negotiate priority he can protect himself to a considerable extent by agreeing to subordinate his lease only to mortgages that meet certain standards. In this way he can prevent his lease from becoming subordinate to a mortgage so onerous that foreclosure is assured. If the lessee is a tenant of the entire premises, he may seek to limit prior mortgages to those which have annual requirements including taxes and operating costs that do not exceed gross rent.[46] If he has a clause in his lease which allows him to cure defaults, he will then be able to prevent a foreclosure.

Another way that the lessee can protect himself, as suggested above, is by obtaining a nondisturbance clause[47] protecting him from eviction after a foreclosure as long as he honors the lease. Depending upon the wording of the agreement, he may have the option to remain under the lease or to treat it as destroyed. If the lessee has this option, he may prefer this position to having his lease superior to the mortgage. However, a mortgage which is technically senior will still have priority over conflicting provisions in the lease. For example, the lease may require the landlord to use fire insurance proceeds for rebuilding, while under the provisions of the mortgage the proceeds could be used to pay off part of that mortgage. The lessee should make sure that the agreements in the lease with regard to fire insurance, condemnation awards and removal of fixtures will be honored by the mortgagee.[48]

44. See Committee on Leases, Drafting Shopping Center Leases, 2 Real Property, Probate and Trust Journal 222, 247 (No. 2 Summer 1967).

45. Hyde, The Real Estate Lease as a Credit Instrument, 20 Bus.Law. 359, 392 (1965).

46. M. Friedman, Preparation of Leases, 61 (1962).

47. A clause in the lease which contains a covenant of quiet enjoyment will not keep the foreclosure of a superior mortgage from cutting off the lessee's right of possession. 220 West 42 Associates v. Ronbet Newmark Co., 53 A.D.2d 829, 385 N.Y.S.2d 304 (1976), modified 40 N.Y.2d 1000, 391 N.Y.S.2d 107, 359 N.E.2d 701. Only a clause to which the mortgagee is a party will guarantee nondisturbance.

48. M. Friedman, supra note 46 at 64; Committee on Leases, supra note 44 at 247.

Often subordination clauses in form leases state only that the lease will be subordinate to all present and future mortgages on the property. Earlier, this section pointed out that a subordination agreement in a purchase money mortgage must put limitations on future construction loans in order to be enforceable. Reasoning by analogy from the purchase money situation, a court might require that a subordination agreement in a lease contain language limiting future mortgages to terms which the lessor-mortgagor is reasonably likely to be able to perform. If a lease contains a clause subordinating the lease to a future mortgage which is not adequately described or limited, the tenant may be able to successfully attack the subordination clause on the grounds that it is (1) too indefinite to enforce, (2) unjust and unreasonable, or (3) invalid under the Statute of Frauds.[49]

There are two points at which a tenant may be able to attack a subordination clause in his lease: while the lease is still executory and after a foreclosure. If the tenant successfully attacks the subordination clause while the lease is still executory, the court might declare the lease void. After a foreclosure, the only reason a tenant will wish to attack the clause will be to restore the priority of his lease so that it will not be cut off by the foreclosure. If the subordination clause is so indefinite that it has exposed the tenant to unreasonable risk, a court may be willing to reinstate the priority of the tenant's lease. The tenant may be more likely to succeed if he was required to sign a form lease. If he had the opportunity to bargain for the terms of his lease with the help of counsel, the court may not be as sympathetic to his cause. The value of his leasehold may also make a difference in whether the court considers the subordination clause a material term.[50]

49. See text at notes 13 to 37, supra.

50. In valuing a leasehold on commercial property many factors must be considered, including the bonus value of the lease (the present value of the difference between the fair market value of the lease and the rent), the value of the location to the tenant's business, and the value of the improvements which the tenant has made on the property.

§ 12.10 Improper Disbursement of Loan Proceeds

Once a construction loan is obtained, the distribution of loan funds becomes a critical concern of all parties interested in the project, since improper disbursement can result in non-payment of subcontractors and material suppliers and the collapse of the entire project. The potential for severe economic loss emphasizes the importance of care on the part of the construction lender.

Suppose, for example, that the construction lender fails to supervise the course of construction and advances more money than the construction progress warrants. Suppose also that the owner or general contractor who receives the advances diverts them to other projects or to personal use. If the amount of the construction loan accurately reflected the cost of construction, diversion of funds will cause the project to go unfinished and the subcontractor to go unpaid. When the owner-borrower defaults on the loan, the lender will foreclose. In the usual case, the lender's lien will be superior to the mechanics' liens filed by unpaid subcontractors and the lender will take the proceeds of the sale.[51] The lender will also have priority over a land vendor who subordinated his interest to enable the developer to secure a construction loan.[52] Other parties may be injured as well. The surety on the performance bond (if any) will be liable for the losses resulting from the non-completion.[53] Purchasers of interests in the project may be unable to realize their expectations. Finally, any guarantors on the construction loan may be liable to the lender for the default.

Given the catastrophic consequences that can result from improper disbursement of the funds by construction lenders, the question of lender liability naturally arises. In a preceding section of this chapter it was observed that lenders can suffer a partial loss of priority in many jurisdictions if their loan disbursements are found to be "optional" instead of "obligatory." [54] This section will focus on other theories used by courts to grant relief to parties injured by improper loan distributions. It should be observed, however, that cases denying relief to injured parties are numerous; unless express conditions of the loan agreement have been breached by the lender, most jurisdictions are unwilling to impose liability for wrongful distribution of loan proceeds.[55]

Express Agreement

The most widely accepted theory upon which relief is granted from improper loan disbursements is that the lender has breached an express agreement requiring disbursements to be made in a particular manner. A typical agreement of this sort requires the lender to see that its advances go only to construction purposes. If the lender fails

51. See § 12.7, supra.

52. See § 12.9, supra.

53. See § 12.2, supra.

54. § 12.7, supra.

55. See e. g., Carlsberg Resources Corp. v. Cambria Sav. & Loan Ass'n, 413 F.Supp. 880 (W.D.Pa.1976), affirmed 554 F.2d 1254 (C.A.Pa.1977); Weiss v. Brentwood Sav. & Loan Ass'n, 4 Cal.App.3d 738, 84 Cal.Rptr. 736 (1970); Gill v. Mission Sav. & Loan Ass'n, 236 Cal.App.2d 753, 46 Cal.Rptr. 456 (1965); Drobnick v. Western Federal Sav. & Loan Ass'n, 479 P.2d 393 (Colo.Ct.App., 1970); First Conn. Small Business Investment Co. v. Arba, Inc., 170 Conn. 168, 365 A.2d 100 (1976); Kennedy v. Betts, 33 Md.App. 258, 364 A.2d 74 (1976); Forest Inc. v. Guaranty Mortgage Co., Inc., 534 S.W.2d 853 (Tenn. App.1975); Fandel, Inc. v. First of Denver Mortgage Investors, 522 S.W. 2d 721 (Tex.Civ.App.1975) (per curiam); National Bank of Wash. v. Equity Investors, 81 Wash.2d 886, 506 P.2d 20 (1973), appeal after remand 83 Wash.2d 435, 518 P.2d 1072; 42 Yale L.J. 980 (1933); Grenada Ready-Mix Concrete, Inc. v. Watkins, note 68 infra.

to meet this obligation, a cause of action will lie. Thus, in the context of an agreement between a construction lender and a subordinating vendor, the rule has been stated: "where * * * the construction mortgagee expressly agrees with the subordinator to see to it that the proceeds of his loan will be applied to construction of the improvement he will be held to his agreement and will lose his priority as to any advance not going to construction." [56]

The above-stated rule was applied in Albert & Kernahan, Inc. v. Franklin Arms, Inc.,[57] in which the insolvency of the debtor prompted a priority fight between two mortgagees. The first mortgagee, a construction company, had agreed to subordinate its lien to that of the second mortgagee, a construction lender. The construction lender, in turn, had expressly agreed that loan distributions would be appropriated to construction expenses. The priority dispute centered on substantial advancements made by the lender that were used for non-construction purposes, the subordinated lienor contending that the lender's priority should not be absolute. The court upheld the conditional nature of the subordination agreement, finding that the construction lender had priority only to the extent that advances went to construction expenses.

An express agreement was also made by the construction lender in Modesto Lumber Co. v. Wylde.[58] In extending a building loan to the owners of residential property, the lender guaranteed that no claim would become a lien on the property and that the construction contractor would not be paid until all claims for labor and materials were satisfied. In fact, the lender disbursed funds directly to the contractor, instructing him to apply the funds to the accounts of materialmen. The contractor did not do so and the materialmen were not paid. In the ensuing litigation, a trial court awarded damages to the materialmen and allowed them to have two liens against the owner's property. The landowners were granted a personal judgment against the lender. On appeal, the court discharged one lien and reduced the amount of the other, but upheld the lender's liability to the owner to the extent of the materialmen's lien. The court reasoned that "the loan association accepted a trusteeship to disburse these funds first to the laborers and materialmen and the balance to the contractor. It fairly appears that the loan association paid sums direct to the contractor." [59]

It should be observed that while the express agreement approach to lender liability is effective, its utility is rather limited. One reason is that the lender will often have made no express agreement to disburse funds in any particular manner. Even if the loan agreement

56. Cambridge Acceptance Corp. v. Hockstein, 102 N.J.Super. 435, 439, 246 A.2d 138, 140 (1968) (per curiam).

57. 104 N.J.Eq. 446, 146 A. 213 (1929).

58. 217 Cal. 421, 19 P.2d 238 (1933).

59. Id. at 428, 19 P.2d at 240.

contains a provision on the manner of disbursement, however, the borrower may not be the party harmed by improper disbursal. Indeed, in the typical case, subordinating vendors and subcontractors have the most to lose when improper disbursements are made; but when the loan agreement is with the owner or general contractor, these third parties find it difficult to succeed in an action against the lender.[60] Relief has been granted by some courts in spite of these problems, but usually upon the next theory discussed below.

Conditional Subordination

A second theoretical approach to the problem of improper disbursements stresses the notion of conditional subordination. Under this theory, the focus is on the agreement by which a land vendor subordinates his interest to that of a subsequent lender. If the agreement is conditional on application of loan proceeds to construction costs, some courts will protect the lender's priority only to the extent disbursements go to construction. As might be expected, not all courts accept the theory.[61]

An example of conditional subordination can be seen in the 1962 decision in Collins v. Home Savings & Loan Association.[62] There a land vendor agreed to subordinate his interest to a "construction loan for the purpose of constructing on each lot a dwelling house with the usual appurtenances." [63] This provision was contained in the seller's deed of trust, which was recorded before the construction loan was obtained. At the request of the title company the vendor signed a subsequent subordination provision that identified more accurately the trust deeds to which his interest was subordinated. However, the second provision did not contain the limiting language of the provision in the vendor's trust deed. When the project failed, the construction lender foreclosed and sold the property to third parties. The subordinating vendor then sued the lender, alleging that three of the disbursements were for non-construction purposes and therefore not within the terms of the subordination agreement. The lender's defense was that there was no requirement in the subsequent subordination agreement that disbursements go to any particular purpose. Despite the failure of the second subordination provision to repeat the conditions of the first, judgment was for the vendor. The court

60. See, e. g., United States v. Chester Heights Associates, 406 F.Supp. 600 (D.S.C.1976); Ross v. Continental Mortgage Investors, 404 F.Supp. 922 (E.D.La.1975); Lampert Yards, Inc. v. Thompson-Wetterling Const. & Realty, Inc., 302 Minn. 83, 223 N.W.2d 418 (1974); Forest, Inc. v. Guaranty Mortgage Co., Inc., 534 S.W.2d 853 (Tenn.App.1975).

61. Some courts refuse to allow the vendor to recover under this theory when the subordination conditions appear in the vendor's trust deed, but not in the lender's trust deed. See e. g., Gill v. Mission Sav. & Loan Ass'n, 236 Cal.App.2d 753, 46 Cal.Rptr. 456 (1965); Fandel, Inc. v. First of Denver Mortgage Investors, 522 S.W.2d 721 (Tex.Civ.App.1975) (per curiam).

62. 205 Cal.App.2d 86, 22 Cal.Rptr. 817 (1962).

63. Id. at 89, 22 Cal.Rptr. at 819.

observed that the lender had actual as well as constructive knowledge of the language in the earlier subordination clause. It also suggested that the two subordination provisions were "executed contemporaneously" and should be read together. Finally, the court noted that it was possible to infer "that the only reason for respondents' subordination of their lien was the expectation that if payments were advanced by the appellant solely for construction purposes, the liens superior to their own would increase in value only as the property under development enjoyed a corresponding increase in value because of the accompanying progress in the work of construction." [64] The court concluded that subordination conditions were unsatisfied and that the vendor's lien retained its priority. Because the property had been sold to third parties, damages were allowed against the lender for the principal amount of the vendor's deed of trust plus interest. It is noteworthy that this result was not one of partial priority; rather, the vendor's entire lien was held superior to that of the lender for purposes of awarding damages.[65]

A similar approach was taken in the later case of Miller v. Citizens Savings & Loan Association.[66] *Miller* also involved a priority dispute between a subordinated land vendor and a construction lender. The vendor included a subordination clause in his deed of trust that imposed various restrictions on the use of the construction loan proceeds, restrictions it claimed were violated by a substantial payment made to the developer and retained by it for its own purposes. It appeared, however, that four days after executing the original agreement, the vendor had entered into subsequent subordination agreements with the lender directly, which agreements contained no restrictions. The lender argued, as did the lender in *Collins,* that since the subsequent subordination agreements did not restrict the uses to which the loan proceeds could be put, any use was permitted. The court rejected this contention. As in *Collins,* the court read the subordination agreements together. It was observed that

> "subordination agreements are in the nature of a mutual enterprise, wherein the vendor provides the land, the purchaser the 'know how' and the purchaser's lending agency the capital, for the mutually beneficial purpose of developing the land and disposing of it. * * * Typically the loan proceeds are to be used for purposes which will promote the mutual enterprise and which will either enhance the ven-

64. Id. at 99, 22 Cal.Rptr. at 825.

65. The court did not reveal the reason for this particular result, but it did point out that the amount of the improper disbursements was greater than the value of the vendor's deed of trust. As a general proposition, absolute priority or damages would appear to be in order when partial priority results in no benefit to the vendor, i. e., when the foreclosure sale would provide no excess over that portion of the lender's lien given priority under the terms of the conditional subordination.

66. 248 Cal.App.2d 655, 56 Cal.Rptr. 844 (1967).

> dor's equity in case he must foreclose his lien, or will provide funds from which he will be paid. A subordination agreement should be construed, unless it expressly provides otherwise, as permitting the loan proceeds to be used only for such purposes." [67]

The court concluded that the lender was aware of the limitations in the subordination agreement, that the disputed payment to the developer was outside the terms of the agreement, and that the lender's priority was limited to disbursements that met the conditions of subordination.

Additional complexities arise when the subordination agreement is implicit—as when the vendor purposefully postpones the recordation of his interest until the lender's lien is recorded. In such a circumstance, any conditions to the "agreement" are implicit as well. What should be the consequences of the lender's disbursement of loan proceeds to nonconstruction purposes? This was the issue facing the court in Middlebrook-Anderson Co. v. Southwest Savings & Loan Association.[68] There the plaintiff agreed to sell 28 lots to developers, with part of the purchase price to be secured by a deed of trust. It was understood that the deed of trust was to be second to a construction loan the developers would obtain. In order to have first priority, the lender recorded its trust deeds first. Loan funds were disbursed, and construction began, but the money ran out before the project was completed. When the developer abandoned the project, the lender foreclosed, purchasing the property itself.[69] The vendor was "wiped out" by the foreclosure, and brought suit, complaining that the lender had permitted the developers to use $300,000 of the loan disbursements for non-construction purposes. In consequence, the vendor argued, it was entitled to a restoration of priority and damages. The cause of action depended, of course, on a conclusion that the agreement to take a second trust deed constituted a subordination agreement—otherwise there was no priority to be restored. A subordination agreement was found to exist, the court ruling "that the duties owed by a lender to a seller under a formal subordination agreement do not differ from the duties owed by a lender to a seller when the lender obtains priority over the seller under an agreement by the seller to record after the lender." [70] The lender's main defenses were

67. Id. at 663–664, 56 Cal.Rptr. at 851.

68. 18 Cal.App.3d 1023, 96 Cal.Rptr. 338 (1971). For a discussion of this case see Note, Purchase Money Subordination Agreements in California: An Analysis of Conditional Subordination, 45 So.Cal.L.Rev. 1109 (1972). Cf. Grenada Ready-Mix Concrete, Inc. v. Watkins, 453 F.Supp. 1298 (N.D. Miss.1978), rejecting the theory of *Middlebrook-Anderson.*

69. Ultimately, the property was sold to third parties.

70. 18 Cal.App.3d at 1029, 96 Cal.Rptr. at 341. For a contrary view, see Spaziani v. Millar, 215 Cal.App.2d 667, 30 Cal.Rptr. 658 (1963); Miller, Regalia & Starr, Subordination Agreements in California, 13 U.C.L.A.L.Rev. 1298 (1966).

that it had no duty to supervise the loan distributions and that there was no privity of contract between it and the vendor. These defenses, held the court, were insufficient to prevent a trial on the merits.

The court was persuaded that there were "strong public policy reasons to protect the seller in subordination situations." [71] To be enforceable, a subordination clause "must contain terms that will define and minimize the risk that the subordinating liens will impair or destroy the seller's security." [72] Given the lender's superior ability to prevent loan misappropriations and its greater ability to absorb loss, the court ruled that an implied agreement to disburse loan proceeds for construction purposes "should be spelled out from the lender's alleged actual knowledge of the provisions of the seller's lien in general, and of the subordination therein in particular." [73] Furthermore the court said:

> "In the superior position of a financial institution constantly engaged in professional construction lending, *Southwestern* had no reason to believe their trust deed conferred any lien to which the fee was subordinate other than to the extent of money spent for construction purposes. Its loan under the circumstances cannot be viewed other than as subject to the fair application of the construction funds. Accordingly, we conclude that such lien as the trust deed might have conferred on the lender should not be advanced or preferred over the seller." [74]

Breach of Duty of Care

The theories of recovery considered thus far have focused on lender liability arising out of the breach of express agreements or reversal of priority for failure to meet conditions in subordination agreements. These theories are not helpful, of course, when there has been no express agreement or facts giving rise to conditional subordination. In such a circumstance, relief must be had on another basis, if at all. A third approach has been taken by some courts: lenders have occasionally been found liable for improper disbursals

71. 18 Cal.App.3d at 1036, 96 Cal.Rptr. at 346. In a subsequent case the public policy requiring protection of subordinating sellers persuaded a California Court to rule that lender and borrower may not make modifications in their loan agreement without the knowledge and consent of the subordinating seller if the modifications materially affect his rights. Gluskin v. Atlantic Sav. & Loan Ass'n, 32 Cal.App.3d 307, 108 Cal. Rptr. 318 (1973).

72. 18 Cal.App.3d at 1036, 96 Cal.Rptr. at 346; Handy v. Gordon, 65 Cal.2d 578, 55 Cal.Rptr. 769, 422 P.2d 329 (1967)); see § 12.9, supra.

73. Id. at 1038, 96 Cal.Rptr. at 347.

74. Id., 96 Cal.Rptr. at 347. A subsequent decision carved out an exception to the *Middlebrook-Anderson* rule when the subordinating vendor is also a part owner of the purchaser and participates in the construction project. Woodworth v. Redwood Empire Sav. & Loan Ass'n, 22 Cal. App.3d 347, 99 Cal.Rptr. 373 (1971).

because they have breached a duty of care. The chief difficulty with this approach is in finding a duty on the part of the lender.[75]

One variation on the breach of duty theme may be seen in Fikes v. First Federal Savings & Loan Association.[76] The case involved a foreclosure action by the lender of a construction loan. *Fikes,* who owned an unrecorded equitable interest [77] in the project, challenged the lender's priority on the ground that the developer diverted loan disbursements to other projects during the course of construction, and did so with the lender's knowledge. The court recognized the validity of the equitable interest asserted, and found that the lender had knowledge of his existence before construction funds were loaned. The central issue facing the court was whether a lender has a duty to protect such third party interests of which it has knowledge.[78] The lender argued that no such duty existed because there was no privity of contract between it and Fikes. The court rejected his contention and held that a duty did exist. It founded the duty in equity.

The court observed that when the plaintiff allowed the developer to take legal title to the property, Fikes had the reasonable expectation that First Federal would perform its role as interim construction lender in a conventional manner. If First National had disbursed the construction loan proceeds according to normal secured-lending practices, the property which Fikes had contracted to buy would have been enhanced in value." [79] By failing to follow such ordinary disbursement procedures, First Federal breached its duty to Fikes.[80] In consequence of this breach, the court ruled that the lender's security interest encompassed only those funds spent for construction.

A similar result was reached in Cambridge Acceptance Corporation v. Hockstein.[81] In that case the subordinated land vendor challenged a foreclosure action brought by the construction lender's assignee, alleging that the loan disbursements were expended for nonconstruction purposes. Unable to find an agreement between owner and lender that limited subordination to funds advanced for construc-

75. Courts frequently hold that a lender owes no duty of care in loan disbursements to parties lacking contractual privity or a fiduciary relationship with the lender. See e. g., Ross v. Continental Mortgage Investors, 404 F.Supp. 922 (E.D.La.1975); Lampert Yards, Inc. v. Thompson-Wetterling Constr. & Realty Inc., 302 Minn. 83, 223 N.W.2d 418 (1974); Forest Inc. v. Guaranty Mortgage Co. Inc., 534 S.W.2d 853 (Tenn.App. 1975). See also Grenada Ready-Mix Concrete, Inc. v. Watkins, 453 F.Supp. 1298 (N.D.Miss.1978), rejecting a duty of care to a "subordinated" ground lessor.

76. 553 P.2d 251 (Alaska 1975).

77. The equitable interest arose out of an earnest money agreement between Fikes and the property owner's agent. Fikes allowed the developer to have legal title in order to facilitate construction financing. The arrangement was entered into on the lender's advice. Id. at 256.

78. Id. at 260.

79. Id. at 261.

80. Id.

81. 102 N.J.Super. 435, 246 A.2d 138 (1968) (per curiam).

tion, the court said that there was at most an "intent and expectation" on the owner's part that the subordination would be to a construction loan. The court then noted the general view that "absent an express stipulation between the subordinator and the construction lender conditioning the scope of the subordination, diversion of construction money by the borrower from its contemplated use will not dislodge the advanced lienor from his bargained-for priority in the absence of collusion with the mortgagor in diverting the money from its purpose." [82] Despite the general rule, judgment was for the landowner. Equitable principles, said the court, required the construction lender "to make and administer the loan in the conventional manner of a construction lender rather than mask what is essentially a loan on the general credit and reliability of the borrower and the security of the land value as a construction loan, and act accordingly in disbursing the funds." [83] The lender failed to observe this standard. It was "totally oblivious of and seemingly disinterested in what the borrower actually did with the money." [84] Because the landowner was equitably entitled to rely on the expectation that the lender would comply with conventional practices, the lender's failure to do so estopped it from asserting the subordination of the owner's interest.

A breach of duty analysis allowed the construction contractor to have relief against a lender in Cook v. Citizens Savings & Loan Association.[85] The contractor in *Cook* agreed with the landowner to furnish labor and materials for building. Financing was arranged by the owner with the defendant lending institution. Following construction, the lender disbursed the loan proceeds. Most of the disbursements went to the landowner; the landowner did not pay the contractor. Upon default on the loan, the lender foreclosed and sold the property to a third party. The contractor sued, contending that it was entitled to judgment against the lender because it failed to use reasonable care to see that the disbursements went to discharge liens for labor and material. The court said that "[a]s a lender paying out construction funds, Citizens should have used reasonable diligence to see that the funds were actually used in payment of the materials or other costs of construction. Citizens totally failed to discharge its duty in disbursing the loan proceeds." [86] Because of the breach, the court ruled that the contractor's lien attached to the proceeds of foreclosure.[87]

82. 102 Id. at 438, 246 A.2d at 140.

83. Id. at 440, 246 A.2d at 141.

84. Id. 246 A.2d at 141.

85. 346 So.2d 370 (Miss.1977).

86. Id. at 372.

87. The court did not expressly identify the source of the lending institution's duty but cited an earlier case relying on the theory that a construction lien should be given priority only to the extent disbursements are actually used in construction. See Southern Life Ins. Co. v. Pollard Appliance Co., 247 Miss. 211, 150 So.2d 416 (1963). This theory, in turn, reflects equitable considerations. See Weiss, Drayfous & Seiferth, Inc. v. Natchez Inv. Co., Inc., 166 Miss. 253, 260, 140 So. 736, 738 (1932).

Other cases dealing with breach of duty analysis could also be noted,[88] but one in particular deserves mention. In Commercial Standard Insurance Co. v. Bank of America [89] the court used a breach of duty analysis that focused more on the policy considerations and the need to protect the plaintiff than on any strict search for duty. The issue was whether the lender could be liable to the surety on a performance bond for improperly disbursing loan proceeds to a construction contractor. The surety, which was forced to cover the losses on the project when the contractor defaulted, sought to be subrogated to the landowner's claims against the lender for negligent disbursement of loan proceeds. The court held that the surety could be subrogated to the owner's claims. It also found that inasmuch as the lender had agreed to disburse loan proceeds in accordance with the value of construction progress, the lender owed the owner a duty to exercise reasonable care. The lender contended, however, that even if it owed a duty to the owner, it owed none to the surety. The court's examination of this duty question reflected a negligence analysis founded in policy considerations. "Duty" observed the court "is not sacrosanct in itself, but only an expression of the sum total of those considerations of policy which lead the law to say that the particular plaintiff is entitled to protection." [90] The policy considerations considered were:

> "the foreseeability of harm to the plaintiff, the degree of certainty that the plaintiff suffered injury, the closeness of the connection between the defendant's conduct and the injury suffered, the moral blame attached to the defendant's conduct, the policy of preventing future harm, the extent of the burden to the defendant and consequences to the community of imposing a duty to exercise care with resulting liability for breach, and the availability, cost, and prevalence of insurance for the risk involved." [91]

After analyzing these factors in the context of the facts alleged, the court imposed a duty on the lender, running to the surety, to exercise reasonable care in disbursing loan proceeds.

Third Party Beneficiary

One of the major barriers to recovery for potential plaintiffs in the situation of improper loan disbursements is the lack of contractual privity between plaintiff and lender.[92] In addition to the ap-

88. See, e. g., Radunich v. Basso, 235 Cal.App.2d 826, 45 Cal.Rptr. 824 (1965); Westland Homes Corp. v. Hall, 193 Neb. 237, 226 N.W.2d 622 (1975).

89. 57 Cal.App.3d 241, 129 Cal.Rptr. 91 (1976).

90. Id. at 248, 129 Cal.Rptr. at 95 (quoting Dillon v. Legg, 68 Cal.2d 728, 734, 69 Cal.Rptr. 72, 76, 441 P.2d 912, 916 (1968)).

91. Id., 129 Cal.Rptr. at 95 (quoting Rowland v. Christian, 69 Cal.2d 108, 70 Cal.Rptr. 97, 443 P.2d 561 (1968).

92. See note 83 supra.

proaches already considered that have sometimes overcome a lack of privity defense, the third party beneficiary theory may be quite helpful. Basically, the theory permits a third person to enforce a promise made for his benefit even though he is a stranger to the contract.[93]

The plaintiff most likely to benefit from an attempted use of the third party beneficiary theory is a subordinated land vendor. While there may be a question in some jurisdictions whether parties to a construction loan agreement *intend* to benefit a subordinating vendor,[94] it is clear that the vendor is in fact a beneficiary of such agreement. Given the circumstances and equities involved in a typical subordination situation, it is likely that some courts would be responsive to the theory's use. Certainly those courts which have accepted the "common enterprise" view of the subordination agreement could approve of this theoretical approach.

It should be observed that no court has yet granted recovery on a third party beneficiary theory to a party injured by lender negligence. One court rejected the theory's application when asserted by an injured materialman as a defense to the lender's foreclosure action.[95] The court observed that successful assertion of such a third party claim required a demonstration that the "contracting parties intended to create a direct, not incidental or consequential benefit to the third party." [96] The court did not find such a demonstration. While this obstacle may be difficult to overcome in many jurisdictions, it would not appear to be impossible, particularly for a subordinating vendor. At least one case has suggested the legitimacy of such a cause of action.[97]

In conclusion, we suggest that the courts have been excessively parsimonious in applying the third party beneficiary concept, and in implying a duty by construction lenders to disburse funds in a reasonably careful manner. It is clear that subordinated vendors and mechanics' lien claimants rely heavily on the construction lender's care and competence, and the lender is usually fully aware of their reliance.[98] While the lender should not be held to be a guarantor of

93. 17 Am.Jur.2d Contracts § 302 (1964).

94. See United States v. Chester Heights Associates, 406 F.Supp. 600 (D.S.C.1976).

95. Id.

96. Id. at 606–07.

97. See Middlebrook-Anderson Co. v. Southwest Sav. & Loan Ass'n, 18 Cal. App.3d 1023, 1038, 96 Cal.Rptr. 338,

98. See Note, 45 U.Cin.L.Rev. 492 (1976), discussing Gardner Plumbing, Inc. v. Cottrill, 44 Ohio St.2d 111, 338 N.E.2d 757, 73 O.O.2d 757 (1975). The Gardner case involved an attempt by the owner-mortgagor to assert a breach of a duty under agency theory by a construction lender which disbursed funds to the general contractor without requiring lien affidavits from him. The court rejected the agency notion and refused to impose liability on the lender. Cf. Falls Lumber Co. v. Heman, 114 Ohio App. 262, 181 N.E.2d 713, 19 O.O.2d 165 (1961), in which an agency was implied from the lender's statement that it "would take care of things."

non-diversion of the funds, neither should he be permitted to assert a first claim on the real estate in cases in which his own failure to observe reasonable and accepted practices have permitted a diversion to the detriment of the junior lienors. Indeed, the owner himself, if not a party to the improper diversion, should be similarly placed in a position to reduce the construction lender's lien pro tanto to the extent of the diversion.

§ 12.11 Lender Liability for Construction Defects or Other Wrongful Acts of Contractors

If a lender becomes more than ordinarily involved in a construction project, its additional activities may form the basis for liability for negligent or illegal acts which it commits. The seminal case in this regard is Connor v. Great Western Savings and Loan Association.[99] This 1969 decision by the California supreme court, which generated considerable concern and commentary,[1] held a construction lender liable to subdivision home purchasers for construction defects in their homes. In *Connor* an inexperienced and undercapitalized construction company borrowed construction funds from Great Western Savings and Loan. In addition to lending these funds, Great Western "warehoused" the land upon which the subdivision was to be constructed, purchasing it in bulk and reselling it to the developer as he was able to use it. The lender was also granted a right of first refusal to make the permanent loans to subdivision homebuyers. The agreement between lender and developer provided that if Great Western met the terms of a competing lender and still lost the loan, the developer would have to pay Great Western the fees it otherwise would have earned.[2] Great Western reviewed the developer's plans, but failed to follow its usual procedure and examine the foundation specifications. When the defectively constructed foundations later cracked, the purchasers brought suit against several defendants, including Great Western. In reversing a judgment of nonsuit against Great Western, the California supreme court said:

> Great Western became much more than a lender content to lend money at interest on the security of real proper-

99. 69 Cal.2d 850, 73 Cal.Rptr. 369, 447 P.2d 609 (1969).

1. See e. g., Annot., Financing Agency's Liability to Purchaser of New Homes or Structures for Consequences of Construction Defects. 39 A.L.R.3d 247 (1971); Note, the Expanding Scope of Enterprise Liability, 69 Colum.L.Rev. 1084 (1969); Comment, New Liability in Construction Lending: Implications of Connor v. Great Western Sav. & Loan, 42 So. Cal.L.Rev. 353 (1969); Comment, Liability of the Institutional Lender for Structural Defects in New Housing, 35 U.Chi.L.Rev. 739 (1968); 6 Houston L.Rev. 580 (1969); 5 Real Property, Prob. & Tr.J. 495 (1970).

2. This sort of referral arrangement may be an illegal tying agreement under the Sherman Act; see Fortner Enterprises, Inc. v. United States Steel Corp., 394 U.S. 495, 89 S.Ct. 1252, 22 L.Ed.2d 495 (1969).

> ty. It became an active participant in a home construction enterprise. It had the right to exercise extensive control of the enterprise. Its financing, which made the enterprise possible, took on ramifications beyond the domain of the usual money lender.[3]

Because of this extensive involvement in the subdivision project, the court found that the lender had a duty to purchasers to exercise reasonable care in preventing defective construction. In so ruling, the court created a new theory of construction lender liability.

Numerous courts have examined the *Connor* theory since its articulation, but the great majority have distinguished *Conner*, permitting lender defendants to avoid liability.[4] The distinction has usually been based on the lack of extensive involvement of the lender in the project, although neither *Connor* nor its progeny make it very clear just how far a lender's activity must go to move within the zone of liability. Perhaps most courts would track the facts of *Connor* itself, requiring both land warehousing and a permanent loan referral scheme, or some similarly intimate involvement. Although one court has suggested that the *Connor* theory represents a minority view,[5] several decisions have adopted the *Connor* rationale—or at least suggested that it might be applied—to subject lenders to liability in a variety of circumstances; rather surprisingly, few of them have involved physical defects in new construction as *Connor* did.

In Jemison v. Montgomery Real Estate and Company [6] a Michigan home purchaser who had abandoned her home as uninhabitable sued the real estate broker and the mortgagee for fraudulent misrepresentation in the sale. The plaintiff alleged that the lender knew

3. 69 Cal.2d at 864, 73 Cal.Rptr. at 376, 447 P.2d at 616 (1969).

4. Drake v. Morris Plan Co., 53 Cal. App.3d 208, 125 Cal.Rptr. 667 (1976) (no lender liability for wrongful death for financing sale of automobile for incompetent unlicensed driver); Fox & Carskadon Financial Corp. v. San Francisco Sav. & Loan Ass'n, 52 Cal.App.3d 484, 125 Cal.Rptr. 549 (1975) (no lender liability to apartment building purchaser who lost equity in foreclosure); Skerlec v. Wells Fargo Bank Nat. Ass'n, 18 Cal.App.3d 1003, 96 Cal.Rptr. 434 (1971) (no lender liability in tort to plaintiff injured in collision where lender knew automobile purchaser could not comply with financial responsibility laws); Bradler v. Craig, 274 Cal.App. 2d 466, 79 Cal.Rptr. 401 (1969) (no liability in lender for construction defects in house in the absence of extraordinary lender involvement in the project); Callaizakis v. Astor Development Co., 4 Ill.App.3d 163, 280 N.E.2d 512 (1972) (no lender liability to condominium purchasers for structural defects in the absence of *Connor*-like facts); Bill Stremmel Motors, Inc. v. IDS Leasing Corp., 89 Nev. 414, 514 P.2d 654 (1973) (financing agent not liable for acts of equipment seller unless knows of wrongful acts and induces others to utilize services of the seller); L. A. Christiansen v. Philcent Corp., 226 Pa.Super. 157, 313 A.2d 249 (1973) (no lender liability to home purchasers for construction defects in absence of *Connor*-like facts). *See also* Flamingo Drift Fishing, Inc. v. Nix, 251 So.2d 316 (Fla. App.1971) (lender's employment of inspector to supervise construction of fishing vessel did not impose obligation on bank toward the purchaser).

5. See Wright v. United States, 428 F. Supp. 782, 789 (D.Mont.1977).

6. 396 Mich. 106, 240 N.W.2d 205 (1976). The facts are reported at 47 Mich.App. 731, 210 N.W.2d 10 (1973).

she was on welfare and knew that she was relatively uneducated and commercially inexperienced. She further alleged that the lender both knew that the realtor was unscrupulous and was aware of facts giving rise to the fraud. Relying on *Connor,* the plaintiff concluded that since the lender "knew or should have known all of these facts, it made itself an integral and necessary part of the fraudulent transaction when it entered into the mortgage loan agreement with plaintiff."[7] Reversing the appellate court, the Michigan supreme court indicated that these allegations stated a cause of action against the lender.

Another application of the *Connor* rule was suggested in Morroco v. Felton.[8] In that case, a New Jersey landlord brought a summary dispossession action against several tenants. The tenants responded by filing to remove the dispossession action and by suing the landlord and mortgagees for breach of an implied warranty of habitability. The court focused on procedural matters, but it observed by way of dicta that, under the *Connor* rationale, liability for maintaining decent dwellings may extend to the lender. "[I]t may well be necessary," said the court, "to join third parties. Especially where the property in question is heavily mortgaged, some determination on the mortgagee's liability appears appropriate."[9]

Without explicitly relying on *Connor,* a federal court has recently ruled that construction lenders can be liable for fraud in connection with the purchase of subdivision lots. In Timmrock v. Munn,[10] 328 plaintiffs alleged fraud in the sale of subdivision lots, arguing that investment contracts were involved and that a violation of federal securities laws had occurred. They also claimed violations of the Interstate Land Sales Full Disclosure Act.[11] The plaintiffs alleged that the bank which had financed the project's construction had entered into an accord with the developers and had allowed itself to be held out to the public as the financial backer of the project. In moving to dismiss the action under the Disclosure Act, the bank contended that section 1709 of the Act limited actions to those brought against developers and their agents. The bank claimed it was neither. Responding to this defense, the court noted that a bank would not be subject to the Act in the normal course of its business, but that if it went beyond this, the bank could be liable.[12] The court ruled that

7. 210 N.W.2d at 15 (dissenting opinion).

8. 112 N.J.Super. 226, 270 A.2d 739 (1970).

9. 270 A.2d at 743.

10. 433 F.Supp. 396 (N.D.Ill.1977).

11. 15 U.S.C.A § 1701 et seq. (1970).

12. Essentially the same rule was suggested in Zachery v. Treasure Lake of Georgia, Inc., 374 F.Supp. 251 (N.D.Ga.1974). In *Zachery,* the court found that only a lender-borrower relationship existed between the lender and the developer. The lender was therefore not liable for misrepresentation under the Interstate Land Sales Full Disclosure Act. It is noteworthy that even a public financing agency can be found to be a developer. See California Housing Finance Agency v. Elliot, 17 Cal.3d 575, 131 Cal.Rptr. 361, 551 P.2d 1193 (1976).

the "plaintiffs are therefore entitled to attempt to show that the Bank exceeded the normal scope of financing practices and actively participated in and aided the advancement of a fraudulent scheme, or otherwise assisted in the luring of purchasers for an allegedly dubious project." [13]

Lender liability could arise in other contexts as well.[14] Tort actions might be brought against lenders heavily involved in construction projects when construction defects contribute to personal injuries.[15] Governmental agencies might cite lenders for building code violations if they go beyond the usual scope of financing in connection with a non-complying structure. Creative plaintiffs could imagine other approaches.[16] The potential for lender liability under a *Connor* theory is real.[17] Even though the case has been frequently distinguished, its theory has been occasionally applied to impose liability on financial institutions who operate outside the scope of normal lending activity.

13. 433 F.Supp. at 406.

14. A similar theory of close-connectedness has been used to prevent financial institutions from achieving holder in due course status. See, e. g., Commercial Credit Corp. v. Orange County Machine Works, 34 Cal. 2d 766, 214 P.2d 819 (1950); see § 5.29 supra.

15. For a case rejecting application of the *Connor* rule in such a situation, see Wright v. United States, 428 F. Supp. 782 (D.Mont.1977).

16. A borrower might argue that his payment to a construction lender of a fee to cover the cost of inspection, or the presence of a clause conditioning loan disbursements upon inspection, has the effect of rendering the lender liable for negligent or inadequate inspections. Thus far, however, this argument has failed. See Meyers v. Guarantee Sav. and Loan Ass'n, 79 Cal.App.3d 307, 144 Cal.Rptr. 616 (1978); Rice v. First Federal Sav. and Loan Ass'n, 207 So.2d 22 (Fla.App. 1968), certiorari denied 212 So.2d 879.

17. The California legislature made a somewhat ambiguous attempt to reverse or limit *Connor:*

> A lender who makes a loan of money [for construction purposes] * * * shall not be held liable to third persons for any loss or damage occasioned by a defect in the * * * property * * * unless such loss or damage is a result of an act of the lender outside the scope of the activities of a lender of money or unless the lender has been a party to misrepresentations with respect to such * * * property.

West's Ann.Cal.Civ.Code, § 3434. The statute may be read as merely restating the result in *Connor*, but if this is its intent it is superfluous. In any event it is hardly a model of legislative drafting, and adds nothing to the clarity of the law in California.

§§ 12.12–13.0 are reserved for supplementary material.

CHAPTER 13

FINANCING CONDOMINIUMS AND COOPERATIVES

Table of Sections

§ 13.1 An Overview of Condominiums and Cooperatives

This chapter will deal with legal problems relating to the financing of condominiums and cooperatives. While space does not permit a detailed treatment of the non-financing aspects of these forms of ownership, a rudimentary overview of the legal relationships involved will preface discussion of the central topic.[1]

Both condominiums and cooperatives are legal formats for "unit ownership"—that is, the ownership of a physically defined portion of a larger parcel of (usually improved) real property. In the majority of cases, the "unit" is a residential apartment in a multifamily housing project. Condominiums are much more tightly controlled by state legislation than are cooperatives, and in recent years many states have amended their condominium statutes to permit the creation of condominiums in non-residential property, including commercial and industrial buildings, and even on unimproved land.[2] There are no

1. The most complete and useful treatment of such non-financing areas is P. Rohan & M. Reskin, Condominium Law & Practice (1976). Other works include D. Clurman & E. Hebard, Condominiums and Cooperatives (1969); A. Ferrer & K. Stecher, Law of Condominium (1967); P. Rohan & M. Reskin, Cooperative Housing Law and Practice (1975); and K. Romney, Condominium Development Guide (1974). An excellent current summary is found in Symposium on the Law of Condominiums, 48 St.John's L.Rev. 677 (1974).

2. The model act on which many early American statutes were based used the term "apartment", presumably implying residential use; see Federal Housing Administration, Model Statute for the Creation of Apartment Ownership § 2(a), reprinted in G. Nelson & D. Whitman, Real Estate Finance and Development 781 (1976) [hereinafter cited as FHA Model Act]. Examples of much broader definitions which permit non-residential uses include Alaska Stat. § 34.07.450(1) (1962); Okla.Stat. tit. 60, § 503(b) (Supp.1976); Va.Code § 55–79.2(a) (1950). See P. Rohan & M. Reskin, Condominium Law and Practice § 5.01[2] (1976). On non-residential condominiums, see generally, D. Clurman, The Business Condominium (1973); Goldstein, Lipson, Rohan & Shapiro, Commercial and Industrial Condominiums: An Overall Analysis, 48 St. John's L.Rev. 817 (1974); Shapiro,

significant legal barriers to non-residential cooperative ownership, although it is quite rare.

In most cases the owner of a condominium or cooperative unit is also a participant in some organization of owners which has responsibility for the operation, maintenance, and management of the "common areas"—features of the building or project which are used or available for use by all unit owners, such as lobbies, stairwells, elevators, grounds and landscaping, and often recreational facilities. The principal distinctions between condominiums and cooperatives are discussed below.

The Condominium

The term "condominium" is variously used to refer to the underlying concept, the building, or the individual unit; in this article, it refers to the building. In a condominium, each owner holds fee simple title to his unit directly. In addition, he and his fellow unit owners each own undivided fractional shares in the common areas of the project as tenants in common. Management and maintenance of these common facilities are performed by an owners' association, which may be incorporated or unincorporated.[3] The fractional shares in the common areas and the vote of each member of the association are assigned on some equitable basis, such as the number of square feet in the unit or its proportionate cost of the original construction.[4] The association may assert a lien on each unit to enforce the owner's obligation to pay his share of the assessments levied by the association for management, maintenance, insurance, reserves for replacements, and the like.[5]

There is little question that a form of unit ownership similar to the condominium concept can be developed by careful structuring of documents in the absence of an authorizing statute. This has been done in many countries and continues today in England.[6] However, every jurisdiction in the United States has enacted a condominium

Commercial Condominiums; Significant Tax Benefits Possible If Properly Structured, 41 J. Taxation 46 (1974); Shapiro, Commercial Condominiums: Tax Considerations for Unit Purchasers And The Association, 41 J. Taxation 204 (1974).

3. The present trend seems to be incorporation of associations. See Hyatt, Condominium and Home Owner Associations: Formation and Development, 24 Emory L.J. 977 (1975); Jackson, Why You Should Incorporate a Homeowners Association 3 Real Est.L.J. 311 (1975); Krasnowiecki, Townhouses with Homes Association: A New Perspective, 123 U.Pa.L. Rev. 711 (1975).

4. See Reichman, Residential Private Governments: An Introductory Survey, 43 U.Chi.L.Rev. 253 (1976).

5. See Jackson, Homeowners Associations: Remedies to Enforce Assessment Collections, 51 L.A.B.J. 423 (1976); Anthony v. Brea Glenbrook Club, 58 Cal.App.3d 506, 130 Cal. Rptr. 32 (1976) (planned unit development).

6. See 1 P. Rohan & M. Reskin, Condominium Law and Practice, ch. 4 (1976); Leyser, The Ownership of Flats—A Comparative Study, 7 Int'l & Comp. L.Q. 31 (1958).

statute which attempts to regularize procedures, spell out the duties and obligations of the unit owners and the association, provide for such eventualities as damage, destruction, and condemnation of the condominium, and provide legal confirmation of the association's lien rights against delinquent unit owners. The statutes also provide for separate property tax assessment on each unit and prohibit partitioning of the common areas. Most American statutes were enacted during the 1960–1970 period, and were based heavily on model legislation drafted by the Federal Housing Administration.[7] The statutes were helpful in standardizing relationships and protecting unit owners from some forms of overreaching, but they were unnecessarily restrictive in many respects and a "second generation" of statutes, which generally provide far greater flexibility in the legal structuring of the development, as well as more extensive consumer protection, has begun to be enacted.[8]

The Cooperative

In a cooperative the entire project, including the individual units and the common areas, is owned by a single corporation (often organized on a non-profit basis).[9] Persons who purchase units in the cooperative receive, as evidence of their interests, two documents: a "proprietary lease", indicating the member's right of possession in the particular apartment, and a stock certificate, evidencing ownership of a share or shares in the corporation. The documents usually provide that ownership of the stock and the tenant's interest in the proprietary lease are inseparable.

In most cooperatives, each apartment owner has a single vote, rather than a vote apportioned by value or size as with condominiums. The functions of the corporation are similar to those of the owners' association in a condominium, but are more extensive. Since

7. See note 2 supra.

8. Leaders in this movement include Fla.Stat.Ann. §§ 718.101–.508 (Supp. 1977), discussed in Comment, 8 U. Mich.J.L.Ref. 387 (1975) and 27 U.Miami L.Rev. 451 (1973); Utah Code Ann. §§ 57–8–1 through 57–8–36 (1953 & Supp.1977); Va.Code §§ 55–79.39–.103 (Supp.1977), discussed in Comment, 9 U.Richmond L.Rev. 135 (1974) and Johnakin, A Second Generation of Condominium Statutes, Lawyers Title News, May-June 1974, at 3. See generally Cannella, Recent Innovations in State Condominium Legislation, 48 St.John's L.Rev. 994 (1974).

9. Although corporate ownership of cooperatives is by far the most common format, trust or tenancy-in-common ownership are also possible and have been used occasionally. P. Rohan & M. Reskin, Cooperative Housing Law and Practice § 201 (1975). I.R.C. § 216(b)(1)(c), which permits deduction of mortgage interest and property taxes by cooperative owners, is satisfied only if "no stockholder * * * is entitled to receive any distribution not out of earnings and profits of the corporation except on a complete or partial liquidation of the corporation." See the description of Co-op City by the Court in United Housing Foundation, Inc. v. Forman, 421 U.S. 837, 840, 95 S.Ct. 2051, 2054, 44 L.Ed.2d 621, rehearing denied 423 U.S. 884, 96 S.Ct. 157, 46 L.Ed.2d 115 and 423 U.S. 884, 96 S.Ct. 157, 46 L.Ed.2d 115 (1975).

the cooperative corporation owns the project, it will normally be the mortgagor on one or more blanket mortgages covering the building. The "rent" paid by tenants under their proprietary leases must be sufficient to cover the cost of servicing this debt and the property taxes on the project in addition to such management, maintenance, and other expenses and reserves as would be expected in a condominium. Both condominum [10] and cooperative unit owners are entitled to deduct the portion of their monthly payments attributable to mortgage interest and real estate taxes, although this privilege is available to cooperative members only if at least 80% of the gross income of the corporation is derived from payments by tenant-stockholders.[11]

10. Rev.Rul. 64–31, 1964–1 C.B. 300.

11. See I.R.C. § 216, which imposes numerous other requirements on co-ops in addition to the 80% test. The treatment of the portion of a co-op member's monthly payment which is attributable to amortization on the blanket mortgage raises difficult tax problems. Often the co-op and its members will agree that this amount is to be treated as additional contribution to capital, and hence not income to the corporation; this is attractive, since the corporation is a taxable entity, and may otherwise owe federal tax on its income. This approach has been successful in avoiding tax at the corporate level in several cases; see, e. g., Lake Forest, Inc. v. Commissioner, 22 T.C.M. 156 (CCH) (1963). However, the members may also wish to assert that the amorization component of each monthly payment is income for purposes of the 80% rule, thus maximizing the amount of income the co-op can receive from outside sources (e. g., commercial rental space, vending and laundry machines) while still qualifying under § 216. The Court of Claims has held that the co-op and its members can agree to either capital or income treatment of the amortization payments but cannot have it both ways; see Eckstein v. U. S., 452 F.2d 1036 (Ct.Cl.1971). See Miller, Tax Problems of the Housing Cooperative under the 80% Income Rule, 18 Prac.Law. 81 (No. 4, Apr. 1972), which also discusses the other requirements which § 216 imposes on the legal structure of co-ops.

A radically different approach was used by the Tax Court in Park Place, Inc. v. Commissioner, 57 T.C. 767 (1972), which held that mortgage amortization, property tax, maintenance, and apparently mortgage interest components of payments made by co-op members to the corporation are not taxable income to it—and that the corporation has no offsetting deduction when it pays out these items—despite the fact that the same items *are* income for purposes of the 80% rule of § 216. The Tax Court thus gave the members the best of both worlds; whether this view will prevail over *Eckstein* remains to be seen.

This issue may become somewhat less important as a result of an amendment to I.R.C. § 216(c), made by § 2101(b) of the Tax Reform Act of 1976, which expressly authorizes cooperatives to claim depreciation deductions on their real estate; the Tax Court had rejected such a claim in *Park Place.* Apparently this deduction is available even if individual tenant-shareholders are also claiming depreciation on their own units because they are being used in a trade or business or for the production of income. At least in the early years of ownership of new buildings, depreciation will usually more than offset mortgage amortization thus minimizing or eliminating taxable income even if the amortization payments are regarded as income. For older and long-held buildings, the conflict between *Eckstein* and *Park Place* will still require resolution.

Condominiums have no 80% test to meet, and they normally make no assessments upon members for mortgage interest or amortization. However, both cooperatives and condominium associations may collect general operating reserves or reserves for future replacements or improve-

For federal tax purposes a cooperative member is treated much like the owner of a condominium or a detached house, assuming the requirements of I.R.C. section 216 are met. But for many other purposes the question remains: Is the cooperator's interest real or personal property? Since the cooperative is a unique kind of hybrid, answers to this question vary, depending on the view the courts take of the underlying policies. The characterization of the interest may be relevant for a wide variety of reasons, including the doctrine of restraints on alienation, rent control, ad valorem taxes, transfer taxes, conveyancing doctrines, construction of wills and of intestacy and judgment lien statutes, availability of title insurance, institutional financing,[12] summary eviction proceedings to members, and determination of the proper procedures for registering or recording transfers and creations of security interests, whether under the Uniform Commercial Code or realty recording acts. The answers of the courts in these contexts are far from uniform,[13] although there is no reason

ments in amounts exceeding the offsetting deductions of the current year's expenditures. Several theories have been developed (and accepted by the Commissioner) under which these reserves may escape taxation at the association or corporate level; one such theory is that, if earmarked specifically for replacements or improvements rather than general operations or repairs, they are contributions to capital; another is that the association is merely an agent of the members in holding these funds until they need to be expended. *See* Concord Village, Inc. v. Commissioner, 65 T.C. 142 (1975); Rev.Rul. 75–370, 1975–2 C.B. 25; Rev.Rul. 75–371, 1975–2 C. B. 52; Frank, IRS Takes Harsh Position on Exempting Condominium and Homeowners' Associations, 44 J. Taxation 306 (1976).

It may also be possible for a condominium or cooperative corporation to qualify for tax-exempt status under I.R.C. § 501(c)(4) as a "civic league." However, in Rev.Rul. 74–99, 1974–1 C.B. 131, the Commissioner seems to have limited application of § 501(c)(4) to associations which (1) bear a reasonably recognizable relationship to an area recognizable as a governmental subdivision or a district thereof; (2) perform no exterior maintenance on privately-owned residences; and (3) own and maintain only facilities which are used and enjoyed by the general public, such as streets and parks. Obviously, many associations far exceed these limited activities, and hence will not be deemed tax-exempt.

I.R.C. § 528, added by § 2101 of the Tax Reform Act of 1976, allows homeowners associations in condominiums and planned unit developments to elect a limited form of tax-exempt status. Cooperatives are not eligible for this election, and a variety of limiting criteria must be met. Moreover, if the election is made, only "exempt function income", defined as membership dues, fees, and assessments, is exempt. Income from use charges for facilities, such as swimming pools, and from other sources is taxable, and the corporate surtax exemption is denied to electing associations. Thus the election could be quite disadvantageous in some cases, and non-electing associations will presumably be relegated to the pre-1976 arguments discussed above if they wish to shelter their excess income from taxation. See Cowan, Working With New Rules for Condominiums, Cooperatives, and Homeowners Associations, 46 J. Taxation 204 (1977).

12. Whether cooperative financing involves real or personal property under the rules of financial regulatory agencies, and the procedures for perfecting liens on cooperative members' interests, are discussed in the text accompanying § 13.6, note 12, infra.

13. See Comment, Legal Characterization of the Individual's Interest in

why the interest of a cooperative member should not be treated on a par with a condominium unit owner—as the owner of real property—for most purposes.

It is apparent that each member of a cooperative is somewhat more reliant upon the financial strength and honesty of his or her fellow members than is a condominium unit owner. If many members of a cooperative default, it may be impossible to meet the regular debt service payments on the blanket mortgage, which may consequently be foreclosed. In a condominium, by contrast, each unit owner arranges his own permanent financing on his apartment, and defaults by one's neighbors in the payment of monthly assessments, while possibly endangering the solvency of the owners' association, cannot directly trigger foreclosure by a lender of the unit belonging to a non-delinquent owner. On the other hand, it is probably easier for the member's organization to evict a delinquent owner and to realize on the security of his unit for unpaid assessments in a cooperative than in a condominium.[14]

Condominiums and cooperatives share many of the same economic and social advantages: economies of scale in the initial cost and maintenance of recreation, parking, and other community facilities, the potential for competent management of the common areas, and the advantages of security and social contact which result from relatively high-density occupancy, as well as the concomitant problems.[15] Since the advent of condominium statutes in most American jurisdictions, lending institutions and developers (and consequently consumers) have tended to prefer condominiums in most jurisdictions, and relatively few new cooperatives are being built.

§ 13.2 Financing Condominiums and Cooperatives

Condominium and cooperative financing differ from one another in important respects. A condominium project is much like a subdi-

a Cooperative Apartment: Realty or Personalty, 73 Colum.L.Rev. 250 (1973); P. Rohan & M. Reskin, Cooperative Housing Law and Practice, § 2.01[5] (1975).

14. The cooperative can treat the delinquent member as a tenant and use unlawful detainer or other summary process to evict him; Sun Terrace Manor v. Municipal Court, 33 Cal. App.3d 739, 108 Cal.Rptr. 307 (1973); Green v. Greenbelt Homes, Inc., 232 Md. 496, 194 A.2d 273 (1963). See Rohan, Cooperative Housing: An Appraisal of Residential Controls and Enforcement Procedures, 18 Stan.L. Rev. 1323 (1966), questioning whether such a severe remedy should be available for minor defaults or violations of the co-op's rules. In a condominium, by contrast, the usual remedy is foreclosure of the association's lien on the unit, an action which normally enjoys no calendar preference and may take many months to complete. In either case, or course, the association must follow its own rules and bylaws, and may also be subject to local statutes or ordinances; see Clydesdale, Inc. v. Wegener, 372 A.2d 1013 (D.C.1977).

15. See Comment, Community Living Condominium Style: Bed of Roses—Or Bed or Thorns?, 6 Univ.W.L.A.L. Rev. 121 (1974).

vision of detached houses; financing of construction is usually independent of the permanent or long-term financing of the sales of individual units.[16] The construction loan is typically secured by a blanket mortgage on the entire property, with provision for the release of each individual unit from that mortgage as the units are sold by the developer to customers; the "partial release clause" in the construction mortgage will spell out the circumstances under which units will be released and the amount which must be applied toward retirement of the construction indebtedness for each unit sold.[17] The permanent mortgages placed on individual units by their purchasers are usually arranged by the developer through a single lender, which may or may not be the mortgagee on the construction loan.[18] In theory, unit purchasers can obtain long-term loans from institutions which have had no prior contact with the project, but this is much more difficult than in subdivisions of detached houses; many lenders will be reluctant to undertake an extensive review of the documents which relate to a condominium if they expect to make only one or a few loans on units in that project.[19]

16. See Pfeiler, Condominium Financing: Some Legal Basics, 38 U.S. League of Saving A Legal Bull. 249, 255–62 (1972) [hereinafter cited as Pfeiler]. Like most subdivision lenders, the condominium construction lender will usually require that a "take-out" or permanent loan commitment be obtained from another lender (or the permanent loan department of the same institution) before approving the construction loan. See Fegan, Condominium Financing, 48 St.John's L.Rev. 799 (1974) [hereinafter cited as Fegan].

17. A common provision requires "presales" (executed contracts of sale to customers) on some fixed percentage of the units (say, 35% to 75%) before the construction lender will release the lien on any of the units. See Vishny, Financing the Condominium, 1970 Ill.L.F. 181 (1970). Similarly, the permanent lender may refuse to disburse funds until a specified percentage of the units have been presold; Fegan, supra note 16. The Federal Housing Administration generally requires that 80% (in value) of the units be presold before unit titles can be transferred and FHA mortgage insurance issued; see 24 C.F.R. 234.26(c)(3) (1977).

In imposing such requirements, lenders are concerned that they not be committed to financing the project as a condominium until they have substantial evidence of consumer demand; if the demand does not materialize, they may insist that the building be converted to rental use.

18. As an alternative to financing unit sales with new permanent mortgages, it is theoretically possible for the construction lender to take a separate mortgage on each unit, and to convert those mortgages to permanent status by loan assumptions as the units are sold to customers. This procedure is fairly common in some areas of the nation with subdivision development, but is not widely used with condominiums. It arguably violates § 14 of the FHA Model Act, supra note 2, which provides: "At the time of the first conveyance of each apartment, every mortgage and other lien affecting such apartment * * * shall be paid and satisfied of record * * *." There is no policy reason to prohibit assumptions of construction loans by unit purchasers, and the Model Act should not be so construed.

19. Such loans are sometimes termed "spot mortgages", and many lenders avoid them; their reluctance makes it extremely difficult for the original permanent lender to diversify its portfolio by declining to make resale financing available as the units turn over later. See Gose, Strum & Zinman, Real Estate Financing Tech-

Cooperatives are also financed with construction mortgages, but there are generally no individual loans to those who purchase the units when construction is completed.[20] Instead, the construction loan may simply be converted to a permanent loan by the mortgagee—which means that it will begin to draw regular (usually monthly) payments of amortization and interest. At that point the construction loan may also be sold by the original mortgagee to another investor, particularly if the construction lender is a type of institution that prefers to avoid long-term mortgages. Alternatively, the cooperative corporation may obtain a new blanket loan from a permanent lender and use the proceeds to discharge the construction loan. In either event, the permanent mortgage on a cooperative project is a blanket mortgage covering the entire property. Unit purchasers make down payments equal to the difference between the unit's market sales value and its pro-rata share of the blanket mortgage; in effect, they assume their shares of the mortgage.

The subsequent resale of an individual unit by one occupant to another also involves different treatment in condominiums than in cooperatives. In a condominium unit sale the existing mortgage may be assumed, taken subject to, or paid off by the unit purchaser with the proceeds of a new loan he has arranged, just as in the sale of a detached house. By contrast, the sale of a cooperative unit amounts to an implicit "assumption" by the purchaser of that unit's pro rata share of the blanket mortgage on the project. Hence the cash paid by the purchaser of a resale cooperative unit may represent three components: (1) the amortization of the blanket mortgage which has occurred since payments were commenced on it; (2) the original unit purchaser's down-payment; and (3) any increase in value which may have occurred since the project was completed due to inflation or to improvements.[21]

Obviously, the longer the project is occupied the higher the cash required by a resale purchaser is likely to be, and the greater the dif-

niques: What Now?, 9 Real Prop., Prob. & Trust J. 617, 634 (1974). Spot mortgages are likely to become much easier to obtain as a result of the actions of the Federal National Mortgage Association and the Federal Home Loan Mortgage Corporation, which in 1978 greatly streamlined their requirements for the purchase of mortgages on units in existing condominium projects in which control of the owners' association has been vested in the residents for at least two years: see note 99a, infra, and accompanying text.

20. Berger, Condominium: Shelter on a Statutory Foundation, 63 Colum.L. Rev. 987 (1963).

21. Some cooperatives limit the resale price by bylaw to the original down payment made by the seller, and others allow him to recoup only his improvements, his share of the mortgage amortization achieved, and some cost-of-living adjustment factor. See FHA Model Form of Bylaws § 8(d), reproduced in J. Krasnoweicki, Housing and Urban Development 317, 323 (1969); National Comm'n. on Urban Problems Building the American City 137 (1968). Many cooperatives impose no restrictions on resale prices at all.

ficulty the seller can anticipate in finding a buyer with sufficient cash and a willingness to invest it in the unit. The seller may be willing to take a promissory note from the purchaser in lieu of some part of this cash, and may be able to secure such a note with an interest in some real or personal property belonging to the purchaser. But an installment sale by the unit owner may jeopardize the standing of the purchaser under I.R.C. section 216.[22]

Additional problems arise if the installment seller desires a security interest in the unit. Under one approach, the purchaser may pledge his stock and assign his interest in the proprietary lease to the seller as security; this may be satisfactory, but many sellers may feel that the legal protection available from such a scheme is inferior to that which a mortgage would give them. Two barriers to the use of a conventional legal mortgage are the lack of a separate, reliable legal description of the unit, and the fact that the legal title is held by the cooperative corporation rather than the occupants of the unit. In addition, many cooperatives impose rights of first refusal or other forms of restrictions on the resale of units which might make it difficult for a secured party to realize on the security, no matter what form it takes.

It would be possible to reduce cash requirements for cooperative resale buyers if institutional lenders were willing to make "second" loans on the security of cooperative units. Any such loans would clearly be subordinate to the existing blanket first mortgage on the entire project, since there is normally no provision in such mortgages for the release of individual units from the lien's coverage. Institutional lenders could take pledges and assignments of the stock and leased on the units as security. There is no doubt that such a method is legally workable, although subject to the same uncertainties as purchase-money financing by vendors mentioned in the foregoing para-

22. I.R.C. § 216(b)(2) defines a "tenant-shareholder" as one "whose stock is fully paid-up in an amount" reasonably related to the unit's share of the corporation's equity in the project. The applicable regulation, Treas. Reg. § 1.216–1(e) (1977), appears to say that this relationship is to be determined "as of the date of the original issuance of the stock". Arguably, an installment sale would qualify if the purchaser made a cash payment equal to the unit's share of the original equity, but this is not clear. Alternatively, the purchaser might structure the transaction so as to "fully pay" for the *stock* with cash, but to pay some additional amount, by way of a promissory note, for the assignment of the *proprietary lease.* The difficulty with this argument is that the stock and lease are invariably required by their own terms or the applicable corporate charter or bylaws to be held by the same person. In sum, whether any installment sale can qualify under § 216 is problematic. This is unfortunate, since there seems to be no policy reason whatever to make the tax benefits of § 216 hinge on an all-cash sale. See Miller, Tax Problems of the Housing Cooperative Under the 80% Income Rule, 18 Prac. Lawyer 81 (No. 4, Apr. 1972).

Since an installment purchaser is arguably not a "tenant-shareholder" it is entirely conceivable that a single installment sale could so reduce the total income from tenant-shareholders that the cooperative would cease to qualify under the 80% test of § 216.

graph. Moreover, whether the regulatory agencies which supervise institutional lenders will recognize such loans as secured, rather than as mere personal loans, is doubtful in many jurisdictions.[23] These financing problems tend to be reflected in large cash requirements for entry into cooperatives, and consequently limit access to relatively high-income purchasers.

It is quite possible that the corporation might decide to refinance the original blanket mortgage on the project; this might be done because the original mortgage is of the balloon type and has reached maturity,[24] because lower interest rates have become available, or because additional cash is needed for repairs or improvements. This last objective might also be achieved by the placement of a second blanket mortgage on the property without disturbing the first. It is apparent that either refinancing or additional financing can result in higher monthly assessments on the members than they anticipated when they joined the cooperative. If an appropriate vote of the directors or members is forthcoming, the added assessments will be imposed on all members, whether they agree with the decision or not.[25] Thus, each member's financial future lies to some extent in the hands of his neighbors; a situation which some might think uncomfortable, and which is largely avoided by the condominium form of ownership.[26]

23. See § 13.6, notes 9–13, infra and accompanying text.

24. While most buildings newly constructed for cooperative use are financed with fully-amortized mortgages, it is not unusual to find a balloon mortgage on a building which is converted from ordinary rental to co-op use. Indeed, if the interest rate on the existing mortgage is significantly below current rates at the time of conversion, it would be foolish to refinance at the time of conversion notwithstanding the balloon feature of the old loan. See Offering Statement, 72–84 Barrow Street, reprinted in 2A P. Rohan & M. Reskin, Cooperative Housing Law and Practice, at 245, 288 app. (1975).

25. For example, the Standard Form Cooperative Bylaws published by the New York Attorney General provide, at Art. III, sec. 7:

> The Board of Directors shall have discretionary power to * * * determine the cash requirements of the Corporation to be paid as aforesaid by the shareholder-tenants under their respective proprietary leases. Every such determination by the Board of Directors shall be final and conclusive as to all shareholder-tenants * * *.

See P. Rohan & M. Reskin, Cooperative Housing Law and Practice 24.67 app. (1975). Similar language is found in most proprietary leases. The decision-making power of the Board is generally very broad, and could even extend to a resolution to sell the project and distribute the proceeds to the members. See Anderson, Cooperative Apartments in Florida: A Legal Analysis, 12 U.Miami L.Rev. 13, 35 (1957).

26. But not completely. Even in a condominium, it is possible for the owners' association to levy larger-than-expected assessments to cover extravagant improvements to the recreational facilities or other common areas. Since title to common areas is held by the unit owners in tenancy in common, the association cannot mortgage them. Nonetheless, the assessments themselves are liens on the units, whether particular owners approve of the expenditures or not. In some cases, condominium bylaws may place an upper limit on assessment amounts.

One should not assume that permanent financing is always essential to the sale of either condominiums or cooperatives. Especially in retirement developments, all-cash purchases are quite common, since many buyers have just sold larger detached houses, often at substantial gains. Retirees usually wish to reinvest these funds and find the purchase of a condominium or cooperative unit a convenient way of doing so. Moreover, federal income tax on the gain from the sale of the previous house may be avoided entirely if the new unit costs at least as much as the sales price of the house sold.[27] This benefit is available whether a condominium or a cooperative unit is purchased, and does not depend on the presence or absence of mortgage financing on the new unit.

§ 13.3 Construction Financing of Condominiums

Although the financing of condominium construction is much like subdivision financing, there are important differences.[28] The documentation of a condominium project is much more complex, its marketability more speculative (at least, from the perspective of many institutional lenders), and the risk of loss it presents in the event of failure correspondingly greater.

Every new condominium project begins with site selection and acquisition. Developers commonly use their own capital to pay the cost of necessary land options. Before applications for institutional financing can be made, however, other costs must be incurred; surveys, engineering and market studies, and architects' fees, for example. These may be financed by use of the developer's cash or the contributions of his business associates, or through unsecured debt. In some cases these expenses are reimbursed out of the first draw of funds on the construction loan.

Upon exercise of the land option, the developer may be expected to pay the full cash price of the land to the seller. Often, however, the seller can be persuaded to sell on an installment basis and to accept a minimal initial cash payment. This installment indebtedness will usually be secured by a mortgage, and it will be necessary for the seller to subordinate his lien to that of the construction loan,[29] since virtually all construction lenders, as a matter of policy or the requirements of their governmental regulatory agencies, insist on first prior-

27. I.R.C. § 1034, which permits this deferral of gain, applies whether the old or the new residence is a condominium or a cooperative; see I.R.C. § 1034(f); Rev.Rul. 64–31, 1964–1 C.B. 300. If a cooperative unit is purchased, the unit's proportional share of the project's mortgage indebtedness is included in the purchase price for purposes of qualifying under § 1034; see Rev.Rul 60–76, 1960–1 C.B. 296.

28. Good general discussions of condominium construction financing include K. Romney, Condominium Development Guide ch. 7 (1974); Fegan, supra note 16; Pfeiler, supra note 16.

29. Subordination by vendors is discussed in Note, Purchase Money Subordination Agreements in California: An Analysis of Conditional Subordination, 45 S.Cal.L.Rev. 1109 (1972); see § 12.9, supra.

ity for the construction mortgage. Unless it is to be paid off from the proceeds of the construction loan, the land seller's subordinated mortgage (like the construction mortgage) must contain a partial release clause enabling the sale of individual units free of the lien.

When the land has been optioned and the necessary background studies completed, the developer is ready to apply for a construction loan. This submission is usually more comprehensive than would be expected in a detached-house subdivision, and the developer may seek the assistance of a mortgage loan broker in preparing and presenting it to prospective construction lenders. Such lenders will be particularly interested in the developer's own financial position, prior condominimum experience, and reputation; they will also analyze the market demand information, architectural and engineering work, and general demographic and locational data submitted by the developer. In many cases the construction lender will make no commitment until permanent financing has been arranged for the sales of units; hence, the developer will make a similar submission of information to prospective permanent lenders, who are generally concerned with the same factors. The permanent financing commitment is not only a prerequisite to construction financing in many cases, but comprises a powerful marketing tool as well, especially if it ties the permanent lender to a fixed interest rate in a rising interest market.

A project does not become a condominium until some basic document—usually termed a master deed, declaration, or plan of unit ownership—is executed by the owners of the real estate and filed for record. This master deed describes the project, the individual units, and the common areas; it assigns weights to each unit for voting and assessment purposes; it provides for a lien on the units to secure the assessments; and it may contain such covenants as a right of first refusal upon resale by a unit owner.[30] The master deed may be filed whenever the owners desire, but in many cases the construction lender will insist that filing be delayed until some fixed percentage of the units have been "presold"—that is, until prospective unit purchasers have paid earnest money deposits and signed purchase agreements on them. On the other hand, no conveyances by deed of units can occur until the master deed has been filed.[31] Given these constraints, the filing usually occurs sometime towards the end of the construction period.

Construction loan mortgages on condominium projects can be insured by the Federal Housing Administration (FHA) under section

30. Some writers have questioned whether such a clause may constitute an unreasonable restraint on alienation or may violate the Rule Against Perpetuities. Neither result seems justifiable or probable. See 1 (pt. 2) P. Rohan & M. Reskin, Condominium Law and Practice § 10.03 (1976). The FHA approved form of master deed does not contain a right of first refusal.

31. See 24 CFR 234.26(d)(1) (1977) (F.H.A.-insured condominium mortgages).

234(d) of the National Housing Act.[32] This insurance coverage, which is not generally available on construction loans in detached-house subdivisions, is not particularly attractive to most developers. The principal amount of the loan may be as high as 90% of the "replacement cost" of the project,[33] in substance, this means the actual cost of land and improvements.[34] By contrast, conventional construction loans are rarely made for more that 75% or 80% of value, but "value" as calculated by the conventional lender may be as high as the total retail sale price of the units which will generally exceed the project's cost by a substantial margin.[35] Thus, conventional construction financing may actually be for as much or more money than FHA-insured financing. The only other significant advantage of an FHA-insured construction mortgage is that the developer is assured that FHA mortgage insurance will also be available on the permanent loans on individual units as they are sold.[36]

Unfortunately FHA-insured construction loans have numerous disadvantages. FHA regulations impose dollar limits on the mortgage amount per unit, and effectively eliminate luxury or even high-middle-income projects.[37] The developer must enter into a regulatory agreement with FHA which may significantly limit his discretion in managing the construction and marketing of the project.[38] FHA mortgage insurance premiums must be paid in addition to interest, fees, and discounts charged by the lending institution. Moreover, FHA processing of multifamily mortgage insurance applications has the reputation of being slow and cumbersome, and FHA minimum property standards with respect to some construction features may appear excessive to some developers.

In light of these problems, it is not surprising that there has been relatively little construction lending under the section 234 program. An internal study of FHA's condominium activity has recommended major changes in the program, but they would require legislative action and have not been seriously considered by Congress at

32. 12 U.S.C. § 1715y (Supp. V 1975); applicable regulations are found at 24 CFR 234.1ff (1977).

33. 12 U.S.C.A. § 1715y(e)(2) (1970).

34. 24 CFR 234.505(h) (1977).

35. See K. Romney, Condominium Development Guide § 7.04 (1974).

36. Loans on individual units in a project not previously covered by an FHA blanket mortgage are insurable by FHA only if the project contains eleven or fewer units, National Housing Act § 234(c), 12 U.S.C.A. § 1715y (c) (Supp. V 1975). An internal study of condominium financing by the Federal Housing Administration has criticized this requirement as unnecessarily restrictive. See U.S. Dep't of Housing and Urban Development, Condominium Study (1975).

37. The limits have been increased on several occasions. At this writing they range from $19,500 for a no-bedroom unit in a low-rise building to $43,758 for a unit with four or more bedrooms in an elevator building. The elevator-building limits may be increased by as much as 50% in high cost areas. 24 CFR 234.525–.530 (1977).

38. 24 CFR 234.26(f) (1977).

this writing.[39] Despite FHA's early influence in the promulgation of state condominium legislation, it has become a minor factor in condominium financing.[40]

Developers of condominium projects sometimes do not complete construction. Failure to do so may result from poor planning and management of the construction work, inadequate budgeting, unanticipated increases in costs, weather problems, strikes, or weak market acceptance of the project. Abandonment will invariably constitute a default under the terms of the construction loan mortgage, and the lender may elect to foreclose. In this setting there are usually unpaid workmen, subcontractors, or suppliers who are entitled to file mechanics' liens. In addition, the prospective purchasers of units in the project will have signed contracts of sale and made down payments or earnest money deposits with the developer; some such contracts may have been executed before construction began, and some afterward. These three groups, the construction lender, mechanics' lienors, and vendees often find themselves adverse to one another in respect to rights in the real estate.

Such problems are not unique to condominium developments; they also occur with speculative subdivisions and other types of construction. We discuss them here because condominiums have frequently been defaulted upon during construction in recent years, and because condominium statutes sometimes contain provisions which bear on these disputes. The problem of priorities as between construction lenders and mechanics' lien claimants will not be covered in this article.[41] Suffice it to say that, in general, the relative priority of the lender and the lien claimant will depend on the language of the mechanics' lien statute, the timing of commencement of work on the project vis-a-vis the recordation of the construction mortgage, and the question of whether the advances made by the construction lender were optional or obligatory.[42]

Priority as Between Construction Lender and Vendees

A difficult conflict may arise with respect to earnest money deposits or down payments (the terms are used here synonymously) collected from intended unit vendees before and during the construction period. If these funds, which may be very substantial, are available for current use by the developer, they may help him solve serious cash

39. U.S. Dep't of Housing and Urban Development, HUD-FHA Condominiums: Their Future (1975).

40. During the first half of the 1970's, F.H.A. blanket condominium mortgages never reached an annual rate of 10,000 units, and was only 1277 units in 1975. See U.S. Dep't of Housing and Urban Development, 1975 Statistical Yearbook 120 (1976).

41. See generally Note, Construction Lending—General Contractor v. Lender, 54 N.C.L.Rev. 952 (1976).

42. See Kratovil & Werner, Mortgages for Construction and the Lien Priorities Problem—the "Unobligatory" Advance, 41 Tenn.L.Rev. 311 (1974).

shortage problems, but at high risk to the vendees.[43] The FHA[44] and the statutes of a few states[45] require that such deposits be escrowed pending completion and transfer of title of the individual units, making them inaccessible to the developer. Such provisions are highly desirable. Where this is not the law, a problem arises in situations in which the developer has invaded the deposits and subsequently abandons the project prior to completion; the unit purchasers may well be left with only their personal rights of action against the developer (who is often insolvent). Even if the construction lender forecloses and completes construction, the original unit subscribers may have neither the right to complete their purchases by paying the remainder of the original contract price, nor the right to a return of their deposits.

This issue may be characterized as one of priority as between the purchase contracts and the construction mortgage. The contract vendee has, under the law of most states, an equitable lien on the realty to secure the return of his down payment if the vendor fails to complete the contract.[46] The difficulty is that the lien's enforceability is constrained in two respects: first, it may be subordinate to preexisting liens, such as the construction mortgage, if it arises after that mortgage is recorded; and second, it is not enforceable even against a subsequent mortgagee or purchaser who has no notice of the existence of the vendee's contract.[47] The latter constraint may not be a serious problem in most cases; seldom will a construction lender grant a loan without first asking about preconstruction sales activity, and the developer will ordinarily be eager to inform the lender of the contracts which have been signed.[48] The matter is

43. See Damian, Condominium Development: Representing the Developer, in Condominium Development 35, 61 (Prac.Law Inst.1971).

44. See FHA Subscription and Purchase Agreement Form No. 3279, cl. 1, reprinted in 1 P. Rohan & M. Reskin, Condominium Law and Practice § 9.-04[6] (1976).

45. See, e. g., Va.Code § 55–79.95 (Supp.1977); Fla.Stat.Ann. § 718.202 (Supp.1977) (permitting the developer to use the money to defray construction costs if the contract of sale so provides). See Note, Recent Innovations in State Condominium Legislation, 48 St. John's L.Rev. 994, 999 (1974); Note, Florida Condominiums—Developer Abuses and Security Law Implications Create a Need For a State Regulatory Agency, 25 U.Fla.L. Rev. 350, 358 (1973). The better approach is to prohibit by statute all developer use of deposit funds; the significance of contract language permitting his use of deposits is unlikely to be understood by lay purchasers.

46. Gribble v. Stearman & Kaplan, Inc., 249 Md. 289, 239 A.2d 573 (1968). See Generally Annot., 43 A.L.R.2d 1384 (1954).

47. National Indemnity Co. v. Banks, 376 F.2d 533 (C.A.Miss.1967); Mihranian, Inc. v. Padula, 134 N.J.Super. 557, 342 A.2d 523 (1975).

48. See Wayne Bldg. & Loan Co. v. Yarborough, 11 Ohio St.2d 195, 228 N.E.2d 841 (1967); Palmer v. Crews Lumber Co., Inc., 510 P.2d 269 (Okla. 1973). These cases suggest that it is sufficient that the subsequent lender knows a contract has been executed, whether or not he is aware of the terms of the contract, the vendee's identity, or the amount of any downpayment made.

more difficult if the purchase contract is signed after the construction mortgage has been recorded. In State Savings and Loan Association v. Kauaian Development Co.,[49] the Hawaii Supreme Court drew a distinction between subscription agreements entered into before and after the creation of the construction mortgage. Agreements executed after the mortgage were obviously subordinate to it, the court thought, apparently because of the constructive notice the public records imparted to vendees, while those executed before the mortgage recordation had priority. However, the court observed that even prior subscription agreements could be made subordinate to the mortgage by express language of subordination, which could be placed in the purchase contract or in a separate document signed by the vendee. The court did not discuss the degree of specificity that would be necessary in such clauses, nor whether it would require that they be intelligible to the laymen signing them.

As a consequence of the *Kauaian* reasoning, most purchase agreements in use now probably contain subordination language,[50] a foreclosing construction lender would thus appear to be free to disregard the agreement and sell the unit to another purchaser and would have no obligation to return the deposit to the contract vendee.

However, the enforceability of such subordination clauses may be open to serious doubt. The purchaser will ordinarily be entirely unsophisticated, and is unlikely to have any concept of the significance of the clause. In addition, the clause will seldom contain details of the proposed construction financing to which the vendee is being asked to subordinate. By analogy to the cases involving so-called "automatic" subordination of purchase-money financing by land vendors to developers, it might well be argued that such subordinations by contract vendees are too vague or too unfair to enforce.[51]

Even a contract vendee who signed his contract after the construction mortgage was recorded, or who has executed a valid subordination clause, might nonetheless manage to persuade a court of

49. 50 Hawaii 540, 445 P.2d 109 (1968).

50. See, e. g., Olympic Towers Purchase Agreement, reprinted in 1A P. Rohan & M. Reskin, Condominium Law and Practice, 118.17 app. (1976):

> The Purchaser agrees that all terms and provisions of this contract are and shall be subject and subordinate to the lien of any building loan mortgage heretofore or hereafter made and any advances heretofore or hereafter made thereon and any payments or expenses already made or incurred or which hereafter may be made or incurred, pursuant to the terms thereof, or incidental thereto, or to protect the security thereof, to the full extent thereof without the execution of any further legal documents by the Purchaser. This subordination shall apply whether such advances are voluntary or involuntary and whether made in accordance with the building loan schedule.

51. See Handy v. Gordon, 65 Cal.2d 578, 422 P.2d 329, 55 Cal.Rptr. 769 (1967); Grooms v. Williams, 227 Md. 165, 175 A.2d 575 (1961). Cf. Starr v. Mooslin, 14 Cal.App.3d 988, 92 Cal. Rptr. 583 (1971), holding an attorney liable for malpractice in incompetently drafting a subordination agreement. See generally § 12.9, supra.

his priority. If the developer's default is traceable in part to the failure of the construction lender to monitor and supervise the progress of the project as its documents gave it the right to do, or if the lender negligently permitted the developer to divert loan funds away from the project, the vendee might argue that he is the third party beneficiary of the construction loan agreement, and that the proper remedy for the lender's breach of that agreement is a loss of priority for the construction loan.[52] Depending on the facts, an argument against the lender's priority may also be based on estoppel. If the lender has reviewed and approved the sales price schedule and the purchase agreement forms, has supplied the developer with criteria for qualifying prospective purchasers in respect to income, credit worthiness, and the like, and has mandated the pre-completion sale of some fixed number of units as a condition of the construction loan agreement, a court might well find the lender estopped by its extensive involvement in the vendor-vendee relationship to deny the priority of the vendee's lien.[53]

52. See Planters Lumber Co. v. Wilson Co., 413 S.W.2d 55 (Ark.1967), elevating a mechanics' lien above a construction mortgage to the extent the mortgage proceeds were not used on the project; Middlebrook-Anderson Co. v. Southwest Sav. & Loan Ass'n, 18 Cal.App.3d 1023, 96 Cal.Rptr. 338 (1971), in which a vendor of land who held a subordinated purchase-money deed of trust had his priorities elevated above that of the construction lender on this theory; Kennedy v. Betts, 33 Md.App. 258, 364 A.2d 74 (1976); Cambridge Acceptance Corp. v. Hockstein, 102 N.J.Super. 435, 246 A.2d 138 (1968). But see Pope Heating & Air Cond. Co. v. Garrett-Bromfield Mortgage Co., 29 Colo.App. 169, 480 P.2d 602 (1971), holding a subordination agreement unconditional and binding despite diversion of construction loan funds; Forest Inc. v. Guaranty Mortgage Co., 534 S.W.2d 853 (Tenn.Ct.App.1975) (semble); See also Falls Lumber Co. v. Heman, 114 Ohio App. 262, 181 N.E.2d 713 (1961), in which a construction lender was held liable in tort to a contract vendee for its failure to disburse construction funds in accordance with the applicable statute, thereby permitting mechanics' liens to be filed against the property; cf. Gardner Plumbing, Inc. v. Cottrill, 44 Ohio St.2d 111, 338 N.E.2d 757 (1975). See generally § 12.10 supra.

53. Cf. Fikes v. First Fed. Sav. & Loan Ass'n, 533 P.2d 251 (Alaska 1975), holding a construction lender's lien limited to funds actually spent on construction and not diverted, as against the claim of a prior contract vendee of which the lender had knowledge; Tucson Fed. Sav. & Loan Ass'n v. Sundell, 106 Ariz. 137, 472 P.2d 6 (1970) (semble) in which the court relied on the fact that the vendee had no knowledge of the construction mortgage. No cases have been found in which the estoppel argument has been raised by a junior vendee. The tendency of courts to protect contract vendees against the literal language of subordination clauses they have signed is illustrated by First Fed. Sav. & Loan Ass'n v. Ott, 285 So.2d 695 (Fla.App.1973), in which the developer refinanced the original construction loan with the same lender; the court refused to enforce the subordination agreement in vendee's contract and she was permitted to take free of the refinanced mortgage. In Security Nat. Bank v. Village Mall at Hillcrest, 85 Misc.2d 771, 382 N.Y.S.2d 882, 889 (1976), the Attorney General of New York argued that the construction lender's lien should be subordinated to the liens of contract vendees because the lender had (1) modified the construction loan agreement without recording the modification, (2) participated in a public offering of the condominium project without making the required disclosures to offerees under New York law, (3) participated in a violation of the statutory provisions al-

An alternative approach for the vendee might be based on an analogy to the cases which have permitted subcontractors and materials suppliers to assert an equitable lien on any undisbursed portion of the construction loan funds if the usual mechanics' lien remedies are unavailing to them.[54] In equity, the contract vendee would seem to have as strong a moral claim to these funds as do those who have invested labor and materials, at least if construction has been completed without exhausting the construction loan account and the vendee's deposit has been used for construction purposes. Unfortunately, this argument may be ineffective in those jurisdictions which have codified the equitable lien concept without including contract vendees among its beneficiaries. New York, for example, has created a statutory trust consisting of the down payments of contract vendees.[55] However, they may recover their funds after the developer's default only if they have not been used in improving the property; in addition, the usual classes of mechanics' lien claimants have first priority on the trust funds.[56] This approach seems entirely inadequate to protect the vendees, although it may be better than no protection at all.

As a matter of policy, it is entirely reasonable to impose on the construction lender a duty to return vendees' deposits in cases in which the lender had played an active role in approving or supervising the developer's marketing program. The lender is far better able than the vendee to investigate the developer's solvency, experience, and reliability, and to spread the risk of the developer's default. Moreover, any construction lender wishing to avoid this risk may easily do so merely by requiring that all deposits by vendees be placed in escrow. The law should not permit developers (and construction lenders) to rely upon vendees' down payments as a means of financ-

lowing vendees' deposits to be used only for improvements, and (4) charged usurious interest rates. The court found that triable issues of fact were involved and denied summary judgment on the merits of these claims.

54. See Swinerton & Walberg Co. v. Union Bank, 25 Cal.App.3d 259, 101 Cal.Rptr. 665 (1972); J. G. Plumbing Inc. v. Coastal Mortgage Co., 329 So. 2d 393 (Fla.App.1976); Crane Co. v. Fine, 221 So.2d 145 (Fla.1969). As a result of statutory change the remedy is apparently no longer available in California; see Boyd & Lovesee Lumber Co. v. Modular Marketing Corp., 44 Cal.App.3d 460, 118 Cal.Rptr. 699 (1975). A similar remedy, known as the "stop notice", is available by statute in a few states, but probably could not be asserted by contract vendees. See Comment, Mechanics' Liens: The "Stop Notice" Comes to Washington, 49 Wash.L.Rev. 685 (1974). See § 12.6 supra.

55. McKinney's N.Y. Lien Law § 71–a (1966).

56. See Security Nat. Bank v. Village Mall at Hillcrest, Inc., 85 Misc.2d 771, 382 N.Y.S.2d 883, 889 (1976); Glazer v. Alison Homes Corp., 62 Misc.2d 1017, 309 N.Y.S.2d 381 (1970). The latter case, though sound in policy, seems to go quite beyond the statutory language and permits contract vendees to assert a lien on funds which were wrongfully diverted by the developer from construction loan proceeds, although the opinion concedes that mechanics' liens would have a superior claim to these funds.

ing construction; doing so is an indicator that the developer is dangerously underfunded, and a lender who actively countenances such a procedure should be held accountable to the vendees for their loss.[57]

Priority as Between Mechanics' Lien Claimants and Vendees

The rights of mechanics' lien claimants in condominium projects raise problems similar to, but more intricate than, those of claims made on subdivision lots. Even if the work was done or the materials supplied on only a single lot or unit, the matter is not simple. It is clear enough that if the vendee enters into his contract of purchase after the work has been completed and the lien filed of record, the lien will have priority and the vendee will take subject to it.[58] This means that if the developer (or his general contractor) are unavailable for recovery, as is all too common, the unit vendee will suffer the loss unless he is protected by an owner's policy of title insurance.

If the vendee acquires legal title by deed to the unit or lot after the work has been done and the lien has "attached",[59] but before the lien is filed of record, he may be entirely innocent of any actual knowledge of the lien's attachment. A few jurisdictions, mostly in the South, protect bona fide purchasers in this situation, granting them priority over the lien.[60] Most states, however, hold the vendee's interest subject to the lien, either on the ground that even BFP's are subject to mechanics' liens [61] or that the very fact of construction ac-

57. In some respects the matter is similar to Connor v. Great Western Sav. & Loan Ass'n, 69 Cal.2d 850, 73 Cal.Rptr. 369, 447 P.2d 609 (1969), in which a construction lender was held liable to home purchasers for its failure to adequately supervise the construction of houses with serious structural defects. Although *Connor* has not been widely followed, see Callaizakas v. Astor Developer Co., 4 Ill.App.3d 163, 280 N.E.2d 512 (1972), the case of diversion of vendees' downpayments seems an especially appealing one for application of the concept, since developers' marketing programs are so generally superintended by construction lenders, particularly in condominium projects.

58. United Accounts, Inc. v. Larson, 121 N.W.2d 628 (N.D.1963); Annot., 85 A.L.R. 927, 928 (1933).

59. The exact time at which priority attaches varies among jurisdictions. Many fix it as of the day the first work is done on the overall construction project, and others on the date the lien claimant first performed his work. Less popular rules attach the lien at the time the general contract or the claimant's contract is entered into or recorded, or when the notice of lien is filed of record. Under all of these rules except the last-mentioned, a lien may attach without any clear evidence of the claim appearing in the public records. The lien must usually be "perfected" by filing of record within some fixed period after the work is completed, and is then said to "relate back" to the attachment date. See R. Kratovil, Modern Mortgage Law and Practice § 214 (1972); 4 American Law of Property § 16.106F (A. J. Casner ed. 1952). See generally § 12.4, supra.

60. See, e. g., Ky.Rev.Stat. § 376.010 (Supp.1976); Walker v. Valley Plumbing Co., 370 S.W.2d 136 (Ky.1963); First State Bank v. Stacey, 37 Tenn. App. 223, 261 S.W.2d 245 (1953); Wood v. Barnes, 420 S.W.2d 425 (Tex. Ct.App.1967); Comfortcraft Heating, Inc. v. Salamone, 19 App.Div. 760, 241 N.Y.S.2d 581 (1963); Bryant v. Ellenburg, 106 Ga. 510, 127 S.E.2d 468 (1962).

61. Schrader Iron Works, Inc. v. Lee, 26 Cal.App.3d 621, 103 Cal.Rptr. 107 (1972); State Sav. & Loan Ass'n v.

tivity on the land imparts notice of the potential filing of liens, and thus negates BFP status.[62] Moreover, owner's title insurance coverage is unlikely to assist the purchaser on these facts; many policies expressly exclude coverage for unfiled liens.

Suppose the vendee's contract of purchase predates the attachment of the lien, even though the conveyance by deed occurs later. May he argue that his vendee's lien created by execution of the contract has chronological, and thus legal, priority over the mechanics' liens? In Wayne Building & Loan Co. v. Yarborough,[63] the Ohio Supreme Court so held, although the vendee was given priority only to the extent of down payments made before the liens attached at the commencement of the work; the vendee had no priority as to further payments he made on the contract after work began. The decision appears to place no emphasis on whether the lien claimants had notice of the executed contract of purchase at the time they began their work, but such notice would presumably strengthen the vendee's position. Thus, in one Texas case the lien claimants were permitted priority for work done up to the time they learned of the executed contract, but not thereafter.[64] However, the existence of the purchase contract has been fatal to the vendee in several decisions in which courts have seen it as clearly establishing the vendee's position as an equitable "owner", and thus a member of the class of persons whose interests were subject to mechanic's liens.[65]

As these cases suggest, the relationship of vendees' and lien claimants' rights is uncertain and confused, although the lienors have usually prevailed. The courts have vacillated between the traditional desire to protect good faith purchasers and to enhance the reliability of the public records, on the one hand, and the wish to construe the lien statutes liberally to aid lien claimants, on the other. One major defect in the system lies in its failure to require potential

Kauaian Devel. Co., 50 Hawaii 540, 445 P.2d 109, 123 (1968); Metropolitan Water Co. v. Hild, 415 P.2d 970 (Okla.1966). See generally G. Thompson, real property § 5218 n. 69 (1957).

62. The knowledge of work in progress may be actual or constructive. See Guaranty Pest Control, Inc. v. Commercial Inv. & Devel. Corp., 288 Ala. 604, 264 So.2d 163 (1972); Capital Bank § Trust Co. v. Broussard Paint & Wallpaper Co., 198 So.2d 204 (La.App.1967); Clark Certified Concrete Co. v. Lindberg, 216 Md. 576, 141 A.2d 685 (1958); J. R. Meade Co. v. Forward Constr. Co., 526 S.W.2d 21 (Mo.App.1975); H. Tiffany, Real Property § 1578 (1939); Annot., 50 A.L.R.3d 944 (1973).

63. 11 Ohio St.2d 195, 228 N.E.2d 841, 849–50 (1967).

64. Stone v. Pitts, 389 S.W.2d 601 (Tex.Civ.App.1965). The lienor's knowledge of the vendee's interest may also be used to compel him to include the vendee as an "owner" in the notice of lien, and failure to do so may exculpate the vendee. See F. M. Sibley Lumber Co. v. Gottesman, 314 Mich. 60, 22 N.W.2d 72 (1946); cf. Oklahoma Hardware Co. v. Townsend, 494 P.2d 326 (Okla. 1972). See Annot., 48 A.L.R.3d 153 (1973).

65. Home Carpet, Inc. v. Bob Antrim Homes, Inc., 210 N.W.2d 652 (Iowa 1973); Toler v. Satterthwaite, 200 Kan. 103, 434 P.2d 814 (1967).

lien claimants to record some public notice as a condition of *attachment* (rather than mere perfection) of the lien. But even a change in the law in this respect would not fully protect purchasers, since they rarely examine the public records or obtain title reports before signing purchase agreements and making deposits. In essence, the contest is between two claimants neither of whom has taken any formal step to give the world notice of his lien, and each of whom is at least dimly aware of the other's potential existence. On these facts it would be arbitrary to make priorities turn on which interest "attached" first, as by lien claimant's first work or the vendee's execution of a contract. Given the almost universal lack of sophisticated residential unit buyers, and the alternative methods open to lien claimants, who are generally well aware of the risks, to safeguard their interests,[66] the preferable approach to this dilemma (short of comprehensive legislative reform) is to recognize a prior vendee's lien for all deposits paid prior to the time the purchaser learns not merely that work has been done on the land, but that delinquent payments are owed to potential lien claimants.

Assuming that a condominium unit purchaser is subject to mechanics' liens, other questions arise. If the work was done or the materials supplied for several units, the common areas, or the entire project, what interests are subjected to the lien? Most of the courts which have dealt with the issue have held that the common areas as such are not lienable.[67] Often this result follows from express language in the condominium statutes involved; the common areas have no independent legal existence apart from the units to which they are appurtenant.[68] Hence a lien claimant who has performed work only on common areas would be expected to file the lien on the individual units—presumably all of them—whose owners had rights in the common facilities in question. A further problem for the lien claimant is raised if some of the units have been conveyed by the developer at the time he hires the lien claimant-to-be. The vendees of these units

66. Subcontractors and materialmen may verify the developer's credit standing, may contact the construction lender to determine whether the project is on schedule and funds available, may insist on immediate payment in cash, or may confine their business activities to developers who have payment bonds. None of these steps may be completely effective or feasible, but they place the potential lien claimant in a considerably stronger position than contract vendees.

67. See, e. g., Country Village Heights Condominium v. Mario Bonito Inc., 79 Misc.2d 1088, 363 N.Y.S.2d 501 (1975); Stevens Constr. Co. v. Draper Hall, Inc., 73 Wis.2d 104, 242 N.W.2d 893 (1976). But see Plateau Supply Co. v. Bison Meadows Corp., 31 Colo.App. 205, 500 P.2d 162 (1972); E. D. McGillicuddy Constr. Co. v. Knoll Recreation Ass'n, 31 Cal.App.3d 891, 107 Cal.Rptr. 901 (1973). The *Stevens* case concludes that liens on the common areas are impermissible even though the lien claimants commenced their work before the condominium declaration was recorded, and thus at a time when the building was not subject to the condominium statute.

68. FHA Model Act § 9(a), supra note 2; A. Ferber & K. Stecher, Law of Condominium § 117 (1967).

might argue that they cannot be held subject to the lien because they neither contracted for nor consented to the work done.[69] It is likely, however, that they would be held to have consented, or be estopped from denying their consent, if the work in question benefitted common areas in which they had rights and which they expected to use.

If work is performed on numerous units, the common areas, or the project as a whole, is a lien claimant required to apportion the lien among all of the affected units and satisfy it from each of them only on a pro rata basis? If the law does not compel this result, the claimant obviously has power to create great injustice among unit owners by "picking on" some while favoring others. This issue has risen frequently in the subdivision context, and the courts have almost uniformly held that, if the lien is susceptible of reasonable apportionment, then apportionment is required.[70] In a condominium, apportionment would seldom be difficult to calculate, since the units are even more likely to be of similar value and have similar construction than subdivision houses. Moreover, many condominium statutes expressly provide that a lien on more than one unit can be satisfied and discharged by pro rata payment by each unit owner.[71] One court has interpreted such language as applicable only when the lien is incurred by one or more individual unit owners, rather than by a developer,[72] but this construction seems strained and inequitable. Whatever the source of the lien, it should be dischargable as to any unit when its owner pays his share; this seems to be the prevalent view.

Mechanics' liens and the assessments of an owners' association may interrelate in at least two ways. It is common for the association to begin functioning and collecting assessments prior to the completion of some phases of the project. If this occurs, a contest may arise as to priority between the mechanics' liens and the association's lien for unpaid assessments. This matter may be resolved by reference to the jurisdiction's condominium statute. Many statutes provide that the assessment lien is superior to all liens except ad valorem

69. See, e. g., Romito Bros. Elec. Constr. Co. v. Frank A. Flannery, Inc., 40 Ohio St.2d 79, 320 N.E.2d 294 (1974). The New York statute permits the filing of a lien on an individual unit only if the work was requested by the owner of the unit or was for emergency repairs. See Country Village Heights Condominium v. Mario Bonito, Inc., 79 Misc.2d 1088, 363 N.Y.S.2d 501 (1975).

70. Apportionment of mechanics' liens required in Weaver v. Harland, 176 Va. 224, 10 S.E.2d 547 (1940). See also West's Ann.Cal.Civ.Code, § 3130 (1974); Del.Code tit. 25, § 2713 (1974).

71. FHA Model Act, § 9(b), supra note 2; A. Ferber & K. Stecher, Law of Condominium § 117 (1967).

72. E. D. McGillicuddy Constr. Co. v. Knoll Recreation Assoc., 31 Cal.App.3d 891, 107 Cal.Rptr. 901 (1973); the court did not explain why allocation of the lien on a pro rated basis among unit owners was impractical. The opinion seemed to rely upon the fact that all purchasers had owner's title insurance coverage—a consideration which seems both irrelevant and improper.

taxes and the first mortgage on any unit.[73] However, a New York court, apparently contradicting the statutory formulation, has given priority to the mechanics' liens on the ground that the association's liens do not come into existence and acquire a priority date until some notice or action to enforce them is filed.[74]

The New York statute expands the rights of mechanics' lien claimants in another fashion as well, granting them, for work done on common areas, a lien on funds collected by the owner's association.[75] This remedy was apparently thought necessary because of the impermissibility of liening the common areas directly, the difficulty of proving that unit owners requested the work done on common areas, and the cumbersomeness of apportionment of the lien among a large number of individual units. From the lienor's viewpoint this remedy is probably superior to merely filing an action to collect the debt owed. In cases in which the association itself requested the work done the procedure is reasonable, but if the work was done at the developer's request, it is difficult to see the fairness of imposing on the association the duty of repaying it.

§ 13.4 Financing Conversions to Condominium and Cooperative Status

Rental apartment buildings are frequently converted to condominium status. The converter may be the original landlord, or the building may be sold to an intermediary who will handle the conversion and marketing process. Often some remodeling and refurbishing of the apartments, lobby, and recreational facilities is necessary. The financial rewards of the conversion can be extremely attractive, since buildings often sell for as much as 33 to 40 percent more than their previous value as rental properties.[76] For landlords who find themselves beset with rising costs for maintenance and utilities, complaints from tenants, and the growing influence of rent control ordinances, conversion may seem an ideal way out of an uncomfortable position.[77]

73. See FHA Model Act § 23(a), supra note 2; A. Ferber & K. Stecher, Law of Condominium § 128 (1967). A few statutes expressly grant priority to mechanics' liens; see Idaho Code § 55–1518 (1976); N.C.Gen.Stat. § 47A–22(a) (1966); Wis.Stat.Ann. § 703.23 (1)(a) (West Spec.Supp.1977).

74. See Security Nat. Bank v. Village Mall at Hillcrest, 85 Misc.2d 771, 382 N.Y.S.2d 882, 896 (1976); cf. McKinney's N.Y. Real Prop. Law § 339–z (Supp.1967).

75. McKinney's N.Y. Real Prop. Law § 339–*l*(2) (1967).

76. See Jaskol, A Lender Looks at Condominium Conversions, 4 Real Est.Rev. 70 (No. 1, 1974); Nat'l Assoc. of Home Builders, Now Is the Time for a Good Condominium Conversion, N.A.H.B.J.-Scope (June 4, 1973). On the treatment of the sale profit as capital gain or ordinary income, see Shapiro & Lemiech, Tax Planning the Condominium Conversion–Analysis of Capital Gain Possibilities, 1 J.Real Est.Tax. 184 (1974).

77. 1 P. Rohan & M. Reskin, Condominium Law & Practice § 3A.01 (1976).

At the same time, conversion is a risky business.[78] Marketing of the converted apartments may be slow, especially if numerous other buildings are being converted or new condominiums built in the same market. It is usually desirable to keep the unsold units rented, but vacancies often grow when the tenants know that the building is being converted. On the other hand, in many buildings the existing tenants cannot afford the purchase prices of the converted units, and hence are forced out of their longtime residences; they may oppose the conversion bitterly and in some jurisdictions their opposition will constitute a legal barrier.[79] Detailed discussion of these problems is beyond the scope of the present treatment, but they must be considered carefully by any lender who is asked to finance a conversion.

Occasionally an apartment building owner is able to manage a conversion without resort to new blanket financing, but this can be accomplished only if the existing mortgage lender is agreeable. If the mortgage contains a due-on-sale clause, the lender must waive it. The lender must also be willing to join in the condominium declaration, and must modify the existing mortgage documents by inserting a partial release clause, thereby permitting the sale of individual units free of the blanket lien. Often the lender is uninterested in taking these steps, or will do so only in return for financial concessions which the converter finds unacceptable. The alternate approach for the converter is to obtain an interim loan from a different lender which will contain the necessary language, and whose proceeds will be used to pay off the existing loan. The attractiveness of this technique will depend on numerous factors, including the interest rate and other costs associated with the interim loan, and the prepayment penalty which may be demanded by the old lender.

Interim loans to finance conversions usually do not require regular principal amortization, but do require the reduction of the principal by some agreed amount for each condominium unit sold, much in the same manner as blanket construction loans on subdivisions.[80] They are usually limited to 75 or 80 percent of the property's value *as a condominium,* but if this would result in a loan approaching 100 percent of the value as a rental project, the interim lender will often require some cash investment by the converter, thus limiting the loan to, perhaps, 90 percent of the rental value. In any event, the "value" on which the loan is based will generally include the cost of the renovations which the converter plans to make. A portion of the interim

78. See Moss, Checklist for Successful Condominium Conversions, 5 Real Est. Rev. 116 (No. 3, 1975).

79. See e. g., McKinney's N.Y.Gen. Bus.Law § 352–e(2) (1976–77) (requiring approval of Attorney General and 35% of existing tenants); Condominium Conversion Ban extended, Wash. Post, Oct. 16, 1974, at A1, col. 6, and numerous other articles in the same period.

80. See Fantini, A Practical Primer for Analyzing Condominium Conversions, 34 The Mortgage Banker 48 (Aug. 1973); Reppe, Winning Over the Condominium Lender, 5 Real Est. Rev. 104 (No. 2, 1975).

loan may even be disbursed in installments as these improvements are put in place, as with a construction loan.

The interim lender is intensely concerned with the converter's cash flow projections for the conversion period. The building must generate enough cash to cover interest payments on the interim loan as well as the usual operating, maintenance, and management costs of a rental building, and the converter's obligation to pay assessments to the new owners' association. Since a shortfall can easily result in default and foreclosure of the interim mortgage, the interim lender must be confident that it can complete the conversion successfully if necessary.

Conversion of rental buildings to cooperatives is far less common nationally than conversion to condominiums, but it has been a frequent occurrence in new York. The motivations for a cooperative conversion are much the same as have been discussed above; avoidance of rent control and high costs, and the opportunity to make a substantial profit.[81] However, the financing problems are much simpler since, absent a due-on-sale clause, the agreement of the existing lender is generally unneeded, and the conversion can proceed without his participation. Often the outstanding balance on the existing financing will be too low to make conversion feasible. In such cases the existing loan may be refinanced, or if its interest rate is so low that it is worth preserving, a wrap-around second mortgage may be arranged to provide cash for refurbishing the building and to lower the required down payments of the apartment purchasers. Separate original, interim, and permanent loans are not necessarily required, however; if the original financing on the rental building is satisfactory, there is usually no reason that it cannot be carried through the conversion period and become the permanent financing for the cooperators.

§ 13.5 Permanent Financing of Condominium Units

Permanent mortgage loans on condominium units can generally be made by institutional lenders on the same terms as loans on detached houses or other buildings. However, the permanent lender on a condominium unit must be concerned with many factors which are unimportant or entirely irrelevant in the financing of subdivision houses.[82] Most of these factors are related to the importance of the owner's association and the common areas to the success (and thus the future security value) of the project. While the discussion which

81. See P. Rohan & M. Reskin, Cooperative Housing Law & Practice § 6.02 (1975); Richards v. Kaskel, 32 N.Y.2d 524, 347 N.Y.S.2d 1, 300 N.E.2d 388 (1973).

82. See generally Jackson, Attorneys for Lenders: What You Should Check in Condominium and PUD Documentations, (pts. 1 & 2) 4 Barrister 47 (Winter), 55 (Spring) (1977) [hereinafter cited as Jackson]; Waldron, Curtain May Soon Rise on Act Two of Condominium Problems, 37 Mortgage Banker 27 (Nov. 1976); Pfeiler, supra note 16.

follows concentrates on the permanent lender's concerns, construction lenders should also be cognizant of the factors mentioned, since they may be forced into a permanent lending role in the event of the developer's default on the construction loan or the permanent lender's refusal to honor its loan commitment. Indeed, unit purchasers themselves should be equally mindful of these problem areas, although they are often insufficiently sophisticated to realize the potential dangers.

Certain precautions are particularly significant to the permanent lender if it finances the sale of some units while other units or the common areas are still under construction or remain in the developer's hands. Obviously, the unit being financed should itself be completed. To ensure that the project will be successfully marketed as a condominium, many permanent lenders impose a "pre-sale requirement"; that is, they will refuse to close any loans until the developer has entered into binding sale contracts for some fixed percentage of the units.[83] The permanent lender will also be legitimately concerned with the developer's financial ability to complete the project, and may wish to verify that sufficient funds remain in the construction loan account for this purpose.

The payment of assessments to the association for unsold units can also pose a problem. Many statutes make no distinction between sold and unsold units, and require that assessments be collected uniformly from all. This approach seems unreasonable from the developer's viewpoint, since unoccupied units obviously contribute little or nothing to certain variable costs of the association's operations; for example, they supply no users for the swimmer pool, tennis courts, or equestrian trails. On the other hand there are many fixed costs which are independent of the number of users. A fair resolution of this problem would be to require a somewhat smaller assessment for units still owned by the developer than are paid for occupied units. While a two-level assessment system is not permitted under many statutes, the same result may be achieved if the developer pays a full assessment but is entitled to reimbursement of a portion from the other owners under a separate contract. Alternatively, the developer might pay the full assessment amounts and attempt to recover his outlays through higher sale prices for the later-sold units.[84] In any event, the permanent lender should ascertain that the developer is obligated to pay a fair share of the costs of operating the association during the marketing period and that he has the financial strength to do so; his default might result in deteriorating physical facilities or a financially weakened or even insolvent association. The lender might even require a cash deposit from the developer to secure these payments.

83. See Vishny, Financing the Condominium, 1970 U.Ill.L.F. 181, 190.

84. See Wolfe, How to Set Up a Homeowners Association So It Works For (Not Against) You, House & Home 74 (Sept. 1974).

The permanent lender must also be concerned with the developer's attempts to retain control over the association until most of the units have been sold. Often this is accomplished by creating two classes of stock, attached to unsold and sold units respectively, with the former having a greater voting power. For example, if the first class has three votes per share and the second only one vote per share, the developer can maintain effective control until the project is three-fourths sold. This degree of retention of control is probably reasonable to protect the developer against the enactment of rules or procedures which would retard his sales.[85] The permanent mortgagee, however, may refuse to lend if the period of developer control will extend past the three-fourths sales mark, and may also insist on the fixing of an outside date by which control must pass to the unit owners irrespective of the number of sales.

Virtually every important aspect of the association's ongoing functions concerns the permanent lender, since operational inadequacies may be reflected in diminished security value of the units. Questions on which the lender will need to be satisfied include the following: Is membership in the association automatic? Has a lien for unpaid assessments been created by proper language in the declaration or master deed? Has the association established a reasonable budget, supported by adequate assessment amounts? Is the assessment delinquency rate reasonably low? Have adequate reserves for repairs and replacements been set up, with provision that they not be used except for specified items? Has a competent management firm been hired if the project is large enough to justify it? Is the project subject to unreasonable management contracts or recreational facility leases? Is an independent annual audit made of the association's books? Has adequate blanket insurance been arranged for the common areas and exteriors of units, with provision for increased coverage to match inflation?

Many permanent lenders insist on certain types of protection in the condominium documentation. For example, the lender may want: notice from the association of default in assessments by any of its mortgagors; exemption (if the lender becomes the owner of a unit through foreclosure) from the usual clause giving the association a right of first refusal or other right to control the subsequent transfer of the unit, and from any restriction on leasing of units; notice of cancellation of any insurance policies on the project; the right to examine the association's books at reasonable times; notice of association meetings and the right to attend; notice of any substantial loss or damage to common areas; and the right to vote on, or even to veto, such major policy decisions as the hiring or firing of a management firm, amendments to the declaration or bylaws, expansion or

85. Id. at 83. A few statutes expressly limit the period of developer control; see, e. g., Fla.Stat.Ann. §§ 718.-301 (condominiums), 719.301 (cooperatives) (Supp.1977).

contraction of the project, or use of hazard insurance proceeds other than for repairs.

Finally, the lender will probably wish to redraft its usual mortgage and note forms to add special provisions relating to condominiums.[86] These revisions will usually include covenants by the mortgagor to pay his association assessments when due, to notify the lender of any delinquency notices received from the association, and to abide by all provisions of the condominium's declaration, bylaws, and rules. The documents may require that assessments be paid to an escrow or impound account. The mortgagor may also be required to covenant not to vote in favor of major policy changes in the project without the mortgagee's consent. Failure of the association to maintain adequate insurance coverage may be made a condition of default, and the lender may reserve the right to pay delinquent assessments and to charge them against the mortgagor's loan balance.

Authority of Lenders, Insurers, and Investors

There is little controversy concerning the power of lenders to make permanent mortgage loans on condominium units. Both federally-chartered and state-chartered institutions are generally permitted to treat them as the equivalent of single-family houses,[87] although the lending powers of state-chartered institutions are a matter of state law and some variations exist.[88]

The Federal Housing Administration (FHA) insures permanent mortgages on condominium units under the same general terms and conditions as mortgages on detached houses, but if the project has more than eleven units, insurance on permanent mortgages is available only if the project has previously been covered by an FHA-insured project mortgage.[89] Thus large numbers of projects are ineligible because they were constructed with conventional financing.

The Veteran's Administration (VA) was first given authority to guarantee loans on condominium units in 1970, but could do so only

86. Pfeiler, supra note 16, at 261; Condominium Rider, FNMA/FHLMC, Uniform Instrument 6/75; Grosser, Making the Loan Commitment, in Community Ass'n Institute, Summary of Proceedings, First Nat. Conference on Community Ass'ns 66 (1976).

87. See, e. g., 12 CFR 7.2195 (1977) (Ruling of the Comptroller of the Currency: condominiums treated as real estate for lending by national banks); 12 CFR 541.10 (1977) (Federal Home Loan Bank Board definition of "single-family dwelling" includes condominium units for purposes of lending by federal savings and loan associations).

88. Many state statutes dealing with institutional lending powers make no reference to condominiums, apparently relying instead on their respective condominium acts to establish that condominium units are to be treated as other dwellings. Some statutes deal specifically with loans on condominium units, and may establish somewhat different lending criteria than apply to detached houses. See, e. g., West's Ann.Cal.Fin.Code § 7153.1 (1977).

89. National Housing Act § 234(c), 12 U.S.C.A. § 1715y(c) (Supp. V 1977); 24 CFR 234.26(a) (1977).

when at least one unit in the project had been insured by FHA.[90] In 1975 this statutory limitation was dropped, and the VA now guarantees such loans regardless of prior FHA involvement.[91] VA imposes a number of requirements to protect its interests,[92] including the escrowing of earnest money deposits by developers, a seventy percent presale requirement (which may be reduced to fifty-one percent in special circumstances), and limitations on reservations of rights by developers (such as the leasing of common areas to the association and the retention of a veto over the association after unit owners obtain majority control). In addition, VA regards projects as unacceptable if they prohibit leasing of units for six months or more, or impose a right of first refusal upon resale.[93] As with FHA, the terms of the VA loan guarantee are identical to those on detached houses.[94]

Both the Federal National Mortgage Association (FNMA) and the Federal Home Loan Mortgage Corporation (FHLMC) purchase permanent mortgage loans on condominium units. If a project has been the subject of an FHA condominium project mortgage, neither of these secondary market agencies is further concerned with the documentation; however, if construction was conventionally financed, FNMA and FHLMC impose a number of stringent requirements on the documentation and on certain operational aspects of the project as well.[95] The two agencies have similar, but not identical, requirements; they are too numerous to be summarized here, but generally deal with the issues and concerns discussed earlier in this section.[96] FNMA will not purchase condominium mortgages in excess of ninety percent of the unit's value, while FHLMC will buy ninety-five percent mortgages. The two agencies also differ in their procedures for purchase of condominium unit mortgages. FNMA must receive full information on the project and approve it before any individual unit mortgages will be purchased,[97] an essential element of the initial submission is an attorney's opinion verifying that the documents meet

90. Veterans Housing Act of 1970, § 3, 84 Stat. 1108 (current version at 38 U.S.C.A. § 1810(d) (1970).

91. Veterans Housing Act of 1974, Pub.L. No. 93–569, § 3, 88 Stat. 1863 (adding 38 U.S.C.A. § 1810(a)(6) (Supp. V 1975) and repealing 38 U.S. C.A. § 1810(d) (1970)).

92. See Policies and Procedures, Condominium Loans Under 38 U.S.C.A. § 1810(A)(6), 40 Fed.Reg. 21794 (1975).

93. The latter requirement is imposed only on condominiums established after December 31, 1976; see 41 Fed. Reg. 44039 (1976).

94. 38 CFR 36.4358 (1976).

95. Examples include the completion of common area improvements, the adequacy of reserves for repairs and replacements, 80 percent occupancy by year-round residents, a 70 percent pre-sale requirement (which may be reduced to 51 percent by special approval), and a power in the association to terminate any management contract upon 90 days notice. See FHLMC, Sellers Guide Conventional Mortgages § 3.207; FNMA, Conventional Selling Contract Supplement § 502.03.

96. See text at notes 77–80, supra; see generally Jackson, note 82 supra.

97. FNMA, Conventional Selling Contract Supplement § 502.03(d).

FNMA's criteria.[98] FHLMC, by contrast, does not give prior approvals. Instead, it requires that the originating lender submit, with the first unit loan sold to FHLMC, a certification that the documents meet FHLMC's requirements.[99] An attorney's opinion must be obtained, but may simply be retained in the lender's files. If the project is operating successfully, and control of the association has been in the hands of the residents for at least two years, both FNMA and FHLMC greatly relax their requirements.[99a]

An obvious concern to permanent lenders is the priority of the mortgage loan as against the lien of the owner's association for unpaid assessments. A large majority of the state statutes follow the FHA Model Act in providing that the lien is subordinate to any "first mortgage of record"; [1] other statutes subordinate the lien to all mortgages.[2] Obviously, under such statutes the mortgagee or other purchaser at a foreclosure sale is not subject to any liability for the assessment delinquencies of the former mortgagor, and mortgage foreclosure wipes out the association lien as to such amounts.[3] However, the real covenant which imposes the lien continues to run with the land, and assessments which accrue after the mortgage foreclosure do become the liability of the foreclosure purchaser, secured by the association's lien.

Subordination of the association's lien to the first mortgage as described above is generally thought advantageous to lenders, and FHLMC, FNMA, FHA and VA all require it.[4] It is clearly undesirable from the viewpoint of the association and its other members, since they will usually have to withstand an unusually heavy assessment to make up the delinquency of the foreclosed unit owners [5] in the long run, a series of such incidents could endanger the solvency of the association, to the detriment of unit owners and mortgagees alike. At present, however, the preference of mortgagees for priority seems well-established. Little thought seems to have been given to the con-

98. See Guide Form for Attorney's Opinion (Condominium Project), FNMA Form 1037.

99. FHLMC, Sellers' Guide Conventional Mortgages § 3.207.

99a. See FHLMC, Sellers' Guide Conventional Mortgages § 3.207 (change 7/1/78); FNMA, Conventional Selling Contract Supplement § 502.07 (1978).

1. FHA Model Act § 23(a), supra § 13.1 note 2; Va.Code § 55–79.85 (Supp. 1977) (first mortgages "securing institutional lenders").

2. See, e. g., Utah Code Ann. § 57–8–20 (1950); Brask v. Bank of St. Louis, 533 S.W.2d 223 (Mo.App.1976).

3. FHA Model Act § 23(b), supra § 13.1 note 2.

4. FHLMC, Sellers' Guide Conventional Mortgages § 3.207(c); FNMA, Conventional Selling Contract Supplement § 502.03(b)(2)(b); Veterans Administration, Policies and Procedures, Condominium Loans, 40 CFR 21794, § 5(c); FHA Master Deed, Form No. 3276, § 19, HUD HANDBOOK 4265.1, App. 8.

5. The FHA Model Act § 23(b), supra § 13.1 note 2, specifically authorizes the charging of such deficiencies against all unit owners, but the language is probably unnecessary.

sequences of a deed in lieu of foreclosure. Such deeds may be construed not to disturb subordinate liens, so the association would appear to emerge entirely unscathed.[6] In a sense this is probably unfortunate, since it serves as an incentive for the lender to employ foreclosure, a decision which is usually more costly and time-consuming for all parties.

In an effort to avoid assessment defaults, some permanent mortgage lenders require their mortgagors to pay their assessments into an impound, reserve, or escrow account similar to those customarily maintained for taxes and insurance; the lender then remits the sums collected to the association on a regular basis. Many lenders are unenthusiastic about this technique, however, since it involves much more frequent payouts than are necessary for tax and insurance funds, and since the assessment lien, unlike taxes and assessments, is usually subordinate to the mortgage. Nonetheless, collection of assessments by the lender is generally a useful and desirable means of discouraging delinquencies and stabilizing the association's cash flow.

§ 13.6 Permanent Financing of Cooperative Units

Traditionally the only permanent financing involving a cooperative project was its blanket mortgage. In most respects lenders have viewed blanket mortgages as similar to loans on rental apartment buildings, although they have been concerned to some extent with the governance, internal procedures, and financial stability of cooperative corporations. Permanent blanket mortgages (as well as construction loans) on cooperative projects can be insured by FHA under section 213 of the National Housing Act.[7] Loan-to-value ratios may be as high as ninety-eight percent, a feature which makes section 213 more attractive than conventional loans, which are generally limited to eighty percent of value. While the time and complexity of processing under section 213 reduces its usefulness, the program has been fairly active in those jurisdictions in which cooperatives are popular.[8]

In recognition of the low foreclosure and loss experience of cooperatives, the Federal Home Loan Bank Board in 1975 amended its regulations to permit federally-chartered savings and loan associa-

6. See Note, 31 Mo.L.Rev. 312 (1966) (discussing priority of deeds in lieu). Cf. Alden Hotel Co. v. Kanin, 88 Misc.2d 546, 387 N.Y.S.2d 948 (1976).

7. 12 U.S.C.A. § 1715e (1970 & Supp. V 1975).

8. From the initiation of the § 213 program in 1950 through 1975, project mortgages on 116,155 units were insured. The states in which use of the program was heaviest were (in order of decreasing use) California, New York, Florida, Arizona, Michigan, Illinois and New Jersey. California and New York were roughly equal in participation, and together accounted for 57 percent of the units. See U.S. Dep't of Housing and Urban Development, 1975 Statistical Yearbook 134 (1976). Participation has generally dropped off sharply in recent years.

tions to make loans up to ninety-five percent of the project's value;[9] the previous limit had been eighty percent. The regulations require completion of construction, presale of ninety percent of the value or purchase price of the units, and owner-occupancy. The cooperative itself must maintain both general operating reserves and reserves for replacements in the same amounts as are required by the FHA section 213 program,[10] and if the loan-to-value ratio exceeds ninety percent, either private mortgage insurance or a specific reserve fund maintained by the lender is required.[11]

Until recently, permanent institutional financing of individual cooperative units was unavailable; subsequent purchasers of the units either paid cash, obtained personal loans from external sources, or gave promissory notes to unit sellers to cover the non-cash portion of the purchase price. However, at least four states, New York, Illinois, New Jersey, and California,[12] now expressly authorize financial institutions to make loans on the security of individual cooperative units. In the absence of such legislation, the authority to do so would be dubious in most jurisdictions, since the security is a pledge of the borrower's shares of stock and an assignment of his proprietary lease, and hence is not clearly a real estate loan.[13] The New York statutes were first enacted in 1971, and have undergone a series of liberalizing amendments.[14] In their original form, they placed severe limits on the permissible maturity and loan-to-value ratio, but both of these terms are now permitted to be as generous as on loans made to owner-occupants of single-family homes. The interest rate on cooperative loans is allowed to exceed that established by the usury statute for home loans by one and one-half percent, presumably as

9. 40 Fed.Reg. 44,125 (1975) (codified in 12 CFR 545.6–1(b)(1)(iii), 545.6–7(b) (1977). Note, however, that this regulation has nothing to say about loans on the security of individual co-op units, which the FHLBB General Counsel has ruled are *not* loans secured by first liens and therefore are generally ineligible as investments by federal savings associations; FHLBB Opinion, June 10, 1976, reported in 10 F.H.L.B.B.J. 37 (No. 6, 1977).

10. See 24 CFR 213.30 (1977).

11. This fund is in addition to the reserves maintained by the cooperative itself and must equal 1 percent of the outstanding principal balance of the blanket mortgage. This provision also applies to loans exceeding 90 percent of value on detached houses, but is little used in such cases because of the wide availability of private mortgage insurance. See 12 CFR 545.6–1(a)(5) (1977).

12. McKinney's N.Y. Banking Law §§ 103(5) (banks), 235(8–a) (savings banks), 380(2–a) (savings and loan associations) (1976–77); Smith-Hurd Ill.Ann.Stat. ch. 32, § 791(d) (1977); N.J.Rev.Stat. § 17:2–6; West's Ann.Cal. Financial Code § 7133.4.

13. See Federal Deposit Ins. Corp. v. Evans, No. 75–C–1947 (E.D.N.Y. April 14, 1976), summarized in 4 Condominium Report 6 (No. 6, July 1976), holding the security interest in a cooperative stock and lease to be personal property and properly foreclosed under Article 9 of the Uniform Commercial Code.

14. See Goldstein, Institutional Purchase Money Financing of Cooperative Apartments, 46 St.Johns L.Rev. 632 (1972).

an incentive to lenders to enter this relatively untested field. In addition, when a loan is made to finance the sale of a cooperative unit, the sale price is deemed to be the appraised value for purposes of computing the loan-to-value ratio; thus, an even larger loan might be made on a cooperative unit than a house of similar actual value.

Institutional financing of individual cooperative units was given further impetus by section 4(b) of the Emergency Home Purchase Act of 1974, which added a new subsection (n) to Section 203 of the National Housing Act.[15] It authorized FHA to insure individual unit loans in buildings subject to a blanket mortgage insured under section 213. Under FHA's regulations the loan must be secured by a first lien on the corporate stock certificate and the occupancy certificate or proprietary lease.[16] The loan maturity is limited to twenty years, and the loan may not exceed the difference between the FHA appraisal value of the unit and the unit's share of the blanket mortgage. Thus, the regulations recognize that a unit purchaser is always taking, in effect, subject to the blanket mortgage.

The proper method of foreclosure of a lender's security interest in the stock and lease which represent a cooperative unit is still uncertain in most jurisdictions. In Federal Deposit Ins. Corp. v. Evans,[17] the court concluded that the lender held a security interest in personal property which could be properly foreclosed by private sale under section 9–504 of the Uniform Commercial Code. The court rejected the cooperative member's argument that such a sale violated due process if not preceded by a hearing, a conclusion consistent with most decisions on the validity of power-of-sale foreclosures of real estate mortgages.[18] But the applicability of the U.C.C. is by no means clear, and the ambiguity is disturbing to many lenders. A statutory foreclosure procedure is needed in those states in which cooperatives are used extensively.

It is possible that the efforts of FHA, the Federal Home Loan Bank Board, and the state legislatures will make cooperatives more popular than heretofore. However, neither VA nor the two quasi-federal secondary market entities, FNMA and FHLMC, have programs to insure or purchase cooperative unit loans. In most areas of the nation condominiums are better understood, and their financing can be handled with only minor modifications of standard real estate

15. 12 U.S.C.A. § 1709(n) (Supp. V 1975).

16. 42 Fed.Reg. 40,430 (1977), 24 CFR 203.43c. Neither the statute nor the regulations explain precisely what documentation will be necessary to establish a first lien on the unit ownership; this issue is left to state law, although there are few if any state decisions on the point. Even New York law is unclear as to whether UCC or real estate recording is appropriate to perfect the lien; see P. Rohan & M. Reskin, Cooperative Housing Law & Practice § 2.01(5) (1975).

17. Federal Deposit Ins. Corp. v. Evans, No. 75–C–1947 (E.D.N.Y. April 14, 1976).

18. See Note, 41 Mo.L.Rev. 278 (1976).

security instruments. Moreover, the problems with which lenders have become increasingly concerned in condominium unit financing, such as developer control and contributions, adequacy of reserves, the impact of rights of approval and first refusal, and the soundness of the association's major policy decisions, are all equally relevant in cooperative unit financing. From the financing viewpoint, cooperatives thus have no advantages and several disadvantages over condominiums. Hence, condominiums will probably continue to eclipse cooperatives as the preferred means of unit ownership.

*

TABLE OF CASES

References are to Pages

A

B

C

E

F

G

H

K

L

M

N

O

P

S

T

U

W

Y

Z

INDEX

References are to Pages

WEST PUBLISHING CO